T0394595

Christian-Muslim Relations
A Bibliographical History

History of Christian-Muslim Relations

Editorial Board

David Thomas
University of Birmingham
Tarif Khalidi
American University of Beirut
Gerrit Jan Reinink
University of Groningen
Mark Swanson
Lutheran School of Theology at Chicago

Volume 11

Christian-Muslim Relations
A Bibliographical History

Volume 1 (600-900)

Edited by
David Thomas and Barbara Roggema

with Juan Pedro Monferrer Sala, Johannes Pahlitzsch
Mark Swanson, Herman Teule, John Tolan

BRILL

LEIDEN • BOSTON
2009

Arts & Humanities Research Council

This project is supported by a grant from the Arts and Humanities Research Council.

front cover illustration: This shows a detail of a mosaic on the Umayyad Mosque in Damascus. Built on the site of the Church of St John the Baptist between 706 and 715, it occupies a position that for a time was shared by Christian and Muslim worshippers. The detail comes from a photograph taken by Stefan Heidemann.

This book is printed on acid-free paper.

Christians and Muslims have been involved in exchanges over matters of faith and morality since the founding of Islam. Attitudes between the faiths today are deeply coloured by the legacy of past encounters, and often preserve centuries-old negative views.

The History of Christian-Muslim Relations, Texts and Studies presents the surviving record of past encounters in authoritative, fully introduced text editions and annotated translations, and also monograph and collected studies. It illustrates the development in mutual perceptions as these are contained in surviving Christian and Muslim writings, and makes available the arguments and rhetorical strategies that, for good or for ill, have left their mark on attitudes today. The series casts light on a history marked by intellectual creativity and occasional breakthroughs in communication, although, on the whole beset by misunderstanding and misrepresentation. By making this history better known, the series seeks to contribute to improved recognition between Christians and Muslims in the future.

Library of Congress Cataloging-in-Publication Data

Christian Muslim relations : a bibliographical history / edited by David Thomas & Barbara Roggema ; with Juan Pedro Monferrer-Sala, Johannes Pahlitzsch, Mark Swanson, Herman Teule and John Tolan.

p. cm. — (The history of Christian-Muslim relations, ISSN 1570-7350 ; v. 11)
Includes index.
ISBN 978-90-04-16975-3 (hardback : alk. paper)
1. Christianity and other religions—Islam. 2. Islam—Relations—Christianity. 3. Christianity and other religions—Islam—Bibliography. 4. Islam—Relations—Christianity—Bibliography. I. Thomas, David. II. Roggema, Barbara. III. Monferrer Sala, Juan Pedro. IV. Title. V. Series.

BP172.C4196 2009
016.2612'7—dc22

2009029184

ISSN 1570-7350
ISBN- 978 90 04 16975 3

Copyright 2009 by Koninklijke Brill NV, Leiden, The Netherlands.
Koninklijke Brill NV incorporates the imprints Brill, Hotei Publishing, IDC Publishers, Martinus Nijhoff Publishers and VSP.

All rights reserved. No part of this publication may be reproduced, translated, stored in a retrieval system, or transmitted in any form or by any means, electronic, mechanical, photocopying, recording or otherwise, without prior written permission from the publisher.

Authorization to photocopy items for internal or personal use is granted by Brill provided that the appropriate fees are paid directly to The Copyright Clearance Center, 222 Rosewood Drive, Suite 910, Danvers, MA 01923, USA.
Fees are subject to change.

PRINTED IN THE NETHERLANDS

CONTENTS

Foreword vii

Abbreviations xiii

David Thomas, *Introduction* 1

Jaakko Hämeen-Anttila, *Christians and Christianity in the Qurʾān* 21

Claude Gilliot, *Christians and Christianity in Islamic exegesis* 31

Suleiman A. Mourad, *Christians and Christianity in the Sīra of Muḥammad* 57

David Cook, *Christians and Christianity in ḥadīth works before 900* 73

David M. Freidenreich, *Muslims in canon law, 650-1000* 83

David M. Freidenreich, *Christians in early and classical Sunnī law* 99

Works on Christian-Muslim relations 600-900 115

Index of names 923

Index of works 944

FOREWORD

David Thomas

Christian-Muslim Relations, a Bibliographical History 1 (*CMR1* to give it its acronym) is the first part of a general history of relations between Christians and Muslims as this is recorded in written sources. This history is intended to cover the whole span from the early seventh century to the present, and will include all continents. *CMR1* takes in the first nine hundred years from 600 to 1500, while *CMR2*, *CMR3* and the other histories will take in the five hundred years from 1500 to 2000 and after. While *CMR1* covers the area of what may conveniently, if rather loosely, be called the extended Mediterranean basin, the other histories will follow Muslims and Christians as they have carried their faiths to the different parts of the world and recorded their attitudes about one another and their mutual encounters in new circumstances.

This is certainly an ambitious project. Its demands are intensified by the decision to include fully documented descriptions of all the known works within its scope. The descriptions are designed to provide a starting point for scholarly investigation into the works and their authors, and also into whatever relationships exist between them. The project is more than a single individual or group could accomplish. But the leaders of the project have been able to draw upon the expertise of the wider scholarly community, made available with ready generosity, and have been assisted by leading authorities in bringing together entries on the works from the history of Christian-Muslim relations which reflect current scholarship. Naturally, this scholarship does not stand still, and so the project leaders welcome updates on details of the entries in due course, together with additions and corrections where, despite all best efforts, there are omissions and mistakes.

CMR1 is divided into three volumes which represent the periods 600-900, 900-1200 and 1200-1500. Within each volume there is an initial essay that surveys relations between the faiths in the period, followed by a series of essays on works that are of main importance to Christian-Muslim relations but do not fit easily into the format adopted for entries on individual works. In *CMR1* volume one, these essays cover the Qurʾān, the biography of the Prophet Muḥammad, Ḥadīth, *tafsīr* and Christian and Muslim legal works, always focussing on elements that bear on relations between the faiths. As will be readily seen, these topics have been chosen for treatment in this manner because, while they include information of fundamental importance for the attitudes of Muslims and Christians towards one another as these developed, each of the individual elements of which they are made up – scattered verses of the Qurʾān, isolated incidents in Muḥammad's life, sayings of his distributed through voluminous ḥadīth collections, individual comments by Qurʾān commentators, and single legal statements amid large bodies of rulings and regulations – presents only a tiny part of a picture that is more complete when all are brought together.

Following the initial and topical essays, which will, of course, differ in theme in succeeding volumes of *CMR1*, come the entries that make up the bulk of the work. And here something should be said about the criteria that have been used to determine what should and should not be included in the bibliographical history. Since it is concerned with relations between Christians and Muslims, inclusion was decided according to whether a work is written substantially about or against the other faith, or contains significant information or judgements that cast light on attitudes of one faith towards the other. Thus, apologetic and polemical works are, by their very nature, included, while large synthetic historical and geographical works, such as are known in this period, are often not, even though they may refer to the other in passing. Only works that contribute in a major way towards building a picture of knowledge about the one by the other and of attitudes between them were chosen for inclusion.

These principle criteria were easily applicable in many cases, but they proved difficult to apply in a significant minority of instances. The project leaders have therefore taken an inclusive approach, especially with respect to works from the earliest years that may contain only a small but insightful detail, and also to works that are no longer extant and whose contents can only be inferred from a title or reference by a later author. It is possible that future discoveries will either confirm the leaders' decisions or show that they have been too inclusive.

The difficulty of applying the set criteria in this period is increased by the fact that many of the works that might appear to be related to Christian-Muslim relations have survived only in fragments or not at all. Thus, for example, among Muslim Arabic works it was decided to include entries on all works about the prophethood of Muḥammad, the *dalāʾil al-nubuwwa*, 'proofs of prophethood', genre, most of which are now known only from their titles or a brief reference, because of the strong likelihood that they contained responses to Christian accusations and maybe discussions of proof texts from the Bible, even though some later surviving examples do not. But it was decided to exclude works that appear to have been concerned to validate the status of prophets in general, often entitled *ithbāt al-rusul*, 'confirmation of messengers', on the grounds that these probably had a wider scope than defenses of Muḥammad as prophet, being collections of arguments against opponents who rejected the need for intermediaries between the human and divine. There is no telling whether any or all of them may have made reference to Christian accusations specifically against Muḥammad or employed proof texts from Christian scripture, but in light of the available evidence, it was considered that on balance this was unlikely.

Fine-tuned judgments such as these characterized a number of discussions within the project group, with the uppermost consideration always being that a work must substantially be about or against the other, or must cast clear light on interfaith attitudes. The result is the series of entries that make up this volume.

Each entry is divided into two main parts. The first is concerned with the author, and it contains basic biographical details, an account of his main intellectual activities and writings, the main primary sources of information about him, and the latest works by present day authors on him and his intellectual involvements and achievements. Without seeking to be exhaustive, this section contains sufficient information for a reader to pursue further details about the author and his general activities.

The second part of the entry is concerned with the works of the author that are specifically devoted to the other faith. And here a measure of completeness is attempted. This part is sub-divided according to the number of the author's works included. In each sub-division a work is named, and then in two important sections its contents are briefly described and its significance in the history of Christian-Muslim relations is appraised. There follow sections on the manuscript witnesses of the work (where a recent edition or study provides an authoritative list of these, this is cited instead of a complete list being given), published editions and translations, and lastly studies of it. It is intended that these will be completely up to date at the time of going to press.

With this coverage, *CMR1* should provide sufficient information to enable a researcher to identify a work, appreciate its importance, and locate it and studies of it. Researchers will also be assisted in locating each work in the history of Christian-Muslim relations by virtue of the principle adopted of placing each as far as is possible in the historical progression of relations between the faiths. Thus, a work written in Greek may come before a work written in Syriac, which may be followed by a Muslim Arabic work, which in turn will be followed by a Latin work. The project leaders decided upon this arrangement at the outset, rather than grouping works according to religious tradition or language, so that some sort of development in dealings between the faiths might become discernible. (The final decision about the ordering of works was made by the project Director, and responsibility for this, with what may seem arbitrariness in places, lies with him.) Of course, proximity between works in the bibliography is definitely not an indication of any necessary direct relationship between them, let alone influence (though this may sometimes be deducible from internal or external evidence). What it does is provide a gauge of relations between the faiths in any stretch of time, though it must always be considered only a rough guide, and its limitations should be particularly borne in mind in the case of anonymous works or works by little-known authors which can only be allocated to a general period, and even more in the case of works the dating of which is debated and disputed.

It has to be remembered that this record of encounters between Muslims and Christians represents only a partial picture. By definition, it reflects the preoccupations of literary, usually scholarly, castes which included the elites of society, for whom engagement with the religious other served a variety of purposes in addition to descriptive accounts of their beliefs and arguments against them. The wider populations of different social strata hardly appear in these records as any more than background groups, and so their interactions can only be perceived fragmentarily. The kinds of relations experienced at, say, artisan or village level may have differed markedly from what is detectable in and deducible from the works listed here. These latter form only a partial picture, though one that is influential and formative, and undeniably authentic.

The composition of this history has been undertaken by a host of individual contributors, who readily and often enthusiastically accepted the invitations of the project leaders. The project was led by Juan Pedro Monferrer Sala (Iberian Arabic texts), Johannes Pahlitzsch (Greek texts, succeeding Emmanouela Grypeou after the first year), Barbara Roggema (Research Fellow; Armenian, Georgian, Coptic, Slavonic),

Mark Swanson (Christian Arabic and Coptic texts), Herman Teule (Syriac texts), David Thomas (Director, and Muslim Arabic texts), and John Tolan (Latin texts). Particular advice was given by Thomas Burman, Maribel Fierro, Robert Hoyland, Maria Mavroudi and Samir Khalil Samir. And in addition, Carol Rowe gave practical help in the form of careful copy editing, Alex Mallett was indispensable at the proof stage, and the staff editors at Brill gave constant encouragement. The project team are deeply indebted to everyone who contributed in one way or another.

The project was funded by a grant made by the Arts and Humanities Research Council of the United Kingdom. This is acknowledged with gratitude.

As has been said, strenuous efforts have been made to ensure the information given in each entry is both accurate and complete, though it would be not only arrogant but also unrealistic to claim that these efforts have succeeded entirely and in every instance. Details (hopefully only minor) must have been overlooked, new works will have come to light, new editions, translations and studies will have appeared. The project leaders therefore invite corrections, additions and updates, which will be incorporated into *CMR1* in the on-line version and in further editions. Details of these should be sent to the project Director, Professor David Thomas, University of Birmingham, UK, d.r.thomas.1@bham.ac.uk.

ABBREVIATIONS

AB
Analecta Bollandiana

Assemani, *BO*
J. Assemani, *Bibliotheca orientalis clementino-vaticana*, 3 vols, Rome, 1719-28

Baumstark, *GSL*
A. Baumstark, *Geschichte der syrischen Literatur*, Bonn, 1922

BHG
F. Halkin (ed.), *Bibliotheca Hagiographica Graeca*, Brussels, 1957

Brockelmann, *GAL*
C. Brockelmann, *Geschichte der arabischen Literatur*, 2 vols and 3 supplements, Leiden, 1937-49

BSOAS
Bulletin of the School of Oriental and African Studies

BZ
Byzantinische Zeitschrift

CSCO
Corpus Scriptorum Christianorum Orientalium

DOP
Dumbarton Oaks Papers

EI2
Encyclopaedia of Islam, 2nd ed.

EI3
Encyclopaedia of Islam, 3rd ed.

EQ
Encyclopaedia of the Qurʾān

Flórez, *España Sagrada*
E. Flórez et al., *España Sagrada. Theatro geographico-historico de la iglesia de España*, 56 vols, Madrid, 1747-1961

Fritsch, *Islam und Christentum im Mittelalter*
E. Fritsch, *Islam und Christentum im Mittelalter. Beiträge zur Geschichte der muslimischen Polemik gegen das Christentum in arabischer Sprache*, Breslau, 1930

Gil, *CSM*
I. Gil, *Corpus Scriptorum Muzarabicorum*, 2 vols, Madrid, 1973

Graf
G. Graf, *Catalogue de manuscrits arabes chrétiens conservés au Caire*, Rome, 1934 (followed by MS number)

Graf, *GCAL*
G. Graf, *Geschichte der christlichen arabischen Literatur*, 5 vols, Vatican City, 1944-53

Hoyland, *Seeing Islam*
R. Hoyland, *Seeing Islam as others saw it. A survey and evaluation of Christian, Jewish and Zoroastrian writings on early Islam*, Princeton NJ, 1997

Ibn al-Nadīm, *Fihrist*
Ibn al-Nadīm, *Kitāb al-fihrist*, ed. M. Riḍā-Tajaddud, Tehran, 1971

ICMR
Islam and Christian-Muslim Relations

Kaḥḥāla
ʿU. Kaḥḥāla, *Muʿjam al-muʾallifīn. Ṭarājim muṣannifī l-kutub al-ʿarabiyya*, 15 vols, Damascus, 1957-61

JAOS
Journal of the American Oriental Society

JSAI
Jerusalem Studies in Arabic and Islam

JSS
Journal of Semitic Studies

MGH
Monumenta Germaniae Historica

MIDEO
Mélanges. Institut Dominicain d'Études Orientales du Caire

MW
The Muslim World

Nasrallah, *HMLEM* ii.2
J. Nasrallah, *Histoire du mouvement littéraire dans l'église melchite du Ve au XXe siècle. Contribution à l'étude de la littérature arabe chrétienne, volume II.2: 750-Xe s.*, Louvain, 1990

OC
Oriens Christianus

OCP
Orientalia Christiana Periodica

ODB
The Oxford Dictionary of Byzantium

Pd'O
Parole de l'Orient

PG
Patrologia Graeca

PL
Patrologia Latina

PO
Patrologia Orientalis

PMBZ
Prosopographie der mittelbyzantinischen Zeit

REB
Revue des études byzantines

REI
Revue des études islamiques

RHR
Revue de l'histoire des religions

RSO
Rivista degli studi orientali

Sbath, *Fihris*
P. Sbath, *al-Fihris (catalogue de manuscrits arabes)*, Cairo, 1938-40

Sezgin, *GAS*
F. Sezgin, *Geschichte des arabischen Schrifttums*, 13 vols to date, Leiden, 1967-

al-Sharfī, *al-Fikr al-Islāmī*
ʿA.-M. al-Sharfī, *al-Fikr al-Islāmī fī l-radd ʿalā l-Naṣārā ilā nihāyat al-qarn al-rābiʿ/ʿāshir*, Tunis, 1986

Simaika
M.P. Simaika and Y. ʿAbd al-Masih, *Catalogue of the Coptic and Arabic manuscripts in the Coptic Museum, the Patriarchate, the principal Churches of Cairo and Alexandria and the monasteries of Egypt*, 2 vols, Cairo, 1939 (followed by MS number)

al-Ṭabarī, *Taʾrīkh*
Abū Jaʿfar Muḥammad al-Ṭabarī, *Taʾrīkh al-rusul wa-l-mulūk/Annales quos scripsit Abu Djafar Mohammed ibn Djarir at-Tabari*, ed. M. de Goeje et al., 15 vols, Leiden, 1879-1901

Tolan, *Saracens*
J. Tolan, *Saracens. Islam in the medieval European imagination*, New York, 2002

Van Ess, *TG*
J. van Ess, *Theologie und Gesellschaft im 2. und 3. Jahrhundert Hidschra*, 6 vols, Berlin, 1991-97

VV
Vizantinskij Vremennik

Watt, *Formative period*
W.M. Watt, *The formative period of Islamic thought*, Edinburgh, 1973

ZDMG
Zeitschrift der Deutschen Morgenländischen Gesellschaft

Introduction

David Thomas

The period covered in this volume, 600-900, is arguably the most important period in relations between Christianity and Islam, because in these centuries Christians and Muslims first became acquainted with one another's beliefs and religious claims, and began to shape attitudes that have continued to exert strong influence to the present.[1] It is also a period in which, under the first great Islamic empires, followers of the two faiths lived closely together and learned from one another in ways that had lasting effects on both.[2] While many of the details of relations between the two faiths in these important centuries

[1] To date, the most complete bibliography of Christian-Muslim relations is R. Caspar et al., 'Bibliographie du dialogue islamo-chrétien', *Islamochristiana* 1 (1975) 125-81; 2 (1976) 188-95; 3 (1977) 255-56; 4 (1978) 247-49 (texts from this period). See also G. Anawati, 'Polémique, apologie et dialogue islamo-chrétiens, positions classiques médiévales et positions contemporaines,' *Euntes Docete* 22 (1969) 375-452; M. Steinschneider, *Polemische und apologetische Literatur in arabischer Sprache zwischen Muslimen, Christen und Juden, nebst Anhängen verwandten Inhalts*, Leipzig, 1877, remains important. For Christian Arabic works, see the bibliographies provided by H. Teule and V. Schepens in *Journal of Eastern Christian Studies* 57 (2005) 129-74; 58 (2006) 265-300; 61 (2009) (forthcoming); G. Graf, *Geschichte der christlichen arabischen Literatur*, 5 vols, Vatican City, 1945-1953 (*GCAL*), remains the basic reference work (the part on East Syrian authors is translated by J. Sanders, *La littérature nestorienne*, Heemstede, 1985). In the notes to this Introduction, citations are usually limited to works that have appeared in the last few decades, apart from books with continuing significance and those with good bibliographies on the topics they cover.

[2] For general surveys, see R. Armour Sr, *Islam, Christianity and the West*, New York, 2002; R. Fletcher, *The cross and the crescent*, London, 2002; H. Goddard, *A history of Christian-Muslim relations*, Edinburgh, 2000; W.M. Watt, *Muslim-Christian encounters, perceptions and misperceptions*, London, 1991.

The experiences of Christians living under Islam are traced comprehensively by S. Griffith, *The church in the shadow of the mosque*, Princeton NJ, 2008. See also H. Teule, *Les Assyro-chaldéens*, Turnhout, 2008; I. Gillman and H.J. Klimkeit, *Christians in Asia before 1500*, Richmond, 1999; R. Le Coz, *Histoire de l'Église d'Orient. Chrétiens d'Irak, d'Iran et de Turquie*, Paris, 1995; B. Landron, *Chrétiens et musulmans en Irak. Attitudes nestoriennnes vis-à-vis de l'Islam*, Paris, 1994; S.H. Moffett, *The history of Christianity in Asia. Vol. I: Beginnings to 1500*, New York, 1992.

For Muslim attitudes towards Christianity, see J. Waardenburg, *Muslims and others. Relations in context*, Berlin, 2003; L. Ridgeon (ed.), *Islamic interpretations of Christianity*, Richmond, 2001; J. Waardenburg (ed.), *Muslim perceptions of other religions*, Oxford, 1999; A. Bouamama, *La littérature polémique musulmane contre le christianisme depuis ses origines jusqu'au XIIIe siècle*, Algiers, 1988.

are lost to time (many permanently, some perhaps waiting to be recovered), what remains shows how closely related they were, and thus suggests how vigorously they strove to accentuate their respective characters.[3] The history of this period is largely one of controversy and confrontation, though behind this lies a less aggressive story of shared living and reciprocal borrowing of both knowledge and wisdom.[4]

The beginnings of Christian-Muslim relations are, of course, to be found in the Qur'ān and life of the Prophet Muḥammad. Two essays devoted to these, and another two devoted to the commentary tradition in which the verses referring to Christianity in Muslim scripture were interpreted and reflected upon, and to the sayings attributed to Muḥammad that are either about Christianity or apparently framed on Gospel and Christian teachings, follow this Introduction. They show how close the connections were between the Prophet and his proclamation on the one hand, and on the other the Christian world that impinged on Islam in its origins.

Precisely what Muḥammad knew about Christianity and its teachings remains unclear.[5] It appears that Christians and Christian communities were very much in evidence in Arabia during his lifetime, in the coastal settlements of the Arabian Gulf, in the south from where a deputation of Christians from the town of Najrān is said to have come to him in Medina, and in the north along the borders of the Byzantine

---

A comprehensive account of Christian and other attitudes towards Muslims is to be found in R. Hoyland, *Seeing Islam as others saw it. A survey and evaluation of Christian, Jewish and Zoroastrian writings on early Islam*, Princeton NJ, 1997.

[3] For editions and studies of texts relating to the relations between the two sides, see volumes in the series *The history of Christian-Muslim relations*, ed. D. Thomas et al., Leiden, 2003-; *Eastern Christian texts*, ed. S. Griffith et al., Provo UT, 2002-; *Corpus Islamo-Christianum*, ed. L. Hagemann and R. Glei, Wiesbaden, 1987-. See also B. Roggema, M. Poorthuis and P. Valkenberg (eds), *The three rings. Textual studies in the historical trialogue of Judaism, Christianity and Islam*, Leuven, 2005; J.-M. Gaudeul, *Encounters and clashes. Islam and Christianity in history*, Rome, 1984, 2000[2]; Y.Y. Haddad and W.Z. Haddad (eds), *Christian-Muslim encounters*, Gainsville FL, 1995; S.K. Samir and J. Nielsen (eds), *Christian Arabic apologetics during the Abbasid period (750-1258)*, Leiden, 1994; N.A. Newman, *The early Christian-Muslim dialogue. A collection of documents from the first three Islamic centuries (632-900 A.D.), translations with commentary*, Hatfield PA, 1993.

[4] See C. Adang, 'Theological rationalism in the medieval world of Islam', *Medieval Encounters* (forthcoming); more generally, R.W. Bulliett, *The case for Islamo-Christian civilization*, New York, 2004, pp. 1-45.

[5] C. Gilliot, 'Reconsidering the authorship of the Qur'ān. Is the Qur'ān partly the fruit of a progressive and collective work?', in G.S. Reynolds (ed.), *The Qur'ān in its historical context*, London, 2008, 88-108.

and Sasanian empires,[6] but a Christian presence in the Ḥijāz and his native Mecca is less easy to identify. Hints in his early biography suggest immediate connections through the figure of Waraqa ibn Nawfal, his wife's cousin, and individuals he knew within the town.[7] And his assumption that Ethiopia would be a safe refuge for his most vulnerable followers away from the clutches of his Quraysh opponents in the first years of Islam is again indicative of awareness and appreciation of the people of this Christian country, but such details are no more than hints, and their full significance remains open to interpretation. Some would say they indicate considerable indebtedness to Christianity on his part, while others remain more circumspect.

It is the same with the Qurʾān. The fact that it has within it a great deal of detailed information about Christians, including monks and priests, and their beliefs about the Trinity, Incarnation and person of Jesus is undeniable. And it seems just as clear that it assumes an advanced degree of knowledge of Abraham, Moses and other biblical figures, about whom it tends to comment rather than narrate, as though contributing to an ongoing conversation concerning the meaning and importance of their deeds and words. But exactly how this relates to contemporary Christian beliefs, doctrines and teachings has long been the object of investigations that have so far not yielded much that lies beyond dispute.[8]

What cannot be disputed is that Christianity is integral to the biography of Muḥammad and to the Qurʾān, not a major element in either, maybe, but always present in both, sometimes admired and often disdained. In the centuries that followed the Prophet's death, the details gathered in these two main sources became an object of study and fuel for thought as Muslims sought ways to understand and deal with their religious neighbours.

---

[6] I. Shahīd, *Byzantium and the Arabs in the sixth century*, Washington DC, 1995.

[7] I. Shahīd, 'Islam and *Oriens Christianus*: Makka 610-622 AD', in E. Grypeou, M. Swanson and D. Thomas (eds), *The encounter of eastern Christianity with early Islam*, Leiden, 2006, 9-31.

[8] S. Griffith, 'Christian lore and the Arabic Qurʾān. The "Companions of the Cave" in *Sūrat al-kahf* and in Syriac Christian tradition', in Reynolds, *The Qurʾān in its historical context*, 109-37; S.K. Samir, 'The theological Christian influence on the Qurʾān', in Reynolds, *The Qurʾān in its historical context*, 141-62; C. Gilliot, 'Creation of a fixed text', in J.D. McAuliffe (ed.), *The Cambridge companion to the Qurʾān*, Cambridge, 2006, 41-57; H. Motzki, 'Alternative accounts of the Qurʾān's formation', in McAuliffe, *The Cambridge companion to the Qurʾān*, 59-75.

Within a hundred years from the time of Muḥammad, Muslim rule had been extended from the Arabian peninsula west through Egypt and North Africa and into Spain, north through the eastern provinces of the Byzantine Empire to the Taurus mountains, east through Mesopotamia and Persia, and on towards Central Asia and India. Extensive populations of Christians of varying Christological confessions were made subject to the caliph, and it would have become increasingly normal throughout the period covered here for Muslims to meet Christians on an almost daily basis, to have some awareness of the various ecclesiastical hierarchies, to know the churches and monasteries in their vicinity, and to have some recognition of their subjects' various beliefs and practices. It would also have been a pressing practical necessity to make arrangements for allocating a place to them within the Islamic polity.

In the two centuries or so before the time of Muḥammad the Byzantine Empire had been split by differences over Christology that the church councils of the fifth century had not only failed to settle but had actually exacerbated. Groups that rejected the conciliar formulas had been marginalized and increasingly discriminated against. This was especially the case with the Copts in Egypt and substantial parts of the Christian population in Syria, who professed a miaphysite Christology that challenged the two natures formula accepted at Chalcedon. The Christians of the Persian Empire came more and more under suspicion of being the followers of Nestorius, former bishop of Constantinople, who had been condemned at the Council of Ephesus for his outspoken diophysite Christology. Although contemporary sources record that they called themselves Nestorians, which is also the name found in Muslim treatises on Christians, the Persian Christians themselves vigorously denied allegiance to Nestorius' Christology, but in the eyes of both the followers of Chalcedon and the miaphysites they were considered as heretical. There are some hints in later sources that maybe the Syrian and Coptic miaphysites greeted the coming of Islam as a deliverance from imperial oppression, though this remains a disputed question which requires exploration in more detail. In the case of the Persian Christians, who had been persecuted by the Sasanian emperors, there were initially no strong feelings against the new Muslim conquerors, though there are also a few examples of loyalty to the Sasanian dynasty.[9]

[9] W. Baum and D. Winkler, *The church of the East. A concise history*, New York, 2003; V. Déroche, *Entre Rome et l'Islam. Les chrétientés d'orient, 610-1054*, Paris, 1996.

Other Christians appear to have looked on the seventh-century Muslim invasions as temporary, sometimes interpreting them according to biblical categories as divine punishment or signs of the end time, though also recognizing in the faith of the Muslims continuity with Old Testament forms of piety and even with Abraham.[10] But these attitudes were complemented and largely replaced by others as they became better acquainted with their new rulers, and were compelled by circumstances to see that Damascus and then Baghdad, rather than Constantinople, were the new centres to which they must look and from which their lives were regulated.

In these early centuries of Islam, more is known about encounters and mutual influence between followers of the two faiths in urban than in rural settings. There are signs that in parts of the new empire Christians were hardly aware of new rule or a new faith, apart from demands for tax. In other parts outside the cities there would be greater awareness of new landlords, though not necessarily of a significant new faith. But in the cities the story must have been rather different. Here Muslims and Christians would have encountered one another on a daily basis in commercial, professional, legal and social contexts, and would have been conscious of differences between them from an early stage. Calls to prayer by both Muslims and Christians, displays of crosses on Christian buildings, and processions on Christian holy days were open reminders and sources of friction which sometimes required the authorities to step in. But such points of clear difference may for many have been only minor irritants in lives that followed similar routines and occasioned only marginal interest in matters of divergent faith and religious observance.[11]

Muslim historians and legal theorists attributed the series of regulations that governed formal relations with Christians and other People of the Book to the second Caliph ʿUmar ibn al-Khaṭṭāb, who is supposed to have laid down the conditions for capitulation of cities taken over by his generals. The precise form that the 'Pact of ʿUmar' took in the period before 900 is not known from extant documents (see below the entry on The Pact of ʿUmar), though there can be little doubt that, as well as the specific taxes that applied, Christians, Jews and others were also obliged to keep their faith to themselves, to

[10] Griffith, *Church in the shadow of the mosque*, ch. 2.

[11] See M. Gervers and R.J. Bikhazi (eds), *Conversion and continuity. Indigenous Christian communities in Islamic lands, eighth to eighteenth centuries*, Toronto, 1990.

distinguish themselves by their dress, and to acknowledge some measure of separation from Muslims.[12] Whether or not the measures detailed were systematically enforced over periods of time, as opposed to being sporadically invoked at points of political and social crisis, they must always have served to remind the subject communities of their position, and have given cause for apprehension in interactions with their Muslim neighbors.[13] An essay devoted to Muslim legal measures towards their Christian and other client subjects, and another covering Christian legislation regarding Islam, follow this Introduction.

Despite these discriminatory measures, interactions, at least on a professional level, were frequent and presumably beneficial to both Muslims and Christians. The case of medical doctors is maybe symptomatic: by virtue of the inheritance from Hellenistic times maintained in Christian centres of learning, medicine in the Islamic world in this period was the province of Christians, and was entirely their preserve. The fact that the Bakhtīshūʿ family of Jundisābūr formed a veritable dynasty of personal physicians to a succession of caliphs serves to show how the Muslim ruler turned to a subject community for necessary expertise, and was obliged to do so because this was guarded from outside inquiry. Other professions, such as financier, apothecary and ranks within the bureaucratic service, were also typically practised by Christians.

One of the most important public services performed by Christians under both Umayyad and ʿAbbasid rule in this period was that of translating texts from Greek and Syriac into Arabic.[14] Works of

---

[12] See R. Hoyland (ed.), *Muslims and others in early Islamic society*, Aldershot, 2004, particularly the essay by A. Noth, 'Problems of differentiation between Muslims and non-Muslims, re-reading the "Ordinances of ʿUmar" (*al-shurūṭ al-ʿumariyya*)', 103-24 (first published in German in *JSAI* 9 (1987) 290-315); Y. Friedmann, *Tolerance and coercion in Islam. Interfaith relations in the Muslim tradition*, Cambridge, 2003. The earlier studies of A. Fattal, *Le statut légal des non-musulmans en pays d'Islam*, Beirut, 1958, and A.S. Tritton, *The caliphs and their non-Muslim subjects. A critical study of the covenant of ʿUmar*, London, 1930, remain important.

[13] Bat Ye'or (pseudonym), *Islam and dhimmitude. Where civilizations collide*, Madison NJ, 2002, together with the same author's earlier books, contains much relevant documentation on the position of Christians and Jews under Islam, though the accompanying interpretations bear clear anti-Islamic bias.

[14] See C. D'Ancona, 'Greek into Arabic: Neoplatonism in translation', in P. Adamson and R.C. Taylor (eds), *The Cambridge companion to Arabic philosophy*, Cambridge, 2004, 10-31; D. Gutas, *Greek thought, Arabic culture. The Graeco-Arabic translation movement in Baghdad and early ʿAbbasid society (2nd-4th/8th-10th centuries)*, London, 1998; M. Salama-Carr, *La traduction à l'époque ʿAbbaside. L'école de Hunayn ibn Ishaq et son importance pour la traduction*, Paris, 1990.

science, including astronomy, medicine and mathematics, and in addition works of philosophy, were thus made available to an Arabic-speaking readership, and became accessible at a time when they could be used to assist in formulating, refining and in part answering questions about the nature of faith and reality that were being explored in intellectual circles under Muslim patronage. And it is clear that the Christian translators of such works, among whom Ḥunayn ibn Isḥāq (d. 873) is acknowledged as the most systematic, were intimate with the people for whom they worked and collaborated closely with them. The philosopher Abū Yūsuf al-Kindī (d. 870) serves to exemplify this. He led a circle of Muslims and Christians who shared a passion for the discipline that was being called by the borrowed name *falsafa*, who cooperated on translations, and who exchanged intellectual concepts in activities of cross fertilization that maybe typified the best of interfaith cooperation in this period.[15]

Such joint efforts in intellectual striving are not far from the more confrontational exchanges that were held in formal settings in this period under the auspices of caliphs or nobles.[16] In such meetings representatives of different viewpoints, including Christian scholars and ecclesiastical leaders (as well as Jewish representatives and others), were invited to examine matters of faith from their various standpoints and expected to silence their opponents by the force of their arguments. In some respects an intellectual exercise, these meetings exemplify both the closeness between representatives of the faiths and the differences between them. It is a matter worthy of note that they were able to make use of the same argumentative logic in order to express and address points of major doctrinal disagreement.

Within the lands of the eastern caliphate, church life continued with order and even vigor. The main denominations of Chalcedonians, Syrian Orthodox and the followers of the Church of the East, known to Muslims (and also often among themselves) as Melkites, Jacobites and Nestorians, may have sought to accentuate the differences between themselves for apologetic purposes as they felt pressure from Islam to identify themselves and the beliefs they stood for.[17] And

---

[15] G. Endress, 'The circle of al-Kindī. Early Arabic translations from the Greek and the rise of Islamic philosophy', in G. Endress and R. Kruk (eds), *The ancient tradition in Christian and Islamic Hellenism*, Leiden, 1997, 43-76.

[16] H. Lazarus-Yafeh et al. (eds), *The majlis. Interreligious encounters in medieval Islam*, Wiesbaden, 1999.

[17] Griffith, *Church in the shadow of the mosque*, ch. 6.

under Islamic rule there was now some equality between them, with no one denomination enjoying government support, as had previously been the case with the Chalcedonians. But they were by no means downtrodden, and the patriarch of the Church of the East, whose residence was moved to Baghdad in early ʿAbbasid times, was a presence at court. The caliphs often took a keen interest in the election of these leading churchmen, whose support could be significant to their peaceful rule, and were occasionally drawn into the rivalries between candidates.[18] When it is considered that a number of caliphs were accustomed to spend time in monasteries, where gardens, vineyards and their produce were an attraction, it is not unlikely that they knew about ecclesiastical politics from the inside.[19]

In Egypt, the Muslim conquest of the early 640s at first worked to the advantage of the anti-Chalcedonian Copts. This is epitomized in a famous scene from *The History of the patriarchs of Alexandria*, where the Arab general, ʿAmr ibn al-ʿĀṣ, restores to his position the Coptic Patriarch Benjamin, who has spent ten years in Upper Egyptian monasteries evading agents of the Chalcedonian Emperor Heraclius (see below the entry on 'George [Jirja] the Archdeacon').[20] (While a Chalcedonian 'Melkite' community continued to exist in Egypt, it gradually declined in size and importance.) In the early centuries, periods of relative calm in relations between the Christian population and their Muslim rulers alternated with times of trial. From the point of view of the Arab authorities, Egypt was a rich prize from which wealth was to be extracted, resulting on the one hand in heavy and often onerous tax demands (which in the eighth and ninth centuries led to frequent tax revolts in which both Christians and Muslims participated), but on the other hand in an indispensable role in government bureaucracies for the Christian agricultural and financial experts who facilitated the production and flow of wealth. In such a system, the heads of *dhimmī* communities, such as the Coptic patriarch, served in the eyes of the Muslim governors principally as tax administrators – and sometimes as ready sources of funding. At key points in the history of these com-

---

[18] W.G. Young, *Patriarch, shah and caliph*, Rawalpindi, 1974.

[19] H. Kilpatrick, 'Monasteries through Muslim eyes: the *Diyārāt* books', in D. Thomas (ed.), *Christians at the heart of Islamic rule. Church life and scholarship in ʿAbbasid Iraq*, Leiden, 2003, 19-37.

[20] Later instalments within this period from *The history of the patriarchs of Alexandria* are treated in the entries on 'Yūḥannā (John) the Deacon' and 'Yūḥannā (John) the Writer'.

munities, however, important Christian individuals who served in government ministries provided resources for funds, administrative ability, and access to the highest government officials.[21]

The complexity of early Christian-Muslim relations in Egypt is reflected in the wide range of Christian assessments of the Arabs in the Coptic texts surveyed in this volume, from fairly positive to apocalyptically negative.[22] The community that is today called the Coptic Orthodox Church was shaped in decisive ways during the early Islamic period, as it assumed a specifically 'Coptic' identity and developed a rich hagiographical literature, with considerable emphasis on martyrdom, in response to the vicissitudes of life within the *Dār al-Islām* and what was, by the ninth century, more than a trickle of converts to Islam.[23]

Further west in the Iberian peninsula, the burgeoning Arab-Muslim culture of the Umayyad state in al-Andalus proved a potent attraction to Christians and other non-Muslims.[24] So much so that religious and cultural distinctions were often blurred as people sought to follow what was most fashionable in thought and physical appearance.[25] As Spain gradually changed culturally and religiously, some Latin Christians began to feel that the world they grew up in was disappearing.[26] This partly explains the phenomenon of the succession of more than 50 Christians who brought execution on themselves by publicly denying Muḥammad. Their actions have plausibly been interpreted in part as gestures against the upsurge of Islam, and as reminders to

---

[21] A good introduction to these matters is C.F. Petry (ed.), *The Cambridge history of Egypt*, i, *Islamic Egypt, 640-1517*, Cambridge, 1998. See especially the chapters by H. Kennedy, 'Egypt as a province in the Islamic caliphate, 641-868', 62-85; and T.G. Wilfong, 'The non-Muslim communities. Christian communities', 175-97. See also M.N. Swanson, *The Coptic papacy in Islamic Egypt*, Cairo, forthcoming.

[22] In addition to specific entries below, see also see the relevant sections in Hoyland, *Seeing Islam*.

[23] See A. Papaconstantinou, 'Historiography, hagiography, and the making of the Coptic "Church of the Martyrs" in early Islamic Egypt', *DOP* 60 (2006) 65-86, pp. 69-73; M.S.A. Mikhail, *Egypt from late antiquity to early Islam: Copts, Melkites, and Muslims shaping a new society*, Los Angeles CA, 2004 (Diss. University of California, Los Angeles).

[24] See A. Christys, *Christians in al-Andalus (711-1000)*, Richmond, 2002; K.B. Wolf, 'Christian views of Islam in early medieval Spain', in J. Tolan (ed.), *Medieval Christian perceptions of Islam*, New York, 1996, 85-108.

[25] See J.P. Monferrer-Sala, 'Les chrétiens d'al-Andalus et leurs manifestations culturelles', in G. Saupin et al. (eds), *La tolérance. Colloque international de Nantes, mai 1998. Quatrième centenaire de l'édit de Nantes*, Rennes, 1999, 363-70.

[26] J.P. Monferrer-Sala, 'Los cristianos arabizados de al-Andalus', in M.J. Viguera (ed.), *Historia de Andalucía. III. Andalucía en al-Andalus*, Seville, 2006, 226-34.

fellow believers of the differences between themselves and Muslims and the need to remain true to their own ways.[27] They were not the only Christian martyrs under Islam in this period,[28] but they are the best known. All in all, Christians retained their position in Andalusian Muslim society in the pre-900 period, taking part in translation work[29] as well as polemical disputes.[30] This was different from the situation after the fall of the caliphate of Cordova, when al-Andalus was gradually left without a noticeable Christian presence.

The available evidence about Christians living under Muslim rule in this period thus points, not unexpectedly, to relations that were dominated by a regulatory code according to which their lives as *Ahl al-dhimma* or *Dhimmī*s were restricted in fact or principle, but were frequently close in professional matters, where Muslims were glad to use Christian expertise and Christians were ready to give it.

There were undoubtedly conversions. Stories of members of the caliph's family becoming Christians, and even of the ʿAbbasid Caliph al-Maʾmūn (d. 833) being a covert Christian, must be treated circumspectly, but they are surely indicative of a current from Islam to Christianity. It is unlikely to have been strong, and was undoubtedly submerged beneath the flow in the other direction. The Umayyad Caliph ʿUmar II's (d. 720) order requiring his provincial governors not to prevent Christians and others converting tells an intricate story of local officials wishing to maintain tax levels by retaining the numbers of *Dhimmīs* paying them, and of the pious caliph putting faith above income. And it also suggests that conversions were inspired by financial and social considerations as much as by purely religious ones. It is very difficult to say with any accuracy what shifts from Christianity to Islam there may have been in this period beyond the fact that conversions did take place.[31] Perhaps the very vigor of controversialist writings between Christians and Muslims that is documented in this

---

[27] J.A. Coope, *The martyrs of Córdoba. Community and family conflict in an age of mass conversion*, Lincoln NE, 1995; K.B. Wolf, *Christian martyrs in Muslim Spain*, Cambridge, 1988. For an explanation of the accounts of these martyrdoms as 'literary-propaganda', see J.P. Monferrer-Sala, 'Mitografía hagiomartirial. De nuevo sobre los supuestos mártires cordobeses del siglo IX', in M. Fierro (ed.), *De muerte violenta. Política, religión y violencia en al-Andalus*, Madrid, 2004, 415-50.

[28] Griffith, *Church in the shadow of the mosque*, pp. 147-51.

[29] *Kitāb Hurūšiyūš (Traducción árabe de las Historiae adversus paganos de Orosio)*, ed. M. Penelas, Madrid, 2001.

[30] M. de Epalza, 'Notes pour une histoire des polémiques anti-chrétiennes dans l'Occident musulman', *Arabica* 18 (1971), 99-106.

[31] R. Bulliet, *Conversion to Islam in the medieval period. An essay in quantitative*

volume serves to show that Christians were by no means cowed by the circumstances in which they found themselves, but had the intellectual means and communal support to respond to questions and criticisms with confidence. They were evidently on the defensive, but they did not see themselves as at all defeated; they knew that they had to explain their faith to Muslims and to encourage fellow Christians to adhere to it, but they did so with energy, open confidence, and sometimes a measure of disdain.

Knowledge of Islam among Christians outside the Muslim world was limited. With regard to Byzantium, the relationship between the empire and Islam was marked by on-going hostilities down to the end of the ninth century. Following the Muslim conquest of Syria and Egypt in the 630s and 640s, the Umayyads even came close to destroying it. They laid siege to Constantinople several times, and their last failed attempt in 717 had the positive outcome of a mosque being built in the city. With the transfer of the capital of the caliphate to Iraq under the ʿAbbasids, this aspiration was no longer of prime importance, and was replaced by a state of continuous warfare between the two empires in the Anatolian borderlands. Only with the decline of the ʿAbbasid caliphate from the middle of the ninth century did Byzantium achieve the upper hand in this struggle.[32]

Despite these hostilities, embassies were exchanged on a regular basis, and these were not confined to negotiations over matters of war and peace. Thus, the Umayyad Caliph al-Walīd (705-15) requested Byzantine assistance in rebuilding the mosques in Medina and Damascus, a Byzantine ambassador is said to have introduced watermills in Baghdad in the second half of the eighth century, and the ʿAbbasid Caliph al-Maʾmūn (813-33) allegedly requested the Emperor Theophilus (829-42) to send the mathematician Leo the Philosopher to Baghdad in order to profit from his great learning. In addition, a kind of literary genre was formed by the various invitations of caliphs to emperors to embrace Islam, it often being the convention for such a letter to be written upon a new caliph's accession to

history, Cambridge MA, 1979, and more briefly, Bulliet, *The case for Islamo-Christian civilization*, pp. 18-24.

[32] In general see R.-J. Lilie, 'Byzanz und der Islam. Konfrontation oder Koexistenz?', in E. Piltz (ed.), *Byzantium and Islam in Scandinavia*, Jonsered, 1998, pp. 13-26; J.F. Haldon and H. Kennedy, 'The Arab-Byzantine frontier in the eighth and ninth centuries. Military organization and society in the borderlands', *Zbornik Radova Vizantoloskog Instituta* 19 (1980) 79-116.

the throne, though also on other occasions.[33] Examples are the letter written on behalf of Hārūn al-Rashīd to Constantine VI (see the entry on Ibn al-Layth), who seems to have replied to this invitation, the correspondence between Leo III and ʿUmar II (q.v.), and the letter of al-Mutawwakil to Michael III.[34]

Thus, in the course of the eighth and ninth centuries cultural and economic connections were developed, and a means of practical accommodation was established. There are even signs that Byzantium looked on the Arabs as equals of a kind. This attitude is expressed in the letter of the Patriarch of Constantinople, Nicholas Mysticus, to the emir of Crete in 908: 'There are two lordships, that of the Saracens and that of the Romans, which stand above all lordships on earth.... For this very reason alone, they ought to be in contact and brotherhood, and not, because we differ in our lives, habits and religion, remain alien in all ways to each other.'[35]

These two aspects of Byzantine-Muslim relations correspond to two different attitudes in historiographical and polemical literature. On the one hand, authors writing in the Byzantine empire, such as Theophanes (d. 818) (q.v.), adhered to the view that the infidel 'Ishmaelites' were an instrument of God's chastisement sent to punish such errors as Heraclius' espousal of monothelitism, or iconoclasm, which Theophanes regarded as a borrowing from the Umayyads. Nicetas of Byzantium (q.v.), from the latter part of the ninth century, whose works became classics of Byzantine anti-Islamic polemic, adopted an equally contemptuous attitude, and dismissed 'Maomet's Bible' as inspired by a demon.[36] And the existence of formulas of ritual abjuration for converts from Islam to Christianity (q.v.) from the mid and

---

[33] See A.T. Khoury, *Les théologiens byzantins et l'Islam. Textes et auteurs (viiie-xiiie s.)*, Louvain, 1969, pp. 200-1.

[34] C. Versteegh, 'Die Mission des Kyrillos im Lichte der arabo-byzantinischen Beziehungen', *ZDMG* 129 (1979) 233-62, p. 233 (a letter from Hārūn al-Rashīd to Nicephorus I), p. 241 (al-Mutawakkil's letter to Michael III).

[35] A. Kaplony, *Konstantinopel und Damaskus: Gesandtschaften und Verträge zwischen Kaisern und Kalifen 639-750. Untersuchungen zum Gewohnheits-Völkerrecht und zur interkulturellen Diplomatie*, Berlin, 1996; H. Kennedy, 'Byzantine-Arab diplomacy in the Near East from the Islamic conquests to the mid-eleventh century', in S. Shephard and S. Franklin (eds), *Byzantine diplomacy*, London, 1992, 133-43; N.M. El Cheikh, *Byzantium viewed by the Arabs*, Cambridge MA, 2004; *Nicholas I, Patriarch of Constantinople. Letters*, ed. and trans. R.J.H. Jenkins and L.G. Westerink, Washington DC, 1973, letter 1, 2.

[36] S. Griffith, 'Byzantium and the Christians in the world of Islam. Constantinople and the church in the Holy Land in the ninth century', *Medieval Encounters* 3 (1997) 231-65, p. 261. A.T. Khoury, *Apologétique byzantine contre l'islam (VIIIe-XIIIe. s.)*, Altenberge, 1982.

late ninth century is symptomatic of the enmity stirred up by open warfare at this time. On the other hand, day to day contact with Muslims produced a more informed and sometimes more conciliatory approach. It could be argued that John of Damascus' categorization of the new faith as a Christian heresy places it higher than Judaism or paganism, and in stories about the heroic life of the Byzantine-Muslim frontier that are transmitted in saints' lives and particularly the epic *Digenēs Akritēs*, which although later certainly contains material from the ninth and tenth centuries, Muslims are effectively accepted as equals to Christians and chivalrous opponents.[37]

In Europe north of the Pyrenees, there was little knowledge of or interest in Islam. When authors there spoke of Saracens, they usually presented them either as savage idolaters or on the contrary as quasi-Christians. After his travels to Jerusalem in the 680s, Arculf Bishop of Gaul describes the Umayyad Caliph Muʿāwiya as a quasi-Christian who recognizes Jesus as Saviour (see the entry on Adomnán of Iona). In Italy in the ninth century, papal documents present the *Saraceni* or *Agareni* as barbarous, violent, infidel invaders, responsible (among other things) for the sack of Rome in 847. Yet when one reads between the lines of the papal polemics, it becomes apparent that various southern Italian cities were forming economic and military alliances with the Aghlabids of Ifrīqiyā – and successfully resisting popes' attempts to extend their hegemony into southern Italy. The European chroniclers who described the advances of Muslim armies in Spain, Italy and Provence showed little or no interest in the religious beliefs of the invaders.

It is quite evident that Christians and Muslims began to explore the differences between them in matters of faith from an early stage.[38] For while records from the first century of encounters are relatively sparse, the first works that can be accessed in any numbers show well formed attitudes and clearly defined positions indicative of a tradition

[37] In addition to Griffith, 'Byzantium and the Christians', see also E.M. Jeffreys, 'The image of the Arabs in Byzantine literature', in *The 17th Byzantine Congress. Major papers*, New Rochelle NY, 1986, 305-23; V. Christides, 'Byzantium and the Arabs. Some thoughts on the spirit of reconciliation and cooperation', in A. Hohlweg (ed.), *Byzanz und seine Nachbarn*, Munich, 1996, 131-42.

[38] Griffith, *Church in the shadow of the mosque*, pp. 35-44. The topics of controversialist encounters are summarized in P. Khoury, *Matériaux pour servir à l'étude de la controverse théologique islamo-chrétienne de langue arabe du VIIIe au XIIe siècle*, 6 vols (vol. 6 has 3 parts), Würzburg and Altenberge (vol. 6, parts 2 and 3 publ. Altenberge), 1989-2002.

of arguments in which the main issues were already identified and the respective positions already established. They show that followers of the two faiths had explored the possibilities and problems between them and had seen what could and could not be agreed.

Put simply, a not atypical Christian attitude towards Islam in the pre-900 period was that it was a spurious message invented by a self-seeking miscreant. This was based on the tacit assumption that in Jesus Christ was to be found the last and all-sufficient revelation from God, so that anything claimed as a fresh revelation afterwards must be wrong and criminally intended. Such a message was obviously unpalatable to Muslims, and it is not surprising that in this period the most scathing criticisms of Muḥammad and the Qurʾān were written either in Greek, which few if any Muslims could read, or under a pseudonym, which would safeguard anonymity. The authors whose works are preserved in Arabic, while denying Muslim claims about Muḥammad, often found diplomatic ways of attributing to him some goodness and divine recognition. This is maybe best exemplified in the celebrated remark of the Patriarch Timothy I (q.v.) before the Caliph al-Mahdī in their meeting in 782-83, that Muḥammad 'walked in the path of the prophets, and trod in the track of the lovers of God', a two-edged judgement that could be taken as approval but was almost certainly not intended as simple endorsement.[39]

These Christian rejections of Islam must be situated within an extensive literature that reflects attempts to defend Christian doctrines and to explain them to Muslim minds. It shows that Christians were placed on the defensive as Muslim reflection on the Qurʾān, allied with principles that had become accessible through translations of works from the Greek, and stimulated or maybe influenced by encounters with Christian concepts and argumentative techniques,[40] caused them to elaborate their own theological thinking and evolve clear principles of faith. Thus, for example, while in previous times Christians had been accustomed to discussing how God was triune and how his divinity became incarnate in Christ, now they were being made to explain whether these two doctrines of the Trinity and

[39] See S.K. Samir, 'The Prophet Muḥammad as seen by Timothy I and some other Arab Christian authors', in D. Thomas (ed.), *Syrian Christians under Islam. The first thousand years*, Leiden, 2001, 75-106.

[40] For a concise account of differing views about Christian influence on theological thinking in Islam, see G.S. Reynolds, *A Muslim theologian in the sectarian milieu. ʿAbd al-Jabbār and the critique of Christian origins*, Leiden, 2004, pp. 21-28.

Incarnation were logically viable, and how God could rationally be portrayed in these ways.

There are clear signs that, from the early ninth century onwards, Christian theologians who were born Arabic speakers and knew the currency of Muslim theological debate accepted the challenge presented by their counterparts, and in partly defensive, partly creative employment of concepts and methods native to Muslim theological debate demonstrated how their main doctrines were not only viable in the terms agreed but also inescapable if reason was to be maintained. In some ways the explanations of these Arab Christians amount to new theology as they capitalized upon the logic they borrowed to maintain the beliefs and understandings of faith they had inherited.[41]

While making use of ideas and methods from Islamic theological thought, Christian theologians continued to employ methods of explanation inherited from the past. Metaphors of the Trinity and Incarnation that Church Fathers of old had honed recur in many works (and prove easy targets for Muslim opponents), and biblical texts familiar from pre-Islamic times also appear for support and confirmation. What Muslims would have made of these is seriously open to question, though to Christians who read them they would have provided encouragement from ancient and unimpeachable authorities, and confirmation that their faith could be upheld in new circumstances by teachings that had stood the test of time.

Christians used not only the Bible in defence of their beliefs but also on occasion the Qurʾān, judiciously interpreted according to their own dogmatic principles.[42] But this made little impression on Muslims who by ʿAbbasid times, at least, had established on the basis of the Qurʾān that the scriptures currently held by Christians and Jews were not the original messages revealed to Jesus and Moses but corrupt forms of these. Christians presented arguments against such accusations, often pointing out that the wide geographical distribution of the texts of their scripture, among which was uniformity, prohibited any

[41] See Griffith, *Church in the shadow of the mosque*, pp. 60-68; and also collected articles on this theme by Griffith, *The beginnings of Christian theology in Arabic. Muslim-Christian encounters in the early Islamic period*, Aldershot, 2002. See also S. Rissanen, *Theological encounter of Oriental Christians with Islam during early Abbasid rule*, Åbo, Finland, 1993.

[42] See S.H. Griffith, 'The Qurʾān in Arab Christian texts. The development of an apologetical argument: Abū Qurrah in the *majlis* of al-Maʾmūn', *Pd'O* 24 (1999) 203-33.

centralized conspiracy to make changes, but to little avail. The Bible proved a risky text to use in debate.

Muslims, for their part, appear to have come to a set of attitudes towards Christians and their faith at an early stage. To the extent that this is articulated in polemical literature, it began with the Bible, or specifically the Gospel. Some authors implied that, while the text itself remained unaffected by time, Christian interpretations had distorted its true meaning and laid over it doctrines that a proper reading could not sustain. And they often proceeded to show how the Bible, when it was read without presuppositions, actually supported the Qur'ān-based view of Jesus and God, and also looked to the coming of Islam. Others took a more dismal view – that the text itself was corrupt. One of these, Abū ʿUthmān al-Jāḥiẓ (d. 869) (q.v.), explained that not all the authors of the historical Gospels had actually known Jesus and may have lied in what they wrote, and others pointed to the apostle Paul as a wilful perverter of Christian origins.

On the basis of their belief that Christian scripture had been misused or misrepresented, Muslims pointed to the main Christian doctrines of the Trinity and Incarnation as misguided portrayals of God and of his way of relating to the world. Clearly guided by their own Qur'ān-based doctrine of strict monotheism, theological minds often went to great lengths to expose logical shortcomings and incoherences in these doctrines, subjecting them to extensive analyses based on general principles of rationality. It is difficult to be clear about the major theological trends in Muslim examinations of Christian beliefs in the pre-900 period, though if the works that survive are at all typical, it appears that these two doctrines were the main subject of Muslim refutations of Christianity.

The difficulty in being clear about Muslim theological attitudes in this period arises from the fact that only a tiny fraction of the works that are known to have been written during this time actually survive. More or less every Muslim theological thinker of note from the eighth and ninth centuries is credited with a work against Christianity, as well as one or more other faiths, though nearly all of these have been lost. But if they, or the majority of them, resembled the surviving works from this and succeeding centuries in focussing on the two main Christian doctrines and paying considerably less attention to the atonement or other key Christian beliefs, they suggest a particular attitude on the part of Muslim theologians towards Christianity.

This was that it primarily served to show what could happen when the central truths of religion were ignored: notions became distorted and fell into logical disarray and disorder. Thus, writings about Christianity would have served to warn Muslims about the alternatives to *tawḥīd*, the absolute monotheism stressed at this time, and the dangers of transgressing it, as much as to show Christians the aberrance of their faith. Polemic and apologetic were intimately intertwined.

A major theme alongside this heavy emphasis upon Christian doctrine and the corruption of scripture was the insistence upon the Qurʾān-based narrative of salvation featuring chosen messengers sent with revealed messages to different communities and all pointing to the coming of Muḥammad. Muslims made strenuous efforts to show how biblical books actually foretold him and his community, if only they were read aright, and also wrote in defence of his prophetic claims, pointing to the progress of history and of his own character and miraculous acts.

The 'proofs of prophethood' literature became an identifiable genre in the eighth and ninth centuries, and the surviving examples show that a significant element, maybe the most significant element, behind its inception was the desire to prove the claims of Muḥammad to non-Muslims, particularly Christians.[43] Connected to this was a motif that occurs in this period and recurs in many works from later centuries, which was to meet Christian claims that Jesus' divinity is proved by his miracles with similar examples from the actions of other biblical figures for whom Christians make no comparable claims. The information that fed such comparisons must have come from Christians or former Christians themselves, and provides an example among others of the degree of intellectual intimacy sometimes attained between followers of the two faiths. Of course, this did not prevent harsh disagreements, either of the doctrinal kind referred to above, or of a more spiritual kind, such as over the Christian customs of facing east in prayer, kissing icons, honouring saints' bones or venerating the cross.

Given that there was intimacy of a kind, it would follow that Christian and Muslim theologians influenced each other. Whether the kind

[43] See Reynolds, *A Muslim theologian in the sectarian milieu*, pp. 178-83; C. Adang, *Muslim writers on Judaism & the Hebrew Bible from Ibn Rabban to Ibn Hazm*, Leiden, 1996, pp. 139-91.

of Muslim theological thinking that came into flower in this period under the leadership of mainly Muʿtazilī minds was influenced in its formation by Christians, or whether this new thinking was stimulated and challenged to elaborate its own character by encounters between religious thinkers from the two faiths, remains a matter of debate. But whatever the involvement of Christians, either as teachers or stimulators, it is difficult not to see any involvement at all. The very forms of Muslim theological argumentative presentation reflecting the question and answer style of Syriac antecedents testify to this.[44]

But it is not only a matter of Muslims following Christians in the development of the form and content of theological debates. The Arabic-speaking Christian theologians who in the early ninth century took up the challenge of articulating their doctrines in language and forms that Muslims would appreciate are examples of Christians responding to Muslim leads. And maybe the move from the former languages of intellectual and religious discourse, Greek and Syriac, to Arabic is another clear sign of the ascendancy of Islam and the impossibility of Christians remaining indifferent to it. This move happened at different rates among Christian in different parts of the Islamic world, but by the middle of the ninth century it had clearly gathered sufficient pace for the demand for Arabic translations of the Bible to be acutely felt in many parts of the Islamic empire. It has long been argued that Christian scripture was available in Arabic at an early stage, even before Islam, though in the absence of the necessary evidence this has not gained widespread acceptance.[45] Nevertheless, the need for Arabic scriptures in Christian communities in the ninth century is expressive of a shift that proved unchangeable. The dominance of Islamic Arab culture was palpable, and just as Muslims could not ignore Christians, neither could Christians ignore Muslims. Their dogmatic stances led them to hostility and confrontation, while their intellectual and cultural attainments led them to a measure of collaboration and sharing. The latter part of this period, when Christians still retained cultural and intellectual confidence, and Muslims

---

[44] See M. Cook, 'The origins of *kalām*', *BSOAS* 43 (1980) 32-43.

[45] The standard study on this remains S.H. Griffith, 'The Gospel in Arabic. An inquiry into its appearance in the first Abbasid century', *Oriens Christianus* 69 (1985) 126-67. See also S.H. Griffith, 'From Aramaic to Arabic. The languages of the monasteries of Palestine in the Byzantine and early Islamic periods', *DOP* 51 (1997) 11-31 (repr. in Griffith, *The beginnings of Christian theology in Arabic*, X).

increasingly discovered confidence in their own genius, was thus a time of sharing and of boundary setting. In later times the sharing sadly diminished to vanishing point, while the boundaries and the images of the other beyond those that were first set in this period persisted and grew with menacing vigor.

Christians and Christianity in the Qurʾān

Jaakko Hämeen-Anttila

For Muslims, who regard the Qurʾān as the Word of God, the possibility of any human influence on it is excluded, and the question of Christian presence in the Arabian peninsula in the early seventh century is irrelevant for understanding its origins or contents. On the other hand, early Western authors often dismissed it without further analysis as no more than a concoction of materials taken from Christian and Jewish sources.[1]

More serious study of the Qurʾān in the West was given impetus in the nineteenth century by T. Nöldeke's *Geschichte des Qorāns*, published in 1860.[2] Since then, the qurʾānic references to Christianity and Christians have been closely studied, often in connection with the traditional accounts of the life of Muḥammad. Similarities between the Qurʾān and Christian works have led scholars to speculate on the Prophet's possible Christian sources, informants or environment.[3]

---

[1] But see T. Burman, *Reading the Qurʾān in Latin Christendom, 1140-1560*, Philadelphia PA, 2007, for a demonstration of the impartiality and sensitivity with which medieval Christian translators often approached the text.

[2] Later, Nöldeke, with his students F. Schwally (Parts I-II), and G. Bergsträsser and O. Pretzl (Part III), completely reworked the book for a second German edition, which remains an irreplaceable tool for qurʾānic studies: T. Nöldeke, *Geschichte des Qorāns*, 3 vols, Leipzig, 1909-38.

[3] The current state of qurʾānic studies has been reviewed in several recent articles. Especially noteworthy are those collected in G.S. Reynolds (ed.), *The Qurʾān in its historical context*, London, 2008. J.D. McAuliffe (ed.), *The Cambridge companion to the Qurʾān*, Cambridge, 2006, and A. Rippin (ed.), *The Blackwell companion to the Qurʾān*, Oxford, 2006, also contain useful articles. Several articles in the *EQ* are also relevant, especially S. Griffith's 'Christians and Christianity'. The three collections of articles edited by Ibn Warraq, *The origins of the Koran*, 1998; *What the Koran really says. Language, text, and commentary*, 2002; *The quest for the historical Muhammad*, 2006 (all published in Amherst NY) contain useful reprints of earlier, and some more recent, articles in an easily available form. The introductions by Ibn Warraq are also useful, although not as well informed as the articles in Reynolds' *Qurʾān*. They also tend to favor revisionist viewpoints.

On the question of Christian, or Jewish, informants of Muḥammad, see also C. Gilliot, 'Les "informateurs" juifs et chrétiens de Muḥammad. Reprise d'un problème traité par Aloys Sprenger et Theodor Nöldeke', *JSAI* 22 (1998) 84-126, and also his 'Le Coran,

The term used for Christians is *Naṣārā* (sing. *Naṣrānī*), mostly in connection with, or in contrast to, *Hūd* or *Yahūd*, 'Jews'. The term probably derives from the Syriac *Naṣrāyē* ('Christians'), but it may also have been associated with Nazareth and with the Arabic etymology of the radicals *n.ṣ.r.*: in Q 61:14 the disciples identify themselves as 'the helpers of God' (*anṣār Allāh*).[4] The later term *Masīḥī* is not used in the Qur'ān, but Christ is frequently called *al-Masīḥ*.[5] Very often both Jews and Christians are grouped under the general term *ahl al-kitāb*, 'People of the (holy) book'. All these terms come mainly in the sūras traditionally dated to the Medinan period. In earlier, Meccan sūras Christian presence is hardly felt, except in Medinan additions. On qur'ānic evidence, it would seem that the environment of the first sūras was not infused with Christianity.[6]

In the Qur'ān, it is often difficult to distinguish between polemics against polytheists and polemics against Christians who believe in

---

fruit d'un travail collectif?', in D. de Smet, G. de Callatay and J.M.F. van Reeth (eds), *Al-Kitāb. La sacralité du texte dans le monde de l'islam*, Brussels, 2004, 185-231. For the Qur'ān in general, see also N. Robinson, *Discovering the Qur'an. A contemporary approach to a veiled text*, London, 1996. For Muḥammad, see also H. Motzki (ed.), *The biography of Muḥammad. The issue of the sources*, Leiden, 2000.

[4] For the etymology of the term, see Griffith, art. 'Christians'. For an attempt to connect it with the Nazoraeans, see most recently F. de Blois, 'Naṣrānī (Nazōraios) and ḥanīf (ethnikos): Studies on the religious vocabulary of Christianity and of Islam', *BSOAS* 65 (2002) 1-30. For an earlier bibliography, see A. Jeffery, *The foreign vocabulary of the Qur'ān*, Baroda, 1938, pp. 280-81. The standard study of Christians in the Qur'ān and its commentaries is J.D. McAuliffe, *Qur'ānic Christians. An analysis of classical and modern exegesis*, Cambridge, 1991. Of more limited value are the first chapters of H. Goddard, *A history of Christian-Muslim relations*, Edinburgh, 2000.

[5] Christ is also called *al-Masīḥ ibn Maryam*, or *al-Masīḥ ʿĪsā ibn Maryam*. It is not clear whether *al-Masīḥ* was understood as a personal name or an epithet. It seems probable that the term is not used in a clearly defined sense in the Qur'ān: the first audience may well have been uncertain about its meaning.

[6] It should be emphasized that biographical passages speaking of Muḥammad's early contacts with Christians aim at showing that he was accepted as a prophet by Christians who might be regarded as authorities (Waraqa ibn Nawfal, the monk Baḥīrā, etc.). Their historical accuracy is questionable. Likewise, references to the images of Jesus and Mary in the sanctuary of the Kaʿba are doubtful. The origins of the sanctuary as a place of monotheistic worship were an issue, and to prove it later theologically motivated commentators sought testimonials to support their claims. For a study of these images, see S. Bashear, 'The images of Mecca: a case-study in early Muslim iconography', *Le Muséon* 105 (1992) 361-77. For an attempt to see the early career of Muḥammad in terms of Arabian paganism, see J. Hämeen-Anttila, 'Arabian prophecy', in M. Nissinen (ed.), *Prophecy in its ancient Near Eastern context*, Atlanta GA, 2000, 115-46.

God having a son, as for example in *Sūrat al-ikhlāṣ* (112.). After Arab paganism lost its relevance, these passages came to be seen as references to Christians. The general nature of references to Christianity should be kept in mind when analyzing the possible theological meaning of qurʾānic passages relating to Christianity. In a text which does not clearly distinguish between Jews and Christians, fine theological distinctions should not be expected.[7]

In one instance, Q 5:47, the Qurʾān uses a specific term *Ahl al-Injīl*, 'People of the Gospel', to denote Christians. Other terms related to Christianity are *al-ḥawāriyyūn*, 'the disciples' or 'the apostles' (of Jesus), and *ruhbān*, 'monks', with the abstract noun *rahbāniyya* (Q 57:27 'monasticism'). None of the uses of these terms suggests close familiarity with Christianity. The term *ḥanīf*, occurring in the singular or plural (*ḥunafāʾ*), seems to refer to some kind of Abrahamic proto-monotheism in the qurʾānic worldview. Its connection to the Syriac term *ḥanpē*, 'pagan', 'renegade', is a matter of some controversy.[8]

Most commonly, Christian themes come up in the Qurʾān through the persons of Jesus and Mary.[9] As with other qurʾānic narratives, their stories are told in general, as if referring to something already known to the audience. It is probable that the main outline of Jesus' life was common knowledge in the Arabian peninsula, although one cannot rule out the possibility that the qurʾānic revelations were supplemented by oral explanations, or that the interest in religious questions was heightened, particularly in Mecca, because of the activity of the Prophet, or that the activity of the Prophet was triggered by such a heightened interest.

Jesus is defined as a prophet and messenger (Q 5:75) and as a man, not as the Son of God (e.g. Q 3:59). These two extremes define the limits of all later Islamic teachings concerning him. Christian doctrines

---

[7] See also S.K. Samir, 'The theological Christian influence on the Qurʾān, a reflection', in Reynolds, *Qurʾān*, 141-62.

[8] A good overall discussion of the term is found in C. Gilliot, 'Muḥammad, Le Coran et les "contraintes de l'histoire"', in S. Wild (ed.), *The Qurʾan as text*, Leiden, 1996, 3-26.

[9] For Jesus in the Qurʾān, see G. Parrinder, *Jesus in the Qurʾān*, London, 1965; H. Räisänen, *Das koranische Jesusbild*, Helsinki, 1971; N. Robinson, *Christ in Islam and Christianity*, Albany NY, 1991; J. Hämeen-Anttila, *Jeesus, Allahin profeetta*, Helsinki, 1998; and T. Khalidi, *The Muslim Jesus. Sayings and stories in Islamic literature*, Cambridge MA, 2001. Mary is also discussed in several of these sources, in addition to which, see (though it is somewhat unsatisfactory), S.A. Mourad, 'Mary in the Qurʾān. A reexamination of her presentation', in Reynolds, *Qurʾān*, 163-74.

about Jesus are explicitly refuted: he is not the third of three (Q 5:73) nor God (Q 5:17), nor was he crucified (Q 4:157).[10] The Qur'ān says very little about his ministry as a teacher and healer (Q 3:49, 5:110), centering instead on his miraculous birth and his last days. What falls between these two are rather stereotyped sayings, thematically common to other qur'ānic prophets as well, and not specifically Christian or specific to the Islamic Jesus.[11]

References to Christian history are also sparse. The story of the Seven Sleepers, which was well-known in late Antiquity, is told in *Sūrat al-kahf* (18:9-26), but it falls under the heading of folklore more than religion properly speaking.[12] The identification of *aṣḥāb al-ukhdūd*, 'the people of the trench' (Q 85:4) with the murderers of the martyrs of Najrān in the incident that is dated to 523, is less than certain. The single reference to Byzantines (*al-Rūm*) in Q 30:2, *ghulibat al-Rūm*, 'the Byzantines have been defeated', sums up the documented knowledge in the Qur'ān of the Christian world. And even here there is no complete clarity because, while the standard reading suggests this passage is pro-Byzantine, there is a variant, *ghalabat al-Rūm*, 'the Byzantines have defeated', which turns the tables, making the passage anti-Byzantine and, hence, anti-Christian. This ambivalence symbolizes the general situation in the Qur'ān.

Read synchronically, the Qur'ān seems remarkably undecided as to how to view Christians. Jesus, his disciples and Mary are sympathetic characters but in Islamicized garb. Monks are regarded positively in Q 5:82, but together with monasticism, they are criticized in other verses (Q 9:31-34). The same ambivalence is exhibited towards Christians in general. In Q 2: 62, they are promised a reward in the afterlife –

[10] Q 5:17 has often been overinterpreted. Nothing implies that Muḥammad had detailed knowledge of Christian theology, and the sentence *inna Allāha huwa l-Masīḥ* seems best understood as a topicalization of *Allāh*, not as a refined theological statement. For the purposes of modern religious dialogue, there have been attempts to show that it is not necessary to interpret Q 4:157 as explicitly denying the crucifixion, though on philological grounds this is improbable.

[11] See J. Hämeen-Anttila, 'Sayings recontextualized: Jesus' teachings in Islamic tradition', in A. Laato and J. van Ruiten (eds), *Rewritten Bible reconsidered*, Åbo, 2008, 271-87.

[12] Most recently studied by S. Griffith, 'Christian lore and the Arabic Qur'ān. The "Companions of the Cave" in Sūrat al-kahf and in Syriac Christian tradition', in Reynolds, *Qur'ān*, 109-37. For a similar study of Syriac legendary material in the Qur'ān, see K. van Bladel, 'The Alexander legend in the Qur'ān 18:83-102', in Reynolds, *Qur'ān*, 175-203.

the passage has sometimes been taken to show Christianity as a religion leading to salvation, though the standard interpretation does not favor this – but in Q 9:29 the believers are exhorted to fight them until they pay the *jizya*.[13]

This ambivalence may be due in part to a development in Muḥammad's relations with Christians. Passages which discuss Jews and Christians seem to fall chronologically into a scheme where both religions are first viewed in positive terms; then later Jews start to be criticized and, finally, this critique extends to Christians as well. Such a scheme should not be taken too rigidly, however, but only as a rough outline of the development. The difficulties in dating qur'ānic verses, even relatively, should not be underestimated.

That the Qur'ān was revealed in a context where Christianity was known is proved beyond doubt by its contents and by its vocabulary, which contains a large number of lexemes of Syriac and Geʿez origin.[14] This has led to speculation concerning the strength and exact nature of the Christian influence. Perhaps the most influential early study was that of R. Bell.[15] In recent decades, some attempts have been made

[13] Note that in the Qur'ān only Jews, not Christians, are accused of corrupting the Scripture (*taḥrīf*).

[14] Rather surprisingly, there is no satisfactory etymological dictionary of the Qur'ān. Jeffery's *Foreign vocabulary*, was a valiant effort but is now outdated. M.R. Zammitt, *A comparative lexical study of qur'ānic Arabic*, Leiden, 2002, is merely a list of words with possible Semitic equivalences. A.A. Ambros, *A concise dictionary of Koranic Arabic*, Wiesbaden, 2004, and E.M. Badawi and M.A. Haleem, *Arabic-English dictionary of qur'anic usage*, Leiden, 2008, contain little new etymological material. Other existing dictionaries of the Qur'ān are also far from satisfactory. See in addition A. Mingana, 'Syriac influence on the style of the Koran', *Bulletin of the John Rylands Library* 11 (1927) 77-98.

[15] R. Bell, *The origin of Islam in its Christian environment*, Edinburgh, 1926. The spread of Christianity in the area of Arabia has been researched, among others, by I. Shahīd in a series of studies: *Byzantium and the Arabs in the fourth century*, Washington DC, 1984; *Byzantium and the Arabs in the fifth century*, Washington DC, 1989; *Byzantium and the Arabs in the sixth century*, 3 vols, Washington DC, 1995-2002 (in progress); 'Islam and *Oriens Christianus*', in E. Grypeou et al. (eds), *The encounter of eastern Christianity with early Islam*, Leiden, 2006. See also J.S. Trimingham, *Christianity among the Arabs in pre-Islamic times*, London, 1979; R. Hoyland, *Arabia and the Arabs from the Bronze Age to the coming of Islam*, London, 2001; J. Retsö, *The Arabs in Antiquity*, London, 2003; T. Hainthaler, *Christliche Araber vor dem Islam*, Louvain, 2007. For the Jewish environment, see G.D. Newby, *A history of the Jews of Arabia*, Columbia SC, 1988, and M. Lecker, *Muslims, Jews and pagans. Studies on early Islamic Medina*, Leiden, 1995. For Jewish influence on the Qur'ān, see A. Katsch, *Judaism in Islam*, New York, 1954, and C.C. Torrey, *Jewish foundations of Islam*, New York, 1967.

to find radically new contextualizations for the birth of Islam. These attempts should be seen in the light of a general uneasiness with the received history of early Islam. The self-repeating Islamic historiography long held a place as uncontested fact until studies by I. Goldziher, J. Schacht, A. Noth and others showed that the Islamic tradition tends to harmonize and simplify earlier reports that were originally variegated and even contradictory. The credibility of Islamic historiography was undermined by these scholars, and since the 1970s their work has led to various revisionist views of the events in the seventh century. This revisionist scholarship has been represented most notably by J. Wansbrough, P. Crone and M. Cook,[16] who see Islam as developing in an environment radically different from that which traditional history claims. For Wansbrough, the polemical style of many passages in the Qur'ān shows that the text was born in an environment professing Christianity (and Judaism). This sectarian milieu is the real environment of the qur'ānic text which he sees slowly developing into what it is today, finding its final form only in the ninth century. Likewise, Crone and Cook move the setting of nascent Islam from the Arabian peninsula to the area of Greater Syria and Iraq. Their work is based on a close reading of non-Muslim literary sources and the use of admittedly scanty archaeological evidence. Both the strength and weakness of their proposal lie in a complete change of viewpoint: instead of Muslim literary sources, which they declare are radically untrustworthy, they turn to the independent, but meagre, non-Muslim tradition.

G. Lüling started working with the Qur'ān in the 1960s. His main thesis has been that the present text is a palimpsest which still shows traces of pre-Islamic Christian hymns. Lüling sees the Qur'ān as consisting of four partly overlapping levels: remnants of a strophic Christian hymnal; parts of the same as edited and Islamicized in Muḥammad's time; Islamic material composed in Muḥammad's time; and, lastly, a post-Muḥammad edition of the earlier levels, detecting this by adhering to the *rasm*, or the bare consonantal form without

[16] J. Wansbrough, *Qur'ānic studies. Sources and methods of scriptural interpretation*, Oxford, 1977; J. Wansbrough, *The sectarian milieu. Content and composition of Islamic salvation history*, Oxford, 1978, reprinted, Amherst NY, 2006; P. Crone and M. Cook, *Hagarism. The making of the Islamic world*, Cambridge, 1977. For a discussion of Wansbrough, see the articles in H. Berg (ed.), 'Islamic origins reconsidered: John Wansbrough and the study of early Islam', *Method and Theory in the Study of Religion* 9/1 (special issue), 1997.

diacritics, but modifying the readings within the limits imposed by this *rasm*.[17]

In order to reconstruct parts of the earlier levels, Lüling tackles passages in the Qurʾān which are difficult to understand in their present form, and re-reads them by redefining the meaning of crucial words with the help of Arabic, or even Semitic, meanings of the root and, when necessary, ignoring the vowels and the diacritical signs and conjuring new meanings from the *rasm*. This heuristic method produces what he believes to be fragments of Christian liturgical texts, datable to about a century before Muḥammad, buried under later layers. He also claims that the Arabian peninsula was heavily Christianized in Muḥammad's time, and that traces of this Christian Arabia were only later effaced. The pre-Islamic Christian community was divided into Unitarians and Trinitarians, and the qurʾānic references to *mushrik*s ('associationists', usually understood to refer to contemporary pagans) should be read as criticizing the Trinitarians. He also interprets the pagan gods and goddesses of the tradition as references to a Christian cult of saints, identifying, among others, the three 'daughters' of *Allāh* in the Qurʾān (Q 53:19-21) as local manifestations of the Virgin Mary. But his failure to address the question of why the frequent invocations of these goddesses in pre-Islamic inscriptions are never accompanied by the use of Christian symbolism is indicative of an unwillingness to discuss contrary evidence, and this lessens the credibility of his studies.

Lüling's work has been noted in the scholarly world, but his results have failed to gain general acceptance.[18] Less attention has been paid to the Arabic works of J. Azzi, partially translated into French.[19] Azzi

[17] See especially his *Über den Ur-Qurʾān. Ansätze zur Rekonstruktion vorislamischer christlicher Strophenlieder im Qurʾān*, Erlangen 1974; *Der christliche Kult an der vorislamischen Kaaba*, Erlangen, 1977; *Die Wiederentdeckung des Propheten Muhammad. Eine Kritik am "christlichen" Abendland*, Erlangen, 1981; *A challenge to Islam for reformation. The rediscovery and reliable reconstruction of a comprehensive pre-Islamic Christian hymnal hidden in the Koran under earliest Islamic reinterpretations*, Delhi, 2003, the last being the modified English version of Lüling, *Ur-Qurʾān*.

[18] For a dispassionate but mildly favorable evaluation, see Ibn Rawandi (pseudonym), 'On Pre-Islamic Christian strophic te[x]ts in the Koran. A critical look at the work of Günter Lüling,' in Ibn Warraq, *What the Koran really says*, 653-710. See also reviews of his books by G.R. Hawting, *JSS* 27 (1982) 108-12, S. Günther, *Al-Qantara* 16 (1995) 485-89, and M. Rodinson, *Der Islam* 54, (1977) 321-25.

[19] Abū Mūsā l-Ḥarīrī (= J. Azzi), *Nabī l-raḥma*, Beirut, 1990; *Qass wa-nabī*, Beirut, 1991; and J. Azzi, *Le prêtre et le Prophète*, trans. from Arabic M.S. Garnier, Paris, 2001.

has endeavored to link Islam with the Ebionites. In brief, he sees Waraqa ibn Nawfal as the priestly leader of a Meccan Ebionite community, who chose Muḥammad as his successor. While Azzi is not without scholarly predecessors in claiming a link between early Islam and the Ebionites,[20] his theory suffers from a selective reading of the sources, which undermines his credibility.

On a more scholarly level, Y.D. Nevo, partly in collaboration with J. Koren, has proposed another radical model for the birth of Islam. His main thesis is that Islam evolved slowly in a situation where a major part of the population remained pagan but the ruling élite was monotheistic in a primitive, Judaeo-Christian way (cf. *ḥanīf*). Nevo's theory is partly based on controversial archaeological evidence.[21]

In his 1999 monograph, G.R. Hawting also tackles the term *shirk*, 'associationism', 'idolatry'.[22] Like Lüling, but on firmer philological ground, Hawting sees internal monotheist polemics lurking behind the use of this term, but in contrast to Lüling, he situates this in a Mesopotamian, rather than a Ḥijāzian, environment.[23] His main idea is that the terms *shirk* and *mushrik* were originally used polemically against fellow monotheists but were later misunderstood as references to polytheists, and the whole run of events was reinterpreted as having taken place on the Arabian peninsula. Hawting's book is full of insightful and well-documented ideas, even for those who cannot agree with his main theory.

Very much in the same vein as Azzi and Lüling is the latest sensational study of the Qur'ān by the pseudonymous C. Luxenberg.[24]

---

[20] Bell, *Origin*; C.D.G. Müller, *Kirche und Mission unter den Arabern in vorislamischer Zeit*, Tübingen, 1967; M.P. Roncaglia, 'Éléments Ébionites et Elkésaites dans le Coran', *Proche-Orient Chrétien* 21 (1971) 101-26; and Trimingham, *Christianity*.

[21] See Y.D. Nevo and J. Koren, 'Methodological approaches to Islamic studies', *Der Islam* 68 (1991) 87-107; Y.D. Nevo, 'Towards a prehistory of Islam', *JSAI* 17 (1994) 108-41; and Y.D. Nevo and J. Koren, *Crossroads to Islam. The origins of the Arab religion and the Arab state*, Amherst NY, 2003.

[22] G.R. Hawting, *The idea of idolatry and the emergence of Islam. From polemic to history*, Cambridge, 1999.

[23] P. Crone, *Meccan trade and the rise of Islam*, Oxford, 1987, effectively shows that the role played by Mecca in early and pre-Islamic times is in need of re-evaluation.

[24] See C. Luxenberg, *Die Syro-Aramäische Lesart des Koran. Ein Beitrag zur Entschlüsselung der Koransprache*, Berlin, 2000, Köthen, 2007^3. English version: *The Syro-Aramaic reading of the Koran. A contribution to the decoding of the language of the Koran*, Köthen, 2007.

Luxenberg[25] explains that his aim has been to clarify the obscure passages in the Qurʾān. This he does by first referring to the classical commentary by al-Ṭabarī and to the dictionary *Lisān al-ʿarab*. Next, he studies homonymous roots in Syro-Aramaic. If these do not shed additional light, he tries to find a suitable meaning for the Arabic word by changing its diacritical marks and, if necessary, again looking for possible Syro-Aramaic roots. This failing, he translates the Arabic 'back' into Syro-Aramaic and peruses Classical Syriac dictionaries for this purpose and, as a last resort, tries considering the Arabic orthography as misread Karshūnī, i.e., Arabic written in Syriac characters. According to these methods, virtually any passage of the Qurʾān is open to new interpretations. The semantic ranges of both Arabic and Syro-Aramaic roots are considerable, and taking into account the similar-looking consonants, without their diacritics, any Arabic word can easily be read as Syriac, with a satisfactory meaning to the text. The book would be better discussed within the framework of Muslim-Christian polemics.[26]

The present state of qurʾānic studies is, in a sense, postmodern. After the initial shock of the 1970s, when it was fully realized that the traditional sources cannot always be relied upon, the scholarly world has started building the image anew, now giving full attention to non-Muslim literary sources, archaeological evidence, and linguistic analysis. It is obvious that the more sensational attempts are failures. Yet it is also clear that a new picture is emerging, and will become clearer when improbable or impossible alternatives are ruled out and the traditional history is tested against independent sources.

Perhaps the least extensively studied group of sources is, rather surprisingly, the corpus of non-religious and non-historical Arabic texts, especially poetry, which has its own serious problems concerning authenticity and dating, yet is to a large extent free of religious

[25] Luxenberg, *Lesart*, pp. 23-30 (= *Reading*, pp. 22-29).

[26] Luxenberg and his supporters have also published three collected volumes of articles, all printed in Berlin, viz. C. Burgmer (ed.), *Streit um den Koran. Die Luxenberg-Debatte: Standpunkte und Hintergründe*, 2004, 2007[3]; K.-H. Ohlig and G.-R. Puin (eds), *Die dunklen Anfänge. Neue Forschungen zur Entstehung und frühen Geschichte des Islam*, 2005; and K.-H. Ohlig (ed.), *Der frühe Islam. Eine historisch-kritische Rekonstruktion anhand zeitgenössischer Quellen*, 2007. For critical assessments of his work, see the reviews in *Journal of Qurʾanic Studies* 5 (2003) 92-97 (F. de Blois); *Arabica* 50 (2003) 381-93 (C. Gilliot); *JSAI* 28 (2003) 377-80 (S. Hopkins); *Critique: Revue générale des publications françaises et étrangères* 671 (2003) 232-51 (R. Brague).

biases. Some use of this material has been successfully made,[27] but a systematic comparison between pre-Islamic and early Umayyad verse and the Qur'ān will undoubtedly either corroborate or refute many theories concerning the authenticity of the qur'ānic text and its Christian environment and the spread of Christianity on the pre-Islamic Arabian peninsula.[28]

---

[27] See especially P. Crone and M. Hinds, *God's Caliph. Religious authority in the first centuries of Islam*, Cambridge, 1986.

[28] Poets such as Umayya ibn Abī l-Ṣalt who are too closely related to religious topics form the least independent source, but even a poetess such as al-Khansāʾ would be worth detailed analysis.

Christians and Christianity in Islamic exegesis

Claude Gilliot

Introduction

Great efforts have been made to shed light on the conudrums of the Arabic Qurʾān, both linguistically, lexically and philologically,[1] and thematically and historically.[2] In recent decades the tendency has been to consider that it belongs, at least in part, within the textual or discursive framework of the early Christian or patristic eras, or the world of late antiquity.[3] Indeed, pre-Islamic Arabia 'was not isolated

The author is thankful to Jan Van Reeth, who read a first draft of this chapter and suggested corrections and additions.

[1] A. Mingana, 'Syriac influence on the style of the Kuran', *Bulletin of the John Rylands Library* 11 (1927) 77-98 (repr. in Ibn Warraq (ed.), *What the Koran really says. Language, text and commentary*, Amherst NY, 2002, 171-92); C. Luxenberg, *Die Syro-Aramäische Lesart des Koran. Ein Beitrag zur Entschlüsselung der Koransprache*, Berlin, 2000, 2007[3] (trans. *The Syro-Aramaic reading of the Koran. A contribution to the decoding of the language of the Koran*, Berlin, 2007); G. Lüling, *Über den Ur-Qurʾān. Ansätze zur Rekonstruktion vorislamischer christlicher Strophenlieder im Qurʾān*, Erlangen, 1974 (trans. with modifications *A challenge to Islam for reformation. The rediscovery and reliable reconstruction of a comprehensive pre-Islamic Christian hymnal hidden in the Koran under earliest Islamic reinterpretations*, Delhi, 2003); see the accompanying essay on Christians and Christianity in the Qurʾān for further references.

[2] A. Geiger, *Was hat Mohammed aus dem Judenthume aufgenommen*, Bonn, 1833, Leipzig, 1902[2] (trans. F.M. Young, *Judaism and Islam*, Madras, 1898, New York, 1970). For other studies, see M. Schöller, art. 'Post-enlightment academic study of the Qurʾān', in *EQ*; C. Gilliot and P. Larcher, art. 'Language and style of the Qurʾān', in *EQ*.

[3] S.H. Griffith, 'Christian lore and the Arabic Qurʾān. The "Companions of the Cave" in Sūrat al-kahf and in Syriac Christian tradition', in G.S. Reynolds (ed.), *The Qurʾān in its historical context*, London, 2007, 109-37, p. 109. A. Neuwirth, 'Psalmen – im Koran neu gelesen (Ps 103 und 104)', in D. Hartwig et al. (eds), *"Im vollen Licht der Geschichte." Die Wissenschaft des Judentums und die Anfänge der Koranforschung*, Würzburg, 2008, pp. 157-89. Neuwirth has also called attention several times to the process of codification and canonization of the Qurʾān within the liturgy: 'Vom Rezitationstext über die Liturgie zum Kanon. Zu Entstehung und Wiederauflösung der Surenkomposition im Verlauf der Entwicklung eines islamischen Kultus', in S. Wild (ed.), *The Qurʾān as Text*, Leiden, 1996, pp. 69-105 (trans. T. Herzog, 'Du texte de récitation au canon en passant par la liturgie. A propos de la genèse de la

from the main currents of world culture and religion',[4] as appears in the striking continuity between the sources of the Qur'ān on Jesus, Mary, Christianity and related topics, and the sources employed by the earliest Muslim commentators.

The sources of the Qur'ān on Jesus and Christianity

It is important to emphasize, as some scholars have pointed out, that the Christianity known among the Arabs in pre-Islamic times[5] 'was largely of the Syrian type, whether Jacobite or Nestorian'.[6] The question has been raised of whether the religious community on which Muḥammad relied for his information might be related to the Elkesaite movement[7] or Manicheism.[8] Manicheism was introduced to

---

composition des sourates et de sa redissolution au cours du développement du culte islamique', *Arabica* 47 (2000) 194-229).

[4] J.W. Sweetman, *Islam and Christian theology*, 4 vols in 2 parts, London, 1945-67, i.1, p. 1.

[5] On Christianity among the pre-Islamic Arabs, see R. Bell, *The origin of Islam in its Christian environment*, London, 1926, pp. 2-63; H. Charles, *Le christianisme des Arabes nomades sur le limes...*, Paris, 1936; R. Dussaud, *La pénétration des Arabes en Syrie avant l'islam*, Paris, 1955; T. Andrae, *Les origines de l'islam et le christianisme*, trans. J. Roche, Paris, 1955, pp. 15-38; J.S. Trimingham, *Christianity among the Arabs in pre-Islamic times*, London, 1979; E. Rabbath, *L'Orient chrétien à la veille de l'islam*, Beirut, 1980; A. Havenith, *Les Arabes chrétiens nomades au temps de Mohammed*, Louvain-la-Neuve, 1988; S.B. al-ʿĀyib, *al-Masīḥiyya l-ʿarabiyya wa taṭawwuruhā*, Beirut, 1997, 1998²; M. Piccirillo, *L'Arabie chrétienne*, trans. E. Schelstraete and M.-P. Duverne, Paris, 2002. For religion in al-Ḥīra, see ʿA. ʿAbd al-Ghanī, *Tārīkh al-Ḥīra fī l-jāhiliyya wa-l-Islām*, Damascus, 1993, pp. 471-95. For the importance of relations between Mecca and al-Ḥīra, see M.J. Kister, 'Al-Ḥīra. Some notes on its relations with Arabia', *Arabica* 15 (1968), 143-69; C. Gilliot, 'Une reconstruction critique du Coran ou comment en finir avec les merveilles de la lampe d'Aladin?', in M. Kropp (ed.), *Results of contemporary research on the Qur'ān*, Beirut, 2007, 33-137, pp. 66-67.

[6] A. Jeffery, *The foreign vocabulary of the Qur'ān*, Baroda, 1938, pp. 20-21.

[7] A. Sprenger, *Das Leben und die Lehre des Moḥammad*, 3 vols, Berlin, 1869², i, pp. 30, n. 1, 32-42, 91-102; ii, pp. 208, 232; A. von Harnack, *Lehrbuch der Dogmengeschichte*, 3 vols, Tübingen, 1909-10², ii, pp. 535-37; G. Luttikhuizen, *The revelation of Elchasai*, Tübingen, 1985, pp. 9-10; J. Van Reeth, 'La zandaqa et le prophète de l'Islam', in *Incroyance et dissidences religieuses dans les civilisations orientales*, Brussels, 2007, 67-79, p. 67.

[8] R. Simon, 'Mānī and Muḥammad', *JSAI* 21 (1997) 118-41, p. 134: 'Both Manicheism and Islam assert the seriality of prophets'; Andrae, *Les origines de l'islam*, p. 209; K. Ahrens, *Muhammed als Religionsstifter*, Leipzig, 1935, pp. 130-32; M. Sfar, *Le Coran, la Bible et l'Orient ancien*, Paris, 1998, pp. 408-25 (ch. 11, '*Aḥmad*, le prophète

al-Ḥīra, a town with which Mecca had close relations,[9] in about 272,[10] and a plausible hypothesis is that 'Islam's first appearance was [as] a non-conformist off-shoot of Manicheism'.[11] Mani's prophetic understanding of himself as an equal partner of the Paraclete, as promised by Jesus, even perhaps as the Paraclete himself, was eschatological (in this respect Muḥammad resembled him),[12] and Islamic authors recorded that he claimed to be the Seal of the Prophets,[13] a term applied to Muḥammad in the Qur'ān (Q 33:40). For T. Andrae, who has made the most systematic investigation of Muḥammad's indebtedness to Syrian Christianity, 'the eschatological piety' of Muḥammad and of the Qur'ān[14] are deeply influenced[15] by this form of Christianity, and especially by Syrian monasticism. He has shown the 'evident relations between the language of the Koran and that of the Christian churches in Syria'. In the same way, A. Mingana has demonstrated that the proper names of biblical personages found in the Qur'ān are given in their Syriac form,[16] coming from the Peshitta, the text of the Bible used in Syriac-speaking areas. J. Bowman has gone further and, pointing to the presence of Monophysites in Najrān and among confederate

---

manichéen'). On the presence of Manicheism in Arabia at the time of Muḥammad, see G. Monnot, 'L'histoire des religions en Islam, Ibn al-Kalbī et Rāzī', *RHR* 188 (1975) 23-34 (repr. in Monnot, *Islam et religions*, Paris, 1986, 27-38, p. 33, quoting Ibn al-Kalbī [q.v.]); M. Gil, 'The creed of Abū 'Āmir', *Israel Oriental Studies* 12 (1992) 9-57; Van Reeth, 'La zandaqa', pp. 67-70.

[9] According to Ibn 'Abbās, quoted by Ibn al-Kalbī, Manicheism (*zandaqa*) was brought to Mecca by Qurayshites who used to go to al-Ḥīra for business and met Christians there; Monnot, *Islam et religions*, p. 33; cf. Kister, 'al-Ḥīra'.

[10] M. Tardieu, 'L'arrivée des manichéens à al-Ḥīra', in P. Canivet and J. Rey-Coquais (eds), *La Syrie de Byzance à l'islam VIIe-VIIIe siècles*, Damascus, 1992, 15-24, p. 18.

[11] Gil, 'The creed of Abū 'Āmir', p. 22; Sfar, *Le Coran, la Bible et l'Orient*, pp. 408-25; Van Reeth, 'La zandaqa', p. 68.

[12] G. Stroumsa, 'Aspects de l'eschatologie manichéenne', *RHR* 198 (1981) 163-81.

[13] Al-Shahrastānī, *Livre des religions et des sectes*, trans. D. Gimaret and G. Monnot, 2 vols, Paris, 1986, i, p. 662: Mani said, 'Then the Seal of Prophets shall come to the land of the Arabs' (probably an interpolation in favor of Muḥammad); H. Puech, *Le Manichéisme*, Paris, 1949, p. 146, n. 248; M. Tardieu, *Le Manichéisme*, Paris, 1981, pp. 19-27; J. Ries, 'Les Kephalaia. La catéchèse de l'église de Mani', in D. de Smet, G. de Callatay and J.M.F. Van Reeth (eds), *Al-Kitab: la sacralité du texte dans le monde de l'islam*, Brussels, 2004, 143-53, pp. 143-8.

[14] Andrae, *Les origines de l'islam*, pp. 67-199, 107, 145, 190, 204; T. Andrae, 'Zuhd und Mönchtum', *Le Monde Oriental* 25 (1931) 296-327, p. 298.

[15] The terms 'borrowing', 'allusion', 'interpretation' and 'influence' are preferable to 'intertextuality', which is rarely defined.

[16] Mingana, 'Syriac influence', pp. 81-82.

Arab tribes, such as the Ghassanids, has explained the prophetology and biblical awareness exhibited in the Qurʾān by the hypothesis that Muḥammad was in contact with Jacobites ('Monophysites'), who used the Syriac *Diatessaron*[17] together with other texts in addition to the canonical Gospels,[18] and that he freely edited these texts for his own purposes.[19]

J. Van Reeth has shown in detail that a number of features of Jesus and Christianity in the Qurʾān can be explained by a connection between the Qurʾān and the *Diatessaron*. For example, Q 48:29 combines the two Gospel pericopes of Mark 4:26–27 and Matthew 12:23: 'Such is their likeness in the Torah and their likeness in the Gospel – like as sown corn that sendeth forth its shoot and strengtheneth it and riseth firm upon its stalk, delighting the sowers – that He may enrage the disbelievers with (the sight of) them. God hath promised, unto such of them as believe and do good works, forgiveness and immense reward.' This is the same combination that appears in the *Diatessaron*, seen in the Middle Dutch translation that was made of it from a lost Latin translation in the thirteenth century, and in the Arabic translation of it.[20]

Van Reeth does the same with the qurʾānic stories of the infancy of Mary (Q 3:35–48), John the Baptist (Q 19:3), and Jesus (Q 3:37, 19:22-26), showing again that 'the Koran witnesses to the tradition of the *Diatessaron*'.[21] Even if the *Diatessaron* does not explain all the qurʾānic details about the life of Jesus, 'In referring to the *Diatessaron*

---

[17] On the *Diatessaron*, see T. Baarda, *Essays on the Diatessaron*, Kampen, 1994; W. Petersen, *Tatian's Diatessaron*, Leiden, 1994.

[18] J. Bowman, 'Holy scriptures, lectionaries and the Qurʾān', in A. Johns (ed.), *International congress for the study of the Qurʾān, Canberra (May 1980)*, Canberra, 1983², 29-37; J. Bowman, 'The debt of Islam to Monophysite Syrian Christianity', *Nederlands Teologisch Tijdschrift* 19 (1964-65), 177-201 (repr. in E. MacLaurin (ed.), *Essays in honour of Griffiths Wheeler Thatcher*, Sydney, 1967, 191-216), summarized by Griffith, 'Christian lore', p. 112.

[19] L. McDonald, 'The integrity of the biblical canon in light of its historical development', *Bulletin for Biblical Research* 6 (1996) 95-132, p. 121; R. Casey, 'The Armenian Marcionites and the Diatessaron', *Journal of Biblical Literature* 57 (1938) 185-94.

[20] C. de Bruin, *Diatessaron Leodiense*, Leiden, 1970, p. 92, §§ 93-94; A. Marmardji, *Diatessaron de Tatien, texte arabe*, Beirut, 1935, pp. 159-60.

[21] J. Van Reeth, 'L'évangile du prophète', in D. de Smet et al., *Al-Kitab*, 155-74, p. 163. On the possible influence of the *Diatessaron* and the apocryphal Gospels on the Qurʾān, see J. Gnilka, *Qui sont les chrétiens du Coran?*, trans. C. Ehlinger, Paris, 2008, 101-9.

as Mani had done before him, the Prophet Muhammad could emphasize the unity of the Gospel. Moreover he came within the scope of the posterity of Marcion, of Tatian and Mani, all of whom wanted to establish or re-establish the true Gospel, in order to take hold of its original meaning. They thought themselves authorized to do this work of textual harmonization because they considered themselves the Paraclete that Jesus had announced.'[22]

While comparisons between references to Mary, Jesus and so on in the Qurʾān, and in the New Testament Apocrypha,[23] the New Testament, the *Diatessaron* and the Peshitta have been noted,[24] there is also continuity between these possible sources, and above all the Apocrypha, and the earliest Muslim Qurʾān commentaries.

The early exegetes

The works of most of the earliest commentators, from the seventh and eighth centuries, have not survived, but many of their interpretations are transmitted in later commentaries with chains of authorities. Chief among them are: ʿAbdallāh ibn ʿAbbās (known as Ibn ʿAbbās, d. c. 687);[25] Saʿīd ibn Jubayr (d. 713); Mujāhid ibn Jabr (d. 722); ʿIkrima (d. 723), a freeman of Ibn ʿAbbās; al-Ḍaḥḥāk ibn Muzāḥim (d. 723), who was active in Transoxiana; ʿAṭāʾ ibn Abī Rabāḥ (d. 732) (all so far are considered pupils of Ibn ʿAbbās); Ḥasan al-Baṣrī (d. 728); Muḥammad

[22] Van Reeth, 'L'évangile du prophète', p. 174; cf. R. Simon, 'Mānī and Muḥammad', *JSAI* 21 (1997) 118-41, p. 134: 'Both Manicheism and Islam assert the seriality of prophets'; Andrae, *Les origines de l'islam*, p. 209; Ahrens, *Muhammed als Religionsstifter*, pp. 130-32.

[23] E.g. J. Elliott, *The apocryphal New Testament. A collection of apocryphal Christian literature in an English translation*, Oxford, 1993; J. Elliott, *The apocryphal Jesus. Legends of the early church*, Oxford, 1996; A. Terian (ed.), *The Armenian Gospel of the Infancy. With three early versions of the Protoevangelium of James*, Oxford, 2008; F. Bovon and P. Geoltrain (eds), *Écrits apocryphes chrétiens*, Paris, 1997.

[24] W. Rudolph, *Die Abhängigkeit des Qorans von Judentum und Christentum*, Stuttgart, 1922; H. Speyer, *Die biblischen Erzählungen im Qoran*, Hildesheim, 1931, 1988², pp. 449-58; K. Ahrens, 'Christliches im Koran. Eine Nachlese', *ZDMG* 84 (1930) 15-68; D. Sidersky, *Les origines des légendes musulmanes dans le Coran et dans les vies des prophètes*, Paris, 1933, pp. 135-54; B. Pirone, 'La tradizione dei testi evangelici nell'ambiente formativo di Muhammad', in R. Tottoli, (ed.), *Corano e Bibbia*, Brescia, 2000, 133-75. See also Van Reeth's article noted above.

[25] C. Gilliot, art. 'Ibn ʿAbbās', in *EI3*; C. Gilliot, 'Portrait "mythique" d'Ibn ʿAbbās', *Arabica* 32 (1985) 127-83; M. Lidzbarski, *De propheticis, quae dicuntur, legendis arabicis prolegomena*, Leipzig, 1893, pp. 41-44.

ibn Kaʿb al-Quraẓī (d. 736);[26] Qatāda ibn Diʿāma (d. 736); al-Suddī al-Kabīr (d. 746), the Kufan popular storyteller; al-Rabīʿ ibn Anas (d. c. 756) of Basra, who was active in Transoxiana;[27] Muḥammad ibn al-Sāʾib al-Kalbī (d. 763, the father of Hishām ibn al-Kalbī, [q.v.]), whose exegesis is often dependent on Ibn ʿAbbās.

From the mid eighth century onwards there are several commentators whose works are extant: Muqātil ibn Sulaymān (d. 767),[28] who was active in Transoxiana; the Yemenite Maʿmar ibn Rashīd (d. 770), in the version of ʿAbd al-Razzāq al-Ṣanʿānī (d. 827),[29] with a tendency to legal exegesis; the Basran Yaḥyā ibn Sallām (d. 815);[30] the Basran of Jewish origin Abū ʿUbayda Maʿmar ibn al-Muthannā (d. 821);[31] and the Kūfan grammarian al-Farrāʾ Yaḥyā ibn Ziyād (d. 822).[32]

To these may be added some others who were not exegetes *stricto sensu*, but whose reports are transmitted in later commentaries: Kaʿb al-Aḥbār (Hebrew *ḥāber*, d. c. 652),[33] a Yemeni Jew who converted[34] to Islam in about 638.[35] He probably came to Medina during the caliphate of ʿUmar and, together with others, transmitted Judaeo-Christian material to Ibn ʿAbbās.[36] His narratives (or those attributed to him) comprise Judaeo-Christian and Judaeo-Islamic traditions.

Wahb ibn Munabbih (d. 732),[37] 'the Manetho of the South Arabians', a Yemeni of Persian origin, probably born Muslim, who draws as

---

[26] As a young boy he was rescued when 600 or 900 men of the Banū Qurayẓa were executed by Muḥammad in Medina.

[27] On these commentators, see C. Gilliot, art. 'Exegesis of the Qur'ān: classical and medieval', in *EQ*.

[28] M. Plessner and A. Rippin, art. 'Muqātil b. Sulaymān', in *EI2*; C. Gilliot, 'Muqātil, grand exégète, traditionniste et théologien maudit', *Journal Asiatique* 279 (1991) 39-92; Muqātil ibn Sulaymān, *Tafsīr*, ed. ʿA.M. Shiḥāta, 5 vols, Cairo, 1980-89.

[29] ʿAbd al-Razzāq, *Tafsīr*, ed. M. ʿAbduh, 3 vols, Beirut, 1999.

[30] Yaḥyā ibn Sallām, *Tafsīr*, ed. H. Shalabī, 2 vols, Beirut, 2004 (*sūras* 16-37 only).

[31] Abū ʿUbayda, *Majāz al-Qurʾān*, ed. F. Sezgin, 2 vols, Cairo, 1954-62.

[32] Farrāʾ, *Maʿānī l-Qurʾān*, ed. A.Y. Najātī and M. al-Najjār, 3 vols, Beirut, 1955-63.

[33] M. Schmitz, art. 'Kaʿb al-Aḥbār', in *EI2*; I. Wolfensohn, *Kaʿb al-Aḥbār und seine Stellung im Ḥadīt und in der islamischen Legendenliteratur*, Gelnhausen, 1933; Lidzbarski, *De propheticis*, pp. 31-40.

[34] On storytellers and converts, see R. Tottoli, *Biblical prophets in the Qurʾān and Muslim literature*, Richmond, 2002, pp. 86-96.

[35] But see M. Perlmann, 'A legendary story of Kaʿb al-Aḥbār's conversion to Islam', in *Joshua Starr memorial volume*, New York, 1953, 85-99; M. Perlmann, 'Another Kaʿb al-Ahbār story', *Jewish Quarterly Review* 45 (1954) 48-58.

[36] Wolfensohn, *Kaʿb al-Aḥbār und seine Stellung*, pp. 42-47.

[37] R. Khoury, art. 'Wahb ibn Munabbih', in *EI2*; van Ess, *TG* ii, pp. 702-5; Lidzbarski, *De propheticis*, pp. 44-54; R.G. Khoury, *Wahb b. Munabbih*, Wiesbaden, 1972.

often as not on Ibn ʿAbbās. Wahb was the first of a long line of Islamic scholars or authors who transmitted 'biblical' narratives. One of the works attributed to him is *Kitāb al-mubtadaʾ wa-qiṣaṣ al-anbiyāʾ* ('The beginning and stories of the prophets'),[38] whose contents are scattered through later works. He is credited by later sources with a commentary on the Qurʾān, though he probably did not compose one; rather, later exegetes, such as al-Ṭabarī and al-Thaʿlabī, incorporated into their own commentaries elements from him of the kind that were later called *isrāʾīliyyāt* (*judaica*, i.e. 'Jewish' exegetical material),[39] though these included not only Jewish or supposedly Jewish material, but also Christian or supposedly Christian material, accounts regarded as history, edifying narratives, and fables or legends from folklore, allegedly (but sometimes actually) borrowed from Jewish, Christian, or other sources. Many Islamic scholars rejected them, though others drew on them, albeit with reluctance. It is worth noting that almost all the commentators named above transmitted material of this kind, and that almost all later commentators made copious use of it.

Muḥammad ibn Isḥāq, known as Ibn Isḥāq (d. 767),[40] the author of the best known Life of Muḥammad, is not considered an exegete, but he gives many accounts which are related to exegesis. His grandfather was possibily a Christian, which might explain his interest in Jewish and Christian material.

Of these, Ibn ʿAbbās, Kaʿb al-Aḥbār, Wahb ibn Munabbih and Ibn Isḥāq in particular transmitted Judaeo-Christian elements,[41] and 'introduced them into the faith and literature of Islam'.[42] In their turn, Abū ʿUbayda Maʿmar ibn al-Muthannā and al-Farrāʾ Yaḥyā ibn Ziyād, who both died at the very beginning of the ninth century, introduced the study of grammar and linguistics and elements of rhetoric and stylistics, contributing to the doctrine of the inimitability (*iʿjāz*) of the Qurʾān, and, in the case of al-Farrāʿ, the examination of the *variae lectiones* (*qirāʾāt*).[43]

---

[38] Khoury, *Wahb b. Munabbih*, pp. 232-46.

[39] On this term, see G. Vajda, art. 'Isrāʾīliyyāt', in *EI2*; J. Dammen McAuliffe, *Qurʾānic Christians. An analysis of classical and modern exegesis*, Cambridge, 1991, p. 29, n. 41.

[40] Lidzbarski, *De propheticis*, pp. 54-57.

[41] Lidzbarski, *De propheticis*, p. 30.

[42] N. Abbott, 'An Arabic papyrus in the Oriental Institute. Stories of the Prophets', *Journal of Near Eastern Studies* 5 (1946) 169-80, pp. 170-71 (with no reference to Ibn Isḥāq).

[43] Gilliot, 'Exegesis of the Qurʾān', pp. 108-10.

'Nazarenes' and others

For the Islamic representation of 'Christians' and 'Christianity', the exegesis of Q 28:52-55 is decisive: 'Those to whom We gave the Scripture before it, they believe in it...', and especially 'Even before it we were of those who surrender [unto Him?] (*muslimīn*)'.[44] In themselves, these verses are allusive with no specific reference to 'Christians'. But according to Mujāhid, they refer to 'the Muslims (*maslama*) among the People of the Book', or according to al-Ḍaḥḥāk, 'people among the People of the Book who believed in the Torah and in the Gospel (*injīl*). Then they encountered Muḥammad and believed in him'. Sometimes names of individuals are given, such as the Jews ʿAṭiyya al-Quraẓī,[45] Abū Rifāʿa and ʿAbdallāh ibn Salām, and Salmān al-Fārisī, the Zoroastrian turned Christian.[46] For others, such as Muqātil, the occasion of the revelation of Q 28:52 was the coming of 40 men of 'the People of the Gospel' to Medina with Jaʿfar ibn Abī Ṭālib when he returned from Ethiopia,[47] and eight from Syria.[48] Yaḥyā ibn Sallām gives two interpretations: the verse was revealed concerning those of the People of the two Books who believed, or concerning the Jew Rifāʿa (ibn Samawʾal) al-Quraẓī, of the Banū Qurayẓa who was spared when his tribe was executed in Medina[49] – 'This verse was revealed concerning ten Jews, of which I am one.'[50] It is clear that, in the religious imagination of the commentators, the true Christians are Muslims, and that Muslims are the true followers of Jesus: 'People of the religion of Jesus

---

[44] Sprenger, *Das Leben und die Lehre des Moḥammad*, ii, pp. 379-82; McAuliffe, *Qurʾānic Christians*, pp. 240-57.

[45] On him, see Ibn al-Athīr, *Usd al-ghāba fī maʿrifat al-ṣaḥāba*, ed. M. Fāyid et al., 7 vols, Cairo, 1963, 1970², iv, p. 46, no. 3689: 'the young lads who were beardless were not killed'; Ibn Isḥāq, *Sīrat rasūl Allāh*, ed. F. Wüstenfeld, Göttingen, 1858-60, pp. 688-92; trans. A. Guillaume, *The life of Muhammad*, Karachi, 1955, pp. 463-65.

[46] Al-Ṭabarī, *Tafsīr al-Qurʾān*, ed. M. al-Saqqā and A.S. ʿAlī, 30 vols, Cairo, 1954-57, xx, pp. 88-89. (Hereafter, al-Ṭabarī, *Tafsīr* = al-Ṭabarī, *Tafsīr al-Ṭabarī: Jāmiʿ al-bayān ʿan taʾwīl al-Qurʾān*, ed. M.M. Shākir and A.M. Shākir, 16 vols, Cairo, 1954-68, which goes as far as Q 14:27. For the remainder of the Qurʾān, references are to the complete edition of al-Saqqā and ʿAlī = al-Ṭabarī, *Tafsīr*, ed. al-Saqqā).

[47] According to Saʿīd ibn Jubayr they were Ethiopians; Sprenger, *Das Leben und die Lehre des Moḥammad*, ii, pp. 380-81.

[48] Muqātil, *Tafsīr*, on Q 28:52.

[49] On Muḥammad's execution of 600 to 900 men of the Banū Qurayẓa, see Ibn Isḥāq, *Sīra*, pp. 688-92/Guillaume, *Life*, pp. 463-65.

[50] Yaḥyā ibn Sallām, *Tafsīr*, ii, p. 599. On Rifāʿa ibn Samawʾal al-Quraẓī, see Ibn Isḥāq, *Sīra*, p. 692/Guillaume, *Life*, p. 466.

are the Muslims (*al-muslimūn*, those who submit to God) above all the religions.'[51]

With regard to Q 2:62,[52] 'And those who are Jews, and Christians (*Naṣārā*), and Sabeans, whoever believeth in God and the Last Day and doeth right, surely their reward is with their Lord...', three etymologies of *Naṣārā* are given. According to the first, which is based on the Arabic root *n.ṣ.r*, Christians are called this because of their support (*nuṣra*) and mutual assistance for each other;[53] the second, represented by Qatāda, Ibn ʿAbbās, and Ibn Jurayj,[54] associates them with Nazareth (*al-Nāṣira*); and the third is based on Q 61:14, in which Jesus asks, 'Who will be my helpers (*anṣār*) for God?'[55] Some exegetes explain this verse by means of a story related by al-Suddī, which preserves memories of the religious syncretism of late antiquity. As Salmān, a young nobleman from Gundishāpūr, was hunting with the local prince one day, they came upon a man who was reading a book and weeping.[56] When he explained that this was the Gospel revealed to Jesus, the two 'submitted themselves to God' (*aslamā*, 'became Muslims'), and Salmān joined a community of monks (*ruhbān*), distinguishing himself by the severity of his ascetic practices. He accompanied the head of the community to Jerusalem, and studied there. When he came to see that prophetic marvels were events of the past,

---

[51] Muqātil, *Tafsīr*, on Q 3:55.

[52] See S. Khalil, 'Le commentaire de Tabari sur Coran 2/62 et la question du salut des non-musulmans', *Annuli dell'Istituto Orientale de Napoli* 11 (1980), 555-617.

[53] Al-Ṭabarī, *Tafsīr*, ii, pp. 143-45; McAuliffe, *Qurʾānic Christians*, p. 95; 'A. Charfi, 'Christianity in the Qurʾān commentary of al-Ṭabarī', *Islamochristiana* 6 (1980) 105-48, p. 133.

[54] Al-Ṭabarī, *Tafsīr*, ii, p. 145, according to the Meccan Ibn Jurayj (d. 767), whose grandfather Gregorius (Jurayj) was a *mawlā* of the Umayyads; ʿA. ʿAlī et al., *Al-Naṣārā fī l-Qurʾān wa-l-tafāsīr*, Amman, 1998, p. 34; McAuliffe, *Qurʾānic Christians*, p. 95; M Ayoub, *The Qurʾan and its interpreters*, 2 vols, Albany NY, 1984 and 1992, i, p. 109. See the discussion on Nazarenes, Nazôrenes, Christians by Gnilka, *Qui sont les chrétiens du Coran?*, pp. 31-39.

[55] Al-Ṭabarī, *Tafsīr*, ii, p. 145; McAuliffe, *Qurʾānic Christians*, p. 95.

[56] In Syrian monasticism, the 'mourners' (*abilē*) were an ascetic elite associated with the Beatitude: 'Blessed are those who mourn...' (Matthew 5:4); see D. Caner, *Wandering, begging monks. Spiritual authority and the promotion of monasticism in late antiquity*, Berkeley CA, 2002, p. 51, n. 2. Muḥammad had evidently been in contact with such men, as seen in Q 5:82-83: '... There are among them priests and monks. When they listen to that which hath been revealed to the Messenger, thou seest their eyes overflow with tears.' Muḥammad knew anchorite practices, and had probably engaged in them himself before his revelations; E. Beck, 'Das christliche Mönchtum im Koran', *Studia Orientalia* (Helsinki) 13 (1946) 1-29, p. 7.

he grew sad, but the head of the community told him that a prophet was soon to arise among the Arabs. While he was returning from Jerusalem, Salmān was captured by Arabs and sold into slavery. Then he heard that a prophet had arrived in Medina. He hurried to the city, and there described to Muḥammad the prayerful community in which he had lived. The Prophet replied: 'They are among the people destined for Hell', upon which Salmān professed belief in Muḥammad and his teachings.[57]

The early commentators also preserve elements of cultural memory concerning the beginnings of Christianity and some of its characteristics in late antiquity, together with theological and mythical representations of a clearly Islamic character. One of the crucial passages is Q 57:27, 'Then We caused our messengers to follow in their footsteps; and We caused Jesus, son of Mary, to follow, and gave him the Gospel, and placed compassion and mercy in the hearts of those who followed him. But monasticism (*rahbāniyya*) they invented – We ordained it not for them – only seeking God's pleasure, and they observed it not with right observance. So We give those of them who believe their reward, but many of them are evil-livers.'[58] In his commentary, Muqātil suggests a clear syntactical distinction in the qurʾānic text between 'compassion and mercy', the two direct objects of the predicative sentence, and 'monasticism', commenting: 'Then He [God] introduces a new sentence.'[59] For him, the 'monasticism' (asceticism) of his time does not correspond to that of the followers of Jesus at the beginning of Christianity, or at least to the conception he has of this way to life,[60] because 'After Jesus son of Mary the number of polytheists

[57] Al-Ṭabarī, *Tafsīr*, ii, pp. 150-55; Ayoub, *The Qurʾan and its interpreters*, i, pp. 110-12; ʿAlī, *Al-Naṣārā*, pp. 36-37; McAuliffe, *Qurʾānic Christians*, pp. 105-6; cf. Ibn Isḥāq, *Sīra*, pp. 137-43/Guillaume, *Life*, pp. 95-98 (a very different account from Ibn ʿAbbās); Muqātil, *Tafsīr*, i, p. 112. See further G. Levi Della Vida, art. 'Salmān al-Fārisī', in *EI2*, Suppl.; K. Tröger, 'Muhammad, Salman al-Farisi und die Islamische Gnosis', in H. Bethge et al. (eds), *For the children, perfect instruction. Studies in honor of H.-M. Schenke*, Leiden, 2002, pp. 247-54.

[58] See H. Çinar, *Maria und Jesus im Islam. Darstellung anhand des Korans und der islamischen kanonischen Tradition unter Berücksichtigung der islamischen Exegeten*, Wiesbaden, 2007, pp. 160-63.

[59] Muqātil, *Tafsīr*, iv, p. 246.

[60] P. Nwyia, *Exégèse coranique et langage mystique*, Beirut, 1970, pp. 52-56. On the different intrepretations of this verse by Western scholars, see S. Sviri, '*Wa-rahbānīyatan ibtadaʿūhā*. An analysis of traditions concerning the origin and evaluation of Christian monasticism', *JSAI* 13 (1990) 195-208, pp. 195-201.

increased; they defeated the believers and humiliated them. The believers isolated themselves, they dwelt in hermitages, and this lasted long. Some of them returned to the religion of Jesus and invented Christianity (*Naṣrāniyya*), so God says: "They invented monasticism", they devoted themselves to God's service (or, they practised celibacy, *tabattalū*) [...]. They did not observe what I have commanded [...], when they became Jews and Christians (or, called themselves so). Some of them however remained faithful to the religion of Jesus until they reached the times of Muḥammad.'[61] Here asceticism in itself is not condemned; what is condemned is the way of practising it, celibacy for instance, and the theological doctrines 'invented' by the Nazarenes (*Naṣrāniyya*). Asceticism (*raḥbāniyya*) could not be condemned because Muḥammed is said to have practised a form of spiritual retreat before the time of Islam, probably under the influence of Manicheism and Judaeo-Christianity, which itself was influenced by Manicheism and gnosticism.

The attitude demonstrated in this account is partly based on the qurʾānic and Islamic dogma of the distortion or falsification (*taḥrīf*) of the scriptures by Jews and Christians, as presented by Ibn ʿAbbās:[62] 'After Jesus, kings[63] distorted the Torah and the Gospel. The king summoned people to choose between death and relinquishing their reading of their books, except what had been distorted. A group of them chose to live on pillars,[64] others to roam about wandering, eating what beasts eat, others built monasteries in the deserts, digging wells and growing herbs. Each group was imitated by others, but they became polytheists. When Muḥammed came, only a few of them remained. Then the hermits descended from their cells, the cenobites came out of their convents, and the roaming monks came back from their wandering, and all of them believed in him and gave credence to him.

[61] Muqātil, *Tafsīr*, iv, p. 246.

[62] Al-Ṭabarī, *Tafsīr*, ed. al-Saqqā, on Q 57:27; C. Gilliot, 'Exégèse et sémantique institutionnelle dans le Commentaire de Tabari', *Studia Islamica* 77 (1993) 41-94, pp. 73-74 (al-Thaʿlabī, *Tafsīr*, ix, pp. 248-49, borrows this tradition from al-Ṭabarī); Sviri, '*Wa-rahbānīyatan ibtadaʿūhā*', pp. 205-6 (here from al-Ḥakīm al-Tirmidhī [fl. 930], *Nawādir al-uṣūl*, ed. A.ʿA. al-Sāyiḥ and S. al-Jumaylī, 2 vols, Cairo, 1988, i, pp. 224-25); McAuliffe, *Qurʾānic Christians*, p. 264 (summarized); Charfi, 'Christianity in the Qurʾān commentary of al-Ṭabarī', p. 139.

[63] The reference is often made to Constantine.

[64] On the stylites in pre-Islamic poetry, see I. Goldziher, '"Säulenmänner" im Arabischen', *ZDMG* 55 (1901) 503-8, pp. 504-5 (repr. in Goldziher, *Gesammelte Schriften*, Hildesheim, 1967, iv, 309-14, pp. 310-11).

These have a twofold recompense' (Q 57:28). A slightly different report is attributed to Ibn Masʿūd, another Companion of Muḥammad.[65]

To the 'monasticism' (asceticism) of the Christians is opposed the 'monasticism' of Islam, according to a tradition transmitted from Muḥammad by the Companion Anas ibn Mālik: 'Every prophet has his monasticism, the monasticism (asceticism) of this community (Islam) is holy war (*al-jihād fī sabīl Allāh*).'[66] However, there is a tension between rejecting forms of asceticism such as Christian monasticism, on the the one hand, and an attraction towards asceticism, on the other. Muḥammad and other members of the Quraysh are said to have practised times of spiritual retreat (*taḥannuth*) before the coming of Islam,[67] and ten of his Companions are said to have been tempted by what were considered within Islam to be 'extreme' forms of asceticism. Among them,[68] the following names are given (on Q 5:87): ʿUthmān ibn Maʿẓūm, ʿAlī, Ibn Masʿūd, and al-Miqdād ibn al-Aswad. According to Mujāhid, they practised celibacy (*tabattalū*), they wore 'monks' habits' (*musūḥ*), they wanted to roam around (*al-siyāḥa*) like wandering monks, they abstained from certain foods, and they wanted to castrate themselves.[69] It should be noted that the qurʾānic *ḥanīfiyya* has been associated with Manicheism, Sabeanism,[70] etc. According to al-Kalbī (d. 763), 'The Sabeans are people between the Jews and the Nazarenes; they confess God, shave the middle of their heads and they castrate themselves (*yajubbūna madhākīrahum*)'.[71] Significantly, the first Muslims themselves were called Sabeans by the pagans of Mecca and Medina.[72]

---

[65] Al-Ṭabarī, *Tafsīr*, xxvii, pp. 239-40 (trans. in Gilliot, 'Exégèse et sémantique', pp. 72-74); McAuliffe, *Qurʾānic Christians*, p. 265 (summarized); Charfi, 'Christianity in the Qurʾān commentary of al-Ṭabarī', pp. 139-40.

[66] Ibn Ḥanbal, *Musnad*, 6 vols, Cairo, 1895, iii, p. 266, cf. iii, p. 82; ed. A.M. Shākir, 22 vols, Cairo, 1945, 1990², xi, p. 278, no. 13742, cf. x, p. 257, no. 11713.

[67] M.J. Kister, 'Al-taḥannuth. An inquiry on the meaning of a term', *BSOAS* 31 (1968) pp. 223-36.

[68] Muqātil, *Tafsīr*, i, pp. 498-99, gives the ten names.

[69] Al-Ṭabarī, *Tafsīr*, x, p. 519, no. 12387. Other accounts are given from ʿIkrima, Ibn ʿAbbās, Ibn Zayd, etc.; al-Ṭabarī, *Tafsīr*, x, pp. 514-21; cf. al-Bukhārī, *Ṣaḥīḥ*, 67, *Nikāḥ* 9.

[70] Gil, 'The creed of Abū ʿĀmir', pp. 13-15; G. Monnot, 'Sabéens et idolâtres selon ʿAbd al-Jabbār', *MIDEO* 12 (1974) 13-48 (repr. in Monnot, *Islam et religions*, 207-27).

[71] Al-Thaʿlabī, *Tafsīr*, i, p. 209, on Q 2:61. Cf. Muqātil, *Tafsīr*, i, p. 112; al-Qurṭubī, *Tafsīr*, i, p. 434, according to al-Ḥasan al-Baṣrī; al-Jaṣṣāṣ, *Aḥkām al-Qurʾān*, 3 vols, Istanbul, 1916-19, iii, p. 91; Sprenger, *Das Leben und die Lehre des Moḥammad*, ii, pp. 579, 388-89.

[72] J. Wellhausen, *Reste arabischen Heidentums*, Berlin, 1897, pp. 237-38.

The origins and early divisions of Christianity

The most common historical, or pseudo-historical, and theological explanation given by the early commentators concerning the divisions between the followers of Jesus after 'he was raised up to heaven by God' is the following: they were split into two, three, or four groups (the 'infidels'), while another group (the true 'Muslims'), remained 'faithful' to Jesus. But they were oppressed by the other groups, or by two of them, until Islam was sent again by God through Muhammad.

According to Ibn ʿAbbās, after Jesus was raised up to heaven, 'his followers divided into three groups [a fourth is sometimes mentioned, those who say that Jesus is "one of three Gods"[73] together with God and Mary;[74] in some versions they are called the "Israelite Christians", and their religion "the religion of the emperor", *dīn al-malik*].[75] One group, the Jacobites, said, "God was among us as long as He willed, then he ascended to Heaven." Another, the Nestorians, said, "The son of God was among us as long as He wished, then [God] caused him to ascend to Him." Another, the Muslims, said, "[Jesus] was the servant of God, and His messenger for as long as He willed, then God caused him to ascend to Him." The two unbelieving groups gained ascendancy

---

[73] They were 'the Israelites who were the kings of the Nazarenes', evidently a confusion; Ibn ʿAsākir, *Taʾrīkh madīnat Dimashq*, ed. M. Amrawī and ʿA. Shīrī, 80 vols, Beirut, 1995-2001, xlvii, pp. 478-79; S. Mourad, 'Jesus according to Ibn ʿAsākir', in J. Lindsay (ed.), *Ibn ʿAsākir and early Islamic history*, Princeton NJ, 2001, 22-43, pp. 30-31.

[74] Cf. Q 5:116: 'O Jesus, son of Mary, didst thou say unto mankind: Take me and my mother for two gods beside God?'; Charfi, 'Christianity in the Qurʾān commentary of al-Ṭabarī', p. 132. On this assertion, see C.E. Sell, *The historical development of the Qurʾān*, London, 1909, p. 172. On the Collyridians ('cake-eaters'), whose worship of Mary is sometimes thought to be related to this verse, see H. Wace, and W.C. Piercy (eds), *A dictionary of Christian biography and literature to the end of the sixth century AD*, art. 'Collyridians'.

[75] Ibn al-Jawzī, *Al-muntaẓam fī taʾrīkh al-umam wa-l-mulūk*, ed. M. ʿAbd al-Qādir ʿAṭā', 17 vols, Beirut, 1992, ii, p. 41; P. van Koningsveld, 'The Islamic image of Paul and the origin of the Gospel of Barnabas', *JSAI* 20 (1996), 200-28, pp. 204-5. Four groups of learned Jews discussing Jesus after his ascension are also presented in an account by Muḥammad al-Quraẓī, but without mention of denominations. One says that he was born after his mother had committed 'an ungodly act' (*ghayr ṣāliḥ*); Ibn al-Jawzī, *Muntaẓam*, ii, p. 40; van Koningsveld, 'The Islamic image of Paul', p. 204.

over the Muslim group and destroyed it. Islam remained in eclipse until God sent Muḥammad.'[76]

According to Muqātil, 'The Nazarenes divided into three groups over Jesus: the Nestorians said that he is God's son, the Jacobites (*al-Yaʿqūbiyya*) that he is God, and the Melkites (*al-Malkāniyyūn*) "God the third of three" (Q 5:73).'[77]

Ibn Jurayj (d. 767) reports in more detail that the leaders of the three groups who split were Decius (Daqyūs),[78] Nestorius and Mār Yaʿqūb. The followers of the last (Jacobites) said that Jesus is God, who came down to earth, caused to live or caused to die as he willed, and then rose to heaven. The followers of the second (Nestorians) said that Jesus is the son of God. The followers of the first, 'the Israelites, kings of the Christians' (Melkites), said that Jesus is 'the third of three', that is 'Allāh is God, he is God, his mother is God'. The fourth group were the 'Muslims' (of the time), who said that Jesus was 'the servant, the messenger, the spirit (*rūḥ*), and the word (*kalima*) of God'. These groups fought each other, and they overcame the 'Muslims'.[79]

A particular group of 'Christians', or better 'Children of Israel', hearers or disciples of Jesus, or Jews,[80] is presented by some exegetes

[76] Al-Ṭabarī, *Tafsīr*, ed. al-Saqqā, xxviii, p. 92, on Q 61:14; Ibn ʿAsākir, xlvii, p. 475; Mourad, 'Jesus according to Ibn ʿAsākir', p. 30 and n. 21.

[77] Muqātil, *Tafsīr*, ii, p. 628, on Q 19:37. Al-Ṭabarī, *Tafsīr*, x, p. 482, on Q 5:73, also mentions the three groups, but has *al-Yaʿqūbiyya* and *al-Malikiyya*, and on p. 484, on Q 5:74, *al-Yaʿqūbiyya* only. Cf. Charfi, 'Christianity in the Qurʾān commentary of al-Ṭabarī', pp. 140-41. It is worth noting that the *mutakallim* al-Māturīdī (d. 944) does not name Christian groups in his commentary, *Taʾwīlāt ahl al-sunna*, ed. F.Y. al-Khaymī, 5 vols, Beirut, 2004.

[78] For Decius (r. 249 to 251), see al-Masʿūdī, *Murūj al-dhahab*, ed. C. Pellat, 7 vols, Beirut, 1966-79, ii, p. 39, § 729/*Les prairies d'or*, trans. C. Pellat, 5 vols, Paris, 1962-97, ii, p. 273, where he is known as the persecutor of the Christians. In Ibn Jurayj's account, there is probably some confusion with Constantine or one of his successors.

[79] Al-Ṭabarī, *Tafsīr*, ed. al-Saqqā, xvi, pp. 83-84, on Q 19:34; Charfi, 'Christianity in the Qurʾān commentary of al-Ṭabarī', pp. 140-41. Qatāda gives a similar account, but without mentioning Decius; al-Ṭabarī, *Tafsīr*, xvi, p. 86, on Q 19:37. He adds an argument of the 'Muslims': Jesus ate and slept, God did not – at this time the Jacobites appeared and the 'Muslims' were killed. For him this is an explanation of Q 3:21.

[80] On 'a people who sinned by violating the Sabbath' (Jews), and their punishment of being transformed into apes or pigs, see I. Lichtenstadter, '"And become ye accursed apes"', *JSAI* 14 (1991) 153-75. On Q 5:65 and 7:163-66, and particularly 7:166, 'Be ye apes despised and loathed', see al-Ṭabarī, *Tafsīr*, xiii, pp. 179-202; on Q 2:65, see al-Ṭabarī, *Tafsīr*, ii, pp. 167-73; Ayoub, *The Qurʾan and its interpreters*, i, pp. 113-16; W.M. Brinner, *Lives of the prophets*, Leiden, 2002, pp. 482-84 (trans. of al-Thaʿlabī *ʿArāʾis al-majālis fī qiṣaṣ al-anbiyāʾ*, hereafter referred to as Thaʿlabī-Brinner; a more

to explain other passages of the Qurʾān, with polemical arguments against Jews and Christians or Judaeo-Christians. So, on Q 5:78: 'Those of the Children of Israel who went astray were cursed by the tongue of David, and of Jesus, son of Mary; that was because they rebelled and used to transgress', Muqātil[81] says that these people ate from the [descended] table and did not believe, so Jesus cursed them, like those who had violated the Sabbath (*aṣḥāb al-sabt*), or the Sabbath-breakers. They were 5,000[82] (other versions have 330), and God transformed them into pigs (other versions have apes, or apes and pigs).[83] It is worth noting that alone among the early commentators Mujāhid interprets this transformation figuratively: 'They were not transformed, but it is a parable which God made for them (the Jews of Medina)', or 'Their hearts were transformed; they were not transformed into apes, but it is a parable which God made for them, like "the ass carrying books" (Q 62:5).'[84]

Some early reports anticipate later Muslim polemics against Paul as the most important founder of the so-called Christian 'evident unbelief' (*kufr mubīn*). The ʿAbbasid historiographer Sayf ibn ʿUmar (q.v.) discusses Paul's 'adverse influence' on early Christianity in the context of the conspiracy that led to the assassination of the Caliph ʿUthmān. He adduces an account about Paul[85] as a parallel to that of a Jew of Ṣanʿāʾ, ʿAbdallāh ibn Sabaʾ,[86] who is said to have converted to Islam in the time of ʿUthmān and then led people astray with doctrines which

accurate translation is H. Busse, *Islamische Erzählungen von Propheten und Gottesmännern*, Wiesbaden 2006, hereafter referred to as Thaʿlabī-Busse – although al-Thaʿlabī died in 1035, he transmits early material).

81 Muqātil, *Tafsīr*, i, p. 496, on Q 2:77-78; al-Ṭabarī, *Tafsīr*, ii, pp. 229-30, on Q 5:114. Cf. Thaʿlabī-Brinner, pp. 664-72; Thaʿlabī-Busse, pp. 501-4; B. Wheeler, *Prophets in the Quran. An introduction to the Quran and Muslim exegesis*, London, 2002, pp. 309-10; Charfi, 'Christianity in the Qurʾān commentary of al-Ṭabarī', pp. 120-21.

82 Matthew 14:21. The longer accounts have reminiscences of the institution of the Eucharist (Matthew 26:26-29 and parallels), of the multiplication of loaves (Matthew 14:15-21; Matthew 15:32-37 and parallels), of Acts 10:11-16, or 1 Corinthians 10:1-13; Çinar, *Maria und Jesus im Islam*, pp. 163-70.

83 Cf. Matthew 8:28-34 and parallels, the story of Jesus casting out demons and casting them into pigs.

84 Al-Ṭabarī, *Tafsīr*, ii, pp. 172-73, nos 1143-44, on Q 2:65; Ayoub, *The Qurʾan and its interpreters*, i, p. 114.

85 Sayf ibn ʿUmar, *Kitāb al-ridda wa-l-futūḥ*, ed. Q. al-Sāmarrāʾī, Leiden, 1995, pp. 132-35.

86 Sayf ibn ʿUmar, *Kitāb al-ridda wa-l-futūḥ*, pp. 135-38; al-Ṭabarī, *Tārīkh*, ii, 2941-44/*The History of al-Ṭabarī*, xv, trans. R.S. Humphreys, Albany NY, 1990, pp. 145-48; M. Hodgson, art. "ʿAbd Allāh b. Sabaʾ", in *EI2*.

became the basis of the dissensions between Shīʿī and Sunnī Islam.[87] Sayf transmits this narrative from ʿAṭiyya (who could be either the commentator Abū Rawq ʿAṭiyya ibn al-Ḥārith al-Hamdānī, or ʿAṭiyya ibn Yaʿlā al-Ḍabbī), who transmitted it from Yazīd al-Faqʿasī, who can be estimated to have died around 708 (this is interesting information for the antiquity of this tradition among the northern Arabian tribe of Asad).

After Jesus had been raised up by God, his followers were 700 (or 700 families). Paul, the king at this time, urged that they should be killed, but they managed to escape. So Paul devised a trick: he put on the clothes worn by Jesus' followers and went to find them. He was captured by them, but he told them he had met Jesus, who had taken away his hearing, sight and reason.[88] He promised to serve the cause of the followers and to teach them the Torah and its regulations. He had four visions, by means of which he convinced the followers that the direction of prayer was east, all food was permissible, and all forms of violence (*jihād*) and revenge were abolished.[89] He reserved the third vision for a group of four, Jacob, Nestor, Malkūn,[90] and the 'believer'.[91] After asking this group several questions, Paul said, 'I declare that God has manifested (*tajallā*) Himself to us, but has then withdrawn from sight (*iḥtajaba*)'. One of them said that Paul was right, the second that it was God and Jesus was His Son, and the third, 'No! But he is the third of three: Jesus as son, his father, and his mother.' But the 'believer' cursed them and insisted that Paul had come to mislead them, and, urging his own followers to remain faithful to the true teaching of Jesus, he departed with them. Paul urged the other three to fight the 'believer' and his followers, but they fled to Palestine (al-Shām), where they were taken captive by the Jews. They asked the Jews to let them live in caves, on mountain tops and in hermitages, and to wander (*nasiḥū*) through the countryside, and their offspring introduced innovations (*biḍaʿ*) in religion (with a quotation of

---

[87] Van Koningsveld, 'The Islamic image of Paul', p. 202.

[88] Cf. Acts, 9:1-9.

[89] Cf. Matthew 5:38-42; Romans 12:17; 1 Peter 3:9, with quotations taken from these texts or others: 'Do not repay evil for evil'; 'If anyone slaps you on a cheek, turn to him the other also'; 'If anyone takes some of your clothes, give him the rest'.

[90] In Terian, *Armenian Gospel of the Infancy*, pp. 48 and 55, one of the Magi, 'kings of the Persians', is called Melkon.

[91] Van Koningsveld, 'The Islamic image of Paul', p. 204, rightly notes that he is 'gnostically referred as the "Believer"'.

Q 57:27: '[...] But monasticism they invented...'). A small remnant of the followers of the 'believer', who 'became the uppermost' (Q 61:14), escaped to the Arabian peninsula, where 30 of them lived as monks (or hermits), saw Muḥammad, and believed in him.

This tradition, as far as is known, does not appear in any of the classical Qurʾān commentaries, although the whole passage is taken up by the Andalusī Muḥammad al-Qaysī (fl. 1309) in one of his anti-Christian treatises.[92]

According to Ibn Isḥāq,[93] 'The Christians assert that [...] among the apostles of Jesus (*ḥawāriyyūn*) and followers who were sent after them were the apostle Peter and Paul, who was a follower and not an apostle; they went to Rome. Andrew and Matthew were sent to the country whose people are man-eaters, a land of blacks,[94] Thomas was sent to Babylonia in the east, and Philip to Qayrawān and Carthage in North Africa. John went to Ephesus, the city of the youths of the cave, and James to Jerusalem, that is Aelia, Bayt al-Maqdis. Bartholomew (Ibn Tulmā/Talmā) was sent to Arabia, namely the Ḥijāz, and Simeon to the lands of the Berbers in Africa. Judas was not sent as an apostle, but his place was taken by Ariobus[95] 'after the latter had perpetrated his deed.'[96]

According to Qatāda, Jesus sent two disciples to Antioch, but people there did not believe in them, so he sent a third to support them.[97]

---

[92] See P. van Koningsveld and G.A. Wiegers, 'The polemical works of Muḥammad al-Qaysī and their circulation in Arabic and Aljamiado among the Mudejars in the fourteenth century', *Al-Qantara* 15 (1994) 163-99, pp. 168-69.

[93] Al-Ṭabarī, *Tārīkh*, i, pp. 737-38/*The History of al-Ṭabarī*, iv, trans. M. Perlmann, Albany NY, 1987, p. 123; cf. Ibn Isḥāq, *Sīra*, p. 972/Guillaume, *Life*, p. 653; Thaʿlabī-Brinner, p. 673.

[94] Cf. *The Acts of Philip* in *The apocryphal New Testament*, trans. M.R. James, Oxford, 1924, p. 32: 'And John was there also, and said to Philip: Andrew is gone to Achaia and Thrace, and Thomas to India and the wicked flesh-eaters, and Matthew to the savage troglodytes. And do thou not be slack, for Jesus is with thee. And they let him depart'; Bovon and Geoltrain, *Écrits apocryphes chrétiens*, p. 1217; *Acts of Thomas*, in Elliott, *The apocryphal New Testament*, pp. 447-48. *Acta Andreae et Matthiae in urbe anthropophagorum* (*Acts of Andrew and Matthias*, a text very close to the dawn of Islam, 4th or 5th century), 1-3, in the city of Myrmidonia, in Elliott, *The apocryphal New Testament*, pp. 283-84.

[95] In Acts 1:26 this is Matthias. Compare with the list given in *The Acts of Philip* VIII, in Bovon and Geoltrain, *Écrits apocryphes chrétiens*, pp. 1262-63.

[96] Wheeler, *Prophets*, p. 308, wrongly translates: 'Judas, who was not a disciple, went to Ariobus'.

[97] Al-Ṭabarī, *Tafsīr*, ed. al-Saqqā, xxii, p. 155, on Q 36:12. According to Wahb: God

According to the Yemeni Shuʿayb (ibn al-Aswad) al-Jabāʾī al-Janadī (d. after 723), the names of these two disciples were Simon and John, and the third was Paul.[98]

Mary

Since the exegetical traditions on Mary and Jesus are well known,[99] only a few representative early traditions need be mentioned here.

It has often been noted that the presentation in the Qurʾān of Mary's birth and childhood is a 'borrowing' from and an adaptation of the *Protoevangelium of James* (or other similar direct or indirect sources).[100] We find further features from the same 'source(s)' or others in early commentaries on Q 3:35. According to Ibn Isḥāq, 'Zachariah and ʿImrān[101] married two sisters, Zachariah marrying the mother

sent three messengers to Antioch whose Pharaoh was the idolatrous Abṭīḥās; their names were Ṣādiq, Maṣdūq and Salūm (figurative names for 'faith'); al-Ṭabarī, *Tafsīr*, xxii, p. 156.

[98] Ibn Abī Ḥātim al-Rāzī, *Tafsīr*, ed. A.M. al-Ṭayyib, 10 vols, Mecca, 1997, x, p. 3192, no. 18050. It is said of this Shuʿayb (who is one of Ibn Isḥāq's authorities) that 'he had read the books', meaning in this context books of the Jews and Christians, and that he was an expert on 'apocalyptic and battle literature (*malāḥim*)'.

[99] See D. Wismer, *The Islamic Jesus. An annotated bibliography of sources in English and French*, New York, 1977; Thaʿlabī-Brinner, pp. 622-80; al-Kisāʾī, *The tales of the prophets of al-Kisāʾī*, trans. W.M. Thackston, Boston MA, 1978, pp. 326-36 (al-Kisāʾī, who was active before 1200, is probably a pseudonym); Wheeler, *Prophets*, pp. 297-320; R. Tottoli, *The stories of the prophets by Ibn Muṭarrif al-Ṭarafī*, Berlin, 2003, pp. 161-74; A. Ferré, 'La vie de Jésus dans Tabari', *Islamochristiana* 5 (1979), 7-29; Charfi, 'Christianity in the Qurʾān commentary of al-Ṭabarī'; N. Robinson, *Christ in Islam and Christianity. The representation of Jesus in the Qurʾān and the classical Muslim commentaries*, Basingstoke, 1991; N. Robinson, art. 'Jesus', in *EQ*; N. Akin, *Untersuchungen zur Rezeption des Bildes von Maria und Jesus in den frühislamischen Geschichtsüberlieferungen*, Edingen-Neckarhausen, 2002 (Diss. University of Heidelberg); Çinar, *Maria und Jesus im Islam*; B. Stowasser, art. 'Mary', in *EQ*; A. Rippin, art. 'John the Baptist', in *EQ*; S. Karoui, *Die Rezeption der Bibel in der frühislamischen Literatur am Beispiel der Hauptwerke von Ibn Qutayba (gest. 276/889)*, Heidelberg, 1997.

[100] Rudolph, *Die Abhängigkeit des Qorans*, p. 77; *The Protoevangelium of James* 7:2; 8:1, in Elliott, *The apocryphal New Testament*, p. 60.

[101] At first glance, one might assume that in identifying Mary as the daughter of Amram and sister of Aaron the Qurʾān confuses Mary with Miriam, the sister of Aaron and Moses (Exodus 6:18, 20; Numbers 26:59); R. Tottoli, art. 'ʿImrān', in *EQ*; J.S. Jaspis, *Koran und Bibel. Ein komparativer Versuch*, Leipzig, 1905, p. 55; G. Parrinder, *Jesus in the Qurʾān*, London, 1965, p. 64; H. Räisänen, *Das koranische Jesusbild*, Helsinki, 1971, p. 18; G. Lauche, *Die koranische Umdeutung und Verkürzung des*

of John [the Baptist], and ʿImrān the mother of Mary, though ʿImrān died while his wife was pregnant with Mary. It has come to us that that the wife of ʿImrān was barren until she reached old age. ʿImrān and his family were people of high esteem with God. While she was sitting one day in the shade of a tree, Anna (Ḥannah) saw a bird feeding its young.[102] She yearned for offspring in the same way, and prayed to God to grant her a child. God answered her prayers, and she conceived Mary. Shortly afterwards, ʿImrān died. When his wife became aware of her pregnancy, she vowed to dedicate the child in her womb to the service of God. The custom was that such a child would worship God and serve the Temple in total isolation from all worldly affairs.'[103]

In the Qurʾān Mary is called 'sister of Aaron (Hārūn)' (Q 19:28). Of course, many people in Mecca and Medina would have known that this was false, and a *pia fraus* had to be found. When one of Muḥammad's Companions, who had been asked about this by the Christians of Najrān, raised it, Muḥammad is supposed to have explained, 'People used to be called by the names of those who were before them!'[104]

According to a prophetic tradition, 'Every child is touched by Satan's attack at his birth, whereupon the child cries out.' The only exception was Mary, 'for when [her mother] bore her, she said: "I crave Thy protection for her offspring from Satan the outcast"' (Q 3:36).[105] According to Qatāda and others, neither Mary nor Jesus was touched by Satan's attack at their birth.[106]

---

biblischen Jesusbildes in seiner soteriologischen Bedeutung, Giessen, 1983, pp. 36-38. But it has been shown by S. Mourad, 'Mary in the Qurʾān: a reexamination of her presentation', in Reynolds, *The Qurʾān in its historical context*, 163-74, pp. 163-66, 172, that her identification as Amram's daughter and Aaron's sister 'are meant to highlight her biblical heritage'; for instance, 'It is on the basis of her Aaronic lineage that Mary could serve in the Temple.'

[102] *The Protoevangelium of James* 3:1, in Elliott, *The apocryphal New Testament*, p. 58; Terian, *Armenian Gospel of the Infancy* 1:9, p. 5; Sidersky, *Les origines des légendes musulmanes*, p 137.

[103] Al-Ṭabarī, *Tafsīr*, vi, p. 330, no. 6858; Ayoub, *The Qurʾan and its interpreters*, ii, 93; cf. al-Ṭabarī, *Tārīkh*, i, pp. 710-12/*History*, iv, pp. 102-3. See also Ibn Isḥāq, *Sīra*, pp. 406-7/Guillaume, *Life*, pp. 274-76; Wheeler, *Prophets*, pp. 297-98; Tottoli, *The stories of the prophets by Ibn Muṭarrif al-Ṭarafī*, pp. 161.

[104] Al-Ṭabarī, *Tafsīr*, ed. al-Saqqā, xvi, p. 78; Charfi, 'Christianity in the Qurʾān commentary of al-Ṭabarī', pp. 111-12.

[105] Al-Ṭabarī, *Tafsīr*, vi, p. 336, no. 6884; Charfi, 'Christianity in the Qurʾān commentary of al-Ṭabarī', p. 112; Ayoub, *The Qurʾan and its interpreters*, ii, p. 94.

[106] Thaʿlabī-Brinner, p. 624; Thaʿlabī-Busse, pp. 471-72.

Many details are given about Mary's guardian (Q 3:37: 'And [God] made Zachariah her guardian'). According to al-Suddī, 'Those who wrote the Torah' were disputing about the custody of Mary, and they decided to casts lots[107] for her. They went to the Jordan and threw in their pens (*aqlām*). Zachariah's pen stood firm above the water, while the pens of the others were swept away.[108] The choice of pens for casting lots in this account denotes a theological intention, because in the Qurʾān Zachariah is preordained by God for the custody of Mary: 'When they threw their pens [to know] which of them should be the guardian of Mary' (Q 3:44). In Islamic mythology the *qalam* (Greek *kalamos*, Latin *calamus*) was one of the first of God's creations, and has to do with predestination and the writing of human acts.[109]

In relation to the verse, 'Whenever Zachariah went into the sanctuary where she was, he found that she had food' (Q 3:37), the commentators give many explanations of what this was:[110] 'He found grapes out of season in a great basket' (Ibn Jubayr, Mujāhid), 'summer fruits in winter and winter fruits in summer' (al-Ḍaḥḥāk, Qatāda), 'Zachariah shut seven doors upon her, but when he entered, he found summer fruits in winter and winter fruits in summer' (al-Rabīʿ ibn Anas).[111] Zachariah said: 'The one who brings these fruits to Mary is able to make my wife fertile and to give me a boy from her.'[112]

---

[107] Cf. Terian, *Armenian Gospel of the Infancy*, 3:3, p. 14.

[108] Al-Ṭabarī, *Tafsīr*, vi, pp. 349-50, no. 6904; Ayoub, *The Qur'an and its interpreters*, ii, p. 99; Thaʿlabī-Brinner, p. 625; Charfi, 'Christianity in the Qurʾān commentary of al-Ṭabarī', pp. 112-13.

[109] According to Ibn ʿAbbās, the first thing God created was the Preserved Tablet (*al-lawḥ al-maḥfūẓ*), then he created the Pen (*qalam*); Kisāʾī-Thackston, p. 5; C. Gilliot, 'Mythe et théologie: calame et intellect, prédestination et libre arbitre', *Arabica* 45 (1998) 151-92.

[110] Al-Ṭabarī, *Tafsīr*, vi, pp. 254-57; ʿAbd al-Razzāq, *Tafsīr*, i, pp. 390-91; Ibn Abī Ḥātim al-Rāzī, *Tafsīr*, ii, p. 640.

[111] Al-Ṭabarī, *Tafsīr*, vi, pp. 354-55; Ayoub, *The Qur'an and its interpreters*, ii, p. 100; Charfi, 'Christianity in the Qurʾān commentary of al-Ṭabarī', p. 133; Thaʿlabī-Brinner, pp. 625-26; Thaʿlabī-Busse, pp. 472-73; Kisāʾī-Thackston, p. 327. Cf. *The Protoevangelium of James* 8:1, in Elliott, *The apocryphal New Testament*, p. 60, where she is fed by the hand of an angel; *Coptic history of the Virgin*, quoted by W. St Clair-Tisdall, *The original sources of the Qurʾān*, London, 1905, pp. 159-60 (from F. Robinson, *Coptic aprocryphal Gospels*, Cambridge, 1896, p. 15); Terian, *Armenian Gospel of the Infancy* 3:1, p. 13; Rudolph, *Die Abhängigkeit des Qorans*, p. 76, refers only to *The Protoevangelium of James*, not the Qurʾān itself.

[112] Muqātil, i, p. 273, the only interpretation he gives.

Ibn Isḥāq continues the story of Mary: 'Later her guardian was Jurayj, the ascetic (*al-rāhib*), a carpenter of the sons of Israel. The arrow came out to him so he took her, Zachariah having been her guardian beforehand. A grievous famine befell the sons of Israel and Zachariah was unable to support her, so they cast losts to see who should be her guardian. "And thou wast not with them when they disputed" i.e. about her (Q 3:44).'[113] The same account is found in al-Thaʿlabī's *Stories of the prophets* (though the attribution is dubious), still attributed to Ibn Isḥāq, except that this time it is Joseph the Carpenter who casts lots and gains responsibility for Mary.[114]

Jesus' birth and childhood

The qur'ānic narratives about Jesus' birth under a palm-tree and the words of the baby Jesus (Q 19:23-26) are very similar to the Pseudo-Gospel of Matthew: 'And the pangs of childbirth drove her (i.e. Mary) unto the trunk of a palm-tree… (Q 19:23) [Jesus said to her]: 'And shake the trunk of the palm-tree toward thee, thou wilt cause ripe dates to fall upon thee' (Q 19:25). However, this Latin text, *Liber de infantia* (chs 20-21, in Elliott, *The Apocryphal New Testament*, pp. 95-96) is from the eighth or ninth century and cannot be the direct source of the Qur'ān, so both must have a common source. According to the *Liber de infantia* the incident of the baby Jesus speaking took place in Egypt, but in the Qur'ān it occurred when Mary gave birth. The origin of the 'mistake' (Egypt/Bethlehem) could have its origin in one of the 'wild readings' of the tradition of the Diatessaron, an instance of such being the Middle Dutch translation: 'They found a shed made of twigs in a street' (De Bruin, *Diatessaron*, 16-17; Van Reeth, 'L'évangile du Prophète', pp. 165-66). Elsewhere Van Reeth has called attention to the influence of Manicheism on the qur'ānic presentation of the eucharist: 'Eucharistie im Koran', in M. Gross and K.-H. Ohlig (eds), *Schlaglichter. Die beiden ersten islamischen Jahrhunderte*, Berlin, 2008, 457-60). Early Muslim exegetes took material from the same common source, as well as from other sources (Muqātil, *Tafsīr*, ii, p. 625; al-Ṭabarī, *Tafsīr*, xvi, pp. 63-73).

[113] Ibn Isḥāq, *Sīra*, p. 407/Guillaume, *Life*, p. 275 (al-Ṭabarī, *Tafsīr*, vi, p. 356-57, gives this in a more amplified form from Ibn Isḥāq).

[114] Thaʿlabī-Brinner, p. 626.

According to Wahb ibn Munabbih, at Jesus' birth, 'Wherever idols were worshipped, the idols were toppled and turned upside down.'[115] Many other miracles which Jesus performed (or as the Muslim commentators describe them, miracles performed by God through Jesus, or upon him with the permission of God) during his childhood, whether or not mentioned by the Qur'ān, are described at length, such as speaking in his cradle (Q 19:29-30: 'I am the servant of God'),[116] creating birds from clay (Q 3:49),[117] etc. According to Ibn Isḥāq, 'When Jesus was about nine or ten years old, his mother sent him to school. But whenever the teacher taught him anything as he used to do with youths, he found that Jesus already knew it. The teacher exclaimed, "Do you not marvel at the son of this widow? Every time I teach him anything, I find that he knows it far better than I do." '[118]

The Kūfan al-Suddī al-Kabīr, interpreting 'And I announce unto you what ye eat and what ye store up in your houses' (Q 3:149), asserts, 'When Jesus grew into a young boy, his mother committted him [to teachers] to study the Torah. When he was playing with the youths of the village, he used to tell them what their parents were doing',[119] or he told them what they would be eating at home.[120] It should be noted that the Khurasānī exegete Muqātil ibn Sulaymān (d. 767), who obviously also knew such narratives, is content with a sum-

[115] Al-Ṭabarī, *Tārīkh*, i, p. 727/*History*, iv, p. 115; al-Ṭabarī, *Tafsīr*, vi, p. 341, no. 6894, on Q 3:36; Ayoub, *The Qur'an and its interpreters*, ii, p. 94; ʿAbd al-Razzāq, *Tafsīr*, i, pp. 390-92; Thaʿlabī-Brinner, p. 643; cf. *The Gospel of Pseudo-Matthew* 23, in Elliott, *The apocryphal New Testament*, p. 96; Bovon and Geoltrain, *Écrits apocryphes chrétiens*, p. 140; Terian, *Armenian Gospel of the infancy* 15:16, 16:4, pp. 72, 76; *The Arabic infancy Gospel* 11-12, in Elliott, *The apocryphal New Testament*, p. 103.

[116] Al-Ṭabarī, *Tafsīr*, ed. al-Saqqā, xvi, pp. 79-80; al-Thaʿlabī, vi, pp. 213-14. Cf. *The Arabic infancy Gospel* 1, in Elliott, *The apocryphal New Testament*, p. 102; Bovon and Geoltrain, *Ecrits apocryphes chrétiens*, p. 227.

[117] N. Robinson, 'Creating birds from clay. A miracle of Jesus in the Qur'ān and in classical Muslim exegesis', *MW* 79 (1989) 1-13. Cf. Ibn Isḥāq, in al-Ṭabarī, vi, pp. 425-26, no. 7086; Ayoub, *The Qur'an and its interpreters*, ii, p. 141; Charfi, 'Christianity in the Qur'ān commentary of al-Ṭabarī', p. 119; also Bovon and Geoltrain, *Écrits apocryphes chrétiens*, 197.

[118] Al-Ṭabarī, *Tafsīr*, vi, p. 433, no. 7099, on Q 3: 49; cf. *The infancy Gospel of Thomas*, Greek text A § 6, Greek text B § 6, Latin text § 6, in Elliot, *The apocryphal New Testament*, pp. 76-77; also Bovon and Geoltrain, *Écrits apocryphes chrétiens*, pp. 198-201.

[119] Al-Ṭabarī, *Tafsīr*, vi, p. 433, no. 7100; Ayoub, *The Qur'an and its interpreters*, ii, p. 142.

[120] Al-Ṭabarī, *Tafsīr*, vi, pp. 434-35, no. 7107.

mary of them without chains of authority,[121] as is the case throughout his commentary.

According to Wahb, 'When Jesus was twelve years old, God revealed to his mother in Egypt, where she had fled from her people after giving birth to him, "Take him back to Syria." She did as she was commanded. She was with him in Syria until he became 30 years of age. The period of his prophethood was only three years, after which God took him up to him.' Al-Ṭabarī continues, 'Wahb further claimed that more than 3,000 diseased people often came together to Jesus to be healed. Those who were able to come to him did so, and he himself went to those who were unable to walk. Jesus used to cure them by means of prayers to God.'[122]

The Christians, and especially Paul, as we have seen, are accused of distorting the scripture brought by Jesus (*taḥrīf*),[123] and abolishing the laws he had enjoined from God. However, exegetes differ regarding the things that Jesus made lawful for the Children of Israel. For some of them, the laws of Jesus were 'more lenient' than those of Moses, even though he came to confirm the Mosaic Law. For Wahb, 'Jesus was a follower of the law of Moses. He observed the Sabbath and faced Jerusalem in prayer. He said to the Children of Israel, "I have not come to call you to disobey even one word of the Torah.[124] I have come only to make lawful for you some of the things which were before unlawful and to relieve you of some of the hardships." '[125] According to al-Rabīʿ ibn Anas (on Q 3:50), 'The Law with which Jesus came was much more lenient than that which Moses brought. In the Torah revealed by Moses the flesh of the camel and the fats (*thurūb*) were forbidden. But they were permitted by the law revealed by Jesus; the spur of the rooster, fats, kinds of fish or of birds that have no claws.'[126]

---

[121] Muqātil, *Tafsīr*, i, p. 277, on Q 3:49.

[122] Al-Ṭabarī, *Tafsīr*, vi, pp. 431-32, on Q 3:49; Ayoub, *The Qur'an and its interpreters*, ii, pp. 141-42.

[123] H. Lazarus-Yafeh, art. 'Taḥrīf', in *EI2*; R. Caspar, and J.M. Gaudeul, 'Textes de la tradition musulmane concernant le taḥrīf (falsification) des écritures', *Islamochristiana* 6 (1980) 105-48.

[124] Cf. Matthew 5:17-19.

[125] Al-Ṭabarī, *Tafsīr*, vi, p. 438, no. 7111; Ayoub, *The Qur'an and its interpreters*, ii, p. 149.

[126] Al-Ṭabarī, *Tafsīr*, vi, p. 439, no. 7113, or according to Qatāda, no. 7112; Ayoub, *The Qur'an and its interpreters*, ii, p. 146; Thaʿlabī-Brinner, p. 656.

The development of exegesis

The development of exegesis on Christians and Christianity follows the general development of qur'ānic exegesis. The traditions mentioned above on Jesus, Christians, and Christianity belong to the 'formative period' of exegesis.[127] Then came an intermediate and decisive stage, with the introduction of grammar and linguistics (from the second half of the eighth century), and elements of rhetoric and stylistics (ninth and tenth centuries),[128] and also the rules of the transmission of ḥadīth, the beginnings of 'sectarian' exegesis (Khārijīs, Shī'īs, etc.),[129] the introduction by some theologians (Khārijīs, Zaydīs, Mu'tazilīs, Ḥanafīs, Ḥanafī-Māturīdīs, Ash'arīs, etc.) of dialectical theology (*kalām*),[130] and the rejection of this theology by others (proto-Ḥanbalīs, Ḥanbalīs, Mālikīs, etc.). In addition, there was the influence of anti-Christian polemic in the newly conquered territories. At the beginning, Muslims had traditions about Christianity but no explicitly constituted theological system.[131] In the eighth and ninth centuries in Kūfa and elsewhere their theology was partly constructed in contact with, and in reaction against, 'dualist' Christians, Marcionites and Ḍaysanites (Bardesanites), and Manicheans.[132]

Most of the great exegetical works, such al-Ṭabarī's (d. 923) commentary, took over many of the exegetical accounts referred to above, although an author such as al-Ṭabarī often gives his own position after quoting them. The Mu'tazila did not pay so much attention to the traditions transmitted, and preferred to argue rationally,[133] according to the principle of the oneness of God (*tawḥīd*). Somewhat like the Mu'tazila, the Sunnī theologian and exegete al-Māturīdī (d. 944) is reluctant to base his choices on exegetical traditions, preferring to

[127] Gilliot, 'Exegesis of the Qur'ān', pp. 104-8.

[128] Gilliot, 'Exegesis of the Qur'ān', pp. 108-10.

[129] Gilliot, 'Exegesis of the Qur'ān', pp. 116-18.

[130] Gilliot, 'Exegesis of the Qur'ān', pp. 114-16.

[131] D. Thomas, *Anti-Christian polemic in early Islam. Abū 'Īsā al-Warrāq's 'Against the Trinity'*, Cambridge, 1992, pp. 3-8.

[132] Van Ess, *TG* i, pp. 416-36.

[133] I. Goldziher, *Die Richtungen der islamischen Koranauslegung*, Leiden, 1920, 1970[3], pp. 107-8, rightly remarks that the 'rationalistic' stance of the early exegete Mujāhid was appreciated by the Mu'tazila (cf. his comment cited above, that the transformation of Jews and Christians into apes or pigs was meant figuratively not literally).

employ his own theological ideas:[134] on Q 19 (Mary), for instance, he refers to very few traditions.[135]

However, the majority of Qur'ān commentaries continue to the present to transmit the exegetical traditions of early Islam on 'Christians' and 'Christianity' with the same polemical (sometimes with more polemical) bias against them. And these traditions are usually accepted as true by the majority of Muslims, including scholars.

Conclusion

The treatment of the Nazarenes and Nazarism in the Qur'ān and in Islamic exegesis is ambiguous. On the one hand, it includes laudatory tones and narratives,[136] but on the other, 'direct or indirect criticism constitutes the largest category'.[137] The 'good' Nazarenes are two types, those who remained 'Muslims' and those who became Muslims. Those who are supposed to have remained 'Muslims' constituted a very interesting category in the Muslim imagination, even if they were few in number according to most accounts. They remained faithful to the *islām* (submission to God and His 'books') of Abraham, Moses, Jesus and other prophets, waiting for the 'praised one' (Muḥammad), or the 'most laudable one' (Aḥmad) (Q 61:6),[138] the Paraclete[139] who is announced by Jesus in the Gospel of John; to Ibn Isḥāq, 'the *Munaḥḥamana* in Syriac is Muḥammad, in Greek he is the Paraclete'. The second type of 'good' Nazarenes is represented by those who, being Christians, 'submit' (*aslamū*) themselves to God and His messenger. Both types are witnesses to the 'truth' of Islam, because

---

[134] M. Mustafizur Rahman, *An introduction to al-Maturidi's Ta'wilat ahl al-sunna*, Dacca, 1981, pp. 91-93. A good example is given in C. Gilliot, 'L'embarras d'un exégète musulman face à un palimpseste. Māturīdī et la sourate de l'Abondance (*al-Kawthar*, sourate 108)', in R. Arnzen and J. Thielmann (eds), *Words, texts and concepts cruising the Mediterranean sea. Dedicated to Gerhard Endress*, Leuven, 2004, 33-69.

[135] Al-Māturīdī, *Ta'wīlāt ahl al-sunna*, iii, pp. 257-82.

[136] Emphasized by McAuliffe, *Qur'ānic Christians*, p. 4: in her study, her choice consists of 'positive allusions to the Christians' in the Qur'ān and exegesis.

[137] McAuliffe, *Qur'ānic Christians*, p. 4. For a list of criticisms, see Charfi, 'Christianity in the Qur'ān commentary of al-Ṭabarī', pp. 134-38.

[138] Al-Ṭabarī, *Tafsīr*, ed. al-Saqqā, xxviii, p. 87, a declaration attributed to Muḥammad himself.

[139] Ibn Isḥāq, *Sīra*, pp. 149-50/Guillaume, *Life*, pp. 103-4. For the claim that the original name of the Prophet of Islam was not Muḥammad, see Gilliot, 'Reconstruction', p. 77, n. 304.

they recognized the 'proofs of prophethood' (*dalāʾil al-nubuwwa*) in Muḥammad and in the message delivered to him.[140] But the 'bad' Nazarenes, who are 'going astray' (*ḍāllūn*)[141] and leading others astray (*muḍillūn*), 'who are polytheists/associationists (*mushrikūn*)', are also adduced as proofs a contrario of Muḥammad's 'prophethood'.

To paraphrase the declaration of Muqātil, who actively engaged in *jihād* and interpreted the Qurʾān to his fellow *mujāhidūn*, one could say that for Islam, 'the true Jews and Christians are the Muslims'. But to tell the truth, Christians do not consider themselves 'People of the Book', because it is not a book that is the core of their faith but Christ.

---

140 A. Schlatter, 'Die Entwicklung des jüdischen Christentums zum Islam', *Evangelisches Missions-Magazin*, NF 62 (1918), 251-64, p. 254. In the hagiographical traditions of his life, Muḥammad appears as a parallel to the Jesus of the church, with a miraculous birth, sinlessness, ascension, etc.

141 Right from the beginning of the Qurʾān (Q 1:6-7), 'those who go astray' designate the Christians, and 'those who earn Thine anger' the Jews, according to several traditions attributed to Muḥammad, and for the majority of the exegetes, e.g. al-Ṭabarī, *Tafsīr*, i, pp. 193-95, 185-88; cf. Muqātil, i, p. 36: 'The religion of the polytheists, that is the Christians', 'The Jews with whom God is angry, so he transformed them into apes and pigs'.

Christians and Christianity in the *Sīra* of Muḥammad

Suleiman A. Mourad

The books on the *Sīra* (life and career) of Muḥammad feature a number of references to Christianity and Christian groups who came into contact, directly or indirectly, with the prophet of Islam. Such references include descriptions of encounters and disputations that Muḥammad had with Christians, sermons he delivered about Christianity, and letters that he sent to Christian rulers. Undoubtedly, there is a problem with the historicity of some or all of these encounters and stories in that no contemporary written documents attesting to their occurrence have survived. Indeed, we only find them in books authored in the late eighth or ninth century. The need for some skepticism is especially pronounced given that this material was employed in discourses on the legitimization of Islam and its prophet, as well as in Muslim polemics and disputations against Christians; some of these stories were either made up or were heavily edited to suit the objectives of medieval Muslim scholars and polemicists.[1]

[1] The issue of the authenticity and reliability of Muslim accounts of pre- and early Islamic history has divided the field of Islamic studies into three camps, representing the descriptive approach (accepting the narrative as it is without any serious scrutiny), the source-critical approach (admitting that there are some problems related to reliability and transmission but that the overall picture can still be reconstructed), and the skeptical approach (rejecting the narrative altogether as unreliable and unreconstructable). For an excellent examination of the main views and scholars behind these three categorizations, especially as they relate to *Sīra* literature, see F.M. Donner, *Narratives of Islamic origins. The beginnings of Islamic historical writing*, Princeton NJ, 1998, pp. 1-31. An essential study that highlights the problematic nature of early Islamic historical narrative is P. Crone and M. Cook, *Hagarism. The making of the Islamic world*, Cambridge, 1977. Even though it has been discredited in many circles and some of its points are no longer tenable, it remains necessary reading. Another important source is J. Wansbrough, *The sectarian milieu. Content and composition of Islamic salvation history*, Oxford, 1978. This should be read in conjunction with A. Rippin, 'Literary analysis of *Qur'ān*, *tafsīr* and *Sīra*. The methodologies of John Wansbrough', in R.C. Martin, ed., *Approaches to Islam in religious studies*, Tucson AZ, 1985, 151-63, which emphasizes the relevance of Wansbrough's essential theory regarding the problem of deriving historical knowledge from Qur'ān and *Sīra*. The two works

Another issue that relates to the unreliability of *Sīra* stories about Christians and Christianity is that several of them seem to be merely attempts to provide an exegesis of particular verses in the Qur᾿ān. Indeed, as seen in some of the cases discussed below, one comes across qur᾿ānic citations in a number of such stories. Thus, the *Sīra* does not provide independent verification or authentication of the historicity of these stories.[2]

The early sources in which we find these stories range from specific books written about the life and career of Muḥammad to major surveys of pre-Islamic and Islamic history. The earliest source we possess is *The Life of the Messenger of God* (*Sīrat rasūl Allāh*) by Ibn Isḥāq (d. 767), which is preserved almost in its entirety in the work with the same title by Ibn Hishām (d. 833). This is the major resource for material about Muḥammad's encounter with Christianity and Christians. We also possess the *Book of wars* (*Kitāb al-maghāzī*) by al-Wāqidī (d. 823), which provides a narrative of the battles and raids in which Muḥammad and his followers were involved. Although this work includes a few references to encounters with Christians, these are limited, as its title implied, to events associated with particular battles or raids. A third important source for the life and career of Muḥammad is the *Book of the great generations* (*Kitāb al-ṭabaqāt al-kubrā*) by Ibn Sa῾d (d. 845), a disciple of al-Wāqidī. Other works from the first two centuries of Islam are only extent as quotations in later works. The principle source for these is the famous *History of*

---

by W.M. Watt, *Muhammad at Mecca*, Oxford, 1953, and *Muhammad at Medina*, Oxford, 1956, remain basic surveys in English for the career of Muḥammad as represented in the Islamic tradition. The article 'Sīra' by W. Raven in *EI2* provides an excellent concise survey of the *Sīra* genre as well as the problem of its reliability, and lists a number of valuable modern studies on several aspects of the *Sīra*.

Regarding the methodology of transmission of history in early Islam, including *Sīra* literature, the reader should consult G. Schoeler, *The oral and the written in early Islam*, trans. U. Vagelpohl, ed. J.E. Montgomery, London, 2006.

On religious life in Arabia before the coming of Islam, incorporating archaeological findings and a variety of Islamic and non-Islamic sources, see R.G. Hoyland, *Arabia and the Arabs. From the Bronze Age to the coming of Islam*, London, 2001, pp. 139-66.

[2] This issue has been raised in several modern studies. Besides some of the references mentioned in n. 1, see also the discussions in W. Raven, 'Some early Islamic texts on the Negus of Abyssinia', *JSS* 33 (1988) 197-218, and A. Rippin, 'Muḥammad in the Qur᾿ān: Reading scripture in the 21st century', in H. Motzki (ed.), *The biography of Muhammad. The issue of the sources*, Leiden, 2000, 298-309.

messengers and kings (*Ta'rīkh al-rusul wa-l-mulūk*) by al-Ṭabarī (d. 923), and to a lesser degree *The pedigrees of aristocrats* (*Ansāb al-ashrāf*) by al-Balādhurī (d. 883), which discusses the genealogies of aristocratic Arab families and tribes essentially of Mecca and Medina.

The material about encounters between Muḥammad and Christians exhibits some interesting features. First, it reflects an effort on the part of early Muslim scholars (and one might argue that this could also have been one of the major preoccupations of Muḥammad and his early followers) to show that the authenticity and veracity of Muḥammad's claim to prophethood were evident to those learned in the Christian scripture.[3] In other words, Muḥammad exhibited all the signs of a true prophet, and Christian scripture foretold his coming. One finds this emphasized in almost every legend of encounters between Christians and Muḥammad and his followers: when they see him or he is described to them, they know in their hearts that he is a true prophet, the one they have been expecting. But as can be seen below in the cases of the bishop of Najrān and the Byzantine Emperor Heraclius, they are not always able to profess this publicly for various reasons, such as fear of loss of status in their communities, persistence in their belief, or their own wickedness and malice. Indeed, the theme of a Christian ruler acknowledging the truthfulness of Islam and its beliefs, in the face of objections from his clergy and generals, is repeated in almost every story of an encounter between Muslims and a Christian ruler. It must be treated as a literary topos inserted into these legends to demonstrate that the veracity of Muḥammad's prophethood and the soundness of the teachings of Islam were evident to the leaders of the Christians. Second, we also notice in many of the stories that the narrative is made to prophesy the victory of Islam, whether the success of Muḥammad and his followers in defeating their enemies in Arabia as proclaimed by the Negus, or the victorious conquests of Syria and defeat of the Byzantines as proclaimed by Heraclius.

Given the scarcity of the sources, we are not in a position, apart from what has been said already, to assess the changes in approach or emphasis on the part of the early Islamic sources and authors to this

---

[3] For a discussion of early Muslim belief that Muḥammad's prophethood is attested and foretold in Christian and Jewish scriptures, see U. Rubin, *The eye of the beholder. The life of Muḥammad as viewed by the early Muslims. A textual analysis*, Princeton NJ, 1995, pp. 21-43.

material on Christianity and Christians in the *Sīra* of Muḥammad. We may add the comment that a few accounts feature material identical to that in the Gospels or exhibit a fair understanding of problematic issues within Christian theology. It cannot, however, be established whether these instances resulted from direct access to texts, or involved Christian converts to Islam or Christian informants.[4]

The sections below examine the main encounters between Christians and Muḥammad and his followers that are found in the *Sīra*, along with any references to and discussion of Christianity, and possible references to material from the Gospels that occur in the *Sīra* text.

The Introduction of Christianity to Najrān

According to one of the legends related by Ibn Isḥāq, Christianity was introduced to Najrān through a Christian ascetic named Faymiyūn, who was captured and sold into slavery there.[5] At that time, the people used to worship a palm-tree. The ascetic became known among them for his spirituality and night vigils, and one day his owner asked him to produce a miracle so that the people of Najrān would leave their religious customs and follow him. Faymiyūn prayed to God that the palm-tree they worshiped should be cursed: a strong wind came and uprooted it, and the people of Najrān became Christians.[6]

---

[4] For studies of the similarity between Gospel and Sīra materials, see I. Goldziher, 'The Ḥadīth and the New Testament', in Goldziher, *Muslim Studies*, trans. C.R. Barber and S.M. Stern, 2 vols, London, 1967-1971, ii, 346-62. For the availability of the New Testament in Arabic in early Islam, see S.H. Griffith, 'The Gospel in Arabic: An inquiry into its appearance in the first Abbasid century', *OC* 69 (1985) 126-67; and G. Lecomte, 'Les citations de l'Ancien et du Nouveau Testament dans l'œuvre d'Ibn Qutayba', *Arabica* 5 (1958) 34-46.

[5] Nöldeke suggests that Faymiyūn is from the Greek name Euphemion; see T. Nöldeke, *Geschichte der Perser und Araber zur Zeit der Sasaniden*, Leiden, 1879, p. 177, n. 3. A. Moberg, however, points to the similarity between the Faymiyūn story and that of the Persian Christian martyr Pethion; on this, see J. Ryckmans, 'Le christianisme en Arabie du Sud préislamique', in *Accademia Nazionale dei Lincei. Atti del Convegno internazionale sul thema l'Oriente christiano nella storia della civilità*, Rome, 1964, pp. 441-42.

[6] Ibn Hishām, *Al-sīrat al-nabawiyya*, ed. I. al-Saqqā et al., 4 vols, Beirut, 1990, i, pp. 28-30/*The life of Muhammad. A translation of Isḥāq's Sīrat rasūl Allāh*, trans. A. Guillaume, Karachi, 1967, pp. 14-16; al-Ṭabarī, *Ta'rīkh al-rusul wa-l-mulūk*, Beirut, 1991, i, pp. 434-35/*The History of al-Ṭabarī*, Albany NY, 1985-99, v, pp. 193-202.

A different version of this story has it that Faymiyūn came to Najrān and lived in a tent in a village where the chief sorcerer of Najrān resided. ʿAbdallāh ibn al-Thāmir, the son of one of the notables, started to come to Faymiyūn instead of going to study with the sorcerer, and learned from the ascetic the religion of 'Islam'. It was ʿAbdallāh ibn al-Thāmir who introduced and spread Christianity in Najrān. Then the Jewish king of Yemen, Dhū Nuʾās, invaded Najrān in the hope of converting its people to Judaism, but they refused and were massacred, thrown in a trench (*ukhdūd*) and burnt. Hence the reference in Q 85:4-9: 'Cursed be the diggers of the Trench, who lighted the consuming fire and sat around it to watch the faithful being put to the torture. Nor did they torture them for any reason save that they believed in God, the mighty, the praised one.' Among those killed that day was ʿAbdallāh ibn al-Thāmir.[7]

The massacre of the people of Najrān was allegedly the reason for the Abyssinian invasion of Yemen,[8] and the subsequent failed attempt on the part of the Abyssinian army to capture Mecca. Irrespective of the historicity of this event, the sources on the life of Muḥammad place it in the year of the elephant (*ʿām al-fīl*), that is the year he was born, which according to the Islamic tradition corresponds to 570.[9] Here too, a qurʾānic reference is adduced to confirm the 'historicity' of the event, which reads, 'Have you not considered how God dealt with the army of the elephant? Did He not confound their stratagem and send against them flocks of birds which pelted them with clay-stones, so that they became like the withered stalks of plants which cattle have devoured?' (Q 105)[10]

---

[7] Ibn Hishām, *Sīra*, i, pp. 30-31/*The Life of Muhammad*, pp. 16-18; al-Ṭabarī, *Taʾrīkh*, i, p. 435/*The History of al-Ṭabarī*, v, p. 202.

[8] On the martyrs of Najrān, see I. Shahīd, *The martyrs of Najrān. New documents*, Brussels, 1971.

[9] The dating of this event (i.e. year of the elephant) can only be established approximately around the year 550; see L.I. Conrad, 'Abraha and Muhammad. Some observations apropos of chronology and literary topoi in the early Arabic historical tradition', *BSOAS* 50 (1987) 225-40.

[10] Ibn Hishām, *Sīra*, i, pp. 32-47/*The Life of Muhammad*, pp. 18-30; al-Ṭabarī, *Taʾrīkh*, i, pp. 436-44/*The History of al-Ṭabarī*, v, pp. 212-25. See also al-Balādhurī, *Ansāb al-ashrāf*, ed. M. Hamidullah, Cairo, 1987, pp. 67-69.

Muḥammad's encounter with Baḥīrā the monk

Probably the most important story of encounters between Christians and Muḥammad is that of Baḥīrā the monk.[11] It is said that when Muḥammad was a young boy, he accompanied his uncle Abū Ṭālib, one of the notables of Mecca, on a trading trip to Syria. The Meccan caravan stopped on the outskirts of the city of Buṣra, south of Damascus, near the cell of a Christian monk named Baḥīrā. The monk, who had never before paid any attention to Meccan traders, noticed an extraordinary phenomenon occurring around the boy Muḥammad (depending on which story one reads, it was either a cloud following him or a tree bending its branches to shade him). He spoke to the boy and was further perplexed as he realized he was not talking to an ordinary person. So the monk proceeded to examine Muḥammad's body, and he noticed a mole between the boy's shoulders. This was the final proof that, according to what the monk had learned regarding the descriptions of prophethood, Muḥammad was to become a prophet. Baḥīrā informed Abū Ṭālib that he was to take the boy back to Mecca and protect him, especially from the Jews, who would conspire to kill the boy if they found out about him.[12]

A variant version of this story identifies the monk as Nestorius and gives the age of Muḥammad as 25.[13]

The description of Muḥammad in the Gospel

Besides the legend of Baḥīrā, there is the story that says Muḥammad is described in the Gospel.[14] This claim, to which there is a vague reference in the Qur'ān (Q 7:157), is first articulated in the *Sīra* of Ibn

[11] On Baḥīrā, see A. Abel, art., 'Baḥīrā', in *EI2*, which includes helpful references. For an analysis of the legend of Baḥīrā's encounter with Muḥammad, see also Rubin, *Eye of the beholder*, pp. 49-52, and B. Roggema, *The legend of Sergius Baḥīrā*, Leiden, 2009, ch. 2.

[12] This story and variant versions are recorded in Ibn Hishām, *Sīra*, i, p. 147/*The Life of Muhammad*, pp. 79-81; Ibn Sa'd, *Kitāb al-ṭabaqāt al-kubrā*, Beirut, 1958, i, pp. 120-21; al-Ṭabarī, *Ta'rīkh*, i, pp. 519-20/*The History of al-Ṭabarī*, vi, pp. 44-46. See also al-Balādhurī, *Ansāb*, i, pp. 96-97.

[13] Ibn Sa'd, *Ṭabaqāt*, i, 130-31.

[14] For an examination of Ibn Isḥāq and his use of this Gospel narrative, see Griffith, 'The Gospel in Arabic', pp. 137-43; A. Guillaume, 'The version of the Gospels used in Medina c. A.D. 700', *Al-Andalus* 15 (1950) pp. 289-96; and J. Schacht,

Isḥāq.[15] It says that in the Gospel of John, Jesus foretells the coming of the *Munaḥḥamanā* as a messenger from God. The quotation reads,

> Whoever hates me hates the Lord also. If I had not done among them the works that no one else did, they would not have sinned. Now they are covetous and think they can prevail over me and the Lord. For the word that is written in the Law has to be fulfilled: 'They hated me without a cause'. But when the *Munaḥḥamanā* comes, whom God will send to you from the Lord, the Holy Spirit who comes from the Lord, he will testify about me. You too are to testify because you have been with me from the beginning. I have said these things to you to keep you from despair.[16]

Then Ibn Isḥāq explains that *Munaḥḥamanā* is a Syriac word that means Muḥammad, and in Greek it means *Parakletos* (Paraclete).

This quotation is taken verbatim from John 15:23-16:1, apart from the very minor difference that, in John, Jesus refers to God as 'my Father', whereas in Ibn Isḥāq's version, God is referred to as 'the Lord' (*al-rabb*). It is worth noting that the *Munaḥḥamanā*/Paraclete, which is also mentioned in John 14:16, 14:26 and 16:7-15, is clearly identified there with the Holy Spirit, and, very interestingly, this also seems to be the case in Ibn Isḥāq's version.[17]

Migration of Muḥammad's followers to Abyssinia

Another encounter with Christians occurs at the migration to Abyssinia of a number of Muḥammad's followers, among them ʿUthmān ibn ʿAffān, the son-in law of Muḥammad and third caliph of Islam.

'Une citation de l'Evangile de S. Jean dans la Sira d'Ibn Ishaq', *Al-Andalus* 16 (1951), pp. 489-90.

[15] Ibn Saʿd devotes a small section to the description of Muḥammad in the Bible and Gospel, showing that he was unaware of Ibn Isḥāq's story; see *Ṭabaqāt*, i, pp. 360-63.

[16] Ibn Hishām, *Sīra*, i, pp. 187-88/*The Life of Muhammad*, pp. 103-4.

[17] The editor of Ibn Hishām's *Sirā* adds the particle of conjunction 'and' in order to distinguish between *al-Munaḥḥamanā* and the Holy Spirit. But clearly this addition does not make any sense in the text. For a discussion of Ibn Isḥāq and his use of this Gospel narrative, see Griffith, 'The Gospel in Arabic', pp. 137-43; and Guillaume, 'Version of the Gospels', pp. 289-96. I do not agree with Griffith and Guillaume that Ibn Isḥāq in this particular case means by the word *al-nāmūs* the angel Gabriel, for the sentence clearly points to something that is written in a text called *al-nāmūs*, meaning the Hebrew scripture; indeed, 'they hated me without a cause' occurs in Psalms 35:19 and 69:4.

They fled the difficulties and persecutions they were facing in Mecca, and the reason for choosing Abyssinia was that its Negus (*al-najāshī*, the title for King) was a pious Christian who ruled with justice and compassion; this persuaded the Muslims that he would protect them and treat them well.[18] But the leaders of Mecca sent on their heels two envoys to the Negus to request that he expel the Muslims from his realm and turn them over to the Meccans. The Negus held court and questioned the followers of Muḥammad about their beliefs. The Muslims read to him verses from Q 19, which caused the Negus to weep. He said to them: 'By God, this and what Jesus proclaimed could only have come from the same source', and he refused to turn them over to the Meccan envoys. But then the Meccan envoys conspired and requested the Negus to ask the Muslims about their views about Jesus, which he did. The Muslims replied by reciting Q 4:171, which affirms that Jesus is God's servant and messenger, His spirit, and His word which He cast into the Virgin Mary, the chaste. The Negus approved of this despite the objection of his clergy and generals, whom he expelled from his court as a result of this disputation.[19]

In a variant tradition, which narrates the circumstances of the conversion of the famous ʿAmr ibn al-ʿĀṣ to Islam, it is said that ʿAmr, who was the Meccan envoy, asked the Negus to hand over the leader of the Muslim immigrants so that he could kill him. The Negus struck ʿAmr on the nose, causing it to bleed, and said angrily, 'Do you have no shame! You dare ask me to hand over to you the envoy of the messenger of God who is visited by the angel Gabriel (*al-nāmūs al-akbar*), who used to come to Moses and Jesus son of Mary!' ʿAmr asked the Negus about the truthfulness of Muḥammad's religious claims and the Abyssinian ruler affirmed that it was the truth and that soon Muḥammad would have dominion over those who opposed him.[20] Then ʿAmr stretched out his hand and asked the Negus to accept his conversion to Islam, which the Abyssinian monarch gladly did, and rewarded ʿAmr generously.[21]

---

[18] For an examination of early Muslim stories about the Negus, see Raven, 'Some early Islamic texts on the Negus'. See also E. van Donzel, art. 'al-Nadjāshī', in *EI2*.

[19] Ibn Hishām, *Sīra*, i, pp. 255-69/*The Life of Muhammad*, pp. 146-53.

[20] This story of the Negus identifying the angel Gabriel as the *nāmūs* who also used to come to Moses and Jesus is similarly attested in the story of Waraqa ibn Nawfal, cousin of Muḥammad's wife Khadīja, when he was told about Muḥammad receiving revelation; see Rubin, *Eye of the beholder*, pp. 106-10.

[21] Al-Wāqidī, *Kitāb al-maghāzī*, ed. M. Jones, 3 vols, Beirut, 1984, ii, p. 743.

Delegation of Christians from Abyssinia

According to Ibn Isḥāq, a delegation of about 20 Christian men came from Abyssinia to meet Muḥammad in Mecca. They questioned him, and after he had answered all their queries, he recited to them verses from the Qurʾān. The minute they heard the recitation, their eyes overflowed with tears. They realized that he was indeed the one mentioned in their scripture. They converted to Islam and went back to their country. Ibn Hishām remarks that others say that this Christian delegation was from Najrān, adding that the verses Q 28:52-55 refer to them.[22]

Delegation from the Christians of Najrān

Shortly before the year 622, a delegation from the Christians of Najrān came to Medina to visit Muḥammad. It comprised 60 people, led by the two chiefs ʿAbd al-Masīḥ, nicknamed al-ʿĀqib, and al-Ayham, nicknamed al-Sayyid. Also in the delegation was the Bishop Abū Ḥāritha, who upon seeing Muḥammad revealed to his brother Kūz (or Kurz) that Muḥammad was indeed the prophet they were awaiting. But for fear that the privileges and rewards his priestly position brought him and his family would be taken away, the bishop confided to his brother that he could not proclaim this in public. The brother converted to Islam at a later point.[23]

The delegation from Najrān met with Muḥammad in the mosque of Medina. Ibn Isḥāq records their belief: 'They uphold that Jesus is simultaneously God, Son of God, and part of the Trinity (*thālith thalātha*).' He adds that they justify their saying 'Jesus is God' on the basis that he raised the dead, cured the sick, foretold the future, and created birds from clay that came to life after he breathed into them (though this was only possible because of God's command) for Jesus was made a sign (*āya*) to humanity, a reference to Q 19:21. As for their belief that Jesus is the Son of God, they justify it on the basis that no human is known to have fathered him, and that he spoke while still an infant in the cradle, which no child has ever done. As for their belief that Jesus is part of the Trinity, they justify it on the basis that God

[22] Ibn Hishām, *Sīra*, ii, pp. 25-26/*The Life of Muhammad*, pp. 179-80.
[23] Ibn Hishām, *Sīra*, ii, pp. 162-63/*The Life of Muhammad*, pp. 270-71.

uses the first person plural in scripture when He says: 'We have done', 'We have commanded', 'We have created', 'We have determined'. Had He been one, He would have used the first person singular: 'I have done', 'I have determined', 'I have commanded', 'I have created'. In their view, this proves that God, Jesus and Mary form a Trinity.[24]

The prophet invited the delegation to convert to Islam, and their leaders replied that they were already Muslims long before Muḥammad was even born. Muḥammad accused them of lying, saying, 'You cannot be Muslims since you ascribe a son to God, worship the cross, and eat pork.' They asked him, 'Who is his (Jesus') father then?' But Muḥammad did not answer them. As a result of this confrontation, several verses of the Qur'ān were revealed to him, forming the first 80 verses or so of *Sūra* 3 (*Āl ʿImrān*). They affirm the oneness and unity of God, recount the annunciation to Mary of Jesus, confirm the nature of Jesus, and challenge some of the beliefs that Christians uphold about him.

The next day, Muḥammad met again with the leaders of the delegation and informed them of what had been revealed to him. They asked to be allowed to deliberate among themselves, and when they did, their leader, ʿAbd al-Masīḥ, told them that if they insisted on holding on to Christianity and to their beliefs about Jesus, they ought to conclude a peace treaty with Muḥammad and return to Najrān, for they were certain that he was indeed a true prophet with a genuine message.[25]

Letters to Christian kings

Ibn Isḥāq's *Sīra* also relates that Muḥammad wrote to several Christian rulers calling them to accept Islam. These included the Byzantine Emperor Heraclius, the Negus of Abyssinia, the governor of Egypt in Alexandria al-Muqawqis, and al-Ḥārith ibn Abī Shāmir, the King of the Ghassānids in Syria. These letters were supposedly sent in 628, the same year in which Muḥammad concluded a temporary peace treaty with the Meccans; Ibn Isḥāq does not actually relate their content. The Prophet spoke to his followers warning them of divisions and discord similar to those that had taken place among the disciples and followers of Jesus when he delegated them to proclaim his message to the

[24] Ibn Hishām, *Sīra*, ii, p. 164/*The Life of Muhammad*, pp. 271-72.

[25] Ibn Hishām, *Sīra*, ii, pp. 165-70/*The Life of Muhammad*, pp. 272-77. A much shorter version of this story is recorded in Ibn Saʿd, *Ṭabaqāt*, i, pp. 357-58.

world. Those delegated to nearby places were happy, but those delegated to distant places protested. Jesus complained to God, and God caused each of the disciples to speak only the language of the people to whom he was delegated; hence the discord among Christians.[26] Ibn Isḥāq also lists the names of the disciples and where each one of them was sent: Peter and Paul, who was not among the disciples of Jesus, to Rome; Andrew and Matthew to the land whose inhabitants eat humans; Thomas to Babylon; Philip to Carthage; John to Ephesus, the town of the Sleepers of the Cave (mentioned in Q 18); Jacob to Jerusalem; Bartholomew (Son of Thelma) to Arabia; Simon to the land of the Berbers (North Africa); Judas, who was not a disciple and replaced Judas Iscariot (no place is indicated). This story of the discord that befell Jesus' disciples certainly takes its origin from the commissioning of the 11 disciples in Matthew 28:16-20.

To return to the letters that Muḥammad sent to the Christian kings and rulers, only al-Ṭabarī relates their contents; the other sources simply say that Muḥammad sent letters. The most extensive discussion is given to Muḥammad's letter to Heraclius,[27] and the exchange that took place between the emperor and Muḥammad's envoy, named Duḥya ibn Khalīfa al-Kalbī. The letter reads:

> In the name of God, the merciful and compassionate. From Muḥammad, the messenger of God, to Heraclius, the emperor of the Byzantines (*ʿaẓīm al-Rūm*). Peace on whoever follows true guidance. Convert to Islam and you shall be saved (*aslim taslam*). Convert to Islam and God shall give you your reward doubled. But if you turn away, let the sins of the wicked ploughmen (*al-akkārūn*) be upon you.[28]

---

[26] Ibn Hishām, *Sīra*, iv, pp. 192-93/*The Life of Muhammad*, pp. 652-53; al-Ṭabarī, *Taʾrīkh*, ii, p. 128/*The History of al-Ṭabarī*, viii, p. 99.

[27] For an examination of this letter and Muslim views of Heraclius as an ideal ruler, see N.M. El-Cheikh, *Byzantium viewed by the Arabs*, Cambridge MA, 2004, pp. 42-46. For arguments against the letter's authenticity, see R.B. Serjeant, 'Early Arabic prose', in A.F.L. Beeston et al. (eds), *The Cambridge history of Arabic literature. Arabic literature to the end of the Umayyad period*, Cambridge, 1983, pp. 114-53; and S. al-Jaburi, 'The Prophet's letter to the Byzantine Emperor Heraclius', *Hamdard Islamicus* 1 (1978) 36-50. In favor of its authenticity, see M.Hamidullah, 'La lettre du Prophète à Héraclius et le sort de l'original', *Arabica* 2 (1955) 97-110; and M.Hamidullah, *Six originaux des lettres diplomatiques du Prophète de l'islam. Etude paléographique et historique des lettres du Prophète*, Paris, 1985, pp. 149-72.

[28] Al-Ṭabarī, *Taʾrīkh*, ii, p. 130/*The History of al-Ṭabarī*, viii, p. 104.

The 'wicked ploughmen' is an evident allusion to Jesus' parable of the wicked tenants in Matthew 21:33-41, which speaks of tenants who leased a vineyard but then refused to honor the terms of the lease and killed the owner's envoys and his son, and their sins earned them 'a miserable death.' In other words, by alluding to Jesus' parable, the letter is emphasizing that those entrusted with the leadership of God's people are under obligation to honor God's commandments, and when they refuse to do so, God will subject them to a miserable punishment.

When Heraclius received the letter – he was in Jerusalem, though other accounts place him in Emesa (Ḥims) – he was anxious to learn more about Muḥammad and his message, especially since he had been shown in a dream that the nation of the circumcision would become victorious. The person who is said to have informed Heraclius about Muḥammad was none other than Abū Sufyān, then Muḥammad's archenemy. Heraclius inquired about Muḥammad's background and characteristics, as well as the types of people who followed him, and then said to Abū Sufyān, 'If you have told me the truth about him (Muḥammad), he shall surely wrest away this very ground under my feet. I only wish I were with him so that I could wash his feet.' Heraclius wrote to a learned Byzantine who was knowledgeable in Hebrew, informing him of the news about Muḥammad. The learned man replied, 'He is indeed the prophet whom we are expecting. There is no doubt about that. You must follow him and believe in what he says.' Then Heraclius held court and summoned his generals. He told them that he had received a letter from Muḥammad calling the emperor to his religion, and assured them that Muḥammad was indeed the prophet they were expecting and about whom they had read in their scriptures. Heraclius appealed to them to accept Muḥammad and follow him so that they would be saved in this world and the next. But when he saw their negative reaction and was afraid, Heraclius retracted, saying that he had only meant to test their allegiance and steadfastness. He then called for Diḥya, Muḥammad's envoy, and informed him that Muḥammad was indeed a true messenger, whom the Byzantine Christians had been expecting and about whom they had read in their scripture, though, for fear that the Byzantines would harm him, Heraclius could not convert. He asked Diḥya to give the news of Muḥammad to Bishop Ṣaghāṭir, who had more popularity and authority among the Byzantines than the emperor. When Ḍiḥya did so, Ṣaghāṭir confirmed what the emperor had affirmed to the envoy, went out to the church and proclaimed his conversion to Islam, saying, 'I am attesting that there is no god but God and that Aḥmad is his servant and messenger.' The crowd turned on Ṣaghāṭir and killed him. Later, when Heraclius marched from Syria to Constantinople, he convened his generals and advised them either to give up Syria to Muḥammad or to pay him a poll-tax (*jizya*) so that the prophet and the Muslims would leave them in peace, but they refused.[29]

Another letter that Muḥammad sent was to the Ghassānid King al-Ḥārith ibn Abī Shāmir in Damascus. The letter reads: 'Peace on whoever follows true guidance and accepts it. I call you to believe in God, the one with no partners, so that your dominion is retained for you.' When it was read to al-Ḥārith, he arrogantly shouted out, 'Who can dare wrest away my kingdom. It is I who shall wrest his (Muḥammad's kingdom)!'[30]

Muḥammad also wrote to the Negus of Abyssinia, calling him to Islam.[31] The letter reads:

> In the name of God, the Merciful and Compassionate. From Muḥammad, the messenger of God, to the Negus al-Aṣḥam, king of Abyssinia. Peace with you. I praise before you God, the King, the most holy, the Peace, the Keeper of faith, the Watcher, and bear witness that Jesus son of Mary is the spirit of God and word from Him that He cast into Mary, the chaste, goodly and virgin, so that she conceived him. For God has created him from His spirit and breathed into him, similar to the way He created Adam by His hand and breathed into him. I call you to God, the one with no partners, and to persist in His obedience. I also call you to follow me and believe in what has been revealed to me. For I am the messenger of God, and have sent you my cousin Ja'far along with a group of Muslims. If he reaches you, accept what he brings and do not be haughty. I call you and your army to God. I am simply proclaiming and offering sincere advice. Accept my advice. Peace on whoever follows true guidance.

The Negus wrote back to Muḥammad:

> In the name of God, the Merciful and Compassionate. To Muḥammad, the messenger of God, from the Negus al-Aṣḥam ibn Abjar. Peace on

[29] Al-Ṭabarī, *Ta'rīkh*, ii, p. 128-31/*The History of al-Ṭabarī*, viii, p. 100-7. See also the shorter variant version in al-Wāqidī, *Maghāzī*, iii, pp. 1018-19; and Ibn Sa'd, *Ṭabaqāt*, i, p. 259.

[30] Ibn Sa'd, *Ṭabaqāt*, i, p. 261; Al-Ṭabarī, *Ta'rīkh*, ii, p. 131/*The History of al-Ṭabarī*, viii, pp. 107-8.

[31] For a discussion of the correspondence between Muḥammad and the Negus, see Hamidullah, *Six originaux des lettres diplomatiques*, 135-48.

> you, O prophet of God, and God's mercy and blessings; it is this God, other than Whom there is no god, Who has guided me to Islam. I have received your letter, O messenger of God, especially that part where you mention Jesus. By the Lord of the sky and earth, Jesus is exactly what you say. I attest to what you have sent us and have acknowledged it before your cousin and his companions. Indeed, I bear witness that you are the messenger of God, speaking the truth and confirming the truth. I have sworn allegiance to you before your cousin, and converted before him to the faith of the submission to God, Lord of creation. I am sending to you my son Arhā ibn al-Aṣḥam ibn Abjar, for I only have power over myself. If you desire me to come to you, I will, O messenger of God. I truly bear witness that what you say is the truth, and peace upon you, O messenger of God.[32]

Muḥammad also wrote to al-Muqawqis, King of the Copts, calling him to convert to Islam, but al-Muqawqis refused and sent the prophet some gifts, including the slave girl Māriya whom Muḥammad married. We are not told the content of this letter.[33]

Conclusion

The importance of these references to Christians and Christianity in the *Sīra* of Muḥammad, as this presentation has shown, is not that they establish the historical record. Even if some aspects of these encounters or sermons did actually take place, the early Muslim sources mention them for specific apologetic and polemical objectives, not for their historicity. Moreover, one should not ignore the impact these stories were to have on later Muslim generations in terms of shaping their understanding of and attitude towards Christianity.

First, the stories are employed to validate Muḥammad's claim to be a prophet and legitimize Islam as a religious tradition following on after Christianity. Given a common polemical Christian position at the time, that the coming of Muḥammad was not foretold by Christianity, Muslim scholars were eager to 'find', or at least allege, that references to him abounded in Christian scripture and other religious texts (although they do not name any of them apart from the Gospel). The

[32] Al-Ṭabarī, *Ta'rīkh*, ii, p. 131-32/*The History of al-Ṭabarī*, viii, pp. 109-10.

[33] See Ibn Sa'd, *Ṭabaqāt*, i, pp. 260-61; al-Ṭabarī, *Ta'rīkh*, ii, p. 134/*The History of al-Ṭabarī*, viii, p. 114. For the text of the letter to al-Muqawqis, see Hamidullah, *Six originaux des lettres diplomatiques*, pp. 95-108.

so-called 'description' of Muḥammad in these texts makes Christians such as the monk Baḥīrā capable of recognizing Muḥammad's prophetic status even when he was a young boy. Moreover, many a notable Christian figure witnesses to the veracity of Muḥammad's claim, and acknowledges that he was the one the Christians were waiting for, as we have seen with the Negus, Heraclius, and the leaders of Najrān. They attest to Muḥammad's prophethood and his message despite the objection of their respective clergy and generals. Only greed, fear of loss of status and prestige, or dogged determination to remain Christian holds them back from actual conversion to Islam.

Second, the material as a whole condemns the Christians, with the exception of a few, for their rejection of Muḥammad and Islam. As can be seen in almost every story of encounter with Christians, what they reject is not a novelty or an idea alien to them. Rather, they readily deny a firmly established Christian belief, that Muḥammad is proclaimed in their own books and teachings. One can see how such condemnation would be very useful in Muslim anti-Christian polemics, in that it exposes those who remain Christians by refusing to follow Muḥammad and convert to Islam as not true Christians after all.

Third, some of the stories about Christianity and Christians in the *Sīra* were employed to proclaim the victory of Islam. Again, both the Negus and Heraclius have no doubt that Muḥammad and his followers will be victorious over their many enemies, in Arabia and elsewhere. Interestingly, these proclamations are placed in the context of exchanges that Muḥammad's envoys had with the Negus and Heraclius as a result of the prophet's letters calling them to convert to his religion. In other words, the letters and the statements by the two monarchs anticipate the triumph of the early Islamic conquests.

Christians and Christianity in *ḥadīth* works before 900

David Cook

The *ḥadīth* literature presents Christianity as a dangerous theological opponent to Islam. However, the attitude towards Christians is far more nuanced. It ranges from the outright hostility and warfare described in the apocalyptic literature to the awe and respect towards the monastic community (cf. Q 5:81-2) that is to be found in the ascetic literature. For the most part, Christians are in the background (compared with Jews) because the personal contact between the Prophet Muḥammad and individual Christians was comparatively limited. Thus, while a great many literary *ḥadīth* are inherited from Christianity, most of these are not ascribed, and there are few personal contacts described in the literature.

Early *ḥadīth* fragments and collections

The earliest *ḥadīth* fragments and collections date from approximately the middle of the eighth century. Among these collections, that of Hammām ibn Munabbih (d. 752) stands out. In his collection, Christians are given a status that indicates some possibility of salvation. The first tradition in the collection reads as follows:

> We [Muslims] are the last, the first on the Day of Resurrection – despite the fact that they were given the book prior to us, but they differed concerning it, while we were given the book after them. This will be their day, that was ordained for them, but they differed concerning it, but God guided us to it. They will be followers to us, the Jews tomorrow, and the Christians the following day.[1]

This tradition would seem to reflect the comparatively positive views of Christians (as opposed to Trinitarian Christianity) that can be

---

[1] Hammām ibn Munabbih, *Ṣaḥīfa*, ed. R.F. ʿAbd al-Muṭṭalib, Cairo, 1985, p. 20 (no. 1), cf. Q 2:213, 3:19, 4:157; al-Bukhārī, *Ṣaḥīḥ*, ed. ʿAbdallāh ibn Bāz, Beirut, 1991, i, p. 238 (no. 876).

found in the Qurʾān (e.g. 5:82-83), and perhaps allows for salvation for the Christians on the Day of Resurrection.

Similarly, in the early ascetic collection of Asad ibn Mūsā (d. 827),

> The most noble of God's creation is Abū l-Qāsim [Muḥammad], and paradise is in heaven, while hell is on earth (*al-nār fī l-arḍ*). When the Day of Resurrection arrives, God will gather the creation together, community by community (*ummatan ummatan*), prophet by prophet, until Aḥmad and his community will be last of the group in place. Then He will place a bridge over Gehenna… and the Prophet and the righteous (*ṣāliḥūn*) will pass over, and the angels will meet them, and give them their places in paradise – on both your left and right, until finally he [Muḥammad] ends up in front of his Lord, and a chair to the right of God is given to him. Then a caller will call out, 'Where are Jesus and his community?' He will begin [to come], and his community – righteous and libertine – will follow him. When they reach the bridge, God will blot out His enemies' sight, and they will fall off it left and right. The prophet [Jesus] will be saved together with the righteous (*ṣāliḥūn*) with him, and the angels will meet them, and give them their places in paradise – on both your right and left, until finally he [Jesus] ends up in front of his Lord, and a chair is given him to the other [left] side. Then the prophets and communities follow them, and the last of them is Noah.[2]

While the primacy of the Muslim community is affirmed in this tradition, the possibility of the salvation of Christians is not ruled out. However, one should note that other traditions in Asad ibn Mūsā contradict this conclusion.[3]

Other early *ḥadīth* collections (pre-canonical) are usually of a highly legal nature and contain little reference to Christianity or to Christians. This is the case with regard to al-Shaybānī (d. 805), Ibn Wahb al-Qurashī (d. 812-13), and Abū Dāwūd al-Ṭayālisī (d. 819-20).

Apocalyptic and ascetic literature

The earliest level of apocalyptic and ascetic literature in Islam closely overlaps with the *ḥadīth* fragments described above and contains most of the materials referencing Christianity or citations from the

[2] Asad ibn Mūsā, *Kitāb al-zuhd*, ed. R.G. Khoury, Wiesbaden, 1986, p. 66; also ʿAbdallāh ibn al-Mubārak, *Musnad*, ed. M.ʿU. Muḥammad, Beirut, 1991, p. 56 (no. 116).

[3] E.g. Asad ibn Mūsā, *Zuhd*, p. 71.

New Testament. Only one major apocalyptic work, that of Nuʿaym ibn Ḥammād al-Marwazī (d. 844), fits within the time period. For the most part, Nuʿaym collected in the region of Syria, and should be considered as the chief repository of the Umayyad and early ʿAbbasid apocalyptic heritage, most of which did not enter the canonical collections. A great many of Nuʿaym's collection, *Kitāb al-fitan*, details the apocalyptic battles to occur between the Byzantine Christians and the Syrian Muslims.

Relations between Muslims and Christians in the apocalyptic literature are seen through this polemical lens. There is a strong paranoid atmosphere concerning Christians in Nuʿaym, especially those in Syria, as they may betray the Muslims due to their religious loyalty towards the Byzantines. In one account, churches and Christians will be burnt in Ḥimṣ (Emesa) because of their treachery.[4] This suspicion is also common towards Christian Arab tribes such as Taghlib, Salīḥ and Tanūkh (all resident in Syria or northern Iraq) about whom there are numerous prophecies concerning their treachery during the apocalyptic battles.[5] There are no direct citations from the New Testament in Nuʿaym (although paraphrases from the Hebrew Bible, such as Isaiah 11:1-6 appear).[6]

The Muslim ascetic (or *zuhd*) literature has close connections with Christians and Christian ideas. In general, its sources can be traced to the following origins: general, edifying stories of saints and holy men and women; wisdom and ascetic sayings of Jewish, Christian, Greek, Iranian or general Middle Eastern provenance; or *ḥadīth* of the Prophet Muḥammad or stories of his Companions. The second category can contain both authentic and apocryphal sayings of Jesus or citations from the New Testament. Ascetic literature is usually organized according to topic and can contain unique information concerning the social relations between Muslims and Christians.

In the early collection of ʿAbdallāh ibn al-Mubārak (d. 797) can be found the following account:

> I [Sila ibn Ushaym al-ʿAdawī] went out among some of the villages of the River Tīrā,[7] riding on my beast sometimes, washing in the water,

---

[4] Nuʿaym ibn Ḥammād al-Marwazī, *Kitāb al-fitan*, ed. S. Zakkār, Beirut, 1993, pp. 277, 279.

[5] Al-Marwazī, *Fitan*, pp. 259-60.

[6] Al-Marwazī, *Fitan*, pp. 346, 359.

[7] In northern Iraq.

> and I rode along a dam – rode for a day without finding anything to eat, and it was oppressive to me. A non-Arab (*ʿilj*) met me, carrying on his back something, and I said, 'Put it down', and he put it down and it was cheese. So I said, 'Feed me from it', and he said, 'Certainly, if you like, but it has pork fat in it.' When he said that, I left it and went on my way. Then I met another, and he was carrying food around his neck, and I said, 'Feed me from it.' He said, 'This is a provision for such and such a number of days, and if you take from it, you will harm me and starve me…' [8]

Although it is not entirely certain whether the 'non-Arab' was a Christian, the fact that he was making use of pork fat is indicative. Ibn al-Mubārak's collection contains a large number of New Testament citations or paraphrases,[9] and an even larger number of sayings ascribed to Jesus.[10]

Other *zuhd* materials are equally copious in biblical sayings. For example, the Kūfan Wakīʿ ibn al-Jarrāḥ (d. 812-13) cites 2 Thessalonians 3:10 to say 'Let each man work as he is able; no one knows the length of his life.'[11] Other similar sayings, some ascribed to Jesus but most unascribed, appear in Wakīʿ.[12] Early writers, such as al-Muʿāfā ibn ʿImrān al-Mawṣilī (d. 801)[13] and the *ḥadīth* collector Abū Dāwūd al-Sijistānī (d. 889) (q.v.),[14] contain equally random citations. Some of these are accurate citations of the New Testament, but most are paraphrases. Some examples include a paraphrase from Matthew 5:7, 3, 8:

> It is written in the Gospels: Blessed are those who are mutually compassionate because of me – they will receive mercy on the Day of

---

[8] ʿAbdallāh ibn al-Mubārak, *Kitāb al-zuhd wa-l-raqāʾiq*, ed. Ḥ. al-Raḥmān al-Aʿẓamī, Beirut, n.d., p. 297 (no. 865).

[9] See D. Cook, 'New Testament citations in the ḥadīth literature and the question of early Gospel translations into Arabic', in E. Grypeou, M. Swanson and D. Thomas (eds), *The encounter of Eastern Christianity with early Islam*, Leiden, 2006, 185-223, pp. 194, 195, 208, 209, 213-14.

[10] See T. Khalidi, *The Muslim Jesus*, Harvard, 2001, pp. 51-66.

[11] Wakīʿ ibn Jarrāḥ, *Kitāb al-zuhd*, ed. ʿA.ʿA. al-Faraywāʾī, 3 vols, Riyadh, 1994, ii, p. 498 (no. 237).

[12] Wakīʿ ibn Jarrāḥ, *Zuhd*, i, p. 399 (no. 166), ii, p. 616 (no. 339), iii, pp. 809 (no. 499), 843 (no. 522); Jesus' sayings at i, pp. 259 (no. 31), 350 (no. 125), ii, p. 519 (no. 255).

[13] Al-Mawṣilī, *Kitāb al-zuhd, wa-yalīhi Musnad al-Muʿāfā ibn ʿImrān al-Mawṣilī*, ed. ʿA.Ḥ. Ṣabrī, Beirut, 1999.

[14] Abū Dāwūd al-Sijistānī, *Kitāb al-zuhd*, ed. Abū Tamīm Yāsir ibn Ibrāhīm ibn Muḥammad and Abū Bilāl Ghunaym ibn ʿAbbās ibn Ghunaym, Hilwan: Dar al-Mishkat, 1993.

> Resurrection. Blessed are the humble because of me – they will be lifted up to the pulpits of power on the Day of Resurrection. Blessed are the pure…[15]

Unfortunately this selection is cut off. But, unusually for the *zuhd* literature, the citation is both reasonably accurate – although the order of the verses is considerably garbled – and actually ascribed to the Gospels. In general, material from the Sermon on the Mount or non-canonical sayings that at least have the form of the Beatitudes have a good chance of acceptance in the *zuhd* literature.

Overall, there is little mention of Christianity *per se* in the *zuhd* literature, but there are frequent notices of monks (*ruhbān*), general ascetics (*nussāk*) or pre-Islamic Christian Arabs (*ʿibād*) who usually preach a generalized undifferentiated monotheism. Eventually, many of these ascetic sayings were absorbed into the Ṣūfī canon.

Ibn Abī l-Dunyā (d. 894-95)

The Baghdadī court moralist Ibn Abī l-Dunyā (q.v.) must receive a separate treatment. Ibn Abī l-Dunyā's scope was vast, and only those of his numerous works which mention sayings, stories and references to Christianity and to Christians will be covered here. In essence, Ibn Abī l-Dunyā offers his readers stories and sayings on every aspect of life. Those materials germane to Christianity are preserved in books on general asceticism and specific ascetic practices, such as denial of food, weeping, silence, contemplation of death, and hope. There are also biographical materials about saints, including St Anthony.[16]

Ibn Abī l-Dunyā's citation of sayings is very uneven. Most of the Jesus sayings are non-canonical, as is noted by Khalidi.[17] In general Jesus is portrayed in terms of sayings, interactions with his disciples, or being questioned by random followers. Citations from the New Testament appearing in Ibn Abī l-Dunyā are usually much less exact than those appearing in earlier *zuhd* materials. A good example of this tendency is the citation of Matthew 6:19-21, which in Ibn al-Mubārak reads: "ʿAbdallāh ibn Masʿūd said, "Whoever can place his treasure in

---

[15] Al-Sijistānī, *Zuhd*, p. 32 (no. 2); the editor notes that the text is unreadable for a line after this.

[16] Ibn Abī l-Dunyā, *Al-wajal wa-l-tawaththuq bi-l-ʿamal*, ed. M.K. Ramaḍān Yūsuf, Beirut, 1997, pp. 27-28.

[17] Khalidi, *Muslim Jesus*, pp. 108-24.

heaven, let him do so, where moth-worms cannot eat it and where thieves cannot reach it, for the heart of every man is with his treasure.'"[18] The citation is ascribed to the qur'ānic reader Ibn Mas'ūd, but the translation is extremely close to the Gospel original. In Ibn Abī l-Dunyā, on the other hand, we read:

> Jesus son of Maryam said, 'Do not take this world as a master lest this world take you as slaves. Store up your treasure with the One who will not lose it. For the possessor of a treasure fears disaster for it, but when the possessor of the treasure is God, then there is no need to fear a disaster for it.'[19]

Thus, while the ascription to Jesus is a change from Ibn al-Mubārak, the actual text is changed to the point where it is only loosely connected to the New Testament.

Ibn Abī l-Dunyā only rarely cites materials mentioning Christians specifically. Some punishment stories relating to the Jews and Christians going astray in the past are adduced (along with the *topos* of metamorphosis into pigs and apes) as a warning to Muslims not to fall into the same trap.[20] There are a number of descriptions of the conquest of the Byzantines by the Muslims (or the punishment of the Byzantines for their treatment of the Jews), or the destruction of their beautiful buildings as a punishment.[21] While there are long discourses ascribed to St Anthony in the *Kitāb al-wajal*, most of the sayings are ascetic sayings ascribed to Jesus. All in all, Ibn Abī l-Dunyā is a rich treasure for comparative work.

Ḥadīth after 815 until the rise of the canonical collections

The principal collections from this period are those of Ibn Abī Shayba (d. 849-50)[22] and 'Abd al-Razzāq al-Ṣan'ānī (d. 827).[23] Both had comparatively little contact with Christianity, as Ibn Abī Shayba was Kūfan and 'Abd al-Razzāq collected in the Yemen. Despite the distance, there

---

[18] Ibn al-Mubārak, *Zuhd*, p. 223 (no. 633).

[19] Ibn Abī l-Dunyā, *Kitāb al-zuhd*, ed. E. Almagor, Jerusalem, 1984, pp. 11-12 (no. 31).

[20] Ibn Abī l-Dunyā, *Al-'uqūbāt*, ed. M.K. Ramaḍān Yūsuf, Beirut, 1996, p. 220 (no. 347).

[21] Ibn Abī l-Dunyā, *'Uqūbāt*, p. 172 (no. 266); Ibn Abī l-Dunyā, *Qiṣar al-amal*, ed. M.K. Ramaḍān Yūsuf, Beirut, 1997, pp. 175-76 (no. 262).

[22] Ibn Abī Shayba, *Kitāb al-muṣannaf*, Bombay, 1983.

[23] 'Abd al-Razzāq al-San'ānī, *al-Muṣannaf*, ed. Ḥ. al-Raḥmān al-A'ẓamī, Beirut, 1983.

are a number of legal *ḥadīths* in both collections that concern Christians, including what happens to a Christian who kills a Muslim, what is the blood price of a Christian, and what is the inheritance of a Christian whose father is Muslim. But most of the questions deal with either conversion of Christians to Islam (or vice versa) or issues related to marriage and sexual relations between Muslims and Christians (free or slave), or between Christians and other protected communities such as Jews or Zoroastrians. There is little, if any, citation of the teachings of Jesus in ʿAbd al-Razzāq.

Ibn Abī Shayba, on the other hand, contains not only this legal material but also a number of biblical or pseudo-biblical citations. In his material on pre-Islamic prophets, he cites

> Jesus son of Mary said to the disciples, 'Do not take a fee from those you teach other than that which you have given me. O salt of the earth! Do not be corrupted, since everything if it is corrupted can be treated with salt, but if the salt is corrupted there is no treatment.'[24]

This is very obviously from Matthew 5:13. Although it is not precise, it gives enough of the original to strongly suggest that a direct translation is the source. Similarly Matthew 19:21-23: 'Jesus son of Mary said to one of his followers who was rich, "Give your possessions to charity", and he disliked this. Jesus said, "Rich people will not enter paradise".'[25] Once again, this citation, while not incorrect, suppresses a good deal of biblical material.

While most of the citations that are ascribed to Jesus in Ibn Abī Shayba have the flavor of the Beatitudes, they are not to be found in the Gospel text. A good example is the following:

> Jesus son of Mary said, 'Do not speak overmuch in matters other than the mention of God most high, for your hearts will harden, and the hard heart is far from God. But do not (try to) learn, do not look at the sins of the people as though you are lords, but look at them as though you are servants. For people are two (types) of men: the tested and the forgiven. And so have mercy on the tested, and praise God about the forgiven.[26] (compare Matthew 7:1-5)

Some of the apparent New Testament citations are not ascribed to Jesus but to Muḥammad, such as the following:

[24] Ibn Abī Shayba, *Muṣannaf*, xiii, p. 197 (no. 16088).
[25] Ibn Abī Shayba, *Muṣannaf*, xiii, p. 196 (no. 16084).
[26] Ibn Abī Shayba, *Muṣannaf*, xiii, p. 193 (no. 16077).

> The Messenger of God said, 'Every believer who gives food to a hungry believer will be fed by God from the produce of paradise; every believer who gives a thirsty believer to drink will be "given to drink from a sealed wine" (Q 83:25); every believer who clothes a naked believer will be clothed by God with the green (clothing) of paradise.[27] (compare Matthew 26:34-36)

The material in Ibn Abī Shayba has a close connection through the preceding citations to the *zuhd* literature that was common throughout Iraq and Syria at the time.

Canonical Sunnī collections

Compared with the attention given to the Jews, Christians receive few references in the canonical *ḥadīth* collections.[28] In general, as in the Qur'ān (cf. 5:82), individual Christians, such as Waraqa ibn Nawfal,[29] the Negus of Ethiopia[30] or even Heraclius, Emperor of Byzantium,[31] or occasionally groups of Christians, such as delegations from Najrān and Syria,[32] receive positive portrayals. Most of these personalities are receptive to the message of Islam and facilitate its delivery, or at least are not disrespectful of it. This positive attitude is not extended to groups who hold to theological opinions that allow God to have partners (*shirk*) such as Trinitarian Christianity. However, Christians and Jews are frequently lumped together in traditions which criticize them for taking the graves of their prophets as places of worship (most probably also an attack upon similar practices in Islam).[33]

Just as with the ascetic literature, a number of New Testament paraphrases are to be found in the canonical collections. One example is the paraphrase of the parable of the workers from Matthew 20:1-16:

---

[27] Ibn Abī Shayba, *Muṣannaf*, xiii, p. 234 (no. 16202).

[28] Compare A.J. Wensinck, *Concordance et indices de la tradition musulmane. Les six livres, le Musnad d'al-Dārimī, le Muwaṭṭa' de Mālik, le Musnad de Aḥmad ibn Ḥanbal*, Leiden, 1936, s.v. *Naṣārā, Naṣrānī* with s.v. *Yahūd, Yahūdī.*

[29] Al-Bukhārī, *Ṣaḥīḥ*, i, p. 4 (no. 3).

[30] Al-Bukhārī, *Ṣaḥīḥ*, iv, pp. 297-98 (nos. 3877-82); Muslim, *Ṣaḥīḥ*, Beirut: Dār al-Jīl, n.d., vii, pp. 187-88.

[31] Al-Bukhārī, *Ṣaḥīḥ*, i, pp. 6-8 (no. 7).

[32] See my 'Aṣḥāb al-ukhdūd', forthcoming in *JSAI*.

[33] Al-Bukhārī, *Ṣaḥīḥ*, i, p. 129 (no. 435), very commonly cited; Wensinck, *Concordance*, s.v. *Naṣārā*.

> The Messenger of God said, 'Your end will only be like those communities who passed before you, like between the afternoon and the sunset. A parable of you and the Jews and the Christians is that of a man who hired workers and said, "Who will work for me until the middle of the day for a *qīrāṭ*?" So the Jews worked until the middle of the day for a *qīrāṭ*. Then he said, "Who will work from the middle of the day till the late afternoon for two *qīrāṭs*?" And the Christians worked. Then he said, "Who will work from the late afternoon prayers until the sunset for four *qīrāṭs*? But you who work from the late afternoon prayers until the sunset for four *qīrāṭs*, are only receiving the wage double." So the Jews and the Christians were angered, and said, "We have worked more and received less!" He said, "Have I refused any of your rightful due?" They said, "No." He said, "This is my generosity given to whom I wish." '[34]

This selection is a good example of the reworking of Gospel materials in the *ḥadīth* literature. While the overall framework of the parable remains the same, it is nowhere ascribed to Jesus; the five groups of the Matthew version are reduced to three and identified with the Jews, the Christians and the Muslims, and the story is given a marked eschatological tone that is not present in the biblical version.

However, compared with the ascetic literature, few New Testament citations are as easily identifiable as this one. Work remains to be done on a much more likely source for the many sayings in the *ḥadīth* literature, which is the huge corpus of pious sayings and stories associated with saints, Church Fathers and especially lives of ascetics. It is very likely that when probed carefully and systematically, these sources will reveal a rich correlation between the Christianity of late antiquity and early Islam (most probably again through the medium of the *zuhd* literature). Among prominent saints, only St George is mentioned.[35]

Conclusion

Generally speaking, the form of the *ḥadīth* literature does not easily lend itself to direct New Testament citations or to frequent references to Christianity. Most of the Gospel quotations have the typical form of beginning with *Ṭūbā* ('Blessed be…') that is associated with the Beatitudes. On the other hand, few of the citations ascribed to Jesus

---

[34] Al-Bukhārī, *Ṣaḥīḥ*, i, p. 157 (no. 557), iii, pp. 68-9 (nos. 2268-9, 2271).

[35] Al-Bukhārī, *Ṣaḥīḥ*, iv, p. 169 (no. 3436).

are actually attested from the Bible. More are derived from apocryphal gospels, but the majority appear to be unique Muslim creations. Far more references to Christians and citations from Christian sources are found in those *ḥadīth* or ascetic-apocalyptic collections that come from Syria than those that come from Iraq or further east, while those such as ʿAbd al-Razzāq from the Yemen contain little of this material. In general, the most surprising fact about the material relating to Christianity in the *ḥadīth* literature is how little there is of it. Given that during this period Christianity was the most obvious and persistent opponent of Islam, the material dealing with it is sparse.

Muslims in canon law, 650-1000

David M. Freidenreich

Scholars have devoted considerable attention to the place of Christians and Jews in Islamic law (see the following essay), as well as to the place of Jews in Christian legal literature. References to Muslims in Christian legal sources have not received comparable treatment. The present essay seeks to remedy this situation by surveying all such references dating from the seventh to the tenth centuries.[1] For reasons that will become clear in the paragraphs that follow, however, this essay doubtless falls short of the comprehensive coverage to which it aspires.

Canon law, the religious law of the Church, is an amorphous body of normative literature whose contents and contours differ from one Christian community to the next. Each major branch of Christianity developed its own corpus of canon law literature, in languages as varied as Latin, Greek, Syriac, Armenian, and Coptic. Many Greek texts from the first Christian millennium entered into Latin and Syriac legal corpora, but for the most part theological and linguistic divides prevented the dissemination of normative texts from one branch of Christianity to another. This essay focuses primarily on legal literature in Latin, Greek, and Syriac, which is to say the canon law of the Roman Catholic, Greek Orthodox (Chalcedonian), Syrian Orthodox (Jacobite), and Church of the East (Nestorian) traditions. The fact that other branches of Christianity receive less attention reflects both the author's linguistic limitations and the emphases of canon law scholarship more broadly.

Medieval Catholic authorities define the authoritative sources of canon law as scripture, normative statements of Church Fathers, canons promulgated by councils of bishops, and papal decrees. Normative statements by other ecclesiastical authorities, frequently in the form of responsa, figure prominently in the Eastern canon law traditions, and secular laws, especially from the Roman Empire, sometimes enter into

[1] On Muslims in Eastern (Greek and Syriac) canon law literature from 1000-1500, and Muslims in Western (Latin) canon law literature from 1000-1500, see later volumes.

canon law as well. Not every normative statement from an authoritative source, however, found its way into compilations of canon law; the classification of such statements for academic purposes as falling within or beyond the bounds of canon law depends on a decision by the researcher compiling these statements. The present study includes references to a few such normative statements, but for reasons of sheer practicality focuses primarily on material found in legal compilations. For the same reason, this survey focuses almost exclusively on texts that exist in modern printed editions, thus ignoring a considerable proportion of canon law literature.

It is not always evident that any given statement about non-Christians in canon law refers specifically to Muslims. In addition to using such terms as 'Saracens', 'Hagarenes', and 'Arabs', Christian authorities regularly refer to Muslims as 'pagans', 'gentiles', and 'barbarians'; the latter terms, of course, are also used with reference to other non-Christian communities.[2] The variety and imprecision of these references further complicate efforts toward comprehensive coverage, even with the aid of digital search engines and prior surveys.[3] The present survey includes

[2] In Latin legal sources, the predominant term for Muslims is *sarracen** (sometimes *saracen**), although *agaren** is also attested. Latin canon law sources also refer to Muslims as *pagan**. Greek sources similarly employ *sarakēn**; the term *hagarēn** is unattested in legal literature from the period 650-1000 but appears in non-legal sources from this period and in later legal texts. The Greek term *barbar** is also employed in reference to Muslims, as is *ethnik** ('gentile'). Syriac sources make no use of the term 'Saracen', employing *mhaggrā** ('Hagarene' or simply 'Muslim') instead. These sources often refer to Muslims as *ḥanp** (translated in this essay as 'pagan', although 'gentile' is also appropriate) and, in canons that address Muslims in their capacity as overlords, as *ṭayyā** ('Arab'). On Syriac terms for Muslims, see S.H. Griffith, *Syriac writers on Muslims and the religious challenge of Islam*, Kottayam, 1995, pp. 8-14.

Terminology that refers to Muslims is inconsistent even within texts ascribed to an individual author. Pope Hadrian I, for example, refers to Muslims as Saracens, Hagarenes, and pagans in different letters; see W. Gundlach (ed.), *Codex Carolinus*, in E.L. Dümmler et al. (eds), *Epistolae Merowingici et Karolini aevi*, 6 vols, Berlin, 1892 (*MGH Epistolae* 3), i, pp. 584, 588-89, 636, 643. All these letters are discussed in M. Rouche, 'Le pape face à l'islam au VIIIe siècle', *Mélanges de la Casa de Velázquez* 32 (1996) 205-16; several are also addressed later in this essay.

[3] Electronic search engines employed in the preparation of this study include the *Library of Latin texts*, *MGH* and the *Thesaurus linguae Graecae*. In addition, the author conducted full-text searches of the *Decretum* of Gratian, ed. E. Friedberg, *Corpus iuris canonici*, Leipzig, 1879-81, i (electronic resource publicly available online through Columbia University Libraries); the *Decretum* of Ivo of Chartres, *Patrologia Latina* database, 161; and the *Decretum* of Burchard of Worms, *Patrologia Latina* database, 140.

all canon law statements known to its author that plausibly refer to Muslims, while consistently indicating the precise term used for the non-Christians in question; it does not include laws that reflect an Islamic milieu but contain no direct reference to Muslims.[4]

Two distinctions derived from the study of Jews in canon law literature and non-Muslims in Islamic legal literature further our own terminological precision when examining references to Muslims in Christian sources. Scholars of Christian attitudes toward Judaism helpfully distinguish between 'Jewish law', laws that developed within the Jewish tradition, and 'Jewry law', Christian laws relating to Jews.[5] Similarly, we ought to distinguish 'Islamic law' from 'Saracen law'; this essay focuses exclusively on the latter, whereas the essay that follows addresses the former. Nurit Tsafrir, in her study of Islamic law regarding non-Muslims ('*dhimmī* law'), draws a further distinction between regulations imposed upon non-Muslims (e.g., clothing that Christians must wear) and regulations that apply to Muslims themselves (e.g., Christian food that Muslims may not eat).[6] This distinction between what we may call 'imposed law' and 'reflexive law' also exists within Christian Jewry law. Christian Saracen law from the seventh to the tenth centuries, in contrast, is exclusively reflexive in its orientation. This orientation, while unsurprising in light of the political dynamics of the period under consideration, is significant nevertheless because it highlights the fact that Christian authorities felt a need to respond to – and erect internal defenses against – perceived threats posed by Muslims. Only in later centuries do some Christian authorities seek to impose Saracen law onto Muslims themselves.

These collections from the mid-twelfth, early twelfth, and early eleventh centuries respectively, preserve a large number of canons from earlier centuries. When a canon appears in more than one of them, generally only the latest collection is cited here.

Of particular value for the study of Eastern sources are M. Penn, 'Syriac sources for the study of early Christian-Muslim relations', *Islamochristiana* 29 (2003) 59-78; Hoyland, *Seeing Islam*; A. Vööbus, *Syrische Kanonessammlungen. Ein Beitrag zur Quellenkunde*, Louvain, 1970.

[4] I would be grateful to receive information about relevant sources absent from this survey, and I wish to thank Robert Somerville for his comments on an earlier draft of the essay.

[5] On this terminological distinction, see G. Kisch, *The Jews in medieval Germany. A study of their legal and social status*, Chicago IL, 1949, p. 7.

[6] N. Tsafrir, *Yaḥas ha-halakhah ha-muslemit kelapei datot aḥerot: 'Inyanei sheḥiṭah ve-nisu'in*, Jerusalem, 1988 (MA Diss. The Hebrew University), p. 2; I am grateful to the author for sharing this unpublished work. Tsafrir applies the term '*dhimmī* law' solely to laws imposed on non-Muslims.

Christian Saracen law of the seventh to the tenth centuries may be divided into two broad categories: laws that respond to Muslims as bearers of power, and laws that seek to regulate interaction between Christians and Muslims. Laws in the former category treat Muslims in political terms, as invaders or overlords; laws in the latter category treat Muslims in religious terms, as non-Christians most often imagined to be pagans. A subset of the latter category addresses situations in which a person or object crosses the border between these two religions. This essay surveys each of these categories in turn and concludes with a brief comparison of the places occupied by Muslims and by Jews in early medieval canon law.

Muslims as bearers of power: Invaders and overlords

Christians first encountered Muslims as invaders. Bishops convened in Constantinople by Justinian II at the Council in Trullo of 692 respond to these 'barbarian invasions' in several canons. They reiterate the requirement that bishops meet annually in provincial synods while acknowledging that barbarian incursions may prevent more frequent gatherings (c. 8), they demand that clerics who fled their churches in the wake of barbarian incursions return to their posts once the situation has calmed down (c. 18), and they praise John, Bishop of Cyprus, for migrating with his community to Christian territory because of 'barbarian attacks', thus freeing themselves 'from slavery to the gentiles [*ethnikēs… douleias*]' (c. 39).[7] The Fourth

[7] Text: H. Ohme (ed.), *Das Konzil Quinisextum*, Turnhout, 2006 (with introduction and German trans.); 'The canons of the Council in Trullo in Greek, Latin and English', in G. Nedungatt and M. Featherstone (eds), *The Council in Trullo revisited*, Rome, 1995, 41-186. On canons 8, 18, and 39, see Ohme, *Konzil Quinisextum*, pp. 126-28, 135; F.R. Trombley, 'The Council in Trullo (691-692). A study of the canons relating to paganism, heresy, and the invasions', *Comitatus* 9 (1978) 1-18, pp. 11-13. Although a number of the canons from the Council in Trullo entered into the Latin canon law tradition, these canons were not among them; see P. Landau, 'Überlieferung und Bedeutung der Kanones des Trullanischen Konzils im westlichen kanonischen Recht', in Nedungatt and Featherstone, *The Council in Trullo revisited*, 215-27. Canon 39 clearly relates to the Arab conquest of Cyprus, but Muslims were not the only 'barbarians' to attack Byzantine territories in the seventh century; the authors of these canons may also have had Slavic invaders in mind.

The Council in Trullo is closely associated with the Third Council of Constantinople (680-81). The proceedings of that council, which did not produce its own set of canons, include the text of a letter by Sophronius, Patriarch of Jerusalem (d. 638)

Council of Constantinople (869-70) similarly acknowledges 'pagan invasions', along with illness, as valid grounds for a bishop to ignore the summons of his patriarch.[8]

Christian authorities in Latin Europe also responded to the military threat posed by Muslim invaders.[9] Several of these responses appear in Gratian's *Decretum* (c. 1140), the most authoritative collection of early medieval canon law within the Catholic tradition.[10] St Boniface, in a letter dated to 746-47, attributes the Saracen invasion of Spain, Provence, and Burgundy to the loose sexual mores of Christians in those regions, and he warns Christians in England and elsewhere to avoid the same fate.[11] An account by Pope Leo IV (r. 847-55), describing his evacuation of the Christian population of Rome in the face of the Saracen sack of 846, appears in the *Decretum* as an exemplar of how priests ought to eschew the use of armed force (C. 23 q. 8

(q.v.), describing the Saracen conquest of that city, and a call for an immediate attack on the 'impious Saracens'; text in R. Riedinger (ed.), *Concilium universale Constantinopolitanum tertium* (*Acta conciliorum oecumenicorum*, series 2, ii.1-2), Berlin, 1990, pp. 492, 614. The Lateran Council of 649 also cites part of a letter by Sophronius, and the closing prayer of its third session seeks divine salvation from 'the tyranny of the powerful, the insolence of the Persians, and, especially, the arrogance of the Saracens'; text in R. Riedinger (ed.), *Concilium Lateranense a. 649 celebratum* (*Acta conciliorum oecumenicorum*, series 2, i), Berlin, 1984, pp. 40, 172.

[8] G. Alberigo et al. (eds), *Decrees of the Ecumenical Councils*, trans. N.P. Tanner, London, 1990, p. 180. The canons of this council, originally produced in Greek, survive in full only in a contemporary Latin trans.

[9] The trope of Saracens as enemies of the Christians appears several times in Carolingian legal literature. See the capitulary of the Holy Roman Emperor Lothair I regarding a military expedition against 'the enemies of Christ, the Saracens and Moors' (October 846), in A. Boretius and V. Krause (eds), *Capitularia regum Francorum*, 2 vols, Hannover, 1883-97 (*MGH Leges* 2), ii, pp. 65-68. Louis the Pious (in 815 and 816) and Charles the Bald (in 844) both refer to the 'most cruel' Saracens in the prefatory remarks that accompany legal texts addressed to Christian refugees from Spain; see i, pp. 261-64; ii, pp. 258-60.

[10] The first portion of the *Decretum* consists of 'distinctions' (D.) and canons (c.), while the second portion consists of hypothetical legal 'cases' (C.), 'questions' associated with those cases (q.) and canons; the citations that follow refer to this organizational structure.

[11] D. 56 c. 10; the complete letter appears in M. Tangl (ed.), *Die Briefe des heiligen Bonifatius und Lullus*, Berlin, 1916 (*MGH Epistolae selectae* 1) pp. 146-55; E. Emerton (trans.), *The letters of Saint Boniface*, 1940, 102-8. Similarly, Pope Zacharias I warned the Franks in 745 that they would not succeed in defeating their pagan enemies until their priests, following Boniface's teachings, cleansed themselves of unchastity and ceased serving as soldiers (Tangl, pp. 125-27; Emerton, pp. 89-91). On these letters, see Rouche, 'Le pape', p. 211.

c. 7). Other canons justify the use of such force. Among the numerous acts of penance which Pope Nicholas I (r. 858-67) imposes upon those who kill members of their own family, such individuals may not bear arms; an exception, however, is granted to those who bear arms against pagans.[12] Nicholas is also lenient regarding clerics who, in self-defense, kill pagans (D. 50 cc. 5-6).[13] Similarly, Pope Stephen V (r. 885-91) excuses Christians who commit murder while in Saracen captivity (D. 50 c. 38).

The presence of Muslim political authorities in close geographical proximity to Latin Christian communities prompted Nicholas to remind priests to assign acts of penance judiciously, lest sinners 'in desperation' flee to pagan territory.[14] In Iraq, Muslim political authority posed more imminent concerns. The synod convened in 676 by George I, Catholicos of the Church of the East, instructed Christians awaiting judgment not to turn to judges from outside the Church (c. 6).[15] The Metropolitan Timothy I (d. 823) (q.v.) cites the fact that

---

[12] Ivo of Chartres, *Decretum*, Book 10, cc. 33, 163, 173, 180. Gratian's *Decretum* contains Ivo's c. 173 (C. 33 q. 2 c. 15), which refers solely to matricide. Ivo ascribes c. 163, the only one of these canons not authored by Nicholas I, to the Council of Tribur (895), but a footnote in Migne's text notes that this canon was first promulgated at 'the Council of Worms'; there were several such councils, one of which took place in 866, during Nicholas' reign. Canon 175, also ascribed to the Council of Tribur, addresses the proper penance for accidentally killing Christian captives in the course of attacking their pagan captors. Ivo's *Decretum* also includes two statements ascribed to Pope John VIII (r. 872-82) exhorting armed resistance to Saracens (Book 10, cc. 68, 71).

The *Decretum* of Burchard of Worms cites several of the canons that appear in Ivo's later compilation. Burchard also incorporates Nicholas' exception to the prohibition against bearing arms into his *Corrector*, a brief penitential manual within the *Decretum* (Book 19, ch. 5; *PL* 140, col. 953).

[13] Nicholas was actively involved in missionary efforts among the Bulgars, whom he may have in mind in addition to or instead of Muslims in this canon and those discussed in the prior note.

[14] C. 26 q. 7 c. 3; this canon is an extract from a letter written in 864 to a bishop in Aquitaine.

[15] J.B. Chabot, *Synodicon orientale*, Paris, 1902, pp. 219-20; trans. (French) pp. 484-85. Also noteworthy in this context is c. 19 (pp. 225-26/489-90), which instructs Christians responsible for collecting the poll tax and other tributary payments on behalf of Muslim overlords not to exact such payments from bishops. On these texts, see Hoyland, *Seeing Islam*, pp. 193-94; M.G. Morony, 'Religious communities in late Sasanian and early Muslim Iraq', *Journal of the Economic and Social History of the Orient* 17 (1974), pp. 125-28 (repr. in R. Hoyland (ed.), *Muslims and others in early Islamic society*, Aldershot, 2004); and the entry 'Ghiwargis I' in this volume. Hoyland, *Seeing*

Christians turn to foreign courts, claiming that they cannot resolve their disputes within the Church, as a reason for promulgating a new collection of 99 canons; c. 12 explicitly forbids recourse to such courts.[16] The Syrian Orthodox Patriarch Ignatius of Antioch (r. 878-83) addresses Christians who, after being assigned appropriate punishments by Christian authorities for their transgressions, ask 'secular rulers, Arab generals, or Christian thugs' to coerce clerics into relaxing these penalties. Ignatius warns such audacious flouters of the law that Jesus will not absolve them of their guilt.[17]

Canonists also address situations in which Muslims interfere in Christian affairs without the solicitation of Christians. The Syrian Orthodox Jacob of Edessa (d. 708) (q.v.), by far the most prolific pre-1000 legal authority on the subject of Muslims, responds leniently to a query regarding a cleric who, pressed into the defense of a besieged city by its Arab rulers, kills one of the invaders scaling the walls.[18]

Islam, p. 194, n. 70, notes that an unedited canon by Jacob of Edessa also exhorts Christians not to use secular authorities or pagans as judges; an abridged version of this canon, referring to clerics who appeal to the judgment of 'outsiders', appears in A. Vööbus (ed.), *The Synodicon in the West Syrian tradition*, 2 parts in 4 vols, Louvain, 1975 (*CSCO* 367-68, 375-76), i/1, p. 272 (ed.), i/2, p. 247(trans.), c. 24.

[16] 'Canones Timothei', in J. Labourt, *De Timotheo I Nestorianorum patriarcha*, Paris, 1904, pp. 52, 57-58. A. Fattal, 'How dhimmīs were judged in the Islamic world', in Hoyland, *Muslims and others in early Islamic society* (trans. of 'Comment les Dhimmis étaient jugés en terre d'islam', *Cahiers d'histoire égyptienne* 3 [1951] 321-41) p. 85, observes that Timothy's successor, among other Eastern Christian authorities, excommunicated Christians who turned to Muslim judges.

[17] Canon 4 of the synod convened by Ignatius (878), in Vööbus, *Synodicon*, ii/1, p. 53 and ii/2, p. 57 (trans.).

[18] Responsum 80 to Addai, as translated from unpublished manuscripts by Hoyland (*Seeing Islam*, p. 606). See also the previous question in which a cleric, out of work and facing hunger, joins a band of soldiers (whose religious affiliation is unidentified) for the duration of the famine; Hoyland does not translate Jacob's answer, but implies on p. 162 that Jacob is lenient in this situation as well. An abbreviated form of responsum 80 appears in Gregorius Barhebraeus, *Nomocanon*, ed. P. Bedjan, Paris, 1898, p. 42; the question and answer, both formulated slightly differently, also appear in Vööbus, *Synodicon*, i/1, pp. 268-69 and i/2, p. 244 (trans.) as responsum 51. See also Vööbus, *Syrische Kanonessammlungen*, p. 279, n. 61.

On these and other responsa by Jacob of Edessa regarding Muslims, see the entry on Jacob in this volume and the bibliography cited there. Jacob of Edessa authored approximately 200 surviving legal responsa, most of which were addressed to Addai, a priest, or to John the Stylite of Litarb. Unfortunately, no single text contains all of these responsa, and numbering consequently differs from one manuscript to another. Hoyland employs a uniform numbering system incorporating canons from a variety of sources.

In a similarly lenient ruling that may also have Muslim overlords in mind, Pope Stephen V allows those who have been mutilated against their will by Norman captors, slave masters, doctors, or pagans to become priests (Gratian, *Decretum*, D. 55 c. 11).

The canon law collection of Gabriel of Basra (composed 884-91), a metropolitan within the Church of the East, requires the eucharist to be celebrated on an altar but allows for alternatives in periods of oppression; the reign of the ʿAbbasid Caliph al-Mutawakkil (r. 847-61) is cited as an example.[19] Jacob of Edessa similarly allows for dispensing with proper eccesiastical procedure in this regard when one is in 'a town of barbarian pagans' where there is no altar.[20]

Christian–Muslim interaction: Muslims as non-Christians

Ancient spokesmen for Christian orthodoxy conceptualized outsiders as belonging to one of three categories – heretics, Jews, and pagans – although they frequently blurred the distinctions between these groups.[21] It is unsurprising, therefore, that Christian authorities thinking within traditional categorical boxes regarded Muslims as pagans: they clearly were neither Jews nor heretical Christians. It is also no surprise that

This essay cites both Hoyland's numbers and those found in Vööbus' edition of the *Synodicon*, the most accessible and most complete collection of Jacob's responsa.

[19] H. Kaufhold, *Die Rechtssammlung des Gabriel von Baṣra und ihr Verhältnis zu den anderen juristischen Sammelwerken der Nestorianer*, Berlin, 1976, pp. 286-89 (Syriac with German trans.); see also p. 50. I am grateful to Barbara Roggema for drawing to my attention this and other relevant passages from Gabriel's work.

[20] Responsum 1 in the first letter to John the Stylite found in Vööbus, *Synodicon*, i/1, p. 234 and i/2, p. 216 (trans); Hoyland identifies this as 'Letter II' or 'B'). H. Teule, 'Jacob of Edessa and canon law', in R.B. ter Haar Romeny (ed.), *Jacob of Edessa and the Syriac culture of his day*, Leiden, 2008, 83-100, p. 97, n. 70, states that Jacob does not refer to Muslims as 'pagans' (*ḥanpē*); I am grateful to the author for providing a pre-publication copy of this essay. Teule may be correct in general, but I am not convinced that this rule applies in all cases. Manuscript variations occasionally affect the terminology used to refer to non-Christians (an example appears in n. 44 below), and in some cases it is quite possible that Jacob refers to Muslims as 'pagans' because that is the term used in the source underlying Jacob's opinion (see, for example, n. 25 below). This survey therefore includes responsa referring to pagans that could plausibly be directed toward Muslims.

[21] On these categories in the pre-Islamic Near East, see A. Cameron, 'Jews and heretics. A category error', in A.H. Becker and A.Y. Reed (eds), *The ways that never parted. Jews and Christians in late antiquity and the early Middle Ages*, Tübingen, 2003, 345-60.

even Christians who were familiar with the monotheistic tenets of Islam treated Muslims as equivalent to pagans for legal purposes. These authorities applied to Christian-Muslim relations the same reflexive restrictions that already existed to regulate Christian-pagan (and Christian-Jewish) relations: Christians may not share meals with non-Christians or consume non-Christian foodstuffs of ritual significance, they may not engage in sexual intercourse with non-Christians, and they may not adopt distinctive practices associated with non-Christian communities.[22]

Precisely because of the continuity between Saracen law and laws regarding other groups of non-Christians, however, it is sometimes impossible to determine with certainty that restrictions articulated in Islamic lands in fact refer to Muslims rather than members of other religious communities. A letter by Athanasius of Balad, Syrian Orthodox Patriarch of Antioch (dated to 684), illustrates this ambiguity.[23] Athanasius decries the fact that Christian men take part in pagan feasts, that Christian women are sexually intimate with pagans, and that Christians eat the meat of pagan sacrifices; such behavior, Athanasius asserts, contravenes the Apostolic Decree of Acts 15:29. According to a title appended to this letter by an eighth-century copyist, Athanasius refers specifically to 'the sacrifices of the Hagarenes'. It is quite possible that Athanasius himself had Muslims in mind when penning this letter, but we cannot be certain.

Several Christian authorities from the seventh to the tenth centuries rearticulate traditional prohibitions regarding the food of non-Christians in contexts that implicitly or explicitly address Muslims. Jacob of Edessa affirms the prohibition against Syrian Orthodox clerics sharing meals with heretics but, citing grounds of necessity, he excuses those clerics ordered by heretical rulers to partake of a common meal. Jacob then extends the same exemption to clerics imposed upon them by an 'emir', taking for granted that commensality between

[22] On Christian prohibitions against commensality with non-Christians and the consumption of non-Christian foodstuffs, see D.M. Freidenreich, *Thou shalt not eat with them. Foreigners and their food in Jewish, Christian, and Islamic law*, Berkeley CA, forthcoming, a revision of *Foreign food. A comparatively-enriched analysis of Jewish, Christian, and Islamic law*, New York, 2006 (Diss. Columbia University).

[23] On Athanasius of Balad and this letter, with complete bibliography, see the entry in this volume.

clerics and Muslims is normally forbidden.[24] Jacob does, however, permit Christians to eat the meat of animals which pagans slaughter in non-sacrificial contexts when meat prepared by Christians is unavailable, citing Paul's words on the subject in 1 Corinthians 10:25.[25] The Armenian Synod of Partaw (768) addresses the proper penance for one who, by accident or out of necessity, consumes the impure meat of 'the impious', a term which in this canon is apparently synonymous with pagans (c. 22).[26] In two letters sent to clerics in Spain, Pope Hadrian I (r. 772-95) (q.v.) bemoans the fact that 'many who call themselves Catholics carry on public life with Jews and unbaptized pagans, sharing in food and drink alike and also straying into error in several ways while saying that they are not defiled'.[27]

Sexual intercourse with non-Christians is a subject addressed frequently by Christian authorities in the lands of Islam. The Nestorian Synod of George I condemns unions with 'pagans' in strong terms (c. 14), as does the Armenian Synod of Partaw (c. 11).[28] George, the Syrian Orthodox Patriarch of Antioch, prohibits marrying one's daughter to a pagan, a Muslim, or a Nestorian, and forbids both

---

[24] Responsa 56-57 to Addai, in T.J. Lamy, *Dissertatio de Syrorum fide et disciplina in re eucharistica*, Leuven, 1859, pp. 154-57 (with Latin trans.), and A.P. de Lagarde (ed.), *Reliquiae iuris ecclesiastici antiquissimae*, Leipzig, 1856, pp. 139-40; French and German translations of these works are listed in the entry in this volume on Jacob of Edessa. Teule, 'Jacob of Edessa and canon law', understands the issue at hand to be specifically one of association with secular rulers, but see also responsum 53, which offers a similar condemnation of commensality between orthodox and heretical clerics.

[25] Responsum 17 in the second letter to John the Stylite found in Vööbus, *Synodicon*, i/1, p. 254 and i/2, p. 232 (trans); Hoyland identifies this as 'Letter I' or 'A').

[26] I rely here on the translation of A. Mardirossian, 'Les canons du Synode de Partaw (768)', *Revue des Études Arméniennes* 27 (1998-2000) p. 126. Mardirossian, p. 131, understands this canon to refer specifically to *ḥalāl* meat. J.P. Mahé raises this as a possibility but seems to prefer to interpret the canon as referring to the meat of animals regarded by Armenian Christians as impure ('L'église arménienne de 611 à 1066', in G. Dagron, P. Riché and A. Vauchez (eds), *Histoire du christianisme des origines à nos jours. Tome IV: Éveques, moines et empereurs (610-1054)*, Paris, 1993, p. 478, n. 278).

[27] Gundlach, 'Codex Carolinus', pp. 636, 643; on this text, see Rouche, 'Le pape', pp. 213-14. Hadrian's concern about commensality with pagans is atypical of Latin authorities from this period, who tend to focus solely on shared meals with Jews. These letters, to the best of my knowledge, did not find their way into canon law literature.

[28] Synod of George I, in Chabot, *Synodicon orientale*, pp. 223-24 (trans., p. 488); Synod of Partaw, in Mardirossian, 'Synode de Partaw', p. 124.

the father who does so and his daughter from entering the church (cc. 12-13).[29] Jacob of Edessa, however, permits offering communion to Christian women who marry Hagarenes, lest they choose to convert to Islam.[30]

In addition to their efforts to prevent commensual sharing and sexual intercourse between Christians and Muslims, Christian authorities in or near Islamic lands sought to prevent their followers from adopting practices deemed to be 'non-Christian'. Justinian II convened the Council in Trullo for the express purpose of uprooting 'any remnant of gentile or Jewish perversity' within the Church;[31] although the canons from this council that refer to pagans do not appear to refer to Muslims, it seems likely that at least some canons from Syriac-language synods during our period do have Islamic practices in mind. Several councils from both the Syrian Orthodox Church and the Church of the East specifically forbid the adoption of pagan funeral customs, and a number of the relevant canons also condemn the adoption of pagan dress or hair styles.[32] It is unclear whether or not

---

[29] Vööbus, *Synodicon*, ii/1, p. 4 and ii/2, p. 5 (trans.). Canon 23 from the synod of Patriarch John III (846) imposes the same penalty for marriage to pagans, Jews, and Magians; see ii/1, p. 44 (trans. ii/2, p. 47). See also responsum 7 of Sewira (c. 850), described in Vööbus, *Syrische Kanonessammlungen*, p. 300, n. 7. Pope Hadrian also decries sexual relations with Jews and pagans in the letters cited in n. 27.

[30] Responsum 75 to Addai, translated in Hoyland, *Seeing Islam*, pp. 604-5; see also Barhebraeus, *Nomocanon*, p. 41, trans. in Hoyland, p. 163. Jacob also recommends the imposition of lighter penalties for acts of interfaith adultery if doing so will lead the unbeliever towards faith in Christ; see responsum 69 to Addai, in de Lagarde, *Reliquiae*, p. 143; Lamy, *Dissertatio*, pp. 166-69.

[31] Nedungatt and Featherstone, 'Canons of the Council in Trullo', p. 53. The 'gentile perversity' which this council addresses includes the swearing of pagan oaths (c. 94) and what in modern times would be considered carnival behavior: keeping bears, causing deception and mischief, fortune-telling, acrobatics, and the like (cc. 61, 71).

[32] Syrian Orthodox prohibitions against the adoption of pagan funeral customs appear in the canons of the Antiochene Patriarchs John III (c. 22), Ignatius (cc. 8-9), and Dionysius II (r. 896-909, c. 23); see Vööbus, *Synodicon*, ii/1, pp. 44, 55, 63 and ii/2, pp. 47, 59, 67-68 (trans.). Jacob of Edessa allows Christian women to attend the funeral processions of Jews or 'pagans of Ḥarrān' when doing so out of a spirit of love or neighborliness, and raises no objection to the presence of such non-Christians at Christian funeral processions (responsa 62-63 to Addai, in de Lagarde, *Reliquiae*, p. 141; Lamy, *Dissertatio*, pp. 162-63; see also Barhebraeus, *Nomocanon*, p. 70); Jacob does not address Muslims in this context. On Syrian Orthodox prohibitions against pagan customs, see also Vööbus, *Syrische Kanonessammlungen*, p. 213. For sources from the Church of the East, see the following note.

these councils had Muslim practices in mind. Of particular interest is Gabriel of Basra's statement on the subject, which singles out, among other practices, hiring a woman 'who is called a *nawwāḥa*' to wail at a funeral. Gabriel employs an Arabic term in an otherwise Syriac text, which may indicate that he regards this practice as common to Muslims; Islamic authorities, however, also condemned this practice as pagan, and it is possible that Christian and Muslim jurists of the period saw themselves fighting a common battle against an entrenched folk custom.[33] Dionysius I (Patriarch of Antioch, r. 817-45) forbids Christians from practicing circumcision, a practice he associates with pagans as well as Jews.[34] A synod convened in southern Italy around the year 900 prohibits clerics and priests from having sex with female slaves, sneering that those who do so 'observe the law and custom of the Hagarenes, whose pseudo-prophet Muameth, who is called by the incorrect name Machameta, is said to have taught that one may licitly enjoy any maid-servant, however she is acquired'.[35]

Jacob of Edessa explains that church doors must be locked during the eucharistic service lest Hagarenes mock the holy mysteries,[36] though he allows and even encourages priests to offer blessed objects to Hagarenes and pagans in need of healing, explaining in one version of this responsum that these objects constitute a demonstration of Christianity's power.[37] Jacob also allows priests to teach the children of Hagarenes when necessity demands.[38]

---

[33] Kaufhold, *Rechtssammlung des Gabriel von Baṣra*, pp. 294-97; Kaufhold suggests that Gabriel here paraphrases canons 9 and 18 of the Synod of George I (Chabot, *Synodicon orientale*, pp. 221-22, 225; trans. pp. 486, 489). On Islamic attitudes towards this practice, see T. Fahd, art. 'Niyāḥa' in *EI2*.

[34] Canon 5 of Dionysius' synod of 817, in Vööbus, *Synodicon*, ii/1, p. 30 and ii/2, p. 33 (trans.).

[35] *Capitula Casinensia*, c. 9, in P. Brommer, R. Pokorny and M. Stratmann (eds), *Capitula episcoporum*, 4 vols, Hannover, 1995 (*MGH*), iii, p. 326.

[36] Responsum 9 in the first letter to John the Stylite found in Vööbus, *Synodicon*, i/1, p. 237 and i/2, p. 219 (trans., which misleadingly suggests that Jacob refers specifically to former Christians).

[37] Responsum 6 in the first letter to John the Stylite found in Vööbus, *Synodicon*, i/1, p. 249 and i/2, pp. 228-29 (trans.); see also responsum 3 in K.-E. Rignell, *A letter from Jacob of Edessa to John the Stylite of Litarab concerning ecclesiastical canons*, Malmö, 1979, pp. 52-53, along with Rignell's discussion of this responsum, pp. 83-84.

[38] Responsum 58 to Addai, in de Lagarde, *Reliquiae*, p. 140; Lamy, *Dissertatio*, pp. 158-59; see also Barhebraeus, *Nomocanon*, p. 380, n. 1. In the following responsum, Jacob states that there is no harm in priests teaching Jews and Ḥarrānian pagans how to read by using the Psalms and other scriptural texts.

Crossing the line between Islam and Christianity

A number of legal sources address procedures related to people or objects crossing the boundary separating Christianity and Islam. The Greek Orthodox Church, apparently in the ninth century, developed a lengthy Ritual of Abjuration (q.v.) to be recited by those who renounce Islam in favor of Christianity. The convert anathematizes the Saracen religion, 'Moamed also known as Mouchoumet', along with a number of his wives, descendants, and successors, the Qur'ān, Mecca, and even 'the God of Moamed', along with a substantial number of specific teachings ascribed to Islam. The title of the surviving texts of this ritual refers to Saracens who 'return' to Christianity, implying that most converts to Christianity were originally Christians, but Daniel J. Sahas observes that some aspects of the ritual seem to have new Christians in mind.[39] Jacob of Edessa addresses the scenario of re-conversion in two canons. He prohibits the rebaptism of a Christian who 'becomes a Hagarene or a pagan' and then repents, apparently because Jacob believes that such a person never really ceased being a Christian and that the original act of baptism retains its force.[40] And for the same reason, it would seem, he allows priests to accept deathbed confessions from such lapsed Christians and to bury them, although he prefers the penitent to be brought before the bishop for the determination of an appropriate penance.[41]

The transfer of objects from Christians to Muslims or back is filled with legal significance. The Nestorian Metropolitan 'Ishobokht (d. 780) addresses in various permutations the issue of inheritance when the

---

[39] D.J. Sahas, 'Ritual of conversion from Islam to the Byzantine Church', *Greek Orthodox Theological Review* 36 (1991) 57-69. The text of the ritual of abjuration appears in *PG* 140, cols 124-36; a critical edition of the anathemas was prepared by E. Montet, 'Un rituel d'abjuration des musulmans dans l'église grecque', *RHR* 53 (1906) 145-63. On this ritual, see also Hoyland, *Seeing Islam*, pp. 517-18; J. Meyendorff, 'Byzantine views of Islam', *DOP* 18 (1964) pp. 123-25 (repr. in M. Bonner (ed.), *Arab-Byzantine relations in early Islamic times*, Aldershot, 2004, pp. 225-27), and also the bibliography cited in the entry below.

[40] Responsum 15 in the second letter to John the Stylite found in Vööbus, *Synodicon*, i/1, p. 253 and i/2, pp. 231-32 (trans.). Hoyland (*Seeing Islam*, pp. 162-63) translates the version of this responsum (which he numbers as A13) preserved in Barhebraeus, *Nomocanon*, p. 22.

[41] Responsum 21 to Addai, in Vööbus, *Synodicon*, i/1, p. 261 and i/2, p. 238 (trans.); Hoyland, *Seeing Islam*, p. 162, numbers this reply as 116.

children or spouse of a Christian has converted out of the faith or when the heirs of a pagan are Christian converts.[42] Timothy I rules that a bequest by a Christian to a Muslim should be honored only if the Muslim is God-fearing and no God-fearing Christians live in the vicinity.[43] On the subject of ritual objects, Jacob of Edessa rules that portable altars which pagans have used as platters for their own food and thus profaned may no longer be used for the Eucharist, although they may be washed and put to secular use by clerics.[44] Similarly, cloth embroidered with the 'Hagarene profession of faith' may not be used for sacral purposes.[45] Jacob does not, however, believe that the possession of Christian relics by Muslims renders them profane, as he reports that he repatriated a Greek Orthodox relic returned to him by Hagarenes from among the spoils of war.[46]

The distinct places of Muslims and of Jews in canon law

The *Liber pontificalis* (q.v.) reports that Pope Zacharias (r. 741-52) interceded to prevent Venetian merchants from selling fellow Christians into slavery to 'the pagan people in Africa... judging it wrong for those washed by Christ's baptism to be the slaves of pagan peoples'.[47] Pope Hadrian I also objects to the practice of selling Christians

---

[42] Cited in Kaufhold, *Rechtssammlung des Gabriel von Baṣra*, pp. 160-61.

[43] C. 75, in Labourt, *De Timotheo I*, pp. 80-81. The following canon permits Christian courts to accept the testimony of pious Muslims. (Labourt does not provide the Syriac original, so it is unclear what terms Timothy uses to refer to Muslims in these canons.)

[44] Responsum 25 to Addai, in Lamy, *Dissertatio*, pp. 126-29, and de Lagarde, *Reliquiae*, p. 128. Note that responsum 26 to Addai addresses marble altars that have been broken by 'enemies'. In the text of Lamy and de Lagarde, q. 25 refers to 'Arabs' and the answer to 'pagans'. Slightly different versions of this responsum, whose texts refer solely to 'pagans', appear as number 42 to Addai in Vööbus, *Synodicon*, i/1, p. 266 and i/2, p. 242 (trans.), and number 3 to John the Stylite in Rignell, *Letter from Jacob of Edessa*, pp. 60-63; see also Barhebraeus, *Nomocanon*, p. 14. On the altars in question, see the discussion in Rignell, pp. 95-96.

[45] Barhebraeus, *Nomocanon*, p. 12, discussed in Hoyland, *Seeing Islam*, p. 161.

[46] Responsum 23 in the first letter to John the Stylite found in Vööbus, *Synodicon*, i/1, pp. 243-44 and i/2, p. 224 (trans.).

[47] L. Duchesne (ed.), *Le Liber pontificalis*, Paris, 1886, p. 433; R. Davis (trans.), *The lives of the eighth-century popes*, Liverpool, 1992, p. 47 (the cited trans. is by Davis). On the *Liber pontificalis*, see the entry in this work; on this passage and the letter cited in the following note, see Rouche, 'Le pape', pp. 212-13.

into slavery to Saracens.[48] In doing so, Zacharias and Hadrian apply in a new manner the long-standing prohibition against the sale of Christians as slaves to Jews.[49] For the most part, however, canon law sources from the period 650-1000 do not equate Muslims and Jews directly; Saracen law and Jewry law correspond to one another only to the extent that both Muslims and Jews are non-Christians. Medieval Christian authorities, however, regard Jews as more than merely non-Christians: they portray Jews as anti-Christians, foils set in diametrical opposition to Christianity in the service of Christian self-definition. For that reason, Christian authorities are especially concerned about the phenomenon of 'judaizing', the adoption by Christians of Jewish practices.[50] Christians do not grant Muslims comparable symbolic significance and do not employ terms such as 'paganizing', 'saracenizing', or the like.

Agobard, Archbishop of Lyons (r. 816-40), pointedly declares that Jews are more abhorrent than either biblical unbelievers such as the Amalekites and Midianites or contemporary unbelievers such as 'Hagarenes, who are known by the incorrect term Saracens'.[51] We have observed that Jacob of Edessa disapproves of commensality with Muslims but allows Christians to eat the meat they slaughter in non-sacrificial contexts. Jacob, however, prohibits consumption of all foods touched by 'the impure hands of the Jews'; with an exception for cases of necessity, he declares, those who eat such food 'shall be cast out from the Church of God and from association with the faithful as one who

[48] See the letter of 776 from Hadrian to Charlemagne, numbered 59 in *Codex Carolinus*, pp. 584-85. To the best of my knowledge, no statement by either of these popes regarding slavery to Muslims appears in canon law literature.

[49] On laws regulating Jewish slave ownership, see W. Pakter, *Medieval canon law and the Jews*, Ebelsbach, 1988, pp. 84-142. An interdiction against selling Christian slaves to non-Christians – apparently Muslims no less than Jews – also appears in c. 77 of Timothy I's collection; see Labourt, *De Timotheo I*, p. 81.

[50] On the history of this term, see S.J.D. Cohen, *The beginnings of Jewishness. Boundaries, varieties, uncertainties*, Berkeley CA, 1999, pp. 176-97; R. Dán, '"Judaizare". The career of a term', in R. Dán and A. Pirnát (eds), *Antitrinitarianism in the second half of the sixteenth century*, Budapest, 1982, 25-34. On the charge that Muslims themselves judaize, see D.M. Freidenreich, 'Sharing meals with non-Christians in canon law commentaries, circa 1160-1260. A case study in legal development', *Medieval Encounters* 14 (2008) 41-77.

[51] Agobard, *De Iudaicis superstitionibus* 21, in L. Van Acker (ed.), *Agobardi Lugdunensis: Opera omnia*, Turnhout, 1981 (Corpus Christianorum Continuatio Mediaevalis 52), pp.215-16. The term 'Saracen' is incorrect, according to various medieval Latin authorities, because Muslims descend from Hagar, not from Sarah.

is impure and despised and abominable, and they shall be numbered among the Jews until they purify themselves through repentance'.[52] The kind of charged, impurity-oriented rhetoric, which Agobard, Jacob, and many other Christian authorities employ with respect to the Jews, is not applied to Muslims in legal documents from the period under consideration here. Muslims are significant in the context of canon law both because of their military might and political power and because they constitute non-Christians with whom Christians interact. However, Christian authorities neither define Christianity in opposition to Islam nor do they ascribe symbolic significance to Muslims as they do to Jews.

[52] Responsum 3 to Thomas, in Vööbus, *Synodicon*, i/1, pp. 257-58; cf. trans., i/2, p. 235.

Christians in early and classical Sunnī law

David M. Freidenreich

Islamic law devotes considerable attention to regulations related to Christians, who comprised a significant minority population within the medieval Islamic Near East. Such regulations appear in numerous areas of law, and every compendium or treatise that addresses one or more of these areas is likely to address Christians. Comprehensive documentation of references to Christians in Islamic legal literature, of the sort attempted in the preceding essay on Muslims in canon law, is therefore practically impossible. Such an endeavor is also of questionable utility because different law books often cover the same ground in very similar ways. The present essay seeks instead to sketch Sunnī laws relating to Christians in broad strokes and to direct readers to relevant secondary scholarship for further details and for citations of the most important primary sources. Shīʿī laws regarding Christians differ in significant ways from their Sunnī counterparts and therefore merit separate treatment.[1]

The place of Christians and other non-Muslims in Islamic (primarily Sunnī) law has received considerable attention within academic scholarship. Antoine Fattal's *Le statut légal des non-Musulmans en pays d'Islam*, a general survey, retains its value as an entry point into the study of this subject. It has been supplemented and often surpassed by a variety of more focused studies, of which Yohanan Friedmann's *Tolerance and coercion in Islam* deserves particular mention. A number of works, including Fattal's and especially Mark R. Cohen's *Under crescent and cross*, devote considerable attention to comparing medieval Islamic laws governing non-Muslims with their counterparts in Roman, Sasanid, and Christian sources. Placed in this context rather than viewed against the backdrop of twenty-first-century Western norms, the laws expressed in medieval Islamic sources appear commonplace and even relatively benign; non-Muslims subject to these laws, of course, surely did not see them as such.[2]

---

[1] Essays surveying classical Shīʿī law and departures from classical approaches to Christians among Sunnī and Shīʿī authorities appear in later volumes.

[2] A. Fattal, *Le statut légal des non-Musulmans en pays d'islam*, Beirut, 1958;

The literature on minorities in Islamic law, although strong in many other respects, generally neglects to consider change over time in regulations regarding non-Muslims. This tendency, which the present essay makes no attempt to rectify, is due in part to the significant challenges associated with efforts to date legal works and normative statements ascribed to what scholars call the 'early' or formative period of Islamic law, roughly the first three Islamic centuries.

The onset of the 'classical' period of Sunnī law, which extends beyond the year 1500, occurs in the tenth Christian century with the crystallization of four schools of Sunnī legal thought named after and oriented toward the teachings of eighth- or ninth-century 'founders'. The differences between these schools with respect to numerous aspects of jurisprudential theory and legal substance result in sometimes significant differences in their respective laws regarding Christians, differences that medieval and modern scholars alike duly note and discuss. In most cases, the authors of legal compendia and treatises were private citizens rather than government functionaries. These works, therefore, express normative ideals that did not necessarily receive support from the coercive powers of the state. Indeed, as an essay in a later volume discusses, Muslim political authorities at times treated their Christian subjects in ways that contravened the norms articulated in classical legal sources, sometimes to the benefit of these subjects and sometimes to their detriment.

Y. Friedmann, *Tolerance and coercion in Islam. Interfaith relations in the Muslim tradition*, Cambridge, 2003; M.R. Cohen, *Under crescent and cross. The Jews in the Middle Ages*, Princeton NJ, 1994, esp. pp. 52-74. Much of Cohen's discussion of Jews in the Islamic world applies to Christians as well.

Scholars and others concerned about the contemporary rise of radical political Islamic movements have written numerous works on the treatment of non-Muslims within Islamic law. Representative of this genre, in its title and contributors, is R. Spencer (ed.), *The myth of Islamic tolerance. How Islamic law treats non-Muslims*, Amherst NY, 2005; Bat Ye'or, Mark Durie, Ibn Warraq, David G. Littman, Daniel Pipes, and Robert Spencer each wrote multiple essays in this volume. Works by advocates of political Islam paint a much more sympathetic picture of Islamic laws regarding non-Muslims; see, for example, M.S. Chaudhry, *Non-Muslim minorities in an Islamic state*, Lahore, 1995. Neither camp offers a sufficiently nuanced portrait of this subject matter, and for this reason the present essay steers clear of both. For a valuable analysis of the historiography of minorities (principally Jews) in the Islamic world, see Cohen, *Under crescent and cross*, pp. 3-14.

The present essay highlights the manner in which Sunnī authorities classify Christians.[3] Most laws treat Christians as non-Muslims, no different from Jews, Zoroastrians, Hindus, and other '*dhimmīs*', the term for religious minorities to which we will return. Some treat Christians as 'Scripturists' ('People of the Book'), adherents of a religion based on a divinely revealed scripture; as such, Christians are classified alongside Jews and Muslims.[4] This distribution pattern encapsulates the place of Christians within the worldview of Sunnī jurists: Christians are inferior to Muslims yet they, along with Jews, merit a limited degree of parity with Muslims. Hardly any laws treat Christians in a class alone, and those that do make clear that the authors of early and classical Sunnī legal literature generally perceive Christianity as posing nothing more than a theoretical challenge for Muslims. In the wake of European Christian military conquests, especially in the Iberian peninsula, some Muslim authorities developed a more defensive posture regarding Christians than is manifest in classical texts; an essay in a later volume addresses this development.

Christians as *dhimmīs*

A sizeable majority of Islamic law regarding Christians treats the latter as *dhimmīs* – more formally, *ahl al-dhimma*, 'people subject to a guarantee of protection'. This term applies solely to non-Muslims living in lands governed by Muslims who accept the authority of their Muslim overlords; it thus excludes both rebellious non-Muslims and non-Muslims who live outside the Islamic world, including those who reside temporarily in Muslim lands for trade or other purposes.[5] Some

[3] On the classification of non-Muslims, see also Y. Friedmann, 'Classification of unbelievers in Sunnī Muslim law and tradition', *JSAI* 22 (1998) 163-95, revised and expanded in his *Tolerance and coercion*, pp. 54-86.

[4] The familiar term 'People of the Book' is a literal trans. of the Arabic phrase *ahl al-kitāb*. Most legal sources employ the term *kitābī*, which refers to an individual member of one of these peoples. For ease of reference, I translate *kitābī* as 'Scripturist'. To my knowledge, this term was coined by N. Robinson; Friedmann, in contrast, employs the tongue-twisting term 'Scriptuary', perhaps inspired by the French 'Scripturaire' used by Fattal.

[5] No legal protection is granted to rebellious non-Muslims, such as those who support foreign invaders, or to non-Muslims resident in the territory of foreign enemies. A handful of laws address non-Muslim visitors to Muslim lands and non-Muslims who reside in foreign domains with which Muslims have negotiated an armistice. Other laws address the status of Muslims who dwell outside the Islamic world

jurists limit the protection associated with *dhimmī* status to Jews and Christians; others extend that protection to most or virtually all other non-Muslims as well.[6] Conversion to Islam frees the convert from the obligations incumbent upon *dhimmī*s, and jurists often seek to insure that the act of conversion redounds to the convert's advantage.

Islamic law obligates Muslim authorities to abstain from acts of hostility toward *dhimmī*s, to accord them various rights, and to protect them from attack by Muslims or foreigners. It further grants to *dhimmī*s, including the slaves and wives of Muslim masters, the right to freely exercise their religion in private.[7] *Dhimmī*s, in turn, must acknowledge their subservience to Muslim authorities and adhere to Islamic laws governing *dhimmī*s. Non-Muslims who refuse to accept these terms or who renege on their commitments forfeit the right to live as non-Muslims in the lands of Islam. Enforcement of *dhimmī* obligations was generally entrusted to the *muḥtasib*, the government official responsible for ensuring public morality.[8]

Chief among the obligations incumbent upon *dhimmī*s is payment of the *jizya*, a qurʾānic obligation which Muslim jurists classically understand to refer to an annual poll tax imposed solely upon non-Muslims.[9] Jurists offer two distinct interpretations of the *jizya*, each of

---

or enter foreign lands temporarily for the purpose of trade; on this subject, discussed in greater detail in an essay in a later volume, see K. Abou el Fadl, 'Islamic law and Muslim minorities. The juristic discourse on Muslim minorities from the second/eighth to the eleventh/seventeenth centuries', *Islamic Law and Society* 1 (1994) 141-87.

[6] On the legal conception of 'dhimmitude', to use the term coined by Bat Ye'or, see Fattal, *Statut légal*, pp. 71-84. On the category of *ahl al-dhimma* and its scope, see Friedmann, *Tolerance and coercion*, pp. 54-55, 58-69, 72-83; Fattal, *Statut légal*, pp. 160-63; see also Y. Friedmann, 'The temple of Multān. A note on early Muslim attitudes to idolatry', *Israel Oriental Studies* 2 (1972) 176-82.

[7] Some of the ramifications of this right are explored by Friedmann, *Tolerance and coercion*, pp. 187-90; R. Marston Speight, 'The place of Christians in ninth-century North Africa, according to Muslim sources', *Islamochristiana* 4 (1978) 47-65, pp. 53, 59. The latter essay surveys references to non-Muslims in the *Mudawwana*, the foundational compendium of Mālikī law ascribed to Saḥnūn (d. 854).

[8] See A. García-Sanjuán, 'Jews and Christians in Almoravid Seville as portrayed by the Islamic jurist Ibn ʿAbdūn', *Medieval Encounters* 14 (2008) 78-98; G. Weigert, 'A note on the muḥtasib and ahl al-dhimma', *Der Islam* 75 (1998) 331-37. García-Sanjuán translates and analyses the relevant extracts from Ibn ʿAbdūn's manual for the *muḥtasib*; relevant extracts from other Andalusian works of this genre appear in C. Melville and A. Ubaydli, *Christians and Moors in Spain. Vol. 3, Arabic sources (711-1501)*, Warminster, 1992, pp. 112-15.

[9] Q 9:29. The original meaning of this verse has been subject to considerable scholarly debate, whose major players include M.M. Bravmann, C. Cahen, M.J. Kister,

which accounts for different details in the laws governing its payment. On the one hand, this tax constitutes a fee for services rendered to *dhimmīs* by Muslims: the right to live as non-Muslims in Islamic territories, exemption from military service, and the protection provided by Muslim soldiers. For this reason, jurists generally exempt women, minors, slaves, and the infirm from the *jizya* payment, as Muslims in these categories are exempt from military service. (Authorities differ over whether and to what degree the tax applies to indigent *dhimmīs*.)[10] On the other hand, the *jizya* constitutes a penalty imposed upon non-Muslims on account of their refusal to embrace Islam. This notion underlies the widespread norm of exacting payment of the *jizya* in humiliating circumstances.[11] *Dhimmīs* are also required to pay distinctive property taxes and to pay taxes on commercial transactions at a higher rate than Muslims.[12]

The inferiority of *dhimmīs* to their Muslim overlords exemplified in the humiliation associated with payment of the *jizya* is reinforced

---

and U. Rubin. Ibn Warraq (ed.), *What the Koran really says: Language, text, and commentary*, Amherst NY, 2002, pp. 343-86, helpfully anthologizes (and, where necessary, translates from the French original) the relevant essays and notes on this subject, which first appeared in *Arabica* 9, 10, 11, 13 and 14, and *Der Islam* 70.

[10] In addition to the primary references cited in the following note, see E. Alschech, 'Islamic law, practice, and legal doctrine. Exempting the poor from the jizya under the Ayyubids (1171-1250)', *Islamic Law and Society* 10 (2003) 348-75.

[11] On the *jizya*: Cohen, *Under crescent and cross*, pp. 56, 68-72; Fattal, *Statut légal*, pp. 264-91. See also Speight, 'Place of Christians', pp. 54-55, and the references in the following note. On the humiliating nature of this tax as administered in seventh- and eighth-century Syria and Iraq, see also C.F. Robinson, 'Neck-sealing in early Islam', *Journal of the Economic and Social History of the Orient* 48 (2005) 401-41. The Banū Taghlib, an Arab Christian tribe, reportedly objected to payment of the *jizya* precisely because of the humiliation involved in its payment, humiliation which the tribesmen felt ought not to be imposed upon Arabs; see n. 43.

[12] Fattal, *Statut légal*, pp. 292-313. On tax administration in general and taxes imposed upon non-Muslims in particular, see M.G. Morony, *Iraq after the Muslim conquest*, Princeton NJ, 1984, pp. 99-124. The *Kitāb al-kharāj* of Yaʿqūb Abū Yūsuf (d. 798), an early treatise on Islamic tax law by one of the 'founders' of the Ḥanafī school of jurisprudence, contains several chapters regarding the taxation and treatment of *dhimmīs* and exists in a variety of modern editions and translations; see the entry 'Abū Yūsuf' in this volume. Relevant extracts from the *Kitāb al-kharāj* appear in N. Stillman, *The Jews of Arab lands. A history and source book*, Philadelphia PA, 1979, pp. 159-61; for another source that recounts the manner in which *jizya* was paid during the thirteenth century, see p. 180. A different extract from the *Kitāb al-kharāj* and other relevant sources on the status of non-Muslims appear in B. Lewis (ed.), *Islam from the Prophet Muhammad to the capture of Constantinople*, 2 vols, New York, 1974, ii (*Religion and society*), pp. 217-35.

through a variety of laws. Many of these appear in the so-called 'Pact of 'Umar', which purports to be a set of surrender terms proposed by Christians to the second Caliph, 'Umar ibn al-Khaṭṭāb (r. 634-44); jurists ultimately applied the terms in this pact to all *dhimmī*s, overriding local capitulation agreements. Scholars dismiss the association of this pact with 'Umar but find in its contents and form elements that reflect eighth- and ninth-century historical realities, including extant capitulation treaties and common caliphal administrative practices.[13] Among the terms of the Pact of 'Umar, Christians obligate themselves to show deference to Muslims by rising when Muslims wish to sit and refraining from building homes higher than those of Muslims. Christians must provide hospitality to traveling Muslims, may not shelter foreign spies, and may not strike Muslims, nor may they purchase slaves whose service ought to benefit Muslims.[14] Christians further agree not to ride horses or to bear arms, both symbols of elevated social status, and commit themselves to wear their traditional clothing and not to adopt Muslim styles of dress, honorific titles, or Arabic signets; these practices, which may have originally been meant to preserve the distinction between Muslims and the majority population, ultimately became signs of humiliation as well.[15]

---

[13] See the entry '*Pact of 'Umar*' in this volume, and the references cited there. Milka Levy-Rubin, author of this entry, elsewhere challenges scholarly consensus by arguing that the restrictions found in the Pact of 'Umar were in fact regularly and effectively enforced by medieval Muslim rulers; see M. Levy-Rubin, 'From early harbingers of *shurūṭ 'Umar* to its systematic enforcement', in *Border crossings. Interreligious interaction and the exchange of ideas in the Islamic Middle Ages*, ed. D.M. Freidenreich and M. Goldstein, Philadelphia (forthcoming), and also her forthcoming book on this subject. On the supersession of local treaties, see also H.E. Kassis, 'Some aspects of the legal position of Christians under Mālikī jurisprudence in al-Andalus', *Pd'O* 24 (1999) pp. 114-16.

[14] On the last of these restrictions, see Cohen, *Under crescent and cross*, pp. 64-65.

[15] On regulations governing the clothing worn by Christians, see Cohen, *Under crescent and cross*, pp. 62-64; Fattal, *Statut légal*, pp. 96-112; I. Lichtenstadter, 'The distinctive dress of non-Muslims in Islamic countries', *Historia Judaica* 5 (1943) 35-52; A.S. Tritton, *The caliphs and their non-Muslim subjects. A critical study of the Covenant of 'Umar*, London, 1930, 1970[2], pp. 115-26. On both clothing restrictions and the right to ride animals, see also E. Ashtor, 'The social isolation of ahl adh-dhimma', in *Pal Hirschler memorial book*, Budapest, 1949, 74-85 (repr. in *The medieval Near East. Social and economic history*, London, 1978). Restrictions governing the clothing and riding practices of non-Muslims appear consistently in medieval accounts of an edict promulgated by the Caliph 'Umar ibn 'Abd al-'Azīz, with whom some scholars associate the Pact of 'Umar itself; see Levy-Rubin, 'From early harbingers', and Levy-Rubin's forthcoming book. On the question of why Christians would commit themselves to

Various legal sources also prohibit Muslims themselves from adopting the mannerisms of non-Muslims, especially in matters of dress and ritual, and instruct Muslims to refrain from greeting non-Muslims in the same manner that they greet fellow believers.[16] Jurists from Andalusia express particular concern about the differentiation of Muslims and Christians.[17] This elevated concern is often manifest in differences of opinion between members of the Mālikī school of jurisprudence, dominant in Andalusia and North Africa, and jurists affiliated with other Sunnī schools.

Laws regarding *dhimmī*s exemplify the dictum, 'Islam is superior and cannot be superceded'.[18] For this reason, Islamic law prohibits *dhimmī*s from serving in positions of authority over Muslims, whether as public officials, members of the military, or owners of Muslim slaves; the law also restricts commercial interactions in which a Muslim might become inferior to a *dhimmī*.[19] According to one authority,

---

seemingly humiliating restrictions, see M.R. Cohen, 'What was the Pact of 'Umar? A literary-historical study', *JSAI* 23 (1999) 100-57, pp. 129-30, and, with particular attention to matters of dress, A. Noth, 'Abgrenzungsprobleme zwischen Muslimen und Nicht-Muslimen. Die "Bedingungen 'Umars (aŝ-Ŝurūṭ al-'Umariyya)" unter einem anderen Aspekt gelesen', *JSAI* 9 (1987) 290-315 (trans. M. Muelhaeusler, 'Problems of differentiation between Muslims and non-Muslims. Re-reading the "Ordinances of 'Umar (*al-shurūṭ al-'Umariyya*)"', in R. Hoyland (ed.), *Muslims and others in early Islamic society*, Aldershot, 2004, 103-24.

[16] See M.J. Kister, '"Do not assimilate yourselves...": *lā tashabbahū*', *JSAI* 12 (1989) 321-71 (repr. in Hoyland, *Muslims and others*). Kister emphasizes that these prohibitions originated in the early period of Islamic law. It is noteworthy that most of the prohibitions Kister adduces address practices associated with Judaism or pre-Islamic Arabian religion and only a small number relate specifically to Christian practices. On the proper greetings to offer non-Muslims and proper interaction with one's non-Muslim neighbor, see also Cohen, *Under crescent and cross*, pp. 131-32; H.E. Kassis, 'Arabic-speaking Christians in al-Andalus in an age of turmoil (fifth/eleventh century until AH 478/AD 1085)', *Al-Qanṭara* 15 (1994) 401-50, pp. 405-7.

[17] See J.M. Safran, 'Identity and differentiation in ninth-century al-Andalus', *Speculum* 76 (2001) 573-98; see also García-Sanjuán, 'Jews and Christians'; Kassis, 'Legal position of Christians'.

[18] *Ṣaḥīḥ al-Bukhārī* (Vaduz, Liechtenstein: Jam'iyyat al-Makniz al-Islāmī, 2000), 23.79. This *ḥadīth* is adduced by Friedmann, *Tolerance and coercion*, p. 35, and A. Fattal, 'How dhimmīs were judged in the Islamic world', in Hoyland, *Muslims and others*, p. 89, both of whom cite the tradition as appearing in 23.80. (The latter essay is a trans. by S. Pickford, of 'Comment les dhimmis étaient jugés en terre d'islam', *Cahiers d'Histoire Egyptienne* 3 (1951) 321-41.)

[19] The prohibition against *dhimmī*s in public office, rooted in numerous qur'ānic verses and *ḥadīth*s, was often ignored by rulers in the interest of expediency. Jurists differ over the legitimacy of employing *dhimmī*s in the military. See Friedmann,

Muslims ought not to perform menial labor on behalf of *dhimmī*s or allow themselves to be treated by non-Muslim physicians.[20]

The principle that Muslims should not be subject to the authority of non-Muslims underlies a number of inequities in the administration of justice in Islamic law. Legal proceedings involving a Muslim and a *dhimmī* must be held in an Islamic court, although *dhimmī*s are entitled to turn to their own judicial authorities for internal matters.[21] When the accused is a Muslim, *dhimmī*s are not allowed to offer testimony against him; some jurists reject the legitimacy of testimony by *dhimmī*s in all circumstances on the grounds that non-Muslims are presumed to be untrustworthy as witnesses.[22] Some jurists value the worth of Muslims and non-Muslims differently for the purpose of assessing penalties in cases of murder or bodily injury; others assert that payment of the *jizya* entitles *dhimmī*s to equal treatment under the law in this respect.[23] Islamic law denies *dhimmī*s the right to inherit from relatives who converted to Islam; authorities differ over whether Muslims are entitled to inherit from non-Muslim relatives and whether *dhimmī*s of different confessions may inherit one from another.[24]

Islamic law seeks to create a society that makes manifest the supremacy of Islam, and to this end it curtails the public display of non-Muslim religious life even as it allows non-Muslims to practice their own religions. Several of the terms of the Pact of ʿUmar relate specifically to religious matters. Chief among these is the rule that Christians may not build new churches, monasteries, or other religious buildings, and that they may not restore any such buildings that fall into

Tolerance and coercion, pp. 36-37; Cohen, *Under crescent and cross*, pp. 65-68; Fattal, *Statut légal*, pp. 232-63; see also Tritton, *Caliphs and their non-Muslim subjects*, pp. 18-36. On commercial interactions between Muslims and non-Muslims, see Fattal, *Statut légal*, pp. 144-50; Speight, 'Place of Christians', pp. 59-60.

20 García-Sanjuán, 'Jews and Christians', pp. 84-86.

21 Islamic law also governs cases involving *dhimmī*s of different confessions and cases in which the parties choose to turn to a Muslim judge. See Fattal, 'How dhimmīs were judged'; see also Speight, 'Place of Christians', pp. 61-62.

22 Friedmann, *Tolerance and coercion*, pp. 35-36; Fattal, 'How dhimmīs were judged', pp. 98-102; Speight, 'Place of Christians', pp. 60-61.

23 Friedmann, *Tolerance and coercion*, pp. 39-53; Fattal, *Statut légal*, pp. 113-18; see also Speight, 'Place of Christians', pp. 60-61. One example of differential penalties is referred to below in n. 36.

24 Friedmann, *Tolerance and coercion*, pp. 55-58; Fattal, *Statut légal*, pp. 137-42; see also Speight, 'Place of Christians', pp. 55-56. On the rights of *dhimmī*s to establish endowments, see Fattal, *Statut légal*, p. 143.

ruin or are located in Muslim neighborhoods. This rule, however, was not regularly enforced, and jurists developed a variety of exceptions and qualifications to it.[25] Christians agree not to proselytize and not to prevent Christians from converting to Islam. The Pact of ʿUmar also obligates Christians to refrain from holding public religious ceremonies and displaying religious symbols publicly, to beat the wooden clappers of their churches (the local equivalent of church bells) very quietly, not to raise their voices when praying, and to direct their funeral processions away from Muslim populations.[26] These regulations collectively serve to minimize the visible 'footprint' of Christianity within the Islamic world. Sunnī authorities, however, generally do not impose distinctively Islamic norms on *dhimmī*s. Thus, for example, Christians may not sell wine among Muslims but they may purchase, possess, and consume it themselves, even when married to Muslim husbands;[27] similarly, *dhimmī*s may engage in interest-generating commercial activities among themselves. Violating Islamic norms of blasphemy, however, nullifies the terms of the *dhimma* and merits capital punishment.[28]

Because of Islam's supremacy over all religions, including those previously revealed by God, conversion from Islam to Christianity or any other religion is strictly forbidden, as is Muslim participation in Christian festivals.[29] Whereas born Christians are eligible for *dhimmī*

---

[25] Kassis, 'Legal position of Christians', pp. 118-25; Cohen, *Under crescent and cross*, pp. 58-60; Fattal, *Statut légal*, pp. 174-203; see also Tritton, *Caliphs and their non-Muslim subjects*, pp. 37-77. On legal attitudes towards the presence of non-Muslim residents and their religious institutions in Muslim neighborhoods, see M. Levy-Rubin, '*Shurūṭ ʿUmar* and its alternatives. The legal debate on the status of the *dhimmī*s', *JSAI* 30 (2005) 170-206; Ashtor, 'Social isolation', pp. 85-88.

[26] Fattal, *Statut légal*, pp. 203-11; see also Tritton, *Caliphs and their non-Muslim subjects*, pp. 100-14.

[27] On this and other regulations guaranteeing non-Muslim wives freedom of religion, see Friedmann, *Tolerance and coercion*, pp. 188-90; S.A. Spectorsky, 'Women of the People of the Book. Intermarriage in early *fiqh* texts', in B.H. Hary, J.L. Hayes and F. Astren (eds), *Judaism and Islam: Boundaries, communication and interaction. Essays in honor of William M. Brinner*, Leiden, 2000, 269-78, p. 274. Some authorities, however, prohibit all *dhimmī*s from possessing or consuming wine; see Levy-Rubin, 'From early harbingers'.

[28] See Safran, 'Identity and differentiation', pp. 588-97; A. Turki, 'Situation du "tributaire" qui insulte l'islam, au regard de la doctrine et de la jurisprudence musulmanes', *Studia Islamica* 30 (1969) 39-72; Fattal, *Statut légal*, pp. 122-24.

[29] Concern about participation in Christian festivals is especially prevalent in Andalusian and North African sources. See Safran, 'Identity and differentiation', p. 581;

status, converts to Christianity from Islam are ineligible for this status and are therefore liable to the death penalty if they refuse to re-embrace Islam. Some authorities similarly forbid conversion from one non-Muslim religion to another on the grounds that one may not choose any religion over Islam. Forced conversion of non-Muslims is generally forbidden, and some jurists therefore allow non-Muslims who converted out of duress to return to their original religion. Jurists do, however, condone the compulsory conversion of non-Muslim women, minors, and prisoners of war in various circumstances.[30] Islamic law defines the offspring of marriages between Muslim men and Christian women as Muslims. Some jurists infer from this that the offspring of mixed marriages among *dhimmīs* are to be affiliated to the religion of their father, but most affiliate such children to the superior of the parents' faiths; in the latter case, the child of a Zoroastrian father and Christian mother is a Christian.[31]

Non-Muslims may not reside in the region of Mecca and Medina, in accordance with the last will of the Prophet; jurists differ over whether this prohibition extends to the entirety of the Arabian peninsula, and whether it applies to visitors. Many jurists specifically prohibit non-Muslims from entering the precincts of the Kaʿba in Mecca, and some extend this prohibition to all mosques.[32] Proceeds from *zakāt*, the alms tax obligatory upon Muslims, may not be given to non-Muslims who would otherwise qualify for such aid, although Muslims are welcome to give other forms of charity to non-Muslims.[33] Various authorities prohibit non-Muslims from possessing or studying the Qurʾān or other sacred Islamic texts, a prohibition sometimes associated with the assertion that non-Muslims are impure.[34]

R.M. Speight, 'Muslim attitudes toward Christians in the Maghrib during the Faṭimid period, 297/909-358/969', in Y.Y. Haddad and W.Z. Haddad (eds), *Christian-Muslim encounters*, Gainesville FL, 1995, 180-92, pp. 185-86; H.E. Kassis, 'Muslim revival in Spain in the fifth/eleventh century: Causes and ramifications', *Der Islam* 67 (1990) 78-110, pp. 85-86.

[30] Friedmann, *Tolerance and coercion*, pp. 106-59; Safran, 'Identity and differentiation', pp. 585-88; Fattal, *Statut légal*, pp. 163-69.

[31] Friedmann, *Tolerance and coercion*, pp. 174-75; Speight, 'Place of Christians', pp. 58-59. On the status of children when one parent converts to Islam, see M. Shatzmiller, 'Marriage, family, and the faith: Women's conversion to Islam', *Journal of Family History* 21 (1996) 235-66, pp. 247-48.

[32] Fattal, *Statut légal*, pp. 85-93.

[33] Speight, 'Place of Christians', p. 57.

[34] Fattal, *Statut légal*, pp. 144, 148-49, 159. Some jurists also express concern about

Islamic legal literature tends to regard non-Muslims as impure, but jurists vigorously debate the reason for this status and its implications for Muslim-*dhimmī* interactions. Sunnīs generally hold that non-Muslims are impure by virtue of their failure to perform the purification rituals necessary to restore the state of purity that is disrupted by any number of normal events. These jurists also speak of the beliefs of non-Muslims as 'impure' in a metaphorical sense. Some Sunnīs, however, hold that non-Muslims are intrinsically, and not merely circumstantially, impure on account of their beliefs. This minority opinion is especially prominent among jurists from Andalusia and North Africa, who tend to refer specifically to the impurity of Christians; scholars have suggested that social factors distinctive to the region may underlie this position. Even these jurists, however, do not regard the impurity of non-Muslims as grounds for stringent measures separating Muslims from non-Muslims of the sort that ultimately developed in some Shīʿī circles; Muslims who come into contact with non-Muslims in a state of impurity are simply enjoined to perform the necessary act of ablution before engaging in ritual activity.[35] Consequently, the notion that non-Muslims are impure does not interfere with Sunnī laws that permit certain forms of intimacy between Muslims and People of the Book, permissions associated with the fact that Christians and Jews adhere to divinely revealed Scriptures.

Christians as Scripturists

Islamic laws that treat Christians as *dhimmīs* tend to impose rules and restrictions on the activity of non-Muslims. Laws that treat Christians as Scripturists, in contrast, are primarily reflexive in nature: they regulate what Muslims themselves may or may not do in matters that

Christians teaching either the Qurʾān or prior revelations to Muslims; see Speight, 'Muslim attitudes', p. 185. On the impurity of non-Muslims, see the references in the following note.

[35] Z. Maghen, 'Strangers and brothers. The ritual status of unbelievers in Islamic jurisprudence', *Medieval Encounters* 12 (2006) 173-223; J.M. Safran, 'Rules of purity and confessional boundaries. Mālikī debates about the pollution of the Christian', *History of Religions* 42 (2003) 197-212; M.H. Katz, *Body of text. The emergence of the Sunnī law of ritual purity*, Albany NY, 2002, pp. 157-67; see also Safran, 'Identity and differentiation', pp. 581-83. On Shīʿī conceptions of non-Muslim impurity and its implications, see Maghen's essay and the essay on Christians in early and classical Shīʿī law in a later volume.

relate to non-Muslims. Laws that fall into this latter category may still profitably be labeled '*dhimmī* law' – analogous to Christian 'Jewry law' and 'Saracen law' – as they presume the inferiority and subservience of the Christians (and Jews).[36] These laws, however, emphasize the relatively elevated status of Christians and Jews among non-Muslims. Whereas the laws surveyed in the previous section express a binary distinction between Us and Them (1 and 0), laws that treat Christians as Scripturists reveal that Muslim jurists embraced a more complex system for classifying foreigners, one in which Christians and Jews are, in mathematical terms, less than 1 but greater than 0.

This intermediate status is given numerical expression by some jurists in their discussion of the blood-money that is due in certain cases to the surviving relatives of a murder victim. According to jurists of the Mālikī and Ḥanbalī schools, the amount of the blood-money when the victim is a Christian or Jew is either 4,000 or 6,000 dirhams, whereas when the victim is a Zoroastrian or another type of non-Muslim the payment due is only 800 dirhams. (The blood-money for a Muslim victim is 12,000 dirhams.) Other jurists hold that the value of the blood-money is identical, regardless of the affiliation of the victim; one jurist, Ibn Ḥazm, holds on technical grounds that no blood-money is paid when the victim is a non-Muslim.[37]

Most legal discussion of Christians as Scripturists stems from the qurʾānic verse:

> Permitted to you this day are the good things, and the food of those who were given the Book is permitted to you, and your food is permitted to them. So are the chaste women among the believers and the chaste women among those who were given the Book before you, provided you give them their dowries and take them in chastity, not in wantonness or as mistresses. If anyone denies the faith, his work shall be of no avail to him, and in the Hereafter he will be among the losers. (Q 5:5)

Sunnī interpreters and jurists uniformly understand the term 'food' (*ṭaʿām*) in this verse as referring to all foodstuffs that God has not prohibited, including permissible meat, the subject of the preceding

---

[36] On the terms 'imposed law', 'reflexive law', 'Jewry law', and 'Saracen law', see the companion essay on canon law in this volume, which observes that Christian Saracen law from ca. 650 to 1000, unlike Jewry law from the period, was exclusively reflexive in its nature.

[37] Friedmann, *Tolerance and coercion*, pp. 47-50.

verses. Animal slaughter was regarded as a divinely prescribed ritual activity in Near Eastern antiquity. For this reason, the declaration that the slaughter practices of 'the believers' and the slaughter practices of 'those who were given the Book' are equally valid indicates that Christians and Jews, no less than Muslims themselves, act in accordance with authentic divine revelations.[38] The meat of animals slaughtered by Zoroastrians, in contrast, is forbidden for consumption by Muslims. The permission of meat prepared by Scripturists expresses the affinity – indeed, the parity – of Jews, Christians, and Muslims.[39]

The limits to this parity, however, become apparent as Q 5:5 continues. 'Chaste women among those who were given the Book before you' are no less suitable for marriage than 'chaste women among the believers' because all come from communities committed to an authentic Scripture; idolatrous women, in contrast, are unfit marriage partners (Q 2:221). Nevertheless, a Muslim woman may not marry a Christian or Jewish man because a Muslim wife may not be subservient to a non-Muslim husband.[40] Sunnī jurists, who regard such a union as a serious breach of the proper social order, prescribe severe punishments for *dhimmīs* who transgress this norm, and they require married women who convert to Islam to separate from their non-Muslim husbands if the husbands do not follow suit.[41] Q 5:5 and the legal discussions that develop

---

[38] Some authorities, however, require that Christian butchers slaughter animals under Muslim supervision to ensure that the butchers do in fact follow divine dictates in this manner. In addition to the references cited in the following note, see Fattal, *Statut légal*, p. 97.

[39] See D.M. Freidenreich, *Thou shalt not eat with them: Foreigners and their food in Jewish, Christian, and Islamic law*, Berkeley CA, forthcoming, a revision of *Foreign food. A comparatively-enriched analysis of Jewish, Christian, and Islamic law*, New York, 2006 (Diss. Columbia University). See also N. Tsafrir, 'The attitude of Sunnī Islam toward Jews and Christians as reflected in some legal issues', *Al-Qanṭara* 26 (2005) 317-28; M.K. Masud, 'Food and the notion of purity in the *fatāwā* literature', in M. Marín and D. Waines (eds), *Alimentacion de las culturas Islamicas*, Madrid, 1994, 89-110; Speight, 'Place of Christians', pp. 57-58. Masud focuses primarily on modern interpretations of early and classical opinions regarding Christian meat.

[40] Nor, according to many jurists, may a Muslim free man marry a non-Muslim slave woman: the incongruity in status between the superior man and the doubly inferior woman is too great. (Muslim men may marry Muslim slave women.) See the primary references cited in the following note.

[41] On laws governing interfaith marriage, see Friedmann, *Tolerance and coercion*, pp. 160-93; Spectorsky, 'Women of the People of the Book'; Shatzmiller, 'Marriage, family, and the faith'; see also Tsafrir, 'Attitude of Sunnī Islam', pp. 228-32; Speight, 'Place of Christians', pp. 58-59. On Mālikī disapproval of such marriages, even while

around it strike a careful balance between the legitimation of Christianity and Judaism on the one hand and the affirmation of Islam's superiority on the other. The former principle, no less than the latter, is crucial to the self-definition of Islam that emerges from these texts: Islam stands in continuity with its predecessor religions even as it constitutes the culmination and climax of God's unfolding revelation.

The theological and definitional issues at stake in the permission of Christian meat and Christian wives become clear in legal discussions of borderline Christian communities. Some jurists limit the application of these permissions to *dhimmīs*: only Christians who acknowledge the superiority of Islam may be granted a limited degree of parity with Muslims.[42] The Banū Taghlib, a large and powerful Arab Christian tribe at the time of the Arab conquest, attracts particular attention in the legal literature and becomes paradigmatic of Arab Christians in general.[43] Most Sunnī authorities treat the Banū Taghlib as Christians even if they might be ignorant of their religion's tenets or latecomers to the faith. Some, however, express antipathy toward the Taghlibīs and refuse to extend to them the permissive laws that apply to other Christians, apparently out of a sense that all Arabs ought to embrace the teachings of God's Messenger to the Arabs. Others limit these permissive laws to Christians whose ancestors converted to Christianity before the time of Muḥammad. Pre-Islamic converts, after all, associated themselves with the best form of religion then in existence, but those who converted to Christianity after the time of Muḥammad rejected their obligation to believe not only in

---

acknowledging their permissibility, see also Safran, 'Identity and differentiation', pp. 583-84.

[42] Freidenreich, *Foreign food*, p. 295. This position, advanced solely by jurists affiliated with the Mālikī school, constitutes another instance of a restrictive attitude toward Christians distinctive to Andalusian and North African legal sources. Similarly, Mālikīs express greater opposition to Muslim patronage of non-Muslim butchers and are the only Sunnī jurists who question the permissibility of wild animals killed by Christian hunters.

[43] On the Banū Taghlib, see M. Lecker, 'Tribes in pre- and early Islamic Arabia', in Lecker, *People, tribes and society in Arabia around the time of Muḥammad*, Aldershot, 2005, XI, pp. 34-47. On the legal status of this and other groups of Arab Christians, see Friedmann, *Tolerance and coercion*, pp. 60-69; on payment of the *jizya* by Taghlibīs, see also Fattal, *Statut légal*, pp. 274-75. N. Tsafrir, *Yaḥas ha-halakhah ha-muslemit kelapei datot aḥerot: 'Inyanei sheḥiṭah ve-nisu'in*, Jerusalem, 1988 (MA diss. The Hebrew University), pp. 16-29, helpfully traces the history of normative traditions regarding Arab Christians in general and the Banū Taghlib in particular.

God but also in his final Prophet. The Shāfiʿī jurist Yaḥyā ibn Sharaf al-Nawawī (d. 1277) draws a further distinction between those whose ancestors embraced Christianity before that religion was corrupted and those whose ancestors converted between the time of its corruption and the revelation of the Qurʾān. As Muslim jurists themselves did not know when Christianity became corrupted, this distinction is of no practical value and reflects the scholastic nature of much of the discussion regarding laws that treat Christians as Scripturists. These laws serve first and foremost to express Sunnī ideas regarding the relationship between Islam and its predecessor religions.[44]

The focus of Islamic legal discourse regarding Christians on issues of theoretical rather than practical relevance is also apparent in the only legal discussion known to this author that treats Christians not as *dhimmī*s or Scripturists but rather as believers in the divinity of Christ.[45] Islamic law requires Muslim butchers to invoke the name of God over the act of animal slaughter, and Muslim jurists presume that idolatrous butchers invoke the name of a being other than God. These jurists also discuss the status of meat prepared by a Christian butcher who invokes the name of Christ. As no Christian source indicates that Christian butchers actually engaged in this practice, it would seem that these discussions are scholastic in their orientation, designed to probe the degree to which Islam's legitimation of Christianity excuses Christians from the basic principles of Islamic monotheism.[46]

The debate regarding meat from animals slaughtered in the name of Christ is surprisingly vigorous, with prominent Sunnī authorities lining up on both sides of the argument. Most jurists express serious reservations about the permissibility of such meat, but even those who prohibit its consumption are careful to preserve the permissibility in principle of meat prepared by Christians. The symbolic significance of this permission, embodying as it does the affinity between Islam and its predecessor traditions, is evidently of considerable

[44] Yaḥyā ibn Sharaf al-Nawawī, *Rawḍat al-ṭālibīn*, 5 vols, Beirut, 2000, v, pp. 474-75. See Freidenreich, *Thou shalt not eat with them*.

[45] On this subject, see Freidenreich, *Thou shalt not eat with them*; see also D.M. Freidenreich, 'Five questions about non-Muslim meat. Toward a new appreciation of Ibn Qayyim al-Ǧawziyyah's contribution to Islamic law', *Oriente Moderno* (forthcoming); Tsafrir, 'Attitude of Sunnī Islam', pp. 323-28.

[46] Of more practical relevance are parallel discussions regarding meat prepared for Christian feast days; opinions regarding such meat tend to match those regarding the meat of animals slaughtered in the name of Christ.

importance to Sunnī jurists. Muḥammad ibn ʿAbdallāh ibn al-ʿArabī (d. 1148), who goes so far as to permit Muslim consumption of chickens which Christians slaughter in a manner that contravenes Islamic law, captures the logic that motivates Sunnī jurists to bend over backwards in their efforts to permit Christian meat: 'Greater respect is accorded to [Christians] than to idolaters because they adhere to God's Book and cling to the coat tails of prophets.'[47] Even as they seek to ensure the absolute superiority of Islam and its adherents over all others, Sunnī jurists are careful to express in limited ways the relatively elevated status of Christians and Jews as People of the Book.

---

[47] Muḥammad ibn ʿAbdallāh ibn al-ʿArabī, *Aḥkām al-Qurʾān*, ed. ʿAlī Muḥammad al-Bajāwī, Cairo, 1957, on Q 5:5. For another example of Ibn al-ʿArabī's permissive attitude toward restrictions associated with Christians, see J.D. McAuliffe, 'Legal exegesis: Christians as a case study', in L. Ridgeon (ed.), *Islamic interpretations of Christianity*, New York, 2001, pp. 67-69. With the exception of jurists from Andalusia and North Africa, Ibn al-ʿArabī among them, Muslim authorities generally assume that Christian slaughter practices conform to those of Muslim butchers. Judging by the laws found in the *Nomocanon* of the Syrian Orthodox Gregory Barhebraeus (d. 1286) (ed. P. Bedjan, Paris, 1898, pp. 458-67), this assumption appears to be accurate.

Works on Christian-Muslim Relations
600-900

Doctrina Iacobi nuper baptizati

Unknown author

DATE OF BIRTH Unknown
PLACE OF BIRTH Unknown
DATE OF DEATH Unknown
PLACE OF DEATH Unknown

BIOGRAPHY —

MAIN SOURCES OF INFORMATION

Primary —

Secondary —

WORKS ON CHRISTIAN-MUSLIM RELATIONS

Didaskalia Iakōbou neobaptistou, 'Doctrina Iacobi nuper baptizati', 'Teachings of Jacob, the newly baptized'

DATE 634 (Hoyland, p. 58) / 640s (Déroche and Dagron, p. 247) / 7th c. (Speck, pp. 268-69)
ORIGINAL LANGUAGE Greek

DESCRIPTION

The *Doctrina Jacobi* is an anti-Jewish treatise purportedly composed in Africa in 634 against the background of Heraclius' order to compel all Jews to convert to Christianity. The text consists of a fictitious dialogue between the Jewish merchant Jacob and his cousin Justus, who was from Palestine. During a business trip to Carthage, Jacob was forcibly baptized, but he was soon convinced of the truth of the Christian faith. When his cousin Justus arrived from Palestine, they engaged in a discussion about Christianity and Judaism.

In the course of the discussion Justus says that he has received a letter from his brother in Palestine mentioning a 'prophet', who was coming with the 'Saracens' proclaiming the advent of the anointed one and claiming that he had the keys of paradise. These events aroused messianic expectations among the Jews of Palestine, who were eager to free themselves from Byzantine rule, and they 'mixed' with the Arabs. However, the letter points out that the new prophet must be false, 'for prophets do not come armed with a sword', and, 'there was no truth to be found in the so-called prophet, only the shedding of men's blood.' (Déroche and Dagron, §§ 16-17, pp. 208-13).

The *Doctrina* is not a work of historiography. Rather, it contains the standard themes of Christian-Jewish polemic and also quite strong novelistic elements (Speck). The date of the work is disputed. While Déroche and Dagron ('Juifs et Chrétiens', p. 247) believe that it was written in the 640s, Hoyland (*Seeing Islam*, p. 58) tends to accept 634 as the actual date of its completion. However, for Speck ('Doctrina Jacobi', pp. 268-69), it is questionable whether the work is a unified text at all. While agreeing that its various parts should be dated to the 7th century, he is of the opinion that a redactor put the work together in the 9th or 10th century. Déroche and Dagron (p. 57), hold the view that the *Doctrina* is the work of a single author but admit that it has been transmitted 'in an irremediably altered form'.

SIGNIFICANCE

The *Doctrina Jacobi* is remarkable for the importance it attaches to eschatology in the debate with the Jews against the background of the decline of Byzantine rule in the Near East in the 7th century. Despite the discussion of its dating, the *Doctrina* is one of the earliest references to Islam in Greek sources. As in Maximus the Confessor's letter to Peter Illustrios from about the same time (Epistle 14, *PG* 91, cols 537-41), the Arab conquest is seen as a sign of the coming end of times and the Arabs are depicted as violent and creating anarchy. According to Crone and Cook (*Hagarism*, p. 4), the 'startling thing about the Doctrina' is that the 'core of the Prophet's message… appears as Judaic messianism'. Whether this is an actual reflection of the original Islamic doctrine is questionable. The whole story of the prophet of the 'Saracens' has rather to be seen in the context of the refutation of the messianic Jewish interpretation of the events of the time.

MANUSCRIPTS

MS BNF – Coislin 299 (10th or 11th c.)

MS Florence, Biblioteca Medicea Laurenziana – Plut. 9, 14v (10th or 11th c.)

For fragments, the abbreviated recension and translations into Slavonic and Arabic, see V. Déroche and G. Dagron, 'Juifs et Chrétiens dans l'Orient du VIIe siècle', in *Travaux et Mémoires* 11 (1991) 17-273, pp. 48-55

EDITIONS AND TRANSLATIONS

Déroche and Dagron, 'Juifs et Chrétiens dans l'Orient du VIIe siècle', pp. 69-219 (edition and French trans.)

N. Bonwetsch, 'Doctrina Iacobi nuper baptizati', *Abhandlungen der königlichen Gesellschaft der Wissenschaften zu Göttingen, philologisch-historische Klasse*, NF. 12/3 (1910)

STUDIES

S. O'Sullivan, 'Anti-Jewish polemic and early Islam', in D. Thomas (ed.), *The Bible in Arab Christianity*, Leiden, 2007, 49-68

D. Olster, 'Letteratura apocalittica ebraica e cristiana nel VII secolo. Un raro caso di "dialogo" ebraico-cristiano', in A. Lewin, *Gli ebrei nell'impero romano. Saggi vari*, Florence, 2001, 279-93

V. Déroche, 'Polémique anti judaïque et émergence de l'islam (7e-8e s.)', *REB* 57 (1999) 141-61

H. Suermann, 'Juden und Muslime gemäß christlichen Texten zur Zeit Muḥammads und in der Frühzeit des Islams', in H. Preissler and H. Stein (eds), *Annäherung an das Fremde. XXVI. Deutscher Orientalistentag*, Stuttgart, 1998, 145-54

Hoyland, *Seeing Islam*, pp. 55-61

P. Speck, 'Die Doctrina Jacobi nuper baptizati', in Speck, *Varia VI. Beiträge zum Thema Byzantinische Feindseligkeit gegen die Juden im frühen siebten Jahrhundert*, Bonn, 1997, 267-439

D. Olster, *Roman defeat, Christian response and the literary construction of the Jew*, Philadelphia PA, 1994

A. Cameron, 'The Byzantine reconquest of North Africa and the impact of Greek culture', *Graeco-Arabica* 5 (1993) 153-65

Déroche and Dagron, 'Juifs et Chrétiens dans l'Orient du VIIe siècle', pp. 17-68, 220-73

P. Crone and M. Cook, *Hagarism. The making of the Islamic world*, Cambridge, 1977, pp. 3-6, 152-56

W.E. Kaegi, 'Initial Byzantine reactions to the Arab conquest', *Church History* 38 (1969) 139-49

Johannes Pahlitzsch 2008

Sophronius, Patriarch of Jerusalem

'the Sophist'

DATE OF BIRTH Between 550 and 580, most probably c. 560
PLACE OF BIRTH Damascus
DATE OF DEATH 11 March 638
PLACE OF DEATH Jerusalem

BIOGRAPHY

Sophronius, son of Myro and Plynthas, who were Greek-speaking but of Syrian origin, was born in Damascus, a city which he praises for its Hellenistic culture and long philosophical tradition. He was a teacher of rhetoric (whence 'sophist'), author, monk (tonsured c. 584-85), theologian and hymnographer (like his compatriots Andrew of Crete [d. c. 720] and John of Damascus [d. 749]), and also patriarch of Jerusalem (634-38).

Early in his life and as a lay person he attached himself to the monastery of Theodosius in Palestine, where he became a life-long disciple and close associate of John Moschus, or Eucratas. The two undertook extensive journeys (578/79-619) which brought them to Egypt, Sinai, Palestine, North Africa and Rome in an effort to support the Orthodox against monophysitism, as well as monoenergytism and monothelitism, which had recently been raised as compromise doctrines and supported by Patriarch Sergius of Constantinople and the Emperor Heraclius. In those travels they visited mainly monastic centers, where they engaged in collecting anecdotes, sayings and advice on spiritual struggles and saintly life from spiritual masters they encountered. The collection formed an anthology on spirituality known as *Leimōn* ('Spiritual meadow'), or *Pratum spirituale*.

In an early and lengthy stay in Alexandria (578-83), Sophronius delved further into Greek philosophy and rhetoric. In the North African monastery of Eucratas, named after Moschus, he met other Easterners including Maximus the Confessor (580-662) who, driven away by the Persian invasions (614-28), had regrouped there. While in Rome, Moschus died (619) and Sophronius undertook the task of bringing back the body of his mentor for burial at the monastery of Theodosius. There he edited Moschus' *Leimōn*, wrote the *Life* of John the Almsgiver, Patriarch of Alexandria (d. 620), and composed a number of poems in a classical style (*anakreontika*) for which he became known, including one (no. 14) on the Persian sack of Jerusalem.

In 634, an already elderly Sophronius was insistently called by clerics, monks and pious laymen to occupy the patriarchal throne of Jerusalem (634-38), which had been vacant for two years. Following a lengthy Arab siege (636-37), the awareness of the adverse repercussions a violent conquest could have on the holy places and on the Christian population led Sophronius to surrender Jerusalem, an act which at his own request he completed with the Caliph ʿUmar in person in 638. Later historians make this a solemn and congenial encounter between the youthful but pious caliph and the ascetic patriarch, who died shortly afterwards.

Sophronius represents the kind of Christian priest and ascetic that the Qurʾān praises (Q 5:82) for humility, and the type of person who Muslim traditions suggest influenced Muḥammad during his formative years. The life and works of Sophronius provide significant information and comment on the context of the emergence of Islam, the first wave of the Arab conquests, and the earliest meetings between Christians and Muslims.

Of Sophronius' many and diverse writings (*PG* 87.3 cols. 3147-4014), particular mention should be made of the *Synodical Letter* that he sent to Sergius and the patriarchal synod of Constantinople on the occasion of his consecration as Patriarch of Jerusalem; the *Christmas Oration* that he delivered from the Church of the Theotokos in Jerusalem; and his sermon on the *Holy Baptism* or *Epiphany*. In all these three writings, and in a progressively graphic way, he makes reference to the progressive Arab conquests, the destruction, and the sufferings of the Christians which he attributes to their behavior, because they have sinned against God and deviated from the right faith and conduct. To some lesser extent, the *Leimōn* of John Moschus, to which Sophronius contributed and which he edited, contains information and intimations on encounters and relations between Christian monks and Arabs in the regions in which the two travelled.

MAIN SOURCES OF INFORMATION

Primary

N.F. Marcos, *Los thaumata de Sofronio*, Madrid, 1975 (= *PG* 87.3, cols 3424-3696)

John Moschus, *Leimōn* (*Pratum spirituale*) *PG* 87, cols 2852-3112 (= T. Stauroniketianos, *Ioannes Moschos, Leimonarion. Eisagogika-metaphrase-scholia*, Hagion Oros, 1983; J. Wortley, *The spiritual meadow (Pratum spirituale) by John Moschos (also known as John Eviratus)*, Kalamazoo, 1992)

C. de Boor, *Theophanis Chronographia*, 2 vols, Leipzig, 1883-85 (repr. Hildesheim, 1963, 1980), i, pp. 330, 336-40

See also the works of Sophronius discussed below.

Secondary

D.J. Sahas, 'The face to face encounter between Patriarch Sophronius of Jerusalem and the Caliph 'Umar ibn al-Khaṭṭāb: friends or foes?', in E. Grypeou, M. Swanson and D. Thomas (eds), *The encounter of Eastern Christianity with early Islam*, Leiden, 2006, 33-44

D.J. Sahas, 'Why did Heraclius not defend Jerusalem, and fight the Arabs?', *Échos de l'Orient* 24 (1999) 79-97

Hoyland, *Seeing Islam*, pp. 67-73

D.J. Sahas, 'Saracens and Arabs in the *Leimon* of John Moschos', *Byzantiaka* 17 (1997) 121-38

D. M. Olster, *Roman defeat, Christian response and the literary construction of the Jew*, Philadelphia PA, 1994, pp. 99-115

A. Papadakis, art. 'Sophronios', in *ODB*

H. Busse, ''Omar b. al-Ḫaṭṭāb in Jerusalem', *JSAI* 5 (1984) 73-119

J. M. Duffy, 'Observations on Sophronius' *Miracles of Cyrus and John*', *Journal of Theological Studies* 35 (1984) 71-90

H. Chadwick, 'John Moschus and his friend Sophronius the Sophist', *Journal of Theological Studies* 25 (1974) 41-74

C. von Schönborn, *Sophrone de Jérusalem. Vie monastique et confession dogmatique*, Paris, 1972

C.G. Bonis, 'Sōphronios Hierosolymōn hos theologos, egkomiastēs kai hymnographos (634-11 Martiou 638)', in *Eucharistērion: timētikos tomos epi tē 45etēridi tēs epistēmonikēs draseōs kai tē 35etēridi taktikes kathegesias Amilka S. Alivizatou*, Athens, 1958, 269-92

T. Nissen, 'Sophronios. Studien II', *BZ* 39 (1939) 89-115

T. Nissen, 'Sophronios. Studien I', *BZ* 37 (1937) 66-85

Sophronios (Eustratiades), 'Sōphronios Patriarchēs Hierosolymōn', *Nea Sion* 29 (1934) 188-93, 241-54, 305-21, 434-42, 481-501

C. Papadopoulos, 'Ta syggrammata tou hagiou Sōphroniou Hierosolymōn', *Nea Sion* 17 (1922) 130-41

I. Phokylides, 'Ioannes ho Moschos kai Sōphronios ho Sophistēs ho kai Patriarchēs Hierosolymōn', *Nea Sion* 13 (1913) 815-36, 14 (1914) 90-97, 185-201

WORKS ON CHRISTIAN-MUSLIM RELATIONS

Ta Synodika tou autou en hosia tē mnēmē Sōphroniou, 'The *Synodika* of the same Sophronius of holy remembrance', '*Epistola synodica*', 'Synodical Letter'

DATE 634
ORIGINAL LANGUAGE Greek

DESCRIPTION
As one of his first acts as patriarch, Sophronius convened a council of local bishops and abbots of monasteries to condemn the heresy of monothelitism to which the Eastern patriarchates (except Jerusalem), the pope and the Emperor Heraclius were aspiring as a means of compromise in the rift between the Chalcedonian Orthodox and non-Chalcedonian Monophysites. He then, and on the occasion of his ascension to the throne, sent a formal *Letter* of credence to Sergius and the synod of bishops of the Patriarchate of Constantinople (hence, *Synodical Letter*), and possibly to Pope Honorius as well.

In this Sophronius expresses his regret for having exchanged the spiritual life of the monastery for the responsibilities of the patriarchal throne in turbulent times, and proceeds with an articulate confession of faith. At the end, and in the context of asking for unity in the Church and for prayers that his flock might persevere, he makes a lengthy reference to the Saracens 'who have now risen up against us unexpectedly and ravage us with… impious and godless audacity'. He concludes with the wish that the 'strong and vigorous sceptre' of the Christian emperors may quickly 'break the arrogance of all the barbarians, and especially of the Saracens' and 'quell their mad insolence'.

SIGNIFICANCE
The *Letter* is an articulate and sophisticated confession of Chalcedonian faith, which reveals both the theological acumen and the superb literary style of its sophist author. It also represents in a graphic manner the reaction of the Palestinian Christians and to a lesser extent of the Byzantine Empire to the first wave of the Muslim conquests during the earliest days, through a contemporary senior ecclesiastical figure. The intellectual, scholar, politician and Patriarch of Constantinople Photius (858-67, 877-86) writes of the *Letter* that 'it is full of piety [i.e. orthodox sentiment] and often innovative in its language, like a colt

exalting in its leaping ability' (*Bibliotheca*, ed. I. Bekker, 2 vols, Berlin, 1824-25, i, p. 286, no. 231).

MANUSCRIPTS

MS Munich, Bayerische Staatsbibliothek - Gr. 186
MS Turin, Biblioteca Nazionale - Gr. 67
MS Ochrid, St Kliment Library - Gr. 84
MS Leiden, Universiteits-Bibliotheek - 60 A
MS Florence, Biblioteca Medicea Laurenziana - Plut. LXXXVI-6
MS Vat - Gr. 1116
MS Mount Athos, Vatopedi Library - 594

EDITIONS AND TRANSLATIONS

Concilium universale Constantinopolitanum tertium concilii, ed. R. Riedinger, Berlin, 1990, pp. 410-94
PG 87.3, cols 3147-3200
G.D. Mansi, *Sacrorum concilium nova et amplissima collectio*, 53 vols, Florence, 1759-74 (repr. Graz, 1960), xi, cols 461-509

STUDIES

Olster, *Roman defeat*, pp. 101-02
R. Riedinger, 'Die Nachkommen der Epistula Synodica des Sophronius von Jerusalem (a. 634; CPG 7635)', *Römische Historische Mitteilungen* 26 (1984) 91-106
Sophronios (Eustratiades), 'Sōphronios Patriarchēs Hierosolymōn'

Tou en hagiois patros hēmōn Sōphroniou archiepiskopou Hierosolymōn logos eis ta theia tou sōtēros genetēlia en hagia Kyriakē katantēsanta kai eis tēn tōn Sarakēnōn ataxian kai phthartikēn epanastasin, 'Sermon of our father Sophronius, Archbishop of Jerusalem, who belongs to the saints, on the divine birthday of the Savior falling on holy Sunday and on the disorder and the destructive rising up of the Saracens', 'Christmas Sermon'

DATE 634
ORIGINAL LANGUAGE Greek

DESCRIPTION

This is an oration which Sophronius delivered at the Church of the Theotokos in Jerusalem on Christmas day, which, as he himself states, had fallen on a Sunday (hence, in the year 634). At such a joyful event, however, Sophronius laments the fact that he and the Christians of Jerusalem are, like Adam, banned from paradise, unable to celebrate the feast at the birthplace of Christ, 'prevented from entering the city by way of the road for fear of the… godless Saracens who have captured the divine Bethlehem… threatening slaughter and destruction if we leave this holy city' – a reference to Jerusalem under siege.

SIGNIFICANCE

The Christmas sermon provides more details on the Arab conquest of Palestine than the *Synodical Letter*. It alludes to the siege of Jerusalem, and to the hardships and sentiments of the Christians in the region. As an orator, Sophronius depicts these themes in a graphic way, while reiterating his conviction and pastoral advice that, should the Christians live in a manner dear and pleasing to God, they would live to 'rejoice over the fall of the Saracen enemy'.

MANUSCRIPTS

MS BNF – Gr. 1171, fols 143r-152r

MS Munich, Bayerische Staatsbibliothek – Gr. 221, fols 199r-210v

EDITIONS AND TRANSLATIONS

J. de la Ferrière, *Sophrone de Jérusalem. Fêtes chrétiennes à Jérusalem*, Paris, 1999, pp. 31-51 (French trans.)

H. Usener, 'Weihnachtspredigt des Sophronios', *Rheinisches Museum für Philologie* 41 (1886) 500-16 (repr. in Usener, *Kleine Schriften*, 4 vols, Berlin, 1990, iv, pp. 162-77)

PG 87.3, cols. 3201-12 (Latin version)

STUDIES

Hoyland, *Seeing Islam*, pp. 70-71

Olster, *Roman defeat*, pp. 106-7

W.E. Kaegi, 'Initial Byzantine reactions to the Arab conquests', *Church History* 36 (1969) 139-49

Tou en hagiois patros hēmōn Sōphroniou archiepiskopou Hierosolymōn logos eis to hagion baptisma, 'Sermon of our father Sophronius, Archbishop of Jerusalem, who belongs to the saints, on Holy Baptism', 'Sermon on Holy Baptism', 'Sermon on Epiphany'

DATE 637?
ORIGINAL LANGUAGE Greek

DESCRIPTION
Sophronius delivered this *Sermon on Holy Baptism* or *Epiphany* on the occasion of the feast of the baptism of Christ. The Arab invasions must have been at an advanced stage, since he describes the predicament of the Christians in the hands of the 'vengeful and God-hating Saracens' in much starker language than before. In a series of rhetorical questions, he wonders 'why so many wars have been waged against us... Why has there been so much destruction and plunder?' As in the previous sermon, Sophronius responds by attributing the sufferings to the behavior of the Christians, who have sinned against God and deviated from the right faith and conduct: 'We are ourselves, in truth, responsible for all these things and no word will be found for our defense.'

SIGNIFICANCE
The *Sermon on Holy Baptism* reflects an advanced stage of the Arab conquests, and a worsened situation for the Christian population in Palestine.

MANUSCRIPTS
MS Mount Athos, Monastery of Dionysios – 228, rla-rmg
MS Mount Athos, Monastery of Dionysios – 228, fols 104-8

EDITIONS AND TRANSLATIONS
De la Ferrière, *Sophrone de Jérusalem. Fêtes chrétiennes à Jérusalem*, pp. 61-86 (French trans.)
A. Gallico, *Le omelie*, Rome, 1991, pp. 188-207 (Italian trans.)
A. Papadopoulos-Kerameus, 'Tou en hagiois patros hēmōn Sōphroniou archiepiskopou Hierosolymōn logos eis to hagion baptisma', *Analekta Hierosolymitikēs Stachyologias* 5, St. Petersburg, 1898 (repr. Brussels, 1963), pp. 151-68

STUDIES

Hoyland, *Seeing Islam*, pp. 71-73
M.B. Krivov, 'On Sophronius' Oration on Baptism' (in Russian), *VV* 41 (1980) 249-51

Daniel J. Sahas 2007

The Panegyric of the three holy children of Babylon

Unknown author

DATE OF BIRTH Unknown
PLACE OF BIRTH Unknown
DATE OF DEATH Unknown
PLACE OF DEATH Unknown

BIOGRAPHY —

MAIN SOURCES OF INFORMATION

Primary —

Secondary —

WORKS ON CHRISTIAN-MUSLIM RELATIONS

Title and beginning of text missing. Modern title: 'The Panegyric of the three holy children of Babylon'

DATE Unknown, perhaps shortly after 640
ORIGINAL LANGUAGE Coptic; the existence of two different versions may indicate that both were translations of a Sahidic text

DESCRIPTION
The text is of a homily that treats a variety of subjects: humanity's fall into sin and refusal to listen to the prophets, necessitating the sending of the Son of God, who became the first martyr; the story of the three holy children of Babylon and of the prophet Daniel; a defense of miaphysite Christology.

In a brief passage in the second part of the homily, the author mentions the Saracens as oppressors who pursue prostitution and massacre and lead people into captivity. The author also mentions that they fast and pray, but by no means commends their religious practice.

SIGNIFICANCE

As Hoyland has pointed out (*Seeing Islam*, p. 121), the emphasis of the text on 'massacre' and 'captivity' may indicate that it was written shortly after the Arab conquest of Egypt. If this is true, the text is significant as counter-evidence to the frequent claim that Egyptian Christians considered the Arab conquest as a liberation from Byzantine rule.

MANUSCRIPTS

MS Vat – Copt. 69, fols 103r-129v (12th c.)

For several fragments, see H. de Vis, *Homélies coptes de la Vaticane*, ii, Copenhagen, 1929 (repr. Louvain, 1990), pp. 60-64

EDITIONS AND TRANSLATIONS

H. Suermann, 'Copts and the Islam of the seventh century', in E. Grypeou, M.N. Swanson and D. Thomas (eds), *The encounter of Eastern Christianity with early Islam*, Leiden, 2006, 95-109, p. 108 (English trans. of the passage referring to the Muslims)

Hoyland, *Seeing Islam*, pp. 120-21 (English trans. of the passage referring to the Muslims)

De Vis, *Homélies coptes*, ii, pp. 64-120 (edition of the Coptic text with French trans.)

STUDIES

Suermann, 'Copts and the Islam of the seventh century', pp. 107-8

Hoyland, *Seeing Islam*, pp. 120-21

P. Crone and M. Cook, *Hagarism. The making of the Islamic world*, Cambridge, 1977, p. 155

Harald Suermann 2008

The Chronicle of Khuzistan

Unknown author

DATE OF BIRTH Unknown
PLACE OF BIRTH Unknown
DATE OF DEATH Unknown
PLACE OF DEATH Unknown

BIOGRAPHY

The author, or authors, of the chronicle belonged to the East-Syrian community.

MAIN SOURCES OF INFORMATION

Primary —

Secondary
See below

WORKS ON CHRISTIAN-MUSLIM RELATIONS

Sharbē medem men qlisastiqē – hānaw dēn tashʿyātā ʿedtānāyātā – wa-d-qosmosṭiqē – hānaw dēn tashʿyātā ʿālmanyātā, 'Some narratives from Qlisastiqē – that is, ecclesiastical histories – and from Qosmostiqē – that is, secular histories'. Modern titles: 'The Chronicle of Khuzistan' (after the probable geographical provenance), 'Anonymous Guidi' (after the name of the first editor)

DATE Mid-7th c., after 652
ORIGINAL LANGUAGE Syriac

DESCRIPTION

This incomplete brief chronicle, covering 23 pages in the Guidi edition, is incomplete at the beginning and the end. In its present form it covers the period between the death of the Persian ruler Hormizd IV (590) and the campaigns of Khālid ibn al-Walīd (d. 642).

The work consists of two unequal parts. The first is a chronological account of ecclesiastical and political events, such as the succession of the East-Syrian patriarchs and the Persian and Byzantine rulers, monastic and dogmatic issues, and the Persian raids into Byzantine territory, including Jerusalem and Alexandria. In his description of the reign of Yazdgird, the author includes a brief reference to the Ishmaelites, their leader Muḥammad and the first successes against the Byzantines and the Persians, e.g. the capture of Maḥozē, the traditional residence of the East-Syrian catholicos.

The author of this first part may have been the East-Syrian Metropolitan Elias of Merv, as suggested by P. Nautin (1982). It is followed by an 'Appendix' (only three pages in Guidi's edition), different in style from the first part, of heterogeneous character and consisting of notes rather than of a consistent narrative. This appendix is defective at the beginning: an allusion in the first line indicates that the author, or authors, intended to write a continuation of an earlier history, which is, however, lost.

The 'Appendix' describes the capture of Bēt Lapaṭ (Gundishāpūr), al-Sūs (including the robbery of the tomb of the prophet Daniel) and Tushtar, and briefly mentions the activities of Abū Mūsā l-Ashʿarī (foundation of Basra, conquests), Saʿd ibn Abī Waqqāṣ (foundation of Kūfa) and Khālid ibn al-Walīd (in Syria, Palestine and Egypt). It ends with a passage about the Dome of Abraham and worship in Mecca, followed by a brief geographical survey of some Arabian cities and regions.

SIGNIFICANCE

The chronicle is an early East-Syrian description of the Muslim conquests of one of the heartlands of the East-Syrian Church. It contains a theological interpretation of the Muslim successes, explaining that their victory comes from God. Muslims are seen as descendants of Abraham, based on their tradition of worship at the Dome (*qubtā*, Kaʿba) of Abraham.

MANUSCRIPTS

MS Baghdad, Chaldean Monastery – 509 (13th-14th c.)
MS Vat – Borg Syr. 82 (19th c., pp. 669-89)
MS Mingana – Syr. 47 (Alqosh, 1907, fols 139v-151v)
MS Mingana – Syr. (Alqosh, 1932, fols 354v-366v)

EDITIONS AND TRANSLATIONS

B. Haddad, *Al-taʾrīkh al-ṣaghīr. Al-qarn al-sābiʿ li-l-milād*, Baghdad, 1976 (edition and Arabic trans.)

I. Guidi, *Chronica minora*, 2 vols, Paris, 1903 (*CSCO* 3-4), i, pp. 15-39 (edition), ii, pp. 15-32 (Latin trans.).

Th. Nöldeke, 'Die von Guidi herausgegebene syrische Chronik übersetzt und commentiert', *Sitzungsberichte der philos.-hist. Classe der kaiserl. Akademie der Wissenschaften* 128 (1893) 5-48 (German trans.)

I. Guidi, 'Un nuovo testo syriaco sulla storia degli ultimi Sassanidi' in *Actes du VIIIe congrès international des orientalistes*, Leiden, 1891, 5 parts in 2 vols, i/2, pp. 3-36 (edition)

STUDIES

C.F. Robinson, 'The conquest of Khuzistan: a historiographical reassessment', *BSOAS* 67 (2004), 14-40

Hoyland, *Seeing Islam*, pp. 182-89

H. Suermann, 'Orientalische Christen und der Islam: christliche Texte aus der Zeit von 632-750', *Zeitschrift für Missionswissenschaft und Religionswissenschaft* 67 (1983) 120-36, pp. 130-31

P. Nautin, 'L'auteur de la "chronique anonyme de Guidi": Elie de Merw', *RHR* 199 (1982) 302-13

J. Moorhead, 'The earliest Christian theological response to Islam', *Religion* 11 (1981) 265-74

S.P. Brock, 'Notes on some texts in the Mingana Collection', *JSS* 14 (1969), 205-26, p. 221

C. Cahen, 'Note sur l'accueil des chrétiens d'orient à l'Islam', *RHR* 166 (1964) 51-58

Herman G.B. Teule 2008

Ishoʿyahb III of Adiabene

DATE OF BIRTH c. 580
PLACE OF BIRTH Quplānā (Qaplān) (in Adiabene, between Kirkuk and Mosul)
DATE OF DEATH 659
PLACE OF DEATH Monastery of Bēt ʿAbē

BIOGRAPHY

Originating from a rich family, Ishoʿyahb studied at the theological school of Nisibis, though left as part of a group of students in protest against the heretical position of its rector, Ḥnānā (d. 596). He later became a monk in the newly established monastery of Bēt ʿAbē, where he became the disciple of its first abbot, Mār Yaʿqūb. In 628, he was elected bishop of Niniveh-Mosul. In this capacity, he was one of the members of the official delegation sent by the Persian Queen Boran to the Emperor Heraclius. A few years later, he was appointed metropolitan of Erbil; this must have taken place before 637, because in this year he was an eye witness to the Muslim conquest of the region of Adiabene, including Erbil. In 649, he was elected patriarch of the Church of the East, and took up residence in Seleucia-Ctesiphon, where he stayed till a few months before his death, which occurred in the monastery of Bēt ʿAbē.

As metropolitan of Erbil, he had to combat the presumed doctrinal errors of Sahdonā, Bishop of Maḥozē, who was an advocate of the doctrine of one *qnomā* ('hypostasis') in Christ (against the traditional Nestorian position of two *qnomē*).

He was respected by the Muslim leaders in the region of the former Persian capital, from whom he obtained fiscal concessions for his community, but towards the end of his life he was imprisoned by ʿAdī ibn al-Ḥārith ibn Ruwaym, the Muslim governor of Bahurasir, the region west of Seleucia-Ctesiphon, who tried to extort money from him. As patriarch, he was confronted with a schism by the bishops of Fars and Qaṭar, who refused to recognize the authority of the see of Seleucia-Ctesiphon. In the later tradition, he is known for his liturgical reforms.

Ishoʿyahb composed several doctrinal, paranetic, hagiographic and ascetic writings, some of which are lost.

MAIN SOURCES OF INFORMATION

Primary

Ishoʿyahb's own letters: R. Duval, *Ishoʿyahb Patriarchae III liber epistularum*, 2 vols, Paris, 1904-5 (*CSCO* 11-12)

E.A.W. Budge, *The Book of governors. The* Historia monastica *of Thomas, Bishop of Margâ A.D. 840*, 2 vols, London, 1893, i, pp. 69-80 (Syriac text); ii, pp. 123-79 (trans.)

ʿAmr ibn Mattā, *Kitāb al-majdal* in H. Gismondi (ed.), *Maris Amri et Slibae. De patriarchis Nestorianorum commentaria*, 4 parts in 1 vol., Rome, 1896-99, ii (*Maris textus arabicus*), p. 62; i (*Maris versio latina*), p. 55

Ṣalībā ibn Yuḥannā al-Mawṣilī, *Kitāb asfār al-asrār* in Gismondi, *Maris Amri et Slibae. De patriarchis Nestorianorum commentaria*, iv (*Amri et Slibae textus versio arabica*), pp. 56-57; iii (*Amri et Slibae textus versio latina*) pp. 32-33

Gregory Barhebraeus, *Ecclesiastical chronicle*: J.B. Abbeloos and T.J. Lamy, *Gregorii Barhebraei chronicon ecclesiasticum*, 3 vols, Paris, 1872-77, iii, pp. 130-32

ʿAbdishoʿ bar Brikhā, *Catalogus librorum*, in Assemani, *BO* iii/1, pp. 113-43

Secondary

Hoyland, *Seeing Islam*, pp. 174-82

J.-M. Fiey, 'Išoʿyaw le Grand. Vie du Catholicos nestorien Išoʿyaw III d'Adiabène (580-690)', *OCP* 35 (1969) 305-33; *OCP* 36 (1970) 5-46

Baumstark, *GSL*, pp. 197-98

WORKS ON CHRISTIAN-MUSLIM RELATIONS

Ktābā d-buyyāʾē awkit d-egrātā, 'Consolations' (i.e. letters)

DATE 628-59

ORIGINAL LANGUAGE Syriac

DESCRIPTION

After his consecration as bishop, Ishoʿyahb conducted a lively correspondence with various individuals (monks, fellow bishops, the patriarch) on a variety of subjects. Two letters give information about the Muslim presence in the territories of the Church of the East: Letter 48, addressed to some monks and written when he was bishop of Mosul, hence before 637, and Letter 14 during his time as Catholicos (hence composed after 649), addressed to Simeon, the dissenting bishop of Rev Ardashir in Fars.

SIGNIFICANCE

Letter 48 is the earliest East-Syrian text in which the suggestion is made that Nestorian Christology would be more compatible with Muslim views on Christ than the miaphysite teaching. It is probably also the earliest Syriac text to use the designation *mhaggrē* for Muslims.

Letter 14 to Simeon of Rev Ardashir ascribes the Arab dominion over the world to God's providence. In this letter, the Catholicos takes a positive attitude towards 'the Arabs' who 'praise our faith' (Christianity in general or the Nestorian creed?), and denounces the weakness of some Christians who convert to Islam, not under Muslim pressure, but for financial reasons.

MANUSCRIPTS

MS Vat. – Syr. 157 (incomplete, 124 fols, 10th c.),
MS Mosul, Chaldean Patriarchate 112 (1696) (now possibly in Baghdad, Chaldean Patriarchate)
MS Mardin, Chaldean Bishopric – 78 (1868)
MS Leeds, Collection Wallis Budge – Syr. 4.1 (1888)
MS Alqosh, Notre-Dame des Semences – 172 (1894)
MS Baghdad, Chaldean Monastery – Syr. 515 (1894; contains the title indicated above)
MS BNF – Syr. 336 (1896)
MS Baghdad, Chaldean Monastery – Syr. 516 (1901)
MS Baghdad, Chaldean Monastery – Syr. 517 (1902)
MS Vat. – Syr. 493 (1909)

EDITIONS AND TRANSLATIONS

Duval, *Išoʿyahb Patriarchae III liber epistularum*, (edition and Latin trans.): Letter 48, i, pp. 92-97, ii, pp. 71-74; Letter 14, i, pp. 247-55, ii, pp. 179-84

P. Scott-Moncrieff, *The Book of consolations or the Pastoral epistles of Mâr Îshô-yahbh of Kûphlânâ in Adiabene*, London, 1904 (edition of the letters written by Ishoʿyahb as bishop of Mosul, based solely on the manuscripts of Budge)

E.A.W. Budge, *The Book of governors. The* Historia monastica *of Thomas, Bishop of Margâ A.D. 840*, 2 vols, London, 1893, ii, pp. 132-47, 154-74 (Letter 14: pp. 154-58)

STUDIES

O. Ioan, 'Arabien und die Araber im kirchenleitenden Handeln des Katholikos Patriarchen Ischoʿjahb III. (649-659)', in M. Tamcke and A. Heinz (eds), *Die Suryoye und ihre Umwelt*, Münster, 2005, 43-58

M. Tamcke, 'The Catholicos Ischoʿjahb III and Giwargis and the Arabs', in R.J. Mouawad (ed.), *Les transmetteurs de civilisations, L'expérience du Bilad El-Sham à l'époque omeyyade, Patrimoine Syriaque*, 2 vols, Antelias 2005, i, 199-210
Hoyland, *Seeing Islam*, pp. 174-82
S.P. Brock, 'Syriac views of emergent Islam' in G. Juynboll, *Studies on the first century of Islamic society*, Carbondale, 1982, 9-21, pp. 14-16 (repr. in S.P. Brock, *Syriac perspectives on late antiquity*, London, 1984)
W.G. Young, *Patriarch, shah and caliph*, Rawalpindi, 1974, pp. 85-99
Fiey, 'Išoʿyaw le grand'

Herman G.B. Teule 2007

'Fredegar'

Pseudo-Fredegar

DATE OF BIRTH Unknown, probably 7th c.
PLACE OF BIRTH Unknown, but somewhere in Francia
DATE OF DEATH Unknown, probably 7th c.
PLACE OF DEATH Unknown

BIOGRAPHY

Nothing more is known about the author than what can be deduced from his world chronicle, which he wrote c. 660.

MAIN SOURCES OF INFORMATION

Primary —

Secondary

R. Collins *Die Fredegar-Chroniken*, Hannover, 2007, pp. 1-81 (*MGH Studien und Texte* 44)

WORKS ON CHRISTIAN-MUSLIM RELATIONS

Title uncertain. Conventional title: *Fredegarii chronicon*, 'Chronicle of Fredegar'

DATE c. 660
ORIGINAL LANGUAGE Latin

DESCRIPTION

This is a world chronicle from the creation up to 642 in five books or sections. One of the Western sources closest in date to the Arab conquests, its fifth book includes short accounts of the campaigns in the reigns of the Byzantine emperors Heraclius (r. 610-41) and Constans II (r. 642-68), promising a fuller account of the latter at the appropriate point in the narrative, which, however, ends abruptly with events in Francia in the year 642.

SIGNIFICANCE

Two short sections of the final book of this work refer to conquests of imperial territory by the Arabs, here referred to as 'Saracens' or 'Hagarenes'. The author thought they came from a region north of the Caspian called Ercolia, and that the conflict resulted from a campaign Heraclius launched against them. He was aware of their subsequent conquests of Jerusalem and Egypt, but shows no knowledge of Islam or anything to do with their religion.

MANUSCRIPTS

These are fully listed in Collins, *Die Fredegar-Chroniken*, pp. 55-75. Seven manuscripts (one destroyed in 1944) and one fragment are recorded, of which the earliest dates to 714/15. The others can be dated to the 8th to 10th centuries, except for one of c. 1500. All come from eastern France or south-western Germany and northern Switzerland.

EDITIONS AND TRANSLATIONS

Full list in C. Straw and R. Collins, *Historical and religious writers of the Latin West. Gregory the Great and Fredegar*, Aldershot, 1996, pp. 132-33

Frédégaire, *Chronique des temps mérovingiens. Livre IV et continuations. Texte latin selon l'édition de J. M.Wallace-Hadrill*, trans. O. Devillers and J. Meyers, Turnhout, 2001

The fourth book of the Chronicle of Fredegar, ed. and trans. J.M. Wallace-Hadrill, London, 1960

Chronicarum quae dicuntur Fredegarii Scholastici Libri IV, ed. B. Krusch, Hannover, 1888, pp. 1-193 (*MGH Scriptores rerum Merovingicarum* 2)

STUDIES

Collins, *Die Fredegar-Chroniken*; see pp. ix-xiii for a full bibliography

J. Flori, *L'Islam et la fin des temps. L'interprétation prophétique des invasions musulmanes dans la chrétienté médiévale*, Paris, 2007, 175-77

Hoyland, *Seeing Islam*, pp. 216-19

Straw and Collins, *Historical and religious writers*, pp. 134-38

E. Rotter, *Abendland und Sarazenen. Das okzidentale Araberbild und seine Enstehung im Frühmittelalter*, Berlin, 1986, pp. 145-82

Roger Collins 2007

The History of Sebeos

Sebēos, pseudo-Sebeos

DATE OF BIRTH Unknown
PLACE OF BIRTH Unknown
DATE OF DEATH Unknown, after 655 and probably after 661
PLACE OF DEATH Unknown

BIOGRAPHY

Nothing is known for certain about the anonymous author of the *History* attributed to Sebeos. Given the repeated recourse to biblical imagery and vocabulary, as well as the apocalyptic apprehensions evident within the text, it is highly likely that he was a cleric. It used to be argued that the author should be identified as Sebeos, bishop of the Bagratunik', a signatory to the Canons of the Council of Dvin in 645. This important church council, however, does not feature in the *History*. Far from displaying exclusively pro-Bagratuni sympathies, the text focuses as much, if not more, attention upon the rival Mamikonean family, not least in describing Hamazasp Mamikonean, the leading prince of Armenia in 655, as 'a lover of reading and learning'. He was also 'a virtuous man in every respect'. Significantly this eulogy appears at the very end of the work and implies that Hamazasp may have been its original sponsor. This sets the fragmentary Mamikonean traditions outlined at the start of the text in sharper focus; evidently the author was associated in some way with the Mamikonean house. The text generally reflects a miaphysite perspective, although a less hostile presentation towards duophysite theology may also be discerned in some passages. This suggests that certain elements within the Armenian Church may have responded more positively to monoenergism and monotheletism than has been appreciated hitherto. It is possible that the author was none other than the anonymous bishop who, according to the text, defied the Emperor Constans II in 653. The narrative contains a vivid, apparently first-hand account of that bishop's private audience with Constans II in Dvin. Since the work includes correspondence sent by and received in the name of more than one Catholicos, the head of the Armenian Church, he must have had access to the archives of the Catholicosate. This again intimates that the author was a senior cleric. He is known only through this work.

MAIN SOURCES OF INFORMATION

Primary

G.V. Abgaryan, *Patmut'iwn Sebēosi*, Yerevan, 1979, pp. 64-177

Secondary

A. Yakobean, 'Sebiosi patmut'ean hatuatsabazhanman khndirĕ ew Zuart'nots'i tachari kaṛuts'man masin glukhĕ', *Handēs Amsoreay* 119 (2005) 213-70

T.W. Greenwood, 'Sasanian echoes and apocalyptic expectations. A re-evaluation of the Armenian History attributed to Sebeos', *Le Muséon* 115 (2002) 323-97

J.D. Howard-Johnston, 'Armenian historians of Heraclius. An examination of the aims, sources and working-methods of Sebeos and Movses Daskhurantsi', in G.J. Reinink and B.H. Stolte (eds), *The reign of Heraclius (610-641). Crisis and confrontation*, Leuven, 2002, 41-62

R.W. Thomson and J.D. Howard-Johnston, *The Armenian History attributed to Sebeos*, 2 vols, Liverpool, 1999 (*Translated Texts for Historians* 31)

R.W. Thomson, 'The defence of Armenian Orthodoxy in Sebeos', in I. Sevcenko and I. Hutter (eds), *AETOΣ Studies in honour of Cyril Mango*, Stuttgart, 1998, 329-41

R.G. Hoyland, *Seeing Islam*, pp. 124-32

R.G. Hoyland, 'Sebeos, the Jews and the rise of Islam', in R.L. Nettler (ed.), *Medieval and modern perspectives on Muslim-Jewish relations*, Oxford, 1995, 89-102

C. Gugerotti, *Sebeos. Storia*, Verona, 1990

A.N. Tēr Ghewondyan, 'Sebēosi erkĕ orpes 7-rd dari merdzavor Arevelk'i patmut'yan aghbyur', *Patmabansirakan Handēs* 120 (1988/1) 121-31

D. Frendo, 'Sebeos and the Armenian historiographical tradition in the context of Byzantine-Iranian relations', *Periteia* 4 (1985) 1-20

J.-P. Mahé, 'Critical remarks on the newly-edited excerpts from Sebēos', in T.J. Samuelian and M.E. Stone (eds), *Medieval Armenian culture*, Chico CA, 1984, 218-39

M.K. Krikorian, 'Sebēos, historian of the seventh century', in T.J. Samuelian (ed.), *Classical Armenian culture*, Chico CA, 1982, 52-67

Z. Arzoumanian, 'A critique of Sebēos and his *History of Heraclius*, a seventh-century document', in Samuelian, *Classical Armenian culture*, 68-78

L. Shahinyan, 'Sebēosi Patmut'yanĕ kits' Ananun heghinaki mi telekut'yan ev harakits' harts'eri masin', *Lraber* (1980/2) 83-99

H. Hübschmann, 'Zur Geschichte Armenien und der ersten Kriege der Araber aus dem Armenischen des Sebēos', repr. in *Revue des études arméniennes* 13 (1978-79) 313-53

P. Ananean, *Sebēosi Patmut'ean grk'i masin k'ani mĕ Lusabanut'iwnner*, Venice, 1973

G.V. Abgaryan, 'Dardzeal Sebēosi masin', *Banber Matenadarani* 10 (1971) 425-74
M. Grigorean, 'Ditoghut'iwnner ew srbagrut'iwnner Sebiosi patmagrots' bnagrin vray', *Handēs Amsoreay* 81 (1967) 417-22; 82 (1968) 101-18, 203-12, 281-92, 485-98; 83 (1969) 199-214, 335-50; 84 (1970) 433-50; 85 (1971) 47-60, 439-62
G.V. Abgaryan, *Sebēosi Patmut'yunē ev Ananuni ạreltsvatsē* , Erevan, 1965
G.V. Abgaryan, 'Remarques sur l'histoire de Sébéos', *Revue des études arméniennes* 1 (1964) 203-15
N. Akinean, 'Sebēos episkopos Bagratuneats' ew iwr Patmut'iwnn i Herakł', *Handēs Amsoreay* 37 (1923) 1-9, 97-105, 220-27, 328-41, 396-420

WORKS ON CHRISTIAN-MUSLIM RELATIONS

Patmut'iwn Sebēosi, 'The History of Sebeos'

DATE In or shortly after 655, with short updating notices appended to the conclusion, advancing the chronological scope to 661
ORIGINAL LANGUAGE Armenian

DESCRIPTION

The work offers a wide-ranging overview of Near Eastern history between 572 and 661. The final third of the text, comprising 41 pages of Abgaryan's critical edition, records the emergence and expansion of a new and dynamic Islamic polity. It sketches key beliefs, tracing them back to Muḥammad, a preacher and legislator and, intriguingly, the 'path of truth'. In particular, Abraham is stressed as a common ancestor whilst the members of the community are defined repeatedly as the sons or children of Ishmael and occasionally as Hagarenes. Claims for territory are justified in terms of Abraham's divinely-sanctioned inheritance. Intriguingly, there is no attempt to refute or rebut these beliefs, other than a terse rejection of these demands by the Byzantine Emperor Heraclius.

Two interpretations are advanced to explain the extraordinary transformation in the political and religious landscape of the Near East. The first associates the Islamic conquests with an unsuccessful Jewish uprising in Edessa. Those held responsible were expelled into the desert from where they made contact with the children of Ishmael. Their discussions did not immediately bear fruit and it required Muḥammad's intervention to establish a firm alliance. This seems to be explaining the extraordinary successes of the Islamic community through the precipitant actions of a familiar, non-Christian agency, namely the Jews. The second interpretation is apocalyptic in character, viewing the kingdom of Ishmael as the fourth beast of Daniel's vision (Daniel 7:23) which 'will consume the whole earth'. One passage even describes Muʿāwiya as servant of the Antichrist, suggesting that the last days were now underway. This is, in all likelihood, the earliest apocalyptic text to contemplate the rise of Islam.

Far from being abstract or largely theoretical, these interpretations are set in a precisely defined, chronologically articulated historical context. The work offers a detailed, coherent account of the Islamic conquests across Byzantine and Sasanian territories; the initial thrusts into Armenia have a very small part to play and it is only towards the end of the work that greater attention is paid to Armenian affairs. The narrative does not downplay the violence associated with those conquests. At the same time, it also confirms the use of negotiated settlements, preserving the outline of a treaty agreed between Muʿāwiya and the leading Armenian prince of his day, Tʿēodoros Ṛshtuni, in 653. Even if the precise terms have been reconstructed by the author, it reveals that members of the Christian and Muslim elites were able to agree terms and establish working relationships with one another. There is no thought of conversion; indeed Muʿāwiya agrees not to send *amirs* or soldiers into Armenia unless requested. He also swears 'by the great God' not to be false.

The work also affords insight into the structure of the Islamic polity. Amṛ/ʿUmar is named as 'king' of the children of Ishmael and is described as not going on campaign to the east. By contrast, Muʿāwiya is titled 'prince of Ishmael', indicating an executive but lesser rank. The work thereby confirms the existence of a clear, operational chain of command. One of the *scholia* inserted at the end of the work purports to give an account of the first Arab civil war (*fitna*). It diverges from Islamic tradition in several respects but coincides as well. As a contemporary Christian perspective on the present conflict within the Muslim world, it merits close attention, although the possible influence of Daniel 7:24 should not be ignored.

Finally the work offers a short description of conditions inside Jerusalem following its capitulation. It records Jewish building work on the Temple mount until the eviction of the Jews by the Muslims, following which they began to construct a place of prayer at the base of the Temple mount. It also records the desecration of the Muslim prayer hall and the subsequent investigation of the crime and adjudication by the prince of Jerusalem, who is described as Jewish. This account reveals ongoing antagonism between the Christian and Jewish communities of Jerusalem as well as the presence of a separate Muslim community, with its own elite – the witness of the crime is one of the 'great ones of Ishmael'.

SIGNIFICANCE

The significance of this work lies in its breadth of historical vision, its early date of composition and its unaltered state. As soon as it became clear that the world was not on the brink of destruction, and that the compiler had been mistaken in his apocalyptic expectation, the work was rendered obsolete. As a near-contemporary account, it merits serious attention. It does, however, perceive and project the present times in unmistakably eschatological terms. The view of the recent past and the present day was shaped by this apprehension of the future. These need to be recognized when exploiting its version of events; there is a tendency to stress violent confrontation, and Muslim success, and to downplay or ignore Byzantine and Sasanian countermeasures, as these do not fit easily into the predetermined sequence of the last days.

MANUSCRIPTS

MS Yerevan, Matenadaran – 2639 (1672)

EDITIONS AND TRANSLATIONS

R.W. Thomson and J.D. Howard-Johnston, *The Armenian History attributed to Sebeos*, 2 vols, Liverpool, 1999 (*Translated Texts for Historians* 31) (trans. with introduction, notes and commentary)

C. Gugerotti, *Sebeos. Storia*, Verona, 1990 (Italian trans. and commentary)

R. Bedrosian, *Sebeos' History*, 1985, at http://rbedrosian/seb1.htm (trans. and brief introduction)

G.V. Abgaryan, *Patmut'iwn Sebēosi*, Yerevan, 1979 (critical edition)

F. Macler, *Histoire d'Héraclius*, Paris, 1904 (French trans. and brief notes)

STUDIES

Greenwood, 'Sasanian echoes and apocalyptic expectations'

Howard-Johnston, 'Armenian historians of Heraclius'

Hoyland, *Seeing Islam*, pp. 124-32

Hoyland, 'Sebeos, the Jews and the rise of Islam'

Mahé, 'Critical remarks on the newly-edited excerpts from Sebēos'
Krikorian, 'Sebēos, historian of the seventh century'
Arzoumanian, 'A critique of Sebēos and his *History of Heraclius*'
Abgaryan, 'Remarques sur l'histoire de Sébéos'

Tim Greenwood 2007

The Maronite Chronicle

Unknown author

DATE OF BIRTH Unknown
PLACE OF BIRTH Unknown
DATE OF DEATH Unknown
PLACE OF DEATH Unknown

BIOGRAPHY

The author of this chronicle probably belonged to the Maronite community, as is suggested by an important passage in the chronicle itself.

MAIN SOURCES OF INFORMATION

Primary
E.-W. Brooks, *Chronica Minora II*, Paris, 1904 (*CSCO* 4), pp. 43-74, esp. p. 70
Hoyland, *Seeing Islam*, p. 135

Secondary
See below

WORKS ON CHRISTIAN-MUSLIM RELATIONS

Title unknown. Modern titles: *Chronicon Maroniticum*, 'The Maronite Chronicle'

DATE 2nd half of 7th c., after 665
ORIGINAL LANGUAGE Syriac

DESCRIPTION
This incomplete brief chronicle consists of 14 folios in its present state of conservation, and covers events from Alexander the Great to 665/66. The period from the end of the 4th century to the conflict between ʿAlī and Muʿāwiya is missing.

The work has been ascribed to Qays al-Mārūnī (Lammens) and Theophilus of Edessa (Breydy). In the case of Qays, the period which is covered in the Maronite Chronicle is different from that covered by Qays, who moreover probably wrote in Arabic; in the case of Theophilus, the reconstruction of his chronicle shows that this work is different from that. The author of this work belonged to the Maronite community, as is suggested by a passage in the chronicle itself. There are indications that he was an eyewitness of the events described at the end of the chronicle, which suggests that he wrote some time in the second half of the 7th century, since 665 is the last year recorded.

SIGNIFICANCE

The chronicle describes the period between 658-665/66 and deals with the conflict between ʿAlī and Muʿāwiya, the latter's attitude towards Jerusalem and his interest in intra-Christian discussions, and Arab raids into Byzantine territory. It gives Syriac translations of certain Muslim concepts.

MANUSCRIPTS

MS BL – Add. 17.216 (fol. 1 is preserved in MS St Petersburg, Russian National Library – New Syriac series 1 (8th-9th c.))

EDITIONS AND TRANSLATIONS

A. Palmer, *The seventh century in the West-Syrian chronicles*, Liverpool, 1993, pp. 29-35 (trans.)

J.-B. Chabot, *Chronica Minora II*, Paris, 1904 (*CSCO* 4), pp. 35-57 (Latin trans. of Brooks' edition)

Brooks, *Chronica Minora II*, pp. 43-74 (edition)

F. Nau, 'Opuscules maronites', *Revue de l'Orient Chrétien* 4 (1899) 318-28 (French trans.)

Th. Nöldeke, 'Zur Geschichte der Araber im 1. Jahrh. d.H. aus syrischen Quellen', *ZDMG* 29 (1875) 89-98 (partial edition and German trans.)

STUDIES

H. Teule, 'Syriac historiography', in Centre d'Etudes et de Recherches Orientales (ed.), *Nos sources. Arts et littérature syriaques*, Antelias, 2005, pp. 326-27

Hoyland, *Seeing Islam*, pp. 135-39

L. Conrad, 'The conquest of Arwād: a source-critical study in the historiography of the early medieval Near East', in A. Cameron and L. Conrad (eds), *The Byzantine and early Islamic Near East I. Problems in the literary source material*, Princeton NJ, 1992, 317-401, pp. 322-36

M. Breydy, 'Das Chronikon des Maroniten Theophilus ibn Tuma', *Journal of Oriental and African Studies* 2 (1990) 34-46

M. Breydy, *Geschichte der Syro-Arabischen Literatur der Maroniten vom VII. bis XVI. Jahrhundert*, Opladen, 1985, pp. 130-38

S.P. Brock, 'Syriac sources for seventh-century history', *Byzantine and Modern Greek Studies* 2 (1976) 17-36, pp. 18-19 (repr. in S.P. Brock, *Syriac perspectives on late antiquity*, London, 1984)
H. Lammens, 'Qays al-Mārūnī aw aqdam taʾrīkh li-l-katabat al-Mawārina', *Al-Mashriq* 2 (1899) 265-68
S. Ronzevalle, 'Lā Qays wa-lā Thāwufīl', *Al-Mashriq* 2 (1899) 451-60

Herman G.B. Teule 2008

The Chapters of the miracles, 19

Unknown

DATE OF BIRTH Unknown, probably early 7th c.
PLACE OF BIRTH Unknown, probably Palestine
DATE OF DEATH Unknown, probably late 7th c.
PLACE OF DEATH Unknown, probably Palestine

BIOGRAPHY

Although the author of this story is unknown, another story within the same cluster of short narratives refers to Michael, priest of 'our lavra of Mār Saba'. On the basis of this, Flusin, pp. 18-19, has raised the possibility that the whole collection was produced in this famous monastic community to the east of Jerusalem. If this is correct, we may assume that the author of the story in question was also a monk there.

MAIN SOURCES OF INFORMATION

Primary —

Secondary —

WORKS ON CHRISTIAN-MUSLIM RELATIONS

Untitled story no. 19 in 'The Chapters of the miracles' in the appendix to the Georgian version of John Moschus' *Spiritual meadow*

DATE Mid-7th c.?
ORIGINAL LANGUAGE Greek

DESCRIPTION

This brief didactic story is found in an appendix to the Georgian translation of John Moschus' *Spiritual meadow*, among 30 short stories all believed to have been composed in Greek, then translated into Arabic and later into Georgian. Some of them, including this one, have only survived in Georgian. Others, which also survive in their Greek original, show that the translation closely follows the original. Among the 30 stories, there is a cluster of 19 pieces which have some sort of unity and all deal with events between the early 600s and the 660s. It seems that the collection was made soon after the time of the Byzantine Emperor Constans II (d. 668) by someone in the monastery of Mar Saba.

It is not known who wrote story 19 in the Georgian appendix, but it is presented on the authority of a certain Theodore, archdeacon of the church of St Theodore just outside Jerusalem, in the time of Patriarch Sophronius (638-41). It tells how the 'impious Saracens' settled in Jerusalem, cleared the area of the Capitol (*Kapitolion*, probably on the Temple Mount) and began to build a mosque there. Theodore's story revolves around a certain John, also from the church of St Theodore, a stone-cutter who was hired to work on the mosque. When Patriarch Sophronius heard about John's collaboration with the Arab settlers, he pressurized him to abandon the project on 'the spot cursed by Christ' (cf. Luke 13:34). John then swore 'by the holy cross' never to work there again, only to take up his tasks in secret two days later. Once his deceit was uncovered, he was excommunicated. In response, he tried to make his way into the church by force, with the help of his Arab companions. Some days later he was injured when he fell off the roof of a monastery, where he was doing restoration work. Theodore then advised him to seek healing from St Theodore, but this helped him only temporarily and eventually he died of his wounds. In the final exhortation, the narrator asserts that it was ignoring the commands of the patriarch and showing contempt for the Holy Spirit that led to such a terrible death.

SIGNIFICANCE

This narrative, best labeled as 'anti-hagiography', is striking because it shows that as early as the mid-7th century, just a few decades after the Muslim conquest, there was an apologetic impulse among Christians in Palestine, who were apparently already confronted with the problem of divided loyalty within the community, here exemplified through the story of a man whose religious beliefs did not prevent him from seeking employment in the new Muslim community. In this respect, it stands in sharp contrast to the detached account of Muslim building activity on the Temple Mount by Adomnán of Iona (q.v.), based on the report of the pilgrim Arculf from Gaul, who was in Jerusalem around the same time as our author.

MANUSCRIPTS

MS Mt Athos, Iviron Monastery – Georgian 9 (977)

EDITIONS AND TRANSLATIONS

B. Flusin, 'L'esplanade du Temple à l'arrivée des arabes d'après deux recits byzantins', in J. Raby and J. Johns, *Bayt al-Maqdis. ʿAbd al-Malik's Jerusalem*, Oxford, 2 vols, 1991, i, 17-31 (repr. of edition by Abuladze)

G. Garitte, ' "Histoires édifiantes" géorgiennes', *Byzantion* 36 (1966) 396-423, pp. 414-16 (Latin trans.)

I. Abuladze, *Ioane Moshi. Limonari*, Tbilisi, 1960, pp. 100-2 (edition)

STUDIES

S.H. Griffith, *The church in the shadow of the mosque*, Princeton NJ, 2008, pp. 26-27

A. Kaplony, *The Ḥaram of Jerusalem, 324-1099. Temple, Friday Mosque, area of spiritual power*, Stuttgart, 2002, pp. 182-84, 208-12

Hoyland, *Seeing Islam*, pp. 62-64

B. Flusin, 'L'Esplanade du Temple à l'arrivée des arabes'

C. Mango, 'The Temple Mount, AD 614-638', in Raby and Johns, *Bayt al-Maqdis*, i, 1-16

B. Flusin, 'Les premières constructions musulmanes sur l'Esplanade du Temple selon deux "récits édifiants" byzantins', *Revue des études grecques* 101 (1988) xxiv-xxvi

G. Garitte, 'La version géorgienne du Pré spirituel', *Mélanges Eugène Tisserant II*, Rome, 1964, 171-85, pp. 181-82

Barbara Roggema 2008

Ghiwarghis I

DATE OF BIRTH Unknown
PLACE OF BIRTH Kafrā, province of Bēt Gāwāyā in Bēt Garmay (Northern Iraq)
DATE OF DEATH 680/81
PLACE OF DEATH Ḥīra

BIOGRAPHY

Born into a noble family, Ghiwarghis was sent by his parents to take charge of their estates in the country of Margā, where he became attracted to monastic life and became monk in the Monastery of Bēt ʿAbē. He caught the attention of Ishoʿyahb, bishop of Mosul-Nineveh, and when the latter became patriarch of the Church of the East as Ishoʿyahb III (q.v.), he made Ghiwarghis metropolitan of Irbil. Shortly before his death, Ishoʿyahb suggested the name of 'his disciple Ghiwarghis' to the future electors of the new patriarch. The brief note on Ghiwarghis in the *Kitāb al-majdal* (11th c.?) also mentions him as metropolitan of Gundishāpūr. Ghiwarghis took up office as patriarch in 660/61. He is the author of some liturgical *memrē* and a remarkable Christological letter, originally written in Persian but preserved in Syriac, addressed to a certain Mina, '*chorepiskopos* in the land of the Persians'. In 676, he convened an important synod on the island of Diren in the Arabian Gulf, which reunited the Metropolitan of Bēt Qaṭrāyē and five bishops of Arabian dioceses.

MAIN SOURCES OF INFORMATION

Primary

'Ecclesiastical histories' by Athqen, quoted by Thomas of Margā (q.v.): E.A.W. Budge, *The Book of governors. The* Historia monastica *of Thomas, Bishop of Margâ A.D. 840*, 2 vols, London, 1893, i, pp. 80-85, 88-89, ii, 179-86, 207-09

ʿAmr ibn Mattā, *Kitāb al-majdal* in: H. Gismondi, *Maris Amri et Slibae. De patriarchis Nestorianorum commentaria*, 4 parts in 1 vol., Rome, 1896-99, ii (*Maris textus arabicus*) p. 63; i (*Maris versio latina*) p. 55

Ṣalībā ibn Yuḥannā al-Mawṣilī, *Kitāb asfār al-asrār* in: Gismondi, *Maris Amri et Slibae. De patriarchis Nestorianorum commentaria*, iv (*Amri et Slibae textus versio arabica*), p. 57; iii (*Amri et Slibae textus versio latina*), p. 33

J.-B. Chabot, *Synodicon orientale ou recueil de synodes nestoriens*, Paris, 1902, pp. 227-45 (Syriac text), 490-514 (Latin trans.)

Secondary
Hoyland, *Seeing Islam*, pp. 192-94
Baumstark, *GSL*, p. 208
O. Braun, *Das Buch der Synhados oder Synodicon orientale*, Stuttgart, Vienna, 1900 (repr. Amsterdam, 1975), pp. 331-33

WORKS ON CHRISTIAN-MUSLIM RELATIONS

Sunhados d-qaddishā (…) Mār Ghiwarghis
'Synod of the holy (…) Mār Ghiwarghis'

DATE 676
ORIGINAL LANGUAGE Syriac

DESCRIPTION
A number of canons issued during this synod contain references to the Islamic environment of the church in east Arabia. Canon 6 is possibly one of the earliest admonitions to Christians not to bring their differences and conflicts to Muslim courts. Canon 14 forbids Christian women to marry foreign *ḥanpē*, again an allusion to the Muslims. Canon 19 stipulates that Christians entrusted by the Muslim authorities with the collection of the *jizya* and *kharāj* should exempt the bishop.

SIGNIFICANCE
The Synodical canons of Diren belong to the first official decisions of the Church of the East to regulate the interaction of its believers with Muslims and Muslim authorities.

MANUSCRIPTS
MS Baghdad – Chaldean Monastery – Syr. 509 (previously, MS Notre-Dame des Semences – 169 = Scher 90, before 14th c.)
MS Siirt, Chaldean Bishopric – 65.2 (17th/18th c.)
MS BNF – Syr. 332 (1895)
MS Vat – Syr. Borg. 82
MS Vat – Syr. 598 (previously, MS Mardin, Chaldean Bishopric – 49, 1871)

EDITIONS AND TRANSLATIONS
J.-B. Chabot, *Synodicon orientale ou recueil de synodes nestoriens*, pp. 215-26, 480-90 (edition and trans.)

O. Braun, *Das Buch der Synhados oder Synodicon orientale*, Stuttgart, Vienna, 1900 (repr. Amsterdam, 1975), pp. 333-48 (trans.)

STUDIES

Hoyland, *Seeing Islam*, pp. 192-94

Herman G.B. Teule 2007

Adomnán of Iona

Adamnan, Adomnanus, Adamnanus

DATE OF BIRTH c. 625
PLACE OF BIRTH County Donegal, Ireland
DATE OF DEATH 704
PLACE OF DEATH Iona Abbey, Scotland

BIOGRAPHY

Adomnán was an Irish monk, who in 679 became the Abbot of Iona, the foremost Irish monastery in Scotland. He is best known as the author of a life of Saint Columba, founder of Iona, and of a treatise of law, the *Cain Adomnan*.

MAIN SOURCES OF INFORMATION

Primary

Bede, *Ecclesiastical history of the English people*, ed. J. McClure and R. Collins, Oxford, 1994

Betha Adamnain: Life of Saint Adamnan, ed. and trans. M. Herbert and P.Ó Riain, Dublin, 1988

Secondary —

WORKS ON CHRISTIAN-MUSLIM RELATIONS

De locis sanctis, 'On the holy places'

DATE c. 680
ORIGINAL LANGUAGE Latin

DESCRIPTION

The work consists of a description of the holy sites of Jerusalem and Palestine: it is a treatise of sacred geography for use as an exegetical aid. Adomnán's principle source is an oral informant named Arculf, a bishop from Gaul who traveled to the Holy Land in the 670s and who described the sites he visited. Arculf presents the Saracens' 'king Mavias' (the Umayyad Caliph Muʿāwiya, r. 661-80) as a quasi-Christian who invokes Christ as savior and who builds a 'church' in Damascus.

He describes a primitive prayer house (*orationis domum*) on the Temple Mount, the site of the future al-Ḥaram al-Sharīf. He describes this house as 'poorly constructed' (*uili fabricati*) on top of ruins; he says however that it could hold 3,000 people.

The description and the date seem to match neither the Dome of the Rock nor the al-Aqṣā mosque; Adomnán may be the unique testimony to an earlier, temporary mosque constructed on the site.

SIGNIFICANCE

Arculf, through Adomnán, provides a rare glimpse of Jerusalem between the Muslim conquest of 638 and the construction of the Dome of the Rock in 692. Bede, in his own *De locis sanctis,* reworks Adomnán's text and reproduces many of his descriptions, including that of the prayer house on the Temple Mount.

MANUSCRIPTS

For the four extant manuscripts, which are all from the 9th century, see Wilkinson, p. 193.

EDITIONS AND TRANSLATIONS

H. Donner, *Pilgerfahrt ins Heilige Land. Die ältesten Berichte christlicher Palästinapilger (4.-7. Jh.)* , Stuttgart, 1979, pp. 315-421 (German trans.)

J. Wilkinson, *Jerusalem pilgrims before the Crusades*, Warminster, 1977, pp. 93-116 (English trans., with Arculf's drawings of floor plans of Jerusalem's holy sites on pp. 191-97)

Itineraria et alia geographica, ed. P. Geyer et al., 2 vols, Turnhout, 1965 (*Corpus Christianorum Series Latina* 175-76), i, pp. 175-234 (edition)

Adamnan, *De locis sanctis*, ed. and trans. D. Meehan, Dublin, 1958 and 1983 (*Scriptores latini hiberniae* 3) (edition and trans.)

Arculf, *Eines Pilgers Reise nach dem heiligen Lande (um 670)*, trans. P. Mickley, 3 parts in 2 vols, Leipzig, 1917 (German trans.)

STUDIES AND SIGNIFICANT REFERENCES

J. Tolan, 'Le pèlerin Arculfe et le roi Mavias: la circulation des informations à propos des «Sarrasins» aux VIIe-VIIIe siècles, de Jérusalem à Iona et Yarrow', in P. Henriet and J. Ducos (eds), *Passages. Déplacements des hommes, circulation des textes et identités dans l'Occident médiéval*, Toulouse, 2009

T. O'Loughlin, *Adomnán on the holy places. The perception of an insular monk on the locations of the biblical drama*, London, 2007

T. O'Loughlin, 'Adomnan and Arculf. The case of an expert witness', *Journal of Medieval Latin* 7 (2007) 127-146

M. Gorman, 'Adomnán's 'De locis sanctis': the diagrams and the sources', *Revue bénédictine* 116 (2006) 5-41

M. Dietz, *Wandering monks, virgins, and pilgrims. Ascetic travel in the Mediterranean world, A.D. 300-800*, University Park PA, 2005, pp. 194-200

O. Limor, 'Pilgrims and authors. Adomnán's "De locis sanctis" and Hugeburc's "Hodoeporicon Sancti Willibaldi"', *Revue bénédictine* 114 (2004) 253-75

K. Scarfe Beckett, *Anglo-Saxon perceptions on the Islamic world*, Cambridge, 2003, pp. 44-46, 51-53, 69-71 and *passim*

A. Kaplony, *The Ḥaram of Jerusalem, 324-1099. Temple, Friday mosque, area of spiritual power*, Stuttgart, 2002, pp. 207-12

D. Woods, 'Arculf's luggage: the sources for Adomnán's *De locis sanctis*', *Ériu* 52 (2002) 25-52

Tolan, *Saracens*, pp. 72-73

T. O'Loughlin, 'Palestine in the aftermath of the Arab conquest: the earliest Latin account', in R.N. Swanson (ed.), *The Holy Land, holy lands, and Christian history*, Woodbridge, 2000, 78-89

Hoyland, *Seeing Islam*, pp. 220-23

E. Rotter, *Abendland und Sarazenen. Das okzidentale Araberbild und seine Enstehung im Frühmittelalter*, Berlin, 1986, pp. 31-42 and passim

P. Geyer, *Adamnanus II. Die handschriftliche Überlieferung der Schrift* De locis sanctis, Erlangen, 1897

John Tolan 2007

Athanasius of Balad

DATE OF BIRTH Unknown
PLACE OF BIRTH Balad
DATE OF DEATH 11 Elul (September) 687
PLACE OF DEATH Unknown

BIOGRAPHY

Athanasius, who belonged to the Syrian Orthodox Church, was a student of Severus Sebokht at the monastery of Qenneshrē, where he studied Greek. Next, he moved to the monastery of Bēt Malkā in Ṭūr ʿAbdīn. Michael the Syrian calls him 'Interpreter of the Scriptures'. Beside his exegetical activities, he occupied himself with translating from Greek the *Isagoge* of Porphyry, an anonymous introduction to the art of logic and, possibly, some letters of Severus of Antioch. He is known as the author of a liturgical *sedrā* and wrote corrections to the Syriac translation of the homilies of Gregory of Nazianzus made at the beginning of the 7th century. In 684, he was elected patriarch. In this capacity, he issued canonical rulings against Christians participating in Muslim festivals (see below) and an interdiction to allow East-Syrians and other heretics to receive baptism or holy communion.

MAIN SOURCES OF INFORMATION

Primary

Chronicle of Zuqnīn: J.-B. Chabot, *Incerti auctoris Chronicon Pseudo-Dyonysianum vulgo dictum,* Louvain, 1933, 1952² (*CSCO* 104), p. 154; French trans. R. Hespel, *Incerti auctoris Chronicon Pseudo-Dyonysianum vulgo dictum*, Louvain, 1989 (*CSCO* 507), p. 116; English trans. A. Harrak, *The Chonicle of Zuqnīn,* parts III and IV A.D. 488-775, Toronto, 1999, pp. 147-48; A. Palmer, *The seventh century in the West-Syrian chronicles*, Liverpool, 1993, p. 60.

Chronicle of 846: E.W. Brooks, *Chronicon anonymum ad A.D. 846* in *Chronica minora*, Paris, 1904 (*CSCO* 3) Paris, 1904, p. 230; Latin trans. J.B. Chabot, *Chronica minora*, Paris, 1904 (*CSCO* 4), p. 175; English trans. Palmer, *The seventh century*, p. 82

Kitāb al-majdal, ed. and trans. H. Gismondi, *Maris, Amri et Slibae. De patriarchis nestorianorum commentaria, pars prior: Maris textus arabicus et versio Latina*, Rome, 1899, p. 65, Latin trans. p. 57

Chronicle of Michael the Syrian: J.-B. Chabot, *Chronique de Michel le Syrien*, 4 vols, Paris, 1899-1910, iv, p. 752; trans. ii, pp. 470, 471, 474; iii, p. 449
Gregory Barhebraeus, *Ecclesiastical Chronicle*: J. Abbeloos and T. Lamy, *Gregorii Barhebraei Chronicon ecclesiasticum*, Paris, 1872, i, pp. 289-90

Secondary
Hoyland, *Seeing Islam*, pp. 147-49
O. Schrier, 'Chronological problems concerning the Lives of Severus bar Mašqā, Athanasius of Balad, Julianus Romāyā, Yoḥannān Sābā, George of the Arabs and Jacob of Edessa', *OC* 75 (1991) 62-90
A. Vööbus, *Syrische Kanonessammlungen. Ein Beitrag zur Quellenkunde*, 2 vols, Louvain, 1970 (*CSCO* 307, 317), i (a), pp. 200-2
Baumstark, *GSL*, pp. 256-67, 276-77

WORKS ON CHRISTIAN-MUSLIM RELATIONS

Egartā d-ṭubtānā Atanāsius paṭriarkā meṭul hāy d-lā nēkul (')nāsh kristyānā min debḥē da-Mhaggrāyē hālen d-hāshā aḥidin, 'The Letter by the blessed Patriarch Athanasius on that no Christian should eat of the sacrifices of those Hagarenes who are now in power' (This title was probably added by later copyists and is not original.)

DATE 684
ORIGINAL LANGUAGE Syriac

DESCRIPTION
As patriarch, Athanasius felt obliged to react against the practices of Christians participating in meals with pagans, *ḥanpē*, and eating from their sacrifices – possibly meaning ritually slaughtered meat – and Christian women marrying pagans. It is not certain whether *ḥanpē* had already by this period become a designation for Muslims. From the title of the letter, possibly added by the compiler of the canonical collections into which this letter came to be inserted, it is clear that, at least according to the later tradition, Athanasius had Muslims particularly in mind. His letter is addressed to the *chorepiskopoi* (bishops responsible for the rural regions, not precisely defined) and to 'inspectors', who are asked to act with prudence towards these Christians, to remind them of the ecclesiastical laws and, if necessary, to deny them holy communion. Women especially were to refrain from eating from

pagan sacrifices and put an end to their illegal relationships. They were to be admonished to have the children of these unions baptized; and if they behaved in a Christian way, they were to be allowed to receive communion.

The date of the letter, 684, is found in a marginal note in most manuscripts.

SIGNIFICANCE

This brief letter (35 lines in Nau's edition) gives insight into a seemingly current practice among members of the Syrian Orthodox Church of mixed marriages with pagans, possibly Muslims, and participation in pagan (Muslim?) festivals. The fact that the addressees of the letter are principally *chorepiskopoi* suggests that this practice was particularly prevalent in rural areas.

The letter was incorporated into a number of important and influential canonical compilations, which suggests that it was still considered to be relevant in later periods. Especially noteworthy is Athanasius' understanding attitude towards woman married to *ḥanpē*.

MANUSCRIPTS

There are nine MSS, of which three are from the 8th/9th century and the others are more recent (from the 16th century onwards); see Vööbus, *Syrische Kanonessammlungen*, p. 200.

EDITIONS AND TRANSLATIONS

Hoyland, *Seeing Islam*, p. 148 (partial English trans.)

Vööbus, *Syrische Kanonessammlungen*, p. 201 (paraphrasing German trans.)

F. Nau, 'Littérature canonique syriaque inédite', *Revue de l'Orient Chrétien* 14 (1909) 113-30, pp. 128-30 (edition based on MS BNF – Syr. 262, a canonical compendium, and French trans.)

STUDIES

Hoyland, *Seeing Islam*, pp. 147-49

Vööbus, *Syrische Kanonessammlungen*, pp. 200-2

Herman G.B. Teule 2008

The Apocalypse of Pseudo-Ephrem

Unknown author

DATE OF BIRTH Unknown, probably early 7th c.
PLACE OF BIRTH Unknown
DATE OF DEATH Unknown, probably late 7th c.
PLACE OF DEATH Unknown

BIOGRAPHY

Virtually nothing is known about the author of this *memrā* that is incorrectly ascribed to Ephrem the Syrian (d. 373). He was writing between 640 and 680 and was probably a Chalcedonian, although his ecclesiastical affiliation cannot be determined with absolute certainty.

MAIN SOURCES OF INFORMATION

Primary —

Secondary —

WORKS ON CHRISTIAN-MUSLIM RELATIONS

Mēmrā d-qāddishā mār(y) Aprēm, malpānā sūryāyā, ʿal ḥartā w-shullāmā w-dīnā w-tbaʿt w-ʿal Bēt Agōg w-Magōg w-ʿal Mshiḥā daggālā, 'The Sermon of the holy lord Ephrem, the Syrian teacher, on the end and completion, the judgment and exaction, on Gog and Magog and on the false Messiah'. Modern title: 'The Apocalypse of Pseudo-Ephrem'

DATE Between 640 and 692
ORIGINAL LANGUAGE Syriac

DESCRIPTION
The apocalypse stems from the time before the Muslim invasion, but a chapter concerning the Arabs was added to the original text

(in the modern edition about 11 pages, of which the addition is about 2 pages). Reinink argues that the entire text was reworked by a later redactor.

The chapter on the Arabs can be summarized as follows (ll. 83-167): the Arabs rise up from the desert before the end of times, which is characterized by the unleashing of Gog and Magog, the re-establishment of the Roman Empire, the coming of the Antichrist and the end of time itself. The Arabs are described as descendants of Abraham through Hagar. They are seen as the messengers of the Antichrist, devastating the country but also building roads.

Since no measures of oppression other than tax collection are mentioned, some scholars are inclined to believe that this chapter must have been written immediately after the conquest, but the allusions to an eventual period of peace and to the construction of roads may indicate the Umayyad period, more particularly the end of the 7th century, when similar apocalypses were composed, notably the *Apocalypse of Pseudo-Methodius* (q.v.). However, the *Apocalypse of Pseudo-Ephrem* is much less detailed than similar contemporary writings.

This Syriac text should not be confused with the Latin *Sermo de fine mundi*, an eschatological text that circulated in medieval Europe, attributed sometimes to Ephrem and sometimes to Isidore of Seville. The Latin *Sermo* contains no references to Islam and shows no clear link with this Syriac apocalypse.

SIGNIFICANCE

It is in all likelihood the oldest Syriac apocalypse on the Arabs, and one of the earliest texts to interpret the Arab invasion within the framework of the Christian-Byzantine scheme of history. It also makes a moral point: the Arabs are sent because of the sins of the Christians.

MANUSCRIPTS

MS Vat – Syr. 566, fols 232r-237r (1472)

MS Dublin, Trinity College – B 5.19, fols 67-89 (1625)

EDITIONS AND TRANSLATIONS

H. Suermann, *Die geschichtstheologische Reaktion auf die einfallenden Muslime in der edessenischen Apokalyptik des 7. Jahrhunderts,* Frankfurt a. M., 1985, pp. 12-33 (copy of the Syriac text with German trans.)

E. Beck, *Des heiligen Ephraem des Syrers Sermones III*, Louvain 1972 (*CSCO* 320-21), pp. 60-71 (edition) 79-94 (German trans.)

T.J. Lamy, *Sancti Ephraem Syri Hymni et Sermones*, 4 vols, Mechelen, 1882-1902, iii, pp. 187-212 (edition and Latin trans.)

STUDIES

H. Suermann, 'The use of biblical quotations in Christian apocalyptic writings of the Umayyad period', in D. Thomas (ed.), *The Bible in Arab Christianity*, Leiden, 2007, 69-90

H. Möhring, *Der Weltkaiser der Endzeit. Entstehung, Wandel und Wirkung einer tausendjährigen Weissagung*, Stuttgart, 2000, pp. 55-56

Hoyland, *Seeing Islam*, pp. 260-67

G.J. Reinink, 'Pseudo-Ephraems "Rede über das Ende" und die syrische eschatologische Literatur des siebten Jahrhunderts', *Aram* 5 (1993) 437-63

Suermann, *Die geschichtstheologische Reaktion*, pp. 111-29

B. McGinn, *Visions of the end. Apocalyptic traditions in the middle ages*, New York, 1979, p. 60

K. Czeglédy, 'The Syriac legend concerning Alexander the Great', *Acta orientalia Academiae Scientiarum Hungarica* 7 (1957) 231-49, pp. 239-40

K. Czeglédy, 'Monographs on Syriac and Muhammedan sources in the literary remains of M. Kmosko', *Acta orientalia Academiae Scientiarum Hungarica* 4 (1955) 21-90, pp. 34-38

A.R. Anderson, *Alexander's gate, Gog and Magog, and the inclosed nations*, Cambridge MA, 1932, pp. 15-19

F. Kampers, *Alexander der Große und die Idee des Weltimperiums in Prophetie und Sage*, Freiburg i. B., 1901, pp. 74-75

W. Bousset, 'Beiträge zur Geschichte der Eschatologie', *Zeitschrift für Kirchengeschichte* 20 (1899) 103-31, 261-90, pp. 113-31

E. Sackur, *Sibyllinische texte und Forschungen. Pseudomethodius, Adso und die Tiburtinische Syballe*, Halle a. S. 1898, pp. 36-39

W. Bousset, *Der Antichrist in der Überlieferung des Judentums, des neuen Testaments und der alten Kirche. Ein Beitrag zur Auslegung der Apokalypse*, Göttingen, 1895, p. 37

Th. Nöldeke, rev. of Lamy's edition, *Wiener Zeitschrift für die Kunde des Morgenlandes* 4 (1890) 245-54

Th. Nöldeke, *Beiträge zur Geschichte des Alexanderromans*, Vienna, 1890, pp. 31-32

Harald Suermann 2008

The Apocalypse of Pseudo-Methodius (Syriac)

Unknown author, Pseudo-Methodius of Patara/of Olympos

DATE OF BIRTH Unknown; probably c. 650
PLACE OF BIRTH Unknown
DATE OF DEATH Unknown; probably late 7th or early 8th c.
PLACE OF DEATH Unknown

BIOGRAPHY

There is almost no information available about the life of the author. Even those points that can be deduced from the *Apocalypse* itself are scanty and their interpretation is uncertain. He was a Syrian, possibly a monk, who might have lived in the city of Sinjār east of Mosul or on the adjacent ridge, as the preamble of the work indicates. His ecclesiastical or confessional affiliation is also unclear; perhaps he avoided any reference to Christological controversies in order to emphasize the unity of Christendom rather than updating internal differences, as he felt his days were a decisive period in salvation history. Recent research, however, tends to assume that he belonged to the Syrian Orthodox minority living in the former Persian border region.

MAIN SOURCES OF INFORMATION

Primary —

Secondary

G.J. Reinink, *Die syrische Apokalypse des Pseudo-Methodius*, 2 vols, Louvain, 1993 (*CSCO* 540-41), ii, pp. vii-xi, xxv-xxix

WORKS ON CHRISTIAN-MUSLIM RELATIONS

Mēmrā ʿal yubbālā d-malkē w-ʿal ḥarat zabnā, 'Homily on the succession of kings and on the end of time'. Modern title: 'The Apocalypse of Pseudo-Methodius'

DATE Probably 691/92
ORIGINAL LANGUAGE Syriac

DESCRIPTION

The text comprises 14 books, covering 78 pages in Reinink's critical edition and up to 36 pages in manuscript. It purports to record in homiletical form the revelations received by Methodius, bishop of the Lycian city of Olympos (d. c. 311) when, as is implied in statements made in the preamble, he lived in the Sinjār mountains. Methodius of Olympos was apparently chosen as the pseudonymous 'author' of the Apocalypse because of his millenarist ideas and his martyrdom (Reinink, *Die syrische Apokalypse*, ii, pp. vi-vii).

As the original title indicates, the text covers the whole of history from Adam to the end of the world, conceived as a political history of a succession of kingdoms. The main purpose is to prove that the (Christian) Graeco-Roman empire from Alexander the Great up to the Byzantine emperors of the author's own days formed one and the same kingdom, namely the fourth and last kingdom according to the Danielic scheme. The text consists of two main parts, a 'historical', retrospective one (1,1-10,6) and a 'prophetic', projective and eschatological section (11,1-14,14).

The prophetic part comprises a sequence of *vaticinia ex eventu*, covering the decay of the Persian empire and the Arab-Muslim conquests (11,1-13,11), and an array of eschatological prophecies starting with the rise of the 'King of the Greeks' (*malkā d-Yaunāyē*) and his defeat of the Muslim empire and ending with the second coming of Christ.

Pseudo-Methodius follows the *Cave of treasures*, dividing history into different millennia, of which the seventh and last, as is explicitly stated in 11,1 at the opening of the prophetic part of the apocalypse, began with the end of the Persian Empire. A second periodization is applied to the last millennium, namely its division into 'year-weeks', which again follows that of the Book of Daniel.

Besides this 'chronographical scheme', there is a 'typological scheme' (Reinink, *Die syrische Apokalypse*, ii, pp. xxxi-vi). It follows an *Urzeit-Endzeit* pattern which connects the events of the historical part of the apocalypse with those of its prophetic part, thereby lending the author's argument and predictions a particular historico-theological conclusiveness. According to this pattern, the author connects the Arab-Muslim rule of his period to that of the Midianites (Judges 6-8) in the fifth millennium, who are likewise identified as 'Sons of Ishmael' (5,1-9). The rule of the Ishmaelites is thus demonstrated to be like that of the Midianites over Israel, merely a temporary chastisement and not a state of affairs destined to persist. Like Gideon in the Book of Judges, the King of the Greeks will rise up and vanquish the Sons of Ishmael after ten year-weeks, when they dare to declare that the Christians had no savior, and subsequently reign in Jerusalem and punish infidels and apostates (11,1-13,18). Another *Urzeit-Endzeit* typology concerns the original and final emperors of the fourth kingdom, Alexander the Great and the King of the Greeks. The principal purpose in connecting the two is to prove the inherent invincibility of the fourth kingdom and its imminent rise to world domination, which will shape the last period of world history and put an end to Muslim rule.

Gog and Magog, the eschatological peoples who had once been enclosed beyond the 'Gates of the North' by the founder of the fourth kingdom, will be released and they will overrun the world during the reign of its last emperor. After their defeat by an angel, the fourth kingdom will come to an end. The King of the Greeks will go up to Calvary, place his crown on the cross, which will be taken up to heaven, and pass away, thereby fulfilling Psalm 68:32 (Peshitta 68:31), 'Kūsh will hand over its power to God'. This is followed by the reign of the Antichrist.

The 'Kingdom of the Christians' which 'betakes itself to the Cross' is thus stylized as the *Katechon* of 2 Thessalonians 2:6-7 (9,9-10,2). To prove the persistence of the fourth kingdom up to these future events, the author has to evince its unity. He does this by constructing a genealogical connection between the (fictitious) dynasties of Alexander, and those of Byzantium and Rome, all of which go back to Kūshyat, a Kushite progenitress. Therefore, the King of the Greeks will be of Kushite descent himself; however the last emperor will not, as some of the author's contemporaries seem to have expected (8,7), be a king of Kūsh. If the name Kūsh, as has been suggested recently (Greisiger), refers to Nubia (rather than Ethiopia), this genealogical construction shows that Syrian Christians derived strong eschatological hopes from the successful resistance of the Christian Nubian kingdoms to the Arab-Muslim expansion in the Nile valley.

Pseudo-Methodius depicts the Arab-Muslim domination as a repressive pagan regime which will lead many (false) Christians to apostasy and in this respect act as a cleansing force to separate the sheep from the goats. This rhetoric was obviously meant to inspire perseverance in the audience to withstand the temptation to convert to Islam. As Reinink and others have reconstructed the setting of the Apocalypse, the sense of crisis among Christians which provoked this type of rhetoric originated in the policies of the Umayyad Caliph ʿAbd al-Malik. The tax burden for non-Muslims was greatly increased as a result of the caliph's fiscal reform of 691-92 in Mesopotamia (Brock, 'Syriac views'). The crushing of the rebellion of al-Mukhtār (685-87) dashed the hopes Syrian Christians had cherished of the imminent downfall of Muslim rule. They were faced, furthermore, with the religio-political propaganda of ʿAbd al-Malik, who claimed the Muslims' right to Jerusalem and built the Dome of the Rock on the Temple Mount. These developments challenged the traditional view of history, which the author was at pains to sustain.

The *Apocalypse of Pseudo-Methodius* draws widely on sources from the Syriac literary tradition, notably the *Alexander legend* (an addition to the Syriac *Alexander romance*), the *Julian romance*, and the *Cave of treasures*. An influence of Jewish Messianic concepts on the text has been suggested (Alexander, 'The medieval legend'; Suermann, *Die geschichtstheologische Reaktion*, 208-12; Suermann, 'Der byzantinische Endkaiser'), but vehemently denied by Reinink ('Die syrischen Wurzeln', and elsewhere). However, a comparative study of Pseudo-Methodius and contemporary Jewish apocalyptic texts is a desideratum.

The concepts and motifs deployed in the *Apocalypse of Pseudo-Methodius* are substantially shaped by the author's objective of refuting Islam's claims to political and religious primacy. This is not carried out by means of an elaborated anti-Islamic polemic but by addressing fellow Christians to persuade them that the obvious success and prosperity of the Umayyad caliphate was not a sign of its predestined victory and that conversion to Islam would mean leaving behind the only true faith.

SIGNIFICANCE

The *Apocalypse of Pseudo-Methodius* was widely circulated among West and East-Syrian Christians only shortly after its composition, and was soon translated into Greek and from Greek into Latin. An early adaptation from Edessa is to be found in the so-called *Edessene Apocalypse*, and Pseudo-Methodius also influenced the *Gospel of the twelve Apostles* and the *Legend of Sergius Baḥīrā* (see the entries in this volume). Furthermore, the text left its traces in a number of medieval Syriac works, and in Christian Arabic, Coptic, Ethiopic and Armenian literature. A Coptic translation has also been proved to have existed (Martinez, 'The King of Rūm', p. 254). The Greek and Latin versions of the *Apocalypse* were exceedingly widespread in the Byzantine and Latin west and profoundly shaped the eschatological expectations and the image of the Muslims among the respective Christian communities.

MANUSCRIPTS

For the Syriac manuscripts, see the descriptions and discussion in Reinink, *Apokalypse*, i, pp. xiv-xxi

EDITIONS AND TRANSLATIONS

G.J. Reinink, *Die syrische Apokalypse des Pseudo-Methodius*, 2 vols, Louvain, 1993 (*CSCO* 540-41) (edition and trans.)

S.P. Brock, 'Two related apocalyptic texts dated AD 691/2', in A.N. Palmer, *The seventh century in the West-Syrian chronicles*, Liverpool, 1993, 222-50, esp. pp. 230-42 (trans. of chapters 11-14)

F.J. Martinez, *Eastern Christian apocalyptic in the early Muslim period. Pseudo-Methodius and Pseudo-Athanasius*, Washington DC, 1985 (Diss. Catholic University of America), pp. 58-121, 122-205 (edition and trans.)

H. Suermann, *Die geschichtstheologische Reaktion auf die einfallenden Muslime in der edessenischen Apokalyptik des 7. Jahrhunderts*, Frankfurt, 1985, pp. 34-85 (edition and trans.)

P.J. Alexander, *The Byzantine apocalyptic tradition*, Berkeley CA, 1985, pp. 36-51 (trans.)

STUDIES

L. Greisiger, 'Ein nubischer Erlöser-König: Kūš in syrischen Apokalypsen des 7. Jahrhunderts', in S.G. Vashalomidze and L. Greisiger (eds), *Der Christliche Orient und seine Umwelt*, Wiesbaden, 2007, 189-213

G.J. Reinink, 'Alexander the Great in seventh-century Syriac "apocalyptic" texts', *Byzantinorossica* 2 (2003) 150-78 (repr. in G.J. Reinink, *Syriac Christianity under late Sasanian and early Islamic rule*, Aldershot, 2005)

P. Bruns, 'Endzeitberechnungen in der syrischen Kirche', in W. Geerlings (ed.), *Der Kalender. Aspekte einer Geschichte*, Paderborn, 2002, 122-39 (esp. pp. 132-34)

G.J. Reinink, 'Heraclius, the new Alexander. Apocalyptic prophecies during the reign of Heraclius', in G.J. Reinink and B.H. Stolte (eds), *The reign of Heraclius (610–641). Crisis and confrontation*, Louvain, 2002, 81-94

J.P. Monferrer Sala, 'Mēmrā del Pseudo Metodio y Yōntōn, el cuarto hijo de Noé. Notas a propósito de un posible origen de la leyenda oriental llegada a Hispania en el s. VII', in *Miscelánea de estudios árabes y hebraicos. Sección árabe-islam* 50 (2001) 213-30

G.J. Reinink, 'Early Christian reactions to the building of the Dome of the Rock', *Xristiansky Vostok* 2 (2001) 227-41 (repr. in Reinink, *Syriac Christianity*)

W. Kaegi, 'Gigthis and Olbia in the Pseudo-Methodius Apocalypse and their significance', *Byzantinische Forschungen* 26 (2000) 161-67

B. McGinn, *Antichrist. Two thousand years of the human fascination with evil*, New York, 2000, pp. 89-94

H. Möhring, *Der Weltkaiser der Endzeit. Entstehung, Wandel und Wirkung einer tausendjährigen Weissagung*, Stuttgart, 2000 (esp. pp. 54-104)

W. Witakowski, 'The eschatological program of the apocalypse of Pseudo-Methodios. Does it make sense?', *Rocznik Orientalistyczny* 53 (2000) 33-42

A.M. Guenther, 'The Christian experience and interpretation of the early Muslim conquest and rule', *ICMR* 10 (1999) 363-78 (esp. pp. 370-71)

B. McGinn, *Visions of the end. Apocalyptic traditions in the Middle Ages*, New York, 1998², pp. 70-76

R.G. Hoyland, *Seeing Islam*, pp. 263-67

G.J. Reinink, 'Pseudo-Methodius and the Pseudo-Ephremian 'Sermo de fine mundi', in R. Nip et al. (eds), *Media Latinitas*, Steenbrugis, 1996, 317-21

A. Caquot, 'Le Kebra Nagast et les Révélations du Pseudo-Méthode', in C. Lepage, (ed.): *Études éthiopiennes. Actes de la Xᵉ conférence internationale des études éthiopiennes*, Paris, 1994, 331-35

Brock, 'Two related apocalyptic texts dated AD 691/2', esp. pp. 222-26

Reinink, *Die syrische Apokalypse* (introductory chapters in both volumes)

G.J. Reinink, 'Neue Erkenntnisse zur syrischen Textgeschichte des "Pseudo-Methodius"', in H. Hokwerda, E.R. Smits and M.M. Woesthuis (eds), *Polyphonia Byzantina*, Groningen, 1993, 83-94

W.E. Kaegi, *Byzantium and the early Islamic conquests*, Cambridge, 1992, pp. 137-38, 233, 234

G.J. Reinink, 'Pseudo-Methodius. A concept of history in response to the rise of Islam', in A. Cameron and L.I. Conrad (eds), *The Byzantine and early Islamic Near East. I. Problems in the literary source material*, Princeton, NJ, 1992, 149-87 (repr. in Reinink, *Syriac Christianity*)

G.J. Reinink, 'The romance of Julian the Apostate as a source for seventh century Syriac apocalypses', in P. Canivet and J.-P. Rey-Coquais (eds), *La Syrie de Byzance à l'Islam. VIIe-VIIIe siècles*, Damascus, 1992, 75-86 (repr. in Reinink, *Syriac Christianity*)

R.L. Wilken, *The land called holy. Palestine in Christian history and thought*, New Haven, 1992, pp. 240-46

G.J. Reinink, 'Der edessenische "Pseudo-Methodius"', *BZ* 83 (1990) 31-45 (repr. in Reinink, *Syriac Christianity*)

F.C. Martinez, 'The king of Rūm and the king of Ethiopia in medieval apocalyptic texts from Egypt', in W. Godlewski (ed.), *Coptic Studies. Acts of the Third International Congress of Coptic Studies*, Warsaw, 1990, 247-59

A. Caquot, 'L'Éthiopie dans les Revelationes du Pseudo-Méthode et dans le livre éthiopien de la Gloire des Rois', *Revue de la Société Ernest Renan* n.s. 39 (1989/90) 53-65

M.V. Krivov, 'Apocalypse of Pseudo-Methodius of Patara as a source on history of Ethiopia', in A.A. Gromyko (ed.), *Proceedings of the Ninth International Congress of Ethiopian Studies*, Moscow, 1988, 111-17

G.J. Reinink, 'Pseudo-Methodius und die Legende vom römischen Endkaiser', in W. Verbeke, D. Verhelst and A. Welkenhuysen (eds), *The use and abuse of eschatology in the Middle Ages*, Louvain, 1988, 82-111 (repr. in Reinink, *Syriac Christianity*)

F.J. Martinez, 'The apocalyptic genre in Syriac. The world of Pseudo-Methodius', in H.J.W. Drijvers (ed.), *IV Symposium Syriacum*, Rome, 1987, 337-52

H. Suermann, 'Der byzantinische Endkaiser bei Pseudo-Methodios', *OC* 71 (1987) 140-55

G.J. Reinink, 'Tyrannen und Muslime. Die Gestaltung einer symbolischen Metapher bei Pseudo-Methodios', in H.L.J. Vanstiphout et al. (eds), *Scripta signa vocis. Studies about scripts, scriptures, scribes and languages in the Near East*, Groningen, 1986, 163-71

Martinez, *Eastern Christian apocalyptic in the early Muslim period*, pp. 2-57

P.J. Alexander, *The Byzantine apocalyptic tradition*, Berkeley, CA, 1985, pp. 13-60

Suermann, *Die geschichtstheologische Reaktion*, pp. 129-61

G.J. Reinink, 'Die syrischen Wurzeln der mittelalterlichen Legende vom römischen Endkaiser', in M. Gosman and J. van Os (eds), *Non nova, sed nove*, Groningen, 1984, 195-209

A. Cariotoglou, 'Pseudo-Méthode de Patara. 'Le temps de l'apostasie et du châtiment des fils d'Ismael'. Commentaire sur les chapîtres de l'Apocalypse du Pseudo-Méthode relatifs aux Arabes, leur histoire et leur religion', *Graeco-Arabica* 2 (1983) 59-68

G.J. Reinink, 'Der Verfassername "Modios" der syrischen Schatzhöhle und die Apokalypse des Pseudo-Methodios', *OC* 67 (1983) 46-64

S.P. Brock, 'Syriac views on emergent Islam', in G.H.A. Juynboll (ed.), *Studies on the first century of Islamic society*, Carbondale, 1982, 1-21 (repr. in S.P. Brock, *Syriac perspectives on late antiquity*, London, 1984) (esp. pp. 17-9)

G.J. Reinink, 'Ismael, der Wildesel in der Wüste. Zur Typologie der Apokalypse des Pseudo-Methodios', *BZ* 75 (1982) 336-44

S. Gero, 'The Legend of the fourth son of Noah', *Harvard Theological Review* 73 (1980) 321–30

P.J. Alexander, 'The medieval legend of the last Roman emperor and its Messianic origin', *Journal of the Warburg and Courtauld Institutes* 41 (1978) 1-15

J. Wortley, 'The literature of catastrophe', *Byzantine Studies / Études Byzantines* 4 (1977) 1-17

A. Vööbus, 'Discovery of an unknown Syrian author. Methodios of Peṭrā', *Abr-Nahrain* 17 (1976/77) 1-4

S.P. Brock, 'Syriac sources for seventh-century history', *Byzantine and Modern Greek Studies* 2 (1976) 17-36 (repr. in S.P. Brock, *Syriac perspectives on late antiquity*, London, 1984), esp. pp. 34-35

P.J. Alexander, 'Psevdo-Mefodiy i Efiopiya, *Antichnaya Drevnost'i Sreditionie Veka*', *Sbornik* 10 (1973) 21-27 (repr. (with additional remarks) in P.J. Alexander, *Religious and political history and thought in the Byzantine Empire*, London, 1978)

P.J. Alexander, 'Byzantium and the migration of literary works and motifs. The legend of the last Roman emperor', *Medievalia et humanistica* n.s. 2 (1971) 47-68 (repr. in Alexander, *Religious and political history*)

P.J. Alexander, 'The Syriac original of Pseudo-Methodius' apocalypse', in D. Sinor (ed.), *Proceedings of the Twenty-Seventh International Congress of Orientalists*, Wiesbaden, 1971, 106-7

P.J. Alexander, 'Medieval apocalypses as historical sources', *American Historical Review* 73 (1968) 997-1018

A.R. Anderson, *Alexander's gate, Gog and Magog, and the inclosed nations*, Cambridge MA, 1932, pp. 44-57

M. Kmosko, 'Das Rätsel des Pseudomethodius', *Byzantion* 6 (1931) 273-96

F. Nau, 'Révélations et légendes. Methodius, Clement, Andronicus', *Journal asiatique* sér. 11, 9 (1917) 415-71 (erroneously identifies the Edessene Apocalypse as the Syriac original of the Apocalypse of Pseudo-Methodius)

Lutz Greisiger 2007

The Edessene Apocalypse

Unknown author

DATE OF BIRTH Unknown; probably mid-7th c.
PLACE OF BIRTH Unknown
DATE OF DEATH Unknown; late 7th to early 8th c.
PLACE OF DEATH Unknown

BIOGRAPHY

There are no biographical data available about the author of this anonymous fragmentary work. It appears from the text itself that he was a monk residing in a monastery in the Edessa area.

MAIN SOURCES OF INFORMATION

Primary —

Secondary —

WORKS ON CHRISTIAN-MUSLIM RELATIONS

Original title unknown. Modern titles: 'The Edessene Apocalypse', 'The Edessene Pseudo-Methodius' or 'The Edessene apocalyptic Fragment'

DATE Shortly after 692 (alternatively, late 13th c.)
ORIGINAL LANGUAGE Syriac

DESCRIPTION
The text of the *Edessene Apocalypse* is fragmentary and its actual title is not preserved. The most comprehensive extant fragment covers 7 pages in manuscript, and Nau's critical edition takes up 9 pages. The text is closely related to the *Apocalypse of Pseudo-Methodius* (q.v.), which led its editor to the conclusion that it was the Syriac version of the then known Greek text of Pseudo-Methodius. When Kmosko announced the rediscovery of the real Syriac original of Pseudo-Methodius, it became clear that Nau's text was in fact a distinct work

based on the actual Pseudo-Methodius. The author, most probably a Syrian Orthodox monk from one of the monasteries in the vicinity of Edessa, apparently aimed at interpreting and adapting that apocalypse according to the traditions of his own community.

On the basis of the codicological evidence, it seems evident that, unlike the *Apocalypse of Pseudo-Methodius*, the historical introduction to the *Edessene Apocalypse* either was very short or perhaps did not exist at all, and that the original text consisted of the 'prophetic' section only, indicating that its author was concerned exclusively with the apocalyptic predictions of his *Vorlage*.

The dating of the text has been subject to some debate. The date given in the text for the defeat of the Muslims by the last emperor and the establishment of the Christian empire which would continue to the end of time is 'at the end of 694 years'. Depending on the calendar era to be applied, the *terminus ante quem* has been dated to 683 (Nau), 694 (Suermann, Reinink) or 1294/5 (Martinez), with Reinink arguing convincingly for 694.

The depiction of the events leading up to the end to which the author considers himself a witness begins with the hardships resulting from the clashes between the 'Sons of Hagar' in the east, most probably referring to the turmoil of ʿAbdallāh ibn al-Zubayr's revolt and the second civil war (see also the entry on John bar Penkāyē). As the author says, these are predicted in the apocalyptic passage in Matthew 24:7: 'For nation shall rise against nation, and kingdom against kingdom and there shall be famines, and pestilences, and earthquakes, in diverse places.' In the remaining one and a half year-weeks the Sons of Hagar steal all the valuables and belongings of the people, causing great distress among them – most likely an allusion to ʿAbd al-Malik's tax reform of 691/92 in Mesopotamia. Soon afterwards, the 'king of the Greeks' will set out against the Sons of Hagar from the west, supported by his son who will wage a similar campaign from the south, and their enemies will flee from them and gather in Babel and then proceed to the city of Makka (*MKH*), where the king of the Greeks will defeat them. There follows a description of peace and abundance, which will prevail in his empire and continue for 208 years, before Gog and Magog are let loose from behind the mountains of Armenia and will be destroyed by angels. In contrast to the text in Pseudo-Methodius, the 'Son of Perdition' (*bar abdānā*) will arrive during the reign of the king of the Greeks and will be vanquished by Enoch and Elijah. Only after that will the king of the Greeks abdicate by placing his crown upon the cross, which will ascend to heaven. He and all creatures on earth will die before the resurrection of the dead, the second coming of Christ and the Last Judgment.

SIGNIFICANCE

The *Edessene Apocalypse*, though much shorter than the prophetic part of the *Apocalypse of Pseudo-Methodius*, contains several new motifs adapted from Pseudo-Methodius and some that are peculiar to it and not to be found in Pseudo-Methodius (Reinink, pp. 40-45). At the same time the author, in many cases, makes only brief allusions to such motifs, obviously assuming his audience is familiar with the predictions of Pseudo-Methodius, which attests to the extraordinarily rapid dissemination of these prophecies within the Syriac-speaking world in the last decade of the 7th century. So the *Edessene Apocalypse* is another witness to the sense of crisis that Syrian Christians were obviously experiencing due to ʿAbd al-Malik's political success and the intensification of the pressure put on the non-Muslim communities within the Islamic empire during his reign.

MANUSCRIPTS

For a description and discussion of the two extant manuscript-fragments see Nau, pp. 423-25, and Reinink, p. 31, nn. 1-5.

EDITIONS AND TRANSLATIONS

S.P. Brock, 'Two related apocalyptic texts dated AD 691/2', in A.N. Palmer, *The seventh century in the West-Syrian chronicles*, Liverpool, 1993, 222-50, esp. pp. 244-50

F.J. Martinez, *Eastern Christian apocalyptic in the early Muslim period: Pseudo-Methodius and Pseudo-Athanasius*, Washington DC, 1985 (Diss. Catholic University of America) pp. 222-31, 232-46 edition and trans.)

H. Suermann, *Die geschichtstheologische Reaktion auf die einfallenden Muslime in der edessenischen Apokalyptik des 7. Jahrhunderts*, Frankfurt, 1985, pp. 86-97 (reprint of the text after Nau with trans.)

F. Nau, 'Révélations et légendes. Methodius. – Clement. – Andronicus', *Journal asiatique*, sér. 11, 9 (1917) 415-71 (erroneously identifies the Edessene Apocalypse as the Syriac original of the *Apocalypse of Pseudo-Methodius*)

STUDIES

L. Greisiger, 'Ein nubischer Erlöser-König: Kūš in syrischen Apokalypsen des 7. Jahrhunderts', in S.G. Vashalomidze and L. Greisiger (eds), *Der Christliche Orient und seine Umwelt*, Wiesbaden, 2007, 189-213

G.J. Reinink, 'Early Christian reactions to the building of the Dome of the Rock in Jerusalem', *Xristianskij Vostok* 2 (2001) 227-41 (repr. in G.J. Reinink, *Syriac Christianity under late Sasanian and early Islamic rule*, Aldershot, 2005)

Hoyland, *Seeing Islam*, pp. 267-70

Brock, 'Two related apocalyptic texts dated AD 691/2', 222-50, esp. pp. 243-44

G.J. Reinink, Der edessenische 'Pseudo-Methodius', *BZ* 83 (1990) 31-45 (repr. in Reinink, *Syriac Christianity*)

Martinez, *Eastern Christian apocalyptic*, pp. 206-21

Suermann, *Die geschichtstheologische Reaktion*, pp. 162-74

M. Kmosko, Das Rätsel des Pseudomethodius, *Byzantion* 6 (1931) 273-96 (esp. pp. 285-86, 296, proving that the fragment edited by Nau is not the Syriac original of Ps.-Methodius)

Lutz Greisiger 2007

John bar Penkāyē

Yōḥannān bar Penkāyē, John of Penek (Fenek)

DATE OF BIRTH Unknown, probably 1st half of 7th c.
PLACE OF BIRTH Penek (west-Syriac: Fenek; Greek: Pinaka; Latin: Phaenicha in Gordyene (Syriac Bēt Qardū); now Finik or Finuk)
DATE OF DEATH Unknown; late 7th or early 8th c.
PLACE OF DEATH Unknown

BIOGRAPHY

Born at an unknown date in Penek (Fenek, on the left bank of the Tigris, north of Gāzartā (Jazīrat ibn ʿUmar, now Cizre), east of Ṭūr ʿAbdīn), John belonged to the Church of the East and was a monk in the monastery of John of Kāmūl under abbot Sabrīshōʿ. He later moved to the Monastery of Mār(y) Bassīmā.

MAIN SOURCES OF INFORMATION

Primary

Neṣḥānā d-ʿal ṭūbānā Mār(y) Yōḥannān bar Penkāyē d-hū sābā rūḥānāyā, 'Eulogy on the blessed Mār(y) Yōḥannān who is a spiritual elder', in A. Scher, 'Notice sur la vie et les œuvres de Yoḥannan bar Penkayé', *Journal asiatique* sér. 10, 10 (1907) 161-78 (edition of a short *Eulogy on John*, pp. 162-64)

I.E. Rahmani, *Studia Syriaca seu collectio documentorum hactenus ineditorum ex codicibus Syriacis*, 4 vols, Monte Libano, 1904-9, i, pp. 3-6, 64-65

E. Sachau, *Verzeichniss der syrischen Handschriften der Königlichen Bibliothek zu Berlin*, 2 vols in 1, Berlin, 1899, pp. 554-55

Secondary

T. Jansma, 'Projet d'édition du Keтâbâ deRêš Mellê de Jean bar Penkaye', *L'Orient Syrien* 8 (1963) 87-106, pp. 89-92

WORKS ON CHRISTIAN-MUSLIM RELATIONS

Ktābā d-rēsh mellē, 'The Book of main points'

DATE Between 686 and 693
ORIGINAL LANGUAGE Syriac

DESCRIPTION

The *Ktābā d-rēsh mellē*, subtitled *History of the world of time*, is an outline of world history (the title is a literal translation of the Greek *kephalaiōsēs istoria*) from creation to the author's days, dedicated to his friend Sabrīshōʿ. The work comprises 15 books of which the five covered by Mingana's edition (10-15) fill 171 pages; in the manuscripts the whole work fills c. 400 pages. Only the concluding passages of Book 14 and Book 15, where the author treats contemporary history and Muslim rule, are relevant to Christian-Muslim relations.

The author's aim in his historiographical endeavor was, as he states at the beginning of Book 11, 'to demonstrate what God has done for us in His grace and what we against Him have presumed to do in our wickedness'. The theme of his work is religious instruction rather than historical information. As a consequence of this agenda, John bar Penkāyē's view of history is centered on ecclesiastical history, especially that of his own church. John deploys a kind of dialectical scheme of history according to which godly conduct on the part of believers is ensured by persecution, whereas religious peace inevitably leads to deviation from the apostolic faith and to moral turpitude. The latter occurred in the Byzantine Empire, where under the rule of Christian emperors theological strife and the theopaschite heresy became prevalent. In contrast, the continual persecution of Christians in the Persian Empire made them live in a godly manner and abide by the Orthodox Nicene faith and creed. In this view, the Arab conquests formed a part of the divine plan and were designed to punish both the Byzantines for their teaching and their attempt to impose the theopaschite heresy on orthodox Christians, and the Sasanids for persecuting Christians.

Book 14 ends with a short account of the end of the Persian Empire and the rise of the 'kingdom of the sons of Hagar', who have been called by God to 'hold the Christians in honor' and to treat the monks with particular care. God's providential relationship with the Muslim conquerors is evidenced by their monotheism and their ability to conquer almost the entire world 'not using weapons of war or human means', while still committing carnage and enslaving the peoples in the conquered lands.

Book 15 starts with a very short summary of pre-Islamic history. When the heretical Christians showed no sign of repentance, even after ominous earthquakes and eclipses, God sent 'the Barbarian kingdom' to chastise His people. The Muslims are characterized as relentless and cruel. Although they acted as God's vengeance for the misconduct of Christians, they were to be punished as well. That was why God divided their kingdom right from the beginning into an eastern and a western part, whose 'kings' struggled for dominance until Muʿāwiya came to power and subdued the eastern kingdom. Muʿāwiya is described as a righteous ruler. He granted religious freedom and merely demanded tribute from his non-Muslim subjects. Under his rule there was unparalleled peace. This allowed for a rallying of heretics, who propagated their theopaschite doctrine among the Christians, and also for immorality among the ecclesiastical and secular authorities of the author's own community. God thereupon brought about portents and natural disasters, political disturbances and an increase in tribute.

After Muʿāwiya's reign, his son 'Yazdīn' (i.e. Yazīd I, 680-83) ascended to the throne but his tyranny was soon ended by God. After him 'Zubayr' (ʿAbdallāh ibn al-Zubayr) turned against the 'westerners'. War was waged against him, and in the course of this his adversaries battled against him in the city 'where their sanctuary was' (i.e. Mecca) and 'they even burnt their own sanctuary'. This war caused persistent instability.

Subsequently, a war broke out between the western and eastern rulers competing for control over Nisibis and causing 'great unrest in Mesopotamia'. Shortly after the westerners' victory, the eastern commander campaigned against ʿĀqōlā (Kūfa) with the support of John of Dāsen, then metropolitan of Nisibis. The pro-Umayyad governor of Iraq, 'Bar Ziyāt' (ʿUbayd Allāh ibn Ziyād), in turn promised John of Dāsen that, if he supported him, he would depose the Catholicos Ḥnānīshōʿ the exegete (686-93). However, al-Mukhtār, leader of the easterners, mustered an army of 13,000 slaves who, though all lightly-armed foot soldiers, defeated his army on the river Ḥāzir (a tributary of the Greater Zab, east of Mosul), and Ḥnānīshōʿ only barely escaped. These slaves bore the name of *shurṭē* (from Arab. *shurṭa*, 'chosen men'), 'signifying their zeal for righteousness'.

Al-Mukhtār's slave-soldiers in Nisibis, discontented with the leadership of their former commander, Abraham's (Ibrāhīm ibn al-Ashtar) brother (ʿAbd al-Raḥmān), rebelled, slew him, and appointed 'an emir from among themselves, whose name was Abūqārib (i.e. Abū Qārib)'. This in turn provoked the *ʿĀqōlāyē* (the faction under Ibrāhīm ibn al-Ashtar at Kūfa) to rebel against al-Mukhtār and they finally defeated and killed him and many of his slave allies. However, the Nisibene faction was strengthened by numerous volunteers and continued successfully to oppose the *ʿĀqōlāyē*.

At this point, John bar Penkāyē explains that since God did not see His people repent, He was 'enraged against us: henceforth it was not through tyrannical kings... but He began to wage war with us Himself'. Here the apocalyptic part of the *Ktābā d-rēsh mellē* is heralded, signaled also by biblical quotations connected to the eschaton (notably Matthew 24:7). The means of God's war was great plagues and famines, such as that of the year 67 (686/7), the 'beginning of the pangs', the first of seven chastisements 'for our sins'. John therefore concludes by saying that he was 'aware that the end of ages has arrived for us', 'everything written (in the Scriptures) has been fulfilled', 'only one thing is missing for us: the advent of the Deceiver (*maṭʿyānā*, i.e. the Antichrist)'. He predicts that God-sent *shurṭē* 'will be the cause of the destruction of the Ishmaelites' and themselves will be dispersed in the world to their former peoples and 'they will become their awakeners'. And 'even more bitter afflictions than these' are held in store: a distant people (apparently Gog and Magog) is 'striving to undo the Byzantine kingdom and... to dominate everyone'. The author predicts that after earthquakes and eclipses and 'the whole earth' being 'filled with the blood of mankind', another catastrophe will occur, 'an evil hidden in good, like poison in honey', an image probably symbolizing the Antichrist.

SIGNIFICANCE

John bar Penkāyē's history mirrors the perception of early Muslim rule among the north-Mesopotamian monastic elite of the Church of the East and is, in this respect, a unique source. The author does not elaborate very much on Muslim rule as God's disciplinary measure for His people; in his eyes, God's most severe punishments take the form of natural disasters. The Muslims are depicted as rather restrained rulers who even temporarily – by means of their indifference and tolerance – give way to laxity and deviation among the Christians. The author also provides a particular local perspective on the rebellion of al-Mukhtār and internal Umayyad strife and gives historical information about these political events that is otherwise unavailable.

Little is known about the reception of this work. Although the *Life* of John bar Penkāyē is extant in manuscripts of Syrian Orthodox provenance, his history was probably not known in that community. It seems to have been copied exclusively in monasteries of the Church of the East.

MANUSCRIPTS

For a description of the extant manuscripts, see Jansma, 'Projet d'édition du K^e^tâbâ d^e^Rêš Mellê', pp. 96-100, and Kaufhold, 'Anmerkungen zur Textüberlieferung der Chronik des Johannes bar Penkāyē', *OC* 87 (2003) 65-79

EDITIONS AND TRANSLATIONS

S.P. Brock, 'North Mesopotamia in the late seventh century. Book XV of John Bar Penkāyē's Rīš Mellē', *JSAI* 9 (1987) 51-75 (repr. in S.P. Brock, *Studies in Syriac Christianity*, Aldershot, 1992) (trans. of end of Book 14 and of Book 15)

A. Mingana, *Sources Syriaques I. Mšiḥa-Zkha (texte et traduction), Bar-Penkayé (texte)*, Leipzig, 1908, 1-202 (edition of Books 10-15, with a trans. of Book 15)

STUDIES

G.J. Reinink, 'East-Syrian historiography in response to the rise of Islam. The case of John bar Penkaye's *Ktābā d-rēš mellē*', in J.J. van Ginkel, H.L. Murre-van den Berg and T.M. van Lint (eds), *Redefining Christian identity. Cultural interaction in the Middle East since the rise of Islam*, Leuven, 2005, 77-89

K. Pinggéra, 'Nestorianische Weltchronistik. Johannes Bar Penkāyē und Elias von Nisibis', in M. Wallraff (ed.), *Julius Africanus und die christliche Weltchronik*, Berlin, 2005, 263-83

P. Bruns, 'Von Adam und Eva bis Mohammed. Beobachtungen zur syrischen Weltchronik des Johannes bar Penkaye', *OC* 87 (2003) 47-64

H. Kaufhold, 'Anmerkungen zur Textüberlieferung'

G.J. Reinink, 'Paideia. God's design in world history according to the east Syrian monk John bar Penkaye', in E. Kooper (ed.), *The medieval chronicle II*, Amsterdam, 2002, 190-98 (repr. in G.J. Reinink, *Syriac Christianity under late Sasanian and early Islamic rule*, Aldershot, 2005)

Hoyland, *Seeing Islam*, pp. 194-200

M. Albert, 'Une centurie de Mar Jean bar Penkayē', in *Mélanges Antoine Guillaumont*, Genève, 1988, 143-51

G.J. Reinink, 'Pseudo-Methodius und die Legende vom römischen Endkaiser', in W. Verbeke, D. Verhelst and A. Welkenhuysen (eds), *The use and abuse of eschatology in the Middle Ages*, Louvain, 1988, 82-111 (repr. in Reinink, *Syriac Christianity*)

S.P. Brock, 'North Mesopotamia in the late seventh century'

H. Suermann, 'Das arabische Reich in der Weltgeschichte des Jôḥannàn bar Penkàjē', in P.O. Scholz and R. Stempel (eds), *Nubia et Oriens Christianus*, Cologne, 1987, 59-71

R. Abramowski, *Dionysius von Tellmahre, jakobitischer Patriarch von 818-845. Zur Geschichte der Kirche unter dem Islam*. Leipzig, 1940, (repr. Nendeln, 1966), pp. 5-8

Jansma, 'Projet d'édition du K^{e}tâbâ d^{e}Rêš Mellê'

P. de Menasce, 'Autour d'un texte syriaque inédit sur la religion des Mages', *BSOAS* 3 (1938) 587-601

P.G. Sfair, 'Il nome e l'epoca d'un antico scrittore siriaco', *Bessarione* 31 (1915) 135-38

P.G. Sfair, 'Degli scritti e delle dottrine di Bar Pinkaie', *Bessarione* 31 (1915) 290-309

Scher, 'Notice sur la vie et les œuvres de Yoḥannan bar Penkayè'

A. Baumstark, 'Eine syrische Weltgeschichte des siebten Jahrh[undert]s', *Römische Quartalschrift für christliche Alterthumskunde und für Kirchengeschichte* 15 (1901) 273-80

Lutz Greisiger 2007

The Apocalypse of Shenute

Unknown author

DATE OF BIRTH 7th c.
PLACE OF BIRTH Unknown, presumably Egypt
DATE OF DEATH After c. 695
PLACE OF DEATH Unknown, presumably Egypt, possibly at the Monastery of St Shenute (the 'White Monastery')

BIOGRAPHY

Nothing is known of the author of a pseudonymous apocalyptic text beyond what can be gathered from the text itself.

MAIN SOURCES OF INFORMATION

Primary —

Secondary —

WORKS ON CHRISTIAN-MUSLIM RELATIONS

No original title. Modern titles: 'The Apocalypse of Shenute', 'The Apocalypse in the Arabic life of Shenute', 'The first (Arabic) Apocalypse of Shenute', 'The Prophecy of Christ to Shenute', 'The Vision of Ps.-Shenute', 'ApocShen I'

DATE Approximately 695
ORIGINAL LANGUAGE Coptic or Greek

DESCRIPTION

This short historical apocalypse is preserved as part of an Arabic and an Ethiopic version of the *Life of Shenute*, and consists of a prophecy of Christ to this Coptic saint (d. 464) about the end of time. The prophecy includes references to the Sasanian occupation of Egypt (619-29), the rule of Cyrus al-Muqawqis (631-42), and the Arab conquests. In addition, an historical passage enclosed in the Antichrist Legend – and generally unnoticed by scholars – gives a brief account of Muslim rule, mentioning harassment of the population, the wrongful gathering of possessions, and people abandoning Christ's church owing to oppression.

The text gives the impression of having been written to counter the threat of conversion to Islam. Implicitly comparing the Muslim rulers with the Antichrist, who attempts to lead the world astray by pretending to be Christ yet who soon reveals himself to be a terrible oppressor, the text aims to stigmatize the Muslims as evil and treacherous and to deny their religious claims. At the same time, by holding up the example of 'the pure ones' who will resist the Deceiver's terror and temptations and thus earn God's eternal reward, the text encourages the believers not to abandon their faith but to endure in the face of present trials.

One of the last clearly historical allusions in the text is the statement that the Arabs will 'rebuild the Temple that is in Jerusalem', which most probably refers to the construction of the Dome of the Rock, begun or completed in 691-92. This and the absence of any reference to the refugee problem that started to afflict Egyptian society around the turn of the century suggest that the work was written in the 690s, perhaps shortly after Governor ʿAbd al-ʿAzīz's tax reform of 693-94 mentioned by Eutychius (*Eutychii annales*, i, p. 41), which, together with Islam's growing religious and political assertiveness, may have caused fears of a major outbreak of apostasy. It has recently been suggested that the apocalypse was written even earlier, shortly after the Arab conquest of Egypt (Hoyland, *Seeing Islam*, pp. 281-82), but the details of Muslim rule as well as the allusion to the Muslims' denial of Christ's crucifixion, which testifies to some knowledge of Islamic tenets, makes such an early date of composition rather doubtful.

The apocalypse was most likely composed by a Coptic miaphysite author in Shenute's 'White Monastery' in Middle Egypt. Its Arabic version shows signs of having been translated from the Coptic, which was probably also the original language of the work, although, in view of its early date of composition, one cannot exclude the possibility of a Greek original. The Ethiopic version, which is secondary to the Arabic, depends on an Arabic *Vorlage* that differs from the extant Arabic textual material. It is unclear when the prophecy was inserted into the *Life*. The apocalypse was strongly influenced by the third-century Egyptian *Apocalypse of Elijah*, and it is closely related to a passage in the *Homily on the wedding feast at Cana* attributed to Patriarch Benjamin I (r. 626-65) (Müller, *Homilie über die Hochzeit zu Kana*, pp. 232-35).

While it is the oldest known Coptic miaphysite apocalypse from the Islamic period, the work has hardly left a trace in later Coptic apocalyptic literature.

SIGNIFICANCE

This much-neglected work is the oldest Coptic apocalypse from the Islamic period that has survived, and a rare contemporary witness to one of the first turning points in Coptic-Muslim relations. It is one of the earliest Coptic miaphysite literary sources to mention, and respond to, conversion of Copts to Islam and to contain information on Islamic doctrine, notably the denial that Christ was crucified.

MANUSCRIPTS

Arabic:

MS Cairo, Coptic Museum – 97 (Hist. 470), fols 30v-33v (dated 1365; short version with considerable number of variants)

MS Monastery of Macarius – 397 (Hag. 13), fols 203v-210v (dated 1550)

MS Monastery of St Anthony – Hist. 142, pp. 64-82 (dated 1689)

MS Cairo, Coptic Patriarchate – 654 (Hist. 59), fols 150v-156v (dated 1741)

MS Al-Muḥarraq Monastery – 9.28, fols 28v-36v (dated 1752)

MS BNF – Ar. 4888, fols 27v-34r (dated 1885)

MS Al-Muḥarraq Monastery – 9.29, fols 80v-89r (19th c.)

MS BNF – Ar. 4787, fols 32r-41r (19th c.)

MS Monastery of St Anthony – Hist. 132, fols 31v-40r (dated 1911)

Amélineau, *Monuments*, i, pp. 338-51 (edition to be treated as distinct witness due to the uncertainty about the identity of MSS used and the methodology)

Ethiopic:

See Colin, *Version éthiopienne*, i, pp. v-vi

EDITIONS AND TRANSLATIONS

J. van Lent, *Coptic apocalyptic writings from the Islamic period*, Leiden, forthcoming (Diss. Leiden University) (critical English trans. from Arabic)

G. Colin, *La version éthiopienne de la vie de Schenoudi*, 2 vols, Louvain, 1982 (*CSCO* 444-45), i, pp. 17-27; ii, pp. 11-18 (edition and French trans. from Ethiopic)

E. Amélineau, *Monuments pour servir à l'histoire de l'Égypte chrétienne aux IVe, Ve, VIe, et VIIe siècles*, 2 vols, Paris, 1888-95, i, pp. 338-51 (edition and French trans. from Arabic; does not conform to modern standards)

STUDIES

J. van Lent, *Coptic apocalyptic writings*

M.N. Swanson, 'Folly to the *ḥunafā'*. The Crucifixion in early Christian-Muslim controversy', in E. Grypeou, M. Swanson and D. Thomas (eds), *The encounter of Eastern Christianity with early Islam*, Leiden, 2006, 237-56, p. 239

H. Suermann, 'Koptische arabische Apocalypsen', in R.Y. Ebied and H.G.B. Teule (eds), *Studies on the Christian Arabic heritage*, Leuven, 2004, 25-44, pp. 39-40

S.J. Davis, *The early Coptic papacy. The Egyptian Church and its leadership in late Antiquity*, Cairo, 2004, p. 114

H. Suermann, 'Koptische Texte zur arabischen Eroberung Ägyptens und der Umayyadenherrschaft', *Journal of Coptic Studies* 4 (2002) 167-86, p. 182

J. van Lent, *Koptische apocalypsen uit de tijd na de Arabische verovering van Egypte*, Leiden, 2001, pp. 15-17

Hoyland, *Seeing Islam*, pp. 279-82

D. Frankfurter, *Elijah in Upper Egypt. The apocalypse of Elijah and early Egyptian Christianity*, Minneapolis MN, 1993, pp. 25-26, 225

J.-M. Rosenstiehl, *L'apocalypse d'Élie*, Paris, 1972, pp. 40-42

Graf, *GCAL* i, p. 463-64

A.J. Butler, *The Arab conquest of Egypt and the last thirty years of the Roman domination*, Oxford, 1902, 1978^{2}, pp. 87-88, 188-89

Amélineau, *Monuments*, i, pp. lii-lix

Eutychii patiarchae Alexandrini annales, ed. L. Cheikho, B. Carra de Vaux and H. Zayyat, 2 vols, Beirut, 1906-9 (*CSCO* 50-51)

C.D.G. Müller, *Die Homilie über die Hochzeit zu Kana und weitere Schriften des Patriarchen Benjamin I. von Alexandrien*, Heidelberg, 1968

Jos van Lent 2008

Symeon of Samosata

Symeon at the dictation of Joseph, disciple of Theoduṭe

DATE OF BIRTH Unknown
PLACE OF BIRTH Samosata
DATE OF DEATH Unknown
PLACE OF DEATH Unknown

BIOGRAPHY

Symeon (Shemʿun) describes himself as a priest and precentor and says that he wrote the *Life of Theoduṭe* (Greek: *Theodotos*; d. 698) in his native city, Samosata, at the dictation of the priest Joseph, who was the disciple of Theoduṭe and a monk of the monastery of Zuqnīn outside the city of Āmīd (Amida). No more is known about the life of Symeon.

MAIN SOURCES OF INFORMATION

Primary
See below

Secondary
See below

WORKS ON CHRISTIAN-MUSLIM RELATIONS

Tashʿītā awkīt neṣḥānē d-qaddīshā mār(i) tʾwdwṭʾ epīsqupā d-āmīd mdī(n)tā, 'The Story or heroic deeds of the holy one, my lord Theoduṭe, bishop of the city of Āmīd/Amidaʾ. Modern title: 'The Life of Theoduṭe of Āmīd'

DATE Shortly after 698
ORIGINAL LANGUAGE Syriac

DESCRIPTION
The *Life*, which is unpublished, will be divided in the first edition, which is being prepared by the author of the present article, into just

over 100 sections averaging 500-1,000 words in translation. The most striking aspect of Christian-Muslim relations in this text is the total absence from most of these sections of any reference to them: the Arab conquest – and then only the siege of Nisibis – is only mentioned because the author wants to explain where the governor of Ṭūr ʿAbdīn acquired the injury which prevented him from entering the monastery of Qartmīn to do honour to the Christian saint who is the subject of the narrative. The first mention of the Arabs is in Section 23, where we read that Theoduṭe 'redeemed many (Syrian Orthodox) souls (prisoners of war?) from the Arabs and from the Romans (the Byzantine authorities in Anzitene)'. In Section 27 we learn of an apparently abortive attempt on the part of the governor (referred to by the Syriac form of the Greek word *arkhōn*) of Samosata, a certain *Elusṭriyā* (Greek *illustrios*, cf. Latin *illustris*) of *Ḥārān* (Ḥarrān / Carrhae), acting through his Christian slave, Sergius, to tax (presumably on behalf of the Arab government) the poor people and the monks of the region of Claudia, west of the Euphrates and east of the mountain now called Nemrut Dağı. (This section is translated in full in Palmer, 'Āmīd'.) From Section 33 we learn that the region of Claudia was administered by Yuḥannān (John), a Christian deputy (referred to by the Syriac form of the Greek word *epitropos*) of the governor of Samosata, who was himself neither an Arab nor a Muslim, to judge by his name. In Section 35 we learn that the Christian population of Byzantine Anzitene lived in terror of a furtive invader (from Arab territory) called *Gydr* (vocalisation unknown). From Sections 43 and 46 we learn the names of the governors of Mayperqaṭ (Martyropolis) and Dara: Esṭarṭī (Greek *Eustratios*?) and Elusṭriyā (Greek *illustrios*, *cf.* Latin *illustris*), respectively. The latter, who is perhaps a Chalcedonian Christian, promises the Syrian Orthodox Theoduṭe that the monastery which he is inviting him to build in the territory of Dara will be exempt from the king's (i.e. the caliph's) capitation tax (referred to by the Syriac cognate of the Arabic *jizya*): 'I shall pay it out of my own income (lit. 'house')'. The only direct encounter between Theoduṭe and the Arab authorities is described in Section 58 (translated in full in Palmer, 'Āmīd'). Here we learn that the Arab (unnamed) who was in authority in Amida and its region examined Theoduṭe in the mosque of that city before he was ordained bishop to ascertain whether he was secretly an ally of the Romans in the neighbouring region of Anzitene. In the process of this examination, which must have ended in an acquittal, it is alleged that Theoduṭe was kicked by this man. There is a reference to the Arab cavalry stationed there. The *Mahgrāyē* (Christians converted to Islam?) of Amida, it is claimed, as well as the Christians (both Syrian Orthodox and others), gave alms to Theoduṭe for the redemption of prisoners of war held by the Romans (Section 66). Theoduṭe disapproved of clergy accepting the post of deputy governor (*epitropos*) or 'bursar' (*salarā*, assuming this to be a Syriac contraction of the Greek *sakellarios*) in the secular administration (Section 72). In Section 74 we read that the *aḥīd shūlṭānā d-kūlāh madnḥā*, the man who held power over the entire east (of the Arabs' empire), gave the following instructions about Theoduṭe in a letter sent to Amida: 'I command that the laws of the (Christian population of the) city of Amida and of all its region be given into the hands of that righteous man (...) for I have heard that he has no respect of persons.'

SIGNIFICANCE

This text supplies a perspective which is usually denied us: that of the ordinary Syrian Orthodox inhabitants of the towns, villages and monasteries of the regions around the upper Euphrates and Tigris rivers which the Arabs had conquered. The fact that the witness who dictated it did not feel confident to write it means, provided Symeon has taken down a text close to that which was dictated to him (as some anomalies suggest), that we are hearing the words of a semi-literate man. Both of the men who were involved in its genesis were clerics, and their purpose was to establish a claim to sanctity on behalf of Joseph's dead master and to use this to make permanent, if possible, certain rights enjoyed by him during his lifetime as head of the monastery he founded and bequeathed by him to Joseph as his successor. The very anonymity of the two Arab officials referred to – the governor of Amida and the governor of the eastern part of the Arab empire, including Amida – is reassuring: a fictional account would have supplied names. The nomenclature of those governors and their deputies, and of tax-collectors who are named and their titles confirms an early date, when Greek was still the language of government in matters of taxation and when being a Muslim was not yet a requirement for holding office. For the rest, the *Life* of Theoduṭe suggests that the religion of the Arab conquerors was a matter of indifference to those engaged in writing a story intended for wide dissemination among the Syrian Orthodox faithful. This implies that conversion to Islam was not yet a frequent occurrence, for otherwise a Christian priest would inveigh against Islam. On the other hand, the *Mahgrāyē* who entrusted to the Syrian Orthodox bishop a financial contribution for the redemption of

Christian prisoners of war were presumably ex-Christians related to these unfortunates, since *ahgar*, in Syriac, means 'to adopt Islam'.

MANUSCRIPTS

MS Damascus, Syrian Orthodox Patriarchate - 12/17-18, fol. 58v-69v (12th c.)

MS Jerusalem, Monastery of St Mark (1733) (Arabic trans. in Syriac script (Karshūnī) made from the Syriac MS listed above. It was copied by Bishārā of Mardin when the Syriac archetype was apparently still complete. The Syriac MS is now damaged and the Arabic is helpful in determining which words to supply in the numerous small lacunae.)

EDITIONS AND TRANSLATIONS

No edition has yet been published, though one is in preparation by the author of this article. Certain passages relevant to Christian-Muslim relations have been translated in Palmer, *Monk and mason*, esp. p. 76 (fol. 67v.1-2), p. 165 (fol. 60v.2) and p. 168 (fol. 68v.2); Palmer, 'Āmid', esp. pp. 113-16 (Section 27), 124-25 (Section 58) and in Hoyland, *Seeing Islam*, esp. p. 157 (Section 108). J. Tannous is preparing a trans. of the Karshūnī text, to be published jointly with the Syriac edition.

STUDIES

A. Palmer, 'Āmīd in the seventh-century Syriac Life of Theoduṭe', in E. Grypeou, M.N. Swanson and D. Thomas (eds), *The encounter of Eastern Christianity with early Islam*, Leiden, 2006, 111-38

Hoyland, *Seeing Islam*, pp. 156-60

A. Palmer, 'The Garšuni version of the *Life* of Theodotus of Amida', *Pd'O* 16 (1990-91) 253-60

A. Palmer, *Monk and mason on the Tigris frontier. The early history of Ṭur 'Abdin*, Cambridge, 1990, pp. 88-91, 165-68

A. Palmer, 'Semper vagus: the anatomy of a mobile monk', in *Studia Patristica* 18 (1989) 255-60

A. Palmer, 'Saints' lives with a difference: Elijah on John of Tella (d. 528) and Joseph on Theodotos of Amida (d. 698)', in H.J.W. Drijvers et al. (eds), *IV Symposium Syriacum 1984: Literary genres in Syriac literature*, Rome, 1987, 203-16

A. Vööbus, 'Discovery of an unknown Syrian author: Theōdūṭē of Amid', *Abr Nahrain* 24 (1986) 196-201

A. Vööbus, 'Découverte de la biographie de Théodote d'Amid par Šem'ōn de Samosate', *Le Muséon* 89 (1976) 39-42

Andrew Palmer 2008

The Passion of the sixty martyrs of Gaza

Unknown author

DATE OF BIRTH Unknown
PLACE OF BIRTH Unknown
DATE OF DEATH Unknown
PLACE OF DEATH Unknown

BIOGRAPHY —

MAIN SOURCES OF INFORMATION

Primary —

Secondary —

WORKS ON CHRISTIAN-MUSLIM RELATIONS

Passio sexaginta martyrum qui passi sunt a Sarracenis, 'The Passion of the sixty martyrs who suffered under the Saracens'; *Legenda Sancti Floriani et sociorum suorum*, 'The Story of Saint Florian and his companions' (the original Greek title is lost)

DATE Mid-7th c.
ORIGINAL LANGUAGE Greek

DESCRIPTION
The original Greek text seems to have described the execution of sixty Byzantine soldiers who refused to convert to Islam following their capture in Gaza, probably in 639. An Arab commander called Ammiras, perhaps identifiable as ʿĀmir ibn ʿAbdallāh ibn al-Jarrāḥ, ordered the execution of a first group of ten in Jerusalem on 11 November, while an Arab commander called Ambrus, perhaps identifiable as ʿAmr ibn al-ʿĀṣ, ordered the execution of the second group of fifty in Eleutheropolis on 17 December. The Patriarch of Jerusalem, Sophronius, had urged the soldiers not to convert to Islam, and he seems to

have been executed shortly afterwards in circumstances which may have included the collapse of the first mosque on the Temple Mount.

The original Greek account is not extant, but the Latin texts entitled *The Passion of the sixty martyrs* and *The Story of Saint Florian and his companions* seem to derive from it by separate routes of transmission, and bear close witness to its structure and content. Unfortunately, neither text is without problems. The former clearly represents a direct translation from a Greek text, but this Greek text, or its translation, seems not to have included the full sequence of events, but to have ended with the execution of the fifty soldiers in Eleutheropolis rather than with that of Sophronius in Jerusalem. In contrast, the latter text clearly represents a severe reworking of an older Latin text rather than of a Greek original, but it points to the conclusion of the original narrative with the death of Sophronius, although it refers to him not as Sophronius, but as 'Florianus'.

SIGNIFICANCE

The original Greek text seems to have preserved a unique account of several key events in the history of the Muslim conquest of Palestine and the early Muslim occupation of Jerusalem. Its importance lies in the fact that it appears to be a very early account of these events, probably contemporary, and as such pre-dates the Syriac author (usually identified as Theophilus of Edessa [q.v.]) whose work underlies the main surviving sources for this period (e.g. Theophanes the Confessor, Agapius, Michael the Syrian, the *Chronicle of 1234*). Most importantly, it seems to contradict this Syriac author on issues such as the date of the surrender of Gaza to the Muslims and the circumstances surrounding the death of the Patriarch Sophronius.

MANUSCRIPTS

MS Vat, Archivio del Capitolo di S. Pietro – lat. A. 5 (alias D), fols 222-223v (dated 1000-1100) (sole manuscript of *The Passion of the sixty martyrs who suffered under the Saracens*)

MS Bologna, Biblioteca Universitaria – MS 2134, fols 109r-112r (dated 1350-1450) (*The Story of Saint Florian and his companions*)

MS Rome, Accademia Nazionale dei Lincei, Biblioteca – codex 64 (alias 40. F. 1), fols 98-99v (dated 1400-1500) (*The Story of Saint Florian and his companions*)

EDITIONS AND TRANSLATIONS

H. Delehaye, '*Passio sanctorum sexaginta martyrum*', *AB* 23 (1904) 289-307 (the only edition of the Latin testimonies to the original Greek text)

D. Woods, 'The 60 martyrs of Gaza and the martyrdom of Bishop Sophronius of Jerusalem', *Aram* 15 (2003) 129-50 (repr. in M. Bonner (ed.), *Arab-Byzantine relations in early Islamic times*, Aldershot, 2004) (the only trans. of these Latin texts)

STUDIES

Woods, 'The 60 martyrs of Gaza and the martyrdom of Bishop Sophronius of Jerusalem', pp. 129-44

Hoyland, *Seeing Islam*, pp. 347-51

G. Huxley, 'The sixty martyrs of Jerusalem', *Greek, Roman and Byzantine Studies* 18 (1977) 369-74

A. Guillou, 'Prise de Gaza par les Arabes au VIIe siècle', *BCH* 81 (1957) 396-404

J. Pargoire, 'Les LX soldats martyrs de Gaza', *EO* 8 (1905) 40-43

David Woods 2007

Anastasius of Sinai

DATE OF BIRTH Unknown, 1st half 7th c.; probably c. 630
PLACE OF BIRTH Amathus, Cyprus
DATE OF DEATH Unknown, c. 700
PLACE OF DEATH Unknown

BIOGRAPHY

Except for a short entry in the *Synaxarion of Constantinople* on the date of his commemoration by the Byzantines, 21 April, all the biographical data concerning Anastasius of Sinai has to be gleaned from allusions in his works, especially in his two collections of stories discussed below.

He was born in the first half of the 7th century in Amathus, a town in the south of Cyprus, and started his ecclesiastical career under the protection of the local bishop, John. He left Cyprus soon after the Arab conquest of the island in 649, and set out for the Holy Land. There, he became a monk at the monastery on Mt Sinai during the lifetime of the abbot John Climacus. He had various roles in the monastic community, especially that of steward of the hospice, probably because of his medical knowledge, which he displays in his works. He was also ordained priest at some point, according to the way he is named in many manuscripts: 'priest and monk of Mt Sinai'. He may have been chosen by his fellow monks to become abbot of the monastery towards the end of his life, though firm evidence for this is lacking. The date and place of his death are not known, but he must have died around 700, or shortly after.

When he was not staying on Mt Sinai, Anastasius is known to have been a great wayfarer, traveling through the provinces of Egypt, Palestine and Syria under Muslim rule. He seems to have been given some kind of missionary responsibility, and as an indefatigable itinerant controversialist he participated in public debates to refute Monophysitism and Monothelitism and to defend the Chalcedonian cause. His travels also put him in contact with the moral and practical problems of Christians living under the Muslim yoke, and when he could, he would comfort Christians who suffered hardship, both in his writings and by acts of charity.

Anastasius' main period of literary activity spans the last third of the 7th century, possibly into the very first years of the 8th century. From the evidence that can be gleaned from his works, he seems to have written many of them in the peace of his cell on Mt Sinai. The exact corpus that can be genuinely ascribed to Anastasius of Sinai has been the subject of unending scholarly debate. However, as Anastasian studies have been rapidly developing over recent decades and his works are being critically edited in modern editions, the canon of works generally accepted as being authentic is gradually being settled. It comprises some 15 works that range across a large variety of genres: apologetics and controversy, theology and exegesis, homiletic and ascetic literature.

In addition to his two main and widely circulated works, the *Hodegos* and the *Erotapokriseis*, as well as his collections of *Narrationes*, all of which are discussed below, he had an important role as a preacher, close to ten sermons and homilies being attributed to him: *On the holy Mass*, *On Psalm 6* or *On repentance*, *On the Transfiguration*, *On the Passion of Christ* or *On Good Friday* (unedited), *On New Sunday* or *On the Apostle Thomas* (unedited), *On Palm Sunday* (unedited), possibly a sermon *On the deceased*, sometimes attributed to Ephrem the Syrian, and another attributed to John Chrysostom, *On false prophets*, as well as other homilies preserved only in Arabic. He is also the author of theological treatises, the *Three homilies on the creation of man* 'in the image and likeness of God', of several *opuscula* against the Monothelites and the Monophysites, of an allegorical commentary on the *Hexaemeron* and of a treaty against the Jews.

Two false identifications of Anastasius occurred in medieval times. In his *Annals*, the historian Saʿīd ibn Baṭrīq identified Anastasius, the author of the *Sermon on Psalm 6*, with the Armenian general Vahan, who is said to have fled to Mt Sinai after being defeated by the Arabs at the battle of Yarmūk in 636. The general chronology of Anastasius' life renders this claim untenable. The confusion between Anastasius of Sinai and his homonyms, the two patriarchs of Antioch, Anastasius I (559-70, 593-98) and Anastasius II (599-609), who were never monks on Mt Sinai, has been more difficult to disentangle, as all these figures were confused as early as the 9th century by Nicephorus I, Patriarch of Constantinople. Ever since, the question of how many Anastasioi had to be differentiated has been at the centre of scholarly investigation, and Sakkos has distinguished up to seven different authors with the same name, although his theory has been severely criticized.

MAIN SOURCES OF INFORMATION

Primary

Synaxarion of Constantinople, in H. Delehaye, *Propylaeum ad acta sanctorum Novembris*, Brussels, 1902, cols 617-18

J.M. Featherstone, *Nicephori patriarchae Constantinopolitani refutatio et eversio definitionis synodalis anni 815*, Turnhout, 1997 (*Corpus Christianorum Series Graeca* 33), p. 174

M. Breydy, *Das Annalenwerk des Eutychios von Alexandrien. Ausgewählte Geschichten und Legenden kompiliert von Saʿīd ibn Baṭrīq um 935 A.D.*, Louvain, 1985 (*CSCO*, 471-72), i, p. 136; ii, p. 115

Secondary

PMBZ, 268

A. Kazhdan, art. 'Anastasios of Sinai', in *ODB*

Clavis Patrum Graecorum, ed. M. Geerhard, Turnhout, 1974-2003, iii, pp. 453-65, Supplementum, pp. 442-45, and Addenda, pp. 45-46 (nos. 7745-81)

H.-G. Beck, *Kirche und theologische Literatur im byzantinischen Reich*, Munich, 1959, pp. 442-46

C.A. Kuehn and J.D. Baggarly, *Anastasius of Sinai. Hexaemeron*, Rome, 2007 (*Orientalia Christiana Analecta* 278), pp. xiii-xxiii

M.-H. Congourdeau, 'Médecine et théologie chez Anastase le Sinaïte, médecin, moine et didascale', in V. Boudon-Millot and B. Pouderon (eds), *Les Pères de l'Église face à la science médicale de leur temps*, Paris, 2005, 287-97

M. Bibikov, 'Die vergleichende Textologie einiger Werke von Anastasius Sinaites nach den ältesten Handschriften (*Mosquensis, Museum Historicum, olim Bibliotheca Synodalis 265 (Vladimir 197)* und *Guelferbytanus, Gudianus gr. 53*) und Ausgaben', in B. Janssens, B. Roosen and P. van Deun (eds), *Philomathestatos. Studies in Greek and Byzantine texts presented to Jacques Noret for his sixty-fifth birthday*, Louvain, 2004, 1-9

J.A. Munitiz, 'Anastasios of Sinai. Speaking and writing to the people of God', in M.B. Cunningham and P. Allen (eds), *Preacher and audience. Studies in early Christian and Byzantine homiletics*, Leiden, 1998, 227-45

Hoyland, *Seeing Islam*, pp. 92-103

Nasrallah, *HMLEM* ii.2, pp. 85-90

W.E. Kaegi, *Byzantium and the early Islamic conquests*, Cambridge, 1992, pp. 221-23, 231-35

J.F. Haldon, 'The works of Anastasius of Sinai. A key source for the history of seventh-century east Mediterranean society and belief', in A. Cameron and L.I. Conrad (eds), *The Byzantine and early Islamic Near East. I. Problems in the literary source material*, Princeton NJ, 1992, 107-47

S.N. Sakkos, *Peri Anastasiōn Sinaitōn*, Thessaloniki, 1964

M. Richard, 'Anastase le Sinaïte l'Hodegos et le monothélisme', *REB* 16 (1958) 29-42 (repr. in Richard, *Opera minora*, 3 vols, Turnhout, 1977, iii, no. 63)

T. Spáčil, 'La teologia di s. Anastasio Sinaita', *Bessarione* 26 (1922) 157-78; 27 (1923) 15-44

J.B. Pitra, 'Anastasiana', in *Iuris Ecclesiastici Graecorum*, 2 vols, Rome, 1864-68, ii, 238-94

J.B. Kumpfmüller, *De Anastasio Sinaita*, Würzburg, 1865

WORKS ON CHRISTIAN-MUSLIM RELATIONS

Hodegos, 'Guidebook'. Conventional title: *Viae dux*

DATE Unknown, probably around 680-90
ORIGINAL LANGUAGE Greek

DESCRIPTION
The *Hodegos*, considered as Anastasius' main opus (320 pp.), is a handbook of argumentation and refutation of heresies, especially Monophysitism and Monothelitism, and a guide to Chalcedonian orthodoxy. There has been much discussion over its author and the date of composition. Sakkos, partly followed by Chrysos, has argued that the author is to be identified with Anastasius II, Patriarch of Antioch, martyred in 609. This claim has been convincingly refuted by, among others, a recent editor (Uthemann, *Viae Dux*, CCVI-XI) who concludes, after Richard, that the different parts of the *Hodegos* were written between the 630s and 681, and combined into a single work with the author's scholia between 686 and 689. However, the early date for the redaction of some parts does not rest on solid evidence or fit with the life history of Anastasius, so it would be better to assume that the work as a whole was compiled between the 680s and 690s.

The book is composed of 24 chapters of various forms: among others, a short history of the main heresies and councils, refutations of various heresies, and a transcript of theological debates between heretics and orthodox. The two first chapters, probably later additions, contain a summary of recommendations for novice defenders of orthodoxy and a series of simplified theological definitions.

SIGNIFICANCE
Although the author of the *Hodegos* is mainly concerned with refuting Monophysitism, the work contains incidentally some of the earliest Greek references to Islamic doctrine, when referring to the 'false notions' that the Muslims profess about Christ in collusion with the Monophysites. It also gives evidence for the diffusion of qur'ānic

teachings among Christians and for the existence of real theological disputations between Christians and Muslims in the late 7th century.

MANUSCRIPTS

See K.-H. Uthemann, *Anastasii Sinaitae Viae dux*, Turnhout, 1981 (*Corpus Christianorum Series Graeca* 8), pp. xxxii-lxiv, with a useful index by Uthemann, 'Eine Ergänzung zur Edition von Anastasii Sinaitae *Viae Dux*: Das Verzeichnis benutzter und zitierter Handschriften', *Scriptorium* 36 (1982) 130-33

EDITIONS AND TRANSLATIONS

Uthemann, *Anastasii Sinaitae Viae dux*

PG 89, cols 35-310

STUDIES

Hoyland, *Seeing Islam*, pp. 92-95

S.H. Griffith, 'Anastasius of Sinai, the *Hodegos* and the Muslims', *Greek Orthodox Theological Review* 32 (1987) 341-58

A.D. Kartsonis, *Anastasis. The making of an image*, Princeton NJ, 1986, pp. 40-67

K.-H. Uthemann, 'Sprache und Sein bei Anastasios Sinaites. Eine Semantik im Dienst der Kontroverstheologie', *Studia Patristica* 18 (1985) 221-31

S.H. Griffith and R. Darling, 'Anastasius of Sinai, the Monophysites and the *Qur'an*', in *Eighth Annual Byzantine Studies Conference*, Chicago, 1982, p. 13

K. Alpers, 'Die Etymologiensammlung im Hodegos des Anastasios Sinaites, das Etymologicum Gudianum (Barb. gr. 70) und der cod. Vind. theol. gr. 40', *Jahrbuch der Österreichischen Byzantinistik* 34 (1984) 55-68

Uthemann, 'Eine Ergänzung zur Edition von Anastasii Sinaitae *Viae Dux*'

E. Chrysos, 'Neōterai ereunai peri Anastasion Sinaiton', *Kleronomia* 1 (1969) 121-44

Sakkos, *Peri Anastasion Sinaiton*

M. Richard, 'Anastase le Sinaïte l'Hodegos et le monothélisme', *REB* 16 (1958) 29-42 (repr. in Richard, *Opera minora* iii, no. 63)

Diegēmata psychōphelē kai steriktika genomena en diaphorois topois epi tōn hēmeterōn chronōn, 'Edifying and supportive tales which occurred in various places in our times'. Conventional title: *Narrationes*

DATE Unknown, c. 690
ORIGINAL LANGUAGE Greek

DESCRIPTION
The first editor of this collection of edifying stories, Nau, used a manuscript containing only nine stories and the general prologue. From what can be reconstituted using other manuscripts and translations into Arabic, the original collection contained at least 28 stories (50 pp.), very much in the spirit of the narratives found in the *Pratum Spirituale* of John Moschus. Anastasius collected all these stories during his travels between Cyprus, Damascus, Jerusalem, Sinai, and Egypt, and the events they describe took place between the first half and the last decade of the 7th century. Around 690, at the time of the construction of the Dome of the Rock in Jerusalem, which is referred to as an event contemporaneous with the composition of the work, these stories were compiled into a loose framework with a marked apologetic aim. Indeed, the author declares in the introduction to one of the stories that he collected over 30 stories relating miracles and prodigies that happened in his times, but decided to write down only those that 'pertain to the faith of the Christians and bring support to our captive brothers'.

The stories are meant to encourage and support his fellow believers undergoing hardships under Muslim rule, especially prisoners of war, captives and slaves, and to preserve them from apostasy. Anastasius' main aim is to defend Christianity against Islam by illustrating the importance and the power of the external signs of Christian faith: the eucharist, the cross, the icons, the saints. By contrast, he denigrates Muslims, calling them 'associates of the demons', and to the Islamic *shahāda* he retorts with a recurring Christian profession of faith: 'There is no other God than the God of Christians'.

In his early years as a monk on Mt Sinai, Anastasius also compiled another collection of 39 stories about monks and hermits living in the deserts around Mt Sinai in the late 6th and 7th centuries. It supplies documentary evidence for the history of the monastic community of

Mt Sinai before and just after the Arab conquests, but the Arabs are only mentioned incidentally.

SIGNIFICANCE

This collection is one of the early apologetic works entirely dedicated to the defense of Christian faith facing Islam. Its main interest lies in the insight it gives into many aspects of day-to-day Christian-Muslim relations in the first half-century after the Muslim conquests.

MANUSCRIPTS

MS Vat – Gr. 2592, fols 123-135v, 174v-182 (10th c.)
MS BNF – Gr. 1596, pp. 381-95 (11th c.)
MS Jerusalem, Greek Orthodox Patriarchate – Holy Sepulchre 113, fols 217v-241 (1672)

Many other manuscripts contain only one or more stories (cf. A. Binggeli, *Anastase le Sinaïte. Récits sur le Sinaï et récits utiles à l'âme. Edition, traduction, commentaire*, 2 vols, Paris, 2001 [Diss. Université Paris IV])

EDITIONS AND TRANSLATIONS

A new edition is being prepared by A. Binggeli, the only available edition to date being:

F. Nau, 'Le texte grec des Récits utiles à l'âme d'Anastase (le Sinaïte)', *OC* 3 (1903) 56-90 (edition of stories 1-2, 5-6, 12, 14-17, 20, 27)

Dispersed editions of individual stories:

A. Reichert, 'Eine Fluchtburg christlicher Sarazenen bei Pharan im südlichen Sinai. Archäologische Anmerkungen zu einer hagiographischen Anekdote des Anastasios Sinaites', in M. Krause and S. Schaten (eds), *ΘΕΜΕΛΙΑ. Spätantike und koptologische Studien. Peter Grossmann zum 65. Geburtstag*, Wiesbaden, 1998, 273-88 (German trans. of story 8)

B. Flusin, 'L'Esplanade du Temple à l'arrivée des Arabes, d'après deux récits byzantins', in J. Raby and J. Johns (eds), *Bayt al-Maqdis. 'Abd al-Malik's Jerusalem*, Oxford, 1992, 17-31 (edition and French trans. of story 7)

F. Halkin, 'La vision de Kaïoumos et le sort éternel de Philentolos Olympiou', *AB* 63 (1945) 56-64 (repr. in Halkin, *Études d'épigraphie grecque et d'hagiographie byzantine*, London, 1973) (edition and French trans. of story 15)

F. Nau, 'Le texte grec des récits du moine Anastase sur les saints pères du Sinaï', *OC* 2 (1902), 58-89 (pp. 87-89: edition of story 8)

STUDIES

A. Binggeli, 'Un nouveau témoin des *Narrationes* d'Anastase le Sinaïte dans les *membra disjecta* d'un manuscrit sinaïtique' (Sinaiticus MG 6 + MG 21)', *REB* 62 (2004) 261-68

Binggeli, *Anastase le Sinaïte. Récits sur le Sinaï et récits utiles à l'âme*

Hoyland, *Seeing Islam*, pp. 99-102

P. Speck, 'Das Teufelsschloss. Bilderverehrung bei Anastasios Sinaites?', in T. Pratsch (ed.), *Varia V*, Bonn, 1994, 293-309

C. Faraggiana di Sarzana, 'Il *Paterikon Vat. gr.* 2592, già di Mezzoiuso, e il suo rapporto testuale con lo *Hieros. S. Sepulchri gr.* 113', *Bollettino della Badia greca di Grottaferrata* n.s. 47 (1993) 79-96

B. Flusin, 'Démons et Sarrasins. L'auteur et le propos des *Diègèmata stèriktika* d'Anastase le Sinaïte', *Travaux et Mémoires* 11 (1991) 381-409

C.P. Kyrris, 'The admission of the souls of immoral but humane people into the *limbus puerorum*, according to the cypriote abbot Kaioumos (VIIth century A.D.) compared to the Quran's *al 'Araf*', *Revue des études sud-est européennes* 9 (1971) 461-77

P. Canart, 'Nouveaux récits du moine Anastase', in *Actes du XIIe congrès international d'études byzantines*, 3 vols, Belgrade, 1964, ii, 263-71

P. Canart, 'Une nouvelle anthologie monastique. Le *Vaticanus graecus* 2592', *Le Muséon* 75 (1962) 109-29

Eroteseis kai apokriseis peri diaphorōn kephalaiōn genomenai ek diaphorōn prosōpōn pros ton abban Anastasion on tas lyseis epoiēsato ouk ex autou all'ek pollēs peiras, 'Questions and Answers on different subjects asked by different people to Abba Anastasius, who gave the answers not from himself but from long experience'. Conventional titles: *Erotapokriseis, Quaestiones et responsiones*

DATE Unknown, probably c. 700

ORIGINAL LANGUAGE Greek

DESCRIPTION

The original collection, consisting of 103 questions and answers, was first reconstituted by Richard and edited by Munitiz (165 pp.). The earlier edition by Gretser (reproduced in *PG*), which comprises 154 questions, is a compilation of different collections of *Erotapokriseis*, of which only questions 75-141 are genuine; *florilegia* of patristic citations, which did not exist in the original collection, were appended to many questions in this amplified collection. The collection is organized in a somewhat haphazard fashion: the connections between questions dealing with similar themes are often lacking, there are many repetitions, and the overall structure is not apparent; likewise, the questions vary in length from a few lines to a few pages, while question 28 constitutes in itself a short treatise on providence and predestination. These observations have brought the recent editor to suggest that the collection could have been compiled and edited by one of Anastasius' disciples after his death (Munitiz, *Quaestiones et responsiones*, p. 1). In any case the material it contains is authentic and goes back to the last third of the 7th century.

The *Erotapokriseis* cover a very wide range of topics and themes. Some treat theological or exegetical questions, others medical and natural science matters, but most of them appeal to the everyday preoccupations of Christians, especially those that have some connection with matters of religious observance. The situation of Christians living under Muslim rule is naturally of particular concern to Anastasius. To all these questions, he always answers in a very pragmatic way that contrasts with the more dogmatic positions reflected in the conciliar regulations.

SIGNIFICANCE

Besides the fact that the *Erotapokriseis* gives precious insight into the mental framework of Christians in the 7th century, their beliefs and concerns, and their day-to-day practice of faith, it is also one of the earliest works to refer explicitly to the beliefs of the Muslim Arabs, such as Satan's refusal to bow down to Adam (Q 2:34). Moreover, some themes, such as the question of predetermination, providence and God's responsibility in human death, have direct parallels in the Qurʾān.

MANUSCRIPTS

See J.A. Munitiz and M. Richard, *Anastasii Sinaitae quaestiones et responsiones*, Turnhout, 2006 (*Corpus Christianorum Series Graeca* 59), pp. xix-xlix

EDITIONS AND TRANSLATIONS

Munitiz and Richard, *Anastasii Sinaitae quaestiones et responsiones*

PG 89, cols 311-824

STUDIES

J.A. Munitiz, 'In the steps of Anastasius of Sinai. Later traces of his *Erotapokriseis*', in Janssens, Roosen, and van Deun, *Philomathestatos*, 435-54

J.A. Munitiz, 'Anastasian *Questions and answers* among the Sinai new finds', *REB* 60 (2002) 201-9

J.A. Munitiz, 'The predetermination of death. The contribution of Anastasios of Sinai and Nikephoros Blemmydes to a perennial Byzantine problem', *DOP* 55 (2001) 9-20

J.A. Munitiz, 'Anastasios of Sinai's teaching on body and soul', in L. James (ed.), *Desire and denial in Byzantium*, Aldershot, 1999, 49-56

Hoyland, *Seeing Islam*, pp. 95-98

D. Krausmüller, 'God or angels as impersonators of saints. A belief and its context in the "Refutation" of Eustratius of Constantinople and in the writings of Anastasius of Sinai', *Gouden Hoorn/ Golden Horn* 6 (1998-99) 5-16

Munitiz, 'Anastasios of Sinai. Speaking and writing to the people of God', pp. 235-42

Haldon, 'The works of Anastasius of Sinai', pp. 129-47

G. Dagron, 'Le saint, le savant, l'astrologue. Étude de thèmes hagiographiques à travers quelques recueils de "Questions et réponses" des Ve-VIIe siècles', in *Hagiographie. Cultures et sociétés (IVe-VIIe siècles)*, Paris, 1981, 143-55 (repr. in Dagron, *La romanité en Orient. Héritages et mutations*, London, 1984)

M. Richard, 'Les véritables Questions et réponses d'Anastase le Sinaïte', *Bulletin de l'Institut de Recherche et d'Histoire des Textes* 15 (1967-68) 39-56 (repr. in Richard, *Opera Minora*, 3 vols, Turnhout, 1977, iii, no. 64)

R. Paret, 'Un parallèle byzantin à Coran, XVIII, 59-81', *REB* 26 (1968) 137-59

A. Binggeli 2008

The Letter of Leo III in Ghewond

Unknown author

DATE OF BIRTH Unknown
PLACE OF BIRTH Unknown
DATE OF DEATH Unknown
PLACE OF DEATH Unknown

BIOGRAPHY —

MAIN SOURCES OF INFORMATION

Primary —

Secondary
See below

WORKS ON CHRISTIAN-MUSLIM RELATIONS

Correspondence between ʿUmar II and Leo III

DATE Unknown
ORIGINAL LANGUAGE Probably Greek

DESCRIPTION

The authenticity of the exchange of correspondence between the Caliph ʿUmar II and the Byzantine Emperor Leo III preserved in the History of Ghewond (q.v. for biographical details) has long been a matter of contention. It remains unresolved. Some scholars, notably Gerö, maintain that the correspondence was originally composed in Armenian and so cannot be genuine. He contends that the scriptural citations and allusions are far closer to the Armenian Bible than the Greek Septuagint, and also that Leo III's 'pathetic remarks' in recognition of the earthly success of the caliphate at the conclusion of his letter 'ring true in the mouth of an Armenian, whose land has been ravaged and subjected by the Arabs; but the same words certainly do not sound well coming from Leo who has just decisively frustrated the great Muslim attack on Constantinople' (Gerö, *Byzantine iconoclasm*, p. 170). Other scholars have persisted in their belief that the correspondence was originally in Greek, although there is a division of opinion as to whether the letter was written by Leo III before the first period of Iconoclasm (Meyendorff), or whether it should be dated to the second half of the 9th century (implied, but not overtly stated by Jeffery).

Following Gerö, there can be little doubt that the short letter from the Caliph ʿUmar II to Leo III contained in Ghewond's *History* is a reconstruction. This letter, which should not be confused with the Arabic letter of pseudo-ʿUmar II to Leo III (q.v.), is based exclusively upon those passages in the reply ascribed to Leo III which cite or paraphrase passages from ʿUmar's original. But it does not follow that Leo III's letter can also be dismissed. This long letter contains an apology for Christianity in response to Muslim polemic, as well a range of arguments against Islamic beliefs and rituals, the Qurʾān and Muḥammad. Mahé has recently judged Gerö's contention that this letter was an original Armenian composition as 'faible', arguing that the proximity of certain biblical quotations and allusions to the Armenian Bible rather than the Septuagint may well be the result of voluntary harmonization, either by the translator or by a later copyist. Moreover, Mahé praises Akinean's excellent study which demonstrates that the text displays unequivocal signs of having been translated from Greek. Quite apart from the frequent use of words clearly borrowed from Greek, *paraklitos* and *ewkʿaristē*, instead of the expected and commonly used Armenian words *mkhitʿarich* and *gohanam*, Mahé also refers to the presence of unusual calques from Greek and the literal translation of Greek phrases. For Mahé, Akinean's study proves that Leo III's letter was originally composed in Greek.

A number of other features of the letter also deserve brief mention. First, the letter is set in the context of previous correspondence, although this is described as concerning worldly affairs rather than spiritual matters. It seems improbable that such an incidental comment would have been invented. Second, the letter addresses a series of specific questions and comments raised by ʿUmar II, rather than itself setting the agenda for the controversy. Third, the text refers to 'the holy *paraklitos*, that is *mkhitʿarich*' (Ezean, p. 58), giving the Greek first and then the Armenian equivalent by way of explanation. This short passage supports the view that the letter was originally in Greek. Earlier (Ezean, p. 52), when it states, 'we call the Pentateuch *Nomos*', it gives the Greek term. Elsewhere, it records how the Gospel of Jesus Christ had spread 'from the civilizations of the Greeks and the

Romans to the furthest barbarians' (Ezean, p. 61). This is a surprising statement to include if the letter was an original Armenian composition, for it is almost an article of faith for Armenian authors to maintain that the Armenian nation was the first to embrace Christianity, during the reign of Trdat I, prior to the conversion of Constantine I. Intriguingly, the same sentence refers to it being 'more or less 800 years since Christ appeared'. This system of calculating time by reference to the birth of Christ was not commonly used in Armenia, judging by the surviving colophons, inscriptions and chronicles. Indeed, there is very little evidence that such a chronology was employed in Armenia before the 10th century. Earlier, the letter states that '...as you say, it is 100 years, more or less, since the time when your religion appeared' (Ezean, p. 60). This is clearly a *hijra* date, a chronological system also unattested in Armenian texts until the 10th century. Finally, when discussing the languages in which the Gospel has been spread, the letter privileges Greek above all others, indicating 'first, (the language) of us Greeks' (Ezean, p. 62). All these items collectively point to a Greek original.

This prompts two further questions. When was the original letter written, and in what circumstances could it have been translated into Armenian? The letter betrays some signs of an early date. It maintains, for example, that the Qur'ān was composed by ʿUmar (ibn al-Khaṭṭāb), Abu Turab (that is, ʿAlī) and Salmān the Persian (Ezean, p. 58). An early 8th-century date would suit such a controversial statement, as would the *hijra* date mentioned previously. It also correctly names ʿUmar II's paternal uncle as Muḥammad, noting that on one occasion he had sacrificed a camel and decapitated a number of Christians, mixing their blood in sacrifice (Ezean, p. 89). On the other hand, the letter cites several Muslim sects: Kʿōzi, Sabari, Tʿorapi, Kntri, Murji, Basghi, the impious Jahdi and the Hariwri. Arguably, the Kʿōzi could be identified as the Khawārij or Kharijīs, the Tʿorapi as followers of an ʿAlid sect, the Turābiyya, the Murji as the Murjiʾa, the Basghi as followers of Wāṣil ibn ʿAṭāʾ, who died in 748, the Jahdi as followers of Abū ʿAmr ibn Baḥr al-Jāḥiẓ (although this is contentious), and the Hariwri as Khārijīs from the town of Ḥarūra. Although several 9th-century sects appear in the list, it is not impossible that these were added at a later date.

The letter would certainly suit an early 8th-century context. However, the fact that Leo seems to respond to pseudo-ʿUmar's letter (q.v.), which modern scholars generally date to the second half of the

8th century or later, militates against this. The date of the original Greek composition thus remains unresolved. That being so, when and why was it translated? If one prefers the traditional late 8th-century date for the composition of the *History* of Ghewond (q.v.), this proves to be problematic, for there is no strong evidence for strong ties between Constantinople and the Armenian Church after 730. However, if one accepts a late 9th-century date, the problem disappears, for we know of several letters exchanged between Photius, Patriarch of Constantinople, and various Armenian correspondents in the 850s, 860s and 870s, including letters originally in Greek which survive only in Armenian. This would seem to be an appropriate context in which a letter from Leo III to ʿUmar II could be unearthed and translated into Armenian. It is highly likely that Photius was himself of Armenian descent.

This letter would have offered him a sophisticated authority of unimpeachable pedigree with which to confront and refute Muslim teaching, which was arguably making significant inroads into the Armenian flock in the 9th century. Although rightly incorporated into the *History* of Ghewond in the reign of ʿUmar II, its translation into Armenian may well belong to the second half of the 9th century, perhaps during the patriarchate of Photius, although this remains conjectural.

SIGNIFICANCE

If one accepts the above, the letter from the Caliph ʿUmar II in Ghewond's *History* cannot be genuine, but is composed of fragments from such a letter which were cited by Leo III in his reply to ʿUmar. However, the letter from Leo III to ʿUmar II gives some indication of being genuine, and as such is fully deserving of sustained study. Arguably, it provides a vitally important witness to Christian-Muslim relations at the start of the 8th century, one that has been unduly neglected. It reveals Muslim attitudes to and interpretations of the Bible, and Christian knowledge of the Qurʾān.

MANUSCRIPTS

MS Yerevan, Matenadaran – 1902 (? late 13th c.)

EDITIONS AND TRANSLATIONS

J.-M. Gaudeul, *La correspondance de ʿUmar et Leon (vers 900)*, Rome, 1985, pp. 40-97

Z. Arzoumanian, *History of Lewond, the eminent vardapet of the Armenians*, Philadelphia, 1982 (trans. with brief commentary)

A. Ter-Ghevondyan, *Ghevond Patmut'yun*, Yerevan, 1982 (modern Armenian trans. and commentary)

A. Jeffery, 'Ghevond's text of the correspondence between ʿUmar II and Leo III', *Harvard Theological Review* 37 (1944) 269-332 (English trans. with intro. and notes, repr. in A. Newman, *The early Muslim-Christian dialogue*, Hatfield PA, 1993, pp. 63-98)

K. Ezean, *Patmutʿiwn Ghewondeay metsi vardepeti Hayotsʿ*, St Petersburg, 1887, pp. 43-99 (edition)

STUDIES

T.W. Greenwood, 'Failure of a mission? Photius and the Armenian Church', *Le Muséon* 119 (2006) 123-67

K. Kościelniak, 'Polemika muzułmańsko-chrześcijańska na podstawie korespondencji przypisywanej kalifowi umajjadzkiemu ʿUmararowi II (†720) i cesarzowi bizantyjskiemu Leonowi III (†741)', *Folia historica Cracoviensia* 8 (2002) 97-105

M. van Esbroeck, 'La politique arménienne de Byzance de Justinien II à Léon III', *Studi sull' Oriente Christiano* 2 (1998) 111-20

A. Kaplony, *Konstantinopel und Damascus. Gesandschaften und Verträge zwischen Kaisern und Kalifen 639-750. Untersuchungen zum Gewohnheits-Völkerrecht und zur interkulturellen Diplomatie*, Berlin, 1996, pp. 207-37

J.-P. Mahé, 'Le problème de l'authenticité et de la valeur de la Chronique de Łewond', in Centre de Recherches d'Histoire et de Civilisation Byzantines, *L'Arménie et Byzance: Histoire et culture*, Paris, 1996, 119-26

B. Martin-Hisard, 'L'Empire byzantin dans l'œuvre de Łewond', in *L'Arménie et Byzance*, 135-44

R.G. Hoyland, 'The correspondence of Leo III (717-41) and ʿUmar II (717-20)', *Aram* 6 (1994) 165-77 (repr. in Hoyland, *Seeing Islam*, pp. 490-501)

J.-M. Gaudeul, 'The correspondence between Leo and ʿUmar: ʿUmar's letter re-discovered?', *Islamochristiana* 10 (1984) 109-57

G. Gerö, *Byzantine Iconoclasm during the reign of Leo III with particular attention to the oriental sources*, Louvain, 1973, Appendix 2, pp. 153-71: 'The authenticity of the Leo-Umar correspondence'

A.T. Khoury, *Les théologiens byzantins et l'Islam. Textes et auteurs (VIIIe-XIIIe s.)*, Louvain, 1969, pp. 200-18

J. Meyendorff, 'Byzantine views of Islam', *DOP* 18 (1964) 115-32

N. Adontsʿ, 'Ghewond ew Khorenatsʿi, kʿnnutʿiwn H.N. Akineani tesutʿean', *Hayrenik* 11:8 (1933) 79-90, 11:9 (1933) 120-26

N. Akinean, 'Ghewond erets' patmagir: matenagrakan-patmakan usumnasirut'iwn mě', *Handēs Amsoreay* 43 (1929) 330-48, 458-72, 593-619, 705-18 (repr. in Akinean, *Matenagrakan hetazotut'iwnner*, Vienna, 1930, iii)

Tim Greenwood 2007

John of Nikiou

Yuḥannā, nicknamed 'al-Mudabbir' (Ethiopic: Yoḥannəs Mädäbbär) = John (bishop) of Nikiou/Nikiu

Date of birth Unknown, before the middle of the 7th c.
Place of birth Unknown
Date of death Soon after 700
Place of death Unknown

BIOGRAPHY

The very scant information available about John's personal circumstances is found in the almost contemporary Coptic *Life of Patriarch Isaac* (d. 692/93), attributed to Bishop Mēna of Nikiou (q.v.), who was John's successor as bishop of Nikiou, and also in the later Arabic *History of the Patriarchs of Alexandria* (q.v.). The part of this work that deals with John is likely to have been written by Mawhūb ibn Manṣūr ibn Mufarrij, an Alexandrian layman in the entourage of Patriarch Cyril II (late 11th c.) who made use of much older Greek and Coptic documents. The reference to John is found in a section that probably harks back to his contemporary Jirjā the Deacon (q.v.).

From these two sources it can be inferred that at an unknown date John, clearly a monk, was appointed (Monophysite) bishop of Nikiou (Greek *Nikíon/Nikíou(s)*, Arabic *Naq(i)yūs/Niq(i)yūs*, Ethiopic *Näqiyus/Niq(ə)yus*, Coptic *Pshati*, Arabic *Ibshādī*; see Timm, *Das christlich-koptische Ägypten*), a town in the south-western Nile delta, most likely at the site of today's Kawm Mānūs, a 'tell' partly occupied by the village of Zāwiyyat Razīn.

Again at an unknown date, he became visitor (Coptic *apotritēs*, Greek **apot(ē)rētēs*, 'inspector' [?]: cf. *epitērētēs*, 'superintendent', 'overseer') to the monasteries of Upper Egypt, thus occupying a leading position within the ecclesiastical hierarchy. He was present, with other important Egyptian bishops, at the death of Patriarch John (III) of Samannūd (2 February 689), and he must have played a significant role in the turbulent election of the latter's successor – his assistant Isaac (February 690). Against the unexpected choice of deacon George (Jirjā) from Sakhā made by the synod gathered for that election, John of Nikiou supported the late patriarch's candidate Isaac.

After governor ʿAbd al-ʿAzīz ibn Marwān had granted formal investiture to Isaac at Fusṭāṭ (Babylon, nowadays a quarter of Cairo), John and his colleague Bishop Gregory of al-Qays, inspector for the monasteries of Lower Egypt, accompanied the new patriarch to Alexandria.

On account of his reputation as an expert in canon law, under the patriarchate of Simon (692/93-700) John became *mudabbir* or '(general) overseer' of all the monasteries of Egypt (hence his Ethiopic nickname *Mädäbbär*, glossed there with *śäraʿi*, 'administrator', 'moderator'). In this capacity, he apparently displeased his fellow Egyptian bishops, who were indeed vexed by his harshness. John's career ended when he was held responsible for the death of a monk whom he had severely disciplined for the rape of a nun at Wādī Ḥabīb. He was then deposed and also suspended from the priesthood. Possibly after this incident and his ensuing retirement as a simple monk, he wrote a universal *Chronicle* following conventional Byzantine patterns. He must have died shortly after 700, not necessarily in his former diocese.

MAIN SOURCES OF INFORMATION

Primary

D.N. Bell, *Mena of Nikiou. The life of Isaac of Alexandria and The martyrdom of Saint Macrobius*, Kalamazoo MI, 1988, 43-94, p. 64 (trans.)

Sāwīrus ibn al-Muqaffaʿ, *History of the Patriarchs of the Coptic Church of Alexandria*, ed. and trans. B. Evetts, 4 vols, Paris, 1904-14, iii [*Agathon to Michael I (796)*], pp. 274, 276, 286-88 (= pp. 20, 22, 32-34)

E. Amélineau, *Histoire du patriarche copte Isaac*, Paris, 1890, pp. 49-50 (edition and trans.)

Secondary

S. Weninger, art. 'John of Nikiou', in S. Uhlig et al. (eds), *Encyclopaedia Aethiopica*, Wiesbaden, 2003-

P.M. Fraser, art. 'John of Nikiu', in A.S. Atiya (ed.), *The Coptic Encyclopaedia*, New York, 1991

M. Rodinson, 'Notes sur le texte de Jean de Nikiou', in Accademia Nazionale dei Lincei, *IV Congresso Internazionale di Studi Etiopici (10-15 aprile 1972)*, 2 vols, Rome, 1974, ii (*Sezione linguistica*), 127-37

Graf, *GCAL* i, pp. 470-72

R. Aubert, 'Jean, évêque monophysite de Nikiou', in A. Baudrillart et al. (eds), *Dictionnaire d'histoire et géographie ecclésiastiques*, Paris, 1912-

WORKS ON CHRISTIAN-MUSLIM RELATIONS

Title unknown. Title (traditional) of Ethiopic translation: *Mädäbbär*, i.e. '(Chronicle of John) Mädäbbär'. Modern title (only found in scholarly literature): 'Chronicle of John of Nikiou' and 'Epitome of the general history of John of Nikiou'

DATE c. 700
ORIGINAL LANGUAGE Coptic

DESCRIPTION

This is a world history from Adam to the return from exile of Patriarch Benjamin of Alexandria in 644, i.e. in the author's own time. The *Chronicle* includes references to ancient Egypt and sections on Hellenistic and early Roman history, but mainly focuses on the Christian Roman Empire, with a distinctive penchant for martyrdom and persecution, down to the conquest of Egypt by ʿAmr ibn al-ʿĀṣ in 640-42 and the years immediately following.

Divided into 122 chapters (the sequel, not numbered, to chapter cxxii in Zotenberg's edition is actually chapter cxxiii of Charles' translation), and preceded by a summary listing of chapter headings, the text only survives in a defective Ethiopic (Gəʿəz) version made in 1601, under Negus Yaʿəqob/Mäläk Sägäd II, from an Arabic *Vorlage*. Produced at the order of Yaʿəqob's wife Maryam Śəna (Mäläk Mogäsa) and the then chief commander of the Ethiopian troops Atnatewos ('Athanasius'), this translation had an explicitly moral purpose, 'for the sake of the soul' (cxxii[i], 1), within the context of the Monophysite-Catholic controversy that was inflaming the country at that time. As a reaction to the long-standing (and soon after successful) attempts by the Jesuits to convert the Ethiopian court, John's text was supposed to typify the evil and punishment inflicted by God upon those who abandoned the true faith, i.e. Monophysite Christianity. Thus, the history of 7th-century Egypt turned out to be, 'if not a formidable warning, then in any case a sufficiently unequivocal and quite timely hint' to 17th-century Ethiopia (Chernetsov, 'The role of Catholicism', p. 206; cf. Pennec, *Des Jésuites au royaume du Prêtre Jean*, p. 297, n. 286).

Following the arguably usual protocol of an Egyptian translator (not fully proficient in Gəʿəz) whose work was then revised by a native Ethiopian, this version of the *Chronicle*, attested to date in four MSS (see below), and itself traditionally known as *Mädäbbär* (Conti Rossini, 'Manoscritti', p. 624 = *Note*, p. 666, and idem, 'Notice', p. 207 = *Notice*, p. 193), was made by the obscure 'deacon Gabriel the Egyptian (*Qəbəryal Gəbṣawi*, Arabic **Jabriyāl al-Qibṭī*), son of the martyr John of Qalyūb (*Yoḥannəs zä-Qäl(ə)yub*)', i.e. a parishioner of the latter's church at Qalyūb in the southern Nile delta (see Crum, 'Christian Egypt', p. 208, and Rodinson, 'Notes', pp. 129-30, 132-33; on Gabriel's possible historical personality, cf. Ricci, 'Letterature', pp. 840-41), and by the learned *abba* Məhərka Dəngəl, who would later have a change of heart and become a supporter of the Jesuit mission and author/redactor of the first part of the *Chronicle* of Negus Susənyos/Mäläk Sägäd III (1607-32), of whom he was then teacher and confessor (Toubkis, 'Məhərkä Dəngəl').

The Arabic *Vorlage*, which has not yet been found (in spite of the claim by Amélineau, *Histoire*, p. xxiv, n. 1: see Crum, 'Christian Egypt', p. 53, and Rodinson, 'Notes', p. 130, n. 16), was in turn a translation, produced at an unknown time, from an original that is no longer extant, and is variously thought to have been either a mixture of Greek and Coptic passages (Zotenberg, 'Mémoire', pp. 451, 456-57 = *La chronique*, pp. 1, 6-7), or an entirely Coptic text (Nöldeke, review of Zotenberg, *Chronique*, p. 1367, and Crum, review of Charles, *The Chronicle*, pp. 207-8; cf. Graf, *GCAL* i, p. 471, and Rodinson, 'Notes', p. 131), or else a Greek text later turned into Coptic (Orlandi, *Elementi*, p. 109). The most likely hypothesis is that the original was Coptic, because Greek was the language of the Melkites and thus unfitting for a Coptic bishop, and also because there is no trace of John of Nikiou's work or name in Byzantine literature (Fraser, 'John of Nikiou', pp. 1366-67).

The two subsequent translations, especially that from Arabic into Ethiopic (due to the complicated protocol described above), have ostensibly obscured the original narration. As for the extant Ethiopic version, major events of the years 610-40 – i.e. the Sassanian conquest, occupation and evacuation of Egypt, and the preliminary phases of ʿAmr's military campaigns, as well as Emperor Heraclius' attempt to reconcile Monophysites and Chalcedonians through Monotheletism – are missing in the relevant chapters cvii-xxii(i). There is a symptomatic lack of match, in terms of figures and content, between chapters lxvi-cxviii and their initial summary listing, in which they correspond to headings lxv-cvxii (see Zotenberg, 'Chronique', p. 349, n. 4 = *Chronique*, p. 229, n. 4). Proper names are often distorted, and defy efforts to restore them plausibly (see Rodinson, 'Notes', pp. 131-37; Fiaccadori,

'Māsidis', pp. 117-21). It is not easy to judge whether the chapter sequence was already confused in the textual tradition of the original or, as seems more probable, the confusion just occurred in the several intermediary stages – Arabic and Gəʿəz versions and their copies – between the original and the *Chronicle* in its present Ethiopic form, with its style 'simple, naive and disjointed in places' (Fraser, 'John of Nikiou', p. 1367).

A new, critical edition of the *Chronicle* is hence a scholarly desideratum, not only because Zotenberg's text is full of shortcomings and problems (like his translation, to which Charles's is heavily indebted), but also because he could not take into account the valuable MSS d'Abbadie 31 (= 209) and Conti Rossini 27, both later entries to this complicated dossier (see Rodinson, 'Notes', p. 133-35, and Fiaccadori, 'Māsidis', pp. 117-19; cf. below).

As a universal chronicle, John's work is obviously dependent on earlier Byzantine writings of this kind, such as the sources common to the extant *Chronicles* of John Malalas (d. after 574) and John of Antioch (early 7th century) and to the *Chronicon Paschale* (in the 630s) – all of which contribute to the retrieval of John of Nikiou's original narrative, at least for the parts that overlap. Yet, apart from its broad universal scheme and its annalistic form, John of Nikiou's *Chronicle* is, to a large extent, a work completely different from them, full of otherwise unknown noteworthy details. It also abundantly draws on Greek historians such as Socrates Scholasticus (d. after 439) for ecclesiastical matters, and Procopius (fl. 550s) and Agathias (d. c. 580), whose authority on the Vandalic and the Persian wars he openly acknowledges (chapter xcii, 20-21), for the reign of Justinian. Other peculiar additions, such as earthquake records (Guidoboni, *Catalogue*), betray John of Nikiou's acquaintance with further sources and documents (see Fiaccadori, 'Māsidis'). He also employs local and oral accounts (Rodinson, 'Notes', p. 129) for both contemporary and earlier events (as far back as the reign of Emperor Maurice, 582-602), while the part on ancient Egypt shows striking similarities with the Coptic *Cambyses Romance* (as we know it from the 8th-century papyrus fragment first published by Möller, 'Zu den Bruckstücken'), a 5th/6th- or better 6th/7th-century literary text that follows closely the Pharaonic past (see Cruz-Uribe, 'Notes'), which is also in keeping with John's ethnicity and his nationalistic bias, quite often surfacing vis-à-vis both the old Byzantine (pro-Melkite) masters and the Arab (Islamic) newcomers.

If much of John's information is untrustworthy, the final chapters of his book (ciii-xxii[i]) are of major historical interest. They portray the twilight of Byzantine Egypt under the reigns of Phocas (602-10) and the 'impious' Heraclius (610-41, with the omissions above), the fall of Egypt to the Arabs being openly attributed to the latter's anti-Monophysite persecutions, enacted by the Melkite Patriarch Cyrus. Several utterances against those who 'divided Christ into two natures' (cxxii[i], 4; Charles, *The Chronicle*, p. 202) show that, to some extent, John blames the Chalcedonians for the invasions, which God brought on as punishment. This is not to say, however, that he depicts the Coptic population as welcoming the Arabs, for on the contrary he condemns those who collaborated with them and followed 'the detestable doctrine of the beast, this is, Mohammed' (cxxi, 10; Charles, *The Chronicle*, p. 201). This and other similar statements at the end of the *Chronicle* can hardly be considered as later interpolations (*pace* Hoyland, *Seeing Islam*, pp. 152-56), since, far from being detached, they seem to underscore, in rather a dramatic way, the general attitude displayed in the text.

The last part of the surviving Ethiopic version is definitely 'corrupt, full of lacunae and dislocated' (Fraser, 'John of Nikiou', p. 1367). Yet, once its actual meaning is disentangled, a number of significant points come to light, and can be seen to bear the authoritative impact of eyewitness testimony (Kaegi, 'Egypt'). They include details about the piecemeal conquest of the country by ʿAmr, the very first years of Islamic rule, and the state of contemporary Christian-Muslim relations, as well as the bitterness of a Coptic bishop not really at ease with either the Byzantines or the Arabs, but equally disappointed by both.

SIGNIFICANCE

However mutilated and confused it is, the *Chronicle* remains the only direct, and therefore independent and reliable, source for the Arab conquest of Egypt and its immediate aftermath, anticipating by almost two centuries the earliest and quite contradictory Muslim accounts, and assuming pride of place over them. The *Chronicle* reveals an unmistakable Christian, or rather Coptic, point of view, especially through its focus on theodicy, in that it views history in terms of divine reward and punishment.

Significantly, the final part of the work, which bemoans 'the horrible deeds by the Muslims, impossible to describe', has recently been translated into Arabic by an Egyptian Muslim scholar (ʿAbd al-Jalīl,

Ta'rīkh Miṣr) as a document giving 'a Coptic perspective on the Islamic conquest' (the subtitle of the book) that is worthy of attention: the Arab invasion of Egypt was to free the Coptic Church from the long-standing Byzantine yoke.

MANUSCRIPTS

MS BNF – Éth. 123 (= 146, late 17th c.), fols 62r-138v (see [Zotenberg], *Catalogue*, 222-49, pp. 223-41 § 2)

MS BL – Or. 818 (= cccxci, first half of the 18th c.), fols 48r-102v (see Wright, *Catalogue*, 297-314, pp. 300-9 § II)

MS BNF – d'Abbadie 31 (= 209, late 17th c.), fols 104r-64v (see Conti Rossini, 'Notice', pp. 207-8 = *Notice*, pp. 193-94 § VI)

MS Rome, Accademia Nazionale dei Lincei – Conti Rossini 27 (20th c.), fols 1r-120r (see Strelcyn, *Catalogue*, pp. 100-2, p. 100 § I)

EDITIONS AND TRANSLATIONS

Ta'rīkh Miṣr li-Yūḥannā l-Niqyūsī. Ru'ya qibṭiyya li-l-fatḥ al-islāmī, trans. ʿUmar Ṣābir ʿAbd al-Jalīl, Cairo, 2000 (Arabic trans. of chapters on the conquest of Egypt with introduction)

Oriental sources concerning Nubia, coll. and trans. G. Vantini, Heidelberg and Warsaw, 1975, 30-35 (excerpts on Nubia and Ethiopia from Charles's English trans.)

F. Altheim and R. Stiehl, *Christentum am Roten Meer*, 2 vols, Berlin, 1971-73, i, pp. 356-89 (German trans., with commentary, of the chapters on the conquest of Egypt)

Y. Kamal, *Monumenta cartographica Africae et Aegypti*, 5 vols, [Cairo], 1926-51, iii (*Époque arabe*), 1, fols 493r-496r (repr., ed. F. Sezgin, Frankfurt a.M., 1987, III, Reihe D, Bd. 3, 3, pp. 21-27: 'Jean, évêque de Nikiou'; excerpts on Egypt, Nubia and Ethiopia, with portions of chapter summary listing, from Zotenberg's edition and trans.)

The Chronicle of John (c. 690 A.D.), Coptic Bishop of Nikiu; being a history of Egypt before and during the Arab conquest, trans. R.H. Charles from Zotenberg's edition of the Ethiopic version, London, 1916 (repr. Amsterdam, 1981)

'Chronique de Jean, évêque de Nikiou', ed. and trans. H. Zotenberg, *Notices et extraits des manuscrits de la Bibliothèque Nationale et autres bibliothèques* 24/1 (1883) 125-608 (repr. *Chronique de Jean, évêque de Nikiou*, ed. and trans. H. Zotenberg, Paris, 1883)

Studies

D. Toubkis, art. 'Məhərkä Dəngəl, in *Encyclopaedia Aethiopica*

S. Emmel, 'Coptic literature in the Byzantine and early Islamic world', in R.S. Bagnall (ed.), *Egypt in the Byzantine world 300-700*, Cambridge MA, 2007, 83-102, pp. 88, 96

P.M. Sijpesteijn, 'The Arab conquest of Egypt and the beginning of Muslim rule', in Bagnall, *Egypt in the Byzantine world*, 437-59, pp. 440, 442

W. Witakowski, 'Ethiopic universal chronography', in M. Wallraff (ed.), *Julius Africanus und die christliche Weltchronistik*, Berlin, 2006, 285-301, pp. 288-89 ('John of Nikiou')

G. Fiaccadori, 'Māsidis (Giovanni di Nikiou, *Chron.* XC 54-60)', in G. Fiaccadori, A. Gatti and S. Marotta (eds), *"In partibus Clius". Scritti in onore di Giovanni Pugliese Carratelli*, Naples, 2006, 113-35 (with bibliography)

J.-M. Carrié, 'Jean de Nikiou et sa *Chronique*: une écriture "égyptienne" de l'histoire?', in N. Grimal and M. Baud (eds), *Événement, récit, histoire officielle. L'écriture de l'histoire dans les monarchies antiques*, Paris, 2004, 155-71

F.J. Martinez, 'La literatura apocalíptica y las primeras reacciones cristianas a la conquista islámica en Oriente', in G. Anes y Álvarez de Castrillón (ed.), *Europa y el Islam*, Madrid, 2003, 143-222, pp. 167-72

W.E. Kaegi, *Heraclius. Emperor of Byzantium*, Cambridge MA, 2003, pp. 8, 59-60, 86, 91, 294

H. Pennec, *Des Jésuites au royaume du Prêtre Jean (Éthiopie). Stratégies, rencontres et tentatives d'implantation 1495-1633*, Lisbon, 2003, p. 297, n. 286

G. Lusini, 'L'Église axoumite et ses traditions historiographiques (IVe-VIIe siècle)', in B. Pouderon and Y.-M. Duval (eds), *L'historiographie de l'Église des premiers siècles*, Paris, 2001, 541-57, pp. 542, 546-49

W.E. Kaegi, 'Egypt on the eve of Muslim conquest', in *The Cambridge History of Egypt*, 2 vols, Cambridge, 1998, i (*Islamic Egypt 640-1517*, ed. C.F. Petry), 34-61

A. Ducellier, *Chrétiens d'Orient en Islam au moyen age. VIIe-XVe siècle*, Paris, 1996, pp. 27-49, 61-63 (*Cristiani d'Oriente e Islam nel Medioevo. Secoli VII-XV*, trans. S. Vacca, Turin, 2001, pp. 5-29, 45-47)

Hoyland, *Seeing Islam*, pp. 152-56 and *passim*

E. Guidoboni, *Catalogue of ancient earthquakes in the Mediterranean area up to the 10th century*, Rome, 1994, pp. 262-63, 274-75, 314-21, 337-38, 348-49, nos. 151, 155, 203, 220, 230

S.B. Chernetsov, 'The role of Catholicism in the history of Ethiopia of the first half of the 17th century', in C. Lepage (ed.), *Actes de la xe conférence internationale des études éthiopiennes (24-28 août 1988)*, i, Paris, 1994, 205-12

W.E. Kaegi, *Byzantium and the early Islamic conquests*, Cambridge MA, 1992, pp. 91, 213

B. Radtke, *Weltgeschichte und Weltbeschreibung im mittelalterlichen Islam*, Beirut, 1992, p. 133

S. Timm, *Das christlich-koptische Ägypten in arabischer Zeit*, 6 vols, Wiesbaden, 1984-92, iii (*G-L*), pp. 1132-40 ("Ibšādī")

A. Carile, 'Giovanni di Nikius, cronista bizantino-copto del VII secolo', *Felix Ravenna* (4th ser.) 121-22 (1981, pub. 1983), 103-55 (repr., with variants, in *Byzántion. Aphiérōma stòn Andréa N. Stráto*, 2 vols, Athens, 1986, ii, 353-98)

M. Rodinson, 'Éthiopien et sudarabique', *Annuaire de l'École pratique des hautes études – Histoire et philologie* 1974-75, 209-47, pp. 242-43 ('Le chapitre 51 de Jean de Nikiou')

S. Strelcyn, *Catalogue des manuscrits éthiopiens de l'Accademia Nazionale dei Lincei*, Rome, 1976

Rodinson, 'Notes sur le texte de Jean de Nikiou'

T. Orlandi, *Elementi di lingua e letteratura copta*, Milan, 1970

E. Cruz-Uribe, 'Notes on the Coptic Cambyses Romance', *Enchoria* 14 (1986) 51-56

L. Ricci, 'Letterature dell'Etiopia', in O. Botto (ed.), *Storia delle letterature d'Oriente*, 4 vols, Milan, 1969, i, 809-911, pp. 840-41

E. Cerulli, *La letteratura etiopica. Con un saggio sull'Oriente cristiano*, Milan, 1968³, p. 176

H. Ludin Jansen, *The Coptic story of Cambyses' invasion of Egypt. A critical analysis of its literary form and its historical purpose*, Oslo, 1950

P. Peeters, *Orient et Byzance. Le tréfonds oriental de l'hagiographie byzantine*, Brussells, 1950, p. 173, n. 2

I. Guidi, [*Breve*] *storia della letteratura etiopica*, Rome, 1932, p. 84

Graf, *GCAL* i, p. 471

W.E. Crum, review of Charles, *The Chronicle* (1916), *Journal of Egyptian Archaeology* 4 (1917) 207-9

W.E. Crum, 'Christian Egypt', *Journal of Egyptian Archaeology* 4 (1917) 47-57

C. Conti Rossini, 'Notice sur les manuscrits éthiopiens de la Collection d'Abbadie', *Journal asiatique* 11ᵉ sér., 6 (1915), 189-238 (repr. *Notice sur les manuscrits éthiopiens de la collection d'Abbadie*, Paris, 1914, pp. 203-252)

A.J. Butler, *The Arab conquest of Egypt and the last thirty years of the Roman dominion*, ed. P.M. Frazer, Oxford, 1902, 1978², p. liii and *passim*

G. Möller, 'Zu den Bruchstücken des koptischen Kambysesromans', mit einer Bemerkung von H. Schäfer, *Zeitschrift für ägyptische Sprache und Altertumskunde* 39 (1901) 113-16

C. Conti Rossini, 'Manoscritti ed opere abissine in Europa', *Rendiconti della Reale Accademia dei Lincei*, sc. mor., ser. v, 8 (1899) 606-37 (repr. *Note per la storia letteraria abissina*, Rome, 1900, pp. 48-79)

K. Krumbacher, *Geschichte der byzantinischen Litteratur von Justinian bis zum Ende des Oströmischen Reiches (527-1453)*, Munich, 1897² (repr. New York, 1958), 403-4

Th. Nöldeke, reviews of Zotenberg, *La chronique* (1879) and *Chronique* (1883), *Göttingische Gelehrte Anzeigen* 1881, 587-94; 1883, 1364-74

H. Zotenberg, 'Mémoire sur la chronique byzantine de Jean, évêque de Nikiou', *Journal asiatique* 7ᵉ sér., 10 (1877) 451-517; 12 (1878) 245-347; 13 (1879) 291-386 (repr. *La chronique de Jean, évêque de Nikiou*, Paris, 1879)

[H. Zotenberg], *Catalogue des manuscrits éthiopiens (gheez et amharique) de la Bibliothèque Nationale*, Paris, 1877

W. Wright, *Catalogue of the Ethiopic manuscripts in the British Museum acquired since the year 1847*, London, 1877

Gianfranco Fiaccadori 2008

Mēna of Nikiou

DATE OF BIRTH Unknown, approximately 660
PLACE OF BIRTH Unknown
DATE OF DEATH Unknown, approximately 720
PLACE OF DEATH Unknown

BIOGRAPHY

Nothing is known about Mēna's life other than that he was from the monastery of St Macarius, and that he became bishop of Nikiou after John of Nikiou was deposed.

MAIN SOURCES OF INFORMATION

Primary

Sāwīrūs ibn al-Muqaffaʿ, *History of the patriarchs of the Coptic Church of Alexandria*, ed. and trans. B. Evetts, 3 vols, Paris, 1904-14, iii (*Agathon to Michael I (796)*) (PO 5), p. 34

Secondary

D.N. Bell, *Mena of Nikiou. The life of Isaac of Alexandria, The martyrdom of Saint Macrobius*, Kalamazoo MI, 1988, pp. 26-30

WORKS ON CHRISTIAN-MUSLIM RELATIONS

Phbios mpinishti mpatriarchēs ethouab ouoh piarchēepiskopos nte tinishti mpolis Rakoti abba Isaak eafhistorin mmof ndje phē ethouab abba Mēna piociōtatos nepiskopos nte tipolis Pshati, 'The Life of the great and holy patriarch and archbishop of the great city of Rakoti (Alexandria), Abba Isaac, related by saint Abba Mēna, the most reverend archbishop of the city of Pshati', 'The Life of Abba Isaac'

DATE Around 700
ORIGINAL LANGUAGE Coptic

DESCRIPTION

The text relates the life of Isaac: his childhood and desire for the monastic life; his embrace of that life in Scetis; his service as secretary to the Coptic Patriarch John of Samannūd (680-90); and finally his own election to the patriarchate (in which he served from 690 to 692). The portion of the text that deals with Isaac as patriarch emphasizes his relationship with the Muslim 'king' or emir (i.e. the Umayyad governor) ʿAbd al-ʿAzīz. Various episodes in the text are not without allusions to the miraculous. For example, the text reports that the emir was initially ill-disposed towards the Christians, but his respect for the patriarch grew after he saw the patriarch at the altar, surrounded by a flame; the patriarch later explained that he was in close contact with God at the time. On another occasion, when the patriarch was attempting to reconcile two Christian Nubian kings, he was accused of conspiracy against the Muslims and arrested. When brought in before the emir, however, he was accompanied by St Peter and St Mark. The emir, seeing them, was in great fear – and released the patriarch. Another episode stresses the patriarch's quick wit. He was asked, as a test, to eat with the emir without making the sign of the cross over the food (as was his custom). The patriarch, however, cleverly made the sign of the cross without the emir noticing. When this was later pointed out to the emir, he acknowledged the intelligence of the patriarch. Ultimately, good relations between the two leaders were established: just before Isaac died, the emir asked him to build a church in Ḥilwān.

In spite of the miraculous elements in the account, on the whole *The life of Isaac* conveys an accurate impression of the atmosphere of Christian-Muslim relations in late 7th-century Egypt. The story occupies about 30 pages in the English translation; about a quarter of them deal with Muslims and Muslim-Christian relations.

There is no direct connection between this *Life of Isaac* and the Life of Isaac found in *The History of the Patriarchs*.

SIGNIFICANCE

The text is a witness to the relationship that existed between the Coptic patriarch and the Muslim governor in late 7th-century Egypt, and gives some idea of the general state of Christian-Muslim relations at the time.

MANUSCRIPTS

MS Vat – Copt. 62, fols 211-242 (19th c.)

EDITIONS AND TRANSLATIONS

D. Bell, *Mena of Nikiou. The life of Isaac of Alexandria* (English trans. based on the edition by Porcher)

E. Porcher, *Vie d'Isaac, patriarche d'Alexandrie de 686 à 689*, (PO 11), 301-90 (edition and French trans.)

E. Amélineau, *Histoire du patriarche copte Isaac*, Paris, 1890 (edition and French trans.)

STUDIES

H. Suermann, 'Copts and the Islam of the seventh century', in E. Grypeou, M.N. Swanson and D. Thomas (eds), *The encounter of Eastern Christianity with early Islam*, Leiden 2006, 95-109, pp. 106-7

Hoyland, *Seeing Islam*, pp. 149-52

Harald Suermann 2008

The Gospel of the twelve Apostles

Unknown author

DATE OF BIRTH Unknown; probably 1st half of or mid-7th c.
PLACE OF BIRTH Unknown
DATE OF DEATH Unknown; late 7th or early 8th c.
PLACE OF DEATH Unknown

BIOGRAPHY

Nothing is known about the life of the anonymous author. He was probably a monk living in or near Edessa. Apart from the very scanty hints to be gathered from the *Gospel of the twelve Apostles* itself, no further information is available about the author.

MAIN SOURCES OF INFORMATION

Primary —

Secondary —

WORKS ON CHRISTIAN-MUSLIM RELATIONS

Ēwangelīyōn d-treʿsar shlīḥē qaddīshē w-gelyānau(hy) d-kul-ḥad ḥad menhōn, 'The Gospel of the twelve holy Apostles and the revelation of each one of them'. Modern title: 'The Gospel of the twelve Apostles'

DATE Between 692 and 705
ORIGINAL LANGUAGE Syriac

DESCRIPTION

The Gospel of the twelve Apostles fills 22 pages in the manuscript and 21 pages in Harris's edition. The text is composed of four parts, beginning with the *Gospel* itself, which is a summary of the four canonical Gospels and the beginning of Acts, complemented by an apocalyptic prophecy (c. 10 pp.). The following three parts constitute the apocalypses of Shemʿōn Kēpā (Simon Peter, 3 pp.), Yaʿqōb (James, 2 pp.) and Yōḥannān (John, 7 pp.).

The first part of the text is a recapitulation of the Gospel story up to Jesus' appearance with the Apostles after his crucifixion, with an emphasis on the appointment of the Apostles and the spiritual power this conferred. The Apostles' question about the time of redemption and Jesus' rejection (Acts 1:6-7) appears in a somewhat extended form, preceded by a lengthy prayer by the Apostles and supplemented by their appointment to speak 'of those things that are and those that are to come' through the power of the Holy Spirit. After Jesus' ascension the Apostles pray for this revelation. The texts that follow record their revelations, which are said to be inspired by the Spirit.

Each of the three apocalypses deals with a specific theme. Peter's is concerned with the church and the true faith. The majority of Christians are viewed as living in sin and unbelief; there is only a small group of true believers who do not 'divide our Lord'. It is predicted that this state of affairs will get worse until Monophysite orthodoxy vanishes completely, leaving behind a doomed church with no prospect of salvation. At the end, however, there will be a great reversion to the true faith and the consequent redemption of the believers.

The apocalypse of James (James son of Zebedee is conflated with James the brother of the Lord) deals with Jerusalem, the destruction of the Temple, the reign of Constantine, and the True Cross. Its theme is the victory of Christianity and the rejection of Jewish claims to Jerusalem, the central locus of salvation history. The concluding passage of this apocalypse contains a prophecy about 'a man from his (i.e. Constantine's) seed' who will establish a world empire of peace and godliness and in whose time redemption awaits the true believers – a prediction which resembles that of the final sentence of the apocalypse of Peter.

The subject matter of the apocalypse of John (John son of Zebedee is identified as John the Evangelist and author of the Book of Revelation) is Islamic rule. Here, the Danielic scheme of the four empires is adapted to the altered political situation as the author conceives it: their order of appearance is given as Rome, Persia, Media and Arabia. In the author's view the Roman empire cannot be the fourth and last empire, as in the traditional exegesis which only shortly before was still being advocated by an apocalyptist such as Pseudo-Methodius (q.v.). After the reign of Constantine, who had ruled the world by the sign of the Holy Cross, later Roman rulers were sinful, evil and godless. God therefore transferred power to Persia, then Media, and then sent 'a mighty wind, the southern one', i.e. the Arabs, to 'subdue Persia and devastate Rome'. They are described as 'a people of deformed aspect and their appearance and manners like those of women'. They are given into the hand of a warrior whom they call a prophet. Among rational contemporaries, he is predicted to cause merely derision and head-shaking.

God has appointed these 'people of the South' to subdue the whole world. According to the promise God gave to Abraham concerning his son Ishmael (Genesis 17:20), twelve kings will arise from them. The Arabs will take many captives and plunder the whole world and impose heavy tribute on the peoples under their rule, who suffer great distress. Among the oppressed there are many who join the oppressors and take advantage of their rule. These converts are condemned as 'hypocrites and men who know not God, and regard not men, except prodigals, fornicators and men wicked and revengeful'.

The oppression will increase with each new king until, after one and a half year-weeks, 'the earth shall be moved concerning them (i.e. the Arabs), and God shall require the sins of men from their hands. And the south wind shall subside and God shall bring to naught their covenant with them'. God will split them into two parties who will wage war against each other, 'and much blood shall be shed at the fountain of waters' – probably an allusion to the battle at Mecca in 692 between the troops of ʿAbd al-Malik and his rival Ibn al-Zubayr. Then a Byzantine emperor, 'the man from the North' (obviously the same king who is predicted in the apocalypse of James) will arise, assemble all the peoples of the world and defeat the Muslims. They will suffer great distress 'and the Lord shall cause the wind of the South to return to his place… and without war they will be laid waste, and unto all generations of the world there shall not be among them any who holds a weapon and stands up in battle'.

SIGNIFICANCE

The Gospel of the twelve Apostles presents a somewhat simplified and updated version of the eschatological expectations voiced by earlier Syriac apocalyptic writings of the same period (see the entries on Pseudo-Methodius, the *Edessene Apocalypse* and John bar Penkāyē). It is a witness, therefore, to the persistence of the strategy Syrian Christians deployed to cope with Muslim rule in the second half of the 7th century. However, it also indicates an abatement of the apocalyptic tension when that rule had become firmly established and could no longer be seen as a temporary episode. In the *Gospel*, emphasis has shifted to dissociation from non-Monophysite Christians and Judaism, and to admonition of the author's own community to abide by the true faith and not to convert to Islam.

Nothing is known about the impact of the work on later Syriac or other Christian literature(s). Considering the fact that it survives in a single extant manuscript, this impact cannot have been very great.

MANUSCRIPTS

For a description of the only extant manuscript (probably mid-8th c.), see Harris, *The Gospel of the twelve Apostles*, pp. 7-11 and Drijvers, 'The Gospel', pp. 189-91.

EDITIONS AND TRANSLATIONS

H. Suermann, *Die geschichtstheologische Reaktion auf die einfallenden Muslime in der edessenischen Apokalyptik des 7. Jahrhunderts*, Frankfurt, 1985, pp. 98-109 (text of the Apocalypse of John after R.J. Harris with trans.)

R.J. Harris, *The Gospel of the twelve Apostles together with the apocalypses of each one of them, edited from the Syriac Ms. with a translation and introduction*, Cambridge, 1900 (edition and trans.; repr. Piscataway, 2003)

STUDIES

Hoyland: *Seeing Islam*, pp. 267-70

H.J.W. Drijvers, 'Christians, Jews and Muslims in northern Mesopotamia in early Islamic times. The Gospel of the twelve Apostles and related texts', in P. Canivet and J.-P. Rey-Coquais (eds), *La Syrie de Byzance à l'Islam. VIIe-VIIIe siècles*, Damascus, 1992, 67-74 (repr. in H.J.W. Drijvers, *History and religion in late antique Syria*, Aldershot, 1994)

H.J.W. Drijvers, 'The Gospel of the twelve Apostles: A Syriac apocalypse from the early Islamic period', in A. Cameron and L.I. Conrad (eds), *The Byzantine and early Islamic Near East, I. Problems in the literary source material*, Princeton NJ, 1992, 189-213 (repr. in H.J.W. Drijvers, *History and religion in late antique Syria*, Aldershot, 1994)

Suermann, *Geschichtstheologische Reaktion*, pp. 175-91

Harris, *Gospel of the twelve Apostles*, pp. 7-24

Lutz Greisiger 2007

Jacob of Edessa

DATE OF BIRTH Around 640
PLACE OF BIRTH ʿAyndēbā, in the land of Gumah, near Antioch
DATE OF DEATH 708
PLACE OF DEATH Monastery of Tell ʿAdē

BIOGRAPHY

Jacob of Edessa was a Syrian Orthodox monk and bishop of Edessa. He studied ecclesiastical sciences (Bible, Fathers of the Church) in his native region and became a monk in the monastery of Qenneshrin, a centre of learning on the west bank of the Euphrates, where he studied Greek. He perfected his knowledge of Greek in Alexandria, where he stayed for some time before settling in Edessa. He was appointed bishop of the city in 684, but resigned after four years in protest against the liberal interpretation of ecclesiastical canons by the patriarch and his fellow bishops. For a short period, he retired to the monastery of St Jacob of Qayshum, where he composed two treatises on the observance of ecclesiastical law. At the invitation of monks in the monastery of Eusebona, he agreed to teach Greek and biblical exegesis there, but after 11 years he was forced to leave on account of the anti-Greek mentality of some of the brothers. Subsequently, he stayed for nine years in the monastery of Tell ʿAdē, where he revised the Syriac text of the Old Testament. In 708, he was reinstated as bishop of Edessa, but died four months later in the monastery of Tell ʿAdē.

Jacob of Edessa is especially known for his grammatical and exegetical work as well as his legislative activity. In addition, he continued the ecclesiastical history of Eusebius of Caesarea, recording events up to his own time.

MAIN SOURCES OF INFORMATION

Primary

Jacob of Edessa's *Chronicle* (see below)

Anonymous *Vita*, preserved in the Chronicle of Michael the Syrian: *Chronique de Michel le Syrien*, ed. and trans. J.-B. Chabot, 4 vols, Paris, 1899-1910 (repr. Brussels, 1963), iv, pp. 445-46; ii, pp. 471-72

Gregory Barhebraeus, *Ecclesiastical Chronicle*: J. Abbeloos and Th. Lamy, *Gregorii Barhebraei Chronicon ecclesiasticum*, 3 vols, Paris, 1872-77, i, pp. 289-94
Brief references are also found in:
Chronicle of Zuqnīn: J.-B. Chabot, *Incerti auctoris Chronicon Pseudo-Dionysianum vulgo dictum*, 2 vols, Paris, 1933 (*CSCO* 91, 104), ii, pp. 155-56
Chronicon ad annum 819, ed. A. Barsaum, in J.B. Chabot, *Anonymi auctoris Chronicon ad annum Christi 1234 pertinens*, 2 vols, Paris, 1916-20 (*CSCO* 81-82), i, p. 14
Chronicon anonymum ad A.D. 846: E.W. Brooks, *Chronica minora*, Paris, 1904 (*CSCO* 3) Paris, 1904, p. 233
Chronicle of Elias of Nisibis: E.W. Brooks, *Eliae Metropolitae opus chronologicum*, 2 vols, Paris, 1909-10 (*CSCO* 62-63), i, p. 158

Secondary
R.B. ter Haar Romeny (ed.), *Jacob of Edessa and the Syriac culture of his day*, Leiden 2008
D. Kruisheer and L. Van Rompay, 'A bibliographical clavis to the works of Jacob of Edessa', *Hugoye* 1 (1998)
Hoyland, *Seeing Islam*, pp. 160-67
O. Schrier, 'Chronological problems concerning the lives of Severus bar Mašqā, Athanasius of Balad, Julianus Romāyā, Yoḥannān Sābā, George of the Arabs and Jacob of Edessa', *OC* 75 (1991) 62-90
H. Drijvers, art. 'Jakob von Edessa', in *Theologische Realenzyklopädie* 16, Berlin, 1987
Baumstark, *GSL*, pp. 248-56

WORKS ON CHRISTIAN-MUSLIM RELATIONS

Letters

DATE Unknown
ORIGINAL LANGUAGE Syriac

DESCRIPTION
During his life, Jacob entertained a lively correspondence with other ecclesiastics on various subjects (Church Law, the Bible, etc). In some letters, he touches on issues related to the Muslim presence among the faithful of his community. In this respect, his correspondence, both juridical and non-juridical, with the priest Addai and John the Stylite of Litarbā has some importance.

In the present survey, Jacob's answers to his correspondents are distinguished from ecclesiastical canons in the strict sense of the word (see below), though in the later tradition (up to the 13th century),

Syrian Orthodox canonists reworked these *responsa* into canons and inserted them as such into the juridical compilations, such as Barhebraeus' *Nomocanon* (these are discussed in the present section rather than in the survey of canons below). The difference between *responsa* and canons is that the first indicate the context of the problems, whereas the latter are abstract injunctions.

SIGNIFICANCE

Though not exclusively dealing with Islam, Jacob's correspondence with Addai and John the Stylite of Litarbā reflects some of the problems with which the faithful and the Church leadership were confronted in their contacts with the Islamic world, such as official relations with Muslim governors, desecration of altars by Muslims, giving blessings or instruction to Muslims, the problem of apostasy and repentance and the issue of rebaptism, military service and the direction of prayer.

In his non-juridical letters to John the Stylite, Jacob of Edessa briefly presents the Muslim view of Christ and discusses the Muslim direction of prayer.

MANUSCRIPTS

1– Correspondence with Addai, first set of Questions and Answers; most important manuscripts:

MS Mardin, Syr. Orth. – 310, fols 178r-189v (8th c.), cf. Vööbus, *Synodicon*)
MS Harvard, Houghton Library – Syr. 93, fols 1-16v (8th-9th c.)
MS BNF – Syr. 62, fols 273r-284v (9th c.)
MS BL – Add. 14,631, fols 49r-52v (9th-10th c.)
MS BL – Add. 17,215, fols 23r-25v (10th-11th c.)
MS Damascus, Syrian Orthodox Patriarchate – 8/11 (1204, cf. Vööbus, *Synodicon*)
MS Vat – Borg. Syr. 133, fols 69r-73v (1224)
MS Cambridge – 2023, fols 259r-275v (13th c.)
MS Charfeh, Charfeh monastery – 234, fols 1r-20r (18th c.)
MS Birmingham, Mingana – Syr. 8, fols 215r-30r (1911)

2– Correspondence with Addai, second set of Questions and Answers; most important manuscripts:

MS Mardin, Syr. Orth. – 310, fols 195v-199r
MS Harvard, Houghton Library – Syr. 93, fols 25r-33v
MS Cambridge – 2023, fols 277v-281r
MS Birmingham, Mingana – Syr. 8, fols 236r-239v

For additional manuscripts, see A. Vööbus, *Syrische Kanonessammlungen. Ein Beitrag zur Quellenkunde*, 2 vols, Louvain, 1970 (*CSCO* 307, 317), i (b), pp. 273-84

3– Juridical correspondence with John the Stylite of Litarbā – two sets of Questions and Answers; most important manuscripts of set 1 (17 *responsa*):

MS Harvard, Houghton Library – Syr. 93, fols 37a-44b
MS Damascus, Syrian Orthodox Patriarchate – 8/11, fols 98a-102a
MS Cambridge – 2023, fols 285a-291a

For other manuscripts, see Vööbus, *Syrische Kanonessammlungen*, i (b) pp. 290-293

4– Juridical correspondence with John the Stylite of Litarbā – two sets of Questions and Answers; most important manuscript of set 2 (27 *responsa*):

MS Damascus, Syrian Orthodox Patriarchate – 8/11, fols 93r-98r
Ms BL Add. 14,493 basically offers a selection from the *responsa* to Addai and John

5– Non-juridical letters to John the Stylite; from the corpus of 16 letters sent to John, letters 5 and 13 are important:

MS BL – Add. 12,172, fols 87b-91r, 124r

EDITIONS AND TRANSLATIONS

Correspondence with Addai:

A. Vööbus, *The Synodicon in the West Syrian tradition*, 2 parts in 4 vols, Louvain, 1975 (*CSCO* 367-68, 375-76), i, pp. 258-69 (edition), ii, pp. 235-44 (trans.)

F. Nau, *Les canons et les résolutions canoniques de Rabboula, Cyriaque d'Amid, Jacques d'Edesse, Georges des Arabes, Cyriaque d'Antioche, Jean III, Théodose d'Antioche et des Pères*, Paris, 1906, pp. 38-66 (French trans.)

C. Kayser, *Die Canones Jacob's von Edessa übersetzt und erläutert* Leipzig, 1886, pp. 11-33 (German trans.)

T.J. Lamy, *Dissertatio de Syrorum fide et disciplina in re eucharistica* Louvain, 1859, pp. 98-171 (edition and Latin trans.)

P. de Lagarde, *Reliquiae iuris ecclesiastici antiquissimi syriace* Leipzig, 1856, pp. 117-44 (edition)

Juridical correspondence with John the Stylite of Litarbā:

Vööbus, *The Synodicon in the West Syrian tradition*, i, pp. 233-54 (edition), ii, pp. 215-33 (trans.)

Non-juridical correspondence with John the Stylite of Litarbā:

Letter 5:

F. Nau, 'Lettre de Jacques d'Edesse sur la généalogie de la Sainte Vierge', *Revue de l'Orient Chrétien* 6 (1901) 512-31 (partial trans.)

Letter 13:

Hoyland, *Seeing Islam*, pp. 565-66 (partial trans.)

P. Crone and M. Cook, *Hagarism. The making of the Islamic world*, Cambridge, 1977, p. 173 (partial trans.)

General:

K. Rignell, *A letter from Jacob of Edessa to John the Stylite of Litarb concerning ecclesiastical canons*, Lund, 1979 (edition and trans. of a selection of *responsa* to Addai and John, found in MS BL Add. 14,493)

STUDIES

H. Teule, 'Jacob of Edessa in the West Syrian canonical tradition', in Ter Haar Romeny (ed.), *Jacob of Edessa and the Syriac culture of his day*, 83-100

R. Hoyland, 'Jacob of Edessa on Islam', in G.J. Reinink and A.C. Klugkist, *After Bardaisan. Studies on continuity and change in Syriac Christianity*, Louvain, 1999, 149-60

Hoyland, *Seeing Islam*, pp. 160-67, 565-67, 601-10

W. Selb, *Orientalisches Kirchenrecht*, 2 vols, Vienna, 1981-89, ii (*Die Geschichte des Kirchenrechts der Westsyrer (von den Anfängen bis zur Mongolenzeit)*, pp. 117, 124-27

M. Cook, *Early Muslim dogma. A source-critical study*, Cambridge, 1981, ch. 15, 'An Epistle of Jacob of Edessa', pp. 145-52

Crone and Cook, *Hagarism*, pp. 11-12, 173

Vööbus, *Syrische Kanonessammlungen*, i (a), pp. 202-16; i (b), pp. 273-86

Canons

DATE Unknown

ORIGINAL LANGUAGE Syriac

DESCRIPTION

Jacob himself issued a set of 30 canons, the majority of which are injunctions for monks and priests and relevant only for members of the Syrian Orthodox Church. A second set of 28 canons, preserved in MS Mardin, Syr. Orth. – 309, is not relevant for this bibliography.

SIGNIFICANCE

Some canons possibly refer to a Muslim context, as can be inferred, for example, from their emphasis on monogamy and the interdiction against lodging appeals with external judges. Muslims are not explicitly mentioned.

MANUSCRIPTS

MS Mardin, Syr. Orth. – 310, fols 191r-195v (8th c.)
MS Harvard, Houghton Library – Syr. 93, fols 18r-25r (8th-9th c.)
MS Damascus, Syrian Orthodox Patriarchate – 8/11, fols 108r-109r (1204)
MS Cambridge – 2023, fols 275v-277v (13th c.)
MS Charfeh, Charfeh Monastery – 73, fols 256r-261v (1911)
MS Damascus, Syrian Orthodox Patriarchate – 8/1, fols 120r-121r (1941)
MS Birmingham, Mingana – Syr. 8, fols 231r-236r (1911)
MS Mardin, Syr. Orth. – 322, fols 184r-190r (recent)
MS Mardin, Syr. Orth. – 327, fols 159v-166r (recent)
MS Mardin, Syr. Orth. – 337, fols 117v-124r (recent)

EDITIONS AND TRANSLATIONS

Vööbus, *The Synodicon in the West Syrian tradition*, i, pp. 269-72 (edition), ii, pp. 245-47 (trans.)

STUDIES

See above

Maktbānut zabnē, 'Chronicle'

DATE 692 (with extension of the chronicle covering the years 692-710)
ORIGINAL LANGUAGE Syriac

DESCRIPTION

This chronicle purports to be a reworking and continuation of Eusebius of Caesarea's *Historia ecclesiastica*. The continuation covers the period from the 21st year of the reign of Constantine until the year 692, with an extension by an anonymous pupil up to the year 710.

SIGNIFICANCE

The chronicle contains some brief notes on Muḥammad, the year of the beginning of the 'Kingdom of the Arabs', and Muslim raids in Palestine, as well as a list of Muslim rulers from Muḥammad to the Umayyad Caliph Yazīd I.

MANUSCRIPTS

MS BL Add. 14,685, fols 1r-23v (10th-11th c.)

EDITIONS AND TRANSLATIONS

A. Palmer, *The seventh century in the West-Syrian chronicles*, Liverpool, 1993, pp. 36-42 (trans.)

E.W. Brooks, *Chronica minora III,* 2 vols, Paris, 1905 (*CSCO* 5-6), i, pp. 261-327 (edition), ii, pp. 199-255 (Latin trans.)

E.W. Brooks, 'The chronological canon of James of Edessa', *ZDMG* 53 (1899) 261-327, 54 (1900) 100-2

STUDIES

H. Teule, 'Syriac historiography' in Centre d'Etudes et de Recherches Orientales (edition), *Nos sources. Arts et littérature syriaque,* Antélias, 2005, pp. 330-31

D. Weltecke, *Die «Beschreibung der Zeiten» von Mōr Michael dem Grossen (1126-1199). Eine Studie zu ihrem historischen und historiographiegeschichtlichen Kontext*, Louvain, 2003 (*CSCO* 594), pp. 183-94

Hoyland, *Seeing Islam*, p. 165

S. Brock, 'Syriac sources for seventh-century history', *Byzantine and Modern Greek Studies* 2 (1976) 17-36, p. 19 (repr. in S.P. Brock, *Syriac perspectives on late antiquity,* London, 1984)

S. Brock, 'Syriac historical writing. A survey of the main sources', *Journal of the Iraqi Academy, Syr. Corp.* 5 (1979-80) 297-326 (repr. in S. Brock, *Studies in Syriac Christianity*, Aldershot, 1992)

Madrāshā (against the Armenians)

DATE Unknown

ORIGINAL LANGUAGE Syriac

DESCRIPTION

This text consists of a series of anti-Armenian remarks addressed to an anonymous pupil.

SIGNIFICANCE

It mentions the circumcision of Muslims and their practice of performing three genuflections (*burkē*) facing southwards during the ritual 'of the sacrifice' (or during prayer?)

MANUSCRIPTS

MS Florence, Biblioteca Medicea Laurenziana – Syr. 62, p. 108 (1360) MS BNF – Syr. 111, fols 192r-193v (16th c.)

EDITIONS AND TRANSLATIONS

Kayser, *Canones*, pp. 3-4 (edition), 34-35 (trans.)

Lamy, *Dissertatio de Syrorum fide*, pp. 209-10 (edition and Latin trans.)

S.E. Assemani, *Bibliothecae mediceae Laurentianae et Palatinae codicum mms orientalium catalogus*, Florence, 1742, pp. XLIX-L (edition and Latin trans.)

STUDIES

Kayser, *Canones*, p. 4

Herman G. Teule 2007

George the Archdeacon

Jirja the Archdeacon

DATE OF BIRTH Mid-7th c.
PLACE OF BIRTH Egypt
DATE OF DEATH Early 8th c.
PLACE OF DEATH Egypt (possibly at the monastery of St Macarius)

BIOGRAPHY

A passing reference and two notices in *The History of the patriarchs of Alexandria* (Evetts, PO 5, pp. 20, 90-91; PO 10, p. 360) allow us to identify the author of one of its sources as Jirja, a monk (probably of the monastery of St Macarius in the Wādī al-Naṭrūn) and archdeacon who was the spiritual son of John III (the 40th Coptic patriarch, 680-89), served as secretary to Simon (42nd patriarch, 692-700), and was spiritual father to a relative who became Patriarch Cosmas I (44th patriarch, 729-30). While at the monastery of St Macarius, he wrote a collection of Lives of the patriarchs, beginning in the 5th century and continuing up to about the year 715, during the patriarchate of Alexander II (43rd patriarch, 704-729).

MAIN SOURCES OF INFORMATION

Primary

Our sole source of knowledge about Jirja the Archdeacon is the historical compilation *Siyar al-bīʿa al-muqaddasa*, 'Lives of the holy Church' or *The History of the patriarchs of Alexandria*. For the published editions of the Arabic appropriation of Jirja's work, written originally in Coptic, see below. In addition, two other notices concerning Jirja and his work are found elsewhere in *The History of the patriarchs*, as follows:

A notice by 'John the Deacon' (q.v.) at the beginning of Life 46, in C.F. Seybold, *Severus ibn al-Muqaffaʿ. Alexandrinische Patriarchengeschichte von. S. Marcus bis Michael I (61-767), nach der ältesten 1266 geschriebenen Hamburger Handschrift im arabischen Urtext herausgegeben*, Hamburg, 1912, pp. 152-53; or B.T.A. Evetts, *History of the patriarchs of the Coptic Church of Alexandria*, III. *Agathon to Michael I (766)*, PO 5 (1909), pp. 90-91; or C.F. Seybold, *Severus Ben al-Muqaffaʿ. Historia patriarcharum Alexandrinorum*, Beirut, 1904 (*CSCO* 52), p. 161.

A notice by 'John the Writer' (q.v.) at the beginning of Life 47, in B.T.A. Evetts, *History of the patriarchs of the Coptic Church of Alexandria*, IV. *Mennas I to Joseph (849)*, PO 10 (1914), pp. 359-60; or Seybold, *Severus Ben al-Muqaffaʿ. Historia patriarcharum Alexandrinorum*, p. 218.

Secondary

J. den Heijer, 'Réflexions sur la composition de *L'histoire des patriarches d'Alexandrie*. Les auteurs des sources coptes', in W. Godlewski (ed.), *Coptic studies*, Warsaw, 1990, 107-13, p. 110

J. den Heijer, *Mawhūb ibn Manṣūr ibn Mufarriğ et l'historiographie copto-arabe. Étude sur la composition de l'*Histoire des patriarches d'Alexandrie, Louvain, 1989 (*CSCO* 513), pp. 7-8, 118-24, 142-45

D.W. Johnson, 'Further remarks on the Arabic history of the patriarchs of Alexandria', *OC* 61 (1977) 103-116, pp. 110-14

WORKS ON CHRISTIAN-MUSLIM RELATIONS

Title unknown, source of *The History of the patriarchs of Alexandria*

DATE About 715 or shortly thereafter
ORIGINAL LANGUAGE Coptic

DESCRIPTION

The Coptic collection of Lives of the patriarchs written by Jirja the Archdeacon was among the sources used in the late 11th century by the Alexandrian deacon Mawhūb ibn Manṣūr ibn Mufarrij and his collaborators as part of their project of compiling an Arabic-language history of the Coptic Orthodox patriarchs (see den Heijer, *Mawhūb*); the copy of Jirja's work was found at the monastery of the Virgin at Nahyā, in Giza. No fragment of the original Coptic has been preserved, so we only know Jirja's work as it was translated and edited. Even its precise extent is not known, but it does appear to be the source for nearly all the text of *The History of the patriarchs of Alexandria* for the 27th to the 42nd patriarchs (477-700), with the exception of an excerpt from the *Book of the consecration of the sanctuary of Benjamin* in Life 38 (see den Heijer, *Mawhūb*, pp. 121-24, 142-45).

The part of *The History of the patriarchs* for which the work of Jirja the Archdeacon is the principle source is a major contributor to our knowledge of the Arab conquest of Egypt, Egyptian Christian reactions to that conquest, and the development of patterns of relationships between Muslim and Christian authorities during the first two generations of Arab rule. Jirja honestly chronicles hardships faced by the Christian community (e.g. the imposition of the *jizya* and attempts to extort money from the patriarch), as well as the increasing role of the Muslim governor in the affairs of the church, including the selection of a patriarch. At the same time, Jirja presents a picture of the ideal relationship between governor and patriarch, best exemplified in the well-known account of the encounter between the Muslim conqueror ʿAmr ibn al-ʿĀṣ and Benjamin, the 38th patriarch (623-62), in which the patriarch preached to and prayed for the governor, and the governor admired the patriarch and confirmed his authority within the Christian community (Evetts, PO 1, pp. 495-97).

SIGNIFICANCE

The collection of Lives written by Jirja (George) the Archdeacon and preserved in edited translation in *The History of the patriarchs* is a critically important and irreplaceable source for our knowledge of Christian-Muslim relations in Egypt in the 60 years or so following the Arab conquest.

MANUSCRIPTS

See den Heijer, *Mawhūb*, pp. 18-27. For the contribution of Jirja, Lives 27-42, the following two MSS might be mentioned. These represent the two different recensions of the work and are the basis for the published editions:

MS Hamburg, Staats- und Universitätsbibliothek Carl von Ossietzky – ar. 304 (1260) ('primitive' recension, published by Seybold, 1912)

MS BNF – ar. 301 (15th c.) ('Vulgate' recension; base manuscript for the editions of Seybold, 1904, and Evetts)

EDITIONS AND TRANSLATIONS

The editions of *The History of the patriarchs of Alexandria*, Lives 27-42 (for which Jirja the Archdeacon is the principal source) are:

Seybold, *Severus ibn al-Muqaffaʿ. Alexandrinische Patriarchengeschichte von. S. Marcus bis Michael I (61-767)* (edition of the 'primitive' recension according to the Hamburg manuscript)

Evetts, *History of the patriarchs of the Coptic church of Alexandria*, II. *Peter I – Benjamin I (661)*, PO 1 (1905), pp. 445-518; III. *Agathon to Michael I (766)*, PO 5 (1909), pp. 1-58 (edition of the 'Vulgate' recension with trans.)

Seybold, *Severus Ben al-Muqaffaʿ. Historia patriarcharum Alexandrinorum*, pp. 84-142 (edition of the 'Vulgate' recension)

STUDIES

Jirja's contribution to *The history of the patriarchs of Alexandria* is discussed in studies such as:

Den Heijer, 'Réflexions sur la composition de l'*Histoire des Patriarches d'Alexandrie*', p. 110

Den Heijer, *Mawhūb ibn Manṣūr ibn Mufarriğ et l'historiographie copto-arabe*, pp. 7-8, 118-24, 142-45

Johnson, 'Further remarks on the Arabic history of the patriarchs of Alexandria', pp. 110-14

The section of *The History of the patriarchs of Alexandria* for which Jirja's history is the primary source is regularly used by those who study the first Islamic century in Egypt, particularly with regard to Christian-Muslim relations. Examples (apart from general histories of the Coptic Orthodox Church) include:

M.N. Swanson, *The Coptic papacy in Islamic Egypt*, Cairo, forthcoming, ch. 1

A. Papaconstantinou, 'Historiography, hagiography, and the making of the Coptic "Church of the Martyrs" in early Islamic Egypt', *DOP* 60 (2006) 65-86, pp. 69-73

H. Suermann, 'Copts and the Islam of the seventh century', in E. Grypeou, M.N. Swanson and D. Thomas (eds), *The encounter of eastern Christianity with early Islam*, Leiden, 2006, 95-109, pp. 98-100

S.J. Davis, *The early Coptic papacy. The Egyptian church and its leadership in late antiquity*, Cairo, 2004, ch. 4

M.S.A. Mikhail, *Egypt from late antiquity to early Islam. Copts, Melkites, and Muslims shaping a new society*, Los Angeles CA, 2004 (Diss. UCLA)

F.R. Trombley, 'Sawīrus ibn al-Muqaffaʿ and the Christians of Umayyad Egypt. War and society in documentary context', in P.M. Sijpesteijn and L. Sundelin (eds), *Papyrology and the history of early Islamic Egypt*, Leiden, 2004, 199-226

J. den Heijer, 'La conquête arabe vue par les historiens coptes', in C. Décobert (ed.), *Valeur et distance. Identités et sociétés en Égypte*, Paris, 2000, pp. 227-45

Hoyland, *Seeing Islam*, pp. 132-35, 149-52, 446-48, 574-90

M. Martin, 'Une lecture de l'*Histoire des patriarches d'Alexandrie*', *Proche-Orient Chrétien* 35 (1985) 15-36, pp. 16-18

C.D.G. Müller, 'Stellung und Haltung der koptischen Patriarchen des 7. Jahrhunderts gegenüber islamischer Obrigkeit und Islam', in T. Orlandi and F. Wisse (eds), *Acts of the Second International Congress of Coptic Study*, Rome, 1985, 203-13

A.J. Butler, *The Arab conquest of Egypt and the last thirty years of the Roman dominion*, Oxford, 1902 (rev. edition, ed. P.M. Fraser, Oxford, 1978)

Mark N. Swanson 2008

The Apocalypse of Pseudo-Ezra

Unknown author

DATE OF BIRTH Unknown
PLACE OF BIRTH Unknown
DATE OF DEATH Unknown
PLACE OF DEATH Unknown

BIOGRAPHY —

MAIN SOURCES OF INFORMATION

Primary —

Secondary —

WORKS ON CHRISTIAN-MUSLIM RELATIONS

Shēltā d-shēl ʿĀzrā sāprā kad hwā b-madbrā w-talmideh ʿameh da-shmeh Qarpus, 'The Question of Ezra the Scribe, which he asked when he was in the desert with his disciple Carpus', *Ḥezwā da-ḥzā ʿĀzrā sāprā ʿal malkutā d-Ishmaʿlāyē*, 'The Vision of Ezra the Scribe which he saw concerning the kingdom of the Ishmaelites'. Modern title: 'The Apocalypse of Pseudo-Ezra'

DATE Unknown, perhaps early 8th c.
ORIGINAL LANGUAGE Syriac

DESCRIPTION
This brief East-Syrian text (seven pages in the manuscripts and editions) is anonymous and does not give any clear information about its time of composition. It contains the Christian apocryphal revelations to Ezra 'the scribe' in answer to his question to an angel about 'the end of time concerning the Ishmaelites'. Relying heavily upon the biblical Book of Daniel, the Gospels, and Revelation, it deals in

very obscure terms with the events of the first centuries of Islam, using animals to represent the political powers. Organized as a series of visions, in the first part it describes a desert snake coming from the east and oppressing God's people; it has 12 horns on its head and eight small cruel horns on its tail. Then an eagle comes from the south and a viper from the east. Four kings imprisoned on the banks of the Euphrates are unchained, and they sting the viper, which departs. Then begins a war between a lion cub and a bull, chief of the ravens whose country is the east.

The second part begins with a prophecy about an unsuccessful war against Constantinople and the destruction of Damascus for its revolt. Apocalyptic events are then announced: a leopard will come with numerous people from the north to help the lion cub. They will go down to Persia where the lion cub will defeat the ravens and break the bull's three horns. He will then subject the Land of the Promise to tribute. Famine, plague and earthquakes will follow. The lion cub will erect walls around the land of Phoenicia, destroy Damascus and go up to Jerusalem with great ceremony before returning to his own country. After three and a half weeks, a warrior will come with numerous people from the south and will impose peace for three years and seven months. The four winds of heaven will be set in motion, and people will rise up against one another until the earth is covered with spilled blood.

At the end, the angel to whom Ezra asked his question comes back to console him and describes how the Ishmaelites will be destroyed in the last days.

The date of this apocalypse is much disputed. Bousset (pp. 47-49) interprets the animals as the Islamic dynasties: the snake representing the Umayyads, the eagle the ʿAbbasids, the viper the Fāṭimids and the four kings the Turks. Hoyland (p. 278) interprets the lion cub as Heraclius and the bull as Khusrau II, and thinks that the text alludes to the wars between the Fāṭimids and Seljuks or Mamlūks in the 12th-13th centuries, while Chabot (p. 345) opts for the 8th century. The allusion to attacks on Constantinople might suggest a date after one of the unsuccessful sieges of 668-69, or, more likely, 715-17.

SIGNIFICANCE

This text seeks to give Syriac-speaking Christians answers about the end of the Muslim empire, though very obscurely, or at least to promise the end of Muslim rule at the *eschaton*. It belongs to the genre of the historical apocalypses that were written in Syriac at the very beginning of the Muslim era, and it was transmitted together with other apocryphal texts, including in two MSS the *Testimonies about our Lord's dispensation*. Before the development of a controversialist literature in which arguments in defense of Christian dogma were provided against Muslim objections, these texts sought to console Christians who had become the subjects of a new empire and religion, and promised the end of that kingdom in the not too distant future.

MANUSCRIPTS

MS BL – Add. 25,875, fols 54r-57v (1709-10)
MS Vat – Syr. 164, fols 69v-73v (1702)
MS Berlin, Staatsbibliothek – Sachau 131, fols 142r-146r (1862)
MS BNF – Syr. 326, fols 1v-5v (19th c.?)

EDITIONS AND TRANSLATIONS

F. Baethgen, 'Beschreibung der syrischen Handschrift Sachau 131 auf der Königlichen Bibliothek zu Berlin', *Zeitschrift für die Alttestamentliche Wissenschaft* 6 (1886) 200-10 (edition and trans.)

J.-B. Chabot, 'L'apocalypse d'Esdras touchant le royaume des Arabes', *Revue sémitique* 2 (1894) 242-50 (edition of MS BNF – Syr. 326, collated with edition of Baethgen), 333-46 (trans. and commentary)

STUDIES

W. Bousset, *Der Antichrist in der Überlieferung des Judentums, des Neuen Testaments u. der alten Kirche*, Göttingen, 1895, pp. 47-49 (trans. *The Antichrist legend. A chapter in Christian and Jewish folklore*, Atlanta GA, 1999)

Hoyland, *Seeing Islam*, pp. 276-78

J.-C. Haelewyck, *Clavis apocryphorum veteris testamenti*, Turnhout, 1998, p. 186

L.E. Iselin, 'Apocalyptische Studien (Die Apocalypse des Esra in syrischer Sprache von Prof. Baethgen veröffentlicht)', *Theol. Zeitschrift aus der Schweiz* (1887) 60-64

Assemani, *BO* ii, p. 498, iii pt. i, p. 282

Muriel Debié 2008

Testimonies of the prophets about the dispensation of Christ

Unknown author

DATE OF BIRTH Unknown
PLACE OF BIRTH Unknown
DATE OF DEATH Unknown
PLACE OF DEATH Unknown

BIOGRAPHY —

MAIN SOURCES OF INFORMATION

Primary —

Secondary —

WORKS ON CHRISTIAN-MUSLIM RELATIONS

Sāhdwātā da-nbiyē d-ʿal mdabbrānuteh da-mshiḥā, 'Testimonies of the prophets about the dispensation of Christ'

DATE Unknown, probably c. 720
ORIGINAL LANGUAGE Syriac

DESCRIPTION
In the guise of a collection of prophecies made by figures in the Hebrew Bible, this East-Syrian text is a kind of *vademecum* of what is to be known about the dispensation of Christ and the sacraments of baptism and the eucharist. It addresses an anonymous reader and has a strong anti-Jewish flavor. At the same time, it tackles issues that are the subject of controversy with Islam, such as the direction of prayer – the religion of the Syrian Christians is said to be the best, because they pray facing the east as did Adam and everyone after him until the confusion of tongues. Against the prophethood of Muḥammad, it states that 'there is no other Messiah in truth than Christ'.

The text seeks to show that the Christians are the new chosen people, the Jews having been deprived of the Promise since they did not listen to the prophets and did not receive Christ. And, possibly as a deterrent against conversion to Islam, it tries to comfort Christians and convince them that they possess the true and most excellent religion and should not 'abandon the path of justice'.

Testimonies relies heavily upon the *Apocalypse of Pseudo-Methodius* (q.v.), which it openly cites as one of its sources – Pseudo-Methodius is mentioned twice under the name of Teōdios. From Pseudo-Methodius, *Testimonies* borrowed the idea that divine election passed to the nation of the Syrian Christians, who possessed the true Hope, which is the Cross. This gives a *post quem* dating of after 690-92, the most likely dating for Pseudo-Methodius. However, members of the new religion are never called 'Muslims' but rather 'heathens' or simply 'Arabs', which implies an earlier date for the text, which is not openly a disputation with Islam, unlike the Questions and Answers, letters and dialogues produced from the middle of the 8th century onwards. With *Testimonies* we probably find ourselves in a period of transition, when Christian apologists found the weapons of anti-Jewish polemic to hand and used them to create, little by little, a new defense against the Muslims. This points to a date in the 720s-30s, before more detailed arguments were produced to counteract the then better-known new religion.

SIGNIFICANCE

Testimonies provides its Syrian readers with material to prove that they are the true children and heirs of Abraham, an argument now directed against the Arabs as well as the Jews. In *Testimonies*, we can see the construction of a range of anti-Muslim arguments in process. The prophecies are intended to rebuke the Muslims as much as the Jews. Christians had had centuries of experience of anti-Jewish controversy, but in the early Islamic period they had not yet built arguments to respond to attacks from Muslims.

The *Testimonies* do not look forward to political change or particular eschatological events. Unlike the *Apocalypse of Pseudo-Methodius*, they do not see the defense of Christianity as coming from a Last Emperor, but from Christians living within the Islamic empire and equipped with arguments such as those provided in this text.

MANUSCRIPTS

MS Vat – Syr. 164 (1702), fols 79-109

MS BL – Add. 25,875 (1709-10), fols 58v-77v

EDITIONS AND TRANSLATIONS —

STUDIES

M. Debié, 'Muslim-Christian controversy in an unedited Syriac text. *Revelations and testimonies about our Lord's dispensation*', in E. Grypeou, M. Swanson and D. Thomas (eds), *The encounter of Eastern Christianity with early Islam*, Leiden, 2006, 225-35

M. Debié, 'A Syriac unedited apocalypse. Revelations regarding the dispensation of the Messiah', *The Harp* 18 (2005) 163-71

A. Desreumaux, 'Remarques sur le rôle des apocryphes dans la théologie des Églises syriaques. L'exemple de *testimonia* christologiques inédits', *Apocrypha* 8 (1997) 165-77

A. Desreumaux, 'The prophetical testimonies about Christ. An unedited typological exegesis in Syriac', *The Harp* 8-9 (1995-1996) 133-38

Muriel Debié 2008

The Apocalypse of Pseudo-Methodius (Greek)

Unknown author

DATE OF BIRTH Unknown
PLACE OF BIRTH Unknown
DATE OF DEATH Unknown
PLACE OF DEATH Unknown

BIOGRAPHY Unknown

MAIN SOURCES OF INFORMATION

Primary —

Secondary —

WORKS ON CHRISTIAN-MUSLIM RELATIONS

Tou en hagiois patros hēmōn Methodiou episkopou Patarōn tou martyros logos ēkribomenos peri tēs basileias tōn ethnōn kai eis tous eschatous kairous akribēs apodeixis archomenos apo Adam heōs synteleias kosmou, 'The precise sermon of our Father Methodius, the bishop of Patara, the martyr who is with the saints, about the kingdoms of the nations and the accurate report of the last things, beginning with Adam until the end of the world'. Modern title: 'The Greek Apocalypse of Pseudo-Methodius'

DATE End of 7th c. or early 8th c.
ORIGINAL LANGUAGE Greek redaction of Syriac original

DESCRIPTION
As in the original Syriac version (q.v.), which was written at the end of the 7th century, human history is traced from the expulsion of Adam

and Eve from paradise to the origins of the Byzantine Empire, with the span of history organized according to the typology of the seven millennia.

The text explains the apocalyptic rise of Islam as a punishment against the Christians because of their sins. One of its most important features is the 'legend of the Last Emperor'. The author tells how the Arabs, the conquerors of 'the people of God', will appear, and then a 'Last Emperor of the Greeks', descended from the kings of Ethiopia, unexpectedly awakened from his sleep, will restore Christian power by overthrowing them. He will defeat the 'sons of Hagar', attacking Islamic possessions from the south, the Red Sea, and restore peace and prosperity throughout Palestine (Matt 24:37-38). Then, Gog and Magog will suddenly appear after breaking through the 'gates of the north', but will be defeated by an angel on the plain of Joppe. The Last Emperor will then reign in Jerusalem for ten years before the coming of the Antichrist and his rule of iniquity.

This first Greek translation of the Syriac apocalypse remains faithful to the original throughout, except for a long interpolation at the point where the Arabs are defeated outside Constantinople before the appearance of the last emperor, a clear allusion to the Arab siege of the city in 717/18. This passage does not appear in the other Greek or Latin versions. Another interpolation is a passage from Anastasius of Sinai's *Disputation against the Jews.*

SIGNIFICANCE

The apocalypse is important because it gives Islam a place within the history of salvation. The legend of the last emperor provides both political hope for Christian populations and also a frame in which to understand Islam as part of the history of the end time.

MANUSCRIPTS

For the 15 extant MSS, of which the oldest is from the 14th c., see Aerts and Kortekaas, *Die Apokalypse des Pseudo-Methodius*, i, pp. 38-48

EDITIONS AND TRANSLATIONS

W.J. Aerts and G.A.A. Kortekaas, *Die Apokalypse des Pseudo-Methodius. Die ältesten griechischen und lateinischen Übersetzungen*, 2 vols, Louvain, 1998 (*CSCO* 569-70)

A. Lolos, *Die dritte und vierte Redaktion des Ps.-Methodios*, Meisenheim am Glan, 1978

A. Lolos, Die Apokalypse des Ps.-Methodios, Meisenheim am Glan, 1976

V. Istrin, *Oktrovenia Mefodiia Patarskago I apokrificheskia Videniia Daniila*, Moscow, 1897

STUDIES

W. Brandes, 'Die Belagerung Konstantinopels 717/718 als apokalyptisches Ereignis. Zu einer Interpolation im griechischen Text der Pseudo-Methodios-Apokalypse', in K. Belke et al. (eds), *Byzantina Mediterranea*, Vienna, 2007, 65-91

L. Brubaker and J. Haldon, *Byzantium in the iconoclast era (ca. 680-850). The sources*, Aldershot, 2001, pp. 272-75

W. Kaegi, 'Gightis and Olbia in the Pseudo-Methodius apocalypse and their significance', *Byzantinische Forschungen* 26 (2000) 21-43

A. Külzer, 'Konstantinopel in der Apokalyptischen Literatur der Byzantiner', *Jahrbuch der Österreichischen Byzantinistik* 50 (2000) 51-76

H. Möhring, *Der Weltkaiser der Endzeit*, Stuttgart, 2000, pp. 311-17

P. Ubierna, 'La 'leyenda del última emperador' en Bizancio y en el cercano oriente cristiano (ss. VII-IX). Una instrumentalización del género apocalíptico' in G. Hansen, *Los caminos inexhauribles de la Palabra*, Buenos Aires, 2000, 463-94

Hoyland, *Seeing Islam*, pp. 295-97

D. Olster, art. 'Byzantine apocalypses', in *The Encyclopedia of Apocalypticism*, New York, 1996

W. Kaegi, *Byzantium and the early Islamic conquests*, Cambridge, 1995, pp. 231-35

P. Magdalino, 'The history of the future and its uses. Prophecy, policy and propaganda' in R. Beaton and C. Roueché, *The making of Byzantine history*, London, 1993, 3-34

W. Brandes, 'Endzeitvorstellungen und Lebenstrost in mittelbyzantinischer Zeit (7.-9. Jahrhundert)', *Poikila Byzantina* 11 (1991) 9-62

J. Irmscher and A. Kazhdan, art. 'Methodios of Patara, Pseudo', in *ODB*

W. Brandes, 'Die apokalyptische Literatur' in F. Winkelman and W. Brandes, *Quellen zur Geschichte des frühen Byzanz*, Amsterdam, 1990, pp. 305-22

T. Frenz, 'Textkritische Untersuchungen zu *Pseudo-Methodius*. Das Verhältnis der griechischen zur ältesten lateinischen Fassung', *BZ* 80 (1987) 50-58

F.J. Thomson, 'The slavonic translations of Pseudo-Methodius of Olympus' *Apokalypsis*', *Turnovka Knizhovna Škola* 4 (1985) 143-73
M.V. Krikov, 'Otkrovenie Pseudo-Mefodia Patarskago', *VV* 44 (1983) 215-21
M.V. Krikov, '"Efiopia" v "otkrovenie" Pseudo-Mefodia Patarskago', *VV* 38 (1977) 120-22
S.H. Cross, 'The earliest allusion in Slavic literature to the Revelations of Pseudo-Methodius', *Speculum* 4 (1929) 329-39

Pablo Ubierna 2007

The Apocalypse of Pseudo-Methodius (Latin)

Unknown author

DATE OF BIRTH Unknown, probably 7th c.
PLACE OF BIRTH Unknown
DATE OF DEATH Unknown, probably 8th c.
PLACE OF DEATH Unknown

BIOGRAPHY —

MAIN SOURCES OF INFORMATION

Primary —

Secondary —

WORKS ON CHRISTIAN-MUSLIM RELATIONS

Revelatio S. Methodii de temporibus nouissimis, 'Revelation of St Methodius on the present times'. Modern title: 'The Apocalypse of Pseudo-Methodius'

DATE End of 7th c. or early 8th c.
ORIGINAL LANGUAGE Latin translation from a slightly expanded Greek recension of the Syriac original

DESCRIPTION
The preface of one of the four manuscripts used by Sackur for his edition (MS BNF - Lat. 13348; this is of dubious authenticity) states that this translation was made from Greek into Latin by Peter the monk at the request of his brothers in the monastery. Some linguistic features of the text of this manuscript suggest that he may have been a Syrian or Greek (Sackur, *Sibyllinische texte* , pp. 56, 59).

Like the Syriac and Greek texts, the Latin version of Pseudo-Methodius can be divided in two long sections: first, a historical section from Adam and Eve's expulsion from paradise to Alexander the Great; and second, a prophetic section in which the end of days is announced by the final destruction of Islam at the hands of the Roman emperor and the subsequent coming of Jesus Christ.

SIGNIFICANCE

The Latin version of *Pseudo-Methodius* was an important source-text for Latin historians. It had an immense influence on apocalyptic literature throughout the Middle Ages, testified to by a number of different recensions and nearly 200 surviving manuscripts. Its continuing popularity can also be deduced from the various translations, among which is the *Profecías de San Metodio martyr*, an abbreviated and expurgated version in Romance Castillian, which may represent an older version made from a corrupted text (Vázquez de Parga, 'Algunas notas').

One of the areas where the impact of its apocalyptic thought had particular importance was in the south of the Iberian peninsula among the Arabized Christian communities living under Muslim rule.

MANUSCRIPTS

There are no fewer than 190 manuscripts (Verhelst, *Adso Dervensis*, p. 139, n. 1). Four go back to the 8th century, and one can perhaps be dated to the late 7th c.

EDITIONS AND TRANSLATIONS

C. Carozzi and H. Taviani-Carozzi, *La fin des temps. Terreurs et prophéties au Moyen Âge*, Paris, 1982, 1999^{2}, pp. 99-112 (partial trans.)

W.J. Aerts and G.A.A. Kortekaas, *Die Apokalypse des Pseudo-Methodius. Die ältesten griechischen und lateinischen Übersetzungen*, 2 vols, Louvain, 1998, (*CSCO* Subsidia 97-98) (edition and trans.)

E. Sackur, *Sibyllinische Texte und Forschungen. Pseudomethodius, Adso und die tiburtinische Sibylle*, Halle/Saale, 1898 (the only critical edition based on the four MSS from the 8th c.)

V. Istrin, *Oktrovenia Mefodiia Patarskago I apokrificheskia Videniia Daniila*, Moscow, 1897, pp. 75-83

For later translations, see below under 'studies'

STUDIES

M.W. Twomey, 'The *Revelationes* of Pseudo-Methodius and scriptural study at Salisbury in the eleventh century', in C.D. Wright, F.M. Biggs and T.N. Hall (eds), *Source of wisdom. Old English and early medieval Latin Studies in honour of Thomas D. Hill*, Toronto, 2007, 370-86

K. Scarfe Beckett, *Anglo-Saxon perceptions of the Islamic world*, Cambridge, 2003, pp. 140-64 and *passim*

Tolan, *Saracens*, 46-50 and *passim*

H. Möhring, *Der Weltkaiser der Endzeit, Enstehung, Wandel und Wirkung einer tausendjährigen Weissagung*, Stuttgart, 2000, pp. 97-104, 136-43 and *passim*

Carozzi and Taviani-Carozzi, *La fin des temps*, pp. 17-22

G.H.V. Bunt, 'The Middle English translations of the Revelations of Pseudo-Methodius', in H. Hokwerda, E.R. Smits and M.M. Woesthuis (eds), *Polyphonia Byzantina*, Groningen, 1993, 131-43

M. Laureys and D. Verhelst, 'Pseudo-Methodius, *Reuelationes*. Textgeschichte und kritische Edition. Ein Leuven-Groninger Forschungsprojekt', in W. Verbeke D. Verhelst and A. Welkenhuysen (eds), *The use and abuse of eschatology in the Middle Ages*, Louvain, 1988, 112-36

T. Frenz, 'Textkritische Untersuchungen zur 'Pseudo-Methodios'. Das Verhältnis der griechischen zur ältesten lateinischen Fassung', *BZ* 80 (1987) 50-58

O. Prinz, 'Eine frühe abendländische Aktualisierung des lateinischen Übersetzung des Pseudo-Methodius', *Deutsches Archiv für die Erforschung des Mittelalters* 41 (1985) 1-23

O. Prinz, 'Bemerkungen zum Wortschatz der lateinischen Übersetzung des Pseudo-Methodios', in A. Reinle, L. Schmugge and P. Stotz (eds), *Variorum munera florum*, Sigmaringen, 1985, 17-22

P.J. Alexander, 'The diffusion of Byzantine apocalypses in the Medieval West and the beginnings of Joachimism', in A. Williams (ed.), *Prophecy and millenarianism. Essays in honour of Marjorie Reeves*, London, 1980, 53-106

R. Rudolf, 'Des Pseudo-Methodius 'Revelationes' (Fassung B) und ihre deutsche Übersetzung in der Brüsseler Handschrift Eghenvelders', *Zeitschrift für Deutsche Philologie* 95 (1976) 68-91

D. Verhelst, *Adso Dervensis. De ortu et tempore Antichristi, necnon et tractatus qui ab eo dependunt*, Turnhout, 1976

L. Vázquez de Parga, 'Algunas notas sobre el Pseudo Metodio y España', *Habis* 2 (1971) 143-64 (with an edition by J. Gil of the *excerptum* from MS Real Academia de la Historia - 78, fols 177r-177v)

P. Lehmann, *Aufgaben und Anregungen der lateinische Philologie des Mittelalters*, Stuttgart, 1959, i, pp. 37-38

M.B. Ogle, 'Petrus Comestor, Methodius and the Saracens', *Speculum* 21 (1946) 318-24

C. D'Evelyn, 'The Middle-English metrical version of the *Revelationes* of Methodius with a study of the influence of Methodius in Middle-English', *Publications of the Modern Language Association of America* 33 n.s. 26 (1918) 191-203

F. Pfister, 'Ein kleiner lateinische Texte zur Episode von Gog und Magog', *Berliner philologische Wochenschrift* 35 (1915) 1549-52

Sackur, *Sibyllinische texte und Forschungen*, pp. 3-59

Juan Pedro Monferrer-Sala 2007

The Disputation of Patriarch John

Unknown author

DATE OF BIRTH Unknown
PLACE OF BIRTH Unknown
DATE OF DEATH Unknown
PLACE OF DEATH Unknown

BIOGRAPHY —

MAIN SOURCES OF INFORMATION

Primary —

Secondary —

WORKS ON CHRISTIAN-MUSLIM RELATIONS

Coptic title: not preserved. Arabic: *Sharḥ mujādalat abīnā l-ab al-baṭriyark anbā Yuʾannis baṭriyark Iskandariyya maʿa l-Yahūdī wa-l-Malikī ʿalā ayyām ʿAbd al-ʿAzīz al-malik bi-Miṣr*, 'Explanation of the disputation of our father Patriarch John, patriarch of Alexandria, with the Jew and the Melkite in the days of ʿAbd al-ʿAzīz the king in Egypt'. Modern title: 'The Disputation of Patriarch John'

DATE Unknown, possibly late 7th or early 8th c.
ORIGINAL LANGUAGE Coptic

DESCRIPTION
This text, which survives in a number of fragments in Bohairic (without traces of Sahidic) as well as in Arabic, reports a discussion between the Coptic Patriarch John, a Jew and a Chalcedonian Christian in the presence of ʿAbd al-ʿAzīz, the governor of Egypt. Graf identifies

the patriarch as John III, who held office between 677 and 686, and ʿAbd al-ʿAzīz as the Umayyad governor of Egypt from 685-705.

The stage for the discussion is set when a silver box from the estate of a recently-deceased Jew is shown to the governor, to whom the patriarch is paying a courtesy call. The box contains a piece of wood – which a miracle proves to be a fragment of the True Cross. The governor offers it to the patriarch, who purchases it from him for 3,000 dinars.

Later, at the governor's command, the patriarch has a discussion with a Jew and a (diophysite) Melkite Christian about the true religion, in the course of which both convert to the patriarch's miaphysite Christian faith. This is followed by a discussion between the governor and the patriarch about how, if God is in heaven, the eucharistic elements can be the body and blood of Christ. Finally, when the governor claims that a robber was crucified on the cross rather than Christ, the patriarch rebukes the governor for taking the 3,000 dinars he paid for the relic of the cross. The governor declares himself defeated in the debate, honors the patriarch, and gives him leave to depart.

SIGNIFICANCE

The account is obviously not a matter-of-fact report of a discussion but rather a hagiographical piece that includes several details of miracles. It is a witness to three themes in the early controversy between Christians and Muslims: the recognition of the true religion, the eucharist, and the crucifixion of Christ.

If the text reflects an actual encounter between John III and ʿAbd al-ʿAzīz, it could be datable to late 7th or early 8th century. In this case, it would be one of the earliest texts of Christian-Muslim controversy to treat the theme of the bodily presence of Christ in the eucharist. However, the possibility of a later date has been noted by S. Noble, whose treatment of the disputation in collaboration with S.J. Davis and B. Orfali is forthcoming.

MANUSCRIPTS

For the four Bohairic fragments from one single MS, see:

H.G. Evelyn White, *The monasteries of the Wadi 'n Natrûn*, New York, 1932, i, p. 171

Arabic text:

MS BNF – Ar. 215 (1590), fols 186r-202v

MS BNF – Ar. 4881, fols 138r-167r (19th c.)

MS Cairo, Coptic Museum – theol. 236 (Simaika 54, Graf, 132), fols 96v-132v (16th c.)

MS Cairo, Coptic Patriarchate – theol. 216 (Simaika, 342, Graf, 369), fols 164r-199r (1729)

MS Cairo, Coptic Patriarchate – theol. 86 (Simaika, 420, Graf, 469), fols 69v-63r (1790)

EDITIONS AND TRANSLATIONS

Evelyn White, *The monasteries of the Wadi 'n Natrûn*, i, pp. 171-75 (edition and English trans. of the Bohairic fragments)

An edition and English trans. of the Arabic version by S.J. Davis, S. Noble and B. Orfali is forthcoming.

STUDIES

S. Noble, 'A disputation over a fragment of the True Cross. A text from the history of inter-religious relations in medieval Egypt', *American Oriental Society. Abstracts 2007*, p. 25

H. Suermann, 'Copts and the Islam of the seventh century', in E. Grypeou, M.N. Swanson and D. Thomas (eds), *The encounter of Eastern Christianity with early Islam*, Leiden, 2006, 95-109, pp. 104-6

H. Suermann, 'Koptische Texte zur arabischen Eroberung Ägyptens und der Umayyadenherrschaft', *Journal of Coptic Studies* 4 (2002) 167-86, pp. 177-79

Graf, *GCAL* i, pp. 478-80

Harald Suermann 2008

The Arabic Homily of Pseudo-Theophilus of Alexandria

Unknown author

DATE OF BIRTH Unknown, perhaps 7th c.
PLACE OF BIRTH Unknown, presumably Egypt
DATE OF DEATH Unknown, perhaps early 8th c.
PLACE OF DEATH Unknown, presumably Egypt

BIOGRAPHY

Nothing is known of the author of this pseudonymous prophetic text beyond what can be gathered from the text itself.

MAIN SOURCES OF INFORMATION

Primary —

Secondary —

WORKS ON CHRISTIAN-MUSLIM RELATIONS

Maymar qālahu al-ab al-mukarram bi-kull nawʿ abīnā anbā Tāʾufīlus baṭriyark al-madīna l-ʿaẓīma l-Iskandariyya min ajl al-kawkabayn al-munīrayn Buṭrus wa-Būlus wa-min ajl al-tawba wa-ayḍan min ajl anbā Atanāsīyūs al-lābis al-rūḥ, 'A sermon delivered by the father honored in every way, our father Abba Theophilus, patriarch of the great city of Alexandria, about the two brilliant stars Peter and Paul, about repentance, and also about Abba Athanasius, the Spirit-bearer (*pneumatophoros*)'. Modern titles: 'Arabic homily in honor of Peter and Paul', 'The Arabic homily of Pseudo-Theophilus of Alexandria'

DATE Unknown, perhaps late 7th c. or early 8th c.
ORIGINAL LANGUAGE Coptic or Greek

DESCRIPTION

Probably composed for the occasion of the feast of SS Peter and Paul, this sermon contains eulogies of these saints as well as some miracle stories located in Rome and involving the corpses of Peter and Paul speaking. The most important of these stories, a revelatory dialogue between St Peter and Bishop Athanasius of Alexandria (d. 373), is set during the latter's exile in Rome. It deals with the future fate of Egypt and its inhabitants and includes passages on Arab rule and Islam.

This dialogue begins with a short prophecy *ex eventu* in which St Peter relates how Athanasius' see will be the only one to remain firm in the true faith, and how God will then remove the Byzantines from the land of Egypt and establish 'a strong nation that will have care for the churches of Christ and will not sin against the faith in any way'. Rather ambivalently, this nation, in which we recognize the Arabs, will at the same time serve as God's instrument for chastising the people of Egypt on account of their sins; but this chastisement will be short and those who remain steadfast in the faith will receive eternal salvation.

The work continues with a series of questions and answers between Peter and Athanasius about those who will be excluded from the Kingdom of Heaven. The first group alluded to are the Muslims, described as 'the nations', who serve God but not the Son and the Holy Spirit and who are not baptized and do not receive communion. They will be excluded even if they fast 'every two days or each year' (*yawmayn yawmayn aw sanata sanata*), and pray day and night without interruption. Special attention is given to the many Christians who renounce their faith in Christ and mix with the Muslims, claiming thus to serve God, as well as those who still recognize Christ but only silently in their thoughts, out of fear of 'the people'. The main message of the work is thus clear: do not assimilate to Islam but remain true to the chosen anti-Chalcedonian Coptic Church and its teachings. In addition, the special interest in baptism demonstrated throughout the sermon may suggest that the work was written against a background of some conflict over this Christian sacrament.

There are hardly any historical references that help date the sermon; suggested dates, varying from the 7th to the 9th century, are based on supposition. Perhaps the likeliest date, first proposed by Frend but without explanation (*Rise*, p. 355; 'Nationalism', p. 21), is the late 7th or early 8th century. Some considerations are:

The ambivalent description of Arab rule, as both respectful of Christianity and oppressive, fits particularly well in this period, when

Egyptian Christians could look back on a relatively calm first 50 years of Muslim domination, but also saw the first effects of a changing attitude of Muslim rulers towards their Christian subjects, manifest in the fierce tax measures and heightened religious assertiveness documented for the period. The repeated emphasis on the brevity of the 'chastisement' may exclude the possibility that the text was written much later (unless the author wanted to express hope that the remaining chastisement would be short).

A date of composition halfway through the first century of Muslim rule in Egypt would also explain the text's slightly 'nationalistic' or chauvinistic flavor (sensed in the recurring glorification of the land of Egypt and its anti-Chalcedonian orthodox inhabitants and also in St Peter's praise of Athanasius and his see), given that, in this century of immense political change the Church of Alexandria appears to have been concerned with the definition of a particularly Egyptian anti-Chalcedonian (miaphysite) Christian identity (see A. Papaconstantinou, 'Historiography, hagiography, and the making of the Coptic "Church of the martyrs" in early Islamic Egypt', *DOP* 60 (2006) 65-86).

While the Islam-related passages may at first glance suggest a later period when the Islamization of Egyptian society was well advanced, they are not at all out of place in the late 7th or early 8th century, as apostasy to Islam then became, for the first time, a serious issue in Eastern Christian writings; for Egypt, see e.g. the apocalypse in the Arabic *Life of Shenute* (q.v.). This early period would also be a fitting context for the rather simplistic characterization of Islamic doctrine and practice, which implies that Islam is merely a Christian heresy or, rather, a variant of Judaism, indicating perhaps a still superficial knowledge of Islam or else a subtle polemic against the politico-religious propaganda of Caliph ʿAbd al-Malik (r. 685-705) and his son al-Walīd I (r. 710-15), which asserted Islam's superiority over Christianity.

Although the text itself attributes the sermon to Patriarch Theophilus of Alexandria (r. 385-412), the real author must have been later. This applies not only to the passages related to Arab rule and Islam but also to the rest of the sermon, given that the former are clearly integral to and amount to almost half of the text, thus suggesting that the sermon was written at one time, and dates in its entirety from the Islamic period. Even if older textual material was used, it is doubtful that it came from Theophilus' pen (*pace* Hoyland, *Seeing Islam*, p. 172), since the narrative framework of the sermon contains an important chronological error (Athanasius' stay in Rome during the papacy of Liberius; see Fleisch, 'Homily', p. 375) that is unlikely to have been made by Theophilus, who was Athanasius' pupil. It may well be, therefore, that this sermon was ascribed to Theophilus only because his name lent credibility and authority to stories involving his master Athanasius.

It has recently been argued that the Arabic text of the sermon was translated from Coptic (Groddek et al., *Ein wildes Volk*, pp. 23, n. 52, 206-7). This may well have been the original language of the work, although, in view of the early date of composition suggested above, one cannot exclude the possibility of a Greek original. However, the arguments in favor of the Greek put forward by Fleisch ('Homélie', 375) are weak.

SIGNIFICANCE

This little-known sermon may be one of the oldest writings of the Coptic Orthodox community to contain information on Islamic doctrine and to describe, and respond to, the religious challenge of Islam. The sermon is also important as a witness to the early Coptic tradition which has a positive attitude towards the initial period of Muslim rule, for which see also, e.g., the biography of Benjamin I, in the *History of the patriarchs of Alexandria*, which was perhaps originally written in the same period (probably by George the Archdeacon [q.v.]), as well as later Coptic apocalyptic writings such as the *Apocalypse of Samuel* and the *Letter of Pisentius*.

MANUSCRIPTS

MS BNF – ar. 4771, fols 200v-225r (19th c)

MS Aleppo, Naṣrī Wakīl Collection – 276 (inaccessible MS in a private collection; Sbath, *Fihris*, i, p. 39)

EDITIONS AND TRANSLATIONS

H. Fleisch, 'Une homélie de Théophile d'Alexandrie en l'honneur de St Pierre et de St Paul', *Revue de l'Orient Chrétien* 30 (1935-36) 371-419 (edition and trans.; errata in *Mélanges de l'Université Saint Joseph* 28 (1948-50) 351-52)

STUDIES

J. van Lent, *Coptic apocalyptic writings from the Islamic period*, Leiden, forthcoming (Diss. Leiden University)

D. Groddek et al., *Ein wildes Volk ist es.... Predigt (Ps.-Athanasius) über Lev 21,9, Ex 19, 22, den Erzengel Michael und das Weltende unter arabischer Herrschaft*, Altenberge, 2004 (Corpus Islamo-Christianum, Series Coptica 1), pp. 23-26, 206-7

S.J. Davis, *The early Coptic papacy. The Egyptian Church and its leadership in Late Antiquity*, Cairo, 2004, pp. 120-21

F.J. Martinez, 'La literatura apocalíptica y las primeras reacciones cristianas a la conquista islámica en Oriente', in G. Anes y Álvarez de Castrillón (ed.), *Europa y el Islam*, Madrid, 2003, 143-222, pp. 172-73, n. 63

H. Suermann, 'Koptische Texte zur arabischen Eroberung Ägyptens und der Umayyadenherschaft', *Journal of Coptic Studies* 4 (2002) 167-86, pp. 182-83

Hoyland, *Seeing Islam*, pp. 121, n. 16, 172, 469, n. 47

E. Wipszycka, 'Le nationalisme a-t-il existé dans l'Égypte byzantine?', *Journal of Juristic Papyrology* 22 (1992) 83-128, pp. 92-93

W.H.C. Frend, 'Nationalism as a factor in anti-Chalcedonian feeling in Egypt', in S. Mews (ed.), *Religion and national identity*, Oxford, 1982, 21-45, pp. 21-22

W.H.C. Frend, *The rise of the Monophysite movement. Chapters in the history of the church in the fifth and sixth centuries*, Cambridge, 1972, pp. 354-55

Graf, *GCAL* i, p. 317

Fleisch, 'Homélie de Théophile', pp. 374-75

Jos van Lent 2008

Movsēs Daskhurantsʿi / Movsēs Kaghankatuatsʿi

Movsēs Dasxurancʿi / Movsēs Kałankatuacʿi

DATE OF BIRTH Unknown
PLACE OF BIRTH Unknown
DATE OF DEATH Early 10th c.
PLACE OF DEATH Unknown

BIOGRAPHY

Traditionally, two names have been associated with the composition entitled *History of Aghuankʿ* (*History of Ałuankʿ/Albania)*: Movsēs Daskhurantsʿi and Movsēs Kaghankatuatsʿi. Movsēs Daskhurantsʿi was first named as the compiler of the work by Mkhitʿar Gosh at the end of the 12th century, whilst Kirakos Gandzaketsʿi (d. 1271) asserted that Kaghankatuatsʿi was responsible. This double identification has generated considerable debate and produced several ingenious solutions. The work itself does not specify the name of the compiler, but in Book II, ch. 11, a passage refers to 'the village of the great district of Kaghankatukʿ, which is in the same province of Uti from which I come as well'. Elsewhere, the text mentions Kaghankatukʿ in five places. However, other commentators have noted that this excerpt connects the author with the province of Uti rather than Kaghankatukʿ. Moreover, there are at least three other passages written in the first person from the perspective of different individuals, and this use of the first person is not confined to the editorial voice. In other words, whilst the excerpt may reveal the origin of the author of the passage, it tells us nothing about the compiler of the whole work. Mkhitʿar's attribution to Movsēs Daskhurantsʿi (i.e. of Daskhurēn) is earlier, but there is still a gap of two centuries between the proposed date of compilation and this reference. At this distance in time and in the absence of any further evidence, a conclusive identification of the compiler is impossible and he must remain anonymous.

The identity of the compiler is not wholly obscure, however. His decision to focus upon Aghuankʿ, that is Caucasian Albania, to the east of historical Armenia, suggests an affinity with that country. Two fundamental historical themes emerge from the work: the kings and princes of Aghuankʿ, and the establishment and development of the separate Church of Aghuankʿ. Moreover, although the sponsor of the compilation is not specified, one Sahak Sevada, prince of Khachʿēn, is portrayed as 'a searcher of literature' and someone who 'appointed leading scribes to his household' (III.23). These scholarly tendencies resonate with the description of Hamazasp Mamikonean in the *History* attributed to Sebeos (q.v.). Arguably Sahak Sevada commissioned the *History of Aghuankʿ* from one of these scholars attached to his household in Khachʿēn, located to the east of Siwnikʿ. Sahak Sevada is presented at the zenith of his power, fighting against Smbat I Bagratuni. Smbat was executed in 914. Another Armenian History, that of John Catholicos/Yovhannēs Draskanakerttsʿi, records that Sahak Sevada and his son were blinded in 919 by Smbat's son, Ashot II Erkatʿ. Arguably, the *History of Aghuankʿ* was compiled at the very start of the 10th century, probably before 914 and almost certainly before 919. Several brief notices were added subsequently, extending the coverage to the end of the 10th century. Tellingly, the earliest allusion to a text entitled *History of Aghuankʿ*, occurs in a letter composed by the Catholicos of Armenia, Anania Mokatsʿi, in around 958. This tallies with the above reconstruction. The compiler can only be approached through the study of this text.

MAIN SOURCES OF INFORMATION

Primary

Movsēs Kaghankatuatsʿi, *Patmutʿiwn Aghuanitsʿ ashkharhi*, ed. V. Aṛakʿelyan, Erevan, 1983

Secondary

J.D. Howard-Johnston, 'Armenian historians of Heraclius. An examination of the aims, sources and working-methods of Sebeos and Movses Daskhurantsi', in G.J. Reinink and B.H. Stolte (eds), *The reign of Heraclius (610-641): crisis and confrontation*, Leuven, 2002, 41-62

T.W. Greenwood, *A History of Armenia in the seventh and eighth centuries*, Oxford, 2000 (Diss. University of Oxford)

A. Akopyan (Hakobyan), *Albaniia-Aluank v greko-latinskhikh i drevnearmianskikh istochnikakh*, Yerevan, 1987; reviewed by P. Donabedian, 'Une nouvelle mise au point sur l'Albanie du Caucase', *Revue des études arméniennes* 21 (1988-89) 485-95

S.V. Smbatjan, *Movses Kalankatyatsi. Istoriia strani Aluank*, Yerevan, 1984 (Russian trans.)

N. Akinean, *Movsēs Daskurantsʿi (kochʿuats Kaghankatuatsʿi) ew ir Patmutʿiwn Aghuanitsʿ*, Vienna, 1970
M. Grigorean, 'Movsēs Kaghankatuatsʿwoy Patmutʿiwnĕ', *Handēs Amsoreay* 77 (1963) 9-24
C.J.F. Dowsett, *The History of the Caucasian Albanians by Movsēs Dasxuranci*, London, 1961
N. Adontsʿ, 'Kʿnnutʿiwn Movsēs kaghankatuatsʿu', *Anahit* 10/3 (1939) 69-78; 10/4-5 (1939) 22-31; 10/6 (1939) 4-9; 11/1-3 (1940) 20-29

WORKS ON CHRISTIAN-MUSLIM RELATIONS

Patmutʿiwn Aghuanitsʿ ashkharhi, 'History of Aghuank''

DATE Compiled early 10th c., incorporating 7th and early 8th c. elements

ORIGINAL LANGUAGE Armenian

DESCRIPTION

The *History of Aghuankʿ* can be accessed through Aṛakelyan's modern critical edition and Dowsett's older English translation. It is a composite text which was put together in the early 10th century. This relatively late date of compilation does not mean that it did not exploit and preserve much older materials, and herein lies the value of the text. Following a familiar Armenian historiographical convention, it is divided into three books. On the basis of contents alone, Book I is irrelevant, being limited to the period from the Flood to the end of the fifth century. However, several passages are drawn from other extant Armenian texts, and these offer invaluable insight into the editorial processes of selection, extraction, abridgement and reworking. Having established the editorial approach to those texts which have survived, it follows that the compiler adopted the same working methods as those underlying sources which have not survived. Close textual scrutiny suggests that the compiler elected to retain the structure and language of his sources, abridging and combining passages where appropriate without rewriting them. There is little evidence that he merged extracts from different sources, preferring to exploit one source at a time.

Book II is primarily focused upon 7th-century history. The general consensus of opinion among scholars is that the rich, detailed historical narrative embedded in Book II derives from contemporary or near-contemporary sources which have not been repeatedly revised or rewritten. There is, however, significant disagreement over the literary vehicles in which this material was preserved. Howard-Johnston accepts Akopyan's proposition that the 7th-century material arrived in the hands of the compiler already conjoined. This postulated source, called the *684 History* by Akopyan, is re-designated by Howard-Johnston as the *682 History*, on the basis that this is the terminal date of its coverage. Both infer that the abrupt conclusion to the work was caused by the irruption of the Khazars in 685. They disagree, however, over the exact make-up of this postulated source. Zuckerman and Greenwood, on the other hand, adopt a slightly more conservative approach, defining clusters of material but shying away from bundling them together into a late 7th-century compilation. The preservation of a single 7th-century compilation, whatever its title, within the *History of Aghuankʿ* remains conjectural and has yet to be proved. This has not deterred scholars from citing material from the *682 History*, thereby giving the rather misleading impression that a new late 7th-century source has been unearthed.

Book II explores the dramatic events of the 7th century from an unashamedly Aghuan perspective. The devastating intervention of Turkic forces in the late 620s is given particular attention. It is only with the mustering of Albanian forces for service in the Sasanian army in the campaigns which culminated in the battle of Qādisiyya (6 January 638) that the narrative mentions Muslim forces (II.18). Thereafter they feature prominently. Initially they are described in hostile terms, on one occasion as the 'cruel scourge of the south'. In response, the prince of Aghuankʿ, Juanshēr, joined a confederation of Caucasian clients carefully put together by Constans II. When this unraveled in the aftermath of the first *fitna*, and Constans II ventured westwards to Sicily, Juanshēr switched sides and came to terms with Muʿāwiya (II.27), who is described as the 'king of the south' and 'the conqueror of the world'. Juanshēr undertook two journeys to Damascus and was richly rewarded on both occasions (II.27 and 28). These detailed descriptions offer significant insights into the court at Damascus and Muʿāwiya's approach to the control of his northern territories. Entirely unrelated to the above, the final three chapters in Book II (II.50-52) record a pilgrimage to Jerusalem in the 630s; a topographical description of the holy sites in Jerusalem, including the dimensions of buildings and distances between them; and a list of Aghuan monasteries (or rather, hostels) in Jerusalem, their location and changes in ownership – the majority are 'now' held partly or wholly by Arabs.

Book III is very different in character. It opens with a hostile account of Muḥammad's prophetic inspiration – identifying an Arian, Baḥīrā, as his teacher – and a long account of alleged teaching on marriage and divorce. Intriguingly, the account contains Arabic rather than Armenian months. This introduces a freestanding caliphal sequence, extending to the accession of the Caliph al-Wāthiq in 842 (III.2). This is different from that employed within the *History of Ghewond.* These opening chapters have no obvious link with Aghuankʿ, but they do provide a broad historical context for the material which follows.

Book III chapters 3-11 chart the circumstances surrounding the deposition of the Aghuan catholicos Nersēs Bakur at the very start of the 8th century by his Armenian counterpart Eghia, including the terms of the settlement that was eventually achieved. Whilst this might appear to be little more than a local dispute between two rival churches, it has an intriguing political dimension, for the chapters purport to preserve an exchange of letters between Eghia and the 'conqueror of the universe and *amir momin*,' ʿAbd al-Malik. Conventionally this is dated to between 703, when Eghia became Catholicos, and October 705, when ʿAbd al-Malik died. Eghia stated that he held the country of Armenia in obedience to the lordship of ʿAbd al-Malik and requested the caliph's permission to punish Nersēs, who had reached an understanding with the Byzantine emperor. 'Abd al-Malik replied positively to the '*jatʿlkid* of the nation of Armen', giving Eghia authority to arrest Nersēs and sending one of his faithful servants with numerous forces in support. He requested that Nersēs and his accomplice, Queen Spram, be sent to the royal court to be humiliated as a warning to other rebels. A subsequent synod at Partaw (Bardhaʾa) issued a declaration which is dated 'the 85th year of the Arabs'; significantly 85 AH equates to 14 January 704 – 2 January 705 and thus corroborates the date proposed above. Finally, a separate document, containing the names – and presumably signatures – of those Albanian nobles who had accepted the confession established by the Council of Partaw, was apparently lodged in the *dīwān* (or registry) of ʿAbd al-Malik. There can be little doubt that the sheaf of documents found in these chapters is authentic, although exactly how an exchange of correspondence between Eghia and ʿAbd al-Malik came to be preserved in such an Albanian historical compilation remains obscure. One solution could be to interpret this exchange as demonstrating the political rather than the ecclesiastical authority under which Eghia was acting – in other words, he moved against Nersēs with the approval of the caliph. The letters therefore sanction the canons and other documents which emanated from the subsequent church council.

Book III chapters 15-22 are very different in character and tone. They display a chronicle style of composition, with terse notices, covering predominantly secular matters – largely military engagements and administrative dispositions in Caucasian Albania – and organized by reference to the Armenian era dating system. They advance rapidly from the middle of the 7th century down to the first decade of the 10th century. The notices are brief and usually hostile. For example, the text avers that the earth refused to accept the loathsome body of Muḥammad ibn Marwān, vomiting up his corpse three times. There is also a short account of the martyrdoms of two brothers, Mankik and Mirdazat, perhaps in 711. The coverage of the 9th century is more detailed, offering several important insights into the activities of Bābak. The character of the notices and their chronological precision suggest that they derive from a single chronicle which may have been put together at the start of the 10th century.

SIGNIFICANCE

The significance of this work for Christian-Muslim relations lies in its description of the evolving relationship between the nascent Islamic polity and the Aghuan elite, from initial hostility to accommodation and reciprocity. The account of Juanshēr's visit to Damascus in the time of Muʿāwiya is unexpected and striking. So too is the involvement of ʿAbd al-Malik in the tussle between the Armenian and Albanian churches at the start of the 8th century. The preservation of an appeal to ʿAbd al-Malik from the head of the Armenian Church and his response in an Armenian composition has not perhaps been given the recognition it deserves, although Robinson has noted it in passing without identifying the source (Robinson, *ʿAbd al-Malik*, p. 80). Arguably, the invective against Muḥammad dates from a later period – perhaps the mid-9th century – but deserves comparison with other hostile biographies found in Christian sources. The three chapters on Jerusalem, one securely dated to the later 630s, are also of interest. Overall the text illustrates a transition from initial resistance and mutual recognition to a later antipathy towards Islam in the early decades of the 8th century, illustrated by the elements dating from the later 9th and early 10th centuries. The moment of transition however is hidden.

MANUSCRIPTS

Chapter 3.i of Akopyan's 1987 monograph offers a full survey of the manuscript tradition. There are 28 extant manuscripts, divided by Akopyan into two groups, 7 lost manuscripts and 5 postulated manuscripts. The oldest is MS Yerevan, Matenadaran – 1531 (1289)

EDITIONS AND TRANSLATIONS

Smbatjan, *Movses Kalankatyatsi. Istoriia strani Aluank* (Russian trans.)

Movsēs Kaghankatuats'i, *Patmut'iwn Aghuanits' ashkharhi*, ed. V. Aṛak'elyan, Erevan, 1983

C.J.F. Dowsett, *The History of the Caucasian Albanians by Movsēs Dasxuranci*, London, 1961 (English trans. with brief introduction and even briefer notes)

STUDIES

Howard-Johnston, 'Armenian historians of Heraclius'

Greenwood, *A History of Armenia in the seventh and eighth centuries*

S.G. Klyashtornij, 'Moisei Kalankatyiskii o verovanyakh drevnetiorskskikh plemen', *Patmabanasirakan Handēs* 150 (1999/1) 290-300

Akopyan (Hakobyan), *Albaniia-Aluank v greko-latinskhikh i drevnearmianskikh istochnikakh*

A. Akopyan, 'O khronologii posleditionikh sobetii v 'Istorii 684 goda', *Kavkaz i Vizantija* 6 (1988) 24-36

A. Hakobyan, 'Movsēs Kaghankatvats'u Aghvanits' patmut'yan dzeṛagrerë', *Banber Matenadarani* 15 (1986) 110-44

S. Smbatyan, 'Erku chshgrtum Movsēs Kaghankatvatsu' "Aghvanits' ashkharhi patmut'yan" bnagrum' *Patmabanasirakan Handēs* (1973/1) 185-94

H. Svazyan, 'Movsēs Kaghankatvatsu' "Aghvanits' ashkharhi patmut'yan" aghbyurnerë', *Patmabanasirakan Handēs* (1972/3) 195-206

S. Smbatyan, 'Mi k'ani chshgrtumner Movsēs Kaghankatvatsu' "Aghvanits' ashkharhi patmut'yan" bnagri mej', *Patmabanasirakan Handēs* (1972/1) 174-92

Akinean, *Movsēs Daskurants'i (koch'uats Kaghankatuats'i) ew ir Patmut'iwn Aghuanits'*

Grigorean, 'Movsēs Kaghankatuats'woy Patmut'iwnë'

Adonts', 'K'nnut'iwn Movsēs kaghankatuats'u'

V. Hats'uni, 'Movsēs Kaghankatuats'in k'aprēr VII darun', *Bazmavēp* 95 (1937) 268-75

Tim Greenwood 2007

The Disputation between a monk of Bēt Ḥālē and an Arab notable

Unknown author

DATE OF BIRTH Unknown
PLACE OF BIRTH Unknown
DATE OF DEATH Unknown, probably 8th c.
PLACE OF DEATH Unknown, probably Iraq

BIOGRAPHY —

MAIN SOURCES OF INFORMATION

Primary —

Secondary —

WORKS ON CHRISTIAN-MUSLIM RELATIONS

Drāshā da-hwā l-ḥad men Ṭayyāyē ʿam iḥidāyā ḥad b-ʿumrā d-Bēt Ḥālē 'The disputation that took place between one of the Arabs and a certain monk from the monastery of Bēt Ḥālē'. Modern title: 'The Disputation between a monk of Bēt Ḥālē and an Arab notable' (with slight variants)

DATE Probably 720s
ORIGINAL LANGUAGE Syriac

DESCRIPTION
This East-Syrian religious disputation between a monk and an Arab, which covers only 8 folios in the accessible manuscript, is one of the oldest surviving examples of the disputation genre of Christian apologetics vis-à-vis Islam. It is presented as a report of a live encounter and cast in the format of 'question-and-answer'.

The monk's Arab interlocutor is referred to as a notable from the entourage of 'governor Maslama'. The reference to a governor with this name in all likelihood means that the disputation was set in the 720s when Maslama, son of the Umayyad Caliph ʿAbd al-Malik, was governor of Iraq. There were two monasteries with the name Bēt Ḥālē, one close to Mosul, also known as Dayr al-Ṭīn, and the other close to al-Ḥīra, also known as Dayr Mār ʿAbdā. If the disputation took place in the former, it could have been as early as 710 when Maslama became governor of Mesopotamia. If, on the other hand, it was the monastery in southern Iraq, then it is more likely that the debate was situated in the 720s, after Maslama had been appointed there as well.

Although the name of the monk is not mentioned in the text, ʿAbdīshō bar Brīkā (d. 1318) mentions a treatise of Abraham of Bēt Ḥālē against the Arabs (Assemani, *BO* iii/1, p. 205). Following the theory of Baumstark that this is a reference to this disputation, Reinink ('Lamb', p. 110) has suggested the author could be the Abraham who is mentioned as a pupil of John Azraq, bishop of al-Ḥīra in the early 8th century (J.-B. Chabot, *Le livre de la chasteté composé par Jésusdenah, évêque de Basrah*, Rome, 1896, pp. 40, 47, 51, 61). It is perhaps strange, however, that his name does not appear in the disputation itself. If the work mentioned by ʿAbdīshō is indeed our text, then it is just as likely that ʿAbdīshō or someone before him attributed it to Abraham.

Obviously, issues concerning the precise location and time of the disputation are only worth discussing if one assumes that there is a historical reality behind this carefully polished disputation in its literary form. This cannot be known for certain. Nevertheless, it needs to be determined whether the text goes back to the time which the setting reflects. As Reinink has claimed, there are no real reasons to suspect that the work was written much later. On the contrary, the urge to deal with the pressing question of why God supports the Muslims by giving them lasting political and military might may well have arisen in response to the political success and propaganda of the Marwānids at that time. Hoyland and Szilágyi are somewhat more hesitant on account of the reference in the *Disputation* to Sergius Baḥīrā, whose double name does not feature in other texts until later. But it is difficult to imagine why after the ʿAbbasid revolution an author would want to create a historical framework for his debate that features an Umayyad. The early Muslim period would have been a more obvious choice for an archaized setting, and moreover one would expect better known protagonists to enhance the historical verisimilitude.

A number of scholars who do not doubt the early 8th century date have drawn attention to the *Disputation* as the oldest non-Muslim text to mention the Qurʾān. This is interesting not only in and of itself, but also because the author seems to think that *Sūrat al-baqara*, 'The Cow', is a separate scripture from the Qurʾān. He also mentions a scripture with the name *ghīghī* (?), which could be a reference to *Sūrat al-ʿankabūt* ('The spider', in Syriac *ghwāghī*) or to *Injīl*, the Arabic Gospel. Either way, the relevant passage (fol. 6r) could refer to a pre-canonical stage of the Qurʾān, which is why it has received attention from scholars researching the early history of the Qurʾān. It has to be noted, however, that another passage in the *Disputation* shows the author's awareness of the Qurʾān as the principal scriptural source of Islam (fol. 1r).

The Disputation shares many of its themes with other texts of this genre. Among the classic points of contention between Muslims and Christians that feature in it are the worship of icons and relics, the direction of prayer, the validity of the laws of the Torah, the Trinity, the Incarnation, the crucifixion of Christ, and the authority of scriptural proofs.

The answers of the monk to the Muslim's questions are well-crafted. Reinink has shown that the author draws on Syriac biblical exegesis to construct his arguments, for example in his typological explanation of Genesis 22, which he uses as a defense against the Muslim charge that Christians disobey the commandment of Abrahamic sacrifice. A striking example of this is the monk's assertion that the Qurʾān's concept of Christ as 'the Word of God and His Spirit' can be traced back to Muḥammad's knowledge of the Gospel of Luke. According to the author, the qurʾānic understanding of Christ reflects the annunciation to Mary: 'The Holy Spirit will come upon you, and the power of the most High will overshadow you' (Luke 1:35). His argument is only comprehensible in the light of the exegesis of Ephrem the Syrian, who understood 'the power of the most High' as 'the Word'.

When the Muslim is confronted with this alleged echo of Luke in the Qurʾān, he tacitly acknowledges that the Qurʾān does not dismiss belief in Christ as Son of God, but proceeds to ask why Muḥammad did not preach this belief in clear terms. The monk answers that Muḥammad received a simplified religious instruction in monotheism from Sergius Baḥīrā, which was more fitting for a pagan nation than a full-blown Christian catechesis. In other words, the Christian apologetic argument of the spiritual 'immaturity' of the Jews is reused here to explain the monotheism of Islam.

This idea that Muḥammad brought the Arabs half-way to the truth also forms the background of the final passage of the debate in which the Muslim asks whether the sons of Hagar will go to heaven. The monk asserts that Christ promised grace in the afterlife, far removed from the torment of hell, to those who do good works. Yet the kingdom of heaven is a place reserved for the sons of Baptism. Here, and elsewhere in the text, one notices the tendency of the apologist to make the differences between Islam and Christianity look minimal and at the same time to maintain the idea that the whole truth is found only through Christian teachings.

SIGNIFICANCE

From a historical point of view the text is significant because, if it is indeed a product of the early 8th century, it is one of the oldest Christian apologetic works vis-à-vis Islam, and the earliest Christian text to show familiarity with the existence of the Qur'an, its contents and its importance as a source of law for Muslims. The debate would also be the earliest Christian text to make mention of Sergius Baḥīrā, the alleged religious teacher of Muḥammad.

Another interesting aspect of the debate is the similarity between its apologetic arguments and those found in texts from the other eastern Christian communities. Several of its arguments are also found in John of Damascus (Roggema, *Sergius Baḥīrā*, pp. 110-12) and Theodore Abū Qurra (Griffith, 'Disputes with Muslims', p. 260). Given the fact that these two Melkite thinkers belonged to another Christian community and lived in other areas, one can deduce that apologetic arguments were already circulating widely among Christians in the Muslim world in the 8th century. Other noteworthy elements of the text, on the other hand, are exclusive to the East-Syrian response to Islam, notably the rather positive appraisal of Muḥammad as a pious man who tried to convert his people to monotheism.

MANUSCRIPTS

MS Diyarbakr, Chaldean Archbishopric – 95 (early 18th c.?) (this is the conventional reference; in 1969, however, it was present in the Chaldean Episcopal Library of Mardin; see Reinink, 'Political power', p. 158. – this is the only MS that has been accessed by Western scholars)

MS Mardin, Chaldean Bishopric 82 (1890) (inaccessible)

MS Seert, Chaldean Bishopric – 112 (seen by A. Scher and dated by him to the 15th c.; probably lost)

(A fourth witness is/was probably MS Alqosh, Notre-Dame des Semances – 144; undated, 19th c. hand. The 6th text in this MS is described by A. Scher, 'Notice sur les manuscripts syriaques conserves dans la bibliothèque du convent des chaldéens de Notre Dame des Semences', *Journal asiatique* 8 (1906) 55-82, p. 76, as 'controverse entre un arabe et un moine'.)

EDITIONS AND TRANSLATIONS

There is no published edition or translation. Lengthy sections in translation can be found in the secondary literature cited below.

STUDIES

G.J. Reinink, 'The veneration of icons, the cross, and the bones of the martyrs in an early East-Syrian apology against Islam', (forthcoming)

K. Szilágyi, 'Muḥammad and the monk. The making of the Christian Baḥīrā legend', *JSAI* 34 (2008) (in press)

B.H. Roggema, *The Legend of Sergius Baḥīrā. Eastern Christian apologetics and apocalyptic in response to Islam*, Leiden, 2008

S.H. Griffith, 'Christians, Muslims, and the image of the One God. Iconophilia and iconophobia in the world of Islam in Umayyad and early Abbasid times', in B. Groneberg and H. Spiekermann (eds), *Die Welt der Götterbilder*, Berlin 2007, 347-80

G.J. Reinink, 'Bible and Qur'an in early Syriac Christian-Islamic disputation', in M. Tamcke (ed.), *Christians and Muslims in dialogue in the Islamic Orient of the Middle Ages*, Beirut, 2007, 57-72

G.J. Reinink, 'Political power and right religion in the East-Syrian Disputation between a monk of Bēt Ḥālē and an Arab notable', in E. Grypeou, D.R. Thomas and M. Swanson (eds), *The encounter of Eastern Christianity with early Islam*, Leiden, 2006, 153-69

G.J. Reinink, 'Following the doctrines of the demons. Early Christian fear of conversion to Islam', in J.N. Bremmer, W.J. van Bekkum and A.L. Molendijk (eds), *Cultures of conversion*, Leuven, 2006, 127-38, pp. 135-37

A.-L. de Prémare, ''Abd al-Malik b. Marwān et le processus de constitution du Coran', in K.-H. Ohlig and G.-R. Puin, *Die dunklen Anfängen. Neue Forschungen zur Entstehung und frühen Geschichte des Islam*, Berlin, 2005, 179-210, pp. 184-85, 201-2

G.J. Reinink, 'The lamb on the tree. Syriac exegesis and anti-Islamic apologetics', in E. Noort and E. Tichelaar (eds), *The sacrifice of Isaac. The Aqedah (Genesis 22) and its interpretations*, Leiden, 2002, 109-24

R.G. Hoyland, 'The earliest Christian writings on Muḥammad. An appraisal', in H. Motzki (ed.), *The Biography of Muḥammad. The issue of the sources*, Leiden, 2000, pp. 276-97

S.H. Griffith, 'Disputing with Islam in Syriac. The case of the Monk of Bêt Ḫâlê and a Muslim Emir', *Hugoye* 3 (2000) [article 10]

Hoyland, *Seeing Islam*, pp. 465-72

S.H. Griffith, *Syriac writers on Muslims and the religious challenge of Islam*, Kottayam, 1995

G.J. Reinink, 'The beginnings of Syriac apologetic literature in response to Islam', *OC* 77 (1993) 165-87, pp. 186-87

S.H. Griffith, 'Disputes with Muslims in Syriac Christian texts. From Patriarch John (d. 648) to Bar Hebraeus (d. 1286)', in B. Lewis and F. Niewöhner (eds), *Religionsgespräche im Mittelalter*, Wiesbaden, 1992, 251-73, pp. 259-61 (repr. in Griffith, *The beginnings of Christian theology in Arabic*, Aldershot, 2002)

P. Crone and M. Cook, *Hagarism. The making of the Islamic world*, Cambridge, 1977, pp. 12-13, 17-18, 163, 167

P. Jager, 'Intended edition of a disputation between a monk of the monastery of Bet Ḥale and one of the Ṭayoye', in H.J.W. Drijvers (ed.), *IV Symposium Syriacum 1984*, Rome 1987, 401-2

Baumstark, *GSL*, p. 211

Barbara Roggema 2008

The Apocalypse of Pseudo-Athanasius

Unknown author

DATE OF BIRTH Unknown, probably 2nd half of the 7th c.
PLACE OF BIRTH Unknown, probably Egypt
DATE OF DEATH Unknown, probably 1st half or beginning of the 2nd half of the 8th c.
PLACE OF DEATH Unknown, probably a monastery in the Fayyūm

BIOGRAPHY

The author ascribed his text to the famous church father and archbishop Athanasius of Alexandria (c. 295-373), but the authorship is in fact unknown. The author is known solely through his composition, the so-called *Apocalypse of Pseudo-Athanasius*. It is certain that he was a Copt living as a monk in an Egyptian monastery in the first half of the 8th century. As such, he learned biblical texts and much about the ecclesiastical canons that were followed in the Coptic Church. His knowledge about the historical Athanasius derives from Coptic hagiographical writings about the church fathers. In addition, we can say that he fought for the miaphysite creed of the Copts, as well as against the members of all other denominations and putative adversaries within his own church, accusing or suspecting them of being heretics.

Many texts written in the 7th and 8th centuries are ascribed to authors of the 4th and 5th centuries. At that time, not only single texts but entire cycles were attributed to prominent persons, including Athanasius. There is therefore a possibility that the author composed other pseudepigraphical texts, but this cannot be ascertained.

MAIN SOURCES OF INFORMATION

Primary
See below

Secondary
See below

WORKS ON CHRISTIAN-MUSLIM RELATIONS

The Apocalypse of Pseudo-Athanasius (Modern title)

DATE Between approximately 715 and 744
ORIGINAL LANGUAGE Coptic

DESCRIPTION
The *Apocalypse* occupies 51 pages in the most important and most complete manuscript, MS New York, Pierpont Morgan Library – M 602, fols 51v-76v. Only 11 pages, fols 68v-73v, deal directly with the Muslims and the conditions in Egypt under their rule. However, allusions to Arab rule can be found throughout the text.

The untitled text is a sermon addressed to the clergy and monks of Egypt. Written between 715 and 744, during the Umayyad caliphate, it attempts to explain the situation of the Copts during this period. The author's belief is that God was sending punishments to the world because of the sins of the priests and monks who were misleading the people by their evil words and deeds. Following the Council of Chalcedon, all churches denied the correct faith, except the (miaphysite) church of Egypt, the see of St Mark, which alone would stand fast.

The author interprets the course of history by using the pattern of apocalyptic eschatology and many allusions to biblical texts. He describes a succession of four empires corresponding to the pattern of the four beasts of the apocalypse in Daniel 7: 1-27. The first beast signifies the Roman empire, and the second the Byzantine empire. After this, only the Coptic Church would remain true to God's ways, and as a punishment for their deeds, God would send the Persians, the third beast, but because 'the Persians transgressed the Law, and the impiety of the inhabitants of the earth (multiplied) beyond measure', He would soon end their rule. Finally, He would give power to the Arabs, 'the fourth beast which the faithful prophet Daniel saw, more terrible than all the (other) beasts which were before it, consuming, crushing, trampling the others with its feet'. But owing to the 'sins of the priests and monks', the Coptic people would not return to the true faith and righteous deeds. God would therefore bring upon them pestilence, wars and natural disasters, first upon Egypt, then upon the entire world. These would be the 'labor pains of the end', announcing the dominion of the Antichrist, followed by the last judgment.

The text is a sermon, and its aim is not only to draw a particular picture of history, but also to effect a change in the thinking and behavior of its audience. Thus, at the beginning, it presents the author's picture of the ideal church, and then, in the form of *vaticinia ex eventu*, his descriptions and criticism of the situation within the Coptic Church during the period of Umayyad rule in Egypt. Furthermore, throughout the text he calls for a general change in the lives of the clergy and monks, and advocates ethical rigor.

The most important manuscript also contains two passages about the Archangel Michael, but these are later insertions.

The work mentions the Arab conquest of Egypt and describes the situation of the Copts under Muslim rule during the formative period of Islam, including references to monetary reforms, censuses, land measuring campaigns which resulted in high taxation, economic difficulties, the expulsion of people from their homes, famines and plagues. The Arabs are described as savage, merciless and avaricious, but the author's polemic is nevertheless always directed against his own people, because he interprets these conditions as the consequence of the Copts' impious behavior.

If nothing apart from the title of the main manuscript was known, it might be taken as a lost work by the historical Athanasius, originally written in Greek. However, its *vaticinia ex eventu* show that it is later, and its style indicates that its original language was definitely Coptic (see Witte, 'Der koptische Text', pp. 123-29).

SIGNIFICANCE

This work is one of the rare literary witnesses to the Coptic reaction to the Arab conquest of Egypt and Muslim rule there during the formative period of Islam. Although it does not contain any discussion of Islamic faith and practice, it illustrates how a Copt interpreted the fundamental historical changes that had taken place in his country, and especially in the everyday life of its inhabitants.

The work was very popular. We possess manuscripts in Coptic and in various Arabic translations. Furthermore, it is likely to have influenced other Coptic or Copto-Arabic writings, especially the *Apocalypse of Samuel of Qalamūn* and an untitled Coptic poem (see Witte, *Die Sünden der Priester und Mönche*, pp. 55-57, Groddek et al., *Ein wildes Volk ist es*, p. 233).

MANUSCRIPTS

A complete survey of all known manuscripts, with a detailed description of all those that are accessible, their value for the reconstruction of the original text, and their entries in printed catalogues, followed by a textual history, is given in Witte, *Die Sünden der Priester und Mönche*, pp. 8-9 (common sigla), 12-61 (catalogue entries, descriptions), 62-70 (text history) and 71 (stemma). A short survey is given in Groddek et al., *Ein wildes Volk ist es*, pp. 13-21.

Manuscripts are known in two languages:

a) Coptic:

The oldest, most complete and most important witness to the work is in MS New York, Pierpont Morgan Library – M 602 (9th c., Coptic), fols 51v-76v

This manuscript is the basis of all editions, but pages have suffered some damage throughout the codex and there are therefore many lacunae in the text. Two other short fragments, the first comprising one folio and the second comprising one page, are known.

b) Arabic translations:

Several manuscripts are accessible, with two unrelated translations (for the stemma, see Witte, *Die Sünden der Priester und Mönche,* p. 71). The most important manuscripts of these two different translations are:

(i) MS Birmingham, Mingana – Syr. 461 (19th c., Karshūnī), fols 70v-93r

(ii) Jirjis Bek Yaʿqūb, *Rasāʾil dīniyya qadīma,* Cairo, 1925, pp. 40-52 (a printed early 20th-century edition). This publication is the sole example of this translation. Its editor has not indicated the source, so it should be assessed in the same way as an actual manuscript.

The other accessible Arabic manuscripts are not relevant for the reconstruction of the original text, although they are useful for illustrating the work's continuing importance and influence.

EDITIONS AND TRANSLATIONS

D. Groddek, T. Lindken and H. Schaefer, *Ein wildes Volk ist es... Predigt (Ps.-Athanasius) über Lev 21,9, Ex 19,22, des Erzengel Michael und das Weltende unter arabischer Herrschaft*, Altenberge, 2004 (Corpus Islamo-Christianum. Series Coptica 1) (edition of the Coptic text [partly in cooperation with Witte] with German trans., introduction and a revised text of Jirjis Bek Yaʿqūb, *Rasāʾil dīniyya qadīma*, pp. 40-52, with German trans. by H.H. Biesterfeld)

B. Witte, *Die Sünden der Priester und Mönche. Koptische Eschatologie des 8. Jahrhundert nach Kodex M 602 pp. 104-154 (ps. Athanasius) der Pierpont Morgan Library*, Altenberge, 2002 (edition of the Coptic text [partly in collaboration with Groddek] with German trans.; includes quotations from the two most important Arabic manuscripts where there are lacunae in the Coptic text; volume with commentary in preparation)

F.J. Martinez, *Eastern Christian apocalyptic in the early Muslim period: Pseudo-Methodius and Pseudo-Athanasius*, Washington DC, 1985 (Diss. Catholic University of America) (Coptic text, transcription of MS Birmingham, Mingana – Syr. 461, with English trans.)

T. Orlandi, 'Esortazioni al clero; sui tempi finali; sulla dominazione araba', in T. Orlandi (ed.), *Omelie copte*, Turin, 1981, 71-91 (Italian trans., with a short introduction)

Yaʿqūb, *Rasāʾil dīniyya qadīma*, pp. 40-52 (source MS not indicated; Christian Arabic orthography; frequent printing errors)

H. Hyvernat, *Bibliothecae Pierpont Morgan codices coptici photographicae expressi. Tomus 25. Codex M 602*, Rome, 1922, pp. 104-54 (facsimile edition; difficult to read; folio numbers consistently one number too high)

STUDIES

H. Kaufhold, review of B. Witte, *Die Sünden der Priester und Mönche*, in *OC* 87 (2003) 245-47

S. Richter and G. Wurst, 'Referat über die Editionen koptischer literarischer Texte und Urkunden von 2000 bis 2002', *APF* 49 (2003) 127-62 – with review of B. Witte, *Die Sünden der Priester und Mönche*, pp. 144-45

W. Beltz, 'Ethos und Ordination - zum Problem des rituellen und moralischen Wohlverhaltens der koptischen Kirche im 8. Jahrhundert', in W. Beltz (ed.), *Die koptische Kirche in den ersten drei islamischen Jahrhunderten. Beiträge zum gleichnamigen Leucorea-Kolloquium 2002*, Halle, 2003, 29-39

H. Suermann, 'Die Apokalypse des Ps.-Athanasius: Ein Beispiel für die koptische Auseinandersetzung mit der islamischen Herrschaft im Ägypten der Ummayyadenzeit', in Beltz, *Die koptische Kirche in den ersten drei islamischen Jahrhunderten*, 183-98

H. Suermann, 'Koptische Texte zur arabischen Eroberung Ägyptens und der Umayyadenherrschaft', *Journal of Coptic Studies* 4 (2002) 167-86

J.P. Monferrer Sala, 'Literatura apocalíptica cristiana en árabe. Con un avance de edición del Apocalipsis árabo-copto del Pseudo Atanasio', *Miscelánea de Estudios Árabes y Hebraicos* 48 (1999) 231-54

B. Witte, 'Das Ende der Zeiten. Apokalyptische Elemente in einer koptischen Homilie des 8. Jahrhunderts', in W. Beltz (ed.), *Zeit und Geschichte in der koptischen Frömmigkeit bis zum 8. Jahrhundert*, Halle, 1998, 119-27

J. van Lent, 'Les apocalypses coptes de l'époque arabe. Quelques reflexions', in M. Rassart-Debergh (ed.), *Études coptes V*, Louvain, 1998, 181-95

Hoyland, *Seeing Islam*, 282-85

J. van Lent, 'An unedited Copto-Arabic apocalypse of Shenute from the fourteenth century. Prophecy and history', in S. Emmel et al. (eds), *Ägypten und Nubien in spätantiker und christlicher Zeit*, 2 vols, Wiesbaden, 1999, ii, 155-68

B. Witte, '"Sur la négligence". Einige Bemerkungen zu einem Fragment aus dem Weißen Kloster', in S. Emmel et al. (eds), *Ägypten und Nubien in spätantiker und christlicher Zeit*, ii, 209-16

T. Orlandi, 'Koptische Literatur', in M. Krause (ed.), *Ägypten in spätantik-christlicher Zeit*, Wiesbaden, 1998, 117-47

T. Orlandi, 'Letteratura copta e cristianesimo nazionale egiziano', in A. Camplani (ed.), *L'Egitto cristiano. Aspetti e problemi in età tardo-antica*, Rome, 1997, 39-120

B. Witte, 'Der koptische Text von M 602 f. 52 – f. 72 der Pierpont Morgan Library – wirklich eine Schrift des Athanasius?', *OC* 78 (1994) 123-30

W.E. Kaegi, *Byzantium and the early Islamic conquests,* Cambridge, 1992, pp. 208-9, 225-27

T. Orlandi, art. 'Literature, Coptic', in A.S. Atiya et al. (eds), *The Coptic encyclopedia*, New York 1991, v, pp. 1450-60

F.J. Martinez, 'The King of Rum and the King of Ethiopia in medieval apocalyptic texts from Egypt', in W. Godlewski (ed.), *Coptic studies. Acts of the Third International Congress of Coptic Studies,* Warsaw, 1990, 247-59

L. MacCoull, 'The strange death of Coptic culture', *Coptic Church Review* 10 (1989) 35-45

T. Orlandi, 'Coptic literature', in B.A. Pearson and J.E. Goehring (eds), *The roots of Egyptian Christianity*, Philadelphia, 1986, 51-81

T. Orlandi, 'Un testo copto sulla dominazione araba in Egitto', in T. Orlandi and F. Wisse (eds), *Acts of the second international congress of Coptic studies,* Rome, 1985, 225-33

(Bekir) Bernd (Karl-Heinz) Witte, 2007

The Martyrdom of Vahan

Author uncertain, probably Abraham, also known as Artavazd

DATE OF BIRTH Unknown, probably 1st half of the 8th c.
PLACE OF BIRTH Unknown
DATE OF DEATH Unknown, probably 2nd half of the 8th c.
PLACE OF DEATH Unknown

BIOGRAPHY

It is unclear from the *Martyrdom* whether the author was Abraham, or an unnamed monk from the unspecified monastery of which Abraham was abbot. Together they visited Vahan's martyrium in Ruṣāfa seven years after Vahan's death (i.e. in 744).

MAIN SOURCES OF INFORMATION

Primary —

Secondary —

WORKS ON CHRISTIAN-MUSLIM RELATIONS

Oghbkʾ vasn chʿareatsʾ Ashkharhis Hayotsʾ ew Vkayabanutʿiwn srboyn Vahanay Goghtʾnatsʿwoy, 'Lament on the evils that befell the land of the Armenians and the martyrdom of holy Vardan from Goghtʾn'. Modern title: 'The Martyrdom of Vahan'

DATE 744
ORIGINAL LANGUAGE Armenian, possibly based on a Greek or Arabic version.

DESCRIPTION
Vahan, son of Khosrov the lord of Goght'n, was taken as a child to Damascus with other Armenian prisoners in the reign of al-Walīd

I and raised as a Muslim. The prisoners were released by ʿUmar II, and Vahan returned to the province of Goght'n as its lord, later withdrawing to the desert as a hermit. In the reign of Hishām he declared his Christianity before the caliph in Ruṣāfa, and was eventually put to death on 17 March, 737 (27 Mareri, 186 Armenian style) according to the *Martyrdom*. The *Synaxarion* (G. Bayan, *Le synaxaire arménien,* PO 5-21, 1909-30) gives the date of his commemoration as 28 Areg (= 28 March).

According to the *Martyrdom*, the information was given to Abraham by Greeks at the caliph's court. The late copy of a colophon (MS Venice, Armenian 231 (1860), from MS BNF – Arm. 180 (14th c.)) suggests there was a Greek text from an Arabic original.

References to Vahan's martyrdom are also to be found in Armenian historical sources, such as the History of Thomas Artsruni (q.v.) (T'ovma Artsruni, *Patmut'iwn Tann Artsruneats'*, St Petersburg 1887, p. 252; trans. R.W. Thomson, *Thomas Artsruni, History of the house of the Artsrunik'*, Detroit 1985, pp. 314-15)

SIGNIFICANCE

This is an important account of Muslim attacks on Armenia in the 8th century, with information about Christians at the Umayyad court.

MANUSCRIPTS

MS Erevan, Matenadaran – 5607 (12th c.)

MS Jerusalem, St James Armenian Patriarchate – 97 (1328), fols 410v-427r

MS Jerusalem, St James Armenian Patriarchate 3152 (1384), fols 158r-175r

MS New Julfa (Isfahan), Armenian Library 229 (16th c.), fols 67r-75r

The manuscripts used for the two printed editions are not specified. In addition, there are innumerable brief accounts in synaxaria and miscellanies in all major Armenian collections.

For the titles, see P. Peeters, *Bibliotheca Hagiographica Orientalis*, Brussels 1910 (repr. 1954), pp. 267-68. The longer text is item 1235, the shorter text is item 1236.

EDITIONS AND TRANSLATIONS

J.A. Gatteyrias, 'Elégie sur les malheurs de l'Arménie et le martyre de saint Vahan de Koghten. Episode de l'occupation arabe en Arménie, traduit pour la première fois de l'arménien littéral, sur l'édition des RR. PP. Méchitaristes', *Journal asiatique* 16 (1880) 177-214

Oghbk' vasn ch'areats' Ashkharhis Hayots' ew Vkayabanut'iwn srboyn Vahanay Goght'nats'woy, in *Sop'erk' Haykakank'* 13, Venice 1854, 1-59 (with an abbreviated version on pp. 61-91)
I.B. Aucher, *Liakatar Vark' ew Vkayabanut'iwnk' Srbots'*, 12 vols, Venice 1810-15, i, pp. 188-216

STUDIES

Hoyland, *Seeing Islam*, pp. 373-75
V. Hovhannesean, 'Vahan Goght'nats'ii hetk'erum vray', *Bazmavep* (Venice) 111 (1953) 70-77
L. Alishan, *Yushikk' Hayreneats' Hayots'*, 2 vols, Venice 1870, ii, pp. 129-200 (a rhetorical retelling, not a learned study)

Robert W. Thomson 2008

The Chronicle of 741

Author unknown

DATE OF BIRTH Unknown, probably late 7th or early 8th c.
PLACE OF BIRTH Unknown
DATE OF DEATH Unknown, after 744
PLACE OF DEATH Unknown

BIOGRAPHY —

MAIN SOURCES OF INFORMATION

Primary —

Secondary —

WORKS ON CHRISTIAN-MUSLIM RELATIONS

The original title, assuming there was one, is lost. Conventional titles: *Chronicle of 741*, *Chronica Byzantia-Arabica* ('Byzantine-Arabic Chronicle'), *Continuatio Byzantia-Arabica* (being a continuation of John of Biclar's *Chronicle*). The most accurate title is *Chronica Hispana-Orientalia ad annum 724*.

DATE After 724, the last date referred to in the text, and possibly after the reign of al-Walīd II (r. 743-44)
ORIGINAL LANGUAGE Latin (*CHO*), Greek or possibly Syriac (*CO*)

DESCRIPTION
The text opens with the death of the King of the Visigoths, Recared (601), whose reign is described in the final section of John of Biclar's *Chronicle*. The anonymous compiler also inserts details of Iberian history, for which he draws exclusively on Isidore of Seville's *Historia Gothorum*. A precise account of the battle of Tolosa in 721, taken from an unknown source, is also included at the end. But the 'Spanish

affairs', as Hoyland calls them, only represent about a tenth of the contents of the work, and seem to have been interpolated rather artificially into the framework of another chronicle devoted to affairs of the east. The final combination of this *Chronica Orientalia* (*CO*) and the details of affairs in Iberia forms the Latin *Chronica Hispana-Orientalia* (*CHO*).

No events after 724 are referred to, apart from the mention of the caliphate of the Umayyad al-Walīd II (r. 743-44). This could have been inserted later, and thus the *CO* must have been redacted soon after 724, and the final *CHO* compiled after 743-44.

The *CO* is focused on the eastern Mediterranean (Constantinople, Syria and Egypt) and shows great knowledge of the history of Byzantium, including its emperors and its relations with the Arabs. This is the reason for Dubler's assertion that it was based on Byzantine sources, though this has not been proved, and it is surprising that the *CO* does not give evidence of a pro-Byzantine bias. The description of the wars between 'Romans' and 'Saracens' remains fairly neutral, except for its disapproval of Maslama ibn ʿAbd al-Malik's slaughter of the inhabitants of Pergamum during the reign of Sulaymān ibn ʿAbd al-Malik (715-17).

The *CO* deals mainly with the development of the Islamic state from Muḥammad to the Umayyads. The author is not only fully informed about Umayyad dynastic history, but also shows great admiration for various figures, including Muḥammad, ʿUmar ibn al-Khaṭṭāb (r. 634-44), Muʿāwiya (r. 660-80) ʿAbd al-Malik (r. 685-705), al-Walīd I (r. 705-15) and ʿUmar II (r. 717-20). His chronicle is evidently biased towards the Umayyads, since, as Collins points out, he deliberately avoids any mention of the reign of ʿAlī (656-61). His allegiance to the Marwānids is also made clear by his stern condemnation of the revolt of ʿAbdallāh ibn Zubayr. In referring to Damascus as the capital of the Arabs from the time of the battle of Gabītha-Yarmūk in 636, and not after Muʿāwiya's accession, the *CO* affirms the continuity of Damascus as a political center from the Byzantine era to the new Arab empire. This is a clue to its Syrian origin.

In spite of his Umayyad-centered viewpoint, the author of the *CO* is not a Muslim. Even though he shows great respect for Muḥammad, he says that his status as prophet was invented by his followers. The birth of Islam is also presented as a 'rebellion' against the Byzantines. The *CO* never defends Islamic faith, and the author seems to think that Mecca is in Mesopotamia – 'in the desert between Ur, the city of the Chaldeans, and *Carras*, the city of Mesopotamia' (*Carrhae* or Ḥarrān in the upper Jazīra). It can be assumed, with Collins, that the author of the *CO* was a Christian, and this chronicle seems to be a rather enthusiastic portrayal of the powerful Umayyad empire through the eyes of a non-Muslim subject.

Various hypotheses may be advanced concerning the author of the *CO*. His Syrian pro-Umayyad tone suggests that he is a Syrian Christian. His attitude does not reveal a real commitment to the Byzantine cause, yet he disapproves of the Pergamum slaughter and records the Arab campaigns against Constantinople as inglorious events. Following Mommsen, he could be Syrian Orthodox ('Monophysite'). And if he was a Melkite, he was nevertheless deeply influenced by Umayyad imperial ideology.

Although Arabic was still little used among Syrian Christians in the early 8th century, the Latin text transcribes Arabic names well. Hoyland posits a Syriac original, translated into Greek and then into Latin (the *Apocalypse of Pseudo-Methodius* [q.v.] went through the same process). But García Moreno convincingly shows that certain geographical terms, such as *Kazaniam* for *Azania*, the Greek name for Somalia, could only have come from a Greek source translated into Latin. It may thus be concluded that the *CO* was originally written in Greek by a Monophysite or Melkite Syrian Christian who was committed to the Umayyad cause, soon after 724.

A few other hypotheses can be discarded. García Moreno suggests the *CO* was written in Egypt, but this is unpersuasive since the chronicle only gives a brief and distanced narration of the conquest of this region. On the basis of the above arguments, neither does the evidence support the conclusions of Dubler, who tries to reconcile the Iberian with the eastern and Byzantine contents of the final compilation by arguing that the author of the *CHO* was a Christian convert to Islam who had been born on the Mediterranean coast of the Iberian peninsula, where Byzantine influence had been strongest during the 6th century. Against this, the evidence indicates that the *CHO* compilation expresses neither a Byzantine nor a Muslim point of view.

The remaining problem is to identify who the final compiler of the *CHO* was. The chronicle was composed in al-Andalus after 743-44, but not necessarily by a local scholar. The use of the Hispanic material seems to be dictated by Isidore of Seville's *Historia Gothorum*, since after the reference to Suintila's reign (621-31) it suddenly disappears. The lack of interest in Iberian matters is undisguised: the fall of the Visigothic state and the conquest of *Hispania* are described so allusively that they seem to have little importance for the author. For many scholars, this is proof that the author was not 'Spanish'.

Dubler has noted that the description of the conquest of Tripolitania and Ifrīqiyā shows greater interest on the author's part. The *wālī* of Egypt, ʿAbdallāh ibn Saʿd, is described as 'bloodthirsty' and his raids are said to have caused the ruin of the whole area. His victory against the Byzantine governor Gregory at the battle of Sbeitla in 647 (wrongly dated by the author to 665), is attributed to the flight of Moorish troops and reported as destroying all the 'African nobility' (*omnis decoritas Africæ*). Thus, a passing but nevertheless severe judgment makes the 'Moors' responsible for the defeat at Sbeitla and the ruin of the Maghrib. This, according to Collins and García Moreno, could imply that the *CHO* compiler might be a Christian from Ifrīqiyā or North Africa settled in al-Andalus. The Christian community of Ifrīqiyā was at the crossroads of Greek and Latin cultures, and a local scholar could have completed and translated into Latin the earlier *CO* to form the *CHO*. However, the *CHO* is far from being centered on North Africa, and the suggestion of Maghribī authorship must remain hypothetical.

Martín has suggested that the *CHO* was composed by a senior Umayyad functionary in al-Andalus, along with a 'Mozarab'. But the *CHO* bears no hint of a Muslim hand, and it can hardly have been commissioned by the ruling house. In fact, the original *CO* was apparently adopted and translated without any change, apart from being slightly 'hispanicized' for a Christian pro-Umayyad milieu interested in the affairs of the east. This could be the key to this complex history. The original *CO* could have been brought to al-Andalus by a Syrian Monophysite or Melkite group, and there translated from Greek into Latin in response to local Christian demand. From the 8th to the 9th centuries, several clues about the circulation and translation of eastern Christian sources in al-Andalus have been detected. The aim of the *CHO* was certainly to complement local historiography with details of events in the east, and the final compilation probably reflects the opinion of a pro-Umayyad milieu, perhaps the ruling elite, for whom the conquest was justified by the desire to form a powerful empire with al-Andalus a part.

The *Chronicle of 754* (q.v.), which is based on a quite similar outline to this, can be regarded as an exact counterpart to the *CHO*. This echoes the ideological division of the Christian community in al-Andalus that was later documented in the 9th-century debate about Islamic domination.

SIGNIFICANCE

The *Chronica Byzantia-Arabica*, along with the *Chronicle of 754*, is one of the earliest sources of Iberian history following the Arab conquest. However, it appears to have had a limited circulation, probably because it conveyed a positive view of Umayyad rule. It constitutes valuable evidence of the intellectual relations that existed between the Christians of al-Andalus and eastern Christians under Islamic rule.

MANUSCRIPTS

The *CHO* is known as part of a lost *codex* from Soria (Castilla). It was among the parts that were copied by two 16th-century Spanish humanists, Juan Bautista Pérez (1537-97), canon of Toledo, and Juan de Mariana (1536-1623). It thus survives only in 16th-century copies, preserved in four different manuscripts. The *Codex Soriensis* contained a number of chronicles, including the *Chronicle of Alfonso III* (q.v.), which was completed after 883. Juan Bautista Pérez suggests that it was written in Visigothic script and says it seemed 'very old', being copied between the end of the 9th and 12th centuries.

EDITIONS AND TRANSLATIONS

J.C. Martín, 'Los Chronica Byzantia-Arabica', *e-Spania* (June 2007), http://e-spania.revues.org/document329.html (revised Spanish trans.)

J.J. Batista Rodríguez and R. Blanco Silva, 'Una crónica mozárabe a la que se ha dado en llamar *Arábigo-bizantina de 741*. Un comentario y una traducción', *Revista de Filología de la Universidad de la Laguna* 17 (1999) 158-66 (Spanish trans.)

Hoyland, *Seeing Islam*, pp. 611-30 (English trans.)

Gil, *CSM* i, pp. 7-14

T. Mommsen (ed.), *Chronica minora saec. IV. V. VI. VII*, 3 vols, Berlin, 1892-98, ii, pp. 334-68 (*MGH Auctores antiquissimi* 9, 11, 13)

Flórez, *España Sagrada*, vi, pp. 430-41

STUDIES

Martín, 'Los Chronica Byzantia-Arabica', pp. 1-18

L.A. García Moreno, 'Elementos de tradición bizantina en dos *Vidas de Mahoma* mozárabes', in I. Pérez Martín and P. Bádenas de la Peña (eds), *Bizancio y la Península Ibérica. De la antigüedad tardía a la edad moderna*, Madrid, 2004, 250-60

Tolan, *Saracens*, pp. 78-83
A. Christys, *Christians in al-Andalus (711-1000)*, Richmond, 2002, pp. 35-51
Batista Rodríguez and Blanco Silva, 'Una crónica mozárabe'
Hoyland, *Seeing Islam*, pp. 423-27, 611-30
M. Huete Fudio, *La historiografía latina medieval en la Península Ibérica*, Madrid, 1997, p. 3
R. Collins, *The Arab conquest of Spain 710-797*, Oxford, 1989, pp. 53-57
J.E. López Pereira, *Estudio crítico sobre la Crónica Mozárabe de 754*, Zaragoza, 1980, pp. 96-99, 116-17
M.C. Díaz y Díaz, 'La historiografía hispana desde la invasión árabe hasta el año 1000', in M.C. Díaz y Díaz, *De Isidoro al siglo XI. Ocho estudios sobre la vida literaria peninsular*, Barcelona, 1976, 203-34, pp. 205-7
C.E. Dubler, 'Sobre la Crónica arábigo-bizantina de 741 y la influencia bizantina en la Península Ibérica', *Al-Andalus* 11 (1946) 283-349
Mommsen, *Chronica minora*, ii, pp. 323-33
T. Nöldeke, 'Epimetrum', in Mommsen, *Chronica minora*, ii, pp. 368-69

Cyrille Aillet 2008

Peter of Damascus

DATE OF BIRTH Unknown
PLACE OF BIRTH Unknown
DATE OF DEATH After 743/44
PLACE OF DEATH Yemen

BIOGRAPHY

Peter was metropolitan of Damascus in the first half of the 8th century. John of Damascus wrote his *Contra Jacobitas* on his behalf (Kotter, iv, p. 109), and he was also the recipient of John's *Libellus de recta sententia* (*PG* 94, col. 1421A). According to Theophanes and Michael the Syrian, the Caliph al-Walīd II (r. 743-44) ordered that Peter should have his tongue cut out and be exiled to Yemen (*Arabia Felix*) because he did not abstain from 'reproving the impiety of the Arabs and Manichees'. Despite having no tongue, he was still able to recite the liturgy aloud. He died in Yemen at an unknown date.

The historicity of Peter's martyrdom is disputed. According to Peeters, the story of his martyrdom refers rather to his homonym Peter of Capitolias (q.v.). Peeters even denies that Peter of Damascus existed at all.

MAIN SOURCES OF INFORMATION

Primary

C. de Boor, *Theophanis Chronographia*, 2 vols, Leipzig, 1883-85, p. 416

J.-B. Chabot, *Chronique de Michel le syrien, patriarche jacobite d'Antioche (1166-1199)*, 4 vols, Paris, 1899-1910, ii, p. 506

J.-B. Chabot, *Chronicon anonymum ad annum Christi 1234 pertinens*, Louvain, 1937 (repr. 1952) (*CSCO* 109), p. 245

B. Kotter, *Die Schriften des Johannes von Damaskos*, 6 vols, Berlin, 1969-88, iv, pp. 101, 109

C. Mango and R. Scott, *The Chronicle of Theophanes Confessor. Byzantine and Near-Eastern history AD 284-813*, Oxford, 1997, pp. 577-79

Secondary

PMBZ no. 5999

J. Nasrallah, 'Dialogue islamo-chrétien à propos de publications récentes', *REI* 46 (1978) 121-51, pp. 124-27

P. Peeters, 'Glanures martyrologiques', *AB* 58 (1940) 104-25, pp. 123-25
P. Peeters, 'La Passion de S. Pierre de Capitolias (+ 13 janvier 715)', *AB* 57 (1939) 299-333

WORKS ON CHRISTIAN-MUSLIM RELATIONS

A treatise against Islam, title unknown

DATE Unknown
ORIGINAL LANGUAGE Greek

DESCRIPTION
It is uncertain whether this work ever existed. Khoury (*Les théologiens byzantins*, p. 40), though without giving any reference, states that 'it is said' Peter wrote a now lost treatise against Islam in Arabic. But he doubts this, since he follows Peeters' argument that Peter of Damascus should be identified with Peter of Capitolias (q.v.). In contrast, Nasrallah ('Dialogue islamo-chrétien', p. 126) mentions that the work is transmitted in a Greek manuscript from Sinai, though without giving its title or number. Nasrallah also says (*Histoire*, p. 78) that Peter wrote a treatise against the Manicheans and Islam, though it seems that this statement is based on a misreading of the *Chronicle* of Theophanes Confessor, which Nasrallah cites as a reference here. Following Kamil's catalogue, Nasrallah refers to MS Sinai – Gr. 443 (erroneously referred to as 343) as a manuscript containing various texts by Peter. This manuscript, however, contains an ascetic work entitled *Anamnēsis tēs idias psychēs* (Gardthausen, no. 443; Hoyland, pp. 358-59), which is better known as *Hypomnesis pros tēn heautou psychen* (Beck, p. 644). According to Gardthausen, two other composite MSS which contain selections of *ascetica* (no. 464) and sayings of the Fathers (no. 466) also include unspecified writings by Peter. However, according to Beck (p. 644), the author of these ascetic texts is another Peter of Damascus, who should be dated to either 1096-97 or 1156-57.

SIGNIFICANCE
If this text ever existed, it would be one of the earliest treatises on Islam in Greek. Furthermore, it would be particularly interesting to compare it with John's of Damascus's short chapter on Islam in his *De haeresibus*, especially since John is known to have written at least one polemical text on behalf of Peter.

MANUSCRIPTS

MS Sinai – Gr. 464 or 466?

EDITIONS AND TRANSLATIONS —

STUDIES

Hoyland, *Seeing Islam*, pp. 359-60

Nasrallah, *HMLEM* ii.2, pp. 77-78

Nasrallah, 'Dialogue islamo-chrétien', pp. 124-27

M. Kamil, *Catalogue of all manuscripts in the Monastery of St. Catharine on Mount Sinai*, Wiesbaden, 1970, p. 88, no. 667 (443)

A.T. Khoury, *Les théologiens byzantins et l'islam. Textes et auteurs (8.-13. s.)*, Louvain, 1969, p. 40

H.-G. Beck, *Kirche und theologische Literatur im byzantinischen Reich*, Munich, 1959, p. 644

V. Gardthausen, *Catalogus codicum graecorum Sinaiticorum*, Oxford, 1886, nos. 443, 464 and 464

Johannes Pahlitzsch 2008

Historia vel Gesta Francorum

Unknown author

DATE OF BIRTH Unknown, probably 8th c.
PLACE OF BIRTH Unknown
DATE OF DEATH Unknown, probably 8th c.
PLACE OF DEATH Unknown

BIOGRAPHY

The compiler, who may have been a monk, was working on the orders of Count Childebrand and his son Count Nibelung, members of the Carolingian ruling house. Nothing is known about him except what can be deduced from his text.

MAIN SOURCES OF INFORMATION

Primary —

Secondary

R. Collins, *Die Fredegar-Chroniken*, Hannover, 2007, pp. 82-145 (*MGH Studien und Texte* 44)

WORKS ON CHRISTIAN-MUSLIM RELATIONS

Historia vel Gesta Francorum, 'The History or deeds of the Franks'

DATE c. 751
ORIGINAL LANGUAGE Latin

DESCRIPTION

This work was compiled soon after 751, using the five-book world chronicle of 'Fredegar' (q.v.), recast into a three-book format with excision of some of its contents and addition of new materials, including a unique narrative of events in Francia in the years from c. 727 to 751. A continuation to this, covering the period from 754 to 768, was added sometime before the end of the 780s, probably by a different author.

SIGNIFICANCE

This provides some near contemporary narrative of the Muslim conquests and raids into Aquitaine and Provence in the 720s and 730s, and the Frankish resistance to them, including Charles Martel's victory at Poitiers. The author refers to the Muslims, whom he calls Saracens – not distinguishing between Arabs and Berbers – as 'perfidious' and as 'infidels'. This is in the context of their burning churches. He gives no indication of any knowledge of Islam itself, and the accounts of the campaigns are brief.

MANUSCRIPTS

Fully listed in Collins, *Die Fredegar-Chroniken*, pp. 96-130

There are seven almost complete manuscripts and two fragments, as well as a far more numerous body of extracts and excerpts. The earliest dates to the second quarter of the 9th century, and most are of mid-9th to early 11th century date, with one from c. 1500. Most come from a small area of southern Germany and northern Switzerland, but with a subgroup of western French origin.

EDITIONS AND TRANSLATIONS

Full list in C. Straw and R. Collins, *Historical and religious writers of the Latin West. Gregory the Great and Fredegar*, Aldershot, 1996, pp. 132-33

There is no complete edition, but the sections containing the 8th-century material can be found in:

Frédégaire, *Chronique des temps mérovingiens. Livre IV et continuations. Texte latin selon l'édition de J.M. Wallace-Hadrill*, trans. O. Devillers and J. Meyers, Turnhout, 2001

The Fourth Book of the Chronicle of Fredegar, ed. and trans. J.M. Wallace-Hadrill, London, 1960

Chronicarum quae dicuntur Fredegarii Scholastici Libri IV, ed. B. Krusch, Hannover, 1888 (*MGH Scriptores rerum Merovingicarum* 2)

STUDIES

Full list in Collins *Die Fredegar-Chroniken*, pp. ix-xiii

Roger Collins 2007

John of Damascus

Johannes Damascenus

DATE OF BIRTH Unknown, c. 675
PLACE OF BIRTH Damascus
DATE OF DEATH Unknown, probably before 754
PLACE OF DEATH Monastery of Mār Saba, near Jerusalem

BIOGRAPHY

Only a little of the available information about John's life can be accepted with confidence, because his medieval biographies are heavily hagiographical and contain much legendary and anecdotic material. The few reliable facts are as follows: John was born about 675 or earlier in Damascus into a Christian family of the Byzantine rite (Melkites). His grandfather, Manṣūr ibn Sarjūn, played an important role in the negotiations with the Muslim rulers of Damascus in 635, and his father Sarjūn was a high ranking official, maybe even minister of finance under Muʿāwiya (r. 661-80). John himself was also a member of the financial administration, at least under the Umayyad Caliphs ʿAbd al-Malik (r. 685-705) and perhaps al-Walīd I (r. 705-15). When the Caliph ʿUmar II (r. 717-20) prohibited *dhimmīs* from holding high positions in government unless they converted to Islam, John retired from office and entered the famous monastery of Mār Saba near Jerusalem, where he lived until the end of his life and devoted himself to studying and writing.

John of Damascus's main work is the *Fount of Knowledge* (*Pēgē gnōseōs*), a compendium of all theological (Christian) knowledge up to his time. He was not so much an original thinker as a great collector and compiler of the patristic tradition, and his principle was 'to say nothing of my own' (*Epistola dedicatoria*, line 60; Kotter, i, p. 53). The *Pēgē* is dedicated to Bishop Cosmas of Maiouma (d. after 743), John's adoptive brother, and is divided into three parts: the *Capita philosophica* ('Best of Greek philosophy', also called *Dialectica*; Kotter, i), the *De haeresibus* ('On heresies'; Kotter, iv), and the *Expositio fidei* ('Explanation of the true faith'; Kotter, ii). The structure of the work is therefore clearly climactic. In the first part, dialectical philosophy is considered as the instrument by which to gain knowledge by using human reason; this is by no means perfect knowledge, which is God's alone, but serves as a basis that needs to be supplemented. In the second, the errors and distortions of human reason extended beyond its limits, i.e., the false opinions of the philosophers and erroneous religious beliefs that can be attributed respectively to the wrong interpretation of divine revelation and to human invention, are discussed in 100 chapters called 'heresies'. The collection is an odd conglomeration and contains such varied 'heresies' as, e.g., Platonism, Judaism, and Arianism. Ancient philosophical schools, the religion of ancient Israel (including, however, some Jewish sects), and Christian heresies are treated in the same way. John is clearly comparing apples with oranges, so to speak, so it is not surprising that Islam is also seen not as an independent religion, but as a (Christian) heresy (see below). The third part, the *Expositio fidei* (also containing 100 chapters), deals with the main articles of orthodox faith laid down in the '*symbolon*': God and the Trinity, visible and invisible creation, Christ and salvation, baptism, the veneration of the cross, of relics and of icons, prayer, the eucharist, the Virgin as *Theotokos*, scripture, and finally the resurrection. Like the whole *Pēgē*, the *Expositio fidei* is not an innovative theological work but a comprehensive explanation of what the orthodox fathers believed.

Besides the *Pēgē gnōseōs*, which was evidently completed after 743, John wrote numerous minor works, e.g., an introduction to elementary philosophical terms (*Introductio elementaris*), three orations against iconoclasm (*Contra imaginum calumniatores*), polemical works against Nestorians, Manichaeans, and others, many homilies, and some hagiographical writings (according to Theophanes the Confessor, these included an account of the martyrdom Peter of Capitolias [q.v.] at the hands of Muslims). A version of the Barlaam-and-Joasaph romance is probably falsely attributed to him. All these works (including doubtful and spurious ones) have been edited by Kotter.

MAIN SOURCES OF INFORMATION

Primary

Anonymous 9th-century Arabic Life, *Sīrat al-qiddīs Yūḥannā l-Dimashqī l-aṣliyya taṣnīf al-rāhib Mīkhā'īl al-Sam'ānī al-Anṭākī*, with an 11th-century prologue by a certain Michael, a monk of the monastery of St Symeon, Antioch, in C. Bacha, *Biographie de saint Jean Damascène. Texte original arabe*, Harissa, 1912. Greek trans. by John, Patriarch of Jerusalem, in *PG* 94, cols 429-90; cf. G. Graf, 'Das arabische Original der *Vita* des hl. Johannes von Damascus', *Der Katholik* 12 (1913) 164-90 and 320-31 (German trans.)

Anonymous 11th-c. *Vita Marciana* in M. Gordillo, 'Damascenica, I. Vita Marciana', *OC* 8 (1926) 60-68
Life by John Merkouropoulos, Patriarch of Jerusalem, in A. Papadopoulos-Kerameus (ed.), *Analekta Hierosolymitikēs Stachylogias*, 5 vols, Brussels, 1963, iv, pp. 271-302
Anonymous 13th century Life, in Papadopoulos-Kerameus, *Analekta Hierosolymitikēs Stachylogias*, iv, pp. 305-50
Sermon on St John of Damascus by Constantine Akropolites, in *PG* 140, cols 812-85 (with biographical elements)

Secondary
I. Rochow, *Die Legende von der abgehauenen Hand des Johannes Damaskenos*, Frankfurt am Main, 2007, pp. 1-24
B. Flusin et al. (eds), *Giovanni di Damasco. Un padre al sorgere dell'Islam*, Magnano, 2006
A. Louth, *St John Damascene. Tradition and originality in Byzantine theology*, Oxford, 2002
V.S. Conticello, art. 'Jean Damascène', in *Dictionnaire des philosophes antiques*, Paris, 1989-
A. Kazhdan, *A history of Byzantine literature (650-850)*, Athens, 1999, pp. 75-93
PMBZ, no. 2969
R. Glei and A.T. Khoury, *Johannes Damaskenos und Theodor Abū Qurra, Schriften zum Islam*, Würzburg-Altenberge, 1995, pp. 9-36 (introduction by Khoury)
M.-F. Auzépy, 'De la Palestine à Constantinople (VIIIe-IXe siècles): Étienne le Sabaïte et Jean Damascène', *Travaux et Mémoires* 12 (1994) 183-218
R. Le Coz, *Jean Damascène. Écrits sur l'Islam*, Paris, 1992, pp. 21-65
Nasrallah, *HMLEM* ii.2, pp. 115-85
D.J. Sahas, *John of Damascus on Islam. The 'Heresy of the Ishmaelites'*, Leiden, 1972, pp. 3-48

WORKS ON CHRISTIAN-MUSLIM RELATIONS

Peri haireseōn, 'On heresies, ch. 100', 'De haeresibus, cap. 100'

DATE The precise date of composition is unknown. It is part of the *Pēgē gnōseōs* that was completed after 743, but it is possible that several chapters were written earlier.
ORIGINAL LANGUAGE Greek

DESCRIPTION
Chapter 100 of *De haeresibus* is the last of the group of 100 heresies that form the second part of the *Pēgē gnōseōs*. Earlier numberings that count 101 or even more chapters must be rejected for reasons of

uniformity and traditional use of the 'century' number. Some scholars have doubted the authenticity of Ch. 100 on various grounds, but these are insufficient to deny the authorship of John of Damascus (see, e.g., Le Coz, pp. 183-98). The chapter comprises eight pages (Kotter, iv, 60-67) and is probably incomplete, because the ending is rather abrupt. But even in its present form, Ch. 100 is the longest and most important in the whole *De haeresibus*, for it deals with Islam, the so-called 'heresy of the Ishmaelites' (referring to Ishmael, son of Hagar) or 'Saracens' (which John explains is from *Sara-kenē* – Sarah is empty: because Sarah was childless, Abraham begot a son with Hagar the servant woman).

John begins Ch. 100 by remarking that this heresy, a forerunner of the Antichrist, was still influential in his own time, that initially the Ishmaelites were idolators, and that Muḥammad, influenced by an Arian monk, claimed falsely that a scripture had been sent down to him from heaven.

He refers to a few of the main doctrines of Islam: that God is one and the creator of all things, that Christ is the word of God (*kalimat Allāh*) and a spirit from Him (*rūḥ minhu*), was son of Mary (confounded with Miriam, sister of Moses and Aaron), and was not crucified nor the son of God. He goes on to talk about Muḥammad: his mission was not foretold by earlier prophets and there were no witnesses to authenticate it because he received his revelations when he was asleep, which does not accord with the rules of Islamic law.

John goes on to reject Muslim polemics against Christians as 'associators' (*mushrikūn*) of other beings with God, and argues that while Muslims revile Christians as idolators who worship the cross, they themselves worship the black stone of the Kaʿba.

He devotes a large part of the chapter to polemics against Islamic marriage law and sexual behavior, with excerpts from *sūra* 4 (*Women*) and other parts of the Qurʾān, in particular a supposed *sūra*, which he calls *The She-Camel of God*. This is not found in the Qurʾān, although a sacred she-camel (*nāqa*) is mentioned in Q 7:73-79; 26:141-49, etc.; John is probably referring to popular legends here.

Short references to *sūra* 5 (*The Table Spread*) and *sūra* 2 *(The Cow)* follow. And finally John briefly mentions laws on circumcision (although circumcision is not mentioned in the Qurʾān) and food. The text breaks off here, seeming to be incomplete.

It is remarkable that John of Damascus regards Islam (though he never uses the term) as a Christian heresy originating from

Muḥammad's contact with an Arian monk, a detail probably taken from the legend of the monk Baḥīrā (q.v.). In consequence of this, he understands qurʾānic Christology, which depicts Christ as the 'word of God and a spirit from Him', as a form of logos- and pneuma-theology, though this bears some resemblances to later Christian apologetic explanations intended for Muslims. Nevertheless, his account of Islam is predominantly polemical: he refers to its dubious mode of revelation, pagan rites at the Kaʿba, marriage and divorce law based mainly on sexual desires, and the fabulous character of many passages in the Qurʾān.

SIGNIFICANCE

As the earliest known Christian document to deal with Islam in some detail, the significance of Ch. 100 of *De haeresibus* can hardly be overestimated. It formed the image of Islam, at least in the Greek world, for many centuries, and exerted wider influence among Christian readers. Later writings often only develop and enrich the motifs laid down in the Damascene's description of Islam, especially when dealing with the topics mentioned above. With regard to apologetics, the main themes treated are the Trinity, Christology, and soteriology. With regard to polemics, the person of Muḥammad, the nature and composition of the Qurʾān, and the supposed inclination of Muslims to bodily desires (including the rather 'earthly' eschatology) remained important topics in Christian-Islamic disputation.

MANUSCRIPTS

For a complete list of manuscripts, see Kotter, iv, pp. 11-18.

EDITIONS AND TRANSLATIONS

R. Glei and A.T. Khoury, *Johannes Damaskenos und Theodor Abū Qurra, Schriften zum Islam*, Würzburg-Altenberge, 1995 (*Corpus Islamo-Christianum, Series Graeca* 3), pp. 73-83 (Greek text from Kotter, with German trans.)

R. Le Coz, *Jean Damascène. Écrits sur l'Islam*, Paris, 1992 (*Sources Chrétiennes* 383), pp. 209-27 (Greek text from Kotter, with French trans.)

P.B. Kotter, *Die Schriften des Johannes von Damaskos*, 5 vols, Berlin, 1969-88, iv, *Liber de haeresibus, Opera polemica*, pp. 60-67 (After Kotter's death, there was a long delay in publishing the last volume, containing spurious works. The second half of the sixth volume, prepared by Robert Volk, appeared in 2006; the first half has not yet appeared.)

D.J. Sahas, *John of Damascus on Islam. The 'Heresy of the Ishmaelites'*, Leiden, 1972, pp. 132-41 (Appendix I: Greek text from *PG* 94, cols 764-73, with English trans.)

Earlier editions and translations are listed in Kotter, iv, pp. 15-17

STUDIES

S.H. Griffith, 'Giovanni di Damasco e la chiesa in Siria all'epoca degli Omayyadi', in Flusin, *Giovanni di Damasco*, pp. 21-52

D.J. Sahas, 'L'Islam nel contesto della vita e della produzione letteraria di Giovanni di Damasco', in Flusin, *Giovanni di Damasco*, pp. 87-115

A. Argyriou, 'Perception de l'Islam et traductions du Coran dans le monde byzantine grec', *Byzantion* 75 (2005) 25-69

M. Beltran, 'Los atributos divinos en Juan de Damasco y su influencia en el islam', *Collectanea Christiana Orientalia* 2 (2005) 25-42

A. Davids and P. Valkenberg, 'John of Damascus. The heresy of the Ishmaelites', in B. Roggema, M. Poorthuis and P. Valkenberg (eds), *The three rings. Textual studies in the historical trialogue of Judaism, Christianity and Islam*, Louvain, 2005, 71-90

I. Pochoshajew, 'Johannes von Damaskos: De Haeresibus 100', *Islamochristiana* 30 (2004) 65-75

Louth, *St John Damascene*, pp. 76-83

P. Valkenberg, 'John of Damascus and the theological construction of Christian identity vis-à-vis early Islam', *Jaarboek Thomas Instituut te Utrecht* 20 (2001) 8-30

P. La Spisa, 'Una citazione di Giovanni Damasceno in Sulaymān ibn Ḥasan al-Ġazzi', *Pd'O* 27 (2002) 85-105

O. Knorr, 'Zur Überlieferungsgeschichte des "Liber de haeresibus" des Johannes von Damaskus (um 650 – vor 754)', *BZ* 91 (1998) 59-69 (with harsh criticism of Kotter's edition)

Hoyland, *Seeing Islam*, pp. 480-89

A. Louth, *A Christian theologian at the court of the caliph. Some cultural reflections*, London, 1995 (Inaugural Lecture, Goldsmiths College, 24 November, 1994)

D.J. Sahas, 'Cultural interaction during the Umayyad period: the "circle" of John Damascenus', *Aram* 6 (1994) 35-66

D.J. Sahas, 'John of Damascus on Islam. Revisited', *Abr-Nahrain* 23 (1984-85) 104-118

Full bibliographies of older works can be found in Glei and Khoury, Le Coz, Kotter, iv, and Sahas.

Reinhold F. Glei 2007

The Chronicle of 754

Unknown author

DATE OF BIRTH Unknown, probably early 8th c.
PLACE OF BIRTH Unknown, probably Spain
DATE OF DEATH Unknown, after 754
PLACE OF DEATH Unknown, probably Spain

BIOGRAPHY

Nothing is known about the author other than what can be deduced from the text itself. He appears to have been a mid-8th century Latin Christian cleric living under Muslim rule somewhere in al-Andalus.

MAIN SOURCES OF INFORMATION

Primary —

Secondary —

WORKS ON CHRISTIAN-MUSLIM RELATIONS

Continuatio Hispana, *Continuatio Isidoriana Hispana*, 'Mozarabic Chronicle of 754', 'Hispanic Chronicle of 754', 'The Chronicle of 754'

DATE 754
ORIGINAL LANGUAGE Latin

DESCRIPTION

This is an anonymous chronicle covering Mediterranean history from the accession of Heraclius in 610 to 754, apparently conceived as a continuation of Isidore of Seville's *Chronica majora*. Faithful to the 'universal chronicle' tradition established by Eusebius, the author treats Byzantine, Arab and Iberian history simultaneously, dating all entries in terms of the reigning emperors, caliphs, and kings or governors. The bulk of the chronicle is dedicated to the history of al-Andalus and the Maghrib from the arrival of the Muslims to 754.

SIGNIFICANCE

No other contemporary chronicles in any language cover the pre-Umayyad period (711-56) of Andalusian history. Hence this is a key source on this period. The author depicts the Muslim conquest of Spain as a catastrophe of epic proportions, but he goes on to give a fairly dispassionate account of Andalusian history, recounting the military and political careers of the peninsula's Muslim rulers. He is clearly familiar with recent Arab history, both in the east and the Maghrib, and he no doubt spoke and read Arabic. This has led some historians to suppose that he was in the entourage of the Cordovan emirs. At any event he carefully avoids any mention of the religion of Spain's new rulers.

MANUSCRIPTS

MS BL – Egerton 1934 + MS Madrid, Biblioteca de la Real Academia de la Historia – 81 (9th c.)

MS Madrid, Biblioteca de la Universidad Complutense – 116, Z, 46 (13th c.)

MS BNF – Arsenal 982 (14th c.)

EDITIONS AND TRANSLATIONS

K.B. Wolf, *Conquerors and chroniclers of early medieval Spain*, Liverpool, 1990, 1999^{2}, pp. 111-60 (English trans.)

J.E. López Pereira, *Crónica mozárabe de 754*, 2 vols, Zaragoza, 1980, i, pp. 24-131 (edition with facing Spanish trans.)

Gil, *CSM* i, pp. 15-54 (Latin edition)

T. Mommsen (ed.), *Chronica minora saec. IV. V. VI. VII*, 3 vols, Berlin, 1892-98, ii, pp. 323-69 (*MGH Auctores antiquissimi* 9, 11, 13) (Latin edition)

STUDIES

A. del Castillo Alvarez and J. Montenegro Valentín, 'La expedición de Abd al-Malik ibn Qatan al-Fihri a los "Pirinaica iuga" en el anónimo mozárabe de 754', *Hispania. Revista española de historia* 64 (2004) 185-202

A. Christys, *Christians in al-Andalus*, Richmond, 2002, pp. 28-51

Tolan, *Saracens*, pp. 78-85

Wolf, *Conquerors and chroniclers of early medieval Spain*, pp. 25-42

Hoyland, *Seeing Islam*, pp. 423-27

C. Cardelle de Hartmann, 'The textual transmission of the Mozarabic chronicle of 754', *Early Medieval Europe* 8 (1999) 13-29

J.E. López Pereira, 'Interpoblaciones en la historiografía Hispano-Latina Medieval. El caso de la crónica mozárabe de 754', in Colegio Universitario de Toledo, *Toledo y Carpetania en la Edad Antigua*, Toledo, 1990, 279-90

R. Collins, *The Arab conquest of Spain: 710-797*, Oxford, 1989, pp. 17-112

G.V. Sumner, 'The mozarabic chronicle of 754 and the location of the Berber victory over the army of Kultüm', *Al-Qantara* 1 (1980) 443-46 (Spanish version: 'La crónica mozárabe de 754 y la localización de la victoria bereber sobre el ejército de Kultum', *Boletín de la Real Academia de la Historia* 180 (1983) 351-54)

López Pereira, *Crónica mozárabe de 754*, ii, pp. 9-117

G.V. Sumner, 'El perdido Códice Alcobaciense y la Crónica Mozárabe de 754', *Boletín de la Real Academia de la Historia* 177 (1980) 343-46

A.M. Sales Montserrat, *Estudios sobre el latín hispánico. La Crónica mozárabe del 754*, Barcelona, 1975 (Diss. University of Barcelona)

M. Barceló Perello, 'La primerenca organització fiscal d'Al-Andalus, segone la "Crònica del 754"', *Faventia. Revista de filologia clàssica* 2 (1972) 231-62

Kenneth B. Wolf 2007

Theophilus of Edessa

Theophilus bar Tuma, Thawfīl al-Rūmī

DATE OF BIRTH 695 or shortly before
PLACE OF BIRTH Unknown, probably Edessa
DATE OF DEATH 15 July 785
PLACE OF DEATH Unknown, probably Baghdad

BIOGRAPHY

Theophilus accompanied the ʿAbbasid Caliph al-Mahdī as astrologer on some of his military campaigns before the year 768, probably the campaigns to Khurāsān and Ṭabaristān (758-59). Thereafter, he became al-Mahdī's chief astrologer in Baghdad. According to Barhebraeus, he belonged to the Maronite community, which seems improbable on account of his presumed Edessene origins. Dionysius of Tell-Maḥrē (q.v.) (quoted by Michael the Syrian) portrays him as a Chalcedonian, which finds some confirmation in the fact that he was much interested in Byzantine history and was well versed in Greek classical literature.

He is the author of a number of scientific works, especially on astrology, composed in Greek (listed in Breydy, *Geschichte*, pp. 135-36) but also partially known to later Muslim authors on astronomy. According to Barhebraeus (*Chronicon Syriacum*, p. 127), he translated the 'two books' of Homer into Syriac, in which language he also composed a 'wonderful chronological work' (see below). It is not certain whether the Syriac translation of Galen's *On the method of maintaining good health*, ascribed by Ḥunayn ibn Isḥāq (q.v.) to a certain Theophilus of Edessa, was made by this Theophilus.

According to Barhebraeus, he died 20 days before al-Mahdī.

MAIN SOURCES OF INFORMATION

Primary

Chronique de Michel le Syrien, ed. and trans. J.-B. Chabot, 4 vols, Paris, 1899-1910, iv, p. 378, ii, p. 358

A. Vasiliev, *Agapius (Maḥbūb) of Manbidj. Kitāb-al-ʿunwān*, Paris, 1911 (PO 8), p. 525

Ibn al-Qifṭī, *Taʾrīkh al-ḥukamāʾ*, ed. J. Lippert, Leipzig 1903, p. 109

Gregorius Barhebraeus, *Chronicon Syriacum*, ed. P. Bedjan, Paris, 1890, pp. 126-27
E.A. Wallis Budge, *The Chronography of Gregory Abû'l-Faraj*, 2 vols, London, 1932, Amsterdam, 1976², i, pp. 116-17
Gregory Barhebraeus, *Mukhtaṣar taʿrīkh al-duwal*, ed. A. Salihānī, Beirut, 1890, 1958², pp. 219-20

Secondary
L.I. Conrad, 'Varietas Syriaca. Secular and scientific culture in the Christian communities of Syria after the Muslim conquest', in G.J. Reinink and A.C. Klugkist (eds), *After Bardaisan. Studies on continuity and change in Syriac Christianity in honour of Professor Han J.W. Drijvers*, Louvain, 1999, 85-105, pp. 91-92
Hoyland, *Seeing Islam*, pp. 400-9
Sezgin, *GAS* vii, pp. 49-50
M. Breydy, 'Das Chronicon des Maroniten Theophilus ibn Tuma', *Journal of Oriental and African Studies* 2 (1990) 34-46
M. Breydy, *Geschichte der syro-arabischen Literatur der Maroniten vom VII. bis XVI. Jahrhundert*, Opladen, 1985, pp. 132-38
Baumstark, *GSL*, pp. 341-42
F. Cumont and F. Boll, *Catalogus codicum astrologorum graecorum. Codicum romanorum*, 12 vols, Brussels, 1898-1936, v, pp. 229-38

WORKS ON CHRISTIAN-MUSLIM RELATIONS

Ktābā d-maktab zabnē, 'Chronography'. Modern title: 'Syriac Common Source'

DATE Shortly after 754
ORIGINAL LANGUAGE Syriac

DESCRIPTION
The work is not extant. Its title is known through Barhebraeus (*Chronicon Syriacum*, p. 127). A partial reconstruction is possible on the basis of the quotations from this chronicle found in the works of three later historiographers. The Syrian Orthodox Dionysius of Tell-Maḥrē (q.v.) used it as a source. Although his own chronicle is no longer extant, it in its turn is partially preserved in the works of Michael the Syrian and the *Chronicle of 1234*. In his *Chronographia*, the Byzantine author Theophanes the Confessor (q.v.) also used a version of Theophilus' chronicle, which was more developed and translated into Greek by a continuator. The third historian to have preserved part of his work is the Chalcedonian Agapius of Manbij in his Arabic universal history known as the *Kitāb al-ʿunwān*.

The original chronicle as far as it is used by these three authors covers the period between 589 and 754. It consists of a chronological ordering of events and describes the early Muslim conquests, the wars against the Byzantines, the Persians and the Armenians, and the later raids in Syria, Mesopotamia, Asia Minor and Palestine. The chronicle devotes attention to the diploma given by the Caliph ʿUmar I to the Patriarch of Jerusalem Sophronius. It also contains incidental references to the demolition and reconstruction of churches and the construction of mosques, and makes mention of the epistolary exchanges between Muslim and Byzantine rulers. Theophilus was also interested in Islamic teachings, as appears, for example, from his description of the Muslim conceptions of paradise.

SIGNIFICANCE

It is difficult to make an assessment of the importance of this chronicle as such, since we only have access to it through the three authors mentioned above, who each extracted and used Theophilus for their own presentation of events. Through these extracts, Theophilus has survived and was read by later generations of Syrian Orthodox and Chalcedonian (both Greek- and Arabic-speaking) readers.

For the later period, Theophilus gives an eye-witness account of the struggles between the last Umayyads and the early ʿAbbasids. His brief (or maybe later abbreviated) notes mainly describe internal Muslim political events, give information on intra-Byzantine struggles or developments, the succession of emperors, Muslim-Byzantine relations, and natural phenomena. Little information is given about the position of the Christians under Muslim rule, although there are references, for example, to Sophronius of Jerusalem and Peter of Capitolias, the martyred metropolitan of Damascus under al-Walīd II. Theophilus' description of Muḥammad's life and teachings, including his call to monotheism, his journeys to Palestine, and his promise of a carnal paradise, are echoed in later chronicles.

MANUSCRIPTS —

EDITIONS AND TRANSLATIONS

Hoyland, *Seeing Islam*, pp. 631-71 (partial reconstruction in English)

STUDIES

L.I. Conrad, 'The *mawālī* and early Arabic historiography', in M. Bernards and J. Nawas (eds), *Patronate and patronage in early and classical Islam*, Leiden, 2005, 370-425

L.I. Conrad, 'Heraclius in early Islamic kerygma', in G.J. Reinink and B.H. Stolte (eds), *The reign of Heraclius (610-641). Crisis and confrontation*, Louvain, 2002, 113-56

Hoyland, *Seeing Islam*, pp. 400-9

L.I. Conrad, 'The Arabs and the Colossus', *JRAS* 6 (1996) 165-87

A. Palmer and R.G. Hoyland, *The seventh century in the West-Syrian Chronicles*, Liverpool, 1993, pp. 96-98

L.I. Conrad, 'The conquest of Arwād. A source-critical study in the historiography of the early medieval Near-East', in A. Cameron and L.I. Conrad (eds), *The Byzantine and early Islamic Near East I. Problems in the literary source material*, Princeton NJ, 1992, 317-401

Herman G.B. Teule 2008

The Proto-fourteenth vision of Daniel

Unknown author

DATE OF BIRTH 8th c.
PLACE OF BIRTH Unknown, presumably Egypt
DATE OF DEATH 760s or later
PLACE OF DEATH Unknown, presumably Egypt

BIOGRAPHY

Nothing is known of the author of this pseudonymous apocalyptic text beyond what can be gathered from the (reconstructed) text itself.

MAIN SOURCES OF INFORMATION

Primary —

Secondary —

WORKS ON CHRISTIAN-MUSLIM RELATIONS

Title unknown. Modern title: 'The proto-fourteenth vision of Daniel', 'Proto-14Dan'

DATE After 750, perhaps in the 760s
ORIGINAL LANGUAGE Coptic or Greek

DESCRIPTION

The *Proto-fourteenth vision of Daniel* is not extant, but evidence for it is provided by two apocalyptic writings that are probably both recensions of this work. The best-known one is the *Fourteenth vision of Daniel*, a historical apocalypse added to the biblical Book of Daniel in several bilingual Copto-Arabic manuscripts, and in its extant form probably dating from the late 12th or early 13th century. The other recension is partly preserved in an unedited 14th-century apocalyptic sermon in Arabic attributed to the Coptic saint Shenute. Referred to in the present volume as the *Prophecy of the nineteen Muslim kings* (q.v.), it may date back to as early as the reign of the ʿAbbasid Caliph al-Amīn (809-13).

A comparative analysis of the two recensions suggests that the original work was fairly similar to the extant *Fourteenth vision*, which itself is modeled after Daniel 7 and contains a prophecy about a succession of 19 Muslim kings, the tenth to the 19th of whom are described. The last of these kings is killed by another, called Pitourgos, 'the Turk', after which, at the end of time, a last Roman emperor will free Egypt from Muslim dominion. The precise contents of the original remain difficult to reconstruct, and its historical interpretation is hampered by the fact that the descriptions of the kings' reigns are very cursory, stylized, and obscure. It is generally assumed that it was written shortly after 750, in reaction to the fall of the Umayyad dynasty, but this date is perhaps slightly too early. The 17th king clearly stood for the last Umayyad Caliph, Marwān II (r. 744-50) originally, and the 18th apparently for the first ʿAbbasid caliph, al-Saffāḥ (r. 750-54), while several indications in the text suggest that the 19th king, rather than symbolizing a fictitious ruler or belonging exclusively to a later redaction, originally represented the Caliph al-Manṣūr (r. 754-75). Conjecturally, then, the *Proto-fourteenth vision* was written against the background of the Coptic revolts of the 760s, with the aim of explaining the course of history and providing hope that Muslim rule would soon end, and thus calling for endurance rather than violent resistance. At the same time, it does not seem to have contained any details of Coptic-Muslim relations or to have responded to the doctrinal challenges of Islam. It has been proposed that the text also served to 'entertain' as much as to edify (van Lent, 'Nineteen Muslim kings', p. 671).

Since we have no Christian Arabic writings from 8th-century Egypt, it seems likely that the *Proto-fourteenth vision* was written in Coptic, a view supported by the existence of a Bohairic Coptic text of the *Fourteenth vision* and clear traces of a Coptic *Vorlage* in its Arabic version, as well as in the Arabic of the other recension. However, due to its early date the possibility that the Coptic was preceded by a Greek original can not be completely ruled out.

The motif of 19 Muslim kings also occurs in an unpublished apocalypse ascribed to Athanasius from the Fāṭimid or early Ayyūbid period, while the description of the 19th king has important parallels in the Fāṭimid *Apocalypse of Samuel* and the *Letter of Pisentius*. In addition, with its allusive and symbolic descriptions of a series of kings, the *Proto-fourteenth vision* stands in the same literary tradition as the apocalypse of the *Legend of Sergius Baḥīrā* (q.v.), the *Apocalypse of Pseudo-Ezra* (q.v.) and similar Eastern Christian apocalyptic works, but there is no indication of a direct relation with any of these. On the other hand, the reference in the *Fourteenth vision* to a last Roman emperor, which most likely already formed part of the original, betrays the influence of the famous *Apocalypse of Pseudo-Methodius* (q.v.).

SIGNIFICANCE

The *Proto-fourteenth vision of Daniel* does not contain the parenetic passages and descriptions of oppression and moral decay that characterize most Coptic apocalyptic literature from the Islamic period, and is closer in style and contents to the apocalyptic texts from Syria and Iraq mentioned above. All the same, it had considerable influence on later Copto-Arabic miaphysite apocalyptic writings. It is the first known Coptic work to have been influenced by the *Apocalypse of Pseudo-Methodius*.

The work testifies to a particular desire for order and a lively interest in the meaning and outcome of history among Copts in the early ʿAbbasid period, when, as is known from other sources, Egypt experienced moments of great political change, social instability, and violence.

MANUSCRIPTS

Fourteenth vision of Daniel:

MS BL – Or. 1314, fols 240r-252r (= British Museum – Copt. 729; dated 1374; Coptic and Arabic; the other MSS are copies from this MS or ultimately depend on it)

MS BNF – Copt. 58, fols 31r-35v (dated 1659; Coptic)

MS BNF – Copt. 2, fols 101r-106v (dated 1660; Coptic and Arabic; copied from the London MS)

MS BNF – Copt. 96, fols 166r-173v (dated 1788; Coptic and Arabic; copied from the London MS)

MS Manchester, John Rylands University Library – Copt. 419, fols 123v-140v (dated 1795; Coptic and Arabic)

Reworking in the apocalyptic sermon of Shenute:

MS BNF – Ar. 6147, fols 72v-74v (dated 1832)

MS Cairo, Franciscan Center of Christian Oriental Studies, Muski – 324, fols 130r-132v (19th c; Arabic)

EDITIONS AND TRANSLATIONS

Fourteenth vision of Daniel:

J. van Lent, *Coptic apocalyptic writings from the Islam period*, Leiden, forthcoming (Diss. Leiden University) (critical English trans. from Coptic and Arabic)

J. van Lent, 'The nineteen Muslim kings in Coptic apocalypses', *Pd'O* 25 (2000) 643-93, pp. 657-61 (partial edition and English trans. from Coptic)

H. Suermann, 'Notes concernant l'apocalypse copte de Daniel et la chute des Omayyades', *Pd'O* 11 (1983) 329-48, pp. 332-38 (reproduction of Macler's trans.)

O.F.A. Meinardus, 'New evidence on the XIVth vision from the History of the Patriarchs of the Egyptian Church', *OCP* 34 (1968) 281-309, pp. 285-307 (repr. of Burmester's trans.)

O.F.A. Meinardus, 'A commentary on the 14th vision of Daniel', *OCP* 32 (1966) 394-449, pp. 411-49 (English trans. from Tattam's edition by O.H.E. Burmester)

C.H. Becker, 'Das Reich der Ismaeliten im koptischen Danielbuch', *Nachrichten von der königlichen Gesellschaft der Wissenschaften zu Göttingen, philologisch-historische Klasse, 1915*, Heft 1, Göttingen, 1916, 7-57, pp. 10-29 (edition and German trans. from Arabic)

F. Macler, *Les apocalypses apocryphes de Daniel*, Paris, 1895, pp. 37-55 (slightly revised: 'Les apocalypses apocryphes de Daniel', *RHR* 33 (1896) 37-53, 163-76, 288-319, pp. 165-76) (French trans. from Coptic)

A. Schulte, *Die koptische Übersetzung der vier großen Propheten*, Münster, 1892, pp. 84-90 (German trans. from Coptic)

H. Tattam, *Prophetae majores in dialecto linguae aegyptiacae memphitica seu coptica cum versione latina*, 3 vols, Oxford, 1852, ii, pp. 387-405 (edition and Latin trans. from Coptic)

J. Bardelli, *Daniel copto-memphitice*, Pisa, 1849, pp. 103-12 (Latin edition from Coptic)

C.G. Woide, *De versione bibliorum aegytiaca*, dissertatio, pp. 141-48 (published posthumously in H. Ford (ed.), *Appendix ad editionem Novi Testamenti Graeci e Codice MS. Alexandrino a Carolo Godofredo Woide descripti…*, Oxford, 1799) (edition and Latin trans. from Coptic)

Reworking in the apocalyptic sermon of Shenute:

Van Lent, 'Nineteen Muslim kings', pp. 673-93 (edition and English trans.; numerous typesetting errors; to be superseded by Van Lent, *Coptic apocalyptic writings*)

STUDIES

J. van Lent, *Coptic apocalyptic writings*

L. DiTommaso, *The Book of Daniel and the apocryphal Daniel literature*, Leiden, 2005, pp. 179-84, 456-58

D. Groddek et al., *Ein wildes Volk ist es.... Predigt (Ps.-Athanasius) über Lev 21,9, Ex 19, 22, den Erzengel Michael und das Weltende unter arabischer Herrschaft*, Altenberge, 2004 (Corpus Islamo-Christianum, Series Coptica 1), pp. 255-58

H. Suermann, 'Koptische arabische Apocalypsen', in R.Y. Ebied and H.G.B. Teule (eds), *Studies on the Christian Arabic heritage*, Leuven, 2004, 25-44, pp. 31-35, 42-43

H. Suermann, 'Die Apokalypse des Ps.-Athanasius. Ein Beispiel für die koptische Auseinandersetzung mit der islamischen Herrschaft im Ägypten der Ummayyadenzeit', in W. Beltz (ed.), *Die koptische Kirche in den ersten drei islamischen Jahrhunderten*, Halle/Saale, 2003, 183-97, pp. 195-96

H. Suermann, 'Koptische Texte zur arabischen Eroberung Ägyptens und der Umayyadenherschaft', *Journal of Coptic Studies* 4 (2002) 167-86, pp. 180-81

J. van Lent, *Koptische apocalypsen uit de tijd na de Arabische verovering van Egypte*, Leiden, 2001, pp. 28-32

Van Lent, 'Nineteen Muslim kings'

H. Möhring, *Der Weltkaiser der Endzeit. Entstehung, Wandel und Wirkung einer tausendjährigen Weissagung*, Stuttgart, 2000, pp. 347-48

J. van Lent, 'An unedited Copto-Arabic apocalypse of Shenute from the fourteenth century', in S. Emmel et al. (eds.), *Ägypten und Nubien in spätantiker und christlicher Zeit*, 2 vols, Wiesbaden, 1999, ii, 155-68, pp. 158-59

J. Iskander, 'Islamization in medieval Egypt. The Copto-Arabic "Apocalypse of Samuel" as a source for the social and religious history of medieval Copts', *Medieval Encounters* 4 (1998) 219-37, pp. 222-24

Hoyland, *Seeing Islam*, pp. 289-90

F. García Martínez, *Qumran and apocalyptic. Studies on the Aramaic texts from Qumran*, Leiden, 1992, 151-52

Suermann, 'Notes'

Meinardus, 'New evidence'

Meinardus, 'Commentary'

Becker, 'Reich'

Macler, 'Apocalypses apocryphes'

Jos van Lent 2008

John the Stylite of Mār Zʿurā at Sarug

DATE OF BIRTH Unknown
PLACE OF BIRTH Unknown
DATE OF DEATH Unknown
PLACE OF DEATH Unknown

BIOGRAPHY

Nothing is known about Mār John, stylite of Mār Zʿurā in Sarug, except his authorship of two works, a grammatical treatise and the disputation discussed below. His name does not feature in other sources, and while Michael the Syrian mentions a monastery with this name in Sarug, where the Patriarch Cyriacus ordained the monk Addai as bishop of Karma, nothing more is known about it. Several scholars have suggested that he may be equated with John the Stylite of Litarb (al-Athārib, near Antioch), who died in 737. He is the author of a treatise in defense of the unity of the divine essence at the end of the 7th century. He also composed a chronicle, which is now lost but which was used by Michael the Syrian. He was a contemporary of Jacob of Edessa (q.v.), with whom he exchanged letters. Jacob's answers to John's questions have been preserved. He also wrote a letter to a certain Daniel, priest of the Arab tribe Tawayo, and other writings may also be attributed to him.

Whether the identification of John the Stylite of Mār Zʿurā with John of Litarb is correct remains a difficult issue, and there are no decisive arguments in favor or against it. Duval believes the two men to be one and the same, whereas Moberg, discussing the authorship of the grammar, hesitates. Because of the Maronite origin of MS BNF Syr. 203, Baumstark assumes that we should expect a Maronite author. However, he identifies the author of the grammar as John of Litarb.

Suermann follows Duval's identification, but Hoyland believes that there are material reasons to question the validity of this assumption. Like Assemani, he claims that the author must have lived in the first half of the 9th century, since John the Stylite's grammatical work appears to rely upon that of Joseph Ḥazzāyā, who is considered nowadays to have lived between 710 and 792. However, Hoyland confuses Joseph Ḥazzāyā with Joseph Hūzāyā, a disciple of Narsai who lived in the second half of the 5th century and the first half of the 6th. It was Joseph Hūzāyā who wrote the grammar, while Joseph Ḥazzāyā wrote on ascetics and mystics (Baumstark, *GSL*, pp. 116-17, 222-23; Ortiz de Urbina, *Patrologia Syriaca*, Rome, 1965, pp. 124, 147-48).

MAIN SOURCES OF INFORMATION

Primary —

Secondary

Hoyland, *Seeing Islam*, pp. 516-17
H. Suermann, 'Bibliographie du dialogue islamo-chrétien (huitième partie). Auteurs chrétiens de langue syriaque [17.6 bis]. Une controverse de Jôhannân de Lîtârb', *Islamochristiana* 15 (1989) 169-74
H. Suermann, 'Une controverse de Jôhannàn de Līṭārb', *Pd'O* 15 (1988-89) 197-213
H. Suermann, 'Ein Disput des Jôhannân von Lîthârb', *CIBEDO. Beiträge zum Gespräch zwischen Christen und Muslimen* 3 (1989) 182-90
I. Peña, P. Castellana and R. Fernandez, *Les stylites syriens*, Milan, 1975, pp. 126-32
Baumstark, *GSL*, pp. 258, 342
Moberg, 'Die syrische grammatik des Johannes Esṭōnājā', *Le monde oriental* 3 (1909) 24-33
R. Duval, *La littérature syriaque des origines jusqu'à la fin de cette littérature après la conquête par les arabes au XIII siècle*, Paris 1899 (repr. Amsterdam 1970), p. 289
Assemani, *BO* iii/1, p. 256

WORKS ON CHRISTIAN-MUSLIM RELATIONS

Qallīl men mamllā d-mār(y) Yūḥannā esṭonāyā d-bēt mār(y) Z'urā qaddishā d-ba-Srug 'Part of the discourse of Mār John the Stylite of Mār Z'urā in Sarug'

DATE Unknown, maybe mid-8th c.
ORIGINAL LANGUAGE Syriac

DESCRIPTION

This text contains a disputation between John and an anonymous antagonist on Christology and God's foreknowledge. Although the antagonist is not explicitly identified as a Muslim, it is suggested indirectly, since he addresses the Jews in the third person.

The first part deals with the doctrines of the Incarnation and the Trinity, which are explained on the basis of biblical arguments. The second part deals with the Incarnation and the unchangeability of

God. It is explained how it can be that God does not change when He becomes man and when He dies, just as the soul does not change at the moment of death. The third part discusses the theme of evil and divine knowledge. The Christian has to answer six embarrassing questions: if God was crucified, would He not be the origin of evil, since He knew that the Jews would crucify Him? And if He had not come, He would also be the origin of evil, making the prophets lie. The second question is about foreknowledge and crucifixion. The third is on foreknowledge and the divine will. The fourth question discusses whether Christ addressed someone more powerful than he, when praying in the garden Gethsemane. The fifth question is whether the death of Christ is good or evil, and the sixth question is about the possibility that God can die.

SIGNIFICANCE

The text discusses some classic points of friction between Muslims and Christians also found in theological literature that is probably contemporary with it. Parallels can be traced in Jacob of Edessa's (q.v.) letter to John of Litarb and the *Dialogue between a Saracen and a Christian* (q.v.), attributed to John of Damascus, especially with regard to the theme of divine foreknowledge and the cause of evil. If one assumes that John of Litarb is indeed the author, it is an example of the theological and philosophical debate as conducted by Christians of various denominations with Muslims in the late 7th and early 8th centuries.

MANUSCRIPTS

MS Paris – Syr. 203 (a collection of Maronite works, dated 1470, copied in a Maronite monastery in Qannubin, Lebanon)

EDITIONS AND TRANSLATIONS

H. Suermann, 'Une controverse de Jôhannàn de Lītārb' (edition and French trans.)

F. Nau, 'Opuscules Maronites', *Revue de l'Orient Chrétien* 4 (1899) 175-226, 318-42, 543-71, pp. 332-35 (French trans.)

STUDIES

Hoyland, *Seeing Islam*, pp. 516-17

Suermann, 'Bibliographie du dialogue islamo-chrétien'

Suermann, 'Une controverse de Jôhannàn de Lītārb'

Suermann, 'Ein Disput des Jôhannân von Lîthârb'

Harald Suermann 2008

John the Deacon

Yuḥannis, Yuʾannis, Yūḥannā
'John the Deacon' is a convenient appellation

DATE OF BIRTH Early 8th c.
PLACE OF BIRTH Egypt, perhaps in Giza
DATE OF DEATH Late 8th c. (after 767)
PLACE OF DEATH Egypt, precise location unknown

BIOGRAPHY

The author of the principal source for *Lives* 43-46 of *The History of the patriarchs of Alexandria* (covering the years 704-67) was a certain Yuḥannis (= John, in the Arabic text also written Yuʾannis or Yūḥannā), a Coptic Orthodox monk and deacon. He was the spiritual son of Bishop Moses (Muwīsīs) of Wasīm in Giza, and loyal servant and companion of Michael (Khāʾīl) I, the 46th patriarch (743-67). John had the trust of Patriarch Michael in delicate diplomatic matters, such as unity negotiations with the Chalcedonians (Evetts, PO 5, pp. 127-31) or in dealing with the representatives of an uncanonically consecrated claimant to the patriarchate of Antioch (Evetts, PO 5, pp. 206-13). He faithfully accompanied the patriarch and Bishop Moses (as well as Bishop Theodore of Miṣr) throughout the troubles of the waning days of the Umayyad caliphate, including their imprisonment by the governor ʿAbd al-Malik (Evetts, PO 5, pp. 134-39) and their captivity and maltreatment at the hands of the Umayyad Caliph Marwān II (r. 744-50), during his final flight from the advancing ʿAbbasids (Evetts, PO 5, pp. 170-88). The text suggests that John eventually became bishop of a small (unnamed) diocese (Evetts, PO 5, pp. 209-11).

MAIN SOURCES OF INFORMATION

Primary

Our sole source of knowledge about John the Deacon is the historical compilation *Siyar al-biʿa l-muqaddasa*, 'Lives of the holy Church', or *The History of the patriarchs of Alexandria*. For the published editions of the Arabic appropriation of John's work, written originally in Coptic, see below. In addition, two other notices concerning John and his work are found elsewhere in *The History of the patriarchs*:

A notice by 'John the Writer' (q.v.) at the beginning of Life 47:

C.F. Seybold, *Severus Ben al-Muqaffa'. Historia patriarcharum Alexandrinorum*, Beirut, 1904 (*CSCO* 52), p. 218; or

B.T.A. Evetts, *History of the patriarchs of the Coptic Church of Alexandria*, iv (*Mennas I to Joseph (849)*), PO 10 (1914), pp. 359-60

A notice by Mawhūb ibn Manṣūr ibn Mufarrij at the end of Life 65:

A.S. Atiya, Y. ʿAbd al-Masīḥ and O.H.E. Khs.-Burmester (eds), *History of the patriarchs of the Egyptian Church, known as the History of the holy Church, by Sawīrus ibn al-Muḳaffaʿ, Bishop of al-Ašmūnīn*, ii/2, Cairo, 1948, pp. 161-62 (edition), 243-44 (trans.)

Secondary

J. den Heijer, 'Réflexions sur la composition de l'*Histoire des patriarches d'Alexandrie*. Les auteurs des sources coptes', in W. Godlewski (ed.), *Coptic studies*, Warsaw, 1990, 107-13, pp. 110-11

J. den Heijer, *Mawhūb ibn Manṣūr ibn Mufarriǧ et l'historiographie copto-arabe. Étude sur la composition de l'*Histoire des patriarches d'Alexandrie, Louvain, 1989 (*CSCO* 513), pp. 8, 118-19, 145-46

WORKS ON CHRISTIAN-MUSLIM RELATIONS

Title unknown, source of *The History of the patriarchs of Alexandria*

DATE About 770
ORIGINAL LANGUAGE Coptic

DESCRIPTION

The Coptic text of the Lives of the 43rd-46th patriarchs written by John the Deacon was among the sources found in the late 11th century by the Alexandrian deacon Mawhūb ibn Manṣūr ibn Mufarrij and his collaborators as part of their project of compiling an Arabic-language history of the Coptic Orthodox patriarchs (see Den Heijer, *Mawhūb*); the copy of John's work was found at the monastery of St Theodore at Manhā in the Fayyūm. No fragment of the original Coptic has been preserved, so we know John's work only as it was translated and edited. It appears to be the principal (or even sole) source for *The History of the patriarchs of Alexandria* for these four patriarchates in the period 704-67.

John the Deacon tells a story of regular oppression on the part of the Muslim governing authorities, patient endurance on the part of saintly patriarchs, and recurring judgment by God, who is ultimately in control of history. His account provides insight into how the Umayyad governors' policies (e.g., with regard to taxes and manpower) were perceived and experienced by the Copts, and mentions the Coptic tax revolts that began in 725. It likewise provides insight into how Coptic Orthodox identity was being shaped in the late Umayyad and early ʿAbbasid periods: John saw his community as one that could expect adversity, but that was called to respond with holy patience and readiness even for martyrdom, in the knowledge that the final victory belonged to God.

A lengthy passage in the biography of Patriarch Michael I (743-67) deals with how he and his entourage, of which John was a member, were caught up in the death throes of the Umayyad dynasty and the final flight of Caliph Marwān II, to which John therefore provides a valuable eyewitness account.

SIGNIFICANCE

The collection of *Lives* written by John the Deacon and preserved in edited translation in *The History of the patriarchs* is a critically important source for our knowledge of Christian-Muslim relations in Egypt in the last half-century of Umayyad rule and the transition to the rule of the ʿAbbasids. In addition, it provides considerable insight into the self-understanding of the Copts (with an emphasis on patient suffering and martyrdom) under Islamic rule at the mid-point of the second Islamic century.

MANUSCRIPTS

See den Heijer, *Mawhūb*, pp. 18-27. For the contribution of John, Lives 43-46, we might mention the following two MSS, which are the basis for the published editions (and which represent two different recensions of the work):

MS Hamburg, Staats- und Universitätsbibliothek Carl von Ossietzky – ar. 304 (1260) ('primitive' recension, published by Seybold, 1912)

MS BNF – ar. 301 (15th c.) ('Vulgate' recension; base MS for the editions of Seybold, 1904, and Evetts)

EDITIONS AND TRANSLATIONS

Seybold, *Severus Ben al-Muqaffaʿ. Historia patriarcharum Alexandrinorum*, pp. 142-217 (edition of the 'Vulgate' recension)

Evetts, *History of the patriarchs of the Coptic Church of Alexandria*, III. *Agathon to Michael I (766)*, PO 5 (1909), pp. 48-215 (edition of the 'Vulgate' recension with trans.)

C.F. Seybold, *Severus ibn al-Muqaffaʿ. Alexandrinische Patriarchengeschichte von. S. Marcus bis Michael I (61-767), nach der ältesten 1266 geschriebenen Hamburger Handschrift im arabischen Urtext herausgegeben*, Hamburg, 1912 (edition of the 'primitive' recension according to the Hamburg manuscript)

STUDIES

For the identification of John's contribution to *The History of the patriarchs of Alexandria*, see:

Den Heijer, 'Réflexions sur la composition de l'*Histoire des patriarches d'Alexandrie*', pp. 110-11

Den Heijer, *Mawhūb ibn Manṣūr ibn Mufarriǧ et l'historiographie copto-arabe*, pp. 8, 96-98, 118-19, 145-46

D.W. Johnson, 'Further remarks on the Arabic history of the patriarchs of Alexandria', *OC* 61 (1977) 103-116, pp. 112-13

The section of *The History of the patriarchs of Alexandria* for which John's history is the principal source is regularly used by those who study 8th-century Egypt, particularly with regard to Christian-Muslim relations and the downfall of the Umayyad caliphate. Examples (apart from general histories of the Coptic Orthodox Church) include:

M.N. Swanson, *The Coptic papacy in Islamic Egypt*, Cairo, forthcoming, ch. 2

M.N. Swanson, 'Folly to the *ḥunafāʾ*: The crucifixion in early Christian-Muslim controversy', in E. Grypeou, M.N. Swanson and D. Thomas (eds), *The encounter of Eastern Christianity with early Islam*, Leiden, 2006, 237-56, pp. 240-43

M.S.A. Mikhail, *Egypt from late antiquity to early Islam. Copts, Melkites, and Muslims shaping a new society*, Los Angeles CA, 2004 (Diss. UCLA)

F.R. Trombley, 'Sawīrus ibn al-Muqaffaʿ and the Christians of Umayyad Egypt. War and society in documentary context', in P.M. Sijpesteijn and L. Sundelin (eds), *Papyrology and the history of early Islamic Egypt*, Leiden, 2004, 199-226

H. Kennedy, 'Egypt as a province in the Islamic caliphate, 641-868', in C.F. Petry (ed.), *The Cambridge history of Egypt*, Cambridge, 1998, i (Islamic Egypt, 640-1517), 62-85, pp. 71-76

Hoyland, *Seeing Islam*, pp. 446-48

M. Martin, 'Une lecture de l'Histoire des patriarches d'Alexandrie', *Proche-Orient Chrétien* 35 (1985) 15-36, pp. 18-20

G. Levi della Vida, 'A Christian legend in Moslem garb', *Byzantion* 15 (1940-41) 144-57, pp. 148-52

E. Amélineau, 'Les derniers jours et la mort du khalife Merouân II, d'après L'histoire des patriarches d'Alexandrie', *Journal asiatique* 11 (1914) 421-49

Original title unknown, *Life* of Patriarch Michael

DATE About 770

ORIGINAL LANGUAGE Coptic

DESCRIPTION

Early in the *Life* of Patriarch Michael (Khā'īl) I (743-67) as it is preserved in *The History of the patriarchs of Alexandria*, its author, John the Deacon, states that, while he would like to have written about Michael's life as a monk (and his miracles) before becoming patriarch, he was concerned for length – and, in any case, he had already written a separate *Life* of Michael (see Seybold, 1904, p. 172; Evetts, PO 5, p. 114; Seybold, 1912, p. 163). This stand-alone *Life* has been lost, but perhaps the *Life* preserved in *The History of the patriarchs* can be considered a précis.

SIGNIFICANCE

Even if we can only guess at the precise contents of this work, the reference to a stand-alone *Life* of Patriarch Michael I (for which we know the author and an approximate date) is a not insignificant addition to our knowledge of Coptic hagiographical literature in the 8th century.

MANUSCRIPTS —

EDITIONS AND TRANSLATIONS —

STUDIES

Den Heijer, *Mawhūb ibn Manṣūr ibn Mufarriǧ et l'historiographie copto-arabe*, p. 146

Mark N. Swanson 2008

Joshua the Stylite of Zuqnīn

Pseudo-Dionysius of Tell-Maḥrē

DATE OF BIRTH Probably early 8th c.
PLACE OF BIRTH Probably in the Jazīra region
DATE OF DEATH Probably shortly after 775
PLACE OF DEATH Unknown, probably the monastery of Zuqnīn near Amida

BIOGRAPHY

The name Joshua the Stylite as the author of the *Chronicle of Zuqnīn* occurs in a colophon inserted by a 9th century Syrian monk in the unique manuscript after the latter restored it, probably in the monastery of the Syrians in Egypt.

Joshua was a Syrian Orthodox priest and stylite who was probably born in the Jazīra region and lived and died there. Since he is called the 'Stylite of Zuqnīn', he must have spent part of his early life in prayer and meditation on the top of a pillar in the open air in or nearby the monastery of Zuqnīn near Amida, modern Diyarbakir. During the early ʿAbbasid period, violence erupted in the Jazīra against stylites, monks, and recluses, and this may have been the reason why he came down from his pillar to live in the monastery where he wrote his universal chronicle.

The evidence indicates that Joshua must have worked as a steward in his monastery. First, he shows a special interest in the prices of commodities and their constant fluctuations as a result of the changing economic policies of the early ʿAbbasids; the striking detail he provides with regard to market prices could only be given by a 'steward' in charge of the monastery budget. Second, he was particularly aware of the politics of his church in the Jazīra, discussing such events as the ordination of bishops and the election of patriarchs. He gathered this information from various sources while travelling within the Jazīra region, which he could not have done under monastic rules if he were a simple monk.

The fact that he had frequent contact with people outside his monastery is corroborated by testimonies on Arab-Byzantine warfare that he personally gathered from Muslim fighters returning from war zones. In his chronicle, Joshua mentions two stewards of Zuqnīn: Dionysius, who became bishop of Ḥarrān in 767/68, and Lazarus, who was steward in the year Joshua completed his chronicle in 775/76. If Joshua did indeed serve in this same position, it must have been sometime between 767 and 775.

After coming down from his pillar, Joshua must have lived in his monastery, spending much time in its library to write his chronicle. The great number of sources he consulted for his work suggests that the library was particularly rich in manuscripts, especially chronicles and histories, and that he had direct and ample access to all these sources.

From Part IV of the *Chronicle of Zuqnīn*, the personal contribution of Joshua the Stylite, one can deduce some aspects of his personality. He was first and foremost deeply committed to his monastic vocation, criticizing fellow monks who owned property instead of 'carrying their crosses and following Christ', and of ecclesiastical leaders who did not serve their flocks responsibly. He was a defender of the poor in Jazīra society regardless of their religious and ethnic affiliations, bitterly criticizing the provincial governor Mūsā ibn Muṣʿab for financially exploiting the peasantry in the early 770s. He was also tolerant: he spoke of the Prophet of Islam with respect, and if he condemned Muslim officials who caused hardship to people it was because they were bad administrators and not merely because they were of a different religion and culture. He reached out to Muslims, seeking from them testimonies 'under oath' with regard to military operations in Byzantine lands, which also suggests that he knew Arabic in addition to his native Syriac. Yet, being a Christian monk, he lamented the conversion of Christian elders and sometimes entire communities to Islam, claiming that they were driven toward apostasy by Satan and not necessarily by physical or financial threat.

Joshua was not known to later generations of readers and writers, apart from the 9th century monk of Zuqnīn who restored his manuscript, which is definitely an autograph.

MAIN SOURCES OF INFORMATION

Primary

The only source for Joshua the Stylite is his chronicle, for which see below.

Secondary
F.R. Trombley and J.W. Watt, *The chronicle of pseudo-Joshua the Stylite*, Liverpool, 2000
A. Harrak, *The Chonicle of Zuqnīn*, Parts III and IV A.D. 488-775, Toronto, 1999
A. Luther, *Die syrische Chronik des Josua Stylites*, Berlin, 1997
W. Witakowski, *Pseudo-Dionysius of Tel-Maḥrē. Chronicle*, Part III, Liverpool, 1996
R. Hespel, *Chronicon anonymum pseudo-dionysianum vulgo dictum, II*, Louvain, 1989 (*CSCO* 507)
W. Witakowski, *The Syriac Chronicle of Pseudo-Dionysius of Tel-Maḥrē: A Study in the History of Historiography*, Uppsala, 1987
J.-B. Chabot, *Incerti auctoris Chronicon Pseudo-Dionysianum vulgo dictum, I*, Louvain, 1949 (*CSCO* 121)
J.-B. Chabot, *Chronique de Denys de Tell-Mahré, Quatrième partie*, Paris, 1895
W. Wright, *The Chronicle of Joshua the Stylite*, Cambridge, 1882
P. Martin, *Chronique de Josué le stylite écrite vers l'an 515*, Leipzig, 1876

WORKS ON CHRISTIAN-MUSLIM RELATIONS

The Chronicle of Zuqnīn, Part IV

DATE 775
ORIGINAL LANGUAGE Syriac

DESCRIPTION
This is the last part of the universal *Chronicle of Zuqnīn* and the personal contribution of its author. It deals with the 7th and 8th centuries, but it concentrates on the period between 750 and 775, the time of the Caliph Abū Jaʿfar al-Manṣūr and the building of Baghdad. It discusses the rapacious economic policies of the early ʿAbbasid caliphate, which turned the Jazīra region, rich in water and human and agricultural resources, into a desolate land as a consequence of excessive taxation and the exploitation of the peasantry and traders. Near the end of Part IV, the chronicler tackles the subject of Muslim-Christian relations, including the sentencing and decapitation of a Christian man of Ḥarrān who was accused of converting to Islam and of recanting.

SIGNIFICANCE
The author was an eyewitness to the economic policies of the early Muslims in the Jazīra, a rich province extending from Takrīt in the south-east to the banks of the upper Euphrates in the west. He describes the formidable tax machine created by the Umayyads and

ʿAbbasids, which consisted of a hierarchy of officers in charge of levies on caliphal property, tithes, alms, and poll taxes from the Muslim and Christian inhabitants. Reforms of the tax system as well as its excesses (violence often accompanied tax collection) are also discussed in great detail. The information related to the economy of the Umayyad and early ʿAbbasid caliphates is not only ample but also unique.

Moreover, much light is shed on the conditions of the large Christian communities that densely populated the Jazīra under Islam during the second half of the 8th century. The region close to the Arab-Byzantine border suffered greatly as a result of seasonal Arab incursions into Byzantine lands. The relations between Muslims and Christians were sometimes tense, if not violent, whereas the contacts between Christian apostates and faithful Christians were marked by mistrust and denigration of each other's religious beliefs.

MANUSCRIPTS

MS Vat – Syr. 162 (Codex Zuqninensis)

EDITIONS AND TRANSLATIONS

Harrak, *The Chonicle of Zuqnīn*

Hespel, *Chronicon anonymum pseudo-dionysianum vulgo dictum*

Chabot, *Incerti auctoris Chronicon*

Chabot, *Chronique de Denys de Tell-Mahré*

STUDIES

A. Harrak, 'Ah! The Assyrian is the rod of My hand! Syriac views of history after the advent of Islam', in J.J. van Ginkel, H.L. Murre-van den Berg and T.M. van Lint (eds), *Redefining Christian identity. Cultural interaction in the Middle East since the rise of Islam*, Leuven, 2005, 45-65

A. Harrak, 'Piecing together the martyrdom of Cyrus of Harran', *AB* 121 (2003) 297-328

A. Harrak, 'The Jazīrah during the Islamic period', in M. Fortin, *Recherches canadiennes sur la Syrie antique / Canadian research on ancient Syria*, Quebec, 2001, 227-34

C.F. Robinson, *Empire and elites after the Muslim conquest. The transformation of Northern Mesopotamia*, Cambridge, 2000, pp. 30-32, 45-49 and *passim*

A. Harrak, 'Arabisms in Part IV of the Chronicle of Zuqnīn', in R. Lavenant (ed.), *VII Symposium Syriacum 1996*, Rome 1998, 469-98

Hoyland, *Seeing Islam*, pp. 409-14

A. Harrak, 'Christianity in the eyes of the Muslims of the Jazīrah at the end of the eighth century', *Pd'O* 20 (1995) 339-57

Y.M. Ishaq, 'The significance of the Syriac chronicle of Pseudo-Dionysius of Tell-Mahre', *Orientalia Suecana* 41/2 (1992-93) 106-18

Witakowski, *The Syriac chronicle of Pseudo-Dionysius of Tel-Mahrē*, esp. pp. 39-58

Y.M. Ishaq, ʿAl-Taʾrīkh al-Zuqnīnī l-manḥūl li-Diyūnīsiyūs al-Talmaḥrīʾ, *Majallat al-majmaʿ al-ʿilmī l-ʿIrāqī. Hayʾat al-lugha l-suryāniyya* 8 (1984) 63-135

C. Cahen, 'Fiscalité, propriété, antagonismes sociaux en Haut-Mésopotamie au temps des premiers ʿAbbāsides d'après Denys de Tell-Mahré', *Arabica* 1 (1954) 136-52

Amir Harrak 2007

The Sixty martyrs of Jerusalem

Unknown author

DATE OF BIRTH Unknown; probably 8th c.
PLACE OF BIRTH Perhaps Palestine
DATE OF DEATH Unknown; probably 8th c.
PLACE OF DEATH Perhaps Palestine

BIOGRAPHY

The anonymous author must have lived in Syria and Palestine and have mastered at least two languages, Syriac and Greek. In an appendix (§ 12) to the main text it is revealed that it was Ioannes the monk who read the original, went 'after a time' on pilgrimage to Jerusalem to venerate the relics of the martyrs, and commissioned the translation of their Martyrdom from Syriac into Greek. The fact that the iconoclast Emperor Leo III (717-41) is styled as 'of pious memory' (§ 4) points to a date after his death but earlier than the Seventh Ecumenical Council in Nicea (787) which condemned Iconoclasm.

MAIN SOURCES OF INFORMATION

Primary
See below

Secondary
See below

WORKS ON CHRISTIAN-MUSLIM RELATIONS

Martyrion tōn hexēkonta neōn martyrōn tōn en tē hagia Christou tou Theou hēmōn polei epi tēs tyrannidos tōn Arabōn martyrēsantōn, 'The Martyrdom of the sixty neo-martyr saints who were martyred in the holy city of Christ our God during the tyrannical rule of the Arabs'

DATE Before 787
ORIGINAL LANGUAGE Syriac (surviving only in a Greek trans.)

DESCRIPTION

The *Martyrdom* (*BHG* 1217) relates the story of seventy Byzantine archons who visited Jerusalem as pilgrims during a seven-year truce concluded between Sulaymān ibn ʿAbd al-Malik and Leo III the Isaurian in 717. Apprehended on the way to Caesarea and imprisoned there in about 724-25, they were tortured to convert to Islam. They all refused to abandon their religion, and three of them requested to be executed next to the Tower of David in Jerusalem. On their way to the holy City, three died and seven apostatized out of cowardice, but these apostates all died of dysentery. The remaining sixty suffered martyrdom by crucifixion and being shot by arrows. They were buried outside the walls of Jerusalem near the Church of St Stephen by a pious Christian named John.

The same story is reproduced in greater detail and with a few significant differences in a second Greek version (*BHG* 1218) composed by Symeon the monk, presbyter and hesychast of the Holy Cave of Lent (*Tessarakonthemeron*) in Jerusalem.

SIGNIFICANCE

The *Martyrdom* exhibits a significant degree of anti-Muslim sentiment, and provides historical detail about Byzantine-Arab relations in the 8th century.

MANUSCRIPTS

MS BNF – Coislin Gr. 303, fols 177-181 (10th c.)

EDITIONS AND TRANSLATIONS

A. Papadopoulos-Kerameus (ed.), 'Mučeničestvo šestidesjati novych svjatych mučenikov', *Pravoslavnij Palestinskij Sbornik* 12.1 (1892), 1-7; with Russian trans. by G. Destunis

STUDIES

PMBZ i (Prolegomena), pp. 111-12

Dumbarton Oaks Hagiography Database Project, Washington DC, 1998, pp. 90-91

Hoyland, *Seeing Islam*, pp. 360-63

A. Kaplony, *Konstantinopel und Damascus. Gesandschaften und Verträge zwischen Kaisern und Kalifen 639-750. Untersuchungen zum Gewohnheits-Völkerrecht und zur interkulturellen Diplomatie*, Berlin, 1996, pp. 353-59

G. Huxley, 'The sixty martyrs of Jerusalem', *Greek, Roman and Byzantine Studies* 18 (1977) 369-74

S. Gero, *Byzantine Iconoclasm during the reign of Leo III*, Louvain, 1973 (*CSCO* 346), pp. 176-81
C. Loparev, 'Vizantijskia žitija sviatych VIII-IX vekov', *VV* 19 (1912) 1-10

Stephanos Efthymiadis 2008

Fī tathlīth Allāh al-wāḥid

Unknown author

DATE OF BIRTH 8th c.
PLACE OF BIRTH Unknown
DATE OF DEATH 8th/9th c.
PLACE OF DEATH Unknown, possibly one of the monasteries of Palestine or Sinai

BIOGRAPHY

The unnamed 8th-century Melkite author is known to us only through his Arabic apology for the Christian faith, preserved in a single manuscript. The depth of biblical and theological knowledge displayed in this apology suggests that its author was a priest and/or monk; its preservation at the Monastery of St Catherine at Mt Sinai suggests a connection with it or with Palestinian monasteries such as Mār Saba or Mār Chariton.

MAIN SOURCES OF INFORMATION

Primary
MS Sinai – ar. 154, fols 99r-139v

Secondary —

WORKS ON CHRISTIAN-MUSLIM RELATIONS

Untitled. Modern title: *Fī tathlīth Allāh al-wāḥid*, 'On the Triune nature of God'

DATE 755 or 788
ORIGINAL LANGUAGE Arabic

DESCRIPTION
This early Arabic Christian treatise, 41 folios long in the unique manuscript (which is incomplete at the end), was somewhat misleadingly called *Fī tathlīth Allāh al-wāḥid* and 'On the Triune nature of God' by its first editor (Gibson, *Arabic version*); in fact it is a wide-ranging

apology for the Christian faith, at a number of points addressed explicitly to Muslims.

The text contains a date of sorts: 746 years after the 'establishment' of Christianity (fol. 110b). Depending on whether this 'establishment' is understood to have taken place at the Incarnation or the Crucifixion, the date converts to 755 (as maintained by Griffith, *Church in the shadow of the mosque*, 89-90, n. 47) or 788 (as maintained by Swanson, 'Some considerations').

It opens with a magnificent prayer full of qurʾānic terms and phrases, which the Christian author uses in a manner that is not at all forced or artificial. The first major section of the text is then dedicated to the defense of the doctrine of the Trinity ('Allāh and his Word and his Spirit') on the basis of scriptures (the author names *al-Tawrāt, al-Anbiyāʾ, al-Zabūr* and *al-Injīl*, and quotes from the Qurʾān as well) and rationally accessible analogies. The second chapter defends a Christian understanding of Christ's work and person. It begins with a survey of salvation/prophetic history from Adam and his Fall under the sway of the devil (Iblīs); through narratives of Noah, Abraham and Lot, Moses, and other prophets; to the annunciation and birth of Christ and an account of how Christ turned the tables on the devil, thereby rescuing Adam and his progeny. Throughout this section, biblical and qurʾānic material is skillfully interwoven; the result is a kind of Christian calque on qurʾānic sequences of messenger stories (see, for example, Q 7 or Q 11). The third and longest chapter is a collection of 34 Old Testament *testimonia* bearing witness to the life of Christ, to baptism, and to the cross. The complex traditions of typological exegesis behind some of these *testimonia* suggest that the treatise can be considered as a work of catechesis addressed to Christians at least as much as a work of apologetic addressed to Muslims.

SIGNIFICANCE

The work is one of the earliest Arabic apologies for Christianity, in particular for Christian Trinitarian and Christological doctrine, in our possession. It is proving to be a rich resource for the study of the Christian apologetic use of the Qurʾān (whether through allusion, quotation, or the adoption of narrative material) as well as for the study of Christian *testimonia* as they were 'redeployed' for conversation and catechesis in the *Dār al-Islām*. The soteriological narrative of the second chapter represents a significant reshaping of traditional materials, such as accounts of Christ's cunning defeat of Satan, for use in a new apologetic environment.

MANUSCRIPTS

MS Sinai – ar. 154, fols 99r-139v

EDITIONS AND TRANSLATIONS

M. Gallo, *Palestinese anonimo. Omelia arabo-christiana dell'VIII secolo*, Rome, 1994 (Italian trans. of Gibson's edition)

M.D. Gibson, *An Arabic version of the Acts of the Apostles and the seven Catholic Epistles from an eighth or ninth century ms. in the Convent of St Katherine on Mount Sinai, with a treatise On the Triune nature of God with translation, from the same codex*, London, 1899 (repr. Piscataway, 2003) (a historically important but incomplete edition and English trans.; Gibson did not transcribe 13 of the 82 pages of text)

STUDIES

S.H. Griffith, *The church in the shadow of the mosque*, Princeton NJ, 2008, pp. 53-57, 89-90, 167-68

M.N. Swanson, 'Apologetics, catechesis, and the question of audience in "On the triune nature of God" (Sinai Arabic 154) and three treatises of Theodore Abū Qurrah', in M. Tamcke (ed.), *Christians and Muslims in dialogue in the Islamic Orient of the middle ages*, Beirut, 2007, 113-34.

M.N. Swanson, 'Beyond prooftexting (2): The use of the Bible in some early Arabic Christian apologies', in D. Thomas (ed.), *The Bible in Arab Christianity*, Leiden, 2007, 91-112

D. Bertaina, 'The development of testimony collections in early Christian apologetics with Islam', in Thomas, *The Bible in Arab Christianity*, 151-73, pp. 162-67

M.N. Swanson, 'Folly to the *ḥunafā*'. The crucifixion in early Christian-Muslim controversy', in E. Grypeou, M.N. Swanson and D. Thomas (eds), *The encounter of Eastern Christianity with early Islam*, Leiden, 2006, 237-56, pp. 243-47

S.H. Griffith, 'The Qur'ān in Arab Christian texts; the development of an apologetic argument. Abū Qurrah in the *mağlis* of al-Ma'mūn', *Pd'O* 24 (1999) 203-33, pp. 214-16

Hoyland, *Seeing Islam*, pp. 502-3

M.N. Swanson, 'Beyond prooftexting. Approaches to the Qur'ān in some early Arabic Christian apologies', *MW* 88 (1998) 297-319, pp. 305-11

S.H. Griffith, 'The view of Islam from the monasteries of Palestine in the early 'Abbāsid period. Theodore Abū Qurrah and the *Summa Theologiae Arabica*', *ICMR* 7 (1996) 9-28, pp. 10-12

M.N. Swanson, *Folly to the* ḥunafāʾ. *The cross of Christ in Arabic Christian-Muslim controversy in the eighth and ninth centuries A.D.*, Cairo, 1995 (*estratto* from dissertation), pp. 22-38

S.K. Samir, 'The earliest Arab apology for Christianity (c. 750)', in S.K. Samir and J.S. Nielsen (eds), *Christian Arabic apologetics during the Abbasid period (750-1258)*, Leiden, 1994, 57-114

M.N. Swanson, 'The cross of Christ in the earliest Arabic Melkite apologies', in Samir and Nielsen, *Christian Arabic apologetics*, 115-45, pp. 129-30.

M.N. Swanson, 'Some considerations for the dating of *Fī tathlīth Allāh al-wāḥid* (Sinai ar. 154) and *al-Ǧāmiʿ wuǧūh al-īmān* (London, British Library or. 4950)', *Pd'O* 18 (1993) 115-41

S.K. Samir, 'Une apologie arabe du christianisme d'époque umayyade?' *Pd'O* 16 (1990-91) 85-106

S.H. Griffith, 'The monks of Palestine and the growth of Christian literature in Arabic', *MW* 78 (1988) 1-28, pp. 18, 21

R. Haddad, *La Trinité divine chez les théologiens arabes (750-1050)*, Paris, 1985, pp. 52-53

Graf, *GCAL* ii, pp. 27-28

J.R. Harris, 'A tract on the triune nature of God', *American Journal of Theology* 5 (1901) 75-86 (repr. in J.R. Harris, *Testimonies*, 2 vols, London, 1916-20, i, pp. 39-51)

Mark N. Swanson 2008

Ioane Sabanisdze

Iovane Sabanisdze (Sabanisʒe)

DATE OF BIRTH Unknown, 8th c.
PLACE OF BIRTH Unknown
DATE OF DEATH Unknown
PLACE OF DEATH Unknown

BIOGRAPHY

Nothing is known about this person except that he lived in Tbilisi, capital of the Kingdom of Kartli, at the end of the 8th century, and that he was a friend of St Abo, of whose martyrdom he was an eye witness. From his works, he seems a highly educated person and refined writer. He probably belonged to the higher ranks of the ecclesiastical hierarchy of Kartli.

MAIN SOURCES OF INFORMATION

Primary

C'amebaj c'midisa da net'arisa moc'amisa Krist'ēsisa Habojsi, romeli ic'ama Kartls šina, kalaksa T'piliss, qelita sark'inoztajta, gamotkumuli Iovane dzisa Sabanisi brdzanebita Krist'ēs mier Samoel Kartlisa k'atalik'ozisajta, in I. Abuladze, *Dzveli kartuli agiograpiuli lit'erat'uris dzeglebi*, 6 vols, Tbilisi, 1963, i, part ii, pp. 46-48 (letters exchanged between Ioane Sabanisdze and the Catholikos Samoel)

Secondary

B. K'ilanava, *Kartuli damc'erlobisa da mc'erlobis sataveebtan*, Tbilisi 1990, pp. 261-80

Š. Oniani, *Iovane Sabanis dze, cxovreba da šemokmedeba*, Tbilisi 1955 (Diss. University of Tbilisi)

WORKS ON CHRISTIAN-MUSLIM RELATIONS

C'amebaj c'midisa da net'arisa moc'amisa Krist'ēsisa Habojsi, romeli ic'ma Kartls šina, kalaksa T'piliss, qelita sark'inoztajta, gamotkumuli Iovane dzisa Sabanisi brdzanebita Krist'ēs mier Samoel Kartlisa k'atalik'ozisajta, 'The Martyrdom of Abo, saint and blessed martyr of Christ, who suffered under the Saracens in Kartli, in the town of Tbilisi, told by Ioane Sabanisdze, by order of Samoel, Catholikos of Kartli in Christ'; short modern title: 'The Martyrdom of Abo of Tbilisi'

DATE 786-90
ORIGINAL LANGUAGE Georgian

DESCRIPTION

The text, which comprises 35 pages in Abuladze's edition with critical apparatus, deals with the life and martyrdom of Abo, a perfumer from Baghdad who came to Georgia and converted to Christianity. Its authenticity is undisputed.

The work consists of two letters exchanged between Ioane Sabanisdze and the Catholicos Samoel, followed by four chapters. The first chapter analyses from an eschatological perspective the effects of Abo's martyrdom on the general economic, political and religious situation of Kartli under Arabic domination. In the exegetical part of this chapter, he makes use of a homily on baptism (Clavis Patrorum Graecorum 3238) by Amphilochius of Iconium (second half of the 4th century).

In the second and third chapters the following phases of Abo's life are described: the imprisonment of Nerse, the regent prince of Kartli, and his meeting with Abo; their return to Kartli; Abo's first contact with the Christians; his flight to Khazaria; his baptism; his flight to Abkhazia and fight against evil; his dialogue with the prince of Abkhazia; his return to Kartli and his meeting with some Arabs in Tbilisi; the historical contextualization of the date of Abo's martyrdom; his first imprisonment and release; the denunciation of Abo as a Christian to the newly appointed emir; his warning to the Christians; his departure from the town; his first debate with the emir; his second imprisonment; his struggle against evil; his preparation for martyrdom; his second debate with the emir; his martyrdom; 'the stunning miracle'. The fourth chapter is a eulogy of Abo in rhyming prose.

SIGNIFICANCE

The work is a rich historical and literary document on Kartli and its neighbouring towns in the second half of the 8th century, which supplements the otherwise scant information in the sources from this period. It illustrates the social, political and cultural aspects of the Arab domination of a Christian country, and represents the first Georgian work that contains clear, polemical, theological arguments against Islam.

The author uses Abo's tragic history to construct the national identity of the Georgian people. He creatively exploits various literary sources in order to produce a distinguished and original work that was to influence subsequent Georgian literary development.

MANUSCRIPTS

MS Sinai – Geo. N. 3. (10th c.)

All other MSS are listed in *C'amebaj c'midisa da net'arisa moc'amisa Krist'ēsisa Habojsi*, p. 46, and in Shurgaia, *Spiritualità*, p. 75. Among these the most important MSS from the 9th-11th century are:

MS Tbilisi, National Centre of Manuscripts – A-1109

MS Tbilisi, National Centre of Manuscripts –19

MS Tbilisi, National Centre of Manuscripts –A-95

MS Sinai – Geo. O. 11

MS Mt Athos, Iviron Monastery – iber. geo. 57

EDITIONS AND TRANSLATIONS

Full bibliography including all earlier editions and translations can be found in G. Shurgaia, *La spiritualità georgiana: Martirio di Abo, santo e beato martire di Cristo di Ioane Sabanisdze*, Rome, 2003 (introduction, Italian trans., commentary, indexes)

Selection of principal editions/trans.:

C'amebaj c'midisa da net'arisa moc'amisa Krist'ēsisa Habojsi, romeli ic'ama Kartls šina, kalaksa T'piliss, qelita sark'inoztajta, gamotkumuli Iovane dzisa Sabanisi brdzanebita Krist'ēs mier Samoel Kartlisa k'atalik'ozisajta, in Abuladze, *Dzveli kartuli agiograpiuli lit'erat'uris dzeglebi*, i, part ii, pp. 46-81 (critical edition)

Drevnegruzinskaja literatura (*V-XVIII vv.*), trans. K'orneli K'ek'elidze, Tbilisi 1982, pp. 99-143 (Russian trans.)

D.M. Lang, *Lives and legends of the Georgian saints*, London, 1956, pp. 116-33 (English trans., repr. 1967)

C'amebaj c'midisa da net'arisa moc'amisa Krist'esi Habojsi, romeli ic'ama Kartls šina, kalaksa T'piliss, qelita sark'inoztajta, gamotkumuli Iovane dzisa Sabanisi, brdzanebita Krist'es mier Samoel, Kartlisa k'atalik'ozisajta, ttuesa ianvarsa z, in K'. K'ek'elidze, *Adrindeli peodaluri kartuli lit'erat'ura*, Tbilisi, 1935, pp. 53-80 (critical edition)

K. Schultze, *Das Martyrium des heiligen Abo von Tiflis*, Berlin, 1905 (Texte und Untersuchungen zur Geschichte der altchristlichen Literatur, Neue Folge, 13:4), pp. 11-41 (unabridged trans. into German according to the edition of the text by P'avle K'arbelašvili)

STUDIES

Shurgaia, *La spiritualità georgiana*

E. Č'elidze, 'Ioane Sabanisdzis lit'erat'uruli c'q'aroebis šesaxeb', in M. Mamac'ašvili (ed.), *Gulani*, Tbilisi 1989, pp. 8-17

R. Siradze, *Kartuli agiografia*, Tbilisi 1987, pp. 49-79

M. van Esbroeck, 'Archéologie d'une homélie sur les Pâques attribuée à Chrysostome ou à Épiphane de Chypre', in M.E. Stone (ed.), *Armenian and biblical studies*, Jerusalem 1976, 165-81

K'. K'ek'elidze, *Geschichte der kirchlichen Georgischen Literatur*, ed. P.M. Tarchnišvili and J. Assfalg, Rome, 1955, pp. 94-95

K'. K'ek'elidze, *Adrindeli peodaluri kartuli lit'erat'ura*, Tbilisi, 1935

Gaga Shurgaia 2008

Pope Hadrian's epistles to Bishop Egila

Hadrian I

DATE OF BIRTH Unknown (8th c.)
PLACE OF BIRTH Rome
DATE OF DEATH 25 December 795
PLACE OF DEATH Rome

BIOGRAPHY

Born into the Roman nobility, Hadrian was pope from 772 to 795 and succeeded in strengthening pontifical authority thanks to his strategy of forming an alliance with Charlemagne. At the beginning of his papacy, the Byzantine Empire was weakened by the iconoclastic crisis and its rule over Italy was challenged by the Lombards. Deprived of its traditional protector, the papacy was now claiming to represent the *imperium* against the growing pressure of the neighboring Lombard kingdom. Under Charlemagne's protection the papacy regained its territorial possessions after the fall of Pavia, the Lombard capital (774), although Charlemagne placed severe limits on pontifical ambitions in Tuscany and Spoleto.

The alliance between Rome and Aachen increased Charlemagne's prestige and legitimacy, which led to his coronation as Holy Roman Emperor in 800. Pontifical authority was also the most effective instrument of territorial expansion, giving religious legitimacy to Carolingian conquests against Eastern pagan peoples and Islamic rule in the Iberian peninsula. Hadrian I and Charlemagne were both involved in the theological controversy against adoptionism, which was condemned as a heresy at the Council of Frankfurt (794). The conflict was mainly directed against Felix (q.v.), Bishop of Urgell, which was then under Carolingian rule, and Elipandus of Toledo, the main see of the church under Islamic rule. The adoptionist controversy thus had political implications, since it provided a justification for Carolingian intervention in the Iberian peninsula and contributed to the alliance with the Asturian monarchy.

Hadrian I himself seems to have shown a great interest in Hispanic matters, and between 785 and 791 he had a legate in al-Andalus. This man, Egila, was to inform the pope about theological and religious matters there and to propagate Roman 'orthodoxy' among the local Christians, who were living in a land dominated by 'pagans'. Egila, however, fell into the 'heresy' and moved beyond the control of the papacy. Nevertheless, Hadrian I maintained his claim to authority over the Spanish church, and in about 785 he wrote two letters to all the Hispanic clergy. Both addressed the 'heresies' which had developed in *Spania*, particularly adoptionism, but also dealt with canonical matters and the question of contact between the faithful and the 'Jews and pagans'.

MAIN SOURCES OF INFORMATION

Primary

Le Liber pontificalis, 2 vols, ed. L. Duchesne, Paris, 1886-92, i, pp. 486-514

'*Codex carolinus*', ed. W. Gundlach, in E. Dümmler et al. (eds), *Epistolae Merowingici et Karolini aevi*, Berlin, 1892, 469-657 (*MGH Epistolae* 3)

Vita Adriani papae, *PL* 96, cols 1167-1203

Hadrian I, *Epistolae, PL* 96, cols 1203-44; *PL* 98, cols 280-438, 1247-92

Secondary

J.C. Picard, art. 'Adrien Ier', in *Dictionnaire historique de la papauté*, Paris, 1994

G. Dagron, P. Riché, A. Vauchez (eds), *Évêques, moines et empereurs (610-1054)*, Paris, 1993, pp. 122-24, 129, 701-6, 720, 731, 750-51, 757-58

R. Schieffer, art. 'Hadrian I', in *Lexicon des Mittelalters*, Munich, 1989

M. Jugie, art. 'Adrien Ier', in *Dictionnaire d'histoire et de géographie ecclésiastiques*, Paris, 1988[2]

D.D. Sefton, *The pontificate of Hadrian I. Papal theory and political reality in the reign of Charlemagne*, Ann Arbor MI, 1975

E. Caspar, *Das Papsttum unter Fränkischer Herrschaft*, Darmstadt, 1956, pp. 35-113 ('Hadrian I. und Karl der Grosse')

O. Bertolini, *Dizionario biografico degli Italiani*, Rome, 1960, i, pp. 312-24

M. Jugie, art. 'Adrien Ier', in *Dictionnaire d'histoire et de géographie ecclésiastiques*, Paris, 1911

H. Hemmer, art. 'Adrien Ier', *Dictionnaire de théologie catholique*, Paris, 1909

L. Duchesne, *Les premiers temps de l'état pontifical*, Paris, 1904, pp. 134-66

P. Jaffé, *Regesta pontificum romanorum*, Leipzig, 1885, i, pp. 289-306

C.J. Héfélé, *Histoire des conciles*, Paris, 1870, iv, pp. 331-51; v, pp. 61-142

WORKS ON CHRISTIAN-MUSLIM RELATIONS

Epistolæ Adriani papæ ad Egilam episcopum, 'Pope Hadrian's epistles to Bishop Egila'

DATE 785-91 (Gundlach)
ORIGINAL LANGUAGE Latin

DESCRIPTION
Hadrian's first letter to Egila reminds him of his mission *in partibus Spaniensis provinciæ*. He has been ordained by Wilcharius, archbishop of the Gauls, as a kind of legate with responsibility for preaching the 'orthodox faith' in Iberian territories under Muslim rule, propagating Roman ecclesiastical legislation, and fighting against local 'heresies'. The deacon Saranus and the monk Victorinus will act as intermediaries between him and the pope. In his epistle, Hadrian I provides arguments which are to be used by Egila in dealing with the dogmatic controversies which were dividing the clergy of al-Andalus.

Hadrian touches on three main questions. The first, also reflected in 8th-century Latin Mozarabic sources, is about the canonical date of Easter, against Christians who were apparently rejecting the computation agreed at the Council of Nicea. The second, also documented by the epistle of Evantius, archdeacon of Toledo in the first part of the 8th century, deals with dietary prohibitions. The pope confirms the freedom to eat any kind of meat, including blood, in response to those who claim that the faithful should follow the Old Testament law of Moses, as was commonly practiced by Jews and Muslims. The third is about predestination, against theologians who claim that the whole of human life, including sins and virtues, is totally preordained by God, thus depriving humankind of free will.

Finally, Egila had apparently reported to the pope that in Muslim *Spania* 'many people, who claimed to be Catholics, [were] living in contact with Jews and unbaptized pagans', sharing food and drink with them, in spite of the obvious risk of being 'contaminated' by their 'various errors'. This confirms that theological debates among Christians in al-Andalus was influenced by contact with Muslims ('pagans'), despite the absence of direct allusions to the new context in 8th-century Latin ecclesiastical texts. The pope also denounces social strategies that involved the forming of matrimonial alliances by local Christian families, who gave their daughters to 'infidels', even though this was prohibited. The local church, according to the pope, was also rejecting canon law by permitting priests to be ordained without being examined, and to be appointed even if they were married.

Egila did not reply to Hadrian's epistle, so the pope sent him a copy taken from the pontifical records. In his second message, Hadrian expresses serious doubt about Egila's loyalty, ordering him to resist heresy and saying that the church could not accept any stain on its reputation. A communication to Hadrian from Charlemagne, through the latter's intermediary in Rome, Peter of Pavia, intimates that Egila's 'deviation' was connected with the adoptionist conflict.

SIGNIFICANCE

These two letters shed light on Carolingian and pontifical interests in al-Andalus at the end of the 8th and beginning of the 9th century. Despite his defeat at the walls of Saragossa in 778, Charlemagne maintained diplomatic contacts with Muslim rebels in the north and continued to make military raids on the eastern frontier of *Tarraconensis*, which finally led to the conquest of Barcelona in 801. Territorial expansion was justified in terms of being both a battle against the infidels and a defense of orthodoxy, which was allegedly threatened in al-Andalus by contact with the infidels. The pope's intervention against heresies extended the legitimacy of the Frankish church, and at the same time restored his own claims to universal moral leadership.

The answer to Egila also uniquely documents the intense doctrinal debate that was taking place within the church in al-Andalus a few decades after the Muslim conquest, and complements contemporary Mozarabic Latin sources. The challenge of living under Muslim rule led the weakened clergy of al-Andalus to consider the various aspects of canon law that affected coexistence, such as those that dealt with sharing food and entering into matrimonial alliances. Coexistence with Islam had theological consequences, both direct and indirect. A minority in the church recommended respect for the Old Testament prohibition against the consumption of blood, a theme that could be linked with the importance of dietary regulations in this context of interreligious contacts.

MANUSCRIPTS

MS Vienna, Österreichische Nationalbibliothek – 449 (*Codex epistolaris carolinus*), a copy of the *Libri Carolini*, made for Willibertus, archbishop of Cologne (870-89)

EDITIONS AND TRANSLATIONS

'*Codex carolinus*', ed. Gundlach, *Epistolæ* 96 and 97, pp. 643-48

Hadrian I, *Epistolæ, PL* 98, cols 333-46 (*Epistolæ* 70 and 71)

P. Jaffé, *Biblioteca rerum Germanicarum*, 6 vols, Paris, 1864-75, iv, pp. 78-79

J.C. Cenni, *Monumenta dominationis pontificiæ*, 2 vols, Rome, 1760, i, pp. 69-70

J. Gretser, *Volumen epistolarum*, Ingolstad, 1613, pp. 95-96

STUDIES

J.C. Cavadini, *The last Christology of the West. Adoptionism in Spain and Gaul (785-820)*, Philadelphia PA, 1993

M. de Epalza, 'Influences islamiques dans la théologie chrétienne médiévale: l'adoptianisme hispanique', *Islamochristiana* 18 (1992) 55-72

J.E. McWilliam, 'The Context of Spanish Adoptionism, a review', in M. Gervers and R. Bikhazi (eds), *Conversion and continuity. Indigenous Christian communities in Islamic lands, 8th to 18th centuries*, Toronto, 1990, 75-88

J.F. Rivera Recio, *El adopcianismo en España (s. VIII)*, Toledo, 1980

R. D'Abadal i de Vinyals, *La batalla del adopcionismo en la desintegración de la iglesia visigoda*, Barcelona, 1949

F.J. Simonet, *Historia de los mozárabes de España*, 4 vols, Madrid, 1897-1903 (repr. 1983), ii, pp. 262-77

Cyrille Aillet 2008

Theodore bar Koni

Theodore bar Konay

DATE OF BIRTH Unknown, 8th c.
PLACE OF BIRTH Unknown
DATE OF DEATH Unknown, late 8th c. or early 9th c.
PLACE OF DEATH Unknown

BIOGRAPHY

According to one of the copyists of Theodore bar Koni's *Book of scholia*, he was a *malpānā* (teacher, doctor) and *rabban* from the land of Kashkar, between Kūfa and Basra. He belonged to the Church of the East, where he was venerated as St Theodore, and composed several writings, including an ecclesiastical history, instructions (ascetic, dogmatic?) and 'funeral discourses' (?, *buyyāē*), which are all lost. His *Book of scholia*, a students' manual, cast in the 'question-and-answer' genre, which deals with exegetical, theological and general ecclesiastical issues, enjoyed a certain popularity up to the end of the 19th century and has been preserved in two different redactions (known as 'of Siirt' and 'of Urmiah'). Memrā 10 contains a refutation of some Muslim theological views.

MAIN SOURCES OF INFORMATION

Primary

Theodore bar Koni, *Eskolyon*, in A. Scher, *Theodorus bar Kōnī. Liber scholiorum*, 2 vols, Paris, 1910-12, (*CSCO* 55, 69), i, p. 3, ii, pp. 3, 350

ʿAbdishoʿ bar Brikhā, *Catalogus librorum*, in Assemani, *BO* iii/1, pp. 198-99

Secondary

S.H. Griffith, 'Chapter ten of the Scholion: Theodore Bar Kônî's apology for Christianity', *OCP* 47 (1981) 158-88

S.H. Griffith, 'Theodore bar Kônî's Scholion. A Nestorian summa contra gentiles from the first Abbasid century', in N. Garsoïan et al (eds), *East of Byzantium: Syria and Armenia in the formative period* Washington DC, 1982, 53-72

R. Hespel and R. Draguet, *Théodore bar Koni. Livre des scolies (recension de Séert)*, 2 vols, Louvain, 1981-82 (*CSCO* 431-32), i (Mimrè I-V), pp. 1-3 (Hespel's introduction)

L. Brade, *Untersuchungen zum Scholienbuch des Theodoros bar Koni; der übernahme des Erbes von Theodoreos von Mopsuestia in der nestorianischen Kirche*, Wiesbaden, 1975

WORKS ON CHRISTIAN-MUSLIM RELATIONS

(*Ktābā d-*)*Eskolyon*, 'Book of scholia', translated as *Liber scholiorum* by the editor

DATE 791/92
Original language Syriac

DESCRIPTION
This is a general biblical, theological and ecclesiastical encyclopedia, written for 'beginners' (students, novices) and addressed to an otherwise unknown exegete, Mār Yoḥannān. Memrā 10 is an apology for the Christian faith, more particularly of the East-Syrian Christological position, and a refutation of a number of objections made by Muslims, called *ḥanpē*, 'pagans'. Like the rest of the work, the apology is cast in the question-and-answer genre. The setting is artificial: a Christian *malpānā*, answering the questions of a Muslim student, who so readily agrees with the way of reasoning of the *malpānā* and his answers that, had he not been prevented by tradition, he would have become a Christian. The refutation deals with Muslim objections and questions concerning the predictions of Christ in the Old Testament, baptism-circumcision, other 'mysteries' (sacraments), such as the eucharist, the veneration of the cross and the crucifixion, the celebration of Palm Sunday, 'Christ, Son of God', and the Trinity.

The manuscripts of the Urmiah redaction contain a long addition on the veneration of the cross in Memrā 9, possibly reflecting Christian-Muslim discussions on this issue.

SIGNIFICANCE
The author offers his students ready-made answers to questions posed by an anonymous representative of the 'pagans'. Despite the artificial setting, the detailed objections and the elaborate answers suggest that Memrā 10 reflects actual Muslim-Christian debates that were taking place in southern Iraq by the end of the 8th century, thus on the one hand giving insight into the Christian perception of Islam and Muḥammad in vogue in the intellectual milieu of the School of Kashkar and, more generally, in the Church of the East, and on the other

into the questions about Christianity and objections to it that occupied the minds of Muslims.

MANUSCRIPTS

Redaction Siirt:

MS BNF – Syr. 366 (10th-11th c.)

MS Siirt 23 (1539, lost)

MS Baghdad, Chaldean Patriarchate (number unknown, previously Diyarbakir 21, 1608)

MS Baghdad, Chaldean Monastery St Antonius – Syr. 80 (previously Alqosh, 1884)

MS BL – Or. Add. 9372 (1891)

MS Paris, Collection *Patrologia orientalis*, previously Pognon (number unknown, 1902)

Redaction Urmiah:

MS Cambridge – Or. 1307 (1896)

MS Berlin, Staatsbibliothek – Or. Quart. 871 (1897)

MS Berlin, Staatsbibliothek – Or. Quart. 1143 (1911)

Redaction unknown:

MS Baghdad, Chaldean Monastery St Antonius – Syr. 81 (1958)

EDITIONS AND TRANSLATIONS

Scher, *Theodorus bar Kōnī. Liber scholiorum*, ii (edition)

Hespel and Draguet, *Théodore bar Koni. Livre des scolies (recension de Séert)*, ii (French trans.)

R. Hespel, *Théodore bar Koni. Livre des scolies (recension d'Urmiah)*, 2 vols, Louvain, 1983 (*CSCO* 447-48) (edition and trans.)

STUDIES

E.C.D. Hunter, 'Interfaith dialogues. The Church of the East and the Abbassids', in S.G. Vashalomidze and L. Greisiger (eds), *Der Christliche Orient und seine Umwelt*, Wiesbaden, 2007, 289-302, pp. 299-301

S.H. Griffith, 'Disputing with Islam in Syriac: The case of the monk of Bêt Ḫâlê and a Muslim emir', *Hugoye* 3 (2000), no. 10

B. Landron, *Chrétiens et musulmans en Irak, attitudes nestoriennes vis-à-vis de l'Islam*, Paris, 1994, p. 53

S.H. Griffith, 'Disputes with Muslims in Syriac Christian texts. From Patriarch John (d. 648) to Bar Hebraeus (d. 1286)', in B. Lewis and F. Niewöhner (eds), *Religionsgespräche im Mittelalter*, Wiesbaden, 1992, 251-73, pp. 259-61 (repr. in Griffith, *The beginnings of Christian theology in Arabic*, Aldershot, 2002)

Griffith, 'Theodore bar Kônî's Scholion. A Nestorian summa contra gentiles'
Griffith, 'Chapter ten of the Scholion'

Herman G.B. Teule 2007

Ibn al-Layth

Abū l-Rabīʿ Muḥammad ibn al-Layth

DATE OF BIRTH 1st half of 8th c.
PLACE OF BIRTH Unknown
DATE OF DEATH c. 819
PLACE OF DEATH Unknown, possibly Kūfa

BIOGRAPHY

Ibn al-Layth is called by Ibn al-Nadīm an 'orator' (*khaṭīb*), 'jurist' (*faqīh*), apologist/theologian (*mutakallim*), 'epistolographer' (*mutarassil*), and 'secretary' (*kātib*). According to one of Ibn al-Nadīm's sources, he was of Persian background, ultimately a descendent of king Darius. Another of his sources calls him a *mawlā* of the Umayyads.

He held high positions under the ʿAbbasid caliphs al-Mahdī, al-Hādī and Hārūn al-Rashīd and was famed for his eloquence and great epistolary style. He first appears in the sources as secretary and advisor to al-Mahdī (according to the historian al-Yaʿqūbī, even as his *wazīr*), who consulted him about the revolt in Khurāsān in 782. In response, Ibn al-Layth wrote a tract on the characteristics of the people of Khurāsān for the caliph, who followed his advice to send his son al-Hādī there to quell the revolt.

For years Ibn al-Layth had a close relationship with the courtier family of the Barmakids. He wrote a work on *belles-lettres* for Yaḥyā l-Barmakī, *Kitāb (ilā) Yaḥyā ibn Khālid fī l-adab*, and a work entitled *Kitāb al-khaṭṭ wa-l-qalam*, 'Calligraphy and the pen', for his son. Later, however, he began to criticize their influence on the caliph, and in revenge they accused him of being a *zindīq*. Hārūn responded by sending him to prison, though he was released and reconciled with the caliph when the Barmakids fell out of favor.

According to al-Ṭabarī he subsequently blackened the Barmakids' name before Hārūn. His *al-Radd ʿalā l-zanādiqa*, 'Refutation of the zindīqs', probably targeted the Barmakids. Chokr (*Zandaqa*, p. 86) suggests that his *Kitāb ʿiẓat Hārūn al-Rashīd*, 'Admonishing Hārūn al-Rashīd', was written in the context of the conflict with the Barmakids.

A work of his with the title *Kitāb al-halīlaja fī l-iʿtibār*, 'The Myrobalan, on contemplation' is quite probably the work named after this fruit which survives in al-Majlisī's *Biḥār al-anwār*, as has been argued by Chokr (*Zandaqa*, pp. 100-2). It is an apology for the belief in one God and His creation of the universe, framed as a discussion between a Muslim *mutakallim* and an Indian doctor. The style is similar to Ibn al-Layth's letter to the Byzantine Emperor Constantine VI, in which it is also argued that the ultimate proof of monotheism can be found in the order of the created world.

In addition to the works already mentioned (all known from the *Fihrist* of Ibn al-Nadīm), Ibn al-Layth also wrote a refutation of the alchemists, of which Abū Bakr al-Rāzī wrote a counter-refutation (Chokr, *Zandaqa*, p. 87). Even though Ibn al-Layth was engaged in the defense of Islam by means of the refutations of others, and was called *mutakallim*, he is never referred to as a Muʿtazilī. Van Ess (*TG* iii, pp. 26-27) has nevertheless been able to point out some similarities between Muʿtazilī ideas and his apologetics.

Al-Yaʿqūbī still mentions Ibn al-Layth in the year 819, which, if correct, means that he lived to a great age.

MAIN SOURCES OF INFORMATION

Primary

al-Yaʿqūbī, *Taʾrīkh*, 2 vols, Beirut: Dār Ṣādir, 1960, ii, pp. 400, 454, 483, 553

al-Ṭabarī, *Taʾrīkh* iii, pp. 668-69

Ibn ʿAbd Rabbihi, *al-ʿIqd al-farīd*, ed. A. Amīn, A. al-Zayn, I. al-Abyārī, 7 vols, Cairo, 1940-53, i, pp. 192, 204-12

Ibn al-Nadīm, *Fihrist*, p. 134

ʿAbd al-Jabbār, *Tathbīt dalāʾil al-nubuwwa*, ed. ʿA.K. ʿUthmān, Beirut, 1966, pp. 77-78

al-Ṣafadī, *Kitāb al-wāfī bi-al-wafayāt*, 29 vols, Leipzig, 1931-, iv, pp. 379-80

Secondary

Van Ess, *TG* iii, pp. 24-27, 31-32, 93

M. Chokr, *Zandaqa et zindīqs en Islam au second siècle de l'hégire*, Damascus, 1993, pp. 85-88, 100-2, 119-20, 124-28, 157-60, 204

Hadi Eid, *Lettre du calife Hârûn al-Rašîd à l'empereur Constantin VI*, Paris, 1992, pp. 15-22

WORKS ON CHRISTIAN-MUSLIM RELATIONS

Risālat Abī l-Rabīʿ Muḥammad ibn al-Layth allatī katabahā li-l-Rashīd ilā Qusṭanṭīn malik al-Rūm, 'The Letter of Abū l-Rabīʿ Muḥammad ibn al-Layth which he wrote for al-Rashīd to the Byzantine emperor Constantine'

DATE c. 796
ORIGINAL LANGUAGE Arabic

DESCRIPTION
The *Risāla* has come down to us through Ibn Abī Ṭāhir Ṭayfūr (d. 893), who included it in volume 12 of his *al-Manthūr wa-l-manẓūm*, and its authenticity has not been questioned by modern scholars. It can be dated with some precision to between 790 and 797. At the time of Hārūn al-Rashīd's accession in 786, the Empress Irene ruled the Byzantine empire on behalf of her young son Constantine VI. Constantine ruled alone from 790 to 797, when he was blinded and deposed by his mother. Since he is the only ruler addressed in the *Risāla*, it must have been written during his short personal reign. In 797 Hārūn renewed the ʿAbbasid campaigns against Byzantium. Since in the *Risāla* the caliph is threatening the emperor with warfare, it is most likely that it was written shortly before this time.

On behalf of Hārūn al-Rashīd, the author reminds Constantine of the time in the early 780s when the Byzantines were paying the ʿAbbasids a sum twice yearly in exchange for a cessation of hostilities. These payments were halted by Constantine and it was a reason for the ʿAbbasids to threaten new campaigns to conquer Byzantium. The *Risāla* emphasizes that if the Byzantine emperor is not willing to convert to Islam, paying tribute is still a better option than warfare. To this end, Ibn al-Layth appeals to the emperor's religious sensitivities, but also argues from a more practical point of view that peace allows one's country to prosper, in particular through trade and agriculture, while a refusal to pay tribute would result in bloodshed for which the emperor would be held personally responsible, since he has been given the choice to avoid it. Interestingly, Ibn al-Layth adds force to this call for a financial settlement of the conflict by appealing to several pacific verses from the Gospels.

This admonishment of the Byzantine emperor provides a framework in which is embedded a refutation of Christianity, combined with a detailed defense of the prophethood of Muḥammad. The *Risāla* incorporates many of the themes of religious controversy between Muslims and Christians in early ʿAbbasid society. The author explicitly appeals to reason, which he considers the unique arbiter in the search for religious truth. In defense of Muḥammad's prophethood, a range of arguments are advanced: Muḥammad fulfills the biblical predictions about him; the qurʾānic predictions regarding the victories of Islam have also been fulfilled; the Qurʾān was already proven to be inimitable during Muḥammad's lifetime, and Muḥammad worked other evidentiary miracles.

At the same time, several contemporary standard arguments of Christians against Islam are refuted. For example, the claim that Muḥammad secretly drew his religious knowledge from a Christian he knew is disproved by the claim that the religion of Islam is too different from Christianity (and from the religions of others with whom he could have had contact). Moreover, if he had frequented a teacher who taught him what to preach, his community would have known about this relationship. Furthermore, being illiterate and unschooled, he could not have known about phenomena such as shooting stars described in the Qurʾān. These must be proof of Muḥammad's miraculous foreknowledge of events. This is one of the few themes in the *Risāla* which were not taken up by later apologists, maybe because it failed to convince (as suggested by Van Ess, *TG* iii, p. 26).

The argument that Muḥammad was primarily driven by unworthy motives such as gaining power, wealth and comfort, is countered by the assertion that both he and his followers suffered frequent physical and mental abuse and yet chose to fight for the advancement of the cause they believed in.

As for Christianity, the author claims that Christians have fallen victim to wrong interpretations of their scripture, which they uncritically accept from their leaders. Ibn al-Layth attacks the belief in the Trinity and the divine Sonship of Jesus both on rational grounds and by means of quotations from the Bible, such as where Jesus calls God 'our Father' in the presence of the disciples, indicating that his own relation to God is comparable to theirs. He also diminishes the value of Christ's miracles by claiming that earlier prophets performed similar miracles, though they were never accorded divinity.

SIGNIFICANCE

The text bears witness to the intense debates regarding the prophethood of Muḥammad in the early decades of the ʿAbbasid caliphate and to the need to respond to an ever more sophisticated anti-Muslim polemic coming from Christians living in *Dār al-Islām*. Van Ess (*TG* iii, p. 24) suggests, for example, that the emphasis on Muḥammad's evidentiary miracles comes as a direct response to the claim, voiced just a decade before by the East-Syrian Patriarch Timothy I (q.v.) to the Caliph al-Mahdī, that Islam came into being without the necessary miracles accompanying it. Many of the arguments in defense of Muḥammad's prophethood advanced in this text can be found in later apologetic works. This may point to the influence of the *Risāla*. On the other hand, it is also possible that Ibn al-Layth's seemingly original arguments in reality reflect an established repertoire of arguments used in the oral disputations of early Islam. In either case, the *Risāla* is a chronological anchor in the history of Muslim apologetic thinking. The supposition that the *Risāla* was read by later apologists is confirmed by ʿAbd al-Jabbār (*Tathbīt*, pp. 77-78), who characterizes it as a solid work of 'proof of prophethood' literature. He also hints at contemporary Muʿtazilī knowledge of it, when he writes that the *Risāla* was dispatched to Byzantium with someone who belonged to the Muʿtazila, 'possibly Muʿammar', (*Tathbīt*, p. 77), i.e. Muʿammar ibn ʿAbbād al-Sulamī (d. 830).

Zaman sees the *Risāla* as an example of proto-Sunnī propaganda, inasmuch as the author tries to portray the truth and success of Islam as tightly connected to the office and power of the caliph. Nothing is known about the reception of the *Risāla* on the Byzantine side, and since Byzantinists did not know about its existence until recently (cf. Rochow), the question of whether the text can be shown to have had an impact on Byzantine politics and attitudes towards Islam and the ʿAbbasid caliphate remains open.

The quotations from the Bible in the text are of particular interest. The *Risāla* contains the earliest collection of biblical testimonia to Muḥammad in Arabic. Although Dunlop and Adang have briefly investigated the issue, it remains difficult to determine whether these go back to a translated version of the Bible, to individually translated verses or to some sort of pre-existing testimonia collection.

MANUSCRIPTS

MS Baghdad, Jāmiʿat al-Ḥikma Adab – 58 (Yaʿqūb Sarkīs Collection), fols 178-204 (917 AH [1511 CE]; MS *de base* of Eid's edition)

MS BL – 1090 N. Add. 18532, fols 85-97 (1092 AH [1681])
MS Cairo, Dār al-Kutub al-Miṣriyya – 581 Adab, fols 135-53 (1297 AH [1879 CE]; MS *de base* of al-Rifāʿī's edition)
MS Cairo, al-Azhar – 464 Abāẓa 7060 (1302 AH [1884 CE])
MS Cairo, Dār al-Kutub al-Miṣriyya – 1860 Adab (1307 AH [1889 CE]; copy of MS Cairo, Dār al-Kutub al-Miṣriyya – 581 Adab; MS *de base* of Ṣafwat's edition)
MS Cairo, al-Azhar – (1752) 18876 (1331 AH [1912 CE])
(Sezgin, *GAS* i, p. 349, notes that there is another manuscript in Medina in an unnamed private collection)

EDITIONS AND TRANSLATIONS

Risālat Abī l-Rabīʿ Muḥammad ibn al-Layth min Hārūn al-Rashīd ilā Qusṭanṭīn malik al-Rūm, ed. K.M. ʿAbduh, Giza, 2006 (not accessed)
Hadi Eid, *Lettre du calife Hârûn al-Rašîd*, Paris, (s.d. [1993]) (handwritten edition with French trans., annotation and introduction)
A.Z. Ṣafwat, *Jamharat rasāʾil al-ʿArab fī ʿuẓūr al-ʿarabiyya l-zāhira*, 4 vols, Cairo, 1937, iii (*al-ʿaṣr al-ʿabbāsī l-awwal*), pp. 252-324 (repr. Cairo, 1971, iii, pp. 217-74)
Risālat Abī l-Rabīʿ Muḥammad ibn al-Layth allatī katabahā li-l-Rashīd ilā Qusṭanṭīn malik al-Rūm. Hiya l-risāla llatī baʿatha bihā l-khalīfa l-ʿabbāsī Hārūn al-Rashīd, ed. A.L. Ḥasan, Cairo, 1936
A.F. al-Rifāʿī, *ʿAṣr al-Maʾmūn*, 3 vols, Cairo, 1928, ii, pp. 188-236 (repr. in M.M. Ḥamāda, *al-Wathāʾiq al-siyāsiyya wa-l-idāriyya li-l-dawla l-ʿabbāsiyya*, Beirut, 1978, pp. 205-57)

STUDIES

N.M. El Cheikh, *Byzantium viewed by the Arabs*, Cambridge MA, 2004, pp. 91-93
I. Rochow, 'Zu den diplomatischen Beziehungen zwischen Byzanz und dem Kalifat in der Zeit der syrischen Dynastie (717-802)', in C. Sodes and S. Tacács, *Novum Millennium. Studies on Byzantine history and culture dedicated to Paul Speck*, Aldershot, 2001, 305-25, pp. 319-20
A.M.H. Shboul, 'Arab Islamic perceptions of Byzantine religion and culture', in J. Waardenburg (ed.), *Muslim perceptions of other religions*, New York, 1999, 122-35, pp. 129-31
M.Q. Zaman, *Religion and politics under the early ʿAbbāsids. The emergence of the proto-Sunnī elite*, Leiden, 1997, pp. 187-88

C. Adang, *Muslim writers on Judaism and the Hebrew Bible from Ibn Rabban to Ibn Hazm*, Leiden, 1996, pp. 21, 111, 143-45, 148, 224, 264-66

Van Ess, *TG* ii, p. 405, iii, pp. 24-27, iv, pp. 611, 633-34

A.M.H. Shboul, 'Arab attitudes towards Byzantium: official, learned, popular', in J. Chrysostomides (ed.), *Kathegetria. Essays presented to Joan Hussey*, Camberley, 1988, 111-18, pp. 116-17

al-Sharfī, *al-Fikr al-Islāmī*, pp. 163-64

D.M. Dunlop, 'A letter of Hārūn al-Rashīd to the Emperor Constantine VI', in M. Black and G. Fohrer (eds), *In memoriam Paul Kahle*, Berlin, 1968, 106-15

Barbara Roggema, 2008

Abū Yūsuf Yaʿqūb

Abū Yūsuf Yaʿqūb ibn Ibrāhīm ibn Ḥabīb al-Anṣārī l-Kūfī

DATE OF BIRTH Unknown, approx. 740
PLACE OF BIRTH Kūfa
DATE OF DEATH 798
PLACE OF DEATH Baghdad

BIOGRAPHY

Abū Yūsuf's origins are obscure, though it is known that he studied under leading legal experts of his day, including Abū Ḥanīfa and Mālik ibn Anas. Since the former died in 767, it is plausible to suppose that Abū Yūsuf was born 20 to 30 years earlier in order to have been old enough to be his student. He was made *qāḍī* in Baghdad under one of the early ʿAbbasid caliphs, and he came to the notice of Hārūn al-Rashīd (r. 786-809), whose high regard is indicated by the title of *qāḍī l-quḍāt* which he conferred on him. He remained close to al-Rashīd for the rest of his life, and in later tradition was sometimes regarded as too readily acquiescent to the caliph's wishes. Among his students were Muḥammad ibn al-Ḥasan al-Shaybānī and Aḥmad ibn Ḥanbal.

Abū Yūsuf followed Abū Ḥanīfa in the main principles of his legal thinking, though tended to rely more than his teacher on prophetic traditions and to be more restrained in the use of reason. His legal thinking is characterized by changes of opinion, the consequence of delivering actual decisions as a judge, and by a polemical attitude towards opposing views.

From a considerable output, only a few of Abū Yūsuf's works have survived. These include comparisons between rival legal views (*Kitāb ikhtilāf Abī Ḥanīfa wa-Ibn Abī Laylā*, 'Disagreement between Abū Ḥanīfa and Ibn Abī Layla'), and also critiques of individual jurists (*Kitāb al-radd ʿalā siyar al-Awzāʿī*, 'Refutation of the opinions of al-Awzāʿī', and *Kitāb al-radd ʿalā Mālik ibn Anas*, 'Refutation of Mālik ibn Anas').

MAIN SOURCES OF INFORMATION

Primary

Ibn al-Nadīm, *Fihrist*, pp. 256-57
al-Khaṭīb al-Baghdādī, *Taʾrīkh Baghdād*, 14 vols, Beirut, 1997, xiv, pp. 245-63
Ibn Khallikān, *Wafayāt al-aʿyān wa-anbāʾ abnāʾ al-zamān*, ed. Iḥsān ʿAbbās, 8 vols, Beirut, 1968, vi, pp. 378-90
Abū Muḥammad ʿAbdallāh al-Yāfiʿī, *Mirʾāt al-janān wa-ʿibrat al-yaqẓān*, 4 vols, Hyderabad, 1337-39 (1918-20), i, pp. 382-88

Secondary

al-Hādī Darqāsh, *Abū Yūsuf al-qāḍī, ḥayāh wa-kitāb al-kharāj, baḥth al-jamāʿī*, Tunis, 1984
Maḥmūd Maṭlūb, *Abū Yūsuf. Ḥayātuhu wa-āthāruhu wa-ārāʾuhu l-fiqhiyya*, Baghdad: Maṭbaʿat Dār al-Salām, 1972
Aḥmad Amīn, *Duḥā l-Islām*, 3 vols, Cairo, 1964, ii, pp. 198-203
J. Schacht, *The origins of Muhammadan jurisprudence*, Oxford, 1950, pp. 44-45
E. Fagnan, *Abou Yousof Yaʿkoub. Le livre de l'impôt foncier (Kitâb el-kharâdj)*, Paris, 1921, pp. ix-xvi

WORKS ON CHRISTIAN-MUSLIM RELATIONS

Kitāb al-kharāj, 'Property tax', *Kitāb al-risāla fī l-kharāj ilā l-Rashīd*, 'The Letter on property tax to al-Rashīd'

DATE Between 786 and 798, though Calder disputes Abū Yūsuf's authorship and dates it to the mid-9th c.
ORIGINAL LANGUAGE Arabic

DESCRIPTION

Since the work was ostensibly written for Hārūn al-Rashīd, it must have been completed between 786, when the caliph succeeded, and 798 when Abū Yūsuf died. If the introduction is at all accurate, it was a practical response to al-Rashīd's request for advice about taxation matters, intended to avoid 'oppression of Muslim or *dhimmī*' and to 'instill loyalty through its fair provisions'. Ibn al-Nadīm, *Fihrist*, p. 257, includes it among the works which Abū Yūsuf dictated to his disciple Bishr ibn al-Walīd, and gives it the title *Kitāb al-risāla fī l-kharāj ilā l-Rashīd*, though it is usually known simply as *Kitāb al-kharāj*. It has the character of a compilation, possibly made at different times, comprising sections on individual and often unrelated taxation elements, and without any clear overall structure.

Calder (particularly pp. 144-52) rejects the traditional attribution. He dates the work to the 9th century, where he claims its contents and concerns match major preoccupations of the brief reign of the Caliph al-Muhtadī (r. 869-70), and he identifies Aḥmad ibn ʿAmr al-Khaṣṣāf (d. 874) as its author. His reattribution has not gained widespread acceptance, and Zaman ('The caliphs', pp. 13-17) in particular draws attention to weaknesses in his arguments.

The work comprises advice on the various forms of taxation currently in force, and how to bring these into conformity with Islamic principles where possible. They include taxes on various kinds of land and produce, granting of pensions, division of booty and miscellaneous levies that were introduced under Islam and also carried over from earlier fiscal structures. The recommendations it contains are based both on precedent, including Qurʾān injunctions, ḥadīth and practices of the first caliphs where these are available, and also on Abū Yūsuf's own practical reasoning, which he is not hesitant to provide.

Among the many recommendations in the work, provisions for Christians among the *dhimmīs* figure in a number of sections. In the 1884 Būlāq edition, which is the basis of Fagnan and Ben Shemesh's translations, these include: the implications of the special concessions made for the tribe of Taghlib, whose power at the time of the Caliph ʿUmar presented a threat to Islam (pp. 68-69); those who are liable for poll-tax (pp. 69-72); the appropriate dress for *dhimmīs* (pp. 72-73); and the treatment of churches, monasteries and crosses (pp. 80-88). In his translation, Ben Shemesh (pp. 84-93) brings together the recommendations which he considers relevant to a work on taxation and omits others as 'improvements' which were inserted in later times, though without fully explaining his reasons (see p. viii).

The details about the treatment of *dhimmīs* in these sections include some that resemble the stipulations of the Pact of ʿUmar, such as restrictions on dress, prohibitions against using saddles, displaying crosses and building new churches and synagogues. There are also a number of references to what appear to be the earlier and current practice of humiliating *dhimmīs* when they pay the *jizya* by making them stand in the sun, beating them, or placing seals on their necks. In line with his overall pragmatic approach to advising the caliph on governing, Abū Yūsuf counsels against such practices and recommends clemency in the treatment of client communities.

SIGNIFICANCE

The work provides a rare glimpse into the legal and social position of Christians and other client communities in Islamic society in the late 8th century. Its references to practices in the treatment of *dhimmīs* hint that certain discriminatory measures had become institutionalized, and were justified on grounds of early Islamic precedents. The general leniency of the advice it contains suggests that Abū Yūsuf disagreed with trends he witnessed around him. In particular, its references to stipulations that appear elsewhere in early forms of what was known as the Pact of ʿUmar are more tolerant and contain fewer individual details than these forms. In following this course, Abū Yūsuf may have been pragmatically recommending a policy that would simplify the task of governing client communities, or else he was expressing a form of pluralistic realism.

MANUSCRIPTS

The fullest list is given in *GAS* i, p. 420, which supersedes *GAL* i, p. 177 (171), and S i, p. 288. It identifies more than 50 MSS, dating from the 15th century onwards. Ben Shemesh (p. viii) suggests that later MSS contain numerous interpolations, though without giving details.

EDITIONS AND TRANSLATIONS

Kitab al-kharadzh. Abu Ĭusuf Ĭaʾkub b. Ibrakhim al-Kufi, trans. (Russian) A.E. Shmidt, St Petersburg, 2001

Kitāb al-kharāj li-Abī Yūsuf Yaʿqūb ibn Ibrāhīm, ed. Ṭāhā ʿAbd al-Raʾūf Saʿd and Saʿd Ḥasan Muḥammad, Cairo: al-Maktaba l-Azhariyya li-l-turāth, 1999

Kitāb al-kharāj li-Abī Yūsuf Yaʿqūb ibn Ibrāhīm, ed. Iḥsān ʿAbbās, Beirut; Dār al-Shurūq, 1985

Kitāb al-kharāj, ed. Maḥmūd al-Bājī, Tunis, 1984

Al-kharāj li-Abī Yūsuf, ed. Muḥammad Ibrāhīm al-Bannā, (Cairo): Dār al-Iṣlāḥ, 1981

Kitāb al-kharāj, Beirut, 1979

Kitab-ul-kharaj / Islamic revenue code, Abu Yusaf, trans. Abid Ahmad Ali (rev. Abdul Hameed Siddiqui), Lahore, 1979

N. Stillman, *The Jews of Arab lands, a history and source book*, Philadelphia, 1979, pp. 159-61

Kitāb al kharāj, Cairo: al-Ṭibāʿa l-Munīriyya, 1976

B. Lewis, ed. and trans., *Islam from the Prophet Muhammad to the capture of Constantinople. II: Religion and society*, New York, 1974, pp. 223-24

Fiqh al-mulūk wa-miftāḥ al-ritāj al-murṣad ʿalā khizānat Kitāb al-kharāj, ed. Aḥmad ʿUbayd al-Kubaysī (with the commentary of ʿAbd al-ʿAzīz ibn Muḥammad al-Raḥbī al-Ḥanafī (d. c. 1770)), Baghdad, 1973

Kitabü 'l-haraç, trans. Ali Özek, Istanbul 1970 (Turkish)

Abū Yūsuf's Kitāb al-kharāj, trans. (partial, with rearrangements) A. Ben Shemesh, Leiden, 1969

Kitāb al-kharāj, (s.l., 1962 or 63)

Kitāb al-kharāj li l-Qāḍī Abī Yūsuf Yaʿqūb ibn Ibrāhīm ṣāḥib al-Imām Abī Ḥanīfa, Cairo: al-Maṭbaʿa l-Salafiyya, 1346 (1927) (reprints with different pagination: 1352 (1933), 1383 (1962), 1392 (1973), Beirut: Dār al-Maʿrifa, 1985)

Al kharadje (impôts fonciers) d'après le livre d'Abou-Youssouf, partial trans. M. Mahmoud, Lyons, 1923

E. Fagnan, *Abou Yousof Yaʿkoub. Le livre de l'impôt foncier* (French trans.)

Abū Yūsuf al-Qāḍī. Il kitab al-kharag o libro de imposte, trans. P. Tripodo, Rome, 1906 (Italian trans.)

Kitāb al-kharāj, Būlāq, 1302 A.H. (1884)

STUDIES

M. Levy-Rubin, '*Shurut ʿUmar* and its alternatives. The legal debate on the status of the Dhimmīs', *JSAI* 30 (2005) 170-206, pp. 182-94

C.F. Robinson, *Empire and elites after the Muslim conquest. The transformation of Northern Mesopotamia*, Cambridge, 2000, pp. 2-6, 9-10 and *passim*

N.M. Siddiqi and S.M. Ghazanfar, 'Early medieval Islamic economic thought, Abu Yousuf's (731-798AD) economics of public finance', in *Medieval Islamic economic thought. Filling the 'great gap' in European economics*, ed. S.M. Ghazanfar, London, 2003, 209-27

ʿIṣma Aḥmad Fahmī Abū Sinna, *Raʾy al-Qāḍī Abī Yūsuf fī l-ḥayāh al-iqtiṣādiyya li-l-dawla l-Islāmiyya fī ʿahd Hārūn al-Rashīd min khilāl Kitāb al-kharāj, 170 H-182 H*, Mecca, 2002

I. ʿAbbās, *Buḥūth wa-dirāsāt fī l-adab wa-l-tārīkh*, 3 vols, Beirut, 2000, i, pp. 72-129

S. Azmi, 'Taxation policy in early Islam: the pioneering contribution of Abu Yusuf', *Muslim and Arab Perspectives* 4 (1999) 263-82

M.Q. Zaman, 'The caliphs, the ʿulamāʾ, and the law. Defining the role and function of the caliph in the early ʿAbbāsid period', *Islamic Law and Society* 4 (1997) 1-36 (repr. in W.B. Hallaq, *The formation of Islamic law*, 2004, Aldershot)

M.Q. Zaman, *Religion and politics under the early ʿAbbāsids. The emergence of the proto-Sunnī elite*, Leiden, 1997, pp. 91-101 and *passim*

N. Calder, *Studies in Muslim jurisprudence*, 1993, pp. 105-60

Aḥmad Ṣādiq Saʿd, *Kitāb al-kharāj li-Abī Yūsuf ibn Yaʿqūb*, (Beirut): Dār al-Farābī: Dār al-thaqāfa l-jadīda, 1988

M.M. Marʿī, *al-Nuẓum al-māliyya wa-l-iqtiṣādiyya fī l-dawla l-Islāmiyya ʿalā ḍawʾ* Kitāb al-kharāj *li-Abī Yūsuf*, Doha: Dār al-Thaqāfa, 1987

Ziaul Haque, *Landlord and peasant in early Islam. A study of the legal doctrine of* muzāraʿa *or sharecropping*, Islamabad, 1977 (see index)

Maṭlūb, *Abū Yūsuf. Ḥayātuhu wa-āthāruhu*, pp. 103-09

Sezgin, *GAS* i, pp. 419-21

Amīn, *Duḥā l-Islām*, ii, pp. 201-03

A. Fattal, *Le statut légal des non-musulmans en pays d'Islam*, Beirut, 1958, partic. pp. 65-66, 175, 271, 276-77, 289, 305

F. Lökkegaard, *Islamic taxation in the classical period with special reference to circumstances in Iraq*, Copenhagen, 1950

A.S. Tritton, *The caliphs and their non-Muslim subjects*, London, 1930, 1970[2]

David Thomas 2008

The Pact of ʿUmar

Unknown author

DATE OF BIRTH Unknown
PLACE OF BIRTH Unknown
DATE OF DEATH Unknown, maybe early 9th c.
PLACE OF DEATH Unknown

BIOGRAPHY —

MAIN SOURCES OF INFORMATION

Primary —

Secondary —

WORKS ON CHRISTIAN-MUSLIM RELATIONS

Shurūṭ ʿUmar or *al-Shurūṭ al-ʿumariyya*; also called *ʿAhd ʿUmar* and *ʿAqd ʿUmar*, 'The Conditions of ʿUmar' or 'The Pact of ʿUmar'

DATE 8th to beginning of 9th c.
ORIGINAL LANGUAGE Arabic

DESCRIPTION

The Pact of ʿUmar is the name given to the canonical text that defines the status of non-Muslims under Muslim rule and the restrictions imposed upon them. The name does not refer to various other documents which attempt to do the same but have not been canonized such as, for example, the document adduced by al-Shāfiʿī (*Kitāb al-umm*, 4 vols, Cairo, 1968, iv, pp. 118-19, trans. B. Lewis, *Islam, from the prophet Muhammad to the capture of Constantinople*, 2 vols, New York, 1974, ii, pp. 219-23) or the one cited by Abū Yūsuf (q.v.) in *Kitāb al-kharāj* (Cairo 1352 A.H. [1933], pp. 138-39).

The document is an agreement allegedly made between the Muslim conquerors, represented by ʿAbd al-Raḥmān ibn Ghanm (d. 697), and the Christians of Damascus or the Jazīra, which was then applied to the *Ahl al-dhimma* in general. The document lists a series of obligations made by the conquered in return for the *amān* given to them by the Muslims. It includes: clauses regarding their obligation to host the Muslims in their houses and churches, and to be loyal to them; a list of restrictive measures regarding their religious customs, such as beating the *nāqūs* lightly, praying quietly, refraining from various public displays (public processions on Christian holidays, funerals, crosses, lights on roads, sale of pigs and wine); clauses regarding their behavior in the presence of Muslims (an obligation to respect them and give them priority on the road as well as in seating, not to be buried next to them, not to peer into their houses, not to own a Muslim slave); a series of clauses regarding the issue of the *ghiyār*, or differentiating signs, including the prohibition on resembling Muslims in appearance, the obligation to wear the *zunnār* (girdle), the prohibition on using saddles, on using Arabic seals, on carrying weapons, and on teaching their children Arabic.

The main reasons for rejecting the traditional attribution of the document to ʿUmar ibn al-Khaṭṭāb is its *Sitz im Leben*, which portrays a state of established co-existence between Muslims and non-Muslim in the cities that is unimaginable during the days of the second caliph himself, and the unacceptable notion that the vanquished asked for such restrictive terms during their surrender, as is stated in the opening sentence of the document. The terms listed in the Pact are also in complete disagreement with the numerous reports regarding the initial surrender agreements made between the Muslims and the various conquered cities and territories.

There is a diversity of opinions amongst scholars regarding the date of the formation of the document. Tritton and Fattal regard it as a product of the *mujtahids* of the 9th century, while Dennett believes that the surrender agreement of Jerusalem stands at its basis, a suggestion that has not been accepted since there is no real resemblance between the two documents. Other scholars, including De Goeje, Salo Baron, Stillman and Zayyat, claim that the ʿUmar who features here is the Umayyad Caliph ʿUmar ibn ʿAbd al-ʿAzīz (r. 717-20), and that the document was forged in his days, although some clauses may have already existed earlier. Others, including Lewis, Noth and Cohen, believe (Noth more exceedingly so) that many of the clauses in the document reflect the conditions of the immediate post-conquest period, although it underwent a process of development and stylization by later historians.

Various *isnād*s attached to different versions of the Pact indicate that the document may be dated to sometime in the 8th century. If we remain within the methodological limitations of recent *isnād* research, these point to the second half of the century, or if we accept the earlier link in the *isnād*, even the first half (see Levy-Rubin, 172; Miller, ch. 5).

The earliest works in which the Pact is cited are Abū Bakr al-Khallāl (d. 923), Ibn Zabr (d. 940) and Ibn al-Murajjā (d. c. 1030-40).

SIGNIFICANCE

The Pact of ʿUmar is a canonical document which sums up the principles applied by the Muslims to the *Dhimmīs*. It replaced the initial agreements that were made individually with conquered cities or regions. These agreements represented a tolerant approach of 'live and let live', demanding in general only the payment of the *jizya* by the conquered communities in return for a promise of security for their lives and property (*amān*), and a guarantee to live according to their ancient customs. *The Pact of ʿUmar* was an attempt which finally succeeded to limit and then dissolve the relevance of these initial agreements, and to replace them with a much more intolerant and restrictive approach. Although there were documents of a similar nature to it in the 8th and beginning of the 9th century, such as those cited by al-Shāfiʿī and by Abū Yūsuf (see above), it seems that by the time at which al-Mutawakkil published his famous edict regarding *Ahl al-dhimma* (al-Ṭabarī, *Taʾrīkh* iii, pp. 1389-90) in the mid-9th century, the Pact had acquired priority over other versions and represented Muslim consensus regarding *Ahl al-dhimma* (Levy-Rubin). From then on it was repeatedly cited and copied by Muslim writers in numerous compositions. Although it was not always systematically or strictly enforced in early times, it seems to have progressively become the accepted norm in later centuries.

MANUSCRIPTS —

EDITIONS AND TRANSLATIONS

Abū Bakr al-Khallāl, *Ahl al-milal wa-l-ridda wa-l-zanādiqa wa-tārik al-ṣalāḥ wa-l-farāʾiḍ min Kitāb al-Jāmiʿ*, ed. I.Ḥ. Sulṭān, 2 vols, Riyadh, 1996, ii, pp. 431-34

Ibn Zabr, in M.R. Cohen, 'What was the Pact of ʿUmar? A literary-historical study', *JSAI* 23 (1999) 100-57, pp. 137-40, 141-42, 145-46 (several versions)

Abū al-Maʿālī al-Musharraf ibn al-Murajjā ibn Ibrāhīm al-Maqdisī, *Faḍāʾil Bayt al-Maqdis wa-l-Khalīl wa-faḍāʾil al-Shām*, ed. ʿŪ. Livne-Kafrī, Shafā ʿAmr [Israel]: Dār al-mashriq li-l-tarjama wa-l-ṭibāʿa wa-l-nashr, 1995, pp. 55-56

Ibn Ḥazm, *Al-muḥallā*, ed. A.M. Shakir, 11 vols, [Cairo, 1928-33] Beirut, 1980, vii, pp. 346-47

Al-Ṭurṭūshī, *Sirāj al-mulūk*, Cairo 1935, pp. 252-53; trans. (German) W. Kallfelz, *Nichtmuslimische Untertanen im Islam: Grundlage, Ideologie und Praxis der Politik frühislamischer Herrscher gegenüber ihren nichtmuslimischen Untertanen mit besonderem Blick auf die Dynastie der Abbasiden (749-1248)*, Wiesbaden 1995, pp. 78-99; trans. (German) A.T. Khoury, *Toleranz im Islam*, Altenberge, 1986, p. 83; trans. N.A. Stillman, *The Jews of Arab lands. A history and source book*, Jewish Publication Society, s.l., 1979, pp. 157-58; trans. Lewis, *Islam*, ii, pp. 217-19; trans. (French) A. Fattal, *Le statut legal des non-musulmans en pays d'Islam*, Beirut, 1958, pp. 60-65

Ibn ʿAsākir, *Taʾrīkh madina Dimashq*, 80 vols, Beirut 1995, ii, pp. 120, 174-79 (includes five different versions of the document); trans. A.S. Tritton, *The caliphs and their non-Muslim subjects*, London, 1930, pp. 5-6

Ghāzī al-Wāsiṭī, in R. Gottheil, 'An answer to the Dhimmīs', *JAOS* 41 (1921) pp. 391 (text), 422-23 (trans.)

Ibn al-Naqqāsh, in M. Belin, 'Fetoua relative à la condition des *zimmis*', *Journal asiatique*, série 4e, 19 (1852) pp. 126-28 (text), 495-500 (trans.)

Ibn Qayyim al-Jawziyya, *Aḥkām Ahl al-Dhimma*, Damascus 1961, pp. 657-62 (two versions); trans. (Hebrew) H. Lazarus-Yafeh, *Sofrim Muslemim ʿal Yehudim ve-Yahadut: ha-Yehudim be-kerev shekhenehem ha-Muslemim*, Jerusalem, 1996, pp. 267-68

A comprehensive list of editions, including many later versions, is given by Miller, *From catalogue to codes*, pp. 395-98

STUDIES

M. Levy-Rubin, '*Shurūṭ ʿUmar* and its alternatives. The legal debate on the status of the *Dhimmīs*', *JSAI* 30 (2005) 170-206

D.E. Miller, *From catalogue to codes to canon: The rise of the petition to ʿUmar among legal traditions governing non-Muslims in medieval Islamicate societies*, Kansas City MO, 2000 (Diss. University of Missouri)

Cohen, 'What was the Pact of ʿUmar?'

Kallfelz, *Nichtmuslimische Untertanen im Islam*, pp. 77-82
M. Cohen, *Under crescent and cross. The Jews in the middle ages*, Princeton NJ, 1994, pp. 52-74, esp. pp. 54-65, 73-74
A. Noth, 'Abgrenzungsprobleme zwischen Muslimen und nicht-Muslimen – die "Bedingungen 'Umar's" (*ash-shurūṭ al-ʿumariyya*) unter einem anderen Aspekt gelesen', *JSAI* 9 (1987) 290-315; trans. M. Muelhaeusler, in R. Hoyland (ed.), *Muslims and others in early Islamic society*, Aldershot, 2004, 103-24
Stillman, *The Jews of Arab Lands*, pp. 25-26
Lewis, *The Jews of Islam*, pp. 24-25
Fattal, *Statut légal*, pp. 60-69
S.W. Baron, *A social and religious history of the Jews*, 2nd ed., Philadelphia, 1957, pp. 97, 129-31, and nn. 10 and 12 on pp. 293-94
D. Dennett, *Conversion and the poll tax in early Islam*, Cambridge MA, 1950, pp. 62-64
E. Strauss (Ashtor), 'The social isolation of Ahl al-Dhimma', in O. Komlos (ed.), *Études orientales à la mémoire de Paul Hirschler*, Budapest, 1950, 73-94
H. Zayyat, 'The distinctive signs of the Christians and Jews in Islam' (Arabic), *Al-Machriq* 43 (1949) 161-252
I. Lichtenstadter, 'The distinctive dress of non-Muslims in Islamic countries', *Historia Judaica* 5 (1943) 35-52
Tritton, *The caliphs and their non-Muslim subjects*, pp. 5-1
M.J. de Goeje, *Mémoire sur la conquête de la Syrie*, Leiden, 1900, pp. 147-48

Milka Levy-Rubin 2008

Felix of Urgell

Feliu d'Urgell

DATE OF BIRTH Unknown
PLACE OF BIRTH Unknown
DATE OF DEATH Uncertain, probably between 811 and 818
PLACE OF DEATH Lyon

BIOGRAPHY

Bishop of Urgell (Catalonia), Felix was a proponent of Adoptionism, the belief that Jesus was God's son through adoption not birth. He was made to abjure this 'heresy' in 792 before Charlemagne's court at Ratisbon and then before the pope in Rome. He was again forced to abjure his Adoptionism at the Council of Aix in 800; deposed from his bishopric, he was imprisoned in Lyons, probably until his death.

MAIN SOURCES OF INFORMATION

Primary

Alcuin, *Liber Alcuini contra haeresim Felicis*, ed. G. Blumenshire, Vatican City, 1980

Secondary

J. Perarnau (ed.), *Jornades internacionals d'estudi sobre el Bisbe Feliu d'Urgel. Crònica i estudis*, Barcelona, 2000

J. Perarnau (ed.), *Feliu d'Urgell. Bases per al seu estudi*, Barcelona, 1999

WORKS ON CHRISTIAN-MUSLIM RELATIONS

Disputatio Felicis cum Sarraceno, 'The Disputation between Felix and a Saracen'

DATE Unknown, before 799
ORIGINAL LANGUAGE Latin

DESCRIPTION

The text is lost or non-existent. Alcuin of York, in a letter to Charlemagne (April-May 799), mentions a *Disputatio Felicis cum Sarraceno* and says that he has looked for it but has not found a copy of it

(Alcuin, *Epistola* 172, in E. Dümmler (ed.), *Epistolae Karolini aevi (II)*, Berlin, 1895, 284-85 [*MGH Epistolae* 4]). Since he frequently refers elsewhere in his letters to Felix of Urgell, it has been assumed not unreasonably that this is the same Felix. This is the only mention of this text, which Perarnau hence classifies among Felix of Urgell's 'scripta dubia'.

SIGNIFICANCE

This is the earliest mention of an anti-Muslim polemical text in Latin.

MANUSCRIPTS —

EDITIONS AND TRANSLATIONS —

STUDIES

See the references in Secondary Sources of Information, above.

John Tolan 2008

The Dialogue between a Saracen and a Christian

Uncertain author

DATE OF BIRTH Unknown
PLACE OF BIRTH Unknown
DATE OF DEATH Unknown
PLACE OF DEATH Unknown

BIOGRAPHY —

MAIN SOURCES OF INFORMATION

Primary —

Secondary —

WORKS ON CHRISTIAN-MUSLIM RELATIONS

Dialexis Sarakēnou kai Christianou, 'The Dialogue between a Saracen and a Christian'

DATE Unknown, probably 2nd half of the 8th c.
ORIGINAL LANGUAGE Greek

DESCRIPTION

This work, which has long been associated with John of Damascus, is a dialogue between a Christian and a Saracen about the cause of good and evil, and the difference between the uncreated Word of God and the created words of God. It explores the subjects of God's omnipotence and man's free will, the uncreated or created nature of God's word, the death of Mary, and the relation of Jesus to John the Baptist.

The work exists in several variations which differ greatly from each other, making a final judgment regarding its authenticity difficult. Some have argued that it is a recapitulation of John of Damascus' teachings, written down in different ways by one or more later scribes. Others have argued that another later author is largely responsible, and still others that it may be by the Damascene himself, but edited by a later redactor. Jugie, followed by Sahas, has proposed the first option, and Griffith has suggested the second, while Le Coz, echoing Kotter, has defended at least the possibility of the third. These views are not far from each other, however, in that they all agree on the possibility of alternative explanations for the work's origin. In any case, what we have now is a composite text, and so it cannot simply be attributed to the hand of John of Damascus.

If the text was written by an author other than John, there is good reason to think that it could be the work of Theodore Abū Qurra (q.v.), or that he at least edited it into the form in which we have it today. Many of the arguments that appear in the text also appear in his corpus, and Griffith has argued that the text follows Abū Qurra's apologetic methodology of adopting positions that had currency in the Islamic milieu, and incorporating them into his own arguments (Griffith, p. 106).

SIGNIFICANCE

How significant one considers the text to be in the context of Christian-Muslim relations depends largely on the level to which one assumes intercultural exchange between Christians and Muslims had taken place by the late 8th or early 9th century. If one posits a high degree of exchange, the text can be viewed as reflecting the development of Islamic theology and Christian response to that theology. If one posits an independent development of Islamic theology (as, for example, do Watt and Griffith, among others), the significance of the *Dialogue* diminishes considerably. One should note that the text was written in Greek, and so was not originally intended to confront Muslims directly.

It does, however, contain some evidence which suggests that it was intended to be used by Christians to refute Muslim arguments. Phrases such as, 'When the Saracen says to you…' appear in several places. It thus provides evidence of the issues that were being addressed between Christians and Muslims in the late 8th and early 9th century.

It is a matter of dispute whether the text gives proof of the influence of Christian ideas on Islam, a Christian reaction and response to Islamic theology already being developed, or an independent expression of Christian ideas relevant to Christians living in an Islamic milieu. Seale and Wolfson argue that the text was very influential in the development of Islamic theology of free will. Other scholars highlight the independent development of Islamic theology, and the existence of the Islamic concept of free will prior to the text's appearance.

Griffith's adduction of Muslim theologians who had previously written concerning the concepts covered in the *Dialogue* cannot be ignored. Whether the *Dialogue* was influential in the further development of Islamic theology or not, it cannot have been the starting point for Islamic ideas regarding free will and predestination.

MANUSCRIPTS

Listed in B. Kotter, *Die Schriften des Johannes von Damaskos*, 5 vols, Berlin, 1969-85 (Patristische Texte und Studien 7, 12, 17, 22, 29, 60), iv, pp. 423-26

EDITIONS AND TRANSLATIONS

S. Karoui, *Johannes von Damaskus. Glaubensgespräch zwischen Christen und Muslimen*, Heidelberg, 2003 (edition with German and Arabic trans.)

R. Glei and A.-T. Khoury, *Johannes Damaskenos und Theodor Abu Qurra. Schriften zum Islam*, Würzburg, 1995 (Corpus Islamo-Christianum. Series Graeca 3), pp. 168-83 (Kotter's edition with German trans.)

R. Le Coz, *Jean Damascène. Écrits sur l'Islam*, Paris, 1992, pp. 228-51 (Kotter's edition with French trans.)

G. Atiya, '*Al-jadal al-dīnī l-masīḥī l-islāmī fī l-ʿaṣr al-umawī wa-atharuhu fī nushūʾ ʿilm al-kalām*', in M.A. al-Bakhit and R. Schick (eds), *Bilād al-Shām during the Umayyad period/ Bilād al-Shām fī l-ʿaṣr al-umawī*, 2 vols, Amman, 1989, i, 407-26, pp. 416-22 (Arabic trans.)

Kotter, *Die Schriften des Johannes von Damaskos*, iv, 419-38 (critical edition with complete survey of manuscripts)

D.J. Sahas, *John of Damascus on Islam. The 'Heresy of the Ishmaelites'*, Leiden, 1972, pp. 142-59 (Migne's edition with English trans.)

PG 96, cols 1336-48

STUDIES

Glei and Khoury, *Johannes Damaskenos und Theodor Abu Qurra. Schriften zum Islam*

Le Coz, *Jean Damascène. Écrits sur l'Islam*

S.H. Griffith, 'Free will in Christian kalam. The doctrine of Theodore Abū Qurrah', *PdO* 14 (1987) 79-107 (repr. in Griffith, *Arabic Christianity in the monasteries of ninth-century Palestine*, Aldershot, 1992)

H.A. Wolfson, *The philosophy of the kalam*, Cambridge MA, 1976, pp. 137, 231-46, 311-12, 607-8, 617

Sahas, *John of Damascus on Islam*

A.-T. Khoury, *Les théologiens byzantins et l'Islam. Textes et auteurs (VIII*[e]*-XIII*[e] *s.)*, Louvain, 1969, pp. 68-82

A. Argyriou, 'Une controverse entre un chrétien et un musulman inédite', *Revue des sciences religieuses* 41 (1967) 237-45

M. Seale, *Muslim theology. A study of origins with reference to the Church Fathers*, London, 1964, pp. 4-12, 16-35, 58-69, 79-81

A. Abel, 'La polémique damascénienne et son influence sur les origines de la théologie musulmane', in *L'élaboration de l'Islam. Colloque de Strasbourg*, Paris, 1961, 61-85

M. Jugie, art. 'Jean Damascène', in *Dictionnaire de theologie catholique*, Paris, 1915-50

C.H. Becker, 'Christliche Polemik und islamische Dogmenbildung', *Zeitschrift für Assyriologie* 26 (1911) 175-95 (repr. in Becker, *Vom Werden und Wesen der islamischen Welt*, Leipzig, 1924-32; English trans. in R. Hoyland (ed.), *Muslims and others in early Islamic society*, Aldershot, 2004)

Peter Schadler 2008

Ḍirār ibn ʿAmr

Abū ʿAmr Ḍirār ibn ʿAmr al-Ghaṭafānī l-Kūfī

DATE OF BIRTH	unknown, c. 730
PLACE OF BIRTH	possibly Kūfa
DATE OF DEATH	unknown, c. 800
PLACE OF DEATH	possibly Basra

BIOGRAPHY

Ḍirār does not figure prominently in biographical works, and little is known for certain about his life. He is associated with scholars who flourished in the late 8th century and is identified among the participants in a debate before Yaḥyā l-Barmakī in the reign of Hārūn al-Rashīd. His date of death can therefore be given roughly as 800, and since he is said to have lived to about 70, he was probably born in about 730. He is linked with Basra in his early life, though he visited Baghdad later. He functioned as *qāḍī* under some of the early ʿAbbasid rulers.

Ḍirār is associated with the Muʿtazila, and particularly with Wāṣil ibn ʿAṭāʾ, the so-called founder of the group, in the generation before him, and with the young Abū l-Hudhayl (q.v.) in the generation after him. But some Muʿtazilīs called him a freethinker and heretic, which in the light of some of his unorthodox ideas is not difficult to understand.

None of his 57 known works survives (Van Ess, *TG* v, pp. 229-31), though the titles indicate that he wrote about many of the major doctrines discussed in his day (among them *Kitāb al-tawḥīd*, 'Divine unity', *Kitāb al-irāda*, 'Divine will', *Kitāb al-qadar*, 'Divine omnipotence', *Kitāb fī l-radd ʿalā Arisṭālīs fī l-jawāhir wa-l-aʿrāḍ*, 'Refutation of Aristotle on substances and accidents'), and joined in disputes between various groups within Islam and outside (including, *Kitāb ʿalā l-Murjiʾa fī l-asmāʾ*, 'Against the Murjiʾa on the [divine] names', *Kitāb al-radd ʿalā l-Khawārij*, 'Refutation of the Kharijites', *Kitāb al-radd ʿalā l-mulḥidīn*, 'Refutation of the atheists', *Kitāb al-radd ʿalā l-zanādiqa*, 'Refutation of the freethinkers'). He wrote a number of works in support of prophethood (among them *Kitāb ithbāt al-rusul*, 'Confirmation of messengers', *Kitāb al-asbāb wa-l-ʿilm ʿalā l-nubuwwa*, 'Occasions and knowledge concerning prophethood', and

Kitāb al-radd ʿalā Maʿmar fī qawlihi inna Muḥammadan rabb, 'Refutation of Maʿmar concerning his teaching that Muḥammad was Lord'), and two on the Qur'an (*Tafsīr al-Qurʾān*, 'Commentary on the Qurʾān', *Taʾwīl al-Qurʾān*, 'Interpretation of the Qurʾān'). Van Ess (*TG* iii, p. 38) suggests that his denial of the reality of God's attributes, which he would probably have expounded in a work such as *Kitāb anna l-asmāʾ lā tuqāsu*, 'That the divine names cannot be explained by analogy', could have been the target of the East-Syrian ʿAmmār al-Baṣrī (q.v.) a few decades later (the latter was attacked by Abū l-Hudhayl (q.v.), who also denied the reality of God's attributes).

Ḍirār's theology can only be partially reconstructed on the basis of inferences from the titles of his works and later quotations and references. He subscribed to a number of Muʿtazilī principles and teachings, particularly the absolute transcendence of God and his immediate control of all things, and the atomist analysis of the created order. But he emphatically diverged from Muʿtazilī principles in holding that the human was not free in performing actions but rather acquired moral responsibility for them. In this doctrine of *kasb* (acquisition) he anticipated Abū l-Ḥasan al-Ashʿarī, with whom it is often associated.

While Ḍirār attracted a number of pupils, his individualist teachings also drew attacks from his younger contemporaries Abū l-Hudhayl and Bishr ibn al-Muʿtamir (q.v.).

MAIN SOURCES OF INFORMATION

Primary

Abū l-Ḥasan al-Ashʿarī, *Maqālāt al-Islāmiyyīn*, ed. H. Ritter, Istanbul, 1930, pp. 166, 174, 281-82, 305, 317, 345, 359, 407, 515, 594

Ibn al-Nadīm, *Fihrist*, pp. 214-15

Abū Manṣūr al-Baghdādī, *Kitāb al-milal wa-l-niḥal*, ed. A. Nader, Beirut, 1970, pp. 147-48

Maḥmūd bin Muḥammad al-Malāḥimī, *Al-muʿtamad fī uṣūl al-dīn*, ed. M. McDermott and W. Madelung, London, 1991, pp. 278, 474, 493, 499

Secondary

Van Ess, *TG* iii, pp. 32-63; v, pp. 229-51

D. Gimaret, *Théories de l'acte humain en théologie musulmane*, Paris, 1980, pp. 64-73

Watt, *Formative period*, pp. 189-95

Sezgin, GAS i, p. 614

Van Ess, art. 'Ḍirār b. ʿAmr, Abū ʿAmr al-Ghaṭafānī al-Kūfī', *EI2*

WORKS ON CHRISTIAN-MUSLIM RELATIONS

Kitāb yaḥtawī ʿalā ʿashara kutub fī l-radd ʿalā ahl al-milal, 'A book comprising ten books on the refutation of the people of the religions'

DATE mid to late 8th c.
ORIGINAL LANGUAGE Arabic

DESCRIPTION
The work is lost, and is known only from Ibn al-Nadīm, *Fihrist*, p. 215, where his reference is probably a description of the work rather than the exact title. It would have been one of the earliest works against other religions known to Muslims at the time, presumably including Christianity.

SIGNIFICANCE
It may have been substantial (though the significance of the term 'book' here must remain unclear), and could have supplied information and arguments for later works.

MANUSCRIPTS —
EDITIONS AND TRANSLATIONS —
STUDIES —

Kitāb al-radd ʿalā l-Naṣārā, 'Refutation of the Christians'

DATE mid to late 8th c.
ORIGINAL LANGUAGE Arabic

DESCRIPTION
The work is lost, and is known only from Ibn al-Nadīm, *Fihrist*, p. 215. It would have been an attack on one or more of the Christian beliefs as Muslims understood them. Given Ḍirār's concerns about the being of God, it possibly included a demonstration that the Trinity, with its implication of multiplicity in the Godhead, cannot be defended in reason.

SIGNIFICANCE
It may have been one of the earliest Muslim theological works written against Christianity.

MANUSCRIPTS —

EDITIONS AND TRANSLATIONS —

STUDIES —

David Thomas 2007

Pseudo-Leo III's first letter to ʿUmar II

Unknown author

DATE OF BIRTH Unknown, 8th c.?
PLACE OF BIRTH Unknown
DATE OF DEATH Unknown, 8th c.?
PLACE OF DEATH Unknown

BIOGRAPHY —

MAIN SOURCES OF INFORMATION

Primary —

Secondary —

WORKS ON CHRISTIAN-MUSLIM RELATIONS

Title unknown, 'Pseudo-Leo III's first letter to ʿUmar II'

DATE Unknown, probably 8th c.
ORIGINAL LANGUAGE Arabic or Greek

DESCRIPTION

Parts of the polemical exchanges that circulated in the form of letters written in the name of the Byzantine emperor Leo III and the Umayyad Caliph ʿUmar II have survived in three different texts. These texts form a Muslim refutation of Christianity that survives in Arabic and Aljamiado, and a Christian reply with an elaborate attack on Islam and a defense of Christianity that survives in Armenian, the former attributed to ʿUmar ibn ʿAbd al-ʿAzīz (r. 717-20) (see entry on Pseudo-ʿUmar II's letter to Leo III) and the latter to the Byzantine Emperor Leo III (r. 717-41) (see the entry on 'Leo's Letter in Ghewond').

In this exchange, it is clear that 'pseudo-Leo' responds to the issues raised by 'pseudo-ʿUmar', but the correspondence reveals that the Muslim was not necessarily the one to initiate it. While in many cases statements about the other party are to be interpreted as general statements about the whole Christian community, in three cases the Muslim author responds directly to issues raised by his Christian correspondent: 'You write to me that in the Psalms of David and the Books of the Prophets you read words concerning 'Īsā which you find true and believe, and you leave aside the witness given by 'Īsā in the Gospel: that he has a Lord, that he adored Him and prayed to Him'; 'you criticize us in your writing for facing the direction of the oratory of Ibrāhīm when we pray'; 'you criticize us in your writing for saying that the inhabitants of Paradise eat, drink, wear clothes and get married'.

In the opening of his letter the Muslim even speaks of several earlier letters: 'You have written to me many letters in which you have treated questions concerning Jesus and your religion'. The possibility that the letter which survives in the Arabic 'Letter of Leo' (SA NF pap. 14) (q.v.) is this earlier letter of Leo must be considered; its discussion of the Fall and the necessity of the Incarnation could be the background of 'Umar's critique of the Christian belief in Satan's might. On the other hand, none of the accessible pages of the Sinai manuscript in which this Arabic 'Letter of Leo' is found contain direct attacks on Islamic doctrine, such as are alluded to here. Although we know nothing else about the exact contents of this lost letter, the mere fact that 'Umar's 'reconstituted letter' was not the first may help to understand better the tenor and choice of topics of his letter.

SIGNIFICANCE

This lost letter is an indication that more letters between 'Leo' and ''Umar' were produced than those that are extant today. The correspondence forms a rare case of a polemical exchange exceeding two letters, and underscores the fact that apologetic and polemical arguments were not only developed within the respective communities but also through direct acquaintance with the critical views of members of the other religion.

MANUSCRIPTS —

EDITIONS AND TRANSLATIONS —

STUDIES

See the entries: 'The Letter of Leo III in Ghewond', 'The Arabic letter of Leo III to 'Umar II' and 'Pseudo-'Umar II's Letter to Leo III'.

Barbara Roggema 2008

The Arabic letter of Leo III to ʿUmar II

Unknown author

DATE OF BIRTH Unknown, perhaps early 8th c.
PLACE OF BIRTH Unknown
DATE OF DEATH Unknown, perhaps late 8th c.
PLACE OF DEATH Unknown, perhaps Palestine or Sinai

BIOGRAPHY

Nothing is known of the actual author of an Arabic text purporting to be a letter of the Byzantine Emperor Leo III (r. 717-41) to the Umayyad Caliph ʿUmar ibn ʿAbd al-ʿAzīz (r. 717-20), other than what can be gathered from the contents of the text itself and the manuscript in which it is fragmentarily preserved (Sinai ar. NF pap. 14). These lead us to think of a Melkite monk or cleric of the mid-8th century, possibly of Palestine or Sinai, who had some Christian biblical and theological formation as well as some familiarity with Islamic vocabulary and teachings.

MAIN SOURCES OF INFORMATION

Primary —

Secondary —

WORKS ON CHRISTIAN-MUSLIM RELATIONS

The untitled text is in the form of a letter, and begins, after a Trinitarian invocation, ʻ*Min Aliyūn malik al-Rūm ilā ʿUmar ibn ʿAbd al-ʿAzīz, amīr al-muʾminīn: Salām*ʼ, ʻFrom Leo, Emperor of the Byzantines, to ʿUmar ibn ʿAbd al-ʿAzīz, Commander of the Faithful: Peaceʼ). Modern title: ʻThe Arabic letter of Leo IIIʼ

DATE Mid to late 8th c.?
ORIGINAL LANGUAGE Arabic

DESCRIPTION

One of the surprises in the publication in 1985 of a checklist of 155 Arabic manuscripts discovered a decade earlier at the Monastery of St Catherine at Mount Sinai (Meïmarēs, *Katalogos*) was the existence of an Arabic 'Letter of Leo' as the second of two works in Sinai ar. NF pap. 14. A photograph of the first two pages of the text (Meïmarēs, *Katalogos*, p. 116, photograph 88) reveals a neat antique *kūfī-naskhī* hand characteristic of the late 9th century. In addition, the present writer is indebted to Prof S. Gerö for sharing copies of some photographs of the manuscript; although incomplete and not always clear, these add about five legible pages in the same *kūfī-naskhī* hand to the two in the photograph published by Meïmarēs.

These seven old pages, while preserving only a fraction of the text, allow us to see the Arabic 'Letter of Leo III' as an apology for Christological doctrine that reflects a very early stage of the Christian-Muslim controversy in Arabic. The author briefly tells the story of Adam's fall and his obedience to Satan, which is overcome by Christ's incarnation. The possibility of God's presence simultaneously in heaven and in a human being is illustrated by analogy with the sun, which is in the heavens but whose power and light is upon the earth and reaches even into small rooms. Christ's divinity is defended with appeals to his authority as revealed in sayings from the Gospels (e.g. Matthew 5:11-16 or 28:18), or in his raising the dead (which is compared to the vision of God's activity in the 'valley of dry bones', Ezekiel 37:1-14, expounded with what is possibly a verbal allusion to Q 75:3).

The anonymous author is not unaware of Islamic vocabulary and doctrine. He writes, he says, in order to answer his correspondent's questions about *al-Masīḥ, ʿĪsā ibn Maryam*, using the qurʾānic name for Jesus; concerning Adam, he says that God 'made him vicegerent over his creation' (*istakhlafahu ʿalā khalqihi*), with an allusion to the qurʾānic witness to Adam as God's *khalīfa* or vicegerent on earth (Q 2:30); speaking of the Incarnation, he refers to 'your Book' and gives a somewhat modified rendering of the qurʾānic description of Jesus as God's 'Word that he sent to Mary and a Spirit from Him' (Q 4:171); and in comparing Christ's authority with that of others sent by God, he mentions not just 'prophets' but displays his knowledge of qurʾānic prophetology with the phrase 'prophets and apostles who were calling the people to God' (*al-anbiyāʾ wa-l-rusul alladhīna kānū yadʿūna l-nās ilā llāh*).

Despite its rather unengaged, impersonal tone, the Arabic 'Letter of Leo' is not without points of interest. It offers a simple scripture-based apology for the doctrine of the Incarnation somewhat reminiscent of the much more fully developed arguments of the ancient apologetic treatise preserved in Sinai ar. 154 (*Fī tathlīth Allāh al-wāḥid*, q.v.). In both texts, humanity's Fall is narrated as a fall under obedience to Satan – interestingly, the author of the most extensive version of the 'Letter of ʿUmar II to Leo III' (q.v.) that is known polemicizes against precisely this point, claiming that Christian soteriological narratives assign too much authority to the devil. Another point of interest, and one that helps locate the Arabic 'Letter of Leo' at a very early stage of exchanges between Christians and Muslims, is that its author appears to believe that quotations of Jesus' sayings from the Gospel of Matthew would have probative force in a work of apologetics; at least in the pages reviewed here, the author shows no awareness of Islamic claims about the falsification of Christian scripture (as in, e.g., the same 'Letter of ʿUmar' just mentioned; Gaudeul, 'Correspondence', pp. 134-36).

SIGNIFICANCE

The significance of the Arabic 'Letter of Leo III' is difficult to assess, given our very limited acquaintance with it. It does not appear to correspond in any direct way to other known texts of the 'ʿUmar-Leo' correspondence (q.v.), although the possibility that it is an early member in a sequence of texts (Leo-ʿUmar-Leo) cannot be discounted. It is also possible that the composition of 'letters of Leo' was something of a standard exercise in early Christian apologetics with respect to Islam. This would help to explain both the multiplicity of such letters and the impersonal tone that we find not only in this Arabic letter, but also in the Latin translation of a Melkite letter of Leo to ʿUmar (described by Gaudeul as 'the draft of an essay in apologetics, an academic exercise'; 'Correspondence', p. 116).

MANUSCRIPTS

MS Sinai – ar. Nouveau Fonds pap. 14 (This is a collection of 90 folios, mostly on paper although 10 are parchment; it comprises two texts in different hands of which the Arabic 'Letter of Leo' is the second.)

EDITIONS AND TRANSLATIONS

All that has been published of the text is a photograph of its first two pages, in I.E. Meïmarēs, *Katalogos tōn neōn arabikōn cheirographōn tēs hieras monēs hagias Aikaterinēs tou orous Sina / / Katālūj al-makhṭūṭāt al-ʿarabiyya l-muktashafa ḥadīthan bi-Dayr Sānt Kātrīn al-Muqaddas bi-Ṭūr Sīnāʾ*, Athens, 1985, p. 116, photograph 88. (Photograph 87 on the same page is of the first text in the manuscript.)

STUDIES

S.H. Griffith, *The church in the shadow of the mosque. Christians and Muslims in the world of Islam*, Princeton NJ, 2008, p. 175 (brief mention of the existence of this text)

R.G. Hoyland, 'The Correspondence of Leo III (717-41) and ʿUmar II (717-20)', *Aram* 6 (1994) 165-77 (repr. in Hoyland, *Seeing Islam*, pp. 490-501, see n. 135), pp. 167-68, n. 11 (brief mention of this text [although the names ʿUmar and Leo are reversed] with a comparison with the Latin 'Letter of Leo')

S.K. Samir, review of Meïmarēs, *Katalogos*, in *OCP* 52 (1986) 441-44 (accessible background information about and evaluation of the Arabic MSS of the *nouveau fonds* at Mt Sinai)

Meïmarēs, *Katalogos*, p. 41 (Greek), p. 43 (Arabic) (brief description of the manuscript)

Mark N. Swanson 2008

Pseudo-ʿUmar II's letter to Leo III

Unknown author

DATE OF BIRTH Unknown, 8th c.?
PLACE OF BIRTH Unknown
DATE OF DEATH Unknown, 8th/9th c.?
PLACE OF DEATH Unknown, probably Syria

BIOGRAPHY —

MAIN SOURCES OF INFORMATION

Primary —

Secondary —

WORKS ON CHRISTIAN-MUSLIM RELATIONS

Title uncertain; according to the Aljamiado manuscripts: *The letter of ʿUmar ibn ʿAbd al-ʿAzīz to Leo, King of the Christian infidels*. Modern title: 'The Letter of ʿUmar II to Leo III'

DATE Unknown, probably mid/late 8th c.
ORIGINAL LANGUAGE Arabic

DESCRIPTION
Several Eastern Christian and Muslim sources from the 9th and 10th centuries make mention of the fact that the Umayyad Caliph ʿUmar ibn ʿAbd al-ʿAzīz (r. 717-20) corresponded with the Byzantine emperor Leo III (r. 717-41) about religion (Kaplony, *Konstantinopel und Damascus*, pp. 207-37). The Armenian *History* of Ghewond (q.v.) contains a fairly long refutation of Islam which the author claims is Leo's reply to a letter by ʿUmar II (q.v.). It is preceded by a short letter containing a list of critical questions about the Christian religion. This is presented as ʿUmar's original letter but is likely to be nothing more than a summary of the issues that Leo addressed in his letter.

There are two texts, however, which may constitute the actual letter, or at least a later redaction of it, to which (pseudo-)Leo responded. The first of these is to be found among a collection of Morisco polemical texts in an early 16th-century Aljamiado manuscript, where it is entitled *Karta de ʿUmar ibn ʿAbd al-ʿAzīz rey de los Keyentes a Lyon rey de los Kristiyanos deskereyentes.* This text, covering 17 folios, contains a heading and a conclusion, and appears to be a well-rounded unity. The second text is a 9th or early 10th century Arabic manuscript of 10 folios, containing a polemical letter from a Muslim to a Christian, in which the names of both writer and addressee are missing (the first part of the text is lost).

J.-M. Gaudeul has made two intriguing discoveries regarding these two texts: they are partly overlapping; the last three folios of the Spanish manuscript agreeing with the first two and a half folios of the Arabic manuscript, and if they are placed alongside Leo's letter in Ghevond's *History* the questions and answers fit 'hand in glove'. They also share three rather peculiar statements and arguments, which is additional proof that they are closely related.

The content of ʿUmar's reconstituted letter is rich and varied in its argumentation against Christianity. It refutes Christ's divinity by asking such critical questions as who ruled the world when Christ was in the womb, and also by means of biblical verses that indicate that Christ had a human nature, such as verses which describe him as hungry, needy and appealing for help to his Lord. The author claims that both the Old and the New Testament have been falsified, and that Christ's original form of worship, including his observance of the Mosaic law, has been corrupted. He also uses the Bible as proof that Christ preached monotheism and predicted the coming of Muḥammad. This technique of holding the Bible against Christianity is used to the full. It is also employed, for example, to prove that there is food and drink in paradise and that God does not disapprove of polygamy.

One section contains a critique of several Christian cultic practices such as the veneration of relics, the cross and images, which are also said to go against scripture. At the same time, Christians are accused of disobeying scriptural commandments such as prostration, loving one's enemy and turning the other cheek.

The letter ends with a brief defense of Muḥammad's prophethood. The possibility that Muḥammad was instructed by secret Christian teachers is dismissed on the grounds that if this were so his religion would have been much closer to Christianity than it is. The Qurʾān is also adduced to show that it refutes this allegation (Q 16:105, 29:48). Muḥammad must have been a true prophet, because he was miraculously successful in bringing a backward idolatrous people to the worship of the one God and an ethical way of life. The fact that Muḥammad's followers were able to conquer territory from two mighty empires, despite being barefoot and unarmed, is presented as an obvious sign of divine support.

Many of the arguments presented in the letter can be found in other polemical texts from the mid-8th century onwards. One particular passage about Christian belief in Satan, on the other hand, contains several original arguments against Christian soteriology. The following points are made: if Christ came to liberate humankind from Satan's realm, it must either be assumed that before his coming God deliberately put them there, including numerous righteous people, in which case God would be unjust, or else Satan had power over God, in which case God is not omnipotent; while Christ led many people to the straight path by vanquishing Satan, he allowed many to keep erring and did not guide everyone to the straight path – again God must be either unjust or powerless; why did Christ not prevent Satan acting against him – when the author exclaims that God is too noble to let Christ endure this, it is evident that he alludes to the qurʾānic denial of the crucifixion. This passage is interesting because the theme of soteriology is often raised by Melkite apologists but rarely responded to by Muslims in their refutations of Christianity. It is also noteworthy because it matches the theme contained in one of the few accessible passages of a 9th century parchment at Sinai that preserves an Arabic letter of Leo to ʿUmar (Sinai Ar. NF pap. 14) (q.v.). This could be an indication of these two texts somehow being related.

A crucial question is whether this reconstructed letter really comes from the pen of the Caliph ʿUmar II, who ruled in the early eighth century. This must be unlikely, since there is no confirmation from other texts that polemical arguments were this well-developed at the time. A *terminus ante quem* is the late 9th/early 10th century, when the Arabic manuscript was produced. Gaudeul regards the date of this manuscript as a likely date of the composition of the letter, but for a variety of reasons this is hard to accept. The *isnād* in the Aljamiado manuscript traces the text back to the late 8th century through three Ḥimsī transmitters of which the oldest died in 798. As Hoyland has rightly pointed out, it is therefore unlikely to be a forged *isnād*, because someone forging it would undoubtedly construct an *isnād* going back to the caliph himself. The death of the oldest transmitter coincides with the comment in Leo's reply that 800 years have passed since the appearance of Christ.

The claim that the text was influenced by several 9th century Muslim polemicists is not convincing (Gaudeul, 'Correspondence', p. 128; Thomas, 'Miracles', p. 225). Not only does one have to take into account the possibility that the influence was the other way around, but the specific examples of supposedly 9th century apologetic arguments are already found in texts from the second half of the 8th century, such as Timothy's *Letter 34* (q.v.) and the Letter of Hārūn al-Rashīd to Constantine VI (see the entry on Ibn al-Layth).

There are some more specific reasons to date the text to the 8th century. First of all, from the 9th century onwards the citation of Q 16:105 and 29:48 in support of Muḥammad's prophethood would be highly surprising, because the opponents of Islam used it to prove precisely the contrary. There is also a lack of the theological terminology commonly that is used in 9th century *kalām* texts. Lastly, the response of Leo is almost certainly from the 8th century.

As Gaudeul has pointed out, there are frequent references in both Leo's and ʿUmar's letters to earlier exchanges, so they may actually be the result of several rounds of debate. Echoes of at least one earlier letter of Leo (q.v.) are detectable in ʿUmar's letter.

SIGNIFICANCE

ʿUmar II's letter to Leo III, as reconstructed by Gaudeul, forms an interesting catalogue of Islamic arguments against Christianity, and is a precursor to the 'proof of prophethood' literature and the more sophisticated interreligious *kalām* of the 9th century. The letter, together with its Christian reply, is evidence of the fact that certain Muslim and Christian apologetic arguments were conceived in direct response to criticisms from the other party.

MANUSCRIPTS

MS Istanbul, Museum of Turkish and Islamic Art – s.n. (9th or 10th c. parchment from Syria containing the acephalous Arabic letter)

MS Madrid, Biblioteca Nacional – 4944, fols 84v-101v (Aljamiado letter, early 16th c.)

MS Madrid, Biblioteca Nacional – 5302 (according to Cardaillac, *La polémique*, p. 7, the same text as 4944)

EDITIONS AND TRANSLATIONS

J.-M. Gaudeul, *La correspondance de 'Umar et Leon (vers 900)*, Rome, 1985, pp. 3-30 (based on Sourdel and Cardaillac)

J.-M. Gaudeul, 'The Correspondence between Leo and 'Umar. 'Umar's Letter re-discovered?', *Islamochristiana* 10 (1984) 109-57 (based on Sourdel and Cardaillac)

D. Cardaillac, *La polémique anti-chrétienne du manuscrit aljamiado N° 4944 de la Bibliothèque Nationale de Madrid*, 2 vols, Montpellier, 1972 (Diss. Univ. Paul Valéry), ii, pp. 194-267 (edition and trans.)

D. Sourdel, 'Un pamphlet musulman anonyme d'époque 'abbāside contre les chrétiens', *REI* 34 (1966) 1-33

STUDIES

K. Kościelniak, 'Polemika muzułmańsko-chrześcijańska na podstawie korespondencji przypisywanej kalifowi umajjadzkiemu 'Umararowi II (†720) i cesarzowi bizantyjskiemu Leonowi III (†741)', *Folia historica Cracoviensia* 8 (2002) 97-105

I. Rochow, 'Zu den diplomatischen Beziehungen zwischen Byzanz und dem Kalifat in der Zeit der syrischen Dynastie (717-802)', in C. Sode and S. Tacács (eds), *Novum Millennium. Studies on Byzantine History and Culture dedicated to Paul Speck*, Aldershot, 2001, 305-25, pp. 309-10

A. Kaplony, *Konstantinopel und Damascus. Gesandschaften und Verträge zwischen Kaisern und Kalifen 639-750. Untersuchungen zum Gewohnheits-Völkerrecht und zur interkulturellen Diplomatie*, Berlin, 1996

M.N. Swanson, *Folly to the ḥunafā'. The cross of Christ in Arabic Christian-Muslim controversy in the eighth and ninth centuries A.D.*, Cairo, 1995 (estratto from diss. PISAI, 1992) pp. 38-40 (includes a new edition and trans. of the critique of Christian soteriological discourse)

R.G. Hoyland, 'The Correspondence of Leo III (717-41) and 'Umar II (717-20)', *Aram* 6 (1994) 165-77 (repr. in Hoyland, *Seeing Islam*, pp. 490-501)

D. Thomas, 'The miracles of Jesus in early Islamic polemic', *JSS* 39 (1994) 221-43

Gaudeul, *La correspondance de 'Umar et Leon*

Gaudeul, 'The Correspondance between Leo and 'Umar'

Barbara Roggema 2008

A Christian Arabic Disputation (PSR 438)

Unknown author

DATE OF BIRTH Unknown, perhaps 8th c.
PLACE OF BIRTH Unknown
DATE OF DEATH Unknown, 8th/9th c.
PLACE OF DEATH Unknown

BIOGRAPHY

We know nothing about the author of an Arabic Christian apologetic text fragmentarily preserved on papyrus, other than the little that can be deduced from the text. Similarities in the text to Melkite apologies such as *Fī tathlīth Allāh al-wāḥid* (q.v.) lead one to think of a Melkite priest or monk who lived towards the end of the 8th century.

MAIN SOURCES OF INFORMATION

Primary —

Secondary —

WORKS ON CHRISTIAN-MUSLIM RELATIONS

Title unknown. Modern title: 'A Christian Arabic disputation (PSR 438)'

DATE Mid or late 8th c.
ORIGINAL LANGUAGE Arabic

DESCRIPTION

The unique manuscript is dated on paleographical grounds by Graf (*GCAL* ii, 26) to the mid or late 8th century (leaving open the possibility that the text was written earlier). Hoyland (*Seeing Islam*, p. 504) is inclined, with some evidence, to a late 8th century date of composition. It consists of dozens of papyrus fragments, painstakingly reassembled; much of the text has been lost (including its beginning and end). Enough remains, however, to reveal an apologetic text that in a number of respects may be compared with the better known *Fī tathlīth Allāh al-wāḥid*: it is a defense of the Trinity (i.e. Allāh and his Word and his Spirit) and of Christ's divinity, drawing both on the Qurʾān and on Old Testament *testimonia*. The best preserved section of the text includes a sequence of five qurʾānic texts (Q 39:4, 90:1-2, 4:171, 2:116 and 43:81) boldly quoted in support of the apologist's case that God has a Son.

SIGNIFICANCE

Christian Arabic Disputation (PSR 438) provides an early witness to Arabic Christian apologetic use of the Qurʾan and biblical *testimonia* in support of Trinitarian and Christological doctrine, and in warding off accusations of *shirk*. Particular points of interest in the text include: its exploitative misreading of the qurʾānic texts listed above, interpreting them to mean something at complete odds with their intention (see Swanson, 'Beyond prooftexting', pp. 302-5); the fact that it gives the names of the qurʾānic *sūra*s that it quotes; its witness to a debate over Q 5:116 (God's question to Jesus, 'Did you say to people, "Take me and my mother as two gods besides God"?'), to which the apologist responds, 'When did this questioning take place? Before (the career of) your apostle, or after?' (see Hoyland, *Seeing Islam*, p. 504, n. 177).

MANUSCRIPTS

P.Heid.Inv.Arab. 438 a-d Recto u. Verso (contemporary papyrologists' designation of the fragments kept at Ruprecht-Karls-Universität Heidelberg, Zentrum für Altertumswissenschaften, Institut für Papyrologie; formerly Heidelberg, Papyrus Schott-Reinhart no. 438)

EDITIONS AND TRANSLATIONS

G. Graf, 'Christlich-arabische Texte. Zwei Disputationen zwischen Muslîmen und Christen', in F. Bilabel and A. Grohmann, *Griechische, koptische und arabische Texte zur Religion und religiösen Literatur in Ägyptens Spätzeit*, Heidelberg, 1934, 1-31, pp. 1-24 (edition of the fragments with German trans.)

STUDIES

M.N. Swanson, 'Beyond prooftexting. Approaches to the Qurʾān in some early Arabic Christian apologies', *MW* 88 (1998) 297-319, pp. 302-5

Hoyland, *Seeing Islam*, p. 504

Graf, *GCAL* ii, p. 26

Graf, 'Christliche-arabische Texte'

Mark N. Swanson 2008

Stephen Manṣūr

Stephen of Damascus, Stephen the Hymnographer, Stephen son of Manṣūr

DATE OF BIRTH Mid-8th c.
PLACE OF BIRTH Unknown, possibly Damascus
DATE OF DEATH c. 807
PLACE OF DEATH Unknown, probably the monastery of Mār Saba

BIOGRAPHY

Little is known of the life of Stephen except that he lived in the second half of the 8th and just into the 9th centuries. We are told in Leontius of Damascus' Arabic *Life of Stephen of Mār Saba* (q.v.) (a different Stephen, not to be confused with Stephen Manṣūr) that he was the author of the *Twenty martyrs of Mār Saba* and that he was a relative of John of Damascus (J. Lamoreaux, *The life of Stephen of Mar Sabas*, 2 vols, Louvain, 1999 (*CSCO* 578-79), ii, pp. 125-26.) The Georgian version of the *Martyrdom* of Romanus (d. 780) indicates that Stephen was also its author (Peeters, 'S. Romain le Néomartyr d'après un document géorgien', p. 407). This same Stephen also wrote a poem in honor of the twenty martyrs, among other poetical works (Blake, pp. 40-42; Nasrallah, pp. 156-57).

The most important source of information about Stephen is the collection of his writings. From these it can be surmised that he was an educated and eloquent Greek speaker who held non-Greeks in derision. The end of the *Twenty martyrs* (ed. Papadopoulos-Kerameus, p. 36) tells of a certain Syriac-speaking Christian who struggled to pronounce Greek properly. Then one night in a vision, a saint came and cleansed his mouth of a sticky yellowish green substance. When he awoke in the morning, the Syrian Christian spoke perfect Greek. This and similar elements in the text reveal Stephen to be a hellenophile to the point of being condescending to non-Greeks (Vila, *Christian martyrs*, p. 327; Vila, 'The struggle over Arabisation', p. 36). Stephen also frequently quotes from the scriptures and from early Christian writers, betraying a significant education in Christian history and thought.

MAIN SOURCES OF INFORMATION

Primary

See *PMBZ* no. 6912

Secondary

D. Vila, 'The struggle over Arabisation in medieval Arabic Christian hagiography', *Al-Masaq* 15 (2003) 35-46

PMBZ no. 6912

J. Timbie, review of J. Lamoreaux, *The Life of Stephen of Mar Sabas*, in *Journal of Early Christian Studies* 8 (2000) 605-6

A. Kazhdan, *A history of Byzantine literature (650-850)*, Athens, 1999, pp. 172-175, 180

D. Vila, *Christian martyrs in the first Abbasid century and the development of an apologetic against Islam* (Diss. St Louis University, 1999), pp. 308-30

M.-F. Auzépy, 'De la Palestine à Constantinople (VIIIe-IXe siècles): Étienne le Sabaïte et Jean Damascène' *Travaux et Mémoires* 12 (1994) 183-218

A. Kazhdan, art. 'Stephen Sabaites', in *ODB*

Nasrallah, *HMLEM* ii.2, pp. 156-57

F. Caraffa, art. 'Stefano il Sabaita, poeta, santo', in *Bibliotheca Sanctorum*

J.-M. Sauget, art. 'Sabaiti', in *Bibliotheca Sanctorum*

G. Garitte, 'Le début de la vie de S. Etienne le Sabäite retrouvée en arabe au Sinaï', *AB* 77 (1959) 332-39

V. Grumel, 'L'ère mondiale dans la date du martyre des vingt moines Sabaïtes', *REB* 14 (1956) 207-8

F. Halkin, 'Saint Théoctiste Moine Sabaïte et Martyr (797)', *AB* 73 (1955) 373-74

G. Garitte, 'Un extrait géorgien de la Vie d'Étienne le Sabaïte', *Le Muséon* 67 (1954) 71-92

R. Blake, 'Deux lacunes combleés dans la Passio XX Monachorum Sabaitarum', *AB* 68 (1950) 27-43

P. Peeters, 'S. Romain le néomartyr († 1 mai 780) d'après un document géorgien', *AB* 30 (1911) 393-427, pp. 405-8

S. Eustratides, 'Stephanos ho poiētēs ho Sabaitēs', *Nea Sion* 28 (1933) 651-73, 722-37; 29 (1934) 3-19, 113-30, 185-87

S. Vailhé, 'Date de la mort de saint Jean Damascène', *Échos d'Orient* 9 (1906) 28-30

David H. Vila 2008

Camebay romanoz axlisa, T'uesa maissa a: camebay cmidisa romanoz axlisa mocamisay, romeli icama mep'obasa ešmakt' msaxowrisa mep'isa mahdissa, romeli aġcera netarman step'ane damaskelman, romeli iqo ert'i mamat'agani lavrisa cmidisa mamisa č'uenisa sabaisa (Georgian), 'The Martyrdom of Romanus the Younger', 'On May 1: The Martyrdom of Saint Romanus the Neomartyr, who was martyred during the reign of the devil's servant King Mahdī, which was described by the blessed Stephen of Damascus, who was one of the monks of the Laura of our holy Father Sabas'

DATE Unknown, probably between 780 and 787
ORIGINAL LANGUAGE Most probably Arabic

DESCRIPTION
The *Martyrdom* of Romanus the Neomartyr was probably written between the saint's execution in 780 and 787. The author praises the double monastery of St Antheousa, which housed monks and nuns, but this is something he would be unlikely to do after the Council of Nicea in 787 condemned double monasteries.

The text survives only in Georgian, which appears to be a translation of a lost Arabic original. The fact that Stephen of Damascus wrote his other works in Greek does not mean he could not have written the *Martyrdom* in Arabic. He came from an ancient Syro-Arab family, and could probably not only speak Arabic but also write it. Griffith considers it possible that he could have written the *Martyrdom* in Arabic, though for Hoyland the pride he took in Greek language and identity point to a Greek original. No Greek version is known, though this can be explained by the fact that the work was composed during the period of Iconoclasm, which it openly criticizes, when Palestinian Christians often used Arabic for works which condemned official policy. Among other examples of such works, Peeters notes the *Life* of John of Damascus, an opponent of Iconoclasm, which was first written in Arabic then translated into Georgian and finally from Georgian into Greek. Furthermore, there is no trace of the saint's cult in the Greek milieu, and he is only commemorated in Georgian calendars.

Georgians often translated hagiographical works from Arabic into Georgian in Palestine during the 8th to 10th centuries. The *Martyrdom* of Romanus the Neomartyr might thus have been translated soon after its original composition. The Georgian version is preserved in two 10th and 11th century manuscripts. It was copied in the monastery of John the Baptist in Parxali from a copy belonging to the monastery of Išxani (both in the historically Georgian region of Tao-Klarjetʿi in present-day Turkey).

The work is not long: its Georgian version covers 22 pages in Khakhanov's edition, and 19 pages in Peeters' Latin translation. It describes how, in about 771, Romanus, of the monastery of Mantineon, was captured by Arabs and taken to the ʿAbbasid Caliph Abū Jaʿfar al-Manṣūr. He was imprisoned with many other Christians, among them Greeks, Georgians and others. Among these was the Archon George, who set the other Greek prisoners against Romanus and his two friends because of their support for icons (here the author appears to portray iconoclast Greeks in a worse light than the Muslims). The iconoclasts tried to kill the three, but the Muslims, together with Assyrians and Franks, saved them. Stephen remarks, 'Then the Saracens, strangers by belief, appeared better than those who considered themselves Christians, and honored the *schema* [monastic habit] of monks and nuns' (Khakhanov, 'Materialy', p. 37, Peeters, 'S. Romain', p. 419). Following this, the Muslim governors allowed an old Christian from Baghdad to take Romanus and his two friends to his own house.

In about 778, in the third year of the reign of the Caliph al-Mahdī, five other Greek monks joined Romanus' group. Later, Jacob, a Greek living in Baghdad who had converted to Islam and wanted to gain favor among the governors, accused Romanus of being a spy who was working for the Byzantines. The caliph questioned Romanus and Jacob, and saw that Romanus was innocent of this. But while he then freed Romanus' friends, he kept Romanus prisoner.

Later, in the spring of 780 during one of his expeditions against the Byzantines, al-Mahdī questioned Romanus again. He made threats to him, and promised him great honor if he converted to Islam, but to no avail. At this time there were some Greek prisoners in the Arab army, who had apostatized out of fear. When they saw how stalwartly Romanus maintained his belief, they repented and asked for his help, whereupon Romanus instructed them. The caliph was furious and accused him of proselytism, and he had him decapitated on 1 May, 780 (Khakhanov, 'Materialy', pp. 36-46; Peeters, 'S. Romain', pp. 420-27).

SIGNIFICANCE

The *Martyrdom* of Romanus the Neomartyr gives a realistic description of the condition of Christian prisoners in Baghdad in the 8th century. It is significant proof of the spread of Arabic among Palestinian Christians, including leading monasteries such as St Sabas. Already in the 8th century Palestinian Christians were composing ideologically important and artistically fine works in Arabic, some of which were translated into Georgian.

The *Martyrdom* of Romanus the Neomartyr was popular in Georgia, because of its anti-Islamic and anti-Iconoclastic sentiments.

MANUSCRIPTS

MS Mount Athos, Iviron Monastery – Georg. 8, fols 273v-293r (10th c.)

MS Tbilisi, Kekelidze Institute of Manuscripts – Georg. A 95, fols 440v-454r (11th c.)

EDITIONS AND TRANSLATIONS

K. Kekelidze, *Etiudebi, vii*, Tbilisi, 1961, pp. 64-75 (Russian trans. of Tbilisi MS)

P. Peeters, 'S. Romain le néomartyr († 1 mai 780)', *AB* 30 (1911), pp. 409-27 (Latin trans., based on Khakhanov's edition)

A. Khakhanov, 'Materialy po gruzinskoĭ agiologii po rukopisiam X veka', *Trudy po Vostokovedeniu izdavaemye Lazarevskim Institutom Vostochnykh Iazikov* 21 (1910) 25-46 (edition of Mount Athos MS)

K. Kekelidze, 'Novootkrytyĭ agiologicheskiĭ pamiatnik ikonoborcheskoĭ ėpokhi', *Trudy kievskoĭ dukhovnoĭ akademii, iun'* (1910) 201-38 (Russian trans. of Tbilisi MS)

STUDIES

E. Gabidzashvili, *Translated works of ancient Georgian literature, Bibliography, 1 (Hagiography)*, Tbilisi, 2004, p. 320, no. 984

M. Nanobashvili, 'The development of literary contacts between the Georgians and the Arabic speaking Christians in Palestine from the 8th to the 10th century', *Aram* 15 (2003) 269-74, p. 272

PMBZ i (Prolegomena), pp. 212-13 and no. 6417

Kazhdan, *A history of Byzantine literature*, pp. 172-175, 180, 187

Vila, *Christian martyrs in the first Abbasid century*, pp. 278-87

S.H. Griffith, 'Christians, Muslims, and neo-martyrs. Saints' lives and Holy Land history', A. Kofsky and G.G. Stroumsa (eds), *Sharing the sacred. Religious contacts and conflicts in the Holy Land. First-fifteenth centuries CE*, Jerusalem, 1998, 163-207, pp. 193-96
Hoyland, *Seeing Islam*, pp. 365-66
Kazhdan, art. 'Stephen Sabaites', in *ODB*
T. Biṭār, *al-Qiddīsūn al-mansiyyūn fī l-turāth al-Anṭākī*, Beirut, 1994, pp. 360-65
S.H. Griffith, 'The monks of Palestine and the growth of Christian Literature in Arabic', *MW* 78 (1988) 1–28, pp. 15-16
Caraffa, art. 'Stefano il Sabaita, poeta, santo'
G. Garitte, *Le calendrier palestino-géorgien du Sinaiticus 34 (Xe siècle)*, Brussels, 1958, pp. 213-14
K'. K'ek'elidze, *K'art'uli nat'argmni agiograp'ia*, Tbilisi, 1957, p. 136, no. 200
K'. K'ek'elidze, *Geschichte der kirchlichen Georgischen Literatur*, ed. P.M. Tarchnišvili and J. Assfalg, Rome, 1955, p. 491, no. 159
P. Devos, 'Le R. P. Paul Peeters (1870-1950), son oeuvre et sa personalité de Bollandiste', *AB* 69 (1951) I-LIX, pp. XX-XXI
Peeters, 'S. Romain le néomartyr († 1 mai 780)'
K'. Kekelidze, 'Novootkrytyĭ agiologicheskiĭ pamiatnik ikonoborcheskoĭ ėpokhi', *Trudy kievskoĭ dukhovnoĭ akademii*, iun' (1910) 201-38

Mariam Nanobashvili 2008

WORKS ON CHRISTIAN-MUSLIM RELATIONS

Exēgēsis ētoi martyrion tōn hagiōn paterōn tōn anairethentōn hypo tōn barbarōn ēgoun Sarakēnōn en tē megistē Laura tou hosiou patros hēmōn Saba, 'An Account of the martyrdom of the holy fathers, slaughtered by the Saracen barbarians in the great monastery of our holy father Saba'. Modern title: 'The Martyrdom of the twenty martyrs of Mār Saba'

DATE c. 800
ORIGINAL LANGUAGE Greek

DESCRIPTION

The text (*BHG* 1200) contains an account of the raid and sack of the monastery of Mār Saba in the year 797 by Arab bedouin. In the modern printed edition, the text consists of 53 paragraphs and is approximately 15,000 words in length. There are two significant lacunae, the second half of paragraph 19 through most of paragraph 20, and the end of paragraph 28 through most of paragraph 29 (Blake, 'Deux lacunes').

The events described in the text took place in the days of Patriarch Elias, while Basil was *hegoumenos* of the monastery. In the process of recounting the events, the author mentions bedouin raids on the monastery of Chariton (§ 5) which was occupied 'for a significant number of days', and on the cities of Jerusalem (§ 4), Gaza, Ascalon, Eleutheropolis, and Sarafian (§ 3) among others, which were 'laid waste', 'left uninhabitable', etc. The 'barbarians' had tried on numbers of occasions to raid the monastery. Each time, God thwarted their evil intentions. Once (§ 7), while on their way to sack the monastery, the bedouin raiders came upon some clay jars full of wine in a nearby field. Then, in a drunken frenzy they turned upon each other and so 'their intent and assembly were confused' as at the tower of Babel. At other times (§ 8), the raiders merely filled their bellies with the food of the monastery and then left.

Finally, just before Easter a gang of 60 raiders surrounded the monastery. Arrows rained down on the holy fathers, until the raiders had emptied their arrow bags. Thirty fathers were wounded, some killed. The raiders demanded a large sum of money, to which the fathers replied that they were poor and had no such sum. A certain medical doctor, Abba Thomas, looked after the injured, but many had been struck with arrows in the face, the back of the head, or the chest and had little hope of survival (§ 14).

A week later, two monks from a neighboring monastery came in the night, having run all the way to the monastery of Mār Saba. There they told the holy fathers that some tribesmen who were friendly to them had informed them that raiders were gathering together and making their way to Mār Saba to destroy the monastery (§ 16). After recounting the death of a number of individual monks in minor skirmishes, it is described how the group of barbarians gathered with the leaders of the monastery and demanded 4000 *nomismata*, to which the holy fathers replied that they had no such money. Realizing that they were not going to get any money from the monks, the 'Godless ones' forced the fathers back into the 'God-built church', which was a deep cave at the monastery that was used as a church (§ 31-32). A fire was started at the mouth of the cave, and many of the monks died from the smoke. Those who fell at the mouth of the cave trying to escape were kicked, beaten and trampled underfoot. The raiders then looted everything they could find in the monastery and, loading up their camels, left the scene. When the smoke cleared, the surviving monks gathered together all the bodies and buried the dead in their bloody clothes, without washing or cleaning them.

§§ 38 through 44 are a defense of the martyrs to any who would doubt that they should be called martyrs, relating various miracles and visions that validated their martyrdom. § 45 is quick to tell us that those who raided the monastery were soon repaid by God, in that a plague struck them and they died so quickly that they could not be properly buried and dogs ate their bodies. The text ends with a mention of a Persian who had converted to Christ and was slandered by a Muslim as having denied God (§ 52). The 'Saracen' king called him to account and after a 'beautiful witness' to Christ, he was struck on the head with a sword. The final paragraph (§ 53) calls down blessings from the blessed Saba on the monastery.

The text still lacks a translation into a western language, though a Russian translation was made in the early 20th century. Besides the Greek original there are several Georgian recensions.

SIGNIFICANCE

One often overlooked element in Christian apologetics and polemics against Islam is the allegation of Muslim violence against Christians (Vila, *Christian martyrs*, pp. 327-30). This text presents the bedouin raiders clearly as Muslims and as violent, 'especially against the Christians' (§ 3) and 'the holy city of Christ our God' (§ 4). This element is also seen when (§ 52) a Persian who came to faith in Christ is put to death by the Saracen king for his 'beautiful witness' to Christ. The text is also important for understanding the social context of the monastery at Mār Saba in the late 8th century. At several points it comments that among the local population around the monastery there were many who harbored ill feelings towards the monks. These 'enemies of Christ and the Church [who] for a long time have been neighbors' (§ 6) joined up with the barbarian raiders to plunder the monastery. Insight can also be gained into the devastation that the raids had on the countryside through the mention of many who abandoned their homes and fled to the cities where they thought that they could be better protected.

MANUSCRIPTS

MS BNF – Coislin 303, fols 99v-125r (10th c.)

For the Georgian recensions and manuscripts, see Blake, 'Deux lacunes', pp. 28-32

EDITIONS AND TRANSLATIONS

A. Papadopoulos-Kerameus, *Syllogē Palaistinēs kai Syriakēs hagiologias*, 2 vols, St Petersburg, 1907-13, i, pp. 1-41

STUDIES

Vila, 'The struggle over Arabisation'

Vila, *Christian martyrs in the first Abbasid century*, pp. 308-30

Hoyland, *Seeing Islam*, pp. 366-67

Auzépy, 'De la Palestine à Constantinople'

Nasrallah, *HMLEM* ii.2, pp. 156-57

R. Blake, 'La Littérature grecque en Palestine au VIIIe siècle', *Le Muséon* 78 (1965) 367-80

Garitte, 'Le début de la vie de S. Etienne le Sabäite'

Halkin, 'Saint Théoctiste Moine Sabaïte et Martyr (797)'

Blake, 'Deux lacunes combleés'

David H. Vila 2008

Abū Nūḥ al-Anbārī

Abū Nūḥ ʿAbd al-Masīḥ ibn al-Ṣalt al-Anbārī

DATE OF BIRTH c. 730
PLACE OF BIRTH Probably in or near al-Anbār
DATE OF DEATH Unknown; he was active in the 780s
PLACE OF DEATH Unknown, perhaps in or near al-Anbār or Baghdad

BIOGRAPHY

As Cabrol has pointed out in her excellent summary of what is known about Abū Nūḥ al-Anbārī ('Une famille', pp. 297-302), his biography is closely interwoven with that of his fellow student and friend who later became the Catholicos Timothy I (q.v.) (728-823, catholicos from 780). They were schooled together in ecclesiastical subjects by the monk Abraham bar Dashandad. Around 769, Timothy received an exemption from the *kharāj* tax for the diocese of Bayt Baghāsh from the governor of Mosul, Mūsā ibn Muṣʿab, for whom Abū Nūḥ served as secretary (*kātib*).

In 780, Abū Nūḥ played a decisive role in Timothy's election to the catholicate. A few years later, the two men worked together to translate Aristotle's *Topics* into Arabic, at the command of the ʿAbbasid Caliph al-Mahdī. Timothy reported to their mutual friend Sergius, Metropolitan of Elam, that Abū Nūḥ did the bulk of the work and that the caliph was pleased with the result (Brock, 'Two letters', pp. 235-36). That letter, from c. 782/3, is the last datable witness that we possess to Abū Nūḥ's career. We do not know how long he lived after that; by the time Thomas of Margā (q.v.) wrote *The Book of governors* (c. mid-9th c.), he could refer to Abū Nūḥ as one 'who rests among the righteous'.

Scattered references indicate that Abū Nūḥ was an author as well as a translator. Thomas of Margā reports that he wrote a *Life* of John of Daylam (presumably in Syriac). The *Catalogue* of ʿAbdīshūʿ of Nisibis (d. 1318) lists a refutation of the Qurʾān (see below), a treatise against the heretics, and other works. It is not clear whether the ʿAbd al-Masīḥ ibn Nūḥ mentioned by Ibn Kabar as the author of a *Book of questions and answers* is to be identified as our author.

MAIN SOURCES OF INFORMATION

Primary

S.P. Brock, 'Two letters of the Patriarch Timothy from the late eighth century on translations from Greek', *Arabic Sciences and Philosophy* 9 (1999) 233-46, pp. 235-37 (English trans. of Timothy's Letter 43, to Pethion, dated 782/3; Syriac text with trans. in O. Braun, 'Briefe des Katholikos Timotheos I', *OC* 2 (1902) 1-32, pp. 4-11; or H. Pognon, *Une version syriaque des aphorismes d'Hippocrate*, Leipzig, 1903, pp. xvi-xix)

E.A.W. Budge, *The book of governors. The* Historia monastica *of Thomas, Bishop of Margâ A.D. 840*, 2 vols, London, 1893, i, p. 97, ii, p. 222

Ibn al-Nadīm, *Kitāb al-fihrist*, ed. G. Flügel, Leipzig, 1871-72; repr. Beirut: Maktabat Khayāṭ, 1966, p. 244

Mārī ibn Sulaymān, *Kitāb al-majdal*, ed. and trans. H. Gismondi, *Maris, Amri et Slibae. De patriarchis nestorianorum commentaria, pars prior: Maris textus arabicus et versio Latina*, Rome, 1899, p. 71

Assemani, *BO* iii, pt. i, p. 212 ('Abdīshū' of Nisibis' book catalogue; English trans. in G.P. Badger, *The Nestorians and their rituals*, London, 1852, ii, 361-79, p. 375)

Shams al-Riʾāsa Abū l-Barakāt ibn Kabar, *Miṣbāḥ al-ẓulma fī īḍāḥ al-khidma*, ed. Samīr Khalīl, Cairo, 1971, p. 326

Secondary

C. Cabrol, 'Une famille de secrétaires nestoriens, les al-Anbārī, sous les premiers Abbassides (750-870)', *Pd'O* 27 (2002) 295-320, pp. 296-302 (with rich bibliography)

C. Cabrol, 'Une étude sur les secrétaires nestoriens sous les Abbassides (750-1258) à Bagdad', *Pd'O* 25 (2000) 407-91 (with much helpful background information, including maps and bibliography)

B. Landron, *Chrétiens et musulmans en Irak*, Paris, 1994, pp. 53-54 (with excellent bibliography)

Graf, *GCAL* ii, p. 118

P. Kraus, 'Zu ibn al-Muqaffa'', *RSO* 14 (1933-34) 1-20, pp. 1-14

WORKS ON CHRISTIAN-MUSLIM RELATIONS

Tafnīd al-Qurʾān, *Shurrāyā d-Qurān*, 'Refutation of the Qurʾān'

DATE Unknown, late 8th or early 9th c.
ORIGINAL LANGUAGE Arabic or Syriac

DESCRIPTION

We know nothing about the contents of this treatise other than what we might expect from its title. While Sbath reports the existence of an

Arabic 'Refutation of the Qurʾān', the *Catalogue* of ʿAbdīshūʿ of Nisibis lists *Shurrāyā d-Qurān*, 'Refutation of the Qurʾān', without indicating that the work was originally in Arabic. This leaves open the possibility that the work was composed in Syriac and then translated into Arabic.

SIGNIFICANCE
Whether originally composed in Syriac or Arabic, this work ranks among the very earliest Christian treatments of the Qurʾān.

MANUSCRIPTS
MS Cairo, Collection of *al-qummuṣ* Armāniyūs Ḥabashī (1297) (inaccessible MS in private collection; see Sbath, *al-Fihris*, Supplément, p. 11, no. 2530)

EDITIONS AND TRANSLATIONS —

STUDIES —

Maqāla fī l-tawḥīd, 'Treatise on the unity (of God)'

DATE Unknown, late 8th or early 9th c.
ORIGINAL LANGUAGE Arabic

DESCRIPTION
We know nothing about the contents of the work apart from what we might expect from its title. We may wonder, however, whether Abū Nūḥ al-Anbārī was the first to exploit Aristotle's definitions of 'the same' (often translated in Arabic as 'the one'), found in the *Topics*, in order to discuss the nature of the unity of God.

SIGNIFICANCE
This is a very early Arabic Christian treatment of the unity of God, and we must hope that a copy can be discovered.

MANUSCRIPTS
MS Cairo, Collection of *al-qummuṣ* Armāniyūs Ḥabashī (inaccessible MS in private collection; see Sbath, *al-Fihris*, Supplément, p. 11, no. 2531)

EDITIONS AND TRANSLATIONS —

STUDIES —

Maqāla fī l-tathlīth, 'Treatise on the Trinity'

DATE Unknown, late 8th or early 9th c.
ORIGINAL LANGUAGE Arabic

DESCRIPTION
We know nothing about the contents of the work apart from what we might expect from its title: an apology for the Christian doctrine of the Trinity, and a defense against accusations of tritheism or *shirk*.

SIGNIFICANCE
This is a very early Arabic Christian apology for the doctrine of the Trinity, and we must hope that a copy can be discovered.

MANUSCRIPTS
MS Cairo, Collection of *al-qummuṣ* Armāniyūs Ḥabashī (inaccessible MS in private collection; see Sbath, *al-Fihris*, Supplément, p. 11, no. 2532)
EDITIONS AND TRANSLATIONS —
STUDIES —

Mark N. Swanson 2008

The affair of the death of Muḥammad

Unknown author

DATE OF BIRTH Unknown, perhaps 8th/9th c.
PLACE OF BIRTH Unknown
DATE OF DEATH Unknown, perhaps 8th/9th c.
PLACE OF DEATH Unknown

BIOGRAPHY —

MAIN SOURCES OF INFORMATION

Primary —

Secondary —

WORKS ON CHRISTIAN-MUSLIM RELATIONS

ʿEltā d-mawteh d-Muḥammad, 'The affair of the death of Muḥammad'

DATE Unknown, perhaps 8th/9th c.
ORIGINAL LANGUAGE Syriac

DESCRIPTION

This short polemical tale is to be found as an appendix to the East-Syrian recension of the *Legend of Sergius Baḥīrā* (q.v.). It relates how the Jew Kaʿb al-Aḥbār told Muḥammad's followers that their prophet was the Paraclete promised by Christ and that on the third day after his death he would rise up and go to heaven, to Christ who sent him. It explains that history proved Kaʿb wrong: when Muḥammad died, his followers prepared his body and placed it in a locked house, only to find the corpse decomposing when they opened the door after three days.

The story was undoubtedly meant to prove that Muḥammad did not fulfill the biblical prophecies about the coming of the Paraclete. It also intimates that the aspects of Islam which were the result of Jewish influence on Muḥammad are to be rejected. At the beginning of the text, it is claimed that Muslims do not know anything about the grave of Muḥammad, because Kaʿb's prediction did not prove true. This is probably a historicizing explanation of why Muslims are prohibited from venerating the dead, and therefore also an implicit defense of the Christian custom of venerating relics and visiting graves.

It cannot be determined when this story was first written down, but the fact that a similar story about Muḥammad's 'failed resurrection' was already being told in Spain in the first half of the 9th century (see 'Istoria de Mahomet'), suggests that anecdotes about this topic were popular early on among Christians living under Islam. The West-Syrian recension of the *Legend of Sergius Baḥīrā* also contains a version of this brief polemical anecdote, fully integrated into the text of the legend.

SIGNIFICANCE

This piece of polemic is an interesting example of Christian 'counter-historical' tales about the rise of Islam, and attests to the concern of Christians in the Muslim world to disprove that the coming of Muḥammad was predicted in the Bible.

MANUSCRIPTS

There are three accessible manuscripts:

MS Berlin, Staatsbibliothek – Sachau 10 (late 17th c.?)

MS Birmingham, Mingana – Syriac 604 (Siirt 1884)

MS Charfet – 841 (formerly 122) (1889)

For inaccessible and lost manuscripts see:

B. Roggema, *The Legend of Sergius Baḥīrā. Eastern Christian apologetics and apocalyptic in response to Islam*, Leiden, 2008, pp. 243-45

EDITIONS AND TRANSLATIONS

Roggema, *The Legend of Sergius Baḥīrā*, pp. 302-3 (and pp. 332-35 for the parallel tale included in the West-Syrian recension of the *Legend of Sergius Baḥīrā*)

STUDIES

K. Szilágyi, 'Muḥammad and the monk. The making of the Christian Baḥīrā Legend', *JSAI* 34 (2008) (in press)

Barbara Roggema 2008

The Confession which Kaʿb al-Aḥbār handed down to the Ishmaelites

Unknown author

DATE OF BIRTH Unknown
PLACE OF BIRTH Unknown
DATE OF DEATH Unknown
PLACE OF DEATH Unknown

BIOGRAPHY —

MAIN SOURCES OF INFORMATION

Primary —

Secondary —

WORKS ON CHRISTIAN-MUSLIM RELATIONS

Tawditā d-ashlem l-Ishmaʿlāyē Kaʿb sāprā – dukhrāneh l-lūttā, 'The Confession which Kaʿb the scribe – cursed be his memory – handed down to the Ishmaelites'

DATE Unknown, 8th/9th c.?
ORIGINAL LANGUAGE Syriac

DESCRIPTION
This brief and somewhat cryptic piece of anti-Muslim polemic is to be found as an appendix to the East-Syrian recension of the *Legend of Sergius Baḥīrā* (q.v.). It describes how the 'Sons of Ishmael' had an idol called al-Kabar, who was the devil ('Iblīs'), and how the worship of this idol resembles the demonic polytheistic and dualistic worship of the Persians, the Ephesians, the Hittites, the Arameans and the ancient Egyptians. The text purports to portray Islam as a continuation of the paganism found among the pre-Islamic Arabs by insinuating firstly that the Arab interest in the stars is a continuation

of Arabian polytheistic worship and betrays Islam's pagan roots, secondly that the Islamic call for prayer proves that the Arabs believe in two gods, God and 'Akbar', who are invoked simultaneously by the muezzin, and thirdly that Islamic ritual slaughter is a form of pagan sacrifice.

This vehement piece of Syriac polemic against Islam stands in sharp contrast with the East-Syrian texts about Islam which maintain that Muḥammad is to be praised for converting his people to the one God, even if Muslims do not recognize the Trinity. It should be noted that the author is not ignorant of Islam's monotheism, since he underscores that Muslims are polytheistic in their worship 'without being aware of it'; in other words, their polytheism is a hidden element of their 'monotheistic' faith.

The title of the text, 'The confession which Kaʿb the scribe handed down to the Ishmaelites', is peculiar. The name refers to Kaʿb al-Aḥbār, but there is no further mention of either Kaʿb or one teaching in particular. However, since he is mentioned in an ensuing polemical piece as the one who instituted the Islamic call for prayer, the corollary may be that Kaʿb al-Aḥbār should be held responsible for the continuing worship of the idol 'Akbar', who is evoked time and again by the muezzin.

The date of the text cannot be determined easily, because the polemical anecdotes about the alleged Muslim worship of 'Akbar' have been popular amongst Christians in the Middle East through the centuries and can still be encountered today. If the text was already included in the oldest East-Syrian redactions of the *Legend of Sergius Baḥīrā*, it may be as old as the 9th century. It could perhaps even date back to the 8th century, since the Christian polemical topos of the Muslim worship of 'Akbar' already features in texts of that time.

SIGNIFICANCE

This brief text is an example of a well-known type of Christian anti-Muslim polemic that views Islam as crypto-polytheism. It shows that the well-known Christian 'rumor' about Muslims secretly or unknowingly worshiping a deity called 'Akbar' besides God was spread not only among Greek and Arabic-speaking Christians but also in the Syriac-speaking communities.

MANUSCRIPTS

There are three accessible manuscripts:

MS Berlin, Staatsbibliothek – Sachau 10 (late 17th c.?)

MS Birmingham, Mingana – Syriac 604 (1884)

MS Charfet – 841 (formerly 122) (1889)

For inaccessible and lost manuscripts see:

B. Roggema, *The Legend of Sergius Baḥīrā. Eastern Christian apologetics and apocalyptic in response to Islam*, Leiden, 2009, pp. 243-45

EDITIONS AND TRANSLATIONS

Roggema, *The Legend of Sergius Baḥīrā*, pp. 298-301 (edition and trans.)

STUDIES

B. Roggema, 'Muslims as crypto-idolaters – a theme in the Christian portrayal of Islam in the Near East', in D. Thomas (ed.), *Christians at the heart of Islamic rule. Church life and scholarship in ʿAbbasid Iraq*, Leiden, 2003, 1-18, esp. pp. 7-8

Barbara Roggema 2008

Leontius of Damascus

DATE OF BIRTH 2nd half of 8th c.
PLACE OF BIRTH Damascus
DATE OF DEATH 1st half of 9th c.
PLACE OF DEATH Perhaps in the monastery of Mār Sabas

BIOGRAPHY

A native of Damascus, Leontius became a monk at the monastery of Mār Sabas toward the end of the 8th century. His spiritual turmoil brought him to Stephen, another monk at the monastery, and through Stephen's teachings and prayers, Leontius received freedom from certain disturbing thoughts. In time, Stephen accepted Leontius as a disciple. Over the course of the next four years, Leontius lived with Stephen, wandered the deserts with him, recorded his teachings, and collected stories about him. Shortly after Stephen's death (31 March 794), Leontius drew up an account of his teacher's life, miracles, and teachings. (In what follows, Leontius' account of Stephen's life is cited first according to the numbering of the paragraphs in the Arabic edition, and then according to the numbering of the paragraphs in the Greek, where extant.)

MAIN SOURCES OF INFORMATION

Primary

Our only source for Leontius' life is the autobiographical account that he included in the last third of his account of Stephen's life (57-82/115-188).

Secondary

PMBZ iv, pp. 223-26

M. Hinterberger, *Autobiographische Traditionen in Byzanz*, Vienna, 1999, p. 130

Nasrallah, *HMLEM* ii.2, pp. 155-59

H.-G. Beck, *Kirche und theologische Literatur im Byzantinischen Reich*, Munich, 1959, pp. 507-08

Graf, *GCAL* i, p. 413, and ii, p. 23

S. Vailhé, 'Les écrivains de Mar-Saba', *Échos d'Orient* 2 (1899) 1-11, 33-47, pp. 40-41

WORKS ON CHRISTIAN-MUSLIM RELATIONS

Biyūs wa-tadbīr abūnā l-qiddīs al-ṭāhir al-muhadhdhab Mār(y) Istāfanus al-sayyāḥ al-fāḍil alladhī kāna fī sīq Abūnā Mār(y) Sābā, 'The Life and conduct of our holy father, the pure and upright Mār Stephen, the virtuous anchorite who dwelt in the lavra of our father Mār Sabas'

DATE Between 800 and 807
ORIGINAL LANGUAGE Greek

DESCRIPTION
The original Greek title of this work has been lost. The title given above is found in the Arabic version.

Stephen of Mār Sabas was born in the year 724 and died on 31 March 794. He spent the greater part of his life practising asceticism in and around the monastery of Mār Sabas, to the southeast of Jerusalem. An account of his life was written within a few years of his death by Leontius of Damascus (*BHG* 1670), who had been a disciple of Stephen for the last few years of the latter's life.

Leontius wrote the *Life* of his spiritual father in Greek. This text is extant in a single 10th-century MS, Coislin Gr. 303, though of the original 15.5 quires, the first three are lacking (it was edited for the *Acta Sanctorum* in 1723 by J. Pien, who based his edition on a copy of the MS made in 1662 by D. Papebroch). In 1954, G. Garitte discovered a Georgian fragment of the *Life*, which had been translated into Georgian by John Zosimus in the 10th century. A few years later, Garitte announced the discovery of two Arabic MSS at Mt Sinai, both dating from the 13th century and both containing a complete Arabic version of the *Life*. A postscript states that Anbā Yanna ibn Iṣṭafān al-Fākhūrī translated the text from Greek into Arabic at Mār Sabas in the year 903.

SIGNIFICANCE
The *Life* of Stephen paints a vivid picture of the state of the monastic institutions of Judaea under the Umayyads and early ʿAbbasids. It also sheds important light on the patriarchate of Jerusalem, pilgrimage to the Holy Land, and the fate of Palestinian Christianity at this time.

Of particular interest are a number of accounts that show Stephen interacting with Muslims, which thus illumine the historical realities of Christian-Muslim relations in this period. Many of these accounts concern the bedouin living near the monastery of Mār Sabas. The monks of Mār Sabas evidently had an uneasy relationship with these tribesmen. They appear in the narrative primarily as bandits and as people to be feared (15/-, 22/17-19, 30/35-39, 50-51/94-98). It was these same bedouin who would sack the monastery shortly after Stephen's death and slaughter many monks, an event that the author of the *Life* himself witnessed and briefly mentions in his narrative (77.5/177).

The Muslim authorities, whether in Baghdad or in Palestine, also appear occasionally in the text. They depose and imprison Elias the Patriarch of Jerusalem (23/19-23 and 33/44-49), and more ominously they are also responsible for the collection of taxes. A number of narratives in the *Life* show the brutality of both the tax burden and the manner of its collection (33/44-49, 55/108-11, 64/133-38), causing Christians to flee from one city to another, as well as to apostasize.

Finally, the *Life* recounts (52/99-102) the conversion of a Muslim to Christianity, on witnessing a miracle performed by Stephen.

MANUSCRIPTS

MS Sinai – new finds, parchment, Ar. 66, fols 1r-2v (10th c.) (the closing folios of the Arabic version of the *Life*)

MS BNP – Coislin Gr. 303, fols 1r-99r (10th c.) (the Greek *unicum*)

MS Sinai – Georgian 6, fols 220r-223r (10th c.) (Georgian fragment, translated from Arabic, corresponding to 72.1-73.5/159-165)

MS Sinai – Ar. 409, fols 22r-160r (1238)

MS Sinai – Ar. 505, fols 94r-202r (13th c.)

MS Tripoli, University of Balamand – 117, fols 138v-140v (1536) (Arabic fragment, corresponding to 72.5-73.5/161-165)

MS BNP – Ar. 139, fols 327r-329v (16th) (Arabic fragment, corresponding to 72.5-73.5/161-165)

EDITIONS AND TRANSLATIONS

J. Lamoreaux, *The Life of Stephen of Mar Sabas*, 2 vols, Louvain, 1999 (*CSCO* 578-79) (edition of the Arabic version, with English trans.)

B. Pirone, *Leonzio di Damasco. Vita di santo Stefano Sabaita (725-794)*, Cairo, 1991 (*Studia orientalia christiana monographiae* 4) = B. Bīrūnī, *Liyyuntiyyus al-Dimashqī. Sīrat al-qiddīs Istāfanus min dayr Mār Sābā (725-793)* (edition of the Arabic version, with Italian trans.)

C. Carta and B. Bagatti, *Leonzio di Damasco. Vita di S. Stefano Sabaita (725-794)*, Jerusalem, 1983 (Italian trans. from the Greek and from Garitte's Latin version of the lost introduction)

G. Garitte, 'Le début de la Vie de S. Étienne le Sabaïte retrouvé en arabe au Sinaï', *AB* 77 (1959) 332-69 (Latin trans. of the lost beginning of the *Life*, from the Arabic)

G. Garitte, 'Un extrait géorgien de la Vie d'Étienne le Sabaïte', *Le Muséon* 67 (1954) 71-92 (edition with Latin trans. of an excerpt of the *Life*, corresponding to sections 72.1-73.5/159-65)

Acta Sanctorum July III (1723), pp. 524-613; 3rd edition, pp. 504-84 (edition with Latin trans. of the Greek *unicum*)

STUDIES

B. Bitton-Ashkelony and A. Kofsky, 'Monasticism in the Holy Land', in O. Limor and G. Stroumsa (eds), *Christians and Christianity in the Holy Land. From the origins to the Latin kingdoms*, Brepols, 2006, 257-91, pp. 289-90

J. Lamoreaux, 'The biography of Theodore Abū Qurrah revisited', *DOP* 56 (2002) 25-40, p. 27 (on the mention of Stephen in the *Passion* of Michael of Mar Sabas)

M.-F. Auzépy, 'Les sabaïtes et l'iconoclasme', in J. Patrich (ed.), *The Sabaite heritage in the Orthodox Church from the fifth century to the present*, Leuven, 2001, 305-14

C. Hannick, 'Hymnographie et hymnographes sabaïtes', in J. Patrich (ed.), *The Sabaite heritage in the Orthodox Church from the fifth century to the present*, Leuven, 2001, 217-228, pp. 223-24

B. Pirone, 'Continuità della vita monastica nell'ottavo secolo. S. Stefano Sabaita', in J. Patrich (ed.), *The Sabaite heritage in the Orthodox Church from the fifth century to the present*, Leuven, 2001, 49-62

Hoyland, *Seeing Islam*, pp. 109-10, 366-67, 482, n. 95, 718

J. Lamoreaux, 'Some notes on a recent edition of the Life of St Stephen of Mar Sabas', *AB* 113 (1995) 117-26

T. Biṭār, *al-Qiddīsūn al-mansiyyūn fī l-turāth al-Anṭākī*, Beirut, 1995, pp. 311-44

M.-F. Auzépy, 'De la Palestine à Constantinople (VIIIᵉ-IXᵉ siècles). Étienne le Sabaïte et Jean Damascène', *Travaux et Mémoires* 12 (1994) 183-218

Y. Hirschfeld, *The Judean desert monasteries in the Byzantine period*, New Haven CT, 1992, p. 248

C. Mango, 'Greek culture in Palestine after the Arab conquest', in G. Cavallo, G. de Gregorio and M. Maniaci (eds), *Scritture, libri e testi nelle aree provinciali di Bisanzio*, 2 vols, Spoleto, 1991, i, 149-60, pp. 150-51

A. Kazhdan and A.-M. Talbot, *Dumbarton Oaks hagiography database*, Washington DC, 1988, pp. 93-94

I. Ševčenko, 'Constantinople viewed from the eastern provinces in the middle Byzantine period', *Harvard Ukrainian Studies* 3-4 (1979-1980) 712-47, pp. 735-36

J.-M. Sauget, *Premières recherches sur l'origine et les caractéristiques des synaxaires melkites (XIe-XVIIe siècles)*, Brussels, 1969 (*Subsidia hagiographica* 45), pp. 141, 179-80, 369-71

G. Garitte, *Le calendrier palestino-géorgien du sinaiticus 34 (Xe siècle)*, Brussels, 1958 (*Subsidia hagiographica* 30), p. 191

R. Blake, 'Deux lacunes comblées dans la *Passio XX monachorum sabaitarum*', *AB* 68 (1950) 27-43, pp. 40-43

Sophronius [Eustratiades], 'Stephanos ho poietes ho Sabaïtes', *Nea Sion* 28 (1933) 594-602, 651-73, 722-37; 29 (1934) 3-19, 113-30, 185-87

I. Phokylides, *Hē hiera laura Saba hēgiasmenou*, Alexandria, 1927, pp. 388-400

K. Loparev, 'Vizantijskia žitija sviatych VIII-IX vekov', *Vizantiĭskiĭ vremennik* 17 (1910) 1-223; 18 (1911) 1-147; 19 (1912) 1-151; (on the *Life*, 19 (1912) pp. 19-33)

I. Phokylides, 'Peri Stephanou tou sabaïtou kai thaumatourgou kai peri tēs en tē laura tou hagiou Saba sphagēs', *Nea Sion* 10 (1910) 64-75

S. Vailhé, 'Date de la mort de saint Jean Damascène', *Échos d'Orient* 9 (1906) 28-30

A. Ehrhard, 'Das griechische Kloster Mar-Saba in Palaestina', *Römische Quartalschrift für christliche Altertumskunde und Kirchengeschichte* 7 (1893) 32-79, pp. 49-50

John C. Lamoreaux 2007

The Prophecy of the nineteen Muslim kings

Unknown author

DATE OF BIRTH 8th c.
PLACE OF BIRTH Unknown, presumably Egypt
DATE OF DEATH Early 9th c.
PLACE OF DEATH Unknown, presumably Egypt

BIOGRAPHY

Nothing is known of the author of this pseudonymous apocalyptic text beyond what can be gathered from the (reconstructed) text itself

MAIN SOURCES OF INFORMATION

Primary —

Secondary —

WORKS ON CHRISTIAN-MUSLIM RELATIONS

Untitled. Modern title: 'The Prophecy of nineteen Muslim kings in the fourteenth-century Copto-Arabic Apocalypse of Shenute'

DATE Perhaps between 809 and 813, or shortly afterwards
ORIGINAL LANGUAGE Coptic or Greek

DESCRIPTION

This political prophecy is preserved in a fourteenth-century Arabic apocalyptic sermon attributed to the Coptic saint Shenute, but most of it clearly dates to an earlier period. It deals with a succession of nineteen Muslim 'kings' following after the prophet Muḥammad. The kings are first enumerated by name, after which the text continues with cursory and obscure descriptions of the reigns of the last nine, from the Umayyad Caliph Sulaymān (r. 715-17) up to and including the ʿAbbasid Caliph al-Amīn (r. 809-13) – who was actually the twenty-fourth caliph. The prophecy bears a strong resemblance to the well-known Copto-Arabic *Fourteenth Vision of Daniel*, and, indeed, analysis shows that both are recensions of the same work, the *Proto-fourteenth vision of Daniel* (q.v.), an early ʿAbbasid historical apocalypse which is now lost. The prophecy under consideration here remained close to its *Vorlage*, which is why there is little correlation between the contents of its descriptions and what is known about the caliphs they claim to describe. Considering that the last king mentioned is al-Amīn, the reworking may well have taken place during this caliph's reign, perhaps in reaction to the fourth Arab civil war, or shortly afterwards (unless the kings' names were added later, e.g., by the author of the fourteenth-century sermon that includes the prophecy, in which case no date can be given). The prophecy is preserved in Arabic, but there are clear traces of a Coptic *Vorlage*. Coptic was probably also the original language of the work, although, in view of the date of composition suggested, one cannot exclude the possibility of a Greek original.

SIGNIFICANCE

This prophecy is an important source for the reconstruction of the early-ʿAbbasid *Proto-Fourteenth Vision of Daniel*. The text does not deal with Islam as a religion but as a political entity that is bound to fall apart. It provides evidence for apocalyptic speculation among Copts during the fourth Arab civil war.

MANUSCRIPTS

MS BNF – ar. 6147, fols 72v-74v (dated 1832)

MS Cairo, Franciscan Center of Christian Oriental Studies, Muski – 324, fols 130r-132v (19th century; Arabic)

EDITIONS AND TRANSLATIONS

J. van Lent, *Coptic apocalyptic writings from the Islamic period*, Leiden, forthcoming (Diss. Leiden University) (critical English trans.)

J.M. van Lent, 'The nineteen Muslim kings in Coptic apocalypses', *Pd'O* 25 (2000) 643-93, pp. 673-93 (edition and English trans.; severely mishandled in the editing process)

STUDIES

J. van Lent, *Coptic apocalyptic writings*

H. Suermann, 'Koptische arabische Apocalypsen', in R.Y. Ebied and H.G.B. Teule (eds), *Studies on the Christian Arabic heritage*, Leuven, 2004, 25-44, p. 41

Van Lent, 'Nineteen Muslim kings'

J. van Lent, 'An unedited Copto-Arabic apocalypse of Shenute from the fourteenth century', in S. Emmel et al. (eds), *Ägypten und Nubien in spätantiker und christlicher Zeit*, 2 vols, Wiesbaden, 1999, ii, 155-68, pp. 158-59

G. Troupeau, 'De quelques apocalypses conservées dans les manuscrits arabes de Paris', *Pd'O* 18 (1993) 75-87, p. 80

Jos van Lent 2008

The Greek Apocalypse of Daniel

Unknown author

DATE OF BIRTH Unknown
PLACE OF BIRTH Unknown
DATE OF DEATH Unknown
PLACE OF DEATH Unknown

BIOGRAPHY —

MAIN SOURCES OF INFORMATION

Primary —

Secondary —

WORKS ON CHRISTIAN-MUSLIM RELATIONS

Diēgesis peri tōn hēmerōn tou Antichristou to pōs mellei genesthai kai peri tēs synteleias tou aiōnos, 'The Account of the days of the Antichrist and how it will be and of the completion of time', *Tou en hagiois patros hēmon Methodiou episkopou logos peri tōn eschatou hēmerōn kai peri tou Antichristou*, 'The Sermon of our father Bishop Methodius who is among the saints, about the last of the days and the Antichrist'. Modern titles: 'The Narration of Daniel about the days of the Antichrist and the end of times', 'The Greek Apocalypse of Daniel', '*Diegesis Danielis*'

DATE Early 9th c.
ORIGINAL LANGUAGE Greek

DESCRIPTION

This text is extant in two manuscripts (14th-16th c.), neither of which actually names Daniel as author. The Montpellier manuscript calls it 'The account of the days of the Antichrist and how it will be and of the completion of time', while the Oxford manuscript identifies Methodius as the author. (According to Berger, *Die griechische Daniel-Diegese*, MS Venice, Bibliotheca Marciana – Grec. VII 22, fols 1-5, preserves another tradition of the apocalypse in which Daniel is named, but Ditommaso, *The Book of Daniel*, p. 131, argues that the Venice manuscript is a copy of *The vision and revelation of the prophet Daniel* and not of this text.)

The text begins with a historical section in which the period from the Emperor Leo III to Irene is presented as a time when power moved from Constantinople to Rome.

The *Apocalypse* itself begins with the vision of an invasion of Asia Minor by four Muslim armies, one from the 'People of Ishmael' and the other three commanded by the 'sons of Hagar'. These will all converge on Constantinople, but when they try to build a bridge to cross to the city the Lord will raise an emperor who was presumed to be dead, and with the help of his two sons he will defeat them. This emperor will then reign for 33 years (36 according to the Oxford manuscript), and will restore peace and rebuild cities and churches.

After him an incestuous emperor from the north will appear, and he will be followed either by a foul, alien woman (Oxford manuscript) or an alien man (Montpellier manuscript). Constantinople will disappear into the sea, with only the column of Constantine still standing (a motif also found in the Andreas Salos Apocalypse), and power will be given to the city of Rome. Finally Daniel, King of the Jews, will reign in Jerusalem, and the Jews will come together in the land of Israel and persecute the Christians. Then the Antichrist will come, and finally the day of judgment will dawn.

These predictions are clearly concerned with the invasion of Asia Minor by the Arabs in 717-18, their siege of Constantinople, and their defeat by Leo III. The theme of the four armies arriving at Chalcedon is referred to in other apocalyptic writings (e.g. P. Alexander, *The oracle of Baalbek. The Tiburtine Sibyl in Greek dress*, Washington DC, 1967, p. 20, and the texts summarized by Liutprand of Cremona [d. c. 972], *Relatio de Legatione Constantinopolitana*, ch. XXXIX), as is the eschatological importance of the coronation of a new emperor in the west (Brandes, 'Tempora periculosa sunt').

Mango ('The Life', pp. 310-13) proposes a date of 716-17 for the original composition of the text, but Berger suggests a date soon after 800, since he identifies the new emperor crowned in the west as Charlemagne, whose coronation took place in that year. Ditommaso (*The book of Daniel*, pp. 130-41) suggests that the figure of the 'foul, alien woman', must be the Empress Irene in the period after her joint rule with Constantine VI, thus in the years 797-802, and dates the work after that.

Regarding the siege of Constantinople and the coming of the second emperor, the text resembles several other Pseudo-Daniel apocryphal texts, such as *Daniel the monk on the city of seven hills* (late 7th or early 8th c.), Pseudo-John Chrysostom's *Sermon on Daniel's vision* (after 827-29), and *Daniel's vision of the last times and the consummation of the world* (867-69).

SIGNIFICANCE

This text is one of the most important Byzantine examples of apocryphal Daniel literature. It places the early 8th century Arab invasions and the siege of Constantinople within the framework of a sequence of eschatological events that will be halted by the appearance of a new emperor.

MANUSCRIPTS

MS Oxford, Bodleian – Canonicianus 19, fols 145-152 (15th c.)

MS Montpellier, Bibliothèque municipale – 405, fols 105r-115 (15th or 16th c)

EDITIONS AND TRANSLATIONS

K. Berger, *Die griechische Daniel-Diegese. Eine altkirchliche Apokalypse*, Leiden, 1976 (standard critical edition of the Greek text with German trans.)

V.M. Istrin and V. Istrin, *Oktrovenia Mefodiia Patarskago I apokrificheskia Videniia Daniila*, Moscow, 1898, pp. 145-50 (edition of the Oxford MS, not very accurate)

F. Macler, *Les apocalypses apocryphes de Daniel*, Paris, 1895, pp. 108-10 (partial French trans. of the Montpellier MS)

G.T. Zervos, 'Apocalypse of Daniel', in J.H. Charlesworth, *The Old Testament Pseudepigrapha*, 2 vols, New York, 1983-85, i, pp. 755-70 (English trans.)

STUDIES

W. Brandes, 'Die Belagerung Konstantinopels 717/718 als apokalyptisches Ereignis. Zu einer Interpolation im griechischen Text der Pseudo-Methodios-Apokalypse', in K. Belke et al. (eds), *Byzantina Mediterranea*, Vienna, 2007, 65-91, pp. 85-86

P. Ubierna, 'L'apocalyptique byzantine au IXe. siècle', in M. Kaplan (ed.), *Monastères, images, pouvoirs et société à Byzance*, Paris, 2006, 207-21

W. Brandes, 'Der Fall Konstantinopels als apokalyptisches Ereignis', in S. Kolditz and R.C. Müller (eds), *Geschehenes und Geschriebenes*, Leipzig, 2005, 433-70

L. Ditommaso, *The Book of Daniel and the apocryphal Daniel literature*, Leiden, 2005, 144-45 (commentary) and 356-59 (notes on MSS and literature)

L. Brubaker and J. Haldon, *Byzantium in the iconoclast era (ca. 680-850). The sources*, Aldershot, 2001, p. 274

W. Brandes, 'Liudprand von Cremona (Legatio cap. 39-41) und eine bisher unbeachtete west-östliche Korrespondenz über die Bedeutung des Jahres 1000 A.D.', *BZ* 93 (2000), 435-63

Hoyland, *Seeing Islam*, 296-307

W. Brandes, '"Tempora periculosa sunt". Eschatologisches im Vorfeld der Kaiserkrönung Karls des Grossen', in R. Berndt (ed.), *Das Frankfurter Konzil von 794*, Mainz, 1997, 49-79

D. Olster, art. 'Byzantine apocalypses', in B. McGinn, J.J. Collins and S.J. Stein, *The Encyclopedia of Apocalypticism*, New York, 1996

K. Berger, art. 'Daniel. II. Danielapokalypsen', in *LThK* (1995)

B. McGinn, *Antichrist. Two thousand years of the human fascination with evil*, San Francisco, 1994, pp. 95-96

P. Magdalino, 'The history of the future and its uses. Prophecy, policy and propaganda', in R. Beaton and C. Roueché, *The making of Byzantine history*, London, 1993, p. 7

F. García Martínez, '4QPseudo Daniel Aramaic and the Pseudo-Danielic Literature', in F. García Martínez, *Qumran and Apocalyptic*, Leiden, 1992, p. 155

G.T. Zervos, art. 'Daniel, Apocalypse of', *The Anchor Bible Dictionary*, New York, 1992

W. Brandes, 'Die apokalyptische Literatur', in F. Winkelman and W. Brandes, *Quellen zur Geschichte des frühen Byzanz*, Amsterdam, 1990, 305-22, pp. 315-16

C. Mango, 'The life of St. Andrew the Fool reconsidered', *Rivista di studi bizantini e slavi* 2 (1982), 297-313, appendix: 'A Daniel apocalypse of 716/17 AD', 310-13 (repr. in C. Mango, *Byzantium and its image*, London, 1984)

A. Vasiliev, *The Russian attack on Constantinople in 860*, Cambridge MA, 1946, p. 161

Istrin and Istrin, *Oktrovenia Mefodiia Patarskago I apokrificheskia Videniia Daniila*, pp. 294-304

Pablo Ubierna 2007

The Martyrdom of Peter of Capitolias

Unknown author

DATE OF BIRTH Unknown
PLACE OF BIRTH Unknown
DATE OF DEATH Unknown
PLACE OF DEATH Unknown

BIOGRAPHY

The anonymous author of the *Martyrdom of Peter of Capitolias* must have been a native of Syria-Palestine, but it is not possible to determine when he lived, since his text is only extant in a Georgian translation preserved in a single 16th-century manuscript. Although his hero saint must have been a historical figure, he presents his biography and martyrdom with a great deal of fictional elaboration and circumstantial detail, especially with regard to the description of his public execution. Since the original text upon which the translation was based is lost, it cannot be determined either whether the author relied, wholly or partly, on a *Martyrdom* of Peter that according to Theophanes the Confessor was written by John of Damascus (q.v.) (*Clavis Patrum Graecorum*, ed. M. Geerhard, Turnhout, 1974-, no. 8100).

MAIN SOURCES OF INFORMATION

Primary —

Secondary

C. Kekelidze (K. K'ek'elidze), 'Žitie Petra novogo, mučenika Kapetolijskogo', *Hristianskij Vostok* 4 (1917) 1-69 (repr. in K'ek'elidze, *Et'iudebi dzveli kartuli lit'erat'uris ist'oriidan*, 13 vols, Tbilisi, 1945-74, vii, pp. 177-223)

WORKS ON CHRISTIAN-MUSLIM RELATIONS

C'(mid)isa da net'arisa m(a)misa č(ue)nisa I(oa)ne monazonisa da xucisa damask'elisa sit'q'(ua)j cx(o) r(e)bisa da γ(ua)c'lta q'(ovla)d d(ide)b(u)lisa P'(e) t're axlisa myd(e)lm(o)c'(a)misa K'ap'et'olelta k(a) l(a)ksa š(in)a c'ameb(u)lisata, 'An Oration of our holy and blessed father John, monk and priest of Damascus, concerning the life and most illustrious deeds of the pious neo-martyr Peter, who was put to death in the city of Capitolias'. Modern titles: 'The Martyrdom of Peter of Capitolias', 'The Life of Peter the Younger, martyr of Capitolias'

DATE Unknown
ORIGINAL LANGUAGE Unknown, perhaps Greek

DESCRIPTION

The *Martyrdom of Peter of Capitolias* (d. 715) survives only in Georgian. It tells the story of a married priest who had one son and two daughters and who devoted himself to the learning of 'the Scripture and the divine lessons'. At the age of 30, he chose to follow an ascetic life, and so his wife agreed to join a convent and their baby daughters were entrusted to a nunnery south-west of the town of Capitolias in Palestinia Secunda and close to the Church of St Savinianos. After installing his 12-year-old son in a separate cell near the Church of the Theotokos in Capitolias and directing him spiritually, Peter lived in a cell as a hermit for the next ten years.

It was then that the desire to be martyred for the faith arose in him and came, in due course, to be fulfilled. He fell sick and hired a Syrian servant named Qaiouma, through whom he sent an invitation to some Muslim leaders. In their presence, he openly professed his faith in Christ and his fierce opposition to Islam. This aroused a wave of anger, but on account of his condition, it was temporarily contained. However, when the saint recovered from his illness and started preaching Christianity in the streets, the Muslim authorities of the town were summoned to the mosque and denounced Peter to 'Umar, son of the Caliph al-Walīd (r. 705-15).

The lieutenant, Zora, who was sent to investigate the matter brought Peter in shackles to ʿUmar. He was then dragged off to the latter's sick father al-Walīd, before whom he determinedly affirmed his Christian faith once again. The ensuing dialogue with the caliph, who was then residing at the monastery of Dayr Murrān, led to Peter's execution. This took place in Capitolias in the presence of a crowd that included the martyr's son and relatives, as well as Jews and Samaritans. The saint's cruel martyrdom (which is related in great detail) lasted for nine days and culminated in the burning of all his remains; the Jews are said to have played a crucial role in this.

Theophanes the Confessor (q.v.) in his *Chronographia* (ed. C. de Boor, pp. 416-17) makes mention of two martyrs under al-Walīd, Peter Bishop of Damascus and Peter of Maiouma. The second, who is said to have served as a *chartoularios* of public taxes, is probably identifiable with Peter of Capitolias: he confessed his Christian faith before prominent Arabs whom he invited to his home when he fell ill. Once his health was restored, he raised his voice to preach Christianity and was chastised with the sword, thus becoming a martyr. According to Theophanes, John of Damascus (q.v.) wrote a eulogy in his honor.

SIGNIFICANCE

The *Martyrdom of Peter of Capitolias* attests to the unusual case of a saint being led to martyrdom because of his own determined zeal rather than through anti-Christian persecution or violent conversion to Islam. All in all, it has the appearance of a hagiographical elaboration of a story of martyrdom with historical touches.

MANUSCRIPTS

MS Kutaisi – Gelati 4, fols 373-389v, copied by the scribe Manuel Inaniklishvili in Gelati monastery in 1565 at the behest of Evdemone Chkhetisdze, Katholikos of Abkhazia (the manuscript is a Menologion for September and October currently held in the Museum of Kutaisi, a town near the monastery)

EDITIONS AND TRANSLATIONS

Kekelidze, 'Žitie Petra novogo, mučenika Kapetolijskogo' (Georgian text with Russian trans.)

P. Peeters, 'La Passion de S. Pierre de Capitolias († 13 janvier 715)', *AB* 57 (1939) 299-333 (summary)

STUDIES

PMBZ no. 5997 (cf. no. 6000)

D. Vila, *Christian martyrs in the first Abbasid century and the development of an apologetic against Islam*, St Louis, 1999 (Diss. St Louis University), pp. 252-60

S.H. Griffith, 'Christians, Muslims, and neo-martyrs. Saints' lives and Holy Land history', in A. Kofsky and G.G. Stroumsa (eds), *Sharing the sacred. Religious contacts and conflicts in the Holy Land. First-fifteenth centuries CE*, Jerusalem, 1998, 184-87

Hoyland, *Seeing Islam*, pp. 354-60

T. Biṭār, *al-Qiddīsūn al-mansiyyūn fī l-turāth al-Anṭākī*, Beirut, 1994, pp. 249-52, 256-57

P. Mendebielle, 'Un martyre dirbed, S. Pierre de Capitolias', *Jerusalem* 27 (1961) 79-87

P. Peeters, 'Glanures martyrologiques', *AB* 58 (1940) 123-25

Peeters, 'La Passion de S. Pierre de Capitolias' *Acta Sanctorum* Oct. II, 494-98

Stephanos Efthymiadis 2008

Theodore the Stoudite

Theodoros ho Stouditēs (Stoudiotēs), Theodore of Stoudios

DATE OF BIRTH 759
PLACE OF BIRTH Constantinople
DATE OF DEATH 11 November 826
PLACE OF DEATH Island of Prinkipo

BIOGRAPHY

Theodore became a monk in 780 in the Sakkoudion monastery in Bithynia, and succeeded his uncle Plato as *hegoumenos* in 794. He opposed the Emperor Constantine VI because of his second marriage, and the Patriarchs Tarasius and Nicephorus I for their religious policies, which he thought conciliatory in the face of iconoclasm. In about 798 he moved to Constantinople, where he restored the Stoudios monastery, but in 809 he was exiled first to the Princes' Islands and in 815 to Metopa, because of his opposition to iconoclasm. He was recalled in 821 by the Emperor Michael II Balbus, but a little later he went into voluntary exile in reaction to the emperor's desire to call a new council to reopen the debate on the question of icons. He went first to Crescens, then to Cape Akritas and finally to the island of Prinkipo.

MAIN SOURCES OF INFORMATION

Primary

Michael the Stoudite, *Vita* B: *PG* 99, cols 233-328 (*BHG* 1754)

Theodoros Daphnopates, *Vita* A: *PG* 99, cols 113-232 (*BHG* 1755)

Vita C: V.V. Latishev, 'Žitie prep. Teodora Studita', *VV* 21 (1914), 258-304 (*BHG* 1755c)

Vita D: T. Matantseva, 'Un fragment d'une nouvelle Vie de saint Théodore Stoudite, Vie D (*BHG* 1755f)', *Byzantinische Forschungen* 23 (1996) 151-63 (*BHG* 1755f)

C. van de Vorst, 'La translation de S. Théodore Studite et de S. Joseph de Thessalonique', *AB* 32 (1913), 50-61 (*BHG* 1756t)

Naukratios the Stoudite, *Encyclical letter*, *PG* 99, cols 1825-49 (*BHG* 1756)

Secondary
R. Cholij, *Theodore the Stoudite. The ordering of holiness*, Oxford, 2002
art. 'Theodoros Studites', in *PMBZ* (with lit.)
T. Pratsch, *Theodoros Stoudites (759-826). Zwischen Dogma und Pragma*, Berlin, 1998
M.-H. Congourdeau, art. 'Théodore Stoudite', in *Dictionnaire de spiritualité*, ed. M.Viller et al., Paris, 1932-95 (with lit.)
G. Fatouros, *Theodori Studitae epistulae*, Berlin, 1992 (*Corpus Fontium Historiae Byzantinae* 31/I), pp. 3*-38*
A. Kazhdan, art. 'Theodore of Stoudios', in *ODB*
H. Beck, *Kirche und theologische Literatur im Byzantinischen Reich*, Munich, 1977, pp. 491-95 (with lit.)

WORKS ON CHRISTIAN-MUSLIM RELATIONS

Stichistikoi logoi kata haireseōn, 'Discourses in verse against heresies'

DATE c. 798/99-808
ORIGINAL LANGUAGE Greek

DESCRIPTION
In a chapter of the *Life* of Theodore, Michael the Stoudite lists the works composed by the saint. Among these there appears one in which 'he enumerated every heresy and rendered them anathema, in (...) pure trimeter verses' (*PG* 99, col. 264c). This work must be compared with *On the heresies and the synods* by Patriarch Germanus I (d. c. 733) and John of Damascus' *On heresies* (q.v.). The latter text (or perhaps the *Anakephalaiōsis* of Epiphanius) must have been Theodore's model for the structure of his work.

Of the writings of Theodore, a single extract is preserved in a collection of anti-Islamic works (MS Mount Athos, Megisti Lavra – Ω 44 [1854]) which, in its present form, dates back to the end of the 14th or the beginning of the 15th century. This collection contains some well-known polemical texts: Riccoldo da Monte Croce's *Libellus contra legem Sarracenorum* in Demetrius Cydones' Greek translation; the chapter on Islam by John of Damascus revised by Michael the Synkellos (q.v.); the entry on Muḥammad by Theophanes the Confessor (q.v.) (found also in *De administrando imperio* of Constantine Porphyrogenitus); the refutation by Euodius (q.v.), and an extract from Bartholomew of Edessa's *Refutation of the Hagarenes*, as well as the extract from Theodore the Stoudite.

In a sequence of verses, Theodore deals with the names by which Muslims are called ('Hagarenes', 'Ishmaelites') and their genealogy, the idolatry of the pre-Islamic Arabs, and Muḥammad's mission. The doctrinal exposition that follows is devoted to: God, Jesus Christ, the story of the 'holy camel', the Islamic paradise, various Muslim practices (rejection of the Jewish Sabbath and Christian baptism, marriage customs, circumcision) and dietary rules.

SIGNIFICANCE

Theodore the Stoudite's verses on the Muslims take up the information in chapter 100 of John of Damascus' *On heresies* devoted to Islam, and the expressions and order of this chapter are followed exactly. The verses are therefore representative of certain Byzantine circles at the beginning of the 9th century, in which the inheritance of John of Damascus was preserved and revived. Theodore the Stoudite's verses seem also to echo other traditions about Islam present in Byzantium at the time, which were sources of new information about the Arabs and Islam. He relies, directly or indirectly, on a Greek version of the Qur'ān, which also appears in other texts of the time and is known from its use in the Qur'ān refutation of Nicetas of Byzantium (q.v.) from the second half of the 9th century.

MANUSCRIPTS

MS Mount Athos, Megistē Laura – Ω 44 (1854), fols 149v-151r (15th c.); for a description of the manuscript, see A. Rigo, 'Niceta Byzantios, la sua opera e il monaco Evodio', in G. Fiaccadori (ed.), *'In partibus Clius'. Scritti in onore di Giovanni Pugliese Carratelli*, i, Naples, 2006, 147-87, pp. 165-67

EDITIONS AND TRANSLATIONS

A. Rigo, 'La sezione sui Musulmani dell'opera di Teodoro Studita contro le eresie', *REB* 56 (1998) 213-30, pp. 228-30 (edition)

STUDIES

Rigo, 'La sezione sui Musulmani'

Antonio Rigo 2008

Theophanes the Confessor

Homologētēs

DATE OF BIRTH c. 760
PLACE OF BIRTH Constantinople
DATE OF DEATH 12 March 818
PLACE OF DEATH Samothrace

BIOGRAPHY

Theophanes came from a noble family. As a young man he became known to the emperor Leo IV (r. 775-80), and in 777/78 he was given the rank of groom (*stratōr*). In 778/79 he married, but he decided to renounce his property and become a monk. He established his wife in a convent, and he himself founded the monastery of Megas Agros on the southern shore of the Sea of Marmora.

In 787 Theophanes attended the Seventh Ecumenical Council. Then in 809/10, when he was 50, he fell ill with a kidney disease and remained bed-ridden for the rest of his life. In 815, when he refused to approve Leo V's (r. 813-20) iconoclastic policy, he was confined under guard in the monastery of Hormisdas, and from there he was transferred to a small cell in the Palace of Eleutherios, where he remained under guard for two years. In 818 he was sent into exile in Samothrace, and he died 23 days after his arrival there. His body was transferred to Hiereia in 820, where it remained for a year, and it was then transferred to Agros and buried in the church.

MAIN SOURCES OF INFORMATION

Primary

Enkomion by Theodore of Studios (*BHG* 1792b), in C. van de Vorst, 'Un panégyrique de S. Théophane le Chronographe par S. Théodore Studite', *AB* 31 (1912) 11-23, and S. Efthymiadis, 'Le panégyrique de S. Théophane le Confesseur par S. Théodore Studite (*BHG* 1792b). Edition critique du texte intégral', *AB* 111 (1993) 259-90

Life of Theophanes by Patriarch Methodios (*BHG* 1787z), in V.V. Latyšev, 'Mefodija patriarcha Konstantinopel'skogo Žitie prep. Feofana Ispoveditionika', *Mémoires de l' academie des sciences de Russie*, 8th sér. 13/4 (1918) 1-44, pp. 1-40

Life of Theophanes the Confessor (*BHG* 1788), in M.I. Gedeon, *Byzantinon Heortologion. Mnēmai tōn apo tou D' mechri tōn mesōn tou IE' aiōnos heortazomenōn hagiōn en Kōnstantinoupolei*, Constantinople, 1899, pp. 290-93

Life of Theophanes the Confessor (*BHG* 1789), in C. de Boor, *Theophanis Chronographia*, 2 vols, Leipzig, 1883-85 (repr. Hildesheim, 1963, 1980), ii, pp. 3-12 (=*PG* 115, cols 19-29)

Life of Theophanes the Confessor (*BHG* 1790), in de Boor, *Theophanis Chronographia*, ii, pp. 13-27 (=*PG* 108, 18-45)

Life of Theophanes the Confessor (*BHG* 1791), in K. Krumbacher, 'Eine neue Vita des Theophanes Confessor', *Sitzungsberichte der philos.-philol. u. hist. Cl. der. K. Bayer. Akad. d. Wiss.*, 1897, i, pp. 389-99 (= V.V. Latyšev (ed.), *Menologii anonymi Byzantini saeculi X quae supersunt: fasciculos duos sumptibus Caesareae Academiae Scientiarum e Codice Mosquensi 376 Vlad.*, 2 vols in 1, St Petersburg, 1911-12, i, pp. 221-29)

Encomium of Theophanes by Theodoros Protasekretis (*BHG* 1792), ed. K. Krumbacher, 'Ein Dithyrambus auf den Chronisten Theophanes', *Sitzungsberichte der philos.-philol. u. hist. Cl. der. K. Bayer. Akad. d. Wiss.*, 1896, pp. 608-18

Synaxarium (*BHG* 1792e), in Latyšev, 'Mefodija patriarcha Konstantinopel'skogo Žitie prep. Feofana Ispoveditionika', pp. 41-44

Secondary

PMBZ no. 8107, and i (Prolegomena), pp. 57-59

Dumbarton Oaks Hagiography Database, Washington DC, 1998, pp. 105-6

C. Mango and R. Scott, *The Chronicle of Theophanes Confessor. Byzantine and Near-Eastern history AD 284-813*, Oxford, 1997, pp. xliv-lii

A. Kazhdan, art. 'Theophanes the Confessor', in *ODB*

J. Gouillard, 'La vie d'Euthyme de Sardes (†831). Une oeuvre du patriarche Méthode', *Travaux et Memoires* 10 (1987) 1-101

J. Gouillard, 'Une oeuvre inédite du patriarche Méthode. La vie d'Euthyme de Sardes', *BZ* 53 (1960) 36-46

E. von Dobschütz, 'Methodios und die Studiten. Strömungen und Gegenströmungen in der Hagiographie des 9. Jahrhunderts', *BZ* 18 (1909) 41-105

J. Pargoire, 'S. Théophane le Chronographe et ses rapports avec S. Théodore Studite', *VV* 9 (1902) 31-102

WORKS ON CHRISTIAN-MUSLIM RELATIONS

Chronographia, 'Chronography'

DATE Between 810 and 814
ORIGINAL LANGUAGE Greek

DESCRIPTION

The *Chronographia* is an extension of the unfinished world chronicle (entitled *Eklogē chronographias*) of George the Synkellos (d. after 810), which covered the period from the creation to the emperor Diocletian (r. 284-305). It makes reference to Christian-Muslim relations in the entries for the years 629/30 to 812/13. In the first of these, which consists of the regnal years of rulers and bishops, the name of the prophet Muḥammad ('leader of the Arabs') is listed second after the name of the Byzantine emperor (Heraclius) and is followed by the names of the three patriarchs of Constantinople, Jerusalem and Alexandria. The names of caliphs, down to the death of the ʿAbbasid Caliph al-Amīn in 813, appear in a similar order in subsequent entries.

Concerning the sources used by Theophanes, for the period between 630 and 750 he depends on a Greek version of the Syriac 'Eastern Source', attributed to Theophilus of Edessa (d. 785) (q.v.). It was probably translated into Greek by a Melkite monk in Palestine, most likely by George the Synkellos, and it reached Constantinople at the time of the destruction of the Palestinian monasteries in 813 (Conrad, 'The conquest of Arwād', p. 332, n. 40). Theophanes also had access to an independent source (Conrad, pp. 11-26), and additional material which was probably the work of the translator/redactor. Theophanes' personal comments are also evident in several entries (Jeffreys, 'Notes towards a discussion', p. 147).

Themes of Christian-Muslim relations feature in the sections dealing with the early Arab conquests, Byzantine-Umayyad and Byzantine-ʿAbbasid warfare, and the measures against Christians (i.e. Chalcedonians) that were taken by Muslim governors and various Umayyad and ʿAbbasid caliphs. Issues of the destruction of churches (ed. de Boor, pp. 452-53), forced conversion, increase of taxes, punishment and torture of civilians (pp. 452-53, 446), the killing of prisoners (pp. 414, 465), the torture and suspension of clergy (pp. 416-17), their transfer to other places after the capture of their cities (p. 382), their deportations (pp. 445, 482, 499), and the imposition of exile on them (the patriarch of Antioch in 756-57, p. 430) are among the most recurrent. Dates of entries are given as years of the world (*Anno mundi*), and do not always correspond to *hijrī* years.

Referring to events occurring in the Christian communities of Syria and Palestine, Theophanes reports that in the early 9th century the anarchy resulting from the civil war between Hārūn al-Rashīd's sons (809-13) caused much hardship to the Christians of Syria, Egypt, and Libya: the churches of Jerusalem and the monasteries of Palestine were made desolate, and in Jerusalem the holy places were profaned (p. 484). He also refers to anarchy in Syria which destroyed the holy places in Syria, Jerusalem and Palestine (p. 499). Many Christians were killed as martyrs, while others fled to Cyprus or Constantinople, and all intellectual life came to a halt (see Griffith, 'Greek into Arabic', pp. 122-23). However, life continued in the monasteries of Judaea, and especially the lavra of Mār Sabas.

Theophanes attributes the Arab victories in Syria, Egypt and Jerusalem mainly to the emperor Heraclius' adoption of the Monothelite heresy (p. 332) and a number of wrong decisions (see Ferber, 'Theophanes' account of Heraclius', p. 39). Theophanes' moral is that the emperor's deviation from the orthodox faith turned God against the Empire and brought about its destruction. In later entries he associates the Arabs with iconoclasm. The iconoclast doctrines of the Umayyad Caliph Yazīd (r. 720-24) were adopted by the Emperor Leo III (r. 717-41), who 'was possessed by an Arab mentality' (p. 410) and is called *sarakēnophrōn* (p. 405). The terminology used for both Leo and the Arabs is the same: they are 'God's enemies', and are criticized for their hostility towards saints, relics and icons (p. 406). In addition, the Arabs are described as 'purveyors of divine punishment', 'deniers of Christ', 'God's enemies', 'impure', and enemies who inflicted all kinds of evils on the Roman state, while Islam is called a malignant, illegitimate and evil doctrine.

Military victories of the Byzantines over the Arabs are attributed to miracles or divine intervention, while acts of Christian impiety usually lead to Arab victories. Success and failure are associated with orthodoxy and heresy. The protective role of the icons is stressed in the expulsion of the Arabs from Nicea in Bithynia. Arab misfortunes in battles, e.g. in the siege of Constantinople, are explained as lessons to be learnt, that Constantinople and the Empire were protected by the Virgin Mary, and that victory happened in vindication of the true believers. So, those Arabs who were saved from defeat had to acknowledge the miraculous signs which they witnessed.

In general, Muslims are described as cowards, who in battle 'withdrew in fear', 'captured (fortresses) by deceit' (p. 409), won their victories through bribery and deception (p. 366), and as transgressors (p. 377). Theophanes considers those Christian prisoners who were converted to Islam as stupid, boorish and impure (p. 402). Holding to the faith and dying as a martyr is praised, and thus Eustathius, son of the patrician Marianus, who was killed in Ḥarrān as a true martyr in the days of the Caliph Hishām (p. 414), and Peter of Maiouma, whose tongue the Caliph Walīd II had amputated for criticizing the impiety of the Arabs and the Manicheans, are examples of Christians martyred in many towns under Muslim rule.

Theophanes' view of the caliphs is generally negative. ʿUmar ibn al-Khaṭṭāb showed 'devilish pretence' when capturing Jerusalem, and his religion is blasphemous; the Umayyad Caliph Yazīd was 'senseless' for the adoption of his measure against the holy images (p. 402); ʿAbd al-Malik's negotiations with Justinian II were questionable (p. 365); a terrible fate awaited those who attempted private or personal diplomacy with the Caliph Muʿāwiya. But sometimes there are positive comments about Muslim rulers, such as on Muʿāwiya rebuilding the church of Edessa (p. 356), and Marwān II allowing Theophylactus to be ordained patriarch of Antioch (p. 421).

Theophanes shows strong anti-Jewish sentiment and blames iconoclasm to some extent on Jewish influences. Jews are 'wretched men', teach 'illicit things', and imparted anti-Christian doctrine to the prophet Muḥammad (p. 333). They advised ʿUmar to take down crosses from the Church of the Ascension on the Mount of Olives to ensure that the mosque on the Temple Mount would not fall. Thus the Muslim builders are 'God's enemies' who 'took down many crosses' (p. 342).

Theophanes informs us of early developments in the caliphate which clearly signaled the emergence of a new Arab-Muslim culture and the gradual Arabization of the Empire. He preserves an account of ʿUmar ibn al-Khaṭṭāb's construction of the mosque on the Temple Mount in Jerusalem (p. 339); Walīd I's (r. 705-15) decree that the registers of public offices should not be written in Greek but in Arabic (p. 376); ʿUmar ibn ʿAbd al-ʿAzīz's (r. 717-20) establishment of a Muslim tax register; and ʿAbd al-Malik's introduction of a new Arab coinage.

Theophanes points out that Christians dominated the administrative professions in the first two or three centuries of Islam. In 758 the Muslims tried to expel Christians from the government chancery but were obliged to entrust them with these duties, because they could not write numbers. John of Damascus' father was reportedly *genikos logothetēs* under the Caliph ʿAbd al-Malik, responsible for the taxation of Christians. Elsewhere, Theophanes asserts that in Egypt as late as the early 8th century Muslim navies recruited most of their crews from the Christian Greek and Coptic populations.

Reports in the *Chronographia* on events of cultural diplomacy between the Umayyad caliphs and the Byzantines are corroborated by Arabic sources. The Caliph al-Walīd, for example, called for workers from Byzantium to help build the mosque of the Prophet in Medina and the Great Mosque in Damascus (Grabar, 'Islamic Art and Byzantium', p. 83), just as Theophanes says.

Theophanes uses Arabic terminology such as *hira* (encampment), *amēraios* and *amēr* (*amīr*), and *Korasenite* (Quraysh). His use of terminology for Arab ships corroborates data from the study of Egyptian papyri (Makrypoulias, *Byzantine ships*); his description of the device of 'Greek fire' used against the Arabs (pp. 353, 354) complements other sources (Haldon, '"Greek fire" revisited', p. 293).

The *Chronographia* sheds light on common Arab-Byzantine practices. It preserves the names of envoys, describes diplomatic protocol and procedures in Byzantine-Umayyad and ʿAbbasid exchanges of embassies (see Vaiou, *Diplomatic relations*), and it is an important source on shipbuilding techniques in early Islam (see Makrypoulias, *Muslim ships*, pp. 181-84), and on Muslim strategy during raids on Cyprus which complement Arab accounts (see Beihammer, p. 61).

The *Chronographia* contains different layers of material and attitudes on Muslims, requiring the accounts to be read as individual pieces and evaluated within wider contexts. The majority of entries on raids and victories for the years 630 to 638 and 642 to 669, which derive from Theophilus of Edessa, are objective. But there are also negative entries, which are generally the expression of Theophanes' iconodule attitude. Adherence to orthodoxy is his main criterion, and the issue of Christian-Muslim conflict takes second place to this. Thus, in conformity with the rhetoric of 9th century Byzantine self-centeredness, he views the Arabs, like the iconoclasts, as enemies of orthodoxy. His perception of them is determined by their 'correct religious stance' rather than 'ethnic affiliation'.

The *Chronographia* was continued during the 10th century, drawing on the continuator of George the Monk and a number of other sources, and producing a series of chronicles known as the *Scriptores post Theophanem*. It served as a source for the author of the *Life* of St Theodore of Chora, as well as for Cedrenus, George Harmatolos (George the Monk) (q.v.), Constantine Porphyrogenitus, Theodosius Melissenus and Zonaras. These authors depended on Theophanes for Muḥammad's genealogy, life and career (see Conrad, pp. 11-20). Theophanes is also the source for some of the information about

Muḥammad in the *Kata Moamed* of Pseudo-Bartholomew (Conrad, pp. 34-36). The Latin translation by Anastasius Bibliothecarius (q.v.) became an important source on Islam in the West.

SIGNIFICANCE

The *Chronographia* is the most important Byzantine source for the history of the Near East for the 7th, 8th and 9th centuries. It is important for the transmission of material from the 'Eastern Source' into mainstream Byzantine tradition, especially as regards the Arab conquests and early Byzantine-Arab relations. It gives valuable information on events in Syria and other lands conquered by the Arabs, and sheds light on the early history of the caliphate, to which it is the earliest testimony in Greek historiography. It also offers insight into the ways in which the Christian communities in Syria and the Arab Muslims perceived one another.

MANUSCRIPTS

MS Vat – Gr. 155 (late 9th, 10th or 11th c.)
MS Oxford – Christ Church, Wake 5 (late 9th c.?)
MS BNF – Gr. 1710 (10th c.)
MS BNF – Gr. 1711 (11th c.)
MS Vat – Gr. 978 (11th/12th c.)
MS BNF – Coislin 133 (12th c.)
MS Vat – Gr. 154 (12th c.) (best MS, according to de Boor)
MS Vat – Barberini 553 (16th c.)
MS BNF – Gr. 1709 (16th c.)
MS Vat – Palat. 395 (16th c.)
MS Munich, Staatsbibliothek – Gr. 391 (16th c.)

For a 10th c. fragment at Basle, Renaissance copies and the early Latin MSS of Anastasius Bibliothecarius, see Mango and Scott, *The Chronicle of Theophanes Confessor*, pp. xcvi-xcviii.

EDITIONS AND TRANSLATIONS

A. Koustenes, *Theophanous Chronographia*, 3 vols, Thessalonica, 2007 (ed. with modern Greek trans.)

Mango and Scott, *The Chronicle of Theophanes Confessor* (trans.)

H. Turtledove, *The Chronicle of Theophanes. An English translation of Anno Mundi 6095-6305 (A.D. 602-813)*, Philadelphia, 1982 (trans.)

L. Breyer, *Bilderstreit und Arabersturm in Byzanz. Das 8. Jahrhundert (717-813) aus der Weltchronik des Theophanes*, Vienna, 1964

C. de Boor, *Theophanis Chronographia*, 2 vols, Leipzig, 1883-85 (repr. Hildesheim, 1963, 1980)

STUDIES

Select bibliography:

J. Haldon, '"Greek Fire" revisited. Recent and current research', in E. Jeffreys (ed.), *Byzantine Style, religion and civilization. In Honour of Sir Steven Runciman*, Cambridge, 2006, 290-325, p. 293

P. Yannopoulos, 'Comme le dit Georges le Syncelle ou, je pense, Théophane', *Byzantion* 74 (2004) 139-45

E. Jeffreys, 'Notes towards a discussion of the depiction of the Umayyads in Byzantine literature', in J. Haldon and L.I. Conrad (eds), *The Byzantine and early Islamic Near East VI. Elites old and new in the Byzantine and early Islamic Near East*, Princeton NJ, 2004, 133-47

A. Beihammer, 'The first naval campaigns of the Arabs against Cyprus (649, 653). A reexamination of the oriental source material', *Graeco-Arabica* 9-10 (2004) 47-68

M. Vaiou, *Diplomatic relations between the Abbasid Caliphate and the Byzantine Empire. Methods and procedures*, Oxford, 2002 (Diss. University of Oxford)

P. Speck, *Kaiser Leon III., die Geschichtswerke des Nikephoros und des Theophanes und der Liber Pontificalis*, Bonn, 2002

B.G. Makrypoulias, 'Muslim ships through Byzantine eyes', in Y.Y. al-Hijji and V. Christides (eds), *Aspects of Arab seafaring. An attempt to fill the gaps of maritime history*, Athens, 2002, 179-90

L. Brubaker and J. Haldon, *Byzantium in the Iconoclast era (680-850). The sources*, Aldershot, 2001, pp. 168-71

P. Yannopoulos, 'Les vicissitudes historiques de la Chronique de Théophane' *Byzantion* 70 (2000) 527-53

A. Kazhdan, *A history of Byzantine literature (650-850)*, Athens, 1999, 219-34

W. Brandes, review of Mango and Scott, *The Chronicle of Theophanes Confessor*, *BZ* 91 (1998) 549-61

R.-J. Lilie, 'Theophanes and al-Ṭabarī on the Arab invasions of Byzantium', in H. Kennedy (ed.), *Al-Ṭabarī. The life and works of a medieval Muslim historian*, Princeton, 1998

R.-J. Lilie et al. (eds), 'Die gemeinsame Vorlage der syrischen Quellen mit Theophanes für die Zeit zwischen 641 und 751', in *PMBZ i* (Prolegomena), pp. 226-34

B. Coulie, P. Yannopoulos and CETEDOC, *Thesaurus Theophanis Confessoris, Chronographia (Corpus Christianorum. Thesaurus Patrum Graecorum)*, Turnhout, 1998

Hoyland, *Seeing Islam*, pp. 428-32

A. Cameron, 'Byzantines and Jews. Some recent work on early Byzantium', *Byzantine and Modern Greek Studies* 20 (1996) 249-74

A. Kaplony, *Konstantinopel und Damaskus. Gesandtschaften und Verträge zwischen Kaisern und Kalifen 639-750*, Berlin, 1996

Y.N. Lyubarskii, 'Concerning the literary technique of Theophanes the Confessor', *Byzantinoslavica* 56 (1995) 317-22

P. Speck, 'Der "zweite" Theophanes. Eine These zur Chronographie des Theophanes', in *Varia* V, Bonn, 1994, 433-83

L.I. Conrad, The conquest of Arwād. A source-critical study in the historiography of the early medieval Near East', in A. Cameron and L.I. Conrad (eds), *Byzantine and early Islamic Near East I. Problems in the literary source material*, Princeton NJ, 1992, 317-401

W.E. Kaegi, *Byzantium and the early Islamic conquests*, Cambridge, 1992

B. Baldwin, 'Theophanes on the iconoclasm of Leo III', *Byzantion* 60 (1990) 426-28

L.I. Conrad, 'Theophanes and the Arabic historical tradition: Some indications of intercultural transmission', *Byzantinische Forschungen* 15 (1990) 1-44

I. Rochow, *Byzanz im 8. Jahrhundert in der Sicht des Theophanes. Quellenkritisch-historischer Kommentar zu den Jahren 717-813*, Berlin, 1989

P. Speck, *Das geteilte Dossier. Beobachtungen zu den Nachrichten über die Regierung des Kaisers Herakleios und die seiner Söhne bei Theophanes und Nikephoros*, Bonn, 1988

H. Kennedy, 'The Melkite church from the Islamic conquest to the Crusades', in *17th International Byzantine Congress*, Washington DC, 1986, 523-42

S.H. Griffith, 'Greek into Arabic. Life and letters in the monasteries of Palestine in the ninth century: the example of the *Summa Theologiae Arabica*', *Byzantion* 56 (1986) 117-38

I. Rochow, 'Zu einigen chronologischen Irrtümern in der "Chronographie" des Theophanes', in J. Hermann, H. Köpstein and R. Müller (eds), *Griechenland - Byzanz - Europa*, Berlin, 1984, 43-49

L.M. Whitby, 'Theophanes' chronicle source for the reigns of Justin II, Tiberius and Maurice (A.D. 565-602)', *Byzantion* 53 (1983) 312-45

L.M. Whitby, 'The Great Chronographer and Theophanes', *Byzantine and Modern Greek Studies* 8 (1982/3) 17-20

I.S. Chichurov, 'Feofan Ispoveditionik. Publikator, Redaktor, Avtor?', *VV* 42 (1981) 78-87
I.S. Chichurov, *Vizantijskie istoriceskie socinenija*, Moscow, 1980, 17-144
I.S. Chichurov, '"Mesto Chronografii" Feofana v rannevizantijskoj istoriograficeskoj tradicii', in *Drevnej·ie gosudarstva na territorii SSSR* Moscow, 1981, 5-146
G. Huxley, 'On the erudition of George the Synkellos', *Proceedings of the Royal Irish Academy* 81 (1981) 207-17
J. Ferber, 'Theophanes' account of the reign of Heraclius', in E. Jeffreys, M. Jeffreys and A. Moffatt (eds), *Byzantine papers. Proceedings of the first Australian Byzantine studies conference*, Canberra, 1981, 32-42
A.N. Stratos, 'The Naval engagement at Phoenix', in A.E. Laiou-Thomadakis (ed.), *Charanis Studies. Essays in honor of Peter Charanis*, New Brunswick, 1980, 229-47
C. Mango, 'Who wrote the chronicle of Theophanes?' *Zbornik radova Vizantološkog Instituta* 18 (1978) 9-18
W. Kaegi, 'The first Arab expedition against Amorion', *Byzantine and Modern Greek Studies* 3 (1977) 19-22
N. Oikonomides, 'Les premiers mentions des themes dans la Chronique de Théophane', *Zbornik radova Vizantološkog Instituta* 19 (1975) 1-8
A.S. Proudfoot, 'The sources of Theophanes for the Heraclian dynasty', *Byzantion* 44 (1974) 367-439
N. Wilson, 'A manuscript of Theophanes in Oxford', *DOP* 26 (1972) 357-60
V. Besevliev, 'Die Berichte des Theophanes und Nikephoros über die Thronwirren in Bulgarien, 763-765', *Jahrbuch der Österreichischen Byzantinistik* 20 (1971) 67-82
N. Pigulevskaya, 'Theophanes' Chronographia and the Syrian Chronicles', *Jahrbuch der Österreichischen Byzantinistik* 16 (1967) 55-60
O. Grabar, 'Islamic Art and Byzantium' *DOP* 18 (1964) 67-88
M. Canard, 'La prise d'Heraclee et les relations entre Harun ar-Rashid et l' Empereur Nicephore I', *Byzantion* 32 (1962) 345-79
G. Arnaldi, art. 'Anastasio Bibliotecario', in *Dizionario biografico degli Italiani*
H.A.R. Gibb, 'Arab-Byzantine relations under the Umayyad caliphate', *DOP* 12 (1958) 219-33
D. Anastasijević, 'Carskij god v Vizanti' [The imperial year in Byzantium], *Seminarium Kondakovianum* 11 (1940) 147-200

V. Grumel, 'L'année du monde dans la Chronographie de Théophane', *Echos d'Orient* 33 (1934) 396-408

G. Ostrogorsky, 'Die Chronologie des Theophanes im 7. und 8. Jahrhundert', *Byzantinisch-neugriechische Jahrbücher* 7 (1928-29) 1-56

D. Tabachovitz, *Sprachliche und text-kritische Studien zur Chronik des Theophanes Confessor*, Uppsala, 1926 (Diss. University of Uppsala)

C. Loparev, 'De S. Theodoro monacho hegumenoque Chorensi', *Zapiski Klassičeskago otdelenija imperatorskogo russkogo arkheologičeskogo obščestva* 1 (1904), suppl. 1-16

E.W. Brooks, 'The sources of Theophanes and the Syriac chroniclers', *BZ* 15 (1906) 578-87

T. Schmit, 'Kahriye Dzami', *Izvestija Russkogo Archeologičeskogo Instituta v Konstantinopole* 11 (1906) 227-79

J. Wellhausen, 'Die Kämpfe der Araber mit den Römäern in der Zeit der Umaijaden', *Nachrichten der Königlichen Gesellschaft der Wissenschaften zu Göttingen Phil.-Hist. Klasse* 4 (1901) 1-34 (English trans by M. Bonner in 'Arab wars with the Byzantines in the Umayyad period', in M. Bonner (ed.), *Arab-Byzantine relations in early Islamic Times,* Aldershot, 2004, 31-64)

K. de Boor, 'Zur Chronographie des Theophanes', *Hermes* 25 (1890) 301-07

J. Classen, *Theophanes Chronographia*, 2 vols, Bonn, 1839-41, ii, pp. 556-668 (notes by F. Combefis)

Maria Vaiou 2008

Sayf ibn ʿUmar

DATE OF BIRTH Unknown
PLACE OF BIRTH Unknown
DATE OF DEATH Possibly 815 but maybe before 800
PLACE OF DEATH Possibly Kūfa

BIOGRAPHY

Nothing is known about the life of Sayf ibn ʿUmar al-Tamīmī, except that he is associated with southern Iraq, and was a writer of historical works. These were used as a main source by Abū Jaʿfar al-Ṭabarī for his *Taʾrīkh al-rusul wa-l-mulūk*, although their accuracy and objectivity were doubted from early times.

MAIN SOURCES OF INFORMATION

Primary
Ibn al-Nadīm, *Fihrist*, p. 106

Secondary
E. Landau-Tasseron, 'Sayf ibn ʿUmar in medieval and modern scholarship', *Der Islam* 67 (1990) 1-26
M. Hinds, 'Sayf b. ʿUmar's sources on Arabia', in *Studies on the history of Arabia. 1. Sources for the history of Arabia*, pt. 2, Riyadh, 1979, 3-16
Sezgin, GAS i, pp. 311-12

WORKS ON CHRISTIAN-MUSLIM RELATIONS

Kitāb al-ridda wa-l-futūḥ, Kitāb al-futūḥ al-kabīr wa-l-ridda, 'The great book of conquests and apostasy wars'

DATE Possibly late 8th c.
ORIGINAL LANGUAGE Arabic

DESCRIPTION
In the section on the assassination of the Caliph ʿUthmān, the work contains a brief account, on the authority of Ibn ʿAbbās, of the way in which Paul corrupted Christian doctrines by persuading three of

his followers, Yaʿqūb, Nasṭūr and Malkūn, of the divinity of Jesus, and sending them into disagreement over the nature of God. Only al-Muʾmin, 'the believer', resisted this as contrary to the true teachings of Jesus. He and his followers fled from the persecution inflicted by the others, and their descendants lived on in Arabia until the time of Muḥammad.

SIGNIFICANCE

This is a very early version of an explanation that is reproduced throughout Islamic history of how Christianity departed from true monotheism, of Paul's part in this, and of a believing remnant that remained true to the original teachings of Jesus which they recognized in the preaching of Muḥammad.

MANUSCRIPTS

MS Riyadh, Imām Muḥammad Ibn Saʿīd Islamic University, fols 127r-129v (no catalogue number, possibly 13th century)

EDITIONS AND TRANSLATIONS

P. van Koningsveld, 'The Islamic image of Paul and the origin of the Gospel of Barnabas', *JSAI* 20 (1996) 200-28, pp. 222-24 (trans.)

Sayf ibn ʿUmar, *Kitāb al-ridda wa-l-futūḥ and Kitāb al-jamal wa-masīr ʿĀʾisha wa-ʿAlī*, ed. Q. al-Samarrai, 2 vols, Leiden, 1995, i, pp. 132-35 (edition), ii, fols 62r-64v (facsimile)

STUDIES

Van Koningsveld, 'The Islamic image of Paul', pp. 200-3

David Thomas 2007

Theodore Abū Qurra

DATE OF BIRTH Mid-8th c.
PLACE OF BIRTH Probably Edessa
DATE OF DEATH Probably after 816
PLACE OF DEATH Perhaps Ḥarrān

BIOGRAPHY

Beyond the few items listed below, little is known about the events of Theodore Abū Qurra's life. He seems to have been a native of Edessa, and was born toward the middle of the 8th century. A Melkite, he was one of the earliest Christians known to have written in Arabic. While it has been suggested that as a young man he was a monk at the Palestinian monastery of Mār Saba, the evidence for this is both slight and dubious (Lamoreaux, 'The biography'). At an unknown date, he was ordained as the bishop of Ḥarrān, an important see just to the south of Edessa. Around 811, Thomas the Patriarch of Jerusalem had one of his Arabic Christological works translated into Greek and sent to the Monophysites of Armenia. According to a late Monophysite source, in about 813 he was deposed from his see by Theodoret, the Melkite Patriarch of Antioch, because of his heretical Christology, though this is hardly likely to have been the case (Lamoreaux, *Theodore Abū Qurrah*, pp. xiii-xv). Sometime between 813 and 817, he went to Armenia to debate with the Monophysites at the court of the Bagratid Prince Ashot Msakeri. Perhaps in 816, he translated into Arabic Pseudo-Aristotle's *De virtutibus animae*. A late text has him meeting the Caliph al-Maʾmūn in Ḥarrān in 829 and participating in a theological debate in his presence, though there are few reasons to trust this source (Lamoreaux, *Theodore Abū Qurrah*, pp. xvii-xviii), much less the later text that claims to be a record of this debate (see the entry below on 'The Debate of Abū Qurra'). The date of his death is unknown. Later authorities remembered him for his polemic against the Manicheans and Jews, his defense of icons, his defense of Melkite Christology against Monophysites and Nestorians, and his polemics against Islam.

Theodore's originally large corpus of writings in Arabic, Greek, and Syriac has been preserved only in part. The history of their transmission is still not well understood, nor in particular the relation between his Arabic works and the Greek fragments ascribed to him. Very nearly all his works also unfortunately still lack critical editions.

Among Theodore's works, a full 30 deal with the challenges of Islam in one manner or another. Sixteen of these are in Arabic and the remainder in Greek. A handful of these works are substantial treatises, but most are quite short, even fragmentary.

Among Theodore's Arabic works that treat Islam, a large number seek to defend Christianity through a comparison of the manner of its propagation with the way in which Islam was propagated. Key for Theodore is that those who first preached Christianity were unable to offer potential converts promises of wealth, power, or pleasures; on the contrary, they could promise only hardship and humility. And yet a great many accepted Christianity. How could this be? Theodore reasons that it could only have happened if its earliest preachers had confirmed their message through the performance of miracles. All this stands in contrast to the other religions of the early medieval Near East, particularly Islam. As Theodore viewed the matter, these other religions were accepted because they offered an ethic that catered to human desire. Converts, for example, might receive political power or wealth, be allowed multiple wives or divorce at will, and so on. And of equal importance, none of these religions, Islam included, could demonstrate that its founder had been attested by miracles.

Another prominent theme in Theodore's writings on Islam is the defense of the reasonableness of Christian doctrine and practice. Not surprisingly, the doctrines of the Trinity and the Incarnation are of paramount concern. On a great many occasions, Theodore seeks to show that neither doctrine contravenes the dictates of reason or the commonly accepted notions about God's attributes. Of near equal importance for Theodore are the defense of free will and of the related topic of the Christian understanding of salvation – that human beings can be saved only through the death of Christ, the eternal Son of God made human. On the matter of Christian practice, subjects of concern include: baptism, the eucharist, and most especially the veneration of icons and the cross.

Theodore's Arabic works seldom mention Islam by name. He speaks instead, obliquely, of 'those who lay claim to faith' or 'those who claim to have a book sent down by God'. However, that Islam is frequently the subject of his concern in his defense of Christianity is confirmed by his subtle use of qurʾānic language and his frequent use of the technical terminology of Muslim theology. The situation is quite different in his Greek works. Here his opponents are almost always explicitly identified as Saracens, Hagarenes, or Arabs. Moreover, the tenor of his arguments is far from subtle, even to the point of accusing the prophet of Islam of moral turpitude, insanity, and willful distortion of the truth or, perhaps most strikingly, of having been possessed by a demon. The remarkably different approaches to Islam evinced by his works in Arabic and Greek might best be explained by reference to the audiences for whom he was writing, and perhaps also by a measure of circumspection and fear.

Taken as a whole, Theodore's works on Islam represent one of the earliest and most detailed defenses of Christianity against the claims of the other faith. Judging from the number of extant manuscripts, his Arabic works seem not to have been widely read or copied in the Middle Ages – perhaps because of the difficulty of their language, or perhaps because they did not have the same appeal as later, more systematic treatises. The situation was far different with his Greek works, which were widely circulated in manuscript form. Most of these Greek works also exist in Georgian translation, and in this form enjoyed an immense popularity. (For the Georgian tradition of Theodore's works, see Tarchnišvili, *Geschichte der kirchlichen georgischen Literatur*, pp. 129, 206, 208-9, 366, 370-71, 375, 380, 385.)

MAIN SOURCES OF INFORMATION

Primary

G. Graf, *Die Schriften des Jacobiten Ḥabīb Ibn Ḫidma Abū Rā'iṭa*, Louvain, 1951 (*CSCO* 130), pp. 65-66, 73, 75-76, 79-80, 82-83, 86, 163 (references to Theodore's Christology, as well as his journey to Armenia)

Nonnus of Nisibis, *Commentary on the Gospel of John*, in A. van Roey, *Nonnus de Nisibe*, Louvain, 1948, pp. 6-9 (trans. of the relevant passage, originally written in Arabic and preserved only in Armenian; without mentioning Theodore by name, the preface to this work makes reference to his visit to Armenia)

L. Cheikho, *Eutychii patriarchae alexandrini annales*, 2 vols, Beirut, 1906-9 (*CSCO* 50-51), ii, p. 64 (that Theodore wrote in defense of icons)

ʿAbd al-Jabbār al-Hamadhānī, *Al-mughnī fī abwāb al-tawḥīd wa-l-ʿadl*, vol. 5, ed. M.M. al-Khuḍayrī, Cairo, 1958, pp. 144-45 (brief mention of a theological argument of Theodore)

The Passion of Michael the Sabaite, in K. Kekelidze (ed.), *Monumenta hagiographica georgica, pars prima. Keimena*, 2 vols, Tbilisi, 1918, i, pp. 165-73; for Latin and English translations, see respectively P. Peeters, 'La passion de S. Michel le Sabaïte', *AB* 48 (1930) 65-98, and M. Blanchard, 'The Georgian version of the martyrdom of Saint Michael, monk of Mar Sabas monastery', *Aram* 6 (1994) 149-63 (this text presents our Theodore as the narrator, perhaps confusing him with Theodore of Edessa; see Lamoreaux, 'The biography', pp. 26-32)

S.K. Samir, 'Un traité nouveau de Sawīrus Ibn al-Muqaffaʿ. La lettre à Abū al-Yumn Quzmān Ibn Mīnā', *Pd'O* 25 (2000) 567-641, pp. 605-6, 614 (brief mention of Theodore as one of the leading Melkite theologians)

Ibn al-Nadīm, *Fihrist*, p. 26 (reading 'Qurrah' for "Izzah') and p. 207 (that Theodore wrote against Nestorius and that he had been refuted by a Muslim)

B. Martin-Hisard, 'La Vie de Jean et Euthyme et le statut du monastère des Ibères sur l'Athos', *REB* 49 (1991) 67-142, p. 86 (on the Life of Euthymius, stating that Theodore's works had been translated from Georgian into Greek; cf. A. Mahé and J.-P. Mahé, *La sagesse de Balahvar*, Paris, 1993, p. 26, who suggest that a textual error underlies this passage)

J.-B. Chabot, *Chronique de Michel le Syrien, patriarche jacobite d'Antioche (1116-1199)*, 4 vols, Paris, 1899-1924, iii, pp. 32-34 (trans.), iv, p. 495 (text)

J.-B. Chabot and A. Abouna, *Anonymi auctoris chronicon ad annum Christi 1234 pertinens*, 4 vols, Paris, 1916, 1920, 1937, 1974 (*CSCO* 81-82, 109, 354), ii, p. 23 (text), iv, p. 16 (trans.) (reference to Theodore's debate before al-Maʾmūn)

R. Thomson, 'The historical compilation of Vardan Arewelcʿi', *DOP* 43 (1989) 125-226, p. 183 (on Theodore's visit to Armenia)

Bar Hebraeus, *Mnorat qudshê*, as cited by Assemani, *BO* ii, p. 292 (that Theodore was one of the first to teach that Christ has two wills)

M. Brosset, *Histoire chronologique par Mkhithar d'Aïrivank, XIIIe S.*, St Petersburg, 1869, p. 83 (on Theodore's visit to Armenia)

Abū l-Barakāt ibn Kabar, *Miṣbāḥ al-ẓulma fī īḍāḥ al-khidma*, ed. S.K. Samir, Cairo, 1971, p. 301 (wrongly identifying Theodore as a Nestorian)

Daniel ibn al-Khaṭṭāb, *Kitāb al-ishrāq fī l-uṣūl al-dīniyya*, as cited in L. Cheikho, *Vingt traités théologiques d'auteurs arabes chrétiens (IXe-XIIIe siècles)*, Beirut, 1920, p. 75 (that Theodore was one of the first to teach that Christ has two wills)

John Kyparissiotes, *Ekthesis stoicheiōdēs tōn rhēseōn theologikōn*, *PG* 152, cols 784, 809 (Latin trans. only); for the Greek text, see Hemmerdinger, 'Le synode réuni par Théodore Abū Qurra contre les manichéens', p. 270 (that Theodore participated in a council against the Manicheans)

Secondary

D. Bertaina, 'The development of testimony collections in early Christian apologetics with Islam', in D. Thomas (ed.), *The Bible in Arab Christianity*, Leiden, 2007, 151-73, pp. 168-71

S. Keating, *Defending the 'People of truth' in the early Islamic period. The Christian apologies of Abū Rā'iṭah*, Leiden, 2006, pp. 35-48, 347-57

S.H. Griffith, 'The church of Jerusalem and the "Melkites". The making of an "Arab Orthodox" Christian identity in the world of Islam (750-1050 CE)', in O. Limor and G. Stroumsa (eds), *Christians and Christianity in the Holy Land. From the origins to the Latin kingdoms*, 2006, 175-204, pp. 198-202

J. Lamoreaux, *Theodore Abū Qurrah*, Provo UT, 2005

S.K. Samir, *Abú Qurrah. Vida, bibliografía y obras*, trans. J. Monferrer Sala, Córdoba, 2005 (augmented trans. of Samir's two pamphlets on Abū Qurrah published in 2000)

M. Beaumont, *Christology in dialogue with Muslims. A critical analysis of Christian presentations of Christ for Muslims from the ninth and twentieth centuries*, Oxford, 2005, pp. 28-43, 93-112

I. Dorfmann-Lazarev, *Arméniens et Byzantins à l'époque de Photius. Deux débats théologiques après le triomphe de l'Orthodoxie*, Louvain, 2004, pp. 68-79

J. Monferrer Sala, 'Una muestra de *kalām* cristiano. Abū Qurra en la sección novena del *Kitāb muŷādalat ma' al-mutakallimīn al-muslimīn fī maŷlis al-Jalīfa al-Ma'mūn*', *Revista española de filosofía medieval* 10 (2003) 75-86

J. Lamoreaux, 'The biography of Theodore Abū Qurrah revisited', *DOP* 56 (2002) 25-40

D. Schon, 'Zur Wahrnehmung des Islam in den Ostkirchen des 9. und 10. Jahrhunderts', *Ostkirchliche Studien* 51 (2002) 29-51, pp. 39-44

D. Thomas, *Early Muslim polemic against Christianity. Abū 'Īsā al-Warrāq's 'Against the Incarnation'*, Cambridge, 2002, pp. 51-54, 78

Y. Maximov, 'Feodor Abu Kurra i ego mesto v istorii ranneĭ pravoslavnoĭ polemiki s islamon', *Bogoslovskiĭ sbornik* 10 (2002) 114-23

J. Lamoreaux, 'Theodore Abū Qurrah and John the Deacon', *Greek, Roman and Byzantine Studies* 42 (2001) 361-86

S.H. Griffith, '"Melkites", "Jacobites" and the christological controversies in Arabic in third/ninth-century Syria', in D. Thomas (ed.), *Syrian Christians under Islam. The first thousand years*, Leiden, 2001, 9-55, pp. 32-34, 36-53

S.H. Griffith, 'The *Life of Theodore of Edessa*. History, hagiography and religious apologetics in Mar Saba Monastery in early Abbasid times', in J. Patrich (ed.), *The Sabaite heritage in the Orthodox Church from the fifth century to the present*, Louvain, 2001, 147-69, pp. 152-54, 157-58

B. Outtier, 'Le Dogmatikon d'Arsène d'Iqalto et ses modèles grecs', *Le Muséon* 114 (2001) 217-26, pp. 221-24

S.K. Samir, *Abu Qurra. al-Mu'allifāt*, Beirut, 2000

S.K. Samir, *Abu Qurra. Sīra wa-l-marāji'*, Beirut, 2000

S.K. Samir, 'Al-jadīd fī sīrat Thāwudūrus Abī Qurra wa-āthārihi', *Al-Mashriq* 73 (1999) 417-49

S.H. Griffith, 'The monk in the emir's *majlis*. Reflections on a popular genre of Christian literary apologetics in Arabic in the early Islamic period', in H. Lazarus-Yafeh et al. (eds), *The majlis. Interreligious encounters in medieval Islam*, Wiesbaden, 1999, 13-65, pp. 38-48

S.H. Griffith, 'The Qur'ān in Arab Christian texts. The development of an apologetical argument. Abū Qurrah in the *mağlis* of al-Ma'mūn', *Pd'O* 24 (1999) 203-33

M. Swanson, 'Beyond prooftexting. Approaches to the Qur'ān in some early Arabic Christian apologies', *MW* 88 (1998) 297-319, pp. 312-14

M. Cacouros, 'La division des biens dans le *Compendium* d'éthique par Abū Qurra et Ibn al-Ṭayyib et ses rapports avec la *Grande morale* et le *Florilège* de Stobée', in A. Hasnawi, A. Elamrani-Jamal and M. Aouad (eds), *Perspectives arabes et médiévales sur la tradition scientifique et philosophique grecque*, Louvain, 1997, 289-318

S.H. Griffith, 'Byzantium and the Christians in the world of Islam. Constantinople and the church in the Holy Land in the ninth century', *Medieval Encounters* 3 (1997) 231-65, pp. 253-57

S.H. Griffith, 'The view of Islam from the monasteries of Palestine in the early 'Abbāsid period. Theodore Abū Qurrah and the *Summa theologiae arabica*', *ICMR* 7 (1996) 9-28

S.H. Griffith, 'Michael, the martyr and monk of Mar Sabas Monastery, at the court of the Caliph 'Abd al-Malik. Christian apologetics and martyrology in the early Islamic period', *Aram* 6 (1994) 115-48

S.H. Griffith, 'Reflections on the biography of Theodore Abū Qurrah', *Pd'O* 18 (1993) 143-70

S. Rissanen, *Theological encounter of oriental Christians with Islam during early Abbasid Rule*, Åbo, 1993, pp. 20-23 et passim

S.H. Griffith, *Theodore Abū Qurrah. The intellectual profile of an Arab Christian writer of the first Abbasid century*, Tel Aviv, 1992

S. Rissanen, 'Der richtige Sinn der Bibel bei Theodor Abu Qurra', in H.-O. Kvist (ed.), *Bibelauslegung und Gruppenidentität*, Åbo, 1992, 79-90

J. Lamoreaux, 'An unedited tract against the Armenians by Theodore Abū Qurrah', *Le Muséon* 105 (1992) 327-41

W. Madelung, 'Al-Qāsim Ibn Ibrāhīm and Christian theology', *Aram* 3 (1991) 35-44

W. Klein, *Die Argumentation in den griechisch-christlichen Antimanichaica*, Wiesbaden, 1991, pp. 229-38

I. Dick, 'La discussion d'Abū Qurra avec les ulémas musulmans devant le calife al-Ma'mūn', *Pd'O* 16 (1990-91) 107-13
S.H. Griffith, 'Islam and the *Summa theologiae Arabica*. Rabīʿ I, 264 A.H.', *JSAI* 13 (1990) 225-64, pp. 227-37, 260-63
S.K. Samir, 'La littérature melkite sous les premiers abbassides', *OCP* 56 (1990) 469-86, pp. 476-81
J. Declerck, 'Le patriarche Gennade de Constantinople (458-471) et un opuscule inédit contre les Nestoriens', *Byzantion* 60 (1990) 130-44
J.-M. Sauget, 'Un homéliaire melkite bipartite. Le manuscrit *Beyrouth, Bibliothèque Orientale 510*', *Le Muséon* 101 (1988) 231-90, p. 256
S.H. Griffith, 'The monks of Palestine and the growth of Christian literature in Arabic', *MW* 78 (1988) 1-28, pp. 22-26
S.H. Griffith, 'A ninth century *Summa theologiae arabica*', in S.K. Samir (ed.), *Actes du deuxième congrès international d'études arabes chrétiennes (1984)*, Rome, 1986, 123-41, pp. 128-36
S.K. Samir, 'La "Somme des aspects de la foi", oeuvre d'Abū Qurrah?' in S.K. Samir (ed.), *Actes du deuxième congrès international d'études arabes chrétiennes (1984)*, Rome, 1986, 93-121
S.H. Griffith, 'Greek into Arabic. Life and letters in the monasteries of Palestine in the ninth century. The example of the *Summa theologiae arabica*', *Byzantion* 106 (1986) 117-38, pp. 124-33, 136-38
S.H. Griffith, 'Stephen of Ramlah and the Christian kerygma in Arabic in ninth-century Palestine', *Journal of Ecclesiastical History* 36 (1985) 23-45, pp. 32-37, 42-44
M. van Esbroeck, 'Le "De sectis" attribué à Léonce de Byzance (CPG 6823) dans la version géorgienne d'Arsène Iqaltoeli', *Bedi kartlisa* 42 (1984) 35-52, pp. 36, 38-39, 44
G. Monnot, 'Les doctrines des chrétiens dans le "Moghni" de ʿAbd al-Jabbār', *MIDEO* 16 (1983) 9-30, pp. 15 and 25 n. 19
S.K. Samir, 'Note sur les citations bibliques chez Abū Qurrah', *OCP* 49 (1983) 184-91
S.K. Samir, 'Thayūdūrus Abū Qurra', *Majallat al-majmaʿ al-ʿilmī l-ʿirāqī* 7 (1983) 138-60
R. Caspar et al., 'Bibliographie du dialogue islamo-chrétien (6)', *Islamochristiana* 6 (1980) 259-99, pp. 290-93
Nasrallah, *HMLEM* ii.2, pp. 104-34
S.H. Griffith, *The controversial theology of Theodore Abū Qurrah (c. 750-c. 820 A.D.). A methodological, comparative study in Christian Arabic literature*, Washington DC, 1978 (Diss. Catholic University of America)
I. Lolašvili, *Arsen Iq'altoeli (cxovreba da moɣvac'eoba)*, Tbilisi, 1978, pp. 112-23
S.K. Samir, 'Théodore de Mopsueste dans le "Fihrist" d'Ibn an-Nadīm', *Le Muséon* 90 (1977) 355-63

M. Richard and M. Aubineau, *Iohannis Caesariensis presbyteri et grammatici opera quae supersunt*, Turnhout, 1977 (*Corpus Christianorum Series Graeca* 1), pp. 113-15

L. Datiašvili, 'Arsen Iq'altoelis targani Teodore Abuk'uras t'rakt'at'isa "Saɣmrtoysa da garešisa pilosoposobisatvis"', in I. Lolašvili (ed.), *Dzveli kartuli lit'erat'ura (XI-XVIII ss.)*, Tbilisi, 1977, 20-40

L. Datiašvili, 'Kartul-bizant'iuri lit'erat'uruli urtiertobas ist'oriidan', *Dzveli kartuli mc'erlobisa da rustvelologiis sak'itxebi* 7-8 (1976) 65-101

J. Nasrallah, 'L'église melchite en Iraq, en Perse et dans l'Asie centrale (3)', *Proche-Orient Chrétien* 26 (1976) 319-53, p. 345

S.K. Samir, 'Les plus anciens homéliaires géorgiens et les versions patristiques arabes', *OCP* 42 (1976) 217-31, p. 229

R. Caspar et al., 'Bibliographie du dialogue islamo-chrétien (1)', *Islamochristiana* 1 (1975) 125-81, pp. 154-56, 170-71

L. Datiašvili, '"Tedore Edeselis Cxovreba" da "Abuk'ura"', *Dzveli kartuli mc'erlobisa da rustvelologiis sak'itxebi* 5 (1973) 144-74

L. Datiašvili, '"Abuk'uras" originalobis sak'itxisatvis', *Macne* 39 (1967) 169-94

M. Kellermann, *Ein pseudoaristotelischer Traktat über die Tugend. Edition und Übersetzung der arabischen Fassungen des Abū Qurra und des Ibn aṭ-Ṭayyib*, Erlangen-Nürnberg, 1965 (Diss. Friedrich-Alexander-Universität)

J. Gauß, 'Glaubensdiskussionen zwischen Ostkirche und Islam im 8.-11. Jahrhundert', *Theologische Zeitschrift* 19 (1963) 14-28, pp. 15-17

I. Dick, 'Un continuateur arabe de saint Jean Damascène. Théodore Abuqurra, évêque melkite de Harran. La personne et son milieu', *Proche-Orient Chrétien* 12 (1962) 209-23, 317-32; 13 (1963) 114-29

B. Hemmerdinger, 'Le synode réuni par Théodore Abū Qurra contre les manichéens (Ḥarrān, 764-765?)', *RHR* 161 (1962) 270

K. K'ek'elidze, *Et'iudebi dzveli kartuli lit'erat'uris ist'oriidan*, 13 vols, Tbilisi, 1945-74, v, pp. 55-57, vi, pp. 18-40

D. Lang, 'St Euthymius the Georgian and the Barlaam and Ioasaph romance', *BSOAS* 17 (1955) 306-25, pp. 315-16

E. Hammerschmidt, 'Einige philosophisch-theologische Grundbegriffe bei Leontius von Byzanz, Johannes von Damaskus und Theodor Abû Qurra', *Ostkirchliche Studien* 4 (1955) 147-57

M. Tarchnišvili, *Geschichte der kirchlichen georgischen Literatur*, Rome, 1955, pp. 129, 206, 208-9, 366, 370-71, 375, 380, 385

Graf, *GCAL* ii, pp. 7-26

R. Walzer, 'New light on the Arabic translations of Aristotle', *Oriens* 6 (1953) 91-142, p. 99 *et passim*

A. Vööbus, *Studies in the history of the Gospel text in Syriac*, Louvain, 1951 (*CSCO* 128), pp. 158-62

A. Abel, 'La portée apologétique de la "vie" de S. Théodore d'Edesse', *Byzantinoslavica* 10 (1949) 229-40

A. van Roey, *Nonnus de Nisibe. Traité apologétique*, Louvain, 1948, pp. 3-22
A. Vasiliev, 'The life of St. Theodore of Edessa', *Byzantion* 16 (1942-43) 165-225, pp. 212-16
H. Beck, *Vorsehung und Vorherbestimmung in der theologischen Literatur der Byzantiner*, Rome, 1937, pp. 40-43
W. Eichner, 'Die Nachrichten über den Islam bei den Byzantinern', *Der Islam* 23 (1936) 133-62, 197-244, pp. 136-38 et passim
A. Tritton, 'The Bible text of Theodore Abu Kurra', *Journal of Theological Studies* 34 (1933) 52-54
P. Kraus, 'Zu Ibn al-Muqaffa'', *RSO* 14 (1933) 1-20, p. 3, n. 3
M. Jugie, 'Quaedam testimonia Byzantinorum de glorificatione humanitatis Christi a primo instanti conceptionis', *Angelicum* 9 (1932) 469-76, pp. 473-75
G. Graf, 'Christliche Polemik gegen den Islam', *Gelbe Hefte. Historische und politische Blätter für das katholische Deutschland* 2 (1926) 825-42, pp. 827-28
A. Guillaume, 'Theodore Abu Qurra as apologist', *MW* 15 (1925) 42-51
A. Guillaume, 'A debate between Christian and Muslim doctors', *Journal of the Royal Asiatic Society, Centenary Supplement* (1924) 233-44
L. Cheikho, *Kitāb al-makhṭūṭāt al-ʿarabiyya li-katabat al-naṣrāniyya*, Beirut, 1924, pp. 23-24
L. Mariès, 'Epikoura = Aboukara', *Revue des études arméniennes* 1 (1920-21) 439-41
L. Mariès, 'Un commentaire sur l'évangile de saint Jean, rédigé en arabe (circa 840) par Nonnos (Nana) de Nisibe, conservé dans une traduction arménienne (circa 856)', *Revue des études arméniennes* 1 (1920-21) 273-96
I. Krachkovskiĭ, 'Ḟedor Abū-Ḳurra u musul´manskikh pisateleĭ IX-X bi͡eka', *Khristianskiĭ vostok* 4 (1916) 302-9
C. Becker, 'Christliche Polemik und islamische Dogmenbildung', *Zeitschrift für Assyriologie* 26 (1912) 175-95
C. Güterbock, *Der Islam im Lichte der byzantinischen Polemik*, Berlin, 1912, pp. 12-16
F. Nau, 'Notice historique sur le monastère de Qartamin, suivie d'une note sur le monastère de Qennešrê', in *Actes du XIVe congrès international des orientalistes (Alger 1905), deuxième partie*, Paris, 1907, 37-135, pp. 66-69
F. Nau, 'Lettre du R. P. Constantin Bacha. Sur un nouveau manuscrit carchouni de la Chronique de Michel le Syrien et sur Théodore Abu-Kurra', *Revue de l'Orient Chrétien* 11 (1906) 102-4
H. Goussen, review of Bacha's editions of works by Theodore, *Theologische Revue* 5 (1906) 148-49
N. Marr, 'Arkaun, mongol´skoe nazvanie khrictian, v cvi͡azi s voprosom ob armi͡anakh-khalkedonitakh', *VV* 12 (1905) 1-68, pp. 8-15, 28, 37

G. Graf, *Die christlich-arabische Literatur bis zur fränkischen Zeit*, Freiburg im Breisgau, 1905, pp. 31-37

WORKS ON CHRISTIAN-MUSLIM RELATIONS

Maymar fī wujūd al-Khāliq wa-l-dīn al-qawīm, 'Treatise on the existence of the Creator and the true religion'

DATE Late 8th or early 9th c.
ORIGINAL LANGUAGE Arabic

DESCRIPTION
Since Cheikho's edition of 1912, this work is generally referred to under the title given above. In the al-Shīr MS from which that edition was made, however, the work is untitled. In the Shuwayr MS, the work is entitled, *Fī ḥaqīqa wujūd Allāh wa-annahu muthallath al-aqānīm wa-ḥaqīqat al-dīn al-masīḥī wa-anna lā dīn fī l-ʿālam ghayrahu qaṭṭ*, 'On the truth of the existence of God and that he a Trinity of hypostases and on the truth of the Christian religion and that there is absolutely no religion in the world other than it'.

This work consists of three (seemingly) independent treatises that have been joined together in the course of transmission. The first (ed. Dick, pp. 173-98) is an attempt to show what the human mind can and cannot discover about God and his attributes on the basis of natural reason alone. The second (ed. Dick, pp. 199-258) seeks to determine which of the religions of the early medieval Near East has the greatest claim to truth. The author begins by imagining that he grew up on a mountain alone and that he then descends to the world of civilization. After meeting adherents of the various religions, including Islam, the author tries to find a methodology to help him discover which of these religions are false, and for what reasons, and which one is true, and for what reasons. The third (ed. Dick, pp. 259-70) examines the various reasons that lead people to accept a religion, and argues that Christianity is true in that it alone was correctly propagated and attested by miracles.

SIGNIFICANCE
This work is one of Theodore's most systematic investigations of theological epistemology and one of his few works in Arabic to deal explicitly with the challenges of Islam.

MANUSCRIPTS

MS Shuwayr, Dayr al-Shuwayr – 215 (formerly 43), 6th work (1532) (cf. J. Nasrallah, *Catalogue des manuscrits du Liban*, 4 vols, Beirut, 1958-70, iii, 223-26, no. 334 [134])

MS al-Shīr, Dayr al-Shīr – 373, pp. 2-59 (late 17th or early 18th c.)

EDITIONS AND TRANSLATIONS

Lamoreaux, *Theodore Abū Qurrah*, pp. 1-25, 41-47, 165-74 (English trans. with numerous conjectural emendations to Dick's edition)

J. Monferrer Sala, '"Apologética racionalista" de Abū Qurrah en el *Maymar fī wujūd al-Ḫāliq wa-l-dīn al-qawīm* II/2,12-14', *Anales del seminario de historia de la filosofia* 22 (2005) 41-56 (Spanish trans. of pp. 240-53 of Dick's edition)

G. Monnot, 'Abū Qurra et la pluralité des religions', *RHR* 208 (1991) 49-71 (trans. of pp. 200-18 in Dick's edition, with important conjectural emendations)

G. Khoury, *Theodore Abu Qurrah (c. 750-820). Translation and critical analysis of his 'Treatise on the existence of the Creator and on the true religion'*, Berkeley CA, 1990 (Diss. Graduate Theological Union)

I. Dick, *Théodore Abuqurra. Traité de l'existence du Créateur et de la vraie religion / Maymar fī wujūd al-Khāliq wa-l-dīn al-qawīm li-Thāwudhūrus Abī Qurra*, Jounieh, 1982 (edition based on the Dayr al-Shīr MS)

I. Dick, *Théodore Abuqurra, évêque melkite de Harran (750?-825?). Introduction générale, texte et analyse du traité De l'existence du Créateur et de la vraie religion*, Louvain, 1960 (Diss. Université Catholique de Louvain) (edition based on the Dayr al-Shīr MS, with a French trans.)

G. Graf, *Des Theodor Abû Ḳurra Traktat über den Schöpfer und die wahre Religion*, Münster, 1913 (German trans. of Cheikho's edition)

L. Cheikho, *Traité inédit de Théodore Abou-Qurra (Abucara), évêque melchite de Harran (ca. 740-820), sur l'existence de Dieu et la vraie religion*, Beirut, 1912 (repr. of the edition published in *Al-Mashriq*)

L. Cheikho, 'Maymar li-Tādurus Abī Qurra fī wujūd al-khāliq wa-l-dīn al-qawīm', *Al-Mashriq* 15 (1912) 757-74, 825-42 (edited from the Dayr al-Shīr MS)

STUDIES

M. Beaumont, "'Ammār al-Baṣrī on the alleged corruption of the Gospels', in D. Thomas (ed.), *The Bible in Arab Christianity*, Leiden, 2007, 241-55 (for parallels to Theodore's arguments in defense of the true religion)

M. Swanson, 'The Trinity in Christian-Muslim conversation', *Dialog. A Journal of Theology* 44 (2005) 256-63, pp. 258-59

B. Roggema, '*Ḥikāyāt amthāl wa asmār* ... King parables in Melkite apologetic literature', in R. Ebied and H. Teule (eds), *Studies on the Christian Arabic heritage*, Louvain, 2004, 113-31

G. Reinink, 'Communal identity and the systematisation of knowledge in the Syriac "Cause of all causes"', in P. Binkley (ed.), *Premodern encyclopaedic texts*, Leiden, 1997, 275-88, pp. 280-81 (on the similarity between Theodore's work and a work composed in the 10th century by a Syrian Orthodox bishop of Edessa)

S.H. Griffith, 'Faith and reason in Christian *kalām*. Theodore Abū Qurrah on discerning the true religion', in S.K. Samir and J. Nielsen (eds), *Christian Arabic apologetics during the Abbasid period (750-1258)*, Leiden, 1994, 1-43

J. Nasrallah, 'Regard critique sur I. Dick, Th. Abû Qurra, De l'existence du Créateur et de la vraie religion', *Proche-Orient Chrétien* 36 (1986) 46-62; 37 (1987) 63-70

I. Dick, 'Le traité de Théodore Abū Qurra de l'existence du Créateur et de la vraie religion', in S.K. Samir (ed.), *Actes du premier congrès international d'études arabes chrétiennes (1980)*, 149-68, Rome, 1982

S.H. Griffith, 'Comparative religion in the apologetics of the first Christian Arabic theologians', *Proceedings of the patristic, medieval, and renaissance conference* 4 (1979) 63-87, pp. 65-66

H. Davidson, 'John Philoponus as a source of medieval Islamic and Jewish proofs of creation', *JAOS* 89 (1969) 357-91, p. 374

G. Klinge, 'Die Bedeutung der syrischen Theologen als Vermittler der griechischen Philosophie an den Islam', *Zeitschrift für Kirchengeschichte* 58 (1939) 346-86, pp. 376-84

P. de Menasce, 'Autour d'un texte syriaque inédit sur la religion des Mages', *BSOAS* 9 (1938) 587-601, pp. 600-1

Maymar yuḥaqqiqu li-l-insān ḥurriyya thābita min Allāh fī khalīqatihi wa-anna ḥurriyyat al-insān lā yadkhulu ʿalayhā l-qahr min wajh min al-wujūh battatan, 'Treatise confirming that human beings have an innate freedom from God in his creation (of them) and that absolutely no compulsion in any manner constrains the freedom of human beings'

DATE Late 8th or early 9th c.
ORIGINAL LANGUAGE Arabic

DESCRIPTION
This treatise investigates the nature of human free will. Theodore seeks to show the error both of those who deny that human beings were created with free will (Muslims) and of those who claim that they have lost their ability to choose freely (Manicheans). He then turns to the problem of God's foreknowledge and argues that such foreknowledge both exists and does not entail compulsion.

SIGNIFICANCE
While Theodore never mentions the Muslims by name in this treatise, they are clearly one of his two major opponents. This is evidenced, in particular, by the qurʾānic allusions he employs in describing their theological position.

MANUSCRIPTS
MS Sinai – Ar. 581 (12th c.). This MS, which is lacking at its beginning and end, is said to contain nine treatises by Theodore, very likely including this one. No copy was made during the Sinai expedition of the early 1950s. It most probably contains the same works as MS Joun, Dayr al-Mukhalliṣ – 392.
MS Tyr, Library of the Greek-Catholic Archbishop – 45, 2nd work, incomplete (1730). Cf. Nasrallah, *Catalogue des manuscrits du Liban*, iii, pp. 120-21. The MSS of this library are believed to have been transferred to Dayr al-Mukhalliṣ during the Lebanese civil war.

MS Joun, Dayr al-Mukhalliṣ – 392 (Haddad), 1st work (1735). It was copied from a MS dated 1051, which was in turn copied from a MS from the monastery of Mār Sabas. This is the MS from which Bacha edited this and the following works. It is not clear whether it is still to be found at Dayr al-Mukhalliṣ. Many MSS were taken when the monastery was pillaged by the Druze in April of 1985, though some, but not all, were apparently returned. It is believed that while they were out of the monastery many of the MSS were microfilmed by the Asad National Library in Damascus.

EDITIONS AND TRANSLATIONS

Lamoreaux, *Theodore Abū Qurrah*, pp. 195-206 (trans.)

P. Pizzi and S.K. Samir, *Teodoro Abū Qurra. La libertà / Thāwudūrus Abū Qurra. Maymar fī al-ḥurriyya*, Turin, 2001 (detailed study of the text, with Italian trans. and re-edition of Bacha's edition [no MSS could be consulted])

G. Graf, *Die arabischen Schriften des Theodor Abû Qurra, Bischofs von Ḥarrān (ca. 740-820)*, Paderborn, 1910, pp. 223-38 (German trans.)

C. Bacha, *Mayāmir Thāwudūrus Abī Qurra usquf Ḥarrān*, Beirut, (1904), pp. 9-22 (edited from the Dayr al-Mukhalliṣ MS)

STUDIES

S. Stroumsa and G. Stroumsa, 'Aspects of anti-Manichaean polemics in late antiquity and under early Islam', *Harvard Theological Review* 81 (1988) 37-58, p. 55 (argues that this treatise is not directed against the Muslims)

S.H. Griffith, 'Free will in Christian *kalām*. The doctrine of Theodore Abū Qurrah', *Pd'O* 14 (1987) 79-107

A. Abel, 'Les sources arabes sur le manichéisme', *Annuaire de l'institut de philologie et d'histoire orientales et slaves* 16 (1961-62) 31-73, pp. 32-33

Maymar yuḥaqqiqu annahu lā yulzamu l-Naṣārā an yaqūlū thalātha āliha idh yaqūlūna l-Āb ilāh wa-l-Ibn ilāh wa-Rūḥ al-Qudus (ilāh) wa-anna l-Āb wa-l-Ibn wa-Rūḥ al-Qudus ilāh wa-law kāna kull wāḥid minhum tāmm ʿalā ḥidatihi, 'Treatise confirming that Christians do not necessarily speak of three gods when they say that the Father is God and the Son is God and the Holy Spirit is God, and that the Father, Son, and Holy Spirit are one God, even though each of them is fully God by himself'

DATE Late 8th or early 9th c.
ORIGINAL LANGUAGE Arabic

DESCRIPTION
This treatise begins with a series of reflections on the motives that lead people to accept or reject a religion and argues against those who would accept a religion that caters to their desires or is characterized by tribal zeal. Theodore then turns to a defense of the Christian doctrine of the Trinity, against those who would either deny that each of the persons is God or claim that Christians worship three gods. His arguments are based on both scripture and reason.

SIGNIFICANCE
This treatise is one of Theodore's most detailed defenses of the doctrine of the Trinity. His opponents are both Jews and Muslims, though the latter are never explicitly named.

MANUSCRIPTS
MS Sinai – New Finds, paper, Ar. 4, 5th work (1191). Cf. Y. Meimaris, *Katālūj al-makhṭūṭāt al-ʿarabiyya al-muktashafa ḥadīthan bi-Dayr Sānt Kātarīn al-muqaddas bi-Ṭūr Sīnāʾ*, Athens, 1985, p. 39. The identification should be considered provisional. The catalogue describes this treatise by Theodore Abū Qurra, Bishop of Ḥarrān, as a defense of the confession of the oneness of God and a refutation of the enemies of Christianity who would disparage this confession.)
MS Sinai – Ar. 581 (12th c.) (see comments on p. 451 above)

MS Shuwayr, Dayr al-Shuwayr – 215 (formerly 43), 2nd work (1532) (see comments on p. 449 above)
MS al-Shīr, Dayr al-Shīr – 373, pp. 99-128 (late 17th or early 18th c.)
MS Tyr, Library of the Greek-Catholic Archbishop – 45, 3rd work (1730) (see comments on p. 451 above)
MS Joun, Dayr al-Mukhalliṣ – 392 (Haddad), 2nd work (1735) (see comments on p. 452 above)

EDITIONS AND TRANSLATIONS

Lamoreaux, *Theodore Abū Qurrah*, pp. 175-93 (English trans.)
Graf, *Die arabischen Schriften*, pp. 133-60 (German trans.)
Bacha, *Mayāmir*, pp. 23-47 (ed. from the Dayr al-Mukhalliṣ MS)

STUDIES —

Maymar fī mawt al-Masīḥ wa-annā idhā qulnā inna l-Masīḥ māta ʿannā innamā naqūlu inna l-Ibn al-azalī l-mawlūd min al-Āb qabla l-duhūr huwa lladhī māta ʿannā lā fī ṭabīʿatihi l-ilāhiyya bal fī ṭabīʿatihi l-insāniyya wa-kayfa yuʿqalu hādhā l-mawt wa-annahu yaḥsunu an yuqālu ʿalā l-Ibn al-azalī fī l-jiha llatī taqūluhu ʿalayhi al-urthūdhuksiyya, 'Treatise on the death of Christ, and that when we say that Christ died for us we say that the eternal Son begotten of the Father before the ages died for us, not in his divine nature, but in his human nature, and how this death is to be understood, and that it is right that it be said of the eternal Son in the manner that Orthodoxy says it of him'

DATE Late 8th or early 9th c.
ORIGINAL LANGUAGE Arabic

DESCRIPTION

This treatise concerns the manner of Christ's death. It argues against the Nestorians that it was not a mere man that died for us. It argues against the Monophysites that it was not God in his divine nature that died for us. It then expounds at some length the Orthodox understanding of how the eternal Son became human and died, that is, in his human nature and not in his divine nature.

SIGNIFICANCE

Judging by the number of extant MSS, this is the most popular of Theodore's Arabic works. While it is primarily a work of inter-Christian polemic, there are occasional asides about Islam: first, with regard to the nature of free will (ed. Bacha, p. 50: on those who say that God 'coerces and compels' human beings to do good and evil and that he created some to be blessed and some to be wretched); secondly, with regard to the nature of God's throne (ed. Bacha, p. 66: 'all those who lay claim to faith'). Theodore's presentation of soteriology is also relevant to Christian-Muslim dialogue, especially his argument that it is only through the death of Christ that human beings can be saved.

MANUSCRIPTS

MS Sinai – Ar. 581 (12th c.) (see comments on p. 451 above)

MS Oxford, Bodleian Library – Roe 26 (Nicholl Chr. Ar. 36), ch. 56 and 57 (late 14th c.) (anonymous fragments in appendix to Yūsuf al-Miṣrī's *Synodicon*)

MS Joun, Dayr al-Mukhalliṣ – s.n. (15th c.) (Bacha, p. 6, notes that there was at this monastery a second MS containing part of this treatise. He does not, however, provide its shelf-mark.)

MS Shuwayr, Dayr al-Shuwayr – 215 (formerly 43), 3rd work (1532) (see comments on p. 449 above)

MS Jerusalem, Greek Orthodox Patriarchate – Holy Sepulcher Ar. 12, fols 244v-248v (1637) (anonymous fragments in appendix to Yūsuf al-Miṣrī's *Synodicon*)

MS Beirut, Bibliothèque orientale – 549, fols 115v-122r (1654) (end of the treatise [ed. Bacha, p. 61], anonymous and without title)

MS al-Shīr, Dayr al-Shīr – 373, pp. 128-55 (17th or 18th c.)

MS Latakia, Library of the Greek-Orthodox Archbishop – 3, fols 108r-112v (1715) (first part of treatise [ed. Bacha, pp. 49-50, 52-58] transmitted anonymously, under the title, *A discourse on the death of the eternal Son and a refutation of the heretics, from the words of the holy fathers and spiritual teachers*; cf. *al-Makhṭūṭāt al-ʿarabiyya fī abrashiyyāt Ḥims wa-Ḥamāh wa-l-Lādhiqiyya li-l-Rūm al-Urthūdhuks*, Beirut, 1994, pp. 92-93, no. 3, and also V. Mistrih, 'Notes sur une collection privée de manuscrits arabes-chrétiens en Syrie', *Studia Orientalia Christiana Collectanea* 23 (1990) 93-137, pp. 115-19, no. 36)

MS Beirut, Bibliothèque orientale – Ar. 516, fols 383-397 (1722) (anonymous fragments, in appendix to Yūsuf al-Miṣrī's *Synodicon*)

MS Tyr, Library of the Greek-Catholic Archbishop – 45, 4th work (1730) (see comments on p. 451 above)

MS Joun, Dayr al-Mukhalliṣ – 392 (Haddad), 3rd work (1735) (see comments on p. 452 above)

MS Denver, Denver Public Library – Lansing Collection 3, pp. 70-80 (1741) (end of the treatise, corresponding to ed. Bacha, p. 61, anonymous and without title; cf. C. Matthews, 'Manuscripts and a Mamlūk inscription in the Lansing Collection in the Denver Public Library', *JAOS* 60 (1940) 370-82, pp. 373-76)

MS Latakia, Library of the Greek-Orthodox Archbishop – 34, fols 31r-44v (18th c.) (nearly the whole of the treatise (ed. Bacha, pp. 49-59, 61-70), transmitted anonymously, under the title, *A discourse on the death of the eternal Son and a refutation of the heretics, from the words of the holy fathers of the sixth holy council*; cf. *al-Makhṭūṭāt al-ʿarabiyya*, pp. 105-6, no. 34, and Mistrih, 'Notes sur une collection privée', pp. 125-27, no. 41)

EDITIONS AND TRANSLATIONS

Lamoreaux, *Theodore Abū Qurrah*, pp. 109-28 (English trans.)

Graf, *Die arabischen Schriften*, pp. 198-223 (German trans.)

Bacha, *Mayāmir*, pp. 48-70 (ed. from the Dayr al-Mukhalliṣ MS)

STUDIES —

Maymar fī taḥqīq al-Injīl wa-anna kullamā lā yuḥaqqiquhu l-Injīl fa-huwa bāṭil, 'Treatise on the confirmation of the Gospel and that everything that the Gospel does not confirm is false'

DATE Late 8th or early 9th c.

ORIGINAL LANGUAGE Arabic

DESCRIPTION

The works opens with a discussion of the reasons that lead people to accept religions that are false. It next argues that Christianity was not accepted for any of these reasons, but because of miracles.

SIGNIFICANCE

That Theodore's primary opponents in this treatise are Muslims is suggested by the rather playful qur'ānic allusions (ed. Bacha, p. 74)

MANUSCRIPTS

MS Sinai – New Finds, parchment, Ar. 12, 5th work (undated, but quite early)

MS Sinai – Ar. 581 (12th c.) (see comments on p. 451 above)

MS Nasrallah – 52, 59v-62v (1568) (current location unknown; it is believed that many of Nasrallah's MSS were sold by his heirs)

MS Joun, Dayr al-Mukhalliṣ – 392 (Haddad), 4th work (1735) (see comments on p. 452 above)

MS Beirut, Bibliothèque orientale – Ar. 549, fols 113r-115v (1654)

MS Denver, Denver Public Library – Lansing Collection 3, pp. 65-70 (1741) (see comments on p. 456 above)

EDITIONS AND TRANSLATIONS

Lamoreaux, *Theodore Abū Qurrah*, pp. 49-53 (English trans.)

Graf, *Die arabischen Schriften*, pp. 128-33 (German trans.)

Bacha, *Mayāmir*, pp. 71-75 (ed. from the Dayr al-Mukhalliṣ MS)

STUDIES —

Maymar ʿalā sabīl maʿrifat Allāh wa-taḥqīq al-Ibn al-azalī, 'Treatise on the way of knowing God and the confirmation of the eternal Son'

DATE Late 8th or early 9th c.

ORIGINAL LANGUAGE Arabic

DESCRIPTION

This treatise begins with a discussion of the various methods whereby God can be known by the human mind, with special attention being given to the knowledge of God through his effects and through what resembles or does not resemble him. Theodore then seeks to show that human reason can discover that God has a Son, one of his own essence and equal to him in every regard.

SIGNIFICANCE

This is a rather generic defense of the Christian doctrine of God. Theodore's opponents, who are never mentioned by name, might equally be Jews or Muslims.

MANUSCRIPTS

MS Sinai – Ar. 581 (12th c.) (see comments on p. 451 above)

MS Nasrallah – 52, 43r-46v (1568) (see comments above)

MS Beirut, Bibliothèque orientale – Ar. 549, fols 98r-102r (1654) (Contrary to L. Cheikho, 'Catalogue raisonné des manuscrits de la Bibliothèque orientale (5)', *Mélanges de l'Université Saint-Joseph* 11 (1926) 193-306, p. 239, and Nasrallah, *HMLEM* ii.2, p. 119, this work is not followed by an unedited appendix. It is, rather, a question of selections from another treatise by Theodore, his work *Against the Armenians*. See J.C. Lamoreaux, 'An unedited tract against the Armenians by Theodore Abū Qurrah', *Le Muséon* 105 (1992) 327-41, and Lamoreaux, *Theodore Abū Qurrah*, 97-101)

MS Joun, Dayr al-Mukhalliṣ – 392 (Haddad), 5th work (1735) (see comments on p. 452 above)

MS Denver, Denver Public Library – Lansing Collection 3, pp. 45-52 (1741) (see comments on p. 456 above)

EDITIONS AND TRANSLATIONS

Lamoreaux, *Theodore Abū Qurrah*, pp. 157-64 (English trans. with numerous corrections to the Arabic on the basis of the Beirut and Denver MSS)

Graf, *Die arabischen Schriften*, pp. 160-68 (German trans.)

Bacha, *Mayāmir*, pp. 75-82 (ed. from the Dayr al-Mukhalliṣ MS)

STUDIES —

Unknown, Questions on the Son of God

DATE Late 8th or early 9th c.

ORIGINAL LANGUAGE Arabic

DESCRIPTION

The original title of this work has been lost. Its three extant selections are entitled: (i) *Maymar fī annahu lā yughfaru (sic) li-aḥad khaṭī'atuhu illā bi-awjāʿ al-Masīḥ allatī ḥallat bihi fī sha'n al-nās wa-anna man lā yu'minu bi-hādhihi l-awjāʿ wa-yuqarribuhā li-l-Āb ʿan dhunūbihi fa-lā maghfirata li-dhunūbihi abadan*, 'Treatise on the fact that no one's sins are forgiven except through the pains that Christ experienced for the sake of human beings and that one who does not believe in these pains and offers them to the Father for the sake of his misdeeds will never have forgiveness for his misdeeds'; (ii) *Maymar fī l-radd ʿalā man yunkiru li-llāh al-tajassud wa-l-ḥulūl fīmā aḥabbu an yaḥulla fīhi (…) wa-annahu fī ḥulūlihi fī l-jasad al-ma'khūdh min Maryam (…)*, 'Treatise in refutation of one who denies that God became a body and dwelt in what he wished to dwell (…) and that in his dwelling in the body taken from Mary (…)' (damage to the MS has rendered parts of the title illegible); (iii) *Maymar yuḥaqqiqu anna li-llāh Ibnan huwa ʿidlahu fī l-jawhar wa-lam yazul maʿahu*, 'Treatise confirming that God has a Son equal to him in essence and eternally present with him'.

The first excerpt argues that human beings are unable to provide recompense for the sins that they have committed. At the same time, God is unable to forgive their sins except through the pains experienced by his Son. The second argues that it is not inappropriate for the eternal Son to dwell in a body. (The text of this second selection has suffered extensively in the course of transmission.) The third seeks to prove that God has a Son, who is eternal and equal to him in all things. This section is accompanied by a lengthy collection of biblical testimonies affirming that God has a Son.

SIGNIFICANCE

No opponents are mentioned by name in the preserved portions of this treatise. Swanson, 'The cross of Christ', pp. 121-25, has established that it is written with a view to answering Muslim objections to the Christian doctrine of salvation.

MANUSCRIPTS

MS Sinai – Ar. 581 (12th c.) (see comments on p. 451 above)

MS Joun, Dayr al-Mukhalliṣ – 392 (Haddad), 6th, 7th and 8th works (1735) (see comments on p. 452 above)

EDITIONS AND TRANSLATIONS

Lamoreaux, *Theodore Abū Qurrah*, pp. 129-49 (English trans.)

Graf, *Die arabischen Schriften*, pp. 169-98 (German trans.)

Bacha, *Mayāmir*, pp. 83-91, 180-86, 91-104 (ed. from the Dayr al-Mukhalliṣ MS)

STUDIES

M. Swanson, 'Apologetics, catechesis, and the question of audience in "On the Triune Nature of God" (Sinai Arabic 154) and three treatises of Theodore Abū Qurrah)', in M. Tamcke (ed.), *Christians and Muslims in dialogue in the Islamic Orient of the Middle Ages*, Beirut, 2007, 113-34 (addresses Abū Qurra's use of the Qurʾān and of Old Testament *testimonia*)

M. Swanson, 'A frivolous God? (*a-fa-ḥasibtum annamā khalaqnākum ʿabathan*)', in D. Thomas and C. Amos (eds), *A faithful presence. Essays for Kenneth Cragg*, London, 2003, 166-83, pp. 168-74 (includes an English trans. of passages from the first excerpt)

M. Swanson, 'Beyond prooftexting. Approaches to the Qur'ān in some early Arabic Christian apologies', *MW* 88 (1998) 297-319, pp. 312-14

M. Swanson, 'The cross of Christ in the earliest Arabic Melkite apologies', in S.K. Samir and J. Nielsen (eds), *Christian Arabic apologetics during the Abbasid period (750-1258)*, Leiden, 1994, 115-45

J. Rivière, 'Un précurseur de saint Anselme. La théologie rédemptrice de Théodore Abû Qurra', *Bulletin de littérature ecclésiastique* 8 (1914) 337-60

Maymar fī taḥqīq nāmūs Mūsā l-muqaddas wa-l-anbiyāʾ alladhīna tanabbaʾū ʿalā al-Masīḥ wa-l-Injīl al-ṭāhir alladhī naqalahu ilā l-umam talāmīdh al-Masīḥ al-mawlūd min Maryam al-ʿadhrāʾ wa-taḥqīq al-urthūdhuksiyya llatī yansubuhā l-nās ilā l-Khalkīdūniyya wa-ibṭāl kull milla tattakhidhu l-Naṣrāniyya siwā hādhī l-milla, 'Treatise on the confirmation of the holy law of Moses and the prophets who prophesied about Christ and the holy Gospel which was transmitted to the nations by the disciples of Christ, born of the pure Mary, and on the confirmation of the orthodoxy that people attribute to Chalcedonianism and the refutation of every religious community that lays claim to Christianity other than this community'

DATE Late 8th or early 9th c.
ORIGINAL LANGUAGE Arabic

DESCRIPTION

This work consists of two independent treatises. The first is a refutation of the Jews. In it Theodore argues that miracles are the primary means of verifying the truth of a religion and that it is because of verifiable miracles that Christianity alone can be established to be true. Theodore further argues that rational arguments are unable to establish the truth of Judaism and that it is only because of Christ that Christians accept Moses and the Torah. The second treatise seeks to establish which of the various Christian sects can rightly lay claim to orthodoxy. He argues that Chalcedonians alone are orthodox, in that they alone adhere to the six ecumenical councils summoned by the Bishop of Rome, which councils alone are thus established to be authoritative.

SIGNIFICANCE

While the first part of this treatise is ostensibly directed against the Jews, many of its arguments are elsewhere applied to the Muslims. Theodore states explicitly (ed. Bacha, p. 150) that the very reasons that led the Jews to accept Moses are being recapitulated at present by that other religion which appeals to the ignorant, offering them an earthly kingdom, political power, polygamy, and divorce.

MANUSCRIPTS

MS Sinai – Ar. 581 (12th c.) (see comments on p. 451 above)

MS Sinai – Ar. 441, fols 233r-255v (1240) (a leaf has been lost between fols 235 and 236, corresponding to ed. Bacha, pp. 145-47)

MS Shuwayr, Dayr al-Shuwayr – 215 (formerly 43), pp. 281-324, (1532) (the treatise is incomplete at its end; see comments on p. 449 above)

MS al-Shīr, Dayr al-Shīr – 372, pp. 166-205 (1719)

MS Joun, Dayr al-Mukhalliṣ – 392 (Haddad), 10th work (1735) (see comments on p. 452 above)

MS al-Shīr, Dayr al-Shīr – 373, pp. 60-99 (late 17th or early 18th c.)

MS Beirut, American University – 230 A96 aA (formerly Maʿlūf 1162), 1st work (s.d.). Cf. Y. Khūrī, *Al-makhṭūṭāt al-ʿarabiyya l-mawjūda fī Maktabat al-Jāmiʿa l-Amrīkiyya fī Bayrūt*, Beirut, 1985, p. 36. The identification is provisional. The catalogue describes this fragment as *Fī l-ʿaqīdat al-Masīḥiyya fī l-majāmiʿ min awrāq Abī Qurra*, 'On the Christian confession concerning the councils, from the pages of Abū Qurra'.

EDITIONS AND TRANSLATIONS

Lamoreaux, *Theodore Abū Qurrah*, pp. 27-39, 61-81 (English trans. of Bacha's edition, with numerous emendations based on a collation of MS Sinai – Ar. 441)

B. Nassif, *On the confirmation of the law of Moses, the Gospel and Orthodoxy. A treatise written in Arabic by Theodore Abū Qurrah, Bishop of Harran (c. 755-c. 829)*, Brookline MA, 1996 (Diss. Holy Cross Greek Orthodox School of Theology) (English trans.)
L. Cheikho, *Vingt traités théologiques d'auteurs arabes chrétiens (IX*[e]*-XIII*[e] *siècles)*, Beirut, 1920, pp. 75-107 (repr. of Bacha's edition)
Graf, *Die arabischen Schriften*, pp. 88-128 (German trans.)
L. Cheikho, *Seize traités théologiques d'auteurs arabes chrétiens (IX*[e]*-XIII*[e] *siècles)*, Beirut, 1906, pp. 56-87 (repr. of Bacha's edition)
C. Bacha, *Un traité des oeuvres arabes de Théodore Abou-Kurra, êvèque de Haran*, Tripoli, Syria, 1905 (repr. of his edition, with French trans.)
Bacha, *Mayāmir*, pp. 140-79 (repr. of his edition)
C. Bacha, 'Maymar fī ṣiḥḥat al-dīn al-masīḥī', *Al-Mashriq* 6 (1903) 633-43, 693-702, 800-09 (ed. from the Dayr al-Mukhalliṣ MS)

STUDIES

B. Nassif, 'Religious dialogue in the eighth century. Example from Theodore Abū Qurrah treatise', *Pd'O* 30 (2005) 333-40
B. Nassif, 'The life of Bishop Theodore Abu Qurrah', *Again* 24 (2002) 20-24 (intro. to the work and English trans. of excerpts)
S.H. Griffith, 'Muslims and church councils. The apology of Theodore Abū Qurrah', *Studia Patristica* 25 (1993) 270-99
S.K. Samir, 'Abū Qurrah (755?-?)', *Encyclopédie Maronite* 1 (1992) 215-17 (on Theodore and the Maronites)
S.K. Samir, 'Abū Qurrah et les Maronites', *Proche-Orient Chrétien* 41 (1991) 25-33
H.-J. Sieben, 'Dtn 17,8-13 als Beitrag des Alten Testamentes zur Theologie des Konzils', *Annuarium historiae conciliorum* 18 (1986) 1-8
H.-J. Sieben, *Die Konzilsidee der alten Kirche*, Paderborn, 1979, pp. 171-91
J. Gouillard, 'L'église d'Orient et la primauté romaine au temps de l'iconoclasme', *Istina* 21 (1976) 25-54, pp. 51-53
H.-J. Sieben, 'Zur Entwicklung der Konzilsidee (VIII). Theodor Abû Qurra über "unfehlbare" Konzilien', *Theologie und Philosophie* 49 (1974) 489-509
J. Gribomont, 'Documents sur les origines de l'église Maronite', *Pd'O* 5 (1974) 95-132, p. 113
C. Kneller, 'Theodor Abucara über Papsttum und Konzilien', *Zeitschrift für katholische Theologie* 34 (1910) 419-27
C. David, *Recueil de documents et de preuves contre la prétendue orthodoxie perpétuelle des Maronites*, Cairo, (1908), pp. 504-6

S. Vailhé, 'L'église Maronite du Ve au IXe siècle', *Échos d'Orient* 9 (1906) 257-68 and 344-51, pp. 349-51
E. Ajam, 'Le monothélisme des Maronites, d'après les auteurs Melchites', *Échos d'Orient* 9 (1906) 91-95, pp. 92-93

Maymar qālahu Anbā Thāwudhūrūs usquf Ḥarrān al-muqaddas wa-huwa Abū Qurra yuthbitu fīhi anna l-sujūd li-ṣūrat al-Masīḥ ilāhinā lladhī tajassada min Rūḥ al-Qudus wa-min Maryam al-adhrāʾ al-muṭahhara wa-ṣuwar qiddīsīhi wājib ʿalā kull Naṣrānī wa-anna kull man ʿaṭṭala min al-Naṣārā l-sujūd li-hādhihi l-ṣuwar innamā taʿṭīluhu jahl bi-mā fī yadayhi min sharaf al-Naṣrāniyya wa-annahu yalzamuhu in waqafa ʿalā dhālika taʿṭīl akthar sarāʾir al-Naṣrāniyya allatī bi-l-īmān al-muhadhdhab kāna qubūl al-Naṣārā iyyāhā min al-sillīḥiyyīn al-muqaddasīn, 'A treatise imparted by the holy Abba Theodore, Bishop of Ḥarrān, that is, Abū Qurra, in which he establishes that prostration to the image of Christ our God (who took flesh from the Holy Spirit and from the pure virgin Mary) and to the images of the saints is incumbent on every Christian; and that every Christian who neglects the veneration of these images does so solely because of ignorance of the nobility of the Christianity that he has received; and that, if he takes this stand, he must (also) neglect the majority of the mysteries of Christianity, which through the faith purified (of all errors) Christians received from the holy apostles'

DATE Sometime after 799
ORIGINAL LANGUAGE Arabic

DESCRIPTION

The title given above is that found in the British Library MS. The Sinai MS offers more or less the same text for the first part, but without the second part from 'and that every Christian…'.

This treatise is a defense of the Christian practice of prostration before icons. It was composed by Theodore at the request of a certain Abba Yannah (John) from Edessa, who had informed Theodore that many Christians were abandoning prostration before icons of Christ and the saints because of the criticism of certain non-Christians 'claiming to have in hand a scripture sent down from God' (ed. Dick, p. 88). That it is a question, at least in part, of Muslim criticisms is manifestly clear from the body of the treatise, not least its use of qurʾānic citations and Prophetic ḥadīth (see the notes to Griffith's translation).

SIGNIFICANCE

This treatise provides important literary evidence for the native iconoclast movement that arose among Christians living under Islam in response to Muslim criticisms. This iconoclast movement is also well attested in the material remains (see R. Schick, *The Christian communities of Palestine from Byzantine to Islamic rule. A historical and archaeological study*, Princeton NJ, 1995).

MANUSCRIPTS

MS BL – Or. 4950, fols 198r-237v (877)

MS Sinai – Ar. 330, fols 315r-356r (10th c.)

EDITIONS AND TRANSLATIONS

S.H. Griffith, *A treatise on the veneration of the holy icons written in Arabic by Theodore Abū Qurrah, Bishop of Harrān (c. 755-c. 830 A.D.)*, Louvain, 1997 (English trans. from Dick's edition)

P. Pizzo, *Teodoro Abū Qurrah. La difesa delle icone. Trattato sulla venerazione delle immagini*, Milan, 1995 (Italian trans. from Dick's edition)

I. Dick, *Théodore Abuqurra. Traité du culte des icônes / Maymar fī ikrām al-ayqūnāt li-Thāwudhūrus Abī Qurra*, Jounieh, 1986 (edition based on both MSS)

G. Graf, *Die arabischen Schriften*, 278-333 (German trans. from Arendzen's edition)

I. Arendzen, *Theodori Abu Ḳurra de cultu imaginum libellus*, Bonn, 1897 (edition of the British Library MS, with Latin trans.)

STUDIES

I. Pochoshajew, 'Abū Ḳurra über die Verehrung christlicher Bilder', *BZ* 101 (2008) 1-21

K. Parry, 'Byzantine and Melkite iconophiles under iconoclasm', in C. Dendrinos et al. (eds), *Porphyrogenita*, Aldershot, 2003, 137-51, pp. 137-39, 142-43

M.-F. Auzépy, 'Les sabaïtes et l'iconoclasme', in J. Patrich (ed.), *The Sabaite heritage in the Orthodox Church from the fifth century to the present*, Louvain, 2001, 305-14

J. Lamoreaux and H. Khairallah, 'The Arabic version of the Life of John of Edessa', *Le Muséon* 113 (2000) 439-60 (on a John of Edessa who has been suggested as the recipient of Theodore's treatise)

S.H. Griffith, 'The Qur'ān in Arab Christian texts. The development of an apologetical argument. Abū Qurrah in the *maǧlis* of al-Ma'mūn', *Pd'O* 24 (1999) 203-33, pp. 219-20 (on the qur'ānic citations in the present work)

P. Pizzo, 'L'Islam e i musulmani nella difesa delle icone di Teodoro Abū Qurrah', *Pd'O* 22 (1997) 667-76

D. Righi, 'Liturgia cristiana e preghiera musulmana in Teodoro Abû Qurrah', in E. Manicardi and F. Ruggiero (eds), *Liturgia ed evangelizzazione nell'epoca dei padri e nella chiesa del Vaticano II*, Bologna, 1996, 291-304 (on the Muslim context for the composition of the treatise)

M. Swanson, 'The cross of Christ in the earliest Arabic Melkite apologies', in S.K. Samir and J. Nielsen (eds), *Christian Arabic apologetics during the Abbasid period (750-1258)*, Leiden, 1994, 115-45, pp. 138-39

S.H. Griffith, 'Theodore Abu Qurrah's On the veneration of the holy icons. Orthodoxy in the world of Islam', *Sacred Art Journal* 13 (1992) 3-19

S.K. Samir, 'Le traité sur les icônes d'Abū Qurrah mentioné par Eutychius', *OCP* 58 (1992) 461-74

S.H. Griffith, 'Images, Islam and Christian icons. A moment in the Christian/Muslim encounter in early Islamic times', in P. Canivet and J.-P. Rey-Coquais (eds), *La Syrie de Byzance à l'islam, VIIe-VIIIe siècles*, Damascus, 1992, 121-38

J. Hatem, review of Dick's edition, *Pd'O* 13 (1986) 387-88 (argues that the treatise is directed primarily against Jews)

S.H. Griffith, 'Theodore Abū Qurrah's Arabic tract on the Christian practice of venerating images', *JAOS* 105 (1985) 53-73

S.H. Griffith, 'Stephen of Ramlah and the Christian kerygma in Arabic in ninth-century Palestine', *Journal of Ecclesiastical History* 36 (1985) 23-45 (on the scribe of the British Library MS, with extensive discussion of Theodore and the present treatise)

I. Dick, 'Thāwudhūrūs Abū Qurra usquf Ḥarrān. Shafā'at al-qiddīsīn wa-wisāṭatuhum', *Nashrat Abrashiyyat Ḥalab li-l-Rūm al-Kāthūlīk* 1-2 (1984) 54-56

S.H. Griffith, 'Eutychius of Alexandria on the Emperor Theophilus and iconoclasm in Byzantium. A tenth century moment in Christian apologetics in Arabic', *Byzantion* 52 (1982) 154-90, pp. 178-83

R. Thomson, 'An eighth-century Melkite colophon from Edessa', *Journal of Theological Studies* n.s. 13 (1962) 249-58, p. 253 (possible mention of the John to whom Theodore addressed this treatise)

J. Blau, 'Über einige christlich-arabische Manuskripte aus dem 9. und 10. Jahrhundert', *Le Muséon* 75 (1962) 101-8, pp. 101-2

J. Blau, 'The importance of middle Arabic dialects for the history of Arabic', in U. Heyd (ed.), *Studies in Islamic History and Civilization*, Jerusalem, 1961, 206-28, p. 208

I. Dick, 'La passion arabe de S. Antoine Ruwaḥ, néo-martyr de Damas († 25 déc. 799)', *Le Muséon* 74 (1961) 109-33, pp. 117-18 (on the mention of the martyrdom of Anthony in this text – key to its dating)

Z. Hassan, 'The attitude of Islam towards painting', *Majallat kulliyyat al-ādāb / Bulletin of the faculty of arts* (Cairo) 7 (1944) 1-15, pp. 9-10 (that the treatise was occasioned by Muslim iconoclasm)

K. Creswell, 'Note on the attitude of Islam towards painting', *Majallat kulliyyat al-ādāb / Bulletin of the faculty of arts* (Cairo) 7 (1944) 16-17 (on the historical context of the treatise)

H. Hirschfeld, review of Arendzen's edition, *Journal of the Royal Asiatic Society* (1898) 653-54 (suggesting that Theodore's biblical citations in this text evince a knowledge of Hebrew)

Maymar yuḥaqqiqu anna dīn Allāh alladhī yaʾkhudhu Allāh bihi l-ʿibād yawm al-qiyāma wa-lā yaqbalu minhum dīnan ghayrahu wa-huwa l-dīn alladhī kharajat bihi l-ḥawāriyyūn ilā aqṭār al-arḍ wa-jamīʿ umam al-dunyā wa-huwa rusul al-Masīḥ rabbinā, 'Treatise confirming that the religion of God, whereby God judges [His] servants on the day of the resurrection, without accepting from them a religion other than it, is the religion that the apostles (that is, the messengers of Christ our Lord) brought to [all] the regions of the earth and to all the nations of the world'

DATE Late 8th or early 9th c.
ORIGINAL LANGUAGE Arabic

DESCRIPTION
This short treatise, which is lacking at its end, summarizes Theodore's views on the characteristics of the true religion. He argues that one can consider that religion alone to be true that has been propagated among all the nations of the world, that was attested by signs and wonders, and that has messengers that instruct the nations in their native tongues.

SIGNIFICANCE
This little treatise never mentions its opponents by name. Parallels with other of Theodore's works make it clear that he is thinking primarily of Jews and Muslims.

MANUSCRIPTS
MS Sinai – Ar. 447, fols 128v-131r (13th c.)
MS Damascus, Greek Orthodox Patriarchate – Ar. 181 (formerly 1616), 10th work (18th c.)
MS Sbath – 1324, 15th work (1773) (This MS seems to be lost. It is not in the Vatican Library with most of Sbath's other MSS, nor is it to be found in the Fondation George et Mathilde Salem in Aleppo.)

EDITIONS AND TRANSLATIONS

Lamoreaux, *Theodore Abū Qurrah*, pp. 55-57 (English trans. of Dick's edition, with variants from the Damascus MS)

I. Dick, 'Deux écrits inédits de Théodore Abuqurra', *Le Muséon* 72 (1959) 53-67, pp. 62-67 (edition of the text from the Sinai MS, with French trans.)

STUDIES —

Suʾila Abū Qurra Anbā Thādhurus usquf Ḥarrān ʿan al-Masīḥ bi-hawāhi ṣuliba am bi-ghayr hawāhi, 'Abba Theodore Abū Qurra, the Bishop of Ḥarrān, was asked about Christ, whether he was crucified willingly or not'

DATE Late 8th or early 9th c.

ORIGINAL LANGUAGE Seemingly Arabic

DESCRIPTION

This short text is an answer to a Muslim who questions Theodore as to whether Christ willed to be crucified, suggesting that had he so willed, then the Jews are to be praised for having crucified him. Theodore argues against this person via an analogy, citing as his example the Muslims who are killed while waging *jihād* against the Christians of Byzantium.

SIGNIFICANCE

This fragment is of unknown provenance. Perhaps it represents a selection from a larger treatise. An identical text has been preserved in Theodore's *Against the outsiders* (see below, pp. 470-71), as well as in Greek *Opusculum* 9 (see below, p. 482). Other versions of this fragment can be found in the *al-Jāmiʿ wujūh al-īmān* (see discussions in Samir and Arbache, cited below) and in Dionysius Bar Ṣalībī (J. Amar, *Dionysius Bar Ṣalībī. A response to the Arabs*, Louvain, 2005 [*CSCO* 614-615], i, pp. 56-59 [edition], ii, pp. 52-54 [trans.]).

MANUSCRIPTS

MS Sinai – Ar. 72, fol. 117r (897)

EDITIONS AND TRANSLATIONS

Lamoreaux, *Theodore Abū Qurrah*, pp. 207-8 (English trans.)

S.K. Samir, 'Kitāb "Jāmiʿ wujūh al-īmān" wa-mujādalat Abī Qurra ʿan ṣalb al-Masīḥ', *Al-Masarra* 70 (1984) 411-27 (includes at pp. 418-19 a re-edition of the fragment and comparison with the parallel text found in *al-Jāmiʿ wujūh al-īmān*)

S.H. Griffith, 'Some unpublished Arabic sayings attributed to Theodore Abū Qurrah', *Le Muséon* 92 (1979) 29-35 (edition and English trans.)

STUDIES

S. Arbache, 'Sentences arabes de Saint Basile', *Le Muséon* 98 (1985) 315-29, p. 315 n. 2 (independently of Samir, discovery that the present fragment is also to be found in *al-Jāmiʿ wujūh al-īmān*)

Untitled, Prayer for al-Maʾmūn

DATE Late 8th or early 9th c.

ORIGINAL LANGUAGE Arabic

DESCRIPTION

This rather curious piece is a short prayer, in rhymed prose, for the Caliph al-Maʾmūn, asking God to grant him wisdom and protection.

SIGNIFICANCE

If this work is actually by Theodore, one wonders if it might not originally have been the preface or conclusion to a larger work, now lost.

MANUSCRIPTS

MS Sinai – Ar. 447, fols 181v-182v (13th c.)

EDITIONS AND TRANSLATIONS

M. Swanson, 'The Christian al-Maʾmūn tradition', in D. Thomas (ed.), *Christians at the heart of Islamic rule. Church life and scholarship in ʿAbbasid Iraq*, Leiden, 2003, 63-92, pp. 66-69, 87-90 (edition and English trans., expressing some doubts about the work's authenticity)

STUDIES

R. Haddad, *La Trinité divine chez les théologiens arabes, 750-1050*, Paris, 1985, p. 55, n. 211 (disputes authenticity)

I. Dick, 'Deux écrits inédits de Théodore Abuqurra', *Le Muséon* 72 (1959) 53-67, p. 54 (disputes authenticity)

Min qawl Thāwudūrus usquf Ḥarrān al-mukannā bi-Abī Qurra ṭaʿana ʿalā l-barrāniyyīn, 'Some statements of Theodore the Bishop of Ḥarrān, known as Abū Qurra, against the outsiders'

DATE Late 8th or early 9th c.
ORIGINAL LANGUAGE Arabic

DESCRIPTION

This work consists of eight small texts against Islam. The first is a dialogue. It takes takes place while Theodore and some other Christians were visiting the Holy Sepulcher. Theodore is approached by some Muslims who ask him whether Christ willed to be crucified. What follows is very nearly identical to Theodore's *About Christ whether he was crucified willingly or not* (see above, p. 468).

The second records a dialogue that is said to have taken place while Theodore and a friend were traveling through the countryside of Syria and attended a wedding festival, at which some Muslims were also present. One of the Muslims asks Theodore what the Christians think about a man who kills his mother and suggests that Christ as God killed Mary by allowing her to die. Theodore responds by arguing that it would have been unjust for Christ not to have allowed her to suffer the fate of all other human beings.

The third text responds to the question how God can be both unseen and seen in the person of the incarnate Christ. Theodore responds that God the Son wrapped himself in a human body through which humans heard his words and saw his deeds.

The fourth text seeks to answer the question: Who came first, Christ or his mother? Theodore explains, in response, how something begotten can still be prior to the one who begot it.

The fifth text is a response to the rather humorous question: If you prostrate yourself to the cross because Christ was crucified on it, why do you not prostrate yourself to the ass because Christ rode on it? Theodore's response centers on the various things that were accomplished through Christ's death on the cross.

The sixth text is an answer to the question of how Christ as God could be contained in his mother's womb.

The seventh seeks to explain in what sense death can be predicated of Christ but not of God. It continues with an extensive discussion of the manner of Christ's death.

The eighth and last text explores how human salvation was accomplished through the death of Christ.

SIGNIFICANCE
This collection would seem to consist of fragments of a number of treatises now lost. It is not known who compiled them or when. A number of these texts are paralleled in *al-Jāmiʿ wujūh al-īmān*. Many of the themes here expounded are also paralleled in others of Theodore's works. The language and theology is unmistakably Theodore's. Much research is required before the relationship between this work, Theodore's other works, and *al-Jāmiʿ wujūh al-īmān* will become clear.

MANUSCRIPTS
MS Damascus, Greek Orthodox Patriarchate – 181 (formerly 1616), 7th work (1561)
MS Sbath 1324, 12th work (1773) (see comments on p. 467)
MS Nagm (P. Sbath, *Al-fihris. Catalogue de manuscrits arabes*, 3 vols, Cairo, 1938, i, p. 25, records that a copy of this treatise was to be found in a MS owned by a certain Paul Nagm, a Greek Catholic priest then living in Aleppo. The present location of this MS is unknown.)

EDITIONS AND TRANSLATIONS
An edition and English trans. are currently being prepared by John C. Lamoreaux

STUDIES —

Al-radd ʿalā lladhīna yaqūlūna inna l-Naṣārā yuʾminū bi-ilāh ḍaʿīf idh yaqūlūna inna al-Masīḥ ilāh wa-innahu luṭima wa-ḍuriba wa-ṣuliba wa-māta wa-qāma, 'The Refutation of those who say that Christians believe in a weak God, in that they say that Christ is God and that he was slapped, struck, crucified, died and rose (again)'

DATE Late 8th or early 9th c.
ORIGINAL LANGUAGE Arabic

DESCRIPTION
This treatise seeks to answer the objection described in its title. Theodore argues that God is possessed of four attributes, justice, goodness, might, and wisdom; that it is because of these four attributes that he allowed his Son to suffer death on the cross; and that only thus could human beings be freed from slavery to the devil.

SIGNIFICANCE
This beautiful little treatise provides one of Theodore's most systematic statements on the necessity of Christ's death and on how that death results in the salvation of humankind. It is directed against unnamed opponents ('the people of ignorance and confusion'), probably both Jews and Muslims.

MANUSCRIPTS
MS Damascus, Greek Orthodox Patriarchate – 181 (formerly 1616), 8th work (1561)
MS Sbath – 1324, 13th work (1773) (see comments on p. 467)
MS Nagm – (see comments on p. 471)

EDITIONS AND TRANSLATIONS
An edition and English trans. are currently being prepared by John C. Lamoreaux

STUDIES —

Al-radd ʿalā lladhīna yaqūlūna inna kalimat Allāh makhlūqa, 'The Refutation of those who say that the Word of God is created'

DATE Late 8th or early 9th c.
ORIGINAL LANGUAGE Arabic

DESCRIPTION
Taking as its starting point the qurʾānic acknowledgment of Christ as the Word of God, this text seeks to explain how this Word was begotten without the physical accouterments of birth and why it is necessary that this Word be eternal like God himself.

SIGNIFICANCE
Theodore's opponents in this text are unnamed. In that they acknowledge Christ to be the Word of God, however, it is clear that they are Muslims. The text also contains unattributed qurʾānic citations.

MANUSCRIPTS

MS Damascus, Greek Orthodox Patriarchate – 181 (formerly 1616), 9th work (1561)

MS Sbath – 1324, 14th work (1773) (see comments on p. 467)

MS Nagm – (see comments on p. 471)

EDITIONS AND TRANSLATIONS

An edition and English trans. are currently being prepared by John C. Lamoreaux

STUDIES —

Kitāb al-radd, 'The Refutation'

DATE Late 8th or early 9th c.

ORIGINAL LANGUAGE Arabic

DESCRIPTION

This treatise consists of a collection of biblical texts designed to refute (i) those who say that Christ is the Word of God, but that he is created and something other than the Creator, (ii) those who say that the Spirit is created, (iii) those who say that Christ cannot be God in that he experienced suffering and death, and (iv) those who say that Christ did not ascend into heaven and take his seat on the throne. Most of the citations are taken from the book of Psalms and from the Minor Prophets.

SIGNIFICANCE

Theodore never names his opponents. Once again, it is probably a question of both Jews and Muslims.

MANUSCRIPTS

MS Damascus, Greek Orthodox Patriarchate – 181 (formerly 1616), 11th work (1561)

MS Sbath – 1324, 16th work (1773) (see comments on p. 467)

MS Nagm – (see comments on p. 471)

EDITIONS AND TRANSLATIONS

An edition and English trans. are currently being prepared by John C. Lamoreaux

STUDIES —

Ek tōn pros tous Sarakēnous antirrhēseōn tou episkopou Theodōrou Charran, to epiklen Aboukara, dia phonēs Ioannou Diakonou, 'Refutations of the Saracens by Bishop Theodore of Ḥarrān, called Abū Qurra, as reported by John the Deacon'

DATE 9th c.? (compiled possibly during the lifetime of Abū Qurra)
ORIGINAL LANGUAGE Greek

DESCRIPTION
This work opens with a short preface from the hand of a certain John the Deacon, who records that in his writings Abū Qurra 'worthily held up to public scorn the impious religion of the Agarenes' and further claims himself often to have been present when Abū Qurra debated with Muslims. He states that assaults on the Church by heretics demand that he record some of what he remembers. There follow nine short treatises (mostly dialogues) recording Abū Qurra's refutations of Muslims. These dialogues correspond respectively to opuscula 18, 19, 21, 22, 23, 24, 32, 20, 25 in Migne's *PG*. Their topics are as follows: that it is because of his lack of miracles that Christians do not accept the prophethood of Muḥammad; that Muḥammad was attested neither by miracles nor by an earlier prophet; that the humble manner of Christianity's first propagation is a confirmation of its truth; that Christian belief in the transformation of the eucharist is not absurd; that Christ remained God even when becoming human; that monogamy is more natural than polygamy; that Christ's sufferings did not touch his divinity; that Muḥammad's manner of receiving prophecy is much the same as that of a demoniac; that God has a Son who shares his essence and is eternal.

SIGNIFICANCE
There are many strong parallels between these works and Abū Qurra's Arabic treatises, so much so that one can very confidently conclude that John the Deacon in part drew directly on Abū Qurra's written works (Lamoreaux, 'Theodore Abū Qurrah and John the Deacon', pp. 375-85).

MANUSCRIPTS
- MS Moscow, National Historical Museum – Sinodal. 394 (Vladimir 231), fols 62r-71r (932) (18-25, 32)
- MS BNF – Gr. 1111, starting at fol. 19v (11th c.) (preface, 18-20, 22, 23 partially, 24 partially, 25, 32)

MS Wolfenbüttel, Herzog-August-Bibliothek – Gud. Gr. 104.2, fols 216v-217r (12th c.) (32)
MS Mount Athos, Monē Batopediou – 236, fols 108r-113r (12th or 13th c.) (preface and 18-24)
MS BNF – Gr. 1301, between fols 332r and 347v (13th c.) (22, 23, 32)
MS Vat – Gr. 2220, fols 293v-295r (1304) (22, 23, 32)
MS Vat – Gr. 1700, fols 38v-39v (1332) (32)
MS Vat – Gr. 402, fols 137v-139v (1383) (22, 23, 32)
MS BNF – Gr. 1258, between fols 389r and 407r (14th c.) (seemingly 22, 23, 32)
MS Wolfenbüttel, Herzog-August-Bibliothek – Gr. 102, fols 27r-32r (14th c.) (18-24)
MS Mount Athos, Monē Megistēs Lauras – *G* 43, fols 146r-end of MS (14th c.) (18, 21, 22, 20, 25, and perhaps others)
MS Meteora, Monē Metamorphōseōs – 578, starting at fol. 14r (14th c.) (18 and perhaps others)
MS Vat – Gr. 840, fols 241v-242r (14th c.) (25 incomplete at end, 32)
MS Vat – Gr. 790, fols 172v-174v (14th or 15th c.) (22, 32)
MS BNF – Gr. 1372, starting at fol. 56r (15th c.) (22 and perhaps others)
MS Florence, Biblioteca Medicea Laurenziana – plut. 55.10, fols 89v-91r (15th c.) (25, 32)
MS Mount Athos, Monē Megistēs Lauras – *L* 135, fols 701v-705v (15th c.) (18-25, 32)
MS BNF – Suppl. Gr. 249, between fols 196r and 213r (1568) (23, 32, and perhaps others)
MS BNF – Gr. 1258, between fols 389r and 407r (16th c.) (22, 23, 32)
MS Munich, Bayerische Staatsbibliothek – Gr. 66, fols 55r-59v (16th c.) (19-24)
MS Athens, Historikē kai Ethnologikē Hetaireia tes Hellados – 71, starting at fol. 139v (17th c.) (21)
MS Vat – Ottob. Gr. 382, fols 78r-86v (17th c.) (19-20, 22-24)
MS Mount Athos, Monē Megistēs Lauras – *K* 128, starting at fol. 270r (18th c.) (22 and perhaps others)
MS BNF – Suppl. Gr. 124, starting at fol. 13r (18th c.) (25)

EDITIONS AND TRANSLATIONS

Lamoreaux, *Theodore Abū Qurrah*, pp. 211-27 (English trans.)

R. Glei and A. Khoury, *Johannes Damaskenos und Theodor Abū Qurra. Schriften zum Islam*, Würzburg, 1995 (*Corpus Islamo-Christianum. Series Graeca* 3), pp. 86-127 (edition and German trans.)

L. Datiašvili, *Teodore Abuk'ura. T'rakt'at'ebi da dialogebi targmnili berdznulidan Arsen Iq'altoelis mier*, Tbilisi, 1980, pp. 94-112 (edition of Georgian trans.)

J. Voorhis, 'The discussion of a Christian and a Saracen', *MW* 25 (1935) 266-73, pp. 272-73 (English trans. of opusculum 18)

(G. Sablukov), 'Protivomusul'manskiīa sochineniīa episkopa Ḟeodora Abukary', *Missioner* 6 (1879) 148-51, 157-59, 172-75, 181-85, 190-93, pp. 158-59 (opusculum 25), 172-75 (opuscula 23, 32, 21), 181-85 (opuscula 22, 18-20, 24) (Russian trans.)

PG 94, cols 1595-98 (opusculum 18), *PG* 97, cols 1543-62 (opuscula 19-25), 1583-84 (opusculum 32, Latin only)

STUDIES

John C. Lamoreaux, 'Theodore Abū Qurrah and John the Deacon', *Greek, Roman and Byzantine Studies* 42 (2001) 361-86

I. Dick, 'Samonas de Gaza ou Sulaïman al-Gazzi. Évêque melkite de Gaza, XIe siècle', *POC* 29 (1980) 175-78, p. 176 (on opusculum 22)

M. Jugie, 'Une nouvelle invention au compte de Constantin Palaeocappa. Samonas de Gaza et son dialogue sur l'eucharistie', in *Miscellanea Giovanni Mercati*, 6 vols, Rome, 1946, iii, 342-59, pp. 353-54 (on opusculum 22)

Theodōrou epiklen Aboukara tōn Karōn episkopou gegonotos, hoti pente echthrous echomen ex hōn hēmas ho Sotēr elytrosato. Kata peusin kai apokrisin, 'By Theodore called Abū Qurrah, Bishop of the Ḥarrānians, That we have five enemies from whom the Savior freed us. By way of question and answer' (opusculum 1)

DATE Late 8th or early 9th c.

ORIGINAL LANGUAGE Greek

DESCRIPTION

This treatise sets out in some detail Abū Qurra's views on soteriology. He explains, first, how human beings fell into various types of slavery and how they are unable to free themselves through repentance. He then recounts how the death of Christ effected their salvation, by 'assuming the curse and condemnation that was owed by us'.

SIGNIFICANCE

Abū Qurra's opponent in this dialogue is specified simply as an 'unbeliever'. It is probably directed at both Jews and Muslims, especially the latter, as is suggested by the numerous strong parallels to the work described above on pp. 458-59.

MANUSCRIPTS

MS Vienna, Österreichische Nationalbibliothek – Phil. Gr. 314, fols 128r-132v (925)
MS Moscow, National Historical Museum – Sinodal. 394 (Vladimir 231), fols 58r-61v (932)
MS Milan, Biblioteca Ambrosiana – sup. Q 74 (Gr. 681), starting at fol. 227r (10th c.) (fragment only, 1469A5-1469B6)
MS Sinai – Gr. 383 (Beneš. 513), fols 151v-153v (10th or 11th c.)
MS Mount Athos, Monē Batopediou – 236, fols 99v-101v (12th or 13th c.)
MS Vat – Gr. 1838, fols 245v-249r (13th c.)
MS BNF – Gr. 1301, between fols 332r and 347v (13th c.)
MS Rome, Biblioteca Vallicelliana – B.53 (Gr. 12), after fol. 93r (13th c.)
MS Ochrid, Nacionalen Muzej – 84 (inv. 86), pp. 65-71 (13th c.)
MS Vat – Gr. 2220, fols 298v-301r (1304)
MS Vat – Gr. 402, fols 144r-148r (1383)
MS Mount Athos, Monē Megistēs Lauras – *G* 43, starting at fol. 142r (14th c.)
MS Mount Athos, Monē Megistēs Lauras – *L* 135, fols 712r-713v (15th c.)
MS BNF – Suppl. Gr. 1090, fol. 252rv (15th c.)
MS Munich, Bayerische Staatsbibliothek – Gr. 66, fols 13r-16r (16th c.)
MS Vat – Ottob. Gr. 382, fols 233v-239r (17th c.)

EDITIONS AND TRANSLATIONS

Lamoreaux, *Theodore Abū Qurrah*, pp. 249-54 (English trans.)
PG 97, cols 1461-70

STUDIES —

Dialogos Theodōrou tou gegonotos episkopou Karōn, to epiklen Aboukara, genomenos pros ton tou dromou Emeses aitesamenon apodexin apodothēnai auto apo logismou hoti esti Theos, 'A Dialogue between Theodore, Bishop of Ḥarrān, called Abū Qurra, and the master of the post of Emesa, who asked him to prove through reason alone that God exists' (opusculum 3)

DATE Late 8th or early 9th c.
ORIGINAL LANGUAGE Greek

DESCRIPTION
A number of topics are treated in this dialogue between Abū Qurra and an unbeliever. It opens with arguments designed to prove that there is a God. These arguments mostly turn on the impossibility of an infinite regress. It next argues that this God must have a co-eternal Son, in that he would not otherwise be capable of knowing himself. The treatise next examines the nature of divine predication and especially the predicate of begetting, which does not entail passions. It then argues that it is improper for God to have begotten more than one Son. Further topics treated include: the reality of free will and why God must have a Spirit.

SIGNIFICANCE
Abū Qurra's primary aim in this treatise is to establish the Christian doctrine of the Trinity in the face of Muslim objections. There are strong parallels between most of the arguments here and Abū Qurra's Arabic works. For details, see the notes to the translation by Lamoreaux.

MANUSCRIPTS
- MS Vienna, Österreichische Nationalbibliothek – Phil. Gr. 314, fols 113r-118r (925)
- MS Moscow, National Historical Museum – Sinodal. 394 (Vladimir 231), fols 45v-50r (932)
- MS Milan, Biblioteca Ambrosiana – sup. Q 74 (Gr. 681), starting at fols 139v and 222r (10th c.) (containing two copies of the work)
- MS BNF – Gr. 1111, starting at fol. 12r (11th or 12th c.)
- MS BNF – Gr. 1301, starting at fol. 332r (13th c.)

MS Vat – Gr. 1838, fols 223v-231r (13th c.)
MS Rome, Biblioteca Vallicelliana – B.53 (Gr. 12), starting at fol. 93r (13th c.)
MS Ochrid, Nacionalen Muzej – 84 (inv. 86), pp. 41-50 (13th c.)
MS Vienna, Österreichische Nationalbibliothek – Theol. Gr. 173, fols 222v-227r (ca. 1300)
MS Vat – Gr. 2220, fols 288r-291v (1304)
MS Vat – Gr. 402, fols 129v-135r (1383)
MS Vat – Gr. 492, fols 192v-198r (13th or 14th c.)
MS Mount Athos, Monē Megistēs Lauras – *G* 43, starting at fol. 131r (14th c.)
MS Wolfenbüttel, Herzog-August-Bibliothek – Gud. Gr. 102, fol. 34r-v (14th c.)
MS Mount Athos, Monē Megistēs Lauras – *L* 135, fols 698r-700r (15th c.)
MS BNF – Suppl. Gr. 1090, fols 237r-241r (15th c.)
MS Munich, Bayerische Staatsbibliothek – Gr. 66, fols 1r-5r, 62r-v (16th c.) (found twice in the MS; the first is incomplete at its end, des. 1493D10)
MS Vat – Ottob. Gr. 382, fols 91r-92r, 211r-218v (17th c.) (found twice in the MS; the first is incomplete at its end, des. 1493D10)
MS Mount Athos, Monē Megistēs Lauras – *K* 128, starting at fol. 131r (18th c.)

EDITIONS AND TRANSLATIONS
Lamoreaux, *Theodore Abū Qurrah*, pp. 229-36 (English trans.)
Glei and Khoury, *Johannes Damaskenos und Theodor Abū Qurra*, pp. 128-45 (edition and German trans.)
PG 97, cols 1491-1504

STUDIES —

Tou autou Theodōrou episkopou Karōn, peri tēs palēs tou Christou meta diabolon, 'By the same Theodore, the Bishop of the Ḥarrānians, On the contending of Christ with the devil' (opusculum 7)

DATE Late 8th or early 9th c.
ORIGINAL LANGUAGE Greek

DESCRIPTION

This treatise is concerned with three topics. Abū Qurra argues, first, that human salvation could not have been accomplished if either God himself had died on the cross or a man alone had died on the cross. Rather, God in the flesh had to die. Second, he argues that God the Word governs and moves his own mind, senses, and faculties. Third, he seeks to answer the question of how Adam fell. He argues that it was the blandishments of pleasures that charmed Adam and led to his fall into unbelief.

SIGNIFICANCE

While this text is directed primarily against the Syrian Orthodox and the Church of the East, it is important in this context because it contains an aside about Islam. In its third section, Abū Qurra likens the factors that led to Adam's fall to the manner in which Islam was propagated by its false prophet. No one would ever have believed in Muḥammad, had not he first offered the blandishments of physical pleasures: booty and spoils, and a law that catered to the desires.

MANUSCRIPTS

MS Vienna, Österreichische Nationalbibliothek – Phil. Gr. 314, fols 119v-121r (925)

MS Moscow, National Historical Museum – Sinodal. 394 (Vladimir 231), fols 50v-52r (932)

MS BNF – Gr. 1111, starting at fol. 225r (11th or 12th c.)

MS Mount Athos, Monē Batopediou – 236, fols 101v-102r (12th or 13th c.)

MS BNF – Gr. 1301, between fols 332r and 347v (13th c.)

MS Vat – Gr. 1838, fols 232r-235r (13th c.)

MS Rome, Biblioteca Vallicelliana – B.53 (Gr. 12), after fol. 93r (13th c.)

MS Ochrid, Nacionalen Muzej – 84 (inv. 86), pp. 51-54 (13th c.)

MS Vienna, Österreichische Nationalbibliothek – Theol. Gr. 173, fols 227v-229r (ca. 1300)

MS Vat – Gr. 2220, fols 292r-293v (1304)

MS Vat – Gr. 402, fols 135v-137v (1383)

MS Vat – Gr. 492, fols 199r-200r (13th or 14th c.)

MS Wolfenbüttel, Herzog-August-Bibliothek – Gud. Gr. 102, fols 1r-3r (14th c.)

MS Mount Athos, Monē Megistēs Lauras – *G* 43, between fols 135r and 137r (14th c.)

MS Mount Athos, Monē Megistēs Lauras – *L* 135, fols 700v-701r (15th c.)

MS BNF – Suppl. Gr. 1090, fols 241v-243r (15th c.)
MS Munich, Bayerische Staatsbibliothek – Gr. 66, fols 5v-7r (16th c.)
MS Vat – Ottob. Gr. 382, fols 220r-223r (17th c.)

EDITIONS AND TRANSLATIONS

Lamoreaux, *Theodore Abū Qurrah*, pp. 237-39 (English trans.)
PG 97, cols 1523-28

STUDIES —

Erōtēsis Arabōn pros Christianon, 'A question of the Arabs to a Christian' (opusculum 8)

DATE Late 8th or early 9th c.
ORIGINAL LANGUAGE Greek

DESCRIPTION

In this short dialogue, Abū Qurra endeavors to explain how Christ and the Holy Spirit can be God without there being more than one God. In arguing that there is a distinction between hypostases and nature, he draws an analogy with the Qur'ān, which exists in multiple copies without there being more than one Qur'ān.

SIGNIFICANCE

The arguments here are also found in Abū Qurra's Arabic works. In particular, one may compare the treatise described on p. 453 (ed. Bacha, pp. 42-43).

MANUSCRIPTS

MS Vienna, Österreichische Nationalbibliothek – Phil. Gr. 314, fol. 121r (925)
MS Moscow, National Historical Museum – Sinodal. 394 (Vladimir 231), fol. 52rv (932)
MS BNF – Gr. 1111, between fols 225r and 230v (11th or 12th c.)
MS Mount Athos, Monē Batopediou – 236, fols 95v-96r (12th or 13th c.)
MS Vat – Gr. 1838, fol. 235r-v (13th c.)
MS BNF – Gr. 1301, between fols 332r and 347v (13th c.)
MS Rome, Biblioteca Vallicelliana – B.53 (Gr. 12), after fol. 93r (13th c.)
MS Ochrid, Nacionalen Muzej – 84 (inv. 86), p. 54 (13th c.)
MS Vat – Gr. 2220, fol. 292r (1304)
MS Vat – Gr. 402, fol. 135v (1383)
MS Vat – Gr. 492, fol. 200r (13th or 14th c.)

MS Mount Athos, Monē Megistēs Lauras – *G* 43, starting at fol. 137r (14th c.)
MS Wolfenbüttel, Herzog-August-Bibliothek – Gud. Gr. 102, fol. 26r (14th c.)
MS Mount Athos, Monē Megistēs Lauras – *L* 135, fol. 701r (15th c.)
MS BNF – Suppl. Gr. 1090, fol. 243rv (15th c.)
MS Milan, Biblioteca Ambrosiana – sup. I 24 (Gr. 457), fol. 295v (15th c.)
MS Munich, Bayerische Staatsbibliothek – Gr. 66, fol. 7r-v (16th c.)
MS Vat – Ottob. Gr. 382, fol. 223r (17th c.)
MS Mount Athos, Monē Megistēs Lauras – *K* 128, starting at fol. 268r (18th c.)

EDITIONS AND TRANSLATIONS

Lamoreaux, *Theodore Abū Qurrah*, p. 239 (English trans.)
Glei and Khoury, *Johannes Damaskenos und Theodor Abū Qurra*, pp. 146-47 (edition and German trans.)
Datiašvili, *Teodore Abuk'ura*, p. 113 (edition and Georgian trans.)
(G. Sablukov), 'Protivomusul'manskii͡a sochinenii͡a episkopa Ḟeodora Abukary', p. 172 (Russian trans.)
PG 97, cols 1527-28

STUDIES —

Erōtēsis Agarēnou pros ton auton, 'A Hagarene's question to the same' (opusculum 9)

DATE Late 8th or early 9th c.
ORIGINAL LANGUAGE Greek

DESCRIPTION

This short text answers a Muslim who asks Abū Qurra whether Christ willed to be crucified, suggesting that had he willed it the Jews are to be praised for having crucified him. Abū Qurra argues against this person via an analogy, citing as his example the Muslims who are killed while waging *jihād* against the Christians of Byzantium.

SIGNIFICANCE

See the comments at 2.11.6.

MANUSCRIPTS

MS Vienna, Österreichische Nationalbibliothek – Phil. Gr. 314, fols 121v-122v (925)

MS Moscow, National Historical Museum – Sinodal. 394 (Vladimir 231), fol. 53r-v (932)
MS Milan, Biblioteca Ambrosiana – sup. Q 74 (Gr. 681), between fols 223v and 225r (10th c.) (fragment only)
MS BNF – Gr. 1111, between fols 225r and 230v (11th or 12th c.)
MS Mount Athos, Monē Batopediou – 236, fol. 96rv (12th or 13th c.)
MS Vat – Gr. 1838, fols 236r-237v (13th c.)
MS BNF – Gr. 1301, between fols 332r and 347v (13th c.)
MS Rome, Biblioteca Vallicelliana – B.53 (Gr. 12), after fol. 93r (13th c.)
MS Ochrid, Nacionalen Muzej – 84 (inv. 86), pp. 54bis-55 (13th c.)
MS Vat – Gr. 492, fols 200v-201v (13th or 14th c.)
MS Vat – Gr. 2220, fol. 295r-v (1304)
MS Vat – Gr. 402, fols 139v-140v (1383)
MS Mount Athos, Monē Megistēs Lauras – *G* 43, between fols 137r and 138r (14th c.)
MS Wolfenbüttel, Herzog-August-Bibliothek – Gud. Gr. 102, fols 26v-27r (14th c.)
MS Mount Athos, Monē Megistēs Lauras – *L* 135, fol. 701v (15th c.)
MS Milan, Biblioteca Ambrosiana – sup. I 24 (Gr. 457), fol. 295v (15th c.)
MS BNF – Suppl. Gr. 1090, fol. 244rv (15th c.)
MS Munich, Bayerische Staatsbibliothek – Gr. 66, fol. 8rv (16th c.)
MS Vat – Ottob. Gr. 382, fols 224r-225r (17th c.)

EDITIONS AND TRANSLATIONS

Lamoreaux, *Theodore Abū Qurrah*, pp. 240-41 (English trans.)
Glei and Khoury, *Johannes Damaskenos und Theodor Abū Qurra*, pp. 150-53 (edition and German trans.)
Datiašvili, *Teodore Abuk'ura*, pp. 114-15 (Georgian trans.)
(G. Sablukov), 'Protivomusul'manskii͡a sochinenii͡a episkopa Ḟeodora Abukary', pp. 172-73 (Russian trans.)
PG 97, cols 1529-30

STUDIES —

Erōtēsis apistou pros ton auton genomenē, 'An unbeliever's question to the same' (opusculum 16)

DATE Late 8th or early 9th c.

ORIGINAL LANGUAGE Greek

DESCRIPTION

Abū Qurra argues in this short treatise that Christ was able both to be hypostatically united to his flesh and to be present in all things, providentially providing for them and governing them.

SIGNIFICANCE

Abū Qurra's opponent is never specified. However, it is very likely a question of a Muslim, as a similar argument can be found in part six of Abū Qurra's *Against the outsiders* (see above, pp. 470-71).

MANUSCRIPTS

MS Vienna, Österreichische Nationalbibliothek – Phil. Gr. 314, fol. 121r-v (925)

MS Moscow, National Historical Museum – Sinodal. 394 (Vladimir 231), fols 52v-53r (932)

MS Milan, Biblioteca Ambrosiana – Sup. Q 74 (Gr. 681), starting at fol. 223v (10th c.)

MS Heidelberg, Universitätbibliothek – Palat. Gr. 281, starting at fol. 172r (1040)

MS BNF – Gr. 1111, between fols 225r and 230v (11th or 12th c.)

MS Escorial, Biblioteca del Real Monasterio de San Lorenzo – R I 15 (Gr. 15), fols 165v-166r (12th c.)

MS Mount Athos, Monē Batopediou – 236, fol. 96r (12th or 13th c.)

MS Vat – Gr. 1838, fols 235v-236r (13th c.)

MS BNF – Gr. 1301, between fols 332r and 347v (13th c.)

MS Rome, Biblioteca Vallicelliana – B.53 (Gr. 12), after fol. 93r (13th c.)

MS Ochrid, Nacionalen Muzej – 84 (inv. 86), pp. 54-54bis (13th c.)

MS Vat – Gr. 492, fol. 200v (13th or 14th c.)

MS Vat – Gr. 2220, fols 291v-292r (1304)

MS Vat – Gr. 402, fol. 135r-v (1383)

MS Mount Athos, Monē Megistēs Lauras – *G* 43, between fols 137r and 138r (14th c.)

MS Vienna, Österreichische Nationalbibliothek – Phil. Gr. 174, fol. 132r (14th c.) (incomplete at end, des. 1541a10)

MS Wolfenbüttel, Herzog-August-Bibliothek – Gud. Gr. 102, fol. 26rv (14th c.)

MS Vat – Gr. 790, fol. 176r (14th or 15th c.) (end lacking, des. 1541A10)

MS Mount Athos, Monē Megistēs Lauras – *G* 135, fol. 701r-v (15th c.)

MS Milan, Biblioteca Ambrosiana – sup. I 24 (Gr. 457), fol. 295v (15th c.)

MS BNF – Suppl. Gr. 1090, fols 243v-244r (15th c.)
MS Munich, Bayerische Staatsbibliothek – Gr. 66, fol. 7v (16th c.)
MS Vat – Reg. Gr. 108, fol. 32r (16th c.) (end lacking, des. 1541A10)
MS Munich, Bayerische Staatsbibliothek – Gr. 104, fol. 288rv (16th c.) (end lacking, des. 1541A10)
MS Escorial, Biblioteca del Real Monasterio de San Lorenzo – Y I 13 (Gr. 252), fol. 169v (16th c.) (end lacking, des. 1541A10)
MS Vat – Ottob. Gr. 382, fols 223v-224r (17th c.)

EDITIONS AND TRANSLATIONS

Lamoreaux, *Theodore Abū Qurrah*, pp. 239-40 (English trans.)
Glei and Khoury, *Johannes Damaskenos und Theodor Abū Qurra*, pp. 148-49 (edition, with German trans.)
PG 97, cols 1539-42

STUDIES —

Ērōtēthē Aboukaras par' apistou, 'Abū Qurra was questioned by an unbeliever' (opusculum 17)

DATE Late 8th or early 9th c.
ORIGINAL LANGUAGE Greek

DESCRIPTION

This short but fascinating dialogue seeks to explain how those who died before Christ can be saved. In particular, it tries to understand how they were able to receive their requisite baptism. Abū Qurra argues that the water that issued from Christ's side at the time of the crucifixion was dissolved into the elements and thus functioned as a baptism for the dead, who had also been dissolved into the elements. This is not to say, however, that all who died before Christ were saved. Rather, only those who had faith in Christ when he descended into hell were able to benefit from the dissolution of the water into the elements.

SIGNIFICANCE

The identity of Theodore's opponents is never specified. In that Abū Qurra is very often concerned to defend Christian soteriology to Muslims, it is possible that here too he is responding to their questions.

MANUSCRIPTS

MS Vienna, Österreichische Nationalbibliothek – Phil. Gr. 314, fols 132v-133r (925)

MS Moscow, National Historical Museum – Sinodal. 394 (Vladimir 231), fols 61v-62r (932)
MS Sinai – Gr. 383 (Beneš. 513), fols 153v-154r (10th or 11th c.)
MS Mount Athos, Monē Batopediou – 236, fols 101v-102r (12th or 13th c.)
MS Vat – Gr. 1838, fol. 249r-v (13th c.)
MS BNF – Gr. 1301, between fols 332r and 347v (13th c.)
MS Rome, Biblioteca Vallicelliana – B.53 (Gr. 12), after fol. 93r (13th c.)
MS Ochrid, Nacionalen Muzej – 84 (inv. 86), p. 71 (13th c.)
MS Vat – Gr. 402, fol. 148rv (1383) (incomplete at end, des. 1544A2)
MS Mount Athos, Monē Megistēs Lauras – *G* 43, between fols 142r and 146r (14th c.)
MS Wolfenbüttel, Herzog-August-Bibliothek – Gud. Gr. 102, fol. 3v (14th c.)
MS Mount Athos, Monē Megistēs Lauras – *G* 135, fol. 713v (15th c.)
MS BNF – Suppl. Gr. 1090, fol. 252r-v (15th c.)
MS Munich, Bayerische Staatsbibliothek – Gr. 66, fols 16r-v, 32v (16th c.) (found twice in MS)
MS Vat – Ottob. Gr. 382, fols 36r-36v, 239v-240r (17th c.) (found twice in MS)

EDITIONS AND TRANSLATIONS

Lamoreaux, *Theodore Abū Qurrah*, p. 254 (English trans.)
PG 97, cols 1541-44

STUDIES

T. Ittig, *Commentatio theologica ad Theodori Abucarae opusculum de baptismo fidelium ante Christi adventum defunctorum per aquam, quae ex eius latere profluxit*, Frankfurt, 1743

Tou autou dialexis apodeiknyousa hoti ho Patēr aei gennai ho de Hyios aei gennatai, 'By the same, A dialogue demonstrating that the Father begets eternally, while the Son is begotten eternally' (opusculum 26)

DATE Late 8th or early 9th c.
ORIGINAL LANGUAGE Greek

DESCRIPTION

This dialogue defends the thesis that the Son was begotten by the Father and that this act of begetting is not to be understood as having taken place within the realm of time. The method of argumentation is entirely philosophical.

SIGNIFICANCE

The participants in this dialogue are a representative of Orthodoxy and an anonymous heretic, whose identity is not specified. While he might be an Arian of sorts or perhaps a Jew, he might equally well be a Muslim. As can be seen from the list of MSS, it is not at all certain that this treatise was written by Abū Qurra. Important MSS, both early and late, also ascribe it to a certain Theodore the Monk or to Theodore of Raithou.

MANUSCRIPTS

MS Milan, Biblioteca Ambrosiana – sup. Q 74 (Gr. 681), starting at fol. 220v (10th c.) (anonymous; incomplete at end, des. 1565A6)

MS Sinai – Gr. 383 (Beneš. 513), fols 155r-156r (10th or 11th c.) (ascribed to Theodore Abū Qurra; incomplete at end, des. 1565A6)

MS Heidelberg, Universitätbibliothek – Palat. Gr. 281, starting at fol. 162r (1040) (anonymous)

MS Genoa, Biblioteca Franzoniana – Mission urbaine, Gr. 27, fol. 293r-v (11th c.) (ascribed to Theodore the Monk)

MS Mount Athos, Monē Batopediou – 236, fol. 2r (12th or 13th c.) (ascribed to a certain Theodore the Monk)

MS Venice, Biblioteca Nazionale Marciana – Gr. 521 (316), fols 196v-197r (13th c.) (ascribed to Theodore the Monk)

MS Wolfenbüttel, Herzog-August-Bibliothek – Gud. Gr. 102, fols 10v-11r (14th c.) (ascribed to Theodore the Presbyter of Raithou)

MS Vienna, Österreichische Nationalbibliothek – Phil. Gr. 174, fol. 126r-127r (14th c.) (anonymous)

MS Venice, Biblioteca Nazionale Marciana – Gr. 154 (398), fols 163r-165r (14th c.) (ascribed to Theodore the Monk)

MS Vat – Gr. 790, fols 169v-171r (14th or 15th c.)

MS Munich, Bayerische Staatsbibliothek – Gr. 66, fol. 38rv (16th c.) (ascribed to Theodore the Presbyter of Raithou)

MS Escorial, Biblioteca del Real Monasterio de San Lorenzo – Y I 13 (Gr. 252), fols 164r-165r (16th c.) (ascribed to Theodore Abū Qurra)

MS Vat – Reg. Gr. 108, fol. 27v (16th c.) (ascribed to Theodore Abū Qurra)

MS Munich, Bayerische Staatsbibliothek – Gr. 104, fols 284r-285r (16th c.) (ascribed to Theodore Abū Qurra)

MS Turin, Biblioteca Nazionale Universitaria – Gr. 316 (C.II.18), starting at fol. 11r (16th c.) (ascribed to Theodore the Philosopher and Bishop of Ḥarrān, called Abū Qurra; this MS was destroyed by fire in 1904)

MS Vat – Ottob. Gr. 382, fol. 36rv (17th c.) (ascribed to Theodore the Presbyter of Raithou)

MS Berlin, Staatsbibliothek – Gr. 80 (Phillipps 1484), starting at fol. 110r (17th c.) (ascribed to Theodore the Monk)

EDITIONS AND TRANSLATIONS

PG 97, cols 1561-66

STUDIES —

Hetera erōtēsis tou autou, 'Another question, by the same' (opusculum 35)

DATE Unknown

ORIGINAL LANGUAGE Greek

DESCRIPTION

This work, a dialogue between a Christian and a Muslim, is concerned first with the origins of evil and the defense of human free will. The author seeks to show the error of the Muslims when they claim that God is the source of both good and evil. The author then turns to the Muslim claim that Jesus is the Word and Spirit of God, and seeks to show that as such the Son is eternal.

SIGNIFICANCE

This work has traditionally been assigned to Abū Qurra, though none of the known MSS actually ascribes it to him. The four extant copies of this work transmit it anonymously, but together with other, authentic works by Abū Qurra. Rather than being a work by Abū Qurra, this seems to be a slightly abbreviated selection from the so-called *Dialexis Sarakenou kai Christianou* (q.v. 'Dialogue between a Saracen and a Christian'), which has traditionally been ascribed to John of Damascus (*Clavis Patrum Graecorum* 8075).

MANUSCRIPTS

MS Venice, Biblioteca Nazionale Marciana – Gr. 521 (316), between fols 168r and 170v (13th c.)

MS Wolfenbüttel, Herzog-August-Bibliothek – Gud. Gr. 102, fols 32r-33r (14th c.)
MS Munich, Bayerische Staatsbibliothek – Gr. 66, fols 59v-61r (16th c.)
MS Vat – Ottob. Gr. 382, fols 86v-89v (17th c.)

EDITIONS AND TRANSLATIONS

Glei and Khoury, *Johannes Damaskenos und Theodor Abū Qurra*, pp. 154-59 (edition and German trans.)
(G. Sablukov), 'Protivomusul'manskiia͡ sochineniia͡ episkopa Ḟeodora Abukary', pp. 190-92 (Russian trans.)
PG 97, cols 1587-92

STUDIES —

Hetera erōtēsis, 'Another question' (opusculum 36)

DATE Unknown
ORIGINAL LANGUAGE Greek

DESCRIPTION

This short work is a dialogue between a Christian and a Muslim. It seeks to establish that God has a Word and that this Word is eternal.

SIGNIFICANCE

See the comments on p. 488.

MANUSCRIPTS

MS Venice, Biblioteca Nazionale Marciana – Gr. 521 (316), between fols 168r and 170v (13th c.)
MS Wolfenbüttel, Herzog-August-Bibliothek – Gud. Gr. 102, fol. 33r-v (14th c.)
MS Munich, Bayerische Staatsbibliothek – Gr. 66, fol. 61r-v (16th c.)
MS Vat – Ottob. Gr. 382, fols 89v-90r (17th c.)

EDITIONS AND TRANSLATIONS

Glei and Khoury, *Johannes Damaskenos und Theodor Abū Qurra*, pp. 160-61 (edition and German trans.)
(G. Sablukov), 'Protivomusul'manskiia͡ sochineniia͡ episkopa Ḟeodora Abukary', p. 192 (Russian trans.)
PG 97, cols 1592-94

STUDIES —

Hetera erōtēsis, 'Another question' (opusculum 37)

DATE Unknown

ORIGINAL LANGUAGE Greek

DESCRIPTION

Again, a short dialogue between a Christian and a Muslim. Two questions are treated: that Mary did not die, and that God did not create anything after the first seven days of creation.

SIGNIFICANCE

See the comments on p. 488.

MANUSCRIPTS

MS Venice, Biblioteca Nazionale Marciana – Gr. 521 (316), between fols 168r and 170v (13th c.)

MS Wolfenbüttel, Herzog-August-Bibliothek – Gud. Gr. 102, fols 33v-34r (14th c.)

MS Munich, Bayerische Staatsbibliothek – Gr. 66, fols 61v-62r (16th c.)

MS Vat – Ottob. Gr. 382, fol. 90r-v (17th c.)

EDITIONS AND TRANSLATIONS

Glei and Khoury, *Johannes Damaskenos und Theodor Abū Qurra*, pp. 162-63 (edition and German trans.)

(G. Sablukov), 'Protivomusul'manskiia͡ sochineniia͡ episkopa Ḟeodora Abukary', p. 192 (Russian trans.)

PG 97, cols 1593-94

STUDIES —

Hetera erōtēsis, 'Another question' (opusculum 38)

DATE Unknown

ORIGINAL LANGUAGE Greek

DESCRIPTION

Again, a short dialogue between a Christian and a Muslim. The author argues that the fact that John the Baptist baptized Christ does not mean that John is greater than Christ.

SIGNIFICANCE

See the comments on p. 488.

MANUSCRIPTS

MS Venice, Biblioteca Nazionale Marciana, Gr. 521 (316), between fols 168r and 170v (13th c.)

MS Wolfenbüttel, Herzog-August-Bibliothek – Gud. Gr. 102, fol. 34r (14th c.)
MS Munich, Bayerische Staatsbibliothek – Gr. 66, fol. 62r (16th c.)
MS Vat – Ottob. Gr. 382, fols 90v-91r (17th c.)

EDITIONS AND TRANSLATIONS

Glei and Khoury, *Johannes Damaskenos und Theodor Abū Qurra*, pp. 164-65 (edition and German trans.)
(G. Sablukov), 'Protivomusul'manskiia͡ sochineniia͡ episkopa Ḟeodora Abukary', pp. 192-93 (Russian trans.)
PG 97, cols 1593-96

STUDIES —

Untitled, 'Truth of the orthodox faith'

DATE Late 8th or early 9th c.
ORIGINAL LANGUAGE Greek

DESCRIPTION

This work seeks to defend the truth of the Orthodox faith against the impiety of the Muslims. The argument is largely philosophical. The main topics treated include: that God has a Son; that God is a Trinity of persons; that God's nature cannot be comprehended; the philosophical and scriptural understandings of the name 'Son'; the Muslim claim that Jesus is the Word and Spirit of God; that God is known both from reason and revelation.

SIGNIFICANCE

Only a single copy of this work would appear to have been preserved. The MS ascribes it explicitly to the 'Blessed Theodore Abū Qurra, the Bishop of Ḥarrān'. The text does not seem to be identical with any other known Greek refutation of Islam, whether by Abū Qurra or anyone else. Further research is needed in order to determine the work's provenance and authenticity.

MANUSCRIPTS

MS Mount Athos, Monē Megistēs Lauras – *L* 135, fols 695r-698r (15th c.)

EDITIONS AND TRANSLATIONS —

STUDIES —

John C. Lamoreaux 2007

The Arabic Sibylline prophecy

Unknown series of redactors

DATE OF BIRTH 8th c.
PLACE OF BIRTH Unknown
DATE OF DEATH 8th-9th c.
PLACE OF DEATH Unknown

BIOGRAPHY

Nothing is known of the anonymous redactors of a sequence of 8th- and early 9th-century recensions of an ongoing Arabic Christian apocalyptic tradition, recently entitled *The Arabic Sibylline prophecy* (Ebied and Young, 'Newly-discovered version'), other than what can be deduced from the texts themselves and the date and provenance of their manuscript witnesses. The oldest manuscript witnesses are found at the Monastery of St Catherine at Mount Sinai. A 'primitive' recension was expanded during or just after the period of turmoil that followed the death of the Caliph Hārūn al-Rashīd (d. 809). There are repeated references to Syria at this point in the expanded text. Taken together, these (rather slight) indications suggest that 'The Arabic Sibylline prophecy' took shape in the hands of Syrian Melkites, perhaps clerics or monks, perhaps at the end of the 8th century and certainly by the beginning of the 9th.

MAIN SOURCES OF INFORMATION

Primary —

Secondary —

WORKS ON CHRISTIAN-MUSLIM RELATIONS

Ḥikmat Sibillā ibnat Harqalus raʾs ḥunafāʾ Afasus, allādhī tanabbaʾat ʿalā l-manẓar allādhī naẓarū hāʾulāʾika l-miʾat rajul fī layla wāḥida, 'The Wisdom of Sibilla, daughter of Heraclius, head of the pagans of Ephesus, which she prophesied concerning the vision that those hundred men saw in a single night'

(This is according to the oldest manuscript, Sinai ar. 461 (9th-10th c.), fol. 34a, although details vary from manuscript to manuscript. The first noun in the title may be *ḥikma* ('wisdom'), *qiṣṣa* ('story'), or *nubuwwa* ('prophesy'), while the name of the prophetess is written in various ways with uncertain vocalization, e.g. Sibilla/Sabilla or Sabīla, ending either in *alif* or *tāʾ marbūṭa*.)

Modern titles: 'The Arabic Sibylline prophecy', 'The oriental Sibylline oracle', and the like

DATE The 'primitive' Arabic recension may date to the 8th c. An expanded recension took shape c. 815.

ORIGINAL LANGUAGE Arabic (although the tradition reworks material known in Latin and Greek)

DESCRIPTION

A Christian apocalyptic legend which has come down to us in a variety of Latin, Greek, Arabic and Ethiopic recensions relates how an elderly prophetess or sibyl interpreted a mysterious dream or vision about nine suns experienced simultaneously by 100 wise men of Rome. According to the sibyl, the nine suns represent the nine ages of humanity, progressing from the darkness of paganism to the appearance of Christ, the reign of Constantine, other historical events important to the redactor of each recension, and finally the eschatological woes and the drama of the End. The legend appears to have taken shape towards the end of the 4th century in Greek, and was soon translated into Latin (see Sackur, *Sibyllinische texte*, on the 'Tiburtine Sibyl') as well as expanded in Greek (see Alexander, *The oracle of Baalbek*). There seems to be little *direct* relationship, however, between these earlier texts and the Arabic Sibylline prophecy.

The oldest manuscript witnesses to the Arabic Sibylline prophecy are from the 9th-10th century (Sinai ar. 461, only one folio) and from the year 1002 (Sinai ar. NF pap. 34, unfilmed and unpublished except for one photograph); these establish the text's first-millennium date and presence in the early Arabic Melkite library. While little comparative study of the recensions of the text has been undertaken since Schleifer, *Erzählungen* in 1908, it may be useful in a provisional way to divide the known texts into three categories:

1. The 'primitive' Melkite recension

A 'primitive' Arabic recension (represented by Schleifer's 'Arab.I'), of Melkite provenance, may date to the 8th century. It does not name Muḥammad and refers only vaguely to 'a people that comes out from the mountains' who will 'possess most of the earth' and be given power over 'the kings of the Byzantines, the Copts and others'. They will reign for an entire Generation – but then rule will return 'to the believers and the Byzantines'.

2. The 'post-Hārūn' Melkite recensions

More detail is found in a set of recensions (the other recensions edited by Schleifer as well as 'Arab. IV' of Ebied and Young, 'Unrecorded Arabic version'), also originally of Melkite provenance, which is characterized by a series of *vaticinia ex eventu* in its 'historical' section that conclude with a clear reference to the struggle over the succession to the Caliph Hārūn al-Rashīd (d. 809). According to most manuscripts of this set, the Seventh Generation closes with the appearance of 'a man from the South' (*rajul min al-tayman*) the 'number of whose name' is 40-8-40-4 (the Arabic letters of 'Muḥammad' read as numerals). The description of the Eighth Generation gives some details of the wars between the Arabs and the Byzantines, possibly including a failed siege of Constantinople. The Caliph Hārūn al-Rashīd (r. 786-809) is described as 'a king who completed 23 years but did not complete 24'. The text mentions embassies to his court from the Franks, general prosperity, his two sons (one named Muḥammad [al-Amīn]), and the breakdown of order after his death.

3. A later recension made by Copts

The above recensions must be distinguished from a recension made by Copts (represented by 'Arab. V' in Ebied and Young, 'Newly-discovered version', and also epitomized in Chapter 70 of al-Mu'taman ibn al-ʿAssāl's 13th-century compendium *Majmūʿ uṣūl al-dīn*). It appears to be of late 11th-century origin: much of its description of the Eighth

Generation is devoted to the Fāṭimids, and especially to events during the reign of the Fāṭimid Caliph al-Mustanṣir (r. 1035-94).

In every recension, Christ is referred to as 'he who was hung upon the cross'. While this appears to be a feature of pre-Islamic recensions of the apocalypse, in the Islamic context it took on a special, assertive significance.

SIGNIFICANCE

The Arabic Sibylline prophecy belongs to the very earliest body of Arabic Christian literature; indeed, its oldest Arabic recension may be the oldest *Arabic-language* Christian apocalyptic work in existence. The ongoing Sibylline tradition functioned to give encouragement and hope to Christians living under Islamic rule, especially during periods of political instability and chaos (such as ensued after the death of Hārūn al-Rashīd in 809).

While originally of Melkite provenance, the tradition spread to other Christian communities, including in Ethiopia (where the Ethiopic version was closely related to the earlier Melkite recension) and in Egypt (where the 'historical' part of the prophecy was rewritten to emphasize the tumultuous events of the later 11th century).

MANUSCRIPTS

See Graf, *GCAL* i, pp. 292-94, to which should be added:

MS Sinai – ar. 461 (9th-10th c.), fol. 34 (only one folio of the text preserved)

MS Sinai – NF pap. 34 (1002) (unfilmed and unpublished except for a single photograph: I.E. Meïmarēs, *Katalogos tōn neōn arabikōn cheirographōn tēs hieras Monēs Hagias Aikaterinēs tou orous Sina*, Athens, 1985, Arabic pp. 50-51 (description of the manuscript), photograph no. 105)

In addition, Ebied and Young add:

MS Leeds, University Library – Arabic 184 (18th c.), fols 7v-13v (a witness to the post-Hārūn Melkite recension)

MS Oxford, Bodleian Library – Huntington 328, fols 154v-160r (a witness to the later recension of the Copts)

EDITIONS AND TRANSLATIONS

It is useful to divide the editions and translations according to the three categories described above:

1. The 'primitive' Melkite recension

J. Schleifer, *Die Erzählungen der Sibylle. Ein Apokryph nach den karschunischen, arabischen und äthiopischen Handschriften zu London, Oxford, Paris und Rom*, Vienna, 1908 (Denkschriften der kaiserlichen Akademie der Wissenschaften in Wien, philosophisch-historische Klasse, LIII, 1), pp. 7-49 (edition), pp. 50-73 (German trans.), 'Arab. I'

R. Basset, *Les apocryphes éthiopiens*, X: *La sagesse de Sibylle*, Paris, 1900, pp. 41-53 (French trans.)

2. The 'post-Hārūn' Melkite recensions

R.Y. Ebied and M.J.L. Young, 'An unrecorded Arabic version of a Sibylline prophecy', *OCP* 43 (1977) 279-307 (edition and English trans. of a text that expands on Schleifer's 'Arab. III', which the editors label 'Arab. IV')

Schleifer, *Erzählungen*, pp. 6-49 (edition of the 'Karschunish', 'Äthiopisch', 'Arab. II' and 'Arab. III' recensions), pp. 50-73 (German trans. of the 'Karschunish' and 'Äthiopisch' recensions)

Basset, *Sagesse*, 27-40 (French trans. of the Ethiopic version), 54-62 (French trans. of a text corresponding to Schleifer's 'Arab. II')

3. A later recension made by Copts

Al-Muʾtaman ibn al-ʿAssāl, *Summa dei principi della religione*, ed. A. Wadi, trans. B. Pirone, 6 vols, Cairo, 1998-2002 (Studia Orientalia Christiana Monographia 6a-b, 7a-b, 8-9), ch. 70, §§ 12-43 (critical edition of al-Muʾtaman's epitome of the text, with Italian trans.)

R.Y. Ebied and M.J.L. Young, 'A newly-discovered version of the Arabic Sibylline prophecy', *OC* 60 (1976) 83-94 (partial edition and English trans. of a witness to this recension of the Copts, which the editors label 'Arab. V')

Ruʾya Sābila al-ḥakīma, (s.l.), (s.d.) (19-page publication from Egypt bearing no publication information; mid-20th c.?)

STUDIES

B. Roggema, *The legend of Sergius Baḥīrā. Eastern Christian apologetics and apocalyptic in response to Islam*, Leiden, 2008, p. 63

M.N. Swanson, 'The Christian al-Maʾmūn tradition', in D. Thomas (ed.), *Christians at the heart of Islamic rule. Church life and scholarship in ʿAbbasid Iraq*, Leiden, 2003, 63-92, pp. 84-85

Ebied and Young, 'An unrecorded Arabic version of a Sibylline prophecy'

Ebied and Young, 'A newly-discovered version of the Arabic Sibylline prophecy'

P.J. Alexander, *The oracle of Baalbek. The Tiburtine Sibyl in Greek dress*, Washington DC, 1967 (edition and English trans. of a Greek recension, with helpful discussion of the history of the tradition in Greek and Latin; see pp. 136-43)

J. Schleifer, 'Die Weisheit der Sibylle. Ein kritischer Beitrag', *Wiener Zeitschrift für die Kunde des Morgenlandes* 24 (1910) 33-50

Schleifer, *Erzählungen*

Basset, *Les apocryphes éthiopiens*, X

E. Sackur, *Sibyllinische texte und forschungen: Pseudomethodius, Adso und die tiburtinische Sibylle*, Halle a.S., 1898

Mark N. Swanson 2008

The Martyrdom of Anthony (Rawḥ al-Qurashī)

Unknown author

DATE OF BIRTH Unknown
PLACE OF BIRTH Unknown
DATE OF DEATH After 25 December 799
PLACE OF DEATH Unknown

BIOGRAPHY

Nothing is known of this author beyond what can be deduced from the text of the *Martyrdom* he composed. He was an Arabic-speaking Melkite Christian, possibly a monk.

MAIN SOURCES OF INFORMATION

Primary

See below, references under Manuscripts, Editions and Translations

Secondary

See below, references under Studies

WORKS ON CHRISTIAN-MUSLIM RELATIONS

The text is untitled, but begins: 'This is the account of the martyrdom of the noble Saint Anthony'; 'The Martyrdom of Anthony (Rawḥ al-Qurashī)'

DATE Early 9th c.
ORIGINAL LANGUAGE Arabic

DESCRIPTION

The text tells the story of Rawḥ al-Qurashī, nephew of the Caliph Hārūn al-Rashīd, who used to witness activities at the Church of St Theodore near his home in Damascus. On occasion, he would enter the church and desecrate the elements, tear down the crosses, and commit other acts of vandalism. One day, infuriated at the sight of an icon of St Theodore, he shot an arrow it, but the arrow turned in mid-air and pierced his hand. Some days later, Rawḥ followed a procession of Christians into the church where he saw the elements of the eucharist transformed into a lamb upon the altar. Later that evening he saw a vision of St Theodore, who commanded him to believe in Christ. Overcome, the young Rawḥ converted to Christianity and followed some Christians to Jerusalem to meet Patriarch Elias. Soon afterwards he was baptized in the river Jordan and was re-named Anthony. After putting on the monk's habit, he returned to Damascus where his identity as a Muslim convert to Christianity became known. As a result, he suffered several imprisonments but also received confirming visions. He was eventually condemned by Hārūn al-Rashīd, and beheaded on the banks of the Euphrates.

The martyrdom account follows a pattern common to the earliest accounts of Christian martyrs under Islam. In this case, however, the protagonist is a Muslim who, after seeing a series of miracles, converts to Christianity; upon his baptism he is given a new name, Anthony. Miracles and dreams play an important role in confirming the truth of Christian faith vis-à-vis Islam.

The text is approximately 1,600 words long in Dick's printed edition. A shorter 'Autobiography' exists in MS Vat-Ar 175, fols 116v-121v. This latter text tells the story of Anthony in the first person and was clearly intended for public reading/performance (see Vila, *Christian martyrs*, pp. 131-40).

SIGNIFICANCE

The Martyrdom of Anthony is one of the more significant hagiographical texts from the first ʿAbbasid century, especially for discerning the nature of Christian-Muslim relations. The themes that are common to texts of this type are all present: conversion of a Muslim to Christianity, confirming miracles, an offer extended to him by a Muslim authority figure to return to Islam, a profession of faith by the Christian, and the eventual martyrdom.

A few additional factors are especially significant. First, the Muslim convert to Christianity is a Muslim of noble birth, a relative of Hārūn al-Rashīd, we are told, and of the tribe of Quraysh. Second, Anthony's 'confession' before his martyrdom seems clearly to be a polemical/apologetic addition to the text (see Vila, *Christian martyrs*, pp. 115-19). Anthony repents of his having participated in Muslim worship (sacrifice on ʿId al-aḍḥā and prayer facing Mecca) and having raided Byzantine lands. These features are informative not only as factors in the account of Anthony, but as indications of the types of issues that Christians in the mid-9th century considered obstacles to conversion to Christianity from Islam. The text asserts that no matter how deeply Muslim one might have been, any obstacles to conversion to Christianity, the true faith, can be overcome. The important thing is to embrace the Christian faith, and the miracles and visions of the story are an aid to this end. Finally, the text is also important for providing insight into Arab Christian polemics against Islam. The Muslims are presented as violent and coercive in their attempt to make Anthony reconvert to Islam. Attempts are even made to bribe Anthony with money and clothing. Similar themes arise in the more traditional apologetics of the period and find their confirmation in the narrative of Anthony.

MANUSCRIPTS

MS Sinai – Ar. 513, fols 363r-372v (10th c.)
MS BL – Or. 5019, fols 100r-103v (10th-11th c.)
MS Sinai – Ar. 445, fols 437r-447v (1233)
MS Sinai – Ar. 448, fols 95v-99r (13th c.)
MS Beirut, Bibliothèque Orientale – 625 (17th c.)

The story was also translated into Ethiopic; see Peeters, 'S. Antoine le néo-martyr'.

The 'Autobiography' of Anthony is contained in:

MS Vat – Arab. 175, fols 122v-127v (14th c.). The Arabic text was translated into Georgian; see Peeters, 'L' autobiographie de S. Antoine'.

EDITIONS AND TRANSLATIONS

E. Braida and C. Pelissetti, *Storia di Rawḥ al-Qurašī. Un discendente di Maometto che scelse di divenire cristiano*, Turin, 2001 (re-edition of the editions of Dick and Peeters, as well as the Latin texts of parallel passages in the *Lives* of St George and St Theodore, with Italian trans.)

B. Pirone, 'Un altro manoscritto sulla vita e sul martirio del nobile qurayshita Rawḥ', in L. Cagni (ed.), *Biblica et Semitica*, Naples, 1999, 479-509 (edition of the text according to BL – Or. 5019, with Italian trans.)

I. Dick, 'La passion arabe de S. Antoine Ruwaḥ, néo-martyr de Damas († 25 déc, 799)', *Le Muséon* 74 (1961) 109-33 (Arabic text of Sinai – Ar. 513, noting some variants from Sinai – Ar. 445 and 448, and French trans.)

P. Peeters, 'S. Antoine le néo-martyr', *AB* 31 (1912) 410-50 (Arabic and Ethiopic editions, based on late and defective manuscripts, with Latin trans.)

STUDIES

C. Foss, 'Byzantine Saints in Early Islamic Syria,' *AB* 125 (2007) 93-119, pp. 109-111

Braida and Pelissetti, *Storia de Rawḥ al-Qurašī* (includes an important introduction listing the attestations of the saint in other Christian and Muslim literature, and reviewing modern studies of the saint, pp. 31-37)

Pirone, 'Un altro manoscritto'

D. Vila, *Christian martyrs in the first Abbasid century and the development of an apologetic against Islam*, St Louis MO, 1999 (Diss. Saint Louis University), pp. 97-140

S.H. Griffith, 'Christians, Muslims, and neo-martyrs. Saints' lives and Holy Land history', in A. Kofsky and G.G. Stroumsa, *Sharing the sacred. Religious contacts and conflicts in the Holy Land, first-fifteenth centuries CE*, Jerusalem, 1998, 163-207, pp. 198-200

S.K. Samir, 'Saint Rawḥ al-Qurašī. Étude d'onomastique arabe et authenticité de sa passion', *Le Muséon* 105 (1992) 343-59

Dick, 'La passion arabe de S. Antoine Ruwaḥ'

P. Peeters, 'L'autobiographie de S. Antoine le néo-martyr', *AB* 33 (1914) 52-63 (summary of a different recension of the story)

Peeters, 'S. Antoine le néo-martyr'

David Vila 2007

Job of Edessa

Job 'the Spotted', Ayyub Urhāyā, Ayyūb al-Ruhāwī 'al-Abrash'

DATE OF BIRTH Unknown, probably c. 760
PLACE OF BIRTH Probably Edessa
DATE OF DEATH Unknown, after 832
PLACE OF DEATH Unknown

BIOGRAPHY

Job of Edessa was a philosopher, physician and translator in Baghdad during the caliphate of al-Maʾmūn. His association with the ʿAbbasid court is evidenced by the fact that he was one of al-Maʾmūn's physicians, at least according to a late source (Yāqūt, *Irshād*). At the opening of his *Book of treasures*, he is called 'chief physician' (*resh asawātā*).

Job's translation activity was predominantly in the field of medicine; the famous physician of the ʿAbbasid family, Jibrīl ibn Bukhtīshūʿ (d. 829), commissioned several translations from him. His specialization seems to have been the work of Galen, at least 36 of whose works he translated from Greek into Syriac. The titles of his translations from Galen are known through Job's younger colleague Ḥunayn ibn Isḥāq (d. 873) (q.v.), who listed Galen's 129 known works and their translators, including himself. He criticized some of Job's translations and called one of them 'incomprehensible'. Nonetheless, they often served as the starting point for Ḥunayn's own translations into Arabic. Ibn al-Nadīm also mentions someone called Job, together with a certain Simʿān, as the translators of the Ptolemaic tables (the so-called *Zīj*) for one of the Barmakids. Several scholars have interpreted this passage in Ibn al-Nadīm's *Fihrist* as a reference to Job of Edessa, but Mingana questioned the correctness of this assumption, on account of the fact that Job's *Book of treasures* does not reveal any knowledge of Ptolemy.

Most of Job's works are lost, but some of their titles are known. One of his works on urine, *Kitāb al-tafsīra fī l-bawl* was used by Muḥammad ibn Aḥmad al-Khwārazmī (d. 997) as a source for his scientific encyclopedia *Mafātīḥ al-ʿulūm*. Another title of a work on urine is given as *Kitāb al-bayān limā yūjibuhu taghayyur al-bawl*. Both of these are mentioned by the 10th-century medical scholar Abū l-Ḥasan Aḥmad al-Ṭabarī. Some other titles are known through Job's own references to them in the extant *Book of treasures* and the *Book of canine hydrophobia*. These are: *The causes of fevers*, *The soul*, *The causes of the coming into existence of the universe from the elements*, *The five senses* and *The essences*. Muṭahhar ibn Ṭāhir al-Maqdisī mentions a *Kitāb al-tafsīr* by Job, which is possibly a reference to the *Book of treasures* or the *Kitāb al-tafsīra fī l-bawl*, rather than to an otherwise unknown work. Al-Birūnī was also familiar with Job's scholarship, but he does not mention any titles (Sezgin *GAS* iii, p. 231).

Considering the fact that Job was active in the entourage of the ʿAbbasid court and had a considerable output, it is surprising that so little is known about his life. His religious affiliation seems to have been the Church of the East, although this is only explicitly stated by Barhebraeus (d. 1286), who describes him as a philosopher 'who followed the doctrine of the Nestorians' in the time of the Patriarch Timothy I (q.v.). Mingana assumed that he had converted from the Melkite or Syrian Orthodox Church to the Church of the East. Presumably this assumption was based on the fact that Job's name suggests that he was from Edessa, a city where few people belonged to the Church of the East. His dates of birth and death are estimates, but Yāqūt still refers to him as being alive in 832, when he served as the personal physician of ʿAbdallāh ibn Ṭāhir, the governor of Khurāsān.

MAIN SOURCES OF INFORMATION

Primary

Ḥunayn ibn Isḥāq, *Risāla ilā ʿAlī ibn Yaḥyā fī dhikr mā turjima min kutub Jālīnūs bi ʿilmihi wa-baʿḍ mā lam yutarjam*, in G. Bergsträsser, *Hunain ibn Ishāq über die syrischen und arabischen Galenübersetzungen*, Leipzig, 1925

Muṭahhar ibn Ṭāhir al-Maqdisī, *al-Badʾ wa-l-taʾrīkh*, ed. C. Huart, 6 parts in 3 vols, Beirut, s.d., i, part i, p. 140

Ibn al-Nadīm, *Fihrist*, pp. 304-5

Yāqūt, *Kitāb irshād al-arīb ilā maʿrifat al-adīb*, ed. D.S. Margoliouth, 7 vols, London, 1907-27, i, p. 122

Ibn Abī Uṣaybiʿa, *ʿUyūn al-anbāʾ fī ṭabaqāt al-aṭibbāʾ*, 2 vols, Cairo (1886), i, pp. 170-71, 204

J.B. Abbeloos and Th. J. Lamy, *Gregorii Barhebraei Chronicon ecclesiasticum*, 3 vols, Paris, 1872-77, ii, p. 181

Secondary

B. Roggema, art. 'Job of Edessa', in G. Kiraz and L. van Rompay (eds), *Encyclopedic dictionary of the Syriac heritage*, Piscataway, 2009

J. Teixidor, *Hommage à Baghdad. Traducteurs et lettrés de l'époque ʿabbaside*, Paris, 2007, pp. 58-63

Yūsuf Ḥabbī, art. 'Ayyūb al-Abrash al-Ruhāwī', in *Muʿjam al-adab al-suryānī*, Baghdad, 1990, i, pp. 272-74

Y. Ḥabbī, 'Ayyūb al-Abrash al-Ruhāwī (AD 9/H. 3)', *Majallat al-majmaʿ al-ʿilmī al-ʿIrāqī* 34 (1983) 124-42

Sezgin, *GAS* iii, pp. 230-31, 315, v, p. 167 , vi, p. 96, viii, p. 168

A. Mingana, *Encyclopædia of philosophical and natural sciences as taught in Baghdad about A.D. 817 or* Book of treasures *by Job of Edessa*, Cambridge, 1935

WORKS ON CHRISTIAN-MUSLIM RELATIONS

Syāmā ḥad b-yad ʿesrā sulughismē kyānāyē da-mḥawwēn ʿal mshiḥā d-Alāhā hu w-barnāshā , 'Treatise containing ten syllogisms taken from the nature of things, which prove that Christ is both God and man', 'Treatise to prove that Christ is both God and man'

DATE Unknown, probably before 817
ORIGINAL LANGUAGE Syriac

DESCRIPTION

This treatise is only known through a later work of Job of Edessa, the *Book of treasures*, in which he briefly explains its content and purpose, as follows: 'Our aim has generally been in all our works to demonstrate our statements from the nature of things. The testimonies taken from the Books are accepted without question by believers only, while non-believers do not accept them. For this reason, we wrote a book containing ten syllogisms taken from the nature of things, which prove that Christ is both God and man, and we added to each of these natural syllogisms many testimonies from all the books of the prophets and the holy Gospel, which demonstrate that Christ is both God and man. We based it on the method of three laws: the natural, the written and the spiritual, a method that points to the Holy Trinity. We quoted many testimonies from the books in it, because it was our aim to do so' (Mingana, p. 458, trans. pp. 278-79 (adapted)).

On the basis of this description, we can conclude that from the point of view of method, this book was not radically different from Job's *Book of treasures*, in which he also takes nature as the prime source of our knowledge of the physical and spiritual world, and then adds testimonies from scripture as auxiliary proof.

SIGNIFICANCE

From the description of this work in the relevant passage in the *Book of treasures*, in which Job explains why he does not allot a primary role to scriptural proofs in his work, it becomes clear that he was searching for a philosophical language that was universally acceptable and by means of which he could confirm the truth of Christianity to Christians and demonstrate it to non-Christians, most of whom, in his milieu, were of course Muslims.

MANUSCRIPTS —

EDITIONS AND TRANSLATIONS —

STUDIES

G.J. Reinink, 'The "Book of nature" and Syriac apologetics against Islam. The case of Job of Edessa's *Book of treasures*', in A. Vanderjagt and K. van Berkel (eds), *The Book of nature in the Middle Ages*, Leuven, 2005, 71-84, pp. 73-74

Syāmā ʿal haymānutā ,'Treatise on faith'

DATE Unknown, probably before 817

ORIGINAL LANGUAGE Syriac

DESCRIPTION

This is another lost apologetic treatise to which Job refers in the *Book of treasures* (Mingana, p. 458, trans. p. 279). He mentions that it treated various aspects of the Christian faith, such as the unitarian and trinitarian nature of God, the necessity of baptism, the eucharist, worship to the east, i.e. apologetic topics of crucial importance to Christians in the Muslim world, but also the existence of God and His creation of the world *ex nihilo*, i.e. issues that were relevant in contemporary debates with the *Dahriyya* , who believed in the eternity of the world.

Job explains in somewhat cryptic terms why he did not use any scriptural proofs in this work, 'since they pertain to the believers and the believers do not miss (their point) and are familiar with them' (*meṭṭul d-hālēn d-mhaymnē (e)nēn w-mhaym(n)ē lā pādin w-yādʿin l-hēn*).

SIGNIFICANCE

Although brief, the passage in which Job of Edessa refers to this work is an interesting reflection on apologetic methods. Following the trend of his time to search for universally acceptable proofs, he alludes to the fact that proofs formulated for 'internal consumption' can be different from those for outsiders. Paradoxically, he seems to suggest that scriptural proofs are of little value to believers, because they already know them; this may suggest that in the case of the other lost apologetic work, in which he *did* include them, he thought them to be of value to outsiders, especially Muslims, not as proof texts *per se*, but as a way to show that the Bible is in agreement with the realities of nature.

MANUSCRIPTS —

EDITIONS AND TRANSLATIONS —

STUDIES

Reinink, 'The "Book of nature" and Syriac apologetics against Islam', pp. 73-74

Ktābā d-simātā, 'Book of treasures'

DATE Probably c. 817

ORIGINAL LANGUAGE Syriac

DESCRIPTION

This extensive work, which covers almost 300 pages in Mingana's translation, comprises a detailed analysis of a wide range of natural phenomena which aims at detecting how the principle characteristics of the elements shape the natural world. The fact that Job states that he hopes to finish the book despite the war that was raging (p. 154), has led Mingana to assume that the work was written during the fourth civil war, i.e. around the year 817.

It is structured in six discourses, moving from an initial exposé of the elements, matter, and the First Cause, to questions regarding aspects of nature pertaining to a range of disciplines, such as metallurgy, meteorology, astronomy and anatomy, and detailed explanations of phenomena specific to classes of animals (e.g. why fish do not have hands or feet) and gender (e.g. why beards grow on men but not on eunuchs). A considerable part of the work is devoted to the senses and colors in light of the question of the distinction between essence and attribute. This part of the book deals with the same topics as some of Job's contemporary Muʿtazilī philosophers, in particular al-Naẓẓām, to whom he alludes as the head of the 'new philosophers' who erroneously conceive of colors, sounds, smells and tastes as essences instead of accidents (Mingana, p. 388, translation pp. 153-54).

Although the author was keen to stress the originality of his work, he reveals a number of his sources, notably Galen, Hippocrates, and Aristotle. According to Mingana, Job's allusion to 'Indian sages' may point to the ancient philosophers and physicians Sharaka and Susruta, often cited by ʿAlī ibn Rabban al-Ṭabarī (q.v.) in his *Firdaws al-ḥikma*. Job also refers to unnamed Persian scholars. However, what remains unclear is how the work relates to the Arabic work, *Kitāb sirr al-khalīqa*, ('The secret of creation', also known as the *Kitāb al-ʿilal*). This extensive cosmological-hermetic work ascribed to Apollonius of Tyana (Arabic Bālinūs) and fundamentally important to medieval alchemy, shows some strong similarities with the *Book of treasures*. Kraus has discovered that their structure is similar, albeit in reverse order, and there are passages which are almost literally the same. The two works perhaps have a common source that integrates part of the work of Nemesius of Emesa's *De natura hominis*. In addition, Lewin has pointed out several parallels between the *Book of treasures* and an Arabic treatise attributed to Proclus, in the form of an overlapping series of questions about human physiology in the style of *problemata physica*. Teixidor discusses the influence of the Cappadocian Fathers on Job and assumes that he was also familiar with the thought of Theodore bar Koni (q.v.).

On account of the programmatic nature of the book, it has been argued that the work should not be labeled an 'encyclopedia', as proposed by Mingana. The author sets out a comprehensive view on the universe and pursues the specific aim of deriving the knowledge of God from the knowledge of nature, with a deeper aim of vindicating the Christian understanding of God and the universe, as Reinink has convincingly shown. Part of the strategy employed towards that aim is the subtle undermining of Islamic theology, in particular its conception of a physical afterlife. Without ever mentioning Islam, the final discourse is a deconstruction of its otherworldly promises. Job shows that the kinds of pleasures promised in the Qurʾān are not only inferior to man's ultimate purpose of the *theoria* of God, but also untenable from the point of physics, since these pleasures involve numerous antagonistic forces between the elements, which cannot exist once the world is dissolved. He also makes clear that the claim of Islamic theologians that the consumption of food in heaven will not lead to waste products, is untenable from the point of view of physics and therefore only acceptable through faith and not through rational inquiry. This is probably meant as a veiled critique of the Muʿtalizīs, with whom Job was in contact in ʿAbbasid circles.

SIGNIFICANCE

The work is an interesting example of how Syriac-speaking Christians in the early ʿAbbasid period formed a link in the chain of transmission of classical science to contemporary Arabic culture, and how, at the same time, they reformulated Christian apologetics in the light of Islamic doctrine. Job's particular focus on the distinction between what should be accepted by faith and what should be accepted through rational inquiry of the physical world is emblematic of the apologetic trend of the time.

Although elements of the *Book of treasures* can be traced in later scientific writings by both Christians and Muslims, Job's arguments against the Islamic doctrines regarding life after death does not seem to have influenced the works of later apologists directly. Nevertheless, the book could well have elicited works in defense of the Islamic afterlife, such as *Against the Christians on felicity and eating and drinking in the hereafter, and against whoever teaches in opposition to this* by Ḥumayd ibn Saʿīd ibn Bakhtiyār (q.v.).

MANUSCRIPTS

MS Harvard, Houghton Library – Syr. 132 (1904, copied in Harput)

MS Mingana – Syr. 559 (1930, copy of a MS in Caesarea from the year 1221 whose current location is unknown)

EDITIONS AND TRANSLATIONS

Van Ess, *TG* vi, pp. 86-94 (German trans. of fragments on the senses and colors, relevant to al-Naẓẓām's philosophy)

Mingana, *Encyclopædia of philosophical and natural sciences* (facsimile edition of MS Mingana – Syr. 559 and (paraphrasing) trans.)

STUDIES

B. Roggema, *The Legend of Sergius Baḥīrā. Eastern Christian apologetics and apocalyptic in response to Islam*, Leiden, 2009, pp. 123-26

G.J. Reinink, 'The "Book of nature" and Syriac apologetics against Islam'
Van Ess, *TG* iii, pp. 44, 333-41, 346, 355-56, 359
U. Weisser, *Das Buch über das Geheimnis der Schöpfung von Ps Apollonios von Tyana*, Berlin, 1980, pp. 55-63
Sezgin, *GAS* iv, pp. 80-81, 156
M. Ullmann, *Die Medizin im Islam*, Leiden, 1970, pp. 101-2
M. Levey, 'Chemical notions of an early ninth century Christian encyclopaedist', *Chymia* 11 (1966) 29-36
B. Lewin, 'Job d'Edesse et son Livre des trésors', *Orientalia Suecana* 6 (1957) 21-30 (the promised sequel to this article has not appeared)
P. Kraus, *Jābir ibn Ḥayyān. Contribution à l'histoire des idées scientifiques dans l'islam*, 2 vols, Cairo, 1942-43, ii (Jābir et la science grecque), pp. 121, 169, 174-75, 274-78
Mingana, *Encyclopædia of philosophical and natural sciences*, pp. xv-xlviii

Barbara Roggema 2008

Ibn al-Kalbī

Abū l-Mundhir Hishām ibn Muḥammad ibn al-Sāʾib al-Kalbī

DATE OF BIRTH Approx. 737
PLACE OF BIRTH Kūfa
DATE OF DEATH 819 or 821
PLACE OF DEATH Kūfa

BIOGRAPHY

Ibn al-Kalbī prided himself on being a student of his own father, Muḥammad ibn al-Sāʾib ibn Bishr al-Kalbī. Since the latter died in 763, and his son must have studied with him long enough to assimilate all the knowledge he attributes to his father, a reasonable date of birth for Ibn al-Kalbī would be 737 (Atallah, p. XIX). The date of his death is variously given as 819 and 821.

Born and brought up in Kūfa, at some point in his mature life he moved to Baghdad, where he taught and may have been attached to the court of the Caliph al-Maʾmūn. Apart from this, little more is known about him.

According to Yāqūt, based on Ibn al-Nadīm, Ibn al-Kalbī wrote more than 150 works. Their titles represent a vast range of topics, including works on the Qurʾān, on Muḥammad and early Islamic history, but primarily on pre-Islamic Arabia, its tribes, their genealogies, lifestyle and customs. Some of his few extant works exemplify these interests: *Jamharat al-nasab*, 'Collected genealogies', *Kitāb al-aṣnām*, 'Idols', and *Nasab al-khayl fī l-jāhiliyya wa-Islām wa-akhbārihā*, 'The genealogies of horses before and under Islam and accounts of them' (these titles appear in various forms), *Kitāb ʿAdī ibn Zayd*, "Adī ibn Zayd', probably containing the poems of the pre-Islamic Christian poet of al-Ḥīra.

One of his surviving (though unpublished) works, *Mathālib al-ʿarab*, 'The shortcomings of the Arabs', which like the *Jamharat al-nasab* was a descriptive account of pre-Islamic Arabian tribes, lists seven tribes that were Christian (Monnot, pp. 28-30).

Some of his works are used extensively by the historian Abū Jaʿfar al-Ṭabarī for events before and during the first years of Islam, particularly his accounts of Persian rulers and Arab tribes, though without mention of any specific titles.

MAIN SOURCES OF INFORMATION

Primary

Ibn Saʿd, *Ṭabaqāt al-kubrā*, 9 vols, Leiden 1905-21, vi, p. 250

Ibn Qutayba, *Kitāb al-maʿārif*, Beirut, 1986, p. 298

Ibn al-Nadīm, *Fihrist*, pp. 108-11

Aḥmad ibn ʿAlī l-Najāshī, *Kitāb al-rijāl*, Tehran, 1950, pp. 339-40

al-Khāṭib al-Baghdādī, *Taʾrīkh Baghdād*, 24 vols, Beirut, 1997, xiv, pp. 45-46

Yāqūt al-Ḥamawī, *Irshād al-arīb alā maʿrifat al-adīb*, ed. D.S. Margoliouth, 7 vols, London, 1923-31, vii, pp. 250-54

Ibn Khallikān, *Wafayāt al-aʿyān wa-anbāʾ abnāʾ al-zamān*, 8 vols, Beirut [s.d.], vi, pp. 82-84

Secondary

T. Khalidi, *Arabic historical thought in the classical period*, Cambridge, 1994, pp. 50-54, 59

I. Shahīd, *Byzantium and the Arabs in the fifth century*, Washington DC, 1989, pp. 233-42

I. Shahīd, *Byzantium and the Arabs in the fourth century*, Washington DC, 1984, pp. 349-66

G. Monnot, 'L'histoire des religions en Islam, Ibn al-Kalbī et Rāzī', *RHR* 188 (1975) 23-34 (repr. in *Islam et religions*, Paris, 1986, 27-38)

W. Atallah, *Les idoles de Hicham Ibn al-Kalbi*, Paris, 1969, pp. XVII-XXVIII

W. Caskel, *Ǧamharat an-nasab. Das Genealogische Werk des Hišām ibn Muḥammad al-Kalbī*, 2 vols, Leiden, 1966, i, pp. 75-80

N. Faris, *The book of idols*, Princeton NJ, 1952, pp. vii-x

R. Klinke-Rosenberger, *Das Götzenbuch. Kitāb al-aṣnām des Ibn al-Kalbī*, Leipzig, 1941, pp. 17-23

WORKS ON CHRISTIAN-MUSLIM RELATIONS

Kitāb al-Ḥīra wa-tasmīyat al-biyaʿ wa-l-diyārāt wa-nasab al-ʿIbād, 'Al-Ḥīra, the names of the churches and monasteries, and the ancestry of "the Faithful"'

DATE Before 819 or 821

ORIGINAL LANGUAGE Arabic

DESCRIPTION

The work is not extant. The title above is that given by Ibn al-Nadīm, *Fihrist*, p. 109 (where the last word is vocalized as *al-ʿabbād*; Flügel gives *al-ʿibādiyyīn*). Yāqūt, who acknowledges the *Fihrist* as his source (*Irshād*, vii, p. 251), shortens it to *Kitāb al-Ḥīra wa-tasmīyat al-biyaʿ wa-l-diyārāt* (p. 253). As this title indicates, the work comprised in part a survey of the Christian religious buildings of the town of al-Ḥīra near the Euphrates, and in part a history of its Christian population. Although al-Ḥīra had largely dwindled away by Ibn al-Kalbī's own day, it had been important in pre-Islamic times. In the 6th century it was the capital of the Christian Lakhmids and the seat of a bishopric of the Church of the East. In the Muslim world it came to be remembered for its poets and the sophisticated culture to which they witnessed.

ʿIbād, 'faithful' or 'worshippers', was the name by which the Christians of the town were particularly known. The *Lisān al-ʿarab* explains that they were originally people from various Arabian tribes who became Christian and chose the epithet *ʿibād* in preference to *ʿabīd*. Dozy (*Supplément aux dictionnaires arabes*) notes that the term was particularly applied to Nestorian Christians.

Like Ibn al-Kalbī's other antiquarian works about pre-Islamic Arabia and its people, this was presumably a descriptive account of this important pre-Islamic city, its main buildings and inhabitants.

Abū Jaʿfar al-Ṭabarī almost certainly makes use of this, or Ibn al-Kalbī's other work on al-Ḥīra referred to below, in the sections of his history concerning the town, where he cites Ibn al-Kalbī as authority though he does not mention any specific work. See particularly his *Taʾrīkh*, i, pp. 821-22, 845-46, and p. 770 for a likely quotation.

SIGNIFICANCE

It was one of the earliest Muslim works on Christian churches and monasteries. If it was descriptive, it stands as a representative example not only of Ibn al-Kalbī's antiquarian interests, but also of a number of works by Muslim authors in the early 9th century that appear to have been purely descriptive accounts of Christian and other non-Muslim beliefs and practices.

It may have been known to Shihāb al-Dīn Aḥmad Ibn Faḍl Allāh al-ʿUmarī (d.1349), who in his *Masālik al-abṣār fī mamālik al-amṣār* (ed. Aḥmad Zakī, Cairo, 1924, i, p. 311) refers to the author of *Diyārāt al-Ḥīra* in his account of Dayr al-Askīm, one of the monasteries of the town.

MANUSCRIPTS —
EDITIONS AND TRANSLATIONS —
STUDIES
Following hints in T. Nöldeke, *Geschichte der Perser und Araber zur Zeit der Sasaniden*, Leiden, 1879, p. XXVII, and G. Rothstein, *Die Dynastie der Laḫmiden in al-Ḥīra*, Berlin, 1899, pp. 50-53, Shahīd, *Byzantium and the Arabs in the fourth century*, pp. 353-57, implies that information about al-Ḥīra cited from Ibn al-Kalbī by al-Ṭabarī, Yāqūt and others comes from this and maybe his other work on the town which is listed below. This is plausible and not unlikely, though in the absence of any specific mention of a title, a categorical identification is not possible.

Kitāb al-Ḥīra, 'Ḥīra'

(Ibn al-Nadīm, *Fihrist*, p. 109, and Yāqūt, *Irshād*, vii, p. 253, list this separately from the preceding work.)

DATE Before 819 or 821
ORIGINAL LANGUAGE Arabic

DESCRIPTION
If this was indeed a separate work from the *Kitāb al-Ḥīra wa-tasmīyat al-biyaʿ wa-l-diyārāt wa-nasab al-ʿIbād*, and not the result of later confusion in listing, one work may possibly have been something like an epitome of the other. Whatever the relationship, this must have been close to the other work in contents.

Together with Ibn al-Kalbī's other work on al-Ḥīra mentioned above, it may have been one of al-Ṭabarī's primary sources in the sections of his *Taʾrīkh* on the town.

SIGNIFICANCE
If a distinct work, and maybe an abbreviated version of *Kitāb al-Ḥīra wa-tasmīyat al-biyaʿ wa-l-diyārāt wa-nasab al-ʿIbād*, it attests to the curiosity shown about this subject in Ibn al-Kalbī's lifetime.

MANUSCRIPTS —
EDITIONS AND TRANSLATIONS —
STUDIES
See the references in Shahīd, Nöldeke and Rothstein cited above.

Kitāb raf ʿĪsā, ʿalayhi al-salām, 'The raising on high of Jesus, peace be upon him'

DATE Before 819 or 821
ORIGINAL LANGUAGE Arabic

DESCRIPTION
The work is not extant. It would have been concerned with Q 4:157-58, where it is stated that Jesus was not killed or crucified but that 'God raised him up to himself', *rafaʿahu Allāh ilayhi*. Like the works among which it is listed by Ibn al-Nadīm, *Fihrist*, p. 109, e.g. *Kitāb Adam wa-wuldihi*, 'Adam and his children', *Kitāb ʿĀd al-ūlā wa-l-akhīra*, "ʿĀd, the beginning and the end', and *Kitāb aṣḥāb al-kahf*, 'The companions of the cave', it would have been primarily an exegetical account or compilation of opinions about the Qurʾān reference. It is likely to have contained some speculation on how Jesus was spared crucifixion, how a substitute replaced him, and who that person was. It probably also contained some discussion of the differences between Muslims and Christians over this event, and maybe some arguments against Christian claims.

SIGNIFICANCE
It may have been among the earliest known Muslim works devoted to the differences between Muslims and Christians over the crucifixion, and either implicitly or explicitly a vindication of the account in the Qurʾān given in the face of Christian criticisms.

MANUSCRIPTS —
EDITIONS AND TRANSLATIONS —
STUDIES —

David Thomas 2008

Timothy I

Ṭīmāte'ōs, East-Syrian patriarch

DATE OF BIRTH	c. 740 (traditional date 727/728)
PLACE OF BIRTH	Ḥazzā (near Arbelā)
DATE OF DEATH	9th January 823
PLACE OF DEATH	Baghdad

BIOGRAPHY

Timothy received a thorough education in the texts of the Church Fathers and the philosophy of Aristotle in the school of Mār Abraham bar Dāshandād in Bāshōsh. When Mār Abraham transferred his school first to Margā and later to the monastery of Mār Gabriel near Mosul, he succeeded his teacher. After 769/70 Timothy was consecrated bishop of Bēt Bagāsh. In 780 he was elected catholicos-patriarch of the East-Syrian Church. His candidacy was highly controversial; the partly contradictory reports mention a total of four other candidates, and Timothy seems to have succeeded by means of bribery. The consecration took place on Sunday, 7 May 780, in the main church of Seleucia-Ctesiphon. The opposition against Timothy continued for about two years, but then several Christians associated with the court of the caliph urged reconciliation. A schism with the ecclesiastical province of Elam lasted for the same time, because the metropolitan had not attended Timothy's consecration. In 782 Timothy held a synod of the patriarchal province, and two synods of the whole East-Syrian Church followed in the years 790/91 and 804/5.

Of Timothy's literary works, one book of law and 59 letters have survived, of which the law book and 45 letters have been published. The contents of the other letters are reported in Bidawid (pp. 34-42), and critical editions with German translation are being prepared by M. Heimgartner. These letters give many interesting insights into how the patriarch managed and administrated his church. In many letters, he asks his correspondents to copy and send books to him. The school of Mār Abraham remained particularly important as a source of information and books from the West-Syrian monastery of Mār Mattai.

Among Timothy's lost works (Putman, p. 21) is a *Book of questions*, which is perhaps the same as his *Disputations* with the Syrian

Orthodox Patriarch George. His *Interpretation of the Theologian* may have been a translation and/or commentary on the works of Gregory of Nazianzus. In addition, ʿAbdīshōʿ mentions a series of synodical decisions that go back to Timothy, though a series of hymns (or sermons?) for the Sundays of the entire church year attributed to him by Barhebraeus seems to have been written by Timothy II (d. 1332). About his *Book of the stars* nothing is known; it has been suggested that it contained a critique of Muslim astrology.

Timothy's most important text for Christian-Muslim relations is Letter 59, the *Disputation* with the Caliph al-Mahdī (see below). Letters 34-36 and 40 (a disputation with an Aristotelian philosopher) also give insight into contemporary debates and the interdependencies of theological and philosophical thought. Time and again Timothy reports on audiences with the caliph – for example, about how he obtained from al-Mahdī (r. 775-85) permission for the reconstruction of numerous churches (Letter 50). In Letter 43 he mentions that in 780/81 al-Mahdī charged him with the translation of Aristotle's *Topics* from Syriac into Arabic. He accompanied the Caliph Hārūn al-Rashīd (r. 786-809) on several journeys and received large amounts of money from him for various purposes (Letter 8). Around the year 800, the vacancy in the metropolitan see of Nisibis caused a kind of 'investiture controversy' between the patriarch and this caliph (Letters 21, 22, 54 and 57).

Timothy's transfer of the patriarchal see from Seleucia-Ctesiphon to Baghdad allowed closer cooperation between patriarch and caliph. Within the church he established a legal system, incorporating a hierarchical structure of bishop-metropolitan-patriarch, for cases between Christians (Letters 53 and 55-57).

These letters attest to the fact that Timothy carried out his office in an exemplary manner by combining great loyalty with diplomatic skills. But they also show that the Caliphs al-Mahdī and Hārūn acted with a real sense of responsibility.

Timothy died on Saturday 9 January 823 at the age of about 85. He was buried in the Klīlīshōʿ monastery in Baghdad.

MAIN SOURCES OF INFORMATION

Primary

Texts by Timothy (apart from those discussed in detail below):

F. Briquel Chatonnet et al., 'Lettre du patriarche Timothée à Maranzekhā, évêque de Ninive', *Journal Asiatique* 288 (2000) 1-13 (trans. of Letter 26)

S. Brock, 'Two letters of the Patriarch Timothy from the late eighth century on translation from Greek', *Arabic Sciences and Philosophy* 9 (1999) 233-46 (trans. of Letters 43 and 48)
T. Darmo, *Letters of Patriarch Timothy I 778-820 A.D.*, Trichur, 1982 (edition of Letters 3-41 based on the Trichur manuscript alone)
R. Bidawid, *Les lettres du patriarche nestorien Timothée I. Étude critique avec en appendice La lettre de Timothée I aux moines du Couvent de Mār Mārōn (traduction latine et texte chaldéen)*, Rome, 1956 (*Studi e Testi* 187) (edition and Latin trans. of Letter 41)
E. Sachau, *Syrische Rechtsbücher*, 3 vols, Berlin, 1907-14, ii (Richterliche Urteile des Patriarchen Chenânîschô, Gesetzbuch des Patriarchen Timotheos, Gesetzbuch des Patriarchen Jesubarnun)
O. Braun, *Timothei Patriarchae I epistulae*, 2 vols, Paris, 1914-15 (*CSCO* 74-75; repr. 1953) (edition and Latin trans. of Letters 1-39)
O. Braun, 'Briefe des Katholikos Timotheos I', *OC* 3 (1903) 1-15 (edition and trans. of Letters 15-17 and extracts of 18)
H. Pognon, *Une version syriaque des Aphorismes d'Hippocrate*, 2 vols, Leipzig, 1903, i (edition and trans. of Letters 43 and 48)
O. Braun, 'Briefe des Katholikos Timotheos I', *OC* 2 (1902) 1-32 (edition and trans. of Letters 9, 13 and 43)
O. Braun, 'Zwei Synoden des Katholikos Timotheos I', *OC* 2 (1902) 283-311 (edition and trans. of Letter 50)
J.-B. Chabot, *Synodicon orientale ou recueil de synodes nestoriens*, Paris, 1902, pp. 599-608 (edition and trans. of Letter 50)
O. Braun, 'Ein Brief des Katholikos Timotheos I über biblische Studien des 9. Jahrhunderts', *OC* 1 (1901) 299-313 (editon and trans. of Letter 47)
J.E. Manna, *Morceaux choisis de littérature araméenne / al-Murūj al-nuzhiyya fī ādāb al-lughat al-Arāmiyya*, 2 vols, Mosul, 1901 (repr. Baghdad, 1977) (edition of Letters 5, 10, 16, 17, 27 and extracts of Letters 26 and 42)

For further letters quoted or mentioned by other writers see Bidawid, *Lettres*, pp. 44-50

Other writers on Timothy:

Thomas of Margā, *The book of governors*, Ch. 4, 3-5, in P. Bedjan, *Liber superiorum seu historia monastica auctore Thoma, episcopo Margensi*, Paris, 1901, pp. 198-202
Chronicle of Elias of Nisibis: E.W. Brooks, *Eliae Metropolitae opus chronologicum*, 2 vols, Paris, 1909-10 (*CSCO* 62-63), i, pp. 32, 87; ii, pp. 58, 184 (exact dates of ordination and death)

Mārī ibn Sulaymān, *Kitāb al-majdal*, in H. Gismondi, *Maris Amri et Slibae. De patriarchis Nestorianorum Commentaria*, 4 parts in 1 vol., Rome, 1896-99, ii (*Maris textus arabicus*), pp. 71-75; i (*Maris versio latina*), pp. 63-66; German trans. in P. Kawerau, *Christlich-arabische Chrestomathie aus historischen Schriftstellern des Mittelalters*, 3 vols, Louvain, 1976-77 (*CSCO* 370, 374, 385), ii, pp. 90-107

Ṣalībā ibn Yuḥannā al-Mawṣilī, *Kitāb asfār al-asrār*, in Gismondi, *Maris Amri et Slibae. De patriarchis Nestorianorum Commentaria*, iv (*Amri et Slibae textus versio Arabica*) pp. 64-66 ; iii (*Amri et Slibae textus versio Latina*) pp. 37-38

ʿAbdishoʿ bar Brikhā, *Catalogus librorum*, in Assemani, *BO* iii, pt. 1, pp. 158-62 (list of writings by Timothy)

ʿAbdīshōʿ bar Brīkhā, *Collectio canonum synodicorum*, ed. and trans. A. Assemani, in A. Mai, *Scriptorum veterum nova collectio e vaticanis codicibus*, 10 vols, Rome, 1825-1838, x, pp. 62, 65-66, 69, 78, 140-41, 143-45, 159-60, 163-67 (materials relating to Timothy's synods)

Gregory Barhebraeus, *Ecclesiastical Chronicle*, ed. J. Abbeloos and T. Lamy, *Gregorii Barhebraei Chronicon ecclesiasticum*, 3 vols, Paris, 1872-77, iii, cols 165-76 and 177-84 (littered with anecdotes)

Secondary

V. Berti, 'Libri e bibliothece Cristiane nell'Iraq dell'VIII secolo. Una testimonionza dell'epistolario del patriarca siro-orientale Timotheo I (727?-823)', in C. d'Ancona (ed.), 'The Libraries of the Neoplatonists', Leiden, 2007, pp. 307-17

V. Berti, *Contesto formativo e vita culturale di Timoteo I, Patriarco della chiesa siro-orientale nell'Iraq dell'VIII secolo*, Padua, 2005 (Diss. Università degli Studi di Padova)

V. Berti, 'Cristiani sulle vie dell'Asia tra VIII e IX secolo. Ideologia e politica missionaria di Timoteo I', *Quaderni di Storia Religiosa* 13 (2006) 117-56

M. Heimgartner, *Die Disputation des ostsyrischen Patriarchen Timotheos (780-823) mit dem Kalifen Al-Mahdi*, Halle/Saale, 2006 (Diss. Martin-Luther-Universität Halle-Wittenberg), pp. 1-26 (on Timothy and his letters in general)

H. Suermann, 'Timotheos I und die Asienmission', in M. Tamcke (ed.), *Syriaca II. Beiträge zum 3. Deutschen Syrologen-Symposium*, Münster, 2004, 193-202

H. Suermann, 'Timotheos I', in W. Klein (ed.), *Syrische Kirchenväter*, Stuttgart, 2004, 152-67

W. Hage, 'Kalifenthron und Patriarchenstuhl. Zum Verhältnis von Staat und Kirche im Mittelalter', in W. Breul-Kunkel and L. Vogel (eds), *Rezeption und Reform. Festschrift Hans Schneider*, Darmstadt, 2001, 3-17

M. Tamcke, art. 'Timotheos I', in *Lexikon für Theologie und Kirche*, Freiburg im Breisgau, 1993-2001[3]

H. Suermann, 'Timothy and his concern for the School of Bašoš', *The Harp* 10 (1997) 51-58
W. Schwaigert, art. 'Timotheos I', in *Biographisch-Bibliographisches Kirchenlexikon*, ed. F. Bautz, Hamm, Westphalia, 1970-
S. Rissanen, *Theological encounter of Oriental Christians with Islam during early Abbasid rule*, Åbo, 1993
T.R. Hurst, *The Syriac letters of Timothy I (727-823). A study in Christian-Muslim controversy*, Washington DC, 1986 (Diss. Catholic University of America)
P. Petitmengin and B. Flusin, 'Le livre antique et la dictée', in E. Lucchesi and H.D. Saffrey (eds), *Antiquité païenne et chrétienne. Mémorial André Festugière*, Geneva, 1984, 247-62 (important for Letter 47)
W. Selb, *Orientalisches Kirchenrecht*, 2 vols, Vienna, 1981-89, i (*Die Geschichte des Kirchenrechts der Nestorianer*), pp. 166-67, 192-201
H. Putman, *L'Église et l'Islam sous Timothée I (780-823). Étude sur l'Église nestorienne au temps des premiers 'Abbāsides avec nouvelle édition et traduction du dialogue entre Timothée et al-Mahdi*, Beirut, 1975 (with an edition by S.K. Samir of one of the Arabic recensions of the Disputation with al-Mahdī, and a French trans. by Putman)
W.G. Young, *Patriarch, shah, and caliph*, Rawalpindi, 1974, pp. 128-54 (with translations of passages from many letters)
Bidawid, *Les lettres du patriarche nestorien Timothée I* (fundamental study)
Graf, *GCAL* ii, 114-18
E. Tisserant, art. 'Timothée Ier', in *Dictionnaire de théologie catholique*, Paris, 1909
Baumstark, *GSL*, pp. 217-18
H. Labourt, *De Timotheo I Nestorianorum patriarcha et christianorum orientalium condicione sub Chaliphis Abbasidis*, Paris, 1904
O. Braun, 'Der Katholikos Timotheos I und seine Briefe', *OC* 1 (1901) 138-52

Martin Heimgartner 2007

WORKS ON CHRISTIAN-MUSLIM RELATIONS

To Sergius, Letter 40

DATE Probably 782-3
ORIGINAL LANGUAGE Syriac

DESCRIPTION
This letter, which is one of Timothy's earliest, reports a debate on religion at the court of the caliph between Timothy and an unnamed

notable well-versed in the philosophy of Aristotle. The latter is called *mlilā*, which is the Syriac rendering of *mutakallim*, and, although it is not stated explicitly that he is a Muslim, it is clear that he represents the Muslim *mutakallimūn*. After a brief introduction in which Timothy, like his contemporary Theodore bar Kōnī (q.v.), refers to the Muslims as 'the new Jews', the first section of the debate develops around the question of how God can be known. While the Muslim posits certain positive categories by which God can be comprehended, also found in the Qur'ān, Timothy asserts that since God is simple and infinite, unlike humans, He can only be described in terms that define the absolute difference between Him and humans.

Despite this, Timothy's argument builds on the attributes of God which the Muslim has posited in order to assert that the attributes of 'seeer' and 'knower' are eternal, not separate from God's essence, and are to be identified with the Son and the Holy Spirit. After Timothy has demonstrated the existence of three divine hypostases by means of these arguments, the Muslim asks whether there is also scriptural proof. As in his debate with the Caliph al-Mahdī, the patriarch then adduces not only biblical but also qur'ānic verses as testimony.

The discussion then moves on to the topic of the Incarnation. In response to the 'Aristotelian's' question how God could become a body, Timothy refers to earlier occasions when God became visible in the physical world without changing or becoming limited in space. The worship of Christians is not directed to the body in which God appeared, but to the divine essence that dwelt in it. His defense contains a clear polemical thrust when he compares the worship of the Divine in a rational body with turning oneself in devotion to a stone in a fixed location (a clear reference to Muslim prayer directed towards the Ka'ba), and he portrays the worship to the 'image of God' as superior to the worship of 'lifeless, non-rational stones'.

The discussion continues with the issues of the veneration of the cross and Christ praying. The fact that several standard points of Muslim polemic against Christianity are referred to in this final section has led Hanna Cheikho to question the integrity of the letter. But Hurst has rightly argued that, although the beginning is more philosophical, the letter as a whole exhibits the principal themes of Christian apologetic of the time, and was therefore quite probably composed as one whole.

The session is terminated abruptly by the Aristotelian, with an agreement to continue at some future time. Timothy closes the Letter by promising to continue his correspondence with Sergius on these topics, and Bidawid (*Lettres*, p. 63) surmises that Letter 59, containing the report of the debate with al-Mahdī, is this continuation.

SIGNIFICANCE

Besides the well-known Letter 59, which is the report of the debate with the Caliph al-Mahdī, this letter is Timothy's best known apologetic tract. It shows that during the earliest stages of interest in Aristotelian philosophy in ʿAbbasid Iraq, knowledge of it was put to use in interreligious debate. The letter also reveals the tension between scriptural and rational demonstrations in apologetic debates, which can be traced in other apologetic texts of this era.

MANUSCRIPTS

MS Baghdad, Chaldean Monastery – 509 (formerly MS Alqosh, Notre Dame des Semences – 169, 13th or 14th c.; all other MSS derive directly or indirectly from this manuscript)

Copies of Baghdad 509:

MS Vat – Borgia Syr. 81 (shortly before 1869)

MS Vat – Syr. 605 (1874) (basis of the editions of H. Cheikho and Hurst)

MS BL – Or. 9361 (1889)

MS Baghdad, Chaldean Monastery – 512 (formerly MS Notre-Dame des Semences – 170) (1894)

MS Mingana – Syr. 587 (1932)

Copies of Baghdad 512:

MS Trichur, Archiepiscopal library (catalogue no. unknown; 1897; Letters 3-59; used by Darmo for his edition)

MS Church of Karamlaiss (near Mosul) – 39 (1904)

For a description of the manuscripts, including a number of lost MSS and corrections to Bidawid's inventory, see Cheikho, *Dialectique*, pp. 43-52.

EDITIONS AND TRANSLATIONS

H. Cheikho, *Dialectique de la langage sur dieu. Lettre de Timothée I (728-823) à Serge*, Rome, 1983 (edition and trans.)

Darmo, *Letters of Patriarch Timothy I 778-820 A.D.*, pp. 227-74 (edition based on the Trichur MS)

T. Hurst, *Letter 40 of the Nestorian Patriarch Timothy I (727-823). An edition and translation*, Washington DC, 1981 (MA Diss. Catholic University of America)

STUDIES

S.H. Griffith, 'The Syriac letters of Patriarch Timothy I and the birth of Christian *kalām* in the Muʿtazilite milieu of Baghdad and Baṣrah in early Islamic times', in W.J. van Bekkum, J.W. Drijvers and A.C. Klugkist (eds), *Syriac polemics. Studies in honour of Gerrit Jan Reinink*, Louvain, 2007, 103-32, esp. pp. 105-15

T.R. Hurst, *The Syriac letters of Timothy I (727-823). A study in Christian-Muslim controversy*, Washington DC, 1986 (Diss. Catholic University of America)

Cheikho, *Dialectique de la langage sur dieu*

Barbara Roggema 2008

Letter 59 (Disputation with the Caliph al-Mahdī); incipit of oldest manuscript: *Tub dilēh kad dīlēh d-mār Ṭīmātē'ōs qāṭōlīqā drāshā da-ʿbad lwāt Mahdī 'amīrā da-mhaymānē b-sharbā d-haymānūtā da-kresṭyānūtā ba-znā d-shū'ālā wa-dpūnāy petgāmā*, 'And now the disputation of the same Catholicos Mār Timothy with Mahdī, the Commander of the Faithful, about Christianity in the form of question and answer'

DATE 782/83

ORIGINAL LANGUAGE Syriac

DESCRIPTION

Letter 59, the so-called *Disputation* (*drāshā*) or *Dialogue* or *Apology*, is a conversation on religion, which Timothy held in Arabic with the Caliph al-Mahdī (r. 775-85) in Baghdad on two days of the year 782/83. Afterwards he wrote down the conversation in the form of a record from memory ('*Gedächtnisprotokoll*') in a letter to a friend, though it was probably composed with a larger audience in mind. This text is a theological tractate in Syriac in the form of a dialogue.

The plan of the text has a circular structure: the most important themes are the doctrine of the Son of God and of the two natures (chs 2-3 and 20, following Heimgartner's numbering), the Trinity (chs 4 and 16-19), the significance of Muḥammad and the question of the continuity of *Heilsgeschichte* between Christianity and Islam (chs 7-8, 10, 13-15). Between these main blocks, various other themes have been integrated, such as circumcision (ch. 5), the direction of prayer (ch. 6), the significance of the cross (ch. 9), the death of Mary (ch. 11) and the question of whether Jesus was 'good' (ch. 12). The introduction (ch. 1) is addressed to the recipient of the letter; the text ends with the 'parable of the pearl' (ch. 21).

At several points, Timothy refers to themes that were discussed in Islamic theological circles at the time, such as the meaning of the word *al-Ṣamad* in Q 112:2 (ch. 18, 42-44), and the significance of the Islamic comprehension of the oneness of God (*tawḥīd*) (chs 16, 34-35; 17, 10-13). Timothy does not consider Muḥammad to be a prophet, but nevertheless accepts that he was an important teacher of the Arabs (ch. 15). Likewise, the Qurʾān is not a text that can be characterized as revelation, but it can support Christian truth. He makes Muḥammad a 'theologian' of the Trinity: the enigmatic three letters at the head of several *sūras* are interpreted as vestiges of the Trinity, as are the verses in which God is referred to in the plural.

For Timothy, Q 4:171 is the *locus classicus* of qurʾānic Trinitarian doctrine (chs 16, 90 and 19, 20). But the Letter also contains early indications of a Muslim tradition of biblical interpretation: the caliph interprets the Paraclete of John's Gospel as Muḥammad (ch. 7, 16-51), and also sees references to him in Deuteronomy 18:18 (ch. 10, 44-62) and Isaiah 21:6-9 (ch. 8, 23-43, where the rider on the ass is Jesus and the rider on the camel is Muḥammad). There are no Islamic sources to show how far the caliphal figure of the debate conforms in his theological insights to the historical al-Mahdī.

The authenticity of the *Disputation* is certain. Although Nau (pp. 241-46), Graf (pp. 115-16) and Putman (pp. 184-85) have disputed whether it reproduces a conversation that actually took place, a number of reasons confirm that the discussion really did take place. In the first place, Timothy tells us about audiences with the caliph in other letters (8 and 50), while Islamic sources report that from al-Mahdī onwards the tradition of disputations often held at the caliph's command, although usually only between Muslims, became highly important (Van Ess, *TG* iii, pp. 10 and 199). Furthermore, this *Disputation* is unlike manuals that give answers to all the 'frequently asked questions' of Christian-Islamic controversial literature in the form of a fictitious conversation. For the caliph is not depicted as a pupil who asks

Timothy as his teacher, and time and again he is portrayed as cleverer than the patriarch: he scrutinizes and caricatures the explanations given by Timothy, and he is not finally convinced by what he hears.

The *Disputation* became a favorite apologetic text among Syriac and Arabic-speaking Christians of various denominations. It was translated into Arabic several times, and at least four different Arabic recensions of it survive; as far as we know, it is the only one of Timothy's letters that has been translated into Arabic. These translations are distinct recensions that re-work the text in their own ways. Recension A I, from the 14th century at the latest, has been edited by Caspar (Caspar, 'Les versions arabes', pp. 125-50). A further recension from the 16th century (unedited; named by Heimgartner A IV) is an adaptation for Melkite readers: Timothy and al-Mahdī are replaced by Theodore Abū Qurra and al-Maʾmūn (Caspar, 'Les versions arabes', p. 108). Recension A II (unedited), from the 16th century at the latest, mocks al-Mahdī as a naive admirer of Timothy (Caspar, 'Les versions arabes', pp. 110-11). Its aim seems to be not to defend Christianity, but to show its superiority. Recension A III of the late 19th century (Caspar, 'Les versions arabes', pp. 111-12) has been edited by L. Cheikho and Putman. MS Beirut, Bibliothèque orientale - 662, might be the autograph of this recension (Putman, p. 174).

It is not known when the earliest Arabic translation was made, but it seems that the East-Syrian recension of the *Disputation of the Monk Ibrāhīm al-Ṭabarānī* (q.v.) (9th c.) already quotes from it. The oldest surviving manuscript that contains an Arabic translation is to be found in the Cairo Geniza and probably dates from the 11th century (K. Szilágyi, 'Christian books in Jewish libraries. Fragments of Christian Arabic writings from the Cairo Genizah', *Ginzei Qedem* 2 (2006) 107*-62*, pp. 138*-40*).

There is also a very short Syriac recension, represented by MS BNF – Syr. 306, fols 107v-111r (1889); it is edited by Van Roey.

SIGNIFICANCE

The *Disputation* is Timothy's best-known work and must have been of immense interest for Christian-Muslim relations, judging from its reception history. The West-Syrian Dionysius bar Ṣalībī (d. 1171) used it in his work against Islam and quotes it without mentioning the source (Heimgartner, *Disputation*, p. 35), and ʿAbdīshōʿ bar Brīkhā (d. 1318) mentions the *Disputation* with al-Mahdī as the second of the writings by Timothy. The various Arabic recensions from later centuries also bear witness to its continuing popularity among Middle Eastern Christians.

MANUSCRIPTS

MS Baghdad, Chaldean Monastery – 509 (formerly MS Alqosh, Notre Dame des Semences – 169) (13th or 14th c., Letters 1-59, Letter 59 on fols 532r-573r; oldest extant MS; all other MSS derive directly or indirectly from it)

Copies of Baghdad 509:

MS Vat – Borgia Syr. 81 (shortly before 1869; Letters 1-59, Letter 59 on fols 307-396)

MS Vat – Syr. 605 (1874; Letters 2-59)

MS Baghdad, Chaldean Monastery – 512 (formerly MS Notre-Dame des Semences – 170) (1894; Letters 1-59; in this MS and the copies of it the Disputation is no. 59, while in all other manuscripts, so also in Baghdad 509, the Disputation is no. 3. To avoid confusion, the numbering followed here is that of Braun and Bidawid (though not original), which counts the Disputation as Letter 59)

MS BL – Or. 9361 (1889, Letters 1-59, Letter 59 on fols 25r-80r)

MS Mingana – Syr. 17 (shortly before 1900; Letters 59 and 26)

MS Mingana – Syr. 587 (1932; Letters 1-59)

Copies of Baghdad 512:

MS Trichur, Archiepiscopal library (catalogue no. unknown; 1897; Letters 3-59; used by T. Darmo for his edition)

MS Church of Karamlaiss (near Mosul) – 39 (1904; Letters 1-59)

For a description of the manuscripts, including a number of lost MSS and corrections to Bidawid's inventory, see H. Cheikho, *Dialectique*, pp. 43-52.

EDITIONS AND TRANSLATIONS

Heimgartner, *Die Disputation des ostsyrischen Patriarchen Timotheos* (edition and trans.)

A. van Roey, 'Une apologie syriaque attribuée à Élie de Nisibe', *Le Muséon* 59 (1946) 381-97 (edition of the short Syriac recension)

A. Mingana, 'The Apology of Timothy the Patriarch before the Caliph Mahdi', *Bulletin of the John Rylands Library* 12 (1928) 137-298 (edition and trans.; repr. in Mingana, *Woodbrooke Studies* 2, Cambridge, 1928, pp. 1-162; repr. of trans. in N.A. Newman, *The early Christian-Muslim dialogue*, Hatfield PA, 1993, pp. 169-267)

STUDIES

E.C.D. Hunter, 'Interfaith dialogues. The Church of the East and the Abbassids', in S.G. Vashalomidze and L. Greisiger (eds), *Der Christliche Orient und seine Umwelt*, Wiesbaden, 2007, 289-302

Heimgartner, *Die Disputation des ostsyrischen Patriarchen Timotheos*

M. Poorthuis, 'The three rings. Between exclusivity and tolerance', in B. Roggema, M. Poorthuis, P. Valkenberg (eds), *The three rings. Textual studies in the historical trialogue of Judaism, Christianity and Islam*, Leuven, 2005, 257-85 (on the pearl parable, pp. 281-84)

S.K. Samir, 'The Prophet Muḥammad as seen by Timothy I and other Arab authors', in D. Thomas (ed.), *Syrian Christians under Islam. The first thousand years*, Leiden, 2001, 75-106

H. Suermann, 'Der nestorianische Patriarch Timotheos I. und seine theologischen Briefe im Kontext des Islam', in M. Tamcke and A. Heinz (eds), *Zu Geschichte, Theologie, Liturgie und Gegenwartslage der syrischen Kirchen*, Hamburg, 2000, 217-30

S.H. Griffith, 'Disputes with Muslims in Syriac Christian texts from Patriarch John (d. 648) to Bar Hebraeus (d. 1286)', in B. Lewis and F. Niewöhner (eds), *Religionsgespräche im Mittelalter*, Wiesbaden, 1992, 251-73, pp. 262-64

R. Caspar, 'Les versions arabes du dialogue entre le Catholicos Timothée I et le Calife al-Mahdî (IIe/VIIIe siècle) "Mohammed a suivi la voie des prophètes"', *Islamochristiana* 3 (1977) 107-75

Graf, *GCAL* ii, pp. 115-18

E.G. Browne, 'Patriarch Timothy and the Caliph al-Mahdī', *MW* 21 (1931) 38-45

F. Nau, review of Mingana, 'The Apology of Timothy', *RHR* 100 (1929) 241-46

A. Rücker, review of Mingana, 'The Apology of Timothy', *Orientalistische Literaturzeitung* (1929) 109-12

L. Cheikho, '*Al-muḥāwarat al-dīniyya allātī jarat bayna l-khalīfa l-Mahdī wa-Ṭīmāthāwus al-jāthlīq*', *Al-Mashriq* 19 (1921) 359-74, 408-18 (repr. in L. Cheikho, *Trois traités de polémique et de théologie chrétienne*, Beirut, 1923)

Martin Heimgartner 2007

To the priests and faithful of Basra and Hūballaṭ, Letter 34

DATE Unknown, probably between 785 and 789
ORIGINAL LANGUAGE Syriac

DESCRIPTION
This letter is intended to set out how the title 'servant of God' should be properly understood when applied to Christ. It begins with an explanation of how the fact that Christ 'took the form of a servant' (cf. Philippians 2:7) has only a metaphorical meaning, and how the term 'servant' can never be applied to either his divinity or his humanity. Timothy relies on the Bible for a number of arguments that exclude Christ's servantship, for example that if Adam was created free and in God's image (Gen 1:26) so was Christ, and that if he was a lawgiver (Matthew 5) he could not have had a subservient status. In cases where the Bible does use the metaphorical term, it is to reflect his humility, his observance of the law and his self-sacrifice for the redemption of humankind.

This general exposition then leads to a more direct confrontation with Islamic doctrine. In the second part, the letter is shaped as a debate with an unnamed scholar, who, although not explicitly designated a Muslim, certainly expresses Muslim ideas (as in Letter 40). In this section, which contains seven further arguments, Timothy uses the Qurʾān in various ways: it bears witness to the fact that he is the 'Word of God and a Spirit from Him' (Q 4:171), and since 'word and spirit' are of the same nature as their 'cause', Christ must have God's nature; it attests that Christ is with God above all creatures, since God raised him to Himself; it witnesses that Christ gave life to birds and raised the dead, acts that are proof of his divine nature and which were carried out at his own command.

SIGNIFICANCE
This letter is a witness to Timothy's zeal to propagate a clear and correct understanding of Christian, especially East-Syrian, doctrine among the Christians in Iraq, and to provide them with answers to critical questions from Muslims.

MANUSCRIPTS

MS Baghdad, Chaldean Monastery – 509 (formerly MS Alqosh, Notre Dame des Semences – 169) (13th or 14th c., Letters 1-59, oldest extant MS; all other MSS derive directly or indirectly from it)

Copies of Baghdad 509:

MS Vat – Borgia Syr. 81 (shortly before 1869)

MS Vat – Syr. 605 (1874)

MS Baghdad, Chaldean Monastery – 512 (formerly MS Notre-Dame des Semences – 170) (1894)

MS BL – Or. 9361 (1889)

MS Mingana – Syr. 587 (1932)

Copies of Baghdad 512:

MS Trichur, Archiepiscopal library (catalogue no. unknown; 1897; Letters 3-59; used by T. Darmo for his edition)

MS Church of Karamlaiss (near Mosul) – 39 (1904)

For a description of the manuscripts, including a number of lost MSS and corrections to Bidawid's inventory, see H. Cheikho, *Dialectique*, pp. 43-52.

EDITIONS AND TRANSLATIONS

Darmo, *Letters of Patriarch Timothy I 778-820 A.D.*, pp. 93-145 (edition based on the Trichur MS)

Braun, *Timothei Patriarchae I epistulae*, i, pp. 156-205 (edition), ii, pp. 106-40 (trans.)

STUDIES

Griffith, 'The Syriac letters of Patriarch Timothy I', esp. pp. 117-23

T.R. Hurst, 'The epistle-treatise. An apologetic vehicle. Letter 34 of Timothy I', in H.J.W. Drijvers (ed.), *IV Symposium Syriacum 1984*, Rome, 1987, 367-82

Hurst, *The Syriac letters of Timothy I*, pp. 43-60 and *passim*

To Mār Naṣr, Letter 35

DATE Unknown, probably between 785 and 789

ORIGINAL LANGUAGE Syriac

DESCRIPTION

This letter is concerned with the accurate expression of two fundamental Christian doctrines. In the first part, Timothy explains that

Christians believe in one God, who is eternally living and rational. While his living eternally implies He has a Spirit who proceeds from Him eternally, His being rational eternally implies the possession of a Word begotten outside of time. In articulating the doctrine of the Trinity in this way, he makes it comprehensible in terms of the discourse about the divine attributes among his Muslim contemporaries.

The second part of the letter is a reiteration of the refutation of Christ's 'servantship', which Timothy also sets out in more detail in Letter 34. In Letter 35 this discussion is somewhat more succinct and there are fewer references to the Qurʾān. Hurst explains the difference in style and scope as a reflection of the difference in audience. The recipient of the letter, Mār Naṣr, already knows the various arguments: 'he needs only a reasoned and sophisticated discussion of the issues so that he can respond to his Muslim neighbors and encourage his fellow Christians to maintain their faith in Christ'.

SIGNIFICANCE

This letter is another testimony to Timothy's interest in disseminating apologetic arguments among his flock. Like his other works, it shows how Christian arguments were developed to serve as replies to Muslim critiques of Christian doctrine.

MANUSCRIPTS

MS Baghdad, Chaldean Monastery – 509 (formerly MS Alqosh, Notre Dame des Semences – 169) (13th or 14th c., Letters 1-59, oldest extant MS; all other MSS derive directly or indirectly from it)

Copies of Baghdad 509:

MS Vat – Borgia Syr. 81 (shortly before 1869)

MS Vat – Syr. 605 (1874)

MS Baghdad, Chaldean Monastery – 512 (formerly MS Notre-Dame des Semences – 170) (1894)

MS BL – Or. 9361 (1889)

MS Mingana – Syr. 587 (1932)

Copies of Baghdad 512:

MS Trichur, Archiepiscopal library (catalogue no. unknown; 1897; Letters 3-59; used by T. Darmo for his edition)

MS Church of Karamlaiss (near Mosul) – 39 (1904)

For a description of the manuscripts, including a number of lost MSS and corrections to Bidawid's inventory, see H. Cheikho, *Dialectique*, pp. 43-52.

EDITIONS AND TRANSLATIONS

Darmo, *Letters of Patriarch Timothy I 778-820 A.D.*, pp. 145-80 (edition based on the Trichur MS)

Braun, *Timothei Patriarchae I epistulae*, i, pp. 205-38 (edition), ii, pp. 140-64 (trans.)

STUDIES

Griffith, 'The Syriac letters of Patriarch Timothy I', esp. pp. 123-26

Hurst, *The Syriac letters of Timothy I*, pp. 60-63 and *passim*

To Mār Naṣr, Letter 36

DATE Unknown, after Letter 35, probably between 785 and 789

ORIGINAL LANGUAGE Syriac

DESCRIPTION

Like Letter 35, this is addressed to the Christian Naṣr and is again apologetic in nature. Timothy explains that it is written against those who denigrate the majesty of Christ. He does not only mean Muslims here, but also Jews, Manicheans, Arians and Marcionites. Hurst has noted that Timothy's approach is somewhat different from that employed in his apologetic works exclusively against Islam, for here he makes use of proof texts from the Pauline epistles, which are rarely used in confrontation with Muslims. In addition, Timothy goes into the textual variants in the Greek and Syriac versions of the Hebrew Bible, not something one would expect in a discussion with Muslims, who were generally eager to point out that the text of the Bible was corrupt. It is nevertheless clear that Timothy directs part of his letter specifically against Muslim critiques of Christianity, when he mentions 'adversaries' who claim that Christ's birth from a virgin without the seed of a man is no more miraculous than Adam's birth – an argument based on Q 3:59 and used frequently by Muslims. Here Timothy contrasts Adam's genesis 'from the earth', like animals, with Christ's birth 'by divine power'. The former was a birth from an irrational, lifeless entity, while the latter was from an exalted woman chosen by God, living and rational. As in two earlier letters (34 and 35), the Patriarch concludes that Christ cannot be called 'servant'.

Timothy also briefly discusses the veneration of the relics of saints and martyrs, which according to him is a way of worshipping God Himself. Against the background of Islamic criticisms, he not only defends the cult, but also asserts that it is an obligation for Christians to honor the saints.

SIGNIFICANCE

The letter is another example of the Patriarch Timothy's interest in apologetics. He pursues a number of themes that are meant to demonstrate the rationality of Christian doctrine to his coreligionists in terms that would help them to counter the polemic of other religious communities, including heretical Christians and Muslims.

MANUSCRIPTS

MS Baghdad, Chaldean Monastery – 509 (formerly MS Alqosh, Notre Dame des Semences – 169) (13th or 14th c., Letters 1-59, oldest extant MS; all other MSS derive directly or indirectly from it)

Copies of Baghdad 509:

MS Vat – Borgia Syr. 81 (shortly before 1869)

MS Vat – Syr. 605 (1874)

MS Baghdad, Chaldean Monastery – 512 (formerly MS Notre-Dame des Semences – 170) (1894)

MS BL – Or. 9361 (1889)

MS Mingama – Syr. 587 (1932)

Copies of Baghdad 512:

MS Trichur, Archiepiscopal library (catalogue no. unknown; 1897; Letters 3-59; used by T. Darmo for his edition)

MS Church of Karamlaiss (near Mosul) – 39 (1904)

For a description of the manuscripts, including a number of lost MSS and corrections to Bidawid's inventory, see H. Cheikho, *Dialectique*, pp. 43-52.

EDITIONS AND TRANSLATIONS

Darmo, *Letters of Patriarch Timothy I 778-820 A.D.*, pp. 181-210 (edition based on the Trichur MS)

Braun, *Timothei Patriarchae I epistulae*, i, pp. 238-64 (edition), ii, pp. 164-83 (trans.)

STUDIES

Griffith, 'The Syriac letters of Patriarch Timothy I', pp. 126-30

Hurst, *The Syriac letters of Timothy I*, pp. 63-68 and *passim*

Barbara Roggema 2008

Bishr ibn al-Muʿtamir

Abū Sahl Bishr ibn al-Muʿtamir ibn Bishr al-Hilālī

DATE OF BIRTH c. 750
PLACE OF BIRTH Kūfa or Baghdad
DATE OF DEATH 825
PLACE OF DEATH Baghdad

BIOGRAPHY

Bishr ibn al-Muʿtamir was the founder of the Baghdad school of the Muʿtazila, and the main author of its distinctive doctrines. Unusually for his day, he wrote a number of theological works in verse.

His place of birth is uncertain, though in his youth he studied in Basra under pupils of Wāṣil ibn ʿAṭāʾ. When he settled in Baghdad he was imprisoned for a time by Hārūn al-Rashīd, maybe for suspected Rāfiḍī sympathies assumed from his preference for ʿAlī among the Companions of the Prophet. But some years later he found favor under al-Maʾmūn, and was one of the signatories of the caliph's declaration making the Imām ʿAlī l-Riḍā his heir in 817. Bishr died at a great age in Baghdad in 825, respected as an ascetic and devout Muslim.

Ibn al-Nadīm and others list 49 works by Bishr in prose and verse (Van Ess, *TG* v, pp. 283-85). None of them survives, apart from lengthy passages from some of his poems and brief quotations from other works. In addition to what may have been major treatises on topics of theology (*Kitāb taʾwīl mutashābih al-Qurʾān*, 'Interpretation of what is ambiguous in the Qurʾān'; *Kitāb al-tawḥīd*, 'Divine unity'; *Kitāb al-ʿadl*, 'Divine justice'), many of these were directed against other Muslim theologians, and were presumably clarifications of Bishr's own views where they differed from fellow Muʿtazilīs and others (including *Kitāb ʿalā Ḍirār fī l-Makhlūq*, 'Against Ḍirār (ibn ʿAmr) on the Created (Qurʾān)', *Kitāb al-istiṭāʿa, ʿalā Hishām ibn al-Ḥakam*, 'Capacity, against Hishām ibn al-Ḥakam', *Kitāb al-radd ʿalā Abī l-Hudhayl*, 'Refutation of Abū l-Hudhayl' – according to anecdotal evidence, these two leaders of the Baghdad and Basra Muʿtazila had little time for each other). There are also a substantial number against Muslim and non-Muslim sects (*Kitāb al-waʿīd, ʿalā l-mujbira*, 'The divine threat, against the determinists', *Kitāb al-radd ʿalā l-Khawārij*, 'Refutation of the Kharijites', *Kitāb al-radd ʿalā l-Majūs*, 'Refutation of the Zoroastrians', *Kitāb al-radd ʿalā l-Yahūd*, 'Refutation of the Jews').

The main outlines of Bishr's theology are lost. He is usually associated with a particular contribution to the debate over the nature of human action, the doctrine of *tawallud*, that one action can be generated by another, and thus humans can be responsible for the consequences of what they do. And he was also remembered for an attempted solution to the problem of evil, that God can bestow favors on humans in addition to what he has already given them.

MAIN SOURCES OF INFORMATION

Primary

Abū l-Ḥusayn al-Khayyāṭ, *Kitāb al-intiṣār*, ed. and French trans. A. Nader, Beirut, 1957, pp. 51-53, 121-22
Abū l-Ḥasan al-Ashʿarī, *Maqālāt al-Islāmiyyīn*, ed. H. Ritter, Istanbul, 1930, pp. 124, 229, 233-34, 246, 250, 364, 377-78, 401-2, 566
Ibn al-Nadīm, *Fihrist*, pp. 184-85, 205
Abū Manṣūr al-Baghdādī, *Kitāb al-milal wa-l-niḥal*, ed. A. Nader, Beirut, 1970, pp. 107-09
Ibn al-Murtaḍā, *Kitāb ṭabaqāt al-Muʿtazila*, ed. S. Diwald-Wilzer, Beirut, 1988, pp. 52-54

Secondary

Van Ess, *TG* iii, pp. 107-30, v, pp. 283-328
Watt, *Formative period*, pp. 222, 227-28, 237, 239
Sezgin, *GAS* i, p. 615
A.N. Nader, *Le système philosophique des Muʿtazila*, Beirut, 1956, *passim*
Brockelmann, *GAL* S i, pp. 338-39

WORKS ON CHRISTIAN-MUSLIM RELATIONS

Kitāb al-radd ʿalā l-Naṣārā, 'Refutation of the Christians'

DATE early 9th c.
ORIGINAL LANGUAGE Arabic, in verse

DESCRIPTION
The work is mentioned by Ibn al-Nadīm, *Fihrist*, p. 185. It was an attack on one or more of the Christian beliefs as Muslims understood them.

SIGNIFICANCE
It presumably employed similar arguments to those in contemporary attacks, and may have fed later polemical works.

MANUSCRIPTS —
EDITIONS AND TRANSLATIONS —
STUDIES —

Kitāb al-ḥujja fī ithbāt al-nabī ʿalayhi l-salām, 'The Proof in confirmation of the Prophet, peace be upon him'

DATE early 9th c.
ORIGINAL LANGUAGE Arabic

DESCRIPTION
The work, which was written in verse, is mentioned by Ibn al-Nadīm, *Fihrist*, p. 185. It was one of the earliest examples of the 'proofs of prophethood' genre, and it may have listed and commented on biblical proof verses and also refuted arguments from Christians.

SIGNIFICANCE
It presumably employed similar arguments to those in contemporary works, and may have fed later works of this kind.

MANUSCRIPTS —
EDITIONS AND TRANSLATIONS —
STUDIES —

David Thomas 2007

Ṣafwān ibn Yaḥyā

Ṣafwān ibn Yaḥyā Abū Muḥammad al-Bajalī

DATE OF BIRTH Unknown
PLACE OF BIRTH Kūfa
DATE OF DEATH 825
PLACE OF DEATH Medina

BIOGRAPHY

Ṣafwān ibn Yaḥyā was remembered as an agent and defender of the Shīʿī Imamate against the claims of the Sunnī caliphs and their cohorts; as a secretary for encounters between Imāms and various interlocutors; and as a respected companion of Imāms, particularly ʿAlī l-Riḍā, and *ḥadīth* transmitter in the Shīʿī tradition. It is primarily the *ḥadīth* sayings transmitted in his name that are remembered by historians and authors.

The biographical references to Ṣafwān's life do not offer many chronological certainties. Al-Najāshī mentions he was from Kūfa. As an agent for the Shīʿī leadership in the region, he would have collected alms for the Imām and carried out important tasks for the leadership. The biographers recall that Ṣafwān was fervent in his practice of prayer, fasting, and charitable contributions. One undated reference notes that he and two companions entered into a covenant at the Kaʿba, according to which each of them would carry out prayer, fasting, pilgrimage and charity for the other person after that person had died.

As a merchant, Ṣafwān traveled far, though he remained closely connected to the family of the Imāms. According to al-Kashshī, he recorded sayings from the seventh Imām Mūsā l-Kāẓim (d. 799), the eighth Imām ʿAlī l-Riḍā (d. 818), and the ninth Imām Muḥammad al-Jawād (d. 835). He is reported as being present with the Imām al-Riḍā during his stay with the Caliph al-Maʾmūn in Khurāsān in 817-18, when he recorded some of al-Riḍā's conversations. He died in 825 in Medina, and his body was wrapped in a shroud sent by the Imām Muḥammad al-Jawād. He was buried in the Jannat al-Baqīʿ cemetery in Medina with prayers offered by Ismaʿīl ibn Mūsā.

Ṣafwān's literary works reflect his background as a merchant interested in business, as well as his concern for religious ritual and law. According to al-Najāshī, he composed 30 works in total, including books on ritual ablution, prayer, fasting, pilgrimage, charity, marriage, divorce, wills, counsels, buying and selling, and emancipating slaves and management. Ibn al-Nadīm mentions that he wrote on commercial transactions, shares of inheritance, and morals (*ādāb*). Al-Ṭūsī notes that he wrote accounts of Muslim discussions with Christians, and also the *Kitāb Ḥusayn ibn Saʿīd*, and *Masāʾil ʿan Abī l-Ḥasan Mūsā wa-l-riwāyāt*. It is likely that the latter work was preserved in snippets by later Shīʿī compilers, including brief religious dialogue encounters traceable to the early 9th century.

MAIN SOURCES OF INFORMATION

Primary

Ibn al-Nadīm, *Fihrist*, p. 278

Aḥmad ibn ʿAlī l-Najāshī, *Kitāb al-rijāl*, Beirut: Dār al-Aḍwāʾ, 1408 (1988), pp. 439-40

Muḥammad ibn al-Ḥasan al-Ṭūsī, *Ikhtiyār maʿrifat al-rijāl, al-maʿrūf bi-Rijāl al-Kashshī*, ed. M. Taqī Fāḍil al-Maybudī and Abū al-Faḍal al-Mūsawiyān, Tehran, 2004, pp. 552-53, 798-800

Muḥammad ibn al-Ḥasan al-Ṭūsī, *Fihrist al-Ṭūsī*, Najaf: al-Maṭbaʿa al-Ḥaydariyya, 1356 (1937), pp. 83-84

Muḥammad ibn al-Ḥasan al-Ṭūsī, *Rijāl al-Ṭūsī*, Najaf: al-Maktaba wa-l-Maṭbaʿa al-Ḥaydariyya, 1381 (1961), pp. 352, 378

Secondary

G. Riḍā ʿIrfāniyān, *Mashāyikh al-thiqāt*, Najaf: Maṭbaʿat al-Ādāb, 1973

WORKS ON CHRISTIAN-MUSLIM RELATIONS

Kitāb al-Ṣafwānī, 'The book of Ṣafwān'

DATE 817-25

ORIGINAL LANGUAGE Arabic

DESCRIPTION

A brief portion from the work called *Kitāb al-Ṣafwānī* is preserved in al-Majlisī's, *Biḥār al-anwār* ('Oceans of lights') from Ibn Shahrāshūb's (d. 1192) *Manāqib Āl Abī Ṭālib*. It is a paragraph-long discussion between the Imām ʿAlī l-Riḍā and a Christian named Ibn Qurra.

The title is ambiguous. It may refer generically to a work of Ṣafwān ibn Yaḥyā, since he is named as the source for several other discussions in the same chapter in al-Majlisī, including another discussion between the Imām and a Christian named John (Yūḥannā) Abū Qurra (see below). On the other hand, *Kitāb al-Ṣafwānī* may refer to a later author named Abū ʿAbdallāh Muḥammad ibn Aḥmad al-Ṣafwānī (d. 957), who may have preserved Ṣafwān's (or another's) original account. The extent of the original work, or the text of the dialogue between the Imām and Ibn Qurra, is unknown.

The text revolves around the Christian definition of Christ as coming from God (*min Allāh*). Al-Riḍā offers an extended response in the form of a series of questions to argue that his interlocutor's words regarding the relationship between Christ and God are imprecise. He reduces Ibn Qurra to silence after he finishes his line of questioning.

Since the account is only a brief portion from a longer work, it is difficult to assess its relationship to other works by Ṣafwān ibn Yaḥyā. However, the contents of the work are focused upon al-Riḍā and his oratorical skills rather than specifically upon Muslim-Christian apologetics or polemics. In relation to other works, this brief piece takes up a common point of disagreement between Muslims and Christians, namely the identity of Christ in relationship to the unity of God.

SIGNIFICANCE

The text is significant as an indicator of Shīʿī Muslim knowledge of Christian argumentation in Iraq and Central Asia during the early 9th century under the caliphate of al-Maʾmūn. Moreover, it has intrinsic value as one of the few popular Muslim literary dialogues from this historical period pertaining to Christian-Muslim relations, in contrast to the more prevalent intellectual treatises.

The narrative is also valuable for its historical and biographical information. The text depicts al-Riḍā as an adept theologian, a refuter of Christian theology, and a rhetorician who responds to his interlocutors' questions and baffles Ibn Qurra with his logical method.

MANUSCRIPTS —

EDITIONS AND TRANSLATIONS

Muḥammad ibn ʿAlī ibn Shahrāshūb, *Manāqib Āl Abī Ṭālib*, 3 vols, Najaf: al-Maṭbaʿa al-Ḥaydariyya, 1376 (1956), iii, p. 462

Muḥammad Bāqir ibn Muḥammad Taqī al-Majlisī, *Biḥār al-anwār al-jāmiʿa li-durar akhbār al-aʾimma al-aṭhār*, 4 vols, Beirut: Dār al-fiqh li-l-ṭibāʿa wa-l-nashr, 1421 (2001), iv, pp. 432-33

STUDIES —

Jawāb al-Riḍā ʿan suʾāl Abī Qurra ṣāḥib al-jāthlīq, 'Al-Riḍā's reply to the question of Abū Qurra, companion of the patriarch'

DATE 817-825

ORIGINAL LANGUAGE Arabic

DESCRIPTION

The original title, if there was one, and the length of the full work are unknown. Mentioned as a *ḥadīth* attributed to Ṣafwān ibn Yaḥyā, this page-long text is preserved in the *ʿUyūn akhbār al-Riḍā* by Ibn Bābawayh al-Qummī (d. 991/2). The content includes a short discussion between the Imām ʿAlī al-Riḍā (d. 818) and a friend of the patriarch, a Christian named John (Yuḥannā) Abū Qurra.

Abū Qurra asks Ṣafwān to introduce him to al-Riḍā. Upon arrival, Abū Qurra greets al-Riḍā with great respect, and asks him about the authenticity of one religion in relation to the testimonies of another. He argues that since Christians and Muslims both testify that Jesus Christ is Word and Spirit, this claim must be more truthful than the claim the Muḥammad is a prophet, because the two religions do not agree about this.

After asking for Abū Qurra's first name, the Imām al-Riḍā explains to him the traditional Muslim understanding of Jesus. Arguing that Jesus, the Word and Spirit, believed and proclaimed Muḥammad, he challenges John's earlier statement that Muslims and Christians agree that Jesus Christ is Word and Spirit, since they have different underlying assumptions about the titles. The text abruptly ends with al-Riḍā telling his companion Ṣafwān: 'Get up! How have we benefited from this encounter?'

There is an authentic quality in the Christian argument, the Muslim rebuttal, and the abrupt ending to the conversation. However, as with the encounter between al-Riḍā and Ibn Qurra, the focus of the story is upon the Imām's rhetorical acumen. At present, there are no studies of this brief text.

SIGNIFICANCE

This account of a Muslim-Christian encounter illuminates the extent of interreligious knowledge and argumentation during the early 9th century. It also depicts a popular image of Shīʿī interaction with Christian intellectuals at the time.

MANUSCRIPTS —

EDITIONS AND TRANSLATIONS

Muḥammad ibn ʿAlī ibn Bābawayh al-Qummī, *ʿUyūn akhbār al-Riḍā*, Najaf: al-Maṭbaʿa al-Ḥaydariyya, 1390 (1970), p. 232

Al-Majlisī, *Biḥār al-anwār*, iv, pp. 428

STUDIES —

David Bertaina 2008

Al-Qāsim ibn Ibrāhīm

Abū Muḥammad al-Qāsim ibn Ibrāhīm ibn Ismāʿīl ibn Ibrāhīm ibn al-Ḥasan ibn al-Ḥasan ibn ʿAlī ibn Abī Ṭālib al-Rassī

DATE OF BIRTH	Unknown, c. 785
PLACE OF BIRTH	Medina
DATE OF DEATH	860
PLACE OF DEATH	Jabal al-Rass (near Medina)

BIOGRAPHY

Al-Qāsim was educated in Zaydī Shīʿī Islam by his ʿAlid family and in Medinan *ḥadīth* by a nephew of Mālik ibn Anas, the founder of the legal school of Medina. His elder brother Muḥammad headed a revolt in Kūfa, claiming the Zaydī imamate, and was killed in 814. Al-Qāsim was in Egypt at that time, where he studied the Jewish and Christian scriptures and Christian theological and philosophical literature and engaged in debates with Muslim and non-Muslim scholars. It was during his stay in Egypt that he composed his refutation of a Manichaean tract attributed to Ibn al-Muqaffaʿ and his refutation of the Christians (see below). In 826 he came under suspicion of fomenting a revolt and soon thereafter left Egypt. He returned to Medina where he acquired an estate at al-Rass near Dhū l-Ḥulayfa. There he stayed writing religious works and teaching Zaydī visitors until his death. Although there is no evidence that he seriously attempted to lead a revolt, he was later generally recognized as a Zaydī Imam on account of his scholarship.

In his theological teaching, al-Qāsim deviated, under distinct influence of contemporary Christian thought, from earlier Zaydī and predominant Islamic doctrine, most notably in rejecting predestinarian determinism and upholding human free will. In consonance with Christian theology, he asserted in particular the absolute dissimilarity of God to the world of creation and emphasized goodness and generosity as central among the divine attributes as against the emphasis on God's sovereignty and arbitrary will in general Islamic thought. He strictly dissociated God from all evil acts. His refutation of a Manichaean tract ascribed to Ibn al-Muqaffaʿ, probably al-Qāsim's first book, contained many arguments employed by Christian apologists before him. He may have been partly influenced by anti-dualist considerations in adopting the Christian doctrine on human free will. In structure and terminology his theology displays some distinct affinity with that of the Melkite theologian Theodore Abū Qurra (d. c. 830). Within Islam he represented rationalist thought while stressing the authority of the Qurʾān over ḥadīth and oral tradition. His anti-determinist stance has sometimes been attributed to Muʿtazilī influence, especially in view of the far-reaching adoption of Muʿtazilī theology in the later Zaydī tradition. His own writings, however, reflect serious reservations about contemporary Muʿtazilī teaching.

MAIN SOURCES OF INFORMATION

Primary

Abū l-Faraj al-Iṣfahānī, *Maqātil al-ṭālibiyyīn*, ed. Aḥmad al-Ṣaqr, Cairo 1949, pp. 553-56

Abu l-ʿAbbās al-Ḥasanī, *al-Maṣābīḥ*, ed. ʿAbdallāh al-Ḥūthī, Ṣanʿāʾ, 1423 A.H. (2002), pp. 553-66

Ibn al-Nadīm, *Fihrist*, p. 244

Abū Ṭālib al-Nāṭiq bi-l-Ḥaqq, *al-Ifāda fī taʾrīkh aʾimmat al-Zaydiyya*, ed. Muḥammad Yaḥyā ʿIzzān, Ṣanʿāʾ, 1417 A.H. (1996), pp. 114-27

Ḥumayd al-Muḥallī, *al-Ḥadāʾiq al-wardiyya*, ed. al-Murtaḍa ibn Zayd al-Maḥṭūrī l-Ḥasanī, Ṣanʿāʾ, 1423 A.H. (2002), part 2, pp. 1-24

Secondary

B. Abrahamov, *Anthropomorphism and interpretation of the Qurʾān in the theology of al-Qāsim ibn Ibrāhīm*. Kitāb al-Mustarshid, Leiden, 1996

W. Madelung, 'Al-Qāsim ibn Ibrāhīm and Christian Theology', *Aram* 3 (1991) 35-44

B. Abrahamov, *Al-Kasim b. Ibrāhīm on the proof of God's existence*. Kitāb al-dalīl al-kabīr, Leiden, 1990

W. Madelung, 'Imam al-Qāsim ibn Ibrāhīm and Muʿtazilism', in U. Ehrensvärd and C. Toll (eds), *On both sides of al-Mandab. Ethiopian, South-Arabic and Islamic studies presented to Oscar Löfgren*, Stockholm, 1989, 39-47

B. Abrahamov, 'Al-Kāsim ibn Ibrāhīm's argument from design', *Oriens* 29-30 (1987) 259-284

W. Madelung, *Der Imam al-Qāsim ibn Ibrāhīm und die Glaubenslehre der Zaiditen*, Berlin, 1965

M. Guidi, *La lotta tra l'Islam e il Manicheismo*, Rome, 1927

R. Strothmann, 'Die Literatur der Zaiditen', *Der Islam* 2 (1911), 49-60

WORKS ON CHRISTIAN-MUSLIM RELATIONS

Kitāb al-radd ʿalā l-Naṣārā, 'Refutation of the Christians'

DATE Unknown, before 826
ORIGINAL LANGUAGE Arabic

DESCRIPTION
The *Refutation* upholds strict qur'ānic monotheism against Christian trinitarian doctrine on rational grounds. The attribution of a coequal Son and a coequal Holy Spirit to God is inconsistent with his unique divinity and eternal lordship. It is comparable to the philosophical doctrine ascribing to the seven planets shared divinity with God. The conflicting teaching of Melkites, Syrian Orthodox, and the Church of the East concerning the Incarnation and nature of Christ as well as their common doctrines of original sin, redemption, Christ's ascension to heaven and second coming, are described. Christians are accused of false interpretation of their scripture and of greed. The Gospels, especially Matthew and John, are quoted to show that they admit theologically sound interpretation. The final section consists of lengthy quotations, paraphrased in rhymed prose, from the early chapters of Matthew, especially the Sermon on the Mount.

This work is the only known writing of al-Qāsim against Christianity. A work with the title *Kitāb mā ḥaddadat al-Naṣārā min qawlihā qad istaḥsaynā fīhi jāmiʿ uṣūlihi* mentioned by Sezgin (*GAS* i, p. 562) is in fact a section from the *Kitāb al-radd ʿalā l-Naṣārā.*

SIGNIFICANCE
The treatise is the earliest extant *kalām* refutation of Christian theology. It reflects a solid knowledge of contemporary Christian doctrine. Since it was written by a Zaydī sectarian author, it had little influence on later mainstream Muslim polemics against Christianity.

MANUSCRIPTS
MS Milan, Ambrosiana – C 186, fols 78r-86v
MS Milan, Ambrosiana – C 131, fols 86v-97v (1681)
MS Milan, Ambrosiana – F 61, fols 100r-125v (1672)
MS Milan, Ambrosiana – D 468, fols 138r-150v
MS Berlin, Glas. 101, Ahlwardt – 4876, fols 27v-38r (1150)

Numerous other manuscripts are extant in public and private libraries in Yemen. For a listing, see G. Schwarb, S. Schmidtke, and D. Sklare, *Handbook of Muʿtazilite works and manuscripts* (forthcoming).

EDITIONS AND TRANSLATIONS

ʿAbd al-Karīm Aḥmad Jadabān, *Majmūʿ kutub wa-rasāʾil li-l-imām al-Qāsim ibn Ibrāhīm al-Rassī*, 2 vols, Ṣanʿāʾ, 2001, i, pp. 387-442

Al-Qāsim ibn Ibrāhīm, *al-Radd ʿalā l-Naṣārā*, ed. Imām Ḥanafī ʿAbdallāh, Cairo, 2000

I. di Matteo, 'Confutazione contro i Christiani dello Zaydita al-Qāsim b. Ibrāhīm', *RSO* 9 (1921-23) 301-64

STUDIES

D. Thomas, 'Christian theologians and new questions', in E. Grypeou, M. Swanson and D. Thomas, (eds), *The encounter of Eastern Christianity with early Islam*, Leiden, 2006, pp. 259-67

G.S. Reynolds, *A Muslim theologian in the sectarian milieu. ʿAbd al-Jabbār and the critique of Christian origins,* Leiden 2004, see index

D. Thomas, *Early Muslim polemic against Christianity. Abū ʿĪsā al-Warrāq's 'Against the Incarnation'*, Cambridge, 2002, pp. 39-41 and index

D. Thomas, *Anti-Christian polemic in early Islam. Abū ʿĪsā al-Warrāq's 'Against the Trinity'*, Cambridge, 1992, pp. 32-34

Abrahamov, *Al-Kāsim b. Ibrāhīm*, pp. 17-20

al-Sharfī, *al-Fikr al-Islāmī*, pp. 135-36, and index s.v. al-Ḥasanī

E. Fritsch, *Islam und Christentum im Mittelalter*, Breslau 1930, pp. 12-13 and index

Wilferd Madelung 2007

Abū l-Hudhayl al-ʿAllāf

Abū l-Hudhayl Muḥammad ibn al-Hudhayl ibn ʿUbayd Allāh ibn Makḥūl al-ʿAbdī l-ʿAllāf

DATE OF BIRTH Between 748 and 753
PLACE OF BIRTH Basra
DATE OF DEATH Between 840 and 850
PLACE OF DEATH Baghdad

BIOGRAPHY

Abū l-Hudhayl is regarded as one of the greatest theologians of early ʿAbbasid times, and the shaper of many of the main doctrines for which the Muʿtazila became known. He was the leader of the Basra school of the Muʿtazila until he moved to the capital in the early 9th century. In both Basra and Baghdad, he knew other leading thinkers, and was often invited by the Caliph al-Maʾmūn (813-33) (q.v.) to join other exponents of theology, including prominent Christians and other non-Muslims, to debate theological matters. He is one of the few theologians of this period who were well enough known to be the subject of anecdotes (for example, he features in al-Jāḥiẓ's *Kitāb al-bukhalāʾ*, 'Misers').

Abū l-Hudhayl was taught by students of Wāṣil ibn ʿAṭāʾ, who was regarded as the founder of the Muʿtazila, and he emerged as a leading exponent of the reason-based theology of his teachers. In Basra, he himself taught students who became leading exponents of Muʿtazilī ideas. He moved to Baghdad in 818-19, but from about 820 to the end of his life he does not appear to have been very active theologically.

Despite Abū l-Hudhayl's weighty reputation, none of the 56 books listed by Ibn al-Nadīm has survived (Van Ess, *TG* v, pp. 367-69). Their titles show that he wrote on many of the main theological questions of the day. They include: *Kitāb ṣifat Allāh bi-l-ʿadl wa-nafī al-qabīḥ*, 'The attribution of justice to God, and the denial of what is vile'; *al-Istiṭāʿa*, '[Human] Capacity'; *al-Jawāhir wa-l-aʿrāḍ*, 'Substances and accidents'), works against contemporary theologians (such as *Kitāb ʿalā Ḍirār wa-Jahm wa-Abī Ḥanīfa wa-Ḥafṣ fī l-makhlūq*, 'Against Ḍirār (ibn ʿAmr), Jahm (ibn Ṣafwān), Abū Ḥanīfa and Ḥafṣ (al-Fard) on what is created'; *Kitāb ʿalā l-Naẓẓām fī khalq al-shayʾ*

wa-jawābuhu ʿanhu, 'Against (Ibrāhīm) al-Naẓẓām on the creation of the thing, and his reply about it'), and works against opposing groups both within and outside Islam (such as *Kitāb al-radd ʿalā l-qadariyya wa-l-mujbira*, 'Against the proponents of free will and the determinists'; *Kitāb al-imāma ʿalā Hishām*, 'The Imamate, against Hishām (ibn al-Ḥakam)'; *Kitāb ʿalā l-Majūs*, 'Against the Zoroastrians'; *Kitāb ʿalā l-Yahūd*, 'Against the Jews'; *Kitāb al-ḥujja ʿalā l-mulḥidīn*, 'The proof against the heretics').

The main outlines of Abū l-Hudhayl's theology can be reconstructed from quotations in later authors, for whom he is often the representative Muʿtazilī voice. His main contributions included the characterization of God as absolutely one, with none of his attributes as real entities identifiable in addition to his essence (likely to have been a major element in his refutation of the Nestorian ʿAmmār al-Baṣrī), and the description of created being in terms of atoms and accidental attributes, by which change and movement can be explained.

Just as he wrote against contemporary thinkers, so others in turn refuted Abū l-Hudhayl's ideas. Works written against him are known from many contemporary and later theologians, including al-Naẓẓām (q.v.), Bishr al-Muʿtamir (q.v.), Abū ʿAlī l-Jubbāʾī and Abū l-Ḥasan al-Ashʿarī.

MAIN SOURCES OF INFORMATION

Primary

Abū l-Ḥusayn al-Khayyāṭ, *Kitāb al-intiṣār*, ed. and French trans. A. Nader, Beirut, 1957, pp. 15-21, 56-60, 90-92

Abū l-Ḥasan al-Ashʿarī, *Maqālāt al-Islāmiyyīn*, ed. H. Ritter, Istanbul, 1930, pp. 165, 177, 229, 230, 232, 302-3, 311-12, 314-15, 321-22, 363-64, 484-86

Ibn al-Nadīm, *Fihrist*, pp. 203-4

Abū Manṣūr al-Baghdādī, *Kitāb al-milal wa-l-niḥal*, ed. A. Nader, Beirut, 1970, pp. 88-90

Ibn al-Murtaḍā, *Kitāb ṭabaqāt al-muʿtazila*, ed. S. Diwald-Wilzer, Beirut, 1988, pp. 44-49

Secondary

O. Aydınlı, *İslam düşüncesinde aklîleşme süreci. Mutezilenin oluşumu ve Ebu'l-Huzeyl Allaf*, Ankara: Okulu Yayınları, 2001

Ṭ. Akhras, *Abū l-Hudhayl al-ʿAllāf al-muʿtazilī. Ārāʾuhu l-kalāmiyya wa-l-falsafiyya*, Beirut, 1994

Van Ess, *TG* iii, pp. 209-91; v, pp. 367-457

H.S. Nyberg, art. 'Abu 'l-Hudhayl al-ʿAllāf, Muḥammad b. al-Hudhayl b. ʿUbayd Allāh b. Makḥūl', in *EI2*

J. van Ess, 'Abu l-Hudhayl in contact. The genesis of an anecdote', in M.E. Marmura (ed.), *Islamic theology and philosophy. Studies in honor of George F. Hourani*, Albany NY, 1984, 13-30.

R.M. Frank, *Beings and their attributes. The teaching of the Basrian School of the Muʿtazila in the classical period*, Albany NY, 1978, pp. 10-13

Watt, *Formative period*, pp. 219, 225-26, 240, 245-46

R.M. Frank, 'The divine attributes according to the teachings of Abū l-Hudhayl al-ʿAllāf, *Le Muséon* 82 (1969) 451–506 (repr. in R.M. Frank, *Texts and studies on the history of the development and history of* kalām, ed. D. Gutas, 2 vols, Aldershot, 2005-07, ii, no. II)

Sezgin, *GAS* i, pp. 617-18

R.M. Frank, *The metaphysics of created being according to Abû l-Hudhayl al-ʿAllâf: a philosophical study of the earliest* kalām, Istanbul, 1966 (repr. in R.M. Frank, *Texts and studies on the history of the development and history of* kalām)

A.N. Nader, *Le système philosophique des Muʿtazila*, Beirut, 1956

ʿA.M. Ghurābī, *Abū l-Hudhayl al-ʿAllāf. Awwal mutakallim islāmī taʾaththara bi-l-falsafa*, Cairo, 1949

Brockelmann, *GAL* S i, p. 339

WORKS ON CHRISTIAN-MUSLIM RELATIONS

Kitāb al-radd ʿalā ahl al-adyān, 'Refutation of the followers of the religions'

DATE Early 9th c.
ORIGINAL LANGUAGE Arabic

DESCRIPTION
It is mentioned by Ibn al-Nadīm, *Fihrist*, p. 204. It was presumably a general refutation of non-Muslim religions, including Christianity.

SIGNIFICANCE
Given Abū l-Hudhayl's stature, it may have contained original arguments, as well as stock points from contemporary polemic.

MANUSCRIPTS —
EDITIONS AND TRANSLATIONS —
STUDIES —

Kitāb ʿalā l-Naṣārā, 'Against the Christians'

DATE Early 9th c.
ORIGINAL LANGUAGE Arabic

DESCRIPTION
The work is lost, but it is mentioned by Ibn al-Nadīm, *Fihrist*, p. 204. It was presumably a refutation comparable to other works of the time on this topic.

SIGNIFICANCE
Although none are specifically attributed to Abū l-Hudhayl in later works, it may have contained original arguments.

MANUSCRIPTS —
EDITIONS AND TRANSLATIONS —
STUDIES —

Kitāb ʿalā ʿAmmār al-Naṣrānī fī l-radd ʿalā l-Naṣārā, 'Against ʿAmmār the Christian in refutation of the Christians'

DATE Early 9th c.
ORIGINAL LANGUAGE Arabic

DESCRIPTION
The work is lost, but it is mentioned by Ibn al-Nadīm, *Fihrist*, p. 204. It was almost certainly directed in particular against the Nestorian author ʿAmmār al-Baṣrī (q.v.), two of whose works are extant and who shows in them clear knowledge of doctrines like those of Abū l-Hudhayl (and Ḍirār ibn ʿAmr) about the attributes of God. Since its precise contents are unknown, it cannot be linked directly with either of these works, though if it is a reply to one of them, as opposed to another unknown work by ʿAmmār or to ideas he had expressed in debate, this is likely to be the *Kitāb al-masāʾil wa-l-ajwiba*, 'Questions

and answers', probably the earlier of the two, which ʿAmmār maybe wrote at the beginning of al-Maʾmūn's reign and before Abū l-Hudhayl left Basra for Baghdad (see M. Hayek, *ʿAmmār al-Baṣrī, apologie et controverses*, Beirut, 1986, pp. 18-20).

In this work Abū l-Hudhayl is likely to have argued against the doctrine of the Trinity, and ʿAmmār's use of Muslim attributes doctrine to define it. Like Muslim opponents of Abū l-Hudhayl, ʿAmmār argues in his works that the divine attributes are real and distinct from God's essence, and he also privileges the attributes of life (as Spirit) and knowledge (as Son) which, together with the being of God (as Father), give a Trinitarian character to the Godhead. This directly defies Abū l-Hudhayl's own doctrine that the attributes are not identifiable in addition to the essence of God.

SIGNIFICANCE

It suggests a close engagement between Muslim and Christian theologians at this time, and importantly the use of common principles and methods.

MANUSCRIPTS —

EDITIONS AND TRANSLATIONS —

STUDIES —

[*Kitāb fī l-nubuwwa*], 'About prophethood'

DATE Early 9th c.

ORIGINAL LANGUAGE Arabic

DESCRIPTION

The work is lost. It is mentioned only in passing by ʿAbd al-Jabbār (*Tathbīt*, ed. ʿA.K. ʿUthmān, Beirut, 1966, p. 511), together with works of this kind from other authors, including al-Jāḥiẓ (q.v.) and Muḥammad ibn Shabīb (q.v.), in the context of a discussion about miracles of Muḥammad. ʿAbd al-Jabbār refers simply to 'their books which they composed about prophethood concerning miracles which are not in the Qurʾān'.

The original title of the work cannot be known, and there is no obvious candidate among the list given by Ibn al-Nadīm, though the *Kitāb al-ḥujja*, 'The proof', may offer a possibility.

According to ʿAbd al-Jabbār's brief reference, the work and the others mentioned with it contained discussions of the miracles of Muḥammad as these are recorded in the sources of his life and mission, and which are so well attested that they are incontestibly true.

SIGNIFICANCE

The element of the work referred to by ʿAbd al-Jabbār is evidently a justification of Muḥammad's miraculous actions and a defense of them against opponents who deny he performed any. This is a known element in the contemporary debate between Muslims and Christians over his prophetic status and the validation of this by his miracles.

MANUSCRIPTS —

EDITIONS AND TRANSLATIONS —

STUDIES —

David Thomas 2008

ʿAbdīshūʿ ibn Bahrīz

Ḥabīb ibn Bahrīz

DATE OF BIRTH Unknown, mid/later 8th c.?
PLACE OF BIRTH Unknown
DATE OF DEATH Unknown, perhaps shortly before 827
PLACE OF DEATH Unknown, perhaps in or near Mosul, where he was metropolitan

BIOGRAPHY

ʿAbdīshūʿ ibn Bahrīz was an eminent bishop and scholar of the Church of the East, who flourished around the time of the Caliph al-Maʾmūn (r. 813-33) and his Christian physician Jibrīl ibn Bukhtīshūʿ (d. 827). His father's name (Bahrīz) indicates his Persian ancestry; perhaps Ḥabīb was his given name, and ʿAbdīshūʿ, 'servant of Jesus', his name as a cleric.

Ibn Bahrīz was remembered as one of the early translators, from Syriac into Arabic, of works of logic and philosophy (for al-Maʾmūn) and medicine (for Gabriel). He epitomized or excerpted Aristotle's *Categories* and *On interpretation*, and wrote a *Kitāb ḥudūd al-manṭiq* ('Definitions of logic'), which has been preserved (Troupeau, "ʿAbdīšūʿ Ibn Bahrīz et son livre'). As a churchman, he was bishop of Ḥarrān and later metropolitan of Mosul and Ḥazza. He was a liturgical and legal scholar; his Syriac work on marriage and inheritance law has been preserved. He is also said to have written Arabic apologetic works, in controversy with Syrian Orthodox and Melkites and also possibly in response to Muslims' questions about Christian Trinitarian doctrine (see below).

In a vivid paragraph in his *Kitāb al-bayān wa-l-tabyīn*, the great littérateur al-Jāḥiẓ (q.v.) mocked Ibn Bahrīz's ambition to become catholicos: he lacked the height, the sonorous voice, and the abundant beard necessary for the position! Fiey suggests that the fact that Ibn Bahrīz did not become catholicos in 827 may indicate that he died before that date (Fiey, 'Ibn Bahrīz et son portrait', p. 137).

MAIN SOURCES OF INFORMATION

Primary

al-Jāḥiẓ, *Kitāb al-bayān wa-l-tabyīn*, 4 parts, Beirut: Dār al-fikr li-l-jamīʿ, 1968, i, p. 88

al-Jāḥiẓ, *Kitāb al-ḥayawān*, ed. ʿA.S. Hārūn, 8 vols, Cairo, 1938-44, i, pp. 75-76

Ibn al-Nadīm, *Kitāb al-fihrist*, ed. G. Flügel, Leipzig, 1871-1872; repr. Beirut: Maktabat Khayāṭ, 1966, pp. 23-24, 244, 248

Ibn Abī Uṣaybiʿa, *ʿUyūn al-anbāʾ fī ṭabaqāt al-aṭibbāʾ*, ed. Nizār Riḍā, Beirut: Dār Maktabat al-Ḥayāt, 1965, p. 282

Assemani, *BO* iii, pt. i, p. 173 (ʿAbdīshūʿ of Nisibis' book catalogue; English translation in G.P. Badger, *The Nestorians and their rituals*, London, 1852, ii, 361-79, p. 373)

Secondary

G. Troupeau, "Abdīšūʿ Ibn Bahrīz et son livre sur les définitions de la logique (*Kitāb ḥudūd al-manṭiq*)', in D. Jacquart (ed.), *Les voies de la science grecque. Études sur la transmission des textes de l'Antiquité au dix-neuvième siècle*, Geneva, 1997, 135-45 (repr. in G. Troupeau, *Études sur la grammaire et la lexicographie arabes. Recueil d'articles sélectionnés*, Damascus, 2002, 23-33)

B. Landron, *Chrétiens et musulmans en Irak. Attitudes nestoriennes vis-à-vis de l'Islam*, Paris, 1994, p. 60 (with excellent bibliography)

J.-M. Fiey, 'Ibn Bahrīz et son portrait', *Pd'O* 16 (1990-1991) 133-37 (with excellent bibliography)

M.T. Dānishpazhūh, *al-Manṭiq li-Ibn al-Muqaffaʿ. Ḥudūd al-manṭiq li-Ibn Bihrīz*, Tehran 1357 (1978) (with introduction in French and Persian, repr. 1381 [2002])

W. Selb, *ʿAbdīšōʿ bar Bahrīz. Ordnung der Ehe und der Erbschaften sowie Entscheidung von Rechtsfällen*, Vienna, 1970, pp. 13-14 (reviews: R. Köbert, *OCP* 37 (1971) 437-40; H. Kaufhold, *OC* 55 (1971) 224-33)

N. Rescher, *The development of Arabic logic*, Pittsburgh, 1964, p. 100

Graf, *GCAL* ii, 119-20

WORKS ON CHRISTIAN-MUSLIM RELATIONS

Maqāla fī l-tawḥīd wa-l-tathlīth, 'Treatise on the Unity and Trinity (of God)'

DATE Unknown, early 9th c.
ORIGINAL LANGUAGE Arabic

DESCRIPTION

We know nothing about the work other than what the title tells us. It is probably a work of apologetic, justifying Christian worship of a triune God and attempting to demonstrate that this is not tantamount to tritheism. It may have drawn on earlier apologies circulating within the community, e.g. the discussion between the Catholicos Timothy I (in office 780-823) and the Caliph al-Mahdī (see the entry on Timothy I).

SIGNIFICANCE

The greatest significance of this work may lie in the fact that a figure important for the early transmission of Aristotelian logic into Arabic also composed an apology for the Christian understanding of the triunity of God. We do not know whether Ibn Bahrīz drew on Aristotelian categories in his apology, and must hope that a copy will come to light.

MANUSCRIPTS

MS Aleppo, Rizq Allāh Bāsīl Collection

MS Aleppo, al-Khūrī Quṣṭanṭīn al-Khuḍarī Collection

(both are inaccessible MSS in private collections; see Sbath, *al-Fihris*, i, p. 53, no. 413)

EDITIONS AND TRANSLATIONS —

STUDIES —

Mark N. Swanson 2008

A Christological discussion

Unknown author

DATE OF BIRTH Unknown, perhaps later 8th c.
PLACE OF BIRTH Unknown, perhaps Iraq
DATE OF DEATH Unknown, perhaps later 9th c.
PLACE OF DEATH Unknown, perhaps Iraq

BIOGRAPHY

We have no information about the author of a brief report on a Christological discussion that took place in the presence of a Muslim official, other from what can be gleaned from the report itself. Assuming that the meeting did indeed take place and that the report was written soon after the event, we are led to a date in the 820s or shortly thereafter. The space given to Abū Rāʾiṭa's response suggests it was written by someone in his circle, therefore an Iraqi Syrian-Orthodox monk or theologian.

MAIN SOURCES OF INFORMATION

Primary —

Secondary

S. Toenies Keating, *Defending the 'people of truth' in the early Islamic period. The Christian apologies of Abū Rāʾiṭah*, Leiden, 2006, pp. 347-51

WORKS ON CHRISTIAN-MUSLIM RELATIONS

Qīl anna ʿAbd Īshūʿ al-muṭrān al-Nasṭūrī wa-Abī Qurra l-usquf al-Malikī wa-Abī Rāʾiṭa l-Yaʿqūbī ijtamaʿū ʿinda aḥad al-wuzarāʾ, 'It is said that ʿAbd Īshūʿ, the Nestorian metropolitan, Abū Qurra, the Melkite bishop, and Abū Rāʾiṭa, the Jacobite, met before one of the viziers' (first line of the text), 'A Debate between Theodore Abū Qurra, Abū Rāʾiṭa and ʿAbd Īshūʿ'

DATE Unknown, 820s or shortly thereafter
ORIGINAL LANGUAGE Arabic

DESCRIPTION
In this brief account of a meeting before an unnamed Muslim official by representatives from three Christian denominations, each is asked to give a short summary of the teaching of his own church on the Incarnation. It is not an extensive debate; rather, each participant presents the doctrine in a few sentences, emphasizing the description of the relationship between the human and divine in Christ. The vizier finds what they present satisfactory and sends them away.

Two of the three participants are well-known, Abū Rāʾiṭa l-Takrītī (q.v.) and Theodore Abū Qurra (q.v.). The third, identified in the text as "Abdīshūʿ, the Nestorian muṭrān", is probably ʿAbdīshūʿ ibn Bahrīz (q.v.), Metropolitan of Mosul and Ḥazza, who may have died before 827.

The discussion is narrated by an unnamed person. It is difficult to determine in which community the text originated, but it is likely to be associated with the Syrian-Orthodox since it was transmitted in the Coptic community. Furthermore, the answer given by the Syrian-Orthodox theologian Abū Rāʾiṭa is the most complete and extensive of the three.

SIGNIFICANCE
If this account is taken as a record of an historical event, it strengthens the argument that reports of Christian theologians being summoned before Muslim officials were not just hypothetical exercises, but that apologists such as Abū Qurra or Abū Rāʾiṭa based their explanations of their beliefs on actual personal experience.

Secondly, the text clearly lays out the differences between the three Christian communities, revealing that at the center of the conflict was the proper definition of the term *hypostasis*. The unknown editor organized the presentations in such a way as to highlight the differences, indicating he was aware of the root of the problem (Keating, *Defending the 'people of truth'*, pp. 347-51).

MANUSCRIPTS

MS Vat – Ar. 1492 (13th-14th c.), fols 30r-31r

MS Oxford, Bodleian – Hunt. 420 (= Ar. Christ. Uri 38) (1549-50), fols 118r-119r

MS BNF – Ar. 82 (14th c.), fols 95r-97r

EDITIONS AND TRANSLATIONS

S. Toenies Keating, *Defending the 'people of truth'*, pp. 352-57 (edition and trans.)

G. Graf, *Die Schriften des Jacobiten Ḥabīb Ibn Ḫidma Abū Rāʾiṭah*, 2 vols, Louvain, 1951 (*CSCO* 130-31), i, pp. 163-65, ii, pp. 198-200 (edition and trans.)

STUDIES

S. Toenies Keating, *Defending the 'people of truth'*, pp. 347-51

S. Toenies Keating 2008

The Debate of Theodore Abū Qurra

Unknown author

DATE OF BIRTH Unknown, early 9th c.?
PLACE OF BIRTH Unknown
DATE OF DEATH Unknown, late 9th c.?
PLACE OF DEATH Unknown

BIOGRAPHY

The identity of the author or redactor of a text purporting to be the account of a debate between Theodore Abū Qurra (q.v.) and Muslim scholars before the Caliph al-Maʾmūn (q.v.) is unknown. Whether such a debate ever in fact took place is a matter of dispute (see below). It can be suggested that a 9th-century Melkite Christian, probably a monk or cleric, composed a dialogue that had reference to an actual historical debate, and he maybe even included first-hand recollections of what was said in that debate. The author was familiar with Theodore Abū Qurra, his writings, and his style of argumentation, and he had a good knowledge of the Qurʾān.

MAIN SOURCES OF INFORMATION

Primary —

Secondary —

WORKS ON CHRISTIAN-MUSLIM RELATIONS

Mujādalat Abī Qurra maʿa l-mutakallimīn al-muslimīn fī majlis al-khalīfa l-Maʾmūn, 'The Debate of Abū Qurra with Muslim scholars at the court of the Caliph al-Maʾmūn'. Short title: *Mujādalat Abī Qurra*, 'The Debate of Abū Qurra'

DATE Unknown; after 829
ORIGINAL LANGUAGE Arabic

DESCRIPTION

The text of a disputation between Theodore Abū Qurra (q.v.) and Muslim scholars before the ʿAbbasid Caliph al-Maʾmūn is preserved in at least 31 manuscripts in two different recensions, one Melkite and one Syrian Orthodox. Since Theodore Abū Qurra was the Melkite Bishop of Ḥarrān, it would follow that the Melkite recension is the older. The manuscripts of the Syrian Orthodox recension typically make the hero of the debate the Syrian Orthodox 'Bishop Simeon (Shimʿūn) Abū Qurra of Ḥabsannās' (a town between Ṭūr ʿAbdīn and Baghdad); he is also called the 'bishop of Ḥarrān and Nisibis'.

The different recensions and large number of manuscripts make it difficult to assemble a critical edition of the text. Ignace Dick provided the first Arabic edition in a volume privately published in Aleppo, in which the text of the debate occupies 62 pages. This edition is based on five manuscripts (MS BNF – Ar. 215, 198, 70, 71 and MS Jerusalem, Saint Anne – 52, although there is no mention of MSS 70 and 215 in the critical apparatus). Bertaina provides an English trans. based on the oldest witness, a Maronite manuscript following the Melkite recension: MS Vat. – Borg. Ar. 135, dated 1308.

Despite variations, most of the manuscripts of Abū Qurra's debate with Muslim scholars cover the following themes: creation and circumcision, the old and new covenants, the divine status of the Word of God, the status of believers and 'submitters' (i.e., Muslims), the women promised to Muslim men in paradise, Jesus' humanity and divinity, his identity as Spirit and Word of God, the identity of the polytheists in the Qurʾān, the commendation of Christians in the Qurʾān, paradise and eternal life, the Incarnation, the hypostases of God, the Trinity, the human acts of Christ and his divine miracles, the accusation against Christians of polytheism, the voluntary passion of Christ, and the veneration of the Cross. During the conversation, Abū Qurra emphasizes that Jesus is the Spirit and Word of God and that Muslims do not properly interpret their scripture nor understand their Prophet Muḥammad's teaching with regard to Christian beliefs and practices; in fact they have altered their scripture and/or its proper interpretation.

The first historical reference to a debate between Theodore Abū Qurra and Muslim scholars before the Caliph al-Maʾmūn occurs in the 9th-century Syriac chronicle of Dionysisus of Tell Maḥrē (q.v.), which is transmitted in the *Chronicon ad annum Christi 1234 pertinens*. Dionysius was Syrian Orthodox patriarch of Antioch, and occasionally traveled with al-Maʾmūn. He records that in the year 829, al-Maʾmūn journeyed from Baghdad towards Byzantine territory on a war campaign. His entourage stopped in Ḥarrān, where he met with the bishop, Theodore Abū Qurra: 'Theodore, bishop of Ḥarrān, who was called Abū Qurra, had a conversation with al-Maʾmūn. There was a great debate between them about the faith of the Christians. This debate is written in a special book, for anyone who wants to read it' (Chabot, *Chronicon*, p. 23).

Another medieval reference to the text of Abū Qurra's debate is found in the Chapter 7 of Shams al-Riʾāsa Abū l-Barakāt Ibn Kabar's (d. 1324) *Miṣbāḥ al-ẓulma wa-īḍāḥ al-khidma*. In a section of his catalogue devoted to 'Nestorians' and others, he notes the existence of Theodore's 'well-known' debate text (*mujādala maʿrūfa*).

A possible reference to the debate comes from a text that bears witness to the good relationship between Theodore Abū Qurra and the Caliph al-Maʾmūn. The 13th-century MS Sinai – Ar. 447 includes a curious item, the preface of which indicates it is a homily given by Abū Qurra, the bishop of Ḥarrān. The text itself, however, begins with a panegyric for 'the Commander of the Faithful, the *imām* al-Maʾmūn, the victorious leader, the fortunate caliph, the beloved master' (Swanson, 'Christian al-Maʾmūn tradition', p. 67). This is followed by a prayer of Abū Qurra for the caliph. The work may represent a literary commemoration of Theodore Abū Qurra's debate before al-Maʾmūn.

Constantin Bacha, the first modern author to discuss the authenticity of the Abū Qurra debate text, concludes that it shows a great resemblance in thought to Theodore's writings, and does not hesitate to associate it with a real historical event (Bacha, *Un traité*, p. 13). Graf comes to a different conclusion in his study devoted to Theodore Abū Qurra (Graf, *Die arabischen Schriften*, pp. 77-85), pointing out that since the account is written in the third person and that the narrator praises Theodore, he could not have written it himself. He also argues that Theodore's genuine writings differ from it in their explanations of the Christian faith, as well as in matters of style, vocabulary, and use of the Qurʾān, although these and other historical data are insufficient to identify the actual author. For Graf, who was the first to catalogue the various manuscripts of the debate according to their recension (*GCAL* ii, pp. 21-22), the disputation is significant as a work of popular apologetic. It celebrates the authority of Christian scholars and the truth of their Christian faith, and it shows the figure of Abū Qurra emerging as a symbol of identity for Melkite Orthodox Christians.

In contrast, Guillaume argues that the debate text can be accepted as substantially the work of Abū Qurra, written for the benefit of his priests. He notes as signs of the work's historicity that Theodore does not always respond effectively to the Muslim scholars' arguments during the debate and that, while Theodore is named the victor, his Muslim interlocutors also score points in the disputation.

Griffith agrees with Graf in doubting the disputation's attribution to Abū Qurra. He points out that the text belongs to a literary genre of Christian-Muslim dialogues which he terms 'the monk in the emir's *majlis*', and notes the remarkable way in which the account uses the Qur'ān in order to commend the truth of Christianity. Griffith reasons that the narrative is a literary prototype, probably tied to a memorable event centering on the defense of Christianity as the true religion. Its purpose was to discourage conversion to Islam in addition to providing entertainment for its readers and listeners.

In his introduction to the Arabic edition of the debate, Dick sides with Bacha and Guillaume against Graf and Griffith in his belief that the work should be attributed to Abū Qurra. Dick was the first scholar to reference the chronicle of Dionysius of Tell-Maḥrē, which, he argues, reaffirms the historicity of the debate account (see Dick, 'La Discussion', pp. 107-13). For him, the manuscripts offer a mostly faithful redaction and abridgement of what occurred during the debate.

Bertaina has argued that the text is a literary work based upon the recollection of a historical debate, set down or composed by a disciple of Theodore Abū Qurra in the 9th century. There is a literary precedent for this practice of reproducing Theodore's discussions with his adversaries in the writings set down by John the Deacon. The evidence suggests that a 9th-century Melkite who was closely connected with Abū Qurra, his writings, and his style of argumentation (most likely a monk or member of the clergy) created an Arabic literary dialogue that was based upon a real meeting, perhaps even including first-hand memories of the debate, just as we have in the dialogues of Abū Qurra recorded by John the Deacon. Since Theodore did not use the Qur'ān extensively in his other works, the passages of the debate text that include qur'ānic argumentation should be considered the anonymous redactor's most original contribution.

The debate text shares some affinities with Theodore's writings. Parallels between the Greek *opuscula* and the Arabic debate include treatment of the following themes: the characteristics of a true prophet, the Muslim allegation that the scriptures have been corrupted, the allegation that Christ prophesied the coming of Muḥammad, the question of miracles, the reasons for the spread of Christianity, Christological terminology, and the issues surrounding monogamy and polygamy. Among Theodore's authentic Arabic works, there are arguments similar (in some cases identical) to what is found in the debate text, e.g. about the Islamic doctrine of the compulsion of the will, Christ as the Word of God, Christ as the Light begotten of God, God's ability to take a son, analogies for the Trinity, and Christ's voluntary passion.

While Theodore's debate text is unique in its style and presentation, the dialogue is similar to other Christian-Muslim disputations from the ʿAbbasid period. The narrative fits into the genre of 'the monk in the emir's *majlis*', which portrays a Christian overcoming difficult odds to defend his faith before a Muslim leader. Other texts in this genre include the Syriac dialogue between the Patriarch Timothy I and the Caliph al-Mahdī held in 781 (q.v.), the dialogue between Abraham of Tiberias (q.v.) and several Muslims before the emir ʿAbd al-Raḥmān al-Hāshimī in Jerusalem around 820, the conversation between Bishop Elias of Nisibis (975-1046) and the Muslim vizier al-Maghribī in 1026, and the debate between the monk George and several Muslims before the emir al-Malik al-Mushammar in the early 13th century.

SIGNIFICANCE

The Abū Qurra debate is one of the most widely read texts within the genre of medieval Christian-Muslim disputations, to judge from the number of manuscripts and their diversity of provenance. The dialogue demonstrates that, during the development of Christian-Muslim relations in the medieval period, eastern Christians employed the Qurʾān, along with traditional biblical exegesis and Aristotelian thinking, in order to find common terms for Christian-Muslim conversation.

The narrative is valuable for its portrayals of its main characters. Theodore is a master theologian, dialectician and rhetorician who responds to his interlocutors' questions in a rational yet witty manner. The Caliph al-Maʾmūn is interested in philosophical and religious knowledge, actively encourages and is engaged in debates held under his patronage, acts as a just arbiter, and can admire and reward a Christian who holds his own in the debate.

The Abū Qurra debate text had significance for later Christian communities as a catechetical tool for its readers, an apologetic primer for students, and an entertaining story that inculcated Christian sociocultural values and discouraged conversion to Islam. The narrative presented a hagiographical image of Abū Qurra as a symbol of Christian identity and a beacon of hope for future generations. The text's Abū Qurra imparts the conviction that Christian teachings are true: faith accords with reason, is verified through experience, and can be expressed without fear.

MANUSCRIPTS

The manuscripts are listed under three headings: Melkite, Syrian Orthodox, or undetermined (depending on whether the main character is Theodore Abū Qurra, Simeon of Ḥabsannās, or undetermined).

Melkite Recension:

- MS Vat – Borg. Ar. 135, fols 157r-172v (1308, not 1408 as reported in other sources; Karshūnī, Maronite MS, Lebanon)
- MS Charfet – Rahmani 630, pp. 32-56 (14th c.)
- MS BNF – Ar. 70, fols 147v-201v; 206r-v; 208r-215r (15th c.; Syria)
- MS BNF – Ar. 258, fols 236r-247r (15th c.; Syria; text similar to MS Par. Ar. 70)
- MS Charfet – Rahmani 335, pp. 1-35 (15th-16th c.)
- MS BNF – Ar. 71, fols 12v-41v (16th c., Syria; text similar to MS BNF – Ar. 70)
- MS BNF – Ar. 198, fols 21r-82r (16th c.; Egypt; incomplete at end)
- MS BNF – Ar. 215, fols 228v-260v (1590-91; Egypt; text similar to MS BNF – Ar. 70, but with a different preamble)
- MS Jerusalem, Saint Anne – 52, pp. 294-324 (17th c.; Lebanon)
- MS Nasrallah – 2, pp. 45-76 (17th c.; some MSS with the Nasrallah family and others have been sold; location unknown)
- MS BNF – Ar. 6981 (date unknown; uncatalogued)

Syrian-Orthodox Recension:

- MS BNF – Syr. 238, fols 167r-188r (1473; Arabic script, not Karshūnī; the caliph is al-Maʾmūn's father Hārūn al-Rashīd)
- MS Mār ʿAbda Harharaya – 77 (16th-17th c.; Karshūnī; monastery is near Ghazīr, Lebanon)
- MS Berlin, Staatsbibliothek – Sachau 87 (cat. no. 247), fols 1r-47r (1845)
- MS Berlin, Staatsbibliothek – Sachau 111 (cat. no. 199), fols 1v-6v (incomplete)
- MS Birmingham, Mingana – Syr. 190, fols 1r-24r (1874; Karshūnī)
- MS Beirut, Bibliothèque Orientale 670 (1886; only work in MS; 52 pages total; copied by Chaldean and purchased in Mosul; MS dates dialogue to 788)

MS BNF – Ar. 5141, fols 73v-85v (1887; copied in Bahshiqa near Mosul from an old MS)

MS Birmingham, Mingana – Syr. 444, fols 131v-170r (1890; Karshūnī)

MS Beirut, Bibliothèque Orientale 671 (19th c.; only work in MS; 26 pages total)

MS Nasrallah – 5, pp. 1-19 (19th c.)

MS Jerusalem, Saint Mark – 133, pp. 1-22 (date unknown; Abū Qurra Bishop of Ḥarrān from the village of Ḥabsannās)

MS Jerusalem, Saint Mark – 133 (4th work in MS)

MS Mardin, Turkey (uncatalogued, see A. Palmer, *Monk and mason on the Tigris frontier*, Cambridge, 1989, p. 161)

Undetermined:

MS BNF – Syr. 204, fols 1v-25r (17th c.; Karshūnī; Syrian Orthodox MS; Abū Qurra Metropolitan of Ḥarrān)

MS Cairo, Coptic Patriarchate – Lit. 212 (Simaika 420, Graf 537), fols 249v-300v (17th c.; Syrian-Orthodox MS)

MS Cairo, Coptic Patriarchate – Theol. 86 (Simaika 420, Graf 469), fols 127r-159v (1790; Abū Qurra and al-Ma'mūn; Syrian-Orthodox MS)

MS Cairo, Coptic Patriarchate – Theol. 218 (Simaika 331, Graf 465), fols 71r-123r (18th c.; Abū Qurra and al-Ma'mūn; Syrian-Orthodox MS)

MS Aleppo, Sbath – 1004, pp. 243-309 (18th c.)

MS Cairo, Coptic Museum – Supplement 6442 (547) (16th-19th c.; 6 folios total)

EDITIONS AND TRANSLATIONS

D. Bertaina, *An Arabic account of Theodore Abu Qurra in debate at the court of Caliph al-Ma'mun. A study in early Christian and Muslim literary dialogues*, Washington DC, 2007 (Diss. Catholic University of America) (Arabic transliteration of Karshūnī MS Vat – Borg. ar. 135 and an English trans. and study)

J.P. Monferrer-Sala, 'Una muestra de *kalām* cristiano. Abū Qurra en la sección novena del *Kitāb muğādalat maʿa al-mutakallimīn al-muslimīn fī mağlis al-jalīfa al-Ma'mūn*', *Revista Española de Filosofia Medieval* 10 (2003) 75-86 (repr. in J.S. Dueso et al. (eds), *Las raíces de la cultura europea*, Zaragoza, 2004, 207-222) (partial Spanish trans.)

I. Dick, *Mujādalat Abī Qurra maʿa al-mutakallimīn al-muslimīn fī majlis al-khalīfa al-Maʾmūn*, (Aleppo), 1999 (Arabic edition from five MSS; study in Arabic; helpful indices; no trans.)

S.K. Samir, 'Kitāb "Jāmiʿ wujūh al-īmān" wa-mujādalat Abī Qurra ʿan ṣalb al-Masīḥ', *Al-Masarra* 67 (1981) 169-84 (partial text)

STUDIES

S.K. Samir, *Abū Qurrah. Vida, bibliografía y obras*, trans. J.P. Monferrer-Sala, Cordova, 2005, 94-97

M. Swanson, 'The Christian al-Maʾmūn tradition', in D. Thomas (ed.), *Christians at the heart of Islamic rule*, Leiden, 2003, 63-92

J. Grand'Henry, review of Dick, *Mujādalat Abī Qurra maʿa l-mutakallimīn al-muslimīn fī majlis al-khalīfa al-Maʾmūn*', *Le Muséon* 113 (2000) 229-30

S.H. Griffith, 'The Qurʾān in Arab Christian texts; the development of an apologetical argument. Abū Qurrah in the *mağlis* of al-Maʾmūn', *Pd'O* 24 (1999) 203-33

S.H. Griffith, 'The monk in the emir's *majlis*: Reflections on a popular genre of Christian literary apologetics in Arabic in the early Islamic period', in H. Lazarus-Yafeh (ed.), *The majlis. Interreligious encounters in medieval Islam*, Wiesbaden, 1999, 13-65

S.H. Griffith, 'Reflections on the biography of Theodore Abu Qurrah', *Pd'O* 18 (1993) 143-170

S.H. Griffith, *Theodore Abu Qurrah. The intellectual profile of an Arab Christian writer of the first Abbasid century*, Tel Aviv, 1992, pp. 23-25

I. Dick, 'La discussion d'Abū Qurra avec les ulémas musulmans devant le calife al-Maʾmūn', *Pd'O* 16 (1990-91) 107-13

Shams al-Riʾāsa Abū al-Barakāt, *Miṣbāḥ al-ẓulma fī īḍāḥ al-khidma*, ed. S.K. Samir, 2 vols, Cairo, 1970, i, p. 301

Nasrallah, *HMLEM* ii.2, pp. 124-25

J.-M. Fiey and A. Abouna, *Anonymi Auctoris chronicon ad annum Christi 1234 pertinens*, Louvain, 1974, p. 16 (*CSCO* 354) (French trans.)

Graf, *GCAL* ii, pp. 21-22

A. Guillaume, 'Theodore Abu Qurra as apologist', *MW* 15 (1925) 42-51

A. Guillaume, 'A debate between Christian and Moslem doctors', *Journal of the Royal Asiatic Society of Great Britain and Ireland*, Centenary Supplement (1924) 233-44

J.-B. Chabot, *Anonymi Auctoris chronicon ad annum Christi 1234 pertinens*, Paris, 1916 (*CSCO* 82), p. 23
G. Graf, *Die arabischen Schriften des Theodor Abū Qurra, Bischofs von Ḥarrān (ca. 740-820)*, Paderborn, 1910, pp. 77-85

David Bertaina 2008

Abū Zakkār Yaḥyā ibn Nuʿmān

DATE OF BIRTH Unknown, c. 760
PLACE OF BIRTH Unknown, possibly Marw
DATE OF DEATH Unknown, c. 830
PLACE OF DEATH Unknown

BIOGRAPHY

Nothing certain is known about Abū Zakkār Yaḥyā ibn Nuʿmān apart from what is briefly mentioned by ʿAlī l-Ṭabarī (q.v.) in *Kitāb al-dīn wa-l-dawla*. ʿAlī says that Abū Zakkār was his paternal uncle and a Christian, and that he was known in Iraq and Khurāsān for his intellectual acumen and had a following of disciples (ed. Mingana, pp. 124, 129). Since ʿAlī was originally from Marw, that must also have been Abū Zakkār's original home, though there is no way of knowing whether he remained there. Like his nephew, he must have belonged to the Church of the East.

ʿAlī himself died in about 860 at more than seventy years of age (if his own remark about this is to be taken literally), so it is plausible that, since he would have been born in about 780, his uncle would have been born some decades earlier. If Abū Zakkār lived out his natural span, he would probably have died in about 830. Mingana, in his introduction to the translation (pp. xv-xvi), suggests that he may have been the Abū Zakariyā Yaḥyā ibn Māsawayh who was physician to a line of caliphs leading up to al-Mutawakkil, and who died in about 855. This is unlikely since Abū Zakariyā originated from Gundishāpūr (Sezgin, *GAS* iii, 231-36).

In addition to the inter-religious work mentioned below, he probably wrote at least one other, if he is the Yaḥyā ibn Nuʿmān the Christian to whom al-Bīrūnī refers in *Al-athār al-bāqiya* as having composed a book about the Zoroastrians.

MAIN SOURCES OF INFORMATION

Primary

A. Mingana, *The book of religion and empire. A semi-official defence and exposition of Islam written by order at the court and with the assistance of the Caliph Mutawakkil (A.D. 847-861), by Ali Tabari*, Manchester, 1923 (edition), pp. 124, 129

A. Mingana, *The book of religion and empire. A semi-official defence and exposition of Islam written by order at the court and with the assistance of the Caliph Mutawakkil (A.D. 847-861), by Ali Tabari*, Manchester, 1922 (trans.), pp. 147, 152

Abū l-Rayḥān al-Bīrūnī, *Al-athār al-bāqiya ʿan al-qurūn al-khāliya*, ed. E. Sachau, Leipzig, 1878, p. 208

E. Sachau, *The chronology of ancient nations: an English version of the Arabic text of the Athâr-ul-Bâkiya of Albîrûnî*, London, 1879, p. 191

Secondary

Graf, *GCAL* ii, p. 120

A. Mingana, 'Ṭabari's semi-official defence of Islam', *BJRL* 9 (1925) 236-40, p. 240

WORKS ON CHRISTIAN-MUSLIM RELATIONS

Al-radd ʿalā ahl al-adyān, 'Refutation of the followers of the faiths'

DATE early 9th c.

ORIGINAL LANGUAGE Arabic

DESCRIPTION

ʿAlī l-Ṭabarī mentions in his *Kitāb al-dīn wa-l-dawla* (ed. Mingana, p. 124) that Abū Zakkār's work included the point that no one who converted to Islam did so as a result of witnessing a miracle. He also refers to 'an uncle of mine who was one of the learned and eloquent men among Christians' (pp. 44-45), surely the same person, arguing with respect to the claim that the Qur'ān's literary qualities proved Muḥammad's prophethood that rhetoric was not a sign of prophetic status because it was common to all nations.

SIGNIFICANCE

The work was evidently a polemic against Islam, contending in part that it was not supported by divinely inspired miracles, and also a wider polemic against other non-Christian faiths.

It gives evidence of lively and open resistance to the claims of Islam among Christians at this time.

MANUSCRIPTS —

EDITIONS AND TRANSLATIONS —

STUDIES —

David Thomas 2007

Abū Rāʾiṭa l-Takrītī

Ḥabīb ibn Khidma Abū Rāʾiṭa l-Takrītī

DATE OF BIRTH Unknown, probably late 8th c.
PLACE OF BIRTH Unknown, probably in or near Takrīt, Iraq
DATE OF DEATH Unknown, probably soon after 830
PLACE OF DEATH Unknown, possibly in or near Takrīt, Iraq

BIOGRAPHY

Almost nothing is known of Abū Rāʾiṭa himself apart from what can be deduced from his writings and from contemporary accounts of three events (discussed below) with which he is associated. It is fairly certain that he was a layman living in the ancient Christian city of Takrīt, north of Baghdad, and was probably a Syriac-speaker who belonged to the first generation of arabophone Christians in Iraq. His father's name is usually given as 'Khidma' in the literature, but Samir has suggested that the name should perhaps be read as Ḥudhayfa (Swanson, 'A frivolous God?', p. 175). Although some have assumed on the basis of his *nisba*, 'al-Takrītī', that Abū Rāʾiṭa was the Syrian Orthodox (Jacobite) *bishop* of Takrīt, there is no contemporary evidence that this was the case. Rather, he is named in Armenian texts as a *vardapet*, a title given to apologists and teachers of theology. Abū Rāʾiṭa himself uses the equivalent Syriac title, *malpōnō*, when referring to Ephrem the Syrian in his *Iḥtijāj ʿan al-thalāth taqdīsāt li-lladhī ṣuliba ʿannā*, 'Vindication of the *Trisagion* addressed to the one "who was crucified for us"'. As a *malpōnō*, Abū Rāʾiṭa would have been recognized as a theologian, and at the height of his career he had apparently become known as a Christian apologist as far away as Armenia.

Abū Rāʾiṭa belongs to the earliest generation of Christians living under ʿAbbasid rule in Iraq who began to feel the pressure to adapt to the increasing power and influence of the Muslim community. Nine extant texts attributed to him, as well as citations from a writing now lost, reveal the transition of Syriac-speaking Christians to the use of Arabic. He is also one of the first Christians known to have written apologetic literature in Arabic, in an effort to stave off conversions to Islam that were encouraged by new policies favoring Muslims put into place by the ʿAbbasid caliphs. These concerns are clearly reflected in all his writings, both those in defense of Christianity against Islam (listed as separate entries below) and those defending the teachings of his own Syrian Orthodox Church against other Christians. Of the latter, four are extant: *Min al-risāla l-thālitha* (or: *al-thāniya*) *li-Abī Rāʾiṭa l-Takrītī fī l-radd ʿalā l-Malakiyya fī l-ittiḥād*, 'From the third (*or* second) *Risāla* of Abū Rāʾiṭa l-Takrītī in refutation of the Melkites concerning the Union (of the divinity and humanity in Christ); *al-Risāla l-thālitha li-Abī Rāʾiṭa l-Takrītī iḥtijājan ʿan al-thalāth taqdīsāt li-lladhī ṣuliba ʿannā li-Abī l-ʿAbbās al-Baṭrīq Ashūṭ ibn Sinbāṭ min ʿAbdallāh Yasūʿ al-Masīḥ Ḥabīb ibn Khidma*, 'The third *Risāla* of Abū Rāʾiṭa l-Takrītī vindicating the Trisagion addressed to the one "who was crucified for us", to Abū l-ʿAbbās al-Baṭrīq Ashūṭ ibn Sinbāṭ, from the servant of God, Jesus Christ, Ḥabīb ibn Khidma'; *Maqāla li-Ḥabīb ibn Khidma l-maʿrūf bi-Abī Rāʾiṭa l-Takrītī l-Yaʿqūbī fī iḥtijāj ʿan al-thalāth taqdīsāt li-lladhī ṣuliba ʿannā*, 'A treatise of Ḥabīb ibn Khidma, known as Abū Rāʾiṭa l-Takrītī the Jacobite, on the vindication of the Trisagion addressed to the one "who was crucified for us" '; and *al-Risāla l-rābiʿa li-Ḥabīb ibn Khidma l-maʿrūf bi-Abī Rāʾiṭa l-Takrītī al-Yaʿqūbī. Radd ʿalā l-Malakiyya*, 'The fourth *Risāla* of Ḥabīb ibn Khidma, known as Abū Rāʾiṭa l-Takrītī the Jacobite. Refutation of the Melkites'. Although these are intra-Christian apologetic works, one detects an underlying concern in each of them for the importance of correct Christian doctrine for a unified and consistent response to the Muslim community.

Three unrelated traditions mention Abū Rāʾiṭa's activities at the beginning of the 9th century. The first is recorded in several Armenian chronicles referring to an invitation made by the *ishxan* Ashot Smbāt Msaker (r. 804-26) to Abū Rāʾiṭa to come to his court and defend miaphysite teachings against the Melkite Bishop Theodore Abū Qurra (q.v.), who was on a missionary journey to Armenia. According to the accounts, this event can be dated sometime between 815 and 817. Abū Rāʾiṭa was unable to travel to Armenia, but instead sent his relative, Archdeacon Nonnus of Nisibis (q.v.) with a letter of introduction in which Abū Rāʾiṭa himself lays out a defense of the Syrian Orthodox view. At least two, and perhaps all, of his extant letters in defense of miaphysite doctrines are related to this incident.

A second tradition has Abū Rāʾiṭa actually meeting Theodore Abū Qurra (q.v.) and a metropolitan from the Church of the East named ʿAbdīshūʿ, probably ʿAbdīshūʿ ibn Bahrīz (q.v.), and engaging in an exchange before an unnamed Muslim official (q.v. 'A Christological discussion'). If historical, this exchange is probably to be dated to sometime in the 820s.

Abū Rāʾiṭa is also mentioned in the *Chronicle* of Michael the Syrian in connection with a local synod at Reshʿayna in 827/8. Although Michael does not explain Abū Rāʾiṭa's role explicitly, it appears that he supported Nonnus in bringing charges against a bishop who was consequently removed from his see. After this date there is no mention of his activities.

Abū Rāʾiṭa's apologetic project is intended both to give support to fellow Christians under pressure to convert and to provide a clear, consistent explanation of Christianity. His writings concerning Islam are primarily dialectical, offering answers to be used by Christians when responding to questions asked by Muslims about Christian doctrine. In his approach, he draws on Christian scripture, traditional apologetic methods, and principles of Hellenistic philosophy, which was becoming of increasing interest to Muslim scholars. In this connection, it is worth noting that he may be mentioned in Ibn al-Nadīm's list of translators of scientific and philosophical texts into Arabic – that is, if the 'Ibn Rābiṭa' found there is in fact Abū Rāʾiṭa.

In keeping with the practice of most Christian apologists of his day, Abū Rāʾiṭa makes clear allusions to Islam, but usually without explicit references to it or quotations from the Qurʾān or *ḥadīth*. Nonetheless, his presentation of hypothetical questions and corresponding arguments reflects a deep knowledge of Islam and the implications of agreements and disagreements on doctrine. His method was highly regarded by later theologians, and much of his work became the template for such apologists as Nonnus of Nisibis, Yaḥyā ibn ʿAdī, ʿAbdallāh ibn al-Faḍl and others.

MAIN SOURCES OF INFORMATION

Primary

Principal editions of Abū Rāʾiṭa's writings:

S. Toenies Keating, *Defending the 'people of truth' in the early Islamic period. The Christian apologies of Abū Rāʾiṭah*, Leiden, 2006 (with intro. including biographical information, pp. 1-72)

G. Graf, *Die Schriften des Jacobiten Ḥabīb Ibn Ḫidma Abū Rāʾiṭah*, 2 vols., Louvain, 1951 (CSCO 130-131) (edition and German trans.)

Other works:

Ibn al-Nadīm, *Kitāb al-fihrist*, ed. G. Flügel, Leipzig, 1871-1872 (repr. Beirut, 1966), p. 244

R.W. Thompson, *The historical compilation of Vardan Arewelcʿi*, Washington DC, 1989, p. 183

Shams al-Riʾāsa Abū l-Barakāt ibn Kabar, *Miṣbāḥ al-ẓulma fī īḍāḥ al-khidma*, ed. Samīr Khalīl, Cairo, 1971, pp. 18-19 (= *Livre de la lampe des ténèbres de l'exposition (lumineuse) du service (de l'église)*, ed. L. Villecourt, E. Tisserant and G. Weit, PO 20, 575-734 (= fasc. 4), pp. 654-55)

A. van Roey, *Nonnus de Nisibe. Traité apologétique*, Louvain, 1948, pp. 10-11, 14-16

J. Muyldermans, *La domination arabe en Arménie. Extrait de l'Histoire universal de Vardan*, Paris, 1927, pp. 60, 115

J.-B. Chabot, *Chronique de Michel le Syrien*, 4 vols, Paris, 1899-1910, iii, p. 5; iv, p. 507

Mkhithar d'Aïrivank, *Histoire chronologique,* trans. M.-F. Brosset, St Petersburg, 1869, t. 13, fasc. 5, p. 83

Assemani, *BO* ii, p. 154

Secondary

S. Toenies Keating, 'The use and translation of scripture in the apologetic writings of Abū Rāʾiṭa l-Takrītī', in D. Thomas (ed.), *The Bible in Arab Christianity*, Leiden, 2007, 257-74

H. Suermann, 'Ḥabīb ibn Ḫidma Abū Rāʾiṭa. Portrait eines miaphysitische Theologen', *Journal of Eastern Christian Studies* 58 (2006) 221-33

S. Toenies Keating, 'Refuting the charge of *taḥrīf*. Abū Rāʾiṭa (d. ca. 835 CE) and his first *Risāla* on the Holy Trinity', in S. Günther (ed.), *Ideas, images, and methods of portrayal. Insights into classical Arabic literature and Islam*, Leiden, 2005, 41-57

M.N. Swanson, 'A frivolous God? (*a-fa-ḥasibtum annamā khalaqnākum ʿabathan*)', in D. Thomas and C. Amos (eds), *A faithful presence. Essays for Kenneth Cragg*, London, 2003, 166-83, pp. 174-81

S.H. Griffith, '"Melkites", "Jacobites" and the Christological controversies in Arabic in third/ninth-century Syria', in D. Thomas (ed.), *Syrian Christians under Islam. The first thousand years*, Leiden, 2001, 9-55, pp. 49-53

S. Dakkāsh, *Abū Rāʾiṭa l-Takrītī wa-risālatuhu 'Fī l-Thālūth al-muqaddas'. Dirāsa wa-naṣṣ*, Beirut, 1996

H. Suermann, 'Der Begriff *Ṣifah* bei Abū Rāʾiṭa', in S.K. Samir and J.S. Nielsen (eds), *Christian Arabic apologetics during the Abbasid period (750-1258)*, Leiden, 1994, 157-71

H. Suermann, 'Trinität in der islamisch-christlichen Kontroverse nach Abū Rāʾiṭah', *Zeitschrift für Missionswissenschaft und Religionswissenschaft* 74 (1990) 219-29

S.K. Samir, 'Création et incarnation chez Abū Rāʾitah. Étude de vocabulaire', in *Mélanges en hommage au professeur et au penseur libanais Farid Jabre*, Beirut, 1989, 187-236 (with introduction including biographical information, pp. 187-94)

J.-M. Fiey, 'Ḥabīb Abū Rāʾiṭah n'était pas évêque de Takrīt', in S.K. Samir (ed.), *Actes du Deuxième congrès international d'études arabes chrétiennes (1984)*, Rome, 1986, 211-14
S. Daccache, 'Polémique, logique et élaboration théologique chez Abū Rāʾita al-Takrītī', *Annales de Philosophie* 6 (1985) 38-88
R. Haddad, *La Trinité divine chez les théologiens arabes (750-1050)*, Paris, 1985 (see the index for relevant passages)
S.K. Samir, 'Liberté religieuse et propagation de la foi chez les théologiens arabes chrétiens du ixe siècle et en Islam', in *Witness of faith in life and worship*, Tantur, 1981, 93-164, pp. 98-100
S.H. Griffith, 'Ḥabīb ibn Ḫidmah Abū Rāʾiṭah, a Christian *mutakallim* of the first Abbasid century', *OC* 64 (1980) 161-201
Ighnāṭiyūs Afram al-Awwal Barṣawm, *al-Luʾluʾ al-manthūr fī tārīkh al-ʿulūm wa-l-ādāb al-suryāniyya*, Glane, 1987, p. 332

WORKS ON CHRISTIAN-MUSLIM RELATIONS

Risāla li-Abī Rāʾiṭa l-Takrītī fī ithbāt dīn al-naṣrāniyya wa-ithbāt al-Thālūth al-muqaddas, 'A *Risāla* of Abū Rāʾiṭa l-Takrītī on the proof of the Christian religion and the proof of the Holy Trinity', 'On the proof of Christianity and the Trinity'

DATE Unknown, probably between 815 and 825
ORIGINAL LANGUAGE Arabic

DESCRIPTION
This is the longest and most comprehensive of Abū Rāʾiṭa's extant works. Known manuscripts lack the conclusion and the 'Proof of the Holy Trinity' referred to by the copyist in the title.

The *Proof* provides the reader with potential questions and responses to be used in debates with Muslims over the truth of Christianity. As in his other writings, Abū Rāʾiṭa provides arguments from both logic and reason, as well as scriptural proofs. The extant text covers six topics: legitimate and illegitimate reasons to change one's religion; the use of analogy as an aid to understanding the Holy Trinity; biblical witnesses in support of the doctrine of the Trinity; answers to questions about the Incarnation, including the reasons and manner of God's becoming human; biblical witnesses in support of the doctrine of the Incarnation; and Christian practices, including the direction of prayer, the eucharist, abandonment of certain Mosaic laws, and fasting. The text breaks off abruptly before concluding.

SIGNIFICANCE

Following the arguments and structure of Syriac apologetics, this is one of the very first and most comprehensive treatises of its kind written in Arabic by a known person. In this text, Abū Rāʾiṭa briefly lays out arguments that he will address more extensively in other *rasāʾil*, suggesting that it is one of his earliest writings (Keating, *Defending the 'people of truth'*, pp. 73-81).

MANUSCRIPTS

MS Aleppo, Fondation Georges et Mathilde Salem – Sbath 1001 (16th-17th c.), fols 179r-200r

MS Aleppo, Fondation Georges et Mathilde Salem – Sbath 1041 (18th c.)

MS Cairo, Coptic Patriarchate – Theol. 177 (Simaika 320, Graf 534) (undated); the Abū Rāʾiṭa texts are at fols 81r-210r

EDITIONS AND TRANSLATIONS

Keating, *Defending the 'people of truth'*, pp. 82-144 (edition and English trans.)

Graf, *Abū Rāʾiṭah*, i, pp. 131-61 (edition); ii, pp. 159-94 (German trans.)

STUDIES

Keating, *Defending the 'people of truth'*, pp. 73-81

Swanson, 'A frivolous God?', pp. 174-81

Al-risālat al-ūlā fī l-Thālūth al-muqaddas, 'The first *Risāla* : On the Holy Trinity', 'On the Trinity'

DATE Unknown, probably between 815 and 828

ORIGINAL LANGUAGE Arabic

DESCRIPTION

This *risāla* is apparently the first of a group of three which Abū Rāʾiṭa presents as the answer to a request by an unknown fellow Syrian Orthodox. It serves as an introduction to the ensuing proof of the Holy Trinity, as well as to his second *risāla* on the Incarnation and to a third text now lost.

The text begins with a comment on the difficulties faced by one who engages in debate with 'those who differ', and suggestions of how best to proceed. The introduction is followed by a short list of attributes of God affirmed by both Christians and the 'people of the south' (the Muslims), leading into extensive discussion of the definitions of several terms used in the debate. In this section, Abū Rāʾiṭa makes extensive use of the principles of Aristotelian logic and analogy. The treatise concludes with references to scripture and more analogies in defense of the consistency and rationality of Christianity.

SIGNIFICANCE

The *risāla On the Holy Trinity* is perhaps Abū Rāʾiṭa's most important and widely known work. In it he provides a list of *ṣifāt Allāh*, divine attributes, that his opponents claim are a point of agreement. This is perhaps one of the earliest of such lists. In response, he develops a definition of the unity and Trinity of God, using terminology which closely parallels that found in Muslim discussions of the *ṣifāt Allāh*. His approach is adopted by many later theologians, and is especially known through the correspondence of al-Hāshimī and al-Kindī (see the entry on the Apology of al-Kindī), which is probably contemporary with Abū Rāʾiṭa.

At the conclusion of the *risāla*, Abū Rāʾiṭa briefly takes up the accusation of *taḥrīf*, formulating several clear arguments in favor of the authenticity of the Christian scriptures. These arguments provide the lens through which the method of his other writings should be viewed (Keating, *Defending*, pp. 147-63).

MANUSCRIPTS

MS Aleppo, Fondation Georges et Mathilde Salem – Sbath 1042 (14th c.)

MS Aleppo, Fondation Georges et Mathilde Salem – Sbath 1001 (16th-17th c.), fols 85r-104r

MS BNF – Ar. 169 (1654), fols 51v-63v

MS Aleppo, Fondation Georges et Mathilde Salem – Sbath 1041 (18th c.)

MS Cairo, Coptic Patriarchate – Theol. 177 (Simaika 320, Graf 534) (undated)

EDITIONS AND TRANSLATIONS

Keating, *Defending the 'people of truth'*, pp. 164-215 (edition and English trans.)

Dakkāsh, *Abū Rāʾiṭa l-Takrītī wa-risālatuhu fī l-Thālūth al-muqaddas* (edition)

Graf, *Abū Rāʾiṭah*, i, pp. 1-26 (edition); ii, pp. 1-31 (German trans.)

STUDIES

Keating, *Defending the 'people of truth'*, pp. 147-63

Keating, 'Refuting the charge of *Tahrīf*, pp. 41-57

Suermann, 'Der Begriff *Ṣifah* bei Abū Rāʾiṭa', pp. 122-38
Suermann, 'Trinität in der islamisch-christlichen Kontroverse nach Abū Rāʾiṭah', pp. 219-29
Daccache, 'Polémique, logique et élaboration théologique chez Abū Rāʾita al-Takrītī', pp. 38-88
Haddad, *La Trinité*, pp. 55-60, 101-22, 163-73, 198-209

Al-risālat al-thāniya li-Abī Rāʾiṭa l-Takrītī fī l-tajassud, 'The second *Risāla* of Abū Rāʾiṭa l-Takrītī: On the Incarnation', 'On the Incarnation'

DATE Later than the *Risāla l-ūlā*, probably between 815 and 828
ORIGINAL LANGUAGE Arabic

DESCRIPTION
The *risāla On the Incarnation* is written with the same purpose and to the same audience as the *risāla On the Holy Trinity*; it is nearly twice as long.

The treatise begins with a short transitional passage and then immediately addresses the relationship between the Trinity and the incarnate Christ. Abū Rāʾiṭa then turns to the problems of how God enters into creation and why salvation through the Incarnation was necessary. This is followed by his own question of why God sent messengers. The second half of the treatise takes up the possibility of the Divine entering into the limitations of time and space, and concludes with an examination of Christ's knowledge of the future and the question of whether or not he was crucified willingly.

SIGNIFICANCE
In spite of the continuity between the first *risāla* and this second, there are notable differences. Here, Abū Rāʾiṭa's knowledge of Islam is more evident. He makes numerous references to Muslim beliefs concerning prophets, the humanity of Jesus and the crucifixion, without explicitly naming his interlocutors. It is also in this *risāla* that one finds the closest parallels to phrases in the Qurʾān in any of his writings.

Abū Rāʾiṭa adapts traditional Christian defenses of the Incarnation in the Islamic context, demonstrating a special sensitivity to the accusation of *taḥrīf*. Unlike the *risāla On the Holy Trinity*, here he avoids logical proofs and provides very succinct answers to questions, probably on the assumption that his reader is already familiar with them. What is unique is his choice of scriptural proofs, which emphasize prophecies in the Hebrew Bible about the Messiah and consistency within the Gospels themselves.

The scripture citations he provides appear to be his own original translations into Arabic (Keating, *Defending the 'people of truth'*, pp. 217-20).

A brief quotation from this work (asserting that Christ's divinity did not depart from his humanity when he died, but remained united to both body and soul; (see Graf, *Abū Rāʾiṭa*, i, pp. 40-41 [edition]; ii, p. 53 [German trans.], or Keating, *Defending the 'people of truth'*, pp. 182-83) is found in the 11th-century Copto-Arabic *florilegium Iʿtirāf al-ābāʾ*, 'The confession of the Fathers', in which Abū Rāʾiṭa is identified as ʿAnbā Ḥabīb, Bishop of Takrīt'.

MANUSCRIPTS

MS Aleppo, Fondation Georges et Mathilde Salem – Sbath 1001 (16th-17th c.), fols 104v-131v

MS BNF – Ar. 169 (1654), fols 63v-81r

MS Aleppo, Fondation Georges et Mathilde Salem – Sbath 1041 (18th c.)

MS Cairo, Coptic Patriarchate – Theol. 177 (Simaika 320, Graf 534) (undated)

EDITIONS AND TRANSLATIONS

Keating, *Defending the 'people of truth'*, pp. 222-97 (edition and English trans.)

Samir, 'Création et incarnation', pp. 199-215 (partial edition and French trans.)

Graf, *Abū Rāʾiṭa*, i, pp. 27-64 (edition); ii, pp. 37-81 (German trans.)

For the quotation in *Iʿtirāf al-abāʾ*, see:

Iʿtirāfāt al-abāʾ, ed. by a monk of Dayr al-Muḥarraq, Cairo, 2002, p. 391 (edition from manuscripts in the library of Dayr al-Muḥarraq dating to 1785 and 1795)

Graf, *Abū Rāʾiṭa*, i, pp. 160-61, §3 (edition); ii, pp. 195-96 (German trans.)

G. Graf, 'Zwei dogmatische Florilegien der Kopten. B. Das Bekenntnis der Väter', *Orientalia Christiana Periodica* 3 (1937) 345-402, pp. 399 (German trans.)

STUDIES

Keating, *Defending the 'people of truth'*, pp. 217-20

Samir, 'Création et incarnation', pp. 194-98, 216-36

Unknown *risāla* in a set of three *rasāʾil* on the Holy Trinity and the Incarnation

DATE Unknown, later than the *Risāla* on the Holy Trinity and the *Risāla* on the Incarnation, probably between 815 and 828
ORIGINAL LANGUAGE Arabic

DESCRIPTION
The brief entry on Abū Rāʾiṭa in the 11th-century Copto-Arabic *florilegium Iʿtirāf al-ābāʾ*, 'The confession of the Fathers', includes a quotation from the second *risāla On the Incarnation* (see above), which is described as *al-risāla l-thāniya min al-thalāth rasāʾil allatī qālahā fī l-Thālūth al-muqaddas wa-l-tajassud*, 'The second *risāla* from the three *rasāʾil* which he pronounced on the Holy Trinity and the Incarnation'. This title suggests the existence of a third *risāla* (after the first on the Trinity and the second on the Incarnation) – which does not seem to correspond to any known work of Abū Rāʾiṭa and is probably lost. We may assume, however, that it was part of a three-part apologetic whole.

SIGNIFICANCE
We do not know whether the third treatise in this three-treatise sequence repeated or expanded upon Abū Rāʾiṭa's apologetic arguments for the Trinity and the Incarnation in the first two treatises, or whether it went on to other issues (Christian practices, perhaps). In any event, the existence of this additional treatise is a witness to Abū Rāʾiṭa's concern to provide a comprehensive apology for distinctive (Syrian Orthodox) Christian doctrines at a time when many Christians were converting to Islam.

MANUSCRIPTS —
EDITIONS AND TRANSLATIONS —
STUDIES —

Shahādāt min qawl al-Tawrāt wa-l-anbiyāʾ wa-l-qiddīsīn, 'Witnesses from the words of the Torah, the prophets and the saints'

DATE Unknown, probably between 820 and 830
ORIGINAL LANGUAGE Arabic

DESCRIPTION

Extant manuscripts give no title or author for this text, simply beginning with 'Witnesses from the words of the Torah'. It has, however, been included among copies of other writings associated with Abū Rāʾiṭa and has not been attributed to anyone else. Further, most of the passages are found in similar translations throughout his other apologetic writings.

The text itself is a list of approximately 80 brief quotations taken from the Hebrew Bible, none more than ten verses long (according to modern numbering). There is no introductory or concluding text. The passages are arranged into two general categories (without headings) of those that might be used as proof texts for the doctrine of the Trinity and those that support the Incarnation.

The source of the translations is probably the Old Syriac version of the Bible. Inconsistancies and similarities between these translations into Arabic and those in the remainder of Abū Rāʾiṭa's other writings suggest that they are original translations and that no widely accepted translation was available to him at the beginning of the 9th century (Keating, *Defending the 'people of truth'*, pp. 299-306).

SIGNIFICANCE

This text probably represents an early Arabic translation of biblical texts intended for apologetic purposes. It is among the earliest known existing examples of an Arabic *testimonia* list.

MANUSCRIPTS

MS Aleppo, Fondation Georges et Mathilde Salem – Sbath 1001 (16th-17th c.), fols 167v-174

MS BNF – Ar. 169 (1654), fols 94r-98r

MS Aleppo, Fondation Georges et Mathilde Salem – Sbath 1041 (18th c.)

MS Cairo, Coptic Patriarchate – Theol. 177 (Simaika 320, Graf 534) (undated)

EDITIONS AND TRANSLATIONS

Keating, *Defending the 'people of truth'*, pp. 308-33 (edition and English trans.)

Graf, *Abū Rāʾiṭa*, i, pp. 49-104 (edition); ii, pp. 117-26 (German trans.)

STUDIES

Keating, *Defending the 'people of truth'*, pp. 299-306

Keating, 'The use and translation of scripture'

Min qawl Abī Rāʾiṭa l-Takrītī al-Suryānī usquf Nasībīn mustadillan bihi ʿalā ṣiḥḥat al-Naṣrāniyya l-maqbūla min al-dāʿīn al-mubashshirīn bihā bi-l-Injīl al-muqaddas, 'From the teaching of Abū Rāʾiṭa l-Takrītī, the Syrian, Bishop of Nisibis, by which he demonstrates the authenticity of the Christianity received from the Evangelists who called to it by the Holy Gospel', 'The authenticity of Christianity'

DATE Unknown, probably between 815 and 828
ORIGINAL LANGUAGE Arabic

DESCRIPTION

This logical proof is the shortest of Abū Rāʾiṭa's extant writings and is unique both in its form and intended readership. In a few short lines, it offers a proof for the validity of Christianity based on its universal acceptance. Unlike in his other treatises, Abū Rāʾiṭa makes no appeal to scripture in this demonstration. Rather, he argues that 'coercion by the sword' will not bring about true conversion; only miracles can convince both the 'wise' and the 'ignorant'.

The text is transmitted both independently, in one manuscript, and in quotation by medieval authors: ʿAbdallāh ibn al-Faḍl al-Anṭākī in *Kitāb al-manfaʿa*, al-Muʾtaman ibn al-ʿAssāl in *Majmūʿ uṣūl al-dīn*, and Shams al-Riʾāsa Abū l-Barakāt ibn Kabar in *Miṣbāḥ al-ẓulma*. Ibn Kabar mentions that it was written in response to a question by 'one of the Muʿtazila', whom the Sbath manuscript names: Yumāma, probably a mistake for Abū Rāʾiṭa's contemporary Thumāma ibn Ashras al-Baṣrī (d. c. 828).

SIGNIFICANCE

This short text, addressed to a Muʿtazilī *mutakallim*, gives further support to the idea that Abū Rāʾiṭa was actively engaged in debate with Muslims on theological issues. Read alongside his *Proof of the Christian religion*, it sheds light on the pressure being felt by Christians living under ʿAbbasid rule (Keating, *Defending the 'people of truth'*, 335-41). In addition, the quotation of the text by both Melkite and Coptic authors gives some indication of the important place of Abū Rāʾiṭa in the history of Arabic Christian apologetics.

MANUSCRIPTS

MS Aleppo, Fondation Georges et Mathilde Salem – Sbath 1017 (15th c.), p. 14

For MSS of ʿAbdallāh ibn al-Faḍl al-Anṭākī in *Kitāb al-manfaʿa*, begin with Graf, *GCAL* ii, pp. 59-60; Samir, 'Liberté religieuse', points to MS Joun, Dayr al-Mukhalliṣ – 173 (18th c.), fol. 190r

For MSS of al-Muʾtaman ibn al-ʿAssāl in *Majmūʿ uṣūl al-dīn*, Chapter 12, see A. Wadi, *Studio su al-Muʾtaman ibn al-ʿAssāl*, Cairo, 1997, pp. 189-92

For MSS of Shams al-Riʾāsa Abū l-Barakāt ibn Kabar, *Miṣbāḥ al-ẓulma*, begin with Graf, *GCAL* ii, pp. 439-42

EDITIONS AND TRANSLATIONS

Keating, *Defending the 'people of truth'*, pp. 342-45 (edition and English trans.)

B. Pirone, *Al-Muʾtaman ibn al-ʿAssāl. Summa dei principi della religione*, 2 vols, Cairo: Franciscan Centre of Oriental Studies, 1998-2002, i, Ch. 12, §25-27 (Italian trans. of the edition that follows below)

A. Wadi, *Al-Muʾtaman ibn al-ʿAssāl. Majmūʿ uṣūl al-dīn wa-masmūʿ maḥṣūl al-yaqīn*, 2 parts in 4 vols, Cairo: Franciscan Centre of Oriental Studies, 1998-99, i, Ch. 12, §25-27 (critical edition of the text as transmitted by al-Muʾtaman)

Samir, 'Liberté religieuse', pp. 98-100 (edition and French trans. of the text as transmitted by al-Muʾtaman)

Shams al-Riʾāsa Abū l-Barakāt ibn Kabar, *Miṣbāḥ al-ẓulma fī īḍāḥ al-khidma*, ed. S. Khalīl, Cairo, 1971, pp. 18-19 (best edition of *Miṣbāḥ al-ẓulma*)

Graf, *Abū Rāʾiṭa*, i, p. 162 (edition); ii, p. 197 (German trans.)

Abū l-Barakāt ibn Kabar, *Livre de la lampe des ténèbres de l'exposition (lumineuse) du service (de l'église)*, ed. L. Villecourt, E. Tisserant and G. Weit (*Patrologia Orientalis* 20), 575-734 (= fasc. 4), pp. 654-55

L. Cheikho, *Vingt traités théologiques d'auteurs arabes chrétiens, IXe-XIIIe siècle*, Beirut, 1920, p. 146 (Arabic text as transmitted by al-Muʾtaman)

L. Cheikho, *Seize traités théologiques d'auteurs arabes chrétiens, IXe-XIIIe siècle*, Beirut, 1906, p. 124 (Arabic text as transmitted by al-Muʾtaman)

L. Cheikho, 'Un traité de Ḥonein', in C. Bezold (ed.), *Orientalische Studien Theodor Nöldeke gewidmet*, 2 vols, Giessen, 1906, i, pp. 287, 291 (Arabic text as transmitted by al-Muʾtaman with French trans.)

STUDIES

Keating, *Defending the 'people of truth'*, pp. 335-41

Samir, 'Liberté religieuse', pp. 98-100

Risāla lahu ilā man bi-l-Baḥrīn min Naṣāra l-maghrib, 'His *risāla* to those of Baḥrīn, of the Christians of the West', 'Letter to the Christians of Baḥrīn'

DATE Unknown, before the second *risāla On the Incarnation*

ORIGINAL LANGUAGE Arabic

DESCRIPTION

At the end of the 'Second *Risāla*: On the Incarnation', Abū Rāʾiṭa makes a reference to his *risāla* in response to one from the people of Baḥrīn (probably the Syrian Orthodox community of the town of Baḥrīn near Mosul, or, less likely, Baḥrayn), in which he offered an exegesis of Christ's words and deeds in his incarnate humility. While the full text of Abū Rāʾiṭa's *risāla* has not been preserved, two brief quotations from it are found in the 11th-century Copto-Arabic *florilegium Iʿtirāf al-ābāʾ*, 'The confession of the Fathers'. The first quotation stresses the reality of the Incarnation, and quotes John 1:14. The second speaks of Christ's human body as a *ḥijāb*, 'veil', a line of discourse found rather frequently in early Arabic Christian apologies, possibly because it echoes the reference to God speaking from 'behind a veil' (*min warāʾi ḥijābin*) in Q 42:51.

SIGNIFICANCE

The limited information that we possess about this text points to the liveliness of Christological discourse in early 9th-century Syrian Orthodox circles in Iraq, as Christians struggled to find ways to speak of the simultaneous divinity and humanity of Christ in the face of Islamic challenges.

MANUSCRIPTS

For MSS of *Iʿtirāf al-ābāʾ*, see Graf, *GCAL* ii, pp. 321-23. This list must now be expanded with MSS from collections in Egypt, including the two MSS used by the editor of the Dayr al-Muḥarraq edition.

EDITIONS AND TRANSLATIONS

Iʿtirāfāt al-abāʾ, ed. by a monk of Dayr al-Muḥarraq, Cairo, 2002, p. 391 (Arabic text of the quotations from Abū Rāʾiṭa, from manuscripts in the library of Dayr al-Muḥarraq dating to 1785 and 1795)

Graf, *Abū Rāʾiṭa*, i, pp. 160-61, §1-2 (edition); ii, p. 195 (German trans.)

G. Graf, 'Zwei dogmatische Florilegien der Kopten', pp. 398-99 (German trans. of the quotations)

STUDIES —

S. Toenies Keating 2008

The Caliph al-Maʾmūn

Abū l-ʿAbbās ʿAbdallāh ibn Hārūn al-Maʾmūn

DATE OF BIRTH 786
PLACE OF BIRTH Baghdad
DATE OF DEATH 833
PLACE OF DEATH Tarsus

BIOGRAPHY

As his name indicates, ʿAbdallāh ibn Hārūn was the son of the Caliph Hārūn al-Rashīd. Declared second heir after his brother al-Amīn, he established himself as governor of Khurāsān during his brother's caliphate. In 810, tensions between the two erupted into open hostility, and by 813 power had moved away from al-Amīn; he was executed, and al-Maʾmūn was acknowledged as caliph. His control over the empire was finally assured when he left Khurāsān and entered Baghdad in 819.

Al-Maʾmūn actively encouraged intellectual pursuits. He sponsored translations of scientific works into Arabic, and under his rule the sciences flourished and religious thinking reached heights of sophistication. He held debates over matters of belief between representatives of Muslim and non-Muslim traditions, and himself favored Muʿtazili teachings, proclaiming them the official doctrines of the empire in 827, and in 833 instituting the *miḥna*, the 'inquisition', under which public officials had to affirm Muʿtazili views about the Qurʾān. In later centuries, it became conventional for authors of debate texts to set the meetings in al-Maʾmūn's court, and a Christian tradition grew up that he converted to Christianity and was martyred.

Al-Maʾmūn died near Tarsus in Cilicia in 833 while engaged in one of his seasonal campaigns against the Byzantine empire.

MAIN SOURCES OF INFORMATION

Primary

Most primary sources are collected together in A. al-Rifāʿī, *ʿAṣr al-Maʾmūn*, 3 vols, Cairo, 1928

al-Ṭabarī, *Taʾrīkh*, trans. C.E. Bosworth, *The caliphate of al-Maʾmūn 198-213 (813-33)*, Albany NY, 1986

Secondary

M. Cooperson, *Al-Maʾmun*, Oxford, 2005

M. Swanson, 'The Christian al-Maʾmūn tradition', in D. Thomas (ed.), *Christians at the heart of Islamic rule*, Leiden, 2003, 63-92

M. Cooperson, *Classical Arabic biography. The heirs of the prophets in the age of al-Maʾmūn*, Cambridge, 2000

S.H. Griffith, 'The monk in the emir's *majlis*. Reflections on a popular genre of Christian literary apologetics in Arabic in the early Islamic period', in H. Lazarus-Yafeh *et al.* (eds), *The Majlis. Interreligious encounters in early Islam*, Wiesbaden, 1999, 13-66, pp. 38-47

T. el-Hibri, *Reinterpreting Islamic historiography. Hārūn al-Rashīd and the narrative of the ʿAbbāsid caliphate*, Cambridge, 1999

J.A. Nawas, 'The Miḥna of 218 A.H./833 A.D. revisited: an empirical study', *JAOS* 16 (1996) 698-708

D. Sourdel, 'La politique religieuse du calife ʿabbāside al-Maʾmūn', *REI* 30 (1962) 26-48

WORKS ON CHRISTIAN-MUSLIM RELATIONS

Risāla fī aʿlām al-nubuwwa, 'Letter on the signs of prophethood'

DATE before 833

ORIGINAL LANGUAGE Arabic

DESCRIPTION

The work is listed by Ibn al-Nadīm, *Fihrist*, p. 129. The 13th-century Shīʿī scholar Abū l-Qāsim ʿAlī ibn Mūsā ibn Ṭāwūs (d. 1266) mentions in his *al-Ṭarāʾif fī maʿrifat madhāhib al-ṭawāʾif*, Qom, [1400] 1979, p. 424, what must be the same work with the title *Kitāb aʿlām al-rasūl*, and says that in a library in Baghdad he had examined a copy of it made in 865 (see E. Kohlberg, *A medieval Muslim scholar at work: Ibn Ṭāwūs and his library*, Leiden, 1992, p. 106).

It was one of the earliest examples of the 'proofs of prophethood' genre, and it may have listed and commented on biblical proof verses and also refuted arguments from Christians. It may have been inspired by the same motivation that lay behind the letters that al-Maʾmūn is known to have sent to foreign rulers advocating the merits of Islam (El-Hibri, p. 129).

SIGNIFICANCE
It presumably employed similar arguments to those in contemporary 'proofs of prophethood' works, and may have fed later works of this kind.

MANUSCRIPTS —
EDITIONS AND TRANSLATIONS —
STUDIES —

Kitāb fī l-radd ʿalā l-Yahūd wa-l-Naṣārā, 'Refutation of the Jews and Christians'

DATE before 833
ORIGINAL LANGUAGE Arabic

DESCRIPTION
The work is listed by Ibn al-Murtaḍā, *Kitāb ṭabaqāt al-Muʿtazila*, ed. S. Diwald-Wilzer, Beirut, 1988, p. 123, who says that the caliph wrote 'many books', but names only this and a work against the Manicheans.

Van Ess (*TG* iii, p. 202) dismisses it and other works against non-Muslims attributed to al-Maʾmūn as part of the legend that was built up around him as a great defender of Islam.

SIGNIFICANCE
It would have been one of the earliest known Muslim refutations of the two faiths, and presumably included typical polemical arguments used at the time.

MANUSCRIPTS —
EDITIONS AND TRANSLATIONS —
STUDIES
Van Ess, *TG* iii, pp. 201-3

David Thomas 2007

The Apology of al-Kindī

ʿAbd al-Masīḥ ibn Isḥāq al-Kindī (pseudonym)

DATE OF BIRTH Unknown, probably late 8th or beginning of 9th c.
PLACE OF BIRTH Unknown
DATE OF DEATH Unknown, probably 9th c.
PLACE OF DEATH Unknown

BIOGRAPHY

Nothing is known about the life of the author. Even his name, cited for the first time in its entirety by al-Bīrūnī in his *Kitāb al-āthār al-bāqiya* together with the name of his interlocutor, ʿAbdallāh ibn Ismāʿīl al-Hāshimī, seems to be a pseudonym, invented to serve as a counterpart to the name of the Muslim adversary, to encapsulate onomastically the religious antagonism between the descendants of Sarah and the descendants Hagar. Moreover, in the introduction of the Arabic text, the author says explicitly that he chose to omit the names. Although his motive is not mentioned, it was presumably because of the harsh tone of the polemics, and instead the author limits himself to naming the clans to which the Christian and the Muslim belonged: the famous Christian Arab tribe of Kinda and the Banū Hāshim, the tribe of Muḥammad. Al-Tawḥīdī, the first to mention the apologist (Haddad, *La Trinité divine*, 41), does not add any more information regarding the name of the Christian author.

In some of the extant manuscripts, rather than ʿAbd al-Masīḥ we find 'Yūsuf ibn Jirjis' or 'Yaʿqūb', the latter suggesting an identification of the Christian author with the famous Muslim philosopher Abū Yūsuf Yaʿqūb al-Kindī. Other hypotheses for identifying the apologist with known thinkers have been advanced.

Equally problematic is the question of where one should place the author within the panorama of Christian confessions. In the eyes of the majority of modern scholars, he would have belonged to the Church of the East, but others believe he was a Syrian Orthodox, a Melkite, an East-Syrian who converted to the Chalcedonian faith, or even a 'Catholic'. Other scholars have concluded that it is impossible to determine his confessional identity.

MAIN SOURCES OF INFORMATION

Primary

Risālat ʿAbdallāh ibn Ismāʿīl al-Hāshimī ilā ʿAbd al-Masīḥ ibn Isḥāq al-Kindī yadʿūhu bihā ilā l-Islām wa-risālat ʿAbd al-Masīḥ ilā l-Hāshimī yarud-du bihā ʿalayhi wa-yadʿūhu ilā l-Naṣrāniyya, ed. A. Tien, Cairo, 1912, p. 4

al-Tawḥīdī, *Kitāb al-imtāʿ wa-l-muʾānasa*, ed. A. Amin and A. al-Zayn, 3 parts in 1 vol., Beirut, s.d., i, pt i, p. 127

al-Bīrūnī, *Kitāb al-āthār al-bāqiya ʿan al-qurūn al-khāliya*, ed. E.C. Sachau, Leipzig, 1876, p. 205

Secondary

F. González Muñoz, *Exposición y refutación del Islam. La versión latina de las epistolas de al-Hāšimī y al-Kindī*, Coruña, 2005, pp. XLIX-LIV

P.S. van Koningsveld, 'The apology of al-Kindī', in T.L. Hettema and A. van der Kooij (eds), *Religious polemics in context*, Assen, 2004, 69-92

B. Landron, *Chrétiens et musulmans en Irak. Attitudes nestoriennes vis-à-vis de l'islam*, Paris, 1994, pp. 82-85

al-Sharfī, *al-Fikr al-islāmī*, pp. 123, 127-28

R. Haddad, *La Trinité divine chez les théologiens arabes, 750-1050*, Paris, 1985, pp. 40-43

G. Tartar, *Dialogue islamo-chrétien sous le calife al-Maʾmūn (813-834). Les épîtres d'Al-Hāshimī et Al-Kindī*, Paris, 1985, pp. 41-45

G. Troupeau, art. 'al-Kindī, ʿAbd al-Masīḥ', in *EI2*

Sezgin, *GAS* i, pp. 612-13

A. Abel, 'L'Apologie d'Al-Kindī et sa place dans la polémique islamo-chrétienne', in Accademia Nazionale dei Lincei, *Atti del convegno internazionale sul tema: L'Oriente cristiano nella storia della civiltà*, Roma, 1964, 501-23

W. Caskel, 'Al-Kindī: Apología del cristianismo, ed. Don José Muñoz Sendino', *Oriens* 4 (1951) 153-58

J. Muñoz Sendino, 'Apología del Cristianismo', *Miscellanea Comillas* 11-12 (1949) 337-460

M.Th. D'Alverny, 'Deux traductions du Coran au Moyen Age', *Archives d'histoire doctrinale et littéraire du Moyen Age* 16 (1948) 69-131

Graf, *GCAL* ii, pp. 141-45

P. Kraus, 'Beiträge zur islamischen Ketzergeschichte. Das *Kitāb az-zumurrud* des Ibn ar-Rāwandī', *RSO* 14 (1933-34) 93-129, 335-79 (repr. in P. Kraus, *Alchemie, Ketzerei, Apokryphen im frühen Islam. Gesammelte Aufsätze*, Hildsheim, 1994)

E. Fritsch, *Islam und Christentum im Mittelalter*, Breslau, 1930, pp. 4-6

L. Massignon, art. 'al-Kindī, ʿAbd al-Masīḥ', in *EI1*

A. Perier, *Yaḥyā ibn ʿAdī, un philosophe arabe chrétien du Xe siècle*, Paris, 1920

G. Simon, *Der Islam und die christliche Verkündigung. Eine missionarische Untersuchung*, Gütersloh, 1920

WORKS ON CHRISTIAN-MUSLIM RELATIONS

Risālat ʿAbdallāh ibn Ismāʿīl al-Hāshimī ilā ʿAbd al-Masīḥ ibn Isḥāq al-Kindī yadʿūhu bihā ilā l-Islām wa-risālat al-Kindī ilā l-Hāshimī yaruddu bihā ʿalayhi wa-yadʿūhu ilā l-Naṣrāniyya, 'The Letter of ʿAbdallāh ibn Ismāʿīl al-Hāshimī to ʿAbd al-Masīḥ ibn Isḥāq al-Kindī in which he invites him to convert to Islam and the letter of al-Kindī to al-Hāshimī in which he refutes him and invites him to convert to Christianity', 'The Apology of al-Kindī', 'The Correspondence of al-Hāshimī and al-Kindī'

DATE Unknown
ORIGINAL LANGUAGE Arabic (Karshūnī)

DESCRIPTION

Formally the only work attributed to ʿAbd al-Masīḥ al-Kindī and known under the title *Apology*, it consists of two letters of unequal length, one by the Muslim ʿAbdallāh ibn Ismāʿīl al-Hāshimī and the other by the Christian ʿAbd al-Masīḥ ibn Isḥāq al-Kindī. Both letters, however, are to be traced back to the Christian author on the basis of its narrative model and the names of the two alleged authors, as well as the spatial and temporal framework according to which the dispute took place in the court of the illustrious Caliph al-Maʾmūn.

The question of the exact dating of the *Apology* is connected to the problem of the identification of the author or authors. In the course of the 20th century, scholars formulated different hypotheses that were affected by the lack of a critical edition of the Arabic and the fact that the Latin translation was made in the 12th century. Some believe the work originated in the 10th century, because of its supposed borrowings from Ibn al-Rāwandī (d. 910), al-Ṭabarī (d. 923) and Yaḥyā ibn ʿAdī (d. 974). Others have proposed a date as late the 15th century (al-Bakrī, 'Risālat', pp. 29-49). On the basis of internal historical references, a majority of scholars, however, situate the text in the era of the Caliph al-Maʾmūn. This was the hypothesis of Muir ('The Apology of al-Kindy', pp. 1-18), to whom we owe the first translation of the work into a modern European language and its first systematic study. His hypothesis is supported by Casanova, Sendino, Tartar and Samir, even if they do not agree on the exact year when the text was composed. At any rate, the epilogue of the *Apology* refers to the fact that al-Maʾmūn, while in either Marw or Baghdad, became aware of the existence of the letters and ordered them to be read to him.

In the first letter, the Muslim invites the Christian to convert to Islam in cordial and succinct terms (*Risāla*, 1912, pp. 4-27), informing him of the essential aspects of his religion, its precepts and traditions, and calling on him to renounce the veneration of the cross, the doctrine of the Trinity and destructive fasting, in order to embrace the true religion, or, if he persists in refusing, to present a profound exposition of the Christian faith.

In the second letter, al-Kindī refutes every assertion of his interlocutor at great length, in an ironic and at times aggressive tone, simultaneously constructing a refutation of Islam and an apology for Christianity. He not only resorts to the major polemical and apologetic arguments of Muslim-Christian polemic, but he also takes into consideration arguments that are representative of the doctrinal debate in the 9th-century world of Islam, basing his approach on arguments from Muslim and Christian scripture, among others.

After briefly contesting Islam's claim to share the ancestral heritage of Abraham, al-Kindī addresses the various themes of Christian doctrine (*Risāla*, 1912, pp. 28-46). He lays out, for example, the discussion of the divine Unity and Trinity according to a procedure reminiscent of several 9th-century scholars, such as the Muslim philosopher Yaʿqūb al-Kindī (q.v.), the East-Syrian apologist ʿAmmār al-Baṣrī (q.v.), and the Syrian Orthodox theologian Abū Rāʾiṭa al-Takrītī (q.v.). He also introduces the distinction between the essential attributes of God and the attributes deriving from His actions, just as Theodore Abū Qurra (q.v.), ʿAmmār al-Baṣrī and the Muʿtazilite theologians Abū l-Hudhayl (q.v.) and ʿAbbād ibn Sulaymān had done. In the second part (*Risāla*, 1912, pp. 47-144), the author focuses on a refutation of Islam which features favorite themes of the polemicists of the 9th and 10th centuries, such as Muḥammad's alleged instruction by a monk, and his conduct in the affair with Zaynab, i.e. the accusation that he was sexually uncontrolled. By means of such themes, he analyses the religion founded by Muḥammad according to three themes: the messenger, the message, and the reception of the message, in order to (a) demonstrate that Muḥammad, as opposed to Christ and the ancient prophets, was a false prophet whose behavior was violent and morally reprehensible, and therefore in disagreement with divine dignity and lacking the qualities of prophethood, (b) show that the Qur'ān is not only a false scripture, but also a law inspired by the devil, and that it does not set out commandments that are perpetually valid and have been transmitted faithfully without human intervention, (c) assert that people's conversion to Islam should be explained as the result of the attraction of its laws regarding marriage, polygamy, the possession of concubines, and divorce, particularly the practice relating to the *muḥallil*.

In the third section (*Risāla*, 1912, pp. 145-81), which is the truly apologetic part, the author applies the same criteria as in the second, with the obvious aim of proving that Christ is the true teacher whose message contains the highest morality and coherence, and that Christians have followed him out of pure faith. All in all, the discussion aims to prove the internal coherence of the Christian revelation and the contradictory nature of the Islamic revelation, using reason, which is the only criterion that can be applied to verify the foundations of the argumentation advanced by the two interlocutors, as the Muslim had already stated at the end of his letter.

Written in the world of Islam by an oriental Christian, the *Apology* seems to be intended for other Christians, as the author himself explicitly affirms according to the conclusion of two 17th-century manuscripts, which both go back to a manuscript from 1173 (MS Gotha – Ar. 2884 and MS BNF – Syr. 204).

SIGNIFICANCE

As a 'summa' of Islamo-Christian polemical literature, this is the best-known Christian Arabic apology in both east and west. The rich manuscript tradition in Arabic and Latin attests to this fact. It is nevertheless difficult to establish the exact circulation of the text in the Christian east, as well as the circumstances of its arrival and diffusion in the Christian west. The Latin translation was made in the 12th century and included in the *Collectio toletana*. This translation, which became one of the principal sources of knowledge about Islam and its founder in medieval Europe, is divergent from the Arabic as we have it today; it contains many omissions, and also interpolations and reformulations that cannot be traced back to the Arabic text. It is one work with at least two forms, one that came into being in the world of Islam through the pen of a Christian Arab, and one that took shape in the world of the *Reconquista* through the pen of a translator and redactor.

MANUSCRIPTS

Surveys of the extant manuscripts can be found in:

Van Koningsveld, 'The apology of al-Kindī', p. 92

Tartar, *Dialogue islamo-chrétien sous le calife al-Ma'mūn*, pp. 15-17

They list 18 MSS, (including a number in Karshūnī), of which only ten are dated. Of these, the earliest dated ones are from the 17th century; two of these are copies from a 12th-century manuscript. Samir ('La version latine', pp. 41-42) speaks of 21 extant and ten lost manuscripts. He does not provide a list but instead refers to a survey he prepared in 1978, which is as yet unpublished.

EDITIONS AND TRANSLATIONS

González Muñoz, *Exposición y refutación del Islam* (edition of the Latin text with Spanish trans.)

L. Bottini, *Al-Kindī. Apologia del Cristianesimo*, Milan, 1998 (Italian trans.)

N.A. Newman, *The early Christian-Muslim dialogue*. Hatfield PA, 1993, pp. 365-545 (English trans. by Tien, ed. and revised by Newman on the basis of Tien's draft)

Tartar, *Dialogue islamo-chrétien sous le calife al-Maʾmūn* (French trans.)

C. Ciaramella, *L'Apologia di al-Kindi. Il concetto di unicità e trinità di Dio*, Napoli, 1980-81 (BA Thesis, Istituto Universitario Orientale di Napoli, with edition and trans. of the first part of the letter of al-Kindī)

G. Tartar, *Ḥiwār islāmī masīḥī fī ʿahd al-khalīfat al-Maʾmūn (813-834). Risālat al-Hāshimī wa-risālat al-Kindī = Dialogue islamo-chrétien sous le calife al-Maʾmūn (813-834). Les épîtres d'al-Hāšimī et d'al-Kindī*, Strasbourg, 1977 (PhD thesis, Université des Sciences humaines, containing a typewritten edition based on MS Paris, BNF – Syr. 204, MS Paris, BNF – Syr. 205, MS Paris, BNF – Ar. 5141, MS New Haven, Yale Landberg Collection – Ar. 56a, and the 1912 Cairo edition)

ʿAbdullāh valad Ismāʿīl Hāshimī ka khatt mushtamil bar daʿvat-i Islām ba-nām-i ʿAbdulmasīḥ valad Isḥāq Kindī aur ʿAbdulmasīḥ kā javāb Hāshimī kī tardīd aur dīn-i ʿIsavī kī daʿvat par, Luknow, American Mission Press (between 1900 and 1970)

J. Muñoz Sendino, 'Al-Kindī. Apología del cristianismo', *Miscellanea Comillas*, 11-12 (1949) 339-461 (edition of the Latin trans.)

T.J. Scott, *The Apology of al-Kindy, written at the court of al-Maʾmūn, c. A.D. 800, in defence of Christianity against Islam*, Luknow, Methodist Pub. House, 1893

W. Muir, *The Apology of al-Kindy, written at the court of al-Maʾmun (circa A.H. 215; A.D. 830) in defence of Christianity against Islam*, London, 1882 (partial English trans. and first systematic study, repr. 1887 and 1911 by the Society for Promoting Christian Knowledge. Repr. of the study in Newman, *The early Christian-Muslim dialogue*, pp. 365-80)

Risālat ʿAbdallāh ibn Ismāʿīl al-Hāshimī ilā ʿAbd al-Masīḥ ibn Isḥāq al-Kindī yadʿūhu bihā ilā l-Islām wa-risālat al-Kindī ilā l-Hāshimī yaruddu bihā ʿalayhi wa-yadʿūhu ilā l-Naṣrāniyya = The Apology of al-Kindī, ed. A. Tien, London, Turkish Mission Aid Society, 1880 (first edition based on two MSS, one from Constantinople [probably MS Dublin, Chester Beatty - Ar. 4924], and one from Cairo [probably MS Cairo, Dār al-kutub - ʿUlūm al-ijtimāʿiyya 1731], repr., London, Society for Promoting Christian Knowledge, 1885; Cairo, 1895; Cairo, Bible Lands Mission Aid Society 1912; Damascus, 2005 [with brief introduction by the editorial team])

STUDIES

S.K. Samir, 'La version latine de l'Apologie d'al-Kindi (vers 830 ap. J.-C.) et son original arabe', in C. Aillet, M. Penelas and P. Roisse (eds), *¿Existe una identidad mozárabe? Historia, lengua y cultura de los cristianos de al-Andalus (siglos IX-XII)*, Madrid, 2007, 33-82

L. Bottini, 'Al di quà e al di là del Mediterraneo: note sull'Apologia del cristianesimo di al-Kindī' in *Atti del Convegno: La rappresentazione dell'Altro nell'area del Mediterraneo. Storiografia e fonti scritte e orali arabo-musulmane*, special issue of *Alifbâ. Studi arabo islamici e mediterranei* 20 (2006) 71-80

González Muñoz, *Exposición y refutación del Islam*, pp. IX-CXXIV

F. González Muñoz, 'Consideraciones sobre la versión latina de las cartas de al-Hāšimī y al-Kindī', *Collectanea Christiana Orientalia* 2 (2005) 43-70

S.H. Griffith, 'Answering the call of the minaret. Christian apologetics in the world of Islam', in J.J. Van Ginkel, H.L. Murre-van der Berg and T.M. Van Lint (eds), *Redefining Christian identity. Cultural interaction in the Middle East since the rise of Islam*, Leuven, 2005, 91-126

E. Platti, 'Vincent de Beauvais (m. 1264) et ʿAbd al-Masīḥ al-Kindī', in Geneviève Gobillot, Marie-Thérèse Urvoy (eds), *L'Orient chrétien dans l'empire musulman. Hommage au professeur Gérard Troupeau*, Versailles, 2005, 237-49

E. Platti, 'Des Arabes chrétiens et le Coran: pérennité d'une polémique', in D. de Smet, G. de Callataÿ and J.M.F. Van Reeth (eds), *Al-Kitab: la sacralité du texte dans le monde de l'islam*, Brussels, 2004, 333-45

Van Koningsveld, 'The apology of al-Kindī', 69-92

D. Urvoy, 'I testi arabi di polemica confessionale in al-Andalus', in *Lo spazio letterario del Medioevo. 3. Le culture circostanti*, ii (B. Scarcia Amoretti (ed.), *La cultura arabo-islamica*), Rome, 2003, 433-56

S. Stroumsa, *Freethinkers of medieval Islam. Ibn al-Rāwandī, Abū Bakr al-Rāzī, and their impact on Islamic thought*, Leiden, 1999, pp. 193-98

J.V. Tolan, 'Peter the Venerable on the "diabolical heresy of the Saracens"', in A. Ferreiro (ed.), *The Devil, heresy and witchcraft in the Middle Ages. Essays in honor of Jeffrey B. Russell*, Leiden, 1998, 345-67

S.H. Griffith, 'Muḥammad and the monk Baḥīrā: reflections on a Syriac and Arabic text from early ʿAbbasid times', *Oriens Christianus* 70 (1995) 146-74

J. Chorão Lavajo, 'Sources du dialogue islamo-chrétien hispanique', in A. Fodor (ed.), *Proceedings of the 14th Congress of the Union Européenne des Arabisants et Islamisants*, Budapest, 1995, 75-90

N. Daniel, 'Spanish Christian sources of information about Islam (ninth-thirteenth centuries)', *Al-Qanṭara* 15 (1994) 365-84

Landron, *Chrétiens et musulmans en Irak*, pp. 78-88

T.E. Burman, 'The influence of the *Apology of al-Kindī* and *Contrarietas Alfolica* on Ramon Lull's late religious polemics, 1305-1313', *Medieval Studies* 53 (1991) 197-228

P.S. van Koningsveld, 'La apología de Al-Kindî en la España del siglo XII. Huellas toledanas de un "Animal Disputax"', in Congreso internacional de estudios mozarabes, *Estudios sobre Alfonso VI y la Reconquista de Toledo: Actas del II Congreso Internacional de Estudios Mozárabes*, 3 vols, Toledo, 1987-89, iii, 107-29
al-Sharfī, *al-Fikr al-islāmī*, pp. 124-27
Haddad, *La Trinité divine chez les théologiens arabes*, pp. 40-43, 110-113
Tartar, *Dialogue islamo-chrétien sous le calife al-Maʾmūn*, pp. 11-84
C. Farina and C. Ciaramella, 'Per una edizione critica dell'Apologia di al-Kindī', in S.K. Samir (ed.), *Actes du premier congrès international d'études arabes-chrétiennes*, Rome, 1982, 193-206
G. Tartar, 'L'authenticité des épîtres d'al-Hāshimī et d'al-Kindī sous le calife al-Maʾmūn (813-834)', in Samir, *Actes du premier congrès international d'études arabes-chrétiennes*, 207-21
Ch.H. Lohr, 'Ramon Llull, Liber Alquindi and Liber Telif', *Estudios Lulianos* 12 (1968) 145-60
M.Th. D'Alverny, 'La connaissance de l'islam en Occident du IXe au XIIe siècle', in Centro Italiano di Studi sull'Alto Medioevo, *L'Occidente e l'Islam nell'Alto Medioevo*, 2 vols, Spoleto, 1965, ii, 577-602
Abel, 'L'Apologie d'Al-Kindī et sa place dans la polémique islamo-chrétienne'
J. Kritzeck, *Peter the Venerable and Islam*, Princeton, 1964
Caskel, 'Al-Kindī: Apología del Cristianismo'
Muñoz Sendino, 'Apología del Cristianismo'
D'Alverny, 'Deux traductions du Coran au Moyen Age'
M.Ḥ. al-Bakrī, 'Risālat al-Hāshimī ilā l-Kindī, wa-radd al-Kindī ʿalayhā', *Majallat kulliyat al-ādāb* 11,1 (1947) 29-49
Graf, *GCAL* ii, pp. 141-45
U. Monneret de Villard, *Lo studio dell'Islām in Europa nel XII e nel XIII secolo*, Vatican City, 1944, pp. 8-18, 57-58
Brockelmann, *GAL* S i, pp. 344-45
Kraus, 'Beiträge zur islamischen Ketzergeschichte. Das *Kitāb az-zumurrud* des Ibn ar-Rāwandī'
Fritsch, *Islam und Christentum im Mittelalter*, pp. 4-6
L. Massignon, art. 'al-Kindī ʿAbd al-Masīḥ', in *EI1*
H.P. Smith, 'Moslem and Christian polemic', *Journal of Biblical Literature* 45 (1926) 243-45

L. Rost, 'Die Risāla al-Kindīs, eine missions-apologetische Schrift', *Allgemeine Missions-Zeitschrift* 50 (1923) 134-44

Perier, *Yaḥyā ibn ʿAdī, un philosophe arabe chrétien du Xe siècle*

Simon, *Der Islam und die christliche Verkündigung. Eine missionarische Untersuchung*

P. Casanova, *Mohammed et la fin du monde*, Paris, 1913

Muir, *The Apology of al-Kindy*

W. Muir, 'Further notes on the Apology of al-Kindy', *JRAS* 14 (1882) 317-18

W. Muir, 'The Apology of al-Kindy. An essay on its age and authorship', *JRAS* 14 (1882) 1-18

Laura Bottini 2008

The affair of the Qurʾān

Unknown author

DATE OF BIRTH Unknown, perhaps 8th/9th c.
PLACE OF BIRTH Unknown
DATE OF DEATH Unknown, perhaps 8th/9th c.
PLACE OF DEATH Unknown

BIOGRAPHY —

MAIN SOURCES OF INFORMATION

Primary —

Secondary —

WORKS ON CHRISTIAN-MUSLIM RELATIONS

ʿEltā d-Quran, 'The affair of the Qurʾān'

DATE Unknown, probably 8th or 9th c.
ORIGINAL LANGUAGE Syriac

DESCRIPTION

This short polemical tale, which is to be found as an appendix to the East-Syrian recension of the *Legend of Sergius Baḥīrā* (q.v.), deals with the alleged corruption of the text of the Qurʾān during the first century of Islam. It begins with a description of how the Jew Kaʿb al-Aḥbār inserted his beliefs into the scripture originally written by the Syrian monk Sergius Baḥīrā, particularly beliefs about the *lex talionis* and divorce laws. He also allegedly spread the belief in jinn and instituted the call for prayer by the muezzin, thus contravening the Christian custom of the sounding-board which Sergius Baḥīrā had taught Muḥammad.

Next, the tale explains how the Umayyad governor of Iraq, al-Ḥajjāj ibn Yūsuf, investigated the text of the Qurʾān and disapproved of it, since it was 'corrupted and confused and laughable and absurd', and devoid of the fear of God. For this reason, he decided to collect and burn all the copies of the text. He then called a meeting of teachers and priests who explained the Bible to him. He wrote down the parts that pleased him and proceeded to divide the new text into sections, to many of which he gave the names of biblical prophets, as well as names consisting of 'secret letters'. He also gave the name 'Qurʾān' to this 'scripture'.

The note ends with the comment that these events speak for themselves, insinuating that the history of the codification and redaction of the Qurʾān reveals that it is a man-made scripture.

SIGNIFICANCE

This brief piece of polemic is probably the most detailed Christian discussion of al-Ḥajjāj ibn Yūsuf's intervention in the compilation of the text of the Qurʾān, a theme that also features in the *Apology of al-Kindī* (q.v.), the *Disputation of the monk Ibrāhīm al-Ṭabarānī* (q.v.) and the *Letter of Leo III to ʿUmar II* (q.v.). It reveals considerable knowledge among Syriac-speaking Christians about the redaction of the Qurʾān by al-Ḥajjāj ibn Yūsuf, who in early Islamic sources is indeed credited with the division of the Qurʾān into parts and chapters.

MANUSCRIPTS

There are three accessible manuscripts:

MS Berlin, Staatsbibliothek – Sachau 10 (late 17th c.?)

MS Birmingham, Mingana – Syriac 604 (Siirt 1884)

MS Charfet – 841 (formerly 122) (1889)

For inaccessible and lost manuscripts see:

B. Roggema, *The legend of Sergius Baḥīrā. Eastern Christian apologetics and apocalyptic in response to Islam*, Leiden 2009, pp. 243-45

EDITIONS AND TRANSLATIONS

Roggema, *The legend of Sergius Baḥīrā*, pp. 302-9

STUDIES —

Barbara Roggema 2008

The Life of Bacchus the Younger

Author unknown (in MS BNF – Gr. 1553, and MS Mount Athos, Monastery of Docheiariou – 74 the name Stephanos appears in the peroration)

DATE OF BIRTH 2nd half of 8th c.?
PLACE OF BIRTH Unknown
DATE OF DEATH 1st half of the 9th c.?
PLACE OF DEATH Unknown

BIOGRAPHY

The author emphasizes that Bacchus' martyrdom occurred during the reign of Irene and Constantine VI (r. 780-97), thereby grafting a Byzantine perspective upon a Palestinian neo-martyr. It is thus likely that the hagiographer was based in Constantinople and not Palestine. If the name Stephanos as author is to be given credence, he may be identifiable as Stephen the Deacon, the biographer of St Stephen the Younger (*BHG* 1666), which would point to a composition of the *Life* of Bacchus in the early 9th century.

MAIN SOURCES OF INFORMATION

Primary —

Secondary —

WORKS ON CHRISTIAN-MUSLIM RELATIONS

Bios kai athlēsis tou hosiou kai neou martyros Bakchou martyrēsantos en tois chronois hēmōn en Palaistinē epi Eirēnēs kai Kōnstantinou tōn philochristōn kai orthodoxōn hēmōn basileōn, 'The Life and martyrdom of the holy neo-martyr Bacchus the Younger who was martyred in our time in Palestine during the reign of Irene and Constantine, our Christ-loving and orthodox emperors', 'The Life of Bacchus the Younger'

DATE Early 9th c.
ORIGINAL LANGUAGE Greek

DESCRIPTION

The *Life of Bacchus the Younger* (*BHG* 209) relates the biography and martyrdom of a native of Maiouma in Gaza, Palestine (c. 769-87/88). His father, together with his sons, converted to Islam, but his mother remained a crypto-Christian. When the sons were each successively married to Muslim women, the third, named Daḥḥāk (Greek Gelasios), wished to remain unmarried and to convert to Christianity. When the father died, he went to the Church of the Resurrection in Jerusalem and met a monk from the Lavra of St Saba, who took him to his monastery. He was baptized by the abbot and renamed Bacchus, and shortly afterwards he was tonsured as a monk, though, fearing that he might be arrested for his apostasy, he did not remain in any one monastery.

He met his mother in the Church of the Resurrection in Jerusalem and told her about his conversion and tonsure. When she returned to Maiouma she made his conversion known to her other children, and they were baptized as Christians and fled to foreign lands. However, one of them refused conversion because of his Muslim wife, and his wife's family instigated a search for Bacchus. He was caught while praying in the Church of the Resurrection and was dragged off to prison and court. To the questions put to him he kept replying in Greek, 'Alleluia, alleluia, glory to God', and although he was not understood, he refused to speak in Arabic. Finally he was executed and, out of fear of the 'Hagarenes' who dwelt in the desert (i.e., the bedouin), his body was hastily placed in an underground tomb in the Church of Cosmas and Damian.

SIGNIFICANCE

The *Life of Bacchus* attests to conversions from Christianity to Islam and back, Christian shrines and monuments in Palestine, and the experience of Christians under Muslim rule. It also points to the religious significance of the Arabic and Greek languages.

MANUSCRIPTS

MS Chalkē, St Trinity – 88 (81), fols 126v-137v
MS BNF – Gr. 1180, fols 132-141
MS BNF – Gr. 1553, fols 174-184
MS Moscow, Historical Museum – Synodal Library 161 (Vladimir 379), fols 272-282v
MS Mount Athos, Monastery of Docheiariou – 74, fols 374v-393v
MS Brussels – Gr. 18864-18874, fols 217-226v

EDITIONS AND TRANSLATIONS

F. Combefis, *Christi martyrum lecta trias*, Paris, 1666, 61-126 (a new edition with French trans. is in preparation by André Binggeli and Stephanos Efthymiadis)

STUDIES

C. Foss, 'Byzantine saints in early Islamic Syria', *AB* 125 (2007) 93-119, pp. 116-17

D. Vila, *Christian martyrs in the first Abbasid century and the development of an apologetic against Islam*, St Louis, 1999 (Diss. St Louis University), pp. 287-96

S.H. Griffith, 'Christians, Muslims, and neo-martyrs. Saints' lives and Holy Land history', in A. Kofsky and G.G. Stroumsa (eds), *Sharing the sacred. Religious contacts and conflicts in the Holy Land. First-fifteenth centuries CE*, Jerusalem, 1998, 163-207, pp. 196-98

PMBZ i (prolegomena), p. 113 and no. 733

Dumbarton Oaks Hagiography Database, Washington DC, 1998, pp. 28-29

F.A. Demetrakopoulos, 'Hagios Bakchos ho Neos', *Epistēmonikē Epeteris tēs Philosophikēs Scholēs tou Panepistēmiou Athēnōn* 26 (1979) 331-63

C. Loparev, 'Vizantijskia žitija sviatych VIII-IX vekov', *VV* 19 (1912) 33-35

Stephanos Efthymiadis 2008

The Legend of Sergius Baḥīrā

Unknown author

DATE OF BIRTH Unknown, 8th c.?
PLACE OF BIRTH Unknown, probably Iraq
DATE OF DEATH Unknown, 9th c.?
PLACE OF DEATH Unknown, probably Iraq

BIOGRAPHY —

MAIN SOURCES OF INFORMATION

Primary —

Secondary —

WORKS ON CHRISTIAN-MUSLIM RELATIONS

Tashʿitā d-rabban Sargīs, 'The story of Rabban Sergius' (with different subtitles in East- and West-Syrian recensions); modern title: 'The Legend of Sergius Baḥīrā', 'The Baḥīrā legend'

DATE Unknown, probably early 9th c.
ORIGINAL LANGUAGE Syriac

DESCRIPTION

This 'story' is a Syriac polemical legend that seeks to explain the rise of Islam from a Christian perspective. It purports to reveal the influence of a Christian monk on Muḥammad during his early life and the beginning of his mission as prophet, and it exploits the story found in the Muslim biographies of Muḥammad (e.g. Ibn Isḥāq's *Sīra*) about a monk called Baḥīrā who recognized Muḥammad as the true and final prophet.

The legend begins and ends with apocalyptic sections. In the first, Baḥīrā receives a vision on Mt Sinai about the imminent political rise of the 'Sons of Ishmael'. A sequence of rulers, symbolized by heavenly animals in the style of the Book of Daniel, is then revealed, followed by a number of Islamic messianic figures (the Sufyānī, the Qaḥṭānī and two Mahdīs). These are vanquished by a king from the east, who ushers in the rule of the Last Emperor and the second coming of Christ. This vision is repeated in the final section of the legend in the form of a long prophecy, in which the plight of humankind, and of Christians in particular, under the ʿAbbasids ('Sons of Hāshim') is spelled out in greater detail.

The story of the encounter between the monk and Muḥammad is placed between these two apocalypses. The text describes how the monk preached the veneration of the one cross among Christians and diligently removed other crosses from churches and shrines. Persecuted on account of these actions, he fled to Arabia where he recognized the young Muḥammad as the future leader of the Arabs when he saw a miraculous vision appearing over his head (this echoes the Islamic account of the recognition of the young Prophet).

This element in the text reinforces the notion clearly present in the apocalyptic sections that Islam was preordained by God. However, the next section, in which Sergius Baḥīrā teaches Muḥammad about God, is meant to make clear that, as a religion, Islam cannot rival Christianity, because it shows that the Qurʾān is not a revealed book but a compilation of the monk's well-intentioned though simplistic instruction of Muḥammad intended specifically to appeal to the backwardness of his audience. Thus, in order to keep Muḥammad's followers interested, it includes the promise of physical pleasures in the afterlife.

At the same time, the legend strives to make clear that the Christian core of the Qurʾān is nevertheless recognizable, for example when it speaks of Christ as the 'Word of God and a Spirit from Him' (Q 4:171), or when it praises monks and priests for their piety and closeness to the believers (Q 5:82). The legend also claims that the reason why this Christian origin of the Qurʾān is to some extent obscured is because the Jew Kaʿb al-Aḥbār corrupted Sergius Baḥīrā's teaching after his death. In this respect the image of the monk differs in this legend from many eastern and western Christian texts. There he is usually portrayed as a heretical influence on Muḥammad, but here he is not held responsible for the 'flawed' beliefs of the Muslims and is presented as a miracle worker who was chosen by God to receive a vision about the rise of Islam.

The legend is known in two slightly different Syriac recensions, one East-Syrian and the other West Syrian. Most scholars have dated the original composition on which they are based to the time of the

Caliph al-Maʾmūn (r. 813-33) (q.v.), on the grounds that the apocalyptic parts predict that the seventh of the ʿAbbasid rulers will be the last. It is possible that the composition was already by this time an amalgam of earlier polemical tales about Islam (Szilágyi), and there are also signs that the text was updated during the later 9th century (Dickens). The West-Syrian recension is distinguished by an introduction, which attempts to situate the 'mission' of Sergius Baḥīrā in an East-Syrian milieu (Griffith). The East-Syrian recension is somewhat shorter, and all the manuscripts containing this text include three additional polemical tales (see the entries on 'The confession which Kaʿb al-Aḥbār handed down to the Ishmaelites', 'The affair of Muḥammad's death', 'The affair of the Qur'ān').

Compelling arguments in favor of both an East-Syrian and a West-Syrian origin have been advanced, but no definite conclusion about its original milieu has yet been reached. The legend was later reworked into a significantly different Arabic recension which contains many more quotations from the Qurʾān. There is also a hybrid Arabic recension, which consists of a translation of the Syriac legend together with the final part of the long Arabic recension. The Latin recension is based on the two apocalyptic parts only, and was probably translated directly from Syriac (see later volumes for the Arabic and Latin versions).

SIGNIFICANCE

The legend of Baḥīrā gives an insight into how Near Eastern Christians tried to come to terms with the fact that they were dominated by a community whose religion was at odds with their own. It tries to make sense of the religion of Islam by suggesting that it is a simplified version of Christianity suitable for pagan Arabs, and it explains the political rise of Islam as a divinely ordained but limited phase in history.

The text attests to the fact that Syriac-speaking Christians in the 9th century were well acquainted with the Qurʾān and Islamic doctrine, and were creatively using their knowledge about Islam to refute its validity and underscore Christianity's perpetual truth and divine support.

The existence of several recensions and translations is a witness to its popularity among Syriac- and Arabic-speaking Christians.

MANUSCRIPTS

There are eight accessible manuscripts, three of the East-Syrian and five of the West-Syrian recensions. The oldest is probably MS

Birmingham, Mingana – Syr. 71, which is datable to c. 1600. The earliest manuscript of the Latin recension, which is closely related to the Syriac recensions, can be dated to the late 13th century. For a description of the manuscripts, including a number of lost ones, see B. Roggema, *The legend of Sergius Baḥīrā. Eastern Christian apologetics and apocalyptic in response to Islam*, Leiden, 2009, pp. 238-46.

EDITIONS AND TRANSLATIONS

Roggema, *The legend of Sergius Baḥīrā*, pp. 253-99 (edition and trans. of the East-Syrian recension), pp. 311-74 (edition and trans. of the West-Syrian recension)

R. Gottheil, 'A Christian Bahira legend', *Zeitschrift für Assyriologie und Vorderasiatische Archeologie* 13 (1898) 189-242; 14 (1899) 203-68 (*editio princeps* with two recensions printed in parallel, and trans.; superseded by Roggema, *The legend of Sergius Baḥīrā*)

STUDIES

Select bibliography:

K. Szilágyi, 'Muhammad and the monk. The making of the Christian Baḥīrā legend', *JSAI* 34 (2008) (in press)

Roggema, *The legend of Sergius Baḥīrā* (includes a full bibliography)

M. Dickens, *Turkāyē. Turkic peoples in Syriac literature prior to the Seljüks*, Cambridge, 2008 (Diss. University of Cambridge), pp. 120-29

B. Roggema, 'The legend of Sergius-Baḥīrā. Some remarks on its origin in the East and its traces in the West', in K. Ciggaar and H. Teule (eds), *East and West in the Crusader states*, Louvain, 1999, 107-23

S.H. Griffith, 'Muḥammad and the monk Baḥīrā: Reflections on a Syriac and Arabic text from early Abbasid times', *OC* 79 (1995) 146-74 (repr. in Griffith, *The beginnings of Christian theology in Arabic. Muslim-Christian encounters in the early Islamic period*, Aldershot, 2002)

B. Landron, *Chrétiens et musulmans en Irak. Attitudes nestoriennes vis-à-vis de l'Islam*, Paris, 1994, pp. 71-78

S. Gerö, 'The legend of the monk Baḥīrā, the cult of the cross, and iconoclasm', in P. Canivet and J.P. Rey-Coquais (eds), *La Syrie de Byzance à l'Islam, VII*e*-VIII*e* siècles*, Damascus, 1992, 47-58

Barbara Roggema 2008

ʿAmmār al-Baṣrī

DATE OF BIRTH Probably late 8th c.
PLACE OF BIRTH Probably in or near Basra
DATE OF DEATH Unknown, possibly mid-9th c.
PLACE OF DEATH Possibly Iraq

BIOGRAPHY

Nothing is known about ʿAmmār's personal circumstances except that he was associated with the city of Basra and with the East-Syrian Christian community. One datable note about him comes from the *Fihrist* of Ibn al-Nadīm, which mentions that Abū l-Hudhayl al-ʿAllāf (q.v.) wrote 'a book against ʿAmmār the Christian in refutation of the Christians', which is overwhelmingly likely to be against him. Since Abū l-Hudhayl died sometime between 840 and 850, ʿAmmār must have been active at about this time. The evidence of his own works (see below) indicates that he was alive after 838.

MAIN SOURCES OF INFORMATION

Primary

Ibn al-Nadīm, *Fihrist*, p. 204

Abū l-Barakāt ibn Kabar, *Miṣbāḥ al-ẓulma fī īḍāḥ al-khidma*, ed. S. Khalil, Cairo, 1970, p. 298

Secondary

M. Hayek, *ʿAmmār al-Baṣrī. Apologie et controverses,* Beirut, 1977

M. Hayek, "Ammār al-Baṣrī. La première Somme de théologie chrétienne en langue arabe, ou deux apologies du christianisme', *Islamochristiana* 2 (1976) 69-133

WORKS ON CHRISTIAN-MUSLIM RELATIONS

Kitāb al-masāʾil wa-l-ajwiba, 'Questions and answers'

DATE Early 9th c.
ORIGINAL LANGUAGE Arabic

DESCRIPTION

The book is an apology for the Christian faith answering questions Muslims might ask Christians, in four sections: (a) 28 questions and answers about God and the world; (b) 14 about the authenticity of the Christian Gospels; (c) 9 about the Trinity; and (d) 51 about the Incarnation.

While section (a) on God and the world shares with ʿAmmār's Arab Christian contemporary Theodore Abū Qurra (d. c. 830) (q.v.) a concern to defend Christianity as the true religion in the light of Islamic rule, ʿAmmār applies the concept of the reasonableness of the Christian faith, which Theodore employs in this particular argument, to the Muslim rejection of the Christian message in section (b), on the authenticity of the Christian Gospels. This is the most thorough apologetic treatment of the authenticity of the Gospels from an early 9th-century Christian theologian writing in Arabic, which shows that Christians in this period were being accused by some Muslims of corrupting the text of their Gospels and not merely misinterpreting them. Section (c) on the Trinity is a debate on the attributes of God with teachings similar to those of the Muslim *mutakallimūn*, Ḍirār ibn ʿAmr (d. c. 800) (q.v.) and ʿAmmār's Muʿtazilī contemporary Abū Hudhayl al-ʿAllāf (d. between 840 and 850) (q.v.), who wrote a treatise against ʿAmmār. The Trinity of Father, Son and Holy Spirit is defended as 'Being', 'Life', and 'Speech', essential and not accidental to the Creator.

Section (d) on the Incarnation can be compared with *The letter on the Incarnation* by ʿAmmār's contemporary Syrian Orthodox theologian Abū Rāʾiṭa (d. after 830) (q.v.), but is much more substantial. The East-Syrian ʿAmmār presents the union of the will of the Son with that of the Father as the key to the Incarnation. Whereas Abū Rāʾiṭa leaves the impression that the divine nature in Christ was never seriously disturbed by testing, ʿAmmār holds to a genuine dialectic between the divine and human natures in Christ. The greatness of Christ lay in his ability to submit to God's will in all circumstances, and this is what qualifies him to transfer merit to those who fail to submit to God. ʿAmmār's treatment of the cross is unique among his theological contemporaries in arguing that the self-giving of Christ guarantees eternal life for others. His analogies of a prizefighter using up all his strength to defeat an opponent, and of a doctor who wants to demonstrate his ability to heal by swallowing some poison before administering medicine to a patient, are vivid attempts to show that Christ submitted to death in order to raise to life those subject to death. His argument that the death of Christ had to be public in order to reassure others of the reality of his defeat of death in the resurrection is designed to head off the possible Muslim complaint that evidence for the death of Christ hung on the truth-telling of a few people who were keen to promote the story.

The work is addressed to an unnamed caliph (Hayek, *ʿAmmār al-Baṣrī*, p. 93). On the basis of what ʿAmmār says about him, Hayek (*ʿAmmār al-Baṣrī*, p. 17, repeated in 'La première somme', p. 73) proposes that this was al-Maʾmūn (q.v.). Then, making the assumption that this was the work to which Abū l-Hudhayl responded in his *Kitāb ʿalā ʿAmmār al-Naṣrānī fī l-radd ʿalā l-Naṣārā*, he hypothesizes that it must have been written between al-Maʾmūn's accession in 813 and 818, the year in which Abū l-Hudhayl left Basra. While this is plausible, there is no firm reason to think that Abū al-Hudhayl was reacting to this or to ʿAmmār's other surviving work; he may equally have been reacting to arguments he had heard ʿAmmār voice in live debate. Further, a date this early places some distance in time between this work and ʿAmmār's *Kitāb al-burhān*, which dates from 838 or after, even though the two works are thematically related.

SIGNIFICANCE

Among the extant works of early 9th-century Arabic Christian literature, the *Kitāb al-masāʾil wa-l-ajwiba* presents the most thorough defense of a number of Christian teachings, especially the authenticity of the Gospels and the reality of the Incarnation, demonstrating a profound capacity to provide answers to well-understood Muslim objections. Its value was recognized by medieval Copts: al-Ṣafī ibn al-ʿAssāl made an epitome of the work in 1241, and his half-brother al-Muʾtaman quotes from it in Chapter 19 of his *Majmūʿ uṣūl al-dīn*.

MANUSCRIPTS

MS BL – Add. 18998 (formerly BM Ar. 801; dated 1297), fols 44-127

MS Charfeh, Charfeh Monastery, Lebanon – 5/4 (14th c.), fols 76v-96r (epitome by al-Ṣafī ibn al-ʿAssāl)

MS Vat – Ar. 115 (another MS of the epitome)

EDITIONS AND TRANSLATIONS

Hayek, *Apologie et controverses*, pp. 93-265 (edition)

Al-Muʾtaman ibn al-ʿAssāl, *Summa dei principi della religione*, ed. A. Wadi and trans. Bartolomeo Pirone, 6 vols, Cairo, 1998-2002, ch. 19, §§ 16-20 (critical edition of an epitome of a passage from *Kitāb al-masāʾil wa-l-ajwiba*, section (c), question 4; cf. Hayek, *Apologie et controverses*, pp. 162-64)

STUDIES

M. Beaumont, "ʿAmmār al-Baṣrī on the alleged corruption of the Gospels', in D. Thomas (ed.), *The Bible in Arab Christianity*, Leiden, 2007, 241-55

M. Beaumont, *Christology in dialogue with Muslims*, Carlisle, 2005, pp. 73-92

M. Beaumont, "ʿAmmār al-Baṣrī on the Incarnation', in D. Thomas (ed.), *Christians at the heart of Islamic rule*, Leiden, 2003, 55-62

A. Wadi, *Studio su al-Muʾtaman ibn al-ʿAssāl*, Cairo, 1997, pp. 111-13 (on the epitomes by al-Ṣafī ibn al-ʿAssāl)

Van Ess, *TG* iii, pp. 36, 38, 220, 275-76, 340-41; iv, p. 425

M.N. Swanson, *Folly to the Ḥunafāʾ. The cross of Christ in Arabic Christian-Muslim controversy in the eighth and ninth centuries A.D.*, Rome, 1992 (Diss. PISAI), pp. 277-87, 313-86

S.H. Griffith, 'Comparative religion in the apologetics of the first Christian Arabic theologians', *Proceedings of the PMR Conference* 4 (1979) 63-87

S.H. Griffith, 'The concept of *al-uqnūm* in ʿAmmār al-Baṣrī's apology for the doctrine of the Trinity', in S.K. Samir (ed.), *Actes du premier congrès international d'études chrétiennes*, Rome, 1982, 169-91

Hayek, "ʿAmmār al-Baṣrī. La première Somme de théologie chrétienne en langue arabe'

Graf, *GCAL* ii, pp. 210-11

Kitāb al-burhān ʿalā siyāqat al-tadbīr al-ilāhī, 'The Proof concerning the course of the divine economy'; usually abbreviated to *Kitāb al-burhān*, 'The Proof'

DATE After 838
ORIGINAL LANGUAGE Arabic

DESCRIPTION

The *Kitāb al-burhān*, whose title is lacking in the MS but is reported by Abū l-Barakāt ibn Kabar (d. 1324), is an apology for the Christian faith in 12 sections. They cover the full range of issues that Christians needed to defend in the face of Muslim polemic: (1) proofs for the existence of God; (2) criteria for determining the true religion; (3) a defense of the truth of Christianity; (4) the authenticity of Christian scripture; (5) the Trinity; (6) the union of divinity and humanity in Christ; (7) the Incarnation; (8) the crucifixion; (9) baptism; (10) the eucharist; (11) the symbol of the cross; (12) eating and drinking in the afterlife.

The *Kitāb al-burhān* contains condensed versions of arguments concerning the existence of God, the authenticity of the Gospels, the Trinity, and the Incarnation which ʿAmmār presents in his earlier *Kitāb al-masāʾil wa-l-ajwiba*, though with some significant additions. For example, in arguing for Christianity as the true religion he stresses the necessity of miraculous signs as authenticating one religion among many, and not simply the apparent rationality of the belief system. Christianity, for example, demands belief in the virgin birth of the Son of God, his death by crucifixion, his resurrection from the grave, his ascension to heaven, and his return. The human mind does not conceive of such doctrines, so attempting to defend their truth without recourse to the miraculous signs of God's activity is futile. He apparently has in mind here Muʿtazila, such as al-Jāḥiẓ (d. 869) (q.v.) or Abū ʿĪsā l-Warrāq (d. c. 864) (q.v.), who charged Christians with irrationality in their beliefs about Christ.

Another example of additional arguments in the *Kitāb al-burhān* is found in the section on the Incarnation, where ʿAmmār offers four motives for the Incarnation that he believes should appeal to Muslims since they show the generosity of God towards humanity, a doctrine affirmed by Muslims. First, God appeared to humans in a form they could appreciate, as a voice to Abraham and Moses, but as a truly human being in Christ so as to demonstrate the fullness of his generosity. Second, since humans long to see with their natural and not only their spiritual eyes, God condescended to be seen by them. Third, since humans will meet God as judge, it was an act of justice for the judge to make himself known in Christ before the event. Fourth, since God has given rule and authority to humans, it was good for him to become human to demonstrate the appropriate manner of ruling. In these ways, God dispenses with the need for messengers between himself and humanity, a conclusion set to undermine Muslim appeals to the centrality of God's revelation by prophetic speech.

The four sections dealing with Christian teaching and practice that are not discussed in his *Kitāb al-masāʾil wa-l-ajwiba* are on baptism, the eucharist, venerating the cross, and not eating and drinking in the afterlife. Baptism is a symbol of the resurrection guaranteed by Christ and therefore a profound indication of the generosity of God. Similarly, the bread and wine of the eucharist remind the partaker of the same certainty of eternal life achieved through Christ's death. Kissing the cross may be rejected by Muslims, but they kiss the black stone on the Kaʿba in Mecca, and if this should not be understood as a form of *shirk* then Christians should be free from such accusations when kissing the cross. Christians, unlike Muslims, do not anticipate eating and drinking in the afterlife because animal existence will be transcended there.

These additions suggest that the *Kitāb al-burhān* postdates the *Kitāb al-masāʾil wa-l-ajwiba*. It must anyway have been written in or soon after 838, since it appears to allude to an incident during the conquest of Amorion in that year by the Caliph al-Muʿtaṣim, 'a king in our time who left his kingdom with all of his armies for Rome to look for a woman in a fortress' (Hayek, *Apologie et Controverses*, p. 38; on this see pp. 19-20, repeated in 'La première somme', pp. 74-75).

SIGNIFICANCE

This is the earliest known apology for Christianity in Arabic which deals systematically with the major beliefs and practices that gave rise to Muslim criticism of Christians. ʿAmmār's defense relies more on rational arguments than on scripture and tradition, in order to show the reasonableness of the Christian faith.

MANUSCRIPTS

MS BL – Add. 18998 (formerly BM Ar. 801; dated 1297), fols 2r-44r
MS Charfeh, Charfeh Monastery, Lebanon – 5/4 (14th c.), fols 97r-134v (the epitome of al-Ṣafī ibn al-ʿAssāl)
MS Vat – Ar. 115 (another MS of the epitome)

EDITIONS AND TRANSLATIONS

Hayek, *Apologie et Controverses*, pp. 21-90 (edition)

STUDIES

Beaumont, *Christology in dialogue with Muslims*, pp. 67-73, 102-04
D. Thomas, 'Cultural and religious supremacy in the fourteenth century. *The Letter from Cyprus* as religious polemic', *Pd'O* 30 (2005) 297-322, pp. 307-11
D. Thomas, 'Explanations of the Incarnation in early ʿAbbasid Islam', in J.J. van Ginkel, H.L. Murre-Van Den Berg and T.M. van Lint (eds), *Redefining Christian identity. Cultural interaction in the Middle East since the rise of Islam*, Louvain, 2005, 127-49, pp. 140-43

Beaumont, ''Ammār al-Baṣrī on the Incarnation'
P.K. Chalfoun, 'Baptême et eucharistie chez 'Ammār al-Baṣrī', *Pd'O* 27 (2002) 321-34
Wadi, *Studio su al-Mu'taman ibn al-'Assāl*, pp. 111-13
S.H. Griffith, ''Ammār al-Baṣrī's *Kitāb al-Burhān:* Christian *kalām* in the first 'Abbasid century', *Le Muséon* 96 (1983) 145-81
Griffith, 'The concept of *al-uqnūm*'
Griffith, 'Comparative religion'
Hayek, ''Ammār al-Baṣrī. La première Somme de théologie chrétienne en langue arabe', pp. 69-133
Graf, *GCAL* ii, p. 210

Mark Beaumont 2007

Al-Murdār

Abū Mūsā ʿĪsā ibn Ṣubayḥ al-Murdār

DATE OF BIRTH Unknown
PLACE OF BIRTH Unknown
DATE OF DEATH 841
PLACE OF DEATH Baghdad

BIOGRAPHY

One of the early Baghdad Muʿtazila, al-Murdār was a pupil and supporter of Bishr ibn al-Muʿtamir, so presumably slightly younger than the founder of the school. He was known for his asceticism (he left his wealth to the poor), and was compared among the Muʿtazila to a monk among the Christians.

None of al-Murdār's 33 works listed by Ibn al-Nadīm survives (Van Ess, *TG* v, pp. 331-32). He wrote works on some of the main issues debated in his school (among them *Kitāb al-tawḥīd*, 'Divine unity', and *Kitāb al-ʿadl*, 'Divine justice') and particularly on the createdness of the Qurʾān (*Kitāb al-Makhlūq, ʿalā l-Najjār*, 'What is created, against (Ḥusayn) al-Najjār', and *Kitāb khalq al-Qurʾān*, 'The createdness of the Qurʾān'). He also wrote works against other Muslim scholars and groups (including *Kitāb al-qudra ʿalā l-ẓulm, ʿalā l-Naẓẓām*, 'Power over sinning, against (Ibrāhīm) al-Naẓẓām', and *Kitāb al-radd ʿalā l-mujbira*, 'Refutation of the determinists'), and apart from his anti-Christian works wrote two other works against non-Muslims (*Kitāb ʿalā l-aḥbār wa-l-Majūs fī l-ʿadl wa-l-tajwīz*, 'Against the Jewish scholars and Zoroastrians about justice and permission' – Van Ess, *TG* v, 331 reads the last word as *tajwīr*, 'endorsement'; and *Kitāb al-radd ʿalā l-mulḥidīn*, 'Refutation of the atheists').

Al-Murdār followed the main principles of the Muʿtazila, and was particularly known for his aversion to determinism and anthropomorphism.

In his only surviving work, a sermon on the two main Muʿtazilī principles of divine unity and justice, al-Murdār refers to the condemnation in the Qurʾān of God having a son as proof of the reality of human free will, because God could not compel humans to believe something that he himself calls 'a thing most monstrous' (Q 19:89).

MAIN SOURCES OF INFORMATION

Primary
Abū l-Ḥusayn al-Khayyāṭ, *Kitāb al-intiṣār*, ed. and trans. A. Nader, Beirut, 1957, pp. 53-56
Abū l-Ḥasan al-Ashʿarī, *Maqālāt al-Islāmiyyīn*, ed. H. Ritter, Istanbul, 1930, pp. 190, 201, 229, 541, 555-56
Ibn al-Nadīm, *Fihrist*, pp. 206-7
Abū Manṣūr al-Baghdādī, *Kitāb al-milal wa-l-niḥal*, ed. A. Nader, Beirut, 1970, pp. 109-10
Ibn al-Murtaḍā, *Kitāb ṭabaqāt al-Muʿtazila*, ed. S. Diwald-Wilzer, Beirut, 1988, pp. 70-71

Secondary
Van Ess, *TG* iii, pp. 134-42, v, pp. 331-39
J. van Ess, 'Ein Predigt des Muʿtaziliten Murdār', *BEO* 30 (1978) 307-15 (French transl. in *Arabica* 30 (1983) 111-24)
Watt, *Formative period*, 1973, p. 223

WORKS ON CHRISTIAN-MUSLIM RELATIONS

Kitāb al-radd ʿalā l-Naṣārā, 'Refutation of the Christians'

DATE early 9th c.
ORIGINAL LANGUAGE Arabic

DESCRIPTION
This work is mentioned by Ibn al-Nadīm, *Fihrist*, p. 207. It presumably contained arguments similar to those in other Muslim works on this subject written at the time.

SIGNIFICANCE
It may have contributed arguments to later works.

MANUSCRIPTS —
EDITIONS AND TRANSLATIONS —
STUDIES —

Kitāb ʿalā Abī Qurra l-Naṣrānī, 'Against (Theodore) Abū Qurra the Christian'

DATE Early 9th c.
ORIGINAL LANGUAGE Arabic

DESCRIPTION
The work is mentioned by Ibn al-Nadīm, *Fihrist*, p. 207. It was a refutation of one or more works of Theodore Abū Qurra (q.v.), the leading early 9th c. Melkite theologian and bishop of Ḥarrān. If it was written after Abū Qurra's death, it would have appeared in the decade leading up to 841.

SIGNIFICANCE
It shows the cogency and accessibility of Abū Qurra's arguments and responses to points made by Muslims, and may have served to publicize them in Muslim circles, where Abū Qurra was often the only Christian theologian whose name was known.

MANUSCRIPTS —
EDITIONS AND TRANSLATIONS —
STUDIES —

David Thomas 2007

Gregory Dekapolites

DATE OF BIRTH c. 780-90
PLACE OF BIRTH Eirenopolis, Isaurian Dekapolis, Syria
DATE OF DEATH 20 November 842 (or 841, or earlier)
PLACE OF DEATH Unknown (possibly Constantinople)

BIOGRAPHY

The source of information about Gregory is a *Life* written by a certain Ignatius, 'deacon and sacristan of the Great Church of God' (Constantinople), later professor of rhetoric at the patriarchal school of St Sophia, bishop of Nicea from 845, and author of *Lives* of other moderate iconophile personalities such as the Patriarchs Tarasius (784-806) and Nicephorus I of Constantinople (806-15).

He tells how early in his youth Gregory left the world for an ascetic and monastic life. During the reign of the iconoclast Emperor Theophilus (829-42), he embarked on a long expedition defending and supporting the iconophiles. His journeys brought him to Ephesus, Prokonnesus (modern Marmara), Ainos, Christopolis (modern Kavala), Thessaloniki, Corinth, Neapolis, Rome, Syracuse, Otranto, and back to Thessaloniki and Constantinople. The *Life* makes mention of an encounter between Gregory and an Arab Saracen soldier, in which the latter raised his spear to kill Gregory. The soldier's hand instantly became stiff, and Gregory healed his assailant by touching his afflicted hand.

Gregory's only extant writing, a sermon in which he describes the conversion of a Saracen to Christianity and his subsequent martyrdom, is a hagiographical account of a possibly historical Muslim-Christian encounter.

MAIN SOURCES OF INFORMATION

Primary

Bios kai thaumata tou hosiou patros hēmōn Gregoriou tou Dekapolitou syngrapheis hypo Ignatiou diakonou kai skeuophilakos tēs tou Theou megalēs ekklēsias, in F. Dvorník, *La vie de saint Grégoire le Décapolite et les Slaves macédoniens au IXe siècle*, Paris, 1926, pp. 45-75

Secondary
PMBZ i (prolegomena), pp. 87-88
A. Kazhdan and N. Patterson Ševčenko, art. 'Gregory of Dekapolis', in *ODB*
Dumbarton Oaks Hagiography Database, Washington DC, 1998, pp. 47-48
C. Mango, 'On re-reading the life of St Gregory the Decapolite', *Byzantina* 13 (1985) 633-46
H. Grégoire, review of Dvorník, *La vie de saint Grégoire le Décapolite et les Slaves macédoniens au IXe siècle*, in *Byzantion* 7 (1932) 642-45

WORKS ON CHRISTIAN-MUSLIM RELATIONS

Logos historikos Gregoriou tou Dekapolitou, pany ōphelimos kai glykytatos kata polla, peri optasias hēn tis Sarrakēnos pote idōn, episteuse, martyrēsas dia ton Kyrion hēmōn Iēsoun Christon, 'A historical sermon by Gregory Dekapolites; very profitable and most pleasing in many ways, about a vision which a Saracen once had, and who as a result of this believed and became a martyr for our Lord Jesus Christ', 'The Sermon of Gregory Dekapolites'

DATE Unknown
ORIGINAL LANGUAGE Greek

DESCRIPTION
In his sermon Gregory Dekapolites states that the story had been related to him by Nicholas, a high military official (*stratēgos*, head of a Byzantine *theme*) from a Syrian town which the Arabs ('Saracens') call 'Vineyard' (Kurūm?). The emir of the city sent his nephew to oversee some construction work in the local castle, where there was also a splendid church dedicated to St George. The Arab ordered his belongings and his camels to be brought inside. The priests pleaded with him not to desecrate the altar of God, but to no avail, but as the camels were brought in, they all fell dead.

Incensed with rage, the prince ordered the carcasses to be removed from the church, while he remained inside witnessing the service of the preparation of the eucharist, which the priest had started. He saw the celebrant take a child in his hand, slaughter it, cut the body into pieces and place them on a tray. The Arab saw even more clearly four pieces of the body and the blood in the cup at the procession of the Great Entrance. At the invitation to communion, he saw the Christians receiving the body and blood of the child. So after the liturgy he angrily confronted the priest with the abominable 'crime' he had committed. The priest confessed the truth of the mystery, although he himself had not experienced the vision, and he explained to him the meaning of the liturgy.

The prince then asked the priest to catechize and baptize him. The priest, fearing the hostility of the prince's uncle the emir, referred him to the monastery at Sinai where he was baptized by its abbot. There he stayed for three years as a monk, taking the name Pachomius. After receiving permission from the abbot, he returned to the priest who had instructed him, and asked him to teach him how he could see Christ. The priest advised him to go to his uncle the emir, preach Christ to him, and publicly deny Muḥammad and the false faith of the Muslims. But his encounter with uncle was traumatic. The emir demanded that he return to Islam, using various threats and enticements, but the prince was unmoved. So the emir had no choice but to deliver him to his guards, who dragged him out of the city and stoned him to death. Many became Christians when a star came down and rested for 40 days over the place where the martyr had died.

SIGNIFICANCE

This attractive and imaginative story reflects characteristic beliefs of Orthodox Christianity about the nature of the eucharist as the true body and blood of Christ, and not simply an image or symbol, as the iconoclasts of the time maintained. The dismemberment of Christ is reproduced in the *melismos* (dismemberment), a theme in Byzantine iconography. Thus, an iconophile eucharistic theology and spirituality are clearly implied in the text.

The sermon points to an encounter that possibly took place during the reign of 'Umar II (717-20) or Hishām (724-43), not at the theoretical or intellectual level but on the level of lived spiritual experience; indicatively, the adjective 'ecstatic' is repeated several times in the sermon. One may even possibly discern in the story signs of emerging Ṣūfī beliefs and practices among Muslims. The text consistently refers to the Muslims as 'Sarracens', rather than 'Saracens', allowing the possibility that John of Damascus' (q.v.) etymological explanation that the name is derived from Sarrah had become widely accepted.

MANUSCRIPTS

The story is found in two manuscripts in two slightly different versions:

MS BNF – 1190 (dated 1568)

MS Vat – 1130 (16th c.) (ed. Aufhauser)

EDITIONS AND TRANSLATIONS

D.J. Sahas, 'What an infidel saw that a faithful did not. Gregory Dekapolites (d. 842) and Islam', *Greek Orthodox Theological Review* 31 (1986) 47-67, pp. 50-62 (repr. in M.N. Vaporis (ed.), *Orthodox Christians and Muslims*, Brookline MA, 1986) (English trans.)

A.J. Festugière, *Collections grecques de miracles. Saint Thècle, saints Côme et Damien, saints Cyr et Jean (extraits), saint Georges*, Paris, 1971, 259-67 (French trans.)

J.B. Aufhauser, *Miracula S. Georgi*, Leipzig, 1913

Acta Sanctorum 23 April, 3.xlii-xlv (Appendix)

PG 100, cols 1201-12

STUDIES

D. Vila, *Christian martyrs in the first Abbasid century and the development of an apologetic against Islam*, St Louis MO, 1999 (Diss. St Louis University), pp. 296-307

Hoyland, *Seeing Islam*, pp. 383-86

Sahas, 'What an infidel saw that a faithful did not'

D.J. Sahas, *Icon and Logos. Sources in eighth-century iconoclasm*, Toronto, 1986

S. Gero, 'The eucharistic doctrine of the Byzantine iconoclasts and its sources', *BZ* 68 (1975) 4-22

S. Gero, 'Notes on Byzantine iconoclasm in the eighth century', *Byzantion* 44 (1974) 23-42

A.-T. Khoury, *Les théologiens byzantins et l'islam. Textes et auteurs (VIIIe-XIIIe s.)*, Louvain, 1969

Daniel J. Sahas 2007

Al-Naẓẓām

Abū Isḥāq Ibrāhīm ibn Sayyār ibn Hānī l-Naẓẓām

DATE OF BIRTH Latter part of 8th c.
PLACE OF BIRTH Basra
DATE OF DEATH 836 or 845
PLACE OF DEATH Baghdad

BIOGRAPHY

Al-Naẓẓām was born in Basra and lived there until 818, when he was called to Baghdad by al-Maʾmūn. In Basra he is said to have studied under Hishām ibn al-Ḥakam, Abū l-Hudhayl (q.v.) and Ḍirār ibn ʿAmr (q.v.). He in turn was teacher of al-Jāḥiẓ, who regarded him as the most impressive theological and legal scholar of his day, and also probably of Muḥammad ibn Shabīb. Little is known about his life. It is often said that he was only 36 when he died, but this age seems improbably young. There is also disagreement over the date of his death; one of the few certain facts is that this was before 847, because al-Jāḥiẓ (q.v.) in his *Kitāb al-ḥayawān*, which was finished in that year, refers to him as already dead.

Al-Naẓẓām's known works, none of which survives, show that he was fascinated by the nature of the physical world, as well as other matters more readily recognizable as religious. He wrote on the physical particles that according to early Muslim conceptions made up the contingent universe (*Kitāb al-juzʾ*, 'The atom'; *Kitāb al-jawāhir wa-l-aʿrāḍ*, 'Substances and accidents'), and on the nature of the world (*Kitāb al-insān*, 'The human'; *Kitāb khalq al-shayʾ*, 'The creation of the thing'; *Kitāb al-tawallud*, 'Generated effects'; *Kitāb al-ṭafra*, 'The leap'). In addition, he wrote about specifically Islamic concerns (*Kitāb ithbāt al-rusul*, 'Confirmation of messengers'; *Kitāb al-tawḥīd*, 'Divine unity'; *Kitāb al-waʿīd*, 'The divine threat'; *Kitāb al-makhlūq, ʿalā l-mujbira*, 'What is created, against the determinists'), and entered into debate with other Muslims and non-Muslims in the usual way of his times (*Kitāb al-maʿānī, ʿalā Muʿammar*, 'Determinants, against Muʿammar [ibn ʿAbbād]'; *Kitāb al-radd ʿalā aṣḥāb al-ithnayn*, 'Refutation of the followers of dualism'). In turn, his ideas were targeted by many of his contemporaries, including his teacher

Abū l-Hudhayl, his student al-Jāḥiẓ, Bishr ibn al-Muʿtamir (q.v.), al-Murdār (q.v.) and al-Iskāfī (q.v.).

Al-Naẓẓām made studies of Greek physics, and was known for distinctive views about the nature of atoms and accidents and other scientific aspects of the *kalām* to which his works attest. He was particularly remembered for his theory of the 'leap' to explain the movement of atoms.

MAIN SOURCES OF INFORMATION

Primary

Abū l-Ḥusayn al-Khayyāṭ, *Kitāb al-intiṣār*, ed. and French trans. A. Nader, Beirut, 1957, pp. 21-22, 25-45, 95

Abū l-Ḥasan al-Ashʿarī, *Maqālāt al-Islāmiyyīn*, ed. H. Ritter, Istanbul, 1930, pp. 166-67, 173, 225, 229, 268-69, 304, 316-17, 318, 321, 331, 346-47, 358, 365, 378, 404, 555

Ibn al-Nadīm, *Fihrist*, pp. 205-6

Abū Manṣūr al-Baghdādī, *Kitāb al-milal wa-l-niḥal*, ed. A. Nader, Beirut, 1970, pp. 93-102

Ibn al-Murtaḍā, *Kitāb ṭabaqāt al-Muʿtazila*, ed. S. Diwald-Wilzer, Beirut, 1988, pp. 49-52

Secondary

Van Ess, *TG* iii, pp. 296-445; vi, pp. 1-204

Watt, *Formative period*, pp. 219-20, 236, 238, 240, 246

A.N. Nader, *Le système philosophique des Muʿtazila*, Beirut, 1956, *passim*

Sezgin, GAS i, pp. 618-19

WORKS ON CHRISTIAN-MUSLIM RELATIONS

[*Kitāb fī tafḍīl al-tathlīth ʿalā l-tawḥīd*, 'The superiority of Trinity over Unity']

DATE early 9th c.

ORIGINAL LANGUAGE Arabic

DESCRIPTION

The work is not extant, and nothing is known about it apart from one brief mention by Ibn Ḥazm (*Ṭawq al-ḥamāma*, p. 127) on the authority of Ibn al-Rāwandī. The latter remarks that al-Naẓẓām wrote 'a book' (*kitāb*) for a Christian boy to whom he was attracted, which showed the superiority of the Christian over the Islamic doctrine of God. This piece of gossip must be treated with caution, because none of the titles recorded by Ibn al-Nadīm or others who wrote about al-Naẓẓām denotes such a work, and in the light of Ibn al-Rāwandī's unremitting slander of the Muʿtazila (shown spectacularly in al-Khayyāṭ's *Kitāb al-intiṣār*), its truthfulness is clearly suspicious. The very title of the work is uncertain, because Ibn Ḥazm's mention may give no more than a description of its main argument.

Despite this, there are sufficient reports about al-Naẓẓām's thought concerning Christianity to show that he could have written a book about it, and was anyway deeply involved in considerations about the implications of its teachings.

According to ʿAbd al-Jabbār (*Tathbīt dalāʾil al-nubuwwa*, ed. ʿA.K. ʿUthmān, Beirut, 1966, p. 148), he followed others in accepting that Christians taught that God took Mary in the way that a man takes a woman as wife. Ibn al-Murtaḍā (*Ṭabaqāt*, p. 50) mentions that he memorized the Torah, the Psalms and the Gospel, together with interpretation of them (*tafsīruhā*). And more fully, al-Jāḥiẓ (*Radd ʿalā l-Naṣārā*, pp. 29-30) relates how he responded to a well-known comparison suggested by Christians between Jesus as adopted son of God and Abraham as friend of God, *khalīl Allāh* (Q 4:125) on the grounds that in both relationships God showed the human honor and care.

As al-Jāḥiẓ summarizes his view ('with which the scholars of the Muʿtazila agreed'), al-Naẓẓām argues that the term *khalīl*, 'friend', is synonymous with *ḥabīb*, 'dear one', and *walī*, 'intimate', and by analogy the term *walad*, 'son', can be applied to a servant of God in the sense of *tarbiya*, 'upbringing', though not *ḥiḍāna*, 'nursing'. A man might rear a dog, but he could not call it his son, though if he found a child and brought it up he could do so because of the resemblance between them. While there is less closeness between God and a human than between a man and a dog, 'God has more right to make him his son and to relate himself to him'. His argument is that since the title used for the human Abraham denotes intimacy with God, the equally intimate title for the human Jesus can be allowed, as long as this does not entail a physical relationship.

SIGNIFICANCE

This latter argument gives indications that al-Naẓẓām was not entirely disposed against Christians, though in his reply to their comparison he was maybe sagely drawing the sting from this group's polemical ploy.

It is not impossible that this answer formed part of a book on the superiority of the Trinity to *tawḥīd*, though if al-Naẓẓām ever wrote such a work it might have been expected to cause some reactions from his fellow Muslims. There is no record of any.

His reply to this Christian question received much attention in theological circles in the 9th and 10th centuries. References in later works show that a number of Muslims responded to it, including al-Jāḥiẓ himself, Abū ʿAlī al-Jubbāʾī and ʿAbd al-Jabbār. And others probably knew about it, including his pupil Muḥammad Ibn Shabīb (q.v.).

MANUSCRIPTS —

EDITIONS AND TRANSLATIONS

J. Finkel, ed., *Thalāth rasāʾil li-Abī ʿUthmān ʿAmr ibn Baḥr al-Jāḥiẓ*, Cairo, 1962

I.S. Allouche, 'Un traité de polémique christiano-musulmane au ixe siècle', *Hespéris* 26 (1939) 123-55, pp. 145-46 (French trans.)

Van Ess, *TG* iii, pp. 397-99, vi, pp. 138-40 (summary and German trans.)

STUDIES

Van Ess, *TG* iii, pp. 397-99, vi, pp. 138-40 (historical study, and discussion)

David Thomas 2007

Dionysius of Tell-Maḥrē

DATE OF BIRTH Unknown
PLACE OF BIRTH Possibly Edessa
DATE OF DEATH 22 August 845
PLACE OF DEATH Unknown, probably in the neighborhood of the monastery of Qenneshrē, where he was buried

BIOGRAPHY

A member of the rich Tell-Maḥrōyō family from Edessa, Dionysius became a monk of the monastery of Qenneshrē, an important intellectual centre of the Syrian Orthodox Church. In 816 he left Qenneshrē for the monastery of St Jacob of Qayshum, where he made an excellent impression on the local bishop, Theophilus. On two occasions, he was offered episcopal rank, which he declined. Then in 818, against his will, according to his own testimony, he was elected patriarch of the Syrian Orthodox Church by the Synod of Callinicus, convened under the supervision of the Muslim governor Ṭāhir, one of the generals of the ʿAbbasid Caliph al-Maʾmūn.

As patriarch, Dionysius traveled to Baghdad in order to receive his diploma from the Caliph al-Maʾmūn. In general, he maintained excellent relations with the Islamic authorities of various regions, whom he visited regularly, despite the fact that he sometimes felt these visits to be humiliating. On several occasions, the Muslim rulers allowed him to rebuild churches or helped him to settle internal Christian disputes, such as the destruction of churches by the Chalcedonians in Edessa or the occupation of the monastery of Qenneshrē by followers of the heretical anti-patriarch Abiram. Especially noteworthy are his two encounters with the Caliph al-Maʾmūn in 828, the second in the presence of a number of Muslim jurisconsults. The main issue discussed at these meetings was al-Maʾmūn's edict which allowed any group of ten persons or more, if they belonged to one of the confessions that fell under the *dhimmī* regulations, to elect their own leader. This would not only weaken the position of the Christians and other non-Muslims, but also uproot the system of apostolic succession that was in practice in the Syrian Orthodox Church. The caliph gave Dionysius permission to explain the structure of authority in the church, and he pointed out that, like the leadership of the imām in congregational prayer, it posed no threat to the authority of the state.

In 833, he accompanied al-Maʾmun on his campaign to Egypt, where he was impressed by the pyramids and established contacts with Coptic leaders. In 836, he was received by the Caliph al-Muʿtaṣim, who conferred upon him a new diploma. During this visit, he had the opportunity to meet with the Nubian King Ghiwarghi, whose orthodoxy he praised highly.

Dionysius' patriarchate was characterized by his efforts to solve the internal conflicts that divided his church, which he described as 'a multi-headed animal, the governance of which is the art of arts and the science of sciences', and to establish good relations with the Muslim authorities, whom he approached with respect but without fear, judging from his own reports of various encounters, when it was necessary to plead for the Christians or to disagree with the rulers. He is the author of an important chronicle, now lost, except for a number of fragments (see below), a pastoral letter written after his election (*sustatikon*, preserved in the *Chronicle* of Michael the Syrian) and a synodal letter (profession of faith) sent to the Coptic patriarch after the latter's consecration as patriarch (preserved in Arabic in the Copto-Arabic *Book of the confession of the fathers*).

Dionysius was capable of conversing directly with Muslim leaders in Arabic, but was proud of the Syriac – which for him meant Aramaic – identity of his people, called the 'Syrians' (Suryōyē).

MAIN SOURCES OF INFORMATION

Primary

Chronicle of 819: A. Barsaum, *Chronicum anonymum ad A.D. 819 pertinens* in J.-B. Chabot, *Anonymi auctoris chronicon ad annum Christi 1234 pertinens*, Paris, 1920 (*CSCO* 81), p. 21; Latin trans. J.-B. Chabot, *Anonymi auctoris chronicon ad annum Christi 1234 pertinens*, Paris, 1937 (*CSCO* 109), p. 15 (one brief reference)

Chronicle of 846: E.W. Brooks, *Chronicon anonymum ad A.D. 846* in *Chronica minora*, Paris, 1904 (*CSCO* 3) Paris, 1904, p. 238; Latin trans. J.B. Chabot, *Chronica minora*, Paris, 1904 (*CSCO* 4), p. 180

Chronography of Elias of Nisibis, Part i: E.W. Brooks, *Eliae metropolitae Nisibeni opus chronologicum*, 2 parts, Paris, 1909-10 (*CSCO* 62-63), pp. 174-80; Latin trans., pp. 83-85 (mentions Dionysius as one of his sources)

Chronicle of Michael the Syrian: J.-B. Chabot, *Chronique de Michel le Syrien*, 4 vols, Paris, 1899-1910, iv, pp. 378, 500-12 (including the text of the *sustatikon*), 514-20, 522-27, 528-30, 530-32, 538-43, 547; trans.: ii, pp. 357-58; iii, pp. 39-59, 62-70, 76-82, 85-87, 90-93, 104-11, 116

Chronicle of 1234 (Part ii), Secular and Ecclesiastical Chronicle: J.-B. Chabot and A. Abouna, *Chronicon ad annum Christi 1234 pertinens*, Paris, 1920, 1974 (*CSCO* 82, 109), pp. 13, 17, 20-21, 33, 266-274, 315 (French trans. pp. 9, 12, 14-15, 23, 200-6, 236)

Gregory Barhebraeus, *Civil Chronicle*: P. Bedjan, *Maktbānut Zabnē*, Paris, 1890, pp. 129, 139, 145, 148; English trans. E.A. Wallis Budge, *The Chronography of Gregory Abū'l Faraj...Bar Hebraeus*, 2 vols, Oxford, 1932, i, pp. 119, 127, 133, 135

Gregory Barhebraeus, *Ecclesiastical Chronicle*: J.B. Abbeloos and Th. J. Lamy, *Gregorii Barhebraei Chronicon ecclesiasticum*, 3 vols, Paris, 1872-77, i, cols 344-86; ii, cols 189-304 (the same material as is found in the work of Michael the Syrian)

Secondary

Hoyland, *Seeing Islam*, pp. 416-19

J.-M. Fiey, *Chrétiens syriaques sous les Abbassides, surtout à Baghdad*, Louvain, 1980, pp. 68-71

R. Abramowski, *Dionysius von Tellmahre. Jakobitischer Patriarch von 818-845. Zur Geschichte der Kirche unter dem Islam*, Leipzig, 1940

Baumstark, *GSL*, p. 275

WORKS ON CHRISTIAN-MUSLIM RELATIONS

Title unknown. Modern title: 'The Chronicle of Dionysius of Tell-Maḥrē'

DATE After 842/43, probably shortly before his death in 845
ORIGINAL LANGUAGE Syriac

DESCRIPTION

Dionysius' *Chronicle* covered the years between 582, the beginning of the reign of the Greek Emperor Maurice, and 842-3, the deaths of the Greek Emperor Theophilus and the Caliph al-Muʿtaṣim. His carefully arranged work, written at the request of Iwannis, Metropolitan of Dara, was divided into two parts, the first of which dealt with ecclesiastical history and the second with secular history. Each part consisted of eight books, with subdivisions into chapters.

The *Chronicle* itself is lost, but important fragments have survived in the work of Patriarch Michael the Syrian (late 12th c.) and in the *Chronicon ad annum 1234 pertinens*, composed by an anonymous Syrian Orthodox chronicler from Edessa in the early 13th century. In the cases where fragments explicitly attributed to Dionysius are found in the works of both later authors, we may be sure that they derive from Dionysius, because they wrote independently of each other. This allows for a partial reconstruction of his original work. On the other hand, one must bear in mind that both Michael the Syrian and the anonymous chronicler dealt with Dionysius' material in their own personal way, adapting and reworking it to fit their own historiographies and sometimes mixing it with material from other sources.

Dionysius' *Chronicle* is much more than just a continuation of an earlier chronicle; it is based on personal consultation of various sources, general and local, Christian, both Greek-Byzantine and Syriac, and Muslim. In his preface, he indicates his Christian predecessors, but nowhere does he mention which Arabic sources he consulted.

SIGNIFICANCE

The *Chronicle* of Dionysius is our best source of knowledge for the important Chronicle (the 'Syriac common source') of Theophilus of Edessa (q.v.).

Dionysius records a number of developments pertaining to Muslim/Arab history, sometimes interpreted from the perspective of a leader of the most important Christian community in Syria. Thus, he mentions not only the names and deeds of governors, generals and other political leaders, but also their attitude towards Christians in general or his own community in particular.

He describes a number of encounters (official, informal, and juridical) between Muslims and Christians. Especially noteworthy are his accounts of personal encounters with Muslim rulers, as well as the debate between Patriarch John III Sedra with the governor ʿUmayr ibn Saʿd ibn ʿUbayd (see the entry on The Disputation of John and the Emir).

He gives information, both contemporary and based on older sources, on issues such as tax collection, apostasy, the destruction and rebuilding of churches, raids and conquests, protection and persecution of Christians, their social position, and the growing importance of Arabic under ʿAbd al-Malik.

He expresses a certain vision about the power of Islam, which is seen as a chastisement for the sins of the Christians in general or of particular groups of Christians.

On the basis of earlier sources, he describes Muslim beliefs, with allusions to or brief quotations from the Qurʾān, their attitude towards Jesus, their conceptions of paradise, the practice of prayer, marriage and fasting, and the collection of the Qurʾān under ʿUthmān.

MANUSCRIPTS —

EDITIONS AND TRANSLATIONS

A. Palmer, *The seventh century in the West-Syrian chronicles*, Liverpool, 1993, pp. 111-221 (a partial reconstruction, in English trans., of the period between 582 and 718)

The *Chronicle* of Michael the Syrian gives several verbatim (?) extracts from the work of Dionysius: the preface, the introduction to the period of his own pontificate, the end and exordium; see *Chronique de Michel le Syrien*, iv, pp. 378, 503-4, 538-43; trans.: ii, pp. 357-58, iii, pp. 42-44, 104-11

STUDIES

D. Weltecke, *Die «Beschreibung der Zeiten» von Mōr Michael dem Grossen (1126-1199). Eine Studie zu ihrem historischen und historiographiegeschichtlichen Kontext*, Louvain, 2003, pp. 197-205

Hoyland, *Seeing Islam*, pp. 416-19

L. Conrad, 'Syriac perspectives on Bilâd al-Shâm during the ʿAbbasid period' in M.A. al-Bakhit and R. Schick (eds), *Bilād al-Shām during the ʿAbbasid period / Bilād al-Shām fī l-ʿaṣr al-ʿAbbāsī*, 2 vols, Amman, 1991, 1-44, esp. pp. 28-39

R. Hoyland, 'Arabic, Syriac and Greek historiography in the first ʿAbbasid century. An inquiry into inter-cultural traffic', *Aram* 3 (1991) 211-33

Abramowski, *Dionysius von Tellmahre*

Herman G. B. Teule 2008

Michael the Synkellos

DATE OF BIRTH Unknown, c. 760
PLACE OF BIRTH Jerusalem
DATE OF DEATH 4 January 846
PLACE OF DEATH Chora monastery, Constantinople

BIOGRAPHY

According to his own words recorded in his *Life* (q.v.), Michael was of 'Persian', i.e. Arab, origin. At the age of three, he was dedicated as an *anagnostēs* (reader) to the Church of the Resurrection in Jerusalem, at twenty-five he became a monk at the monastery of St Saba, and in 797 (*PMBZ*, no. 5059) or 798 (Cunningham, *Life*, pp. xiv and 137, n. 27) he was ordained priest by the patriarch of Jerusalem. Two years later he returned to St Saba, and in about 800 he accepted Theodorus Graptus (*PMBZ*, no. 7526) and his brother Theophanes (*PMBZ*, no. 8093) as monks and disciples. In about 811 (Cunningham, *Life*, p. xiv, 139, n. 40) or between 808 and 812 (*PMBZ*, no. 5059) he was appointed *synkellos* to the Patriarchate of Jerusalem, and together with the two brothers he moved to the monastery of Spudaioi near the Church of the Resurrection.

Around 812/13, Michael and the brothers were sent to Rome by the Patriarch to take to Pope Leo III (cf. *PMBZ*, no. 4239) letters that referred to the dispute over the *filioque* and also Arab outrages against the church in Palestine. Arriving in Constantinople before July 813 (*PMBZ*, no. 5059), he remained there for a time and was caught up in the controversies that followed the re-introduction of iconoclasm in 815. He was imprisoned for his support of the iconophile party, and exiled outside the city until 843, when under the new regime he was freed and promoted as patriarch. He refused, and was appointed *synkellos* of the new patriarch and also *hegoumenos* of the Chora monastery. He died there less than three years later on 4 January 846.

Regarding the writings ascribed to Michael the Synkellos, it is still not quite clear which of them can be attributed with certainty to the *synkellos* of Jerusalem and Constantinople, because it appears that in the 9th century there were three (Beck, *Kirche und theologische Literatur*, p. 504) or even four (*PMBZ*, no. 5059) individuals bearing the name Michael the Synkellos, with or without the addition 'of Jerusalem' or 'of Constantinople'. The works that can be safely affirmed as belonging to the *synkellos* of Jerusalem and Constantinople are the following (cf. also Cunningham, *Life*, pp. 36-38):

1. *Encomion* of Dionysios Areopagites (*BHG* 556; *PG* 4, cols 617-68)
2. *Martyrdom of the 42 martyrs of Amorion* (according to Kotzampassi, 'To martyrio', pp. 121-24 and *PMBZ*, no. 5059, although Kazhdan, 'Hagiographical notes' [repeated in his *History of Byzantine Literature* (850-1000), pp. 206-9, without reference to Kotzampassi], casts doubts on his authorship; cf. Cunningham, *Life*, p. 37, n. 128)
3. *Methodos peri tēs tou logou syntaxeos*, ed. D. Donnet, *Le traité de la construction de la phrase de Michel le Syncelle de Jérusalem*, Brussels, 1982
4. A letter to his disciples Theodoros and Theophanes Graptos included in his *Life* (ed. Cunningham, ch. 24, pp. 96-98), the authenticity of which, however, is not beyond dispute
5. A translation into Greek of an Arabic text on the profession of the Chalcedonian faith (*PG* 97, cols 1504-21)
6. *Michael Synkellou Ierosolymon libellos peri tes orthodoxou pisteos* (B. de Montfaucon, *Bibliotheca coisliniana*, Paris, 1715, pp. 90-93)
7. Anacreontic verses on the restoration of the icons (C. Crimi, *Michele Sincello. Per la restaurazione delle venerande e sacre immagini*, Rome, 1990, pp. 29-34 [edition], pp. 35-37 [Italian trans.]; cf. ed. T. Nissen, *Die byzantinischen Anakreonteen*, (Sitzungsberichte der Bayerischen Akad. der Wiss., Phil.-hist. Abteilung 3) Munich, 1940, 48-52
8. Four Canons (Stiernon, 'Michel le Syncelle', col. 1197; Stiernon, 'Michele il Sincello', col. 457)

For his possible authorship of a treatise on Islam and Muḥammad, see below.

MAIN SOURCES OF INFORMATION

Primary

See the entry on the *Life* of Michael the Synkellos for editions and translations of this work

Theophanes continuatus, *Chronographia*, ed. I. Bekker, Bonn, 1838, p. 106

John Skylitzes, *Ioannae Skylitzae Synopsis Historiarum*, ed. I. Thurn, Berlin, 1973, p. 63

Joseph Genesios, *Iosephi Genesii regum libri quattuor*, ed. A. Lesmueller and I. Thurn, Berlin, 1978, p. 52
Theodore of Stoudios' Letter 547, in G. Fatouros, *Theodori Studitae Epistulae*, Berlin, 1992
Life of Theophanes Graptos (*BHG* 1793), in A. Papadopoulos-Kerameus, *Analekta hierosolymitikes stachyologias*, 4 vols, St Petersburg, 1891-98, iv, pp. 185-223
Life of Empress Theodora (*BHG* 1731), in A. Markopoulos, 'Bios tes autokrateiras Theodoras', *Symmeikta* 5 (1983) 249-85, p. 262 (repr. in Markopoulos, *History and Literature of Byzantium in the 9th-10th Centuries*, Aldershot, 2004)
On the absolution of Emperor Theophilus (*BHG* 1732), in W. Regel, *Analecta Byzantino-Russica*, St Petersburg, 1891, 19-39, p. 32

Secondary
A. Kazhdan, *A History of Byzantine Literature (850-1000)*, Athens, 2006, pp. 204-9
A. Kazhdan, *A History of Byzantine Literature (650-850)*, Athens, 1999, pp. 257-59
PMBZ, no. 5059 (with bibliography)
S. Kotzampassi, 'To martyrio tōn saranta dyo martyrōn tou Amoriou. Hagiologika kai hymnologika keimena', *Epistēmonikē Epetēris Philosophikēs Scholēs Aristoteleiou Panepistēmiou Thessalonikēs, periodos B', Tmēma Philologias* 2 (1992) 109-53, pp. 121-24
M.B. Cunningham, *The Life of Michael the Synkellos*, Belfast, 1991, pp. 1-42 (with bibliography)
R. Browning and A. Kazhdan, art. 'Michael Synkellos', in *ODB*
C. Crimi, *Michele Sincello. Per la restaurazione delle venerande e sacre immagini*, Rome, 1990, pp. 5-11
S.H. Griffith, 'Greek into Arabic. Life and letters in the monasteries of Palestine in the ninth century. The example of the *Summa theologiae arabica*', *Byzantion* 56 (1986) 117-38, pp. 127-28, 130-31
A. Kazhdan, 'Hagiographical notes', *Byzantion* 56 (1986) 148-70 (repr. in Kazhdan, *Authors and texts in Byzantium*, Aldershot, 1993, no. 14: 'Collective death and individual deeds', 152-59)
N.G. Wilson, *Scholars of Byzantium*, London 1983, pp. 76-78
Donnet, *Le traité de la construction de la phrase de Michel le Syncelle de Jérusalem*
D. Stiernon, art. 'Michel le Syncelle', in *Dictionnaire de Spiritualité*, Paris, 1937-95
D. Stiernon, art. 'Michele il Sincello', in *Bibliotheca Sanctorum*
H. Hunger, *Die hochsprachliche profane Literatur der Byzantiner*, 2 vols, Munich, 1978, i, p. 261, ii, p. 15
V. Laurent, 'Histoire des Pauliciens d'Asie Mineure', *Travaux et Mémoires* 5 (1973) 1-144, pp. 86-87

W. Wolska-Conus, 'De quibusdam Ignatiis', *Travaux et Mémoires* 4 (1970) 329-60, pp. 334-35
H.-G. Beck, *Kirche und theologische Literatur im byzantinischen Reich*, Munich, 1959, pp. 503-4
BHG 556; 1213; 1294a; 1296; 1297
S. Vailhé, 'Saint Michel le Syncelle et les deux frères Grapti', *Revue de l'Orient Chrétien* 6 (1901) 313-32, 610-42
S. Vailhé, Le monastère de Saint-Sabas, *Échos d'Orient* 3 (1899) 18-28, p. 27

WORKS ON CHRISTIAN-MUSLIM RELATIONS

Martyrion tōn hagiōn tessarakonta dyo martyrōn tou Christou Kallistou doukos, Kōnstantinou patrikiou, Theodōrou prōtospathariou kai tēs synodias autōn, syngraphen para Michaēl monachou kai synkellou, 'The Martyrdom of the forty-two holy martyrs of Christ, Callistus the *dux*, Constantine the *patrikios*, Theodorus the *protospatharios* and their companions, written by Michael the monk and synkellos'

DATE After 6 March 845 (the martyrs' death) and before 4 January 846 (Michael's death) (Kotzampassi, 'To Martyrio', pp. 121-24); around 900 or after (Kazhdan, 'Hagiographical notes', pp. 152-53)
ORIGINAL LANGUAGE Greek

DESCRIPTION
After briefly praising the martyrs (Vasilievskij and Nitikin, p. 22), Michael focuses on Callistus (*PMBZ*, no. 3932), describing his virtues as a Christian, military leader and governor, and stressing his extraordinary piety and his devotion to his heavenly Master rather than to the emperor (the iconoclast Theophilus; cf. *PMBZ*, no. 8167). During a battle against the Arabs, he is captured by their Paulician (Manichean) allies and handed over to them. He is taken to Tarsus and put in prison with the Byzantine officers who were captured in Amorion (Vasilievskij and Nitikin, pp. 22-30).

Representatives of the caliph try to persuade the prisoners to convert by offering glory and wealth if they accept and threatening execution if they refuse. But they resist, and are humiliatingly marched to Baghdad to the banks of the river Tigris. Theodorus Craterus (or Carterus; cf. *PMBZ*, no. 7679), one of the generals, is called to convert, but he steadfastly refuses to abandon his beliefs and insults the caliph for his descent from the slave Hagar, and he is beheaded (Vasilievskij and Nitikin, pp. 30-33). Then Callistus makes a long speech to his fellow prisoners to encourage them to die for the love of Christ and to gain eternal life. The caliph's representatives make a second attempt to persuade them to convert, though they all refuse and are beheaded and their bodies thrown into the river. But they are miraculously retrieved and buried (Vasilievskij and Nitikin, pp. 33-35).

The account closes with a prayer to the martyrs, asking them to protect Christians, help the emperor to gain victories against the Arabs, safeguard the empire and strengthen orthodoxy.

Like Sophronius of Cyprus (q.v.) in his version of this episode, Michael the Synkellos does not include any doctrinal arguments, apart from pejorative epithets expressing the mutual contempt of either side for the other's faith.

SIGNIFICANCE

Michael's account typifies the confrontation between Christians and Muslims at this time by employing characterizations familiar from contemporary works, such as *anosios*, 'sacrilegious', and *atheos*, 'atheist', for Muslims in general, and *miaros*, 'sacrilegious', *anomos*, 'lawless', 'rejecting God's law', and *atheos*, 'servant of Satan', for the caliphs. The text also exemplifies the military and political confrontation between the two sides in the 9th century.

MANUSCRIPTS

MS Moscow, Synod Library – 162 (archim. Vladimir catal. 380)

EDITIONS AND TRANSLATIONS

V. Vasilievskij and P. Nikitin, *Skazanija o 42 amorijskich mučenikach*, St Petersburg, 1905, pp. 22-36 (text *G*)

STUDIES

Kazhdan, *A History of Byzantine Literature* (850-1000), pp. 204-9

A. Kolia-Dermitzaki, 'The execution of the forty-two martyrs of Amorion. Proposing an interpretation', *Al-Masaq* 14 (2002) 141-62

PMBZ, no. 5059

Kotzampassi, 'To martyrio tōn saranta dyo martyrōn tou Amoriou'

Cunningham, *The Life of Michael the Synkellos*, p. 37 with n. 128

Kazhdan, 'Hagiographical notes', pp. 152-59

Stiernon, art. 'Michel le Syncelle', in *Dictionnaire de Spiritualité*

V. Laurent, 'Histoire des Pauliciens d'Asie Mineure', pp. 86-87
Beck, *Kirche und theologische Literatur*, pp. 503-4
BHG 1213
Vasilievskij and Nikitin, *Skazanija o 42 amorijskich mučenikach*, pp. 272-79 (commentary by P. Nikitin)
Vailhé, 'Saint Michel le Syncelle et les deux frères Grapti'
R. Abicht and H. Schmidt, 'Quellennachweise zum Codex Suprasliensis, III', *Archiv für slavische Philologie* 18 (1896) 138-55, p. 142

Unknown refutation of Islam

DATE Late 8th or early 9th c.
ORIGINAL LANGUAGE Greek

DESCRIPTION

The refutation of Islam which is included in George the Monk's (q.v.) *Chronicon syntomon* (ed. C. de Boor, *Georgii Monachi Chronicon*, 2 vols, Leipzig, 1904, ii, 697-702; repr. Stuttgart, 1978) should perhaps (possibly in part) be attributed to Michael the Synkellos. In one of the manuscripts of this chronicle (MS BNF – Coislin 305, fol. 312v; cf. ed. de Boor, ii, 699) reference is made in the middle of the section on Islam to Michael the Synkellos' treatment of the topic 'in summary' (*di' epitomēs*). This may mean that George used Michael's summary of a work he had written, though it could also mean that Michael had made a summary of a work written by a third person.

SIGNIFICANCE

See the entry on George the Monk (George Hamartolos).

MANUSCRIPTS

See the entry on George the Monk (George Hamartolos).

EDITIONS AND TRANSLATIONS

See the entry on George the Monk (George Hamartolos).

STUDIES

R. Browning and A. Kazhdan, art. 'Michael Synkellos', in *ODB*
Hunger, *Die hochsprachliche profane Literatur der Byzantiner* i, p. 261
Vasilievskij and Nikitin, *Skazanija o 42 amorijskich mučenikach*, p. 113

Athina Kolia-Dermitzaki 2008

Speraindeo

DATE OF BIRTH Unknown
PLACE OF BIRTH Unknown, probably Cordova or environs
DATE OF DEATH c. 850-51
PLACE OF DEATH Probably Cordova

BIOGRAPHY

Little is known about Speraindeo's life. He taught Eulogius (q.v.) and Paulus Alvarus (q.v.), supporters and main chroniclers of the martyrs' movement among Christians in Cordova, 850-59. His only complete writing that survives is a brief letter written to Paulus Alvarus in the 840s or early 850s in which Speraindeo denounces a group of Christians Alvarus describes as anti-Trinitarians, who believed Jesus was not divine. The anti-Trinitarians may have connections with the Adoptionists in late 8th-century al-Andalus led by Elipandus, Archbishop of Toledo, whose views spread into the Carolingian Spanish March and were vigorously denounced by Alcuin. Adoptionism, while not rejecting Christ's divinity altogether, emphasized his human nature. In de-emphasizing his divinity, the beliefs of the Adoptionists and of the group Speraindeo refutes come close to the beliefs of Muslims about Jesus, and may have been part of a syncretistic movement in al-Andalus that emphasized similarities between Christianity and Islam.

Speraindeo wrote an account, none of which survives, of the deaths of John and Adolphus in 822, the first Cordovan Christians of the era whom the Muslim authorities put to death for making insulting remarks about Islam. Eulogius and Paulus Alvarus regarded them as the earliest of the martyrs, and may have patterned their own accounts of later martyrdoms after Speraindeo's.

A quotation from a lost polemical work against Islam by Speraindeo survives in Eulogius' *Memoriale sanctorum*.

MAIN SOURCES OF INFORMATION

Primary

Contra haereticos in Paul Alvarus, 'Epistula 8', *PL* 115 cols 959-66; Gil, *CSM* i, pp. 203-10

(and see further below)

Secondary

J. Coope, *The martyrs of Córdoba. Community and family conflict in an age of mass conversion*, Lincoln NE, 1995, pp. 46-47

K. Wolf, *Christian martyrs in Muslim Spain*, Cambridge, 1988, pp. 52-53, 63-64

E. Colbert, *The martyrs of Córdoba (850-859). A study of the sources*, Washington DC, 1962, pp. 157-63

F.R. Franke, *Die freiwilligen Märtyrer von Cordova und das Verhältnis der Mozaraber zum Islam (nach den Schriften des Speraindeo, Eulogius und Alvar)*, Münster, 1958

WORKS ON CHRISTIAN-MUSLIM RELATIONS

Title unknown, 'Polemic against Islam'

DATE Unknown, probably 830s or 840s
ORIGINAL LANGUAGE Latin

DESCRIPTION

All that survives of Speraindeo's polemic against Islam is a one-page passage in which he condemns what he understands as the Muslim belief that those who enter paradise (presumably men) will be rewarded with beautiful women as sexual partners. Speraindeo characterizes the Muslim paradise as a brothel, and quotes passages from Matthew and Luke affirming that there will be no marriage in heaven.

Although brief, the passage and the larger work from which it came probably formed the basis for the anti-Islamic polemic of Eulogius and Paulus Alvarus, and possibly of Abbot Samson of Cordova (q.v.). All focus their attacks against Islam on the supposed sensuality and sexual promiscuity of Muslims, to which they contrast the asceticism of true Christians. There may have been Middle Eastern influence on the Cordovan polemicists; John of Damascus (q.v.) also emphasized the alleged sexual depravity of Muslims, and the fact that one of the Christians executed during the martyrs' movement was from the monastery of Mār Saba near Jerusalem, where John was at one time a monk, shows that Cordova had contact with Christians in the Middle East. Another factor in their decision to focus on the presumed sensuality of Islam may be that the Cordovan polemicists regarded the behavior of the Muslim emir and his courtiers, a group known for their less than restrained way of life, as typical of all Muslims.

SIGNIFICANCE

Speraindeo's polemic shaped later Cordovan Christian authors' views of Islam, and may indicate a connection with Middle Eastern Christian polemic.

MANUSCRIPTS

The manuscript of Eulogius's *Memoriale sanctorum* (q.v.) is no longer extant.

EDITIONS AND TRANSLATIONS

The quotation from Speraindeo's polemic against Islam can be found in Eulogius, *Memoriale sanctorum* 1.7, in *PL* 115, col. 745, and Gil, *CSM* ii, pp. 375-76

STUDIES

G. del Cerro Calderón and J. Palacios Royán, *Epistulario de Álvaro de Córdoba*, Cordova, 1997, pp. 8, 93-105

Coope, *The martyrs of Córdoba*, pp. 46-47

Wolf, *Christian martyrs in Muslim Spain*, Cambridge, 1988, pp. 52-53, 63-64

Colbert, *The martyrs of Córdoba*, pp. 157-63

Franke, *Die freiwilligen Märtyrer*

Jessica A. Coope 2007

The Forty-two martyrs of Amorion (BHG 1212)

Unknown author

DATE OF BIRTH Unknown
PLACE OF BIRTH Unknown
DATE OF DEATH Unknown
PLACE OF DEATH Unknown

BIOGRAPHY —

MAIN SOURCES OF INFORMATION

Primary —

Secondary —

WORKS ON CHRISTIAN-MUSLIM RELATIONS

Athlēsis tōn hagiōn kai kallinikōn mb′ martyrōn tou Christou, Kōnstantinou, Theodōrou, Theophilou, Kallistou, Bassoou kai tōn syn autōn teleiōthentōn en Syria hypo tōn atheōn Agarēnōn epi Michaēl kai Theodōras tōn orthodoxōn basileōn, 'The struggle of the forty-two holy and victorious martyrs of Christ: Constantine, Theodorus, Theophilus, Callistus, Bassoēs and those who died with them in Syria at the hands of the godless Hagarenes, under the orthodox Emperors Michael and Theodora', 'The forty-two martyrs of Amorion (*BHG* 1212)'

DATE Probably before January 846 or at the latest before June 847
ORIGINAL LANGUAGE Greek

DESCRIPTION

The account starts with a long introduction praising the act of martyrdom (Vasilievskij and Nikitin, pp. 8-9), and detailing the forty-two martyrs' different origins, their shared virtue and piety, and their bravery and military successes, especially against the Arabs (Vasilievskij and Nikitin, pp. 9-11). The main part of the *Martyrdom* begins with a brief description of the town of Amorion, praise for the Emperor Theophilus and his successful expeditions against the 'sacrilegious' Caliph al-Muʿtaṣim, a short account of the siege and capture of the city in August 838 and the massacre that followed, with a simple hint at a possible act of treason (Vasilievskij and Nikitin, pp. 11-12).

The hagiographer then tells how the forty-two officers were held in difficult conditions for six years (most other versions give seven years), and of the forbearance they showed. When they are finally taken to the Tigris to be executed, there is a great rush of people of all kinds to the river bank (Vasilievskij and Nikitin, pp. 12-13). As in version *P* (q.v.), the main hero is Theodorus Craterus (or Carterus; cf. *PMBZ*, no. 7679), while Bassoēs (*PMBZ*, no. 982) is only named, and there is no mention of the other martyrs who are named in the title of the work.

Before they are executed, a representative of the Caliph al-Wāthiq attempts to lure Theodorus away from his faith, but without diverting the officer from his resolve and from his abhorrence of Islam (Vasilievskij and Nikitin, pp. 13-15). When he is executed, the other officers are eager to follow his example despite a renewed attempt by the caliph's representative (Vasilievskij and Nikitin, pp. 15-17). From the exchanges between them it emerges that they are intent on martyrdom in order to gain eternal life (Vasilievskij and Nikitin, pp. 17-20). They are beheaded and their bodies are thrown into the Tigris, but these are miraculously discovered by the monks of a nearby monastery and buried (Vasilievskij and Nikitin, pp. 20-21; cf. the text of Michael the Synkellos [version *G*] and version *E*).

Like Sophronius (version *D*) and the anonymous author of version *P*, the author of this version (version *B*) praises the iconoclast Emperor Theophilus for his exploits against the Arabs, in contrast to the authors of versions *A*, *G* (Michael the Synkellos), and *Z* (Euodius, q.v.), who are scornful about him. The author of this version is the only one who gives details about the martyrs' physical robustness and their illustrious military career.

SIGNIFICANCE

The *Martyrdom* combines elements of the military and religious confrontation between Byzantium and Islam in the 9th century. It expresses the religious confrontation not by doctrinal arguments but by referring to the benefits of martyrdom and the desire for eternal life, and by using contemptuous terms for Muslims and Islam: *miaros*, 'sacrilegious', *atheos*, 'atheist', *theomachos*, 'enemy of God', and *anomos*, 'lawless', 'not accepting the law of God'.

MANUSCRIPTS

MS Moscow, Synod Library – 173 (archim. Vladimir catal. 378)

EDITIONS AND TRANSLATIONS

V. Vasilievskij and P. Nikitin, *Skazanija o 42 amorijskich mučenikach*, St Petersburg, 1905, pp. 8-21 (version *B*)

STUDIES

A. Kolia-Dermitzaki, 'The execution of the forty-two martyrs of Amorion. Proposing an interpretation', *Al-Masaq* 14 (2002) 141-62

S. Kotzampassi, 'To martyrio tōn saranta dyo martyrōn tou Amoriou. Hagiologika kai hymnologika keimena', *Epistēmonikē Epetēris tēs Philosophikēs Scholēs Aristotēleiou Panepistēmiou Thessalonikēs, periodos B′, Tmēma Philologias* 2 (1992) 109-53

A. Kazhdan, 'Hagiographical notes', *Byzantion* 56 (1986) 148-70 (repr. in Kazhdan, *Authors and texts in Byzantium*, Aldershot, 1993, no. 14: 'Collective death and individual deeds', pp. 152-59)

BHG 1212

Vasilievskij and Nikitin, *Skazanija o 42 amorijskich mučenikach*, pp. 272-79 (commentary by P. Nikitin)

Athina Kolia-Dermitzaki 2008

The forty-two martyrs of Amorion (BHG 1214c)

Unknown author

DATE OF BIRTH Unknown
PLACE OF BIRTH Unknown
DATE OF DEATH Unknown
PLACE OF DEATH Unknown

BIOGRAPHY —

MAIN SOURCES OF INFORMATION

Primary —

Secondary —

WORKS ON CHRISTIAN-MUSLIM RELATIONS

Martyrion tōn hagiōn tou Christou tessarakonta kai dyo martyrōn tōn en Persidi teleiōthentōn, 'The Martyrdom of the forty-two holy martyrs of Christ who died in Persia' (version *P*), 'The forty-two martyrs of Amorion (*BHG* 1214c)'

DATE Probably before January 846 or at the latest before June 847 (Kotzampassi, 'To martyrio', pp. 124-26). According to Halkin (*Hagiologie byzantine*, p. 152), it belongs to a pre-metaphrastic Menologion, i.e. before the 930s-960s, while Kazhdan (*Byzantine literature*, pp. 234-35), dates the text before the 980s.
ORIGINAL LANGUAGE Greek

DESCRIPTION
In a short introduction, the unknown author refers to the descent of the Arabs from the 'slave' Ishmael (a reference to the origin of their religion) and to their hostility and destructive passion against the 'gentle' people (the Christians, i.e. the Byzantines). Then follows

the description of the siege of Amorion (called by the hagiographer 'Theoupolis', i.e. 'City of God' in order to emphasize its Christian character in contrast to its conquerors' faith) and the effective defence of the city by forty-three (a symbolic number) eminent officers sent by the Emperor Theophilus. One of them converts to Islam, reducing their number to forty-two, betrays the others, and opens the way for the sack of the city. The description of this covers almost one third of the narrative.

The officers' seven years of captivity and the hardships they suffer in jail are narrated briefly, while the rest of the text covers the attempts made by the caliph himself to convert each of them separately, their steadfast refusal, their beheading, and finally the disposal of their bodies in the river Tigris and their burial by the Christians. The main heroes among them are Theodorus Craterus (or Carterus; *PMBZ*, no. 7679) and Bassoēs (*PMBZ*, no. 982), and there is special mention of three more, Constantinus Baboutzicus (*PMBZ*, no. 3932), Theophilus (*PMBZ*, no. 8211) and Callistus (*PMBZ*, no. 3932).

In this brief account there is no reference to doctrinal arguments from either side, while the anonymous hagiographer seizes the opportunity to make reference to the victories of the Emperor Theophilus, like Sophronius (version *D* and the unknown author of version *B* (q.v.), in contrast to the authors of versions *A*, *G* (Michael the Synkellos), and *Z* (Euodius [q.v.]), who express themselves scornfully about the Byzantine sovereign.

The present version *P* is closely related to versions *D* and *D1* (Halkin, p. 152; Kotzampassi, pp. 117-20).

SIGNIFICANCE

The account highlights the military-political confrontation between Christians and Muslims, and also indirectly comments on the religious error of the Muslims by including scornful allusions to them and their caliph.

MANUSCRIPTS

MS Patmos, Monastery of St John the Theologian – 736, fols 50v-56 (14th c.)

EDITIONS AND TRANSLATIONS

F. Halkin, *Hagiologie byzantine*, Brussels 1986, pp. 152-60 (no. 12, *Passion inédite des Quarante-deux martyrs d'Amorium*)

STUDIES

A. Kolia-Dermitzaki, 'The execution of the forty-two martyrs of Amorion. Proposing an interpretation', *Al-Masaq* 14 (2002) 141-62

D. Vila, *Christian martyrs in the first Abbasid century and the development of an apologetic against Islam* (Diss. St Louis University, 1999), pp. 330-43

S. Kotzampassi, 'To martyrio tōn saranta dyo martyrōn tou Amoriou. Hagiologika kai hymnologika keimena', *Epistēmonikē Epetēris tēs Philosophikēs Scholēs Aristotēleiou Panepistēmiou Thessalonikēs, periodos B', Tmēma Philologias* 2 (1992) 109-53

A. Kominēs, *Pinakes chronologēmenōn patmiakōn kōdikōn*, Athens 1968, pp. 69-70

BHG 1214c

V. Vasilievskij and P. Nikitin, *Skazanija o 42 amorijskich mučenikach*, St Petersburg, 1905, pp. 272-79 (with commentary by Nikitin)

Athina Kolia-Dermitzaki 2008

Liber pontificalis

Unknown authors

DATE OF BIRTH Unknown
PLACE OF BIRTH Unknown
DATE OF DEATH Unknown
PLACE OF DEATH Unknown

BIOGRAPHY

The *Liber pontificalis* was written by members of the staff of the papal archives; the life of each pope after the year 640 was composed during or shortly after his reign.

MAIN SOURCES OF INFORMATION

Primary —

Secondary —

WORKS ON CHRISTIAN-MUSLIM RELATIONS

Liber pontificalis, 'The Book of Pontiffs'

DATE before 540 and between 638-880s
ORIGINAL LANGUAGE Latin

DESCRIPTION

The book contains institutional biographies of each pope from St Peter to each author's present. The focus is on the institutional history of the Roman see. Each *Life* tells the origin of the pope, the length of his reign, the church regulations he promulgated, the number of bishops, priests, and deacons he ordained, his architectural and artistic patronage, his role in theological controversies, the historical events of his reign, the date and place of his burial, and the length of time before the ordination of his successor.

Muslims (*Saraceni* or *Agareni*) are mentioned when they encroach on papal territory, most notably in the case of the Sack of Rome of 847, described in the *Lives* of Popes Sergius II (chs 44-47, although the end of the account is lost) and Leo IV (chs 7, 32, and 47-55). Muslims are referred to as '*gens nefandissima paganorum*' (Sergius II.44), '*Sarracenis perfidis Deoque contrariis*' (Leo IV.32), '*Satane filii*' (Leo IV.47), '*gens illa pestifer*' (Leo IV.48) and '*s[a]eva gens*' (ibid. 55). Some who were captured after the incursion at the time of Leo IV seem to have been enslaved by the pope (ch. 54). Although the authors clearly recognized that the Saracens were not Christians, there is no mention of Muḥammad or of any details of Muslim beliefs.

SIGNIFICANCE

The *Liber pontificalis* is one of our main sources for Italian history in the 8th and 9th centuries, and as such provides information about Muslim activities in Italy in those centuries.

MANUSCRIPTS

The *Liber pontificalis* has an extremely complex manuscript tradition, with several different recensions, especially for the pre-8th-century parts. The earliest manuscripts date to the late 8th century; see Duchesne, ed., clxiv-ccvi, and Mommsen, ed., lxix-cx.

EDITIONS AND TRANSLATIONS

Le livre des papes. Liber pontificalis (492-891), trans. M. Aubrun, Turnhout, 2007

The Book of Pontiffs (Liber pontificalis). The ancient biographies of the first ninety Roman bishops to AD 715, trans. and comm. R. Davis, Liverpool, 1989 (rev. edition 2000)

The lives of the eighth-century popes (Liber pontificalis). The ancient biographies of nine popes from AD 715 to AD 817, trans. and comm. R. Davis, Liverpool, 1992 (rev. edition 2007)

The lives of the ninth-century popes (Liber pontificalis). The ancient biographies of ten popes from A.D. 817-891, trans. and comm. R. Davis, Liverpool, 1995

Le Liber Pontificalis, 2 vols, ed. L. Duchesne, Paris, 1886-92 (repr. Paris, 1955-57, with vol. 3: *Additions et corrections*, ed. C. Vogel, repr. 1981)

Liber pontificalis, ed. T. Mommsen, Berlin, 1898 (*MGH Gesta Pontificum Romanorum* 1)

H. Geertman, 'Le biografie del Liber pontificalis dal 311 al 535. Testo e commentario,' in H. Geertman (ed.), *Atti del colloquio internazionale Il* Liber Pontificalis *e la storia materiale*, Assen, 2003, 285-355

STUDIES AND SIGNIFICANT REFERENCES

H. Geertman (ed.), *Atti del colloquio internazionale. Il* Liber Pontificalis *e la storia materiale*, Assen, 2003

D.M. Deliyannis, 'A biblical model for serial biography. The Roman *Liber Pontificalis* and the Books of Kings', *Revue bénédictine* 107 (1997) 15-23

E. Rotter, *Abendland und Sarazenen. Das okzidentale Araberbild und seine Enstehung im Frühmittelalter*, Berlin, 1986

T.F.X. Noble, 'A new look at the *Liber Pontificalis*', *Archivium historiae pontificiae* 23 (1985) 347-58

H. Geertman, *More veterum. Il Liber Pontificalis e gli edifici ecclesiastici di Roma nella tarda antichità e nell'alto medioevo*, Groningen, 1975

O. Bertolini, 'Il "Liber Pontificalis"', Centro Italiano di Studi sull'Alto Medioevo, *La Storiografia Altomedievale*, 2 vols, Spoleto, 1970, i, 387-456, 707-10

Deborah M. Deliyannis 2007

Paul Alvarus

Albar, Alvaro

DATE OF BIRTH Unknown, probably early 9th c.
PLACE OF BIRTH Unknown, probably Cordova
DATE OF DEATH Unknown
PLACE OF DEATH Unknown

BIOGRAPHY

What little is known of Alvarus' life comes entirely from his own writings and those of his friend Eulogius of Cordova (q.v.), with whom he studied under Abbot Speraindeo (q.v.). Those of Alvarus' writings for which we have firm dates fall between 840 and 859. He was most likely a noble-born layman and man of letters. In an obscure passage, Alvarus seems to claim Jewish ancestry. The bulk of his corpus is comprised of 20 letters, of which numbers 10-13 refer to events in Cordova during the time of the so-called Cordovan martyrs' movement. He is also the author of a *Life of Eulogius*, which refers to these same events. In addition, Alvarus wrote one anti-Islamic treatise, the *Indiculus luminosus*.

MAIN SOURCES OF INFORMATION

Primary

G. del Cerro Calderón and J. Palacios Royán, *Epistolario de Alvaro de Córdoba*, Cordova, 1997 (Spanish trans.)

F. León Delgado, *Alvaro de Córdoba y la polémica contra el Islam. El Indiculus luminosus*, Cordova, 1996 (Spanish trans.)

Epistolario de Álvaro de Córdoba, ed. P.J. Madoz, Madrid, 1947 (Monumenta Hispaniae Sacra, serie patristica 1), pp. 191-210 (Latin edition)

Gil, *CSM* i, pp. 143-361 (Latin edition of corpus)

PL 121, cols 387-566 (Latin edition of corpus)

Secondary

F. González Muñoz, 'En torno a la orientación de la polémica antimusulmana en los textos latinos de los mozárabes del siglo IX', in C. Aillet, M. Penelas and P. Roisse (eds), *¿Existe una identidad mozárabe? Historia, lengua y cultura de los cristianos de al-Andalus (siglos IX-XII)*, Madrid, 2008, 9-31

I. Pochoshajew, *Die Märtyrer von Cordoba. Christen im muslimischen Spanien des 9. Jahrhunderts*, Frankfurt am Main, 2007
A. Christys, *Christians in al-Andalus 711-1000*, Richmond, 2002, pp. 55-61
L.F. Mateo-Seco, 'Paulo Álvaro de Córdoba. Un personaje símbolo de la cultura mozárabe', in E. de la Lama et al. (eds), *Dos mil años de evangelización. Los grandes ciclos evangelizadores*, Pamplona, 2001, 209-34
J.C. Lara Olmo, 'La polémica de Albaro de Córdoba con Bodón/Eleazar', in C. del Valle Rodriguez (ed.), *La controversia judeo-cristiana en España (desde los orígenes hasta el siglo XIII)*, Madrid, 1998, 131-59
Del Cerro Calderón and Palacios Royán, *Epistolario de Álvaro de Córdoba*, pp. 13-24
F. González Muñoz, *Latinidad mozárabe. Estudios sobre el latín de Albaro de Córdoba*, La Coruña, 1996
F. León Delgado, *Alvaro de Córdoba y la polémica contra el Islam*
J. Vernet, 'El Romano de Alvaro de Córdoba', *Oriens* 35 (1996) 105-10
J. Coope, *The martyrs of Córdoba. Community and family conflict in an age of mass conversion*, Lincoln NE, 1995, pp. 35-54
K. Wolf, *Christian martyrs in Muslim Spain*, Cambridge, 1988
R. Jiménez Pedrajas, 'Las relaciones entre los cristianos y los musulmanes en Córdoba,' *Boletín de la Real Academia de Córdoba de Ciencias, Bellas Letras y Nobles Artes* 80 (1960) 107-246
F.R. Franke, *Die freiwilligen Märtyrer von Cordova und das Verhältnis der Mozaraber zum Islam (nach den Schriften des Speraindeo, Eulogius und Alvar)*, Münster, 1958
C. Sage, *Paul Albar of Córdoba. Studies on his life and writings*, Washington DC, 1943, pp. 1-183

WORKS ON CHRISTIAN-MUSLIM RELATIONS

Vita Eulogii, 'Life of Eulogius'

DATE 854
ORIGINAL LANGUAGE Latin

DESCRIPTION
This is a hagiographical treatment of the life and death of Eulogius of Cordova, Alvarus' friend and co-apologist for the so-called 'martyrs of Cordova'. Eulogius was executed by the Muslim authorities on 11 March 859, for harboring a female convert from Islam to Christianity and encouraging her apostasy. Alvarus followed the well-established conventions of the *passiones*, which described the deaths of Christian martyrs of the Roman period.

SIGNIFICANCE

Though written with a typically apologetic intent, this work provides an important context for Eulogius' involvement in the events surrounding the religiously-motivated executions in Cordova in the 850s.

MANUSCRIPTS

No longer extant. Ambrosio Morales claimed to have worked from two manuscript copies when preparing his edition of Eulogius' works (1574).

EDITIONS AND TRANSLATIONS

P. Herrera Roldán (ed.), *San Eulogio de Córdoba. Obras completas*, Madrid, 2005 (trans.)
Gil, *CSM* i, pp. 331-43
Sage, *Paul Albar of Córdoba*, pp. 185-214 (trans; the *passio* portion of the *Vita* was reprinted in O.R. Constable (ed.), *Medieval Iberia. Readings from Christian, Muslim, and Jewish sources*, Philadelphia, 1997, pp. 51-55)
PL 115, cols 705-20
A. Morales, *Divi Eulogii Cordubensis Opera*, Alcala, 1574

STUDIES

Coope, *The martyrs of Córdoba*, pp. 35-54
Wolf, *Christian martyrs in Muslim Spain*, pp. 551-61
E. Colbert, *The martyrs of Córdoba (850-859). A study of the sources*, Washington DC, 1962, pp. 174-83, 349-53
Sage, *Paul Albar of Córdoba*, pp. 185-89
J. Pérez de Urbel, *S. Eulogio de Córdoba*, Madrid, 1942

Indiculus luminosus, 'A shining declaration'

DATE 854
ORIGINAL LANGUAGE Latin

DESCRIPTION

Like the treatises of Eulogius of Cordova, the first half of the *Indiculus luminosus* seeks to defend the 'Cordovan martyrs' of the 850s from criticism by fellow Cordovan Christians. The second and more interesting half is devoted to biblical exegesis, divided between Daniel's prophecies about the Antichrist and Job's descriptions of Leviathan and Behemoth. In both cases, Alvarus uses his commentaries to disparage Islam and its prophet.

SIGNIFICANCE

Alvarus' exegetical assault on Islam and Muḥammad is the earliest work of this type to appear in the Latin west.

MANUSCRIPTS

MS Cordova, Archive of the Cathedral/Mezquita – BC Cordubensis I (10th c.)

EDITIONS AND TRANSLATIONS

León Delgado, *Alvaro de Córdoba y la polémica contra el Islam*

Gil, *CSM* i, pp. 270-315

PL 121, cols 513-56

STUDIES

León Delgado, *Álvaro de Córdoba y la polémica contra el Islam*

K.B. Wolf, 'Muhammad as Antichrist in ninth-century Córdoba', in M.D. Meyerson and E.D. English (eds), *Christians, Muslims, and Jews in medieval and early modern Spain. Interaction and cultural change*, Notre Dame, 1999, 3-19

Colbert, *The martyrs of Córdoba (850-859)*, pp. 266-304

Kenneth B. Wolf 2007

Al-Iskāfī

Abū Jaʿfar Muḥammad ibn ʿAbdallāh al-Iskāfī

DATE OF BIRTH Unknown, probably mid-8th c.
PLACE OF BIRTH Iskāf
DATE OF DEATH 854
PLACE OF DEATH Baghdad

BIOGRAPHY

Al-Iskāfī's name goes back to the town of Iskāf, between Baghdad and Wāsiṭ. His family originated in Samarqand. He was a Baghdad Muʿtazilī, and a follower of Jaʿfar ibn Ḥarb (d. 850), who encouraged him in his studies contrary to his parents' wishes. He was greatly admired by the Caliph al-Muʿtaṣim (maybe for the ingenuity that is exemplified in his arguments against Christianity, as is shown below), who urged him to promote Muʿtazilī teachings. He lived to a great age.

Al-Iskāfī's numerous works reveal a dedicated Muʿtazilī with a particular interest in the problem of suffering. They include defenses of the key Muʿtazilī doctrine about the Qurʾān (*al-Makhlūq, ʿalā l-mujbira*, 'What is created, against the determinists', *Kitāb ʿalā man ankara khalq al-Qurʾān*, 'Against whoever denies the createdness of the Qurʾān), a defense of the transcendence of God (*Radd ʿalā l-mushabbiha*, 'Refutation of the anthropomorphists'), and one on the problem of the fate of babies in the afterlife (*Kitāb ibṭāl qawl man qāla bi-taʿdhīb al-aṭfāl*, 'Disproving the teachings of those who uphold the punishment of infants'). His only surviving work is *Naqḍ al-ʿUthmāniyya*, 'Refutation of the work on ʿUthmān', a rebuttal of al-Jāḥiẓ's composition in favor of the Caliph ʿUthmān, and he was known for his views about the status of ʿAlī among the Prophet's Companions – in fact, al-Khayyāṭ (*Intiṣār*, p. 76), calls him a leading Shīʿī of the Muʿtazila.

Al-Iskāfī was particularly remembered for his teaching about certain attributes of God such as sight, hearing and generosity, and for his observations about human action and its moral consequences. He regarded the sufferings of hell as a sign of God's mercy because they deterred humans from unbelief.

MAIN SOURCES OF INFORMATION

Primary

Abū l-Ḥusayn al-Khayyāṭ, *Kitāb al-intiṣār*, ed. and French trans. A. Nader, Beirut, 1957, pp. 68-69, 74, 76

Abū l-Ḥasan al-Ashʿarī, *Maqālāt al-Islāmiyyīn*, ed. H. Ritter, Istanbul, 1930, pp. 157, 178, 202, 230, 231, 244, 506-07, 537

Ibn al-Nadīm, *Fihrist*, p. 213

Ibn al-Murtaḍā, *Kitāb ṭabaqāt al-Muʿtazila*, ed. S. Diwald-Wilzer, Beirut, 1988, p. 78

Secondary

Van Ess, *TG* iv, pp. 77-87, vi, pp. 301-12

(Editors), art. 'al-Iskāfī, Abū Djaʿfar Muḥammad b. ʿAbd Allāh', in *EI2*

Watt, *Formative period*, 1973, pp. 224, 238, 241-42

WORKS ON CHRISTIAN-MUSLIM RELATIONS

Radd ʿalā l-Naṣārā, 'Refutation of the Christians'

DATE 1st half of the 9th c.
ORIGINAL LANGUAGE Arabic

DESCRIPTION

This work, of which the title 'Refutation of the Christians' is unlikely to be original, is lost. According to ʿAbd al-Jabbār (*Tathbīt dalāʾil al-nubuwwa*, ed. ʿA.-K. ʿUthmān, 2 vols, Beirut, 1966, i, p. 148; cf. p. 198), it may, together with a number of other works, have referred to the popular Christian belief that God took Mary in the way that a man takes a woman as wife.

It may also have contained two arguments quoted from al-Iskāfī by Abū l-Qāsim al-Kaʿbī l-Balkhī (d. 931), *Awāʾil al-adilla*, excerpts of which are preserved by the Christian Ibn Zurʿa, *Maqāla fī l-tathlīth* (in P. Sbath, *Vingt traités philosophiques et apologétiques d'auteurs arabes chrétiens du IXe au XIVe siècle*, Cairo, 1929, p. 65). In these, al-Iskāfī argues that, if God has a Son, this Son must himself have a son if he too is divine, and that if Jesus was both divine and human and Christians worship him, then they must be committing the sin of worshipping a human being. Arguments of this kind are repeated by ʿAbd al-Jabbār in the name of 'his masters' (*al-Mughnī fī abwāb al-tawḥīd wa-l-ʿadl*, v, ed. M.M. al-Khuḍayrī, Cairo, 1958, p. 86).

SIGNIFICANCE

The work appears to have contained arguments that were part of the common stock of polemic.

MANUSCRIPTS —

EDITIONS AND TRANSLATIONS —

STUDIES —

David Thomas 2007

Abū l-Faḍl ʿAlī ibn Rabban al-Naṣrānī

DATE OF BIRTH Unknown, mid/late 8th c.?
PLACE OF BIRTH Unknown, probably Iraq
DATE OF DEATH Unknown, early/mid-9th c.?
PLACE OF DEATH Unknown, probably Iraq

BIOGRAPHY

According to the (now inaccessible) manuscript of his refutation of Islam, Abū l-Faḍl ʿAlī ibn Rabban al-Naṣrānī ('the Christian') served as secretary to the great East-Syrian ('Nestorian') Catholicos Timothy (q.v.), who was in office from 780 to 823. His name 'Ibn Rabban' ('son of our master') indicates that his father was a recognized teacher of the community. Landron (*Chrétiens et musulmans en Irak*, p. 60) has considered the possibility of identifying him with the well-known convert to Islam and Muslim apologist ʿAlī ibn Rabban al-Ṭabarī (q.v.), but this seems unlikely: the latter's *kunya* was Abū l-Ḥasan, not Abū l-Faḍl. Moreover, ʿAlī l-Ṭabarī spent his early life in Ṭabaristān and only came to Iraq in the 840s.

MAIN SOURCES OF INFORMATION

Primary —

Secondary
B. Landron, *Chrétiens et musulmans en Irak*, Paris, 1994, pp. 59-60
Graf, *GCAL* ii, p. 118
Sbath, *Fihris* i, p. 54

WORKS ON CHRISTIAN-MUSLIM RELATIONS

Kitāb al-burhān, 'The proof'

DATE Unknown, early/mid-9th c.?
ORIGINAL LANGUAGE Arabic

DESCRIPTION
According to Sbath (*Fihris* i, p. 54), the work is a refutation of Islam in three parts, the first concentrating on the Prophet Muḥammad, the second on the Qurʾān, and the third on the Islamic faith in general.

SIGNIFICANCE

We cannot say much about the significance of the work as long as a copy is not available. On the basis of Sbath's description, however, one is struck by the directness with which ʿAlī goes about his polemical task.

MANUSCRIPTS

MS Aleppo, Rizq Allāh Bāsīl Collection (1086/7) (inaccessible MS in a private collection; see Sbath, *Fihris* i, p. 54, no. 418)

EDITIONS AND TRANSLATIONS —

STUDIES —

Mark N. Swanson 2008

Vienna, Papyrus Erzherzog Rainer – Inv. Ar. Pap. Nr. 10.000

Unknown author

DATE OF BIRTH 8th/9th c.
PLACE OF BIRTH Unknown
DATE OF DEATH Not later than 9th c.
PLACE OF DEATH Unknown

BIOGRAPHY

Nothing is known of the author of an extremely fragmentary text known from a single double leaf of papyrus, dated to the first half of the 9th century.

MAIN SOURCES OF INFORMATION

Primary —

Secondary —

WORKS ON CHRISTIAN-MUSLIM RELATIONS

Title unknown

DATE Probably 1st half of 9th c.
ORIGINAL LANGUAGE Arabic

DESCRIPTION

The fragmentary text in our possession is part of a disputation, in which a Christian apologist responds to objections and questions from a Muslim interlocutor. The best preserved of these objections has to do with the Trinity: how can one believe in three divine hypostases without introducing plurality into God? A dilemma-question is also preserved: was Christ God from before his birth, or only afterwards? Either answer leads to conclusions unacceptable to the Muslim controversialist: either a birth or a beginning in time must be predicated of God.

Later in the text, we find the Christian using Genesis 26:4 and Psalm 115:16 as *testimonia* bearing witness to Christ.

Graf dates the unique manuscript to the first half of the 9th century; the text cannot have been written very much earlier.

SIGNIFICANCE

This minor text provides an early Arabic example of a disputation text in which a Muslim controversialist's challenges to Christian doctrine are quoted in full. Even in its fragmentary state, it preserves features characteristic of early Christian-Muslim controversy: the Muslim makes the accusation that the Christian Trinity unacceptably introduces plurality into God; the Muslim poses a dilemma-question regarding Christ's divinity; the Christian employs Old Testament *testimonia* in an argument intended to be convincing to his Muslim interlocutor.

MANUSCRIPTS

P.Vind.Inv.A.P. 10000 (contemporary designation of fragments preserved in Vienna, in the Papyrussammlung of the Österreichische Nationalbibliothek; formerly Vienna, Papyrus Erzherzog Rainer – Inv. Ar. Pap. Nr. 10.000)

EDITIONS AND TRANSLATIONS

G. Graf, 'Christlich-arabische Texte. Zwei Disputationen zwischen Muslîmen und Christen', in F. Bilabel and A. Grohmann, *Griechische, koptische und arabische Texte zur Religion und religiösen Literatur in Ägyptens Spätzeit*, Heidelberg, 1934, 1-31, pp. 24-31 (edition of the fragments with German trans.)

STUDIES

Graf, *GCAL* ii, 26

Graf, 'Christliche-arabische Texte', 24-31

Mark N. Swanson 2008

Ḥafṣ al-Fard

Abū ʿAmr (Abū Yaḥyā) Ḥafṣ al-Fard

DATE OF BIRTH Unknown, mid-8th c.
PLACE OF BIRTH Possibly Egypt
DATE OF DEATH Unknown, mid-9th c.
PLACE OF DEATH Possibly Egypt

BIOGRAPHY

Ḥafṣ al-Fard was probably born in Egypt, and is linked with Egypt at certain points in his life. He traveled to Iraq as a young man, and studied in Basra under Abū l-Hudhayl al-ʿAllāf (d. between 840 and 850) (q.v.) and others. He also became known to a number of leading scholars, including Abū ʿUthmān al-Jāḥiẓ (q.v.), who mentions him in his *Kitāb al-ḥayawān*. He was regarded as Abū l-Hudhayl's intellectual equal, but at some point, presumably before the latter's move to Baghdad in 818-19, he broke with him. This split may have been caused by Ḥafṣ's rejection of key Muʿtazilī teachings, and his acceptance of views put forward by Ḍirār ibn ʿAmr (q.v.), with whom he is often linked in later Muslim tradition.

In Egypt, Ḥafṣ is known to have disputed with the great jurisprudent al-Shāfiʿī, which must have been between 814, when al-Shāfiʿī went there, and his death in 820. In Egypt he also participated in a debate between the Zaydī Imām al-Qāsim ibn Ibrāhīm (d. 860) (q.v.) and a Coptic Christian, which would be between 815 and 826, when al-Qāsim, a native of Medina, was living there.

Ḥafṣ is thought to have died in Egypt. No year is given for his death, though it must have been sometime towards the middle of the 9th century.

Of Ḥafṣ's six works listed by Ibn al-Nadīm (van Ess, *TG* v, p. 252), none has survived. Their titles give some indication of his theological stance, for as well as a general work on theology, *Kitāb al-tawḥīd*, 'Divine unity', he also wrote two works about the Muʿtazilī doctrine of the created Qurʾān, which he evidently opposed, *Kitāb al-abwāb fī l-makhlūq*, 'Chapters on the created', and *Kitāb fī l-makhlūq ʿalā Abī l-Hudhayl*, 'On the created against Abū l-Hudhayl', and an attack against the Muʿtazila, *Kitāb al-radd ʿalā l-Muʿtazila*, 'Refutation of the Muʿtazila'.

Ḥafṣ followed Ḍirār ibn ʿAmr's teaching that the human is not free to perform actions, though he was not remembered for any major contributions to theological thought: al-Ashʿarī cites views he shared with others about the mode in which believers will see God in the afterlife, and about atoms and attributes.

His views attracted refutations from the Muʿtazilīs Abū l-Hudhayl, Bishr ibn al-Muʿtamir (q.v.) and al-Iskāfī (q.v.).

MAIN SOURCES OF INFORMATION

Primary

Abū l-Ḥusayn al-Khayyāṭ, *Kitāb al-intiṣār*, ed. and trans. A. Nader, Beirut, 1957, p. 98

Abū l-Ḥasan al-Ashʿarī, *Maqālāt al-Islāmiyyīn*, ed. H. Ritter, Istanbul, 1930, pp. 216, 317-18, 407-8, 515

Ibn al-Nadīm, *Fihrist*, pp. 229-30

Secondary

Van Ess, *TG* ii, pp. 729-35; v, p. 252

Watt, *Formative period*, pp. 202-03, 248

(Editors), art. 'Ḥafṣ al-Fard, Abū ʿAmr or Abū Yaḥyā', in *EI2*

WORKS ON CHRISTIAN-MUSLIM RELATIONS

Kitāb ʿalā l-Naṣārā, 'Against the Christians'

DATE Unknown

ORIGINAL LANGUAGE Arabic

DESCRIPTION

The work is mentioned by Ibn al-Nadīm, *Fihrist*, p. 230. It presumably contained arguments like those in similar works written in this period.

SIGNIFICANCE

It may have contributed arguments to later Muslim refutations.

MANUSCRIPTS —

EDITIONS AND TRANSLATIONS —

STUDIES —

David Thomas 2007

The Refutation of the Christians

Unknown author

DATE OF BIRTH Unknown
PLACE OF BIRTH Unknown
DATE OF DEATH Unknown
PLACE OF DEATH Unknown

BIOGRAPHY —

MAIN SOURCES OF INFORMATION

Primary —

Secondary —

WORKS ON CHRISTIAN-MUSLIM RELATIONS

Kitāb al-radd ʿalā l-Naṣārā, 'The Refutation of the Christians'

DATE Unknown, perhaps 8th or 9th c.
ORIGINAL LANGUAGE Arabic

DESCRIPTION

This anonymous *Refutation of the Christians* is only known indirectly through the Melkite apology for Christianity entitled *Masāʾil wa-ajwiba ʿaqliyya wa-ilāhiyya* or 'Questions and answers, rational and divine' (q.v.), which is to be found in MS Sinai – Ar. 434, fols 171r-181v. At the opening of this treatise, the author says that he wrote it in response to three critical questions about Christianity put to him by an eminent shaykh from Jerusalem. The shaykh had found these questions in a work with the title *Kitāb al-radd ʿalā l-Naṣārā*.

The questions are: 'Is the eternal Being one of the hypostases?'; 'What verification do you claim for the union [of the human and the divine in Christ]?'; 'What proof is there for the veracity of the claim of verification [of the union of divine and human] from the actions of Christ (and) from what might be affirmed on the basis of what is comparable to the claim?' (Griffith, 'Answers', pp. 286-87). The Melkite apologist characterizes these questions as a hostile attempt 'to confound and to frighten the simple-minded among us, who are not conversant with the Christian sciences of divinity' (Griffith, 'Answers', pp. 284-85).

As Nasrallah and Griffith note, it would be interesting to determine whether this anti-Christian treatise can be identified as one of those of the same name known from elsewhere. Unfortunately, however, almost all the treatises with this title from the first centuries of Islam are lost. Of the surviving works, none appear to contain these questions expressed in the same wording (Griffith, 'Answers', pp. 285-86).

SIGNIFICANCE

This unknown treatise is worth drawing attention to not so much for its contents as for the historical circumstances reflected in the opening of the Melkite response. An intriguing point in the introduction of the Melkite work is the fact that the apologist accuses the Muslim author of the anti-Christian work of trying to undermine the faith of the common people among the Christians. If the Melkite author is right in claiming that this refutation, despite its inclusion of technical terms such as 'hypostatic union', was meant to address a lay audience, it raises the question of what extent polemical works were read outside academic circles.

Furthermore, we may assume that the author of the *Masāʾil wa-ajwiba ʿaqliyya wa-ilāhiyya* was giving a real report of events, or at least did not invent a story that would strike readers as most unusual, when he wrote that a shaykh from Jerusalem had had access to a certain *Refutation of the Christians*, drew some questions from it, and then sent these to him. This shows that polemical arguments were exchanged not only during face-to-face encounters but also in a written form. What is most striking here is the geographical aspect. Most of the early works with the title *Radd ʿalā l-Naṣārā*, 'Refutation of the Christians', were written by Muʿtazilīs in Iraq. An exception is the work of al-Qāsim ibn Ibrāhīm (q.v.), who probably wrote in Egypt. No early works with this title are known from Palestine. So perhaps the shaykh owned a work that had been imported from elsewhere, or perhaps this work was written in Palestine after all, by someone familiar with the contemporary anti-Christian discourse in Iraq.

Either way, the introduction of the *Masāʾil wa-ajwiba ʿaqliyya wa-ilāhiyya* gives us a glimpse of a historical reality that can also be inferred from the actual content of early polemical works. This is that the theological terminology and arguments of early *kalām* traveled widely and became standard among Arabic-speaking Christians and Muslims in all the regions of the Middle East.

MANUSCRIPTS —

EDITIONS AND TRANSLATIONS —

STUDIES

S.H. Griffith, 'Answers for the shaykh: A "Melkite" Arabic text from Sinai and the doctrines of the Trinity and the Incarnation in "Arab orthodox" apologetics', in E. Grypeou, M.N. Swanson and D. Thomas (eds), *The encounter of Eastern Christianity with early Islam*, Leiden, 2006, 277-309

J. Nasrallah, 'Dialogue islamo-chrétien. À propos de publications récentes', *REI* 46 (1978) 121-51, p. 143

Barbara Roggema 2008

Masāʾil wa-ajwiba ʿaqliyya wa-ilāhiyya

Unknown author

DATE OF BIRTH Unknown, possibly 8th/9th c.
PLACE OF BIRTH Unknown, but later had connections with Jerusalem
DATE OF DEATH Unknown, possibly 9th c.
PLACE OF DEATH Unknown, but possibly in or near Jerusalem

BIOGRAPHY

The unknown author was a Melkite priest and monk who wrote an Arabic apology for the Christian faith (preserved in a single manuscript at Mt Sinai) in response to the questions of a Muslim *shaykh* of Jerusalem, possibly in the 9th century.

MAIN SOURCES OF INFORMATION

Primary
MS Sinai – Ar. 434, fols 171r-181v

Secondary —

WORKS ON CHRISTIAN-MUSLIM RELATIONS

Masāʾil wa-ajwiba ʿaqliyya wa-ilāhiyya, 'Questions and answers, rational and divine'. Modern title: 'Answers for the *shaykh*'

DATE Unknown; late 8th- and 9th-c. dates have been suggested
ORIGINAL LANGUAGE Arabic

DESCRIPTION

'Questions and answers, rational and divine' is a fairly short treatise occupying 11 folios of the unique manuscript in which it is found. In it, an anonymous Melkite monk responds to three questions of an unnamed Muslim *shaykh* in the city of Jerusalem, who had gathered them from a (yet unidentified) work entitled *al-Radd ʿalā l-Naṣārā*, 'The Refutation of the Christians'. The three questions address three major areas of Christian-Muslim controversy: the Trinity; the union of divinity and humanity in Christ; and the evidence for the truth of the Christian religion and the divinity of Christ. The author proposes to respond to each question in a double fashion, first from reason and then from scripture. The arguments 'from reason' consist of a variety of theological considerations, along with rationally accessible analogies for the Trinity and the Incarnation, while the arguments *min al-sharʿ*, from written tradition, consist of Old Testament *testimonia*, some New Testament passages (from *al-Injīl*, 'the Gospel', or from *al-ḥawāriyyūn*, 'the disciples'), as well as passages from 'your Book' or 'your Qurʾān'.

In the response to the third question, a number of intriguing references are made: to a book *al-Shāmūth* (*Shmôth*?) of the Rabbinical Jews; to a Jewish group known as the ʿĪsāwiyya; to *al-Sabʿa aḥjār* of Hermes Trismegistos; and to a number of Greek sages, including Hippocrates, Socrates and Parmenides.

R. Haddad has suggested 780 as the approximate date of composition (Haddad, *Trinité divine*, 38), but a 9th century date is perhaps more probable (Griffith, 'Answers', pp. 307-8). The single known copy of the work was made in 1139.

SIGNIFICANCE

The text is an important addition to a small collection of Arabic Melkite treatises from the first generations of Christian apologists who wrote in Arabic. While it cannot be said to be tightly organized (although lacunae in the text and the careless handwriting of the unique manuscript's scribe may mask something of the author's intended structure), it is an interesting repository of ideas – sometimes stated very briefly and without full explanation – for the defense of Christian doctrine in the *Dār al-Islām*. Its use of Old Testament *testimonia* is worthy of note and of comparison with other Christian apologies of the time, while the frequency with which it cites the Qur'an (with what may be seen as an implicit admission of this scripture's authority) is remarkable in a Christian text of this period (Griffith, 'Answers', pp. 302-4).

MANUSCRIPTS

MS Sinai – ar. 434, fols 171r-181v (1137-39)

EDITIONS AND TRANSLATIONS

ʿĪd Ṣalāḥ Saʿd (Eid Salah), *Taḥqīq makhṭūṭ Sin. Ar. 434:* Masāʾil wa-ajwiba ʿaqliyya wa-ilāhiyya *li-muʾallif malakī ghayr maʿrūf*, Cairo, 1994 (B.Th. thesis, Evangelical Theological Seminary in Cairo; Salah's edition of the text will be published with an English trans. by Mark N. Swanson)

STUDIES

S.H. Griffith, *The church in the shadow of the mosque*, Princeton NJ, 2008, p. 83

S.H. Griffith, '*Answers for the shaykh*: A "Melkite" Arabic text from Sinai and the doctrines of the Trinity and the Incarnation in "Arab orthodox" apologetics', in E. Grypeou, M.N. Swanson and D. Thomas (eds), *The encounter of eastern Christianity with early Islam*, Leiden, 2006, 277-309

M.N. Swanson, 'Beyond prooftexting. Approaches to the Qurʾān in some early Arabic Christian apologies', *MW* 88 (1998) 297-319, pp. 301-2

Hoyland, *Seeing Islam*, pp. 504-5

Eid Salah, *Taḥqīq*

R. Haddad, *La Trinité divine chez les théologiens arabes (750-1050)*, Paris, 1985, p. 38

Eid Salah and Mark N. Swanson 2007

Isaac the Presbyter

DATE OF BIRTH Unknown, perhaps mid- to late 8th c.
PLACE OF BIRTH Unknown, perhaps in the region of the Fayyūm
DATE OF DEATH Unknown, perhaps early to mid-9th c.
PLACE OF DEATH Unknown, but probably at the monastery of Qalamūn

BIOGRAPHY

We know nothing of this author other than what we can gather from his *Life of Samuel of Qalamūn*: that he was a monk and priest of the monastery of Qalamūn, who wrote the *Life* some 'four generations' after the saint's death (c. 695). While a 'generation' is not a particularly precise measure of time (25-40 years?), we can probably date the text to the end of the 8th century or first half of the 9th century.

MAIN SOURCES OF INFORMATION

Primary

A. Alcock, *The life of Samuel of Kalamun, by Isaac the Presbyter*, Warminster, 1983

Secondary —

WORKS ON CHRISTIAN-MUSLIM RELATIONS

Pbios auō tpolutia mpenpetouaab neiōt ettaiēu nanankhōritēs auō narkhēmatritēs (sic) *apa Samouēl peiōt ntkinonia etouaab ntparthenos mptoou nkalamōn hmptosh piom*, 'The Life and conduct of our holy and revered father, the anchorite and archimandrite Apa Samuel, the father of the holy community of the Virgin of the mountain of Kalamon in the province of Fayyūm'. Abbreviated title: 'The Life of Samuel of Qalamūn'

DATE Late 8th or 1st half of 9th c.
ORIGINAL LANGUAGE Coptic

DESCRIPTION
The Life of Samuel of Qalamūn tells the story of the saint from his upbringing by wealthy and pious parents in lower Egypt, through his tumultuous career as a monk and organizer of a monastic community at Qalamūn, until his death at the age of 98 on 8 Koiahk (4 December), c. 695. The text, we are told, was written for recitation to the community on the day of the saint's commemoration.

Samuel initially earned his title 'Confessor' by steadfastly rejecting the Chalcedonian Christological formula central to the ecclesiastical policy of the Byzantine Emperor Heraclius (610-641) and his agent Cyrus (appointed archbishop of Alexandria in 631) during the decade prior to the Arab conquest of Egypt (c. 641). When Cyrus sent a military detachment from Alexandria to the monastic settlements of Scetis with a demand that the monks subscribe to what the text calls 'the Tome of Leo', Samuel voiced their resistance and tore up a copy, whereupon he was cruelly beaten and driven out of the region. He and a few disciples made their way south to the monastery of Naqlūn in the Fayyūm, but after a year of peace Cyrus attempted to impose his will on the monks of the Fayyūm as well. Samuel was arrested, beaten, and again driven to the south. Eventually, he was guided to a grove of date palms and a sand-filled church in Qalamūn, where he was to establish the monastery that eventually came to bear his name.

Shortly after his arrival in Qalamūn, Samuel fell into the hands of 'barbarians' (or 'Berbers', also referred to in the Coptic text as 'Masgx', cf. the 'Mazices' of Latin texts and inscriptions), who took him into slavery for three years. Again, despite maltreatment, he remained true to his monastic confession, refusing both his master's sun-worship and his attempts to marry him to a slave girl. Eventually he won his captors' gratitude and reverence by performing miracles of healing – including the cure of his master's wife. Granted his freedom, Samuel returned to Qalamūn where he spent more than half a century building up a thriving monastic community.

It has been noted that, in spite of the fact that Samuel lived for half a century beyond the Arab conquest of Egypt, Muslims are nowhere explicitly mentioned in the text of the *Life*. Vecoli ('Samuel') has recently argued, however, that the entire episode dealing with the Masgx and Samuel's captivity should be read as an exhortation to Egyptian Christians under Islamic rule. Samuel resisted pressure to join in his master's worship (which was apparently monotheistic and involved prostration in particular directions at particular times of day – possibly an allusion to Islamic practice), and refused to compromise his rigorous standards of sexual purity. At the same, time, however, Samuel and his friend John of Scetis (another slave) 'performed the duty of their service well and obeyed their masters according to the flesh in every command', in accordance with 1 Peter 2:18 (Alcock, *Life*, p. 92). Samuel delivered members of his captors' community from their diseases and won their esteem without, it should be noted, converting them to Christianity. Each point would have had relevance for Christians in late 8th- or 9th-century Egypt, as they sought ways of living with Christian integrity under the rule of Muslims, between the extremes of conversion on the one hand and martyrdom on the other.

SIGNIFICANCE

The Life of Samuel of Qalamūn serves as a reminder that inter-religious considerations may lie behind many texts in which the religious Other is not explicitly named: an Islamic *kalām* text may have Christian Trinitarian or Christological doctrine as an unstated, inadmissible limit; a Christian hagiographical text such as that described here may present models of behavior from long-ago or far-away settings, yet be full of practical wisdom for the life and witness of Christians within the *Dār al-Islām*.

The Life of Samuel of Qalamūn was translated from Coptic into Arabic (perhaps by means of a Bohairic recension; Alcock, 'Arabic Life', 382-83). A précis of the story (including the episode of barbarian captivity) is found in the *Synaxarion* of the Coptic Orthodox Church, and is thus read liturgically with great regularity. From Arabic, the work was translated into Ethiopic.

MANUSCRIPTS

1. Coptic MSS

The one complete Coptic MS is:

MS New York, Pierpont Morgan – 578, fols 1-68 (Sahidic with some Fayyumic features)

For a list of fragments (of another Sahidic recension, plus two Bohairic fragments), see Alcock, *Life*, pp. vii-xi, and Lucchesi's review, cols 89-90.

2. Arabic MSS

MS Wādī l-Naṭrūn, Monastery of St Macarius – Hag. 26 (Zanetti 392), fols 2-37(14th c.)

MS Wādī l-Naṭrūn, Monastery of al-Baramūs – (dated 1582-3; used by Yūsuf Ḥabīb)

MS Cairo, Church of Saints Sergius and Bacchus – Theol. 17 (serial no. 120), fols 3v-37v (17th c.)

MS Cairo, Franciscan Center of Christian Oriental Studies – 140, pp. 7-61 (1945)

Abuliff, 'Samuele', p. 929, also mentions a manuscript at Dayr al-Suryān.

3. Ethiopic MSS

MS Halle, Universitäts- und Landesbibliothek – Yb 4°7 (14th-15th c.)

MS BL – or. 689 (15th c.)

MS BL – or. 687-699 (17th-18th c.)

EDITIONS AND TRANSLATIONS

A. Alcock, 'The Arabic life of Anbā Samaw'īl of Qalamūn', *Le Muséon* 109 (1996) 321-45, 111 (1998) 377-404 (edition and trans. of the Arabic version from the Franciscan Center MS)

E. Lucchesi, review of Alcock, *The life of Samuel of Kalamun*, in *Bibliotheca Orientalis* 46 (1989) cols 89-96

A. Alcock, *The life of Samuel of Kalamun, by Isaac the Presbyter* (edition and English trans. of Pierpont Morgan 578 and of fragments of another Sahidic codex, with notes and indices)

T. Orlandi, *Vite di monaci copti*, Rome, 1984, pp. 221-85 (Italian trans. of the Sahidic text from Pierpont Morgan 578)

F.M. Esteves Pereira, *Vida do Abba Samuel do mosteiro do Kalamon*, Lisbon, 1894 (edition and trans. of the Ethiopic version from two MSS)

STUDIES

F. Vecoli, 'Samuel de Qalamoun et la fin de la *parrhèsia* dans l'hagiographie égyptienne', *Proche-Orient Chrétien* 57 (2007) 7-23

Wadi Abuliff, art. 'Samuele il Confessore di Kalamon', in J. Nadal Cañellas and S. Virgulin (eds), *Enciclopedia dei santi. Le chiese orientali*, Rome, 1998-99 (with very extensive bibliography in Arabic as well as European languages)

U. Zanetti, 'Notes sur la Vie de S. Samuel de Kalamon. Versions arabe et éthiopienne – Deux citations de la "prière de la fraction"', *AB* 115 (1997) 147-58 (important observations on the Arabic and Ethiopic recensions)

A. Alcock, art. 'Samū'īl of Qalamūn, Saint', in *The Coptic Encyclopaedia*, ed. A.S. Atiya, 8 vols, New York, 1991

Y. Ḥabīb, *Al-qiddīs anbā Ṣamū'īl al-mu'tarif wa-adyurat al-Fayyūm*, Cairo, 1970

J. Simon, 'Saint Samuel de Kalamon et son monastère dans la littérature éthiopienne', *Aethiopica* 1 (1933) 36-40

P. van Cauwenbergh, *Étude sur les moines d'Égypte depuis le concile de Chalcédoine (451) jusqu'à l'invasion arabe (640)*, Paris, 1914, pp. 39-50, 88-122

Mark N. Swanson 2008

ʿAlī l-Ṭabarī

Abū l-Ḥasan ʿAlī ibn Sahl Rabban al-Ṭabarī

DATE OF BIRTH c. 780
PLACE OF BIRTH Merv
DATE OF DEATH c. 860
PLACE OF DEATH Samarra or Baghdad

BIOGRAPHY

ʿAlī l-Ṭabarī was the son of a physician whose pre-eminence earned him the Syriac title *Rabban*, 'our master'. This has often been mistaken for a Jewish title, but the evidence of ʿAlī's works, and the fact that in his *Kitāb al-dīn wa-l-dawla* (ed. Mingana, p. 124) he refers to his father's brother Abū Zakkār Yaḥyā ibn Nuʿmān (q.v.) as a Christian scholar, identify him clearly as from a Christian family.

ʿAlī says that his father worked in Merv, and he was presumably born there. He himself is first mentioned in the service of Māzyār ibn Qārin, the governor of Ṭabaristān, and was a loyal supporter through the years when Māzyār rose against the central authorities. When the governor was defeated and executed in 840, ʿAlī may have fled to Rayy, but soon afterwards he entered the caliphal service at Samarra, and remained a servant of successive caliphs through the rest of his life.

At some point he converted from his East-Syrian Christianity to Islam. Ibn al-Nadīm (*Fihrist*, p. 354, where he is called Ibn Rabal; cf. p. 378, where he is named ʿAlī ibn Zayd al-Naṣrānī) says this was under al-Muʿtaṣim, and thus before 842. But the comments which ʿAlī makes in his *Kitāb al-dīn wa-l-dawla* (ed. Mingana, p. 144) about al-Mutawakkil's help towards him suggest that he converted during this caliph's reign. In his medical work, *Firdaws al-ḥikma*, 'Paradise of wisdom', which he says he completed in 850, he mentions al-Mutawakkil with civility but none of the warmth of the *Kitāb al-dīn wa-l-dawla*. So it could be that he converted after this date.

In *Kitāb al-dīn wa-l-dawla* (ed. Mingana, pp. 86, 93), ʿAlī mentions his *Radd ʿalā l-Naṣārā*. This is a work which he explicitly wrote as a retraction from Christianity, and he remarks at the beginning that he remained a Christian for the first 70 years of his life (Khalifé and Kutsch, 'Ar-Radd ʿalā-n-Naṣārā', 119). If he meant this literally, he provides an important item for dating, for since the *Kitāb al-dīn wa-l-dawla* must have been written after 847, ʿAlī cannot have converted much earlier without having grown improbably old before writing this work (the 13th-century Copt al-Ṣafī ibn al-ʿAssāl thought he was senile when he converted; Samir, 'Réponse', p. 283). This would give 850 as the approximate date for the *Radd ʿalā l-Naṣārā*, and a few years later for the *Kitāb al-dīn wa-l-dawla*, and it indicates that he was born in about 780. On this computation he must have died in about 860, when he would have reached 80.

Some scholars do not take this important date in the *Radd* literally, but see it as a generalization for 'many' (Adang, *Muslim writers*, p. 23, n. 1). If this is so, ʿAlī would not necessarily have been so old when he converted, and a date around 810 has been given for his birth. This, however, is not entirely free from problems, since he would then have been only 20 when he entered Māzyār ibn Qārin's service, and would have been entrusted as a relatively young man with the major negotiating responsibilities that the historian Abū Jaʿfar Muḥammad ibn Jarīr al-Ṭabarī says the governor laid upon him.

Apart from his two anti-Christian works, ʿAlī is known mainly for scientific writings. Of these the *Firdaws al-ḥikma* was very influential, and was particularly revered by the historian and exegete Abū Jaʿfar Muḥammad ibn Jarīr al-Ṭabarī, who is supposed to have taken down his own copy from ʿAlī's dictation.

MAIN SOURCES OF INFORMATION

Primary

al-Ṭabarī, *Taʾrīkh*, iii, pp. 1276-77, 1283, 1293

Ibn al-Nadīm, *Fihrist*, pp. 354, 378

Ibn al-Qifṭī, *Taʾrīkh al-ḥukamāʾ*, ed. J. Lippert, Leipzig, 1903, p. 231

Secondary

B. Scarcia Amoretti, 'Tratti tipologici delle élites nel III secolo dell'egira. A proposito di ʿAlī ibn Rabban al-Ṭabarī e del suo *Kitāb al-dīn wa ʾl-dawla*', in V. Ruggieri and L. Pieralli (eds), *EUKOSMIA. Studi miscellanei per il 75° di Vincenzo Poggi S.J.*, Soveria Mannelli, 2003, 83-102, pp. 83-95

C. Adang, *Muslim writers on Judaism and the Hebrew Bible, from Ibn Rabban to Ibn Hazm*, Leiden, 1996, pp. 23-27

al-Sharfī, *al-Fikr al-Islāmī*, pp. 128-30, and see index

Sezgin, *GAS* iii, pp. 236-40
M. Bouyges, 'Nos informations sur ʿAliy... aṭ-Ṭabariy', *MUSJ* 28 (1949-50) 69-114
M. Bouyges, "Aliy ibn Rabban al-Ṭabariy', *Der Islam* 20 (1935) 120-21
M. Meyerhof, "Alī ibn Rabban aṭ-Ṭabarī, ein persischer Arzt des 9. Jahrhunderts n. Chr.', *ZDMG* 85 (1931) 38-68

WORKS ON CHRISTIAN-MUSLIM RELATIONS

Al-Radd ʿalā l-Naṣārā, 'Refutation of the Christians'

DATE c. 850
ORIGINAL LANGUAGE Arabic

DESCRIPTION
The work is not complete, though parts of its later sections are quoted by the 10th-century Christian convert to Islam al-Ḥasan ibn Ayyūb, whose work is preserved in Ibn Taymiyya, *al-Jawāb al-ṣaḥīḥ*, and by the 13th-century Copt al-Ṣafī ibn al-ʿAssāl (see Samir, 'Réponse').

It was written to mark ʿAlī l-Ṭabarī's conversion to Islam, and contains his basic objections to Christianity in a series of sections devoted to comparisons between Christian teachings and reason. He examines in some detail verses from the Bible, mainly the Gospels, and the Nicene Creed to show that there are contradictions between them and that they do not stand up to rational scrutiny.

SIGNIFICANCE
The *Radd* is the earliest surviving example of a convert's attitude towards the teachings of his former faith, and of arguments from a Muslim polemicist with intimate knowledge of the doctrines of Christianity.

It contains examples of a number of motifs found in later polemics (e.g. the comparison of the miracles of Jesus and other prophets to show they do not prove his divinity), and attests to the vigor of argumentation in the mid-9th century.

MANUSCRIPTS
MS Istanbul, Suleymaniyye – Šehit Ali 1628, fols 1r-45r (possibly 17th century; see Samir, 'Réponse', p. 289)

EDITIONS AND TRANSLATIONS

ʿAlī ibn Rabban al-Ṭabarī, *al-Radd ʿalā aṣnāf al-Naṣārā*, ed. K.M. ʿAbduh, Cairo, 2005

J.-M. Gaudeul, *Riposte aux chrétiens par ʿAlī al-Ṭabarī*, Rome, 1995 (French trans.)

I.-A. Khalifé and W. Kutsch, 'Ar-Radd ʿalā-n-Naṣārā de ʿAlī aṭ-Ṭabarī', *MUSJ* 36 (1959) 115-48 (edition)

STUDIES

D. Thomas, "Alī Ibn Rabban al-Ṭabarī. A convert's assessment of his former faith', in M. Tamcke (ed.), *Christians and Muslims in dialogue in the Islamic Orient of the Middle Ages*, Beirut, 2007, 137-56

M. Accad, 'The Gospels in the Muslim discourse of the ninth to the fourteenth centuries: an exegetical inventorial table', *ICMR* 14 (2003) 67-81, 205-20, 337-52, 459-79

D. Thomas, 'The miracles of Jesus in early Islamic polemic', *JSS* 39 (1994) 221-43

al-Sharfī, *al-Fikr al-Islāmī*, p. 130 (and see index)

S.K. Samir, 'La réponse d'al-Ṣafī Ibn al-ʿAssāl à la réfutation des chrétiens de ʿAlī al-Ṭabarī', *Pd'O* 11 (1983) 281-328

O. Schumann, *Der Christus der Muslime. Christologische Aspekte in der arabisch-islamischen Literatur*, Cologne, 1975, 1988², pp. 35-47

E. Fritsch, *Islam und Christentum im Mittelalter*, Breslau 1930, pp. 6-12

Kitāb al-dīn wa-l-dawla, 'The Book of religion and empire'

DATE c. 855

ORIGINAL LANGUAGE Arabic

DESCRIPTION

From the time it was first published the authenticity of this work has been disputed, most vehemently by M. Bouyges. But Sepmeijer, Thomas, and Adang have shown that it is undoubtedly ancient and attributable to ʿAlī l-Ṭabarī, and questions of its authorship should be regarded as settled.

It is a defense of the prophetic status of Muḥammad, based on a range of arguments including his and his Companions' virtues, his miracles, and above all predictions of him and his community in various books of the Old and New Testaments, especially in references to Hagar and Ishmael.

SIGNIFICANCE

The work is one of the earliest examples of the *dalāʾil al-nubuwwa*, 'proofs of prophethood', genre, and the most innovative that is known in marshalling evidence from the books of the Bible.

It is difficult to say how original ʿAlī's arguments are, though Adang, *Muslim writers*, pp. 11, 145, suggests possible dependence on Muḥammad ibn al-Layth (q.v.), and it is not unlikely that some of his other arguments are also borrowed. There is also a close, though probably indirect, relationship with Ibn Qutayba's *Dalāʾil al-nubuwwa* (q.v.).

MANUSCRIPTS

MS Manchester, John Rylands Library – 69 (Crawford 631) (1219)

EDITIONS AND TRANSLATIONS

ʿAlī ibn Rabban al-Ṭabarī, *Kitāb al-dīn wa-l-dawla fī ithbāt nubuwwat Muḥammad*, ed. ʿA. Nuwayhiḍ, Beirut, 1973, 1977, 1979, 1982; (Tunis): al-Maktaba l-ʿAtīqa, 1973 (repr. of the Mingana 1923 edition with added footnotes)

A. Mingana, *The book of religion and empire. A semi-official defence and exposition of Islam written by order at the court and with the assistance of the Caliph Mutawakkil (A.D. 847-861), by Ali Tabari*, Manchester, 1923

A. Mingana, *The book of religion and empire. A semi-official defence and exposition of Islam written by order at the court and with the assistance of the Caliph Mutawakkil (A.D. 847-861), by Ali Tabari*, Manchester, 1922 (trans.)

STUDIES

S. Schmidtke, 'Abū l-Ḥusayn al-Baṣrī and his transmission of biblical materials from *Kitāb al-Dīn wa-l-Dawla* by Ibn Rabban al-Ṭabarī. The evidence from Fakhr al-Dīn al-Rāzī's *Mafātīḥ al-ghayb*', *ICMR* 20 (2009) 105-18 (this gives a full list of publications concerning the authenticity of the work)

Thomas, 'A convert's assessment'

C. Adang, 'A rare case of biblical "testimonies" to the Prophet Muhammad in Muʿtazili literature. Quotations from Ibn Rabban al-Ṭabarī's *Kitāb al-dīn wa-l-dawla* in Abū l-Ḥusayn al-Baṣrī's *Ghurar al-adilla*, as preserved in a work by al-Ḥimmaṣī al-Rāzī', in C. Adang, S. Schmidtke and D. Sklare (eds), *A common rationality. Muʿtazilism in Islam and Judaism*, Würzburg, 2007, 297-330

Scarcia Amoretti, 'Tratti tipologici', pp. 96-102
M. Accad, 'The Gospels in the Muslim discourse of the ninth to the fourteenth centuries: an exegetical inventorial table', *ICMR* 14 (2003) 67-81, 205-20, 337-52, 459-79
Adang, *Muslim writers*, pp. 27-30, and see index
al-Sharfī, *al-Fikr al-Islāmī*, pp. 131-35, and see index
D. Thomas, 'Ṭabarī's Book of religion and empire', *BJRL* 69 (1986) 1-7
F. Sepmeijer, *Een Weerlegging van het Christendom uit de 10e eeuw. De brief van al-Ḥasan b. Ayyūb aan zijn broer 'Alī*, Kampen, 1985 (Diss. Free University of Amsterdam), pp. 4-8
M. Bouyges, 'Nos informations sur 'Aliy ... aṭ-Ṭabariy', *MUSJ* 28 (1949-50) 69-114
F. Taeschner, 'Die alttestamentlichen Bibelzitate, vor allem aus dem Pentateuch, in aṭ-Ṭabarî's Kitâb al-Dîn wad-Dawla und ihre Bedeutung für die Frage nach der Echtheit dieser Schrift', *OC* 3 (1934) 23-39
Fritsch, *Islam und Christentum im Mittelalter*, pp. 10-12
A. Guppy, 'The genuineness of aṭ-Ṭabarī's Arabic "Apology"...', *BJRL* 14 (1930) 121-23
D.S. Margoliouth, 'On the 'Book of religion and empire' by Ali b. Rabban al-Tabari', *Proceedings of the British Academy* 14 (1930) 165-82
A. Mingana, 'Kitāb ud dīn wa-d-daulah', *BJRL* 11 (1927) 99-100
D.B. Macdonald, review in *MW* 15 (1925) 210-11
A. Mingana, 'Remarks on Ṭabarī's semi-official defence of Islam', *BJRL* 9 (1925) 236-40
M. Bouyges, *Le Kitab ad-din wa 'd-dawlat n'est pas authentique*, Beirut, 1925
M. Bouyges, *Le 'Kitāb ad-dīn wa'd-dawlat' récemment edité par Mr. A Mingana, est-il authentique? Letter to the Director of the John Rylands Library*, Beirut, 1924
P. Peeters, review of Mingana's edition in *AB* 62 (1924) 200-2
M. Schreiner, 'Zur Geschichte der Polemik zwischen Juden und Mohammedanern', *ZDMG* 42 (1888) 591-675, pp. 642-45

David Thomas 2008

Sophronius, Archbishop of Cyprus

DATE OF BIRTH Unknown
PLACE OF BIRTH Unknown
DATE OF DEATH Unknown
PLACE OF DEATH Unknown

BIOGRAPHY

There is some difficulty over the identification of the author of this account of the martyrdom of the forty-two martyrs of Amorion. According to the manuscript containing the Slavonic version, he was archbishop of Cyprus (Abicht and Schmidt, 'Quellennachweise, III', pp. 143-44; Vasilievskij and Nikitin, *Skazania*, p. 38; cf. Zaimov and Kapaldo, *Suprasalski*, p. 54), while according to MS Vat – Palatinus Gr. 4 ($10^{th}/11^{th}$ c., though Halkin, *Novum Auctarium*, p. 144, dates it to $11^{th}/12^{th}$ c.) he was archbishop of Jerusalem.

Of the possible candidates, Sophronius I of Jerusalem (634-38) (q.v.), who surrendered the city to the Caliph 'Umar, lived two centuries before the martyrs of Amorion, while Sophronius II of Jerusalem lived in the second half of the 11th century (before 1059-after 1064), and Sophronius III of Jerusalem was active around the middle of the 13th century (Grumel, *Chronologie*, pp. 451-52). However, MS Vat – Palatinus Gr. 1476, which contains a mutilated version that does not give the author's name (text *E*), is dated to 890. Thus, Sophronius I is too early, and Sophronius II and III are too late, leaving Sophronius Archbishop of Cyprus as the likely author.

MAIN SOURCES OF INFORMATION

Primary —

Secondary

A. Kazhdan, *A History of Byzantine literature* (850-1000), Athens 2006, pp. 206-7

A. Kazhdan, 'Hagiographical notes', *Byzantion* 56 (1986) 148-70 (repr. in Kazhdan, *Authors and texts in Byzantium*, Aldershot, 1993, no. 14: 'Collective death and individual deeds', pp. 152-59)

F. Halkin, *Novum Auctarium Bibliothecae hagiographicae graecae*, Brussels, 1984

V. Grumel, *La Chronologie,* Paris, 1958
BHG 1209, 1210
R. Abicht, 'Quellennachweise zum Codex Suprasliensis, II', *Archiv für slavische Philologie* 16 (1894) 140-153, pp. 143-44

WORKS ON CHRISTIAN-MUSLIM RELATIONS

Martyrion tōn hagiōn tessarakonta dyo martyrōn, 'Martyrdom of the forty-two holy martyrs' (*BHG* 1209, version *D*), *Martyrion tōn hagiōn kai endoxōn neophanōn martyrōn Theophilou, Theōdorou, Kōnstantinou, Kallistou, Bassoou kai tēs synodias hagiōn ton arithmon tessarakonta dyo*, 'Martyrdom of the holy and glorious newly shining martyrs Theophilos, Theodorus, Constantine, Callistus, Bassoēs and the company of saints numbering forty-two' (*BHG* 1210, version *D* 1), 'The forty-two martyrs of Amorion (Sophronius, Archbishop of Cyprus)'

DATE Before 856 (Kotzampassi, 'To martyrio', pp. 124-27) or after 858 (Kazhdan, 'Hagiographical notes', p. 153; Kazhdan, *A History of Byzantine Literature*, pp. 206-7).
ORIGINAL LANGUAGE Greek

DESCRIPTION
After an introduction praising the inner strength of the martyrs, who chose to die and gain eternal life, Sophronius gives a brief description of the siege and fall of the city of Amorion to the Arabs under the Caliph al-Muʿtaṣim (833-42), and the fate of the captured citizens and soldiers. There follows an account of the attempt by a representative of the new Caliph al-Wāthiq (842-47) to persuade the forty-two Byzantine officers, now in the seventh year of their imprisonment (845), to convert to Islam, (in contrast to the version given by Euodius [q.v.], there is no reference to doctrinal arguments used by either side), their refusal, and their subsequent execution. The final part contains a brief account of a miracle regarding the martyrs' bodies, and a prayer addressed to them by the author, begging for their intercession

on behalf of all Christians, and asking – among other things – for the submission of the Muslims to the Byzantine emperor.

Sophronius attributes leading parts to two of the martyrs, Theodorus Craterus (or Carterus; cf. *PMBZ*, no. 7679) and Bassoēs (*PMBZ*, no. 982) (Kazhdan, 'Hagiographical notes', p. 156, mentions only Theodorus). This is another point of difference between his text and that of Euodios, who does not single out any of the martyrs. In addition, Sophronius praises the Emperor Theophilus for his victories against the Arabs, like the anonymous author of version *B*, but unlike the authors of versions *A* (anonymous), *G* (Michael the Synkellos), and *Z* (Euodius), who are very negative about the emperor (see the relevant entries).

SIGNIFICANCE

The martyrdom indirectly underlines the religious confrontation between Christians and Muslims. It does this by giving emphasis to the hope of the Christian martyrs to gain the afterlife and by calling the Muslims *miaros*, 'sacrilegious', and *atheos*, 'atheist', and the caliphs *anomos*, 'lawless', 'rejecting the law of God' and *atheos*. The text also includes references to the military-political confrontation between the two sides in the 9th century.

MANUSCRIPTS

MS BNF – Gr. 1476 (1) fols 1-2 (version *E*) (copied in 890)
MS Vat – Palatinus Gr. 4 (10th/11th c.)
MS BNF – 1447 (36) fols 394v-95v (11th c.)
MS BNF – 1534 (3) fols 22v-29v (version *D* 1)(12th c.)

EDITIONS AND TRANSLATIONS

I. Zaimov and M. Kapaldo, *Suprasulski ili Retkov sbornik*, Sofia 1982, 54-68 (edition of the Slavonic version)
V. Vasilievskij and P. Nikitin, *Skazanija o 42 amorijskich mučenikach*, St Petersburg, 1905, pp. 38-56 (text *D*), pp. 58-60 (text *E*)
A. Vasiliev, *Grečeskij tekst žitija soroka dvuch amorijskich mučenikov*, St Petersburg, 1898, pp. 9-17 (text *D* 1)

STUDIES

Kazhdan, *A History of Byzantine literature* (850-1000), pp. 206-8
A. Kolia-Dermitzaki, 'The execution of the forty-two martyrs of Amorion. Proposing an interpretation', *Al-Masaq* 14 (2002) 141-62

S. Kotzampassi, 'To martyrio tōn saranta dyo martyrōn tou Amoriou. Hagiologika kai hymnologika keimena', *Epistēmonikē Epetēris tēs Philosophikēs Scholēs Aristotēleiou Panepistēmiou Thessalonikēs, periodos B', Tmēma Philologias* 2 (1992) 109-53, pp. 124-27

Kazhdan, 'Hagiographical notes'

BHG 1209 (texts *D* and *E*); 1210 (text *D* 1)

Vasilievskij and Nikitin, *Skazanija o 42 amorijskich mučenicach*, pp. 272-79 (commentary by P. Nikitin)

Vasiliev, *Grečeskij tekst žitija soroka dvuch amorijskich muchenikov*, p. 6 (version *E*)

R. Abicht and H. Schmidt, 'Quellennachweise zum Codex Suprasliensis, II', *Archiv für slavische Philologie* 18 (1896) 138-55, p. 142

R. Abicht, 'Quellennachweise zum Codex Suprasliensis', *Archiv für slavische Philologie* 15 (1893) 121-337, p. 336

Athina Kolia-Dermitzaki 2008

Eulogius of Cordova

Eulógio of Córdoba, Eulógio of Toledo

DATE OF BIRTH Unknown
PLACE OF BIRTH Cordova
DATE OF DEATH 859
PLACE OF DEATH Cordova

BIOGRAPHY

Eulogius received part of his education from Speraindeo (q.v.), abbot of St Zoylus. He became a deacon, then a priest (dates uncertain) and is known to have traveled as far north as Pamplona. He is best known for his works defending the martyrs of Cordova, forty-nine Christians put to death for blasphemy (in most cases for publicly insulting Islam and its Prophet in a deliberate attempt to provoke the Muslim authorities to make martyrs of them) or for apostasy (in general, the apostates were children of mixed Christian-Muslim marriages who publicly declared their Christianity). In reaction to the martyrs' movement, the emirs ʿAbd al-Raḥmān II and Muḥammad I passed new restrictions against the Christians of Cordova, notably limiting the positions they could hold in the emir's court and ordering the destruction of recently-built churches. The majority of Cordovan Christians were hostile to the martyrs, whom they viewed as troublemaking fanatics.

Eulogius' works (like those of his friend Paulus Alvarus (q.v.)), using traditional hagiographical *topoi*, attempt to prove that the martyrs were indeed saints worthy of veneration. They also sought to prove that Spain's Muslim rulers actively persecuted Christians and that those Christians who fraternized with their infidel rulers compromised their faith. In 852 Eulogius was elected bishop of Toledo, but never set foot in his see. He was arrested in 859 for harboring an apostate and was subsequently condemned for blasphemy and decapitated on 11 March 859. His body was transferred to Oviedo in 884.

MAIN SOURCES OF INFORMATION

Primary
Paulus Alvarus (q.v.), *Vita Eulogii*

Secondary

F. González Muñoz, 'En torno a la orientación de la polémica antimusulmana en los textos latinos de los mozárabes del siglo IX', in C. Aillet, M. Penelas & P. Roisse (eds), *¿Existe una identidad mozárabe? Historia, lengua y cultura de los cristianos de al-Andalus (siglos IX-XII)*, Madrid, 2008, 9-31

I. Pochoshajew, *Die Märtyrer von Córdoba. Christen im muslimischen Spanien des 9. Jahrhunderts*, Frankfurt am Main, 2007

Tolan, *Saracens*, 85-102

M.J. Aldana García, 'Testimonios de la imagen literaria de la guerra en la tradición cristiana y su pervivencia en San Eulogio de Cordova', *Revista agustiniana* 38 (1997) 685-702

P. Herrera Roldán, *Léxico de la obra de S. Eulogio*, Cordova, 1996

J. Coope, *The martyrs of Córdoba: community and family conflict in an age of mass conversion*, Lincoln NE, 1995

P. Herrera Roldán, *Lengua y cultura latinas entre los mozárabes cordobeses del S. IX*, Cordova, 1995

K. Wolf, *Christian martyrs in Muslim Spain*, Cambridge, 1988

D. Millet Gérard, *Chrétiens mozarabes et culture islamique dans l'Espagne des VIIIe-IXe* siècles, Paris, 1984

E. Colbert, *The martyrs of Córdoba (850-59). A study of the sources*, Washington, 1962

F.R. Franke, *Die freiwilligen Märtyrer von Cordova und das Verhältnis der Mozaraber zum Islam (nach den Schriften des Speraindeo, Eulogius und Alvar)*, Münster, 1958

WORKS ON CHRISTIAN-MUSLIM RELATIONS

Memoriale sanctorum, 'In memory of the saints'

DATE 852-56
ORIGINAL LANGUAGE Latin

DESCRIPTION

This is a hagiography of Christian martyrs of Cordova between 850 and 856. Eulogius describes the beginning of the martyr movement, cataloguing the deaths of over forty Christians, and describing their fates in language reminiscent of the hagiography of the martyrs of the early church. He seeks to prove that those who died should indeed be venerated as martyrs, and lambasts those Christians (including much of the Cordovan church hierarchy) who rejected or criticized the martyrs' self-sacrifice. In order to prove that Christians indeed faced persecution similar to that of pagan antiquity, he presents Islam as a heretical sect founded by an impious pseudo-prophet, a 'precursor of Antichrist'. He describes the anti-Christian measures taken by the emirs of Cordova ʿAbd al-Raḥmān II and Muḥammad I as proof that Muslims persecuted Christians. He exhibits extreme animosity towards Muslims and describes the revulsion he feels, for example, when he hears the call of the muezzin.

SIGNIFICANCE

It is a fundamental text that describes the beginnings of the Cordovan martyr movement and defends the martyrs at a time when they provoked sharp dissent within the Christian community of Cordova.

MANUSCRIPTS

There are no extant manuscripts.

One manuscript is attested in Oviedo in the 16th century, when it was discovered by bishop and inquisitor Pedro Ponce de León (Ambrosio de Morales, *La coronica general de España*, ed. B. Cano, 12 vols, Madrid, 1791-92, iii, p. 39); this manuscript subsequently served as the basis of the edition of Eulogius' works by Ambrosio de Morales (see editions below). It was subsequently lost.

EDITIONS AND TRANSLATIONS

San Eulogio de Córdoba, *Obras*, trans. P. Herrera Roldán, Madrid, 2005, 55-166

Obras completas de San Eulogio, trans. M.J. Aldana García, Cordova, 1998, 81-174

Gil, *CSM* ii, pp. 363-459

Obras completas de S. Eulogio, ed. and trans. A.S. Ruig, Cordova, 1959

PL 115, cols 735-818

Sanctorum Patrum Toletanorum opera, ed. F. A. de Lorenzana y Butron, Madrid 1785, ii

Hispania illustrata, ed. A. Schott, 4 vols, Frankfurt 1603-8, iv, pp. 237-302

Sacra Bibliotheca Sanctorum Patrum, ed. M de la Bigne, Paris, 1589, ix, pp. 769-922

Divi Eulogii Cordubensis, martyris, Doctoris et electi Archiepiscopi Toletani opera, ed. A. de Morales, Alcalá de Henares, p. 1574

STUDIES

I. Pochoshajew, *Die Märtyrer von Córdoba*

A. Christys, *Christians in al-Andalus 711-1000*, Richmond, 2002, pp. 53, 68, 73, 76-79

M.J. Aldana García, 'La visión negativa del mundo musulmán en el pensamiento de S. Eulogio: la belleza frente a la fealdad', *Revista agustiniana* 41 (2000) 637-48

M.J. Aldana García, 'Notas sobre la significación del término 'martyrium' en la obra de S. Eulogio', *Revista agustiniana* 40 (1999) 89-102

M.J. Aldana García, 'La polémica teológica Cristianismo-Islam en el 'Memoriale sanctorum' de San Eulogio y su posible influencia oriental', *Alfinge. Revista de filología* 8 (1997) 11-22

Wolf, *Christian martyrs*, pp. 56-60

Documentum martyriale, 'Martyrial document'

DATE 857?

ORIGINAL LANGUAGE Latin

DESCRIPTION

This is an exhortation addressed to Flora and Maria, two Christians imprisoned for apostasy from Islam, urging them to remain steadfast in their Christianity and to endure persecution and martyrdom. Eulogius paints in lurid terms the image of the Muslim oppressor, whom he imagines lusting after innocent Christian virgins. Drawing inspiration from Jerome's writings on virginity, Eulogius promises Flora and Maria an eternal union with their Divine spouse, Christ.

SIGNIFICANCE

It is another important testimony contemporary to the martyr movement.

MANUSCRIPTS

see references to *Memoriale sanctorum* above

EDITIONS AND TRANSLATIONS

PL 115, cols 819-34

San Eulogio de Córdoba, *Obras*, pp. 167-89

Obras completas de San Eulogio, pp. 174-90

Gil, *CSM*, ii, pp. 459-75

STUDIES

Christys, *Christians in al-Andalus*, pp. 56, 76-77

Wolf, *Christian martyrs*, 67-69

Liber apologeticus martyrum, 'Book in defense of the martyrs'

DATE 857-59
ORIGINAL LANGUAGE Latin

DESCRIPTION
Here Eulogius combines a general defense of the martyrs' claim to sanctity with specific hagiographical narratives, in this case involving the passions of Rudericus and Salomon who died on 13 March 857. In the course of this work Eulogius makes passing reference to a new persecution launched by the emir Muḥammad I. He incorporates into this work the *Istoria de Mahomet* (q.v.).

SIGNIFICANCE
This is one of the earliest attempts in Latin to present Muḥammad's biography in order to prove that he is a heresiarch and precursor of the Antichrist.

MANUSCRIPTS
See references to *Memoriale sanctorum* above
EDITIONS AND TRANSLATIONS

San Eulogio de Córdoba, *Obras*, pp. 191-214
Obras completas de San Eulogio, pp. 191-219
Gil, *CSM*, ii, pp. 475-95

John Tolan 2007

The Martyrdom of ʿAbd al-Masīḥ

Unknown author

DATE OF BIRTH Unknown, probably early 9th c.
PLACE OF BIRTH Unknown
DATE OF DEATH Unknown, after c. 860
PLACE OF DEATH Unknown, possibly at Mt Sinai or one of the monasteries of Palestine

BIOGRAPHY

Nothing is known of this author beyond what can be deduced from the text of the *Martyrdom* he composed. He was an Arabic-speaking Melkite Christian and very possibly a monk (perhaps of Mount Sinai).

MAIN SOURCES OF INFORMATION

Primary —

Secondary —

WORKS ON CHRISTIAN-MUSLIM RELATIONS

The manuscript copies are without title but begin: 'This is the story of our father, the holy ʿAbd al-Masīḥ superior of Mount Sinai, who was martyred at al-Ramla' (Sinai Ar. 542), or 'This is the story of ʿAbd al-Masīḥ who was martyred in Ramla under Umayyad rule' (BL Or. 5019). Modern title: 'The martyrdom of ʿAbd al-Masīḥ …' (with various expansions of the name).

DATE Late 9th c.
ORIGINAL LANGUAGE Arabic

DESCRIPTION

The text tells the story of Qays al-Ghassānī (short for Qays ibn Rabīʿ ibn Yazīd al-Ghassānī l-Najrānī), a young Christian man from a family that originally came from Najrān in the south of the Arabian peninsula. Strong in his Christian faith, he set out for Jerusalem at the age of 20, seeking to worship in the holy city. He traveled with a group of Muslims who soon beguiled him and led him into raiding Byzantine territories and even into praying with them. He continued with this life for 13 years. Passing through Syria one day, he entered a church at Baalbek and was converted back to Christianity upon hearing the priest reading the scripture. Qays then set out for Jerusalem and met with the Patriarch Abba John, who sent him to the monastery of Mār Saba where he remained as a monk for five years. He then set out on a tour of various monasteries and settled at Mt Sinai. His devoted service to the monastery, including handling matters of taxation with officials in Ayla (ʿAqaba/Eilat) led him to be appointed *oeconome* over the monastery, a position he held for five years. In time, he felt the need to make a public confession of his apostasy from Islam and return to Christianity, and so he traveled to al-Ramla with two other monks. There he wrote out his story on a piece of paper and threw it into the community mosque, indicating on the note where he might be found. When the Muslims came to look for him 'God blinded them to him', and after three days he returned to Mt Sinai unharmed. Upon his return, he was appointed superior of the monastery, a position he held for seven years. At this stage in the text we are told that ʿAbd al-Masīḥ is the name that our protagonist took upon entering the monastic life.

Problems over the taxation of the monastery led ʿAbd al-Masīḥ to travel to al-Ramla. En route, he was recognized by one of his former Muslim comrades, was arrested by the authorities as an apostate, and was sent to al-Ramla to see the governor. After refusing to recant was beheaded, and his body was taken to a nearby village and thrown into a well and burned. The account ends with a lengthy description of the rescue of ʿAbd al-Masīḥ's remains nine months later. The faithful lowered a monk down into the well and recovered the bones. There is then a scene of the monks disputing over various bones. Finally, the head was returned to Mt Sinai, while other parts were buried, and a forearm and thighbone were kept to bring out for those seeking a blessing from the saint.

The account of the martyrdom of ʿAbd al-Masīḥ follows a pattern common to the genre. A Muslim (who in this case was previously a Christian) converts to Christianity. He is brought before the Muslim authorities and given an opportunity to recant. Upon failing to do so, he is summarily executed. The present text seems to have been written not only to encourage the faithful to stand firm in their faith, but also to encourage those who might have embraced Islam to return to their former faith.

The earlier recension (as in Sinai Ar. 542) dates to the latter part of the 9th century. Although BL Or. 5019 says that events took place 'under Umayyad rule', such an account of events seems unlikely, in light of the issues raised by Griffith ('Arabic account', pp. 344-47), and we are on more solid footing in assuming that the account describes events that transpired in the middle of the 9th century. In any case, the date of the Sinai manuscript, late 9th c., forms a terminus ante quem.

SIGNIFICANCE

As noted by Sidney Griffith in the first serious study of the account of the martyrdom of ʿAbd al-Masīḥ (Griffith, 'Arabic account', p. 333), the text is important for at least three reasons: as a witness in the history of Christian Palestinian manuscripts, both original Arabic compositions and translations from Greek, Syriac, and Georgian; as a witness to ecclesiastical life in the Holy Land between the rise of Islam and the Crusades; and most importantly as a witness to the development of a hagiography of relations between Christians and Muslims. In this latter role, accounts such as this functioned as apologetic texts in their own right, developing themes that are found in the more traditional apologetic treatises of the period. Among the prominent themes in this text is the 'Arabness' of the protagonist, emphasizing the legitimacy of the existence of Arab Christians alongside Arab Muslims. In addition, Swanson ('Martyrdom', p. 124) notes the importance of the text for 'hold(ing) open the door of repentance' for those who had lapsed into Islam and wanted to return to their Christian faith. The text also serves in a more polemical way through the implicit charge that the Muslims were coercive and/or violent in their dealings with non-Muslims, a theme that is also prominent in the more theological apologetic treatises of the day (Vila, 'Christian martyrs', pp. 95-97).

MANUSCRIPTS

MS Sinai– Ar. 542 (late 9th c.), fols 65r-67r
MS BL– Or. 5019 (11th c.), fols 103v-105v

In addition, a 10th-century manuscript (no. 14 in the 1922 catalog of Karl Hiersemann) from Mt Sinai perished in a fire.

Another witness to ʿAbd al-Masīḥ can be found in MS Sinai – Ar. 396, a *Menologion* for the month of November, dated by Kamil (*Catalogue*, 18) to the 13th century. Regrettably, the manuscript was not microfilmed during the Library of Congress/University of Alexandria expedition to Mt Sinai in 1950 and so is not available for study.

EDITIONS AND TRANSLATIONS

S.H. Griffith, 'The Arabic account of ʿAbd al-Masīḥ an-Naǧrānī al-Ghassānī', *Le Muséon* 98 (1985) 331-74 (edition from the Sinai manuscript with English trans. Note the corrections offered in Swanson, 'Martyrdom', 107-8)

Ḥ. Zayyāt, 'Shuhadāʾ al-Naṣrāniyya fī l-Islām', *Al-Mashriq* 36 (1938) 463-65 (edition from the British Library manuscript)

STUDIES

M.N. Swanson, 'The martyrdom of ʿAbd al-Masīḥ, superior of Mount Sinai (Qays al-Ghassānī)', in D. Thomas (ed.), *Syrian Christians under Islam. The first thousand years*, Leiden, 2001, 107-29

D. Vila, *Christian martyrs in the first Abbasid century and the development of an apologetic against Islam*, St Louis MO, 1999 (Diss. Saint Louis University), pp. 140-60

S.H. Griffith, 'Christians, Muslims, and neo-martyrs. Saints' lives and Holy Land history', in A. Kofsky and G.G. Stroumsa, *Sharing the sacred. Religious contacts and conflicts in the Holy Land, first-fifteenth centuries CE*, Jerusalem, 1998, 163-207, pp. 187-93

Hoyland, *Seeing Islam*, pp. 381-83

T. Biṭār, *Al-qiddīsūn al-mansiyyūn fī l-turāth al-Anṭākī*, Beirut, 1994, pp. 293-300

Griffith, 'The Arabic account of ʿAbd al-Masīḥ an-Naǧrānī'

M. Kamil, *Catalogue of all manuscripts in the Monastery of St Catherine, Mt Sinai*, Wiesbaden, 1970

Zayyāt, 'Shuhadāʾ al-Naṣrāniyya fī l-Islām'

David Vila 2007

Thomas of Margā

DATE OF BIRTH Unknown, c. 815
PLACE OF BIRTH Neḥshon, in the region of Bēt Shāronāyē, north eastern Iraq
DATE OF DEATH Unknown, after 860
PLACE OF DEATH Unknown

BIOGRAPHY

When still a youth, Thomas of Margā became a monk at the monastery of Bet ʿAbē in 832. He became *kātobā*, secretary to Catholicos Abraham II (837-50), a former abbot of Bēt ʿAbē. At an unknown date, he was appointed bishop of Margā. There is no evidence that he was also appointed metropolitan of Bēt Garmay, as suggested by Budge, whose assumption is based on an erroneous interpretation of a passage in the *Kitāb al-majdal.*

Thomas is the author of *Histories* (*tashʿyātā*) *of some holy men* (lost), *The Book of governors* and a *History of the monks Cyprian and Gabriel* (in later times inserted into the *The Book of governors*, of which it formed the sixth and last book, though it was composed before it).

MAIN SOURCES OF INFORMATION

Primary

E.A.W. Budge, *The Book of governors. The* Historia monastica *of Thomas, Bishop of Margâ A.D. 840*, 2 vols, London, 1893 (repr. Piscataway, 2003) i, pp. 109-10, 125, 385, 407; ii, pp. 3, 242, 266, 655, 685

Secondary

Hoyland, *Seeing Islam*, pp. 213-15
Budge, *The Book of governors*, i, pp. xxiv-xxvi
Assemani, *BO* iii/1, p. 210

WORKS ON CHRISTIAN-MUSLIM RELATIONS

Tashʿyātā w-sharbē mawtrānē d-ʿal nāshā qaddishē (w-iḥidāyē) da-hwaw b-dār dār b-ʿumrā qaddishā d-Bēt ʿAbē, 'The useful histories and stories on the holy men (and solitaries), who generation after generation lived in the holy monastery of Bēt ʿAbē'. The work is generally known as *Ktābā d-rishānē*, 'The Book of Governors', i.e. the leaders of the monastery of Bēt ʿAbē.

DATE Unknown, but while he was bishop of Margā
ORIGINAL LANGUAGE Syriac

DESCRIPTION
The work contains biographies of the abbots of the monasteries of Bēt ʿAbē and of many other figures of the Church of the East (e.g. Patriarch Ghiwargis I, Timothy I, etc.), covering the period between the late 6th and the mid-9th centuries. It contains important information on the general developments of the East-Syrian Church.

SIGNIFICANCE
The book contains a number of allusions to the Muslim environment, such as the Islamic era, persecution of Christians, the Muslim origin of the monk Shubḥalishoʿ, the exceptionally heavy taxation of Bēt ʿAbē by the governor of Mosul, incidental confiscation of property.

MANUSCRIPTS
MS Diyarbakır, Chaldean Archbishopric – 113 (16th cent.)
MS Vat Syr. 165 (1663)
MS Vat Syr. 381 (incomplete)
MS Vat Syr. 382 (incomplete)
MS BNF Syr. 286 (copy of MS Vat. Syr. 165, incomplete)
MS Baghdad, Chaldean Monastery – Syr. 541 (1701)
MS BL Or. 2316 (17/18th cent., incomplete)
MS Tell-Kayff (Tel-Kēpē), Chaldean Church of the Sacred Heart – 66 (1740)
MS Baghdad, Chaldean Monastery – Syr. 541 (1880)
MS Baghdad, Chaldean Monastery – Syr. 543 (1881)
MS Berlin, Staatsbiliothek – Sachau 77 (1882)

MS Harvard, Houghton Library – Syr. 55 (1888)
2 MSS dated 1888 formerly in the private collection of E.A.W. Budge, present location unknown (London?)

EDITIONS AND TRANSLATIONS

Tūmā Usquf al-Marj, *Kitāb al-ruʾasāʾ. Wa-yatanāwalu akhbār unās fuḍalāʾ ʿāshū fī mukhtalif al-ajyāl fī dayr Bayt ʿAbī al-muqaddas*, trans. A. Abūna, Mosul, 1966 (Arabic trans., repr. 1990)

P. Bedjan, *Liber superiorum seu historia monastica auctore Thoma, epicopo Margensi*, Paris, 1901 (edition)

Budge, *The Book of governors* (edition and trans.)

STUDIES

C.F. Robinson, *Empire and elites after the Muslim conquest. The transformation of Northern Mesopotamia*, Cambridge, 2000, pp. 92-102 and *passim*

C.J. Villagomez, *The fields, the flocks and finances of monks. Economic life at Nestorian Monasteries, 500-850*, Los Angeles, 1998 (Diss. UCLA)

W. Schwaigert, art. 'Thomas von Marga', in *Biografisch-Bibliografisch Kirchenlexikon*, ed. F. Bautz, Hamm, Westphalia, 1970-

W.G. Young, *Patriarch, shah, and caliph*, Rawalpindi, 1974, pp. 106-27

J.-M. Fiey, 'Thomas de Marga. Notule de littérature syriaque', *Le Muséon* 78 (1965) 361-66

Herman G.B. Teule 2008

Abbot Samson

DATE OF BIRTH Unknown
PLACE OF BIRTH Unknown, probably Cordova
DATE OF DEATH 890
PLACE OF DEATH Unknown, probably Cordova

BIOGRAPHY

Samson was abbot of St Zoilus in Cordova, the church and monastery where Eulogius (q.v.) and Paul Alvarus (q.v.) studied under Speraindeo (q.v.). He later became abbot of Pinna Mellaria, also near Cordova and a center of the martyrs' movement of 850-59. In the early 860s he was employed at the emir's court translating letters intended for the Frankish court from Arabic to Latin. For reasons that are unclear, a group of courtiers turned against Samson, accusing him of passing secrets to the Franks. Not only Muslims but prominent Christians connected with the court attacked Samson, and in 862 Bishop Hostegesis of Malaga denounced Samson as a heretic. Two years later, a church council, called by the Muslim emir, renewed the charge of heresy and deposed Bishop Valentius of Cordova, a close friend of Samson's, replacing him with one of Samson's rivals. At that point, Samson fled to Martos, where he wrote his major work, the *Apologeticus*. His other extant works are *De gradibus consanguinitatis tractatulus*, 'On prohibited degrees of kinship', which may be a reaction against Berber and Arab practices of close-kin marriage, and the *Carmina*, three brief epitaphs for churchmen in Cordova.

MAIN SOURCES OF INFORMATION

Primary

Samson of Cordova, *De gradibus consanguinitatis tractatulus*, in Gil, *CSM* ii, pp. 659-64
Samson of Cordova, *Carmina*, in Gil, *CMS* ii, p. 665
(and see further below)

Secondary

J. Coope, *The martyrs of Córdoba. Community and family conflict in an age of mass conversion*, Lincoln NE, 1995, pp. 58-62

G. Casado Fuente, *Estudios sobre el latín medieval español. El abad Samson; Edición crítica y comentario filológico de su obra*, Madrid, 1964
F.J. Simonet, *Historia de los mozárabes de España*, Madrid, 1897, pp. 488-500
Flórez, *España sagrada*, xi, pp. 300-24 (Flórez's study of Samson's life)

WORKS ON CHRISTIAN-MUSLIM RELATIONS

Apologeticus

DATE 864
ORIGINAL LANGUAGE Latin

DESCRIPTION
The *Apologeticus* occupies 152 pages in Gil's edition. Most of the material on Christian-Muslim relations is in the second book of the treatise, which is 101 pages long.

The *Apologeticus* is primarily an attack on two Christians: Hostegesis, Bishop of Malaga, and Servandus, Count of Cordova, both of whom conspired to drive Samson out of Cordova. It is nevertheless relevant to Christian-Muslim relations in that Samson condemns these two men and their supporters for their close relations with Muslims and what he sees as their acceptance of Islamic practices. The treatise includes a theological and a personal attack. Samson lays out his doctrinal argument against Hostegesis, who had accused him of pantheism and of insulting the deity by saying that God is present in all creation, including vermin and places where people are sinning. Samson defends his position largely on the basis of St Augustine's teaching that all creation is good, although various parts of it lack God's perfect goodness to a greater or lesser extent. Since all creation is good, God must be present throughout it. Samson argues that Hostegesis and his followers are anthropomorphists, since they contend that God is in a specific place, in heaven, and is present in his creation only indirectly.

In addition to his theological arguments, Samson also launches a more personal attack against Hostegesis and Servandus. According to Samson, they and their associates held their positions by virtue of their close relationship with powerful Muslims, not through piety or virtue, no doubt a reference to the Umayyads' policy of controlling subject populations by appointing their leaders. The two men's high offices allowed them to extort unjustified taxes and tithes from the Christian community. Servandus's treatment of fellow Christians was so harsh that many of them converted to Islam. Among other ill deeds, he took relics of the Cordovan martyrs from church altars and brought their mutilated bodies to the emir's men, demanding that the Christians who had preserved the bodies against the emir's orders be punished.

However, even more upsetting to Samson than his enemies' treatment of other Christians was the fact that they and their associates adopted what Samson perceived to be Muslim practices. Hostegesis' father, Avurnus, was also a courtier. He had converted to Islam as an adult and been circumcised, an operation which Samson describes in graphic detail. An uncle of Hostegesis had not converted but had been circumcised to be more acceptable to Muslims at court. Samson's disgust with circumcision echoes that of Paul Alvarus (q.v.), who says in his *Indiculus luminosus* that Christians who are circumcised take on the mark of the Antichrist. A 10th-century Christian, Abbot John of St Arnulf, reports that Muslims in Cordova insisted that the Christian men they worked with should be circumcised, suggesting that circumcision had become a test of loyalty for some Christians and Muslims. Samson also associates the court with drinking and sexual excess; two of Servandus's Christian colleagues at court were drunkards and had sexual relationships with the court eunuchs and with various women. Samson's characterization of Christians at the Islamic court as greedy, cruel, and debauched matches Eulogius and Paul Alvarus' stereotypes of Muslims. The Cordovan polemicists of this period regarded courtiers' behavior as typical of Islam, and of Christians who associated with Muslims.

SIGNIFICANCE

Samson's polemic, although aimed primarily at Christians, is of a piece with the Cordovan Christian polemic against Islam. The polemicists of the period equated Islam with their perceptions of Umayyad court culture, and thus with abuse of power, sexual promiscuity, and luxury.

MANUSCRIPTS

MS Madrid, BN – 10:018, fols 89r-180r (9th or early 10th c.)

EDITIONS AND TRANSLATIONS

Apologético del Abad Sansón, ed. J. Palacios Royán, Madrid, 1987 (repr. Tres Cantos: Akal ediciones, 1998)

Gil, *CSM* ii, pp. 506-658

Casado Fuente, *Estudios sobre el latín*

Flórez, *España sagrada* xi, pp. 325-516

STUDIES

Coope, *The martyrs of Córdoba*, pp. 58-62
Casado Fuente, *Estudios sobre el latín*
Simonet, *Historia de los mozárabes*, pp. 488-500
Flórez, *España sagrada* xi, pp. 300-24

Jessica A. Coope 2007

Abū ʿĪsā l-Warrāq

Abū ʿĪsā Muḥammad ibn Hārūn ibn Muḥammad al-Warrāq

DATE OF BIRTH Unknown, probably late 8th c.
PLACE OF BIRTH Unknown
DATE OF DEATH Unknown, probably soon after 864
PLACE OF DEATH Baghdad

BIOGRAPHY

Nothing is known about Abū ʿĪsā's personal circumstances, except that he lived in the Islamic capital, where he is associated with scholars active in the early 9th century. He was closely connected with the heterodox thinker Ibn al-Rāwandī, maybe as his teacher, though the relationship deteriorated into hostility leading to Ibn al-Rāwandī insinuating that he was a dualist. Al-Masʿūdī says he died in the Ramla quarter in 861 (247 A.H.), but his authorship of a report about a renegade killed in 864 contradicts this. Ibn al-Jawzī says he died in 910/11 (298 A.H.) in prison, though he is not linked elsewhere with events after the mid-9th century.

Abū ʿĪsā was originally a Muʿtazilī, but he later converted to a form of Shīʿism, and his works include a number of expositions and defenses of Shīʿī beliefs. His true religious loyalties are unclear, maybe because he himself preferred to question more than he affirmed. He was accused of dualism and atheism, most specifically Manicheism, though this probably arises from his impartial and sometimes sympathetic accounts of dualist and other beliefs, as well as his criticisms of fundamental beliefs about the Qur'ān and Muḥammad. His polemics against a variety of non-Muslim faiths suggest that he remained a monotheist, though probably with strongly critical attitudes.

Abu ʿĪsā is widely known for his writings on non-Muslim beliefs, particularly Persian dualism and Christianity. However, none of his works survives in its original form, and most have disappeared without trace, being known only by their titles and the remarks about some of them by later authors. Fragments from a few are quoted, often without attribution, and the only work that is extant in a form approaching its original is his refutation of Christianity.

His most influential work was the *Kitāb maqālāt al-nās wa-ikhtilāfihim* (on this see below), which was so well known among later authors that it was called simply *Kitāb al-maqālāt* or *kitābuhu*, 'his book'. A notorious work was *al-Gharīb al-mashriqī*, 'The Stranger from the East', which contained searching criticisms of Islamic teachings and of Muḥammad, maybe articulated by Brahmins, and in this category he also wrote other works that may have contained attacks on Muslim beliefs and practices. A second group of works are his expositions and defences of Shīʿī beliefs, among them *Ikhtilāf al-Shīʿa*, 'The differences among the Shīʿa', *al-Imāma*, 'The imamate', and *al-Saqīfa*, 'The shelter' (referring to the debate that took place in the absence of ʿAlī to decide the succession after Muḥammad's death). And a third group are his expositions and refutations of the beliefs of the Jews, dualists, Magians and Christians.

MAIN SOURCES OF INFORMATION

Primary

Abū l-Ḥusayn al-Khayyāṭ, *Kitāb al-intiṣār*, ed. and French trans. A. Nader, Beirut, 1957, pp. 73, 108, 110-11

Abū l-Ḥasan al-Ashʿarī, *Maqālāt al-Islāmiyyīn*, ed. H. Ritter, Istanbul, 1929-30, pp. 33-34, 64, 349

Abū Manṣūr al-Māturīdī, *Kitāb al-tawḥīd*, ed. F. Kholeif, Beirut, 1970, pp. 186-87, 191-92, 198-99, 201, 284

al-Masʿūdī, *Les prairies d'or*, ed. and trans. C. Barbier de Meynard and Pavet de Courteille, 9 vols, Paris, 1861-77, v, pp. 473-74, vi, pp. 57-58, vii, pp. 234-37

al-Masʿūdī, *Kitāb al-tanbīh wa-l-ishrāf*, ed. M.J. de Goeje, Leiden, 1894, p. 396

Ibn al-Nadīm, *Fihrist*, p. 216

ʿAbd al-Jabbār, *Tathbīt dalāʾil al-nubuwwa*, ed. ʿA.-K. ʿUthmān, Beirut, 1966, pp. 128, 129, 232, 371, 374, 407, 414, 508

al-Sharīf al-Murtaḍā, *al-Shāfī fī l-Imāma*, ed. ʿA.Z. al-Ḥusaynī, Tehran, 1986, i, pp. 89-90

Aḥmad ibn ʿAlī l-Najāshī, *Kitāb al-rijāl*, Bombay, 1898-99, pp. 23, 47

Abū Jaʿfar Muḥammad al-Ṭūsī, *Fihrist*, ed. A. Sprenger, *et al.*, Calcutta, 1853-55, pp. 99, 263-64, 586-88

al-Shahrastānī, *Kitāb al-milal wa-l-niḥal*, ed. W. Cureton, London, 1846, p. 188

Ibn al-Jawzī, *al-Muntaẓam fī tārīkh al-mulūk wa-l-umam*, Hyderabad, 1938, vi, p. 102

Secondary

D. Thomas, art, 'Abū ʿĪsā al-Warrāq', in *EI3*

D. Thomas, *Early Muslim polemic against Christianity, Abū ʿĪsā al-Warrāq's 'Against the Incarnation'*, Cambridge, 2002

S. Stroumsa, *Freethinkers of medieval Islam. Ibn al-Rāwandī, Abū Bakr al-Rāzī, and their impact on Islamic thought*, Leiden, 1999
Van Ess, *TG* i, pp. 431-34, iv, pp. 289-94, 296-349 (passim), vi, pp. 430-33, 469-81
D. Thomas, *Anti-Christian polemic in early Islam. Abū ʿĪsā al-Warrāq's 'Against the Trinity'*, Cambridge, 1992
M.J. McDermott, 'Abū ʿĪsā al-Warrāq on the *Dahriyya*', *MUSJ* 50 (1984) 385-402
W. Madelung, 'Abū ʿĪsā al-Warrāq über die Bardesaniten, Marcioniten and Kantäer', in A. R. Roemer and A. Noth (eds), *Studien zur Geschichte und Kultur des Vorderen Orients. Festschrift für Bertold Spuler*, Leiden, 1981, 210-24
W. Madelung, 'Bemerkungen zur imamitischen Firaq-Literatur', *Der Islam* 43 (1967) 37-52
J. van Ess, 'Al-Fārābī and Ibn al-Rāwandī', *Hamdard Islamicus* 3 (1960) 3-15
Sezgin, GAS i, p. 620
Brockelmann, S i, pp. 241-42

WORKS ON CHRISTIAN-MUSLIM RELATIONS

Kitāb maqālāt al-nās wa-ikhtilāfihim, 'The teachings of people and the differences between them'

DATE Unknown
ORIGINAL LANGUAGE Arabic

DESCRIPTION

The work is not extant, but references in later works (see Thomas, *Anti-Christian polemic*, p. 23) suggest it was a descriptive account of the major beliefs known in Abū ʿĪsā's time, among them, Judaism, Christianity, dualist sects, and pre-Islamic Arabian beliefs. There is no sign of any polemical content. Although the date of the work is unknown, it must have been written before *al-Radd ʿalā l-thalāth firaq min al-Naṣārā*, where it is mentioned.

SIGNIFICANCE

It was Abū ʿĪsā's main source for his own *al-Radd ʿalā l-thalāth firaq min al-Naṣārā*, and probably for his other polemical works, and was a major source for later polemicists, particularly its accounts of dualist beliefs (see Thomas, 'Abū ʿĪsā al-Warrāq', pp. 276-83).

MANUSCRIPTS —

EDITIONS AND TRANSLATIONS —

STUDIES

D. Thomas, 'Abū ʿĪsā al-Warrāq and the History of Religions', *JSS* 41 (1996) 275-90

Al-Radd ʿalā l-thalāth firaq min al-Naṣārā, 'The refutation of the three Christian sects' (longer version)

DATE Unknown, but probably mid-9th c.

ORIGINAL LANGUAGE Arabic

DESCRIPTION

The *Radd* is preserved in Yaḥyā ibn ʿAdī's *Tabyīn ghalaṭ Muḥammad ibn Hārūn*, where it is quoted extensively and probably exhaustively in the course of the Christian's response to its arguments. It contains a descriptive introduction to Christian beliefs about the Trinity and Incarnation, together with detailed refutations of the two doctrines as expressed by the Melkites, East-Syrians and Syrian Orthodox. These refutations are based entirely upon the kind of immediate commonsense logic that both Muslims and Christians would share; there is no reference to scriptural proofs.

Ibn al-Nadīm (*Fihrist*, p. 216) lists three versions of the work, *kabīr*, *awsaṭ*, *aṣghar*, 'long, medium and shorter'. Given the length of the work preserved in Yaḥyā ibn ʿAdī's *Tabyīn* and the fact that Yaḥyā ibn ʿAdī took it as the target of his refutation, this is presumably the long version.

SIGNIFICANCE

The *Radd* is the longest and most detailed Muslim attack devoted to the two major Christian doctrines that has survived, and the longest extant pre-14th century anti-Christian polemic. Descriptive accounts and arguments from it influenced anti-Christian polemic for more than a century after its appearance (Thomas, *Anti-Christian polemic*, pp. 42-50; *Early Muslim polemic*, pp. 75-82)

MANUSCRIPTS

MS BNF – Ar. 167 (624/1227)

MS BNF – Ar. 168 (14th c, restored in 994/1586)

MS Vat – Ar. 113 (626/1229)
MS Vat – Ar.114 (712/1312, copy of BNF arabe 167)
MS Cairo, Coptic Patriarchate – 506 (638/1241 copy of Vat ar. 113) (see Thomas, *Anti-Christian polemic*, pp. 51-53)

EDITIONS AND TRANSLATIONS

Thomas, *Anti-Christian polemic* (edition and trans. of the introduction and refutation of the Trinity)

Thomas, *Early Muslim polemic* (edition and trans. of part of the introduction and refutation of the Incarnation)

E. Platti, 'La doctrine des Chrétiens d'après Abū ʿĪsā al-Warrāq dans sa traité sur la Trinité', *MIDEO* 20 (1991) 7-30 (French trans. of the introduction)

E. Platti, *Abū ʿĪsā al-Warrāq, Yaḥyā ibn ʿAdī. De l'Incarnation*, Louvain, 1987 (*CSCO* 490-91) (ed. and French trans. of Yaḥyā ibn ʿAdī's *Tabyīn* incorporating his quotations from Abū ʿĪsā's work)

A. Abel, *Le livre pour la réfutation des trois sectes chrétiennes*, Brussels, 1949 (ed. and French trans. of the introduction and the refutation of the Incarnation)

STUDIES

Thomas, *Early Muslim polemic against Christianity*, pp. 60-82

Thomas, *Anti-Christian polemic in early Islam*, pp. 51-65

E. Platti, 'Les objections de Abū ʿĪsā al-Warrāq concernant l'incarnation et les réponses de Yaḥyā Ibn ʿAdī', *Quaderni di Studi Arabi* 5-6 (1987-88) 661-66

al-Sharfī, *al-Fikr al-Islāmī*, pp. 141-46

Al-Radd ʿalā l-thalāth firaq min al-Naṣārā, 'The refutation of the three Christian sects' (medium version)

DATE Unknown
ORIGINAL LANGUAGE Arabic

DESCRIPTION

It was presumably a summary of the longer version of the *Radd*. The work has not survived, and is only known from Ibn al-Nadīm's list (*Fihrist*, p. 216) where it is referred to as *Kitāb al-radd ʿalā l-Naṣārā l-awsaṭ*, 'The refutation of the Christians, medium version'.

There is a slim possibility that traces of it are to be seen in Abū Bakr al-Bāqillānī's *Kitāb al-tamhīd*, 'Introduction', where the Ashʿarī theologian is clearly following Abū ʿĪsā's *Radd*, but includes a few details that are not found in the extant version; cf. e.g. *Tamhīd* (ed. R.J. McCarthy, Beirut, 1957, pp. 87-88, §§ 154-55) and *Radd* (ed. Thomas, *Early Muslim polemic*, pp. 88-89, §§ 11-12). Unless al-Bāqillānī was inserting his own information at this point, or using an intermediary source, he may have been following either this or the shorter version of the *Radd*, to which Abū ʿĪsā may have added these details.

SIGNIFICANCE
See the account of the significance of the longer version above.

MANUSCRIPTS —
EDITIONS AND TRANSLATIONS —
STUDIES —

Al-Radd ʿalā l-thalāth firaq min al-Naṣārā, 'The refutation of the three Christian sects' (shorter version)

DATE Unknown
ORIGINAL LANGUAGE Arabic

DESCRIPTION
It was presumably a summary of either of the longer versions of the *Radd*. The work has not survived, and is only known from Ibn al-Nadīm's list, (*Fihrist*, p. 216) where it is referred to as *Kitāb al-radd ʿalā l-Naṣārā l-aṣghar*, 'The refutation of the Christians, shorter version'.

As with the medium version of the *Radd*, there is a slim possibility that traces of it are to be seen in Abū Bakr al-Bāqillānī's *Kitāb al-tamhīd*, 'Introduction'.

SIGNIFICANCE
See the account of the significance of the longer version above.

MANUSCRIPTS —
EDITIONS AND TRANSLATIONS —
STUDIES —

Al-Naqḍ ʿalā man uḍīfa ilā l-Yaʿqūbiyya… wa-ʿalā bāqī ṣunūf al-Naṣārā, 'The invalidation of those who are related to the Jacobites … and of other Christian groups'

DATE Unknown
ORGINAL LANGUAGE Arabic

DESCRIPTION
At the end of the *Radd* (see Thomas, *Early Muslim polemic*, pp. 276-77), Abū ʿĪsā declares that he plans a separate work in which he will refute the monophysite sects of the Julianists and Eutychians, together with other sects such as the Maronites, Sabellians, Gregorians, Macedonians, Apollinarians, Arians, Eunomians, Photinians and followers of Paul of Samosata. He does not name this work, and there is no indication that it was ever written (though see the discussion in Thomas, *Early Muslim polemic*, p. 304).

SIGNIFICANCE
Abū ʿĪsā's statement of intention in the *Radd* indicates both that he was aware of the different teachings of minor Christian sects and that knowledge of them was in circulation among Muslims at this time.

MANUSCRIPTS —
EDITIONS AND TRANSLATIONS —
STUDIES —

David Thomas 2007

John the Writer

Uncertain name; Yūḥannā (John) is a possibility. 'John the Writer' is a convenient appellation

DATE OF BIRTH c. 820
PLACE OF BIRTH Egypt
DATE OF DEATH After 866
PLACE OF DEATH Egypt

BIOGRAPHY

The author of the principal source for *Lives* 47-55 of *The History of the patriarchs of Alexandria* (covering the years 767-880) was a Coptic Orthodox monk and a former disciple of the hermit Amūna, who around the year 840 had taught him to write and prophesied that he would be the author of the next section of *The History of the patriarchs* (Evetts, PO 10, pp. 531-32). A little later, he became spiritual son and scribe to Patriarch Yūsāb I (the 52nd patriarch, 831-49), whom he attended even in prison (Evetts, PO 10, pp. 533-34, 543). He also served Patriarch Shenute I (the 55th patriarch, 859-80), who urged him to write his history (Evetts, PO 10, p. 360), a task in which he was engaged in the year 866 ('Abd al-Masīḥ and Burmester, ii/1, p. 31 (Arabic), p. 44 (trans.)).

The identification of this author as Yūḥannā (John) is based on a third-person reference in *The History of the patriarchs* to a Yūḥannā who was scribe to Patriarch Shenute I – but this in what is normally a first-person narrative ('Abd al-Masīḥ and Burmester, ii/1, p. 52 (Arabic), p. 76 (trans.)). While this evidence for the author's name is not decisive, it has become standard in the scholarly literature (Johnson, 'Further remarks'; Den Heijer, *Mawhūb*, and 'Réflexions') to refer to this author as John II in order to differentiate him from the author of the principal source for Lives 43-46, who is referred to as John I. Here we use 'John the Writer' and 'John the Deacon' (q.v.), respectively.

MAIN SOURCES OF INFORMATION

Primary

Our sole source of knowledge about 'John the Writer' is the historical compilation *Siyar al-bīʿa al-muqaddasa*, 'Lives of the holy Church' or *The History of the patriarchs of Alexandria*. For the published editions of the Arabic appropriation of John the Writer's work, written originally in Coptic, see below. In addition, there is an important notice by Mawhūb ibn Manṣūr ibn Mufarrij (q.v.) at the end of Life 65:

A.S. Atiya, Y. ʿAbd al-Masīḥ and O.H.E. Khs.-Burmester (eds), *History of the patriarchs of the Egyptian Church, known as the History of the holy Church, by Sawīrus ibn al-Mukaffaʿ, Bishop of al-Ašmūnīn*, ii/2, Cairo, 1948, pp. 161-62 (Arabic text), pp. 243-44 (English trans.).

Secondary

J. den Heijer, 'Réflexions sur la composition de l'*Histoire des patriarches d'Alexandrie*. Les auteurs des sources coptes', in W. Godlewski (ed.), *Coptic studies*, Warsaw, 1990, 107-13, pp. 111-12

J. den Heijer, *Mawhūb ibn Manṣūr ibn Mufarriǧ et l'historiographie copto-arabe. Étude sur la composition de l'*Histoire des patriarches d'Alexandrie, Louvain, 1989 (*CSCO* 513), pp. 8-9, 66-67, 118-19, 146-49.

D.W. Johnson, 'Further remarks on the Arabic history of the patriarchs of Alexandria', *OC* 61 (1977) 103-116, pp. 110-12

WORKS ON CHRISTIAN-MUSLIM RELATIONS

Title unknown

DATE 866 (for at least part of his work)
ORIGINAL LANGUAGE Coptic

DESCRIPTION

The Coptic text of the *Lives* of the 47th-55th patriarchs by the author we are calling 'John the Writer' was among the sources found in the late 11th century by the Alexandrian deacon Mawhūb ibn Manṣūr ibn Mufarrij and his collaborators as part of their project of compiling an Arabic-language history of the Coptic Orthodox patriarchs (see den Heijer, *Mawhūb*); the copy of this text was found at the monastery of Nahyā in Giza. No fragment of the original Coptic has been preserved, so we know the author's work only as it was translated and edited. It appears to be the principal source for *The History of the patriarchs of Alexandria* for the nine patriarchates in the period 767-880.

The work tells a rather dismal story of the suffering and decline of the Coptic Orthodox church during the ʿAbbasid period in Egypt, which was marked by onerous tax policies and recurrent civil strife. Patriarch Mark II (the 49th patriarch, 799-819) was forced to flee the city of Alexandria, opening a new stage in the relationship between the patriarchs and their city; tax revolts such as the 'Bashmuric' uprising of 831 were crushed with great violence; discriminatory legislation against *dhimmī*s was enacted under the Caliph al-Mutawakkil (r. 847-61); and in the chaos following al-Mutawakkil's death, monasteries were sacked and pilgrimage to the great shrine of St Menas was cut off. At a number of points, the text bears witness to an increased incidence of Copts converting to Islam.

For 'John the Writer', Satan is constantly at work in the world, stirring up trouble for the faithful. It is worth noting in John's account, however, that Satan works through Muslims and also through Christians, just as God is at work through Muslims as well as through Christians. While 'John the Writer' chronicles a difficult period in the history of the Coptic church, he refuses the temptation to apportion blame solely on the basis of religious affiliation.

SIGNIFICANCE

The collection of *Lives* composed by 'John the Writer' and preserved (in edited Arabic translation) in *The History of the patriarchs* is an important contemporary source for our knowledge of the history of the Coptic Orthodox church and of Christian-Muslim relations in Egypt during the ʿAbbasid period.

MANUSCRIPTS

See den Heijer, *Mawhūb*, pp. 18-27. For the contribution of 'John the Writer', Lives 47-55, we might mention the following MSS, which represent the two different recensions of the work:

MS BNF – ar. 303 (14th c.) (contains Lives 49-65, unpublished witness to the 'primitive' recension)

MS BNF – ar. 301 (15th c.) ('Vulgate' recension; base MS for the editions of Lives 47-52 by Seybold, 1904, and Evetts)

MS Cairo, Coptic Museum – Hist. 1 (a) (Simaika 93, Graf 134) (13th-14th c.) ('Vulgate' recension; base MS for the edition of Lives 53-55 by ʿAbd al-Masīḥ and Burmester)

EDITIONS AND TRANSLATIONS

ʿAbd al-Masīḥ and Burmester, *History of the patriarchs of the Egyptian Church*, ii/1, Cairo, 1943 (edition of the 'Vulgate' recension of Lives 53-55, with English trans.)

B.T.A. Evetts, *History of the patriarchs of the Coptic Church of Alexandria*, IV *Mennas I to Joseph (849)*, PO 10 (1914), pp. 357-551 (edition of the 'Vulgate' recension of Lives 47-52, with English trans.)

C.F. Seybold, *Severus Ben al-Muqaffaʿ. Historia patriarcharum Alexandrinorum*, Beirut, 1904 (*CSCO* 52), pp. 217-300 (edition of the 'Vulgate' recension of Lives 47-52)

STUDIES

For the identification of John the Writer's contribution to *The History of the patriarchs of Alexandria*, see:

Den Heijer, 'Réflexions sur la composition de l'*Histoire des patriarches d'Alexandrie*', pp. 110-11

Den Heijer, *Mawhūb ibn Manṣūr ibn Mufarriǧ et l'historiographie copto-arabe*, pp. 8, 66-67, 96-98, 118-19, 145-46

Johnson, 'Further remarks on the Arabic history of the patriarchs of Alexandria', pp. 110-12

The section of *The History of the patriarchs of Alexandria* for which John the Writer's history is the principal source is regularly used by those who study the ʿAbbasid period in Egypt. Examples (apart from general histories of the Coptic Orthodox church) include:

M.N. Swanson, *The Coptic papacy in Islamic Egypt*, Cairo, forthcoming, ch. 3

J. den Heijer, 'Relations between Copts and Syrians in the light of recent discoveries at Dayr as-Suryān', in M. Immerzeel and J. van der Vliet (eds), *Coptic studies on the threshold of a new millennium*, Louvain, 2004, ii, 923-38, pp. 925-29

M.S.A. Mikhail, *Egypt from late antiquity to early Islam: Copts, Melkites, and Muslims shaping a new society*, Los Angeles CA, 2004 (Diss. UCLA)

C. Décobert, 'Maréotide médiévale. Des bédouins et des chrétiens', in C. Décobert (ed.), *Alexandrie médiévale* 2, Cairo, 2002, 127-67

M. Martin, 'Une lecture de l'Histoire des patriarches d'Alexandrie', *Proche-Orient Chrétien* 35 (1985) 15-36, pp. 19-22

Mark N. Swanson 2008

Al-Jāḥiẓ

Abū ʿUthmān ʿAmr ibn Baḥr al-Fuqaymī al-Jāḥiẓ

DATE OF BIRTH c. 776
PLACE OF BIRTH Basra
DATE OF DEATH 869
PLACE OF DEATH Basra

BIOGRAPHY

Al-Jāḥiẓ was born and brought up in Basra, and there learnt the Arabic language and literary skills for which he became celebrated. In *kalām* he was a student of Ibrāhīm al-Naẓẓām, though he did not always agree with his master's views. Even while still a student in the early 800s, al-Jāḥiẓ wrote works that brought him to the attention of the Caliph al-Maʾmūn.

He spent long periods in Baghdad and Samarra, though he always returned to his home town. He made a living by his literary skills, and his books were dedicated to some of the leading court officials of his day.

Nearly 200 of al-Jāḥiẓ's works are known. They range from encyclopedias such as the *Kitāb al-ḥayawān*, 'Animals', and literary essays, to political works in which he favored the ʿAbbasids, and works devoted to religion. These include disputations such as *Kitāb faḍīlat al-Muʿtazila*, 'The excellence of the Muʿtazila', and *Kitāb al-radd ʿalā Abī Isḥāq al-Naẓẓām*, 'Refutation of Abū Isḥāq al-Naẓẓām', typically Muʿtazilī works such as *Kitāb khalq al-Qurʾān*, 'The createdness of the Qurʾān', *Kitāb al-waʿd wa-l-waʿīd*, 'The promise and the threat', and works against non-Muslims such as *Radd ʿalā al-Yahūd*, 'Refutation of the Jews'. He is not known for any distinctive theological opinions, and among immediate successors he was remembered mainly for his pro-ʿAbbasid works, which attracted many rejoinders.

MAIN SOURCES OF INFORMATION

Primary

al-Khaṭīb al-Baghdādī, *Taʾrīkh Baghdād*, 14 vols, Cairo, 1931, xii, pp. 212-22
Ibn ʿAsākir, *Tārīkh madīnat Dimashq*, ed. ʿA.G. ʿAmrawī, Beirut, xlv, 1996, pp. 431-44 (= *Revue de l'Académie Arabe de Damas* 9, 1929, pp. 203-17)

Yāqūt, *Kitāb irshād al-arīb ilā maʿrifat al-adīb*, ed. D. Margoliouth, 7 vols, London, 1907-27, vi, pp. 56-80

Secondary

ʿA. Shalaq, *Al-Jāḥiẓ*, Beirut, 2006

Van Ess, *TG* iv, pp. 96-118; vi, pp. 313-37

C. Pellat, 'Nouvel essai d'inventaire de l'oeuvre Ǧāḥiẓienne', *Arabica* 31 (1984) 117-64

C. Pellat, 'Al-Ǧāḥiẓ jugé par la posterité', *Arabica* 27 (1980) 1-67

C. Pellat, *The life and works of Jāḥiẓ*, trans. D.M. Hawke, Berkeley CA, 1969

C. Pellat, *Arabische Geisteswelt*, trans. W.M. Müller, Zürich, 1967

C. Pellat, 'Ǧāḥiẓiana III. Essai d'inventaire de l'oeuvre Ǧāḥiẓienne', *Arabica* 3 (1956) 147-80

C. Pellat, *Le milieu baṣrien et la formation de Ǧāhiẓ*, Paris, 1953

C. Pellat, 'Ǧāḥiẓ à Baġdād et à Sāmarrā', *RSO* 27 (1952) 47-67

WORKS ON CHRISTIAN-MUSLIM RELATIONS

Kitāb al-ḥujja fī tathbīt al-nubuwwa, 'The Proof about confirmation of prophethood'

DATE before 847
ORIGINAL LANGUAGE Arabic

DESCRIPTION

Since the work is mentioned in the *Kitāb al-ḥayawān* (ed. ʿA.S. Hārūn, 7 vols, Cairo, 1965-69, i, p. 9, vii, p. 200), which was finished by 847 (Pellat, 'Ǧāḥiẓiana', p. 170), it must have been completed before then. Later authors give its title in various forms, though al-Jāḥiẓ himself refers to it twice by the title given above. The work on prophethood by al-Jāḥiẓ which ʿAbd al-Jabbār (*Tathbīt dalāʾil al-nubuwwa*, ed. ʿA.K. ʿUthmān, Beirut, 1966, p. 511) mentions in passing is presumably this.

The work survives in the form of a series of excerpts. In these, Christians and Christianity are mentioned a number of times, particularly at the end of 28 (in Hārūn's numbering of excerpts, pp. 251-52), where al-Jāḥiẓ argues that the miracles performed by Jesus and Paul are proof that they must have held true beliefs because God would not otherwise have bestowed miracles upon them; in 30 (pp. 253-54), where he says that Christians accorded divinity to Jesus out of misguided love; in 38 (pp. 269-70), where he argues that since Christian converts to Islam from diverse places who do not know one another all cite the predictions to Muḥammad in the Bible as reason, the predictions must be there; and in 41 (p. 279), where he argues that just as

Jesus' miracles of healing were intended for a time when medical ability was esteemed, so Muḥammad's miracle of the Qurʾān was intended for a time when rhetoric was valued.

SIGNIFICANCE

It is a rare surviving example of a very popular genre in early Islam, and it gives first-hand information about the contents of such works. It is likely to contain as many arguments original to al-Jāḥiẓ as from the common stock.

MANUSCRIPTS

MS Berlin, Staatsbibliothek – Ahlwardt 5032, fols 100v-101v, 113v-115v (1650) (on the questionable value of this collection of extracts from al-Jāḥiẓ's works, see C. Pellat, 'Notice sur un manuscript arabe de Berlin', *Oriens* 7 (1954) 85-86)

MS Cairo, Dār al-Kutub al-Miṣriyya, 19 *adab* Taymūr (1897)

MS Istanbul, Emamet Hazinesi 1358 (n.d.)

EDITIONS AND TRANSLATIONS

Rasāʾil al-Jāḥiẓ, ed. ʿA.S. Hārūn, 4 vols, Cairo, 1964-79, iii, 223-81 (repr. ʿAlī Abū Malḥim, ed., *Rasāʾil al-Jāḥiẓ*, 3 vols, Beirut, 1987, ii, *al-Rasāʾil al-kalāmiyya – kashshāf āthār al-Jāḥiẓ*, pp. 127-57; repr. M.B. ʿUyūn al-Sūd, *Rasāʾil al-Jāḥiẓ*, 4 vols, Beirut, 2000, iii, *al-Fuṣūl al-mukhtāra min kutub al-Jāḥiẓ*, pp. 171-214)

Pellat, *The life and works of al-Jāḥiẓ*, pp. 39-48 (partial trans.)

Pellat, *Arabische Geisteswelt*, pp. 64-80 (partial trans.)

O. Rescher, *Excerpte und Übersetzungen aus den Schriften des Philologen und Dogmatikers Gāḥiẓ am Baçra*, Stuttgart, 1931, pp. 139-45 (partial trans.)

STUDIES

Van Ess, *TG* iv, pp. 112-15 and *passim*

S. Stroumsa, 'The signs of prophecy. The emergence and early development of a theme in Arabic theological literature', *Harvard Theological Review* 78 (1985) 101-14

C. Pellat, 'Christologie Ǧāḥiẓienne', *SI* 31 (1970), 219-32 (repr. in *Études sur l'histoire socio-culturelle de l'Islam (VIIe-XVe siècle)*, London, 1976)

Al-Radd ʿalā l-Naṣārā, 'Refutation of the Christians'

DATE mid-9th c., possibly before 847
ORIGINAL LANGUAGE Arabic

DESCRIPTION
This work is usually referred to by later authors as simply *al-Radd ʿalā l-Naṣārā*. Al-Jāḥiẓ himself once refers to it as *kitābunā ʿalā l-Naṣārā* (*Kitāb al-ḥayawān*, ed. Hārūn, iv, p. 28), but he also refers to *kitābī ʿalā l-Naṣārā wa-l-Yahūd* (*Kitāb al-ḥayawān*, i, p. 9). These both appear to be descriptions rather than titles, and the latter can plausibly be taken as an account of the scathing criticisms of both Jews and Christians in Islamic society with which the surviving work opens, rather than as a reference to another polemical work now lost.

A work on Christian-Muslim polemic by al-Jāḥiẓ that is mentioned by Brockelmann (*GAL*, S i, p. 240), the *Kitāb ḥujaj al-Naṣārā ʿalā l-Muslimīn*, 'Proofs of the Christians against the Muslims', might appear to be a separate composition that sides with the opponents targeted in the *Radd*. A number of scholars (e.g. M. Allard, 'Les chrétiens à Bagdād', *Arabica* 9 (1962) 375-88, p. 383) have referred to it as such. However, this identification is probably based on a misreading of the one source that may appear to mention this title, Ibn Qutayba's *Kitāb taʾwīl mukhtalif al-ḥadīth* (ed. ʿAbd al-Qādir Aḥmad ʿAṭā, Cairo, 1982, p. 76). This is in a passage where Ibn Qutayba severely criticizes al-Jāḥiẓ's habit of writing in defense of two opposing viewpoints, and accuses him of playing into the hands of Christians and causing Muslims to have doubts about their religion when he cites 'proofs of Christians against Islam' in a book of his. Ibn Qutayba does not refer here to an actual title of a book, and he may well have in mind the Christian arguments against Islam which al-Jāḥiẓ lists in the *Radd*, such as their critique of contradictory ḥadīth.

The *Radd ʿalā l-Naṣārā* has usually been connected with al-Mutawakkil's anti-*dhimmī* measures of 850 (e.g. Pellat, Ǧāḥiẓ à Baġdād', p. 58, n. 1), but there is reason to question this. The dating is based upon Yāqūt (*Irshād*, vi, p. 72), who reports that al-Fatḥ ibn Khāqān, al-Mutawakkil's vizier, wrote to al-Jāḥiẓ to encourage him to complete his *Radd*. This must have been after 847, when al-Mutawakkil came to the throne, and fits well with the anti-*dhimmī* measures he instituted. However, in *Kitāb al-ḥayawān*, which was dedicated to the vizier Ibn al-Zayyāt, al-Jāḥiẓ himself mentions the *Radd* as a work that is already finished. The vizier fell from favor when al-Mutawakkil acceded and died soon afterwards, so according to this the *Radd* must have been completed before 847 (Pellat, 'Ğāḥiẓiana', 170).

There is no clear evidence in the work to support a connection with the caliph. In fact, the stated reason for its composition was a letter from a group of Muslims asking for al-Jāḥiẓ's help to answer a series of questions asked them by some Christians. This private and obscure origin (if it is not a literary ploy) does not fit well with a work that was being solicited as political propaganda. Thus, the *Radd* may well be the work written before al-Mutawakkil's reign which is mentioned in *Kitāb al-ḥayawān*. This would make the other anti-Christian work which ʿAbd al-Jabbār knew (see below) a contender for this semi-official refutation of Christianity.

The *Radd* is extant in the form of ten excerpts of different lengths, edited down from the original by a certain ʿUbayd Allāh ibn Ḥassān (d. 1058; Pellat, 'Nouvel essai', p. 119) before any of the known copies was made. In the first of these, al-Jāḥiẓ lists the Christians' six questions, and then in the second and third he launches into a lengthy account of the social successes and moral failures of Christians living under Muslim rule, together with some comments on Jews. In the following excerpts, he takes up some of the questions posed by the Christians, and discusses others that are found elsewhere in contemporary and later polemic, including an intriguing comparison between Jesus as adopted Son of God and Abraham as friend of God, the title accorded to him in the Qurʾān.

SIGNIFICANCE

The *Radd* contains instructive information about the social and legal conditions of Muslim and Christian relations in ʿAbbasid society. While this is almost certainly exaggerated for effect, it nevertheless gives a unique insight into the mixed urban life of the period and the relative ease with which Christians moved in society.

The work was well-known to Muslims in later times. Abū ʿAlī al-Jubbāʾī and ʿAbd al-Jabbār both made use of it (ʿAbd al-Jabbār, *Mughnī*, v, ed. M.M. al-Khuḍayrī, Cairo, 1958, pp. 107-08, 113, 149, 150-51), while al-Bāqillānī (*Iʿjāz al-Qurʾān*, ed. A. Ṣaqr, Cairo, 1963, p. 248), and probably al-Māturīdī (*Kitāb al-tawḥīd*, ed. F. Kholeif, Beirut, 1970, p. 213), were aware of arguments in it.

MANUSCRIPTS

MS BL Suppl. – 1129 (1877)
MS Cairo, Azhar – 6836 (1895)

MS Cairo, Dār al-kutub al-miṣriyya – 19 *adab* Taymūr (1897)
MS Istanbul, Emamet Hazinesi 1358 (n.d.)

EDITIONS AND TRANSLATIONS

C.D. Fletcher, *Anti-Christian polemic in early Islam. A translation and analysis of Abū ʿUthmān ʿAmr b. Baḥr al-Jāḥiẓ's risāla:* Radd ʿalā al-Naṣārā *(A reply to the Christians)*, Montreal, 2002 (MA thesis, McGill University)

M. ʿA. al-Sharqāwī, *al-Mukhtār fī l-radd ʿalā l-Naṣārā maʿa dirāsa taḥqīqiyya taqwīmiyya*, Cairo, 1984 (based upon Finkel and Hārūn; repr. Beirut, 1991)

Rasāʾil al-Jāḥiẓ, ed. ʿA.S. Hārūn, 4 vols, Cairo, 1964-79, iii, pp. 301-51 (repr., ed. ʿAlī Abū Malḥim, 3 vols, Beirut, 1987, ii, *al-Rasāʾil al-kalāmiyya – kashshāf āthār al-Jāḥiẓ*, pp. 253-89; repr., ed. Muḥammad Bāsil ʿUyūn al-Sūd, 4 vols, Beirut, 2000, iii, *al-Fuṣūl al-mukhtāra min kutub al-Jāḥiẓ*, pp. 231-64)

Pellat, *The life and works of Jāḥiẓ*, pp. 86-91 (partial trans.)

Pellat, *Arabische Geisteswelt*, Zürich, 1967, pp. 141-48 (partial trans.)

I.S. Allouche, 'Un traité de polémique christiano-musulmane au ixe siècle', *Hespéris* 26 (1939) 123-55 (partial trans.)

Rescher, *Excerpte und Übersetzungen*, pp. 40-67 (partial trans.)

J. Finkel, 'A risāla of al-Jāḥiẓ', *JAOS* 47 (1927) 311-34 (partial trans., repr. in N.A. Newman, *The early Christian-Muslim dialogue. A collection of documents from the first three Islamic centuries (632-900 A.D.), translations with commentary*, Hatfield PA, 1993, pp. 685-717, with some additional notes)

Thalāth rasāʾil li-Abī ʿUthmān ʿAmr ibn Baḥr al-Jāḥiẓ, ed. J. Finkel, Cairo, 1926 (repr. Cairo, 1382 [1962]), 10-38

STUDIES

D. Thomas, 'Arab Christianity', in K. Parry (ed.), *The Blackwell companion to Eastern Christianity*, Oxford, 2007, 1-22, pp. 11-14

S. Rissanen, *Theological encounter of Oriental Christians with Islam during early ʿAbbasid rule*, Åbo, 1993, pp. 170-75

M. Erdem, 'Câhiz ve el-Muhtâr fi'r-Redd ala'n-Nasara isimli risalesi', *Ankara Üniversitesi İlâhiyat Fakültesi Dergisi* 31 (1989) 454-74

O. Schumann, *Der Christus der Muslime. Christologische Aspekte in der arabisch-islamischen Literatur*, Cologne, 1988², pp. 46-61

J. Sadan, 'Some literary problems concerning Judaism and Jewry in medieval Arabic sources', in M. Sharon (ed.), *Studies in Islamic history and civilization in honour of Professor David Ayalon*, Leiden, 1986, 353-98, pp. 353-65

al-Sharfī, *al-Fikr al-Islāmī*, pp. 137-40, and see index
Pellat, 'Christologie Ǧāḥiẓienne'
E. Fritsch, *Islam und Christentum im Mittelalter,* Breslau 1930, pp. 13-14

Al-Risālat al-ʿasaliyya, 'The "honey-colored" letter'

DATE mid-9th c., possibly after 847
ORIGINAL LANGUAGE Arabic

DESCRIPTION
ʿAbd al-Jabbār, *Tathbīt*, i, p. 198, knows of this as a separate work from the *Radd*, but it is not mentioned elsewhere, and it has not survived.

SIGNIFICANCE
Its title may include a play upon the yellow waist-band that Christians and other *dhimmīs* were required to wear (though the alternative vocalization *ʿasliyya* would denote 'reviling'). Such a title would have suited a letter written in cooperation with the caliph's re-imposition of the *dhimmī* regulations.

MANUSCRIPTS —
EDITIONS AND TRANSLATIONS —
STUDIES
On the basis of what he suggests are correspondences with al-Jāḥiẓ's *Radd ʿalā l-Naṣārā*, al-Sharfī, *Al-fikr al-Islāmī*, p. 160, identifies the extract published in 1966 by D. Sourdel ('Un pamphlet musulman anonyme d'époque ʿAbbaside', *REI* 34 (1966) 1-33) as part of the *Risālat al-ʿasaliyya*. But that extract is now known to belong to the correspondence attributed to the Emperor Leo III and the Caliph ʿUmar II (q.v.).

David Thomas 2008

Muḥammad ibn Shabīb

Abū Bakr Muḥammad ibn ʿAbdallāh ibn Shabīb al-Baṣrī

DATE OF BIRTH Unknown, probably late 8th c.
PLACE OF BIRTH Unknown
DATE OF DEATH Unknown, mid-9th c.
PLACE OF DEATH Unknown

BIOGRAPHY

Ibn Shabīb was probably born in Basra, but is often mentioned in connection with events in Baghdad. It is generally agreed that he was a student of Ibrāhīm al-Naẓẓām (q.v.), and so he must have known al-Jāḥiẓ (q.v.), who was another of al-Naẓẓām's students. Since al-Naẓẓām was called from Basra to Baghdad in 818, Ibn Shabīb must have studied under him before that date. As a contemporary of al-Jāḥiẓ, it is not unlikely that he died at about the same time as him in the mid-9th century. Ibn al-Nadīm does not include Ibn Shabīb in the *Fihrist*, and little definite was known about him even among Muslims who were his contemporaries. Some thought he was a Murjiʾī, while others thought him a Muʿtazilī. Al-Ashʿarī (*Maqālāt*, pp. 143, 146-47) names him as the leader of a group of Murjiʾī thinkers, but he is best known among later Muslims not for any innovative thinking but for the ideas and information from others which he reports in his main work, the *Kitāb al-tawḥīd*, 'Divine Unity'. Jaʿfar ibn al-Mubashshir (d. 848) refuted his *Kitāb fī l-irjāʾ*, 'The postponement of judgment about the position of sinners', and al-Iskāfī (d. 854) (q.v.) refuted his *Kitāb fī l-waʿīd*, 'The divine threat'. These may be separate works, but could also be parts of the *Kitāb al-tawḥīd*.

MAIN SOURCES OF INFORMATION

Primary

Abū l-Ḥusayn al-Khayyāṭ, *Kitāb al-intiṣār*, ed. and French trans. A. Nader, Beirut, 1957, p. 93

Abū l-Ḥasan al-Ashʿarī, *Maqālāt al-Islāmiyyīn*, ed. H. Ritter, Istanbul, 1930, pp. 137-38, 149, 201

Abū Manṣūr al-Māturīdī, *Kitāb al-tawḥīd*, ed. F. Kholeif, Beirut, 1970, pp. 123-24, 126-29, 137-41, 149, 150, 153-54, 210

Ibn al-Murtaḍā, *Kitāb ṭabaqāt al-Muʿtazila*, ed. S. Diwald-Wilzer, Beirut, 1988, p. 71

Secondary

Van Ess, *TG* iv, pp. 124-31, vi, pp. 338-57

U. Rudolph, *Al-Māturīdī & die sunnitische Theologie in Samarkand*, Leiden, 1997, pp. 178-79

Van Ess, art. 'Muḥammad b. ʿAbd Allāh, called Ibn Shabīb, Abū Bakr', in *EI2*

WORKS ON CHRISTIAN-MUSLIM RELATIONS

Kitāb al-tawḥīd, 'Divine Unity'

DATE Unknown, mid-9th c.
ORIGINAL LANGUAGE Arabic

DESCRIPTION

According to Ibn al-Murtaḍā (*Ṭabaqāt*, p. 71) this was Ibn Shabīb's main work. Its contents are known mainly from quotations and references in al-Māturīdī's *Kitāb al-tawḥīd*, of which it was a main source (assuming that the various references given by the later theologian all derive from this one work).

It contained reports of teachings from dualists, Sabians, Greek philosophers including Aristotle, and also Christians. If it also included the teachings about Islamic issues that other Muslims, such as Jaʿfar ibn al-Mubashshir, al-Iskāfī (q.v.) and al-Ashʿarī attributed to Ibn Shabīb, it would have been one of the earliest known attempts to bring together a range of theological and philosophical matters from both within Islam and outside. It may have contained both descriptions and evaluations of them.

Intriguingly, one of the fragments preserved in this work, in which it is argued that the world must be contingent and therefore temporal, on the grounds that although dissimilar things naturally repel one another they are found combined in the world, recalls the same argument for the contingency of the world given by Ibn Shabīb's Christian contemporary ʿAmmār al-Baṣrī (q.v.) at the beginning of his *Kitāb al-burhān*.

In his refutation of Christianity in his 10th-century *Kitāb al-tawḥīd* (ed. Kholeif, p. 210), al-Māturīdī cites Ibn Shabīb as the source of a teaching from an anonymous group, who are connected in some way with Christianity ('*samiʿtu min muwalladīhim*'), that Christ was son of God by adoption not begetting. This echoes a similar reference made by al-Jāḥiẓ in his *Radd ʿalā l-Naṣārā* (ed. Finkel, p. 25) to Christians who compare Jesus as adopted son of God with Abraham as friend, *khalīl*, of God, according to the designation in the Qurʾān. Al-Jāḥiẓ also mentions a response from al-Naẓẓām to this provocative suggestion (pp. 29-30), and this is summarized without attribution by al-Māturīdī (*Kitāb al-tawḥīd*, p. 213), who could thus have been drawing upon either al-Jāḥiẓ or a putative equivalent account in Ibn Shabīb's work. The explicit reference to Ibn Shabīb by al-Māturīdī and the similarities between al-Māturīdī and al-Jāḥiẓ, together with the historical connection between al-Naẓẓām, al-Jāḥiẓ and Ibn Shabīb, suggest a close relationship between some of the contents of al-Jāḥiẓ's *Radd* and Ibn Shabīb's *Kitāb al-tawḥīd*, and raise the likelihood of dependence on this and maybe other points.

SIGNIFICANCE

The work may be a synthetic treatise of theology, in which disparate elements of debate were brought together. If so, it is the earliest of this kind about whose contents any detailed information is available (and it raises the possibility that at least some of the other lost works from the 9th century with the same title were similar in structure). The presence of elements from non-Muslim beliefs, including Christianity, among discussions of topics from within Islamic thought, suggests they were all treated in relation to one another, and anticipates surviving works from the 10th century in which demonstration of the irrationality of Christianity and other non-Muslim faiths was used in part to underline the truthfulness of Muslim doctrine.

MANUSCRIPTS —

EDITIONS AND TRANSLATIONS —

STUDIES

J.M. Pessagno, 'The reconstruction of the thought of Muḥammad ibn Shabīb', *JAOS* 104 (1984) 445-53

[*Kitāb fī l-nubuwwa*, 'On prophethood']

DATE Unknown, mid-9th c.

ORIGINAL LANGUAGE Arabic

DESCRIPTION

The work is lost. It is mentioned only in passing by ʿAbd al-Jabbār (*Tathbīt dalāʾil al-nubuwwa*, ed. ʿA.K. ʿUthmān, Beirut, 1966, p. 511) together with similar works by other authors, including Abū l-Hudhayl (q.v.) and al-Jāḥiẓ, in the context of a discussion about miracles of Muḥammad. ʿAbd al-Jabbār refers simply to 'their books which they composed about prophethood concerning miracles which are not in the Qurʾān'.

The original title of the work cannot be known.

According to ʿAbd al-Jabbār's brief reference, the work and the others mentioned with it contained discussions of the miracles of Muḥammad as these are recorded in the sources of his life and mission, and which are so well attested that they are incontestibly true.

SIGNIFICANCE

The element of the work referred to by ʿAbd al-Jabbār is evidently a justification of Muḥammad's miraculous actions and a defense of them against opponents who deny he performed any. This is a known element in the contemporary debate between Muslims and Christians over Muḥammad's prophetic status and the validation of this by his miracles.

MANUSCRIPTS —

EDITIONS AND TRANSLATIONS —

STUDIES —

David Thomas 2008

The Passion of St Maximilian

Unknown author

DATE OF BIRTH Unknown
PLACE OF BIRTH Unknown
DATE OF DEATH Unknown
PLACE OF DEATH Unknown

BIOGRAPHY —

MAIN SOURCES OF INFORMATION

Primary —

Secondary —

WORKS ON CHRISTIAN-MUSLIM RELATIONS

Passio Sancti Maximiliani 'The Passion of St Maximilian'

DATE 8th or 9th c.
ORIGINAL LANGUAGE Latin

DESCRIPTION
This passion purports to describe the trial at Tebessa in the Roman province of Africa of a young conscript by the name of Maximilian who refused to accept military service and so was condemned to death on 12 March 295. It is an extremely short work (3-4 pages) whose simplicity has generally led to its acceptance as a reliable account of the death of a genuine Christian martyr in 295.

SIGNIFICANCE
While the passion does not mention Islam, it has recently been argued that it is better understood as an 8th- or 9th-century literary fiction designed to encourage African Christians to resist Muslim rule, in particular, not to pay the *jizya* (Woods, 'St Maximilian and the *jizya*'). The main arguments lie in the similarity between the command that Maximilian should wear a lead seal about his neck and the wearing

of such seals by non-Muslim taxpayers from the mid-8th century onwards, and in the absence of any corroborating evidence for the cult of St Maximilian before the mid-9th century.

MANUSCRIPTS

MS Oxford, Bodleian Library - Fell 3 (S.C. 8687), fols 29v-30r (dated 1000-1200)

MS Avranches, Bibliothèque Municipale - 167, fols 80-81 (dated 1200-1300)

MS Dublin, Trinity College – 171 (B. 1. 16), fols 37-39 (dated 1200-1300)

MS Canterbury, Cathedral Library – 42, fol. 35v (dated 1100-1200)

EDITIONS AND TRANSLATIONS

A.A.R. Bastiaensen et al. (eds), *Atti e passioni dei martiri*, Milan, 1987, pp. 233-45 (edition with Italian trans.)

H. Musurillo, *Acts of the Christian Martyrs II*, Oxford, 1972, pp. 244-49 (edition with English trans.)

E. Di Lorenzo, *Gli Acta S. Maximiliani Martyris*, Naples, 1975 (edition with Italian trans.)

T. Ruinart, *Acta primorum martyrum sincera*, Paris, 1689, pp. 309-11 (edition)

STUDIES

A. Rossi, 'Fabio Vittore: dal sangue dei martiri nascono i padri? Per una rilettura degli "Acta Maximiliani"', *Annali di Scienze Religiose* 10 (2005) 181-218

D. Woods, 'St. Maximilian and the *jizya*', in P. Defosse (ed.), *Hommages à Carl Deroux. V. Christianisme et Moyen Âge, Néo-latin et survivance de la latinité*, Brussels, 2003, 266-76

P. Brock, *The riddle of St Maximilian of Tebessa*, Toronto, 2000

P. Brock, 'Why did St Maximilian refuse to serve in the Roman army ?', *JEH* 45 (1994) 195-209

R. Cacitti, R. 'Massimiliano - un obiettore di coscienza del tardo impero', *Humanitas Brescia* 36 (1980) 828-41

P. Siniscalco, *Massimiliano, un obiettore di coscienza del tardo impero. Studi sulla "Passio S. Maximiliani"*, Turin, 1974

David Woods 2007

The Martyrdom of David of Dwin

Unknown author

DATE OF BIRTH Unknown
PLACE OF BIRTH Unknown
DATE OF DEATH Unknown
PLACE OF DEATH Unknown

BIOGRAPHY —

MAIN SOURCES OF INFORMATION

Primary —

Secondary —

WORKS ON CHRISTIAN-MUSLIM RELATIONS

Khach'azgeats' nahatakn ew k'ajayaght' vkayn K'ristosi , 'The cross-bearing athlete of God and brave martyr of Christ'. Modern title: 'The Martyrdom of David of Dwin'

DATE 8th or 9th c.
ORIGINAL LANGUAGE Armenian

DESCRIPTION
David (Dawitʿ) was an Arab or Persian originally called Surhan, who settled in Armenia in the 660s. He was converted to Christianity and baptized by Catholicos Anastas (661-67). Arrested by the Muslim governor, he refused to revert to Islam and was crucified on 23 Areg. The year is uncertain: 703 or 705. The Synaxarion (G. Bayan, *Le synaxaire arménien, Patrologia Orientalis* 5-21, 1909-30) notes his commemoration on 31 March. His martyrdom is mentioned by John Catholicos (Yovhannes Draskhanakerts'i) in his *Patmut'iwn Hayots'* (see edition Tbilis, 1912, pp. 94-95; trans. in K.H. Maksoudian, *Yovhannes Draskhanakertc'i. History of Armenia*, Atlanta GA, 1987, p. 107).

SIGNIFICANCE

This martyrology is important as a source for the settlement of Muslims in Armenia in the 7th-8th centuries and the interaction between the settlers and the local Armenians.

MANUSCRIPTS

MS Jerusalem, St James Armenian Patriarchate – 1, pt. 3, fols 279r-281v (1418)

MS Vienna, Mekhitarist Library – 2 fols 306r-309r (15th c.)

The manuscripts used for the printed editions are not specified by the editors.

In addition, there are innumerable brief accounts in synaxaria and miscellanies. For the title, see P. Peeters, *Bibliotheca hagiographica orientalis*, Brussels, 1910 (repr. 1954), pp. 57-58, item 246.

EDITIONS AND TRANSLATIONS

Hoyland, *Seeing Islam*, pp. 672-76 (trans. by R.W. Thomson)

Gh. Alishan, *Hayapatum*, 3 vols, Venice, 1901, i, pp. 546-52 (single volume edition, 1901, pp. 240-42)

Sop'erk' Haykakank' 11, Venice 1854, pp. 39-45, and 19, pp. 85-96

I.B. Aucher, *Liakatar Vark' ew Vkayabanut'iwnk' Srbots'*, 12 vols, Venice, 1810-15, vi, pp. 188-216

STUDIES

Hoyland, *Seeing Islam*, pp. 370-73

Robert W. Thomson 2008

Istoria de Mahomet

Unknown author

DATE OF BIRTH Unknown
PLACE OF BIRTH Unknown
DATE OF DEATH Unknown
PLACE OF DEATH Unknown

BIOGRAPHY —

MAIN SOURCES OF INFORMATION

Primary —

Secondary —

WORKS ON CHRISTIAN-MUSLIM RELATIONS

Istoria de Mahomet , 'Story of Muḥammad', *Vita Mahumeti*, 'Life of Muḥammad'

DATE Not later than mid-9th c.
ORIGINAL LANGUAGE Latin

DESCRIPTION
This text contains a brief and polemical life of Muḥammad. It relates Muḥammad's marriage with Khadīja, describes how a golden-mouthed vulture claiming to be Gabriel revealed 'psalms' to Muḥammad, and accuses the Prophet of sexual debauchery. The story also includes the claim that Muḥammad predicted that he would rise from the dead three days after his death. Instead, on the third day dogs desecrated his corpse.

SIGNIFICANCE
This is one of the earliest polemical treatments of Muḥammad in Latin. The text reflects knowledge of the Prophet's biography and a desire to present him as a false prophet and precursor of the Antichrist. Elements standard in Muslim biographies of the Prophet are transformed the better to denigrate him, and the story of his death

and the desecration of his corpse is taken from standard Christian accounts of the Antichrist.

MANUSCRIPTS

The story is not extant as an independent text, but is incorporated into two later texts. Eulogius of Cordova (q.v.) says he discovered the text in the monastery of Leyre (Navarra) in 850; in 857-59, he incorporated it into his *Liber apologeticus martyrum*. It was subsequently recopied in the Asturian *Prophetic chronicle* (883) (*Chronicle of Albelda* [q.v.]).

EDITIONS AND TRANSLATIONS

San Eulogio de Córdoba, *Obras*, trans. P. Herrera Roldán, Madrid, 2005, pp. 203-4

K. Wolf, 'The earliest Latin lives of Muḥammad,' in M. Gervers and R. Bikhazi (eds), *Conversion and continuity. Indigenous Christian communities in Islamic lands, eighth to eighteenth centuries*, Toronto, 1990, 89-101 (repr. in O.R. Constable (ed.), *Medieval Iberia. Readings from Christian, Muslim, and Jewish sources*, Philadelphia, 1997, 48-50)

Y. Bonnaz, *Chroniques Asturiennes (fin IXe siècle)*, Paris, 1987, pp. 5-6 (edition and French trans. of *Cronica profetica*)

D. Millet-Gérard, *Chrétiens mozarabes et culture islamique dans l'Espagne des VIIIe-IXe siècles*, Paris, 1984, pp. 126-27 (French trans.)

Gil, *CSM* ii, p. 483 (edition of Eulogius, *Liber apologeticus martyrum*)

E. Colbert, *The martyrs of Córdoba (850-59). A study of the sources*, Washington, 1962, pp. 336-38 (English trans.)

STUDIES

J. Tolan, *Sons of Ishmael. Muslims through European eyes in the middle ages*, Gainesville, 2008, ch. 2

A. Christys, *Christians in al-Andalus 711-1000*, Richmond, 2002, pp. 62-68

Tolan, *Saracens*, pp. 91-93

R.G. Hoyland, *Seeing Islam*, pp. 512-15

(See also Eulogius of Cordova, above)

John Tolan 2007

Ḥumayd ibn Bakhtiyār

Ḥumayd ibn Saʿīd ibn Bakhtiyār

DATE OF BIRTH Unknown
PLACE OF BIRTH Unknown
DATE OF DEATH Unknown, possibly mid-9th c.
PLACE OF DEATH Unknown

BIOGRAPHY

Ibn al-Nadīm lists Ḥumayd ibn Saʿīd among theologians who may have been Muʿtazilī or Murjiʿī. Since many of these died in the early 10th century, Ḥumayd would appear to have died at the same time. However, Van Ess (*TG* iv, p. 132) identifies him as the Ḥumayd ibn Saʿīd ibn Ḥumayd ibn Baḥr who is mentioned by Abū l-Faraj al-Iṣfahānī as being imprisoned under the Caliph al-Wāthiq (842-47), which means that he may have lived half a century earlier than the *Fihrist* seems to imply.

Among Ḥumayd's 13 known works, none of which is extant, are refutations of Muslim groups, including *Kitāb al-faṣl fī l-radd ʿalā l-mushabbiha*, 'The distinction, in refutation of the anthropomorphists' (Dodge, *The Fihrist of al-Nadīm*, 2 vols, New York, 1970, i, p. 429, reads *faḍl*, 'superiority'), and *Kitāb fīmā aḥdatha baʿḍ al-Muslimīn min al-qirāʾāt wa-wujūhihā*, 'Concerning the readings introduced by some Muslims and their meanings', as well as non-Muslim groups (*Kitāb al-radd ʿalā l-Majūs*, 'Refutation of the Zoroastrians') and a number of works about theological matters (*Kitāb khalq al-Qurʾān*, 'Createdness of the Qurʾān'; *Kitāb nafy al-tajassum ʿan Allāh*, 'Denial that God could take a material form').

MAIN SOURCES OF INFORMATION

Primary

Abū l-Faraj al-Iṣfahānī, *Kitāb al-aghānī*, 24 vols, Cairo (1927-74), xviii, p. 155
Ibn al-Nadīm, *Fihrist*, p. 220 (margin)

Secondary

Van Ess, *TG* iv, pp. 131-33, vi, p. 357

WORKS ON CHRISTIAN-MUSLIM RELATIONS

Kitāb al-radd ʿalā Yūshaʿ Bukht maṭrān Fārs, 'Refutation of Īshōʿbokht, metropolitan of Fars'

DATE Mid-9th c.
ORIGINAL LANGUAGE Arabic

DESCRIPTION
The work is mentioned by Ibn al-Nadīm, *Fihrist*, p. 220 (margin, which reads the last words of the title as *Maṭr Ibn Fāris*, though Fück, 'Neue Materialien zum Fihrist', *ZDMG* 90 (1936) 298-321, p. 308, emends this to 'metropolitan of Fars'). The Christian's name suggests he was an East-Syrian. Fück identifies him as Īshōʿbokht of Rēwardashīr (as does G. Monnot, *Islam et religions*, Paris, 1986, p. 77), although Van Ess (*TG* iv, pp. 132-33) argues that since Īshōʿbokht of Rēwardashīr must have lived more than half a century before Ḥumayd, it is more likely that the latter wrote against another East-Syrian with the same name. The work was presumably a rejoinder to arguments presented by the Christian leader and was maybe part of a continuing debate.

SIGNIFICANCE
The title suggests that Ḥumayd was well acquainted with this Christian's ideas.

MANUSCRIPTS —
EDITIONS AND TRANSLATIONS —
STUDIES —

Kitāb ʿalā l-Naṣārā fī l-naʿīm wa-l-akl wa-l-shurb fī l-ākhira wa ʿalā jamīʿ man qāla bi-ḍiddi dhālika, 'Against the Christians on felicity and eating and drinking in the hereafter, and against whoever teaches in opposition to this'

DATE Mid-9th c.
ORIGINAL LANGUAGE Arabic

DESCRIPTION

The work is mentioned by Ibn al-Nadīm, *Fihrist*, p. 220 (margin). It was evidently a defense of the Islamic view of paradise as a place of sensory pleasures in response to Christian attacks, such as can be found in the near-contemporary Syriac *Legend of Sergius Baḥīrā* (q.v.) and the *Book of Treasures* by Job of Edessa (q.v.), in which it is argued on grounds of physical practicalities that food and drink in paradise are impossible.

SIGNIFICANCE

It maybe shows Ḥumayd's deep involvement in debates with Christians and other non-Muslims.

MANUSCRIPTS —

EDITIONS AND TRANSLATIONS —

STUDIES —

David Thomas 2007

The Life of Antony the Younger

Unknown author

DATE OF BIRTH First half of the 9th c.?
PLACE OF BIRTH Unknown
DATE OF DEATH Second half of the 9th c.?
PLACE OF DEATH Unknown

BIOGRAPHY

The anonymous author comments that he visited Antony shortly before his death, so he must have written the saint's *Life* not too long after 865, probably in Constantinople.

MAIN SOURCES OF INFORMATION

Primary —

Secondary
PMBZ no. 11651

WORKS ON CHRISTIAN-MUSLIM RELATIONS

Bios kai politeia tou hosiou Antōniou tou Neou, 'Life and conduct of the holy Antony the Younger', 'Life of Antony the Younger'

DATE Not long after 865
ORIGINAL LANGUAGE Greek

DESCRIPTION
The *Life* of St Antony the Younger (*BHG* 142) relates the biography of John Echimus (785-865), who was born and brought up in Phossaton in Palestine. After the death of his mother in c. 800, he moved to Attaleia together with his brother and sister, and started a military career in the navy. In 821/22, under Emperor Michael II (820-29) he was made deputy-governor (*ek prosopou*) of the maritime *theme* of Kibyrrhaioton and had his headquarters in Attaleia. In 822/23, he participated in campaigns against the rebel Thomas the Slav (820/21-23), and in 823/24 he spent ten months in Constantinople.

After his return to Attaleia in 824, he defended the city against the threat of an Arab attack by meeting with the Arab commander for negotiations, which took place in Syriac.

Later, he took the monastic habit, changed his name to Antony and lived in several monasteries in Bithynia and Constantinople. In 829/30 he was sentenced to corporal punishment and imprisonment for his role in the quelling of the rebellion of Thomas the Slav. Towards the end of his life, he was very close to the general Petronas, a member of the imperial family, whose victory over the Arabs in 863 at Porson he predicted. Antony died in Constantinople on 11 November 865.

SIGNIFICANCE

The *Life* of St Antony the Younger attests to the use of Syriac in negotiations between a Byzantine and an Arab naval commander. (Although this may well be true, the possibility cannot be excluded that the *Life* confuses Syriac with Arabic.) From the point of view of Muslim-Christian relations, the *Life* is remarkable for the fact that the author does not posit any religious motives for the battles between the Byzantines and the Arabs. Rather, the saint states in his negotiations with the Arab commander that the Byzantine soldiers are going to war simply at the command of the Byzantine emperor, not of their own accord.

MANUSCRIPTS

MS Vienna – Hist. Gr. 31 (28) fols 1r-17r (10th c., ed. Papadopoulos-Kerameus)

MS Athens – Suppl. 534 fols 1-9 (12th c., ed. Halkin)

EDITIONS AND TRANSLATIONS

F. Halkin, 'Saint Antoine le Jeune et Pétronas le vainqueur des Arabes en 863 (d'après un texte inédit)', *AB* 62 (1944) 210-23 (repr. in Halkin, *Saints moines d'Orient*, London 1973, VIII)

A. Papadopoulos-Kerameus, *Syllogē Palaistinēs kai Syriakēs hagiologias*, 2 vols, St Petersburg, 1907-13, i, pp. 186-216

STUDIES

PMBZ no. 534 (Antonios), no. 5929 (Petronas), i (Prolegomena), pp. 57-59

Dumbarton Oaks Hagiography Database Project, Washington DC, 1998, p. 24

E. Malamut, *Sur la route des saints byzantins*, Paris, 1993, pp. 249-51

A. Kazhdan, art. 'Antony the Younger', in *ODB*

N. di Grigoli, art. 'Antonio il Giovane', in *Bibliotheca Sanctorum*, Rome, 1961-70

O. Volk, art. 'Antonios d. Jüngere', in *Lexikon für Theologie und Kirche*, Freiburg im Breisgau, 1993-2001

Halkin, 'Saint Antoine le Jeune et Pétronas le vainqueur des Arabes' *AB* 62 (1944) 187-210; 64 (1946) 256-57

B. Menthon, *Une terre de légendes. L'Olympe de Bithynie. Ses saints, ses couvents, ses sites*, Paris, 1935, pp. 150-56

C. Loparev, 'Vizantijskie žitija sviatych VIII-IX vekov', *VV* 18 (1911) 109-24

Thomas Pratsch 2008

George the Monk

George Hamartolos ('the Sinner')

DATE OF BIRTH Unknown
PLACE OF BIRTH Unknown
DATE OF DEATH Unknown
PLACE OF DEATH Unknown

BIOGRAPHY

All we know about George (Georgios) the Monk is that he was a monk in Constantinople during the reign of Michael III (842-67). His epithet Hamartolos, 'the sinner', which appears in the title of his single work, was a common mark of humility for Byzantine monks. He is the author of a world *Chronicle* which extends from the creation to the end of the second Iconoclastic period (843). He was a staunch supporter of the iconophile cause, and it is perhaps no accident that his *Chronicle*, at least in the majority of manuscripts, is rounded off with the official end of the controversy in 843.

Couched in a simple language and style, it is almost entirely a patchwork made up of earlier sources, some now extant and others not. For the part corresponding to the Byzantine period (4th-8th centuries), it is based chiefly on earlier chroniclers and church historians. Its overall significance as a source is mostly that it records excerpts of texts which are lost today, and also that it covers the period of Second Iconoclasm.

MAIN SOURCES OF INFORMATION

Primary

Georgius Monachus Chronicon, ed. C. de Boor, 2 vols, Leipzig, 1904 (repr. Stuttgart, 1978, with corrections by P. Wirth)

Secondary

A.P. Kazhdan, *A history of Byzantine literature* (850-1000), Athens, 2006, pp. 41-52

A. Karpozelos, *Byzantinoi historikoi kai chronographoi*, 2 vols, Athens, 1997-2002, ii (8th-10th c.), pp. 213-49

D.E. Afinogenov, 'The date of Georgios Monachos reconsidered', *BZ* 92 (1999) 437-47

J.A. Ljubarskij, 'Georgios the Monk as a short-story writer', *Jahrbuch der Österreichischen Byzantinistik* 44 (1994) 255-64

M.A. Monégier du Sorbier, 'Le Vat. gr. 1246 témoin d'une version perdue de la Chronique de Géorgios le Moine', *Revue d'histoire des textes* 19 (1989) 369-79

M.A. Monégier du Sorbier, *Recherches sur la tradition manuscrite de la Chronique de Géorgios le Moine*, Paris, 1985 (Diss. University of Paris I – La Sorbonne)

A. Markopoulos, 'Symbolē stē chronologēsē tou Geōrgion Monachou', *Symmeikta* 6 (1985) 223-31

P. Odorico, 'Excerpta di Giorgio Monaco nel cod. Marc. gr. 501 (= 555)', *Jahrbuch der österreichischen Byzantinistik* 32/4 (1982) 39-48

H. Hunger, *Die hochsprachliche profane Literatur der Byzantiner*, 2 vols, Munich, 1978, i, pp. 347-51

WORKS ON CHRISTIAN-MUSLIM RELATIONS

Chronikon syntomon ek diaphorōn chronographōn te kai exēgētōn syllegen kai syntethen hypo Geōrgiou hamartōlou monachou, 'A compendious chronicle based on various chroniclers and interpreters, gathered together and arranged by George, a sinner monk'. Modern title: 'The Chronicle of George the Monk'

DATE Between 843 and 867
ORIGINAL LANGUAGE Greek

DESCRIPTION

George's *Chronicle* is full of excerpts from the Church Fathers, citations of the Acts of the Church Councils, and anecdotes and stories of varied content. The section which refers to the Prophet Muḥammad at length (ed. de Boor, pp. 697-706) is inserted in the section on the Emperor Constans II (642-68). It repeats Muḥammad's genealogy as sketched in Theophanes the Confessor's *Chronographia* (q.v.), and so Muḥammad is portrayed as a poor man suffering from epilepsy who was hired by a rich woman to take care of her camels and trade with the Arabs in Egypt and Palestine, where he became acquainted with Jewish and Christian teaching. When she was widowed, his patroness became his wife and contributed both to the dissemination of his teachings among other women and the declaration of him as a prophet. The same account was later excerpted by Constantine VII Porphyrogenitus and included in his treatise known as *De administrando imperio* (ch. 14, ed. G. Moravscik and R. Jenkins, pp. 76-78).

According to a note in one of the manuscripts, MS BNF – Coislin 305, fol. 312v (cf. ed. de Boor, ii, p. 699), this section on Muḥammad, or part of it, goes back to an otherwise unknown work summarized (and perhaps composed) by Michael the Synkellos (q.v.).

To this story George appends a long excursus on the heretical character of Muḥammad's ideas; this is partly theological in character, partly mere invective. Briefly referring to the battle of Yarmuk (636), George takes the opportunity to include a long digression on both the promised land and Jerusalem, mourning over the 'sacred territories' taken from the Christians. For this purpose, he draws on both biblical texts and secular authors (such as Flavius Josephus and Aristotle). His sparse use of anti-Muslim theological polemic (cf., ed. de Boor, p. 703), echoing John of Damascus' *On heresies* (q.v.) and Theodore Abū Qurra (q.v.), is noteworthy.

Derogatory attributes applied to the Saracens appear from the beginning, in the preamble, where he counts among the purposes of his account to 'refute' the beliefs of the wicked and ill-minded Saracens, their bestial life and the teachings of the deceiver of the people and pseudo-prophet (ed. de Boor, p. 3). However, Islam is treated in no different terms from any other religious belief or heresy, such as Manicheism or Nestorianism.

Unlike Theophanes the Confessor, his major source, George is not interested in Islamic history: his references to the Arabs are confined to their military campaigns against the Byzantines, such as the sieges of Constantinople in 674-78 and in 717-18 (ed. de Boor, pp. 727-28 and 744-46). Once again following Theophanes, he attributes the outbreak of Iconoclasm to a plot concocted by Iazad (the Caliph Yazīd) and two Jews, whose enmity to icons was adopted by Leo III, then a young man whom they elevated to the Byzantine throne by means of astrology and sorcery; and he records the fall of Amorion in Phrygia (15 August 838), hometown of the Emperor Theophilus (829-42), as a divine punishment for the emperor's iconoclastic policy. The concluding lines of the Chronicle mention the failed naval campaign of the Arabs, who suffered shipwreck in the sea off the *theme* of Kibyrrhaiotai in 842 (ed. de Boor, p. 801).

SIGNIFICANCE

The Chronicle records Byzantine popular views about Islam and its rise; it includes excerpts of Christian anti-Muslim theological polemic; it refers to military conflicts between the Arabs and the Byzantines for the period of the Umayyads and the ʿAbbasids. All in all, it reflects completely hostile sentiments against the Arabs and their religion, which are comparable to those expressed with varying degrees of passion by other Byzantine authors.

MANUSCRIPTS

According to C. de Boor, the Chronicle has been transmitted in two redactions.

1st redaction:

MS BNF – Coislin Gr. 305 (10th-11th c.)

2nd redaction:

MS BNF – Coislin Gr. 310 (10th c.)

MS BNF – Coislin Gr. 314 (13th c.)

MS Escorial – Gr. I Φ I (D) (11th c.)

MS Patmos, Monastery of St John the Theologian – Gr. 7 (E) (11th c.). Excerpts in: MS Venice, Bibliotheca Marciana – Gr. 501 (= 555, 14th c.)

EDITIONS AND TRANSLATIONS

Georgius Monachus Chronicon, ed. de Boor

STUDIES

H.-A. Théologitis, 'La forza del destino. Lorsque l'histoire devient littérature', in P. Odorico, P.A. Agapitos and M. Hinterberger (eds), *L'écriture de la mémoire. La littérarité de l'historiographie*, Paris, 2006, 181-219, pp. 196-219

Kazhdan, *A history of Byzantine literature (850-1000)*, pp. 41-52

D. Afinogenov, 'Le manuscrit grec *Coislin*. 305. La version primitive de la *Chronique* de Georges le Moine', *REB* 62 (2004) 239-46

Karpozelos, *Byzantinoi historikoi kai chronographoi*, ii, pp. 213-49

Afinogenov, 'The date of Georgios Monachos reconsidered'

Ljubarskij, 'Georgios the Monk as a short-story writer'

Monégier du Sorbier, 'Le Vat. gr. 1246'

Monégier du Sorbier, *Recherches sur la tradition manuscrite de la Chronique de Géorgios le Moine*

Markopoulos, 'Symbolē stē chronologēsē tou Geōrgiou Monachou'

Odorico, 'Excerpta di Giorgio Monaco nel cod. Marc. gr. 501 (= 555)'

Hunger, *Die hochsprachliche profane Literatur der Byzantiner*, i, pp. 347-51
A.T. Khoury, *Les théologiens byzantins et l'Islam. Textes et auteurs. VIIIe-XIIIe s.*, Louvain, 1969, pp. 180-86

Stephanos Efthymiadis 2008

Al-ʿUtbī l-Qurṭubī

Abū ʿAbdallāh Muḥammad ibn Aḥmad al-Umawī l-Sufyānī l-ʿUtbī l-Qurṭubī

DATE OF BIRTH 9th c.
PLACE OF BIRTH Cordova
DATE OF DEATH 868/69
PLACE OF DEATH Cordova

BIOGRAPHY

Al-ʿUtbī was born and lived in Cordova, the city in which he followed his legal career. He was a renowned Mālikī scholar (*faqīh*), well versed in Islamic law (*fiqh*) and legal questions (*masāʾil*), and labeled by his biographers as *min ahl al-jihād wa-l-khayr*, 'one of the excellent people struggling for the faith'. His most influential work was *al-Mustakhraja min al-asmiʿa* ('The selection from what is heard'), also known as *al-ʿUtbiyya*.

MAIN SOURCES OF INFORMATION

Primary

Ibn Ḥārith al-Khushanī, *Akhbār al-fuqahāʾ wa-l-muḥaddithīn/Historia de los alfaquíes y tradicionistas de al-Andalus*, ed. M.L. Ávila and L. Molina, Madrid, 1992, pp. 119-21, no. 133

Ibn al-Qūṭiyya, *Taʾrīkh iftitāḥ al-Andalus*, ed. and trans. J. Ribera, Madrid, 1926, no. 96

Ibn al-Faraḍī, *Kitāb taʾrīkh ʿulamāʾ al-Andalus/Historia virorum doctorum Andalusiae*, ed. F. Codera, 2 vols, Madrid, 1891-92, no. 1102

al-Ḥumaydī, *Jadhwat al-muqtabis fī dhikr wulāt al-Andalus*, Cairo, 1966, no. 5

al-Qāḍī ʿIyāḍ, *Tartīb al-madārik wa-taqrīb al-masālik li-maʿrifat aʿlām madhhab Mālik*, ed. M. ibn Tāwīt al-Ṭanjī et al., 8 vols, Rabat, 1983, 2nd edition, iv, pp. 252-54

al-Ḍabbī, *Bughyat al-multamis fī taʾrīkh rijāl ahl al-Andalus*, ed. F. Codera and J. Ribera, Madrid, 1884, no. 9

Ibn ʿIdhārī al-Marrākushī, *al-Bayān al-mughrib fī akhbār al-Andalus wa-l-Maghrib*, ed. G. Colin and E. Lévi-Provençal, 3 vols, Paris, 1930 and Leiden 1948-51, ii, no. 112

Ibn Farḥūn, *Kitāb al-dībāj al-mudhahhab fī maʿrifat aʿyān ʿulamāʾ al-madhhab*, ed. M. al-Aḥmadī, 2 vols, Cairo, 1976, ii, pp. 176-77, no. 15
al-Maqqarī, *Nafḥ al-ṭīb min ghuṣn al-Andalus al-raṭīb*, ed. I. ʿAbbās, 8 vols, Beirut s.d. [1968], i, pp. 603-4
Secondary
A. Fernández Félix, *Cuestiones legales del Islam temprano: la ʿUtbiyya y el proceso de formación de la sociedad islámica andalusí*, Madrid, 2003, pp. 17-61
A. Fernández Felix, 'Biografías de alfaquíes: la generación de al-ʿUtbī', in M.L. Ávila and M. Marín (eds), *Biografías y género biográfico en el Occidente islámico*, Madrid, 1997, 141-75
M. Marín, 'Nómina de sabios de al-Andalus (93-350/711-961)', in M. Marín (ed.), *Estudios onomástico-biográficos de al-Andalus I*, Madrid, 1988, pp. 80, 141, no. 1125
Sezgin, *GAS* i, p. 472
J. López Ortiz, *Le recepción de la escuela malequí en España*, Madrid, 1931, pp. 143-52

WORKS ON CHRISTIAN-MUSLIM RELATIONS

Al-ʿUtbiyya, al-Mustakhraja min al-asmiʿa, 'The ʿUtbiyya', 'The Selection from what is heard'

DATE Before 869
ORIGINAL LANGUAGE Arabic

DESCRIPTION
Al-mustakhraja or *al-ʿUtbiyya* contains legal questions (*masāʾil*) on the authority of Mālik ibn Anas and his pupils, some of which relate to the process of Islamization. The work is preserved in Ibn Rushd al-Jadd, *al-Bayān wa-l-taḥṣīl* (12th c.). Al-ʿUtbī gathered more than 280 *masāʾil* dealing with Christians and Jews, most of which are related to the Christians of al-Andalus. Apart from these, a small number of *masāʾil* refer to the Byzantines (*Rūm*). The material brought together in *al-ʿUtbiyya* allows us to recover some of the legal and religious discussions arising from the contact between Muslims and Christians (as well as other non-Muslim communities), dealing with several aspects of their interaction in the early Islamic period.

The number of questions related specifically to al-Andalus is limited; most of the information deals with the rest of the Islamic world.

SIGNIFICANCE

The work provides detailed information about the process of Islamization, and the legal, social and religious governing the Christian populations, in both al-Andalus and other parts of the Muslim world.

MANUSCRIPTS

There are no complete manuscripts, and only 11 fragments are currently known:

MS El Escorial 612, 2 fols (s.d.)
MS Qayrawān 37, 16 fols (1029)
MS Qayrawān 144, 6 fols (s.d.)
MS Qayrawān 280, 19 fols (s.d.)
MS Qayrawān 282, 29 fols (s.d.)
MS Qayrawān 283, 15 fols (s.d.)
MS Qayrawān 1644, 2 fols (s.d.)
MS Qayrawān 1645, 2 fols (s.d.)
MS Qayrawān = Schacht 220-I-114, 22 pp. (1054/5)
MS Qayrawān = Schacht 212-I-2622, 50 pp. (s.d.)
MS BNF Ar. 6151, 21 fols (s.d.)

EDITIONS AND TRANSLATIONS

Ibn Rushd al-Jadd, *al-Bayān wa-l-taḥṣīl wa-l-sharḥ wa-l-tawjīḥ wa-l-taʿlīl fī l-masāʾil al-mustakhraja*, ed. M. Ḥājjī et al., 20 parts in 19 vols, Beirut, 1988-1991, 2nd edition

STUDIES

J. Safran, 'The sacred and profane in Islamic Cordoba', *Comparative Islamic Studies* 1 (2005) 21-41

A. Fernández Félix, *Cuestiones legales del Islam temprano. La ʿUtbiyya y el proceso de formación de la sociedad islámica andalusí*, Madrid, 2003, pp. 63-294, and especially pp. 433-92 and 549-63 for the *ahl al-dhimma*

J. Safran, 'Rules of purity and confessional boundaries. Maliki debates about the pollution of "the Christian"', *History of Religions* 42 (2003) 197-212

A. Fernández Félix, 'Children on the frontiers of Islam', in M. García Arenal (ed.), *Conversions islamiques. Identités religieuses en islam méditerranéen / Islamic conversions. Religious identities in Mediterranean Islam*, Paris, 2002, 61-72

J. Safran, 'From alien terrain to the abode of Islam. Landscapes of the conquest of al-Andalus,' in J. Howe and M. Wolfe (eds), *Inventing medieval landscapes. Senses of place in the Latin West*, Gainesville FL, 2002, 136-49

J. Safran, 'Identity and differentiation in ninth-century al-Andalus', *Speculum* 76 (2001) 573-98

A. Fernández Félix and M. Fierro, 'Cristianos y conversos al Islam en al-Andalus bajo los omeyas. Una aproximación al proceso de islamización a través de una fuente legal andalusí del s. III/IX', in L. Caballero Zoreda & P. Mateos Cruz (eds), *Visigodos y Omeyas. Un debate entre la Antigüedad Tardía y la Alta Edad Media*, Madrid, 2000, 415-27

M. Ḥājjī, 'al-Mustakhraja li-l-ʿUtbī wa-l-bayān wa-l-taḥṣīl wa-l-muqaddimāt li-Ibn Rushd: akbar ishām andalusī fī l-fiqh', in *Actas del II Coloquio Hispano-Marroquí de Ciencias Históricas: 'Historia, ciencia y sociedad'*, Madrid, 1992, 43-48

M. Muranyi, *Materialen zur mālikitischen Rechtsliteratur*, Wiesbaden, 1984, p. 53

J. Schacht, 'On some manuscripts in the libraries of Kairouan and Tunis', *Arabica* 14 (1967) 225-58, pp. 225, 245-46

Juan Pedro Monferrer-Sala 2007

Muḥammad ibn Saḥnūn

Muḥammad ibn Saḥnūn ibn Saʿīd ibn Ḥabīb al-Tanūkhī

DATE OF BIRTH 817
PLACE OF BIRTH Qayrawān
DATE OF DEATH 870
PLACE OF DEATH Near Qayrawān

BIOGRAPHY

Muḥammad ibn Saḥnūn was a leading Mālikī legal expert of his day in his part of the world. He learnt legal thinking from his father, and also in Medina.

He is credited with almost 100 books on various subjects, and these show his involvement in the main intellectual discussions of the time. They include his encyclopedic *al-Jāmiʿ*, 'The compendium', which covered the branches of intellectual knowledge and jurisprudence, and also polemical works such as *Kitāb al-ḥujja ʿalā l-Qadariyya*, 'The proof against the supporters of free will', *Kitāb al-īmān wa-l-radd ʿalā ahl al-shirk*, 'Faith, and refutation of those who associate others with God', and *Kitāb al-radd ʿalā ahl al-bidaʿ*, 'Refutation of the innovators', which demonstrate his anti-Muʿtazilī stance.

Among the many issues that Ibn Saḥnūn addressed in his legal works were the questions of *jihād* and the ways of dealing with Christians coming from abroad (*al-Rūm* and *al-Ifranj*). He forbade attacks on Christian merchants, but declared that it was legal to seize the goods of other foreign Christians unless they could show that they paid the *jizya* elsewhere (e.g. al-Andalus), and therefore deserved to be protected. Ibn Saḥnūn's biographers relate that he lost his life while defending the Tunisian coast against European pirates.

MAIN SOURCES OF INFORMATION

Primary

Abū l-ʿArab al-Tamīmī, *Ṭabaqāt ʿulamāʾ Ifrīqiyā wa-Tūnis*, Algiers, 1914, pp. 200-15, 280-87, 322

Abū Bakr ʿAbdallāh al-Mālikī, *Riyāḍ al-nufūs fī ṭabaqāt ʿulamāʾ al-Qayrawān wa-Ifrīqiyā*, ed. Ḥ. Muʾnis, Cairo, 1951, pp. 344-60

al-Qāḍī ʿIyāḍ ibn Mūsā, *Tartīb al-madārik wa-taqrīb al-masālik li-maʿrifat aʿlām madhhab Mālik*; ed. A.B. Maḥmūd, 4 vols, Beirut, 1967-68, iii, pp. 104-18

Secondary
Van Ess, *TG* ii, p. 109, iv, pp. 270-71
M. Talbi, 'Theological polemics at Qairawān during the 3rd/9th century', *Rocznik Orientalistyczny* 43 (1984) 151-60
G. Lecomte, art. 'Muḥammad b. Saḥnūn b. Saʿīd b. Ḥabīb al-Tanūkhī', in *EI2*
Sezgin, *GAS* i, pp. 472-73
M. Talbi, *L'émirat aghlabide*, Paris 1966, pp. 534-35 and *passim*
M. Talbi, 'Intérêt des œuvres juridiques traitant de la guerre', *Cahiers de Tunisie* 15 (1956) 280-93

WORKS ON CHRISTIAN-MUSLIM RELATIONS

Kitāb al-ḥujja ʿalā l-Naṣārā, 'The Proof against the Christians'

DATE Mid-9th c.
ORIGINAL LANGUAGE Arabic

DESCRIPTION
The work is lost, and is known only from the reference in *Tartīb al-madārik*. It presumably contained arguments against the main Christian beliefs that conflicted with Islam.

SIGNIFICANCE
The work formed part of Ibn Saḥnūn's refutations of the opponents of Islamic orthodoxy as he saw it, and of an apologetic structure of correct belief.

MANUSCRIPTS —
EDITIONS AND TRANSLATIONS —
STUDIES
Qāḍī ʿIyāḍ, *Tartīb al-madārik* iii, p. 106

David Thomas 2007

Muʿārik ibn Marwān al-Nuṣayrī

Muʿārik ibn Marwān ibn ʿAbd al-Malik ibn Marwān ibn Mūsā ibn Nuṣayr

DATE OF BIRTH	Unknown, 9th c.
PLACE OF BIRTH	Probably Egypt
DATE OF DEATH	Unknown, 9th c.
PLACE OF DEATH	Probably Egypt

BIOGRAPHY

Muʿārik ibn Marwān was the great-great-grandson of Mūsā ibn Nuṣayr, the conqueror of al-Andalus. He is reported to have written a book entitled *Akhbār al-Andalus* ('Historical reports about al-Andalus') dealing with his ancestor's role in this conquest. His place of birth is not known for certain, though M. ʿAlī Makkī suggests that he must have been Egyptian since his great-grandfather Marwān returned east with his father Mūsā ibn Nuṣayr and stopped in Egypt, where the family seems to have settled and where some of its members filled high-ranking posts under the ʿAbbasids. In support of this, the main source of information about Muʿārik for Andalusian biographers was the Egyptian scholar Abū Saʿīd ibn Yūnus (d. 947). However, according to de Gayangos (*History of the Mohammedan dynasties*, i, p. lxxxvi, n. 66) Marwān died in battle in al-Andalus.

MAIN SOURCES OF INFORMATION

Primary

Muḥammad ibn Abī Naṣr al-Ḥumaydī, *Kitāb jadhwat al-muqtabis fī dhikr wulāt al-Andalus*, ed. Muḥammad ibn Tāwīt al-Ṭanjī, Cairo, s.d., p. 317

Abū Bakr ibn al-ʿArabī, *al-ʿAwāṣim min al-qawāṣim fī taḥqīq mawāfiq al-ṣaḥāba baʿda wafāt al-Nabī*, ed. Muḥibb al-Dīn al-Khaṭīb, Cairo, 1371 A.H. (1952), p. 248

al-Ḍabbī, *Bughyat al-multamis fī taʾrīkh rijāl ahl al-Andalus*, ed. F. Codera and J. Ribera, Madrid, 1884, p. 443

Ibn al-Faraḍī, *Kitāb taʾrīkh ʿulamāʾ al-Andalus / Historia virorum doctorum Andalusiae*, ed. F. Codera, 2 vols, Madrid, 1891-92, i, p. 241

Secondary

M.ʿA. Makkī, 'Egipto y los orígenes de las historiografía arábigo-española', *Revista del Instituto Egipcio de Estudios Islámicos* 5 (1957) 157-248, pp. 178, 201-3, 210-20 (English trans. M. Kennedy, in M. Fierro and J. Samsó (eds), *The formation of al-Andalus*, Aldershot, 1998, pp. 193, 216-18, 223-33)

WORKS ON CHRISTIAN-MUSLIM RELATIONS

Al-Imāma wa-l-siyāsa, 'On legitimate political leadership and governance'

DATE 2nd half of 9th c.

ORIGINAL LANGUAGE Arabic

DESCRIPTION

The book is a collection of miscellaneous narratives and traditions on the eastern caliphs from Abū Bakr to Hārūn al-Rashīd, unsystematically arranged, which, given their different styles, seem to be the work of several authors. *Al-Imāma wa-l-siyāsa* has been attributed to Ibn Qutayba (d. 889) (q.v.), and often appears under his name in catalogues, though as early as the 12th century the Seville scholar Abū Bakr ibn al-ʿArabī (d. 1143) expressed his doubts about this authorship. The attribution to Ibn Qutayba has been convincingly rejected in favour of Muʿārik ibn Marwān by de Gayangos, Dozy, de Goeje, Pérès and M. ʿAlī Makkī. However, J. Jabbūr has pointed to Ibn Ḥazm (this is rejected by M.Y. Najm), and Lecomte to Ibn al-Qūṭiyya.

The book is divided into two parts of similar length (197 and 182 pages respectively, in the 1967 Beirut edition), the first ending with the death of Muʿāwiya ibn Abī Sufyān and the second with that of Hārūn al-Rashīd. The material relevant to Christian-Muslim relations in al-Andalus appears in the first part, in the chapter concerned with the period from the Muslim conquest of North Africa and the Iberian peninsula by Mūsā ibn Nuṣayr, down to the separation of al-Andalus from the ʿAbbasid caliphate.

SIGNIFICANCE

Muʿārik ibn Marwān's account of the conquest of al-Andalus abounds in exaggerations and legendary elements, probably meant to convince the reader of the importance of Mūsā's military deeds, the immense treasure he took from the enemy, his honesty in handing this over to the caliph, and the resulting benefits for the public treasury.

As might be expected from an account of the Islamic conquest of al-Andalus written by a descendant of the conqueror, whose main goal is self-assertion, Christians appear as an 'other' whose role is to be used to emphasize the military and theological superiority of Mūsā ibn Nuṣayr and his people.

MANUSCRIPTS

MS Madrid, Real Academia de la Historia - Colección Gayangos 117 (1554)

EDITIONS AND TRANSLATIONS

Ibn Qutayba, *al-Imāma wa-l-siyāsa al-maʿrūf bi-Tārīkh al-khulafāʾ*, Sūsa: Dār al-maʿārif li-l-ṭibāʿa wa-l-nashr, 1997

Ibn Qutayba, *al-Imāma wa-l-siyāsa*, ed. Ṭaha Muḥammad al-Zaynī, Beirut, 1967 (repr. 1981)

F. Codera, *Historia de la conquista de España de Abenalcotía el Cordobés. Seguida de fragmentos históricos de Abencotaiba, etc.*, Madrid, 1926, pp. 105-61

Ibn Qutayba, *al-Imāma wa-al-siyāsa*, ed. M.M. al-Rāfiʿī, Cairo, 1904 (repr. Cairo, 1907, 1909, 1913, 1957, 1960)

P. de Gayangos, *The history of the Mohammedan dynasties in Spain extracted from the Nafhu-t-Tîb min Ghosni-l-Andalusi-r-ratib by Ahmed ibn Makkarî*, London, 1840-43, i, Appendix E, pp. l-xc; ii, Appendix E, pp. iii-viii (repr. Delhi, 1984)

STUDIES

A. Hamori, 'Going down in style. The Pseudo-Ibn Qutayba's story of the fall of the Barmakis', *Princeton Papers in Near Eastern Studies* 3 (1994) 89-125

G. Lecomte, art. 'Ibn Ḳutayba', in *EI2*

M.Y. Najm, 'Kitāb al-imāma wa-l-siyāsa al-mansūb li-Ibn Qutayba – man huwa muʾallifuhu?', *Al-Abhath* 14 (1961) 122-32

J. Jabbūr, 'Kitāb al-imāma wa-l-siyāsa al-mansūb li-Ibn Qutayba – man huwa muʾallifu-hu?: radd ʿalā naqd', *Al-Abhath* 14 (1961) 326-41

M.ʿA. Makkī, 'Egipto y los orígenes de las historiografía arábigo-española', pp. 178, 201-3, 210-20 (English trans. M. Kennedy, in Fierro and Samsó, *The formation of al-Andalus*, pp. 193, 216-18, 223-33)

Brockelmann, *GAL* i, p. 127, S i, p. 187

Delfina Serrano Ruano 2007

Nonnus of Nisibis

Nunā of Nisibis

DATE OF BIRTH Late 8th c.
PLACE OF BIRTH Region of Nisibis
DATE OF DEATH After 862
PLACE OF DEATH Unknown

BIOGRAPHY

Nonnus was a Syrian Orthodox theologian and archdeacon of Nisibis. The Jewish Karaite philosopher Abū Yaʿqūb al-Qirqisānī (10th c.) states that 'Nonnus (Nānā), a physician by training, was much respected by the Christians, because he was an accomplished philosopher' (*Kitāb al-anwār* i, 44), and that Dāwūd ibn Marwān al-Muqammaṣ converted from Judaism to Christianity under his influence.

Nonnus is known for a Christological dispute with the Melkite theologian Theodore Abū Qurra (q.v.), which took place at the court of the Armenian Prince Ashot Msaker between 813 and 817 (see the entry on Abū Rāʾiṭa l-Takrītī, above). At the request of Bagarat Bagratuni, son of Ashot, he wrote (in Arabic) a commentary on the Gospel of John, based on various Syriac sources found in West-Syrian monasteries. His Christological treatise, addressed to the East-Syrian Thomas of Margā (q.v.), was composed in Samarra, where both men lived as prisoners of the Caliph al-Mutawakkil. His two shorter theological letters (in Syriac) and his extensive apologetic treatise (see below) may also have been written during his imprisonment.

Nonnus maintained good relations with Abū Rāʾiṭa (q.v.), who may have been responsible for his education and theological instruction.

MAIN SOURCES OF INFORMATION

Primary

Two unedited letters by Abū Rāʾiṭa, contained in MS BNF – Ar. 169; German transl. by G. Graf in A. van Roey, *Nonnus de Nisibe. Traité apologétique*, Louvain, 1948, pp. 4-5

Introduction to the Commentary on the Gospel of St John (preserved in an Armenian trans., in Kh.H. Črakhean, *Commentary on the Gospel of John by Nonnus, Vardapet of Syria*, Venice, 1920 (in Armenian), pp. 1-13; French trans. in Van Roey, *Nonnus de Nisibe. Traité apologétique*, pp. 6-8

Dionysius of Tell-Maḥrē, preserved in *Chronique de Michel le Syrien*, ed. J.-B. Chabot, 4 vols, Paris, 1899-1910, iii, pp. 29-34, 50, 65; iv, pp. 495-97, 507, 517

Abū Yaʿqūb al-Qirqisānī, *Kitāb al-anwār wa-l-marāqib. Code of Karaite Law*, ed. L. Nemoy, 4 vols, New York, 1939-43, i, p. 44

Secondary

Van Roey, *Nonnus de Nisibe. Traité apologétique*, pp. 1-41

WORKS ON CHRISTIAN-MUSLIM RELATIONS

Mammlā lwāt (')nāsh d-lā awdaʿ shmeh d-sha''el d-men aylēn mḥawwēn Kristyānē l-sagyay alāhē wa-d-mahpekin apayhun min ktābē qaddišē d-ḥad itaw(hy) alāhā... 'Discourse to someone who did not mention his name, who asked on what basis the Christians prove to the polytheists and to those who renounce the holy scriptures that God is one...' Modern title: 'The apologetic treatise of Nonnus of Nisibis'

DATE Probably between 850 and 870, possibly between 858 and 862
ORIGINAL LANGUAGE Syriac

DESCRIPTION

The apologetic treatise of Nonnus is structured as follows: demonstration of God's unity, of the Trinity (the Word and Spirit are essential attributes), and of Christ's divinity, followed by a general defense of Christianity, based on three arguments: the presence of a supra-natural force, notably revealed in miracles, which explains the fact that Christianity was accepted by many people; the Gospel, and not the Old Testament or the Qurʾān is the only perfect Book of God; nature itself, and the natural tendency of human beings to preservation and development, confirms the veracity of the Gospel and its teaching of love and doing good to others.

SIGNIFICANCE

Although Muslims are nowhere explicitly mentioned, the majority of the arguments used by Nonnus are only understandable in a Muslim context, more particularly the intellectual milieu of the *mutakallimūn*. Muslims are indirectly designated as the 'pagans of the present time' (*d-hāshā ḥanpē*) or the 'new pagans' (*ḥadtē d-hānpē*) and credited with having sound opinions concerning Jesus' virginal birth from Mary, the Trinity (Nonnus knows of the Trinitarian interpretation of Q 4:171), Jesus' ascension unto heaven and his second coming. Nonnus offers an original interpretation of Q 4:157 (the denial of the crucifixion), which shows his understanding for the Muslim position. He says that they do not accept the crucifixion because they are people who hold Jesus in great honor. In a different context, however, the Muslims are also called *ḥanpē sāqurin*, 'hostile pagans'.

The author had a good knowledge of the Qur'ān. No direct quotations of it are given, but the treatise contains several allusions to it.

Though defending the miaphysite Christology of his own community, the author mostly positions himself as a defender of Christians in general, not of one specific denomination. He uses the term *Krisṭiānē* for them, but also *Naṣrāyē*, possibly under the influence of the qur'ānic *Naṣārā*.

MANUSCRIPTS

MS BL – Or. 719 (Add. 14,594)

EDITIONS AND TRANSLATIONS

Van Roey, *Nonnus de Nisibe. Traité apologétique*, pp. 1*-72*.

STUDIES

S.H. Griffith, 'Disputes with Muslims in Syriac Christian texts. From Patriarch John (d. 648) to Bar Hebraeus (d. 1286)', in B. Lewis and F. Niewöhner (eds), *Religionsgespräche im Mittelalter*, Wiesbaden, 1992, 251-73, pp. 265-67 (repr. in S.H. Griffith, *The beginnings of Christian theology in Arabic*, Aldershot, 2002)

S.H. Griffith, 'The apologetic treatise of Nonnus of Nisibis', *Aram* 3 (1991) 115-38 (repr. in Griffith, *The beginnings of Christian theology in Arabic*)

Van Roey, *Nonnus de Nisibe. Traité apologétique*, pp. 1-60

Herman G.B. Teule 2007

Al-Kindī

Abū Yūsuf Yaʿqūb ibn Isḥāq al-Kindī

DATE OF BIRTH c. 800
PLACE OF BIRTH Kūfa or Basra
DATE OF DEATH c. 870
PLACE OF DEATH Baghdad

BIOGRAPHY

Al-Kindī traced his ancestry back to the Kinda tribe of Arabia and a Companion of the Prophet Muḥammad. Although born in the south of Iraq – his father was governor of Kūfa – he was educated in Baghdad, and entered the caliphal service while still young. He rose to prominence under al-Muʿtaṣim as tutor to the caliph's son, and he addressed many of his works to one or other of these. He lost favor under al-Mutawakkil, and is supposed to have had his books confiscated for a while. He must have died after 866, because in one of his astrological works he mentions an uprising in this year.

Al-Kindī moved in the most advanced intellectual circles of his day. There are signs in his works of Muʿtazilī interests as well as philosophical preoccupations, among a wide range of intellectual pursuits. His known works, which number nearly 250 (only 40 of these survive), include treatises on astronomy, astrology, natural events, philosophy, mathematics, logic, music and medicine, as well as refutations of Muslim and non-Muslim groups.

MAIN SOURCES OF INFORMATION

Primary

Ibn al-Nadīm, *Fihrist*, pp. 315-20
Ibn al-Qifṭī, *Taʾrīkh al-ḥukamāʾ*, ed. J. Lippert, Leipzig, 1903, pp. 376-78
Ibn Abī Uṣaybiʿa, *ʿUyūn al-anbāʾ fī ṭabaqāt al-aṭibbāʾ*, ed. A. Müller, 2 vols, Cairo, 1882, i, pp. 206-14

Secondary

P. Adamson and P. Pormann, *The philosophical works of al-Kindī*, Karachi, 2009 (forthcoming)
P. Adamson, *Al-Kindī*, Oxford, 2007

G. Endress, 'The circle of al-Kindī. Early Arabic translations from the Greek and the rise of Islamic philosophy', in G. Endress and R. Kruk (eds), *The ancient tradition in Christian and Islamic Hellenism*, Leiden, 1997, 43-76
A.L. Ivry, 'Al-Kindī and the Muʿtazila. A philosophical and political reevaluation', *Oriens* 25 (1976) 69-85
G.N. Atiyeh, *Al-Kindī. The philosopher of the Arabs*, Rawalpindi, 1966
R. Walzer, 'New studies on al-Kindī', *Oriens* 10 (1957) 203-32

WORKS ON CHRISTIAN-MUSLIM RELATIONS

Radd ʿalā l-Naṣārā, 'Refutation of the Christians'

DATE Mid-9th c.
ORIGINAL LANGUAGE Arabic

DESCRIPTION
The work survives as quotations in the refutation made by the 10th-century Syrian Orthodox Yaḥyā ibn ʿAdī, who refers to al-Kindī's *Maqāla fī l-radd ʿalā l-Naṣārā*, 'Treatise on the refutation of the Christians'. While Yaḥyā has undoubtedly reproduced what he thought were the main points, he may well have omitted other parts. G. Endress, *The works of Yaḥyā ibn ʿAdī*, p. 100, suggests the *Radd* was originally part of a longer work, the *Risāla fī iftirāq al-milal fī l-tawḥīd wa-annahum majmūʿūn ʿalā l-tawḥīd wa-kull qad khālafa ṣāḥibahu*, 'Epistle on the difference between the communities about divine oneness and that they all accept divine oneness although they all disagree with each other' (*Fihrist*, p. 319). The abrupt beginning of the *Radd*, *fa-ammā l-qawl fī l-radd ʿalā l-Naṣārā*..., 'as for the refutation of the Christians...', indicating al-Kindī has turned from another topic to this, supports this suggestion.

The work comprises three parts, all of them demonstrating that the doctrine of the Trinity makes the Godhead into a plurality. In the first, al-Kindī shows that each of the Persons must be composite, and so they must be effects of a higher cause; in the second he applies to the Trinity the categories of Porphyry's *Isagoge*, and shows again that the Persons must be composite; and in the third he argues on the basis of Aristotle's *Topics* that however the Trinity is explained as one, it cannot be understood as a single unity. Throughout, he makes explicit use of Greek philosophical concepts, above all the principle that composite entities must be effects and thus contingent.

SIGNIFICANCE

The *Radd ʿalā l-Naṣārā* is the only surviving refutation from this period that is explicitly indebted to Greek philosophy. In using works such as the *Isagoge*, which al-Kindī says 'is hardly ever missing from most of their [Christians'] homes', he evidently intends to construct arguments he expects to be understandable and convincing to Christians.

MANUSCRIPTS

See G. Endress, *The works of Yaḥyā Ibn ʿAdī*, Wiesbaden, 1977, p. 100 (and for dates of the MSS, see pp. 9-19)

EDITIONS AND TRANSLATIONS

Adamson and Pormann, *The philosophical works of al-Kindī* (trans.)

R. Rashed and J. Jolivet, *Oeuvres philosophiques et scientifiques d'al-Kindī*, 2 vols, Leiden, 1997-98, ii *Métaphysique et cosmologie*, pp. 119-27 (edition (reprint of Périer) and French trans.)

A. Périer, 'Un traité de Yaḥyâ ben ʿAdî (1), défense du dogme de la Trinité contre les objections d'al-Kindî', *Revue de l'Orient Chrétien* 22 (1920-21) 3-21 (edition and French trans.) (revised trans. in Périer, *Petits traités apologétiques de Yaḥyâ Ben ʿAdî*, Paris, 1920, pp. 118-28; text repr. in *al-Majalla al-baṭriyarkiyya al-suryāniyya* 9 (1936) 12-22)

STUDIES

Adamson, *Al-Kindī*, pp. 41-42, 99-100

S. Escobar Gómez and J.C. González López, 'La polémica trinitaria entre Yaḥyā ibn ʿAdī y al-Kindī', *Anales del seminario de historia de la filosofía* 23 (2006) 75-97

D. Thomas, *Anti-Christian polemic in early Islam. Abū ʿĪsā al-Warrāq's 'Against the Trinity'*, Cambridge, 1992, pp. 35-37

al-Sharfī, *Al-fikr al-Islāmī*, pp. 136-37

M. Fakhry, *A history of Islamic philosophy*, New York, 1970, 1983^2, pp. 197-201

H. Wolfson, 'The philosopher al-Kindi and Yahya Ibn ʿAdi', in O. Amine (ed.), *Études philosophiques offertes au Dr Ibrahim Madkour*, 2 vols, Cairo, 1974, i, 49-64 (repr. in Wolfson, *The philosophy of the kalam*, Cambridge Mass, 1976, 321-36)

T.J. de Boer, 'Kindī wider die Trinität', in C. Bezold (ed.), *Orientalische Studien Theodor Nöldeke gewidmet*, 2 vols, Gieszen, 1906, i, pp. 279-81

Risāla fī iftirāq al-milal fī l-tawḥīd wa-annahum majmūʿūn ʿalā l-tawḥīd wa-kull qad khālafa ṣāḥibahu, 'Epistle on the difference between the communities about divine oneness and that they all accept divine oneness even though they all disagree with each other'

DATE Mid-9th c.
ORIGINAL LANGUAGE Arabic

DESCRIPTION
The work is lost. Its title, which is listed by Ibn al-Nadīm, *Fihrist*, p. 319, indicates that it was a demonstration of the underlying unity of religions despite the apparent disagreement between them. It very probably included a discussion about the Trinity and how this was at base an expression of divine oneness and maybe a debasement of it. Endress suggests (see above) that this discussion survives as the *Radd ʿalā l-Naṣārā*.

One might speculate that the work was comparable to the lost *Kitāb maqālāt al-nās wa-ikhtilāfihim*, 'The teachings of people and the differences between them', of al-Kindī's contemporary Abū ʿĪsā l-Warrāq (q.v.), which can be shown to have been in all likelihood a descriptive account of the main religions that Arab Muslims would have known in the 9th century, together with some explicit or implicit deductions that they all approximated to, or diverged from, the principle of divine unity (see D. Thomas, 'Abū ʿĪsā al-Warrāq and the history of religions', *JSS* 41 (1996) 275-90).

SIGNIFICANCE
The work was one of a number of possible attempts in al-Kindī's time to relate the religious traditions to one another, and maybe to show how they were connected at various stages of remove to Islam as the supreme expression of divine oneness. It will have placed Christianity in a formal relationship with Islam as an expression of truth but in a distorted form.

MANUSCRIPTS —
EDITIONS AND TRANSLATIONS —
STUDIES —

David Thomas 2007

Nicetas of Byzantium

Niketas Byzantios

DATE OF BIRTH Unknown, probably 1st half 9th c.
PLACE OF BIRTH Unknown, perhaps Constantinople
DATE OF DEATH Unknown, probably late 9th c.
PLACE OF DEATH Unknown

BIOGRAPHY

The only information on the life of Nicetas, who is remembered as *philosophos*, *didaskalos* and *patrikios*, can be gathered from his works and the manuscripts which contain them. A first piece of evidence is supplied by a note found in a group of manuscripts that contain the *Twenty-four syllogistic chapters on the procession of the Holy Spirit* (J. Hergenröther, *Monumenta graeca ad Photium ejusque historiam pertinentia*, Regensburg, 1869, pp. 84-138), according to which Nicetas flourished during the reigns of Michael III and Leo VI, i.e., the years 842 to 912. From the titles of his two replies to the letters of the 'Hagarenes' we know that he responded to the two different missives send by the ʿAbbasid court to Byzantium during the reign of Michael III, i.e., between 842 and 867. In all likelihood, this letter was carried to Constantinople on the occasion of a diplomatic mission, perhaps one that took place either at the end of 855 or 859/60. In this case, the redaction of Nicetas' replies to the letters from the 'Hagarenes' must have taken place around 860. His refutation of the Qurʾān postdates these replies. In the preamble, Nicetas praises imperial policies. His reference to the victories over the Arabs points to either the final years of Michael III (after 863) or the reign of his successor, Basil I (867-86). In favor of the second possibility, it should be remembered that it was Basil I who commissioned Nicetas to reply to the letter of the Armenian sovereign Ashot (between 882 and 883) (*PG* 105, cols 588-665). In addition to writing for Basil I, he wrote also in the name of Patriarch Photius.

His writing of the *Twenty-four syllogistic chapters about the procession of the Holy Spirit* is perhaps to be connected with the writings of Photius on the procession of the Holy Spirit, his letter of 883/84 to the archbishop of Aquileia and, a little later, his *Mystagogia*.

The data that can be extracted from Nicetas' works allow us to determine that he was active mainly between c. 860 and 885. In the course of these 25 years he was able to gain the favor of Michael II and subsequently of Basil I. During this period he was also in close contact with Photius.

The hypothesis advanced by some modern scholars that Nicetas may have been imprisoned at Samarra, where he would have studied Arabic and the Qur'ān, has been proved to be entirely untenable. The *History* of al-Ṭabarī only speaks of an anonymous official with the title of logothete (*logothetes*) who was imprisoned in Lulon (Luʾluʾa) in Cappadocia (Rigo, 'Niceta Byzantios', pp. 183-87).

MAIN SOURCES OF INFORMATION

Primary

Cited in Nicetas' biography

Secondary

A. Rigo, 'Niceta Byzantios, la sua opera e il monaco Evodio', in G. Fiaccadori (ed.), *'In partibus Clius'. Scritti in onore di Giovanni Pugliese Carratelli, Naples*, 2006, 147-87

WORKS ON CHRISTIAN-MUSLIM RELATIONS

Ekthesis kataskeuastikē meta apodeixeōs tou Christianikou dogmatos ek koinōn ennoiōn kai dialektikēs methodou kai physikōn epicheirēmatōn kai syllogistikēs polytechnias proagomenē kai antirrhēsis tēs staleisēs epistolēs ek tōn Agarēnōn pros Michaēl basilea hyion Theophilou epi diabolē tēs tōn Christianōn pisteōs, 'Positive exposition of Christian doctrine, developed from general concepts by means of dialectical method, rational arguments, and multiple syllogistic proofs, followed by a confutation of the letter sent by the Hagarenes to the Emperor Michael, son of Theophilus, in order to slander the Christian faith'

DATE About 860

ORIGINAL LANGUAGE Greek

DESCRIPTION

In his reply to the letter sent to Constantinople by the ʿAbbasid court, Nicetas particularly refutes the points which deny the divinity of Christ and proclaim the oneness of God, as well as those which glorify holy war. In his reply to the denial of Christ's divinity, Nicetas discusses at great length why it is untenable to claim that the one who generates always precedes in time the one who is generated.

SIGNIFICANCE

The letter contains one of the most detailed Byzantine responses to Islamic anti-Christian polemic.

MANUSCRIPTS

MS Vat – Gr. 681, fols 166r-214v (last quarter of 9th c.)

MS Moscow, Historical Museum – Syn. 368 (Vladimir 239) (15th c.), fols 335v-344v

EDITIONS AND TRANSLATIONS

K. Förstel, *Niketas von Byzanz. Schriften zum Islam*, Würzburg, 2000 (*Corpus Islamo-Christianum. Series Graeca* 5), pp. 156-72 (edition with German trans.)

PG 105, cols 807-21

STUDIES

Rigo, 'Niceta Byzantios, la sua opera e il monaco Evodio'

D. Krausmüller, 'Murder is good if God wills it. Nicetas Byzantius' polemic against Islam and the Christian tradition of divinely sanctioned murder', *Al-Masaq* 16 (2004) 163-76

A. Rigo, '*Saracenica* di Friedrich Sylburg (1595). Una raccolta di opere bizantine contro l'Islam', in M. Cortesi (ed.), *I Padri sotto il torchio. Le edizioni dell'antichità cristiana nei secoli XV-XVI*, Florence, 2002, 289-310, pp. 295, 299, 303

Förstel, *Niketas von Byzanz*

A. Kazhdan, art. 'Niketas Byzantios', in *ODB*

K. Versteegh, 'Die Mission des Kyrillos im Lichte der arabo-byzantinischen Beziehungen', *ZDMG* 129 (1979) 233-62

A.T. Khoury, *Les théologiens byzantins et l'Islam. Textes et auteurs. VIIIe-XIIIe s.*, Louvain, 1969, pp. 127-33

H.-G. Beck, *Kirche und theologische Literatur im byzantinischen Reich*, Munich, 1959, p. 530 (with bibliography)

C. Güterbock, *Der Islam im Lichte der byzantinischen Polemik*, Berlin, 1912, pp. 23-33

N. Pokrovskij, *Nikita Vizantijskij kak apologet*, St Petersburg, 1882

Antirrhēsis kai anatropē tēs deuteras epistolēs tēs staleisēs para tōn Agarēnōn pros Michaēl basilea hyion Theophilou epi diabolē tēs tōn Christianōn pisteōs, 'Confutation and refutation of the second letter sent by the Hagarenes to the Emperor Michael, son of Theophilus, in order to slander the Christian faith'

DATE c. 860

ORIGINAL LANGUAGE Greek

DESCRIPTION

This second letter to the Hagarenes reiterates some of the points raised in the first and also introduces new arguments and critical points vis-à-vis Islam. Among other things, Nicetas attacks the Muslim claim that man is not created in the image of God, the 'unnatural' way of life sanctioned by Islamic law, and the permissibility of killing non-monotheists.

SIGNIFICANCE

Together with the first letter, this work forms one of the more detailed Byzantine responses to Islam.

MANUSCRIPTS

MS Vat – Gr. 681, fols 214v-238v (last quarter of 9th c.)

MS Moscow, Historical Museum – Syn. 368 (Vladimir 239), fols 344v-348v (15th c.)

EDITIONS AND TRANSLATIONS

Förstel, *Niketas von Byzanz*, pp. 176-98 (edition with German trans.)

PG 105, cols 821-41

STUDIES

See references to the previous work

Nikēta Byzantinou philosophou programma tēs hypogegrammenēs anatropēs tēs para tou Arabos Mōamet plastographētheisēs biblou, 'Nicetas of Byzantium's foreword to the following refutation of the book forged by the Arab Muḥammad'

DATE c. 870
ORIGINAL LANGUAGE Greek

DESCRIPTION
Nicetas' refutation of the Qur'ān is subdivided into 30 chapters of unequal length. The first, which constitutes approximately one quarter of the entire work, is devoted to the exposition of the Christian faith. Chapters 2 to 17 each deal with a sūra from the Qur'ān (Q 2-18), from which several passages are quoted. Chapter 18 is entitled 'General confutation', i.e. of the rest of the Qur'ān, and quotes some verses from Q 19 to Q 113. In the subsequent chapters, Nicetas dwells upon a number of central points in the controversy between Christians and Muslims, such as the concept of the Word of God, God and the origin of evil, paradise and angels according to Islam, and Muslims and the inheritance of Abraham.

SIGNIFICANCE
Nicetas' refutation of the Qur'ān, even though it forms the basis of the majority of later Byzantine literature about Islam, and pre-eminently the compilations of Euthymius Zygabenus and Nicetas Choniates, has come down in only one manuscript. It was circulated through the epitome made by Euodios the Monk (q.v.) in the last quarter of the 9th century, which was used by Euthymius Zygabenus in his *Panoplia dogmatica*, Chapter 27, which specifically deals with the Muslims.

The refutation of the Qur'ān by Nicetas is also important because it represents a direct and important witness to the existence in 9th-century Byzantium of a (partial) Greek translation of the Qur'ān (cf. the works of Trapp, Versteegh and Argyriou cited below).

MANUSCRIPTS
MS Vat – Gr. 681, fols 1r-165v

EDITIONS AND TRANSLATIONS
Förstel, *Niketas von Byzanz*, pp. 2-152 (edition with German trans.)
PG 105, cols 669-805

STUDIES

Rigo, 'Niceta Byzantios, la sua opera e il monaco Evodio'

A. Argyriou, 'Perception de l'Islam et traductions du Coran dans le monde byzantin grec', *Byzantion* 75 (2005) 25-69, pp. 27, 32-40, 60

Förstel, *Niketas von Byzanz*

A. Rigo, 'Gli Ismaeliti e la discendenza da Abramo nella "Refutazione del Corano" di Niceta Byzantios (metà del IX secolo)', in G. Ruggieri (ed.), *I nemici della Cristianità*, Bologna, 1997, 83-104

K. Versteegh, 'Greek translations of the Qur'ān in Christian polemics (9th century AD)', *ZDMG* 141 (1991) 52-68

E. Trapp, 'Gab es eine byzantinische Koranübersetzung?', *Diptycha* 2 (1980/81) 7-17

Khoury, *Les théologiens byzantins et l'Islam*, pp. 133-62

Antonio Rigo 2008

Israel of Kashkar

DATE OF BIRTH Unknown, probably early 9th c.
PLACE OF BIRTH Unknown, probably Iraq
DATE OF DEATH 872
PLACE OF DEATH Baghdad, monastery of Mār Pethion (Dayr Mār Fathiyūn or al-Dayr al-ʿAtīq)

BIOGRAPHY

Most of the information about Israel of Kashkar's life is found in *Kitāb al-majdal*, under the heading of Enosh, the 48th East-Syrian catholicos. But Israel's name is mentioned before this in connection with the preceding catholicos, Sergius, where it is stated that he appointed 'Israel the interpreter' (*al-mufassir*) bishop of Kashkar. On the basis of this statement, we may fix the *terminus post quem* of his appointment as bishop of Kashkar to 21 July 860, since this is the date when Sergius became catholicos. The epithet 'interpreter' is the only piece of information that perhaps reveals something of his occupation before becoming a bishop. The word *al-mufassir* is ambiguous, since it can mean both commentator and translator as well as interpreter. It nevertheless indicates that Israel was a scholar and a learned monk, perhaps connected with one of the two schools at Kashkar.

The subsequent account of the rivalry between Israel and Enosh for the patriarchal see upon the death of Sergius corroborates the inference that Israel was a scholar and a learned monk. Here it is stated that Israel was worthy of being elected catholicos because of his knowledge (*ʿilm*) and his excellence (*faḍl*). He is also described as intelligent (*fahīm*) and an expert in debate (*ʿālim bi-l-jadal*). His skills in debate are also stressed in the account of his debate with the philosopher Aḥmad ibn al-Ṭayyib al-Sarakhsī (q.v.), where he is pictured as the hero. Gabriel of Basra calls Israel 'custodian of the patriarchal throne' and, in connection with the importance of reading logical texts, quotes him as saying that a teacher who does not study logic is poor and needy.

When he was elected catholicos, problems arose for Israel, because Enosh, the metropolitan of Mosul, also claimed the leadership of the church. Since Enosh had good qualities as well some people sided with him, and a serious conflict arose between the two parties. The leaders lost control of their followers, and a physical fight broke out. Both parties went so far as to seek assistance from the political authorities, who already had trouble with the revolt of the Zanj. The ruler in Baghdad tried to persuade Israel to step down, but this only aggravated the rivalry. The fatal and dramatic climax came when Israel was about to officiate at the eucharist. As he began the liturgy, he was attacked by a follower of Enosh, who so violently squeezed his genitals that Israel fainted. He died 40 days later and was buried in the monastery of Mār Pethion.

Israel's main surviving work is his *Risāla fī tathbīt waḥdāniyyat al-bāriʾ wa-tathlīth khawāṣṣihi*. In addition, passages by him are quoted in *Kitāb al-majdal* (his discussion with Qusṭā ibn Lūqā), in al-Muʾtaman ibn al-ʿAssāl's *Majmūʿ uṣūl al-dīn*, and the report of his debate with al-Sarakhsī also reflects his thought. The work *Kitāb fī uṣūl al-diyāna*, attributed to him by Abū l-Barakāt ibn Kabar, is no longer extant.

MAIN SOURCES OF INFORMATION

Primary

H. Kaufhold, *Die Rechtssammlung des Gabriel von Baṣra und ihr Verhältnis zu den anderen juristischen Sammelwerken der Nestorianer*, Berlin, 1973, pp. 306-07

ʿAmr ibn Mattā, *Kitāb al-majdal* in H. Gismondi (ed.), *Maris Amri et Slibae De patriarchis Nestorianorum commentaria*, 4 parts in 1 vol., Rome, 1896-99, i, p. 81; ii, pp. 73-74, 92

al-Muʾtaman ibn al-ʿAssāl, *Summa dei principi della religione*, ed. A. Wadi, trans. B. Pirone, 6 vols, Cairo, 1998-2002, ch. 6, §§ 26-50 (= *Majmūʿ uṣūl al-dīn*)

Abū l-Barakāt ibn Kabar, *Miṣbāḥ al-ẓulma fī īḍāḥ al-khidma*, ed. S. Khalil, Cairo, 1970, p. 302 (= *Der Katalog der christlichen Schriften in arabischer Sprache von Abū 'l-Barakāt*, edition and trans. W. Riedel, Göttingen, 1902, p. 652)

Secondary

J. Faultless, 'The two recensions of the Prologue to John in Ibn al-Ṭayyib's *Commentary on the Gospels*', in D. Thomas (ed.), *Christians at the heart of Islamic rule. Church life and scholarship in ʿAbbasid Iraq*, Leiden, 2003, 177-98, p. 194

B. Holmberg, '"Person" in the trinitarian doctrine of Christian Arabic apologetics and its background in the Syriac Church Fathers', *Studia Patristica* 25 (1993) 300-07

B. Holmberg, 'The Trinitarian terminology of Israel of Kashkar (d. 872)', *Aram* 3 (1991) 53-81
B. Holmberg, *A treatise on the Unity and Trinity of God by Israel of Kashkar (d. 872)*, Lund, 1989
J.M. Fiey, *Assyrie chrétienne*, 3 vols, Beirut, 1965-68, iii, pp. 178-79
Graf, *GCAL* ii, pp. 155-56

WORKS ON CHRISTIAN-MUSLIM RELATIONS

Risāla fī tathbīt waḥdāniyyat al-bāriʾ wa-tathlīth khawāṣṣihi, 'Epistle on the confirmation of the Unity of the Creator and the Trinity of his properties'

DATE Mid-9th c.
ORIGINAL LANGUAGE Arabic

DESCRIPTION

The treatise covers 11 folios (22 pages) in the oldest manuscript and 70 pages in the modern edition. In the following, paragraph numbers refer to the edition. The treatise may be divided into three major parts. While the first two parts are provided with headings in the manuscripts, the third is introduced without any heading.

After the title (§§ 1-5), which does not really belong to the author's text, and the introduction (§§ 4-14), the first part of the treatise deals with the doctrine of unity (*al-qawl fī l-tawḥīd*), which consists of the three levels of knowledge (§§ 15-57). In this part, the author emphasizes the unreliability of sensual perception (§§ 16-20), of intellectual knowledge (§§ 21-42), and of inferential reasoning (§§ 43-54), and recommends an adherence to revelation as far as a study of the Creator is concerned (§ 54). A lot of doxological material is presented in this part.

The second part deals with the doctrine (or the doctrines) of the one (*al-qawl fī l-wāḥid*; §§ 58-115). It commences with an exposition of the three ways in which 'one' may be said (§§ 59-62). The whole of this part consists of doxological material pertaining to both Greek philosophers and sages (§§ 65-83) and to persons and schools more or less contemporary with the author (§§ 84-115), e.g. the Muʿtazila and Hishām ibn al-Ḥakam (§§ 84-96), and al-Nāshiʾ al-Akbar (§§ 102-118). Most of their doctrines are rejected by the author.

In the third and most extensive part, Israel expounds his own Christian doctrine of divine unity (§§ 119-220). Having presented some introductory statements on the importance of tradition as well as inferential reasoning, the relationship between the Creator and his creation, and God as substance (§§ 119-30), the author develops his doctrine of the Unity and Trinity of God in the form of 12 questions and answers (§§ 131-220).

The first of these questions and answers refers back to the final statement in the author's introduction to this third part, namely, that God is substance (§§ 131-41). Then follow three questions and answers in which the author develops his doctrine that God is one as a species (§§ 142-51).

In the next five questions and answers, the author draws the reader's attention to the two divine attributes of life and reason, which in his philosophical apologia for a Trinitarian doctrine represent the second and third persons of the Trinity (§§ 152-98).

The 10th and 11th questions and answers are devoted to the concepts of hypostasis (*al-qunūm*) and differentia (*al-faṣl*) respectively (§§ 199-203 and 204-14).

In the 12th and final question and answer, the relevance of the Trinitarian analogies of the soul or the human being (with their life and speech) or of the sun (with its heat and light) is discussed (§§ 215-20). This gives the author occasion to emphasize a theme which recurs throughout the treatise – the transcendence of God.

The authenticity of the treatise has been disputed. All six extant manuscripts attribute the treatise to Yaḥyā ibn ʿAdī (d. 974), but a marginal note in the oldest (on which all the other manuscripts depend) mentions 'al-Kaskarī' as the author. The question of authorship is thoroughly discussed in the introduction to the modern edition (see Holmberg, *A treatise*, pp. 17-106), where the attribution to Israel of Kashkar (d. 872) is established.

SIGNIFICANCE

The treatise is important for the discussion on the Unity and Trinity of God. It is a typical *kalām* work, highly philosophical, yet original at the same time. Rare words such as *rasīl* ('counterpart') are employed. The author stresses the transcendence of God, takes a skeptical attitude towards the possibility of knowledge, and discusses the relevance of analogies. Among others, the author refutes the Muʿtazila, al-Nāshiʾ al-Akbar and Hishām ibn al-Ḥakam.

MANUSCRIPTS

MS Eastern Desert, Egypt, Monastery of St Anthony – Theol. 130 (1570 AD), fols 53r-64r

MS Cairo, Coptic Patriarchate – Theol. 184 (1783 AD) (Simaika, 400; Graf, 641), fols 82v-97v

MS Eastern Desert, Egypt, Monastery of St Anthony, Theol. 129 (1788 AD), fols 59v-72v

MS Cairo, Coptic Patriarchate – Theol. 183 (1875) (Simaika, 526; Graf, 642), fols 75v-90r

MS Wādī l-Naṭrūn, Egypt, Monastery of St Bishoi – Theol. 303 (1882 AD), fols 85v-101v

MS Cairo, Franciscan Centre of Christian Oriental Studies – AC 661 (early 20th c.), fols 2r-11r (contains only §§ 119-221)

For a description of the manuscripts, see Holmberg, *A treatise*, pp. 107-29.

EDITIONS AND TRANSLATIONS

Holmberg, *A treatise*, pp. 3*-72* (edition)

STUDIES

Holmberg, 'Trinitarian terminology'

Holmberg, *A treatise*, pp. 17-138

Bo Holmberg 2008

ʿAlī ibn Yaḥyā ibn al-Munajjim

Abū l-Ḥasan ʿAlī ibn Yaḥyā ibn al-Munajjim

DATE OF BIRTH 815/6
PLACE OF BIRTH Baghdad
DATE OF DEATH 888
PLACE OF DEATH Samarra

BIOGRAPHY

Abū l-Ḥasan ʿAlī ibn Yaḥyā ibn al-Munajjim came from a Persian family of renowned astrologers. His grandfather was Abū Manṣūr Abān, who was employed as an astrologer by the ʿAbbasid Caliph al-Manṣūr, while his father, Abū ʿAlī Yaḥyā, worked as an astrologer for the ʿAbbasid Caliph al-Maʾmūn (q.v.) and converted from Zoroastrianism to Islam under the influence of his patron. For the next two centuries the al-Munajjim family had intimate ties with the ruling elite.

Abū l-Ḥasan ʿAlī ibn Yaḥyā was himself the most prominent and beloved boon-companion (*nadīm*) of the Caliph al-Mutawakkil and later also of al-Muntaṣir, al-Mustaʿīn, al-Muʿtazz, al-Muhtadī and al-Muʿtamid, who all admired him for his great learning and wit. The lavish payments he received from the ʿAbbasids allowed him to found the *Khizānat al-ḥikma*, an impressive library and study centre in Karkar, close to Baghdad, which was open to any scholar. He commissioned a study on engineering from Qusṭā ibn Lūqā and a survey of the works of Galen from Ḥunayn ibn Isḥāq (q.v.).

Abū l-Ḥasan ʿAlī ibn Yaḥyā ibn al-Munajjim's greatest achievements were in the field of literature and the theory of music. Among his works are a book on cookery and a book on poets from pre-Islamic and Islamic times called *Kitāb al-shuʿarāʾ al-qudamāʾ wa-l-islāmiyyīn*.

MAIN SOURCES OF INFORMATION

Primary

Muḥammad ibn ʿImrān al-Marzubānī, *Muʿjam al-shuʿarāʾ*, ed. F. Krenkow, Cairo, 1354 A.H. (1935), p. 287
Ibn al-Nadīm, *Fihrist*, pp. 160-61, 353

Yāqūt al-Ḥamawī, *Irshād al-arīb alā maʿrifat al-adīb*, ed. D.S. Margoliouth, 7 vols, London, 1923-31, v, pp. 457-60, 473-76, 486-87
Ibn al-Qiftī, *Taʾrīkh al-ḥukamāʾ*, ed. J. Lippert, Leipzig 1903, pp. 117, 128-29, 200, 363-64
Ibn Abī Uṣaybiʿa, *ʿUyūn al-anbāʾ fī ṭabaqāt al-aṭibbāʾ*, ed. Nizār Riḍā, Beirut, 1965, pp. 274, 329

Secondary
S.M. Toorawa, *Ibn Abī Ṭāhir Ṭayfūr and Arabic writerly culture. A ninth-century bookman in Baghdad*, London, 2005, pp. 118-21 and *passim*
Y.A. al-Sāmarrāʾī, "Alī ibn Yaḥyā al-Munajjim", *Majallat al-majmaʿ al-ʿilmī al-ʿIrāqī* 36 (1986) 201-61
M. Fleischhammer, art. 'al-Munadjdjim, Banū', in *EI2*
J.E. Bencheikh, 'Les secrétaires poètes et animateurs de cénacles aux IIe et IIIe siècles de l'Hégire. Contribution à l'analyse d'une production poétique', *Journal asiatique* 263 (1975) 265-315
S.M. Stern, 'Abū ʿĪsā ibn al-Munajjim's chronography', in S.M. Stern, A. Hourani and V. Brown (eds), *Islamic philosophy and the classical tradition*, Oxford, 1972, 437-66, pp. 437-439
A.G. Chejne, 'The boon-companion in early ʿAbbasid times', *JAOS* 85 (1965) 327-35
M. Fleischhammer, 'Die Banū al-Munağğim. Eine Bagdader Gelehrtenfamilie aus dem 2.-4. Jahrhundert d.H.', *Wissenschaftliche Zeitschrift der Martin-Luther Universität Halle-Wittenberg (Ges.-Sprachw.)* 12 (1963) 215-20

WORKS ON CHRISTIAN-MUSLIM RELATIONS

Al-burhān, 'The Proof'

DATE Before 873
ORIGINAL LANGUAGE Arabic

DESCRIPTION
This work belongs to the genre of 'proofs of prophethood' treatises (of which several were written in the 9th century) by way of an invitation to Islam, sent to Ḥunayn ibn Isḥāq (q.v.) and Qusṭā ibn Lūqā. It is one of the earliest texts to focus heavily on the inimitability of the Qurʾān in the context of the theological-apologetic search for an absolute proof of Muḥammad's prophethood. The author structured his proof around the claim that Muḥammad must have had supernatural certainty about the unique nature of the text of the Qurʾān. Without absolute knowledge that no one could ever rival the style of the Qurʾān, Muḥammad would not have challenged his opponents

to produce a similar text, because it would have been a reckless and imprudent act, while the history of Muḥammad's life shows that he was a wise and blameless person. Some of the arguments used echo the letter written by Muḥammad ibn al-Layth (q.v.) on behalf of the Caliph Hārūn al-Rashīd to the Byzantine emperor. Perhaps Abū l-Ḥasan ʿAlī knew Ibn al-Layth's letter through his acquaintance Ibn Abī Ṭāhir Ṭayfūr (d. 893), who included it in his *al-Manthūr wa-l-manẓūm*. Interestingly, the text contains no theological refutation of Christianity; the author focuses exclusively on his claim that Muḥammad was the true and final prophet of God.

Abū l-Ḥasan ʿAlī's authorship cannot be determined with absolute certainty. The Beirut manuscript does not attribute this text to him but to 'Abū ʿĪsā Yaḥyā al-Munajjim', while the Zahleh manuscript omits the *kunyā*. This calls into question the attribution of this invitation to Islam, since there was no one in the al-Munajjim family with the name Abū ʿĪsā Yaḥyā. Scholars have opted for two different members of this family as possible authors: Abū l-Ḥasan ʿAlī and his son Abū ʿĪsā Aḥmad. Several factors point to the younger candidate. First, his name is more similar and second, Ibn al-Nadīm says (*Fihrist*, p. 353) that, during his stay in Armenia at the end of his life, Qusṭā ibn Lūqā responded to a letter in defense of Muḥammad's prophethood by Abū ʿĪsā ibn al-Munajjim.

Nevertheless, attributing the letter to Abū ʿIsa Aḥmad is problematic. Abū ʿIsa Aḥmad belonged to the generation after Ḥunayn. The dates of his life are unknown, but his father, Abū l-Ḥasan ʿAlī, was born in 815/6, which means that Aḥmad was born in 835 at the earliest (and probably much later since his brothers Yaḥyā and Hārūn were not born till 855 and 865 respectively). This would make Ḥunayn at least 26 years older than Abū ʿĪsā Aḥmad. Since the author speaks of the fatherly affection he feels towards the recipients of his invitation to Islam, he cannot have been Abū ʿĪsā.

In addition, there are specific reasons for attributing it to Abū l-Ḥasan ʿAlī, as R. Haddad has shown. First, he was a close friend and patron of the Christian scholars, so an expression of fatherly affection is much more to be expected from him. Haddad also draws attention to the fact that Ibn Abī Uṣaybiʿa, despite copying the non-existent name of Abū ʿĪsā Yaḥyā from Ibn al-Nadīm elsewhere, lists as one of Ḥunayn's works *Kitāb ilā ʿAlī ibn Yaḥyā, jawāb kitābihi fīmā daʿāhu ilayhi min dīn al-Islām* (*ʿUyūn al-anbāʾ*, p. 274). This title refers without doubt to the father, not to the son.

Nevertheless, Zilio-Grandi apparently assumes that the letter was redacted by Abū ʿĪsā; although she gives no arguments for this, she published the correspondence without Ḥunayn's reply and mentions Abū ʿĪsā Aḥmad ibn al-Munajjim as the author of the Muslim text. Nasrallah is also inclined to attribute the work to Abū ʿĪsā, or else to his brother Abū Aḥmad Yaḥyā (d. 912), whose name also resembles the name in the manuscripts more closely than does his father's. Coincidentally, Fleischhammer ('al-Munadjdjim, Banū') states that Abū Aḥmad Yaḥyā wrote a *Risālat ilā Qusṭā ibn Lūqā wa-Ḥunayn* (referring to Brockelmann, *GAL* S i, 225, where no manuscript reference is given), though the manuscript reference he gives (MS Istanbul – Suleymaniyye – Şehit Ali 2103) is incorrect, since this manuscript contains only Qusṭā ibn Lūqā's *Maqāla fī l-wabaʾ* and two other unrelated works. Since Ibn al-Nadīm, the earliest author who indicates that Abū ʿĪsā wrote a letter to Qusṭā, does not add the name Yaḥyā, the attribution to this second son seems highly unlikely. Moreover, the chronological problem (regarding the 'fatherly affection') is even more awkward here.

Nwiya and Samir have attempted to solve the conundrum by suggesting that two redactions were made: first Abū l-Ḥasan ʿAlī wrote to Ḥunayn, and many years later his son Abū ʿĪsā wrote a reworked version to Qusṭā. Although their reconstruction of events is the most plausible, one further observation can be made. It is possible that the reference in Ibn al-Nadīm to Qusṭā's reply to Abū ʿĪsā's defense of Muḥammad's prophethood refers to an entirely different work. There is no reason to assume that Qusṭā could not have received two treatises in defense of Islam during his lifetime and written two responses. If so, the later manuscript tradition has confused these separate correspondences. That the *incipit* containing the name Abū ʿĪsā Yaḥyā cannot be the original one is clear from the fact that there was no one with such a name. In other words, these words and the rest of the *incipit* could be a later addition by someone who thought this was the letter to which Qusṭā replied from Armenia. It may be shown that this erroneous name found its way into the manuscripts much earlier than the time of the surviving manuscripts by referring to the *Tatimmat ṣiwān al-ḥikma* of the historian ʿAlī ibn Zayd al-Bayhaqī (d. 1169). In that work the name Abū ʿĪsā Yaḥyā appears, together with a few lines from the *Burhān* that has come down to us (M. Meyerhof, "ʿAlī al-Bayhaqī's *Tatimmat ṣiwān al-ḥikma*', *Osiris* 8 (1948) 122-217, p. 167; Zilio-Grandi, pp. 43-46).

One factor that supports the possibility that, if indeed Abū ʿĪsā and Qusṭā did write apologetic treatises to each other, these are not our *Burhān* and its reply is the improbability of Abū ʿĪsā expressing paternal feelings towards Qusṭā, since the latter was at least 15 years older than the former.

SIGNIFICANCE

The *Burhān* reflects the growing importance of the search for proof of the absolute truth of Islam in the early ʿAbbasid period and an important phase in the development of the doctrine of the inimitability of the Qur'an. The letter, together with the two Christian replies to it, forms an example of a truly historical interreligious encounter. It is the product of amicable encounters of Muslims and Christians who lived and worked in the same scholarly and cultural milieu of 9th-century Iraq, and believed that the language of reason was the key to making one's faith understandable to the other.

The fact that ʿAlī ibn Zayd al-Bayhaqī, in 12th-century Iran, quotes from the text is a sign that it was known in later centuries among Muslims, although it only survives in Christian manuscripts.

MANUSCRIPTS

MS Zahleh, Collection Maʿlūf – 1355 (18th c.) (inaccessible manuscript of the 18th c.; cf. J. Nasrallah, *Catalogue des manuscrits du Liban*, 4 vols, Beirut, 1958-70, iv, pp. 24-26)

MS Beirut, Bibliothèque Orientale – Or. 664, fols 217-232 (1876, the only manuscript used by Samir and Nwyia)

MS Damascus, Greek Orthodox Patriarchate – s.n. (recently discovered by Cyrille Cairala; Zilio-Grandi, *Una corrispondenza*, p. 42, n. 6)

EDITIONS AND TRANSLATIONS

J.A. Szymańczyk, *Korespondencja Między Chrześcijaninem a Muzułmaninem*, Krakow, 2005 (Polish trans. based on Samir's edition)

I. Zilio-Grandi and S.K. Samir, *Una corrispondenza islamo-cristiana sull' origine divina dell' Islam*, Turin, 2003 (Italian trans. based on Samir's edition)

S.K. Samir and P. Nwyia, 'Une correspondance islamo-chrétienne entre Ibn al-Munağğim, Ḥunayn ibn Isḥāq et Qusṭā ibn Lūqā', *Patrologia Orientalis* 40 (1981), 524-723 (edition by Samir, French trans. by Nwyia)

STUDIES

Zilio-Grandi and Samir, *Una corrispondenza islamo-cristiana*

Samir and Nwyia, 'Une correspondance islamo-chrétienne'

J. Nasrallah, 'Dialogue islamo-chrétien. À propos de publications récentes', *REI* 46 (1978) 121-51, pp. 134-39

P. Nwyia, 'Un dialogue islamo-chrétien au IXe siècle', *Axes* 9 (1977) 7-22

R. Haddad, 'Ḥunayn ibn Isḥāq apologiste chrétien', *Arabica* 21 (1974) 292-302

Barbara Roggema 2007

Ḥunayn ibn Isḥāq

Abū Zayd Ḥunayn ibn Isḥāq al-ʿIbādī

DATE OF BIRTH 809
PLACE OF BIRTH al-Ḥīra
DATE OF DEATH 873
PLACE OF DEATH Baghdad

BIOGRAPHY

As can be inferred from his *nisba*, al-ʿIbādī, Ḥunayn's father belonged to the Arab Christian community of the ʿIbād in the southern Iraqī town of al-Ḥīra, the provincial capital of the Lakhmids. Ḥunayn started the practice of medicine with his father, who was a druggist. He learned Syriac in al-Ḥīra and was ordained deacon (*shammās*) of the East-Syrian church in that city. He moved to Gundishāpūr, where he learned Persian. Then he went to Baghdad and studied medicine with the famous Christian physician and scholar Yūḥannā ibn Māsawayh, who was the director of *Bayt al-ḥikma* ('The House of Wisdom').

After arguing with his master, Ḥunayn left Baghdad and went to Byzantium, where he improved his knowledge of Greek. When he returned to Baghdad he was reconciled with Yūḥannā ibn Māsawayh, who entrusted him with the translation of Greek works. Thus, by the year 862, when he returned to Baghdad, Ḥunayn had a good command of Arabic, Syriac, Greek and Persian. In Baghdad, he worked in Jibrīl ibn Bukhtīshūʿ's administration and was named physician to the ʿAbbasid Caliph al-Mutawakkil. He also worked as a translator for the caliphs al-Maʾmūn, al-Muʿtaṣim, al-Wāthiq, and al-Mutawakkil.

In the year 854, he was imprisoned for four months as the result of a court intrigue hatched by Bukhtīshūʿ ibn Jibrāʾīl and Isrāʾīl ibn Zakariyyā l-Ṭayfūrī, his rivals in the practice of medicine in Baghdad in those days. They challenged him to spit on an icon before the Caliph al-Mutawakkil, ostensibly to demonstrate that Christians are not idolaters but in reality to expose him as a heretic. How he temporarily fell from favor as a result of this misstep can be read in his purported 'autobiography', which was probably written by one of his disciples.

Ḥunayn was not only a well-known translator from Greek and Syriac into Arabic, but also one of the most prominent Christian scholars of the 9th century. In addition, he was a physician and a teacher of several subjects, including medicine and theology. He had a strong reputation as a master-translator; for example, the Arabic translation of the Septuagint attributed to him was well received among his contemporaries.

As a translator, Ḥunayn was without doubt the decisive link in the transmission of Greek science to the Arabic scientific community; he accomplished this by virtue of the lexical and terminological contribution made by his translations. Notable among the scholars who worked under his supervision are his son Isḥāq ibn Ḥunayn, and his nephew Ḥubaysh ibn al-Ḥasan. Although 260 translations and 100 original works – on medicine, philosophy, astronomy, magic, oneiromancy, theology, mathematics and linguistics – are attributed to Ḥunayn, only a few have come down to us. Among those that survive is his *Nawādir al-falāsifa*, 'Aphorisms of the philosophers', a collection of maxims of ancient philosophers and sages, which has been characterized as an attempt to define a 'commonly accepted ethical framework' for the Christian and Muslim intellectual elite (Griffith, 'Timothy I to Ḥunayn').

Unfortunately, his *Kitāb taʾrīkh al-ʿālam*, 'History of the world', which allegedly covered the whole of history from creation to the 'kings of Islam', is lost. So is his *Kitāb al-nuqaṭ*, 'Diacritical points'. Although Ḥunayn was a native Arabic-speaker and wrote virtually all his works in Arabic, a passage in one of Elijah of Nisibis' *Majālis* reveals that in *Kitāb al-nuqaṭ* Ḥunayn criticized the limited scientific vocabulary of the Arabic language (Graf, *GCAL* ii, pp. 125-26).

The contents of Ḥunayn's lost work entitled *Risāla fī dalālat al-qadr ʿalā l-tawḥīd* can only be surmised. Graf lists this as one of Ḥunayn's apologetic works and translates its title as 'Abhandlung darüber, dass die (in der Welt sich offenbarende göttliche) Macht ein Beweis für die Einzigkeit (Göttes) ist'. Assuming Graf's translation is correct, one can perhaps locate the work within the trend among Muslims and Christians in 9th-century Iraq to use the order of the physical world as the basis for demonstrations of the existence of God and creation. The arguments employed were often directed against dualists and the *dahriyya*. One prominent idea was that, since the elements are naturally at odds with each other, they can only have been brought together by one single force, namely the Creator (Van Ess, *TG* iii,

p. 367, iv, p. 207-9). Since the title indicates that Ḥunayn tried to prove the existence of the one God on the basis of His power, it may be the case that he espoused this or comparable ideas in this lost work. Another of Ḥunayn's lost theological works, *Maqāla fī khalq al-insān wa-annahu min maṣlaḥatihi wa-l-tafaḍḍul 'alayhi ju'ila muḥtājan*, 'Treatise on the creation of man and that it was for his own benefit and out of favor towards him that he was made needy', may equally have been written in response to challenges to the doctrine of monotheism, in particular to the belief in divine goodness and providence.

MAIN SOURCES OF INFORMATION

Primary

Ibn al-Nadīm, *Fihrist*, ed. Yūsuf 'Alī Ṭawīl, Beirut, 1996, pp. 463-64

Ibn Juljul, *Ṭabaqāt al-aṭibbā' wa-l-ḥukamā'*, ed. F. Sayyid, Cairo, 1955, pp. 68-72

Ibn Abī Uṣaybi'a, *'Uyūn al-anbā' fī ṭabaqāt al-aṭibbā'*, ed. N. Riḍā, Beirut, 1965, pp. 257-74

Ibn al-Qifṭī, *Ta'rīkh al-ḥukamā'*, ed. J. Lippert, Leipzig, 1903, pp. 171-77

Barhebraeus, *Mukhtaṣar ta'rīkh al-duwal*, ed. A. Ṣālḥānī, Beirut, 1890, pp. 250-53

al-Baghdādī, Isma'īl ibn Muḥammad, *Hadiyyat al-'ārifīn. Asmā' al-mu'allifīn wa-āthār al-muṣannifīn*, Baghdad, s.d. (repr. Istanbul, 1951), p. 340

Secondary

S.H. Griffith, 'From Patriarch Timothy I to Ḥunayn ibn Isḥāq. Philosophy and Christian apology in Abbasid times. Reason, ethics and public policy', in M. Tamcke (ed.), *Christians and Muslims in dialogue in the Islamic Orient of the middle ages*, Beirut, 2007, 75-98

J. Aßfalg, art. 'Ḥunain ibn Isḥāq', in H. Kaufhold (ed.), *Kleines Lexikon des christlichen Orients*, Wiesbaden, 2007[2]

R. Morrison, art. 'Ḥunayn b. Isḥāq', in *Dictionary of literary biography* cccxi (Arabic literary culture 500-925), Detroit, 2005

M. Cooperson, 'The autobiography of Hunayn ibn Ishaq (809-873 or 877)', in D.F. Reynolds (ed.), *Interpreting the self: Autobiography in the Arabic literary tradition*, Berkeley CA, 2001, 107-18

Ḥunayn ibn Isḥāq, *Fī l-a'mār wa-l-ājāl*, ed. S.K. Samir, Beirut, 2001, pp. 8-11

G. Saliba, 'Competition and transmission of the foreign sciences. Hunayn at the Abbasid court', *Bulletin of the Royal Institute for Inter-Faith Studies* 2 (2000) 85-101

F. Sezgin, *Hunain ibn Ishāq (2. 260). Texts and studies*, 2 vols, Frankfurt, 1996-99 (collection of numerous articles by various scholars)

M. Cooperson, 'The purported autobiography of Hunayn ibn Ishaq', *Edebiyât* 7 (1997) 235-49

A. Dubyān, *Ḥunayn ibn Isḥāq. Dirāsa tārīkhiyya wa-lughawiyya*, Riyadh, 1993
G. Anawati, *Al-Masīḥiyya wa-l-ḥaḍāra al-ʿarabiyya*, Cairo, 1992², pp. 204-9
S.K. Samir, 'Un traité perdu de Ḥunayn ibn Isḥāq retrouvé dans la "Somme" d'Ibn al-ʿAssāl', *Aram* 3 (1991) 171-92
G.C. Anawati and A.Z. Iskander, art. 'Ḥunayn b. Isḥāq', in *Dictionary of scientific bibliography (suppl. 1)*, New York, 1990
L. Cheïkho, *ʿUlamāʾ al-naṣrāniyya fī l-Islām, 622-1300*, ed. C. Hechaïmé, Rome, 1983, pp. 152-56, n. 174
A.Z. Iskandar, 'An attempted reconstruction of the late Alexandrian medical curriculum (based on Hunain b. Ishaq and Ibn Ridwan)', *Medical History* 20 (1976) 235-58
Y. Ḥabbī and N. Ḥikmat, *Jawāmiʿ Ḥunayn ibn Isḥāq fī l-āthār al-ʿulwiyya li-Arisṭū*, Baghdad, 1976
Y. Ḥabbī, *Ḥunayn ibn Isḥāq*, Baghdad, 1974
R. Köbert, 'Zur Ḥunain-Biographie des Ibn Abī Uṣaibiʿa', *Orientalia* 43 (1974) 414-16
ʿA.R. Sāmarrāʾī and ʿA-Ḥ al-ʿAlwajī, *Āthār Ḥunayn ibn Isḥāq*, Baghdad, 1974
S.K. Samir, 'Ḥunayn ibn Isḥāq (wa-l-khalīfat al-Maʾmūn 813-833 m)', *Ṣadīq al-Kāhin* 12 (1972) 193-98 (edition of the text about Ḥunayn's downfall at court from Ibn Abī Uṣaybiʿa)
M. Ullmann, *Die Medizin im Islam*, Leiden, 1970, pp. 115-19
G. Strohmaier, art. 'Ḥunayn b. Isḥāq al-ʿIbādī', in *EI2*
F. Sezgin, *GAS* iii, pp. 247-56
G. Strohmaier, 'Hunain ibn Ishaq und die Bilder', *Klio* 43-45 (1965) 525-33 (repr. in Strohmaier, *Von Demokrit bis Dante. Die Bewahrung antiken Erbes in der arabischen Kultur*, Hildesheim, 1996)
G. Graf, *GCAL* ii, pp. 122-32
L.M. Saʿdi, 'A bio-bibliographical study of Hunayn ibn Ishaq al-Ibadi (Johannitius), 809-877 A.D.', *Bulletin of the History of Medicine* 2 (1934) 409-46
Baumstark, *GSL*, pp. 227-32
K. Merkle, *Die sittensprüche der philosophen "Kitâb Âdâb al-Falâsifa" von Ḥonein ibn Isḥâq in der überarbeitung des Muḥammed Ibn Alî al-Anṣârî*, Leipzig, 1921
G. Bergsträsser, *Ḥunain Ibn Isḥāḳ und seine Schule*, Leiden, 1913

WORKS ON CHRISTIAN-MUSLIM RELATIONS

Maqāla fī l-ājāl, 'Treatise on lifespans', *Kitāb al-ājāl*, 'Book on lifespans', *Fī l-aʿmār wa-l-ājāl*, 'On ages and lifespans', *Kayfiyyat al-iʿtiqād fī l-aʿmār wa-l-ājāl*, 'How to believe in ages and lifespans'

DATE Unknown
ORIGINAL LANGUAGE Arabic

DESCRIPTION

Ḥunayn ibn Isḥāq's *Fī l-aʿmār wa-l-ājāl* is preserved in Ch. 58 of the *Majmūʿ uṣūl al-dīn* ('Encyclopaedia of the fundamentals of religion') by the 13th-century Copto-Arabic author al-Muʾtaman ibn al-ʿAssāl. It deals with the general topic of the limitation (*ḥadd*) of human beings' lives by God, and addresses the question of whether God has prescribed for each human being a particular, immutable 'term' of life (*ajal*).

Ḥunayn does not question the reality of divine foreknowledge (*ʿilm*), nor of the existence of a 'general limitation' (*al-ḥadd al-ʿāmm*) of human life. However, he sets up a chain of dialectical arguments in order to show that divine foreknowledge is *not* the cause of everything that happens (and certainly not the cause of evil!); in particular, God's foreknowledge is not the cause of a human being's death or deliverance from death in particular instances. Thus, there is a role for human thought and prudence with respect to the extension of one's life. Ḥunayn reacts sharply against any fatalistic attitude towards death.

According to Ḥunayn, there is a distinction to be made between the lifespan of plants and animals, which is circumscribed (*ʿumr maḥdūd*), and that of human beings (*al-ḥayawān al-nāṭiq*, 'the rational animal'), which is a gift from God. Ḥunayn presents the biblical data for the general life expectancy of human beings, which in the present 'third generation' is 70 or 80 years (Psalm 90:10). The Bible gives examples of God extending or shortening this life expectancy, however, and human beings play a role through what we today might call 'lifestyle choices': diet, mental and physical exercise, alcohol consumption, and risky behavior.

The work was composed according to the well-known method used in the treatises of *ʿilm al-kalām*; and Ḥunayn's language and the arguments reflect the intellectual milieu of the contemporary Muslim *mutakallimūn*. At the same time, he is capable of using a well-chosen analogy in order to make his meaning clear, or of referring to Galen in order to support a point.

SIGNIFICANCE

Fī l-aʿmār wa-l-ājāl is the first known Christian Arabic treatise that deals with the connection between the concepts 'ages' (*aʿmār*) and 'terms' (*ājāl*) of life and the causal relationship of God's foreknowledge (*ʿilm*) of them. Ḥunayn's aim may be seen as to provide a theological compendium on these matters. At the same time, one should not overlook the apologetic character of the work. While Ḥunayn does not quote the Qurʾān or make explicit reference to Islamic concepts, the term *ajal* is loaded with qurʾānic significance (see Q 6:2 and parallels), and is often associated with the idea that God has allotted every human being a fixed, immutable term of life (cf. Q 3:154). Over and against particular notions of determinism found in Islamic discourse, Ḥunayn defends traditional eastern Christian understandings of human freedom and responsibility – a responsibility which, in the case of the stewardship of a human life, had been provided with useful tools by physicians such as Galen.

MANUSCRIPTS

Ḥunayn's treatise can be found in the following manuscripts of al-Muʾtaman ibn al-ʿAssāl's *Majmūʿ uṣūl al-dīn*:

MS Cairo, Coptic Museum – Theol. 211 (Simaika, 47; Graf, 125) (14th c.)
MS BNF – Ar. 200 (16th c.)
MS Berlin, Staatsbibliothek – Or. 2098 (517) (1655)
MS Cairo, Coptic Patriarchate – Theol. 346 (Simaika, 252; Graf, 318) (before 1677)
MS BL – Or. 1020 (Ar. 1694) (1678)
MS Cairo, Coptic Patriarchate – Theol. 322 (Simaika, 284; Graf, 649) (1724)
MS Wādī l-Naṭrūn, monastery of St Macarius – Theol. 12 (U. Zanetti, *Les manuscrits de Dair Abû Maqâr. Inventaire*, Genève, 1986, no. 283) (18th c.)

MS Cairo, Coptic Patriarchate – Theol. 101 (Simaika, 497; Graf, 650) (1833)
MS Wādī l-Naṭrūn, Monastery of St Macarius – Theol. 10 (Zanetti, no. 281) (1854)
MS Cairo, Coptic Patriarchate – Theol. 287 (Simaika, 540; Graf, 540) (1866)
MS Birmingham, Mingana – Chr. Ar. 54 (64b) (1880)
MS Damascus, Greek Orthodox Patriarchate – 89 (formerly 1526) (1901)
MS Cairo, Coptic Museum – Theol. 399 (Simaika, 87) (1904)
MS Cairo, Coptic Patriarchate – Theol. 308 (Simaika, 563) (1930)

In addition, see MSS 8, 36, 38-45 (all in Egyptian monastic libraries) from the list in A. Wadi, *Studio su al-Muʾtaman ibn al-ʿAssāl*, Cairo, 1997, pp. 189-92; these may contain the whole *Majmūʿ uṣūl al-dīn*, including ch. 58.

EDITIONS AND TRANSLATIONS

Ḥunayn ibn Isḥāq, *Fī l-aʿmār wa-l-ājāl*, ed. S.K. Samir, pp. 35-56 (edition with an introductory bio-bibliographical study in Arabic)
B. Pirone, *al-Muʾtaman ibn al-ʿAssāl. Summa dei principi della religione*, 2 vols, Cairo, 1998-2002, ii, ch. 58 (Italian trans.)
A. Wadi, *al-Muʾtaman ibn al-ʿAssāl. Majmūʿ uṣūl al-dīn wa-masmūʿ maḥṣūl al-yaqīn*, 2 vols in 4 parts, Cairo, 1998-99, ii, ch. 58 (edition)
S.K. Samir, 'Maqāla fī l-ājāl li-Ḥunayn ibn Isḥāq', *Al-Mashriq* 65 (1991) 403-25 (edition based on five manuscripts, with study in Arabic)
See also Wadi, *Studio su al-Muʾtaman ibn al-ʿAssāl*, pp. 193-97, for a list of previous editions.

STUDIES

P. La Spisa, review of Ḥunayn ibn Isḥāq, *Fī l-aʿmār wa-l-ājāl*, ed. S.K. Samir, in *Collectanea Christiana Orientalia* 2 (2005) 540-46
Ḥunayn ibn Isḥāq, *Fī l-aʿmār wa-l-ājāl*, ed. S.K. Samir, pp. 11-34
Van Ess, *TG* iv, pp. 494-97
Samir, 'Un traité perdu de Ḥunayn ibn Isḥāq retrouvé'

Juan Pedro Monferrer-Sala 2007

Kayfiyyat idrāk ḥaqīqat al-diyāna , 'How to discern the truth of a religion' (with variations), *Kitāb ilā ʿAlī ibn Yaḥyā jawāb kitābihi fīmā daʿāhu ilayhi min dīn al-islām* 'A work written to ʿAlī ibn Yaḥyā [ibn al-Munajjim] in response to the work in which he invited him to the religion of Islam'

DATE Unknown
ORIGINAL LANGUAGE Arabic

DESCRIPTION
This text is another of the few works by Ḥunayn that deal exclusively with religion, constituting a defense of Christianity in response to pressure to convert to Islam. The work is known in two different recensions, a shorter one with a personal touch, which was part of a correspondence involving Ibn al-Munajjim and Qusṭā ibn Lūqā, and a longer, more impersonal one.

The latter is a brief explanation of the ways in which truth can be distinguished from falsehood in rather general terms. Ḥunayn deals only indirectly with doctrine here; his arguments are above all historical and psychological, and in his approach he reveals something of his profession as a physician, focusing on the symptoms in order to find the cause of the disease. He lists a number of negative reasons why people accept ideas and reports that are false: they may do so because they are coerced, because they want to be relieved from hardship, because they are eager to gain a higher status, because a malicious person talks them into it, because such a person takes advantage of their ignorance and backwardness, and because people want to adhere to what their close kin believe.

Next he gives a number of ways by which to recognize the truth. It may be discerned on the basis of supernatural signs, or because the external aspects of a religion are visible evidence of the reality of its hidden mysteries. Alternatively, logical demonstration leads to truth, as well as historical investigations into the continuing validity of an assertion through the centuries.

After setting out these guidelines, Ḥunayn goes on to review the history of Christianity in the light of them and concludes that none of the negative reasons are at the basis of its establishment as a religion. Although the word 'Islam' is never used, it is obvious that Ḥunayn wants to turn the apologetic argument of Islam's popularity and rapid spread into an argument *against* its claim to divine support. This becomes particularly clear when he says that the strongest factor in Christianity's claim to truth is the inaccessibility of its doctrines.

In the more personal recension, which is Ḥunayn's response to ʿAlī ibn Yaḥyā ibn al-Munajjim's (q.v.) defense of Muḥammad's prophethood and invitation to Islam, his rejection of Islam emerges more openly. In the prelude to the treatise proper, he accuses Ibn al-Munajjim of being biased in his approach and therefore of making untenable claims about the inimitability of the Qurʾān. He counters Ibn al-Munajjim's claim that Muḥammad was both extraordinarily intelligent and miraculously successful in converting his people by asking whether Muḥammad did not have a great advantage in the fact that his audience was uneducated, leaving open the logical possibility that merely human cleverness was at work. He laments the fact that Ibn al-Munajjim talks of 'proof', without investigating whether his opponent agrees with his premises. With some condescension, he adds that Ibn al-Munajjim had probably not even read the *Book of the proof* to prepare himself for his reasoned defense of Islam. As Samir notes, this *Book of the proof* probably refers to Aristotle's *Posterior analytics*.

Although the two recensions are occasionally mentioned as separate works, it is clear that they are largely the same. There is no clear indication as to whether the shorter recension was the original version, later recast as a response to Ibn al-Munajjim, or whether this shorter recension is an excerpt of the other.

SIGNIFICANCE

This is one of a number of Christian Arabic texts from early ʿAbbasid times that advance the idea that the truth of a religion can be determined by looking at the motives people have for converting or not converting to it. Ḥunayn adopted this idea from the generation of Christian Arabic apologists before him, in particular Theodore Abū Qurra (q.v.), Abū Rāʾiṭa (q.v.) and ʿAmmār al-Baṣrī (q.v.). Ḥunayn's treatise illustrates how the concept of reason was both an instrument and a weapon in the scholarly circles closely associated with the ʿAbbasid court. The treatise must have had a wide circulation, since we find it in several later apologists (Yuḥannā ibn Mīna, Muʾtaman ibn al-ʿAssāl and Abū l-Barakāt ibn Kabar).

MANUSCRIPTS

The 'personal recension' (including Ibn al-Munajjim's *Burhān* and Qusṭā ibn Lūqā's response):

MS Zahleh, Collection Maʿlūf – 1355 (18th c.)

MS Beirut, Université St Joseph – Or. 664 (1876) fols 277-83

MS Damascus, Greek Orthodox Patriarchate – s.n. (recently discovered by Cyrille Cairala; see: I. Zilio-Grandi and S.K. Samir, *Una corrispondenza islamo-cristiana sull'origine divina dell'Islam*, Turin, 2003, p. 42, no. 6)

The 'impersonal recension', mostly in manuscripts of al-Muʾtaman ibn al-ʿAssāl's *Majmūʿ uṣūl al-dīn*:

MS Aleppo, Fondation Georges et Mathilde Salem – Sbath 1589 (1249)

MS Vat – Ar. 103, fols 140v-143v (13th c.)

MS Monastery of St Anthony – 119, Theol. 157 (1339)

MS Aleppo, Fondation Georges et Mathilde Salem – Sbath 1125 (14th c.)

MS Beirut, Université St Joseph – Or. 1089 (573) (14th c.)

MS Cairo, Coptic Museum – Theol. 211 (Simaika, 47; Graf, 125) (14th c.)

MS Aleppo, Fondation Georges et Mathilde Salem – Sbath 1017 (15th c.)

MS Oxford, Bodleian Library – Ar. Chr. Uri 38 (Hunt. 240) (1549/50) (fols 111v-113r, an extract from Ibn al-ʿAssāl's *Majmūʿ uṣūl al-dīn*)

MS Cairo, Coptic Patriarchate – Theol. 104 (Simaika, 239; Graf, 648) (1554)

MS BNF – Ar. 200 (16th c.)

MS Aleppo, Fondation Georges et Mathilde Salem – Sbath 1001 (16th/17th c.)

MS Cairo, Coptic Patriarchate – Theol. 105 (Simaika, 286; Graf, 647) (1643)

MS Berlin, Staatsbibliothek – Or. 2098 (517) (1655)

MS BL – Or. 1020 (Ar. 1694) (1678)

MS Cairo, Coptic Patriarchate – Theol. 322 (Simaika, 284; Graf, 649) (1724)

MS Aleppo, Fondation Georges et Mathilde Salem – Sbath 1040 (1787)

MS Cairo, Coptic Patriarchate – Theol. 102 (Simaika, 421; Graf, 324) (1792)

MS Birmingham, Mingana – Chr. Ar. 53 (64) (19th c.)

MS Cairo, Coptic Patriarchate – Theol. 101 (Simaika, 497; Graf, 650) (1833)
MS Damascus, Greek Orthodox Patriarchate – 107 (formerly 1773) (1858)
MS Beirut, Université St Joseph – Or. 1099 (583) (1860, Karshūnī)
MS Cairo, Coptic Patriarchate – Theol. 103 (Simaika, 468; Graf, 326) (1867)
MS Wādī l-Naṭrūn, monastery of St Macarius – Theol. 11 (Zanetti, no. 282) (1872?)
MS Cairo, Coptic Patriarchate – Theol. 234 (Simaika, 527) (1877)
MS Birmingham, Mingana – Chr. Ar. 54 (64b) (1880)
MS Damascus, Greek Orthodox Patriarchate – 89 (formerly 1526) (1901)
MS Cairo, Coptic Museum – Theol. 399 (Simaika, 87) (1904)
MS Cairo, Coptic Patriarchate – Theol. 308 (Simaika, 563) (1930)
MS Assyut, Library of al-qummuṣ Ayyūb Masīḥa – s.n. (1942)
MS Wādī l-Naṭrūn, Monastery of St Macarius – Theol. 10 (Zanetti, no. 281) (1854)

In addition, see MSS 8, 36, 38-45 (all in Egyptian monastic libraries) from the list in Wadi, *Studio su al-Muʾtaman ibn al-ʿAssāl*, pp. 189-92; these may contain the whole *Majmūʿ uṣūl al-dīn*, including ch. 12. An excerpt from the treatise is also to be found in ch. 6 of Abū l-Barakāt ibn Kabar's *Miṣbāḥ al-ẓulma fī īḍāḥ al-khidma* (cf. Graf, *GCAL* ii, p. 128))

EDITIONS AND TRANSLATIONS

'Personal recension':

J.A. Szymańczyk, *Korespondencja Między Chrześcijaninem a Muzułmaninem*, Krakow, 2005 (Polish trans. on the basis of Samir's edition)
S.K. Samir and P. Nwyia, 'Une correspondance islamo-chrétienne entre Ibn al-Munağğim, Ḥunayn ibn Isḥāq et Qusṭā ibn Lūqā', *Patrologia Orientalis* 40 (1981), 524-723 (edition by Samir of the 'personal recension', French trans. by Nwyia)

'Impersonal recension':

Pirone, *al-Muʾtaman ibn al-ʿAssāl. Summa dei principi della religione*, i, ch. 12 (Italian trans.)
Wadi, *al-Muʾtaman ibn al-ʿAssāl. Majmūʿ uṣūl al-dīn*, i, ch. 12 (edition)

S.K. Samir, 'Maqālat Ḥunayn ibn Isḥāq fī "Kayfiyyat idrāk ḥaqīqat al-diyāna"', *Al-Mashriq* 71 (1997) 345-63 (edition based on the manuscripts from Oxford, Paris and the Vatican, treated as a work separate from the 'personal recension')

P. Sbath, *Vingt traités philosophiques et apologétiques d'auteurs arabes chrétiens du IXe au XIV*e *siècle*, Cairo, 1929, pp. 181-85 (edition based on three MSS in his possession)

L. Cheikho, *Vingt traités théologiques d'auteurs arabes chrétiens, ixe-xiiie siècle*, Beirut, 1920, pp. 143-46 (edition)

L. Cheikho, *Seize traités théologiques d'auteurs arabes chrétiens, ixe-xiiie siècle*, Beirut, 1906, pp. 121-23 (edition)

L. Cheikho, 'Un traité de Ḥonein', in C. Bezold (ed.), *Orientalische Studien Theodor Nöldeke gewidmet*, 2 vols, Giessen, 1906, i, pp. 283-91 (edition and trans. on the basis of two MSS of Ibn ʿAssāl's *Majmūʿ uṣūl al-dīn* in his possession)

STUDIES

Samir, 'Maqālat Ḥunayn ibn Isḥāq fī "Kayfiyyat idrāk ḥaqīqat al-diyāna"'

S.K. Samir, 'Liberté religieuse et propagation de la foi chez les théologiens arabes chrétiens du ixe siècle et en Islam', in *Witness of faith in life and worship*, Tantur, 1981, 63-164, pp. 149-53

Samir and Nwyia, 'Une correspondance islamo-chrétienne', pp. 543-57

P. Nwyia, 'Un dialogue islamo-chrétien au IXe siècle', *Axes* 9 (1977) 7-22

R. Haddad, 'Ḥunayn ibn Isḥāq. Apologiste chrétien', *Arabica* 21 (1974) 292-302

P. Nwyia, 'Actualité du concept de religion chez Ḥunayn Ibn Isḥāq', *Arabica* 21 (1974) 313-17

Graf, *GCAL* ii, pp. 126-28

Barbara Roggema 2008

Al-Jūzajānī

Abū Isḥāq Ibrāhīm ibn Yaʿqūb ibn Isḥāq al-Saʿdī al-Jūzajānī

DATE OF BIRTH Unknown, probably early 9th c.
PLACE OF BIRTH Khurāsān
DATE OF DEATH 870 or 873
PLACE OF DEATH Damascus

BIOGRAPHY

Al-Jūzajānī was originally from Khurāsān and traveled widely in the Muslim world before settling in Damascus. He is primarily known as a scholar and transmitter of *ḥadīth*, from Aḥmad ibn Ḥanbal among others. Some of his works and the traditions he cited in them are known through *ḥadīth* collectors of subsequent generations and also through the works of Muḥammad ibn Jarīr al-Ṭabarī, who used al-Jūzajānī as a source. Al-Ṭabarī may in fact have studied with him in Damascus (Rosenthal, p. 26). Several biographers make mention of his strong anti-ʿAlid stance.

Sezgin has drawn attention to three manuscripts in the Dār al-Kutub al-ẓāhiriyya in Damascus which contain works by al-Jūzajānī, but no studies of these have so far appeared.

MAIN SOURCES OF INFORMATION

Primary

Ibn ʿAsākir, *Taʾrīkh madīnat Dimashq*, 7 vols, Damascus, 1911-32, ii p. 310

al-Dhahabī, *Tadhkirat al-ḥuffāẓ*, ed. ʿAbd al-Raḥmān Yaḥyā al-Muʿallimī, 4 vols, Hyderabad, 1968-70, ii, p. 549

al-Ṣafadī, *Kitāb al-wāfī bi-l-wafayāt*, 29 vols, Leipzig, 1931-, vi, p. 170

Ibn Kathīr, *Al-bidāya-wa-l-nihāya fī l-tārīkh*, 14 vols, Cairo, 1932-33, xi, p. 31

Ibn Ḥajar, *Tahdhīb al-tahdhīb*, 12 vols, Beirut, 1968, i, pp. 181-83

Secondary

F. Rosenthal, *The History of al-Ṭabarī. General introduction and from the Creation to the Flood*, Albany NY, 1989, p. 26

G.H.A. Juynboll, *Muslim tradition. Studies in chronology, provenance and authorship of early* ḥadīth, Cambridge, 1983, p. 239

Sezgin, *GAS* i, p. 135

Kaḥḥāla, i, pp. 128-29
K. Ziriklī, *Al-aʿlām, qāmūs tarājim li-ashhur al-rijāl wa-l-nisāʾ min al-ʿArab wa-l-mustaʿribīn wa-al-mustashriqīn*, 13 vols, Beirut, 1969, i, p. 76

WORKS ON CHRISTIAN-MUSLIM RELATIONS

Amārāt al-nubuwwa, 'Tokens of prophethood'

DATE Before 873
ORIGINAL LANGUAGE Arabic

DESCRIPTION
The contents of the work can only be known after examination of the surviving fragment in Damascus (Sezgin, *GAS* i, p. 135). Like other works of this genre, it may have contained stories about Muḥammad's life which showed divine support for his mission, notably his miracles and prophetic foreknowledge of events, and called for Jews and Christians to acknowledge that Islam abrogated their religions. It may also have contained biblical verses which could be read as predictions of his coming.

SIGNIFICANCE
Although nothing more than the title is known, it points to the widespread apologetic interest that 9th-century Muslim scholars took in formulating the proofs of Muḥammad's prophethood.

MANUSCRIPTS
MS Damascus, Dār al-Kutub al-ẓāhiriyya – Maj. 104, fols 162r-169r (591 A.H. [1195])
EDITIONS AND TRANSLATIONS —
STUDIES —

Barbara Roggema 2008

The Disputation of John and the Emir

Unknown author

DATE OF BIRTH Unknown
PLACE OF BIRTH Unknown
DATE OF DEATH Unknown
PLACE OF DEATH Unknown

BIOGRAPHY —

MAIN SOURCES OF INFORMATION

Primary —

Secondary —

WORKS ON CHRISTIAN-MUSLIM RELATIONS

Egartā d-Mār(y) Yoḥannan paṭriyarkā meṭṭul mamllā d-mallel ʿam amirā da-Mhaggrāyē, 'The Letter of Patriarch John about his disputation with an emir of the Mhaggrāyē'

DATE Unknown, between c. 640 and 874
ORIGINAL LANGUAGE Syriac

DESCRIPTION

This letter purports to be a report in the form of a letter of a disputation between a Syrian Orthodox patriarch named John (Yoḥannan) and an anonymous emir (army commander/governor). The emir interrogates the patriarch on topics such as the integrity of the Bible, the divinity of Christ and the Christian sources of law.

The answers given by the patriarch bear strong resemblance to themes and arguments found in Christian apologetics vis-à-vis Judaism.

The Letter is contained in a unique manuscript written in *serto* in the year 874. The only date in the letter is 'the 9th of May', but on the basis of a note in the *Chronicle* of Michael the Syrian, in a section that all likelihood goes back to 9th century historian Dionysius of

Tell-Maḥrē (q.v.) (*Chronique de Michel le Syrien*, ed. and trans. J.-B. Chabot, 4 vols, Paris, 1910, iv, pp. 421-22) about a disputation between a patriarch named John and an emir called ʿAmru bar Ṣaʿd during the early days of the Caliph ʿUthmān (r. 644-56), the patriarch is identifiable as John Sedra (d. 648) (cf. K. Pinggéra, art. 'JOHANNES I. (III.) von Antiochien ('Johannes Sedra')', in *Biographisch-Bibliographisches Kirchenlexicon* 23 (2004) 734-37) and the emir as ʿUmayr ibn Saʿd al-Anṣārī. The identification of the patriarch is supported by the list of names of ecclesiastical dignitaries present during the disputation, which is mentioned at the end of the letter.

There is no scholarly consensus, however, on the question of whether the letter originates in this early period or whether a later (8th or 9th century) author has retrojected his work onto the 7th century. Scholars who maintain that this text was written in the 640s, do so on the basis that the author seems unaware of the fact that the emir follows a religion that has its own revealed scripture. There is no reference to the Qurʾān; the 'Mhaggraye', as the Arabs are called, are presented as attaching particular value to the Law of Moses. The words 'Muslim' or 'Islam' do not occur in the text. In other words, the text may reflect a phase in what could be called 'proto-Islam'. Moreover, the fact that the debate goes into the question whether the Christians should have legislative autonomy, fits well in the period of the Muslim conquests. In particular, the fact that the Syrian Orthodox patriarch speaks on behalf of all Christians and is praised for his public defense by the Chalcedonians present during the disputation may constitute an attempt to increase the influence of Syrian Orthodox ecclesiastical authorities in the aftermath of the collapse of Byzantine rule in Syria.

Nevertheless, doubts have been raised about the early dating of the text. Crone and Cook note that the emir's final question about inheritance law seems to allude to qurʾānic regulations and since it is unlikely that a Syriac Christian author of the first decade after the Muslim conquests would have knowledge about this, the question may be a later interpolation. Roggema has argued that the way this issue is discussed in the disputation reflects a fair degree of knowledge of Islamic inheritance law and an awareness of the fact that the Qurʾān alone does not suffice as a source for all regulations regarding inheritance. In other words, it could have been chosen to counter the insinuation that Christians follow laws that are not found in the Bible. This points to an 8th or 9th century context, that is, at least for this particular section of the text.

Reinink, followed by Griffith, believes the entire work to be a composition that was probably written in response to the fear of conversion to Islam among Christians in the early 8th century. During this time, when the Umayyad caliphs propagated Islam as the universal religion superior to all other religions, the Christian apologist tried to misrepresent Islam as a latter-day form of Judaism, so as to underscore its inferiority to Christianity. This particular dating has been questioned on the grounds that the text alludes in no way to the threat of conversion (Saadi), and does not, unlike other 8th century disputations, provide model answers to Muslim critique of Christianity, nor does it end in a clear triumph for the Christian (Hoyland). The latter two aspects set the text apart from other Christian apologies vis-à-vis Islam in question-and-answer format.

SIGNIFICANCE

This letter is often considered to be the oldest surviving Christian-Muslim disputation. If indeed the questions of the emir reflect the religious ideas of the Arab conquerors, then the disputation could serve as a source for the doctrines of pre-classical Islam. However, doubts have been raised about the text's date and integrity.

Although the letter has received considerable scholarly attention because of this enigma of its historical context, it does not seem to have been well-known within its own community. There is only one manuscript and the text does not appear to have influenced later apologists.

MANUSCRIPTS

MS BL Add. 17193, fols 73r-75v

EDITIONS AND TRANSLATIONS

A.M. Saadi, 'The letter of John of Sedreh. A new perspective on nascent Islam', *Journal of the Assyrian Academic Society* 11 (1997) 68-84 (edition with three minor differences from Nau's text, with trans.; repr. in *Karmo* 1(1999) 46-64)

N.A. Newman, *The early Muslim-Christian dialogue*, Hatfield, PA, 1993, pp. 24-28 (English trans. of Nau's French trans.)

H. Suermann, 'Orientalische Christen und der Islam. Christliche Texte aus der Zeit von 632-750', *Zeitschrift für Missionswissenschaft und Religionswissenschaft* 67 (1983), 120-36, pp. 122-25 (trans.)

F. Nau, 'Un colloque du Patriarche Jean avec l'Émir des Agaréens et faits divers des années 712 à 716 d'après le MS. du British Museum *add* 17193, avec un appendice sur le patriarche Jean le Ier, sur un colloque d'un patriarche avec le chef des Mages et sur un diplôme qui aurait été donné par Omar à l'Évêque du Tour 'Abdin', *Journal asiatique* ser. 11, 5 (1915), 225-279, pp. 248-64 (edition and translation)

STUDIES

B. Roggema, 'The debate between Patriarch John and an emir of the Mhaggrāyē. A reconsideration of the earliest Christian-Muslim Debate', in Tamcke (ed.), *Christians and Muslims*, 21-39

H. Suermann, 'The Old Testament and the Jews in the dialogue between the Jacobite Patriarch John I and 'Umayr ibn Sa'd al-Anṣārī', in J.P. Monferrer Sala (ed.), *Eastern crossroads. Essays on medieval Christian legacy*, Piscataway, 2007, 131-41

Y.D. Nevo and J. Koren, *Crossroads to Islam. The origins of the Arab religion and the Arab state*, Amherst NY, 2003, 222-29

Hoyland, *Seeing Islam*, pp. 459-65

Saadi, 'The letter of John of Sedreh'

G.J. Reinink, 'The beginnings of Syriac Apologetic Literature in Response to Islam', *OC* 77 (1993) 165-87, pp. 171-85

S.H. Griffith, 'Disputes with Muslims in Syriac Christian Texts: from Patriarch John (d. 648) to Bar Hebraeus (d. 1286)', in B. Lewis and F. Niewöhner, *Religionsgespräche im Mittelalter*, Wiesbaden, 1992, 251-73, pp. 257-59 (repr. in Griffith, *The beginnings of Christian theology in Arabic*, Aldershot, 2002)

S.K. Samir, 'Qui est l'interlocuteur musulman du patriarche syrien Jean III (631-48)?', in H.J.W. Drijvers (ed.), *IV Symposium Syriacum 1984*, Rome, 1987, 387-400

A. Abel, *Le Livre de la réfutation des trois sectes chrétiennes de Abū 'Isā al-Warrāq*, Bruxelles, 1949, p. LV

Nau, 'Un colloque du Patriarche Jean', pp. 225-247, 268-271

H. Lammens, 'A propos d'un colloque entre le patriarche jacobite Jean Ier et 'Amr ibn al-'Aṣī', *Journal asiatique* ser. 11, 13 (1919) 97-110

Barbara Roggema 2008

Anastasius Bibliothecarius

DATE OF BIRTH Unknown
PLACE OF BIRTH Unknown
DATE OF DEATH Between 28 May 877 and 29 March 879
PLACE OF DEATH Rome

BIOGRAPHY

Anastasius was brought up in Rome with Latin as his mother tongue, and acquired some knowledge of Greek at an early age. Created cardinal by Pope Leo IV in 847 or 848, Anastasius joined the imperial party opposed to Pope Leo and was exiled and excommunicated. Upon Leo's death in July 855, Anastasius marched on Rome with an army in an attempt to install himself on the papal throne. After only three days he was deposed by supporters of Benedict III. He was later readmitted to lay communion by Benedict.

Soon after the inauguration of Pope Hadrian II on 14 December 867, Anastasius was elevated to the position of *bibliothecarius Romanae ecclesiae.* Although he fell from grace in 868, we subsequently find him in the close circles of both Emperor Louis II and various popes. During Anastasius' final years, from 876, Pope John VIII was courting Carolingian protection against the Saracen threat to Rome; he died between 877 and 879.

The whole Anastasian corpus consists of works translated from Greek into Latin. These may be divided into three categories: hagiography; Church councils and histories; theological works.

MAIN SOURCES OF INFORMATION

Primary

Ludovici II imperatoris epistola ad Basilium I imperatorem Constantinopolitanum missa, ed. W. Henze, in *Epistolae Karolini Aevi (V)*, Berlin, 1928 (repr. Munich, 1978), 386-94 (*MGH Epistolae* 7) (866)

Annales Bertiniani, trans. J. Nelson, *The annals of St-Bertin*, Manchester, 1991, 143-50 (868)

Liber Pontificalis, ii, ed. L. Duchesne, Paris, 1955^2: *Leo IV*, ch. 92, 129; *Benedictus III*, ch. 6, 141; cc. 8-19, 141-44; *Hadrianus II*, ch. 10, 175, cc. 42-45, 181-2, ch. 60, 184-85 (after 870)

Acta Concilii Constantinopolitani IV, Actio 10 (*PL* 129), col. 148 (871)
Anastasii Bibliothecarii epistolae sive praefationes, ed. E. Perels and G. Laehr, in *Epistolae Karolini aevi (V)*, Berlin, 1928 (repr. Munich, 1978) (*MGH Epistolae* 7), Ep. 2, 399 (858-67), Ep. 5, 403 and 410 (871), Ep. 9, 423 (874), Ep. 13, 433 (23 Mar. 875), Ep. 17, 440 (Jun. 876)

Secondary
R.E. Forrai, 'Anastasius Bibliothecarius and his textual dossiers. Greek collections and their Latin transmission in ninth-century Rome', in S. Gioanni and B. Grevin (eds), *L'Antiquité tardive dans les collections médiévales: textes et représentations VIe-XVIe siecle*, Rome, 2008, 319-37
B. Neil, *Seventh-century popes and martyrs. The political hagiography of Anastasius Bibliothecarius*, Turnhout, 2006, pp. 11-28, 34
P. Allen and B. Neil (eds), *Scripta saeculi VII vitam Maximi Confessoris illustrantia*, Turnhout, 1999 (*Corpus Christianorum Series Graeca* 39)
K. Herbers, *Leo IV. und das Papsttum in der Mitte des 9. Jahrhunderts. Möglichkeiten und Grenzen päpstlicher Herrschaft in der späten Karolingerzeit*, Stuttgart, 1996, pp. 214-224, 227
R. Davis, *The Lives of the ninth-century popes (Liber Pontificalis)*, Liverpool, 1995, pp. 150-51, 170-76, 250-52, 279-82, 289
P. Llewellyn, *Rome in the dark ages*, London, 1971, 1993[2], pp. 268-71, 273, 278
M. McCormick, art. 'Anastasius Bibliothecarius', in *ODB*
G. Arnaldi, 'Anastasio Bibliotecario a Napoli nell'871? Nota sulla tradizione della «Vita Athanasii episcopi neapolitani» di Guarimpoto', *La Cultura* 17 (1980) 3-33
P. Devos, 'Anastase le Bibliothécaire. Sa contribution à la correspondence pontificale. La date de sa mort', *Byzantion* 32 (1962) 97-115
G. Arnaldi, 'Anastasio Bibliothecario', *Dizionario Biografico degli Italiani* 3 (1961) 25-37
A. Lapôtre, *De Anastasio Bibliothecario sedis apostolicae*, Paris, 1885 (repr. in *Etudes sur la papauté au IXe siècle* 1 Turin, 1978, 121-466)

WORKS ON CHRISTIAN-MUSLIM RELATIONS

Chronographia tripertita

DATE 871-74
ORIGINAL LANGUAGE Greek

DESCRIPTION
The *Chronographia tripertita* is made up of excerpts from three ninth-century iconophile sources:

1. Nicephorus of Constantinople's *Chronographikon Syntomon*, a series of date tables for various significant figures in the history of the

world, from Adam and the Jewish patriarchs, to the Byzantine emperors up to Michael III, and empresses of Byzantium up to Eudocia, as well as lists of the books of the Old and New Testaments and Apocrypha. The sections relevant to Christian-Muslim relations are the entries for the 7th-century emperors after the death of Emperor Phocas in 610, especially Heraclius, his son Constantine, and his nephew Constantine;

2. George the Synkellos' *Chronicon*, a history of the world from creation up to the accession of Diocletian (284);

3. Theophanes the Confessor's *Chronographia* (q.v.) a history of the Byzantine empire from the accession of Diocletian up to 813, a continuation of George the Synkellos. From Theophanes' *Chronographia*, Anastasius made brief excerpts of entries up to the death of Theodosius II, and longer ones up to the end of Justinian I's reign, but translated in full the period from the accession of Justin I (Mango and Scott, *The Chronicle*, p. xcvii). Only the first and third parts contain information relevant to Christian-Muslim relations, as George the Synkellos' *Chronicon* finishes in 284. *Chronographia tripertita* was compiled for John the Deacon, court historiographer for John VIII, for inclusion in a larger church history (not surviving).

Anastasius made a very literal translation of Theophanes, albeit with some errors, and for the period regarding Muḥammad and the Arabs he has translated the original in full. For this reason he cannot be said to have been advancing an agenda of his own on either the first two centuries of Islam or its leader. One interesting 'fact' that was not transmitted by all Greek manuscripts but was preserved in the Latin translation was a statement concerning the murder of Muḥammad (*usque ad caedem eius*) (see Mango and Scott, *The Chronicle*, p. 465, n. 2). According to Theophanes, this occurred in AM 6122 (629/30). The catalogue of Arab caliphs supplied by Theophanes, from Muḥammad's successor Abū Bakr to the ʿAbbasid Caliph al-Amīn, also shows some inaccuracies (see Mango and Scott, *The Chronicle*, p. lxxi).

The relevant period of Christian-Muslim relations covered by this history stretches from Muḥammad's death to the final year of the history, 813. Details on the length of the history and the Christian-Muslim elements of its content can be found in Theophanes' *Chronographia* (q.v.). Anastasius made his translation with the interests of the court historiographer, John Immonides, in mind. In his preface to the *Chronographia tripertita*, Anastasius declares that he intended it to form part of a larger ecclesiastical history that John Immonides was compiling (De Boor, *Theophanis Chronographia,* ii, p. 33). The choice of work seems at least in part driven by a similar agenda to the *Collectanea.* The purpose of translating that dossier of documents was to present the monothelite controversy of the 640s to 680s in such a way as to drive a deeper wedge between Rome and the church of Constantinople in his own time, the third quarter of the 9th century. Theophanes' sources included an anti-monothelite tract based partially on Anastasius of Sinai's *Sermo III in 'secundum imaginem'*, but also using material that is common to the *Synodicon vetus* of c. 890 (Mango and Scott, *The Chronicle,* p. lxxxvii). Anastasius' translation of the *Chronographia* of Theophanes was one of very few histories available in Latin offering an account of the Greek empire and its relations with the followers of Islam from 632 to 813, as well as providing a history of the iconoclast controversy from an iconophile perspective.

Anastasius' summary of Nicephorus, Patriarch of Constantinople's *Chronographikon Syntomon* presents very little information relevant to Christian-Muslim relations.

SIGNIFICANCE

The Latin *Chronographia tripertita* was one of the chief early sources for information about Muḥammad and early Islam in Latin Europe between the 9th and early 12th centuries. It was used by Peter the Venerable of Cluny in the composition of two polemical works in the early 12th century: *Summa totius haeresis Saracenorum* and *Liber contra sectam sive haeresim Saracenorum.*

MANUSCRIPTS

Full list presented by Brown, 'The *Chronographia Tripertita*', with two fragmentary additions recently discovered, pp. 132-37. De Boor used three Latin manuscripts for his edition of Anastasius' version: MS Cassinensis–6 (1085), MS Vat – Pal. 826 (9th/10th c.), MS Vat – Pal. 909 (10th/11th c.) (De Boor, *Theophanis Chronographia,* ii, pp. 423-25); and he mentions several others. The oldest surviving manuscript of the Latin version is MS Vat – Pal. 826. Anastasius based his translation on better Greek manuscripts than those that now survive, except for MS Vat – Barb. 553 (16th c.) and MS Vat – Gr. 154 (12th c.), both highly fragmentary but, according to de Boor, preserving the best Greek tradition (de Boor, *Theophanis Chronographia*, i, p. vii; *ibid.* 2, p. 550).

EDITIONS AND TRANSLATIONS

C. de Boor, *Theophanis Chronographia*, 2 vols, Leipzig, 1885, ii, 36-340 (critical edition of the Latin text of the *Chronographia tripertita* including Nicephorus' *Chronographia brevis*, pp. 36-59; George the Synkellos' *Chronicon*, pp. 60-77; Theophanes' *Chronographia*, pp. 77-340; repr. Hildesheim, 1980)

I. Bekker, *Theophanis Chronographia*, ii, Bonn, 1841 (repr. of Fabrotus' edition)

C.A. Fabrotus, *Anastasii Bibliothecarii Historia ecclesiastica sive chronographia tripertita*, Paris, 1649, (*editio princeps* from MS BNF - Lat. 5092 and MS Vat. - Lat. 2013)

STUDIES

P. Chiesa, M. Cupiccia and A. Galli, 'Anastasius Bibliothecarius', in P. Chiesa and L. Castaldi (eds), *La trasmissione dei testi latini del medioevo. Mediaeval Latin texts and their transmission*, Florence, 2005, 87-103, esp. pp. 100-3

C. Mango and R. Scott, *The Chronicle of Theophanes the Confessor. Byzantine and Near Eastern history, AD 284-813*, Oxford, 1997, pp. xcvi-xcix (excellent trans. of the Greek text with reference to the Latin trans. in comprehensive notes)

V. Brown, 'The *Chronographia tripertita* of Anastasius Bibliothecarius. New fragments in Beneventan script at Altamura and Matera', *Altamura* 35 (1993) 131-40

Tolan, *Saracens*, pp. 104, 157, 168

B. Kedar, *Crusade and mission*, Princeton NJ, 1984, 33-34, 206-207

M. Mahdi, review of J. Kritzeck, *Peter the Venerable and Islam*, *Journal of Near Eastern Studies* 24 (1965) 132-36

D. Tabachovitz, 'Sprachliches zur lateinischen Theophanesübersetzung des Anastasius Bibliothecarius', *BZ* 38 (1938) 16-22

R. Otto, 'Mohamed in der Anschauung des Mittelalters. II', *Modern Language Notes* 4/2 (1889) 45-49

C. de Boor, *Theophanis Chronographia*, ii, 401-35

Bronwen Neil 2007

Al-Jāmiʿ wujūh al-īmān

Unknown author

DATE OF BIRTH Unknown, possibly early 9th c.
PLACE OF BIRTH Unknown
DATE OF DEATH Unknown, possibly late 9th c.
PLACE OF DEATH Unknown, perhaps in or near Edessa

BIOGRAPHY

Little is known about the author/editor of a major 9th-century Christian Arabic theological compilation apart from information that can be gleaned from the text itself – the study of which is still in a preliminary state, due in part to the lack of a published edition. Careful study is still required, for example, to determine whether the text is best regarded as the work of a single author (examples of cross-referencing throughout the work are noted by Hoyland, 'St Andrews MS. 14', p. 165), or as a compilation of disparate materials brought together by an editor (suggested by Griffith, e.g. 'The view of Islam', p. 18). Thus, we do not know whether the few temporal and geographical indications scattered through the work give us information about a single author or about individual sources compiled by an editor.

This paucity of information has not hindered scholars from making suggestions about the identity of the author/editor. The 20th century witnessed a slow debate as to whether Theodore Abū Qurra (q.v.) may have been the author of the work (beginning with Maʿlūf and al-Bāshā in 1903 and 1904 respectively; see Samir, 'La "Somme des aspects de la foi", oeuvre d'Abū Qurrah?', or Griffith, 'A ninth century Summa theologiae arabica'). Another suggestion is that Stephen of al-Ramla, the scribe of the best manuscript copy of the work, may have been its author or at least its compiler (e.g., Griffith, 'Stephen', pp. 43-44). The latest scholarship, however, seems content to speak of a 'now unknown author' (Griffith, *Church in the shadow of the mosque*, p. 57).

A debate relevant to the question of authorship has to do with the date of the work. The earliest dated copy, in MS BL Or. 4950, was written in AD 877. Furthermore, the text in this copy of the work contains two indications of a date of composition: in Chapter 21, a statement that the Temple had been destroyed for '800 years and more'; and in Chapter 22, a statement that Judaism had been 'abolished' for 825 years. The former statement seems clearly to indicate a date after 870. The latter statement requires interpretation; a plausible conversion, calculating 825 years from the Crucifixion of Christ (and the rending of the Temple veil) according to the Alexandrian world era, yields a date of 867 (Swanson, 'Some considerations'). However, the numbers given in the text may be subject to error or to 'updating' by scribes; they may belong to different sources; and it is possible that the conversion suggested above is incorrect (e.g., taking the Incarnation rather than the Crucifixion as a starting point yields a date of 834). The present writer thinks of the work as an essential unity (and will speak below of 'the author') and of the early 870s as the date of composition (considering '825 years' to be a round figure reached in the recent past). Hoyland more cautiously speaks of 'a text composed in the mid-ninth century give or take thirty years' (Hoyland, 'St Andrews MS. 14', p. 165).

The 'now unknown' 'mid-ninth century' author was a Melkite Christian, probably a monk and/or priest, who was well-grounded in biblical and patristic studies but who also had a strong knowledge of the Qurʾān and of the debates among contemporary Muslim scholars. He wrote as a pastor, seeking to confront the doctrinal assimilation to Islamic teachings that he encountered within the Christian community. References in Chapters 8 and 17 to Jerusalem as part of 'the land of the West' suggest that the author hailed from some Mesopotamian center of Melkite Christianity, e.g. Edessa or Ḥarrān.

MAIN SOURCES OF INFORMATION

Primary —

Secondary
See below

WORKS ON CHRISTIAN-MUSLIM RELATIONS

Al-Kitāb al-jāmiʿ wujūh al-īmān bi-tathlīth waḥdaniyyat Allāh wa-taʾannus Allāh al-kalima min al-ṭāhira al-ʿadhrāʾ Maryam, 'The Compilation of the aspects of the faith in the Tri-unity of God and the Incarnation of God the Word from the pure one, the Virgin Mary'
Frequent abbreviation: [*al-*]*Jāmiʿ wujūh al-īmān*
Griffith has popularized the title *Summa theologiae arabica*

DATE Before 877 (perhaps by less than a decade)
ORIGINAL LANGUAGE Arabic

DESCRIPTION
Al-Jāmiʿ wujūh al-īmān is a wide-ranging theological/apologetic compilation in 25 chapters. After an introductory chapter that rails against Christians who would avoid distinctive Christian speech about God and Christ so as not to offend Muslims' sensibilities, Chapters 2-3 deal with the unity and Trinity of God, while the next several chapters focus on Christological matters, brought to a conclusion in Chapter 13, a catalogue of Old Testament *testimonia* that bear witness to the Incarnation. This is followed in Chapter 14 by a sharply formulated list of beliefs that exclude those who hold them from being considered Christians. The next several chapters respond to a variety of questions: about passages from the Gospels, especially those that might be used to argue against Christ's divinity (Chapter 17); those posed by 'the monotheists and dualists' – that is, Muslims and Manicheans (Chapter 18); about the true religion, with special emphasis on the place of Judaism (Chapters 19-22); and about prayer (Chapter 23). The work concludes (Chapter 25) with canonical material that discourages Christians from mixing with those outside the faith.

A striking feature of *al-Jāmiʿ* is the sharpness with which the author reacts to those Christians who would assimilate their beliefs to Islamic formulations while claiming to remain within the Christian community. In the first pages of the work, the author characterizes such Christians as 'hypocrites' (*munāfiqūn*) and 'waverers' (*mudhabdhabūn*). Chapter 14, on the doctrines that exclude their holders from the Christian community, insists that a Christian bear testimony (*yashhadu*) that God (*Allāh*) is 'the Father, the Son, and the Holy Spirit', and has no patience with one who says 'Christ is God, but God is not Christ' (perhaps giving heed to Q 5:17; see Griffith, 'Islam and the *Summa*, p. 240). Chapter 23, on prayer, stresses the distinctiveness of Christians' practice: they are to make the sign of the cross whenever and wherever they pray, and are encouraged to make the cross, which represents Christ, a focus for meditation and prayer (Swanson, 'Cross', pp. 140-41).

Throughout the work, the author displays his knowledge of the Qurʾān and of contemporary Islamic debates (see, e.g., Griffith, 'The first Christian *Summa*' and 'Islam and the *Summa*'; Hoyland, 'St Andrews MS. 14', pp. 169-72). Christian doctrines are explained with attention to points of contact in qurʾānic teaching, as when the Incarnation is explained – with an allusion to Q 42:51 – as God's revelation by means of self-veiling (*iḥtijāb*) (Swanson, 'Beyond prooftexting', p. 300), or when Christ's death and resurrection are presented as his freely accepted and divinely arranged demonstration of the reality of the *general* resurrection (Swanson, 'Cross', pp. 126-27). The questions of Chapters 17 and 18 frequently reflect Muslims' concerns or reproduce debate questions that Muslims regularly posed to Christians. (On Chapter 17, see Griffith, 'Arguing from scripture', pp. 47-56. On Chapter 18, see Samīr, 'Kitāb', and Griffith, 'Islam and the *Summa*'.)

SIGNIFICANCE

Al-Jāmiʿ wujūh al-īmān is significant as a compendium of apologetically formulated explanations of Christian doctrines and practices, as well as of responses to particular questions regularly posed by Muslims (and others). More than this, however, it is an eloquent witness to what its author perceived as a crisis in Church life brought about by the assimilation of some Arabic-speaking Christians within the *Dār al-Islām* to Islamic modes of speech and thought, including a self-restriction in doctrinal matters to statements to which Muslims would not object. In response, *al-Jāmiʿ* calls its Christian readers to unembarrassed embrace of distinctive Christian doctrines and practices: God as Trinity, Christ as God, and the cross as aid to and focus for prayer. That it does so in an Arabic idiom that itself shows the impress of qurʾānic speech makes it a not only a landmark in the history of Christian theology in Arabic, but also an intriguing witness to processes of assimilation and differentiation in the encounter of religious communities.

MANUSCRIPTS

For a list of manuscripts and related bibliography, see Samir, 'Date', and add Hoyland, 'St Andrews MS. 14'. The known manuscripts are:

MS London BL – Or. 4950, fols 1r-197v (877; complete except for the first folio)

MS Munich, Bayerische Staatsbibliothek – ar. 1071, 4 fols (9th c.; from Ch. 12-13)

MS Birmingham, Mingana – Chr. Ar. 170 (= Chr. Add. 140; 9th c.; two leaves, one from Ch. 17, Questions 22-23, and one from Ch. 25)

MS St Andrews, University Library – 14 (9th c.; Chs 1b-8, 13-24)

MS Sinai – ar. 330, fols 198r-227r, 283r-308v (10th c.; Chs 12-13, 17)

MS Sinai – ar. 431, fols 97r-167r [10th c.; Chs 3-9, 14-17]

MS Sinai – ar. 483, fols 1a-149a (1178; Chs 3b-25)

MS Sinai – ar. 448, fols 127r-132r (13th c.; Chs 5-8, 11)

MS Beirut, Bibliothèque orientale – 552, pp. 2-47 (1718; Ch. 18)

EDITIONS AND TRANSLATIONS

M.N. Swanson, *Folly to the ḥunafāʾ. The cross of Christ in Arabic Christian-Muslim controversy in the eighth and ninth centuries A.D.*, Cairo, 1995 [*estratto* from dissertation], pp. 54-59 (text and English translation of Ch. 17, Question 25, and a brief passage from Ch. 8)

M.N. Swanson, 'The cross of Christ in the earliest Arabic Melkite apologies', in S.K. Samir and J.S. Nielsen (eds), *Christian Arabic apologetics during the Abbasid period (750-1258)*, Leiden, 1994, 115-45, pp. 125-27 and 140-41 (brief passages with English trans. from Ch. 18, Question 4 and Ch. 23)

[S.]K. Samir, 'Date de composition de la "Somme des aspects de la foi"', *OCP* 51 (1985) 352-87 (includes brief passages with French trans. from Chs 3, 13, 21 and 22)

Samīr Khalīl [Samir], 'Kitāb jāmiʿ wujūh al-īmān wa-mujādalat Abī Qurra ʿan ṣalb al-Masīḥ', *Al-Masarra* 70 (1984) 411-27 (edition of Ch. 18, Question 5)

L. Cheikho (ed.), *Vingt traités théologiques d'auteurs arabes chrétiens*, Beirut, 1920, 108-20 (reproduces the text of L. Maʿlūf, 'Aqdam al-makhṭūṭāt')

A.S. Lewis and M.D. Gibson, *Forty-one facsimiles of dated Christian Arabic manuscripts*, Cambridge, 1907, plate II (photograph of the conclusion of Ch. 25 and the scribe's colophon in BL or. 4950)

L. Cheikho (ed.), *Seize traités théologiques d'auteurs arabes chrétiens (ixe-xiiie siècles)*, Beirut, 1906, 87-99 (reproduces the text of L. Maʿlūf, 'Aqdam al-makhṭūṭāt')

L. Maʿlūf, 'Aqdam al-makhṭūṭāt al-naṣrāniyya al-ʿarabiyya', *Al-Mashriq* 6 (1903) 1011-23 (free transcription of Chapters 5-8)

STUDIES

S.H. Griffith, *The church in the shadow of the mosque*, Princeton NJ, 2008, pp. 52-53, 57-60, 82-83

R.G. Hoyland, 'St Andrews MS. 14 and the earliest Arabic *Summa theologiae*. Its date, authorship and apologetic content', in W.J. van Bekkum, J.W. Drijvers and A.C. Klugkist (eds), *Syriac polemics*, Louvain, 2007, 159-72

S.H. Griffith, 'Arguing from scripture. The Bible in the Christian/Muslim encounter in the Middle Ages', in T.J. Heffernan and T.E. Burman (eds), *Scripture and pluralism. Reading the Bible in the religiously plural worlds of the Middle Ages and Renaissance*, Leiden, 2005, 29-58, pp. 47-56

B. Roggema, '*Ḥikāyāt amthāl wa asmār*... King parables in Melkite apologetic literature', in R. Ebied and H. Teule (eds), *Studies on the Christian Arabic heritage*, Leuven, 2004, 113-31, pp. 118-19, 121-24

M.N. Swanson, 'Beyond prooftexting. Approaches to the Qurʾān in some early Arabic Christian apologies', *MW* 88 (1998) 297-319, pp. 297-300

S.H. Griffith, 'The view of Islam from the monasteries of Palestine in the early ʿAbbāsid period. Theodore Abū Qurrah and the *Summa theologiae arabica*', *ICMR* 7 (1996) 9-28

M.N. Swanson, *Folly to the* ḥunafāʾ*: The cross of Christ in Arabic Christian-Muslim controversy in the eighth and ninth centuries A.D.*, Cairo, 1995 [*estratto* from dissertation], pp. 54-59

M.N. Swanson, 'The cross of Christ in the earliest Arabic Melkite apologies', in S.K. Samir and J.S. Nielsen (eds), *Christian Arabic apologetics during the Abbasid period (750-1258)*, Leiden, 1994, 115-45, pp. 125-27, 140-41

M.N. Swanson, 'Some considerations for the dating of *Fī tathlīth Allāh al-wāḥid* (Sinai ar. 154) and *al-Ǧāmiʿ wuǧūh al-īmān* (London, British Library or. 4950)', *Pd'O* 18 (1993) 115-41

S.H. Griffith, 'The first Christian *Summa theologiae* in Arabic. Christian *kalām* in ninth-century Palestine', in M. Gervers and R.J. Bikhazi (eds), *Conversion and continuity. Indigenous Christian communities in Islamic lands, eighth to eighteenth centuries*, Toronto, 1990, 15-31

S.H. Griffith, 'Free will in Christian kalām. Chapter XVIII of the Summa theologiae arabica', in R. Schulz and M. Görg (eds), *Lingua restituta orientalis*, Wiesbaden, 1990, 129-34

S.H. Griffith, 'Islam and the *Summa theologiae arabica*; Rabīʿ I, 264 A.H.', *JSAI* 13 (1990) 225-64

[S.]K. Samir, 'La literature melkite sous les premiers abbassides', *OCP* 56 (1990) 469-86, pp. 482-83

S.H. Griffith, 'The monks of Palestine and the growth of Christian literature in Arabic', *MW* 78 (1988) 1-28, pp. 24-26 (repr. in S.H. Griffith, *Arabic Christianity in the monasteries of ninth-century Palestine*, Aldershot, 1992, essay III)

Nasrallah, *HMLEM* ii.2, pp. 138-42

S.H. Griffith, 'Greek into Arabic. Life and letters in the monasteries of Palestine in the ninth century. The example of the *Summa theologiae arabica*', *Byzantion* 56 (1986) 117-38 (repr. in Griffith, *Arabic Christianity*, essay VIII)

[S.]K. Samir, 'La "Somme des aspects de la foi", oeuvre d'Abū Qurrah?' in [S.]K. Samir (ed.), *Actes du deuxième congrès international d'études arabes chrétiennes*, Rome, 1986, 93-121 (includes a complete survey of earlier opinions as to whether or not Theodore Abū Qurra was the author, including brief mentions not referenced here, pp. 97-107)

S.H. Griffith, 'A ninth century Summa theologiae arabica', in Samir, *Actes du deuxième congrès*, 123-41 (repr. in Griffith, *Arabic Christianity*, essay IX)

S.H. Griffith, 'Stephen of Ramlah and the Christian kerygma in Arabic in ninth-century Palestine', *Journal of Ecclesiastical History* 36 (1985) 23-45, pp. 42-44 (repr. in Griffith, *Arabic Christianity*, essay VII)

R. Haddad, *La Trinité divine chez les théologiens arabes (750-1050)*, Paris, 1985, pp. 59-62

[S.]K. Samir, 'Date de composition de la "Somme des aspects de la foi"', *OCP* 51 (1985) 352-87

Samīr Khalīl [Samīr], 'Kitāb Jāmiʿ wujūh al-īmān wa-Mujādalat Abī Qurra ʿan ṣalb al-Masīḥ', *Al-Masarra* 70 (1984) 411-27

J. Nasrallah, 'Dialogue islamo-chrétien à propos de publications récentes', *REI* 46 (1978) 121-51, pp. 131-32

J. Blau, 'Über einige christlich-arabische Manuskripte aus dem 9. und 10. Jahrhundert', *Le Muséon* 75 (1962) 101-8, pp. 101-2

Graf, *GCAL* ii, pp. 16-19

Q. al-Bāshā, *Mayāmir Thāwadūrus Abī Qurra usquf Ḥarrān. Aqdam taʾlīf ʿarabī naṣrānī*, Beirut, 1904, pp. 187-90 (rejects attribution of authorship to Theodore Abū Qurra)

L. Maʿlūf, 'Aqdam al-makhṭūṭāt al-naṣrāniyya al-ʿarabiyya', *Al-Mashriq* 6 (1903) 1011-23 (suggests Theodore Abū Qurra as author)

Mark N. Swanson 2009

The Life of Constantine-Cyril

Unknown author

DATE OF BIRTH Unknown, probably 9th c.
PLACE OF BIRTH Unknown
DATE OF DEATH Unknown, 9th or 10th c.
PLACE OF DEATH Unknown

BIOGRAPHY

Constantine was called Cyril in his later life, and he and his brother Methodius are known as the 'apostles of the southern Slavs'. His *Life* was written not long after his death in 869, and the fact that the author was familiar with the details of his youth and used a high literary style has led some scholars to identify him as his brother Methodius. This is plausible, although it cannot be stated with any certainty.

MAIN SOURCES OF INFORMATION

Primary —

Secondary
See below

WORKS ON CHRISTIAN-MUSLIM RELATIONS

Pamet' i Žitie blaženago učitelja našego Kostantina Filosofa prěvago nastav'nika sloven'sku jezyku, 'Memory and life of our blessed teacher Constantine the Philosopher, the first educator of the Slavonic people'. Modern titles: 'The Life of Constantine-Cyril', '*Vita Constantini*'

DATE Between 873 and 880
ORIGINAL LANGUAGE Old Church Slavonic

DESCRIPTION

The *Life* of Constantine-Cyril describes the life of the Christian missionary to the Slavs who became known as St Cyril. Born in 826/27 in Thessaloniki, Constantine was ordained in Constantinople, where he became widely known for his erudition. The greatest achievement for which he is remembered is his mission to Moravia in 863. Here he founded a native church, for which he translated Greek texts into Slavonic and designed the Glagolitic alphabet.

It can be shown that his *Life*, in Old Church Slavonic, was written soon after his death. It is in part inspired by the Greek hagiographical tradition, but nevertheless has unique features, in that it gives much space to Constantine's own works and to four religious disputations in which he took part: with John Grammatikos on iconoclasm, with Muslims at the ʿAbbasid court on Islam and Christianity, with the Khazars on Judaism, and with the Venetians on his introduction of the Slavonic script and the use of Slavonic in the liturgy.

The disputation with the Muslims is described in Chapter 6 of the *Life*, which relates how Constantine is sent by the emperor to the 'Hagarenes' in the company of the court secretary, George. Since Constantine, who is called 'the Philosopher' throughout, is said to have been 24 years old at this time, this mission may have taken place around the year 851, during the reign of al-Mutawakkil, in the period when Samarra was the capital of the ʿAbbasid Empire. Although no place names or personal names are mentioned, and we cannot ascertain whether the scenes described refer to al-Mutawakkil's entourage, the text nevertheless portrays Constantine's interlocutors as members of the ʿAbbasid elite, 'well versed in scholarship, geometry, astronomy and other sciences', who speak in the name of the 'Amerumnin', i.e. the *Amīr al-muʾminīn*, the caliph.

Among the objections which Constantine's Muslim opponents raise is the lack of a unified legal system in Christianity. Constantine replies that Muḥammad, by contrast, introduced a law that is simple to follow, making it too easy to reach the divine realms. They also attack the worship of the Trinity as a kind of polytheism, to which Constantine responds that the prophets had already taught there are three hypostases in the one divine Being, and that even Muḥammad bore witness to this in Q 19:17, 'We sent Our spirit to the Virgin'. The Muslims ask how Christians can justify the use of armed force when Christ had commanded them to 'turn the other cheek', to which Constantine answers that Christians fulfill the command to lay down one's life for one's friend (John 15:13). Lastly, the Muslims ask why the Byzantines do not pay tribute to them in the way that Christ paid tribute to the Romans, but Constantine asserts that Christ's example justifies paying the Romans not the 'Ishmaelites'. Sure of his cultural superiority, Constantine exclaims that Muslims resemble people who boast of having a water bag full of the truth, but do not realize that they are surrounded by the ocean of truth that is Christianity. This is how Constantine claims that 'all the arts have come from us'.

The encounter bears the marks of a literary composition, containing allusions to Gregory of Nazianzus among others, and is structured in the same way as many Greek and Christian Arabic disputation texts, with a conclusion in which the Muslims unsuccessfully attempt to lure their opponent to their faith with offers of precious gifts and then, equally unsuccessfully, try to poison him. This suggests that the whole chapter might have been based on such a disputation text rather than reflecting an actual journey to the ʿAbbasid court. Nevertheless, several scholars take seriously the possibility of a real mission. McCormick (*Origins*, pp. 183-84, n. 39), for example, suggests that Constantine's visit might reflect the historically documented Byzantine-ʿAbbasid diplomatic contacts around the year 855, in which case Constantine would have been slightly older than 24, the age given in the *Life*. Although the historicity of Constantine's encounter with the Muslims cannot be excluded, Vavřinek ('Byzantine polemic', p. 542) explains most cogently why this chapter should be read first and foremost as an integral part of the *Life*'s primary aim to depict Constantine's holiness: 'the three preceding disputations, including that against Islam, which show Constantine as an ardent and competent defender of the true faith, [...] enhance the effect and significance of the fourth polemic in which he defends his own work – the creation of Slavonic literature and liturgy.'

SIGNIFICANCE

The general significance of the work, as has been noted throughout modern scholarship, is the insight it gives into the mission of Constantine-Cyril and Methodius to the Slavs. The section on Islam, although brief, reflects the central issues in Byzantine-Muslim debate in the 9th century: holy war, mutual reproaches of irrationality in theology, and the relationship between imperial power and religious truth. The *Life* is the earliest Slavonic source to contain information on Islam, and it presumably had a role in shaping ideas about Islam in the Slavonic Churches.

MANUSCRIPTS

The numerous manuscripts of the text are listed in:

G. Ziffer, 'La tradizione della letteratura cirillometodiana ("Vita Constantini", "Vita Methodii", "Encomio di Cirillo", "Panegirico di Costantino e Metodio", "Sulle lettere di Chrabr")', *Ricerche slavistiche* 39-40 (1992-93) 263-89, pp. 280-82

See also B.N. Florya, 'Rukopisnaja tradicija pamjatnikov Kirillo-Mefodievskogo cikla (Itogi I zadači izučenija)', in P. Dinekov et al. (eds), *Žitija Kirilla i Mefodija*, Moscow, 1986, pp. 25-33, for a survey of studies in the manuscript tradition.

EDITIONS AND TRANSLATIONS

There are numerous editions and translations, the most important of which are:

Dinekov et al, *Žitija Kirilla i Mefodija*, pp. 42-180 (edition with Russian trans. and facsimiles)

M. Kantor, *Medieval Slavic lives of saints and princes*, Ann Arbor MI, 1983 (English trans.)

J. Schütz, *Die Lehrer der Slawen Kyrill und Method*, St Ottilien, 1985, pp. 23-81 (German trans.)

V. Peri, *Cirillo e Metodio. Le biografie paleoslave*, Milan, 1981 (Italian trans.)

N. Randow, *Die Pannonischen Legenden*, Berlin, 1972 (repr. 1973, 1977), pp. 5-45 (German trans.)

F. Grivec and F. Tomšič, *Constantinus et Methodius thessalonicenses. Fontes*, Zagreb, 1960, pp. 95-143 (edition), pp. 169-213 (Latin trans.)

F. Dvornik, *Les légendes de Constantin et de Méthode vues de Byzance*, Prague, 1933 (repr. 1969), pp. 349-80 (French trans.)

STUDIES

From the vast amount of literature on the *Life*, only studies dealing with Chapter 6 and principle works on the text are cited here. A detailed bibliography can be found in G. Podskalsky, *Theologische Literatur des Mittelalters in Bulgarien und Serbien 865-1459*, Munich, 2000, pp. 274-78.

M. Capaldo, 'Materiali e ricerche per l'edizione critica di "Vita Constantini". 4. Edizione della redazione vaticana', *Ricerche slavistiche* 29 (2005) 63-151

M. Capaldo, 'Materiali e tecniche per l'edizione critica di "Vita Constantini". Testimoni e gruppi di testimoni', *Ricerche slavistiche* 48 (2004) 49-66

G. Delopoulos, 'The Byzantine diplomatic mission of Constantine (St Cyril) to the Arabs in the 9th century', *Journal of Oriental and African Studies* 13 (2004) 361-66

M. McCormick, *Origins of the European economy. Communications and commerce AD 300-900*, Cambridge, 2001, pp. 181-90

V. Vavřinek, 'A Byzantine polemic against Islam in Old Slavonic hagiography', *Graeco-Arabica* 7-8 (1999-2000) 535-42

PMBZ i (prolegomena), pp. 245-47

G. Ziffer, 'Hagiographie und Geschichte. Die altkirchenslavische "Vita Constantini"', in P. Dilg, G. Keil and D.-R. Moser (eds), *Rhythmus und Saisonalität*, Sigmaringen, 1995, 143-45

G. Ziffer, 'Un nuovo gruppo di testimoni (frammentari) della "Vita Constantini": il "gruppo della Paleja"', *Slovo* 44-46 (1994-96) 7-25

G. Ziffer, 'La tradizione russa sud-occidentale della "Vita Constantini"', in M. Ferrazzi (ed.), *Studi slavistici offerti a Alessandro Ivanov*, Udine, 1992, 370-97

G. Ziffer, *Ricerche sul testo e la tradizione della 'Vita Constantini'*, Udine, 1992 (Diss. University of Udine)

G. Ziffer, 'Nota sulla tradizione manoscritta della "Vita Constantini"', *Quaderni Utinensi* 8 (1990) 321-24

G. Ziffer, 'Per la tradizione manoscritta della "Vita Constantini"', *Quaderni Utinensi* 8 (1990) 399-419

V. Vavřinek, 'Altkirchenslawische Hagiographie', in F. Winkelman and W. Brandes (eds), *Quellen zur Geschichte des frühen Byzanz*, Amsterdam, 1990, 297-304, pp. 297-302

K. Versteegh, 'Die Mission des Kyrillos im Lichte der arabo-byzantinischen Beziehungen', *ZDMG* 129 (1979) 233-62

F. Dvornik, 'The embassies of Constantine-Cyril and Photius to the Arabs', in *To honor Roman Jakobson*, 3 vols, The Hague, 1967, i, pp. 569-76 (repr. in F. Dvornik, *Byzantine missions among the Slavs*, New Brunswick NJ, 1970, pp. 285-96)

J. Meyendorff, 'Byzantine views of Islam', *DOP* 18 (1964) 113-32, pp. 130-31

F. Dvornik, 'Constantine-Cyril's religious discussion with the Arabs', in M. Bauerová and M. Štěrbová (eds), *Studia palaeoslovenica*, Prague, 1971, 77-78

H. Schaeder, 'Geschichte und Legende im Werk der Slavenmissionare Konstantin und Method', *Historische Zeitschrift* 152 (1935) 229-255, pp. 232-34

Barbara Roggema 2008

Pope John VIII

DATE OF BIRTH Unknown
PLACE OF BIRTH Unknown
DATE OF DEATH 15 December 882
PLACE OF DEATH Rome

BIOGRAPHY

Nothing is known about John VIII's place and date of birth. According to Petrus Guillermus he was *natione Romanus*. His father's name, *Gundo*, might indicate a Langobardian descent. During the 850s and 860s he was archdeacon of the Roman church. He obviously had profound knowledge of Roman law and held offices in the financial administration and the administration of patrimonies.

On 14 December 872 he was consecrated pope. Three major issues stand out during the ten years of his pontificate, the Aghlabid raids on Rome and southern Italy, the conflicts with Photius and the Eastern Church, and the imperial succession after the death of Emperor Louis II in 875.

John VIII designated and crowned the two Carolingian emperors Charles the Bald in 875 and Charles the Fat in 882. The coronations brought a decisive change in the relations between pope and emperor as henceforth the empire and the imperial succession was bound constitutionally to the pope (Arnold, *Johannes VIII*, pp. 67-109).

A vivid description of the papal court and especially of the intellectual circle round the pope is found in Johannes Hymmonides, *Cena Cypriani*, p. 899, which together with the works of Anastasius Bibliothecarius (q.v.) and Gauderich of Velletri document cultural life during the years of his pontificate, as well as the support it received from the papacy. John VIII died on 15 December 882. The *Annales Fuldenses*, p. 109, suggest that he may have been murdered, but this cannot be verified.

His most important work is the papal record. The original is not extant, but an 11th-century copy containing 314 letters gives the complete record of the last six indictions of the pontificate, September 876-September 882 (Lohrmann, *Johannes VIII.*, pp. 164-65; Arnold, *Johannes VIII.*, pp. 27-37). Letters from the period before September

876 can be found as fragments in canonical collections (Arnold, *Johannes VIII.*, p. 38), especially in the *Collectio Britannica* which contains 55 fragments from the pontificate (Ewald, *Papstbriefe*, pp. 275-414).

MAIN SOURCES OF INFORMATION

Primary

H. Hoffmann, *Die Chronik von Montecassino*, Hannover, 1980 (*MGH Scriptores* 34)

U. Přerovský, *Liber pontificalis nella recensione di Petro Guglielmo e del card. Pandolfo, glossato da Pietro Bohier*, 3 vols, Rome, 1978

F. Grat, J. Vielliard and S. Clémencet, *Annales Bertiniani*, Paris, 1964, pp. 189-251

U. Westerbergh, *Chronicon Salernitanum*, Lund, 1956

V. Federici, *Johannes von Volturno. Chronicon Vulturnense*, 3 vols, Rome, 1925-38 (*Fonti per la storia d'Italia* 58-60)

K. Strecker, *Johannes Diaconus. Versiculi de Cena Cypriani*, Berlin, 1914, pp. 857-900 (*MGH Poetae Latini medii aevi* 4/2)

G. Zucchetti, *Libellus de imperatoria potestate in urbe Roma*, Rome, 1920 (*Fonti per la storia d'Italia* 55), pp. 191-210

B. von Simson, *Annales Xantenses et Annales Vedastini*, Hannover, 1909, pp. 40-82 (*MGH Scriptores rerum Germanicarum in usum scholarum separatim editi* 12)

F. Kurze, *Annales Fuldenses sive Annales regni Francorum orientalis*, Hannover, 1891, pp. 82-109 (*MGH Scriptores rerum Germanicarum in usum scholarum separatim editi* 7)

L. Duchesne, *Liber pontificalis*, 2 vols, Paris, 1886-92, ii

G. Waitz, *Erchempert. Historia Langobardorum Beneventanorum*, in *Scriptores rerum Langobardicarum et Italicarum saec. VI-IX*, Hannover, 1878, pp. 231-64 (*MGH Scriptores rerum Langobardicarum et Italicarum saec. VI-IX*)

Secondary

D. Arnold, *Papst Johannes VIII. Päpstliche Herrschaft in den karolingischen Teilreichen am Ende des* 9. Jahrhunderts, Frankfurt, 2005

N. Cariello, *Giovanni VIII. Papa medioevale (872-882)*, Rome, 2002

C. Modesto, *Studien zur Cena Cypriani und deren Rezeption*, Tübingen, 1992

G. Arnaldi, *Natale 875. Politica, ecclesiologia, cultura del papato altomedievale*, Rome, 1990

C. Leonardi, 'Pienezza ecclesiale e santità nella "Vita Gregorii" di Giovanni Diacono', *Renovatio* 12 (1977) 51-66

G. Arnaldi, 'Giovanni Immonide e la cultura a Roma al tempo di Giovanni VIII', *Bulletino del'instituto storico italiano per il medio evo e archivo Muratoriano* 68 (1956) 33-89

H.K. Mann, *The lives of the popes in the early middle ages*, 18 vols, London, 1902-, 1925², iii (*The popes during the Carolingian Empire*)

A. Lapôtre, *L'Europe et le Saint-Siège à l'époque carolingienne. I: Le pape Jean VIII (872-882)*, Paris, 1895 (repr. in A. Lapôtre, *Etudes sur la Papauté au IXᵉ siècle II*, Turin, 1978, 57-437)

P. Ewald, 'Die Papstbriefe der Britischen Sammlung', *Neues Archiv* 5 (1880) 275- 414; 503-596

WORKS ON CHRISTIAN-MUSLIM RELATIONS

Letters (preserved in the papal record)

DATE 872-82
ORIGINAL LANGUAGE Latin

DESCRIPTION

While no extant papal document is addressed directly to a Muslim recipient, 93 letters in the papal register, including the fragments from the *Collectio Britannica* (Arnold, *Johannes VIII*, pp. 37-45), deal with issues concerning the 'Saracens', including the Aghlabid invasions of the *Patrimonium Petri* and southern Italy, and the relations of the southern Italian rulers with the Saracens. A great number of letters are addressed to the Carolingian rulers, reporting the devastation of the *Patrimonium Petri* caused by the Saracens and asking for help against the Saracen assaults. Although the pope led the papal army into war against the Saracens during the reign of Emperor Louis II (cf. Caspar and Laehr, *Epistolae*, p. 279, n. 11; p. 303, n. 49), he does not seem to have undertaken any military action after 875, but asked the Emperors Charles the Bald and Charles the Fat, the Carolingian kings (cf. Caspar and Laehr, *Epistolae*, p. 1, n. 1; p. 19, n. 22; p. 29, n. 31; p. 31, n. 32; p.,35, n. 36; p. 45, n. 47; p. 51, n. 56; p. 85, n. 89; p. 144, n. 180; p. 154, n. 193; p. 245, n. 278), and the commander of the Byzantine Emperor Basil I (Caspar and Laehr, *Epistolae*, p. 45, n. 47, cf. p. 232, n. 263) for support.

The other letters are addressed to southern Italian rulers, urging them to cancel their pacts and to end any relations with the Saracens (Arnold, *Johannes VIII*, pp. 205-20). For economic and political reasons, Campanian rulers had continued alliances with the Aghlabids since the 830s (Cilento, *Saraceni*, pp. 109-11; Engreen, *Arabs*, pp. 319-24). Their pacts served their mutual interests: on the one hand, the Campanian rulers were able to secure as well as expand their trade relations, while on the other, the Muslims served as mercenaries for rulers in their struggles for power in the changing political pattern of southern Italy, gaining free access to the harbors of the Tyrrhenian coast in return – so that they could start invasions into the hinterland (Citarella, *Medieval trade*).

In his letters John VIII puts pressure on the rulers to break off their alliances by threatening to anathematize them (cf. Caspar and Laehr, *Epistolae*, p. 5, n. 6; p. 38, n. 40; p. 39, n. 41; p. 39, n. 42; p. 49, n. 53; p. 204, n. 230; p. 218, n. 250; p. 241, n. 273; p. 246, n. 279). During the period 876-82, Campanian rulers – bishops as well as dukes – were repeatedly excommunicated (cf. Caspar and Laehr, *Epistolae*, p. 36, n. 37; p. 39, n. 41; p. 214, n. 246; p. 217, n. 249; p. 246, n. 279; p. 264, n. 305; p. 275, n. 4). The pope was able temporarily to build up successful alliances with certain rulers who defended papal interests in southern Italy (cf. Caspar and Laehr, *Epistolae*, p. 2, n. 3; p. 3, n. 4; p. 27, n. 29; p. 28, n. 30; p. 33, n. 34; p. 36, n. 37; p. 38, n. 39; p. 39, n. p. 41; 39, n. 42; p. 44, n. 46; p. 48, n. 51; p. 49, n. 53; p. 134, n. 164; p. 135, n. 165; p. 136, n. 167; p. 137, n. 169; p. 139, n. 172; p. 141, n. 176; p. 217, n. 249). Furthermore, Campanian rulers received large payments to secure the Tyrrhenian coast from assault during the pope's absence (cf. Caspar and Laehr, *Epistolae*, p. 75, n. 79; p. 81, n. 86; p. 192, n. 214; p. 194, n. 217; p. 218, n. 250; Schwarz, *Amalfi*, pp. 29-30). For the same reasons the pope obviously also paid tributes to Muslims, as he mentions in a letter to King Karlmann (cf. Caspar and Laehr, *Epistolae*, p. 85, n. 89).

According to the papal documents, the pope dealt with the 'Saracen question' by asking for military help from the Carolingian rulers and seeking to subject the Campanian rulers to papal authority. These actions correspond closely to Erchempert's description in the *Historia Langobardorum Beneventanorum*.

Whether the often polemical characterization of the 'Saracens' in the papal letters represents common opinion or papal rhetoric cannot be decided because of the paucity of references elsewhere.

SIGNIFICANCE

Pope John VIII's letters, with their descriptions of the Muslims and arguments for resisting them, provide the only continuous documentation of papal actions against the Saracens of this time. Although military activity and papal support for them may indicate systematic mobilization against the Muslims, John VIII can in no way be considered the originator of the idea of crusade (but see Cilento, *Saraceni*, p. 117).

MANUSCRIPTS

MS Vat. Secret Archive – Reg. Vat. I (11th c.)

MS Vat. Secret Archive – Arm. XXXI, t. 1 (16th c.)

EDITIONS AND TRANSLATIONS

E. Caspar and G. Laehr, *Epistolae Karolini aevi (V)* Berlin, 1928 (*MGH Epistolae* 7)

G.D. Mansi, *Sacrorum concilium nova et amplissima collectio*, 53 vols, Florence, 1759-74, xxvii (repr. Graz, 1960)

Ewald, 'Die Papstbriefe der Britischen Sammlung', 275-414; 503-96

PL 126

P. Labbe and G. Cossart, *Sacrosancta concilia ad regiam editionem exacta*, 17 vols, Paris, 1671-72, ix

Conciliorum omnium generalium et provinicialium collectio regia, 37 vols, Paris, 1644, xxiv

A. Carafa, *Epistolae decretalium summorum pontificum*, Rome, 1591, iii

STUDIES

D. Arnold, *Papst Johannes VIII. Päpstliche Herrschaft in den karolingischen Teilreichen am Ende des 9. Jahrhunderts,* Frankfurt a.M., 2005

G. Spinelli, 'Il papato e la riorganizzazione ecclesiastica della Longobardia meridionale', in G. Andenna and G. Picasso (eds), *Longobardia e longobardi nell' Italia meridionale. Le istituzioni ecclesiastiche*, Milan, 1996, 19-43

P. Skinner, *Family power in southern Italy. The duchy of Gaeta and its neighbours, 850-1139*, Cambridge, 1995

H. Taviani-Carozzi, *La principauté lombarde de Salerne (IXe-XIe siècle). Pouvoir et société en Italie lombarde meridionale*, 2 vols, Rome, 1991, i

H. Zielinski, *Die Regesten des Kaiserreichs unter den Karolingern 751-918 (926), vol 3: Die Regesten des Regnum Italiae und der burgundischen Regna, part 1: Die Karolinger im Regnum Italiae 840-887 (888) (Johann Friedrich Böhmer, Regesta Imperii I, 3, 1)*, Cologne, 1991

Arnaldi, *Natale 875. Politica, ecclesiologia, cultura del papato altomedievale*

I. di Resta, 'Il principato di Capua', *Storia del mezzogiorno*, 15 vols, Naples, 1988, ii/1, 147-87

C. Russo Mailler, 'Il ducato di Napoli', *Storia del mezzogiorno*, ii/1, 341-405

G. Sangermano, 'Il ducato di Amalfi', *Storia di mezzogiorno*, ii/1, 279-321
G. Vergineo, *Storia di Benevento e dintorni*, 4 vols, Benevento, 1985-89, i (*Dalle origini mitiche agli Statuti del 1230*)
U. Schwarz, *Amalfi im frühen Mittelalter (9.-11. Jahrhundert). Untersuchungen zur Amalfitaner Überlieferung*, Tübingen, 1978
R. Panetta, *I saraceni in Italia*, Milan, 1973
N. Cilento, *Italia meridionale longobarda*, Milan, 1966, 1971²
D. Lohrmann, *Das Register Johannes' VIII. (872-882)*, Tübingen, 1968
M. Schipa, 'Storia del principato longobardo di Salerno', in F. Hirsch and M. Schipa, *La Longobardia meridionale (570-1077). Il ducato di Benevento. Il principato di Salerno*, Rome, 1968, 87-278
N. Cilento, *Le orgini della signoria capuana nella Longobardia minore*, Rome, 1966
G. Arnaldi, 'Appunti sulla crisi dell'autorità pontifica in età post-carolingia', *Studi Romani* 3 (1961) 492-507
N. Cilento, 'I saraceni nell'Italia meridionale nei secoli IX e X', *Archivio storico per le province Napoletane* 38 (1959) 109-22
F.E. Engreen, 'Pope John the Eighth and the Arabs', *Speculum* 20 (1945) 318-30
L.M. Hartmann, *Geschichte Italiens im Mittelalter*, 4 vols, Gotha, 1897-1915, iii
M. Merores, *Gaeta im frühen Mittelalter (8. bis 12. Jahrhundert)*, Gotha, 1911
J. Gay, *L'italie méridionale et l'empire byzantin. Depuis l'avènement de Basile Iᵉʳ jusqu'à la prise de Bari par les Normands*, Paris, 1904
Lapôtre, *L'Europe et le Saint-Siège à l'èpoque carolingienne*, pp. 57-437
E. Dümmler, *Geschichte des Ostfränkischen Reiches*, 3 vols, Leipzig, 1887-88² (repr. Darmstadt, 1960)
Ewald, 'Die Papstbriefe der Britischen Sammlung', pp. 275-414, 503-596

Dorothee Arnold 2007

The Chronicle of Albelda and *the Prophetic chronicle*

Unknown authors

DATE OF BIRTH Unknown, probably 9th c.
PLACE OF BIRTH Unknown
DATE OF DEATH Unknown, probably late 9th c.
PLACE OF DEATH Unknown

BIOGRAPHY

The author of the *Chronicle of Albeda* was a cleric or a monk from the entourage of Alphonse III of Oviedo (866-910). Gómez Moreno identifies him as a monk from Monte Laturce ('Las primeras crónicas', 565-70), but Sánchez Albornoz argues against this ('El autor de la Crónica').

A particular cluster of texts within the *Chronicle of Albelda* is conventionally identified as the *Prophetic chronicle*. This cluster is the work of a Mozarab cleric or monk who also wrote in Oviedo. Gómez Moreno has identified him as Dulcidius, the Toledan priest who was sent by the king on a mission to Cordova in 883 ('Las primeras crónicas', 588).

MAIN SOURCES OF INFORMATION

Primary —

Secondary

J.I. Ruiz de la Peña Solar, 'La monarquía asturiana (718-910)', in *El Reino de León en la Alta Edad Media*, 11 vols, León, 1988-(1995), iii, 9-127

P. Linehan, *History and the historians of medieval Spain*, Oxford, 1993, pp. 76-127

Y. Bonnaz, *Les chroniques asturiennes (fin IXe siècle)*, Paris, 1987, pp. lvii-lxiii

J.I. Ruiz de la Peña, 'Estudio preliminar', J. Gil Fernández, 'Introducción', in J. Gil Fernández, J.L. Moralejo and J.I. Ruiz de la Peña, *Crónicas asturianas*, Oviedo, 1985, pp. 31-42, 81-105

A. Barbero and M. Vigil, *La formación del feudalismo en la península ibérica*, Barcelona, 1978, pp. 232-78 ('La historiografía de la época de Alfonso III')

C. Sánchez Albornoz, *Investigaciones sobre historiografía hispana medieval (siglos VIII al XII)*, Buenos Aires, 1967, pp. 66-79 ('El autor de la Crónica llamada de Albelda')

M. Gómez Moreno, 'Las primeras crónicas de la Reconquista, el ciclo de Alfonso III', *Boletín de la Academia de la Historia* 100 (1932) 565-628

WORKS ON CHRISTIAN-MUSLIM RELATIONS

Chronica Albendensia, Epitome Ovetensis, Crónica Albeldense, 'The Chronicle of Albelda', 'The Prophetic Chronicle'

DATE The *Chronicle of Albelda*, in all likelihood first put into writing in 881, was redacted in its final form in November 883, the date when it was completed. Sánchez Albornoz ('¿Una crónica asturiana perdida?') thinks it incorporated a 'lost chronicle' from the end of the eighth century.

The redaction of the *Prophetic chronicle* was completed on 11 April 883, and it was immediately incorporated into the final version of the *Chronicle of Albelda*. Together they form one whole, in which the date of the Muslim conquest is cast back to the year 714, on the grounds that 884 is given as the date of the final victory over the Muslims, predicted by the *Prophetic chronicle* to take place after 170 years of Muslim domination (Barbero and Vigil, *La formación*, pp. 240-49).

ORIGINAL LANGUAGE Latin

DESCRIPTION

The *Chronicle of Albelda*, or *Liber Cronice*, is a universal history which forms a heterogenic whole, made up of writings of diverse origins and genres. After a series of short geographical and historical texts, often drawn from classical authors or from Isidore of Seville, one finds the *Ordo gentis Gotorum*. Composed as an extension of the *Historia Gothorum* of Isidore, it continues until the last Visigoth ruler, Roderick, whose reign was disrupted by the Muslim conquest. This account may have been written shortly after 711 in Toledo (Díaz y Díaz, 'La Historiografía hispana', p. 218, n. 30). It is followed by the *Ordo Gotorum obetensium regum*, which runs from Pelagius (?-737) to Alfonso III (866-910) and describes the reigns of the Asturian kings, their *reconquista* or fight against the enemies of their kingdom, Muslims in particular, their restoration and population of conquered areas, and their occasional collaboration with rebelling Muslims.

These historical notices, which are generally brief (with the exception of the one dealing with Alfonso III), provide us with relatively reliable data. Among the best known passages are those dealing with the initial victory of Pelagius over the Muslims (which are less detailed than in the *Chronicle of Alfonso III*), the victories of Alfonso III over the forces of al-Mundhir, and his raids in al-Andalus.

After the closing events, dated to November 883, several additional short texts are to be found, together given the generic name *Prophetic chronicle* since the edition of them by Gómez Moreno ('Las primeras crónicas', pp. 600-9). The first come from the Muslim world, probably from Cordova. Worth mentioning are a genealogy of the 'Saracens', based on Isidore of Seville and on texts from the east which trace the 'Hagarenes' to Abraham's concubine Hagar, and the 'Ishmaelites' to her son Ishmael.

This is followed by the polemical 'anti-hagiographical' account of Muḥammad's life entitled *Istoria de Mahomet* (q.v.), which was composed on the basis of Eastern Christian sources by a Mozarab in the mid-8th century.

In addition, the *Prophetic chronicle* contains an account of the Muslim conquest, a list of Muslim governors and, from 756 onwards, of the 'Kings of the Ishmaelites of Umayyad origin'. Lastly, a text that lists a series of passages from Ezekiel announces that after 170 years Gog will destroy Ishmael, rather than Israel as found in the Bible. The interpretation of this prophecy again takes up Isidorian etymology and brings 'Gog' into relation with the 'Goths': in a complete reversal of roles, Ezekiel predicts the destruction of Ishmael and the restoration of the kingdom of the Goths between 11 November 883 and 11 November 884. As mentioned above, the date of the Muslim conquest is moved to 714 for this reason.

SIGNIFICANCE

This chronicle plays a key role in the forging and transmission of an ideology of Gothic renaissance, what later historians would call *reconquista*, in the face of a demonized Muslim enemy. The text must have been popular, since it is extant in ten medieval and ten modern manuscripts. It is worth noting that in 974/76, the scribe of the *codex Albendensis* (MS Escorial – D.I.2) extends the period of Muslim domination to 270 years, hence announcing victory on the date of 11 November 984.

MANUSCRIPTS

See Gil Fernández, 'Introducción', in *Crónicas asturianas*, 81-105 and Bonnaz, *Les chroniques asturiennes*, xxix-xl

EDITIONS AND TRANSLATIONS

Bonnaz, *Les chroniques asturiennes*, pp. 2-30 (edition and trans. of the *Chronicle of Albelda* and the *Prophetic chronicle*)

Gil Fernández, Moralejo, and Ruiz de la Peña, *Crónicas asturianas*, pp. 151-188 and 223-63 (edition and trans. of the *Chronicle of Albelda* and the *Prophetic chronicle* [incomplete])

M. Gómez Moreno, 'Las primeras crónicas', pp. 600-9 and 622-28 (edition of the *Chronicle of Albelda* and the *Prophetic chronicle*)

A. Huici, *Las Crónicas Latinas de la Reconquista*, 2 vols, Valencia, 1913, i, pp. 113-95 (edition of the *Chronicle of Albelda*)

Flórez, *España Sagrada* xiii, pp. 433-65 (repr. in *PL* 129, cols 1123-46) (edition of the *Chronicle of Albelda* and the *Prophetic chronicle* [incomplete])

STUDIES

H. Sirantoine, 'Le discours monarchique des "Chroniques asturiennes", fin IXe siècle. Trois modes de légitimation pour les rois des asturies', *Monarquía y sociedad en el reino de Léon, de Alfonso III a Alfonso VII*, 2 vols, Léon, 2007, ii, 793-819

J. Flori, *L'Islam et la fin des temps. L'interprétation prophétique des invasions musulmanes dans la chrétienté médiévale*, Paris, 2007, pp. 164-68

J.F. O'Callaghan, *Reconquest and crusade in medieval Spain*, Philadelphia PA, 2003

M. González Jiménez, 'Sobre la ideología de reconquista: Realidades y tópicos', in *Memoria, mito y realidad en la Historia Medieval* (XIV Semana de Estudios Medievales, Nájera, 2002), Logroño, 2003, 151-70

T. Deswarte, *De la destruction à la restauration. L'idéologie du royaume d'Oviedo-León (VIIIe-XIe siècles)*, Turnhout, 2003

P. Henriet, 'L'idéologie de guerre sainte dans le Haut Moyen Age hispanique', *Francia* 29 (2002) 171-220

T. Deswarte, 'La prophétie de 883 dans le royaume d'Oviedo. Attente adventiste ou espoir d'une libération politique?', *Mélanges de science religieuse* (Lille) 58 (2001) 39-56

S. Gouguenheim, *Les fausses terreurs de l'an mil. Attente de la fin des temps ou approfondissement de la foi?*, Paris, 1999, pp. 97-99

A. Rucquoi, 'El fin del milenarismo en la España de los siglos X y XI', in *Milenarismos y milenaristas en la Europa medieval*, Logroño, 1999, 281-304

A.P. Bronisch, *Reconquista und Heiliger Krieg. Die Deutung des Krieges im christlichen Spanien von den Westgoten bis ins frühe 12. Jahrhundert*, Münster, 1998, 2007[2] (trans. *Reconquista y Guerra Santa. La concepción de la guerra en la España cristiana desde los Visigodos hasta comienzos del siglo XII*, Oviedo, 2006)

J. Montenegro and A. Del Castillo, 'De nuevo sobre don Pelayo y los orígenes de la Reconquista', *Espacio, Tiempo y Forma*, 2nd ser. *Historia Antigua* 8 (1995) 507-20

P. Linehan, *History and the historians*, pp. 76-127

J. Montenegro and A. del Castillo, 'Don Pelayo y los orígenes de la Reconquista. Un nuevo punto de vista', *Hispania* 52 (1992) 5-32

J.E. López Pereira 'Continuidad y novedad léxica en las crónicas asturianas', *Akten der I. internationalen Mittellateinerkongresses, Mittellateinisches Jahrbuch* 24-25, Stuttgart, 1991, 295-310

J.M. Mínguez Fernández, *La Reconquista*, Madrid, 1989

R. Collins, *The Arab Conquest of Spain (710-797)*, Oxford, 1989

Ruiz de la Peña, 'Estudio preliminar', and Gil Fernández, 'Introducción', in *Crónicas asturianas*, pp. 31-42, 81-105

D. Millet-Gérard, *Chrétiens mozarabes et culture islamique dans l'Espagne des VIIIe-IXe siècles*, Paris, 1984

G. Martin, 'La chute du royaume visigothique d'Espagne dans l'historiographie chrétienne des VIIIe et IXe siècles. Sémiologie socio-historique', *Cahiers de linguistique hispanique mediévale*, 9 (1984) 207-33

M.C. Díaz y Díaz, *Libros y librerías en la Rioja altomedieval*, Logroño, 1979

J. Gil, 'Judíos y Cristianos en Hispania: s. VIII y IX (Continuación)', *Hispania Sacra* 31 (1978-79) 9-88

J. Gil, 'Los terrores del año 800', in *Actas del Simposio para el estudio de los codices del Comentario al Apocalypsis de Beato de Liébana*, 2 vols, Madrid, 1978, i, pp. 215-47

Barbero and Vigil, *La formación*, pp. 232-78

D.W. Lomax, *The reconquest of Spain*, London, 1978

L.A. García Moreno, *El fin del reino visigodo de Toledo. Decadencia y catástrofe. Una contribución a su crítica*, Madrid, 1975

C. Sánchez Albornoz, *Orígenes de la nación española. Estudios críticos sobre la historia del Reino de Asturias*, 3 vols, Oviedo, 1972-75, ii

M.C. Díaz y Díaz, 'La historiografía hispana desde la invasión árabe hasta el año 1000', in *De Isidoro al siglo XI. Ocho estudios sobre la vida literaria peninsular*, Barcelona, 1976², 203-34 (repr. *La Storiografia altomedievale*, 2 vols, Spoleto, 1970, i, 313-43, pp. 332-33)

L. Vázquez de Parga, 'Algunas notas sobre el pseudo Metodio y España', *Habis* 2 (1971) 143-64

Sánchez Albornoz, *Investigaciones sobre historiografía*, pp. 44-65 ('La crónica de Albelda y la de Alfonso III'), pp. 66-79 ('El autor de la Crónica llamada de Albelda'), pp. 80-96 ('Sobre la autoridad de las Crónicas de Albelda y de Alfonso III') pp. 111-60 ('¿ Una crónica asturiana perdida?')

Sánchez Albornoz, *Despoblación y repoblación en la valle del Duero*, Buenos Aires, 1966

J.A. Maravall, *El concepto de España en la Edad Media*, Madrid, 1954

Gómez Moreno, 'Las primeras crónicas'

Thomas Deswarte 2007

Ibn Qutayba

Abū Muḥammad ʿAbdallāh ibn Qutayba

DATE OF BIRTH 828
PLACE OF BIRTH Kūfa
DATE OF DEATH 889
PLACE OF DEATH Baghdad

BIOGRAPHY

Ibn Qutayba was educated in conservative intellectual circles, and he identified himself as a follower of Aḥmad ibn Ḥanbal. His ideas found favour with the Caliph al-Mutawakkil, and from about 851 he held the post of *qāḍī* under the patronage of the vizier al-Fatḥ ibn Khāqān. He lost this post when the latter fell from favor in 870, and after that mainly devoted himself to writing.

He wrote on a range of topics, mainly *adab*, for which he was primarily known, and religious matters. His *adab* works include *Kitāb adab al-kātib*, 'Etiquette for the secretary', *Kitāb al-shiʿr wa-l-shuʿarāʾ*, 'Poetry and poets', and *Kitāb al-maʿārif*, 'Important information', and his religious works include *Kitāb tafsīr gharīb al-Qurʾān*, 'Commentary on difficulties in the Qurʾān', *Kitāb al-masāʾil wa-l-ajwiba*, 'Questions and answers', and *Kitāb gharīb al-ḥadīth*, 'Difficulties in the ḥadīth'.

There are frequent quotations and references from the Bible in many of his works (see Khalidi, pp. 101-8, for the sayings attributed to Jesus collected in his *ʿUyūn al-akhbār*).

MAIN SOURCES OF INFORMATION

Primary

See the bibliography given by G. Lecomte, art. 'Ibn Ḳutayba' in *EI2*

Secondary

T. Khalidi, *The Muslim Jesus. Sayings and stories in Islamic literature*, Cambridge MA, 2001

S. Karoui, *Die Rezeption der Bibel in der frühislamischen Literatur am Beispiel der Hauptwerke von Ibn Qutayba (gest. 276/889)*, Heidelberg, 1997 (Diss. Ruprecht-Karls-Universität, Heidelberg)

C. Adang, *Muslim writers on Judaism and the Hebrew Bible, from Ibn Rabban to Ibn Hazm*, Leiden, 1996, pp. 30-36
A. Isteero, *ʿAbdullah Muslim ibn Qutayba's biblical quotations and their source. An inquiry into the earliest existing Arabic Bible translations*, Baltimore MD, 1991 (Diss. Johns Hopkins University)
G. Lecomte, *Ibn Qutayba, l'homme, son oeuvre, ses idées*, Damascus, 1965
G. Lecomte, 'Les citations de l'Ancien et du Nouveau Testament dans l'œuvre d'Ibn Qutayba', *Arabica* 5 (1958) 34-46
I. Huseini, *The life and works of Ibn Qutayba*, Beirut, 1950
G. Vajda, 'Observations sur quelques citations bibliques chez Ibn Qutayba', *Revue des études juives* 99 (1935) 68-80

WORKS ON CHRISTIAN-MUSLIM RELATIONS

Dalāʾil al-nubuwwa, 'Proofs of prophethood'

DATE Mid-9th c.
ORIGINAL LANGUAGE Arabic

DESCRIPTION
The original is lost, and its extent and scope can no longer be known. Only relatively short quotations in Ibn al-Jawzī and a few other authors, including Ibn Ḥazm, remain. These include verses from Genesis that are used to show how Islam will abrogate the Jewish law and bring all other dispensations to an end, and also from Isaiah and other prophets from the Hebrew Bible, as well as a few from the Gospels of Matthew and John (the Paraclete verses) that are used to prove that the coming of Muḥammad was foretold.

Many, though not all, of the proof verses resemble texts in ʿAlī l-Ṭabarī's *Kitāb al-dīn wa-l-dawla* (q.v.), suggesting a close though not direct relationship between the two works.

SIGNIFICANCE
The work is an early example of the *dalāʾil al-nubuwwa*, 'proofs of prophethood', genre, in which biblical prooftexts are often adduced to demonstrate the veracity of Muḥammad's mission. The overlap between it and ʿAlī l-Ṭabarī's work suggests both authors were employing similar source material that would have been in open circulation and may have been made available in al-Mutawakkil's court.

MANUSCRIPTS —

EDITIONS AND TRANSLATIONS

Ibn al-Jawzī, *Al-wafā' bi-aḥwāl al-Muṣṭafā*, ed. M. ʿAbd al-Wāḥid, Cairo, 1966, pp. 62-73

Adang, *Muslim writers*, pp. 267-77 (trans. from Ibn al-Jawzī of the passages from the Hebrew Bible, together with some additions from Ibn Ḥazm and Ibn Qayyim al-Jawziyya)

C. Brockelmann, 'Ibn Ǧauzi's Kitāb al-Wafā fī faḍā'il al-Muṣṭafā nach der Leidener Handschrift untersucht', in F. Delitzsch and P. Haupt (eds), *Beiträge zur Assyriologie und semitischen Sprachwissenschaft*, 3 vols, Leipzig, 1898, iii, 2-59, pp. 46-55

STUDIES

J. Bray, 'Lists and memory: Ibn Qutayba and Muḥammad b. Shabīb', in F. Daftary and J. Meri (eds), *Culture and memory in medieval Islam*, London, 2003, 210-31, pp. 214-21

Adang, 'Medieval Muslim polemics against the Jewish scriptures', in J. Waardenburg (ed.), *Muslim perceptions of other religions*, New York, 1999, 143-59, pp. 145-47

Adang, *Muslim writers*, pp. 112-17, 148-50, 159-62, 169-70, 196-97, 225-26, 264-66

Adang, 'Some hitherto neglected biblical material in the work of Ibn Ḥazm', *Al-Masāq* 5 (1992) 17-28

D.S. Margoliouth, 'On the 'Book of religion and empire' by Ali b. Rabban al-Tabari', *Proceedings of the British Academy* 14 (1930) 165-82

David Thomas 2007

Abū Dāwūd al-Sijistānī

Abū Dāwūd Sulaymān ibn al-Ashʿath al-Sijistānī

DATE OF BIRTH 817
PLACE OF BIRTH Sijistān (eastern Iran)
DATE OF DEATH 889
PLACE OF DEATH Basra

BIOGRAPHY

Abū Dāwūd is best known as the compiler of the *Kitāb al-sunan*, one of the six Sunnī canonical collections of ḥadīth. He came from the province of Sijistān in eastern Iran, and after much traveling settled in Basra, where he came to be deeply respected for his learning in his subject. Among his pupils was the ḥadīth compiler Abū ʿĪsā Muḥammad al-Tirmidhī, whose collection was also accepted as one of the canonical *ṣiḥāḥ sitta*.

MAIN SOURCES OF INFORMATION

Primary

al-Khaṭīb al-Baghdādī, *Taʾrīkh Baghdād*, 14 vols, Cairo, 1931, ix, p. 57

al-Nawawī, *Tahdhīb al-asmāʾ wa-l-lughāt*, ed. F. Wüstenfeld, Göttingen, 1842-47, p. 711

Ibn Ḥajar, *Tahdhīb al-tahdhīb*, 12 vols, Hyderabad, 1908-9, iv, pp. 169-73

Hajjī Khalīfa, *Kashf al-ẓunūn ʿan asmā l-kutub wa-l-funūn*, 7 vols, ed. G. Flügel, Leipzig, 1835-58, iii, p. 237

Secondary

C. Melchert, 'The life and works of Abū Dāwūd al-Sijistānī', *Al-Qantara* 29 (2008) 9-44, p. 20

C. Melchert, art. 'Abū Dāwūd al-Sijistānī', in *EI3*

GAS i, pp. 149–52

J. Robson, 'The transmission of Abū Dāwūd's *Sunan*', *BSOAS* 14 (1952) 579-88

Brockelmann, *GAL* i, p. 161

WORKS ON CHRISTIAN-MUSLIM RELATIONS

Dalāʾil al-nubuwwa, 'Proofs of prophethood'

DATE Unknown
ORIGINAL LANGUAGE Arabic

DESCRIPTION
The work is mentioned by Hajjī Khalīfa, *Kashf al-ẓunūn*, iii, p. 237, on the authority of Ibn Ḥajar, *Tahdhīb al-tahdhīb*. While the work may well have largely comprised lists of ḥadīths, it could also have listed and commented on biblical proof verses and also replied to arguments from Christians.

SIGNIFICANCE
It presumably employed similar arguments to those in contemporary works of the kind, and may have both used earlier works and fed later works in the genre.

MANUSCRIPTS —
EDITIONS AND TRANSLATIONS —
STUDIES —

David Thomas 2007

Ritual of abjuration

Unknown author

DATE OF BIRTH Unknown
PLACE OF BIRTH Unknown
DATE OF DEATH Unknown
PLACE OF DEATH Unknown

BIOGRAPHY —

MAIN SOURCES OF INFORMATION

Primary —

Secondary —

WORKS ON CHRISTIAN-MUSLIM RELATIONS

Taxis ginomenē epi tois apo sarakēnōn epistrephousi pros tēn katharan kai alēthē hēmōn tōn christianōn, 'Rite which came about for those from among the Saracens who converted to the pure and true faith of us Christians', 'Ritual of abjuration'

DATE c. 880-90
ORIGINAL LANGUAGE Greek

DESCRIPTION

In the *Euchologion*, the prayer book for the various rituals of the Byzantine Church, there is a rubric that contains a series of abjuration rituals for heretics, Jews and Muslims who convert to Christianity. The texts of these rituals contain a first section devoted to catechisms and liturgical procedures intended for the initiate who wants to embrace Christianity, followed by a series of anathemas against the original faith and a profession of faith to be recited in public by the convert. The oldest core of the collected rituals (for former Manicheans, Paulicians, Athinganoi, Jews, Muslims and others) goes back to the late 9th century.

In the ritual for converts from Islam, two parts can be distinguished. The introductory part, in which the sacramental process that the convert is to follow is defined, reproduces exactly the first section of the ritual for converts from Manicheism. The second part, containing the abjurations, begins with a formula that corresponds to the abjuration rituals for Jews and Athinganoi. This is followed by 22 anathemas, repudiating first Muḥammad, his successors as caliphs and his wives, and then the Qurʾān and doctrines contained in it, such as paradise, angels, Christian scripture and Jesus as a prophet, and thirdly Islamic religious practices, such as marriage customs, divorce, rituals regarding the Meccan sanctuary, the 'holy camel' and prayer. The long profession of faith that follows and the final malediction again duplicate those contained in the anti-Jewish formulas.

The majority of the anathemas (2-3, 5-6, 11-13, 15-22) in the ritual of abjuration are quotations from the anonymous treatise entitled *Against Muḥammad* (*PG* 104, cols 1448-57). Other anathemas in the ritual (1, 4, 7, 10) are summaries of passages from the same treatise. The rest of the ritual is based on Michael the Synkellos (q.v.) and the same Greek version of the Qurʾān as was used by Nicetas of Byzantium (q.v.).

The ritual of abjuration goes back to the 880s, a period of continuous warfare between the Byzantines and the Arabs. The capture of many prisoners led to numerous conversions from Islam to Christianity (as well as vice versa), and the admission of former Muslims into the Church was thus an issue of great importance, leading to the redaction of this ritual for all who wanted to convert.

The text of the ritual was employed by a later redactor as a source for another ritual of abjuration, which is now found in a unique 11th-century manuscript from the area of Sebaste (Sivas).

SIGNIFICANCE

The ritual of abjuration was one of the best known texts about Islam in Byzantium. This is evidenced in the theological discussions of the second half of the 12th century, and led to the publication of a document (*tomos*) by Emperor Manuel I Comnenus in May 1180, in which article 22 of the ritual, where the 'God of Muḥammad' is anathematized, was replaced by a rejection of 'Muḥammad and his inspirer' (Darrouzès, 'Tomos inédit', p. 197; Grumel and Darrouzès, *Les regestes*, no. 1153). Despite this imperial decision, which was approved by the patriarch and the synod, the measure was not applied and the formula contained in the old redaction continued to be used.

MANUSCRIPTS

The ritual of abjuration is preserved in a considerable number of manuscripts of the *Euchologion*, as well as in independent manuscripts, together with the rituals for other converts, such as Jews and Manicheans. It is also found in manuscripts containing collections of heresiographical works. A provisional overview can be found in P. Eleuteri and A. Rigo, *Eretici, dissidenti, Musulmani ed Ebrei a Bisanzio. Una raccolta eresiologica del XII secolo*, Venice, 1993, pp. 19-36.

EDITIONS AND TRANSLATIONS

E. Montet, 'Un rituel d'abjuration des Musulmans dans l'église grecque', *RHR* 53 (1906) 145-63 (partial edition)

PG 140, cols 124-36

STUDIES

A. Rigo, '*Saracenica* di Friedrich Sylburg (1595). Una raccolta di opere bizantine contro l'Islam', in M. Cortesi (ed.), *I Padri sotto il torchio. Le edizioni dell'antichità cristiana nei secoli XV-XVI*, Florence, 2002, 289-310, pp. 307-9

Hoyland, *Seeing Islam*, pp. 517-18

D. Sahas, '"Holosphyros?" A Byzantine perception of "The God of Muhammad"', in Y.Y. Haddad and W.Z. Haddad (eds), *Christian-Muslim encounters*, Gainesville FL, 1995, 109-25

Eleuteri and Rigo, *Eretici, dissidenti, Musulmani ed Ebrei a Bisanzio*, pp. 53-57

A. Rigo, 'Una formula inedita d'abiura per i Musulmani (fine X – inizi XI secolo)', *Rivista di studi bizantini e neoellenici*, N.S. 29 (1992) 163-73

D.J. Sahas, 'Ritual of conversion from Islam to the Byzantine Church', *Greek Orthodox Theological Review* 36 (1991) 57-69

V. Grumel and J. Darrouzès, *Les regestes des actes du patriarcat de Constantinople* I. *Les actes des patriarches*, fasc. II et III, *Les regestes de 715 à 1206*, Paris, 1989[2], no. 1153 (with literature)

A. Argyriou, 'Éléments biographiques concernant le prophète Muḥammad dans la littérature grecque des trois premiers siècles de l'hégire', in T. Fahd (ed.), *La vie du prophète Mahomet*, Paris, 1983, 159-82, pp. 174-75

J. Darrouzès, 'Tomos inédit de 1180 contre Mahomet', *REB* 30 (1972) 187-97

A.-T. Khoury, *Les théologiens byzantins et l'Islam. Textes et auteurs (VIIIe-XIIIe s.)*, Louvain, 1969[2], pp. 186-87

E. Trapp, *Manuel II. Palaiologos, Dialoge mit einem "Perser"*, Wien 1966, pp. 15-16
J. Meyendorff, 'Byzantine views of Islam', *DOP* 18 (1964) 113-32, pp. 123-25 (repr. in *Arab-Byzantine relations in early Islamic times*, ed. M. Bonner, Aldershot, 2004, pp. 225-27)
W. Eichner, 'Die Nachrichten über den Islam bei den Byzantinern', *Der Islam* 23 (1936) 133-62; 197-244, p. 141
H. Lammens, 'Le califat de Yazid Ier', *Mélanges de la Faculté Orientale de l'Université St. Joseph* 6 (1913) 79-267, pp. 186-87
C. Güterbock, *Der Islam im Lichte der byzantinischen Polemik*, Berlin, 1912, pp. 37-38
F. Cumont, 'L'origine de la formule grecque d'abjuration imposée aux Musulmans', *RHR* 64 (1911) 143-50
J. Ebersolt, 'Un nouveau manuscrit sur le rituel d'abjuration des Musulmans dans l'église grecque', *RHR* 54 (1906) 231-32
E. Montet, 'Un rituel d'abjuration des Musulmans'

Antonio Rigo 2008

Ibn Ḥabīb

Abū Marwān ʿAbd al-Malik ibn Ḥabīb ibn Sulaymān ibn Hārūn/Marwān ibn Julhuma ibn ʿAbbās ibn Mirdās al-Sulamī

DATE OF BIRTH c. 790
PLACE OF BIRTH A village near Granada
DATE OF DEATH 852-53
PLACE OF DEATH Cordova

BIOGRAPHY

ʿAbd al-Malik ibn Ḥabīb was born in *kūrat Ilbīra*, a small village near Granada, where he may have started his studies. He was a druggist (*ʿaṭṭār*) like his father, and he had a brother whom he defended against a charge of blasphemy before the judge of Ilbīra. He fathered two sons and a daughter.

At some point Ibn Ḥabīb moved to Cordova, where he studied *ḥadīth* and *fiqh* with three scholars. When he was 33, he spent three years studying in the Middle East in order to further his knowledge. Some time between 825 and 827, he returned to al-Andalus, carrying with him a great number of books. He moved to Cordova for good in 833 at the request of the emir ʿAbd al-Raḥmān II, who made him his legal adviser (*faqīh mushāwar*) on account of his fame. He remained there until his death in 852/3.

Ibn Ḥabīb was a prolific writer. An anonymous informant reports that he composed 'one thousand and fifty books'. Despite this excessive number, the sources only give the titles of 42 works, belonging to different Muslim genres such as qurʾānic exegesis, *ḥadīth, fiqh*, medicine, eschatology and history.

MAIN SOURCES OF INFORMATION

Primary

Ibn Ḥārith al-Khushanī, *Akhbār al-fuqahāʾ wa-l-muḥaddithīn / Historia de los alfaquíes y tradicionistas de al-Andalus*, ed. M.L. Ávila and L. Molina, Madrid, 1992, pp. 245-54, no. 328

al-Zubaydī, *Ṭābaqāt al-naḥwiyyīn wa-l-lughawiyyīn*, ed. Muḥammad Abū l-Faḍl Ibrāhīm, Cairo, 1984, pp. 260-61, no. 203

Ibn al-Faraḍī, *Kitāb taʾrīkh ʿulamāʾ al-Andalus / Historia virorum doctorum Andalusiae*, ed. F. Codera, 2 vols, Madrid, 1891-92, i, pp. 325-28, no. 814
al-Ḥumaydī, *Jadhwat al-muqtabis fī dhikr wulāt al-Andalus*, Cairo, 1966, pp. 282-84
Ibn Khāqān, *Kitāb maṭmaḥ al-anfus wa-masraḥ al-taʾannus fī mulaḥ ahl al-Andalus*, ed. Muḥammad ʿAlī, Beirut, 1983, pp. 233-37
al-Qāḍī ʿIyāḍ, *Tartīb al-madārik wa-taqrīb al-masālik li-maʿrifat aʿlām madhhab Mālik*, ed. Muḥammad ibn Tāwīt al-Ṭanjī et al., 8 vols, Rabat, 1966, 1983[2], iv, pp. 122-42
al-Ḍabbī, *Bughyat al-multamis fī taʾrīkh rijāl ahl al-Andalus*, ed. F. Codera and J. Ribera, Madrid, 1884, pp. 364-377, no. 1063
Ibn al-Khaṭīb, *Al-Iḥāṭa fī ākhbār Gharnāṭa*, ed. Muḥammad ʿAbdallāh ʿInān, 4 vols, Cairo, 1956, iii, pp. 548-53
Ibn Farḥūn, *Kitāb al-dībāj al-mudhahhab fī maʿrifat aʿyān ʿulamāʾ al-madhhab*, ed. M. al-Aḥmadī, 2 vols, Cairo, 1976, ii, pp. 8-15

Secondary
I. ʿAbbās, "Abd al-Malik ibn Marwān wa-dawruhu fī thaqāfat ʿaṣrihi', in I. ʿAbbās, *Buḥūth wa-dirāsāt fī l-adab wa-l-taʾrīkh*, 3 vols, Beirut, 2000, 383-99
J.P. Monferrer-Sala, *ʿAbd al-Malik b. Ḥabīb y el Kitāb waṣf al-firdaws (La descripción del paraíso)*, Granada, 1997, pp. 14-25
B. Ossendorf-Conrad, *Das "K. al-Wāḍiḥa" des ʿAbd al-Malik ibn Ḥabīb. Edition und Kommentar zu Ms. Qarawiyyīn 809/40 (Abwāb al-Ṭahāra)*, Stuttgart, 1994
J. Aguadé, *ʿAbd al-Malik b. Ḥabīb (m. 238/853). Kitāb al-taʾrīj (La historia)*, Madrid, 1991, pp. 15-56
M. Jarrar, *Die Prophetenbiographie im islamischen Spanien. Ein Beitrag zur Überlieferungs- und Redaktionsgeschichte*, Bern, 1989, pp. 110-13

WORKS ON CHRISTIAN-MUSLIM RELATIONS

Kitāb al-taʾrīkh, 'History'

DATE 1st half of 9th c., redacted in 2nd half of 9th c.
ORIGINAL LANGUAGE Arabic

DESCRIPTION
The version of the *Kitāb al-taʾrīkh* which has come down to us is a recension made by Ibn Ḥabīb's pupil Yūsuf ibn Yaḥyā l-Maghāmī in the years 888-91. Together with Ibn Raʾs Ghanama's *History*, the *Kitāb al-taʾrīkh* is one of only two world histories written in al-Andalus known to have survived.

The work deals with a succession of topics: the creation of the world and the stories of the pre-Islamic prophets, the biography of Muḥammad, the orthodox caliphs, the conquest of al-Andalus, together with the eschatological and apocalyptic predictions about the destruction of the Iberian peninsula, the generations of legal scholars and traditionalists and their merits, and finally, a miscellaneous section consisting of a fragment with exegesis of several terms from Mālik's *al-Muwaṭṭa*ʾ and various documents on ascetic subjects.

Of significance for Christian-Muslim relations, the work contains traditions based on eastern Muslim predictions which incorporate material from Jewish and Christian apocalyptic sources.

SIGNIFICANCE

The *Kitāb al-taʾrīkh* is the first Andalusian text that has come down. It contains apocalyptic predictions and eschatological prophecies about Cordova and al-Andalus, together with threats that the Christian population would be slaughtered.

MANUSCRIPTS

MS Oxford, Bodleian Library – 2 (dated 1295/6)

EDITIONS AND TRANSLATIONS

ʿAbd al-Malik ibn Ḥabīb, *Kitāb al-tārīkh*, ed. Sālim Muṣṭafā l-Badrī, Beirut, 1999

Aguadé, *ʿAbd al-Malik b. Ḥabīb*, Madrid, 1991, pp. 13-191 (edition with Spanish introduction)

M.ʿA. Makkī, 'Egipto y los orígenes de las historiografía arábigo-española', *Revista del Instituto Egipcio de Estudios Islámicos* 5 (1957) 157-248, pp. 221-43 (edition of the Arabic fragment related to al-Andalus)

STUDIES

A. Christys, 'The History of Ibn Ḥabīb and ethnogenesis in al-Andalus', in R. Corradini, M. Diesenberger and H. Reimitz (eds), *The construction of communities in the early Middle Ages*, Leiden, 2003, pp. 323-48

J.P. Monferrer-Sala, 'Algo más sobre una profecía relativa a la destrucción de Córdoba (Ibn Ḥabīb, *Taʾrīj*, nos 450-1)', *Qurṭuba* 5 (2000) 281-85

M.I. Fierro, 'Sobre *al-qarmūniyya*', *Al-Qanṭara* 11 (1990) 83-94

Aguadé, *ʿAbd al-Malik b. Ḥabīb*, pp. 77-108

Jarrar, *Die Prophetenbiographie im islamischen Spanien*, pp. 116-25

J. Aguadé, 'El libro del escrúpulo religioso (Kitāb al-waraʿ) de ʿAbd al-Malik b. Ḥabīb,' *Actas del XII Congreso de la Unión de Arabistas e Islamólogos*, Madrid, 1986, 17-34
Makkī, 'Egipto y los orígenes de las historiografía arábigo-española,' pp. 190-97

Juan Pedro Monferrer-Sala 2007

Ibn Abī l-Dunyā

Abū Bakr ʿAbdallāh ibn Muḥammad ibn ʿUbayd ibn Abī l-Dunyā

DATE OF BIRTH 823
PLACE OF BIRTH Baghdad
DATE OF DEATH 894-95
PLACE OF DEATH Baghdad

BIOGRAPHY

Ibn Abī l-Dunyā was known as a literary scholar and ascetic. He was tutor to the future caliphs al-Muʿtaḍid (r. 892-902) and al-Muqtafī (r. 902-908) as well as other ʿAbbasid princes, and was known for his pious life. He spoke out strongly in favor of upright living and against what he saw as moral evils.

He is credited with more than 100 works, among which *Kitāb dhamm al-dunyā*, 'Reproach of the world', and *Kitāb al-taqwā*, 'Piety', indicate the kind of interest that might lead him to collect maxims of Christian monks.

A number of sayings attributed to Jesus are to be found in his works (see Khalidi).

MAIN SOURCES OF INFORMATION

Primary

al-Masʿūdī, *Les prairies d'or*, ed. and trans. C. Barbier de Meynard and Pavet de Courteille, 9 vols, Paris, 1861-77, viii, pp. 209-10

Ibn al-Nadīm, *Fihrist*, pp. 236-67

al-Dhahabī, *Siyar aʿlām al-nubalāʾ*, ed. Shuʿayb al-Arnāʾūṭ and Ḥuṣayn al-Asad, 23 vols, Beirut, 1985, xiii, pp. 401-4

Secondary

T. Khalidi, *The Muslim Jesus. Sayings and stories in Islamic literature*, Cambridge MA, 2001, pp. 108-24

R. Weipert and S. Weninger, 'Die erhaltenen Werke des Ibn Abī d-Dunyā: Eine vorläufige Bestandsaufname', *ZDMG* 146 (1996) 415-55

E. Almagor, *Kitāb dhamm al-dunyā li-Ibn Abī al-Dunyā*, Jerusalem, 1984, pp. 9-15

Ṣ. al-Munajjid, '*Muʿjam muṣannafāt Ibn Abī al-Dunyā*', *Revue de l'Académie arabe de Damas* 49 (1974) 579-94

WORKS ON CHRISTIAN-MUSLIM RELATIONS

Al-muntaqā min kitāb al-ruhbān, 'Selections from The Book of Monks'

DATE Before 894
ORIGINAL LANGUAGE Arabic

DESCRIPTION
The surviving text comprises 24 selections, each reported in the name of an individual, including Wahb ibn Munabbih (d. 728 or 732), all of them brief, and many containing aphoristic comments or answers to questions by monks. A number are framed on recognizable sayings of Jesus.

Ibn Abī l-Dunyā selected them from an earlier unknown work on monks. The exact nature of this work, and of Ibn Abī l-Dunyā's work in which they are gathered, can no longer be known.

SIGNIFICANCE
The collection is an example of works that show the liveliness of contacts between the followers of the two faiths in the early centuries (cf. Mourad), and the respect in which Christian monks were held as sources of wisdom. It also shows that *Maṣīḥiyyāt*, 'sayings of the Christians', were collected alongside *Isrāʾīliyyāt*, 'sayings of the Jews'.

MANUSCRIPTS
MS Rampur, Uttar Pradesh, Raza Library – 335/10, (13th c.?)

EDITIONS AND TRANSLATIONS
Ṣ. al-Munajjed, 'Morceaux choisis du Livre des moines', *MIDEO* 3 (1956) 349-58

STUDIES
S. Mourad, 'Christian monks in Islamic literature: a preliminary report on some Arabic *Apophthegmata Patrum*', *Bulletin of the Royal Institute for Inter-Faith Studies* 6 (2004) 81-98 (this article treats sayings attributed to monks in general though does not refer to this particular collection)

Dalāʾil al-nubuwwa, 'Proofs of prophethood'

DATE Before 894
ORIGINAL LANGUAGE Arabic

DESCRIPTION

The work is listed among Ibn Abī l-Dunyā's works in MS Damascus, Dār al-Kutub al-Ẓāhiriyya – Majmūʿa 42, fols 57-59, and, based upon this, is mentioned by al-Munajjid, '*Muʿjam muṣannafāt Ibn Abī al-Dunyā*', p. 586. It would have been an example of the 'proofs of prophethood' genre, and it may have listed and commented on biblical proof verses and also refuted arguments from Christians.

SIGNIFICANCE

It presumably employed similar arguments to those in contemporary works, and may both have used earlier works and have fed later works of this kind.

MANUSCRIPTS —

EDITIONS AND TRANSLATIONS —

STUDIES —

David Thomas 2007

Ibrāhīm ibn Isḥāq al-Ḥarbī

Abū Isḥāq Ibrāhīm ibn Isḥāq ibn Ibrāhīm ibn Bishr al-Ḥarbī

DATE OF BIRTH 811
PLACE OF BIRTH Merv
DATE OF DEATH 898
PLACE OF DEATH Baghdad

BIOGRAPHY

Al-Khāṭib al-Baghdādī and Ibn al-Qifṭī report al-Ḥarbī recalling that most of his maternal uncles were Christians. He moved from his home town to Baghdad, and there he was a student of Aḥmad ibn Ḥanbal. Like his teacher, he was an opponent of Muʿtazilī doctrines, particularly the createdness of the Qurʾān. He was known as a philologist and collector of ḥadīth, and in his personal life as a man of piety and forbearance.

Among al-Ḥarbī's works are 24 collections of ḥadīth, and compositions on Arabic grammar and practical morality.

MAIN SOURCES OF INFORMATION

Primary

al-Khāṭib al-Baghdādī, *Taʾrīkh Baghdād*, 14 vols, Cairo, 1931, vi, pp. 27-40, no. 3059

Ibn al-Qifṭī, *Inbāh al-ruwāt ʿalā anbāh al-nuḥāt*, ed. M.A. Ibrāhīm, 4 vols., Cairo, 1950-73, i, pp. 155-58, no. 93

Yāqūt, *Muʿjam al-udabāʾ*, 7 vols, ed. I. ʿAbbās, Beirut, 1993, i, pp. 41-50, no. 6

al-Subkī, *Ṭabaqāt al-Shāfiʿiyya al-kubrā*, 10 vols, Cairo, 1964-76, ii, pp. 256-57, no. 26

Secondary

J.-C. Vadet, art. 'Ibrāhīm b. Isḥāḳ, b. Ibrāhīm b. Bis͟hr al- Ḥarbī, Abū Isḥāḳ', in *EI2*

WORKS ON CHRISTIAN-MUSLIM RELATIONS

[*Dalāʾil al-nubuwwa*, 'Proofs of prophethood']

DATE before 898

ORIGINAL LANGUAGE Arabic

DESCRIPTION

A work about proofs of prophethood is mentioned by Ḥājjī Khalīfa, *Kashf al-ẓunūn ʿan asmā l-kutub wa-l-funūn*, 7 vols, ed. G. Flügel, Leipzig, 1835-58, iii, p. 237, though nothing else is known about it. It would have been an example of the genre, and it may have listed and commented on biblical proof verses and also refuted arguments from Christians.

SIGNIFICANCE

It presumably employed similar arguments to those in contemporary works, and may both have used earlier works and fed later works of this kind.

MANUSCRIPTS —

EDITIONS AND TRANSLATIONS —

STUDIES —

David Thomas 2007

Ibn Waḍḍāḥ

Abū ʿAbdallāh Muḥammad ibn Waḍḍāḥ ibn Bazīʿ
al-Umawī l-Marwānī l-Qurṭubī

DATE OF BIRTH 815
PLACE OF BIRTH Cordova
DATE OF DEATH 3 February 900
PLACE OF DEATH Cordova

BIOGRAPHY

Ibn Waḍḍāḥ's grandfather Bazīʿ was a slave soldier, probably a Christian from Oviedo, manumitted by the Cordovan Umayyad emir ʿAbd al-Raḥmān I (r. 756-88). Ibn Waḍḍāḥ's non-Arab origin did not prevent him from entering the world of Islamic scholarship, but it did make him the object of derision on the part of an Arab colleague for his alleged defective knowledge of Arabic.

Ibn Waḍḍāḥ was the first member of his family to devote himself to the pen and not to the sword. He studied with 165 teachers in al-Andalus and during his two trips to the east, visiting Ifrīqiyā (Tunisia), Egypt, Arabia, Syria and Iraq. His first trip took place between 833 and 835 with the aim of contacting pious and devout ascetics (*al-ʿubbād*). His interest in asceticism was followed by some of his Andalusian disciples such as Aṣbagh ibn Mālik (from Cabra), of whom it was said that his companions were like monks (*kāna lahu aṣḥāb ka-l-ruhbān*). In his second trip, started in 845, Ibn Waḍḍāḥ studied mostly law and the science of ḥadīth, and he returned to al-Andalus around 859.

Ibn Waḍḍāḥ was a pious and ascetic man who devoted his life to the spread of religious knowledge. Together with his contemporary Baqī ibn Makhlad, he was the most influential teacher of his generation in both Islamic (Mālikī) law and ḥadīth. Ibn Waḍḍāḥ transmitted many works he had learned during his trips, acting as an agent of Islamicization through the many pupils who came to study with him in Cordova from different areas of the Iberian peninsula. No fewer than 216 students of Ibn Waḍḍāḥ are referred to in the sources, and they were active as scholars, teachers, jurists, traditionists and judges during the caliphal period, when Andalusian society became fully Islamicized (in terms of Muslims becoming the majority of the population and the diffusion of Islamic norms and practices). Among the many works Ibn Waḍḍāḥ transmitted in al-Andalus, there were some that had relevance for the treatment of non-Muslims: al-Fazārī's *Kitāb al-siyar* and al-Walīd ibn Muslim's *Kitāb al-siyar ʿan al-Awzāʿī*, dealing with correct legal conduct during military campaigns, Ibn al-Mubārak's *Kitāb faḍl al-jihād* ('On the excellence of holy war'), and Nuʿaym ibn Ḥammād's *Kitāb al-fitan* ('The trials of the end time').

Ibn Waḍḍāḥ also contributed to the Islamicization of al-Andalus through his transmission of anecdotes dealing with the establishment of Successors of the Prophet (*tābiʿūn*) in the Iberian peninsula and with the localization in al-Andalus of religious events, such as the report that the woman who killed Yaḥyā ibn Zakariyyāʾ (John the Baptist) was from Italica (Seville) and that the people mentioned in Q 18:60-82 (those who refused to provide lodging for Moses and al-Khiḍr) were the inhabitants of Algeciras, a town situated in the Straits of Gibraltar.

Although his legal knowledge was subject to criticism, Ibn Waḍḍāḥ is a central figure in the transmission of the two founding works of western Mālikism, Mālik's *al-Muwaṭṭaʾ* (in the recension (*riwāya*) of Yaḥyā ibn Yaḥyā al-Laythī) and Saḥnūn's *Mudawwana*, the texts of which he corrected. His main contribution to the Mālikī legal school was his attempt to reconcile Mālikī doctrine with prophetic Tradition..

Al-Bunnāhī (= al-Nubāhī), in his work *al-Marqaba al-ʿulyā fī man yastaḥiqq al-qaḍāʾ wa-l-futyā* (Beirut, s.d., p. 33) records that the eastern Mālikī judge Ismāʿīl ibn Isḥāq (d. 895) was asked why Jews could alter (*tabdīl*) their scripture, whereas Muslims could not alter the Qurʾān. His answer was that Q 5:44 proves that the preservation of the text of the Torah was put by God into the hands of the Jews, whereas Q 15:9 proves that the preservation of the Qurʾān is in God's hands, so Muslims cannot alter it. Al-Bunnāhī adds that a Christian asked Ibn Waḍḍāḥ the same question and his answer was the same.

MAIN SOURCES OF INFORMATION

Primary

Ibn Ḥārith al-Khushanī, *Akhbār al-fuqahāʾ wa-l-muḥaddithīn / Historia de los alfaquíes y tradicionistas de al-Andalus*, ed. M.L. Ávila and L. Molina, Madrid, 1992, pp. 122-32, no. 137

Ibn al-Faraḍī, *Kitāb taʾrīkh ʿulamāʾ al-Andalus / Historia virorum doctorum Andalusiae*, ed. F. Codera, 2 vols, Madrid, 1891-92, no. 1134 (Cairo, 1966, no. 1136)

al-Ḥumaydī, *Jadhwat al-muqtabis fī dhikr wulāt al-Andalus*, ed. M. ibn Tāwīt al-Ṭanjī, Cairo, 1952, no. 152
al-Qāḍī ʿIyāḍ, *Tartīb al-madārik wa-taqrīb al-masālik li-maʿrifat aʿlām madhhab Mālik*, ed. M. ibn Tāwīt al-Ṭanjī et al., 8 vols, Rabat, 1966, 1983², iv, 435-40
al-Ḍabbī, *Kitāb bughyat al-multamis fī taʾrīkh rijāl ahl al-Andalus*, ed. F. Codera and J. Ribera, Madrid, 1884, no. 291
al-Dhahabī, *Siyar aʿlām al-nubalāʾ*, ed. Shuʿayb al-Arnāʾūṭ and Huṣayn al-Asad, 23 vols, Beirut, 1985, xiii, pp. 445-46, no. 219
al-Dhahabī, *Tadhkirat al-ḥuffāẓ*, ed. ʿAbd al-Raḥmān Yaḥyā al-Muʿallimī, 4 vols, Hyderabad, 1968-70, ii, pp. 646-48, no. 670
Ibn Farḥūn, *Kitāb al-dībāj al-mudhahhab fī maʿrifat aʿyān ʿulamāʾ al-madhhab*, 2 vols, Cairo, 1972, ii, pp. 179-81

Secondary
L. Molina, 'Un árabe entre muladíes: Muḥammad ibn ʿAbd al-Salām al-Jušanī', *Estudios onomástico-biográficos de al-Andalus. VI*, Madrid, 1994, 337-51 (English trans. 'An Arab among Muwallads: Muḥammad ibn ʿAbd al-Salām al-Khushanī', in M. Marín (ed.), *The formation of al-Andalus. Part 1: History and society*, Aldershot, 1998, 115-128)
M.I. Fierro, 'The introduction of *ḥadīth* in al-Andalus (2nd/8th-3rd/9th centuries)', *Der Islam* 66 (1988) 68-93
M.I. Fierro, 'Bazīʿ, *mawlà* de ʿAbd al-Raḥmān I, y sus descendientes', *Al-Qanṭara* 8 (1987) 99-118
M. Muranyi, 'Das *Kitāb al-siyar* von Abū Isḥāq al-Fazārī. Das Manuskript der Qarawiyyin-Bibliothek zu Fas', *JSAI* 6 (1985) 63-69
Nūrī Muʿammar, *Muḥammad ibn Waḍḍāḥ al-Qurṭubī muʾassis madrasat al-ḥadīth bi-l-Andalus maʿa Baqī ibn Makhlad*, Rabat, 1403/1983
Sezgin, *GAS* i, p. 474
F. Rosenthal, *A history of Muslim historiography*, Leiden, 1952, 1968², p. 521
M. ʿA. Makki, *Ensayo sobre las aportaciones orientales en la España musulmana y su influencia en la formación de la cultura hispano-árabe*, Madrid, 1968, pp. 140, 156, 193-94
Kaḥḥāla xii, p. 94
Makhlūf, *Shajarat al-nūr al-zakiyya fī ṭabaqāt al-mālikiyya*, 2 vols, Cairo, 1950-52, i, p. 76, no. 116
Ziriklī, *Al-aʿlām, qāmūs tarājim li-ashhur al-rijāl wa-l-nisāʾ min al-ʿArab wa-l-mustaʿribīn wa-l-mustashriqīn*, 2nd ed., 10 vols, Cairo, 1954-59, vii, p. 133
Brockelmann, *GAL* S ii, p. 978
F. Pons Boigues, *Ensayo bio-bibliográfico sobre los historiadores y geógrafos arábigo-españoles*, Madrid, 1898, p. 47, no. 7

WORKS ON CHRISTIAN-MUSLIM RELATIONS

Kitāb al-bidaʿ, 'Innovations', *Kitāb al-bidaʿ wa-l-nahy ʿanhā*, 'Innovations and the prohibition of them', *Ittiqāʾ al-bidaʿ*, 'Wariness of innovations'

DATE Probably between 859 and 900
ORIGINAL LANGUAGE Arabic

DESCRIPTION
It includes twelve chapters of uneven length containing prophetic traditions and transmissions from the first generations of Muslims. The material was compiled by Ibn Waḍḍāḥ's pupil Aṣbagh ibn Mālik and consists of what Ibn Waḍḍāḥ heard from his teachers in the east regarding the fact that the religious life of the Muslim community had inevitably undergone a process of gradual corruption (*fasād*) after the passing of the Prophet, so that true Muslims had become rare, innovations were flourishing and traditions disappearing, a process leading to the Last Hour. The 288 transmissions recorded in the *Kitāb al-bidaʿ* deal with the general prohibition of introducing innovations in the rituals and practices of Muslims, as well as with the prohibition of specific innovations such as the use of the rosary, 'following the lore of the Prophet' (*ittibāʿ āthār al-nabī*), and the celebration of non-Muslim festivals. Contact with innovators should be avoided; to walk with a Christian is preferable to doing the same with a heretic (i.e. a Muʿtazilī, cf. ix, p. 21).

SIGNIFICANCE
Ibn Waḍḍāḥ records material concerning the prohibition of celebrations of non-Muslim festivals by Muslims. Part of this material has been preserved not in the extant manuscripts of the *Kitāb al-bidaʿ*, but in al-ʿAzafī's *al-Durr al-munaẓẓam*. In this work, Ibn Waḍḍāḥ is quoted transmitting a tradition from ʿUmar ibn al-Khaṭṭāb stating that Muslims should keep away from the festivals of Jews and Christians. He is also quoted asking the North African jurist Saḥnūn about a custom in al-Andalus in which, during Christian festivals such as the *mīlād* (Nativity of Christ) and the *ʿanṣara* (in the west, birth of St John the Baptist, 24th June), Muslim children visit churches, where they are given presents. Related innovative practices are that the mosque imam accepts presents from children during Christian festivals, that Muslims dress as non-Muslims and that they celebrate

the festivals of *yannayr* (New Year's eve) and the *laylat al-ʿajūz* (the Night of the Old Woman). Ibn Waḍḍāḥ also records material dealing with the religious status of Jerusalem (ix, 22) and the permissibility of deliberately singling out certain mosques to pray in, such as that in Jerusalem (vi, 4a).

MANUSCRIPTS

MS Princeton, Garrett Collection – 070/1

MS Damascus, Dār al-Kutub al-Ẓāhiriyya – 258/1 *ādāb*

EDITIONS AND TRANSLATIONS

M.I. Fierro, *Muḥammad ibn Waḍḍāḥ al-Qurṭubī. Kitāb al-bidaʿ (Tratado contra las innovaciones)*, Madrid, 1988 (2nd edition, based on the Garret and Ẓāhiriyya MSS)

M.I. Fierro, *El "Kitāb al-bidaʿ wa-l-nahy ʿan-hā" de Muḥammad ibn Waḍḍāḥ (siglo III/IX)*, Madrid, 1985 (Diss. Complutense University of Madrid)

Muḥammad ibn Waḍḍāḥ, *al-Bidaʿ wa-l-nahy ʿanhā*, ed. Muḥammad Aḥmad Duhmān, Damascus, 1349 (1930) (repr. Damascus, 1400/1980; Cairo, 1990) (1st edition, based on the Ẓāhiriyya MS)

Later editions (not accessed) by Badr ʿAlī al-Badr, Riyad, 1416/1996; ʿAmr ʿAbd al-Munʿim Sālim, Cairo: Maktabat Ibn Taymiyya, 1416/1996; Muḥammad Ḥasan Ismāʿīl al-Shāfiʿī, Beirut: Dār al-Kutub al-ʿIlmiyya, 1997

STUDIES

J.M. Safran, 'Identity and differentiation in ninth-century al-Andalus', *Speculum* 76 (2001) 573-98

M.I. Fierro, 'The treatises against innovations (*kutub al-bidaʿ*)', *Der Islam* 69 (1992), 204-46

Fierro, *Muḥammad ibn Waḍḍāḥ al-Qurṭubī*

F. de la Granja, 'Fiestas cristianas en al-Andalus (Materiales para su estudio). I: *al-Durr al-munaẓẓam* de al-ʿAzafī', *Al-Andalus* 34 (1969) 1-53, esp. pp. 39-46

Kitāb al-ṣalāt fī l-naʿlayn, 'Praying in sandals'

DATE Probably between 859 and 900

ORIGINAL LANGUAGE Arabic

DESCRIPTION

This lost work dealt with the issue of the permissibility of praying while wearing sandals, an issue debated in the formative period of Islam, with some accepting the practice.

SIGNIFICANCE

M.J. Kister ('Do not assimilate yourselves...: *Lā tashabbahū*', *JSAI* 12 (1989) 321-71) has shown that the issue of the permissibility of praying while wearing sandals was related to the more general issue of *mukhālafat ahl al-kitāb*, i.e. of the need for Muslims to differentiate themselves from Jews and Christians.

MANUSCRIPTS —

EDITIONS AND TRANSLATIONS —

STUDIES

M. Fierro, 'Religious beliefs and practices in al-Andalus in the third/ninth century', *RSO* 66 (1993) 15-33, pp. 27-29

Maribel Fierro 2007

The Debate between Israel of Kashkar and al-Sarakhsī

Author unknown

DATE OF BIRTH Unknown
PLACE OF BIRTH Unknown
DATE OF DEATH Unknown
PLACE OF DEATH Unknown

BIOGRAPHY —

MAIN SOURCES OF INFORMATION

Primary —

Secondary —

WORKS ON CHRISTIAN-MUSLIM RELATIONS

Majlis dhakara[hu] Īliyya muṭrān Naṣībīn ḥaḍarahu Isrāʾīl al-Kaskarī, 'A disputation reported by Elijah, Metropolitan of Nisibis, which Israel of Kashkar attended'. Modern title: 'The Debate between Israel of Kashkar and al-Sarakhsī'

DATE Unknown, probably 2nd half of 9th c.
ORIGINAL LANGUAGE Arabic

DESCRIPTION
This text purports to be a report of a religious debate that took place between the East-Syrian bishop Israel of Kashkar (d. 872, q.v.) and Aḥmad ibn al-Ṭayyib al-Sarakhsī, student of the famous Muslim philosopher and polymath Abū Yūsuf al-Kindī (q.v.). The latter is said to have been the instigator of the disputation, after hearing rumors about the East-Syrian Bishop Israel, reputedly a great scholar and dialectician, who had recently arrived in Baghdad. Al-Kindī is described as urging al-Sarakhsī to take measure of this stranger, because he doubts

that someone who is reputedly intelligent and learned can believe in the irrational doctrines of Christianity.

Al-Sarakhsī then goes out to meet Israel, accompanied by a group of polemicists, among them Jews, Muslims and Muʿtazilīs (who are mentioned separately, as though a group apart from the Muslims).

The first sign of tension between the two men comes at the start, when al-Sarakhsī asks for Israel's *kunyā*, the Arabic name formed by 'Father of' (Abū), and the name of the first son. Israel rejects this familiar Arabic way of addressing people for several reasons, one of which is his claim that it does not have validity in the universal language of reason, which is what should be used in philosophical inquiry.

Next al-Sarakhsī challenges the rationality of Christian doctrine by means of a number of philosophical questions. He asks, for example, if Israel agrees that 8 plus 1 makes 9, insinuating that Christians cannot count when they say that the one Divinity is also three. Israel's counter argument is that even if the total number changes when 1 is added to 8, the essence of the 8 does not change: 'The number merges as a whole in a particular term, but nothing that exists in its essence passes from its nature when the number is taken [and added] to the [other] term' (Moosa, 'A new source', p. 23). Israel advances complicated but convincing philosophical rejoinders to all the Muslim's questions and shows he is more than competent as a logician; his Muslim interlocutor uses the excuse of the afternoon prayer to escape.

Al-Kindī is portrayed as indirectly admitting Israel's triumph when, after receiving a report of the debate, he hangs down his head and forbids al-Sarakhsī to debate with the bishop again. This and similar literary devices, which are intended to show Israel's great learning as well as the superiority of Christianity in philosophical defense of religious truth, serve an apologetic function in this text equal in importance to the actual argumentation.

The debate is presented as a report by an unnamed author who himself knew of the debate through 'Elijah, Metropolitan of the West, who was called ʿAlī ibn ʿUbayd ibn Dāwūd before he became a monk'. In the title of the text in the manuscript, however, his name is given as 'Elijah, Metropolitan of Nisibis'. As Moosa notes, the person in question cannot be the famous 11th-century East-Syrian Elijah of Nisibis, because the Elijah of this text is presented as an eye-witness and the debate takes place during the lifetime of al-Kindī, who died in about

870. The confusion is probably caused by the fact that Elijah of Nisibis was well known for his religious debates with the Muslim *wazīr* Ibn ʿAlī al-Maghribī. The Elijah of our text was in all likelihood the East-Syrian Elijah of Damascus, who was bishop of Jerusalem and metropolitan of Damascus from 893 onwards (Holmberg, *A treatise*, pp. 50-51, 92-93).

The title is also problematic for grammatical reasons; it probably has to be emended as above or else be read as *Majlis dhakara Īliyya muṭrān Naṣībīn ḥaḍrata Isrāʾīl al-Kaskarī*, 'A disputation reported by Elijah, Metropolitan of Nisibis, on behalf of Israel of Kashkar' (Holmberg, *A treatise*, p. 51). Holmberg rejects the first option, because Israel not only attended the disputation but played a main part. However, the anachronistic mention of Elijah of Nisibis in the title probably means that what we have here is a superficial description by a later reader rather than the original title.

SIGNIFICANCE

The debate is a typical example of the genre of literary Christian-Muslim debates in which the fictional setting, including a staged Muslim acknowledgement of Christian triumph, is at least as important as the actual argumentation itself. Holmberg ('Trinitarian terminology') has nonetheless shown convincingly that the philosophical proofs used contain strong thematic and linguistic resemblance to those in Israel's own writings. For this reason, one may regard the text as a reverberation of Israel's voice. Holmberg (*A treatise*, pp. 58, 95) also advances the hypothesis that the work was originally a propaganda pamphlet in support of Israel's candidacy as patriarch. For these reasons, it is more than likely that the text was written during Israel's lifetime.

The text is not known to have circulated widely, as did several better-known texts of this genre. Only one manuscript is presently known, and there are no references to the text in later sources.

MANUSCRIPTS

MS Florence, Biblioteca Medicea Laurenziana – Ar. 299, fols 149v-156r (undated, not before mid-13th c.)

EDITIONS AND TRANSLATIONS

M. Moosa, 'A new source on Aḥmad ibn al-Ṭayyib al-Sarakhsī: Florentine MS Arabic 299', *JAOS* 92 (1972) 19-24 (trans. on pp. 22-24; mistakes in Moosa's trans. are indirectly revealed in Holmberg's studies of the text)

M. Moosa, 'Kitāb fīhi l-shudhūr al-dhahabiyya fī madhhab al-Naṣrāniyya', *Al-majalla l-baṭriyarkiyya l-suryāniyya* n.s. 7 (1969) 189-97, 244-52 (edition in second part, description of manuscript in first part)

STUDIES

G. Troupeau, 'Sur un philosophe de l'école de Bagdad', *Arabica* 40 (1993) 125-26

B. Holmberg, 'The trinitarian terminology of Israel of Kashkar (d. 872)', *Aram* 3 (1991) 53-82

B. Holmberg, *A treatise on the Unity and Trinity of God by Israel of Kashkar (d. 872)*, Lund, 1989, pp. 50-58, 92-96

Barbara Roggema 2008

Euodius the Monk

DATE OF BIRTH Unknown, probably early to middle 9th c.
PLACE OF BIRTH Unknown
DATE OF DEATH Unknown, probably late 9th or early 10th c.
PLACE OF DEATH Unknown

BIOGRAPHY

There is no direct evidence about the life of Euodius. He probably lived in Constantinople, where he was a disciple of Joseph the Hymnographer (Tomadakes, *Iosēph o hymnographos*, pp. 56-57, 99) and a monk in the latter's monastery (though this depends on whether he was the creator of a canon dedicated to Joseph, for while his authorship of this canon is generally accepted, there is insufficient source evidence; see Nikas, *Analecta Hymnica Graeca*). He is the author of a version of the *Martyrdom of the forty-two martyrs of Amorion*, and a refutation of Islam based on Nicetas of Byzantium (q.v.).

MAIN SOURCES OF INFORMATION

Primary —

Secondary

A. Kazhdan, *A history of Byzantine literature (850-1000)*, Athens, 2006, pp. 206-9, 318

A. Rigo, 'Niceta Byzantios, la sua opera e il monaco Evodio', in G. Fiaccadori (ed.) *"In partibus Clius". Scritti in onore di Giovanni Pugliese Carratelli*, Naples, 2006, 147-87, pp. 175-76

PMBZ no. 1682

S. Efthymiades, *Euodios monachos. Oi saranta dyo martyres tou Amoriou*, Athens, 1989, p. 12

A. Kazhdan, 'Hagiographical notes', *Byzantion* 56 (1986) 148-70 (repr. in Kazhdan, *Authors and texts in Byzantium*, Aldershot, 1993), no. 14: Collective death and individual deeds, pp. 152-59

E. Tomadakēs, *Iosēph ho hymnographos. Bios kai ergon*, Athens, 1971, pp. 56-57, 99

C. Nikas, *Analecta Hymnica Graeca*, 13 vols, Rome, 1970, viii (*canones Aprilis*), pp. 390-91

H.-G. Beck, *Kirche und theologische Literatur im byzantinischen Reich*, Munich, 1959, p. 511

BHG 1214
C. Loparev, 'Vizantijskia žitija svjatych VIII-IX vekov', *VV* 17 (1912) 1-224, pp. 76-91

WORKS ON CHRISTIAN-MUSLIM RELATIONS

Martyrion tōn hagiōn tessarakonta dyo tou Christou martyrōn tou Amoriou syngraphen hypo Euodiou monachou, 'The Martyrdom of the forty-two martyrs of Christ of Amorion written by the monk Euodius'

DATE After 855/856 (Kotzampassi, 'To martyrio', p. 127) and probably between 867 and 887 (Nikitin, commentary in Vasilieskij and Nikitin, Skazania, p. 273), or between the 2nd half of the 9th century and the 1st half of the 10th century (Kazhdan, 'Hagiographical notes', 152)
ORIGINAL LANGUAGE Greek

DESCRIPTION
The account in the main text (*Z*), starts with an extensive introduction in which Euodius describes the first appearance and gradual expansion of the Arabs, attributing their capture of Roman provinces, killing of the population and destruction of cities and countryside to the heresies (monotheletism, iconoclasm) introduced and supported by emperors of the 7th-9th centuries (referring by name only to the 'impious' Theophilus, in whose reign the siege of Amorion took place).

An extremely brief account of the siege and fall of Amorion on 15th August 838 (Kolia-Dermitzaki, 'Forty-two martyrs', p. 141, n. 1) is then followed by a detailed description of the hardships of imprisonment in Tarsus of the forty-two captured leaders and other officers of the Byzantine army. The Arabs make strenuous efforts to persuade them to deny their faith, and debates are held between them and Muslim theologians sent by the Caliph al-Muʿtaṣim (r. 833-42), but to no avail (in these debates Euodius furnishes the Christians with arguments borrowed from Nicetas of Byzantium). Finally, after a last attempt to get them to convert by theologians from the new Caliph al-Wāthiq (r. 842-47), they are executed in the seventh year of their imprisonment (6 March 845). The account ends with praise for the martyrs.

It is noteworthy that Euodius treats the martyrs as one group, in contrast to Michael the Synkellos (q.v.) and Sophronius (q.v.), who focus either on single individuals or on parts within the group. This is also the case in the anonymous versions of the martyrdom.

There are two more versions of Euodios' text (*Z*), and a third is an abbreviation:

Version *K*, is part of imperial *Mēnologion* B in MS Mount Athos, Koutloumousiou monastery – 23. This version is almost identical to *Z*, differing only in the epilogue. The epilogue of version *K* has been edited by Kotzampassi, 'To martyrio', pp. 152-53.

Version *M*, in MS Athens, National Library of Greece – 996, differs from versions *Z* and *K* on two points only: the addition of an extensive description of the siege of Amorion, and the omission of the long epilogue contained in these two versions.

Version *A*, the abbreviation (*BHG* 1211), which is contained in imperial *Mēnologion* A, does not include the account of the first appearance and expansion of the Arabs (in the introduction of *Z*), or the explanation that they were sent as punishment for heresy.

SIGNIFICANCE

The account expresses both the military-political and religious nature of the confrontation between Byzantium and Islam in the 9th century, and provides examples of popular Christian and Muslim polemical arguments in refutation of the other religion.

MANUSCRIPTS

Euodios, version *Z*:

MS Moscow, Synod Library – 26 (archim. Vladimir catal. 384)
MS Moscow, Synod Library – 184 (archim. Vladimir catal. 377)
MS Moscow, Synod Library – 161 (archim. Vladimir catal. 379)
MS Munich, Bayerische Staatsbibliothek – 24 (1) fols 11-30v
MS Munich, Bayerische Staatsbibliothek – 524 (1) fols 213-219v, 20, 22v (acephelous *incipit*)
MS Athens, National Library of Greece – 982 (19) fols 155v-170v
MS BNF – 773 (31) fols 403-415
MS BNF – 1500 (11) fols 146-161
MS BNF – 1178 (7) fols 124-135v (acephelous *incipit*)
MS BNF – 1529 (10) fols 121-134
MS BNF – 1604 (1) fols 2-30
MS Vat – 1245 (9) fols 126-140v
MS Vat – 1993 (9) fols 252v-267v

MS Oxford, Bodleian Library – 44 (1) fols 6-21

Version *K*: MS Mount Athos, Koutloumousiou monastery – 23, fols 145-159v

Version *M*: MS Athens, National Library of Greece – 996 (6) fols 45v-58

Version *A*: MS Moscow, Synod Library – 183 (archim. Vladimir catal. 376)

EDITIONS AND TRANSLATIONS

S. Kotzampassi, 'To martyrio tōn saranta dyo martyrōn tou Amoriou. Hagiologika kai hymnologika keimena', *Epistēmonikē Epetēris tēs Philosophikēs Scholēs Aristotēleiou Panepistēmiou Thessalonikēs, periodos B′, Tmēma Philologias* 2 (1992) 109-53, pp. 131-48 (Version *M*)

S. Efthymiades, *Euodios monachos. Oi saranta dyo martyres tou Amoriou* (Modern Greek trans. parallel to the text ed. by Vasilievskij and Nikitin)

V. Latyšev, *Menologii anonymi Byzantini saeculi X quae supersunt fasciculos duos sumptibus Caesareae Academiae Scientiarum e Codice Mosquensi 376 Vlad*, 2 vols in 1, St. Petersburg 1911-12 (repr. Leipzig 1970), i, pp. 190-97 (Version *A* [*alpha*])

V. Vasilievskij and P. Nikitin, *Skazanija o 42 amorijskich mučenikach*, St. Petersburg, 1905, pp. 1-7 (Version *A*), 61-78 (Version *Z*)

Acta Sanctorum, Mart. i, pp. 887-93 (3rd edition, pp. 880-84)

STUDIES

A. Kolia-Dermitzaki, 'The execution of the forty-two martyrs of Amorion. Proposing an interpretation', *Al-Masāq* 14 (2002) 141-62

Kotzampassi, 'To martyrio tōn saranta dyo martyrōn tou Amoriou'

Kazhdan, 'Hagiographical notes'

A.-T. Khoury, *Les théologiens byzantins et l'Islam. Textes et auteurs (VIIIe-XIIIe s.)*, Louvain, 1969, pp. 163-79

BHG 1214 (Euodios' text *Z*), 1211 (Version *A*), 1214a (Version *M*), 1214b (Version *K*)

Vasilievskij and Nikitin, *Skazanija o 42 amorijskich mučenicach*, pp. 272-79 (commentary by Nikitin)

A. Vasiliev, *Grecheskij tekst zhitija soroka dvuch amorijskich muchenikov*, St. Petersburg, 1898, pp. 6-18

R. Abicht and H. Schmidt, 'Quellennachweise zum Codex Suprasliensis, III', *Archiv für slavische Philologie* 18 (1896) 138-55, p. 142

Athina Kolia-Dermitzaki 2008

Euodiou monachou kephalaia tēs pseudōnymou graphēs tou dyssebous Mōamed kai penias, 'Chapters from the forged book of the unbelieving Muḥammad and of destitution'

DATE Last quarter of 9th c.
ORIGINAL LANGUAGE Greek

DESCRIPTION
The *Chapters* by Euodius reproduce the 30 sections of the refutation of the Qur'ān by Nicetas of Byzantium (q.v.) in a concise and more manageable form. Euodius omits the philosophical-theological passages and the demonstration of the Christian faith in Nicetas' original, retaining only Nicetas' polemical arguments against the Muslims (which he also uses in the *Martyrdom of the forty-two martyrs of Amorion*). It must be underlined that, independently of Nicetas, Euodius relates the birth and expansion of Islam to the establishment of monotheletism, following an established pattern which had previously been set by Anastasius of Sinai (q.v.) (*Homilia III de creatione hominis*).

SIGNIFICANCE
Euodius's work presents the information and arguments contained in Nicetas of Byzantium's refutation of the Qur'ān in a briefer and more effective form. These chapters had some influence in Byzantium and, together with Chapter 100 of John of Damascus' *De haeresibus* (q.v.), were used by Euthymius Zygabenus (early 12th c.) for Chapter 28, 'Against the Saracens', of his *Panoplia dogmatica.*

MANUSCRIPTS
MS El Escorial – gr. Ψ.III.8 (463) (13th c.), fols 232r-242r
MS Mount Athos, Megistē Laura – Ω 44 (1854) (15th c.), fols. 123r-128v, 113r-120v, 129r-149v

EDITIONS AND TRANSLATIONS
The work is unedited, but a detailed description is available in Rigo, 'Niceta Byzantios, la sua opera e il monaco Evodio', pp. 168-74

STUDIES
Rigo, 'Niceta Byzantios, la sua opera e il monaco Evodio', pp. 163-82
Khoury, *Les théologiens byzantins et l'Islam*, p. 179, n. 15
E. Trapp, *Manuel II. Palaiologos. Dialoge mit einem 'Perser'*, Vienna, 1966, p. 27

Antonio Rigo 2008

Yūḥannā ibn al-Ṣalt

DATE OF BIRTH Unknown, probably early/mid-9th c.
PLACE OF BIRTH Unknown
DATE OF DEATH Unknown, probably late 9th c.
PLACE OF DEATH Unknown

BIOGRAPHY

Virtually nothing is known about this author. Graf (*GCAL* ii, p. 150) raises the possibility that he is the father of the East-Syrian Catholicos and scholar Ḥanūn ibn Yūḥannā ibn al-Ṣalt (*GCAL* ii, pp. 150-51), which seems likely. If this is right, we may assume that since Ḥanūn was active in the late 9th and early 10th century, Yūḥannā lived in the second half of the 9th century and also belonged to the Church of the East.

The titles of four works of his are known to us only through Paul Sbath, who found them in the private manuscript collection of ʿAbd al-Masīh al-Masʿūdī (d. 1935) from the Baramus monastery in Scetis. Apart from the three titles given below, Sbath also mentions Yūḥannā ibn al-Ṣalt's *Kitāb al-iqnāʿ* ('Persuasion'), against the Jews.

The work on 'astrological medicine' published under his name (F. Klein-Franke, *Iatromathematics in Islam. A study on Yuhanna ibn Salt's book on "Astrological Medicine"*, Hildesheim, 1984), as well as the theological treatises published by Paul Sbath (*Traités religieux, philosophiques et moraux, extraits des oeuvres d'Isaac de Nineve (VIIe siècle) par Ibn al-Salt (IXe siècle)*, Cairo, 1934) are the work of Ḥanūn and not of Yūḥannā.

MAIN SOURCES OF INFORMATION

Primary —

Secondary

S. Rosenkranz, *Die jüdisch-christliche Auseinandersetzung unter islamischer Herrschaft, 7.-10. Jahrhundert*, Bern, 2004, p. 55.
B. Landron, *Chrétiens et musulmans en Irak*, Paris, 1994, p. 88.
Graf, *GCAL* ii, pp. 149-50.

WORKS ON CHRISTIAN-MUSLIM RELATIONS

Kitāb al-burhān, 'The Proof'

DATE Unknown, 2nd half 9th c.?
ORIGINAL LANGUAGE Arabic

DESCRIPTION
This work is a refutation of Islam, according to Sbath, *Fihris*, i, p. 7.

SIGNIFICANCE
Since the work is inaccessible, the precise contents cannot be known, but in all likelihood it followed the trend of 9th-century Arabic Christian treatises against Islam. It is not cited in later works and we may therefore conclude that it had no significant impact on later Christian apologists.

MANUSCRIPTS
MS Cairo – Ṣalīb (inaccessible MS in the private collection of ʿAbd al-Masīḥ Ṣalīb al-Masʿūdī, cf. Sbath, *Fihris* i, p. 7)
EDITIONS AND TRANSLATIONS —
STUDIES —

Kitāb dalīl al-ḥāʾir, 'Guide for the confused'

DATE Unknown, 2nd half of 9th c.?
ORIGINAL LANGUAGE Arabic

DESCRIPTION
An apologetic exposé of the Christian religion, according to Sbath, *Fihris* i, p. 7.

SIGNIFICANCE
The work may have been contained arguments in defense of Christianity that were specifically designed to respond to the challenge of Islamic doctrine, but this cannot be determined until a manuscript can be accessed.

MANUSCRIPTS
MS Cairo – Ṣalīb (inaccessible MS in the private collection of ʿAbd al-Masīḥ Ṣalīb al-Masʿūdī, cf. Sbath, *Fihris* i, p. 7)
EDITIONS AND TRANSLATIONS —
STUDIES —

Kitāb al-hudā, 'Guidance'

DATE Unknown, 2nd half of 9th c.?
ORIGINAL LANGUAGE Arabic

DESCRIPTION
The work is described by Sbath (*Fihris*, i, p. 7) as an exposé of Christian doctrine and ethics. Considering the title, it probably had an apologetic purpose.

SIGNIFICANCE
The work may have contained arguments in defense of Christianity that were specifically designed in response to the challenge of Islamic doctrine, but this cannot be determined until manuscripts become accessible.

MANUSCRIPTS
MS Cairo – Ṣalīb (inaccessible MS in the private collection of ʿAbd al-Masīḥ Ṣalīb al-Masʿūdī, cf. Sbath, *Fihris* i, p. 7)

EDITIONS AND TRANSLATIONS —

STUDIES —

Barbara Roggema 2007

The Life and Passion of Kostanti-Kaxay

An anonymous monk from Kartli (Georgia)

DATE OF BIRTH Unknown, probably 9th c.
PLACE OF BIRTH Probably Kartli (Georgia)
DATE OF DEATH Unknown, probably late 9th c.
PLACE OF DEATH Unknown

BIOGRAPHY

Nothing is known about the author's personal circumstances, except that he was a monk and that he lived during the reign of the Byzantine Empress Theodora (r. 842-67), at the time when Muslims were carrying out persecutions of the Christian population throughout Kartli, Georgia, as can be deduced from his work *The life and passion of Kostanti-Kaxay*.

He was acquainted with Christian literature and used passages of the Greek version, or an otherwise unknown translation, of Gregory of Alexandria's *Life of John Chrysostom*. One can also detect the influence of Aristotle's philosophy and of the Apology of Marcianus Aristides. In addition, the author used Georgian hagiographical works, such as *The Passion of Eustatios of Mcxeta* and Ioane Sabanisdze's *Martyrdom of Abo of Tbilisi*. He also used the letter which the Empress Theodora wrote to Georgians after Kostanti's martyrdom in praise of Kartvelian/Georgian Christianity.

MAIN SOURCES OF INFORMATION

Primary —

Secondary
See below

WORKS ON CHRISTIAN-MUSLIM RELATIONS

Cxorebaj da c'amebaj c'midisa moc'amisa k'ost'ant'isi kartvelisaj, romeli ic'ama babiloelta mepisa dzaparis mier, 'The Life and Passion of the holy martyr Kostanti the Kartvelian, who was tortured by Jaʿfar, King of the Babylonians'. Abbreviated title: 'The Life and Passion of Kostanti-Kaxay'. Latin: '*Vita Constantini Hiberi*'

DATE Probably late 9th c.
ORIGINAL LANGUAGE Georgian (nusxuri script, asomtavruli script and mxedruli script)

DESCRIPTION

The Life of Kostanti-Kaxay is a short work, occupying just nine pages of Abuladze's critical edition. It is a source for the period of Arab rule in eastern Caucasia and the situation in the southwestern Georgian regions during the era of the early Kartvelian Bagratids.

The *Life* traces this Georgian saint from his birth, to his life during the reign of the Byzantine Emperor Michael III and his amassing of considerable wealth, to his public confession of Christianity, his arrest at the advanced age of 85 years, his appearance before the Muslim general Bugha the Elder and his imprisonment in Samarra, his resistance to conversion and ultimately his beheading ordered by the ʿAbbasid Caliph al-Mutawakkil (r. 847-61).

Besides being a monk, the biographer describes himself as a contemporary of Kostanti, saying that the martyr 'lived during our time', when Queen Theodora, the famous Byzantine empress who opposed iconoclasm, reigned as a servant of God (cap.1). In the same passage, Kostanti's biographer also mentions her son Michael III (r. 842-67).

There is no reason to doubt the historical existence of Kostanti-Kaxay in the 9th century, but the date of his received *Life* cannot be determined easily. It could obviously not have been written before his death in 853. Certain internal features, including: the use of the old term Zena–Sopeli, the concept *q'oveli* Kartli, and the absence of the medieval Georgian *koronikon* system in the one instance that a specific date is given, may point to a date in the late 9th century. Scholars disagree about the significance of the last observation: Abashidze is of the opinion that the *koronikon* was widely used by this time and that its absence is puzzling, while Rapp holds that although the *koronikon* had been invented by this time, its application remained relatively sporadic until the 10th/11th century. The final part of the *Life* closely connects Kartli to the Byzantine Empire. This could be another indication of its having been composed during the early Bagratid period (9th/10th century).

Kostanti-Kaxay was well-known throughout Christian Caucasia, his capture and torture by Bugha being confirmed by local sources. There is a stone inscription on the Ateni Sioni cathedral in Kartli, near Gori, which mentions that 'on 5 August, a Saturday, in koronikon 73, the Islamic year 239, Bugha burnt the city of Tbilisi and captured the amir Sahak and killed him. And in the same month, on 26 August, a Saturday, Zirak took Kaxay and his son Tarxuji prisoner' (T'. Barnaveli, *At'enis sionis c'arc'erebi*, Tbilisi, 1957, p. 18). This testifies that it happened between 12 June 853 and 1 June 854.

The Armenian historian Thomas Artsruni was also acquainted with Kostanti, and he confirms the existence of Kostanti in the 9th century (R.W. Thomson, *Thomas Artsruni. History of the house of the Artsrunik'*, Detroit, 1985, pp. 251-52) and his execution, although a striking difference lies in the fact that Artsruni's account mentions two martyrs, Kaxay and his companion Sevordi. Interestingly, another Armenian source of the early 10th century, refers to seven men being martyred under Bugha in 302 of the Armenian era (Yovhannes Drasxanakertc'i, *History of Armenia*, trans. K.H. Maksoudian, Atlanta, 1987, pp. 121-22), which according to Maksoudian agrees with the very year of Kostanti's martyrdom.

Kostanti was canonized by the Georgian Church.

SIGNIFICANCE

Probably composed in the late 9th century, this text traces the life of a Georgian saint who lived during the reign of the Byzantine Emperor Michael III and his mother Theodora and was martyred by the ʿAbbasids after refusing to convert to Islam. It mentions his pilgrimage to Jerusalem and the Jordan, which confirms that Georgians visited these sacred places at the time. The text is also important as a source for the history of Georgian-Byzantine relations.

MANUSCRIPTS

MS Tbilisi, Kekelidze Institute of Manuscripts – A-130, fols 81-85 (copied in 1713 by G. Saginov in the *nusxuri* script)

MS Tbilisi, Kekelidze Institute of Manuscripts – A-170, fols 49-51 (copied in 1733 by the Hierodeacon Ioanne in the nusxuri script)

MS Tbilisi, Kekelidze Institute of Manuscripts – A-176, fols 72-77 (copied in the 18th c. by unknown scribes in the nusxuri script. Some inserted pages belonging to the 17th c.)

MS Tbilisi, Kekelidze Institute of Manuscripts – H-2077, fols 49-51 (copied in 1736 at Suetitsxoveli (Mcxeta) by Archpriest Alexi in nusxhuri script, with asomtavruli table of contents and initial letters; includes images of 26 saints)

MS Tbilisi, Kekelidze Institute of Manuscripts – H-1672, fols 361-369 (copied in 1740 at Sioni (Tbilisi) by Archdeacon Ahron in nusxuri script)

MS Tbilisi, Kekelidze Institute of Manuscripts – H-2121, fols 66-70 (copied in 1748 by a certain Nikolozi in nusxuri)

MS St Petersburg, Institute of Oriental Studies – H-22, fols 51-55 (copied in 1842 by Guruli Swimon Tabidze)

MS Tbilisi, Kekelidze Institute of Manuscripts – S-3637, fols 36-39 (copied in 1838 by Prince Teimuraz in mxedruli script)

EDITIONS AND TRANSLATIONS

M.D. Abashidze and S.H. Rapp Jr, 'The life and passion of Kostanti-Kaxay', *Le Muséon* 117 (2004) 137-73 (repr. of Abuladze's edition with English trans., introduction and annotation)

B. Balxamišvili, 'K'ost'ant'i k'axis mart'vilobis met'aprast'uli redakcia', in *Lit'eraturuli dziebani* 16 (1986) 252-60

N. Vacnadze and K. K'ucia, *Cxorebaj da c'amebaj c'midisa moc'amisa k'ost'ant'isi kartvelisaj, romeli ic'ama babiloelta mepisa dzaparis mier / Zhitie Muchenichestvo sviatogo muchenika Kostanti gruzina, kotoryi byl zamuchen tsarem Vavilonian Dzhafarom*, Tbilisi, 1978, pp. 50-65 (edition), pp. 66-79 (Russian trans.)

I. Abuladze, *Dzveli kartuli agiograpiuli lit'erat'uris dzeglebi*, 6 vols, Tbilisi, 1963, i, part ii, pp. 164-72

S. Q'ubaneišvili, *Dzveli kartuli literaturis krestomatia* I, Tbilisi, 1946, pp. 74-80

P. Peeters, 'De S. Constantino, martyre in Babilonia', *Acta Sanctorum, Novembris*, vi, Louvain, 1925, pp. 541-63 (Latin trans. based on Sabinin's edition)

G.P. Sabinin, *Sakartvēlos samotxe*, St Petersburg, 1882, pp. 363-70 (not a critical edition)

STUDIES

Abashidze and Rapp, 'The life and passion of Kostanti-Kaxay'

D. Rayfield, *The literature of Georgia. A history*, Oxford, 1994, pp. 37-38

Balxamišvili, 'K'ost'ant'i k'axis mart'vilobis met'aprast'uli redakcia'

K'. K'ek'elidze, *Dzveli kartuli lit'erat'uris ist'oria* I, Tbilisi, 1980, pp. 520-22

Vacnadze and K'ucia, *Cxorebaj da c'amebaj c'midisa moc'amisa k'ost'ant'isi kartvelisaj, romeli ic'ama babiloelta mepisa dzaparis mier*

K'. K'ek'elidze, 'K'ost'ant'i K'axi's mart'viloba da vinaoba', *TSU moambe*, 1976, vii, pp. 160-73

E. Cagareišvili, *Sakartveloši buɣa turkis laškrobis sak'itxisatvis, Macne – ist'oriis*, Tbilisi, 1975, iv, pp. 105-14

I. Dzavaxišvili, *Dzveli kartuli saist'orio mc'erloba (V-XVIII)*, Tbilisi, 1945, pp. 86-90 (repr. in Dzavaxišvili, *Txzulebani*, 12 vols, Tbilisi, 1977, viii)

K'. K'ek'elidze, *Konspektivni course istorii drevnegruzinskoiy literaturi*, Tbilisi, 1938, pp. 23-24

P. Peeters, 'De S. Constantino, martyre in Babilonia'

Medea A. Abashidze 2008

Abū l-ʿAbbās ʿĪsā ibn Zayd

DATE OF BIRTH Unknown, early/mid-9th c.?
PLACE OF BIRTH Unknown (probably Iraq)
DATE OF DEATH Unknown, end of 9th c.?
PLACE OF DEATH Unknown (probably Iraq, perhaps in or near al-Anbār or Baghdad)

BIOGRAPHY

Very little is known about this East-Syrian author. The monk Ḥanūn ibn Yūḥannā ibn al-Ṣalt, who outlived him, praised his piety, intellect and generosity, recounted a conversation that Abū l-ʿAbbās had once held with the Catholicos John III bar Narsai (in office 884-92), and related that he himself had borrowed a book of Mār Isḥāq's writings from him (see Sbath, *Traités religieux*, pp. 54-55).

MAIN SOURCES OF INFORMATION

Primary —

Secondary

B. Landron, *Chrétiens et musulmans en Irak*, Paris, 1994, p. 88
GCAL ii, p. 118
Sbath, *Fihris*, Supplément, p. 10
P. Sbath, *Traités religieux, philosophiques et moraux extraits des œuvres d'Isaac de Ninive (VIIe s.) par Ibn as-Salt (IXe s.)*, Cairo, 1934, pp. 54-55 (Arabic text), 109-10 (French trans.)

WORKS ON CHRISTIAN-MUSLIM RELATIONS

Kitāb al-iqnāʿ, 'Persuasion'

DATE Late 9th c.
ORIGINAL LANGUAGE Arabic

DESCRIPTION

Sbath describes the book as a work of Christian apologetic. Until a copy is found, however, we cannot be certain that it was directed towards Muslims.

SIGNIFICANCE

Each small entry of this sort contributes to our sense of the energy that the Arabic-speaking East-Syrian community of the 9th century dedicated to the Christian apologetic enterprise.

MANUSCRIPTS

MS Aleppo, Shukrī Naḥḥās Collection (1267/8) (inaccessible MS in private collection; see Sbath, *Fihris*, Supplément, p. 10, no. 2524)

EDITIONS AND TRANSLATIONS —

STUDIES —

Mark N. Swanson 2008

Abū l-Faraj Saʿīd ibn ʿAlī l-Anbārī

DATE OF BIRTH Unknown, early/mid-9th c.?
PLACE OF BIRTH Probably in or near the town of al-Anbār
DATE OF DEATH Unknown, late 9th c.?
PLACE OF DEATH Unknown, perhaps in or near the town of al-Anbār

BIOGRAPHY

Virtually nothing is known of this author. According to Sbath (*Fihris*, Supplément, p. 10), he was a scholar who belonged to the East-Syrian community and who lived in the 9th century. His *nisba*, al-Anbārī, suggests both a place of origin (the town of al-Anbār) as well as a possible connection with the al-Anbārī family of scholars and civil servants, the best known of whom was Abū Nūḥ al-Anbārī (q.v.).

MAIN SOURCES OF INFORMATION

Primary —

Secondary

B. Landron, *Chrétiens et musulmans en Irak*, Paris, 1994, p. 88
Graf, *GCAL* ii, p. 118
Sbath, *Fihris*, Supplément, p. 10

WORKS ON CHRISTIAN-MUSLIM RELATIONS

Kitāb al-burhān, 'The Proof'

DATE Unknown, 9th c.?
ORIGINAL LANGUAGE Arabic

DESCRIPTION

Like several other Arabic Christian works entitled *Kitāb al-burhān*, this was likely an apology for the Christian faith in response to Muslims' questions and criticisms.

SIGNIFICANCE

We cannot say much about the significance of the work since we do not know its contents. However, its very existence, taken together with other evidence, bears witness to a lively apologetic enterprise among the Arabic-speaking East-Syrian Christian community of Iraq in the 9th century.

MANUSCRIPTS

MS Aleppo, Shukrī Naḥḥās Collection (1281/2) (inaccessible MS in private collection; see: Sbath, *Fihris*, Supplément, p. 10, no. 2525)

EDITIONS AND TRANSLATIONS —

STUDIES —

Mark N. Swanson 2008

Abū l-Khayr ʿĪsā ibn Hibat Allāh

DATE OF BIRTH Unknown, early/mid-9th c.?
PLACE OF BIRTH Unknown, probably Iraq
DATE OF DEATH Unknown, late 9th c.?
PLACE OF DEATH Unknown, probably Iraq

BIOGRAPHY

Virtually nothing is known about this author, identified by Sbath (*Fihris*, Supplément, p. 9) as a 9th-century scholar and member of the East-Syrian community.

MAIN SOURCES OF INFORMATION

Primary —

Secondary
B. Landron, *Chrétiens et musulmans en Irak*, Paris, 1994, p. 88
Graf, *GCAL* ii, p. 119
Sbath, *Fihris*, Supplément, p. 9

WORKS ON CHRISTIAN-MUSLIM RELATIONS

Kitāb al-hidāya, 'Guidance'

DATE Unknown, mid-/late 9th c.?
ORIGINAL LANGUAGE Arabic

DESCRIPTION
Sbath (*Fihris*, Supplément, p. 9) identifies this book as a work of Christian apologetic. It must be a work of some considerable length, as an abridgement of it is also known (see below).

SIGNIFICANCE
We cannot say much about the significance of the work since we do not know its contents. However, its very existence, taken together with other evidence, bears witness to a lively apologetic enterprise among the Arabic-speaking East-Syrian community of Iraq in the 9th century.

MANUSCRIPTS
MS Aleppo, Shukrī Naḥḥās Collection (1294/5) (inaccessible MS in private collection, according to Sbath, *Fihris*, Supplément, p. 9, no. 2520)
EDITIONS AND TRANSLATIONS —
STUDIES —

Kitāb al-kifāya, 'Sufficiency'

DATE Unknown, mid-/late 9th c.?
ORIGINAL LANGUAGE Arabic

DESCRIPTION
According to Sbath (*Fihris*, Supplément, 9), this book is an abridgement of the author's apologetic treatise *Kitāb al-hidāya*.

SIGNIFICANCE
See previous work. The fact that this work is an abridgement of the author's longer treatise suggests that someone valued Abū l-Khayr's apologetic capacity and desired to make it accessible to readers who could not afford or manage the larger book.

MANUSCRIPTS
MS Aleppo, Shukrī Naḥḥās Collection (1294/5) (inaccessible MS in private collection; see Sbath, *Fihris*, Supplément, p. 9, no. 2521)
EDITIONS AND TRANSLATIONS —
STUDIES —

Mark N. Swanson 2008

Ḥadīth Wāṣil al-Dimashqī

Unknown author

DATE OF BIRTH Unknown
PLACE OF BIRTH Unknown
DATE OF DEATH Unknown
PLACE OF DEATH Unknown

BIOGRAPHY —

MAIN SOURCES OF INFORMATION

Primary —

Secondary —

WORKS ON CHRISTIAN-MUSLIM RELATIONS

Ḥadīth Wāṣil al-Dimashqī, 'The Account of Wāṣil al-Dimashqī'

DATE Possibly 9th c.
ORIGINAL LANGUAGE Arabic

DESCRIPTION

The story starts with a certain Bashīr, a Roman who had been captured as a youth by the Muslims 'during the rule of the Umayyads' and showed all signs of converting, but later fled back to Byzantine territory where he was given noble status and possessions. A band of captured Muslims are brought to him and he questions them. One of them, Wāṣil 'from the people of Damascus', an older man and a noble who is versed in *kalām*, at first refuses to answer his questions, but then the two dispute over the status of Christ, with Wāṣil showing that the two spirits in the one body, as Christians believe, must have been at odds, and that Jesus' human traits rule out his divinity.

Bashīr renews the argument the next day, when he brings a priest, who offers to baptize Wāṣil. But Wāṣil reduces the priest to silence, whereupon he is taken to 'the king', who has him dispute with 'the head of the Christians'. Undaunted, Wāṣil argues that, while Christians agree that Jesus was entangled in Mary's womb, they do not allow their priests to have relations with women, and then he compares Jesus with Old Testament figures to show that their miracles were the equal of his and thus prohibit divinizing him but not them. He also exposes the inconsistency in Jesus' allowing Mary to suffer the agonies of witnessing his passion rather than killing her to spare her.

In exasperation, the king has Wāṣil taken to the main church, where he recites the call to prayer, expostulating that it is appropriate to remember God in such a place. Finally, Wāṣil raises the question of worshipping 'what they have made with their own hands', although this has no Gospel warrant. The king then orders such things – icons – to be destroyed, has Wāṣil returned to Damascus, and persecutes his own priests and nobles because they could not withstand the Muslim.

It is not clear by how far the incidents of this story, which is set in Umayyad times, predate the time of composition. Griffith shows that many of the arguments employed by Wāṣil have parallels in 9th-century Christian works, and tentatively suggests a date in that century. He also speculates that Wāṣil may be identified as Wāṣil ibn ʿAṭāʾ (d. 749), the founder of the Muʿtazila, that the Byzantine 'king' may be the emperor Leo III, and more securely he identifies the Byzantine noble Bashīr as the Bēsḗr who appears in accounts from the early 9th century onwards in Christian and Muslim traditions as a Christian who converted to Islam and then back. Intriguingly, this Bashīr/ Bēsḗr is identified in the Greek sources as a supporter of iconoclasm (Griffith, pp. 293-98). There is no mention of this in the Arabic account (assuming the author knew about it), though its absence increases the impact of its climax, where it is Wāṣil's argumentative brilliance alone that forces the emperor to order the destruction of icons.

SIGNIFICANCE

If the work is 9th century, its composition shows how elements from earlier history, including polemical *topoi*, were being combined by this time into literary accounts to prove the superiority of Islam, and the confidence of its proponents, even in the most intimidating and awe-inspiring circumstances. It thus serves to strengthen and encourage Muslims, possibly in the face of Byzantine aggression.

The presence of two fragments among Cairo Genizah finds prompts Szilágyi ('Christian books', p. 129*) to suggest that this and works like it influenced Jewish anti-Muslim polemic.

MANUSCRIPTS

MS Leiden – Oriental 951 (2) fols 22v-25r (early or late 14th c.; see Griffith, 'Bashīr/Bēsér', p. 299)

MS St Petersburg, Russian National Library – Yevr-Arab. II 1543, comprising two fragments, 11th c. (= Griffith edition, pp. 314, 320; see Szilágyi, 'Christian books', p. 128*)

EDITIONS AND TRANSLATIONS

S.H. Griffith, 'Bashīr/Bēsér, boon companion of the Byzantine Emperor Leo III. The Islamic recension of his story in *Leiden Oriental MS* 951 (2)', *Le Muséon* 103 (1990) 293-327, pp. 313-27 (edition and trans., with L.B. Miller)

STUDIES

K. Szilágyi, 'Christian books in Jewish libraries: fragments of Christian Arabic writings from the Cairo Genizah', *Ginzei Qedem* 2 (2006) 107*-162*

Griffith, 'Bashīr/Bēsér', pp. 301-12

M. Steinschneider, *Polemische und apologetische Literatur in arabischer Sprache zwischen Muslimen, Christen und Juden*, Leipzig, 1877, p. 44

David Thomas 2007

Ghewond

Łewond, Lewond

DATE OF BIRTH Unknown
PLACE OF BIRTH Unknown
DATE OF DEATH Unknown
PLACE OF DEATH Unknown

BIOGRAPHY

Nothing is known about Ghewond except that he held the clerical rank of *vardapet*, indicating that he was an unmarried priest with superior theological training who was responsible for doctrinal instruction and the maintenance of orthodox belief. His *History* was sponsored by Lord Shapuh Bagratuni, and a broad sympathy towards the Bagratuni house may be discerned in it. Unlike the *History* attributed to Sebeos (q.v.), however, the final notices do not focus upon the exploits of members of this princely family, making the sponsorship of Shapuh rather hard to fathom. This introduces the vexed subject of when the *History* was compiled and which Shapuh Bagratuni commissioned it.

MAIN SOURCES OF INFORMATION

Primary

K. Ezean, *Patmut'iwn Ghewondeay metsi vardepeti Hayots'*, St Petersburg, 1887

Secondary

T.W. Greenwood, *A History of Armenia in the seventh and eighth centuries*, Oxford, 2000 (Diss. University of Oxford)

J.-P. Mahé, 'Le problème de l'authenticité et de la valeur de la Chronique de Łewond', in Centre de Recherches d'Histoire et de Civilisation Byzantines, *L'Arménie et Byzance. Histoire et culture*, Paris, 1996, 119-26

B. Martin-Hisard, 'L'Empire byzantin dans l'œuvre de Łewond', in *L'Arménie et Byzance*, 135-44

Z. Arzoumanian, *History of Lewond, the eminent vardapet of the Armenians*, Philadelphia, 1982

WORKS ON CHRISTIAN-MUSLIM RELATIONS

Patmutʻiwn Ghewondeay, ʻHistory of Ghewondʼ (excluding the Letter of Leo III to the Caliph ʻUmar II, [q.v.])

DATE Late 8th or late 9th c.
ORIGINAL LANGUAGE Armenian

DESCRIPTION
Traditionally, the *History* has been treated as a product of the late 8th century, largely on the basis of its chronological scope, which extends to the year 789, the identification of its sponsor Shapuh Bagratuni as the shadowy son of Smbat Bagratuni, who was killed in 775, and quite simply in the absence of any other evidence. A minority of scholars, however, argue that the compilation should be re-dated to late 9th century. This requires the sponsor to be identified as a different Shapuh Bagratuni, the compiler of another Armenian History, which is no longer extant but which is thought to have covered the period between 792 and 884. More significantly, the *History* of Ghewond asserts that 'the scepter of kingship shall return very soon to the house of Tʻorgom', i.e. the Armenian nation. Arguably, this is not the prediction of a contemporary late 8th-century author but rather the perception of a late 9th-century author who had witnessed the restoration of an Armenian kingdom – Ashot I Bagratuni was crowned on 26 August 884. This contention is supported by several instances when Bagratuni princes are portrayed as reluctant opponents of the caliph. Such sensitivity is surprising until one remembers that Ashot I received his crown from the caliph; these episodes simultaneously apologize for and justify the conspicuous later 9th-century loyalty of the Bagratuni house to the caliph. This would then make Ghewond's *History* a precursor to Shapuh's lost *History*, sketching the oppression experienced by Armenia in the 8th century and thereby setting the triumph of Ashot I in sharper relief. This re-dating of the text does not mean that the whole text is without historical merit, but it does undermine one longstanding assumption – that the final chapters reflect the perceptions and knowledge of a contemporary and thereby possess a particular significance.

The scope of the *History* extends from the death of Muḥammad in 632 to the depredations suffered by the Armenian church at the hands of a rapacious governor in 789. The coverage is uneven, both chronologically and thematically. Whilst the list of Byzantine emperors is limited to those involved with Armenia in some way, the caliphal sequence is complete and includes several brief character sketches, some surprisingly positive – ʿAbd-al Malik was 'provoked by the evil-minded Satan' but ʿUmar II was 'nobler than all other men of his race'. Intriguingly, the compiler used this sequence as a chronological skeleton upon which he mounted and arranged the other extracts and notices. All other lists of caliphs preserved in Armenian sources are free-standing sequences. It is likely that this underlying list of caliphs was integrated with the sequence of 8th-century Arab governors and administrators of Armenia. Tellingly, this sequence tallies with the numismatic record. Two very detailed notices recording the Khazar raids into the eastern Caucasus in 730 and 764, and the military responses, should probably be associated with this source. The case for such a source, decidedly non-Armenian in character, is strong without being conclusive. Its exploitation may indicate a blurring of cultural and linguistic boundaries as well as a dearth of Armenian historical writing across the relevant period.

Although the *History* does not offer any explicit justification for the writing of history, the work as a whole can be viewed as a commentary on the interaction of Armenians and Muslims across this century and a half of direct engagement. That relationship is portrayed in predominantly, although not exclusively, negative terms, with attention focused upon military operations within Armenia or involving Armenians and the financial burdens imposed upon Armenia. Arab governors tend to be presented as harsh oppressors, eager to extract the maximum return and swift to crush any attempted rebellion. Such passages, which often have the character of laments, may be based upon actual events, but tend to be thoroughly infused with biblical images and allusions, implying substantial reworking and literary development at the expense of historical detail. Other passages report the actions and sometimes the martyrdoms of individual Armenian princes. These may well derive from epic princely biographies and hagiographies, arguably of oral rather than written origin.

Confrontation is, however, only one of the contexts employed in the *History* of Ghewond to outline the engagement of Christians and Muslims. An apologetic tone can be detected in passages reporting the reluctance of members of the Bagratuni house to join various uprisings. Evidently, the Armenian elite was divided between those who believed their best interests were to be served through collaboration and those who saw armed resistance or exile as the only courses of action available to them. Perhaps unintentionally, the *History* of Ghewond attests the different responses within the Armenian elite to the consolidation and extension of control over Armenia at the time of the ʿAbbasids. This can be traced in terms of administrative sophistication and down-reach, and in terms of increasing Arab settlement within Armenia. This more rigorous attitude to the government of Armenia can be contrasted with the more limited regime operated during the Umayyad era, when the leading Armenian princely families retained substantial rights and privileges, not least to collect and remit taxes and to bear arms. The ʿAbbasid reaction to this *laissez-faire* approach may also be linked to the military support given by Armenian princes to Marwān ibn Muḥammad.

Thus, this *History* explores the impact of the Islamic world upon Armenia and Armenians, and the progress of that relationship. Such a composition would have had greatest meaning when the relationship between the caliphate and Armenia was current and ongoing rather than historic, when the ʿAbbasids controlled the whole of Armenia and thus before the Byzantine empire began to make inroads from the west at the start of the 9th century.

The authenticity of the text has been questioned by Gerö. He advanced a radical hypothesis, that the original text comprised a local Armenian chronicle of the late 8th century, which was then substantially reworked between the 11th and 13th centuries by an unknown author who transformed it into a universal history. Gerö does not explain why such a reworking was necessary at this time, nor the highly unusual character of the postulated original work. Mahé has refuted Gerö's interpretation and reiterated the conventional argument that the text has always existed in its present form. Close comparison between the early 11th-century *Universal History* of Stephen of Taron and the *History* of Ghewond confirms that the text of Ghewond available to and exploited by Stephen already possessed much supranational material.

SIGNIFICANCE

Traditionally, the significance of the *History* of Ghewond lay in its purported late 8th-century date and its account of the contemporary devastation of Armenia. The date of composition is no longer secure, however, and there is a very real possibility that the *History* is a late 9th-century composition. There must be significant doubts over the historical accuracy of some parts of the text, which seem to have been heavily reworked, with biblical themes and parallels now to the fore. Nevertheless, the *History* of Ghewond is an important witness to the development of Christian-Muslim relations in the 7th and 8th centuries, from initial confrontation in the conquest era to client management and relative detachment in Umayyad times, and finally to the emergence of an independent provincial administration at the expense of native Armenian princely houses, the majority of which chose to rebel or emigrate rather than suffer a continued and inevitable decline in their fortunes. Although instances of glorious, if futile, resistance prevail, a minority of passages stress cooperation and coexistence, not least by members of the Bagratuni family after the ʿAbbasid take-over. These indicate a wider range of reactions to the arrival of the Muslims than is usually credited.

MANUSCRIPTS

MS Yerevan, Matenadaran – 1902 (? late 13th c.)

EDITIONS AND TRANSLATIONS

R. Bedrossian, *Ghewond's History*, 2006, at http://rberosian.com/ghewint.htm (trans., excluding chs 13 and 14)

Arzoumanian, *History of Lewond* (full English trans. with brief commentary)

A. Ter-Ghevondyan, *Ghevond Patmut'yun*, Yerevan, 1982 (modern Armenian trans. and commentary)

K. Ezean, *Patmutʻiwn Ghewondeay metsi vardepeti Hayotsʻ*, St Petersburg, 1887 (edition)

STUDIES

Greenwood, *History of Armenia*

M. van Esbroeck, 'La politique arménienne de Byzance de Justinien II à Léon III', *Studi sull'oriente cristiano* 2 (1998) 111-20

L.L. Khachʻatryan, 'Grabari dardzavatsayin miavorneri dzevabanakan-kaṛutsʻvatskʻayin tipern ĕst Łewond vardapeti 'Patmutʻiwn' erki', *Lraber* 597 (1998) 178-84

Mahé, 'Le problème de l'authenticité'

Martin-Hisard, 'L'Empire byzantin dans l'œuvre de Łewond'

G. Gerö, *Byzantine iconoclasm during the reign of Leo III with particular attention to the oriental sources*, Louvain, 1973, pp. 153-71 (Appendix 2, 'The authenticity of the Leo-Umar correspondence')

Gh. Alishan, 'Surb Ghewond erētsʻ Vanandatsʻi', *Bazmavēp* 109 (1951) 235-43, 325-30; 110 (1952) 20-26, 78-86

N. Adontsʿ, ʻGhewond ew Khorenatsʿi, kʿnnutʿiwn H.N. Akineani tesutʿeanʼ, *Hayrenik* 11/8 (1933) 79-90; 11/9 (1933) 120-26
N. Akinean, ʻGhewond eretsʿ patmagir: matenagrakan-patmakan usumnasirutʾiwn mĕʼ, *Handēs Amsoreay* 43 (1929) 330-48, 458-72, 593-619, 705-18 (repr. in N. Akinean, *Matenagrakan hetazotutʿiwnner*, III, Vienna, 1930)

Tim Greenwood 2007

The Life of Michael the Synkellos

Unknown author

DATE OF BIRTH 1st half of the 9th c.?
PLACE OF BIRTH Unknown
DATE OF DEATH 2nd half of the 9th c.?
PLACE OF DEATH Unknown

BIOGRAPHY

It used to be thought that the *Life* of Michael the Synkellos was written soon after 850, and that the author, a monk from the Chora monastery in Constantinople, was contemporary with the events he described and possessed detailed material for the second half of Michael's life, including eye-witness accounts. But it is now thought that the *Life* was written some time after Michael's death, probably in the 880s or 890s, and that the author was active in this slightly later period.

MAIN SOURCES OF INFORMATION

Primary
See below

Secondary
See below

WORKS ON CHRISTIAN-MUSLIM RELATIONS

Bios kai politeia kai agōnes tou hosiou patros hēmōn kai homologētou Michaēl presbyterou kai synkellou gegonotos poleōs Hierosolymōn, 'The Life, conduct and struggles of our holy father and confessor Michael, priest and synkellos of the city of Jerusalem'. Modern title: 'The Life of Michael the Synkellos'

DATE 2nd half of the 9th c.
ORIGINAL LANGUAGE Greek

DESCRIPTION

Michael the Synkellos, to whom various works have been attributed, including a Greek grammar, was born in Jerusalem between 758 and 762, the son of non-Greek parents. According to his *Life*, he claimed to be of Persian (i.e. Arab) descent. In any case, he appears to have mastered Arabic, and the translation of a letter written by Theodore Abū Qurra (q.v.) by order of the Patriarch Thomas to the heretical (Monophysite) Armenians (*PG* 97, cols 1504-21) can be safely attributed to him.

At the age of three, he is said to have been entrusted to the Patriarch of Jerusalem to serve in the Church of the Resurrection. After receiving the tonsure and being appointed as lector, he learned grammar, rhetoric and philosophy, as well as poetry and astronomy. According to his *Life*, after his father's death he entered the Monastery of St Saba near Jerusalem at the age of 25, then after ordination as priest in the Church of the Resurrection he retreated to a monk's cell, where he was joined by two brothers, Theodore and Theophanes (from the area of the Moabites). At the age of 50, between about 808 and 811, he was appointed *synkellos* by Patriarch Thomas of Jerusalem, and he moved to the Spudaioi Monastery in Jerusalem with Theodore and Theophanes.

After a synod in Jerusalem in 812 or 813, Michael and the two brothers, together with a third monk, were sent to Constantinople and Rome with letters to Emperor Leo V, Patriarch Theodotus, and Pope Leo III. In the *Life*, the reasons given for this journey were: to take the Patriarch of Jerusalem's reply to the pope's request for advice about the practice among the Franks of including the *filioque* in the creed; to seek financial help from the pope for the patriarch, who was under pressure for money from Muslims in Palestine, and was having to cope with the unrest following the death of the Caliph Hārūn al-Rashīd; and to take a letter from Theodore the Stoudite (q.v.) which objected to the emperor's iconoclastic sympathies. But close examination of the *Life* shows that these reasons for Michael's departure from Jerusalem are fictitious, and are intended to present him as a saint who brings aid to all three churches: the Church of Rome in its arguments against the Franks, the Church of Jerusalem by passing on the request for help from the patriarch to the pope, and the Church of Constantinople by carrying a letter to dissuade them against iconoclasm.

The *Life* does, however, suggest that Michael went on a pilgrimage from Jerusalem via Constantinople to Rome. When he arrived in Constantinople (probably in 814), it seems that he took the side of the iconodules and came under persecution from the Emperors Leo V (813-20), Michael II (820-29) and Theophilus (829-42). A letter from Theodore the Stoudite, from the period of Michael's persecution, praises Michael's steadfastness and urges him to persevere in his stance. The *Life* records that at the end of the conflict over images and the deposition of John Grammaticus in 843, Michael was offered the position of patriarch but refused it out of humility. The new patriarch thereupon appointed him *synkellos* and abbot of the Chora Monastery, where he remained until he died. According to his *Life*, this was on 4 January 846, though since the synaxaries commemorate him on 18, 19 or 20 December, this may actually have been in 845.

SIGNIFICANCE

The *Life* of Michael the Synkellos largely follows conventional hagiographical *topoi*, although it gives valuable information about the situation of Christians in Palestine under Islamic rule in the late 8th and early 9th centuries, their cultural life, churches and monasteries.

MANUSCRIPTS

MS Genoa, Biblioteca Franzioni – Urbani 33 (10th or 11th c.)

MS Mt Athos, Pantokrator Monastery – 13, fols 85-114v (1047) (A)

EDITIONS AND TRANSLATIONS

S.V. Poljakova, *Vizantijskie legendy*, Moscow, 1972, 1994^{2}, pp. 114-39 (Russian trans.), pp. 236-91 (commentary)

M.B. Cunningham, *The Life of Michael the Synkellos*, Belfast, 1991, pp. 44-128 (English trans. facing Smit's edition with minor emendations)

F.I. Smit, *Kachrie Dzami I. Istorija monastyrija Chory. Architektura meceti, mozaiki narfikov*, Sofia, 1906, pp. 227-59

M.I. Gedeon, 'Eklogai apo tēs biographias Michaēl tou Synkellou', *Hellēnikos Philologikos Syllogos, archaiologikon deltion, parartēma tou KD'-KST' tomou* (1896) 23-34 (repr. in Gedeon, *Byzantinon Heortologion. Mnēmai tōn apo tou D' mechri tōn mesōn tou IE' aiōnos heortazomenōn hagiōn en Kōnstantinoupolei*, Constantinople, 1899, 231-42) (excerpts)

STUDIES

C. Sode, 'Creating new saints. The case of Michael the Synkellos and Theodore and Theophanes Graptoi', in E. Kountoura-Galake (ed.), *The heroes of the Orthodox Church*, Athens, 2004, 177-89

C. Sode, *Jerusalem – Konstantinopel – Rom. Die Viten des Michael Synkellos und der Brüder Theodoros und Theophanes Graptoi*, Stuttgart, 2001

PMBZ no. 5059

S.H. Griffith, *A treatise on the veneration of the holy icons written in Arabic by Theodore Abū Qurrah, Bishop of Harrān (C.755-C.830 A.D.)*, Louvain, 1997, pp. 7-11

H. Robins, *The Byzantine grammarians. Their place in history*, Berlin, 1993, pp. 149-63

D.F. Callahan, 'The problem of the "filioque" and the letter from the pilgrim monks of the Mount of Olives to Pope Leo III and Charlemagne. Is the letter another forgery by Adémar of Chabannes?', *Revue bénédictine* 102 (1992) 75-134

Cunningham, *The Life of Michael the Synkellos*, pp. 1-35

C. Mango, 'Greek culture in Palestine after the Arab conquest', in G. Cavallo, G. de Gregorio and M. Maniaci (eds), *Scritture, libri e testi nelle aree provinciali di Bisanzio*, 2 vols, Spoleto, 1991, i, 149-60, pp. 153-56

D. Donnet, *Le traité de la "Construction de la phrase" de Michel le Syncelle de Jérusalem*, Brussels, 1982

E. von Dobschütz, 'Methodios und die Studiten. Strömungen und Gegenströmungen in der Hagiographie des 9. Jahrhunderts', *BZ* 18 (1909) 41-105

Claudia Sode 2008

The Disputation of the monk Ibrāhīm al-Ṭabarānī

Unknown author

DATE OF BIRTH Probably 9th c.
PLACE OF BIRTH Unknown
DATE OF DEATH 9th or 10th c.
PLACE OF DEATH Unknown

BIOGRAPHY

Nothing is known of the anonymous author/redactor of *The Disputation of the monk Ibrāhīm al-Ṭabarānī* beyond what can be deduced from the text (a story set c. 815-20) and the date of the earliest manuscript (10th c.). The author was probably a Melkite Christian, perhaps a monk. He was well-versed in the themes and arguments of Christian-Muslim controversy, and could draw upon both the Bible and the Qurʾān with considerable skill.

An alternative approach to the question of authorship is to consider the story as an essentially historical account, in which case the monk Ibrāhīm al-Ṭabarānī (or 'Abraham of Tiberias') could be the text's author (or the author's principal informant); for a portrait of Ibrāhīm, see Marcuzzo, *Dialogue*, pp. 106-20.

MAIN SOURCES OF INFORMATION

Primary

G.B. Marcuzzo, *Le dialogue d'Abraham de Tibériade avec ʿAbd al-Raḥmān al-Hāšimī à Jérusalem vers 820*, Rome, 1986, pp. 251-533 (text and trans.)

Secondary

Marcuzzo, *Dialogue*, pp. 95-133 (introductions on the historicity of the text and the personalities of its characters).

WORKS ON CHRISTIAN-MUSLIM RELATIONS

Mujādalat al-rāhib al-qiddīs Ibrāhīm al-Ṭabarānī maʿa l-amīr ʿAbd al-Raḥmān ibn ʿAbd al-Malik ibn Ṣāliḥ al-Hāshimī, 'The Disputation of the saintly monk Ibrāhīm al-Ṭabarānī with the emir ʿAbd al-Raḥmān ibn ʿAbd al-Malik ibn Ṣāliḥ al-Hāshimī' (with slight variations in the oldest and best manuscripts). Abbreviated title: *Mujādalat Ibrāhīm al-Ṭabarānī*, 'The Disputation of Ibrāhīm al-Ṭabarānī'

DATE After c. 820, probably later 9th c.
ORIGINAL LANGUAGE Arabic

DESCRIPTION
The text recounts a religious disputation (*mujādala*) that took place in Jerusalem over the course of an unspecified number of days between the monk Ibrāhīm al-Ṭabarānī and a series of interlocutors at the court of the emir ʿAbd al-Raḥmān ibn ʿAbd al-Malik ibn Ṣāliḥ al-Hāshimī. According to the frame story, the emir desires to inquire into Christian beliefs and to this end convenes a group including the (presumably Melkite) patriarch, the East-Syrian Bishop Īliyyā (Elias), three members of the emir's retinue who had converted to Islam (two of them from Christianity), two Jews, and his physician. When this group fails to engage in the desired debate, however, the emir seizes on the incidental presence of the monk Ibrāhīm, who is on pilgrimage to the holy sites. Ibrāhīm boldly debates not only with the emir ʿAbd al-Raḥmān, but also with a succession of Muslim worthies (identified, in turn, as al-Manẓūr ibn Ghaṭafān al-ʿAbsī, the bedouin al-Bāhilī, and a learned pilgrim from Basra).

The monk proceeds to best everyone in debate, and the emir's attitude towards him progresses from early fury and demands that the monk embrace Islam to laughter and admiration of his persuasiveness (§389, where § represents the number of the *verset* in Marcuzzo, *Dialogue*). Toward the end of the debate, Ibrāhīm defends Christians' veneration of the cross with the claim that a Christian could consume poison, expel demons, or even enter fire 'in the name of Christ and with the sign of the cross' (§521). This claim sets up the final scene of the story, in which the monk performs an exorcism and undergoes trials by poison and fire without suffering any harm. This display of divine power leads to the conversion of the two Jews and the re-conversion of the two former Christians; the latter are immediately put to death for their apostasy. Ibrāhīm is briefly imprisoned, but then quietly released by the emir and allowed to go his way.

The discussion between the monk and the Muslims covers many of the topics that were regularly debated between Christians and Muslims in the 9th century, including the true religion and the truth of the scriptures, God as Trinity, the Incarnation and the specifically human activities of Christ, his crucifixion, and Christian veneration of the cross. The monk's arguments draw on a variety of authorities in a rather *ad hoc* fashion. From the Bible we find Old Testament *testimonia* (especially in defense of the Trinity, §§188-209), but also – and perhaps with greater frequency than in other texts of the period – arguments from the New Testament, appealing to Christ's disciples (*al-ḥawāriyyūn*) as truthful witnesses whom the Qurʾān calls *anṣār Allāh* ('helpers of God'; e.g., §§282-84, 414). Biblical arguments are supplemented by analogies; for (unusual) example, the union of the impassible divine Word with suffering humanity in Christ is illustrated by the case of a guardian angel who is unharmed as its human charge – with whom the angel remains without separation – is boiled alive in oil (§§333-49). The text draws on the Qurʾān itself with great frequency (see the extensive qurʾānic index in Marcuzzo, *Dialogue*, pp. 628-29), sometimes in surprising ways. For example, Ibrāhīm responds to a question about how a divine Christ could have submitted to creatures by paying the temple tax (*jizya*; see Matthew 17:24-27) with echoes of Q 9:29 (where the payment of *jizya* is imposed upon subjugated 'People of the Book'); however, according to the monk it is not those who pay the *jizya* in Matthew's account but rather Christ's critics who are 'brought low', *ṣāghirūn* (§409). A little later, Ibrāhīm responds to the assertion that belief in Christ's divinity is refuted by his prayer (since 'God does not pray', §432), and draws attention to Q 33:56, according to which 'God and his angels *yuṣallūna ʿalā* (= "pray upon" or "bless") the Prophet' (§456).

Many of the specific arguments of the text are fairly typical of the literature of the period, as is Ibrāhīm's tone, which is often quite sharply polemical, and not infrequently disparaging with respect to the Jews (see Rosenkranz, *Auseinandersetzung*, pp. 81-84). Some passages in the text, however, are quite striking. Ibrāhīm's evaluation of Muḥammad is remarkable for the period: while denying that Muḥammad was a prophet, the monk is ready to describe him as 'a king in whom God was pleased, and in and by whom God has fulfilled his promise to Abraham in Ishmael' (§110, also 468). Another distinctive formulation found in this text is that, because of the death and resurrection of Jesus, Christians live 'in truth and certainty' of the general resurrection, whereas Muslims merely live 'in hope' of it (§535-45). This assertion makes explicit the apologetic logic behind many early Arabic Christian presentations of Christ's death and resurrection (notably in ʿAmmār al-Baṣrī (q.v.), Ḥabīb Abū Rāʾiṭa (q.v.), and the Melkite compilation *al-Jāmiʿ wujūh al-īmān* [q.v.]), where these events are narrated as a divine demonstration of the reality of the general resurrection.

SIGNIFICANCE

The *Mujādala* offers a textbook example of the genre of Arabic-language Christian apologetic literature that Griffith has described as 'the monk in the emir's *majlis*'. Its extensive use of the Qurʾān deserves careful study, and may indicate the existence of Arabic Christian collections of qurʾānic materials that could prove useful in debate (see, for example, the string of qurʾānic quotations in §121). Its description of Muḥammad anticipates modern Christian attempts to move towards a positive evaluation of his career. And, as the text's treatment of the death and resurrection of Christ shows, the details of its treatment of particular apologetic *topoi* are sometimes distinctive and may shed light on other texts of the period.

Judging from the significant number of manuscripts in which the debate is preserved (or elaborated), the *Mujādala* enjoyed widespread popularity among Arabic-speaking Christians. The original Melkite recension (Marcuzzo's *alpha* recension) was soon expanded and circulated in the Church of the East (Marcuzzo's *beta* recension). The *Mujādala*'s popularity is not surprising, since in an entertaining way it assured Christians within the *Dār al-Islām* that, given the opportunity, their theologians and holy men could hold their own in debate – and thaumaturgy! – with the most skilled opponents that the Muslim authorities could muster.

MANUSCRIPTS

See Marcuzzo, *Dialogue d'Abraham de Tibériade*, pp. 169-208, for a description of the 36 MSS known to him and an analysis that reveals an earlier *alpha* recension and a later and lengthier *beta* recension.

Oldest manuscript of the *alpha* recension (and the base manuscript for Marcuzzo's edition):

MS Sinai, Monastery of St Catherine – ar. 556 (12th c.)

Oldest manuscript of the *beta* recension (and the source of Vollers' trans.):

MS Vollers (10th c.; purchased in Egypt, lost)

See also J. Nasrallah, 'Dialogue islamo-chrétien. À propos de publications récentes', *REI* 46 (1978) 121-51, pp. 134 for MSS unknown to Marcuzzo.

EDITIONS AND TRANSLATIONS

N.A. Newman, *The early Christian-Muslim dialogue. A collection of documents from the first three Islamic centuries (632-900 A.D.), translations with commentary*, Hatfield PA, 1993, pp. 269-353 (English trans. of Vollers' German trans. of a MS of the *beta* recension)

Marcuzzo, *Dialogue d'Abraham de Tibériade* (edition of the *alpha* recension on the basis of six MSS, and French trans. with lexicon and indices)

K. Vollers, 'Das Religionsgespräch von Jerusalem (um 800 D); aus dem arabischen übersetzt', *Zeitschrift für Kirchengeschichte* 29 (1908) 29-71, 197-221 (German trans. of a MS of the *beta* recension)

STUDIES

S. Rosenkranz, *Die jüdisch-christliche Auseinandersetzung unter islamischer Herrschaft*, Bern, 2004, pp. 81-84

S.K. Samir, 'The Prophet Muḥammad as seen by Timothy I and other Arab Christian authors', in D. Thomas (ed.), *Syrian Christians under Islam. The first thousand years*, Leiden, 2001, 75-106, pp. 77-81

S.H. Griffith, 'The monk in the emir's *majlis*. Reflections on a popular genre of Christian literary apologetics in Arabic in the early Islamic period', in H. Lazarus-Yafeh et al. (eds), *The majlis. Interreligious encounters in medieval Islam*, Wiesbaden, 1999, 13-65, pp. 22-37

Hoyland, *Seeing Islam* pp. 501, 519 (where the disputation in MS Mingana 184 should probably be identified as a fragment of *Mujādalat Ibrāhīm al-Ṭabarānī*)

M.M. Bar Asher, review of Marcuzzo, *Dialogue*, in *Revue biblique* 96 (1989) 116-19

Nasrallah, *HMLEM* ii.2, pp. 134-36

A. Charfi, review of Marcuzzo, *Dialogue*, in *Islamochristiana* 13 (1987) 253-55.
Marcuzzo, *Dialogue d'Abraham de Tibériade*
J. van Ess, 'Disputationspraxis in der islamischen Theologie. Ein vorläufige Skizze', *REI* 44 (1976) 23-60, pp. 29-30
G. Vajda, 'Un traité de polémique christiano-arabe contre les Juifs attribué à Abraham de Tibériade', *Bulletin – Institut de recherches et d'histoire des textes* 15 (1967-68) 137-50 (on an anti-Jewish polemic that appears to have been modeled on the *beta* recension of the *Mujādala*)
A. Abel, 'La portée apologétique de la «Vie» de St Théodore d'Edesse', *Byzantinoslavica* 10 (1949) 229-40, p. 232
Graf, *GCAL* ii, pp. 28-30
Vollers, 'Religionsgespräch'

Mark N. Swanson 2008

The Chronicle of Alfonso III

Alfonso III (author or patron)

DATE OF BIRTH c. 848
PLACE OF BIRTH Unknown
DATE OF DEATH 20 December 910
PLACE OF DEATH Zamora

BIOGRAPHY

The two versions of this chronicle (*Rotensis* and *Ovetensis*) are the work of either Alfonso III of Oviedo or a member of his entourage. According to Gómez Moreno ('Las primeras crónicas') and Sánchez Albornoz ('La redacción original'), the king himself wrote the *Rotensis* version. Díaz y Díaz ('La Historiografía hispana', p. 228), on the other hand, believes that Alfonso wrote the *Ovetensis*.

It is currently believed that Alfonso was the instigator and patron of the work in its double version (Bonnaz, *Les chroniques asturiennes*, pp. liii-liv, Ruiz de la Peña, *Crónicas asturianas*, pp. 38-41). These texts are in fact centered on the history of the Asturian royal family and their kingdom. Without any proof, Bonnaz (*Les chroniques asturiennes*, pp. liii-liv and pp. 105-6, n. 1) identifies the redactor of the *Rotensis* version as Dulcidius, the Toledan priest who was sent by the king on a mission to Cordova in 883. In similar fashion, he asserts that the *Ovetensis* was written by Bishop Sebastian of Orense (d. c. 890). Flórez erroneously assumes that it was Sebastian of Salamanca (*España sagrada*, pp. xiii, 464-69).

MAIN SOURCES OF INFORMATION

Primary

Chronicle of Albelda in J. Gil Fernández, J.L. Moralejo and J.I. Ruiz de la Peña *Crónicas asturianas*, Oviedo, 1985, c. xv-12/13 and xix-3, pp. 176-81, 188
Chronicle of Sampiro in J. Pérez de Urbel, *Sampiro. Su crónica y la monarquía leonesa en el siglo X*, Madrid, 1952, pp. 275-308

Secondary

J.I. Ruiz de la Peña Solar, 'La monarquía asturiana (718-910)', in *El Reino de León en la Alta Edad Media*, 11 vols, León, 1988-(1995), iii, pp. 9-127

P. Linehan, *History and the historians of medieval Spain*, Oxford, 1993, pp. 76-127
Y. Bonnaz, *Les chroniques asturiennes (fin IXe siècle)*, Paris, 1987, pp. liii-lvii
Ruiz de la Peña, 'Estudio preliminar', in Gil Fernández, Moralejo, and Ruiz de la Peña, *Crónicas asturianas*, pp. 31-42
M.C. Díaz y Díaz, *Codices visigóticos en la monarquía leonesa*, León, 1983
A. Barbero and M. Vigil, *La formación del feudalismo en la península ibérica*, Barcelona, 1978, pp. 232-78 ('La historiografía de la época de Alfonso III')
M.C. Díaz y Díaz, *De Isidoro al siglo XI. Ocho estudios sobre la vida literaria peninsular*, Barcelona, 1976², 203-34 ('La Historiografía hispana desde la invasión árabe hasta el año 1000') (repr. *La Storiografia altomedievale*, 2 vols, Spoleto, 1970, i, 313-43, pp. 332-33)
C. Sánchez Albornoz, *Investigaciones sobre historiografía hispana medieval (siglos VIII al XII)*, Buenos Aires, 1967, pp. 19-43 ('La redacción original de la crónica de Alfonso III')
M. Gómez Moreno, 'Las primeras crónicas de la Reconquista, el ciclo de Alfonso III', *Boletín de la Academia de la Historia* 100 (1932) 565-628
Flórez, *España Sagrada*, xiii, pp. 464-69

WORKS ON CHRISTIAN-MUSLIM RELATIONS

Chronica Visegothorum, Adefonsi Tertii Chronica, Chronicon Sebastiani, 'Chronicle of Alfonso III' (Version *Rotensis, Rotense* or *Barbare*. Version *Ovetensis, Ovetense, Ad Sebastianum* or *Erudite*)

DATE This chronicle, which runs until the death of Ordoño I in 866, was perhaps undertaken at this ruler's instigation (Gil, *Crónicas asturianas*, pp. 74-75). Sánchez Albornoz ('¿Una crónica asturiana perdida?') suggests that it was inspired by a lost chronicle from the end of the 8th century. A first redaction took place most certainly in 883, before 11 November.

This chronicle is in fact related to the *Prophetic chronicle* contained in the *Chronicle of Albelda* (q.v.) written on 11 April 883, which predicts that the final victory over the Muslims will take place 170 years after their conquest, between 11 November 883 and 11 November 884. Like the *Prophetic chronicle*, the *Chronicle of Alfonso III* places the Muslim conquest in 714 in order to make this victory fall in the year 884 (Barbero and Vigil, *La formación*, pp. 240-49).

A second redaction of the *Chronicle of Alfonso III* was made under Garcia I (910-14) and Ordoño II (914-24). From there on, opinions diverge. According to a number of historians, while both versions date

to the late 9th century, the *Ovetensis* is posterior to the *Rotensis*, which it corrects and adapts in a neo-Gothic manner (Bonnaz, pp. xxviii-xxix). According to Prelog and Gil, however, these two versions are only to be distinguished after the second redaction under Garcia I (910-14). The *Ovetensis*, composed under Garcia I, and the Rotensis, redacted under Ordoño II, are therefore to be traced back to the same earlier version (Prelog, *Die Chronik Alfons III*, pp. lxxx-lxxxv; Gil Fernández, *Crónicas asturianas*, pp. 60-63). A continuation of the *Ovetensis* was composed under Ordoño II on the basis of the *Chronicle of Albelda* (Bonnaz, 'La chronique d'Alphonse III'). On the relationship between the *Chronicle of Alfonso III* and the *Chronicle of Albelda*, including the *Prophetic chronicle*, see Gil Fernández, *Crónicas asturianas*, pp. 101-4.
ORIGINAL LANGUAGE Latin

DESCRIPTION
This chronicle is a series of royal biographies that imitates and continues the *Historia Gothorum* of Isidore of Seville. Starting with Receswinth (653-72), it describes the reigns of the Visigothic kings and, from the Muslim conquest onwards, the Asturian kings. The two versions amount to 36 pages in Gil's edition. This chronicle and the *Chronicle of Albelda* constitute the only contemporary historical sources from the Asturian period (8th-9th c.). After the Muslim conquest, the *Chronicle of Alfonso III* narrates the reigns of Asturian kings, their *reconquista* or struggle against the enemies of their kingdom, in particular the Muslims, as well as their restoration and population of conquered territory, and their occasional collaboration with Muslim rebels. The Muslims are described as the instrument of divine punishment, according to a classical Old Testament model (Wolf, *Conquerors*).

Famous episodes include Alfonso I (739-57) conquering numerous villages, killing all the 'Arabs' and taking the Christians with him (Gil Fernández, *Crónicas asturianas*, Ovetensis c. 13, p. 133) and Ordoño I (850-866) defeating the *muwallad* Mūsā ibn Mūsā of the Banū Qasī, who had rebelled against Cordova and assumed the title 'Third King of Spain' (c. 25-26, pp. 145-48). Muslim chroniclers generally confirm its historical accuracy. For example, the installation of a *muwallad* in Galicia, Maḥmūd, who had rebelled against the emir ʿAbd al-Raḥmān II (822-52), followed by his rebellion against Alfonso II (791-842) are mentioned also by Ibn Ḥayyān and Ibn al-Athīr.

The most detailed episode is the famous victory of Covadonga over the invaders, when Pelagius and his forces, hidden in a cave, defeated their enemies by a miracle. Numerous historians regard this episode as an adaptation of an older account incorporated into the first version of this chronicle (Gómez Moreno, 'Las primeras crónicas', pp. 586-87; Sánchez Albornoz, *Orígenes*, ii, pp. 41-76; Bronisch, *Reconquista*, pp. 382-90), but it is clearly a literary composition which includes many motifs from classical literature, notably from Herodotus (Hook, 'From the Persians to Pelayo'). Moreover, it is directly influenced by martyrologies, in particular those of the saints Facond and Primitif, dated to the late 880s. Redacted in the early 10th century, the account of Covadonga is then incorporated into the chronicle at the time of its second redaction in 910/14. Nevertheless, it relates a historical event to which the Mozarabic *Chronicle of 754* (q.v.) had perhaps already referred (García Moreno, 'Covadonga').

SIGNIFICANCE

The *Rotensis*, along with the *Chronicle of Albelda*, plays a role in the forging and transmission of an ideology of Gothic renaissance, which later historians would call a *reconquista*. The text, transmitted in two medieval and four modern manuscripts, served as a source for many important later Spanish chronicles, such as the *Historia Silense* (1110/20) and the *Chronicle of Nájera* (c. 1180). In the 13th century, it was used together with the *Ovetensis* by Lucas of Tuy for his *Chronicon mundi* (1230/39) and by Rodrigo Jiménez of Rada for his *De rebus Hispaniae* (c. 1240). The *Ovetensis*, which is extant in 13 modern manuscripts, is integrated by Pelagius of Oviedo into his *Liber chronicorum* (1142/1143).

MANUSCRIPTS

Cf. Gil Fernández, 'Introducción', in *Crónicas asturianas*, pp. 45-80; Bonnaz, 'Introducción', in *Les chroniques asturiennes*, viii-xxix; Prelog, *Die Chronik Alfons III*

EDITIONS AND TRANSLATIONS

K.B. Wolf, *Conquerors and chroniclers of early medieval Spain*, Liverpool, 1999², pp. 161-77 (trans. of the *Rotensis*)

Bonnaz, *Les chroniques asturiennes*, 31-59 (edition and trans. of the *Rotensis* and *Ovetensis*)

Gil Fernández, Moralejo, and Ruiz de la Peña, *Crónicas asturianas*, 111-49 and 194-221 (edition and trans. of the *Rotensis* and *Ovetensis*)

J. Prelog, *Die Chronik Alfons III*, Frankfurt am Main, 1980 (edition of the *Rotensis* and *Ovetensis*)

A. Ubieto Arteta, *Crónica de Alfonso III*, Valencia, 1961 (edition of the *Rotensis* and *Ovetensis*)

Gómez Moreno, 'Las primeras crónicas', 609-21 (edition of the *Rotensis*)

Z. García Villada, *Crónica de Alfonso III*, Madrid, 1918

A. Huici, *Las crónicas latinas de la reconquista*, 2 vols, Valencia, 1913, i (edition of the *Ovetensis*)

L. Barrau-Dihigo, 'Une relation inédite du Pseudo-Sébastien de Salamanque', *Revue hispanique* 23 (1910) 235-64 (edition of the *Rotensis*)

Flórez, *Espana sagrada* xiii, 475-89 (repr. in *PL* 129, cols 1111-24) (edition of the *Ovetensis*)

STUDIES

H. Sirantoine, 'Le discours monarchique des "Chroniques asturiennes", fin IXe siecle. Trois modes de légitimation pour les rois des asturies', *Monarquía y sociedad en el reino de Léon, de Alfonso III a Alfonso VII*, 2 vols, Léon, 2007, ii, 793-819

D. Hook, *From Orosius to the Historia Silense. Four essays on the late antique and early medieval historiography of the Iberian peninsula*, Bristol, 2005, pp. 51-95 ('From the Persians to Pelayo. Some classical complications in the Covadonga complex')

F.J. Zabalo Zabalegui, 'El numéro de musulmanes que atacaron Covadonga: los precedentes biblicos de unas cifras simbólicas', *Historia, Instituciones, Documentas* (Universidad de Sevilla) 31 (2004) 715-28

J.F. O'Callaghan, *Reconquest and crusade in medieval Spain*, Philadelphia PA, 2003

M. González Jiménez, 'Sobre la ideología de reconquista: Realidades y tópicos', in *Memoria, mito y realidad en la Historia Medieval* (XIV Semana de Estudios Medievales, Nájera, 2002), Logroño, 2003, 151-70

T. Deswarte, *De la destruction à la restauration. L'idéologie du royaume d'Oviedo-León (VIIIe-XIe siècles)*, Turnhout, 2003

P. Henriet, 'L'idéologie de guerre sainte dans le Haut Moyen Age hispanique', *Francia* 29 (2002) 171-220

Wolf, *Conquerors and chronicles*, pp. 43-56

A.P. Bronisch, *Reconquista und Heiliger Krieg. Die Deutung des Krieges im christlichen Spanien von den Westgoten bis ins frühe 12. Jahrhundert*, Münster, 1998, 2007² (trans. M.D. Hernando, *Reconquista y Guerra Santa: La concepción de la guerra en la España cristiana desde los Visigodos hasta comienzos del siglo XII*, Granada, 2007)
L.A. García Moreno, 'Covadonga, realidad y leyenda', *Boletín de la Real Academia de la Historia* 194 (1997) 353-80
J. Montenegro and A. Del Castillo, 'De nuevo sobre don Pelayo y los orígenes de la Reconquista', *Espacio, tiempo y forma*. 2nd ser. *Historia Antigua* 8 (1995) 507-20
Linehan, *History and the historians*, pp. 76-127
J. Montenegro and A. Del Castillo, 'Don Pelayo y los orígenes de la Reconquista. Un nuevo punto de vista', *Hispania* 52 (1992) 5-32
J.E. López Pereira, 'Continuidad y novedad léxica en las crónicas asturianas', *Akten der I. internationalen Mittellateinerkongresses, Mittellateinisches Jahrbuch* 24-25, Stuttgart, 1991, 295-310
J.M. Mínguez Fernández, *La Reconquista*, Madrid, 1989
R. Collins, *The Arab conquest of Spain (710-797)*, Oxford, 1989
J.M. Caso, 'La fuente del episodio de Covadonga en la Crónica Rotense', in *Studia in honorem Prof. M. de Riquer*, 4 vols, Barcelona, 1986, i, 273-87
Ruiz de la Peña, 'Estudio preliminar', and Gil Fernández, 'Introducción', in *Crónicas asturianas*, pp. 31-42, 45-80
G. Martin, 'La chute du royaume visigothique d'Espagne dans l'historiographie chrétienne des VIIIe et IXe siècles. Sémiologie socio-historique', *Cahiers de linguistique hispanique mediévale* 9 (1984) 207-33
M.C. Díaz y Díaz, *Libros y librerías en la Rioja altomedieval*, Logroño, 1979
J. Gil, 'Judíos y Cristianos en Hispania: s. VIII y IX (Continuación)', *Hispania Sacra* 31 (1978-79) 9-88
Barbero and Vigil, *La formación del feudalismo en la península ibérica*, pp. 232-78
D.W. Lomax, *The reconquest of Spain*, London, 1978
Y. Bonnaz, 'La chronique d'Alphonse III et sa *continuatio* dans le ms. 9880 de la Bibliothèque Nationale de Madrid', *Mélanges de la Casa de Velázquez* 13 (1977) 85-101
L.A. García Moreno, *El fin del reino visigodo de Toledo. Decadencia y catástrofe. Una contribución a su crítica*, Madrid, 1975

C. Sánchez Albornoz, *Orígenes de la nación española. Estudios critícos sobre la historia del Reino de Asturias*, 3 vols, Oviedo, 1972-75, ii

Díaz y Díaz, 'La Historiografía hispana'

C. Sánchez Albornoz, *Investigaciones sobre historiografía*, pp. 19-43 ('La redacción original de la crónica de Alfonso III'), pp. 44-65 ('La crónica de Albelda y la de Alfonso III'), pp. 80-96 ('Sobre la autoridad de las Crónicas de Albelda y de Alfonso III'), pp. 97-108 ('Otra vez sobre la Crónica de Alfonso III'), pp. 111-60 ('¿Una crónica asturiana perdida?'), pp. 161-202 ('El relato de Alfonso III sobre Covadonga'), pp. 217-33 ('El anónimo continuador de Alfonso III'), pp. 235-63 ('De nuevo sobre la crónica de Alfonso III y sobre la llamada Historia silense')

C. Sánchez Albornoz, *Despoblación y repoblación en la valle del Duero*, Buenos Aires, 1966

J.A. Maravall, *El concepto de España en la Edad Media*, Madrid, 1954

Gómez Moreno, 'Las primeras crónicas'

Thomas Deswarte 2007

Al-Īrānshahrī

Abū l-ʿAbbās al-Īrānshahrī

DATE OF BIRTH Unknown
PLACE OF BIRTH Nīshāpūr
DATE OF DEATH Late 9th c.
PLACE OF DEATH Unknown, possibly Nīshāpūr

BIOGRAPHY

Very little is known about this figure, even his full name (*Encyclopedia Iranica* and Aminrazavi 1999 give it as Abū l-ʿAbbās Muḥammad ibn Muḥammad al-Īrānshahrī but do not cite a source), though the few surviving fragments of information suggest he was anything but orthodox. He came from Nīshāpūr, also known as Īrānshahr, and is mentioned by al-Bīrūnī as witnessing a solar eclipse there in 873 (Pines, *Doctrine*, pp. 193-94 n. 1). Al-Bīrūnī also says that he used works of Abū Yaʿlā Muḥammad al-Mismaʿī, known as Zurqān, who died in 891 (*Taḥqīq*, p. 4). If, as Nāṣir-i Khusraw says, he was the teacher of the philosopher Abū Bakr al-Rāzī, who was born in 865, he would have been active in the period 880-895. Although there is no indication of the date of al-Īrānshahrī's death, he is generally placed in the late 9th century. (Monteil, p. 314 n. 6, wrongly says he was alive in 912, the result of a misreading of Minorsky, p. 129.)

Al-Bīrūnī (*Taḥqīq*, p. 4) intriguingly says that al-Īrānshahrī did not believe in any of the religions of his time and invented his own, though he does not expand upon this (cf. Abū l-Maʿālī, ed. Dāneshpazhuh, pp. 306-7). Nāṣir-i Khusraw says he was an important member of the *aṣḥāb al-hayūla*, materialists, a possibility supported by the title of one of his lost works, *Masāʾil al-ṭabīʿa*, 'Questions of natural philosophy' (al-Bīrūnī, *Ifrād*, i, p. 53).

Taking up Nāṣir-i Khusraw's points about the link between al-Īrānshahrī and Abū Bakr al-Rāzī, Meier and Aminrazavi argue that the latter thinker's cosmological teachings about matter, time and space are largely borrowings from al-Īrānshahrī. If this is so (and there are no means of substantiating the link in the present state of knowledge), it confirms al-Īrānshahrī as an individualist who maybe diverged so far from orthodox Muslim views that he was regarded as having rejected them, not unlike his elder contemporary Abū ʿĪsā l-Warrāq (q.v.).

The titles of two other lost works are known, although their meaning and significance remain unclear. These are *Kitāb al-jalīl*, 'The exalted' (?), and *Kitāb al-athīr*, 'The favoured' (?). Al-Bīrūnī, in two of his works, reports from al-Īrānshahrī details about the Indian mountain Meru (*Taḥqīq*, pp. 124 and 126), and also details about feast days in Persia and Armenia (*Āthār*, pp. 222 and 225). But he does not say whether they are taken from these or other of al-Īrānshahrī's unknown works.

MAIN SOURCES OF INFORMATION

Primary

Abū l-Rayḥān al-Bīrūnī, *Taḥqīq mā lil-Hind*, ed. E. Sachau, London, 1887; trans. E. Sachau, *Alberuni's India*, 2 vols, London, 1910

al-Bīrūnī, *Al-āthār al-bāqiya ʿan al-qurūn al-khāliya*, ed. E. Sachau, Leipzig, 1878

al-Bīrūnī, *Ifrād al-maqāl fī amr al-zilāl*, trans. E.S. Kennedy, *The exhaustive treatise on shadows*, 2 vols, Aleppo, 1976

Abū l-Maʿālī Muḥammad ibn ʿUbayd Allāh, *Bayān al-adyān*, ed. H. Reza, *Tārikh-e kāmel-e adyān*, Tehran, 1964 (French trans.: H. Massé, 'Exposé des religions', *RHR* 94 (1926) 17-75)

Abū l-Maʿālī, ed. M.-T. Dāneshpazhuh, 'Bāb-e panjom az ketāb-e *Bayān al-adyān*', *Farhang-e Irān-zamīn* 10, 1962, 282-318

Nāṣir-i Khusraw, *Zād al-musāfirīn*, ed. M.B. al-Raḥmān, Berlin, 1923, pp. 73, 98, 102, 110, 343

Secondary

art. 'al-Īrānshahrī, Abū l-ʿAbbās', in *Encyclopaedia Iranica*, ed. E. Yarshater, London, 1982-

S.H. Nasr with M. Aminrazavi, *An anthology of philosophy in Persia*, 2 vols, New York, 1999, i, 88-90 (drawing on Aminrazavi's 1992 article, though containing translations of relevant passages from Nāṣir-i Khusraw)

S. Stroumsa, *Freethinkers of Medieval Islam*, Leiden, 1999, pp. 12-13, 90-91, 135

S. Pines, *Studies in Islamic atomism*, trans. M. Schwarz, ed. T. Langermann, Jerusalem, [1936] 1997, 41-42

S. Pines, 'La doctrine de l'intellect selon Bakr al-Mawṣilī', in S. Pines, *Studies in the history of Arabic philosophy III*, ed. S. Stroumsa, Jerusalem, 1996, 193-207, pp. 193-34, n. 1

Abū Rayḥān al-Bīrūnī. Le livre de l'Inde, trans. V.-M. Monteil, Arles, 1996

M. Aminrazavi, 'Īrānshahrī: life and views on time and space', *Islamic Studies* 31 (1992) 479-86

F. Meier, 'Der 'Urknall' eine Idee des Abū Bakr ar-Rāzī', *Oriens* 33 (1992) 1-21 (German trans. of passages from Nāṣir-i Khusraw on pp. 11, 12, 13)
G. Monnot, 'Les écrits musulmans sur les religions non bibliques', in Monnot, *Islam et religions*, Paris, 1986, 39-82, pp. 56-57
V. Minorsky, *Sharaf al-Zamān Ṭāhir Marvazī on China, the Turks and India*, London, 1942, p. 129

WORKS ON CHRISTIAN-MUSLIM RELATIONS

Unknown, probably *Kitāb al-maqālāt*, 'Doctrines'

DATE Late 9th c.
ORIGINAL LANGUAGE Arabic

DESCRIPTION
According to al-Bīrūnī (*Taḥqīq*, p. 4), al-Īrānshahrī wrote on the doctrines of the Jews and Christians, and on the contents of the Torah and Gospel. In al-Bīrūnī's opinion, this stood out from similar accounts in contemporary *Maqālāt* works for its objectivity, although al-Īrānshahrī's account of Hinduism left much to be desired, mainly because he drew on Abū Yaʿlā Muḥammad al-Mismaʿī (fl. mid-9th century) for these details.

Nāṣir-i Khusraw (p. 98) refers to a *Kitāb al-maqālāt*, which is very likely to have been the work on which al-Bīrūnī comments.

SIGNIFICANCE
This unknown work appears to have comprised descriptive accounts of the religions of al-Īrānshahrī's time, employing Abū Yaʿlā Muḥammad al-Mismaʿī's lost *Kitāb al-maqālāt*, and maybe resembling Abū ʿĪsā l-Warrāq's *Kitāb maqālāt al-nās wa-ikhtilāfihim*. It may have fed into later Muslim works on Christianity.

MANUSCRIPTS —
EDITIONS AND TRANSLATIONS —
STUDIES —

David Thomas 2008

The Life of Gabriel of Qartmīn

Anonymous monk of the monastery of Qartmīn

DATE OF BIRTH 9th or 10th c.
PLACE OF BIRTH Probably Bēt Qusṭān in Ṭūr ʿAbdīn
DATE OF DEATH Unknown
PLACE OF DEATH Probably monastery of Qartmīn

BIOGRAPHY Unknown

MAIN SOURCES OF INFORMATION

Primary —

Secondary —

WORKS ON CHRISTIAN-MUSLIM RELATIONS

Tashʿītā d-qaddīshā mār(y) Shmūʾēl w-mār(y) Shemʿūn w-mār(y) Gabrīʾēl 'The Story of my lord Samuel and my lord Symeon and my lord Gabriel', the last part of which may be referred to as the 'Life of Gabriel'

DATE Between 758 and 969, though probably 9th c.
ORIGINAL LANGUAGE Syriac

DESCRIPTION
The *Life* of Gabriel of Qartmīn is part of a trilogy which comprises the *Lives* of Samuel of Eshtin and Symeon of Qartmīn, the 4th century founders of the monastery, and that of Gabriel, who died in 648. The author was perhaps a son of Gabriel's village of Bēt Qusṭān, who hoped to add to its fame by linking Gabriel with the founders of the monastery of Qartmīn. In fact, Gabriel's name subsequently eclipsed those of the founders and today the monastery is known as that of Mōr Gabriel, *tout court*.

He must have been writing some time after 758, the date of the original compilation of the *Chronicum anonymum ad A.D. 819 pertinens* (ed. A. Barsaum, in J.-B. Chabot, *Anonymi auctoris chronicon ad annum Christi 1234 pertinens*, Paris, 1920 [*CSCO* 81]), because while this chronicle, which was also compiled (up to 758) at the monastery of Qartmīn, mentions only one miracle of Gabriel restoring a dead body to life (p. 11), the *Life* adds three more. The last of these, of a boy trampled underfoot at Gabriel's funeral, is identified by the writer of the *Life* as Symeon, who became bishop of Ḥarrān from 700 to 734.

He is likely to have written the *Life* before 969, because this is the earliest possible date for the *Life* of Aaron (see A. Palmer, 'Charting undercurrents in the history of the West-Syrian people. The resettlement of Byzantine Melitene after 934', *OC* 70 [1986] 37-68, pp. 61-63), which was influenced by it.

The historical kernel of the *Life* is the record of Gabriel's funeral, to which is appended a summary of his career, together with stories drawn from various Syriac sources (the 6th-century hagiographical work of John of Ephesus, the *Chronicle of Zuqnīn* (q.v.), completed in 775, and the inscription on a monolithic kneading-table installed at the monastery of Qartmīn in 776/767).

One of these added stories, in Chapter 10 (LXVII.17-LXXII.2), connects Gabriel with the monk Yuḥannān Ṭayyāyā ('John the Arab'), whose silver-plated skull continues to draw ailing pilgrims, many of them Muslims, to the burial-vaults of Qartmīn. The *Life* tells how when he was still a Muslim he left a large sum of money with a monk of the monastery. This monk died, but Gabriel briefly restored him to life so that he could tell the Muslim where his money was buried. The Muslim was thereupon converted and himself became a monk. This story is adapted from the record of an event involving the 8th-century Bishop Ḥabīb of Edessa (J.-B. Chabot, *Incerti auctoris Chronicon Pseudo-Dionysianum vulgo dictum, II*, Paris, 1933 (*CSCO* 104), pp. 160-63; trans. A. Harrak, *The Chronicle of Zuqnīn, Parts III and IV, A.D. 488-775*, Toronto, 1999, pp. 153-55).

These borrowings may well have been used to supplement the meagre tradition about Gabriel after the occasion when his body was exhumed in the early 770s to put an end to the plague which was then decimating the community. It was probably at that time that his *Life* was appended to those of the founders, with the addition of a preface which bridges the gap between the 4th and 7th centuries.

An important element in the *Life* as it has come down is a chapter about the supposed treaty that was concluded between Gabriel and the Arab conquerors of northern Mesopotamia. The *Chronicum anonymum ad A.D. 819 pertinens* confirms that Gabriel was enthroned between 1 October 633 and 31 September 634, and the most likely date is 1 May 634. Thus, he was a contemporary of the Caliph ʿUmar ibn al-Khaṭṭāb (634-44), under whom northern Mesopotamia was incorporated into the Arab Empire (al-Balādhurī and al-Khwārizmī date the conquest of Ṭūr ʿAbdīn to 640).

The *Life* (Ch. 12, LXXII) claims that Gabriel received from ʿUmar in person a written assurance that priests and deacons should not pay the poll-tax (if this is the right interpretation of the word *paqrātā*, literally 'vertebrae'), and that monks should be free from the land-tax (here termed *madʿatā*). This alleged assurance also stated that the sounding of the gong for the times of prayer should not be abolished and that anthems might be sung in public funeral processions. But all this is highly suspect. Gabriel is unlikely to have met ʿUmar himself, but rather one of his subordinates, possibly ʿIyāḍ ibn Ghanm, and it is also unlikely that the poll-tax and land-tax were yet distinguished, since there is no such distinction in treaties recorded elsewhere for northern Mesopotamia at this time. Furthermore, the treaty between ʿIyāḍ and the people of Callinicus, as recorded by al-Balādhurī, explicitly abolished the sounding of the gong and the Christian practice of processing in public.

The *Life* of Gabriel was most likely written sometime in the period, in the 9th century, when debates over the stipulations of the so-called *Shurūṭ ʿUmar* (q.v.) were at their most heated (see al-Ṭabarī, *Taʾrīkh* i, pp. 2405-6). All the specific concessions allegedly made to Gabriel in the *Life* read like wishful thinking on the part of the Christians – the concession to sound the gong is clearly formulated as an exception to the rule explicitly laid down in the *Shurūṭ*. In sum, when the inherent implausibility of the treaty allegedly obtained by Gabriel in person from ʿUmar is weighed against the evidence from the *Life* itself, that no narrative of Gabriel's life existed before the late 8th century apart from a brief *curriculum vitae* appended to the record of his funeral, the conclusion has to be that the two men never met.

SIGNIFICANCE

A rural area such as Ṭūr ʿAbdīn would have been included under the treaties made with surrounding cities, though it appears that in the period when the *Life* fabricated this special treaty for Ṭūr ʿAbdīn the practice of sounding the gong for prayer and processing with anthems to the cemetery was still in force in villages where perhaps no Muslims lived. The higher clergy, apparently, were exempt from the poll-tax and the monasteries did not have to pay the land-tax (thanks to Symeon of Ḥarrān, who died in 734, the monastery of Qartmīn had many properties and extensive estates in and around Nisibis). A study of the churches of Ṭūr ʿAbdīn, and notably that of the monastery of St Jacob near the village of Ṣalāḥ (Palmer, *Monk and Mason*, Appendix on inscriptions, pp. 206-8, 212-13), suggests that some of them were rebuilt in the 8th century. If this is true, it provides evidence that the restriction on repairs to existing churches was ineffective in the remote plateau of Ṭūr ʿAbdīn. These exemptions may have been challenged in the late 8th century, no doubt beginning with the manifest iniquity of the monastery of Qartmīn being exempted from the land-tax, which will have grated in the minds of other property and land owners in and around Nisibis. The *Life* of Gabriel is evidence of the strategy adopted by this monastery to answer this challenge. It may well have been unsuccessful, which would help to explain the decline discussed in the final chapter of Palmer, *Monk and mason* (pp. 182-90).

MANUSCRIPTS

MS BL – Add 17,265, fols 74-80, 83-88 (one leaf missing), 89-90 (one leaf missing), 94-105 (one leaf missing), 91-93, 81-82 (three leaves missing, including end of text and colophon) (dated by the script to the 13th c. approximately; see W. Wright, *Catalogue of Syriac manuscripts in the British Museum: acquired since the year 1838*, 3 vols, London, 1870-72, iii, p. 1140). Palmer, *Tashʿītā*, supplements this incomplete MS with the Istanbul and Paris MSS, neither of which was copied directly from it.

MS Istanbul – Yeni 196, fols 99r-113r (referred to by A. Vööbus, 'Important discoveries for the history of the monastery of Qartamīn (sic): new light on the literary traditions regarding its history', *Orientalia Lovaniensia Periodica* 8 (1977) 223-27, as Meryem Ana 7) belongs to the Syrian Orthodox Church of the Mother of God, Karakurumsokağı 20, Tarlabaşı, Beyoğlu.

The Paris MS, pp. 36-60 of a black notebook measuring 222 x 175 mm (formerly [1981] in the keeping of the late François Graffin, SJ), is a copy made by Henri Pognon, probably in 1893, from a MS belonging to Afrem Raḥmānī, Syrian Catholic bishop of Baghdad, 1890-94 (the Raḥmānī MS, which was apparently undated, also contained, amongst other texts, 'The story of Mār(y) Bassus and his sister Susan').

MS Damascus – 9/29; as yet this is unedited. It was described by G.P. Behnām in his *Life of the Patriarch Afrām*, Mosul, 1959, as follows: 'MS 9/29 (of the Syrian Orthodox Patriarchate): three books (bound) in one volume, the first being the Book of Common Prayer (Syriac: *shḥīmā*), while the second is of the stories of Mār Samuel, Mār Symeon and Mār Gabriel. The books were combined in the 16th c. The MS measures 15 x 21 cm.' This description is based on that given in a handwritten Syriac catalogue of the patriarchal manuscript collection (now kept in the monastery of St Ephrem at Maʿarrat Saydnāyā, outside Damascus) by P.Y. Dolabānī. It appears that the hagiographical part of this MS is in Karshūnī. Dolabānī's paraphrase of the *Life* of Gabriel in his *Maktabzabnē d-ʿūmrā qaddīshā d-qarṭmīn* (*sic*), pp. 85-120, is therefore probably based on one of the Mardin MSS. MSS Mardīn 8.257, 8.258, 8.262 and 8.275, signalled by Vööbus, 'Important discoveries', were probably copied directly or indirectly from the Damascus MS when it was at Dayr al-Zaʿfarān near Mardīn.

MS Mosul – 254; according to Vööbus, 'Important discoveries', this differs in its readings from the London MS.

MS BNF – Syr. 375 (Qartmīn trilogy: fols 4v-132v); according to F. Briquel-Chatonnet, 'Note sur l'histoire du monastère de Saint-Gabriel de Qartamīn (sic)', *Le Muséon* 98 (1985) 95-102, p. 96, this resembles the text of Berlin MS Sachau 221 (fols 41v-114r; the *Life* of Gabriel begins on fol. 88v), which differs notably from the London MS.

MS Berlin – Sachau 239; this is in Ṭūrōyō with a parallel Arabic trans.

MS Birmingham, Mingana – Syriac 223, fols 1r-30v; this is in Karshūnī.

EDITIONS AND TRANSLATIONS

A. Palmer, *Monk and mason on the Tigris frontier. The early history of Ṭur ʿAbdin*, Cambridge, 1990, + 2 microfiches, Part One, Sections A-D, esp. B, LV-XCII (revised edition of the *Life* with English trans., based on the same MSS as Palmer, *Tashʿītā*, 1983)

A. Palmer, *Tashʿitā d-qaddishā mār(y) Shmuʾēl w-mār(y) Shemʿūn w-mār(y) Gabriʾēl*, Glane, 1983, pp. 55-92 (first complete edition of the *Life* based on the BL, Istanbul and Paris MSS)

F. Nau, 'Notice historique sur le monastère de Qartamin', in *Actes du XIVème congrès international des orientalistes, Alger 1905*, Part 2, Paris, 1907, Section 2, 1-75 (37-111) (edition and trans. of extracts LV.1-LVIII.2, LVIII.20-LXIII.13, LXIV.18-LXV.9, LXXIV.7-LXXV.3, LXXV.9-14, LXXVIII.18-LXXXII.20, XC.1-XCII.3, based on MS BL – Add 17,265)

H. Pognon, *Inscriptions sémitiques de la Syrie, de la Mésopotamie et de la région de Mossoul*, Paris, 1907, 39-40 (edition and trans. in Pognon's own hand of LIX.19-LXI.4, omitting LX.5-8 and LX.16-LXI.2, based on the Paris MS)

STUDIES

C.F. Robinson, *Empire and elites after the Muslim conquest. The transformation of northern Mesopotamia*, Cambridge, 2000, pp. 15-16 (including passage on Gabriel's negotiations with ʿUmar)

Hoyland, *Seeing Islam*, pp. 39, 42, 121-24, 169-70

Palmer, *Monk and mason*, pp. 13-18, 154-58, 251-52 (index to all comments on the *Life*), 257 (index to all passages on Gabriel)

P.Y. Dolabānī, *Maktabzabnē d-ʿūmrā qaddīshā d-qarṭmīn* (sic) ['History of the holy monastery of Qartmīn'] (in Syriac), Mardin, 1959, pp. 85-120 (paraphrase of the *Life*, probably based on the Damascus MS 9/29), 120-22 (on the Arab conquest)

I. Afrām I Barṣawm, *Al-luʾluʾ al-manthūr fī tārīkh al-ʿulūm wa-l-ādāb al-suryāniyya*, Baghdad, 1943, no. 39

F. Nau, 'Un colloque du patriarche Jean avec l'émir des Agaréens et faits divers ... avec un appendice ... sur un diplôme qui aurait été donné par Omar à l'évêque du Ṭour ʿAbdīn', in *Journal asiatique* 11th s., 5 (1915) 225-79 (based on MS BNF – Syr. 375, which differs from the London MS)

Nau, 'Notice historique sur le monastère de Qartamin'

Andrew Palmer 2008

The Life of John of Edessa

Unknown author

DATE OF BIRTH Unknown, perhaps 8th or 9th c.
PLACE OF BIRTH Perhaps Edessa
DATE OF DEATH Unknown, perhaps 9th or 10th c.
PLACE OF DEATH Perhaps Edessa

BIOGRAPHY

The anonymous author of the *Life of John of Edessa* seems to have been active in about 900, perhaps in Edessa. Beyond this, nothing else about him is known.

MAIN SOURCES OF INFORMATION

Primary —

Secondary

J. Lamoreaux and H. Khairallah, 'The Arabic version of the Life of John of Edessa', *Le Muséon* 113 (2000) 439-60

P. Peeters, 'La passion de S. Michel le Sabaïte', *AB* 48 (1930) 65-98, pp. 85-91

K. K'ek'elidze, 'Zhitie i podvigi Ioanna, katolikosa Urhaĭskogo', *Khristianskiĭ vostok* 2 (1914) 301-48 (repr. with minor additions and corrections in his *Et'iudebi dzveli kartuli lit'erat'uris ist'oriidan*, 13 vols, Tbilisi, 1945-74, vii, pp. 102-35)

WORKS ON CHRISTIAN-MUSLIM RELATIONS

Untitled

DATE Perhaps c. 900
ORIGINAL LANGUAGE Arabic

DESCRIPTION

The *Life of John of Edessa* recounts the saintly bishop's debate and thaumaturgic contest with a certain Phineas the Jew, in the presence of the Caliph Hārūn al-Rashīd (r. 786-809). The text opens with a description of the wicked Jew Phineas, a courtier of the caliph, and how he had turned the caliph against the Christians. When John learns of this, after praying before the image of Christ in Edessa (mandylion), he travels to al-Raqqa to meet with the caliph. Upon John's arrival, the caliph summons him and Phineas to take part in a debate. The debate focuses on passages from the Hebrew Bible that support the doctrine of the Trinity. The caliph eventually finds himself convinced of the truth of the Christian position, and proceeds to present philosophical arguments in favor of the Trinity. Finding himself on the losing side, Phineas challenges John to perform miracles. The text recounts that John cast out a demon, caused Phineas to lose his ability to speak, drank poison without harm, caused Phineas' hand to wither, and lastly raised the caliph's daughter from the dead. Not surprisingly, the caliph was seized by fear and wonder, with the result that he ordered a cessation of hostility against the Byzantines, permitted Christians to practice their faith openly, relieved them of their taxes, and allowed churches to be built throughout his kingdom.

While the text does not mention John's ecclesiastical affiliation, he was probably a Melkite – at least judging from the fact that only they preserved a memory of him. The text can be dated to some time after the reign of Hārūn al-Rashīd, but before its first witnesses. The earliest of these is a liturgy in John's honor, copied by the famous Georgian hymnographer Michael Modrekeli, preserved in MS Tbilisi, Institute of Manuscripts, S-425 (copied between 978 and 988). Whoever the author of the original Georgian liturgy was, it is clear that he made use of a Georgian version of the *Life* of John. This Georgian version, in turn, was translated from Arabic, apparently the language of its composition. The text must therefore have appeared after c. 800 (the reign of Hārūn al-Rashīd) but before c. 975 (the *floruit* of Modrekeli). A date of composition c. 900 seems not unlikely.

The Georgian version of the *Life* is preserved in a single manuscript (MS BL – Add. 11281, copied at the Monastery of the Holy Cross, near Jerusalem, between 1034 and 1042). A complete copy of the Arabic version once existed in a 10th-century Sinai MS. It entered the antiquities market in the 1920s (Hiersemann Katalog 500, no. 14), and was purchased by the Catholic University of Louvain. It did not survive the Second World War, however, being destroyed by fire in 1940 during the German invasion of Louvain. What must have been an index added to this manuscript by a later scribe was excised and sold separately. It ended up in the Mingana Collection (MS Mingana – Chr. Arab. Add. 172, copied in 1287). An additional page from this manuscript has been preserved in MS Mingana – Chr. Arab. Add. 195.

Substantial portions of the Arabic version of the *Life* have been published from the fragments preserved in MS Sinai – Ar. 441, copied in 1287. A complete Arabic version of the *Life* is also said to be extant in a 19th-century manuscript in Dayr al-Mukhalliṣ (2252). It has not yet been published.

SIGNIFICANCE

This text is patently a work of fiction, and the events it recounts never took place. But it is remarkable because it is a fine example of how the telling of stories can function polemically and apologetically, to refute the faith of one's opponents and defend one's own.

MANUSCRIPTS

MS Sinai – s.n. (10th c.) (MS that once contained a copy of the Arabic version, of which the index has survived in MS Mingana – Chr. Arab. Add. 172 and an additional page in MS Mingana – Chr. Arab. Add. 195) (For a brief description of this MS, prepared by A. Baumstark, see K.W. Hiersemann, *Katalog 500. Orientalische Manuskripte. Arabische, syrische, griechische, armenische, persische Handschriften des 7.-18. Jahrhdrts*, Leipzig, 1922, pp. 10-12 and plate VI)

MS BL – Add. 11281, fols 273v-285v (Georgian version copied between 1034 and 1042) (See J. Wardrop's appendix on the Georgian MSS of the British Library in F. Conybeare, *A Catalogue of the Armenian manuscripts in the British Museum*, London, 1913, pp. 397-405)

MS Sinai – Ar. 441, fols. 191r-198r (1287)

MS Joun, Dayr al-Mukhalliṣ – 2252, fols 13v-21r (19th c.) (cited in Haddad, *La Trinité divine*, p. 29)

EDITIONS AND TRANSLATIONS

Lamoreaux and Khairallah, 'The Arabic version of the life of John of Edessa', pp. 450-54 (edition and English trans. of the portions of the text preserved in MS Sinai Ar. 441)

Peeters, 'La passion de S. Michel le Sabaïte', pp. 87-89 (edition and Latin trans. of Ch. 14, from the now lost Sinai MS)

K'ek'elidze, 'Zhitie i podvigi Ioanna, katolikosa Urhaĭskogo', pp. 114-29 (edition of the Georgian version, with Russian trans., as well as an edition and trans. of Modrekili's liturgy in John's honor)

STUDIES

S. Rosenkranz, *Die jüdisch-christliche Auseinandersetzung unter islamischer Herrschaft 7.-10. Jahrhundert*, Bern, 2004, pp. 89-91

H. Khairallah, 'La joute de Jean d'Edesse avec le juif Phinéas', *Chronos* 4 (2001) 63-89

J. Lamoreaux, 'John of Edessa and Phineas the Jew at the court of Harun al-Rashid', *Karmo* 1 (1999) 5-21 (with a detailed summary of the life, based on the Georgian version)

R. Haddad, *La Trinité divine chez les théologiens arabes, 750-1050*, Paris, 1985, pp. 29-30

R. Caspar et al., 'Bibliographie du dialogue islamo-chrétien (6)', *Islamochristiana* 6 (1980) 259-99, p. 294

W. Strothmann, 'Die orientalischen Handschriften der Sammlung Mettler (Katalog Hiersemann 500)', in W. Voigt (ed.), *XIX. deutscher Orientalistentag*, Wiesbaden, 1977, 285-93, pp. 286-87 and 292, n. 31 (on the fate of the Sinai MS purchased by Louvain)

R. Caspar et al., 'Bibliographie du dialogue islamo-chrétien (1)', *Islamochristiana* 1 (1975) 125-81, p. 156

B. Outtier, 'Le sort des manuscrits du "Katalog Hiersemann 500"', *AB* 93 (1975) 377-80, p. 378

K'. K'ek'elidze, *Geschichte der kirchlichen Georgischen Literatur*, ed. P.M. Tarchnišvili and J. Assfalg, Rome, 1955, p. 480

Graf, *GCAL* ii, pp. 25-26

J. Simon, 'Répertoire des bibliothèques publiques et privées d'Europe contenant des manuscrits arabes chrétiens', *Orientalia* NS 7 (1938) 239-64, pp. 252-53 (on the Sinai MS purchased by Louvain)

P. Peeters, 'La passion de S. Julien d'Émèse', *AB* 47 (1929) 44-76, p. 63 n. 1 (on the date of the Sinai MS purchased by Louvain)

John C. Lamoreaux 2007

Peter of Bayt Raʾs

Buṭrus al-Shammās ibn Nasṭās al-Bayt Raʾsī

DATE OF BIRTH Probably 9th c.
PLACE OF BIRTH Unknown, possibly Bayt Raʾs (Capitolias in Transjordan)
DATE OF DEATH Probably 9th c., not later than 10th
PLACE OF DEATH Unknown, possibly Bayt Raʾs (Capitolias in Transjordan)

BIOGRAPHY

A marginal note in the oldest manuscript of *al-Burhān* identifies its author as 'the deacon Peter, son of Anastasius, of Bayt Raʾs' (MS Sinai – ar. 75 (not later than early 10th c.), fol. 102b), although it should be observed that notices in the two 13th-c. manuscripts offer variants on this name and make Peter a bishop. One may think of a 9th-c. Melkite churchman from (or serving in) Bayt Raʾs, Capitolias in the Transjordan. From the contents of his book, he appears to have been well-grounded in Greek patristic theology, Old Testament *testimonia*, and the Christian geography of the Holy Land; and he was not unacquainted with Islamic teaching.

MAIN SOURCES OF INFORMATION

Primary
MS Sinai – ar. 75

Secondary —

WORKS ON CHRISTIAN-MUSLIM RELATIONS

Al-burhān, 'The Proof', *Kitāb al-burhān*, 'The Book of the proof', *Kitāb burhān dīn al-naṣrāniyya*, 'The Proof of the Christian religion'

DATE 9th (or, at the latest, early 10th) c.
ORIGINAL LANGUAGE Arabic

DESCRIPTION

The compilation known as *al-Burhān*, 'The proof' or 'The demonstration', probably dates to the late 9th or early 10th century. The oldest manuscript copy of the work, MS Sinai – ar. 75, fols 102v-222r, preserves a note of the year 1002 in which the elderly Bishop Solomon of Mt Sinai reports that he had inherited the manuscript from his father *and his grandfather* (Swanson, 'Solomon', pp. 95-98), indicating that this manuscript was almost certainly in existence before the mid-10th century.

The compilation consists of four major parts: a major theological treatise followed by three separate catalogues of *testimonia* (Old Testament foreshadowings or witnesses to the career of Christ and to Christian teachings). The theological treatise is a presentation of Christian teaching about God, the Trinity and the Incarnation that is close to (and quotes from) *De fide orthodoxa* by John of Damascus (q.v.); it is concerned to assert and defend (neo-)Chalcedonian positions in a context of intra-Christian debate. All the same, the author is aware of Christian-Muslim apologetic *loci* and alludes to the Qurʾān and uses qurʾānic terminology in an unforced and skilful manner. Of considerable interest is the passage at the end of the treatise about the 'medicines and ointments' that Christ left his followers: (1) Baptism; (2) the Eucharist; (3) the Cross; (4) the Resurrection (and Sunday, the Day of Resurrection); (5) the *qibla* towards the east; (6) 'the traces of Christ and the places of his holiness in the world'; (7) the oil of Chrism. The important list of Palestinian churches and shrines that bear 'the traces of Christ' is interrupted by a brief composition on Christ's Call and Priesthood.

The three *testimonia*-catalogues that fill out the compilation are of different sorts. The first lists Old Testament *types* of Christ and his incarnate career (and by its list of grammatically feminine types of the Virgin Mary, shows itself clearly to be an original composition in Arabic). The second catalogue is a list of 'evidences', Old Testament passages of Christological or Trinitarian apologetic utility, arranged according to biblical book and without commentary. The third catalogue is a list of testimonies to Christ's Incarnation and earthly life, death, burial, resurrection and ascension, arranged in narrative sequence.

It should be noted that Graf misidentified the author of the work as Eutychius, Melkite patriarch of Alexandria. This misidentification held sway until the work of Blau, Haddad and Breydy.

SIGNIFICANCE

In many ways, the compilation is closely related to Greek patristic works: it begins with a quotation from John of Damascus, while the final *testimonia*-catalogue is very similar to one preserved in a Greek text, the pseudo-Athanasian *Quaestiones ad Antiochum ducem*. However, there are numerous qurʾānic allusions and vocabulary items in the theological treatise that is Book I of the compilation (Watt, *Eutychius*, i, pp. iii-iv, and see his index of qurʾānic references, ii, p. 84), among which a striking example is the author's assertion that in his defeat of the Devil the Incarnate Word was proved to be *khayr al-mākirīn*, 'the best of devisers', an epithet used of God himself in the Qurʾān (Q 3:54 or 8:30). While the author does not bring Islamic teachings, practice and history explicitly into his arguments, they are clearly in the background of his assertions (for example) that the resurrection of Christ is the 'ground and verification' of the general resurrection; that Christianity spread through humble messengers supported by signs and wonders, and not by force or wealth or worldly wisdom; that the east as prayer-direction or *qibla* is superior to a *qibla* that is a spatially-limited place; and that Christ's *daʿwa* or call is the final and perfect one (implicitly leaving no room for a later messenger; Samir, 'The Prophet Muḥammad', pp. 82-83).

The various 'catalogues' found in *al-Burhān* are not without significance for the history of Christian-Muslim relations. The list of Palestinian churches and shrines in the 'traces of Christ' passage reflects a Christian community mapping out a Christian sacred geography even within the *Dār al-Islām*. As for the catalogues of Old Testament *testimonia*, they are tools to which Christian apologists regularly resorted in this early stage of the Christian-Muslim encounter.

MANUSCRIPTS

The oldest manuscripts are:

MS Sinai – ar. 75, fols 102-223 (late 9th or early 10th c.)

MS Vat – ar. 491 and 645 (dated 1234; Peter, 'bishop' of Bayt Raʾs, is identified as the brother of Basil the Great and Gregory of Nyssa)

MS Sinai – ar. 441, fols 121-227 (mid-13th c.; a marginal note identifies Peter as 'bishop' of Bayt Raʾs, while a colophon deforms the author's name into Qaṭarī ibn ʿUthmān)

MS Cairo, Coptic Orthodox Patriarchate – Theol. 209 (Simaika 238) (dated 1386; the work is attributed to St Athanasius)

In addition, a copy of *al-Burhān* was probably once present in MS Sinai – ar. 436 (10th c.), to judge from its index.

For other manuscripts, mostly from the 17th century and later (which regularly attribute the work to St Athanasius), see Graf, *GCAL* ii, p. 38, and Nasrallah, *HMLEM* ii.2, p. 144

EDITIONS AND TRANSLATIONS

P. Cachia (ed.) and W.M. Watt (trans.), *Eutychius of Alexandria. The Book of the demonstration (Kitāb al-burhān)*, Louvain, 1961 (*CSCO* 192-93 and 209-10) (edition using the oldest MS as base, and English trans.)

al-Qiddīs Athanāsiyūs al-rasūlī. Kamāl al-burhān ʿalā ḥaqīqat al-īmān, ed. Manassā Yūḥannā, Cairo, 1928 (and frequently reprinted) (The Coptic Orthodox editor freely removed the Chalcedonian 'interpolations' that he found in his source manuscript.)

Yūḥannā Martā, 'Shahādāt ʿarabiyya fī l-mazārāt al-filisṭīniyya', *Al-Mashriq* 5 (1902) 481-88 (from the passage listing Palestinian churches and shrines)

STUDIES

M.N. Swanson, 'Beyond prooftexting (2). The use of the Bible in some early Arabic Christian apologies', in D. Thomas (ed.), *The Bible in Arab Christianity*, Leiden, 2007, 91-112, pp. 99-105

M.N. Swanson, 'Solomon, bishop of Mount Sinai (late tenth century),' in R. Ebied and H. Teule (eds), *Studies on the Christian Arabic heritage*, Leuven, 2004, 91-111, pp. 95-98 (on the oldest manuscript)

B. Roggema, '*Ḥikayāt amthāl wa asmār*... King parables in Melkite apologetic literature', in R. Ebied and H. Teule (eds), *Studies on the Christian Arabic heritage*, Leuven, 2004, 113-31

S.K. Samir, 'The Prophet Muḥammad as seen by Timothy I and other Arab Christian authors', in D. Thomas (ed.), *Syrian Christians under Islam. The first thousand years*, Leiden, 2001, 75-106, pp. 82-83

S.K. Samir, 'al-Turāth al-ʿarabī l-masīḥī l-qadīm wa-l-Islām', in G.N. Nahhas (ed.), *al-Masīḥiyya wa-l-Islām. Mirāyā mutaqābila*, Balamand, 1997, 69-118, pp. 108-13

S.H. Griffith, 'The view of Islam from the monasteries of Palestine in the early ʿAbbāsid period', *ICMR* 7 (1996) 9-28, pp. 20-21

M.N. Swanson, *Folly to the* ḥunafāʾ. *The cross of Christ in Arabic Christian-Muslim controversy in the eighth and ninth centuries A.D.*, Cairo, 1995 (*estratto* from dissertation), pp. 28-30

M.N. Swanson, 'Ibn Taymiyya and the Kitāb al-burhān. A Muslim controversialist responds to a ninth-century Arabic Christian apology', in Y.Y. Haddad and W.Z. Haddad (eds), *Christian-Muslim encounters*, Gainesville FL, 1995, 95-107

R.L. Wilken, *The land called holy. Palestine in Christian history and thought*, New Haven CT, 1992, pp. 252-54

S.K. Samir, 'La littérature melkite sous les premiers abbassides', *OCP* 56 (1990) 469-86, pp. 483-85

S.H. Griffith, 'The monks of Palestine and the growth of Christian literature in Arabic', *MW* 78 (1988) 1-28, pp. 26-28

Nasrallah, *HMLEM* ii.2, pp. 31-34, 143-45

M. Breydy, *Das Annalenwerk des Eutychios von Alexandrien. Ausgewählte Geschichten und Legended kompiliert von Saʿid ibn Batriq um 935 A.D.*, Louvain, 1985 (*CSCO* 471-72), pp. 73-87

R. Haddad, *La Trinité divine chez les théologiens arabes (750-1050)*, Paris, 1985, pp. 63-65

A.M. Makhlouf, 'The Trinitarian doctrine of Eutychius of Alexandria (877-940 A.D.)', *Pd'O* 5 (1974) 5-20

J. Blau, *A grammar of Christian Arabic based mainly on South-Palestinian texts from the first millennium*, 3 vols, Louvain, 1966-67, i, pp. 22-23

Graf, *GCAL* ii, 35-38

G. Graf, 'Ein bisher unbekanntes Werk des Patriarchen Eutychius von Alexandrien', *OC* n.s.1 (1911) 227-44

G. Graf, *Die Philosophie und Gotteslehre des Jahjâ ibn ʿAdî und späteren Autoren*, Münster, 1910, pp. 56-62

Mark N. Swanson

Usṭāth al-Rāhib

The monk Eustathius

DATE OF BIRTH Unknown, possibly early 9th c. (and not later than 10th c.)
PLACE OF BIRTH Unknown, possibly Iraq
DATE OF DEATH Unknown, possibly later 9th c.
PLACE OF DEATH Unknown, possibly Iraq

BIOGRAPHY

Little is known about the monk Eustathius (Usṭāth), author of a wide-ranging Arabic-language apology for the Christian faith, although scattered indications point to a Syrian Orthodox (miaphysite) monk who may have lived in Iraq in the 9th century. His apology is mentioned by at least three authors of the Copto-Arabic tradition: first by the 10th-century author Sāwīrus ibn al-Muqaffaʿ, who made extensive use of Eustathius' apology in his *al-Bayān al-mukhtaṣar fī l-īmān* (and in Chapter Four refers to Eustathius by name as 'our brother'); by al-Nushūʾ Abū Shākir ibn al-Rāhib, in Chapter 16 of his theological compendium *al-Burhān*; and by Shams al-Riʾāsa Abū l-Barakāt ibn Kabar in the catalogue of theological writings that makes up Chapter 7 of his *Miṣbāḥ al-ẓulma fī īḍāḥ al-khidma*. Ibn al-Nadīm in the *Fihrist* and Ibn Abī Uṣaybiʿa in *ʿUyūn al-anbāʾ fī ṭabaqāt al-aṭibbāʾ* both mention someone named Eustathius among the translators of medical, scientific and philosophical works into Arabic; in particular, Ibn al-Nadīm mentions one Eustathius who translated part of Aristotle's *Metaphysica* for the philosopher al-Kindī (q.v.). Whether this translator is the same as the author of the apology, however, is at present a matter of speculation. (See Swanson, 'Eustathius', pp. 123-27. Nasrallah, 'Dialogue', p. 145, thinks that Eustathius the apologist is not to be confused with Eustathius the translator – and points out that he is certainly not to be identified with a Melkite Eustathius who died in 806, as in Sbath, *Fihris*, i, 29.)

MAIN SOURCES OF INFORMATION

Primary

Sāwīrus ibn al-Muqaffaʿ, *Kitāb al-bayān al-mukhtaṣar fī l-īmān*, Chapters 3-5a, ed. Samīr Khalīl, *Risālat al-kanīsa* 8 (1976) pp. 160-65, 200-6, 255-60, 309-16, 371-78, 411-17; p. 378

Ibn al-Nadīm, *Kitāb al-fihrist*, ed. G. Flügel, Leipzig, 1871-72; repr. Beirut: Maktabat Khayāṭ, 1966, p. 244

Ibn Abī Uṣaybiʿa, *ʿUyūn al-anbāʾ fī ṭabaqāt al-aṭibbāʾ*, ed. N. Riḍā, Beirut, 1965, p. 281

al-Nushūʾ Abū Shākir ibn al-Rāhib, *Kitāb al-Burhān*, MS BAV – ar. 104, fols 68v-72r and 181v-188r

Shams al-Riʾāsa Abū l-Barakāt ibn Kabar, *Miṣbāḥ al-ẓulma fī īḍāḥ al-khidma*, ed. Samīr Khalīl, Cairo, 1971, p. 321

Secondary

M.N. Swanson, '"Our brother, the monk Eustathius". A ninth-century Syrian Orthodox theologian known to medieval arabophone Copts', *Coptica* 1 (2002) 119-40

R.S. Burnham, *The* Book of Usṭāth *unearthed. An Arabic Christian apology of the ninth century*', St Paul MN, 2002 (MA thesis, Luther Seminary St Paul)

J. Nasrallah, 'Dialogue islamo-chrétien. À propos de publications récentes', *REI* 46 (1978) 121-51, p. 145

WORKS ON CHRISTIAN-MUSLIM RELATIONS

Kitāb Usṭāth (*al-rāhib*), 'The Book of Eustathius (the monk)', *Kitāb al-bayān*, 'The Exposition'

DATE Possibly 9th (and not later than 10th) c.
ORIGINAL LANGUAGE Arabic

DESCRIPTION

The *Book of Eustathius* claims to be the author's response 'to the one who wrote him asserting the correctness of the doctrine of the *muwaḥḥidūn* and their religions, such as the Jews and their like, and finding fault with the Christians and their religion' (Swanson, 'Eustathius', p. 129). The lengthy (213 folios in the most accessible manuscript) and rather loosely organized apologetic treatise that follows has a roughly Trinitarian shape, with a long central section devoted to various issues of importance in early Christian-Muslim controversy (Burnham, *The* Book of Usṭāth *unearthed*).

The work is usually referred to simply as *Kitāb Usṭāth* (*al-rāhib*), 'The book of Eustathius (the monk)'. Ibn Kabar (*Miṣbāḥ al-ẓulma*, ed. Samīr, p. 321) calls it *Kitāb al-bayān*, 'The book of the exposition', which may well be the original title.

The work is a wide-ranging apology for the Christian faith that deals with many of the challenges posed to Christians by Muslim controversialists, including the accusation of the falsification of Christian scriptures; apparent contradictions in the Gospels; the (in)coherence of Christian speech about the Incarnation, life, crucifixion and death of one confessed to be God; the explanation of Christian divisions; and the meaning of Christian veneration of icons.

SIGNIFICANCE

The *Book of Eustathius* is a significant early witness to Christian apologetic use (and accurate quotation) of the Qur'ān, as well as to Christian apologetic exploitation of 'issues such as the qur'ānic anthropomorphisms, or the paradox of God's predetermination and human capacity, that were hotly debated in the early Islamic centuries by Muslim *mutakallimūn*' (Swanson, 'Eustathius', p. 131).

MANUSCRIPTS

MS Aleppo, Fondation Georges et Mathilde Salem – Sbath 1011 (dated 1301, Dayr Shahrān)
MS Cairo, Coptic Patriarchate – Theol. 129 (Simaika 280; Graf 529) (13th-14th c.)
MS Birmingham, Mingana – Chr. Ar. 52 (A.D. 1876, Dayr al-Anbā Būlā; the most readily accessible of the manuscripts)
MS Cairo, Coptic Museum – Theol. Add. 7 (old register no. 4877, new register no. 124) (A.D. 1876, Dayr al-Anbā Būlā)
MS Cairo, Coptic Patriarchate – Theol. 128 (Simaika 279; Graf 620) (19th c., Dayr Barsūm al-ʿUryān = Dayr Shahrān)

In addition, Paul Sbath mentions two other manuscripts: one (uncatalogued) in his own collection, and one in that of ʿAbd al-Masīḥ Ṣalīb al-Masʿūdī (Sbath, *Fihris*, i, 29, no. 203).

EDITIONS AND TRANSLATIONS

Swanson, 'Eustathius', pp. 136-40 (English trans. of two short passages from Mingana Chr. Ar. 52, fols 146-47 and 199)
Burnham, *The* Book of Usṭāth *unearthed*, pp. 22-85 (edition, English trans. and commentary on a passage from Mingana Chr. Ar. 52, fols 135-47)

STUDIES

Swanson, 'Eustathius'

Burnham, *The* Book of Usṭāth *unearthed*

Karam Lamʿī (Karam Lamei), *Sāwīrus ibn al-Muqaffaʿ (al-qarn al-ʿāshir al-mīlādī). Kitāb al-bayān al-mukhtaṣar fī l-īmān, al-bāb al-awwal, Fī kayfiyyat al-tajassud*, Cairo, 1995 (BTh thesis, Evangelical Theological Seminary in Cairo)

A.Y. Sidarus, *Ibn al-Rahibs Leben und Werk. Ein koptisch-arabischer Enzyklopädist des 7./13. Jahrhunderts*, Freiburg, 1975, pp.112, 133

Eid Salah and Mark N. Swanson 2008

The Martyrdom of Michael of Mār Saba

Unknown author

DATE OF BIRTH Unknown, probably 8th or 9th c.
PLACE OF BIRTH Unknown
DATE OF DEATH Unknown, probably 9th or 10th c.
PLACE OF DEATH Unknown

BIOGRAPHY

The author of this *Martyrdom* does not reveal his identity, but was probably connected with the Monastery of Mār Saba, whose founder and later followers are highly praised in the epilogue.

MAIN SOURCES OF INFORMATION

Primary —

Secondary —

WORKS ON CHRISTIAN-MUSLIM RELATIONS

C'amebaj c'midisa mikaelisi romeli iq'o lavrasac'midi mamisa čuenisa sabajssa, 'The Martyrdom of Saint Michael who was in the great lavra of our holy father Saba' (the original Arabic title is lost)

DATE 9th c. or 10th c.
ORIGINAL LANGUAGE Probably Arabic

DESCRIPTION

The *Martyrdom* is said to have been narrated to the unnamed author by a certain Basil of Mār Saba, which is perhaps an allusion to the Basil who was *hegoumenos* of the monastery at the turn of the 9th century, according to Stephen Manṣūr (q.v.). Basil supposedly heard the story about Michael's martyrdom from Theodore Abū Qurra (q.v.), when he visited him in his cell.

Theodore relates to him how the Umayyad Caliph ʿAbd al-Malik, on a visit to Jerusalem, seeks a Christian knowledgeable in the law. A eunuch of the caliph's wife meets a young Sabaite monk called Michael who is selling his handicrafts in the market. The eunuch brings the young man to the caliph's wife, and she tries to seduce him. He rejects her advances and she then calls for him to be put to the test by the caliph. A religious dispute between the caliph and the young monk follows. The Muslim ruler voices two criticisms, first that monks transgress the laws of the Bible when they refrain from marriage and eating meat, and second that Christians have been led astray by Paul. However, the monk soon gets the upper hand in the dispute and asserts boldly that Muḥammad was an impostor who lured people to his false religion with promises of a carnal afterlife, and that Islam is confined to a geographically limited region while Christianity is spread throughout the world.

After trying to entice him to convert with promises of valuable gifts and a high position in the army, all to no avail, the caliph gives Michael a final choice between conversion and death. Michael chooses to die as a martyr but, miraculously, a cup of poison does not harm him. He is then put to death by the sword, his holiness immediately revealing itself through a series of miraculous events in the days that follow.

The narration, apart from numerous hagiographical motifs, also contains a variety of apologetic commonplaces, such as the presence of a Jew who unknowingly shows himself to be a supporter of Christianity rather than Islam. The plot seems to be inspired by the biblical story of Joseph and Potiphar's wife. As several scholars have noted, the historical framework is anachronistic. The Caliph ʿAbd al-Malik is said to reside in Babylon, a name frequently used for Baghdad, which suggests that the text cannot predate ʿAbbasid times. A reference to the 'martyred ones burnt with fire and cut with the sword' is in all likelihood a reference to the Twenty Martyrs of Mār Saba, who died in 797, and whose martyrdom was described by Stephen Manṣūr (q.v.) – an event that took place a century after ʿAbd al-Malik.

This reference forms a *terminus post quem*, while the oldest manuscript is proof of the fact that the composition had been completed by the 10th century. Griffith has tentatively proposed a date between 797 and 807, on account of the mention of a certain 'Thomas' as one of the great Sabaite figures, 'who furnished teachings for the lavra' (transl. Blanchard, p. 158). According to Griffith, this could well be a reference to the Thomas who became patriarch of Jerusalem in 807. He argues that, since this figure's rank is not mentioned, the text might predate that year. But this argument *e silentio* is not entirely compelling, not only because the correctness of the identification of this Thomas is uncertain, but also because the relevant passage is a flowery panegyric of the legendary figures of the lavra, not a precise record of their achievements. An additional argument against such an early date is perhaps the lightness of its tone. Lamoreaux ('Biography', p. 30) characterizes the debate with the caliph as 'not a little witty and humorous repartee – no doubt offering much pleasure to the original hearers of the text'. It is hard to imagine that such a text was composed only a few years after the ferocious attack on the lavra of Mār Saba that left many monks dead. These events surrounding the twenty martyrs of Mār Saba would have been alive in the mind of any Sabaite author in the early days of the 9th century, and supply the historical material for sober yet vivid and powerful martyrological accounts that could respond more realistically to the challenges facing the community than the overwhelmingly legendary and stylized account of the Martyrdom of Michael of Mār Saba.

The text has been edited from a 10th-century Georgian manuscript and probably survives in at least one other, if not more, Georgian manuscripts, as well as in Slavonic translations (Lamoreaux, 'Biography', pp. 28-29, and n. 19).

A similar story in Greek is incorporated into the *Life* of Theodore of Edessa (*BHG* 1744), which was composed in the 10th century, but this does not mean that the Martyrdom was originally composed in Greek. The Georgian text of the Martyrdom reveals numerous Arabisms, while no clear signs of an original Greek version can be detected (Blanchard, pp. 159-63). This has led a majority of scholars to conclude that the Martyrdom belongs to the corpus of hagiographical works composed originally in Arabic and translated into Georgian quite soon after their composition. Vila, however, draws attention to the possibility of the existence of a Greek account of the martyrdom preceding the Arabic: 'Certainly the story of this faithful martyr would have been passed down from generation to generation at the monastery and would likely have done so in Greek, at least initially' (Vila, *Christian martyrs*, pp. 168-69). This would have been probable if indeed Michael was a true historical early 8th-century martyr, but most scholars doubt that the story has a historical kernel.

SIGNIFICANCE

The *Martyrdom* is a Melkite example of the literary genre of writings which Griffith has entitled 'the monk in the Emir's majlis', combining well-known hagiographical topoi and polemical arguments against Islam to construct a model of resistance to conversion for Christians living in the Muslim world, especially monks. Although the person of Michael and the story of his martyrdom are in all likelihood unhistorical, the text is a witness to the arguments used by Christians and Muslims in early ʿAbbasid times to refute each other's faith.

MANUSCRIPTS

MS Mount Athos, Iviron Monastery – Georgian 57 (10th c.) fols 223r-231r

MS Oxford, Bodleian Library – s.n. (cf. P. Peeters, 'De codice Hiberico Bibliothecae Bodleianae Oxoniensis', *AB* 31 (1912) 301-18, p. 307)

EDITIONS AND TRANSLATIONS

M.J. Blanchard, 'The Georgian version of the Martyrdom of Saint Michael, monk of Mar Sabas Monastery', *Aram* 6 (1994) 149-63, pp. 149-58 (English trans. based on K'ek'elidze's edition)

P. Peeters, 'La Passion de s. Michel le sabaïte', *AB* 48 (1930) 65-98, pp. 66-77 (Latin trans.)

K. K'ek'elidze, *Kartuli agiograpiuli dzeglebi*, 2 vols, Tbilisi, 1918-46, i, pp. 165-73 (edition of MS Mount Athos, Iviron Monastery – Georgian 57)

STUDIES

S. Rosenkranz, *Die jüdisch-christliche Auseinandersetzung unter islamischer Herrschaft, 7.-10. Jahrhundert*, Bern, 2004, pp. 85-88

J.C. Lamoreaux, 'The biography of Theodore Abū Qurrah revisited', *DOP* 56 (2002) 25-40

S.H. Griffith, 'The *Life of Theodore of Edessa*. History, hagiography, and religious apologetics in Mar Saba Monastery in early Abbasid times', in J. Patrich (ed.), *The Sabaite heritage in the Orthodox Church from the fifth century to the present*, Louvain, 2001, 147-69

D. Vila, *Christian martyrs in the first Abbasid century and the development of an apologetic against Islam*, St Louis, 1999 (Diss. St Louis University), pp. 160-77

S.H. Griffith, 'Christians, Muslims, and neo-martyrs. Saints' lives and Holy Land history', A. Kofsky and G.G. Stroumsa (eds), *Sharing the sacred. Religious contacts and conflicts in the Holy Land, first-fifteenth centuries CE*, Jerusalem, 1998, 163-207, pp. 170-80

PMBZ no. 5003, and i (Prolegomena), p. 211
Hoyland, *Seeing Islam*, pp. 379-81
Blanchard, 'The Georgian version of the Martyrdom', pp. 159-63
S.H. Griffith, 'Michael, the martyr and monk of Mar Sabas monastery, at the court of the Caliph ʿAbd al-Malik. Christian apologetics and martyrology in the early Islamic period', *Aram* 6 (1994) 115-48
Nasrallah, 'Dialogue islamo-chrétien à propos de publications récentes', *REI* 46 (1978) 121-51, pp. 132-33
A. Vasiliev, 'The Life of St Theodore of Edessa', *Byzantion* 16 (1942-43) 165-225, pp. 174-76, 210-16

Barbara Roggema 2008

The Martyrdom of Elias of Helioupolis (Elias of Damascus)

Unknown author

DATE OF BIRTH Unknown
PLACE OF BIRTH Unknown
DATE OF DEATH Unknown
PLACE OF DEATH Unknown

BIOGRAPHY

The anonymous author of the *Martyrdom of Elias of Helioupolis (Elias of Damascus)* (*BHG* 578, 579) must have been a native of Syria-Palestine but it is not certain when he lived and in what circumstances he became acquainted with the story of the martyrdom of this Christian saint.

MAIN SOURCES OF INFORMATION

Primary —

Secondary —

WORKS ON CHRISTIAN-MUSLIM RELATIONS

Hypomnēma kath' historian tēs athlēseōs tou hagiou megalomartyros Hēlia tou neou, tou apo Hēlioupolitōn, en Damaskō martyrēsantos, 'Memorial on the basis of an account of the martyrdom of the holy great martyr Elias the Younger, from Helioupolis, who suffered martyrdom in Damascus', 'The Martyrdom of Elias of Helioupolis'

DATE 9th-10th c.
ORIGINAL LANGUAGE Greek

DESCRIPTION

The Martyrdom of Elias (759-79 or 775-95) is the biography of a neo-martyr born to a Christian family in Helioupolis (Baalbek) and trained as a carpenter. Together with his mother and two brothers, he left his native town for Damascus, where for two years he was employed by a Syrian. The latter was converted to Islam by an Arab magnate, and when he gave a dinner party for his son's birthday, Elias was pressured by the guests to renounce his Christian faith, but to no avail. He joined in the eating and dancing, during which a few of the guests conspired surreptitiously to loosen his belt. However, the next morning Elias was accused of having in fact renounced his faith – probably because his loose belt was a sign of his having given up his status as *dhimmī* – and so he was urged by his brother to leave Damascus for Helioupolis until the rumor died down. Having followed his trade in Helioupolis for eight years, Elias, now 20, deemed it safe to return to Damascus, where he opened his own workshop making camel saddles. However, he was denounced out of envy by his former employer and taken to a Muslim official, who invited him to renounce his Christian faith. He was whipped and tortured and then dragged off to the governor of the city, but again he refused to convert to Islam, and he finally suffered martyrdom on 1 February, 779 or 795 (6287 in the Alexandrian era). His body was left hanging for 14 days before being cast into the river Chrysorrhoas (Baradā). Pieces of his relics were collected by pious Christians from Helioupolis, to some of whom the saint appeared in a vision.

SIGNIFICANCE

The Martyrdom of Elias of Helioupolis gives a vivid picture of the daily coexistence of Christians and Muslims in 8th-century Damascus. The settings of the saint's biography and martyrdom are totally secular, in contrast with the overwhelmingly monastic character of Greek hagiography written in the 8th to 10th centuries.

MANUSCRIPTS

MS BNF – Coislin 303 (10th c.), fols 236v-249v

EDITIONS AND TRANSLATIONS

S. McGrath, 'Elias of Heliopolis. The Life of an eighth-century Syrian saint', in J.W. Nesbitt (ed.), *Byzantine authors. Literary activities and preoccupations. Texts and translations dedicated to the memory of Nicolas Oikonomides*, Leiden, 2003, 85-107, pp. 91-107 (English trans. and commentary)

A. Papadopoulos-Kerameus, *Sbornik palestinskoj i sirijskoj agiologii/ Syllogē Palaistinēs kai Syriakēs hagiologies*, 2 vols, St Petersburg, 1907-13, i, pp. 42-59 (repr. Thessaloniki, 2001)

F. Combefis, *Christi martyrum lecta trias*, Paris, 1666, pp. 155-206 (partial edition)

STUDIES

C. Foss, 'Byzantine saints in early Islamic Syria', *AB* 125 (2007) 93-119, pp. 107-9

McGrath, 'Elias of Heliopolis', pp. 85-90

PMBZ nos. 1485 (Elias), 4231 (al-Layth)

D. Vila, *Christian martyrs in the first Abbasid century and the development of an apologetic against Islam*, St Louis, 1999 (Diss. St Louis University), pp. 267-78

Hoyland, *Seeing Islam*, pp. 363-65

Dumbarton Oaks Hagiography Database, Washington DC, 1998, p. 34

C. Loparev, 'Vizantijskia žitija sviatych VIII-IX vekov', *VV* 19 (1912) 36-40

Stephanos Efthymiadis 2008

The Life of Timothy of Kākhushtā

Unknown author

DATE OF BIRTH 9th or 10th c.
PLACE OF BIRTH Perhaps Syria
DATE OF DEATH 9th or 10th c.
PLACE OF DEATH Perhaps Syria

BIOGRAPHY

Little is known about the authors of various recensions of the *Life of Timothy of Kākhushtā*. The earliest version seems to have been written by someone attached to the monastery of the saint, following his death in the early decades of the 9th century (Lamoreaux and Cairala, *Life of Timothy*, p. 27). Later versions, in Arabic, Greek, and Georgian, were written in Antioch after Timothy's remains had been translated there, in the mid-11th century (Lamoreaux and Cairala, *Life of Timothy*, p. 26).

MAIN SOURCES OF INFORMATION

Primary —

Secondary

J. Lamoreaux and C. Cairala, *The Life of Timothy of Kākhushtā*, Turnhout, 2000 (*Patrologia Orientalis* 48.4), pp. 9-33
Nasrallah, *HMLEM* ii.2, p. 165
K. K'ek'elidze, *Et'iudebi dzveli kartuli lit'erat'uris ist'oriidan*, 13 vols, Tbilisi, 1945-74, vi, pp. 276-311 ('T'imote Ant'iok'eli (ucnobi sirieli moɣvac'e VIII sauk'unisa)')
K. K'ek'elidze, *Geschichte der kirchlichen Georgischen Literatur*, ed. P.M. Tarchnišvili and J. Assfalg, Rome, 1955, p. 496
Graf, *GCAL* i, pp. 522-23, ii, p. 474

WORKS ON CHRISTIAN-MUSLIM RELATIONS

Sīrat al-qiddīs al-fāḍil al-nāsik Tīmāthayūs, 'The Life of the holy and virtuous ascetic, Timothy', 'Life of Timothy of Kākhushtā'

DATE 9th or 10th c.
ORIGINAL LANGUAGE Arabic

DESCRIPTION
The *Life of Timothy* is set in the last decades of the 8th century and the early decades of the 9th, in the little-known villages located between Antioch and Aleppo. Timothy was a native of the otherwise unknown village of Kākhushtā. His parents having died while he was still an infant, he was raised by his brothers and sisters. When he was seven years old, a beating at the hands of his eldest brother caused him to flee Kākhushtā. He was taken in by the residents of the nearby village of Kafr Zūmā, where he lived until coming of age, at which point he decided to renounce the world. He traveled to Jerusalem, where he visited the holy sites and eventually received the monastic habit. In time, he returned to Kafr Zūmā, where for many years he lived the life of an enclosed hermit. When he was about 40 years old, he was required to travel to Antioch. On the way, he stopped at Kākhushtā and was persuaded to stay. He began, once again, to live the life of a recluse. In time, his reputation for sanctity grew and he began to receive disciples. By the time Timothy died, a monastery had grown up around his hermitage.

The *Life of Timothy of Kākhushtā* is extant in a number of different recensions. The earliest of these has been partially preserved in MS BNF – Ar. 259. Originally written in Arabic, it seems to have been the monks of his monastery who drew up this first account of Timothy's life. When Timothy's remains were translated to Antioch, in the middle decades of the 11th c., his life was rewritten, its weak Arabic being strengthened and its unadorned narrative being embellished. This recension is preserved in MS Saidnaya, Convent of Our Lady of Saidnaya – 94. This second Arabic version, or one quite similar to it, shortly thereafter served as the basis for a Greek version, now lost. This Greek version, in turn, was almost immediately translated into Georgian. Yet another version of the *Life* has recently come to light in a manuscript in the Greek Orthodox Patriarchate in Damascus. The relation of this recension to the other Arabic versions, as well as to the Georgian version, has yet to be determined.

SIGNIFICANCE

The *Life of Timothy of Kākhushtā* sheds much light on the religious life of the Syrian countryside in the early decades of the ʿAbbasid period. Blake is quite right in observing that 'le tableau que cette Vie trace de la vie religieuse en Syrie est sans pareil' (Blake, 'Littérature grecque', p. 377). (In what follows, Timothy's *Life* is cited first according to the numbering of the paragraphs of the Paris recension, where extant, followed by that of the Saidnaya recension.) Much of the *Life* is concerned with Timothy's day-to-day interactions with the faithful of his monastery, with pilgrims, and with local villagers. Occasionally his life intersected with the broader currents of his time, in particular the exile and imprisonment under Hārūn al-Rashīd of Theodoret, Patriarch of Antioch (§§ 27-28/33-34). Of particular note are Timothy's encounters with Muslims. They cross the stage of his *Life* on a number of occasions: a Muslim from Kākhushtā, whom Timothy punishes for his sexual sins (§ 18/23); a Muslim who converts to Christianity on meeting Timothy (§ 25/31); and Muslim ghazis engaged in plunder of Byzantine territory who have a miraculous encounter with the saint (-/§ 44).

MANUSCRIPTS

MS Saidnaya, Convent of Our Lady of Saidnaya – 94, fols 129v-154v (1396)

MS BNF – Ar. 259, fols 104v-150v (14th c.)

MS Damascus, Greek Orthodox Patriarchate – 394, pp. 79-122 (18th c.)

MS Saidnaya, Convent of Our Lady of Saidnaya – 63, one folio in length, about ten folios from the end of the otherwise unfoliated and undated MS (a fragment of the recension witnessed by Saidnaya 94)

For a list of the Georgian MSS containing the Life, see K'ek'elidze, *Geschichte der kirchlichen Georgischen Literatur*, p. 496.

EDITIONS AND TRANSLATIONS

Lamoreaux and Cairala, *The Life of Timothy of Kākhushtā*, pp. 38-183 (edition of the Arabic versions found in the Paris and Saidnaya MSS, with English trans.)

K. K'ek'elidze, *Et'iudebi dzveli kartuli lit'erat'uris ist'oriidan*, vi, pp. 311-413 (edition of the Georgian version); reprinted from his 'T'imote Ant'iok'eli (ucnobi sirieli moɣvac'e VIII sauk'unisa)', *Enis, ist'oriisa da mat'erialuri k'ult'uris inst'it'ut'i ak'ad. N. Maris sax.* 7 (1940) 1-150

STUDIES

C. Foss, 'Byzantine saints in early Islamic Syria', *AB* 125 (2007) 93-119

Lamoreaux and Cairala, *The Life of Timothy of Kākhushtā*, pp. 9-33

Hoyland, *Seeing Islam*, pp. 113-15, 719-20

B. Tūmā, *Siyar al-qiddīsīn wa-sā'ir al-aʿyād fī l-kanīsa l-urthūdhuksiyya (al-Sinaksār)*, 2 vols, Dūmā, 1992-97, ii, pp. 370-78

B. Tūmā, *al-Qiddīsūn al-mansiyyūn fī l-turāth al-Anṭākī*, Beirut, 1995, pp. 201-23

J.-M. Sauget, *Premières recherches sur l'origine et les caractéristiques des synaxaires melkites (XIe-XVIIe siècles)*, Brussels, 1969, pp. 334-37

R. Blake, 'Littérature grecque en Palestine au VIIIe siècle', *Le Muséon* 78 (1965) 367-80, p. 377

G. Garitte, 'Bibliographie de K. Kekelidze († 1962)', *Le Muséon* 76 (1963) 443-80, p. 457, no. 81, and 472, no. 140q

G. Garitte, 'La passion de S. Élien de Philadelphie (ʿAmman)', *AB* 79 (1961) 412-46, p. 412

G. Garitte, *Le calendrier palestino-géorgien du Sinaiticus 34 (Xe siècle)*, Brussels, 1958, p. 272

M. Tarchnišvili, 'Kurzer Überblick über den Stand der georgischen Literaturforschung', *OC* 37 (1953) 89-99, p. 97

P. Peeters, *Le tréfonds oriental de l'hagiographie byzantine*, Brussels, 1950, p. 22

R. Blake, 'Deux lacunes comblées dans la *Passio XX monachorum sabaitarum*', *AB* 68 (1950) 27-43, p. 28 n. 3

P. Peeters, 'La vie géorgienne de Saint Porphyre de Gaza', *AB* 59 (1941) 65-216, pp. 68-69

V. Beneshevich, 'Bibliographische Notizen und Nachrichten', *Byzantinisch-neugriechische Jahrbücher* 8 (1931) 429-30

H. Delehaye, *Les saints stylites*, Brussels, 1923, p. cxxv

P. Peeters, 'S. Hilarion d'Ibérie', *AB* 32 (1913) 236-69, p. 240

John C. Lamoreaux 2007

Index of Names

Numbers in italics indicate a main entry.

Aaron 48, 49, 298, 893
ʿAbbād ibn Sulaymān 588
ʿAbbasids 519, 521, 544, 557, 560, 567, 578, 601, 602, 622, 703, 704, 706, 710, 732, 740, 741, 751, 753, 762, 766, 768, 776, 788, 800, 801, 829, 853, 854, 869, 870, 912, 914, 921
ʿAbdallāh ibn Faḍl al-Anṭākī 569, 578
ʿAbdallāh ibn Ismāʿīl al-Hāshimī, *see* al-Hāshimī, ʿAbdallāh ibn Ismāʿīl
ʿAbdallāh ibn al-Mubārak 74, 75, 76, 835
ʿAbdallāh ibn Saʿd 287
ʿAbdallāh ibn Ṭāhir 503
ʿAbdallāh ibn al-Thāmir 61
ʿAbdallāh ibn al-Zubayr 173
ʿAbd al-ʿAzīz ibn Marwān 210
ʿAbd al-Jabbār 14, 42, 351, 548-549, 620, 621, 650, 707, 710, 712, 716
ʿAbd al-Malik, caliph 166, 173, 174, 224, 258, 265, 266, 269, 285, 295, 430, 625, 912
ʿAbd al-Malik, governor 317
ʿAbd al-Masīḥ, martyr *684-87*
ʿAbd al-Masīḥ, al-ʿĀqib 65, 66
ʿAbd al-Masīḥ al-Kindī *585-94*
ʿAbd al-Masīḥ ibn Nūḥ 397
ʿAbd al-Raḥmān I, Spanish emir 834
ʿAbd al-Raḥmān II, Spanish emir 679, 681, 825, 884
ʿAbd al-Raḥmān ibn ʿAbd al-Malik al-Hāshimī 560, 877
ʿAbd al-Raḥmān ibn al-Ashtar 178
ʿAbd al-Raḥmān ibn Ghanm 360
ʿAbd al-Razzāq al-Ṣanʿānī 36, 50, 52, 78, 79, 82
ʿAbdīshō bar Brīkā 269
ʿAbdīshūʿ ibn Bahrīz *550-52*, 554, 568
ʿAbdīshūʿ of Nisibis 397, 399
Ablution 109, 536
Abjuration, *see* Ritual of abjuration
Abraham 3, 5, 23, 55, 131, 141, 161, 224, 243, 270, 298, 331, 588, 608, 620, 710, 715, 755, 812, 879
  as friend of God 620, 710, 715
Abraham, Dome of, *see* Dome of the Rock
Abraham II, patriarch 688
Abraham of Bēt Ḥālē 269
Abraham of Tiberias 560, *876-81*
Abraham bar Dāshandād 397, 515
Abraham, known as Artavazd 281, 282
Abū l-ʿAbbās al-Baṭrīq Ashūṭ ibn Sinbāṭ 568
Abū l-ʿAbbās ʿĪsā ibn Zayd *857-58*
Abū ʿAbdallāh Muḥammad ibn Aḥmad al-Ṣafwānī 537
Abū Aḥmad Yaḥyā ibn al-Munajjim *762-67*, 775, 776
Abū ʿAlī al-Jubbāʾī 621
Abū Bakr, caliph 741, 788
Abū Bakr al-Khallāl 362
Abū Bakr al-Bāqillānī, *see* al-Bāqillānī, Abū Bakr
Abū Bakr al-Rāzī 348, 889
Abū l-Barakāt ibn Kabar 397, 558, 578, 607, 758, 776, 907, 909
Abū Dāwūd al-Sijistānī 76, *819-20*
Abū l-Faḍl ʿAlī ibn Rabban al-Naṣrānī 652
Abū l-Faraj Saʿīd ibn ʿAlī al-Anbārī *859-60*
Abū Ḥanīfa 354, 544
Abū Ḥāritha, bishop 65
Abū l-Ḥasan al-Ashʿarī, *see* al-Ashʿarī
Abū l-Hudhayl al-ʿAllāf 371, 372, 532, *544-49*, 588, 604, 606, 618, 619, 656, 657, 716
Abū ʿĪsā l-Warrāq 608, *695-701*, 749, 890, 891
Abū Jaʿfar al-Ṭabarī, *see* al-Ṭabarī, Abū Jaʿfar
Abū l-Khayr ʿĪsā ibn Hibat Allāh *861-62*
Abū Mūsā l-Ashʿarī 131
Abū Nūḥ al-Anbārī *397-400*, 859
Abū Rāʾiṭa l-Takrītī 553, 554, *567-81*, 588, 605, 743, 776, 879
Abū Saʿīd ibn Yūnus 740
Abū Sufyān 68
Abū Ṭālib 62
Abū Yūsuf Yaʿqūb 103, *354-59*, 360, 362

Abū Yūsuf al-Kindī, *see* al-Kindī, Abū Yūsuf
Abū Zakkār Yaḥyā ibn Nuʿmān *565-66*, 669
Abyssinia 58, 61, 63, 64, 65, 66, 69
Adam 69, 125, 164, 201, 211, 242, 245, 249, 331, 378, 480, 514, 527, 530, 788
Adamnan, *see* Adomnán of Iona
Addai 89, 92, 93, 94, 95, 96, 227, 228, 314
Adomnán of Iona 13, 149, 154-56
Adoptionism 338, 339, 341, 365, 633
ʿAdī ibn Zayd 510
Africa 96, 117, 717, *see also* North Africa; Ifrīqiyā
Afterlife 24, 271, 507, 508, 601, 608, 609, 649, 657, 677, 912, *see also* Paradise; Heaven
Agapius of Manbij 191, 306
Agarenes, *see* Hagarenes
Agathias 213
Aghlabids 13, 804, 806
Agobard, archbishop 97, 98
Ahl al-dhimma 6, 8, 10, 85, 89, 101-9, 110, 111, 112, 113, 295, 355, 357, 361, 362, 622, 704, 709, 712, 917
  Dress of 356, 712
  Impurity of 109
  Inheritance 106
  New churches 356
  Religious ceremonies of 107
Ahl al-kitāb 22, 101, 839
Aḥmad ibn ʿAmr al-Khaṣṣāf 356
Aḥmad ibn Ḥanbal 42, 80, 354, 780, 816, 832
Aix, Council of, *see under* Church councils
Akbar 404
Albar, *see* Paul Alvarus
Alcuin of York 365, 366, 633
Alexander the Great 24, 145, 164, 165, 166, 249
Alexander II, patriarch 234
Alexandria 8, 66, 120, 131, 209-11, 219, 226, 234, 235, 253, 256, 257, 258, 259, 274, 317, 318, 321, 428, 665, 687, 702, 703, 704, 792, 852, 903, 917
Alfonso I 884
Alfonso II 884
Alfonso III of Oviedo 288, 811, 812, *882-88*, 884
ʿAlī ibn Abī Ṭālib, caliph 42, 145, 146, 205, 285, 532, 540
ʿAlī l-Riḍā, Imām 532, 535, 536, 538
ʿAlī ibn Rabban al-Ṭabarī 507, 565, 566, 652, *669-74*, 752, 817
ʿAlī ibn Yaḥyā ibn al-Munajjim *762-67*, 775, 776
ʿAlids 205, 540, 780
Aljamiado 47, 375, 381, 382, 383
Alphonse, *see* Alfonso
Altar 90, 96, 220, 228, 499, 615, 693
Alvaro, *see* Paul Alvarus
Amida 186, 187, 188, 322
al-Amīn, caliph 309, 411, 412, 428, 494, 582, 788
ʿĀmir ibn ʿAbd Allāh ibn al-Jarrāḥ 190
ʿAmmār al-Baṣrī 372, 545, 547, 548, 588, *604-10*, 714, 776, 879
Amorion 675, 676, 731, 844, 845, 846, 848
Amphilochius of Iconium 335
ʿAmr ibn al-ʿĀṣ 8, 64, 190, 211, 236
ʿAmru bar Ṣaʿd 783
Anania Mokatsʿ I 262
Anas ibn Mālik 42
Anastas, patriarch 719
Anastasius of Sinai 848
Anastasius Bibliothecarius *786-90*, 804
al-Anbār 397, 857, 859
al-Andalus 9, 10, 47, 62, 63, 102, 104, 105, 107, 109, 112, 114, 286, 187, 288, 302, 303, 338, 340, 341, 633, 735, 736, 738, 740, 741, 812, 825, 826, 827, 834, 835, 837
Anna, *see* Ḥannah
Antheousa, St, monastery of, *see under* Monasteries
Anthony, St 77, 78
Anthony (Rawḥ al-Qurashī) *498-501*
Anthropomorphism 611, 649, 692, 723
Antichrist 142, 161, 165, 179, 182, 183, 246, 275, 298, 414, 415, 647, 681, 683, 693, 721, 722
Antioch 47, 48, 89, 91, 92, 93, 94, 157, 194, 196, 213, 226, 314, 317, 428, 430, 439, 557, 783, 904, 919, 920, 921
Antony the Younger *726-28*
Apocalyptic literature 48, 73, 74-77, 82, 139, 142, 143, 160-62, 163-71, 172-75, 179, 182-85, 222-25, 239-41, 243, 245-48, 249-52, 258, 259, 274-80, 286, 309-13, 411, 412, 414-18, 492, 493, 495, 600, 601, 602, 603, 827
Apocrypha 34, 35, 47, 48, 49, 50, 51, 52, 75, 82, 239, 241, 416, 788, *see also* Gospels, apocryphal
Apollinarians 701
Apollonius of Tyana 507
Apostasy 165, 183, 198, 228, 258, 323, 325, 328, 391, 408, 437, 598, 625, 646, 679, 682, 685, 878

Apostles 16, 23, 47, 67, 166, 194, 222-25, 378, 387, 463, 467, 799, *see also* disciples of Jesus
al-Aqṣā mosque 155
Aquitaine 88, 294
Arab conquests 8, 11, 59, 71, 78, 86, 87, 112, 118, 121, 123, 125, 126, 129, 131, 133, 137, 138, 141, 142, 149, 155, 161, 164, 177, 182, 183, 187, 191, 193, 199, 211, 214, 215, 235, 236, 276, 286, 287, 288, 294, 303, 307, 341, 361, 428, 432, 437, 609, 625, 665, 666
Arabia 2, 25, 27, 31, 32, 33, 36, 46, 47, 58, 59, 67, 71, 105, 112, 131, 151, 152, 223, 290, 404, 438, 510, 512, 601, 746, 834, *see also* Arabian peninsula
Arabian peninsula 4, 21, 23, 26, 27, 28, 30, 47, 108, 685
Arculf, bishop 13, 149, 154, 155
Arians 265, 296, 298, 299, 487, 530
Aristotle 371, 397, 399, 439, 507, 515, 516, 520, 521, 550, 552, 560, 573, 714, 731, 747, 776, 852, 907
Armenia 139, 142, 173, 205, 261, 262, 265, 282, 439, 441, 567, 568, 719, 720, 764, 765, 854, 867, 868, 869, 890
Armenian Bible 203, 204
  Church 139, 206, 266, 867
  Gospel of the Infancy, *see* Gospels, apocryphal
  language 83, 141, 166, 203, 204, 205, 206, 263, 281, 282, 375, 441, 567, 719, 867, 868, 869
Artavazd, *see* Abraham, known as Artavazd
Asad ibn Mūsā 74
Aṣbagh ibn Mālik 834, 837
Ascalon 394
Ascension, church of, *see under* Churches, *see also* Jesus, ascension of
Ascetic literature 73, 74-82, 133, 194, 291, 343
Ascetism 39, 40, 41, 42, 51, 60, 61, 76, 121, 315, 407, 420, 532, 611, 614, 634, 827, 829, 834, 920
al-Ashʿarī, Abū l-Ḥasan 372, 545, 657, 713, 714
Ashʿarīs 54
Ashot I Bagratuni 751, 867
Ashot II Erkatʿ 262
Ashot Smbāt Msaker 439, 568, 743
al-Askīm, Dayr 512, *see under* Monasteries
Associators 298, 738
Athanasius of Alexandria 257, 258, 259, 272, 274, 276
Athanasius of Balad 91, *157-59*
Atheists 371, 611, 631, 638, 677, 695
Athinganoi 821, 822
Attributes of God 372, 440, 448, 472, 520, 529, 540, 545, 547, 548, 572, 573, 588, 605, 649, 657, 760
Augustine, St 692
al-Ayham 65
Ayyūb al-Ruhāwī 'al-Abrash', *see* Job of Edessa
Ayyūb Urhāyā, *see* Job of Edessa
Ayyūbids 310

Baalbek 685, *see also* Helioupolis
Baghdad 6, 8, 11, 77, 305, 324, 335, 354, 371, 391, 392, 397, 408, 502, 510, 515, 516, 522, 532, 544, 548, 557, 558, 567, 582, 583, 588, 611, 618, 622, 631, 649, 656, 669, 695, 706, 713, 746, 757, 758, 762, 768, 816, 829, 832, 840, 857, 912
Bagratids 139, 262, 439, 743, 853, 854, 866, 867, 868, 870
Baḥīrā 22, 62, 71, 166, 265, 269, 270, 271, 298, 299, 310, 401, 402, 403, 404, 595, *600-3*
Baḥrīn 580
al-Balādhurī 59, 61, 62, 894
al-Balkhī, Abū l-Qāsim al-Kaʿbī 650
Banū Taghlib 75, 103, 112, 356
Baptism 92, 95, 117-19, 121, 126, 157, 159, 228, 242, 257, 271, 296, 331, 335, 340, 344, 425, 440, 485, 499, 505, 598, 608, 616, 719, 863, *see also* Jesus, baptism of
Baqī ibn Makhlad 834
al-Bāqillānī, Abū Bakr 700, 710
Baramūs, monastery of, *see under* Monasteries
Barbarians 84, 86, 90, 123, 177, 205, 393, 394, 395, 665, 666
Barcelona 341
Barhebraeus 89, 93, 94, 95, 96, 114, 228, 305, 306, 503, 516
Barmakids 347, 371, 502
Bartholomew, apostle 47, 67
Bartholomew of Edessa 424
Bashīr 863, 864
Basra 36, 90, 94, 131, 343, 371, 527, 532, 544, 548, 604, 606, 618, 656, 706, 713, 746, 757, 819, 877
Basil I, emperor 751, 752, 806
Basil of Mār Saba 911
Bassīmā, Mār(y), monastery of, *see under* Monasteries
Bassoēs, martyr 636, 637, 640, 676, 677
al-Bayhaqī, ʿAlī ibn Zayd 765, 766

Bayt Ra's, *see* Capitolias
Bede, Venerable 155
Behemoth 648
Benedict III, pope 786
Benjamin, patriarch 8, 183, 211, 235, 236, 259
Bēsér, *see* Bashīr
Bēt ʿAbē, *see under* Monasteries
Bēt Ḥālē, *see under* Monasteries
Bēt Malkā, *see under* Monasteries
Bethlehem 51, 125
Bible, 15, 16, 18, 24, 32, 33, 63, 82, 203, 204, 206, 226, 227, 402, 506, 527, 530, 577, 596, 671, 673, 707, 772, 782, 783, 812, 816, 876, 878, 912, *see also* Proof texts, Bible; Hebrew Bible
  Corruption of 16, 530, *see also* Corruption of scripture
  Important citations from:
    Genesis 17:20 224
    Deuteronomy 18:18 523
    Isaiah 21:6-9 523
    Daniel 7:1-27 275
    Daniel 7:23 142
    Daniel 7:24 142
    Matthew 24:7 173, 179
Biblical testimonia *see* Proof texts, Bible
al-Birūnī, Abū l-Rayḥān 503, 565, 585, 889, 890, 891
Bishop of Rome, *see* Pope
Bishr ibn al-Muʿtamir *532-34*, 611, 619, 657
Bishr ibn al-Walīd 355
Bithynia 423, 429, 727
Blood-money 110
Boniface, St 87
Book of Daniel, *see* Daniel, Book of
Book of Revelation, *see* Revelation, Book of
Brahmins 696
Bugha the Elder 853, 854
Byzantine empire 2-3, 4, 11, 12, 13, 59, 66, 67, 78, 86, 118, 123, 129, 131, 137, 141, 146, 164, 167, 177, 179, 187, 193, 214, 215, 224, 246, 257, 275, 285, 286, 307, 322, 323, 325, 338, 349, 351, 428, 429, 431, 500, 558, 582, 640, 677, 685, 727, 729, 731, 732, 735, 754, 764, 783, 788, 801, 821, 822, 845, 854, 863, 864, 868, 869, 899, 921, *see also* Romans

Caliphs, orthodox, *see* Rightly-guided caliphs
Callinicus 894
Callinicus, synod of, *see under* Church councils
Callistus, martyr 630, 631, 636, 640, 676
Capitolias 420, 421, 902, *see also* Peter of Capitolias
Cappadocian Fathers 507
Carthage 47, 67, 117
Catherine, St, monastery of, 193, 198-99, 330, 378, 492, 616, 685
Cedrenus 431
Chalcedon, 415, 421, *see also under* Church councils
Chariton, Mār, monastery of, *see under* Monasteries
Charlemagne, emperor 97, 338, 341, 365, 416
Charles the Bald, emperor 87, 804, 806
Charles the Fat, emperor 804, 806
Charles Martel 294
Childebrand, Count 293
Chora, monastery, *see under* Monasteries
Christ, *see* Jesus Christ
Christology 4, 128, 135, 151, 163, 299, 315, 331, 344, 378, 387, 439, *553-55*, 560, 568, 580, 665, 666, 734, 745, 793, 903
Church buildings 4, 75, 86, 106, 107, 294, 307, 356, 361, 415, 428, 429, 511, 512, 516, 601, 622, 625, 679, 685, 691, 837, 864, 874, 895, 899, 903, 904
  Church of the Ascension 430
  Church of Cosmas and Damian 599
  Church of St George 615
  Church of the Resurrection 470, 873
  Church of St Savinianos 420
  Church of St Stephen 328
  Church of St Theodore 149, 498
  Church of the Theotokos, Capitolias 420
  Church of the Theotokos, Jerusalem 121, 125
  Church of St Zoilus 691
Church councils 4, 83, 88, 93, 94, 196, 691, 730, 786
  Council of Aix 365
  Synod of Callinicus 622
  Council of Chalcedon 4, 275
  Third Council of Constantinople 86
  Fourth Council of Constantinople 86-87
  Synod of Constantinople 121, 123
  Council of Dvin 139
  Council of Frankfurt 338

Council of Nicea 327, 340, 390
Synod of Partaw 92, 265
Council in Trullo 86, 93
Church councils, ecumenical 87, 461
Circumcision 68, 94, 232, 298, 344, 425, 523, 557, 693
Coinage, Arab 430
Columba, St 154
Communion, *see* Eucharist
Constans II, emperor 137, 139, 149, 264, 730
Constantine, martyr 630, 636, 676
Constantine I, emperor 41, 44, 205, 223, 231, 415, 493
Constantine VI, emperor 12, 348, 349, 384, 416, 597, 598
Constantine VII Porphyrogenitus, emperor 424, 431, 731
Constantine-Cyril, *see* Cyril and Methodius
Constantinople 4, 5, 11, 12, 69, 86, 120, 123, 193, 194, 203, 206, 240, 246, 285, 286, 360, 415, 416, 423, 426, 428, 429, 494, 597, 614, 627, 628, 726, 727, 729, 731, 751, 753, 789, 800, 844, 872, 873, 874
Constantinople, Third Council of, *see under* Church councils
Constantinople, Fourth Council of, *see under* Church councils
Constantinople, Synod of, *see under* Church councils
Conversion 5, 10, 36, 64, 68, 71, 79, 95, 102, 107, 108, 142, 166, 183, 184, 188, 205, 243, 323, 408, 421, 428, 499, 500, 559, 561, 567, 578, 589, 598, 599, 614, 666, 669, 670, 671, 676, 685, 686, 693, 695, 704, 707, 719, 743, 762, 775, 776, 784, 792, 821, 822, 823, 845, 853, 854, 857, 863, 864, 877, 878, 893, 912, 914, 917, 921
Conversion, forced 108, 323, 421, 428, 853
Coptic language 166, 182, 183, 209, 211, 212, 213, 219, 234, 235, 253, 256, 259, 275, 276, 277, 309, 310, 311, 317, 318, 321, 411, 412, 665, 666, 667, 703
Coptic Orthodox Church 4, 9, 214, 215, 257, 258, 259, 274, 275, 276, 310, 319, 554, 667, 702, 703, 704, 705
Cordova 10, 303, 633, 634, 635, 645, 646, 647, 679, 680, 681, 691, 692, 693, 734, 810, 812, 825, 827, 834, 882, 884
Cordova, martyrs of 10, 645, 646, 647
Corruption of scripture 17, 41, 53, 379, 573, 574, 909, *see also* Bible, corruption of
Corruption of the Qurʾān 595
Cosmas I, patriarch 234
Cosmas of Maiouma, bishop 295
Cosmas and Damian, Church of, *see under* Church buildings
Covadonga, battle of 884, 885
Creator, God as 298, 448, 473, 605, 759, 760, 769
Crete 12, 120
Cross 5, 17, 66, 99, 149, 165, 174, 198, 220, 223, 224, 243, 254, 296, 298, 323, 331, 344, 356, 361, 382, 430, 440, 459, 470, 472, 480, 495, 498, 520, 523, 557, 588, 601, 605, 608, 609, 719, 794, 877, 878, 903
Veneration of the 17, 296, 344, 382, 440, 520, 557, 588, 601, 608, 878
Crucifixion 24, 183, 184, 223, 254, 270, 298, 316, 320, 328, 331, 344, 383, 468, 470, 471, 482, 485, 514, 567, 568, 574, 608, 719, 745, 792, 878, 909
Crusades 686, 807
Cyprus 86, 193, 198, 429, 431, 631, 675, 676
Cyriacus, patriarch 314
Cyril and Methodius *799-803*
Cyrus, patriarch 182, 214, 665, *see also* al-Muqawqis

Dahriyya 505, 769
dalāʾil al-nubuwwa, *see* Proofs of prophethood
Damascus 5, 11, 62, 69, 154, 198, 240, 264, 266, 281, 285, 290, 291, 295, 298, 307, 360, 388, 406, 420, 421, 431, 452, 498, 499, 731, 780, 781, 842, 863, 864, 916, 917, 920
Great mosque of 431
Daniel, prophet 128, 131, 142, 164, 223, 275, 415, 416, 647
Daniel, Book of 164, 239, 309, 415, 416, 600
David, king and prophet 43, 328, 376
Dāwūd al-Muqammaṣ 743
Ḍaysanites 54
Death 41, 68, 77, 95, 108, 149, 201, 210, 367, 394, 395, 408, 508, 523, 717, 772, 878, *see also* Christ, death of; Muḥammad, prophet, death of
Determinists 532, 540, 541, 545, 611, 618, 649, 773

Devil 331, 379, 390, 403, 472, 479, 589, 904 *see also* Satan
Dhimmī, see Ahl al-dhimma
Dhū Nuʾās 61
Diatessaron 34, 35, 51
Dietary regulations 46, 85, 91, 96, 97, 110, 298, 340, 341, 425, 772
Digenēs Akritēs 13
Ḍirār ibn ʿAmr *371-74*, 547, 605, 618, 656, 657
Diocletian, emperor 428, 788
Dionysius, bishop 323
Dionysius I, patriarch 94, 557
Dionysius II, patriarch 93
Dionysius of Tell-Maḥrē 305, 306, 559, *622-26*, 782-83
Dionysius bar Ṣalībī 468, 524
Direction of prayer 46, 228, 242, 270, 523, 571, 904
Disciples of Jesus 22, 23, 24, 44, 47, 66-67, 77, 79, 350, 460, 662, 878
Divorce 265, 299, 440, 461, 536, 589, 595, 822
Diyarbakir 322
Dome of the Rock 131, 155, 166, 183, 198
Dualism 54, 403, 541, 618, 695, 696, 697, 714, 769, 793
Dulcidius, priest 810, 882
Dvin, Council of *see under* Church councils

Ebionites 28
Edessa 141, 166, 172, 173, 222, 226, 305, 430, 439, 464, 502, 503, 622, 624, 791, 792, 898, 899, *see also* Bartholomew of Edessa; Jacob of Edessa; Job of Edessa; John of Edessa; Theophilus of Edessa
Eghia, patriarch 265
Egila, bishop *338-42*
Egypt 4, 8, 9, 11, 51, 66, 120, 129, 131, 138, 182, 183, 193, 198, 209-15, 220, 234, 235, 236, 253, 254, 256, 257-58, 274, 275-76, 285, 286, 287, 309, 310, 311, 317, 319, 320, 322, 403, 411, 428, 429, 430, 431, 495, 540, 623, 656, 659, 665, 666, 702, 703, 704, 730, 740, 834
Eirenopolis 614
Eleutheropolis 190, 191, 394
Elias, patriarch 394, 408, 499
Elias of Damascus, *see* Elias of Helioupolis
Elias of Helioupolis *916-18*
Elias of Merv 131
Elias of Nisibis, bishop 560
Elijah, prophet 173, 183
Elijah of Damascus 841, 842
Elijah of Nisibis 769, 840, 841, 842
Elipandus of Toledo, archbishop 338, 633
Elkesaites 28, 32
Emesa 68, 75, 478, 507
Emir 12, 91, 178, 220, 303, 335, 336, 559, 560, 615, 616, 625, 635, 679, 681, 683, 691, 693, 782-84, 825, 834, 877, 878, 879, 884, 914
Enoch 173
Enosh, patriarch 757, 758
Ephrem the Syrian 160, 161, 194, 270, 567
Erchempert 807
Eschatology 118, 275, 299, 825, 827
Eternal life 557, 605, 609, 631, 637, 638, 676
Ethiopia 3, 38, 80, 165, 211, 212, 246, 495
Eucharist 45, 51, 90, 92, 93, 94, 96, 157, 158, 159, 198, 204, 242, 254, 257, 296, 344, 440, 474, 499, 505, 571, 608, 609, 615, 616, 758, 786, 903
Euchratas, monastery of, *see under* Monasteries
Eulogius of Cordova 633, 634, 645, 646-47, *679-83*, 691, 693, 722
Eunomians 701
Euodius the Monk 424, 637, 640, *844-48*
Euphrates 187, 188, 226, 240, 324, 499, 512
Eusebius of Caesarea 226, 231, 302
Eusebona, monastery of, *see under* Monasteries
Eustathius 429, *see also* Usṭāth al-Rāhib
Euthymius Zygabenus 755, 848
Eutychians 701
Eutychius 183, 903 *see also* Saʿīd ibn Baṭrīq
Eve 246, 249
Evidentiary miracles 350, 351
Ezekiel, prophet 812
Ezra the Scribe 239

Fall of man 128, 376, 378, 379, 480
Fasting 128, 257, 535, 536, 571, 588, 625
al-Fatḥ ibn Khāqān, vizier 709, 816
Fāṭimids 240, 310, 495
Faymiyūn 60-61
Fayyūm 274, 318, 664, 665
Felix of Urgell, bishop 338, *365-66*

Filioque 627, 873
Flavius Josephus 731
Florian, St 190-91
Food and drink *see* Paradise, food and drink in
France 138
Francia 137, 293
Frankfurt, Council of, *see under* Church councils
Franks 87, 293, 391, 494, 691, 873
'Fredegar' *137-38*, 293
Freethinkers 371
Free will 367, 368, 369, 440, 451, 455, 478, 488, 540, 541, 545, 611, 738
Friend of God, *see* Abraham as friend of God

Gabītha-Yarmūk, *see* Yarmūk, battle of
Gabriel, angel 63, 64, 721
Gabriel, Mār /Mōr, of Qartmīn *892-97*
Gabriel, Mār, monastery of, *see under* Monasteries
Gabriel of Basra 90, 94, 757
Gabriel the Egyptian, deacon 212
Galen 321, 502, 507, 762, 773
Garcia I, king 883, 884
Gauderich of Velletri 804
Gaza 190, 191, 394, 598
Geʿez 25, 211, 212
Gentiles 84, 86
Genuflection 232
George, St 81, 615
George I, patriarch 88, 92, 94
George the Archdeacon 8, 209, *234-38*, 259
George the Deacon, *see* George the Archdeacon
George Hamartolos, *see* George the Monk
George the Monk 431, 560, 632, *729-33*
George the Synkellos 428, 788
Georgian Christianity 390, 852, 854
Georgian language 148, 149, 335, 336, 388, 390, 391, 392, 395, 407, 419, 420, 441, 686, 852, 853, 899, 900, 913, 919, 920, 921
Germanus, patriarch 424
Germany 85, 138, 294
Gethsemane 316
Ghassanids 34, 66, 69
Ghevond, *see* Ghewond
Ghewond *203-8*, 265, 381, *866-71*
Ghiwarghi, Nubian king 623
Ghiwargis I, patriarch *151-53*
Gideon 165
Glagolitic alphabet 800
Gog and Magog 160, 161, 165, 173, 179, 246
Gospel 2, 16, 18, 23, 34, 35, 38, 39, 40, 41, 51, 52, 60, 62, 63, 70, 76, 77, 78, 79, 81, 204, 205, 542, 575, 578, 605, 606, 608, 620, 662, 671, 744, 793, 864, 891, 909
Gospel of Matthew 81, 379, 542, 634, 817
Gospel of Luke 270, 634
Gospel of John 55, 63, 523, 542, 743, 817
Gospels, apocryphal 82
Arabic Infancy Gospel 52
Armenian Gospel of the Infancy 35, 46, 49, 50, 52
Gospel of Barnabas 43
Gospel of the Twelve Apostles 166, 222-25
Infancy Gospel of Thomas 52
Granada 825
Gratian, canon lawyer 84, 87, 88, 90
Gregorians 701
Gregory, governor 287
Gregory of Alexandria 852
Gregory Dekapolites *614-17*
Gregory of Nazianzus 157, 516, 801
Gregory of al-Qays, bishop 210
Gundishāpūr 39, 131, 151, 565, 768

Ḥabīb of Edessa, bishop 893
Ḥabīb ibn Khidma, *see* Abū Rāʾiṭa l-Takrītī
al-Hādī, caliph 347
Ḥadīth vii, viii, 2, 54, 60, 73-82, 105, 356, 464, 535, 538, 540, 541, 569, 709, 780, 816, 819, 820, 825, 832, 834
Hadrian I, pope 84, 92, 93, 96, 97, *338-42*
Hadrian II, pope 786
Ḥafṣ al-Fard 544, *656-57*
Hagar 161, 298, 631, 673, 812
Hagar, sons of 173, 177, 246, 271, 298, 415, 585
Hagarenes 84, 91, 93, 94, 95, 96, 97, 138, 141, 158, 424, 425, 441, 474, 482, 598, 636, 751, 752, 754, 800, 812, *see also* Hagar, sons of; Ishmaelites
al-Ḥajjāj ibn Yūsuf 595, 596
Ḥajjī Khalīfa 820, 833
Hamazasp Mamikonean, prince 139, 262
Ḥammām ibn Munabbih 73

Ḥanafīs 54, 103
Ḥanbalīs 54, 110
Ḥannah 49
ḥanpē 23, 90, 152, 158, 159, 344, 745
Ḥanūn ibn Yuḥannā ibn al-Ṣalt 849, 857
al-Ḥarbī, Ibrāhīm ibn Isḥāq *832-33*
al-Ḥārith ibn Abī Shāmir 66, 69
Ḥarrān 93, 94, 187, 286, 323, 324, 430, 439, 463, 468, 470, 474, 476, 478, 479, 491, 550, 557, 558, 613, 792, 893, 895
Hārūn al-Rashīd, caliph 12, 347, 349, 354, 355, 371, 384, 428, 492, 494, 495, 498, 499, 516, 532, 582, 741, 764, 873, 898, 899, 921
al-Ḥasan ibn Ayyūb 671
Ḥasan al-Baṣrī 35, 42
al-Hāshimī, ʿAbd Allāh ibn Ismāʿīl 585, 587
Ḥazzā 515, 550, 554
Heaven 43, 44, 74, 78, 165, 174, 240, 254, 271, 298, 378, 401, 473, 508, 542, 600, 608, 630, 634, 692, 745, *see also* Paradise
Hebrew Bible 75, 242, 575, 577, 817, 899, *see also* Old Testament
Helioupolis 917, *and see* Baalbek
Hell 40, 74, 271, 485, 649
Heraclius, emperor 8, 12, 59, 66-69, 71, 80, 117, 120, 123, 133, 137, 138, 141, 212, 214, 240, 302, 428, 429, 665, 788
Heraclius, father of the Sibyl 493
Heresy 13, 86, 123, 177, 258, 296, 298, 338, 339, 341, 365, 424, 429, 683, 691, 731, 823, 845, 846
Heretics 4, 90, 91, 92, 133, 157, 177, 178, 196, 274, 371, 397, 439, 474, 487, 531, 545, 601, 622, 681, 691, 731, 768, 821, 837, 873
Herodotus 885
Ḥijāz 3, 28, 47
Hindus 101, 891
Hippocrates 507, 662
al-Ḥīra 32-33, 151, 269, 510, 511, 512, 513
Hishām, caliph 282, 430, 616
Hishām ibn al-Ḥakam 532, 545, 618, 759, 760
Ḥnānīshōʿ 178
Holy camel 298, 425, 822
Holy Land 154, 193, 407, 686, 902
Holy Sepulcher, church of, *see* Church of the Resurrection *under* Church buildings
Holy Spirit 63, 149, 223, 257, 270, 453, 463, 481, 520, 542, 605, 751, 794, *see also* Spirit
Homologētēs, *see* Theophanes the Confessor
Honorius, pope 123
Hormisdas, monastery of, *see under* Monasteries
Hormizd IV 130
Hostegesis, bishop 691, 692, 693
Ḥubaysh ibn al-Ḥasan 769
Ḥumayd ibn Saʿīd ibn Bakhtiyār 508, *723-25*
Ḥunayn ibn Isḥāq 6, 7, 305, 502, 762, 763, *768-79*
Ḥusayn al-Najjār 611
Hypostasis 133, 555, 760

ʿIbād 77, 467, 511, 512, 513, 768
Iberian peninsula, *see* Spain
Iblīs, *see* Devil
Ibn ʿAbbās, ʿAbdallāh 33, 35, 36, 37, 41, 43, 50, 437
Ibn Abī l-Dunyā 77-78, *829-31*
Ibn Abī Shayba 78, 79, 80
Ibn Abī Ṭāhir Ṭayfūr 349, 764
Ibn Abī Uṣaybiʿa 764, 907
Ibn ʿAlī al-Maghribī 560, 842
Ibn al-ʿAssāl, al-Muʿtaman 494, 578, 758, 772, 776
Ibn al-ʿAssāl, al-Ṣāfī 606, 670, 671
Ibn al-Athīr 38, 884
Ibn Bābawayh 538
Ibn Ḥabīb *825-28*
Ibn Ḥajar al-ʿAsqalānī 820
Ibn Ḥazm 110, 619, 620, 741, 817
Ibn Ḥayyān al-Qurṭubī, 884
Ibn Hishām 58, 60, 61, 62, 63, 64, 65, 66, 67
Ibn Isḥāq 37, 38, 40, 47, 48, 49, 51, 52, 55, 58, 60, 62, 63, 65, 66, 67, 600
Ibn al-Jawzī 43, 695, 817
Ibn Kabar, *see* Abū l-Barakāt ibn Kabar
Ibn al-Kalbī, Abū l-Mundhir Hishām 33, 36, *510-14*
Ibn al-Layth, Muḥammad *347-53*, 384, 673, 764
Ibn Mufarrij, Mawhūb ibn Manṣūr 209, 235, 318, 703
Ibn al-Munajjim, *see* Abū Aḥmad Yaḥyā ibn al-Munajjim *and* ʿAlī ibn Yaḥyā ibn al-Munajjim
Ibn al-Muqaffaʿ 540, 907

Ibn al-Murtaḍā 584, 620, 714
Ibn al-Nadīm 347, 348, 355, 373, 502, 510, 512, 514, 532, 533, 534, 536, 544, 546, 547, 548, 583, 604, 611, 612, 613, 620, 656, 657, 669, 698, 700, 713, 723, 724, 725, 749, 764, 765, 907
Ibn al-Qifṭī 832
Ibn Qurra 536, 537, 538
Ibn Qutayba 48, 60, 673, 709, 741, *816-18*
Ibn al-Qūṭiyya 741
Ibn al-Rāwandī 587, 619, 620, 695
Ibn Ra's Ghanama 826
Ibn Rushd al-Jadd 735
Ibn Sa'd 62, 63, 66, 69, 70
Ibn Shahrāshūb 536
Ibn Ṭāwūs 583
Ibn Taymiyya 671
Ibn Waḍḍāḥ *834-39*
Ibn al-Zayyāt, vizier 709
Ibn Zur'a 650
Ibrāhīm *see* Abraham
Ibrāhīm al-Ṭabarānī 560, *876-81*
Iconoclasm 12, 203, 204, 296, 327, 338, 390, 391, 392, 423, 426, 429, 430, 431, 464, 614, 616, 627, 630, 637, 729, 731, 789, 800, 845, 853, 864, 873
Icons 17, 22, 198, 270, 296, 382, 391, 423, 429, 430, 439, 440, 441, 463, 464, 499, 616, 731, 768, 864, 874, 899, 909
al-Ifranj 738
Ifrīqiyā 13, 287, 834, *see also* North Africa
Ignatius, deacon 614
Ignatius of Antioch, patriarch 89, 93
Ikrima 35, 42
Images *see* Icons
Imāms 535, 540, 545, 623, 696, 741-42, 837
'Imrān 48, 49
Incarnation 3, 14, 15, 16, 270, 315, 331, 376, 378, 379, 440, 470, 520, 542, 554, 557, 571, 572, 574, 576-77, 580, 605, 606, 608, 662, 698, 792, 793, 794, 878, 903, 904, 909
Ioane Sabanisdze *334-37*, 852
Ioannes the monk 327
Iona 13, 149, 154
al-Īrānshahrī *889-91*
Iraq 11, 26, 75, 80, 82, 88, 103, 151, 178, 268, 269, 311, 344, 437, 521, 527, 537, 553, 565, 567, 580, 595, 600, 604, 652, 656, 659, 688, 746, 757, 766, 768, 769, 834, 857, 860, 861, 907
Irene, empress 349, 415, 416, 597, 598
'Īsā *see* Jesus
Isaac, Coptic patriarch 209, 210, 219-21
Isaac the Presbyter *664-68*
Isaac of Nineveh 849
'Īsāwiyya 662
al-Iṣfahānī, Abū l-Faraj 723
Isḥāq ibn Ḥunayn 769
Ishmael 142, 143, 224, 298, 639, 673, 812, 879
Ishmael, sons of 141, 142, 164, 165, 415, 600
Ishmaelites 12, 131, 164, 179, 239, 240, 298, 403, 404, 425, 602, 801, 812
'Ishmaelites, heresy of the' 298
Isho'yahb III, patriarch *133-36*, 151
Īshō'bokht of Rēwardashīr, patriarch 95, 724
Isidore of Seville 161, 284, 286, 302, 811, 812, 884
al-Iskāfī, Abū Ja'far Muḥammad *649-51*, 657, 713, 714
Israel 164, 296, 415, 812
Israel of Kashkar *757-61*, 840-43
Isrā'īliyyāt 37, 830
Išxanī, monastery of, *see under* Monasteries
Italy 13, 94, 338, 643, 804, 806, 807
Iwannis, metropolitan 624
'Iyāḍ ibn Ghanm 894

Jacob of Edessa 89, 90, 91, 92, 93, 94, 95, 96, 97, 98, *226-33*, 314, 316
Jacob, merchant 117-19
Jacob, St, of Qayshum/Kayshum, monastery of, *see under* Monasteries
Ja'far ibn Ḥarb 649
Ja'far ibn al-Mubashshir 713, 714
al-Jāḥiẓ, Abū 'Uthmān 16, 205, 548, 550, 608, 618, 619, 620, 621, 649, 656, *706-12*, 713, 715, 716
Jahm ibn Ṣafwān 544
James, apostle 35, 47, 48, 49, 50, 223, 224
Jazīra 286, 322, 323, 324, 325, 360
Jerome, St 682
Jerusalem 13, 39, 40, 47, 53, 67, 68, 120-26, 131, 138, 142, 143, 146, 148, 149, 154, 155, 165, 166, 183, 190, 191, 198, 223, 240, 246, 266, 295, 307, 327-28, 361, 394, 407, 408, 415, 428, 429, 430, 439, 499, 557, 560, 598, 627, 628, 634, 658, 659, 661, 675, 685, 731, 792, 838, 842, 854, 872, 873, 877, 899, 912, 913, 920

Jesus Christ 3, 13-17, 22-24, 32-35, 38-41, 43-49, 51-56, 63-64, 67-70, 74-79, 81, 87, 89, 93, 133, 135, 149, 154, 182, 183, 184, 194, 196, 204, 223, 228, 242, 243, 250, 254, 257, 270, 271, 296, 316, 323, 327, 331, 335, 344, 350, 365, 367, 376, 378, 379, 382, 383, 384, 387, 395, 401, 420, 425, 429, 438, 440, 454, 455, 458, 459, 460, 461, 463, 464, 467, 468, 470, 471, 472, 476, 479, 482, 484, 485, 488, 490, 491, 493, 495, 499, 514, 520, 523, 527, 529, 530, 537, 538, 542, 550, 557, 560, 568, 574, 580, 588, 589, 605, 606, 608, 615, 616, 620, 625, 630, 631, 633, 636, 639, 650, 655, 658, 662, 671, 682, 707, 707-8, 710, 715, 745, 792, 793, 794, 800, 801, 816, 822, 829, 830, 863, 864, 878, 879, 899, 903, 904
  as adopted son of God 620, 710, 715
  as Son of God 44, 46, 63, 65, 66, 270, 350, 365, 440, 715, 719
  as Spirit of God 23, 64, 69, 378, 488, 491, 538, 557
  as Word of God 64, 298, 299, 378, 472, 473, 488, 491, 538, 557, 560, 601
  ascension of 43, 223, 514, 745, 903
  baptism of 96, 126, 490
  birth of 24, 51, 52, 530, 654, 745, 837, *see also* Gospels, apocryphal
  death of 316, 454, 455, 470, 471, 472, 473, 476, 480, 575, 606, 608, 609, 794, 879, *see also* Crucifixion
  divinity of 14, 17, 24, 43, 44, 65, 113, 125, 378, 382, 387, 395, 438, 470, 471, 473, 474, 481, 504, 527, 554, 557, 568, 574, 575, 580, 605, 608, 633, 650, 655, 658, 662, 671, 707, 744, 753, 782, 793, 794, 863, 877, 878
  miracles of 17, 45, 51, 52, 53, 350, 557, 671, 707-8, 864
  resurrection of 471
  second coming of 164, 174, 250, 542, 601
Jews, *see* Judaism
Jibrīl ibn Bukhtīshū‘ 502, 550, 768
jihād 42, 46, 56, 468, 482, 734, 738, 835
Jirja the Archdeacon, *see* George the Archdeacon
jizya 25, 69, 88, 102, 103, 106, 112, 152, 187, 236, 325, 356, 362, 717, 738, 878, 894-95
Job 647
Job of Edessa *502-9*, 725
Job 'the Spotted', *see* Job of Edessa
Johannes Damascenus, *see* John of Damascus
Johannes Hymmonides 804
John, apostle 47, 48, 67, 223, *see also* Gospel of John
John I (III) Sedra, patriarch 625, *782-85*
John III, patriarch of Antioch 93
John III of Samannūd, patriarch 209, 220, 234, *253-55*
John III bar Narsai, patriarch 857
John VIII, pope 88, 786, 788, *804-9*
John of Antioch 213
John the Baptist 34, 48, 367, 835, 837
  John the Baptist, monastery of, at Parxali, *see under* Monasteries
John of Biclar 284
John of Damascus 13, 120, 271, 290, *295-301*, 316, 367, 368, 388, 390, 419, 421, 424, 425, 430, 488, 616, 634, 731, 848, 903, 904
John of Dāsen, patriarch 178
John of Daylam 397
John the Deacon, Coptic historian 234, *317-21*
John the Deacon, disciple of Theodore Abū Qurra 474, 559
John the Deacon, papal historiographer 788
John of Edessa *898-901*
John of Ephesus 893
John of Kāmūl, monastery of, *see under* Monasteries
John of Litarb 89, 90, 92, 94, 95, 96, 227, 228, 314, 316
John of Nikiou *209-18*, 219
John of Penek (Fenek), *see* John bar Penkāyē
John of Qalyūb 212
John of Scetis 666
John the Stylite of Mār Z‘urā at Sarug *314-16*
John the Stylite, *see* John of Litarb
John the Writer 8, 235, *702-5*
John Azraq, bishop 269
John Abū Qurra 537, 538
John Catholicos 262, 719
John Chrysostom 194, 416, 852
John Climacus 193
John Echimus 726
John Grammaticus 800, 874
John Immonides 788
John Malalas 213
John Moschus 120, 121, 148, 198
John bar Penkāyē 173, *176-81*, 224

John Zosimus 407
Joseph, son of Jacob 912
Joseph, priest 186, 188
Joseph the Carpenter 51
Joseph the Hymnographer 844
Joseph Ḥazzāyā 314
Joseph Hūzāyā 314
Joshua the Stylite of Zuqnīn 186, *322-26*
Juanshēr 264, 266
al-Jubbāʾī, *see* Abū ʿAlī al-Jubbāʾī
Judaism 2, 5, 6, 7, 13, 15, 17, 21-25, 26, 36-39, 41-46, 48, 54, 56, 59, 61, 62, 73, 75, 78-81, 83, 85, 86, 90-94, 96-98, 100-3, 105, 106, 110, 111, 112, 114, 117, 118, 141-43, 166, 194, 223, 225, 242, 243, 246, 253, 254, 258, 270, 296, 315, 316, 339, 340, 401, 415, 421, 425, 430, 439, 453, 457, 460, 461, 467, 468, 472, 473, 477, 482, 487, 520, 524, 530, 533, 540, 545, 584,595, 601, 611, 645, 662, 669, 696, 697, 706, 709, 710, 730, 731, 735, 743, 781, 782, 784, 785, 788, 792, 793, 800, 817, 821, 822, 823, 827, 830, 835, 837, 839, 841, 849, 864, 877, 878, 891, 898, 908, 912
Judas, betrayer of Jesus 47, 67
Julianists 701
Justin I, emperor 788
Justinian I, emperor 213, 788
Justinian II, emperor 86, 93, 430
al-Juzajānī *780-81*

Kaʿb al-Aḥbār 36, 37, 401, *403*-5, 595, 601, 602
Kaʿba 108, 298, 299, 520, 535, 609
al-Kabar 403
Karaite 743
Karkar 762
Karlmann, king 807
Karshūnī 29, 189, 587, 590
Kartli 334, 335, 336, 852, 853, 854
Kashkar 343, 344, 757, *see also* Israel of Kashkar
Khadīja 64, 721
Khālid ibn al-Walīd 130, 131
khalīl, *see* Abraham as friend of God
al-Khansāʾ 30
kharāj 103, 152, 355-57, 360, 397
Khārijīs 54, 205, 371, 533
al-Khāṭib al-Baghdādī 832
Khawārij, *see* Khārijīs
al-Khayyāṭ, Abū l-Ḥusayn 620, 649
Khazars 264, 800, 868
Khazaria 335
al-Khiḍr 835
Khurāsān 52, 305, 347, 503, 535, 565, 582, 780
al-Khwārazmī, Muḥammad ibn Aḥmad 502, 894
al-Kindī, ʿAbd al-Masīḥ ibn Isḥāq, *see* ʿAbd al-Masīḥ al-Kindī
al-Kindī, Abū Yūsuf Yaʿqūb 7, 585, 746, 840
Klīlīshōʿ, monastery of, *see under* Monasteries
Kūfa 36, 52, 54, 76, 78, 131, 178, 343, 347, 354, 371, 437, 510, 532, 535, 540, 746, 816
Kūz 54

Lakhmids 512, 768
Last emperor 165, 173, 243, 246, 250, 310, 311, 601
Last Judgement 39, 73, 74, 77, 174, 275, 467
Lazarus, steward 323
Lead seal 356, 717-18
Leo III, emperor 12, *203-8*, 327, 328, 375, *377-80*, 381, 383, 384, 415, 429, 596, 712, 731, 864, 867
Leo III, pope 627
Leo IV, emperor 426
Leo IV, pope 87, 642, 643, 786, 873
Leo V, emperor 426, 873, 874
Leo VI, emperor 751
Leo the Philosopher 11
Leo, *Tome* of 665
Leontius of Damascus 388, *406-10*
Leviathan 647
Lewond/Łewond, *see* Ghewond
Life of Muḥammad, *see* Muḥammad, prophet, biography of
Lombards 338
Lot 331
Lothair I, emperor 87
Louis II, emperor 786, 804, 806
Louis the Pious 87
Lucas of Tuy 885
Luke, apostle 270, *see also* Gospel of Luke
Lyons 97, 365

Macarius, St, monastery of, *see under* Monasteries
Macedonians 701
al-Mahdī, caliph 14, 305, 347, 351, 390, 391, 397, 516, 520, 521, 522, 523, 524, 552, 560
Mahgrāyē, *see Mhaggrāyē*

Maiouma 598, *see also* Cosmas of Maiouma, bishop; Peter of Maiouma, martyr
Magians, *see* Zoroastrians
al-Malik al-Mushammar, emir 560
Mālik ibn Anas 102, 354, 540, 735, 835
Mālikīs 54, 104, 105, 109, 110, 111, 112, 734, 738, 834, 835
Malkūn, follower of St Paul 46, 438
Mamlūks 240
al-Ma'mūn, caliph 10, 11, 439, 469, 502, 510, 524, 532, 535, 537, 544, 548, 550, 556, 557-58, 560, *582-84*, 587, 588, 606, 618, 622, 623, 768
Mandylion 899, *see also* Image
Mani, *see* Manicheism
Manicheans, *see* Manicheism
Manicheism 32, 33, 35, 41, 42, 51, 54, 290, 296, 430, 439, 451, 530, 540, 630, 695, 731, 793, 821, 822, 823
Mankik 266
al-Manṣūr, caliph 310, 324, 391, 762
Manṣūr ibn Sarjūn 295
Mantineon, monastery of, *see under* Monasteries
Manuel I, emperor 822
Manuel Inaniklishvili, scribe 421
Maomet's Bible, *see* Qur'ān
al-Maqdisī, Muṭahhar ibn Ṭāhir 503
Mār Abraham bar Dāshandād, *see* Abraham bar Dāshandād, Mār
Mār(y) Bassīmā, monastery of, *see under* Monasteries
Mār Chariton, monastery of, *see under* Monasteries
Mār Gabriel, monastery of, *see under* Monasteries
Mār Mattai, monastery of, *see under* Monasteries
Mār Naṣr 528-31
Mār Pethion, monastery of, *see under* Monasteries
Mār Saba/Mār Sabas, monastery of, *see* Saba/Sabas, Mār
Mār Ya'qūb, leader of the Jacobites 44
Mār Ya'qūb, abbot 133
Marcianus Aristides 852
Marcion 35
Marcionites 54, 530
Margā 151, 515, *see also* Thomas of Margā
Mariana, Juan de 288
Māriya the Copt 70
Mark, apostle 220, 275
Mark II, patriarch 704
Maronites 701
Marriage 48, 70, 79, 92, 93, 107, 108, 111, 152, 158, 159, 265, 298, 299, 340, 341, 376, 420, 423, 425, 426, 536, 550, 589, 598, 625, 634, 666, 679, 691, 721, 822, 866, 912
Martel, Charles 294
Martyrdom 9, 10, 164, 211, 266, 281-82, 290, 296, 319, 327, 328, 334, 335-36, 388, 390, 391, 392, 393, 395, 419, 420, 421, 430, 498, 499, 597, 598, 614, 628, 630, 633, 637, 638, 639, 666, 675, 676, 677, 682, 684, 686, 719, 844, 845, 846, 848, 852, 854, 868, 911, 912, 913, 914, 916, 917
Martyrs 10, 24, 60, 61, 128, 190-91, 196, 212, 245, 250, 258, 307, 327, 335, 388, 393, 395, 420, 421, 429-30, 499, 530, 582, 598, 615, 616, 630, 631, 633, 634, 636, 637, 639, 645, 646, 647, 666, 675, 676, 677, 679, 680, 681, 682, 683, 684, 691, 693, 717, 719, 844, 845, 846, 848, 853, 854, 912, 913, 916, 917
Marwān II, caliph 310, 317, 319, 430, 869
Marwānids 285
al-Marwazī, Nu'aym ibn Ḥammād 75
Mary, Virgin 22, 23, 24, 27, 32, 34, 40, 43, 48-51, 55, 64, 69, 78, 79, 270, 298, 367, 378, 429, 458-59, 460, 463, 470, 490, 523, 650, 864, 903
al-Masīḥ, *see* Jesus Christ
Maslama ibn 'Abd al-Malik 268-69, 285
al-Mas'ūdī 695
Mattai, Mār, monastery of, *see under* Monasteries
Matthew, apostle 47, 67, *see also* Gospel of Matthew
al-Māturīdī, Abū Manṣūr 44, 54, 55, 710, 714, 715
Maurice, emperor 213, 624
Maximilian, St *717-18*
Maximus the Confessor 118, 120
Māzyār ibn Qārin, governor 669, 670
Mecca 3, 22, 23, 28, 32, 33, 39, 42, 49, 59, 61, 62, 64, 65, 66, 95, 108, 131, 178, 224, 285, 500, 609, 822
Medina 2, 11, 22, 36, 40, 42, 45, 49, 59, 65, 108, 431, 535, 540, 738
Megas Agros, monastery of, *see under* Monasteries
Mēna of Nikiou, bishop 209, *219-21*
Merv 565, 588, 669, 832

Mesopotamia 4, 28, 166, 173, 178, 179, 269, 285, 286, 307, 792, 893, 894
Methodius, bishop 245, 415
Mhaggrāyē 84, 135, 158, 188, 782, 783
Mhaggrē, see Mhaggrāyē
Michael, archangel 276
Michael (Khāʾīl) I, patriarch 317, 319, 321
Michael II, emperor 423, 726, 752
Michael III, emperor 12, 636, 729, 751, 752, 754, 788, 853, 854
Michael of Mār Saba 148, *911-15*
Michael Mondrekeli 899
Michael the Synkellos 424, *627-32*, 637, 640, 677, 731, 822, 846, *872-5*
Michael the Syrian 157, 191, 290, 305, 306, 314, 569, 623, 624, 625, 782
Miracles 60, 148, 198, 220, 254, 257, 321, 336, 350, 351, 384, 395, 406, 408, 429, 440, 448, 456, 460, 461, 474, 499, 500, 530, 548, 560, 566, 578, 601, 608, 631, 637, 666, 671, 676, 707, 744, 864, 885, 893, 899, 912, 921, *see also* Jesus Christ, miracles of; Muḥammad, prophet, miracles of
Mirdazat 266
Miriam 48, 298
al-Mismāʿī 889, 891
Mkhitʿar Gosh 261
Monasteries 4, 8, 41, 106, 120, 123, 148, 149, 172, 173, 179, 187, 188, 193, 209, 210, 249, 264, 269, 274, 281, 322, 323, 330, 356, 392, 394, 428, 429, 511, 512, 598, 637, 665, 666, 684, 685, 704, 727, 743, 844, 874, 895, 919, 920, 921
  Monastery of St Antheousa 390
  Dayr al-Askīm 512
  Monastery of Baramūs 849
  Monastery of Mār(y) Bassīmā 176
  Monastery of Bēt ʿAbē 133, 151, 688, 689
  Monastery of Bēt Ḥālē 268, 269
  Monastery of Bēt Malkā 157
  Monastery of St Catherine *see* Catherine, St, monastery of
  Monastery of Mār Chariton 330, 394
  Monastery of Chora 627, 872, 874
  Monastery of Euchratas 120
  Monastery of Eusebona 226
  Monastery of Mār Gabriel 515, 892
  Monastery of the Holy Cross 899
  Monastery of Hormisdas 426
  Monastery of Iona 154
  Monastery of Išxanī 391
  Monastery of St Jacob of Qayshum 226, 622
  Monastery of St Jacob near Ṣalāḥ 895
  Monastery of John of Kāmūl 176
  Monastery of John the Baptist at Parxali 391
  Monastery of Klīlīshōʿ 516
  Monastery of St Macarius 219, 234
  Monastery of Mantineon 391
  Monastery of Mār Mattai 515
  Monastery of Megas Agros 426
  Dayr Murrān 421
  Monastery of the Virgin at Nahyā 235, 703
  Monastery of Naqlūn 665
  Monastery of Mār Pethion 757, 758
  Monastery of Qalamūn 664, 665, 666
  Monastery of Qartmīn 187, 892, 893, 895
  Monastery of Qenneshrē/Qenneshrin 157, 226, 622
  Monastery of Mār Saba/Mār Sabas, *see* Saba/Sabas, Mār, monastery of
  Monastery of Sakkoudion 423
  Monastery of St Shenute 182, 183
  Monastery of Spudaioi 627, 873
  Monastery of Stoudios 423
  Monastery of the Syrians 322
  Monastery of Tell ʿAdē 226
  Monastery of St Theodore 318
  Monastery of Theodosius 120
  Monastery of St Zoilus 691
  Monastery of Zuqnīn 186, 322, 323
  Monastery of Mār Zʿurā 314
Monasticism 23, 24, 33, 39, 40, 41, 42, 47, 73, 131, 151, 179, 193, 220, 322, 323, 391, 407, 614, 666, 685, 727, 917, 920
Monk of Bēt Ḥālē *268-73*
Monks 3, 23, 24, 39, 41, 42, 47, 77, 120, 133, 134, 148, 151, 154, 163, 172, 173, 176, 177, 186, 187, 193, 194, 198, 209, 210, 222, 226, 230, 234, 249, 274, 275, 276, 281, 293, 298, 317, 321, 322, 323, 327, 330, 377, 386, 390, 391, 394, 395, 406, 408, 423, 426, 428, 439, 492, 498, 499, 553, 556, 559, 588, 598, 611, 616, 622, 627, 634, 637, 661, 664, 665, 684, 685, 688, 689, 702, 729, 757, 792, 810, 829, 830, 834, 841, 844, 852, 853, 857, 872, 873, 876, 892, 893, 894, 907, 912, 913, 914
Monogamy 231, 474, 560
Moors 287

Moses 3, 15, 48, 53, 55, 64, 298, 331, 340, 460, 461, 608, 783, 835
Moses (Muwīsīs) of Wasīm, bishop 317
Mosul 133, 134, 151, 163, 178, 269, 397, 515, 550, 554, 580, 689, 757
Movsēs Daskhurants'i/ Dasxuranc'i *261-67*
Movsēs Kaghankatuats'i/ Kałankatuac'i *261-67*
Mozarab 287, *302-4*, 340, 341, 810, 812, 885
al-Mu'āfā ibn 'Imrān al-Mawṣilī 76
Mu'ammar ibn 'Abbād 351, 618
Mu'ārik ibn Marwān al-Nuṣayrī *740-42*
Mu'āwiya, caliph 13, 142, 145, 146, 154, 178, 264, 266, 285, 295, 430
al-Mudabbir, *see* John of Nikiou
Muḥammad, prophet ix, 2, 4, 9, 14, 17, 21, 22, 24-28, 32-36, 38-44, 47, 49, 55, 56, 73, 74, 79, 112, 121, 131, 141, 204, 231, 242, 265, 266, 270, 271, 285, 298-99, 307, 323, 344, 350, 351, 372, 382-84, 404, 411, 424, 425, 428, 430, 431-32, 438, 441, 474, 480, 494, 510, 523, 538, 557, 588, 595, 600-2, 616, 628, 643, 648, 652, 695, 696, 721, 730-31, 746, 763, 776, 788, 789, 800, 822, 848, 879, 912
  as Seal of the Prophets 33
  biography of vii, 2, 3, 21, 22, 37, *57-72*, 683, 721, 764, 781, 812, 827
  death of 3, 401-2, 602, 696, 788, 867
  his foreknowledge 350
  letters of *66-70*, 764
  miracles of 17, 350, 351, 383, 474, 548, 549, 672, 708, 716, 781
  predictions about 33, 55, *62-63*, 70-71, 79-80, 350, 402, 560, 672-73, 707, 817
  prophethood of, *see* Proofs of prophethood
  sayings of, *see* Ḥadīth
  see also *Munaḥḥamanā*; Paraclete
Muḥammad I, Spanish emir 679, 681, 683, 721
Muḥammad al-Jawād 535
Muḥammad ibn 'Abdallāh Ibn al-'Arabī 114
Muḥammad ibn al-Ḥasan al-Shaybānī 74, 354
Muḥammad ibn Marwān 266
Muḥammad ibn Saḥnūn *738-39*
Muḥammad ibn Shabīb 548, 618, 621, *713-16*
al-Muhtadī, caliph 356, 762
al-Mukhtār 166, 178, 179
Munaḥḥamanā 55, 63
al-Mundhir 812
al-Muntaṣir, caliph 762
Muqātil ibn Sulaymān 36, 52
al-Muqawqis 66, 70, 182
al-Muqtafī, caliph 829
al-Murdār *611-13*, 619
Murji'a 205, 371, 713, 723
Murrān, Dayr, *see under* Monasteries
Mūsā l-Kāẓim, Imām 535
Mūsā ibn Mūsā 884
Mūsā ibn Muṣ'ab 323, 397
Mūsā ibn Nuṣayr 740, 742
al-Musta'īn, caliph 762
al-Mustanṣir, caliph 495
mutakallimūn 44, 347, 348, 520, 556, 578, 605, 745, 773, 909
al-Mu'taḍid, caliph 829
al-Mu'taman ibn al-'Assāl, *see* Ibn al-'Assāl, al-Mu'taman
al-Mu'tamid, caliph 762
al-Mu'taṣim, caliph 609, 623, 624, 637, 649, 669, 676, 746, 768, 845
al-Mutawakkil, caliph 12, 90, 362, 565, 669, 704, 709, 710, 743, 746, 762, 768, 800, 816, 817, 853
Mu'tazila 18, 54, 348, 351, 371, 372, 507, 532, 541, 544, 545, 578, 582, 584, 588, 605, 608, 611, 620, 649, 656, 657, 659, 695, 706, 713, 723, 738, 746, 759, 760, 832, 837, 841, 864
al-Mu'tazz, caliph 762

Nahyā, monastery of the Virgin at, *see under* Monasteries
Najrān 2, 24, 33, 49, 59, 60-61, 65-66, 71, 80, 685
Naqlūn, monastery of, *see under* Monasteries
nāqūs 107, 361
al-Nāshi' al-Akbar 759, 760
Nāṣir-i Khusraw 889, 891
Naṣr, Mār *528-31*
Naṣṭūr, follower of St Paul 438, *see also* Nestorius
al-Nawawī 113
al-Naẓẓām 507, 545, 611, 619, 620, 706, 713, 715
Negus 59, 64, 66, 69, 71, 80, 212
Negus Ya'əqob 211
Neḥshon 688
Nemesius of Emesa 507
Nerse, prince 335

Nersēs Bakur, patriarch 265
Nestorius 4, 44, 46, 62, *see also* Baḥīrā
Nibelung, Count 293
Nicea 429, 614
Nicea, Council of, *see under* Church councils
Nicene creed 177, 671
Nicephorus I, patriarch 194, 423, 614, 787, 789
Nicetas of Byzantium 12, 425, *751-56*, 822, 844, 845, 848
Nicetas Choniates 755
Nicholas I, pope 12, 88
Nicholas, military official 615
Niketas Byzantios, *see* Nicetas of Byzantium
Nīshāpūr 889
Nisibis 133, 178, 187, 516, 557, 895, *see also* ʿAbdīshūʿ of Nisibis; Elias of Nisibis; Elijah of Nisibis; Nonnus of Nisibis
Noah 74, 331
Nonnus of Nisibis 568, 569, *743-45*
North Africa 4, 47, 67, 102, 105, 107, 109, 112, 114, 120, 287, 741, 837, *see also* Ifrīqiyā
Nunā of Nisibis, *see* Nonnus of Nisibis
al-Nushūʾ Abū Shākir ibn al-Rāhib 907

Old Testament 5, 226, 340, 341, 344, 744, 864, 884, 903
Old Testament *testimonia*, *see* Proof texts, Old Testament
Omnipotence 367, 371, 383
Ordoño I, king 883, 884
Ordoño II, king 883, 884
Original sin 542
Oviedo 679, 810, 834, 882, 885

Pachomius 616
Pact of ʿUmar 5, 104, 106, 107, 356, 357, *360-64*
Pagans 13, 22, 23, 27, 28, 42, 84, 86-97, 158-59, 165, 270, 299, 338, 339, 340, 344, 403, 404, 493, 602, 680, 745
Palestine 46, 117-18, 120, 125, 126, 131, 148, 149, 154, 191, 193, 231, 246, 307, 327, 330, 377, 391, 408, 419, 428, 429, 464, 597, 598, 599, 627, 659, 684, 726, 730, 873, 874, 916
Palm Sunday 194, 344
Paraclete 33, 35, 55, 63, 204, 401, 523, 817
Paradise, food and drink in 80, 382, 508, 608, 609, 725
Parmenides 662
Partaw, Synod of, *see under* Church councils
Paul, apostle 32, 45, 46, 47, 48, 53, 67, 92, 256, 257, 437, 438, 530, 707, 912
Paul Alvarus 633, 634, *645-48*, 679, 691, 693
Paul of Samosata 701
Paulicians 630, 821
Pelagius, king 811, 812, 884
Pelagius of Oviedo 885
Pentateuch 204
People of the Book 5, 38, 56, 101, 109, 114, 878, *see also Ahl al-kitāb*
Pérez, Juan Bautista 288
Pergamum 285, 286
Persia 4, 223-24, 240, 639, 890
Persian empire 4, 120, 121, 130, 131, 133, 163, 164, 177, 213, 275, 307, 403, 511
Persian language 151, 768
Persians 4, 36, 46, 60, 87, 151, 205, 347, 395, 507, 550, 627, 695, 719, 762, 873, 885
Peshitta 33, 35, 165
Peter, apostle 47, 67, 220, 223, 256-58, 642
Peter the monk 249
Peter the Venerable 789
Peter of Bayt Ra's, *see* Peter of Capitolias
Peter of Capitolias 290, 291, 296, 307, *419-22*, *902-6*
Peter of Damascus, bishop *290-92*, 421
Peter of Maiouma, martyr 421, 430
Peter of Pavia 341
Peter Illustrios 118
Pethion, Mār, monastery of, *see under* Monasteries
Petrus Guillermus 804
Phineas the Jew 898-99
Phocas I, emperor 214, 788
Phoenicia 240
Photinians 701
Photius, patriarch 123, 206, 751, 752, 804
Pilgrimage 264, 327, 407, 535, 536, 704, 854, 873, 877
Pitourgos 310
Platonism 296
Poison 179, 605, 801, 877, 878, 899, 912
Poitiers 294
Polemics viii, 10, 12, 22, 26, 28, 29, 45, 75, 118, 243, 296, 439, 455, 531, 537, 566, 841, 864

Christian polemic against Islam 12, 13, 70, 166, 243, 258, 276, 291, 298, 299, 336, 351, 366, 375, 376, 395, 401, 402, 403, 404, 424, 439, 455, 499, 500, 520, 585, 588, 589, 595, 596, 600, 602, 633, 634-45, 659-60, 686, 693, 721, 732, 789, 801, 807, 812, 846, 848, 878, 900, 914
Muslim polemic against Christianity 16, 17, 22, 26, 45, 54, 55, 57, 70, 71, 204, 298, 354, 375, 376, 379, 382, 383, 384, 520, 531, 533, 534, 542, 546, 566, 584, 588, 607, 620, 650-51, 653, 659-60, 671, 695, 697, 698, 709, 710, 731, 738, 846, 864, 878
Poll tax, see *jizya*
Polygamy 382, 461, 474, 560, 589
Polytheists 22, 28, 40, 41, 56, 403, 404, 557, 744, 800
Pope 13, 461, 642, 786, 804
Porphyry 157, 747
Prayer 5, 49, 53, 60, 81, 87, 228, 270, 316, 376, 520, 523, 838-39, 878, 904
Christian prayer 17, 40, 46, 107, 123, 223, 236, 242, 296, 322, 331, 361, 406, 535, 558, 571, 598, 631, 676, 793, 794, 821, 894, 899
Muslim prayer 128, 142, 155, 228, 257, 404, 469, 500, 520, 535, 536, 595, 623, 625, 685, 822, 838, 841, 864
Predestination 50, 201, 340
Processions 5, 93, 107, 361, 499, 616, 894
Proclus 507
Procopius 213
Proof texts, Bible ix, 15, 16, 270, 350, 351, 382, 504, 505, 506, 520, 527, 530, 534, 571, 575, 577, 583, 698, 816, 876, 903
Proof texts, Old Testament 331, 387, 655, 662, 793, 878, 902, 903, 904
Proof texts, Qurʾān 58, 61, 298, 331, 383, 387, 451, 459, 464, 472, 520, 527, 558, 559, 560, 602, 625, 662, 755, 794, 876, 879, 903, 904, 909
Proofs of prophethood viii, 56, 71, 350, 351, 371, 382-83, 384, 474, 534, 549, 566, 583, 584, 620, 650, 672, 673, 707, 715, 716, 763, 764, 765, 776, 781, 817, 820, 830, 831, 833
Prophet of Islam, *or* the Prophet, *see* Muḥammad, prophet
Prophetess, *see* Sibyl
Prophethood of Muḥammad *see* Proofs of prophethood
Prophets ix, 14, 34, 37, 39, 51, 55, 74, 80, 114, 118, 128, 194, 242-44, 298, 316, 331, 350, 376, 378, 460, 473, 474, 504, 574, 576, 589, 596, 671, 800, 817, 827, *see also* Jesus Christ as prophet; Muḥammad, prophet
Prostration 382, 463, 464, 470, 666, *see also* Cross, veneration of
Provence 13, 87, 294
Psalms 94, 376, 473, 620, 721
Pseudo-Bartholomew 432
Pseudo-Dionysius of Tell-Maḥrē *322-26*, 893
Pseudo-Ephrem *160-62*
Pseudo-Leo III *375-76*
Pseudo-Methodius 161, *163-71*, 172-74, 223, 224, 243, *245-48*, *249-52*, 286, 311
Pseudo-Theophilus *256-60*
Pseudo-ʿUmar II 204, 376, *381-85*

Qādisiyya, battle of 264
Qalamūn, *see* Samuel of Qalamūn
Qalamūn, monastery of, *see under* Monasteries
Qartmīn, monastery of, *see under* Monasteries, *see also* Gabriel of Qartmīn
al-Qāsim ibn Ibrāhīm *540-43*, 656, 659
Qays al-Ghassānī 685
Qays al-Mārūnī 145
Qenneshrē/Qenneshrin, monastry of, *see under* Monasteries
al-Qirqisānī, Abū Yaʿqūb 743
Qurʾān 12, 25, 108, 109, 113, 201, 204, 205, 206, 270, 271, 298, 299, 331, 350, 356, 372, 383, 387, 397, 398-99, 425, 481, 507, 510, 514, 520, 523, 529, 532, 541, 548, 556, 557, 566, 569, 574, 582, 589, 595, 596, 601, 602, 611, 625, 649, 652, 656, 695, 706, 708, 710, 715, 716, 723, 744, 745, 751, 752, 755, 773, 783, 792, 816, 822, 832, 835, 848, 878, 904
corruption of, *see under* Corruption of scripture
exegesis *31-56*, 372, 825
inimitability of 37, 350, 763, 766, 776
proof texts, *see* Proof texts, Qurʾān
Important citations from:
Q 4:157 24, 73, 745
Q 4:171 64, 378, 387, 523, 527, 601, 745
Q 5:5 110-12
Q 5:82 24, 80, 121, 601
Q 5:116 43, 387
Q 9:29 25, 102, 878
Q 42:51 580, 794

Quraysh 3, 33, 42, 431, 499
Qusṭā ibn Lūqā 758, 762, 763, 764, 765, 775

Rawḥ al-Qurashī, *see* Anthony (Rawḥ al-Qurashī)
al-Rāzī, Abū Bakr, *see* Abū Bakr al-Rāzī
Recared, king 284
Receswinth, king 884
Reconquista 590, 811, 812, 884, 885
Redemption 223, 527, 542
  of prisoners 188, 187
Relics 96, 254, 429, 693, 917
  Veneration of 17, 270, 296, 327, 382, 402, 530
Repentance 95, 98, 177, 179, 194, 228, 256, 391, 476, 499, 686
Resurrection 402
  Day of 73, 74, 77, 174, 296, 467, 794, 879, 903, 904, *see also* Last Judgement
  church of, *see under* Church buildings
  of Jesus Christ, *see* Jesus Christ, resurrection of
Revelation 14, 23, 38, 64, 109, 111, 112, 113, 164, 222, 223, 239, 249, 296, 298, 299, 415, 491, 523, 589, 608, 759, 794
  Book of 223, 239
Riccoldo da Monte Croce 424
Rightly-guided caliphs 827
Ritual of abjuration 12, 95, *821-24*
Roderick, king 811
Rodrigo Jiménez of Rada 885
Romans (Byzantines) 12, 24, 67, 87, 89, 164, 166, 187, 188, 211, 224, 285, 310, 311, 338, 339, 340, 349, 377, 429, 609, 717, 735, 738, 845, 863
Romanus 388, 390, 391-92
Rome, city and empire of 13, 47, 67, 83, 87, 120, 161, 165, 205, 211, 223, 224, 257, 259, 275, 338, 341, 365, 415, 461, 493, 614, 627, 642, 646, 786, 789, 801, 804, 873
al-Rūm, *see* Romans

Saba/Sabas, Mār/St, monastery of 148, 149, 295, 330, 388, 390, 392, 393, 394, 395, 406, 407, 408, 429, 439, 452, 598, 627, 685, 873, 911, 912, 913, *see also* Stephen of Mār Saba; Basil of Mār Saba; Michael of Mār Saba
Sabeans 39, 42, 714
Sabrīshōʿ 176, 177
Sabellians 701
Sabians, *see* Sabeans
Sacraments 242, 257, 344, 822
Saʿd ibn Abī Waqqāṣ 131
Saddles 356, 361, 917
al-Saffāḥ, caliph 310
al-Ṣafī ibn al-ʿAssāl, *see* Ibn al-ʿAssāl, al-Ṣafī
Ṣafwān ibn Yaḥyā *535-39*
Sahak, amir 854
Sahak Sevada, prince 262
Saḥnūn, legal scholar 102, 738, 835, 837
Saʿīd ibn Baṭrīq 194, *see also* Eutychius
Saints 13, 17, 27, 75, 77, 81, 124, 126, 182, 187, 198, 219, 245, 257, 309, 327, 335, 388, 390, 411, 414, 419, 420, 421, 424, 429, 463, 464, 530, 531, 576, 664, 665, 676, 679, 680, 685, 726, 727, 853, 854, 873, 885, 916, 917, 919, 921
Sakkoudion monastery, *see under* Monasteries
Salmān al-Fārisī 38, 39, 40, 205
Salvation 17, 25, 67, 68, 73, 74, 87, 163, 223, 246, 257, 296, 331, 440, 455, 459, 471, 472, 476, 480, 485, 574
Samarra 669, 706, 743, 752, 762, 800, 853
Samoel, patriarch 334, 335
Samosata 186, 187
Samothrace 426
Samson of Cordova, abbot 634, *691-94*
Samuel of Eshtin 892
Samuel of Qalamūn 664, 665
Sandals 838-39
Saracens 12, 13, 84, 85, 86, 87, 88, 91, 95, 97, 110, 117, 118, 123, 124, 126, 128, 138, 149, 154, 190, 285, 294, 298, 316, 335, 365, 367-68, 391, 393, 395, 441, 474, 488, 614, 615, 616, 642, 643, 731, 786, 789, 806, 807, 812, 821, 848
Sarafian 394
Sarah/Sarrah 97, 298, 585, 616
al-Sarakhsī, Aḥmad ibn al-Ṭayyib 757, 758, *840-43*
Sarjūn ibn Manṣūr 295, 430
Sasanians 3, 4, 99, 142, 143, 177, 182, 264
Satan 49, 201, 323, 331, 376, 378, 379, 383, 631, 704, 868, *see also* Devil
Savinianos, St, church of, *see under* Church buildings
Sāwīrus ibn al-Muqaffaʿ 219, 234, 540, 907
Sayf ibn ʿUmar 45, 46, *437-38*
Sbeitla, battle of 287
Scotland 154

Scripture 2, 15, 16, 18, 38, 59, 63, 65, 66, 68, 70, 83, 94, 101, 109, 111, 159, 179, 203, 270, 296, 298, 331, 350, 379, 382, 388, 420, 453, 464, 491, 521, 540, 542, 557, 569, 573, 575, 578, 588, 589, 595, 596, 608, 609, 662, 685, 744, 783, 822, 835, 878, 909, *see also* Corruption of scripture; Proof texts
Seal, *see* Lead seals
Sebaste 822
Sebastian of Orense, bishop 882
Sebastian of Salamanca 882, 883
Sebeos *139-44*, 262, 866
Seleucia-Ctesiphon 133, 515, 516
Seljuks 240
Septuagint 203, 204, 769
Sergius, East Syrian patriarch 757
Sergius, patriarch and friend of Timothy I 397, 519, 521
Sergius, patriarch of Constantinople 120, 121, 123
Sergius, slave 187
Sergius II, pope 642, 643
Sergius Baḥīrā, *see* Baḥīrā
Servandus, count 692, 693
Severus of Antioch 157
Severus Sebokht 157
Sevordi 854
al-Shāfiʿī, Abū Idrīs 360, 362, 656
Shahāda 198
Shapuh Bagratuni 866, 867
Sharaka 507
al-Shaybānī, *see* Muḥammad ibn al-Ḥasan al-Shaybānī
She-camel of God 298, 425, 822
Shenute, St *182-85*, 258, 309, 411
Shenute, St, monastery of, *see under* Monasteries
Shenute I, patriarch 702
Shurūṭ ʿUmar, see Pact of ʿUmar
al-Shurūṭ al-ʿUmariyya, see Pact of ʿUmar
Sibyl 493
Sibylline Prophecy (Arabic) *492-97*
al-Sijistānī, *see* Abū Dāwūd al-Sijistānī
Simeon of Rev Ardashir, bishop 134, 135
Simeon Abū Qurra of Ḥabsannās 557
Simon, apostle 47, 48, 67, 223
Simon, patriarch 210, 234
Sinai 120, 193, 194, 198, 291, 330, 376, 377, 383, 407, 464, *see also* Catherine, St, monastery of
Sīra, see Muḥammad, prophet, biography of
Slaves 40, 60, 70, 78, 79, 86, 90, 94, 96-97, 102, 103, 104, 105, 111, 178, 187, 198, 361, 472, 476, 536, 631, 639, 643, 666, 834
Slavonic 675, 799, 800, 801, 913
Slavs 86
Social interaction x, 5, 6, 10, 75, 104, 109, 111, 311, 336, 340, 357, 395, 625, 710, 736
Socrates 662
Socrates Scholasticus 213
Somalia 286
Son of Perdition 173
Sons of Ishmael, *see* Ishmaelites
Sophronius of Cyprus, archbishop 631, 637, 640, *675-78*, 846
Sophronius I of Jerusalem, patriarch 86, 87, *120-27*, 149, 190, 191, 675
Sophronius II of Jerusalem, patriarch 675
Sophronius III of Jerusalem, patriarch 675
Spain 4, 9, 13, 87, 92, 101, 250, 284, 286, 288, 302, 303, 338, 340, 402, 679, 741, 827, 834, 835
Speraindeo, abbot *633-35*, 645, 679, 691
Spirit 69, 223, 256, 331, 473, 478, 529, 548, 744, 800, 863, *see also* Holy Spirit; Jesus Christ as Spirit of God
Spram, queen 265
Spudaioi, monastery of, *see under* Monasteries
Stephen, monk 406
Stephen V, pope 88, 90
Stephen of Damascus, *see* Stephen Manṣūr
Stephen the Deacon 597
Stephen the Hymnographer, *see* Stephen Manṣūr
Stephen Manṣūr *388-96*, 911, 912
Stephen of al-Ramla 791
Stephen of Mār Saba 388, 406-8
Stephen, St, church of, *see under* Church buildings
Stephen of Taron 869
Stephen the Younger, St 597
Stoudios monastery, *see under* Monasteries
Stylites 41, 322, *see also* John the Stylite; Joshua the Stylite
Suintila, king 286
Sulaymān ibn ʿAbd al-Malik, caliph 285, 328, 411

Sun, analogy of the Trinity with 378, 493, 760
Susruta 507
Switzerland 138, 294
Symeon, bishop of Ḥarrān 893, 895, 896
Symeon the monk 328
Symeon of Qartmīn 892, 893, 895, 896
Symeon of Samosata *186-89*
Synagogues 356
Syrians, monastery of the, *see under* Monasteries 322

al-Ṭabarī, Abū Jaʿfar Muḥammad ibn Jarīr 37, 54, 59, 67, 347, 437, 510, 512, 513, 587, 670, 752, 780
al-Ṭabarī, ʿAlī ibn Rabban, *see* ʿAlī ibn Rabban al-Ṭabarī
Ṭabaristān 305, 652, 669
Taghlib, *see* Banū Taghlib
Takrīt 567
taḥrīf, *see* Corruption of scripture
Tarasius, patriarch 423, 614
Tatian 35
tawḥīd 17, 54, 371, 399, 400, 523, 532, 551, 611, 618, 619, 620, 650, 656, 710, 713, 714, 715, 747, 749, 759, 769
al-Tawḥīdī, Abū Ḥayyān 585
Taxation 5, 8, 10, 103, 108, 161, 166, 173, 183, 187, 188, 258, 276, 319, 324, 355, 356, 408, 421, 428, 430, 625, 685, 689, 692, 704, 718, 869, 878, 894, 895, 899, *see also jizya; kharāj*
Tbilisi 334, 335
Tell ʿAdē, monastery of, *see under* Monasteries
Temple 49, 102, 183, 223, 792, 878
Temple Mount, mosque 142, 149, 155, 166, 191, 430
Testimonia/testimonies, *see* Proof texts
Testimonia catalogues 242-44, 331, 351, 459, 504, 577, 793, 903, 904
al-Thaʿlabī 37, 51
Thawfīl al-Rūmī, *see* Theophilus of Edessa
Theodora, empress 637, 852, 853, 854
Theodore, archdeacon 149
Theodore Abū Qurra 271, 368, *439-91*, *556-64*, 613, 731, 743, 776, 791, 873, 911-12
Theodore of Chora 431
Theodore of Edessa 913
Theodore bar Koni/Konay *343-46*, 507, 520, 524, 541, 554
Theodore of Miṣr, bishop 317
Theodore the Monk 487
Theodore of Raithou 487
Theodore, St 499
Theodore, St, church of, *see under* Church buildings
Theodore, St, monastery of (at Manhā), *see under* Monasteries
Theodore the Stoudite *423-25*, 873, 874
Theodoret, patriarch of Antioch 439, 921
Theodorus Craterus/Carterus 630, 631, 636, 637, 640, 676
Theodorus Graptus 627, 873
Theodosius II, emperor 788
Theodosius Melissenus 431
Theodosius, monastery of, *see under* Monasteries
Theodotus, patriarch 873
Theophanes the Confessor 12, 191, 290, 291, 296, 306, 419, 421, 424, *426-36*, 730, 731, 788, 789
Theophanes Graptus 627, 628, 873
Theophilus, bishop 622
Theophilus, emperor 11, 614, 624, 630, 637, 640, 677, 731, 752, 754, 845, 874
Theophilus, martyr 636, 640, 676
Theophilus of Alexandria, patriarch 258
Theophilus of Edessa 145, 191, *305-8*, 428, 431, 625
Theophilus bar Tuma, *see* Theophilus of Edessa
Theophylactus 430
Theotokos 296, *see also* Theotokos, church of *under* Church buildings
Thessaloniki 614, 800
Thomas, apostle 47, 67, 194
Thomas, patriarch 439, 873, 912-13
Thomas Artsruni 282, 854
Thomas of Margā *688-90*, 743
Thomas the Slav 726, 727
Throne of God 455, 473
Thumāma ibn Ashras 578
Tigris 176, 188, 631, 637, 640
Timothy I, patriarch 14, 88, 89, 96, 97, 351, 384, 397, 503, *515-31*, 552, 560, 652, 689, 769
Timothy II, patriarch 516
Timothy of Kākhushtā *919-22*
al-Tirmidhī 41, 819
Tolosa, battle of 284
Torah 34, 38, 41, 46, 50, 52, 53, 270, 461, 576, 577, 620, 835, 891

Trinity 3, 14, 15, 16, 27, 65, 66, 73, 80, 270, 296, 299, 315, 331, 344, 350, 373, 377, 386, 387, 400, 404, 440, 448, 453, 478, 491, 504, 505, 522, 523, 529, 542, 548, 550, 551, 557, 560, 571, 572, 573, 574, 576, 577, 588, 605, 608, 619, 620, 633, 654, 655, 662, 666, 698, 744, 745, 747, 749, 760, 793, 794, 800, 842, 878, 899, 903, 908
Tripolitania 287
True religion 254, 448, 467, 559, 605, 607, 608, 793, 878
Trullo, Council in, *see under* Church Councils
Ṭūr ʿAbdīn 157, 176, 187, 557, 892, 894, 895
Turks 240, 310

ʿUbayd Allāh ibn Ḥasan 710
ʿUbayd Allāh ibn Ziyād 178
ʿUmar I, *see* ʿUmar ibn al-Khaṭṭāb
ʿUmar II, *see* ʿUmar ibn ʿAbd al-ʿAzīz
ʿUmar ibn ʿAbd al-ʿAzīz, caliph 10, 12, 104, *203-8*, 282, 285, 295, 361, 375, 377-79, 381-84, 430, 596, 616, 712, 867, 868
ʿUmar ibn al-Khaṭṭāb, caliph 5, 104, 285, 361, 430, 837, 894, *see also* Pact of ʿUmar
al-ʿUmarī, Aḥmad ibn Faḍl Allāh 512
ʿUmayr ibn Saʿd al-Anṣārī 625, 783
Umayya ibn Abī l-Ṣalt 30
Umayyads 6, 9, 10, 11, 12, 13, 30, 39, 75, 154, 161, 166, 178, 179, 220, 231, 240, 254, 269, 275, 276, 282, 285-88, 295, 303, 307, 310, 317, 318-19, 324, 325, 347, 361, 375, 377, 381, 407, 411, 428, 429, 430, 431, 595, 684, 686, 692, 693, 732, 784, 812, 834, 863, 864, 869, 870, 912
Union (of the divine and human in Christ) 568, 605, 608, 658, 659, 662, 878
Ur 285
Usṭāth al-Rāhib *907-10*
al-ʿUtbī l-Qurṭubī *734-37*
ʿUthmān, caliph 45, 63, 437, 625, 649, 783

Vahan, general 194
Vahan son of Khosrov *281-83*
Valentius, bishop 691
Veil 580, 792, 794
Virgin Mary, *see* Mary, Virgin
Virgin birth, *see* Jesus, birth of; *see also* Mary, Virgin

Wahb ibn Munabbih 36, 37, 47, 52, 53, 830
al-Walīd I, caliph 258, 281-82, 285, 295, 420, 421, 430, 431
al-Walīd II, caliph 284, 285, 290, 307, 430
al-Walīd ibn Muslim 835
Wakīʿ ibn al-Jarrāḥ 76
al-Wāqidī 58
Waraqa ibn Nawfal 3, 22, 28, 64, 80
al-Warrāq, *see* Abū ʿĪsā al-Warrāq
Wāṣil al-Dimashqī *863-65*
Wāṣil ibn ʿAṭāʾ 532, 544, 864
al-Wāthiq, caliph 265, 637, 676, 723, 768, 845
White Monastery, *see* monastery of St Shenute *under* Monasteries
Wilcharius, archbishop 340
Wonders, *see* Miracles
Word of God 21, 270, 298, 299, 367, 472, 473, 527, 557, 560, 601, 755

Yahūd, *see* Judaism
Yaḥyā al-Barmakī 347, 371, *see also* Barmakids
Yaḥyā ibn ʿAdī 569, 587, 698, 747, 760
Yanna ibn Iṣṭafān al-Fākhūrī 407
Yannah, Abba, of Edessa 464
Yaʿqūb, follower of St Paul 44, 438
Yaʿqūb, Mār, abbot 133
al-Yaʿqūbī 347, 348
Yāqūt 502, 503, 510, 512, 513, 709
Yarmūk, battle of 194, 285, 731
Yazdgird, ruler 131
Yazīd I, caliph 178, 231, 429, 430, 731
Yemen 61, 78, 82, 290
Yuḥannā ibn Māsawayh 768
Yuḥannā ibn Mīna 776
Yuḥannā ibn al-Ṣalt *849-51*
Yuḥannān Ṭayyāyā 893
Yūsāb I, patriarch 702
Yūsuf ibn Jirjis 585
Yūsuf ibn Yaḥyā l-Maghāmī 826

Zachariah 48, 50, 51
Zacharias, pope 87, 96, 97
Zamora 882
Zanj 758
Zaynab 588
Zindīq 347, 371

Zoilus, St, church of, *see under* Church buildings; monastery of, *see under* Monasteries
Zonaras 431
Zoroastrians 38, 79, 101, 108, 110, 111, 533, 545, 565, 611, 723, 762
Zunnār 361
Zuqnīn, monastery of, *see under* Monasteries
Zʿura, Mār, monastery of, *see under* Monasteries

Index of Works

Numbers in italics indicate a main entry.

Abba Theodore Abū Qurra was asked about Christ, whether he was crucified willingly or not, see *Su'ila Abū Qurra Anbā Thādhurus 'an al-Masīḥ bi-hawāhi ṣuliba am bi-ghayr hawāhi* *468-69*
About prophethood, see *Kitāb fī l-nubuwwa* (Abū l-Hudhayl al-'Allāf) *548-49*
Abū Qurra was questioned by an unbeliever *485-86*
Abū l-Rabī' Muḥammad ibn al-Layth which he wrote for al-Rashīd to the Byzantine Emperor Constantine, Letter of *349-53*, 384
Account of Wāṣil al-Dimashqī, see *Ḥadīth Wāṣil al-Dimashqī* *863-65*
Admonishing Hārūn al-Rashīd, see *Kitāb 'iẓat Hārūn al-Rashīd* (Ibn al-Layth) *347*
Affair of the death of Muḥammad *401-2*, 602
Affair of the Qur'ān *595-96*, 602
Against 'Ammār the Christian in refutation of the Christians, see *Kitāb 'alā 'Ammār al-Naṣrānī fī l-radd 'alā l-Naṣārā* (Abū l-Hudhayl al-'Allāf) *547-48*
Against the Christians, see *Kitāb 'alā l-Naṣārā* (Abū l-Hudhayl al-'Allāf) *547*
Against the Christians, see *Kitāb 'alā l-Naṣārā* (Ḥafṣ al-Fard) *657*
Against the Christians on felicity and eating and drinking in the hereafter, see *Kitāb 'alā l-Naṣārā fī l-na'īm wa-l-akl wa-l-shurb fī l-ākhira wa-'alā jamī' man qāla bi-ḍiddi dhālika* (Ḥumayd ibn Bakhtiyār) *724-25*
Against Muḥammad 822
Against the outsiders, see *Min qawl Thāwudūrus ṭa'ana 'alā l-barrāniyyīn* (Theodore Abū Qurra) *470-71*
Alexander legend 166
Alexander romance 166
Amārāt al-nubuwwa (al-Juzajānī) *781*
'alā 'Ammār al-Naṣrānī fī l-radd 'alā l-Naṣārā, Kitāb (Abū l-Hudhayl al-'Allāf) *547-48*
Anamnēsis tēs idias psychēs 291
Anonymous Guidi, see *Chronicle of Khuzistan* *130-32*
Another question (opusculum 36) (Theodore Abū Qurra) *489*
Another question (opusculum 37) (Theodore Abū Qurra) *490*
Another question (opusculum 38) (Theodore Abū Qurra) *490-91*
Another question by the same (opusculum 35) (Theodore Abū Qurra) *488-89*
Answers for the shaykh, see *Masā'il wa-ajwiba 'aqliyya wa-ilāhiyya* 658, 659, *661-63*
Antirrhēsis kai anatropē tēs deuteras epistolēs tēs staleisēs para tōn Agarēnōn pros Michaēl basilea, see *Confutation and refutation of the second letter sent by the Hagarenes to the Emperor Michael* (Nicetas of Byzantium) *754*
Apocalypse of Pseudo-Athanasius *274-80*
Apocalypse of Pseudo-Ephrem *160-62*
Apocalypse of Pseudo-Ezra *239-41*
Apocalypse of Pseudo-Methodius (Syriac) 161, *163-71*, 172, 173, 174, 243
Apocalypse of Pseudo-Methodius (Greek) *245-48*
Apocalypse of Pseudo-Methodius (Latin) *249-52*
Apocalypse of Samuel 259, 276, 310
Apocalypse of Shenute *182-85*, 411
Apologetic treatise of Nonnus of Nisibis *744-45*
Apologeticus (Abbot Samson) 691, *692-94*
Apology of al-Kindī 573, *585-94*, 596
Arabic homily of Pseudo-Theophilus of Alexandria *256-60*
Arabic letter of Leo III to 'Umar *377-80*, 596, 867
Arabic Sibylline prophecy *492-97*

al-asbāb wa-l-ʿilm ʿalā al-nubuwwa, Kitāb (Ḍirar ibn ʿAmr) 371
Athlēsis tōn hagiōn kai kallinikōn mbʿ martyrōn 636-38
al-bayān, Kitāb (Usṭāth al-Rāhib) 908-10
al-bidaʿ, Kitāb (Ibn Waḍḍāḥ) 837-38

Bios kai athlēsis tou hosiou Bakchou, see *Life and martyrdom of the holy Bacchus* 598-99
Bios kai politeia kai agōnes Michaēl presbyterou kai synkellou, see *Life of Michael the Synkellos* 872-75
Bios kai politeia tou hosiou Antōniou tou Neou, see *Life of Antony the Younger* 726-28
Book in defense of the martyrs, see *Liber apologeticus martyrum* (Eulogius of Cordova) 683, 722
Book of main points (John bar Penkāyē) 176-81
Book of the consecration of the sanctuary of Benjamin 235
Book of Eustathius, see *Kitāb al-bayān* (Usṭāth al-Rāhib) 908-10
Book of governors (Thomas of Margā) 397, 688, 689-90
Book of questions (Timothy I) 515
Book of religion and empire, see *Kitāb al-dīn wa-l-dawla* (ʿAlī ibn Rabban al-Ṭabarī) 565, 566, 669, 670, 672-74
Book of scholia (Theodore bar Koni) 343, 344-46
Book of the stars (Timothy I) 516
Book of treasures (Job of Edessa) 502, 503, 504, 505, 506-9, 725
al-burhān, Kitāb (Abū l-Faḍl ʿAlī ibn Rabban al-Naṣrānī) 652-53
al-burhān, Kitāb (Abū l-Faraj Saʿīd ibn ʿAlī al-Anbārī) 859-60
al-Burhān (ʿAlī ibn Yaḥyā ibn al-Munajjim) 763-67, 776
al-burhān, Kitāb (ʿAmmār al-Baṣrī) 607-10
al-Burhān (Peter of Bayt Raʾs) 902-6
al-burhān, Kitāb (Yuḥannā ibn al-Ṣalt) 850
d-buyyāʾē awkit d-egrātā, Ktābā see *Consolations* (Ishoʿyahb III) 134-36

Calligraphy and the pen, see *Kitāb al-khaṭṭ wa-l-qalam* (Ibn al-Layth) 347
Cambyses romance 213
Cʾamebaj cʾmidisa mikaelisi romeli, see *Martyrdom of Michael of Mār Saba* 911-15
Cʾamebaj Habojsi, see *Martyrdom of Abo of Tbilisi* 335-37
Canons (Jacob of Edessa) 89, 90, 91, 93, 95, 96, 97, 222, 230-31
Cave of treasures 164, 166
Chapters, see *Euodiou monachou kephalaia* 848
Chapters of the miracles 19, 148-50
Christian Arabic disputation 386-87
Christmas sermon (Sophronius) 124-25
Christological discussion 553-55
Chronica Albendensia, see *Chronicle of Albelda*
Chronica Byzantia-Arabica 284-89
Chronica Hispana-Orientalia ad annum 724, see *Chronicle of 741* 284-89
Chronica majora (Isidore of Seville) 302
Chronica Orientalia 285
Chronica Visegothorum, see *Chronicle of Alfonso III* 288, 882-88
Chronicle (Dionysius of Tell Mahrē) 559, 624-26
Chronicle (Jacob of Edessa) 231-32
Chronicle of 741 284-89
Chronicle of 754 287, 288, 302-4, 885
Chronicle of 1234, see *Chronicon ad annum Christi 1234 pertinens* 191, 306, 557, 624, 893
Chronicle of Albelda 722, 810-15, 883, 884, 885
Chronicle of Alfonso III 288, 882-88
Chronicle of Fredegar 137-38, 293
Chronicle of George the Monk 431, 632, 729, 730-33
Chronicle of John of Nikiou 210, 211-18
Chronicle of Khuzistan 130-32
Chronicle of Nájera 885
Chronicle of Zuqnīn 322, 323, 324-46, 893
Chronicon ad annum Christi 1234 pertinens 191, 306, 557, 624, 893
Chronicon Geōrgiou hamartōlou monachou, see *Chronicle of George the Monk* 431, 632, 729, 730-33
Chronicon Maroniticum, see *Maronite Chronicle* 145-47
Chronicon Syriacum (Barhebraeus) 305
Chronicum anonymum ad A.D. 819 pertinens 892, 894

Chronographia (Theophanes the Confessor) 291, 306, 427-36, 730, *788-89*
Chronographia tripertita (Anastasius Bibliothecarius) *787-90*
Chronography, see *Chronographia* (Theophanes the Confessor), and *Syriac common source*
Codex Soriensis 288
Collectio toletana 589
Compilation of the aspects of the faith, see *Al-Jāmiʿ wujūh al-īmān* 468, 471, *791-98*, 879
Confession which Kaʿb al-Aḥbār handed down to the Ishmaelites *403-5*, 602
Confirmation of messengers, see *ithbāt al-rusul, Kitāb* (Ḍirar ibn ʿAmr) *371*
Confutation and refutation of the second letter sent by the Hagarenes to the Emperor Michael (Nicetas of Byzantium) *754*
Consolations (Ishoʿyahb III) *134-36*
Continuatio Hispana, Continuatio Isidoriana Hispana, see *Chronicle of 754* 287, 288, *302-4*, 885
Contra Jacobitas (John of Damascus) 290
Correspondence of al-Hāshimī and al-Kindī, see *Risālat al-Hāshimī ilā ʿAbd al-Masīḥ al-Kindī wa-risālat al-Kindī ilā l-Hāshimī* *587-94*
Cxoregaj da cʾamebaj cʾmidisa mocʾamisa kʾostʾantʾisi kartvelisaj, see *Life and passion of Kostanti-Kaxay* *852-56*

dalīl al-ḥāʾir, Kitāb (Yuḥannā ibn al-Ṣalt) *850*
Dalāʾil al-nubuwwa (Abū Dāwūd al-Sijistānī) *820*
Dalāʾil al-nubuwwa (al-Ḥarbī, Ibrāhīm ibn Isḥāq) *833*
Dalāʾil al-nubuwwa (Ibn Abī l-Dunyā) *830-31*
Dalāʾil al-nubuwwa (Ibn Qutayba) 673, *817-18*
De administrando imperio 424, 731
De haeresibus (John of Damascus) 291, 295, *297-301*, 848
De locis sanctis, see *On the holy places* (Adomnán of Iona) *154-56*
Debate between Israel of Kashkar and al-Sarakhsī *840-43*
Debate between Theodore Abū Qurra, Abū Rāʾiṭa and ʿAbd Īshūʿ *554-55*
Debate of Theodore Abū Qurra 439, *556-64*
Dialexis apodeiknyousa hoti ho Patēr aei gennai ho de Hyios aei gennatai, see *Dialogue demonstrating that the Father begets eternally, while the Son is begotten eternally* (Theodore Abū Qurra) *486-88*
Dialexis Sarakēnou kai Christianou, see *Dialogue between a Saracen and a Christian* 316, *367-70*, 488
Dialogos Theodōrou genomenos pros ton tou dromou Emeses aitesamenon, see *Dialogue between Theodore and the master of the post of Emesa* (Theodore Abū Qurra) *478-79*
Dialogue between a Saracen and a Christian 316, *367-70*, 488
Dialogue between Theodore and the master of the post of Emesa (Theodore Abū Qurra) *478-79*
Dialogue demonstrating that the Father begets eternally, while the Son is begotten eternally (Theodore Abū Qurra) *486-88*
Didaskalia Iakōbou neobaptistou *117-19*
Diegēmata psychōphelē kai steriktika genomena en diaphorois topois epi tōn hēmeterōn chronōn, see *Narrationes* (Anastasius of Sinai) 194, *198-200*
Diegesis Danielis, see *Greek apocalypse of Daniel* *414-18*
al-dīn wa-l-dawla, Kitāb (ʿAlī ibn Rabbān al-Ṭabarī) 565, 566, 669, 670, *672-74*
Discourses in verse against heresies (Theodore the Stoudite) *424-25*
Disputatio Felicis cum Sarraceno, see *Disputation between Felix and a Saracen* *365-66*
Disputation against the Jews (Anastasius of Sinai) 246
Disputation between Felix and a Saracen *365-66*
Disputation between a monk of Bēt Ḥālē and an Arab notable *268-73*
Disputation of John and the Emir 625, *782-85*
Disputation of Ibrāhīm al-Ṭabarānī 524, 596, *876-81*
Disputation of Patriarch John *253-55*
Disputation with the Caliph al-Mahdī (Timothy I) 516, *522-26*

Divine Unity, see *Kitāb al-tawḥīd* (Muḥammad ibn Shabīb) 713, *714-15*
Doctrina Iacobi nuper baptizati *117-19*
Doctrines, see *Kitāb al-maqālāt* (al-Īrānshahrī) 696, *891*
Documentum martyriale (Eulogius of Cordova) *682-83*

Edessene Apocalypse 166, *172-75*, 224
Egarta d-Mar(y) Yoḥannan paṭriyarkā, see *Letter of Patriarch John* *782-85*
Egarta d-ṭubtānā Atanāsius paṭriarkā, see *Letter* (Athanasius of Balad) *158-59*
Ek tōn pros tous Sarakēnous antirrhēseōn dia phonēs Ioannou Diakonou, see *Refutation of the Saracens as reported by John the Deacon* (Theodore Abū Qurra) *474-76*
Ekthesis kataskeuastikē meta apodeixeōs tou Christianikou dogmatos, see *Positive exposition of Christian doctrine* (Nicetas of Byzantium) *752-53*
Eltā d-mawteh d-Muḥammad, see *Affair of the death of Muḥammad* *401-2*, 602
Eltā d-Quran, see *Affair of the Qurʾān* *595-96*, 602
Epistle on the confirmation of the Unity of the Creator and the Trinity of his properties, see *Risāla fī tathbīt waḥdāniyyat al-Bāriʾ wa-tathlīth khawāṣṣihi* (Israel of Kashkar) 758, *759*
Epistle on the difference between the communities about divine oneness, see *Risāla fī iftirāq al-milal fī l-tawḥīd* (al-Kindī, Abū Yūsuf) 747, *749-50*
Epistolæ Adriani papæ ad Egilam episcopum, see *Pope Hadrian's epistles to Bishop Egila* *338-42*
Erotapokriseis, see *Quaestiones et responsiones* (Anastasius of Sinai) *200-2*
Erōtēsis Agarēnou pros ton auton, see *A Hagarene's question to the same* (Theodore Abū Qurra) *482-83*
Erōtēsis apistou pros ton auton genomenē, see *An Unbeliever's question to the same* (Theodore Abū Qurra) *483-85*
Erōtēsis Arabōn pros Christianon, see *A Question of the Arabs to a Christian* (Theodore Abū Qurra) *481-82*
Erōtēthē Aboukaras par' apistou, see *Abū Qurra was questioned by an unbeliever* *485-86*
Eskolyon, (Ktābā d-) see *Book of Scholia* (Theodore bar Koni) 343, *344-46*
Euchologion 821, 823
Euodiou monachou kephalaia *848*
Ēvangelīyōn d-treʿsar shlīḥē qaddīshē, see *Gospel of the twelve Apostles* 166, *222-25*
Exēgēsis ētoi martyrion... en tē Laura tou... Saba see *Twenty martyrs of Mār Saba* 388, *393-96*
Exposition, see *Kitāb al-bayān* (Usṭāth al-Rāhib) *908-10*

Fī ḥaqīqa wujūd Allāh, see *Maymar fī wujūd al-Khāliq wa-l-dīn al-qawīm* (Theodore Abū Qurra) *448-50*
Fī tathlīth Allāh al-wāḥid, see *On the Triune nature of God* 330-33
Fihrist (Ibn al-Nadīm) 348, 355, 373, 502, 512, 513, 514, 533, 534, 546, 547, 583, 604, 612, 613, 657, 669, 698, 699, 700, 713, 723, 724, 725, 747, 749, 764, 907
Firdaws al-ḥikma (ʿAlī ibn Rabban al-Ṭabarī) 507, 669, 670
Forty-two martyrs of Amorion (Sophronius, Archbishop of Cyprus) 675, *676-78*
Forty-two martyrs of Amorion (BHG 1212) *636-38*
Forty-two martyrs of Amorion (BHG 1214c) *639-41*
Fount of knowledge (John of Damascus) 295
Fourteenth vision of Daniel 309
Fredegarii chronicon, see *Chronicle of Fredegar* *137-38*, 293

Gospel of the twelve Apostles 166, *222-25*
Great book of conquests and apostasy wars, see *Kitāb al-ridda wa-l-futūḥ* (Sayf ibn ʿUmar) 45, *437-38*
Greek apocalypse of Daniel *414-18*
Guidance, see *Kitāb al-hidāya* (Abū l-Khayr ʿĪsā ibn Hibat Allāh) *861-62*
Guidance, see *Kitāb al-hudā* (Yuḥannā ibn al-Ṣalt) *851*
Guide for the confused, see *Kitāb dalīl al-ḥāʾir* (Yuḥannā ibn al-Ṣalt) *850*

Ḥadīth Wāṣil al-Dimashqī *863-65*
A Hagarene's question to the same (Theodore Abū Qurra) *482-83*
al-halīlaja fī l-iʿtibār, Kitāb (Ibn al-Layth) 347

al-ḥayawān, Kitāb (al-Jāḥiẓ) 618, 656, 706, 707, 709, 710
Hetera erōtēsis, see *Another question* (Theodore Abū Qurra) *489, 490, 490-91*
Hetera erōtēsis tou autou, see *Another question by the same* (Theodore Abū Qurra) *488-89*
Hexaemeron (Anastasius of Sinai) 194
al-hidāya, Kitāb (Abū l-Khayr ʿĪsā ibn Hibat Allāh) *861-62*
Ḥikmat Sibillā ibnat Harqalus, see *Arabic Sibylline prophecy* *492-97*
al-Ḥīra, Kitāb (Ibn al-Kalbī) *513*
al-Ḥīra wa-tasmīyat al-biyaʿ wa-l-diyārāt, Kitāb, see *al-Ḥīra, the names of the churches and monasteries* (Ibn al-Kalbī) *511-13*
Hispanic Chronicle of 754, see *Chronicle of 754* 287, 288, *302-4*, 885
Historia ecclesiastica (Eusebius of Caesarea) 231
Historia Gothorum (Isidore of Seville) 284, 286, 811, 884
Historia Silense 885
Historia vel gesta Francorum, see *History of the deeds of the Franks* *293-94*
History, see *Kitāb al-taʾrīkh* (Ibn Ḥabīb) *826-28*
History of Aghuankʿ 261, 262, *263-67*
History of the deeds of the Franks *293-94*
History of Ghewond 203, 206, 265, 381, *867-71*
History of Sebeos *139-44*
History of the Patriarchs of Alexandria 8, 209, 234, 235, 259, 317, 318, 321, 702, 703r
History of the patriarchs of Alexandria (source of) *235-38*
History of Thomas Artsruni 282
Hodegos, see *Viae dux* (Anastasius of Sinai) *196-97*
'Honey-colored' letter, see *al-Risālat al-ʿasaliyya* (al-Jāḥiẓ) *712*
Hoti pente echthrous echomen ex hōn hēmas ho Sotēr elytrosato, see *That we have five enemies from whom the Savior freed us* (Theodore Abū Qurra) *476-77*
How to discern the truth of a religion, see *Kayfiyyat idrāk ḥaqīqat al-diyāna* (Ḥunayn ibn Isḥāq) *775-79*
al-hudā, Kitāb (Yuḥannā ibn al-Ṣalt) *851*
al-ḥujja ʿalā l-Naṣārā, Kitāb (Muḥammad ibn Saḥnūn) *739*
al-ḥujja fī ithbāt al-nabī, Kitāb (Bishr ibn al-Muʿtamir) *534*
al-ḥujja fī tathbīt al-nubuwwa, Kitāb (al-Jāḥiẓ) *707-8*
Ḥusayn ibn Saʿīd, Kitāb (Ṣafwān ibn Yaḥyā) 536
al-Imāma wa-l-siyāsa (Muʿārik ibn Marwān al-Nuṣayrī) *741-42*

In memory of the saints, see *Memoriale sanctorum* (Eulogius of Cordova) 633, *680-82*
Indiculus luminosus (Paul Alvarus) 645, *647-48*
Innovations, see *Kitāb al-bidaʿ* (Ibn Waḍḍāḥ) *837-38*
Interpretation of the Theologian (Timothy I) 516
Invalidation of those who are related to the Jacobites... and of other Christian groups, see *al-Naqḍ ʿalā man uḍīfa ilā l-Yaʿūbiyya... wa-ʿalā bāqī ṣunūf al-Naṣārā* (Abū ʿĪsā l-Warrāq) *701*
al-iqnāʿ, Kitāb (Abū l-ʿAbbās ʿĪsā ibn Zayd) 849, *857-58*
Isagoge (Porphyry) 157, 747, 748
Istoria de Mahomet 402, 683, *721-22*, 812
ithbāt al-rusul, Kitāb (Ḍirar ibn ʿAmr) 371
Iʿtirāf al-ābāʾ 575, 576, 580
ʿizat Hārūn al-Rashīd, Kitāb (Ibn al-Layth) 347

al-Jāmiʿ wujūh al-īmān 468, 471, *791-98*, 879
Jawāb al-Riḍā ʿan suʾāl Abī Qurra (Ṣafwān ibn Yaḥyā) *538-39*

Kayfiyyat idrāk ḥaqīqat al-diyāna (Ḥunayn ibn Isḥāq) *775-79*
Khachʾazgeatsʾ nahatakn ew kʾajayaghtʾ vkayn Kʾristosi, see *Martyrdom of David of Dwin* *719-20*
al-kharāj, Kitāb see *Property tax* *355-59*
al-khaṭṭ wa-l-qalam, Kitāb (Ibn al-Layth) 347
al-kifāya, Kitāb (Abū l-Khayr ʿĪsā ibn Hibat Allāh) *862*
Kitāb ʿalā ʿAmmār al-Naṣrānī fī l-radd ʿalā l-Naṣārā (Abū l-Hudhayl al-ʿAllāf) *547-48*

Kitāb ʿalā l-Naṣārā (Abū l-Hudhayl al-ʿAllāf) *547*
Kitāb ʿalā l-Naṣārā (Ḥafṣ al-Fard) *657*
Kitāb ʿalā l-Naṣārā fī l-naʿīm wa-l-akl wa-l-shurb fī l-ākhira wa-ʿalā jamīʿ man qāla bi-ḍiddi dhālika (Ḥumayd ibn Bakhtiyār) *724-25*
Kitāb al-asbāb wa-l-ʿilm ʿalā al-nubuwwa (Ḍirar ibn ʿAmr) 371
Kitāb al-bayān (Usṭāth al-Rāhib) *908-10*
Kitāb al-bidaʿ (Ibn Waḍḍāḥ) *837-38*
Kitāb al-burhān (ʿAmmār al-Baṣrī) *607-10*
Kitāb al-burhān (Abū l-Faḍl ʿAlī ibn Rabban al-Naṣrānī) *652-53*
Kitāb al-burhān (al-Anbārī, Abū l-Faraj Saʿīd ibn ʿAlī) *859-60*
Kitāb al-burhān (Yuḥannā ibn al-Ṣalt) *850*
Kitāb dalīl al-ḥāʾir (Yuḥannā ibn al-Ṣalt) *850*
Kitāb al-dīn wa-l-dawla (ʿAlī ibn Rabbān al-Ṭabarī) 565, 566, 669, 670, *672-74*
Kitāb fī l-nubuwwa (Abū l-Hudhayl al-ʿAllāf) *548-49*
Kitāb fī l-nubuwwa (Muḥammad ibn Shabīb) *715-16*
Kitāb al-halīlaja fī l-iʿtibār (Ibn al-Layth) 347
Kitāb al-ḥayawān (al-Jāḥiẓ) 618, 656, 706, 707, 709, 710
Kitāb al-hidāya (Abū l-Khayr ʿĪsā ibn Hibat Allāh) *861-62*
Kitāb al-Ḥīra (Ibn al-Kalbī) *513*
Kitāb al-Ḥīra wa-tasmīyat al-biyaʿ wa-l-diyārāt (Ibn al-Kalbī) *511-13*
Kitāb al-hudā (Yuḥannā ibn al-Ṣalt) *851*
Kitāb al-ḥujja ʿalā l-Naṣārā (Muḥammad ibn Saḥnūn) *739*
Kitāb al-ḥujja fī ithbāt al-nabī (Bishr ibn al-Muʿtamir) *534*
Kitāb al-ḥujja fī tathbīt al-nubuwwa (al-Jāḥiẓ) *707-8*
Kitāb Ḥusayn ibn Saʿīd (Ṣafwān ibn Yaḥyā) 536
Kitāb al-iqnāʿ (Abū l-ʿAbbās ʿĪsā ibn Zayd) 849, *857-58*
Kitāb ithbāt al-rusul (Ḍirar ibn ʿAmr) 371
Kitāb ʿiẓat Hārūn al-Rashīd (Ibn al-Layth) 347
Kitāb al-kharāj see *Property tax* *355-59*
Kitāb al-khaṭṭ wa-l-qalam, (Ibn al-Layth) 347
Kitāb al-kifāya (Abū l-Khayr ʿĪsā ibn Hibat Allāh) *862*
Kitāb al-majdal 151, 688, 757, 758
Kitāb al-maqālāt (al-Īrānshahrī) 696, *891*
Kitāb maqālāt al-nās wa-ikhtilāfihim (Abū ʿĪsā l-Warrāq) 695, *697-98*, 749, 891
Kitāb al-masāʾil wa-l-ajwiba (ʿAmmār al-Baṣrī) 547, *604-7*, 608, 609
Kitāb al-masāʾil wa-l-ajwiba (Ibn Qutayba) 816
Kitāb al-radd (Theodore Abū Qurra) *473*
Kitāb al-radd ʿalā ahl al-adyān (Abū l-Hudhayl al-ʿAllāf) *546-47*
Kitāb al-radd ʿalā Maʿmar fī qawlihi inna Muḥammadan rabb (Ḍirar ibn ʿAmr) *372*
Kitāb al-radd ʿalā l-Naṣārā (Anonymous) *658-60*
Kitāb al-radd ʿalā l-Naṣārā (Bishr ibn al-Muʿtamir) *533-34*
Kitāb al-radd ʿalā l-Naṣārā (Ḍirar ibn ʿAmr) *373-74*
Kitāb al-radd ʿalā l-Naṣārā (al-Murdār) *612*
Kitāb al-radd ʿalā l-Naṣārā (al-Qāsim ibn Ibrāhīm) *542-43*
Kitāb fī l-radd ʿalā l-Yahūd wa-l-Naṣārā (al-Maʾmūn) *584*
Kitāb al-radd ʿalā Yūshaʿ Bukht maṭrān Fars (Ḥumayd ibn Bakhtiyār) *724*
Kitāb fī tafḍīl al-tathlīth ʿalā l-tawḥīd (al-Naẓẓām) *619-21*
Kitāb rafʿ ʿĪsā (Ibn al-Kalbī) *514*
Kitāb al-ridda wa-l-futūḥ (Sayf ibn ʿUmar) 45, *437-38*
Kitāb al-Ṣafwānī (Ṣafwān ibn Yaḥyā) *536-37*
Kitāb al-ṣalāt fī l-naʿlayn (Ibn Waḍḍāḥ) *838-39*
Kitāb sirr al-khalīqa 507
Kitāb al-sunan (Abū Dāwūd al-Sijistānī) 819
Kitāb al-taʾrīkh (Ibn Ḥabīb) *826-28*
Kitāb al-tawḥīd (Muḥammad ibn Shabīb) 713, *714-15*
Kitāb al-ʿunwān (Agapius of Manbij) 306
Kitāb Usṭāth, see *Kitāb al-bayān* (Usṭāth al-Rāhib) *908-10*

Kitāb yaḥtawī ʿalā ʿashara kutub fī l-radd ʿalā ahl al-milal (Ḍirar ibn ʿAmr) *373*
Kitāb (ilā) Yaḥyā ibn Khālid fī l-adab (Ibn al-Layth) 347
Ktābā d-buyyāʾē awkit d-egrātā, see *Consolations* (Ishoʿyahb III) *134-36*
(Ktābā d-)Eskolyon, see *Book of Scholia* (Theodore bar Koni) 343, *344-46*
Ktābā d-maktab zabnē, see *Syriac common source* *306-8*, 625
Ktābā d-rēsh mellē, see *Book of main points* (John bar Penkāyē) *176-81*
Ktābā d-rishānē, see *Book of governors* (Thomas of Margā) 397, 688, *689-90*
Ktābā d-simātā, see *Book of treasures* (Job of Edessa) 502, 503, 504, 505, *506-9*, 725

Legend of Sergius Baḥīrā 166, 310, 401, 402, 403, 404, 595, *600-3*, 725
Legenda Sancti Floriani et sociorum suorum, see *Passion of the sixty martyrs of Gaza* *190-92*
Leimōn (John Moschus) 120, 121
Leo III in Ghewond, Letter of *203-8*
Leo III to ʿUmar II, Letter of *377-80*, 596
Letter (Athanasius of Balad) *158-59*
Letter 34, see *To the priests and faithful of Baṣra and Hūballaṭ, Letter 34* (Timothy I) *527-28*
Letter 35, see *To Mār Naṣr, Letter 35* (Timothy I) *528-30*
Letter 36, see *To Mār Naṣr, Letter 36* (Timothy I) *530-31*
Letter 40, see *To Sergius, Letter 40* (Timothy I) *519-22*
Letter 59, see *Disputation with the Caliph al-Mahdī* (Timothy I) 516, *522-26*
Letter of Abū l-Rabīʿ Muḥammad ibn al-Layth which he wrote for al-Rashīd to the Byzantine Emperor Constantine *349-53*, 384
Letter of Leo III in Ghewond *203-8*
Letter of Leo III to ʿUmar II *377-80*, 596
Letter of Patriarch John *782-85*
Letter of Pisentius 259, 310
Letter of Pseudo-ʿUmar 204, 375, *381-85*
Letter of ʿUmar II to Leo III, see *Letter of Pseudo-ʿUmar* 204, 375, *381-85*
Letter on the signs of prophethood, see *Risāla fī aʿlām al-nubuwwa* (al-Maʾmūn) *583-84*
Letter to the Christians of Baḥrīn, see *Risāla lahu ilā man bi-l-Baḥrīn min Naṣārā l-maghrib* (Abū Rāʾiṭa l-Takrītī) *580-81*
Letters (John VIII, pope) 804, *806-9*
Libellus de recta sententia (John of Damascus) 290
Liber apologeticus martyrum (Eulogius of Cordova) *683*, 722
Liber pontificalis 96, *642-44*
Liber scholiorum, see *Book of Scholia* (Theodore bar Koni) 343, *344-46*
Life and martyrdom of the holy Bacchus *598-99*
Life and passion of Kostanti-Kaxay *852-56*
Life of Abba Isaac (Mēna of Nikiou) *219-21*
Life of Antony the Younger *726-28*
Life of Bacchus the Younger *598-99*
Life of Constantine-Cyril *799-803*
Life of Eulogius (Paul Alvarus) 645, *646-47*
Life of Gabriel of Qartmīn *892-97*
Life of John of Edessa *898-901*
Life of Michael the Synkellos *872-75*
Life of Muḥammad, see *Istoria de Mahomet* 402, 683, *721-22*, 812
Life of Patriarch Michael (John the Deacon) *321*
Life of Peter the Younger, martyr of Capitolias, see *Martyrdom of Peter of Capitolias* *419-22*
Life of Samuel of Qalamūn (Isaac the Presbyter) 664, *665-68*
Life of Shenute 182
Life of Stephen of Mar Sabas (Leontius of Damascus) 388, *407-10*
Life of Theoduṭe of Āmīd *186-89*
Life of Timothy of Kākhushtā *919-22*
Logos historikos Gregoriou tou Dekapolitou, see *Sermon of Gregory Dekapolites* *615-17*

Madrāshā (against the Armenians) (Jacob of Edessa) *232-33*
Mafātīḥ al-ʿulūm (al-Khwārazmī) 502
al-majdal, Kitāb 151, 688, 757, 758
Majlis dhakara[hu] Īliyya muṭrān Naṣībīn ḥaḍarahu Isrāʾīl al-Kaskarī, see *Debate between Israel of Kashkar and al-Sarakhsī* *840-43*
Majmūʿ uṣūl al-dīn (Ibn al-ʿAssāl, al-Muʾtaman) 578, 606, 758, 772
d-maktab zabnē, Ktābā see *Syriac common source* *306-8*, 625

Maktbānut zabnē, see *Chronicle* (Jacob of Edessa) 231-32
Mammlā lwāt (ʾ)nāsh d-lā awdaʿ shmeh d-shaʾʾel, see *Apologetic treatise of Nonnus of Nisibis* 744-45
Maqāla fī l-ājāl (Ḥunayn ibn Isḥāq) *772-74*
Maqāla fī l-tathlīth (Abū Nūḥ al-Anbārī) *400*
Maqāla fī l-tawḥīd (Abū Nūḥ al-Anbārī) *399*
Maqāla fī l-tawḥīd wa-l-tathlīth (ʿAbdīshūʿ ibn Bahrīz) 551-52
al-maqālāt, Kitāb (al-Īrānshahrī) 696, *891*
maqālāt al-nās wa-ikhtilāfihim, Kitāb (Abū ʿĪsā l-Warrāq) 695, *697-98*, 749, 891
Maronite Chronicle 145-47
Martyrdom of ʿAbd al-Masīḥ 684-87
Martyrdom of Abo of Tbilisi 335-37
Martyrdom of Anthony (Rawḥ al-Qurashī) 498-501
Martyrdom of David of Dwin 719-20
Martyrdom of Elias of Helioupolis 916-18
Martyrdom of the forty-two holy martyrs of Christ (Michael the Synkellos) 628, *630-32*
Martyrdom of the forty-two martyrs of Christ of Amorion (Euodius the Monk) 844, *845-47*
Martyrdom of Michael of Mār Saba 911-15
Martyrdom of Peter of Capitolias 419-22
Martyrdom of Romanus the Younger 390-93
Martyrdom of St Michael, see *Martyrdom of Michael of Mār Saba* 911-15
Martyrdom of the sixty neo-martyr saints, see *Sixty martyrs of Jerusalem* 327-29
Martyrdom of the twenty martyrs of Mār Saba, see *Twenty martyrs of Mar Saba* 388, *393-96*
Martyrdom of Vahan 281-83
Martyrial document, see *Documentum martyriale* (Eulogius of Cordova) 682-83
Martyrion tōn hagiōn tou Christou tessarakonta kai dyo martyrōn, see *Forty-two martyrs of Amorion (BHG 1214c)* 639-41
Martyrion tōn hagiōn tessarakonta dyo martyrōn, see *Martyrdom of the forty-two holy martyrs of Christ* (Michael the Synkellos) 628, *630-32*
Martyrion tōn hagiōn tessarakonta dyo martyrōn (BHG 1209, version D) (BHG 1210, version D1), see *Forty-two martyrs of Amorion* (Sophronius, Archbishop of Cyprus) 675, *676-78*
Martyrion tōn hagiōn tessarakonta dyo tou Christou martyrōn tou Amoriou, see *Martyrdom of the forty-two martyrs of Christ of Amorion* (Euodius the Monk) 844, *845-47*
Martyrion tōn hexēkonta neōn martyrōn, see *Sixty martyrs of Jerusalem* 327-29
Masāʾil ʿan Abī l-Ḥasan Mūsā wa-l-riwāyāt (Ṣafwān ibn Yaḥyā) 536
al-masāʾil wa-l-ajwiba, Kitāb (ʿAmmār al-Baṣrī) 547, *604-7*, 608, 609
al-masāʾil wa-l-ajwiba, Kitāb (Ibn Qutayba) 816
Masāʾil wa-ajwiba ʿaqliyya wa-ilāhiyya 658, 659, *661-63*
Maymar ʿalā sabīl maʿrifat Allāh wa-taḥqīq al-Ibn al-azalī (Theodore Abū Qurra) 426-27
Maymar fī mawt al-Masīḥ (Theodore Abū Qurra) 454-56
Maymar fī taḥqīq al-Injīl (Theodore Abū Qurra) 456-57
Maymar fī taḥqīq nāmūs Mūsā l-muqaddas (Theodore Abū Qurra) 460-63
Maymar fī wujūd al-Khāliq wa-l-dīn al-qawīm (Theodore Abū Qurra) 448-50
Maymar qālahu… anba Tāʾufīlus, see *Arabic homily of Pseudo-Theophilus of Alexandria* 256-60
Maymar yuḥaqqiqu anna dīn Allāh huwa l-dīn alladhī kharajat bihi l-ḥawāriyyūn ilā aqṭār al-arḍ (Theodore Abū Qurra) 467-68
Maymar yuḥaqqiqu annahu lā yulzamu l-Naṣārā an yaqūlū thalātha āliha (Theodore Abū Qurra) 453-54
Maymar yuḥaqqiqu li-l-insān ḥurriyya thābita min Allāh (Theodore Abū Qurra) 451-52
Maymar yuthbitu fīhi anna l-sujūd li-ṣūrat al-Masīḥ wājib ʿalā kull Naṣrānī (Theodore Abū Qurra) 463-66
Memoriale sanctorum (Eulogius of Cordova) 633, *680-82*

Mēmrā ʿal yubbālā d-malkē w-ʿal ḥarat zabnā, see *Apocalypse of Pseudo-Methodius* 161, *163-71*, 172, 173, 174, 243
Mēmrā d-qāddishā mār(y) Aprēm, see *Apocalypse of Pseudo-Ephrem* *160-62*
Min qawl Thāwudūrus ṭaʿana ʿalā l-barrāniyyīn (Theodore Abū Qurra) *470-71*
Miṣbāḥ al-ẓulma wa-īḍāḥ al-khidma (Abū l-Barakāt ibn Kabar) 558, 907
Mujādalat Abī Qurra, see *Debate of Theodore Abū Qurra* 439, *556-64*
Mujādalat al-rāhib al-qiddīs Ibrāhīm al-Ṭabarānī maʿa l-amīr ʿAbd al-Raḥmān, see *Disputation of Ibrāhīm al-Ṭabarānī* 524, 596, *876-81*
al-Muntaqā min kitāb al-ruhbān (Ibn Abī l-Dunyā) *830*
al-Mustakhraja min al-asmiʿa (al-ʿUtbī l-Qurṭubī) 734, *735-37*
The Myrobalan, on contemplation, see *Kitāb al-halīlaja fī l-iʿtibār* (Ibn al-Layth) 347

al-Naqḍ ʿalā man uḍīfa ilā l-Yaʿqūbiyya... wa-ʿalā bāqī ṣunūf al-Naṣārā (Abū ʿĪsā l-Warrāq) *701*
Narrationes (Anastasius of Sinai) 194, *198-200*
ʿalā l-Naṣārā, Kitāb (Abū l-Hudhayl al-ʿAllāf) *547*
ʿalā l-Naṣārā, Kitāb (Ḥafṣ al-Fard) *657*
ʿalā l-Naṣārā fī l-naʿīm wa-l-akl wa-l-shurb fī l-ākhira wa-ʿalā jamīʿ man qāla bi-ḍiddi dhālika, Kitāb (Ḥumayd ibn Bakhtiyār) *724-25*
Nicetas of Byzantium's foreword *755-56*
Nikēta Byzantinou philosophou programma, see *Nicetas of Byzantium's foreword* *755-56*
Nineteen Muslim kings, Prophecy of, see *Prophecy of the nineteen Muslim kings* 309, 310, *411-13*
Nomocanon (Barhebraeus) 89, 93, 94, 95, 96, 114, 228
fī l-nubuwwa, Kitāb (Abū l-Hudhayl al-ʿAllāf) *548-49*
fī l-nubuwwa, Kitāb (Muḥammad ibn Shabīb) *715-16*

Occasions and knowledge concerning prophethood, see *Kitāb al-asbāb wa-l-ʿilm ʿalā al-rusul* (Ḍirar ibn ʿAmr) *371*
On the contending of Christ with the devil (Theodore Abū Qurra) *479-81*
On heresies, see *De haeresibus* 291, 295, *297-301*, 848
On the holy places (Adomnán of Iona) *154-56*
On the Holy Trinity, see *al-Risālat al-ūlā fī l-Thālūth al-muqaddas* (Abū Rāʾiṭa l-Takrītī) *572-74*
On the Incarnation, see *al-Risālat al-thāniya li-Abī Rāʾiṭa l-Takrītī fī l-tajassud* *574-75*
On legitimate political leadership and governance, see *al-Imāma wa-l-siyāsa* (Muʿārik ibn Marwān al-Nuṣayrī) *741-42*
On the proof of Christianity and the Trinity, see *Risāla li-Abī Rāʾiṭa l-Takrītī fī ithbāt dīn al-naṣrāniyya wa-ithbāt al-Thālūth al-muqaddas* *571-72*
On prophethood, see *Kitāb fī l-nubuwwa* *548-49*, *715-16*
On the Triune nature of God *330-33*
On the true existence of God, see *Maymar fī wujūd al-Khāliq wa-l-dīn al-qawīm* (Theodore Abū Qurra) *448-50*
Opuscula (Theodore Abū Qurra) 468, 476, 478, 479, 481, 482, 483, 485, 486, 488, 489, 490

P. Vind. Inv.A.P.10.000, see *Vienna, Papyrus Erzherzog Rainer – Inv. Ar. Pap. 10.000* *654-55*
Pact of ʿUmar 5, 104, 106, 107, 356, 357, *360-64*
Pamet' i žitie blaženago učitelja našego Kostantina Filosofa, see *Life of Constantine-Cyril* *799-803*
Panegyric of the three holy children of Babylon *128-29*
Part of the discourse of Mār John the Stylite of Mār Zʿurā in Sarug *315-16*
Passio Sancti Maximiliani, see *Passion of St Maximilian* *717-18*
Passio sexaginta martyrum, see *Passion of the sixty martyrs of Gaza* *190-92*
Passion of St Maximilian *717-18*
Passion of the sixty martyrs of Gaza *190-92*
Patmutʿiwn Aghuanitsʿ ashkharhi, see *History of Aghuankʿ* 261, 262, *263-67*
Patmutʿiwn Ghewondeay, see *History of Ghewond* 203, 206, 265, 381, *867-71*

Patmutʿiwn Sebēosi, see *History of Sebeos* 139-44
Patriarch John, Letter of 782-85
Pbios apa Samouēl, see *Life of Samuel of Qalamūn* (Isaac the Presbyter) 664, *665-68*
Pēgē gnōseōs 295, 296, 297
Peri haireseōn, see *De haeresibus* 291, 295, *297-301*, 848
Peri tēs palēs tou Christou meta diabolon, see *On the contending of Christ with the devil* (Theodore Abū Qurra) *479-81*
Persuasion, see *Kitāb al-iqnāʿ* (Abū l-ʿAbbās ʿĪsā ibn Zayd) 849, *857-58*
Phbios mpinishti mpatriarchēs... Isaak, see *Life of Abba Isaac* *219-21*
Pisentius, Letter of 259, 310
Polemic against Islam (Speraindeo) *634-35*
Pope Hadrian's Epistles to Bishop Egila *338-42*
Positive exposition of Christian doctrine (Nicetas of Byzantium) *752-53*
Pratum spirituale, see *Leimōn* (John Moschus) 120, 121
Prayer for al-Maʾmūn (Theodore Abū Qurra) *469*
Praying in sandals, see *Kitāb al-ṣalāt fī l-naʿlayn* (Ibn Waḍḍāḥ) *838-39*
Profecías de San Metodio martyr 250
The proof, see *Kitāb al-burhān* (Abū l-Faḍl ʿAlī ibn Rabban al-Naṣrānī) *652-53*
The proof, see *al-Burhān* (ʿAlī ibn Yaḥyā ibn al-Munajjim) *763-67*, 776
The proof, see *Kitāb al-burhān* (ʿAmmār al-Baṣrī) *607-10*
The proof, see *al-Burhān* (Peter of Bayt Raʾs) *902-6*
The proof, see *Kitāb al-burhān* (Abū l-Faraj Saʿīd ibn ʿAlī al-Anbārī) *859-60*
The proof, see *Kitāb al-burhān* (Yuḥannā ibn al-Ṣalt) *850*
Proof about confirmation of prophethood, see *Kitāb al-ḥujja fī tathbīt al-nubuwwa* (al-Jāḥiẓ) *707-8*
Proof against the Christians, see *Kitāb al-ḥujja ʿalā l-Naṣārā* (Muḥammad ibn Saḥnūn) *739*
Proof in confirmation of the Prophet, see *Kitāb al-ḥujja fī ithbāt al-nabī* (Bishr ibn al-Muʿtamir) *534*
Proofs of prophethood, see *Dalāʾil al-nubuwwa* (Abū Dāwūd al-Sijistānī) *820*
Proofs of prophethood, see *Dalāʾil al-nubuwwa* (al-Ḥarbī, Ibrāhīm ibn Isḥāq) *833*
Proofs of prophethood, see *Dalāʾil al-nubuwwa* (Ibn Abī l-Dunyā) *830-31*
Proofs of prophethood, see *Dalāʾil al-nubuwwa* (Ibn Qutayba) 673, *817-18*
Property tax (Abū Yūsuf al-Yaʿqūbī) *355-59*
Prophecy of the nineteen Muslim kings 309, 310, *411-13*
Prophetic chronicle *810-15*, 883, 884
Proto-fourteenth vision of Daniel *309-13*, 412
Pseudo-Athanasius, Apocalypse of *274-80*
Pseudo-Ephrem, Apocalypse of *160-62*
Pseudo-Ezra, Apocalypse of *239-41*
Pseudo-Leo's first letter to ʿUmar II 375-76
Pseudo-Methodius, Apocalypse of (Syriac) 161, *163-71*, 172, 173, 174, 243
Pseudo-Methodius, Apocalypse of (Greek) *245-48*
Pseudo-Methodius, Apocalypse of (Latin) *249-52*
Pseudo-ʿUmar, Letter of 204, 375, *381-85*

Quaestiones ad Antiochum ducem 904
Quaestiones et responsiones (Anastasius of Sinai) *200-2*
A Question of the Arabs to a Christian (Theodore Abū Qurra) *481-82*
Questions and answers see *Kitāb al-masāʾil wa-l-ajwiba* (ʿAmmār al-Baṣrī) 547, *604-7*, 608, 609
Questions on the Son of God (Theodore Abū Qurra) *458-60*

al-radd, Kitāb (Theodore Abū Qurra) *473*
al-radd ʿalā ahl al-adyān, Kitāb (Abū l-Hudhayl al-ʿAllāf) *546-47*
Radd ʿalā lladhīna yaqūlūna inna kalimat Allāh makhlūqa (Theodore Abū Qurra) *472-73*
Radd ʿalā lladhīna yaqūlūna inna l-Naṣārā yuʾminū bi-ilāh ḍaʿīf (Theodore Abū Qurra) *471-72*

al-radd ʿalā Maʿmar fī qawlihi inna Muḥammadan rabb, Kitāb (Ḍirar ibn ʿAmr) *372*
Radd ʿalā al-Naṣārā (ʿAlī ibn Rabban al-Ṭabarī) *671-72*
al-radd ʿalā l-Naṣārā, Kitāb (Anonymous) *658-60*
al-radd ʿalā l-Naṣārā, Kitāb (Bishr ibn al-Muʿtamir) *533-34*
al-radd ʿalā l-Naṣārā, Kitāb (Ḍirar ibn ʿAmr) *373-74*
Radd ʿalā al-Naṣārā (al-Jāḥiẓ) *709-12*
Radd ʿalā al-Naṣārā (al-Kindī, Abū Yūsuf) *747-48*
al-radd ʿalā l-Naṣārā, Kitāb (al-Murdār) *612*
al-radd ʿalā l-Naṣārā, Kitāb (al-Qāsim ibn Ibrāhīm) *542-43*
Radd ʿalā al-thalāth firaq min al-Naṣārā (Abū ʿĪsā l-Warrāq) 697, *698-700*
fī l-radd ʿalā l-Yahūd wa-l-Naṣārā, Kitāb (al-Maʾmūn) *584*
al-radd ʿalā Yūshaʿ Bukht maṭrān Fars, Kitāb (Ḥumayd ibn Bakhtiyār) *724*
Radd ʿalā l-zanādiqa (Ibn al-Layth) 347, 371
rafʿ ʿĪsā, Kitāb (Ibn al-Kalbī) *514*
Raising on high of Jesus, see *Kitāb rafʿ ʿĪsā* (Ibn al-Kalbī) *514*
The Refutation, see *Kitāb al-radd* (Theodore Abū Qurra) *473*
Refutation of the Christians, see *Radd ʿalā al-Naṣārā* (ʿAlī ibn Rabban al-Ṭabarī) *671-72*
Refutation of the Christians, see *Kitāb al-radd ʿalā l-Naṣārā* (Anonymous) *658-60*
Refutation of the Christians, see *Kitāb al-radd ʿalā l-Naṣārā* (Bishr ibn al-Muʿtamir) *533-34*
Refutation of the Christians, see *Radd ʿalā al-Naṣārā* (al-Jāḥiẓ) *709-12*
Refutation of the Christians, see *Radd ʿalā al-Naṣārā* (al-Kindī, Abū Yūsuf) *747-48*
Refutation of the Christians, see *Kitāb al-radd ʿalā l-Naṣārā* (al-Murdār) *612*
Refutation of the Christians, see *Kitāb al-radd ʿalā l-Naṣārā* (al-Qāsim ibn Ibrāhīm) *542-43*
Refutation of the followers of the religions, see *Kitāb al-radd ʿalā ahl al-adyān* (Abū l-Hudhayl al-ʿAllāf) *546-47*
Refutation of the Hagarenes (Bartholomew of Edessa) 424
Refutation of Īshōʿbokht, metropolitan of Fars, see *Kitāb al-radd ʿalā Yūshaʿ Bukht maṭrān Fars* (Ḥumayd ibn Bakhtiyār) *724*
Refutation of the Jews and Christians, see *Kitāb fī l-radd ʿalā l-Yahūd wa-l-Naṣārā* (al-Maʾmūn) *584*
Refutation of Maʿmar, see *Kitāb al-radd ʿalā Maʿmar fī qawlihi inna Muḥammadan rabb* *372*
Refutation of the Qurʾān, see *Tafnīd al-Qurʾān* (Abū Nūḥ al-Anbārī) *398-99*
Refutation of those who say that Christians believe in a weak God, see *Radd ʿalā lladhīna yaqūlūna inna l-Naṣārā yuʾminū bi-ilāh ḍaʿīf* (Theodore Abū Qurra) *471-72*
Refutation of those who say that the Word of God is created, see *Radd ʿalā lladhīna yaqūlūna inna kalimat Allāh makhlūqa* (Theodore Abū Qurra) *472-73*
Refutation of the three Christian sects (longer version), see *Radd ʿalā al-thalāth firaq min al-Naṣārā* (Abū ʿĪsā l-Warrāq) *698-99*
Refutation of the three Christian sects (medium version), see *Radd ʿalā al-thalāth firaq min al-Naṣārā* (Abū ʿĪsā l-Warrāq) *699-700*
Refutation of the three Christian sects (shorter version), see *Radd ʿalā al-thalāth firaq min al-Naṣārā* (Abū ʿĪsā l-Warrāq) *700*
Refutations of the Saracens as reported by John the Deacon (Theodore Abū Qurra) *474-76*
Refutation of the zindīqs, see *Radd ʿalā l-zanādiqa* (Ibn al-Layth) 347, 371
d-rēsh mellē, Ktābā see *Book of main points* (John bar Penkāyē) *176-81*
al-Riḍāʾs reply to the question of Abū Qurra, see *Jawāb al-Riḍā ʿan suʾāl Abī Qurra* (Ṣafwān ibn Yaḥyā) *538-39*
al-ridda wa-l-futūḥ, Kitāb (Sayf ibn ʿUmar) 45, *437-38*
Risālat Abī l-Rabīʿ Muḥammad ibn al-Layth allatī katabahā li-l-Rashīd ilā Qusṭanṭīn malik al-Rūm, see *Letter of Abū l-Rabīʿ Muḥammad ibn al-Layth which he wrote for al-Rashīd to the*

Byzantine emperor Constantine 349-53, 384
al-Risāla l-ʿasaliyya (al-Jāḥiẓ) *712*
Risāla fī aʿlām al-nubuwwa (al-Maʾmūn) *583-84*
Risāla fī iftirāq al-milal fī l-tawḥīd (al-Kindī, Abū Yūsuf) 747, *749-50*
Risālat al-Hāshimī ilā ʿAbd al-Masīḥ al-Kindī wa-risālat al-Kindī ilā l-Hāshimī *587-94*
Risāla fī tathbīt waḥdāniyyat al-Bāriʾ wa-tathlīth khawāṣṣihi (Israel of Kashkar) 758, *759*
Risālat ilā Qusṭā ibn Lūqā wa-Ḥunayn 765
Risāla lahu ilā man bi-l-Baḥrīn min Naṣārā l-maghrib (Abū Rāʾiṭa l-Takrītī) *580-81*
Risāla li-Abī Rāʾiṭa l-Takrītī fī ithbāt dīn al-naṣrāniyya wa-ithbāt al-Thālūth al-muqaddas *571-72*
al-Risālat al-thāniya li-Abī Rāʾiṭa l-Takrītī fī l-tajassud (Abū Rāʾiṭa l-Takrītī) *574-75*
al-Risālat al-ūlā fī l-Thālūth al-muqaddas (Abū Rāʾiṭa l-Takrītī) *572-74*
d-rishānē, Ktābā see *Book of governors* (Thomas of Margā) 397, 688, *689-90*
Ritual of abjuration 95, *821-24*

al-Ṣafwānī, Kitāb (Ṣafwān ibn Yaḥyā) *536-37*
al-ṣalāt fī l-naʿlayn, Kitāb (Ibn Waḍḍāḥ) *838-39*
Samuel, Apocalypse of 259, 276, 310
scholia, Book of (Theodore bar Koni) 343, *344-46*
Scriptores post Theophanem 431
Secret of creation 507
Selection from what is heard, see *al-Mustakhraja min al-asmiʿa* (al-ʿUtbī l-Qurṭubī) 734, *735-37*
Selections from The Book of Monks, see *Al-Muntaqā min kitāb al-ruhbān* (Ibn Abī l-Dunyā) *830*
Sermon of the holy lord Ephrem on the end and completion, see *Apocalypse of Pseudo-Ephrem* *160-62*
Sermon of Gregory Dekapolites *615-17*
Sermon on holy baptism (Sophronius) *126-27*
Shahādāt min qawl al-Tawrāt wa-l-anbiyāʾ wa-l-qiddisīn (Abū Rāʾiṭa l-Takrītī) *576-77*
Sharbē medem men qlisastiqē wa-d-qosmosṭiqē, see *Chronicle of Khuzistan* *130-32*
Shenute, Apocalypse of *182-85*, 411
Shining declaration, see *Indiculus luminosus* (Paul Alvarus) 645, *647-48*
Shurrāyā d-Qurān, see *Tafnīd al-Qurʾān* (Abū Nūḥ al-Anbārī) *398-99*
Shurūṭ ʿUmar, see *Pact of ʿUmar* 5, 104, 106, 107, 356, 357, *360-64*
al-Shurūṭ al-ʿUmariyya, see *Pact of ʿUmar* 5, 104, 106, 107, 356, 357, *360-64*
d-simātā, Ktābā see *Book of treasures* (Job of Edessa) 502, 503, 504, 505, *506-9*, 725
Sīrat al-qiddīs al-fāḍil al-nāsik Timāthayūs, see *Life of Timothy of Kākhushtā* *919-22*
sirr al-khalīqa, Kitāb 507
Sixty martyrs of Jerusalem 327-29
Some statements of Theodore against the outsiders, see *Min qawl Thāwudūrus ṭaʿana ʿalā l-barrāniyyīn* (Theodore Abū Qurra) *470-71*
Source of The History of the patriarchs of Alexandria (John the Deacon) *235-28*
Spiritual meadow, see *Leimōn* (John Moschus) 120, 121
Stichistikoi logoi kata haireseōn, see *Discourses in verse against heresies* (Theodore the Stoudite) *424-25*
Story of Muḥammad, see *Istoria de Mahomet* 402, 683, *721-22*, 812
Story of Saint Florian and his companions, see *Passion of the sixty martyrs of Gaza* *190-92*
Sufficiency, see *Kitāb al-kifāya* (Abū l-Khayr ʿĪsā ibn Hibat Allāh) *862*
Suʾila Abū Qurra Anbā Thādhurus ʿan al-Masīḥ bi-hawāhi ṣuliba am bi-ghayr hawāhi *468-69*
Summa theologiae arabica, see *al-Jāmiʿ wujūh al-īmān* 468, 471, *791-98*, 879
al-sunan, Kitāb (Abū Dāwūd al-Sijistānī) 819
Sunhados d-qaddishā (...) Mār Ghiwarghis, see *Synod of the Holy (...) Mār Ghiwarghis* *152-53*
Superiority of Trinity over Unity, see *Kitāb fī tafḍīl al-tathlīth ʿalā l-tawḥīd* (al-Naẓẓām) *619-21*

Synod of the Holy (...) Mār Ghiwarghis 152-53
Synodical Letter (Sophronius) 121, 123-24, 125
Syriac common source 306-8, 625
Syāmā ḥad b-yad ʿesrā sulughismē, see *Treatise containing ten syllogisms* (Job of Edessa) 504-5
Syāmā ʿal haymānutā, see *Treatise on faith* (Job of Edessa) 505-6

Ta synodika Sōphroniou, see *Synodical Letter* (Sophronius) 121, 123-24, 125
fī tafḍīl al-tathlīth ʿalā l-tawḥīd, Kitāb (al-Naẓẓām) 619-21
Tafnīd al-Qurʾān (Abū Nūḥ al-Anbārī) 398-99
al-taʾrīkh, Kitāb (Ibn Ḥabīb) 826-28
Taʾrīkh al-rusul wa-l-mulūk (Abū Jaʿfar al-Ṭabarī) 59, 437
Tartīb al-madārik (Qāḍī ʿIyāḍ) 739
Tashʿītā d-qaddīshā mār(y) Shmūʾēl w-mār(y) Shemʿūn w-mār(y) Gabrīʾēl, see *Life of Gabriel of Qartmīn* 892-97
Tashʿītā d-rabban Sargīs, see *Legend of Sergius Baḥīrā* 166, 310, 401, 402, 403, 404, 595, 600-3, 725
Tawditā d-ashlem l-Ishmaʿlāyē Kaʿb sāprā – dukhrāneh l-lūtā, see *Confession which Kaʿb al-Aḥbār handed down to the Ishmaelites* 403-5, 602
al-tawḥīd, Kitāb (Muḥammad ibn Shabīb) 713, 714-15
Teachings of Jacob, the newly baptized, see *Doctrina Iacobi nuper baptizati* 117-19
Teachings of people and the differences between them, see *Kitāb maqālāt al-nās wa-ikhtilāfihim* (Abū ʿĪsā l-Warrāq) 695, 697-98, 749, 891
Testimonies about our Lord's dispensation, see *Testimonies of the prophets about the dispensation of Christ* 242-44
Testimonies of the prophets about the dispensation of Christ 242-44
That we have five enemies from whom the Savior freed us (Theodore Abū Qurra) 476-77
To Mār Naṣr, Letter 35 (Timothy I) 528-30
To Mār Naṣr, Letter 36 (Timothy I) 530-31
To the priests and faithful of Baṣra and Hūballaṭ, Letter 34 (Timothy I) 527-28
To Sergius, Letter 40 (Timothy I) 519-22
Tokens of prophethood, see *Amārāt al-nubuwwa* (al-Juzajānī) 781
Tome of Leo 665
Tou Sōphroniou archiepiskopou Hierosolymōn logos eis ta theia tou Sōtēros genetēlia, see *Christmas sermon* (Sophronius) 124-25
Tou Sōphroniou archiepiskopou Hierosolymōn logos eis to hagion baptisma, see *Sermon on holy baptism* (Sophronius) 126-27
Treasures, Book of (Job of Edessa) 502, 503, 504, 505, 506-9, 725
Treatise against Islam (Peter of Damascus) 291-92
Treatise confirming that Christians do not necessarily speak of three gods, see *Maymar yuḥaqqiqu annahu lā yulzamu l-Naṣārā an yaqūlū thalātha āliha* (Theodore Abū Qurra) 453-54
Treatise confirming that human beings have an innate freedom from God, see *Maymar yuḥaqqiqu li-l-insān ḥurriyya thābita min Allāh* (Theodore Abū Qurra) 451-52
Treatise confirming that the religion of God is the religion that the Apostles brought to [all] the regions of the earth, see *Maymar yuḥaqqiqu anna dīn Allāh huwa l-dīn alladhī kharajat bihi l-ḥawāriyyūn ilā aqṭār al-arḍ* (Theodore Abū Qurra) 467-68
Treatise containing ten syllogisms (Job of Edessa) 504-5
Treatise in which he establishes that prostration to the image of Christ is incumbent on every Christian, see *Maymar yuthbitu fīhi anna l-sujūd li-ṣūrat al-Masīḥ wājib ʿalā kull Naṣrānī* (Theodore Abū Qurra) 463-66
Treatise on the confirmation of the Gospel, see *Maymar fī taḥqīq al-Injīl* (Theodore Abū Qurra) 456-57
Treatise on the confirmation of the holy law of Moses, see *Maymar fī taḥqīq nāmūs Mūsā l-muqaddas* (Theodore Abū Qurra) 460-63

Treatise on the death of Christ, see *Maymar fī mawt al-Masīḥ* (Theodore Abū Qurra) *454-56*
Treatise on the existence of the Creator and the true religion, see *Maymar fī wujūd al-Khāliq wa-l-dīn al-qawīm* (Theodore Abū Qurra) *448-50*
Treatise on faith (Job of Edessa) *505-6*
Treatise on lifespans, see *Maqāla fī l-ājāl* (Ḥunayn ibn Isḥāq) *772-74*
Treatise on the Trinity, see *Maqāla fī l-tathlīth* (Abū Nūḥ al-Anbārī) *400*
Treatise on the Unity (of God), see *Maqāla fī l-tawḥīd* (Abū Nūḥ al-Anbārī) *399*
Treatise on the Unity and Trinity (of God), see *Maqāla fī l-tawḥīd wa-l-tathlīth* (ʿAbdīshūʿ ibn Bahrīz) *551-52*
Treatise on the way of knowing God and the confirmation of the eternal Son, see *Maymar ʿalā sabīl maʿrifat Allāh wa-taḥqīq al-Ibn al-azalī* (Theodore Abū Qurra) *426-27*
Truth of the orthodox faith (Theodore Abū Qurra) *491*
Twenty martyrs of Mār Saba (Stephen Manṣūr) 388, *393-96*

ʿUmar II to Leo III, Letter of see *Letter of Pseudo-ʿUmar* 204, 375, *381-85*
An Unbeliever's question to the same (Theodore Abū Qurra) *483-85*
unknown risāla (Abū Rāʾiṭa l-Takrītī) *576*
unknown work on Islam (Michael the Synkellos) *632*
al-ʿunwān, Kitāb (Agapius of Manbij) 306
Usṭāth, Kitāb see *Kitāb al-bayān* (Usṭāth al-Rāhib) *908-10*
al-ʿUtbiyya, see *al-Mustakhraja min al-asmiʿa* (al-ʿUtbī l-Qurṭubī) 734, *735-37*
ʿUyūn akhbār al-Riḍā (Ibn Babawayh) 538

Viae dux (Anastasius of Sinai) *196-97*
Vienna, Papyrus Erzherzog Rainer – Inv. Ar. Pap. 10.000 *654-55*
Vita Constantini, see *Life of Constantine-Cyril* *799-803*
Vita Eulogii, see *Life of Eulogius* (Paul Alvarus) 645, *646-47*
Vita Mahumeti, see *Istoria de Mahomet* 402, 683, *721-22*, 812

The Wisdom of Sibilla, daughter of Heraclius, see *Arabic Sibylline prophecy* *492-97*
Witnesses from the words of the Torah, the prophets and the saints, see *Shahādāt min qawl al-Tawrāt wa-l-anbiyāʾ wa-l-qiddisīn* (Abū Rāʾiṭa l-Takrītī) *576-77*

Yaḥyā ibn Khālid fī l-adab, Kitāb (ilā) (Ibn al-Layth) 347